D1107738

Handbook of Spectroscopy
Volume II

Handbook of Spectroscopy

Volume II

Editor

J. W. Robinson
Department of Chemistry
Louisiana State University
Baton Rouge, La

published by:

18901 Cranwood Parkway, Cleveland, Ohio 44128

HANDBOOK OF SPECTROSCOPY
VOLUME II

International Standard Book Number (ISBN)

Complete Set 0-87819-333-2
Volume II 0-87819-332-4

Library of Congress Catalog Card Number 73-77524

PREFACE

The principal objective of this handbook is to provide a readily accessible source of information on the major fields of spectroscopy. Specifically, these fields are NMR, IR, Raman, UV (absorption and fluorescence), ESCA, X-ray (absorption diffraction fluorescence), mass spectrometry, atomic absorption, flame photometry, emission spectrography, and flame spectroscopy.

Because of the considerable quantity of information amassed on these spectroscopic fields, it was necessary to publish the Handbook in two volumes. An attempt was made to select the related subject matter for each volume for ease of use, but it is felt that these are companion volumes.

The book will provide some theoretical information, but is mostly dedicated to providing a reference for the spectroscopic data available on the most important materials in the particular field.

The handbook will be of maximum value to the practicing spectroscopist. Many scientists are experts in one or two fields of spectroscopy, but relative novices in other similar fields. This handbook will be invaluable to people wishing to get information about these other fields.

It will be of particular use to analytical, organic, inorganic chemists or spectroscopists wishing to identify materials or compounds. The book will indicate to him which techniques may provide him with useful information and what kind of information those will provide him and will not provide him. In short, it will be a companion to those spectroscopists who have need to broaden their horizons into the major fields discussed.

Because of space limitations, the Handbook will not provide a complete reference service in all fields, but it will provide the most important information available, thereby providing a reference in breadth.

J. W. Robinson
Louisiana State University

CONTRIBUTORS
for VOLUMES I AND II

David A. Allison, Ph.D.
Department of Chemistry
University of Alberta
Edmonton, Alberta, Canada

Juanita H. Allison, Ph.D.
Department of Chemistry
University of Alberta
Edmonton, Alberta, Canada

Stanley S. Ballard, Ph.D.
Department of Physics
University of Florida
Gainesville, Florida

Eugene P. Bertin, Ph.D.
RCA/David Sarnoff Research Center
Princeton, New Jersey

Norman S. Bhacca, Ph.D.
Department of Chemistry
Louisiana State University
Baton Rouge, Louisiana

L. S. Birks, M.S.
Head, X-Ray Optics Branch
Naval Research Laboratory
Washington, D. C.

J. S. Browder, Ph.D.
Department of Physics
Jacksonville University
Jacksonville, Florida

Dennis B. Brown, Ph.D.
X-Ray Optics Branch
Naval Research Laboratory
Washington, D. C.

Alex Burr, Ph.D.
Physics Department
New Mexico State University
Las Cruces, New Mexico

L. R. P. Butler, Ph.D.
Head, Applied Spectroscopy Division
National Physical Research Laboratory
Council for Scientific and Industrial Research
Pretoria, South Africa

Horacio A. Farach, Ph.D.
Department of Physics and Astronomy
University of South Carolina
Columbia, South Carolina

R. W. Fink, Ph.D.
Department of Chemistry
Georgia Institute of Technology
Atlanta, Georgia

A. G. Gaydon, D.Sc., F.R.S.
Imperial College
London, England

John V. Gilfrich, B.S.
X-Ray Optics Branch
Naval Research Laboratory
Washington, D. C.

Jeanette G. Grasselli, M.S.
The Standard Oil Company (Ohio)
Research and Engineering Department
Cleveland, Ohio

N. J. Harrick, Ph.D.
Harrick Scientific Corporation
Ossining, New York

H. G. C. Human, Ph.D.
Applied Spectroscopy Division
National Physical Research Laboratory
Council for Scientific and Industrial Research
Pretoria, South Africa

R. O. Kagel, Ph.D.
Dow Corning Corporation
Midland, Michigan

Francis W. Karasek, Ph.D.
Department of Chemistry
University of Waterloo
Waterloo, Ontario, Canada

Richard A. Nyquist, B.S.
The Dow Chemical Company
Midland, Michigan

Charles P. Poole, Jr., Ph.D.
Department of Physics and Astronomy
University of South Carolina
Columbia, South Carolina

P. Venugopala Rao, Ph.D.
Department of Physics
Emory University
Atlanta, Georgia

A. E. Sandstrom, Ph.D.
Royal University of Uppsala
Uppsala, Sweden

R. H. Scott, Ph.D.
Applied Spectroscopy Division
National Physical Research Laboratory
Council for Scientific and Industrial Research
Pretoria, South Africa

Professor Kai Siegbahn
Institute of Physics
Uppsala University
Uppsala, Sweden

R. K. Skogerboe, Ph.D.
Department of Chemistry
Colorado State University
Fort Collins, Colorado

A. Lee Smith, Ph.D.
Dow Corning Corporation
Midland, Michigan

R. E. Smith, Ph.D.
Imperial College
London, England

William J. Veigele, Ph.D.
Kaman Sciences Corporation
Colorado Springs, Colorado

J. B. Willis, D.Sc., Ph.D.
Division of Chemical Physics
Commonwealth Scientific and Industrial Research Organization
P. O. Box 160
Clayton, Victoria, Australia 3168

THE EDITOR

J. W. Robinson, B.Sc., Ph.D., is Professor of Chemistry and Chairman of the Analytical Division at Louisiana State University, Baton Rouge, La., U.S.

Dr. Robinson earned his degrees at the University of Birmingham in England (B.Sc., 1949, and Ph.D., 1952). He obtained his American citizenship in 1965.

Dr. Robinson has authored more than 100 publications and has recently written two books, *Undergraduate Instrumental Analysis* and *Atomic Absorption Spectroscopy.* He is Editor of *Spectroscopy Letters* and *Environmental Letters.* He is a former Chairman of the National Society of Applied Spectroscopy and is currently Chairman of both the Gordon Conference and the Louisiana State University International Symposium on Analytical Chemistry. Dr. Robinson is also Director of the Saul Gordon Workshop on Atomic Absorption Spectroscopy.

TABLE OF CONTENTS

Section A

Infrared Spectroscopy

INFRARED SPECTROSCOPY

A. Lee Smith, Dow Corning Corporation

I. SAMPLING

A. Properties of Common Window Materials

Stanley S. Ballard, University of Florida, and James Steve Browder, Jacksonville University

Data are given on the optical and other physical properties of twenty-two materials that may be useful as absorption-cell windows. These materials are listed below, in alphabetical order by their complete names. This table is followed by a listing of the same materials, but in the order of increasing infrared cutoff wavelength, where the cutoff is generally defined as the wavelength for which the external transmittance of a window of specified thickness has dropped to 50%. It should be noted that these cutoff wavelengths are only approximate. This statement is even more true for short-wavelength transmission limits, which are quoted for general information only and without noting the thickness of the samples.

Data on several properties, especially refractive index, are given separately for each material. Then follow comparative tables for six different physical properties in which the several materials are listed, not alphabetically, but in the order of increasing values of that particular property.

Literature references are not given for what might be called routine data, such as can readily be found in the CRC Handbook of Chemistry and Physics, the American Institute of Physics Handbook, and other common data compilations. Many of these data have been previously reported by the present authors in *Applied Optics*, 5, 1873, 1966.

It is realized that crystal quartz is not commonly used as an absorption-cell window, but some of its properties are included in order to emphasize the fact that they differ from the properties of amorphous fused silica, which is the more popular window material and is often erroneously called "quartz."

Other glasses have been developed for use in the infrared, calcium aluminate, with a long-wavelength transmission limit of 5 to 6 μm being perhaps the most successful. However, none of these materials seems to be popular enough to deserve coverage herein. Certain plastics, especially polyethylene, are sometimes used as window materials despite the fact that they show a large number of absorption bands in the infrared region. It did not seem appropriate to treat plastics here.

Among the newest infrared-transmitting materials are the so-called Irtrans, six in number, developed by the Eastman Kodak Company. They are hot-pressed, compacted materials which are microcrystalline aggregates of well-known substances. The pure powder is heated and compacted in a high pressure apparatus to form a blank that is roughly of the size and shape of the desired optical element. The chemical and physical properties of an Irtran are generally similar to those of the basic substance, except that the Irtrans have higher thermal shock resistance and, of course, do not exhibit cleavage. Despite their high melting points, all above 1000°C, their maximum useful temperature may be considerably lower, depending on the nature of the surrounding atmosphere, the length of exposure at the high temperature, etc. As would be expected with such microcrystalline aggregates, the short-wavelength cutoffs are governed by scattering as well as absorption.

As to nomenclature, we are told by various standardizing bodies that we should use micrometer (μm) in place of the historical unit the micron (μ); in the visible region we are told to use nanometer (nm) instead of the millimicron (mμ). These new SI units are being used to an increasing extent, but many will prefer to use the more familiar units to which they have long been accustomed. Temperatures are usually given in °C, although kelvins may be used (K; no longer °K). The kelvin as a temperature interval is exactly equal to the Celsius (centigrade) degree.

Optical materials for which data are given

Arsenic trisulfide glass (As_2S_3)	Potassium bromide (KBr)
Barium fluoride (BaF_2)	Potassium chloride (KCl)
Calcium fluoride (CaF_2)	Sapphire (Al_2O_3)
Cesium bromide (CsBr)	Fused silica (SiO_2)
Cesium iodide (CsI)	Silicon (Si)
Crystal quartz (SiO_2)	Silver chloride (AgCl)
Germanium (Ge)	Sodium chloride (NaCl)
Irtrans 1-6	Thallium bromide-iodide (KRS-5)
Lithium fluoride (LiF)	

1. Transmission Limits

Optical materials, listed in approximate order of increasing infrared cutoff wavelength (defined as the wavelength at which the external transmittance* of a window of listed thickness has dropped to 50%):

Material	IR Transmission Limit, μm	Sample Thickness, mm
Crystal quartz (SiO_2)	3.5	10
Fused silica (SiO_2)	3.6	10
Sapphire (Al_2O_3)	5.0	8
Irtran 5	6.2	12
Lithium fluoride (LiF)	6.2	12
Irtran 1	6.4	12
Calcium fluoride (CaF_2)	7.8	10
Irtran 3	8.7	12
Irtran 2	10.7	12
Arsenic trisulfide glass (As_2S_3)	11.1	5
Irtran 4	15.2	12
Sodium chloride (NaCl)	17	10
Potassium chloride (KCl)	21	10
Irtran 6	23	12
Silver chloride (AgCl)	24	5
Potassium bromide (KBr)	32	4
Thallium bromide-iodide (KRS-5)	38	5
Cesium bromide (CsBr)	40	10
Cesium iodide (CsI)	55	5

NOTE: *Germanium* and *silicon* are not listed because of their low apparent transmittance, due to large surface reflection losses.

2. Refractive Index Tables

Arsenic Trisulfide Glass (As_2S_3)

Synthetic, amorphous.

Specific gravity, 3.198.

Short-wavelength transmission limit, 0.6 μm.

Long-wavelength limit: 50% external transmittance at 11.1 μm for 5-mm thickness.

*External transmittance is the apparent transmittance of a material, uncorrected for reflection losses at the air interfaces.

Arsenic Trisulfide Glass (As_2S_3) (continued)

Wavelength (μm)	Refractive Index (25°C)
0.576960	2.66324
0.6678	2.58083
0.85212	2.50611
1.01398	2.47568
1.52952	2.43803
1.81308	2.42999
1.9701	2.42682
3.4188	2.41374
4.258	2.41013
5.138	2.40671
6.238	2.40221
6.692	2.40035
8.662	2.39035
9.724	2.38342
11.035	2.37365
11.475	2.36944
11.862	2.36577

From Malitson, I. H., Rodney, W. S., and King, T. A., *J. Opt. Soc. Am.*, 48, 633, 1958. With permission.

Barium Fluoride (BaF_2)

Single-crystal, synthetic; cubic, calcium fluoride structure.
Specific gravity, 4.83 at 20°C.
Short-wavelength transmission limit, 0.15 μm.
Long-wavelength limit: 50% external transmittance at 11.5 μm for 9.1-mm thickness.

Wavelength (μm)	Refractive Index (25°C)
0.2536	1.5122
0.28035	1.5067
0.34662	1.4916
0.54607	1.4759
0.767858	1.4708
1.01398	1.4685
1.36728	1.4668
1.52952	1.4662
1.918	1.4649
2.1526	1.4641
2.32542	1.4636
2.576	1.4626
2.673	1.4624
3.2434	1.4602
3.422	1.4594
3.7067	1.4588
5.138	1.4501
5.3034	1.4491
5.343	1.4488
5.549	1.4474
5.7663	1.4459
6.16	1.4436
9.724	1.4209
11.035	1.4142

Adapted from Malitson, I. H., *J. Opt. Soc. Am.*, 54, 628, 1964.

Calcium Fluoride (CaF_2)

Single-crystal, natural or synthetic; cubic structure.
Specific gravity, 3.179 at 25°C.
Short-wavelength transmission limit, 0.13 μm.
Long-wavelength limit: 50% external transmittance at 7.8 μm for 10-mm thickness and at 11.3 μm for 1-mm thickness.

Wavelength (μm)	Computed Index (24°C)
0.6562793	1.43246
0.85212	1.43002
1.01398	1.42879
1.39506	1.42675
1.52952	1.42612
1.81307	1.42478
2.1526	1.42306
2.32542	1.42212
2.4374	1.42147
3.3026	1.41561
3.422	1.41467
3.5070	1.41398
3.7067	1.41229
4.258	1.40713
5.01882	1.39873
5.3034	1.39520
6.0140	1.38539
6.238	1.38200
6.63306	1.37565
6.8559	1.37186
7.268	1.36443
7.4644	1.36070
8.662	1.33500
9.724	1.30756

Adapted from Malitson, I. H., *Appl. Optics*, 2, 1103, 1963.

Cesium Bromide (CsBr)

Single-crystal, synthetic; cubic, cesium chloride structure.
Specific gravity, 4.44.
Short-wavelength transmission limit, 0.22 μm.
Long-wavelength limit: 50% external transmittance at 40 μm for 10-mm thickness.

Wavelength (μm)	Refractive Index (27°C)
0.5	1.70896
1.0	1.67793
2.0	1.67061
3.0	1.66901
4.0	1.66813
5.0	1.66737
6.0	1.66659
7.0	1.66573
8.0	1.66477
9.0	1.66370
10.0	1.66251
11.0	1.66120
12.0	1.65976
13.0	1.65820
14.0	1.65651
15.0	1.65468
16.0	1.65272
17.0	1.65062
18.0	1.64838
19.0	1.64600
20.0	1.64348
21.0	1.64080
22.0	1.63798
23.0	1.63500
24.0	1.63186
25.0	1.62856
26.0	1.62509
27.0	1.62146
28.0	1.61764
29.0	1.61365
30.0	1.60947
31.0	1.60510
32.0	1.60053
33.0	1.59576
34.0	1.59078
35.0	1.58558
36.0	1.58016
37.0	1.57450
38.0	1.56860
39.0	1.56245

Adapted from Rodney, W. S. and Spindler, R. J., *J. Res. NBS,* 51, 123, 1953.

Cesium Iodide (CsI)

Single-crystal, synthetic; cubic, cesium chloride structure.
Specific gravity, 4.526.
Short-wavelength transmission limit, 0.24 μm.
Long-wavelength limit: 50% external transmittance at 55 μm for 5-mm thickness.

Wavelength (μm)	Refractive Index (24°C)
0.500	1.80635
1.00	1.75721
2.00	1.74616
3.00	1.74400
4.00	1.74305
5.00	1.74239
6.00	1.74181
7.00	1.74122
8.00	1.74059
9.00	1.73991
10.0	1.73916
11.0	1.73835
12.0	1.73746
13.0	1.73650
14.0	1.73547
15.0	1.73436
16.0	1.73317
17.0	1.73190
18.0	1.73056
19.0	1.72913
20.0	1.72762
21.0	1.72602
22.0	1.72435
23.0	1.72258
24.0	1.72073
25.0	1.71880
26.0	1.71677
27.0	1.71465
28.0	1.71244
29.0	1.71014
30.0	1.70774
31.0	1.70525
32.0	1.70266
33.0	1.69996
34.0	1.69717
35.0	1.69427
36.0	1.69127
37.0	1.68815
38.0	1.68493
39.0	1.68159
40.0	1.67814
41.0	1.67457
42.0	1.67088

Cesium Iodide (CsI)

Wavelength (μm)	Refractive Index
43.0	1.66707
44.0	1.66312
45.0	1.65905
46.0	1.65485
47.0	1.65051
48.0	1.64602
49.0	1.64139
50.0	1.63662

Computed by Rodney, W. S. from his measurements (see *J. Opt. Soc. Am.*, 45, 987, 1955).

Crystal Quartz (SiO_2)

Natural crystal; hexagonal.
Specific gravity, 2.648 at 25°C.
Short-wavelength transmission limit, 0.12 μm.
Long-wavelength limit: 50% external transmittance for the ordinary ray at 3.5 μm for 10-mm thickness.

Wavelength (μm)	Refractive Index (ordinary ray)	(extra-ordinary ray)
0.185	1.65751	1.68988
0.198	1.65087	1.66394
0.231	1.61395	1.62555
0.340	1.56747	1.57737
0.394	1.55846	1.56805
0.434	1.55396	1.56339
0.508	1.54822	1.55746
0.5893	1.54424	1.55335
0.768	1.53903	1.54794
0.8325	1.53773	1.54661
0.9914	1.53514	1.54392
1.1592	1.53283	1.54152
1.3070	1.53090	1.53951
1.3958	1.52977	1.53832
1.4792	1.52865	1.53716
1.5415	1.52781	1.53630
1.6815	1.52583	1.53422
1.7614	1.52468	1.53301
1.9457	1.52184	1.53004
2.0531	1.52005	1.52823
2.30	1.51561	
2.60	1.50986	
3.00	1.49953	
3.50	1.48451	
4.00	1.46617	
4.20	1.4569	
5.00	1.417	
6.45	1.274	
7.0	1.167	

From Micheli, F. J., *Ann. Physik,* 4, 7, 1902. With permission.

Germanium (Ge)

Single-crystal, synthetic; cubic, diamond structure. Also used in polycrystal form.
Specific gravity, 5.327 at 25°C.
Short-wavelength transmission limit, 1.8 μm.
Long-wavelength limit: transmits well to beyond 15 μm, with absorption bands at 23 μm and 28 μm; transmission recovers partially at about 35 μm and continues to beyond 50 μm into the far infrared to 400 μm (A. Mitsuishi, et al., *Japan. J. Appl. Phys.,* 4 (Suppl. 1), 581, 1965).

Wavelength (μm)	Refractive Index (27°C) Single-crystal	Polycrystal
2.0581	4.1016	4.1018
2.1526	4.0919	4.0919
2.3126	4.0786	4.0785
2.4374	4.0708	4.0709
2.577	4.0609	4.0608
2.7144	4.0552	4.0554
2.998	4.0452	4.0452
3.3033	4.0369	4.0372
3.4188	4.0334	4.0339
4.258	4.0216	4.0217
4.866	4.0170	4.0167
6.238	4.0094	4.0095
8.66	4.0043	4.0043
9.72	4.0034	4.0033
11.04	4.0026	4.0025
12.20	4.0023	4.0020
13.02	4.0021	4.0018

Adapted from Salzberg, C. D. and Villa, J. J., *J. Opt. Soc. Am.,* 48, 579, 1958. Resistivity is about 50 ohm-cm.

Irtran 1

Microcrystalline aggregate of magnesium fluoride (MgF_2).
Specific gravity, 3.18.
Short-wavelength transmission limit, 1.0 μm.
Long-wavelength limit: 50% external transmittance at 6.4 μm for 12-mm thickness and at 7.7 μm for 1-mm thickness.

Irtran 1 (continued)

Wavelength (μm)	Refractive Index					
	Irtan* 1	Irtran* 2	Irtran* 3	Irtran* 4	Irtran* 5	Irtran* 6
1.0000	1.3778	2.2907	1.4289	2.485	1.7227	2.838
1.2500	1.3763	2.2777	1.4275	2.466	1.7188	2.773
1.5000	1.3749	2.2706	1.4263	2.456	1.7156	2.742
1.7500	1.3735	2.2662	1.4251	2.450	1.7123	2.725
2.0000	1.3720	2.2631	1.4239	2.447	1.7089	2.714
2.2500	1.3702	2.2608	1.4226	2.444	1.7052	2.707
2.5000	1.3683	2.2589	1.4211	2.442	1.7012	2.702
2.7500	1.3663	2.2573	1.4196	2.441	1.6968	2.698
3.0000	1.3640	2.2558	1.4179	2.440	1.6920	2.695
3.2500	1.3614	2.2544	1.4161	2.438	1.6868	2.693
3.5000	1.3587	2.2531	1.4141	2.437	1.6811	2.691
3.7500	1.3558	2.2518	1.4120	2.436	1.6750	2.689
4.0000	1.3526	2.2504	1.4097	2.435	1.6684	2.688
4.2500	1.3492	2.2491	1.4072	2.434	1.6612	2.687
4.5000	1.3455	2.2477	1.4047	2.433	1.6536	2.686
4.7500	1.3416	2.2462	1.4019	2.433	1.6455	2.685
5.0000	1.3374	2.2447	1.3990	2.432	1.6368	2.684
5.2500	1.3329	2.2432	1.3959	2.431	1.6275	2.683
5.5000	1.3282	2.2416	1.3926	2.430	1.6177	2.683
5.7500	1.3232	2.2399	1.3892	2.429	1.6072	2.682
6.0000	1.3179	2.2381	1.3856	2.428	1.5962	2.681
6.2500	1.3122	2.2363	1.3818	2.426	1.5845	2.681
6.5000	1.3063	2.2344	1.3778	2.425	1.5721	2.680
6.7500	1.3000	2.2324	1.3737	2.424	1.5590	2.680
7.0000	1.2934	2.2304	1.3693	2.423	1.5452	2.679
7.2500	1.2865	2.2282	1.3648	2.422	1.5307	2.678
7.5000	1.2792	2.2260	1.3600	2.421	1.5154	2.678
7.7500	1.2715	2.2237	1.3550	2.419	1.4993	2.677
8.0000	1.2634	2.2213	1.3498	2.418	1.4824	2.677
8.2500	1.2549	2.2188	1.3445	2.417	1.4646	2.676
8.5000	1.2460	2.2162	1.3388	2.416	1.4460	2.675
8.7500	1.2367	2.2135	1.3330	2.415	1.4265	2.675
9.0000	1.2269	2.2107	1.3269	2.413	1.4060	2.674
9.2500		2.2078	1.3206	2.411		2.674
9.5000		2.2048	1.3141	2.410		2.673
9.7500		2.2018	1.3073	2.409		2.672
10.0000		2.1986	1.3002	2.407		2.672
11.0000		2.1846	1.2694	2.401		2.669
12.0000		2.1688		2.394		2.666
13.0000		2.1508		2.386		2.663
14.0000				2.378		2.660
15.0000				2.370		2.657
16.0000				2.361		2.655
17.0000				2.352		
18.0000				2.343		
19.0000				2.333		
20.0000				2.323		

From *Kodak Pamphlet U-71*, 1972 Revision.

Index of refraction values were experimentally determined at selected wavelengths between 1 and 10 μm. Coefficients of an interpolation formula were established and reduced by least-square methods, and the values computed. All values beyond 10 μm are extrapolated.

**Irtran* is a trade name of the Eastman Kodak Co. These materials are also available under their generic names from other suppliers. Certain of their properties may vary slightly, depending on the conditions of manufacture.

Irtran 2

Microcrystalline aggregate of zinc sulfide (ZnS).
Specific gravity, 4.09.
Short-wavelength transmission limit, 0.7 μm.
Long-wavelength limit: 50% external transmittance at 10.7 μm for 12-mm thickness and at 14.4 μm for 1-mm thickness.

For Refractive Index Data See Above Table.

Irtran 3

Microcrystalline aggregate of calcium fluoride (CaF_2).
Specific gravity, 3.18.
Short-wavelength transmission limit, 0.4 μm.
Long-wavelength limit: 50% external transmittance at 8.7 μm for 12-mm thickness and at 11.2 μm for 1-mm thickness.

For Refractive Index Data See Above Table.

Irtran 4

Microcrystalline aggregate of zinc selenide (ZnSe).
Specific gravity, 5.27.
Short-wavelength transmission limit, 0.5 μm.
Long-wavelength limit: 50% external transmittance at 15.2 μm for 12-mm thickness and at 20.6 μm for 1-mm thickness.

For Refractive Index Data See Above Table.

Irtran 5

Microcrystalline aggregate of magnesium oxide (MgO).
Specific gravity, 3.58.
Short-wavelength transmission limit, 0.4 μm.
Long-wavelength limit: 50% external transmittance at 6.2 μm for 12-mm thickness and at 8.7 μm for 1-mm thickness.

For Refractive Index Data See Above Table.

Irtran 6

Microcrystalline aggregate of cadmium telluride (CdTe).
Specific gravity, 5.85.
Short-wavelength transmission limit, 0.8 μm.
Long-wavelength limit: 50% external transmittance at 23.2 μm for 6-mm thickness and at 29.5 μm for 1-mm thickness.

For Refractive Index Data See Above Table.

Lithium Fluoride (LiF)

Single-crystal, synthetic; cubic, sodium chloride structure.
Specific gravity, 2.639 at 25°C.
Short-wavelength transmission limit, 0.12 μm.
Long-wavelength limit: 50% external transmittance at 6.2 μm for 12-mm thickness and at 8.0 μm for 1-mm thickness.

Wavelength (μm)	Refractive Index
0.1935	1.4450
0.2026	1.4390
0.2100	1.4346
0.302	1.40818
0.4861	1.39480
0.80	1.38896
1.00	1.38711
1.50	1.38320
2.00	1.37875
2.50	1.37327
3.00	1.36660
3.50	1.35868
4.00	1.34942
4.50	1.33875
5.00	1.32661
5.50	1.31287
6.00	1.29745
6.91	1.260
7.53	1.239
8.05	1.215
8.60	1.190
9.18	1.155
9.79	1.109

Data at a temperature of 23.6°C for 0.50 to 6.0 μm from Tilton, L. W. and Plyler, E. K., *J. Res. NBS,* 47, 25, 1951; at 18°C for 6.91 to 9.79 μm from Hohls, H. W., *Ann. Physik,* 29, 433, 1937. With permission.

Potassium Bromide (KBr)

Single-crystal, synthetic; cubic, sodium chloride structure.
Specific gravity, 2.75 at 23°C.
Short-wavelength transmission limit, 0.23 μm
Long-wavelength limit: 50% external transmittance at 32 μm for 4-mm thickness.

Wavelength (μm)	Refractive Index (22°C)
0.404656	1.589752
0.508582	1.568475
0.643847	1.555858
0.706520	1.552447
1.01398	1.54408
1.36728	1.54061
1.7012	1.53901
2.44	1.53733
2.73	1.53693
3.419	1.53612
4.258	1.53523
6.238	1.53288
6.692	1.53225
8.662	1.52903
9.724	1.52695
11.035	1.52404
11.862	1.52200
14.29	1.51505
14.98	1.51280
17.40	1.50390
18.16	1.50076
19.01	1.49703
19.91	1.49288
21.18	1.48655
21.83	1.48311
23.86	1.47140
25.14	1.46324

From Stephens, R. E., Plyler, E. K., Rodney, W. S., and Spindler, R. J., *J. Opt. Soc. Am.*, 43, 111–112, 1953.

Wavelength (μm)	Refractive Index
0.185409	1.82710
0.200090	1.71870
0.250833	1.58979
0.308227	1.54136
0.410185	1.50907
0.508606	1.49620
0.62784	1.48847
0.76824	1.48377
0.88398	1.481422
0.98220	1.480084
1.1786	1.478311
1.7680	1.475890
2.3573	1.474751
2.9466	1.473834
3.5359	1.473049
4.7146	1.471122
5.3039	1.470013
5.8932	1.468804
8.2505	1.462726
8.8398	1.460858
10.0184	1.45672
11.786	1.44919
12.965	1.44346
14.144	1.43722
15.912	1.42617
17.680	1.41403
18.2	1.409
18.8	1.401
19.7	1.398
20.4	1.389
21.1	1.379
22.2	1.374
23.1	1.363
24.1	1.352
24.9	1.336
25.7	1.317
26.7	1.300
27.2	1.275
28.2	1.254
28.8	1.226

Data at a temperature of 15°C for 0.58932 to 17.680 μm from Paschen, F., *Ann. Physik,* 26, 120, 1908; for 18.2 to 28.8 μm from Hohls, H. W., *Ann. Physik,* 29, 433, 1937. With permission.

Potassium Chloride (KCl)

Single-crystal, synthetic; cubic, sodium chloride structure.
Specific gravity, 1.9865 at 28°C.
Short-wavelength transmission limit, 0.21 μm.
Long-wavelength limit: 50% external transmittance at 21 μm for 10-mm thickness and at 23 μm for 5.3-mm thickness.

Sapphire (Al_2O_3)

Synthetic single-crystal of corundum, pure Al_2O_3; hexagonal.
Specific gravity, 3.98.
Short-wavelength transmission limit, 0.17 μm.
Long-wavelength limit: 50% external transmittance at 5.0 μm for 8-mm thickness and at 6.6 μm for 0.5-mm thickness.

Sapphire (Al_2O_3) (continued)

Wavelength (μm)	Refractive Index (ordinary ray)
0.26520	1.83360
0.30215	1.81351
0.404656	1.78582
0.546071	1.77078
0.64385	1.76547
0.706519	1.76303
0.85212	1.75885
1.01398	1.75547
1.12866	1.75339
1.36728	1.74936
1.39506	1.74888
1.52952	1.74660
1.6932	1.74368
1.70913	1.74340
1.81307	1.74144
1.9701	1.73833
2.1526	1.73444
2.24929	1.73231
2.32542	1.73057
2.4374	1.72783
3.2439	1.70437
3.2668	1.70356
3.3026	1.70231
3.3303	1.70140
3.422	1.69818
3.5070	1.69504
3.7067	1.68746
4.2553	1.66371
4.954	1.62665
5.1456	1.61514
5.349	1.60202
5.419	1.59735
5.577	1.58638

Adapted from Malitson, I. H., *J. Opt. Soc. Am.*, 52, 1377, 1962.

Fused Silica (SiO_2)

Amorphous.
Specific gravity, 2.202.
Short-wavelength transmission limit, 0.2 μm.
Long-wavelength limit: 50% external transmittance at 3.6 μm for 10-mm thickness, and at 3.9 μm for 2.85-mm thickness.

Wavelength (μm)	Computed Index (20°C)
0.643847	1.456704
0.894350	1.451835
1.01398	1.450242
1.12866	1.448869
1.3622	1.446212
1.39506	1.445836
1.4695	1.444975
1.52952	1.444268
1.6606	1.442670
1.681	1.442414
1.6932	1.442260
1.70913	1.442057
1.81307	1.440699
1.97009	1.438519
2.0581	1.437224
2.1526	1.435769
2.32542	1.432928
2.4374	1.430954
3.2439	1.413118
3.2668	1.412505
3.3026	1.411535
3.422	1.408180
3.5070	1.405676
3.5564	1.404174
3.7067	1.399389

Adapted from Malitson, I. H., *J. Opt. Soc. Am.*, 55, 1205, 1965.

Silicon (Si)

Single-crystal, synthetic; cubic, diamond structure.
Specific gravity, 2.329 at 25°C.
Short-wavelength transmission limit, 1.2 μm.
Long-wavelength limit: High purity silicon can be used from 1.2 μm to about 15 μm; a deep absorption band occurs at about 9 μm and is followed by a region of lower transmission. The transmission recovers and is good from about 20 μm to 50 μm; it has been measured into the far infrared to 250 μm (A. Mitsuishi et al., *Japan. J. Appl. Phys.*, 4 (Suppl. 1), 581, 1965.

Wavelength (μm)	Refractive Index (26°C)
1.3570	3.4975
1.3673	3.4962
1.3951	3.4929
1.5295	3.4795
1.6606	3.4696
1.7092	3.4664
1.8131	3.4608
1.9701	3.4537
2.1526	3.4476
2.3254	3.4430
2.4373	3.4408
2.7144	3.4358
3.00	3.4320
3.3033	3.4297

Silicon (Si) (continued)

Wavelength (μm)	Refractive Index
3.4188	3.4286
3.50	3.4284
4.00	3.4255
4.258	3.4242
4.50	3.4236
5.00	3.4223
5.50	3.4213
6.00	3.4202
6.50	3.4195
7.00	3.4189
7.50	3.4186
8.00	3.4184
8.50	3.4182
10.00	3.4179
10.50	3.4178
11.04	3.4176

From Salzberg, C. D. and Villa, J. J., *J. Opt. Soc. Am.*, 47, 244, 1957. With permission.

Silver Chloride (AgCl)

Single-crystal, synthetic; cubic, sodium chloride structure.
Specific gravity, 5.589 at 0°C.
Short-wavelength transmission limit, 0.4 μm.
Long-wavelength limit: 50% external transmittance at 24 μm for 5-mm thickness and at 30 μm for 0.5-mm thickness.

Wavelength (μm)	Refractive Index (23.9°)
0.5	2.09648
0.6	2.06385
0.7	2.04590
0.8	2.03485
0.9	2.02752
1.0	2.02239
1.1	2.01865
1.2	2.01582
1.3	2.01363
1.4	2.01189
1.5	2.01047
1.6	2.00931
1.7	2.00833
1.8	2.00750
1.9	2.00678
2.0	2.00615
2.1	2.00559
2.2	2.00510
2.3	2.00465
2.4	2.00424
2.5	2.00386
2.6	2.00351
2.7	2.00318
2.8	2.00287
2.9	2.00258
3.0	2.00230
3.1	2.00203
3.2	2.00177
3.3	2.00151
3.4	2.00126
3.5	2.00102
3.6	2.00078
3.7	2.00054
3.8	2.00030
3.9	2.00007
4.0	1.99983
4.5	1.99866
5.0	1.99745
5.5	1.99618
6.0	1.99483
6.5	1.99339
7.0	1.99185
7.5	1.99021
8.0	1.99847
8.5	1.98661
9.0	1.98464
9.5	1.98255
10.0	1.98034
10.5	1.97801
11.0	1.97556
11.5	1.97297
12.0	1.97026
12.5	1.96742
13.0	1.96444
13.5	1.96133
14.0	1.95807
14.5	1.95467
15.0	1.95113
15.5	1.94743
16.0	1.94358
16.5	1.93958
17.0	1.93542
17.5	1.93109
18.0	1.92660
18.5	1.92194
19.0	1.91710
19.5	1.91208
20.0	1.90688
20.5	1.90149

From Tilton, L. W., Plyler, E. K., and Stephens, R. E., *J. Opt. Soc. Am.*, 40, 540, 1950. With permission.

Sodium Chloride (NaCl)

Single-crystal, synthetic; simple cubic.
Specific gravity, 2.164 at 20°C.
Short-wavelength transmission limit, 0.21 μm.
Long-wavelength limit: 50% external transmittance at 17 μm for 10-mm thickness and at 22 μm for 1-mm thickness.

Sodium Chloride (NaCl) (continued)

Wavelength (μm)	Refractive Index (20°)
0.589	1.54427
0.6400	1.54141
0.7604	1.53682
0.8835	1.55395
0.9033	1.53361
1.0084	1.53206
1.1058	1.53098
1.2016	1.53014
1.3126	1.52937
1.4874	1.52845
1.5552	1.52815
1.6368	1.52781
1.7670	1.52736
2.0736	1.52649
2.1824	1.52621
2.2464	1.52606
2.3560	1.52579
2.6505	1.52512
2.9466	1.52466
3.2736	1.52371
3.5359	1.52312
3.6288	1.52286
3.8192	1.52238
4.1230	1.52156
4.7120	1.51979
5.0092	1.51883
5.3009	1.51790
5.8932	1.51593
6.4825	1.51347
6.80	1.51200
7.0718	1.51093
7.22	1.51020
7.59	1.50850
7.6611	1.50822
7.9558	1.50665
8.04	1.5064
8.8398	1.50192
9.00	1.50100
9.50	1.49980
10.0184	1.49462
11.7864	1.48171
12.50	1.47568
12.9650	1.47160
13.50	1.4666
14.1436	1.46044
14.7330	1.45427
15.3223	1.44743
15.9116	1.44090
17.93	1.4149
20.57	1.3735
22.3	1.3403

From Coblentz, W. W., *J. Opt. Soc. Am.*, 4, 443, 1920. With permission.

Thallium Bromide-Iodide (KRS-5)

Synthetic mixed crystal of thallium bromide and thallium iodide; cubic.
Specific gravity, 7.371 at 16°C.
Short-wavelength transmission limit, 0.5 μm.
Long-wavelength limit: 50% external transmittance at 38 μm for 5.15-mm thickness and at 47 μm for 2-mm thickness.

Wavelength (μm)	Refractive Index (25°C)
0.540	2.68059
1.00	2.44620
1.50	2.40774
2.00	2.39498
3.00	2.38574
4.00	2.38204
5.00	2.37979
6.00	2.37797
7.00	2.37627
8.00	2.37452
9.00	2.37267
10.0	2.37069
11.0	2.36854
12.0	2.36622
13.0	2.36371
14.0	2.36101
15.0	2.35812
16.0	2.35502
17.0	2.35173
18.0	2.34822
19.0	2.34451
20.0	2.34058
21.0	2.33643
22.0	2.33206
23.0	2.32746
24.0	2.32264
25.0	2.31758
26.0	2.31229
27.0	2.30676
28.0	2.30098
29.0	2.29495
30.0	2.28867
31.0	2.28212
32.0	2.27531
33.0	2.26823
34.0	2.26087
35.0	2.25322
36.0	2.24528
37.0	2.23705
38.0	2.22850
39.0	2.21965
40.0	2.21047

Adapted from Tilton, L. W., Plyler, E. K., and Stephens, R. E., *J. Res. NBS*, 43, 81, 1949.

3. Solubility, in Grams per 100 Grams of Water

Material	Solubility	Temperature, °C
Arsenic trisulfide glass (As_2S_3)	insoluble*	
Crystal quartz (SiO_2)	insoluble	
Fused silica (SiO_2)	insoluble	
Germanium (Ge)	insoluble	
Irtran 2	insoluble	
Irtran 4	insoluble	
Irtran 5	insoluble	
Irtran 6	insoluble	
Sapphire (Al_2O_3)	insoluble	
Silicon (Si)	insoluble	
Silver chloride (AgCl)	insoluble	
Calcium fluoride (CaF_2)	0.0017	26
Irtran 3	0.0017	
Irtran 1	0.0076	
Thallium bromide-iodide (KRS-5)	0.05	room
Barium fluoride (BaF_2)	0.17	10
Lithium fluoride (LiF)	0.27	18
Potassium chloride (KCl)	34.7	20
Sodium chloride (NaCl)	35.7	0
Cesium iodide (CsI)	44.0	0
Potassium bromide (KBr)	53.5	0
Cesium bromide (CsBr)	124.3	25

*"Insoluble" means less than 10^{-3} gm/100 gm of water at room temperature.

4. Specific Heat (With Optional Units of Calories per Gram per C°)

Material	Specific Heat	Temperature, °C
Irtran 6	0.045	25
Cesium iodide (CsI)	0.048	20
Cesium bromide (CsBr)	0.063	20
Germanium (Ge)	0.077	25
Irtran 4	0.08	25
Silver chloride (AgCl)	0.0848	0
Potassium bromide (KBr)	0.104	0
Irtran 2	0.12	0
Potassium chloride (KCl)	0.162	0
Silicon (Si)	0.168	25
Sapphire (Al_2O_3)	0.18	25
Crystal quartz (SiO_2)	0.188	12 to 100
Calcium fluoride (CaF_2)	0.204	0
Sodium chloride (NaCl)	0.204	0
Irtran 3	0.21	40
Irtran 5	0.21	0
Fused silica (SiO_2)	0.22	
Irtran 1	0.23	25
Lithium fluoride (LiF)	0.373	10

5. Hardness, in Knoop Number Unless Otherwise Specified

Material	Hardness	Remarks
Potassium bromide (KBr)	5.9	200-g indenter load
Potassium chloride (KCl)	7.0	200-g indenter load
Silver chloride (AgCl)	9.5	200-g indenter load
Sodium chloride (NaCl)	15.2	200-g indenter load
Cesium bromide (CsBr)	19.5	200-g indenter load
Thallium bromide-iodide (KRS-5)	40.2	200-g indenter load
Irtran 6	45	
Barium fluoride (BaF_2)	82	500-g indenter load
Arsenic trisulfide glass (As_2S_3)	109	100-g indenter load
Lithium fluoride (LiF)	110	600-g indenter load
Irtran 4	150	
Calcium fluoride (CaF_2)	158	500-g indenter load
Irtran 3	200	
Irtran 2	355	
Irtran 1	575	(6.0 Moh)
Germanium (Ge)	6.25	Moh number
Irtran 5	640	(6.5 Moh)
Crystal quartz (SiO_2)	741	500-g indenter load
Silicon (Si)	1150	(7 Moh)
Sapphire (Al_2O_3)	1370	1000-g indenter load

6. Melting or Softening Temperature

Material	Temperature, °C
Arsenic trisulfide glass (As_2S_3)	210*
Thallium bromide-iodide (KRS-5)	414.5
Silver chloride (AgCl)	457.7
Cesium iodide (CsI)	621
Cesium bromide (CsBr)	636
Potassium bromide (KBr)	730
Potassium chloride (KCl)	776
Sodium chloride (NaCl)	801
Lithium fluoride (LiF)	870
Germanium (Ge)	936
Irtran 6	1090
Irtran 1	1255
Barium fluoride (BaF_2)	1280
Calcium fluoride (CaF_2)	1360
Irtran 3	1360
Silicon (Si)	1420
Irtran 4	1520
Crystal quartz (SiO_2)	1610
Fused silica (SiO_2)	1710*
Irtran 2	1830
Sapphire (Al_2O_3)	2030
Irtran 5	2800

*Softening temperature.

7. Linear Coefficient of Thermal Expansion in Units of 10^{-6} $(C°)^{-1}$

Material	Expansion Coefficient	Temperature Range, °C
Fused silica (SiO_2)	0.5	20 to 900
Silicon (Si)	4.15	10 to 50
Germanium (Ge)	5.5	25
Irtran 6	5.7	25 to 60
Irtran 2	6.7	25 to 60
Sapphire (Al_2O_3)	6.7 (parallel to c-axis)	50
Irtran 4	7.5	25 to 60
Crystal quartz (SiO_2)	8.0 (parallel to c-axis)	0 to 80
Irtran 1	11.5	25 to 60
Irtran 5	11.5	25 to 60
Irtran 3	19.9	25 to 60
Arsenic trisulfide glass (As_2S_3)	24.6	33 to 165
Silver chloride (AgCl)	30	20 to 60
Lithium fluoride (LiF)	37	0 to 100
Potassium bromide (KBr)	43	20 to 60
Sodium chloride (NaCl)	44	-50 to 200
Cesium bromide (CsBr)	47.9	20 to 50
Cesium iodide (CsI)	50	25 to 50
Thallium bromide-iodide (KRS-5)	58	20 to 100

8. Thermal Conductivity, in Units of 10^{-4} Cal (cm sec $C°)^{-1}$

Material	Thermal Conductivity	Temperature, °C
Arsenic trisulfide glass (As_2S_3)	4.0	40
Thallium bromide-iodide (KRS-5)	13	20
Cesium bromide (CsBr)	23	25
Cesium iodide (CsI)	27	25
Silver chloride (AgCl)	27.5	22
Fused silica (SiO_2)	28.2	41
Irtran 6	98	20
Potassium bromide (KBr)	115	46
Sodium chloride (NaCl)	155	16
Potassium chloride (KCl)	156	42
Irtran 3	190	80
Crystal quartz (SiO_2)	255 (parallel to c-axis)	50
Calcium fluoride (CaF_2)	232	36
Lithium fluoride (LiF)	270	41
Barium fluoride (BaF_2)	280	13
Irtran 4	310	54
Irtran 1	350	56
Irtran 2	370	54
Sapphire (Al_2O_3)	600 (parallel to c-axis)	26
Irtran 5	1040	36
Germanium (Ge)	1400 (n-type)	20
Silicon (Si)	3090 (p-type)	40

9. Far Infrared Window Materials – External Transmittance*

Material (thickness, mm.)	Wavenumber 200	150	100	50	33	Ref.
Germanium (1.6)	25	30	30	45	25	a.
Irtran 1 (2)	–	–	3	27	48	b.
Irtran 2 (2)	–	–	4	32	40	b.
Irtran 3 (2)	–	–	<1	4	23	b.
Irtran 4 (2)	–	–	<1	<1	<1	b.
Irtran 5 (2)	–	–	5	49	55	
Kel-F (1)	<1	55	60	60	60	a.
Polyethylene, high density[1] (3.9)	50	60	70	80	80	c.
Quartz, crystalline[2] (0.4)	60	60	70	70	70	c.
Silicon (1)	50	50	50	50	50	c.
Teflon (1.6)	<1	45	65	–	–	a.

[1] Absorption band at 72 cm^{-1} shifts to 78 cm^{-1} and becomes more intense upon cooling to 164 K.

[2] Absorption band at 128 cm^{-1}. Also may show fringe pattern.

REFERENCES

a. McCarthy, D. E., *Appl. Opt.*, 10, 2539, 1971.
b. McCarthy, D. E., *Appl. Opt.*, 5, 472, 1966.
c. Fateley, W. G., Witkowski, R. E., and Carlson, G. L., *Appl. Spectrosc.*, 20, 190, 1966.

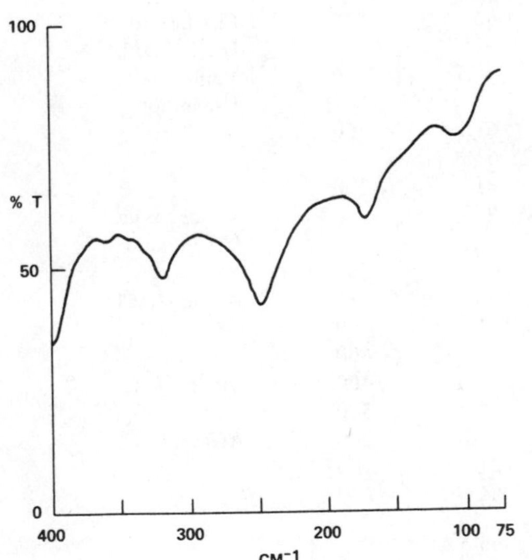

FIGURE 1. External transmittance of 1.5 mm polypropylene.

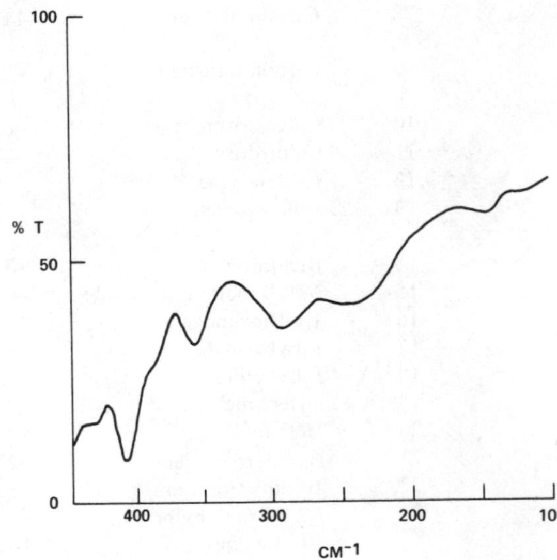

FIGURE 2. External transmittance of 3.2 mm TPX methylpentene polymer.

*Contributed by Dr. Gerald L. Carlson of Mellon Institute of Science, Carnegie-Mellon University, Pittsburgh.

B. Properties of Common Solvents

Only a few common solvents transmit infrared radiation over a wide enough wavelength span to be generally useful. The solvent pair CCl_4-CS_2 forms a useful combination that covers the entire range with only minor interferences. Both these materials have toxic vapors, however, and should be handled only in a chemical fume hood. For scans over more limited wavelength regions, other more polar solvents may be employed. As a rule of thumb, the solvent should have a transmission at least 50%; otherwise, too much energy is lost, and the spectrometer will not respond properly. For quantitative analysis, it is also important to match as closely as possible the refractive index of the solvent with the cell window material; otherwise, interference fringes may appear and will be superimposed on the spectrum.

Spectral traces are shown for the solvents listed in the following table. The samples are all approximately 0.1 mm in thickness. These spectra were obtained on a Perkin-Elmer Model 521, using a NaCl cell from 3800 to 800 cm^{-1} and a CsBr cell from 800 to 250 cm^{-1}. Grating changes occur at 2000 and 630 cm^{-1}. The spectra are meant to show which regions of the spectrum are reasonably clear and are not intended as model spectra of ultra-pure materials. Thus, some minor impurity bands may be seen. It is recommended that the user check his own solvent over the region of interest to confirm its suitability; many solvents contain inhibitors or water, which may interfere with their intended use.

Curve No.	Material	M.P.	B.P.	Maximum Allowable Exposure ppm in Air	Remarks
1	Acetone	−95.3	56.2	1000	Fire hazard.
2	Acetone-d_6				
3	Acetonitrile	−45.7	81.6	20	
4	Benzene	5.5	80.1	10	Vapor toxic. Use in hood.
5	Benzene-d_6				
6	Bromoform	8.3	149.5	0.5	Vapor toxic. Use in hood.
7	*t*-Butanol	25.5	82.2	100	
8	Carbon disulfide	−112	45	20	Fire hazard. Use in hood.
9	Carbon tetrachloride	−23.0	76.7	10	Vapor toxic. Use in hood.
10	Chloroform	−63.5	61.2	50	
11	Chloroform-d_1	−64.1	61.3	–	
12	Cyclohexane	6.5	81	300	
13	Dibromomethane	−52	97	–	Vapor toxic. Use in hood.
14	Dichloromethane	−97	40	500	
15	*N,N*-Dimethylformamide	−61	153	10	Affects NaCl.
16	1,4-Dioxane	11.8	101	100	
17	Ethyl acetate	−83.6	77.1	400	
18	Ethyl ether	−116.2	34.6	400	Fire hazard.
19	*n*-Heptane	−91	98.4	500	
20	Methanol	−93.9	65.0	200	Affects NaCl.
21	Perchloroethylene	−22	121	100	
22	Tetrahydrofuran	−65	64	200	
23	2,2,4-Trimethylpentane (isooctane)	−107	99.2	–	

Refractive Indices of Liquid Benzene at 20°C

λ(μm)	n	λ(μm)	n
2.01	1.479	6.06	1.471
2.09	1.480	6.15	1.468
2.12	1.479	6.24	1.470
2.17	1.477	6.36	1.470
2.19	1.477	6.45	1.464
2.31	1.476	6.90	1.489
2.39	1.475	6.99	1.481
2.42	1.475	7.09	1.476
2.49	1.478	7.25	1.481
2.59	1.478	7.36	1.475
2.68	1.477	7.50	1.473
2.78	1.477	7.57	1.471
2.90	1.476	7.64	1.474
2.95	1.475	7.80	1.472
3.02	1.475	7.94	1.468
3.04	1.475	8.11	1.469
3.09	1.474	8.28	1.466
3.11	1.473	8.34	1.462
3.13	1.472	8.38	1.457
3.16	1.472	8.78	1.472
3.18	1.469	8.86	1.470
3.20	1.466	9.06	1.467
3.33	1.498	9.15	1.464
3.34	1.492	9.25	1.462
3.36	1.489	9.32	1.455
3.38	1.484	9.40	1.452
3.41	1.484	9.42	1.452
3.44	1.482	9.47	1.441
3.46	1.479	10.32	1.473
3.50	1.481	10.47	1.472
3.53	1.480	10.59	1.468
3.62	1.478	10.72	1.466
3.72	1.477	10.84	1.465
3.80	1.477	10.99	1.461
3.91	1.476	11.15	1.461
4.03	1.475	11.29	1.457
4.16	1.475	11.43	1.454
4.26	1.477	11.57	1.449
4.35	1.476	12.00	1.456
4.50	1.475	12.14	1.450
4.56	1.476	12.30	1.445
4.67	1.475	12.46	1.442
4.78	1.474	12.57	1.436
4.90	1.473	12.61	1.434
4.96	1.471	12.75	1.426
5.02	1.468	13.02	1.430
5.18	1.476	13.14	1.419
5.24	1.473	13.29	1.408
5.31	1.471	13.33	1.405
5.37	1.470	13.44	1.399
5.43	1.464	13.71	1.376
5.47	1.453	14.00	1.328[a]
5.58	1.484	14.20	1.272[a]
5.63	1.476	14.40	1.166[a]
5.72	1.477	14.56	1.014[a]
5.79	1.473	14.60	0.984[a]
5.88	1.472	14.70	1.120[a]
5.96	1.469	14.77	1.503[a]

Refractive Indices of Liquid Benzene at 20°C (continued)

λ(μm)	n	λ(μm)	n
14.80	1.752[a]	16.85	1.556
14.84	1.930[a]	17.14	1.550
14.90	2.012[a]	17.46	1.544
15.00	1.928[a]	17.78	1.539
15.06	1.868[a]	18.12	1.534
15.20	1.770[a]	18.46	1.527
15.40	1.691[a]	18.89	1.525
15.60	1.646[a]	19.27	1.520
16.00	1.598[a]	19.73	1.518
16.32	1.575	20.23	1.515
16.61	1.566	20.68	1.512

[a]Calculated points.

Accuracy estimated to be ± 0.003, 2–16 μm; ± 0.005, 16–20 μm.

REFERENCE: Schatz, P. N., *J. Chem. Phys.*, 32, 894, 1960.

Refractive Indices of Liquid CS_2

λ(μm)	n	λ(μm)	n
2	1.582	16	1.610
3	1.575	17	1.608
4	1.566	18	1.607
5	1.548	19	1.605
5.5	1.524	20	1.602
6		21	1.597
7		22	1.594
7.5	1.685	23	1.586
8	1.657	24	1.573
9	1.636	25	
10	1.628	26	
11	1.622	27.6	1.650
12	1.618	28	
13	1.615	29.3	1.634
14	1.614	30	
15	1.612	31.7	1.628

REFERENCE: Wilhelmi, B., *Ann. Phys. Leipzig,* 19, 244, 1967.

Refractive Indices of Carbon Tetrachloride (25 ± 1)°C

λ(μm)	n	λ(μm)	n
2.051	1.444	3.717	1.4425
2.191	1.443	3.582	1.439
2.171	1.445	3.792	1.438
2.353	1.444	4.034	1.438
2.443	1.444	4.369	1.439
2.534	1.441	4.689	1.439
2.639	1.441	5.06	1.438
2.755	1.442	5.11	1.4305
2.877	1.441	5.56	1.431
3.163	1.442	5.85	1.426
3.330	1.443	6.10	1.431
3.513	1.443	6.51	1.437

Refractive Indices of Carbon Tetrachloride (25 ± 1)°C (continued)

λ(μm)	n	λ(μm)	n
6.89	1.430	16.49	1.563
7.03	1.428	17.16	1.549
7.34	1.425	17.47	1.535
7.51	1.424	18.07	1.533
7.68	1.421	18.67	1.529
7.86	1.419	19.35	1.525
8.07	1.422	20.13	1.525
8.28	1.420	20.85	1.517
8.48	1.417	21.67	1.511
8.69	1.413	24.0	1.504
8.91	1.408	25.0	1.497
9.16	1.405	26.0	1.492
9.41	1.401	27.0	1.491
9.62	1.394	28.0	1.491
9.93	1.389	29.0	1.490
10.19	1.380	30.0	1.486
10.46	1.369	30.8	1.491
10.73	1.356	32.0	1.486
10.99	1.339	34.0	1.496
11.21	1.316	35.0	1.494
11.45	1.292	36.0	1.492
11.81	1.226	37.0	1.491
11.95	1.187	38.0	1.490
12.04	1.141	39.0	1.490
14.09	1.717	40.0	1.489
14.29	1.677	42.0	1.489
14.57	1.643	43.0	1.488
14.93	1.618	47.0	≈1.490
15.34	1.593	48.0	≈1.489
15.86	1.575		

Accuracy estimated to be ± 0.003, 2–20 μm; ± 0.005, 20–50 μm.

REFERENCE: Ralajczak, H., *Trans. Faraday Soc.*, 61, 2603, 1965.

Refractive Indices of Cyclohexane at 21.5°

λ (μm)	n
2.0	1.41
2.5	1.41
3.0	1.40
4.0	1.42
5.0	1.41
6.0	1.41

REFERENCE: Kagarise, R. E., *J. Opt. Soc. Am.*, 50, 36, 1960.

Refractive Indices of Dibromomethane (corrected to 20°C)

λ (μm)*	n	λ(μm)*	n
2.020	1.521	6.534	1.509
2.110	1.521	6.799	1.508
2.210	1.521	7.088	1.506
2.303	1.521	7.255	1.508
2.402	1.520	7.554	1.501
2.512	1.520	7.711	1.496
2.612	1.520	7.873	1.491
2.718	1.519	8.010	1.480
2.812	1.520	8.137	1.466
3.017	1.519	8.554	1.581
3.130	1.518	8.642	1.557
3.189	1.517	8.779	1.541
3.218	1.516	9.181	1.527
3.241	1.512	9.931	1.514
3.279	1.530	10.863	1.505
3.297	1.523	11.221	1.503
3.325	1.521	11.578	1.498
3.361	1.522	11.936	1.489
3.393	1.520	12.574	1.568
3.536	1.518	12.946	1.555
3.614	1.519	13.392	1.547
3.821	1.518	13.833	1.534
4.056	1.518	14.250	1.514
4.323	1.518	14.632	1.487
4.758	1.517	14.907	1.446
5.123	1.515	17.82	1.618
5.461	1.514	18.37	1.585
5.848	1.513	19.10	1.561
6.289	1.511		

*Accuracy estimated to be ± 0.001, 2–15 μm; ± 0.003, 15–20 μm.

REFERENCE: Pritchard, W. H. and Orville-Thomas, W. J., *Trans. Faraday Soc.*, 59, 2218, 1963.

Refractive Indices of Dichloromethane
(corrected to 20°C)

λ (μm)	n (obs.)*	λ (μm)	n (obs.)*
2.001	1.413	7.270	1.400
2.371	1.414	7.417	1.395
2.505	1.413	7.569	1.389
2.728	1.414	7.711	1.379
3.020	1.413	8.064	1.442
3.241	1.412	8.176	1.425
3.290	1.418	8.343	1.416
3.315	1.414	8.534	1.409
3.359	1.416	8.765	1.407
3.464	1.413	9.250	1.400
3.502	1.413	9.520	1.397
3.709	1.412	9.794	1.392
3.945	1.411	10.412	1.385
4.731	1.410	10.730	1.378
4.523	1.411	11.461	1.367
4.955	1.409	11.789	1.352
5.387	1.408	12.108	1.333
5.578	1.407	12.392	1.307
5.681	1.407	12.627	1.274
6.132	1.406	15.22	1.519
6.515	1.404	16.30	1.479
6.647	1.402	17.02	1.467
6.779	1.399	17.87	1.459
7.127	1.405		

*Accuracy estimated to be ± 0.001, 2–15 μm; ±0.003, 15–20 μm.

REFERENCE: Pritchard, W. H. and Orville-Thomas, W. J., *Trans. Faraday Soc.*, 59, 2218, 1963.

C. Spectra of Common Solvents

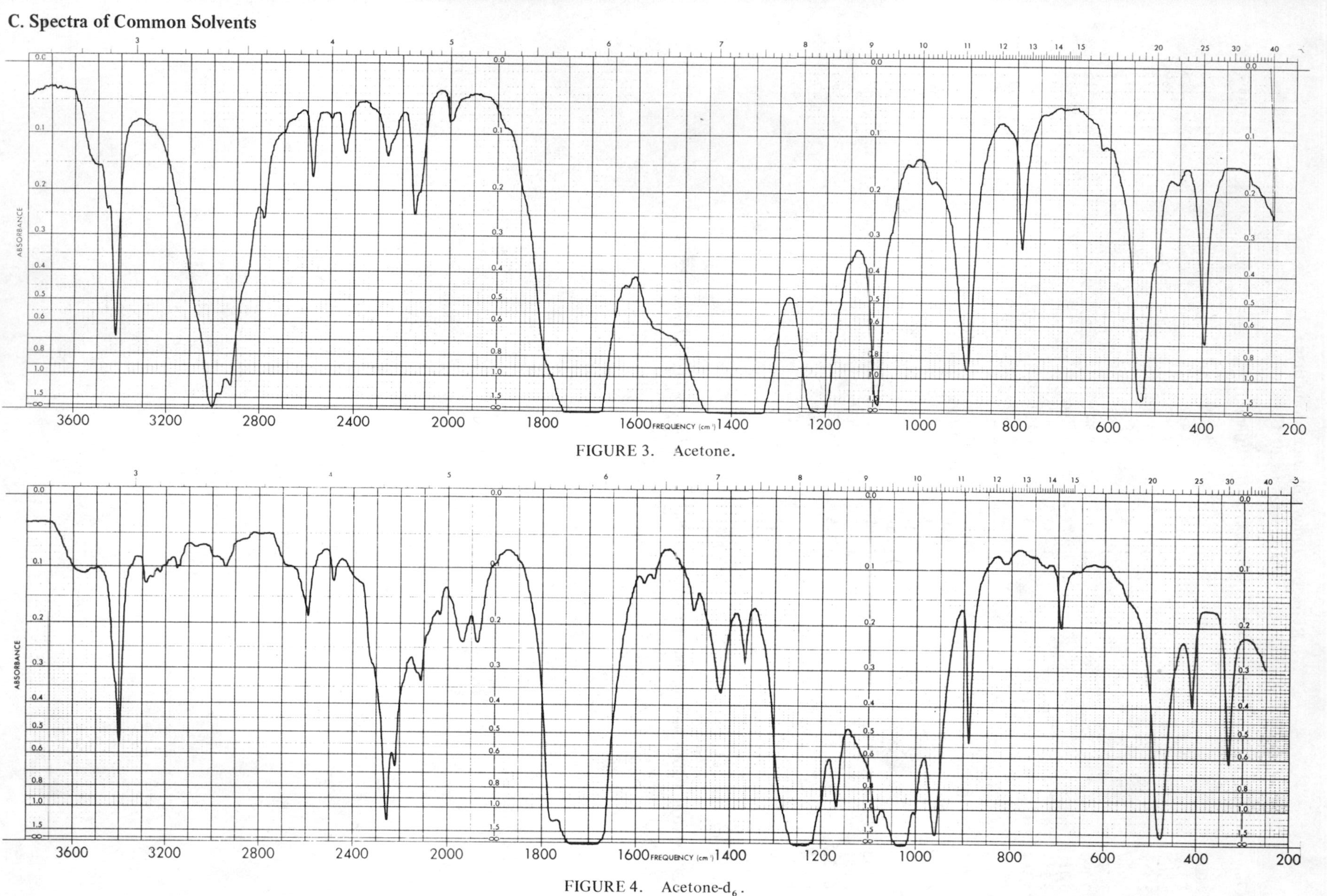

FIGURE 3. Acetone.

FIGURE 4. Acetone-d_6.

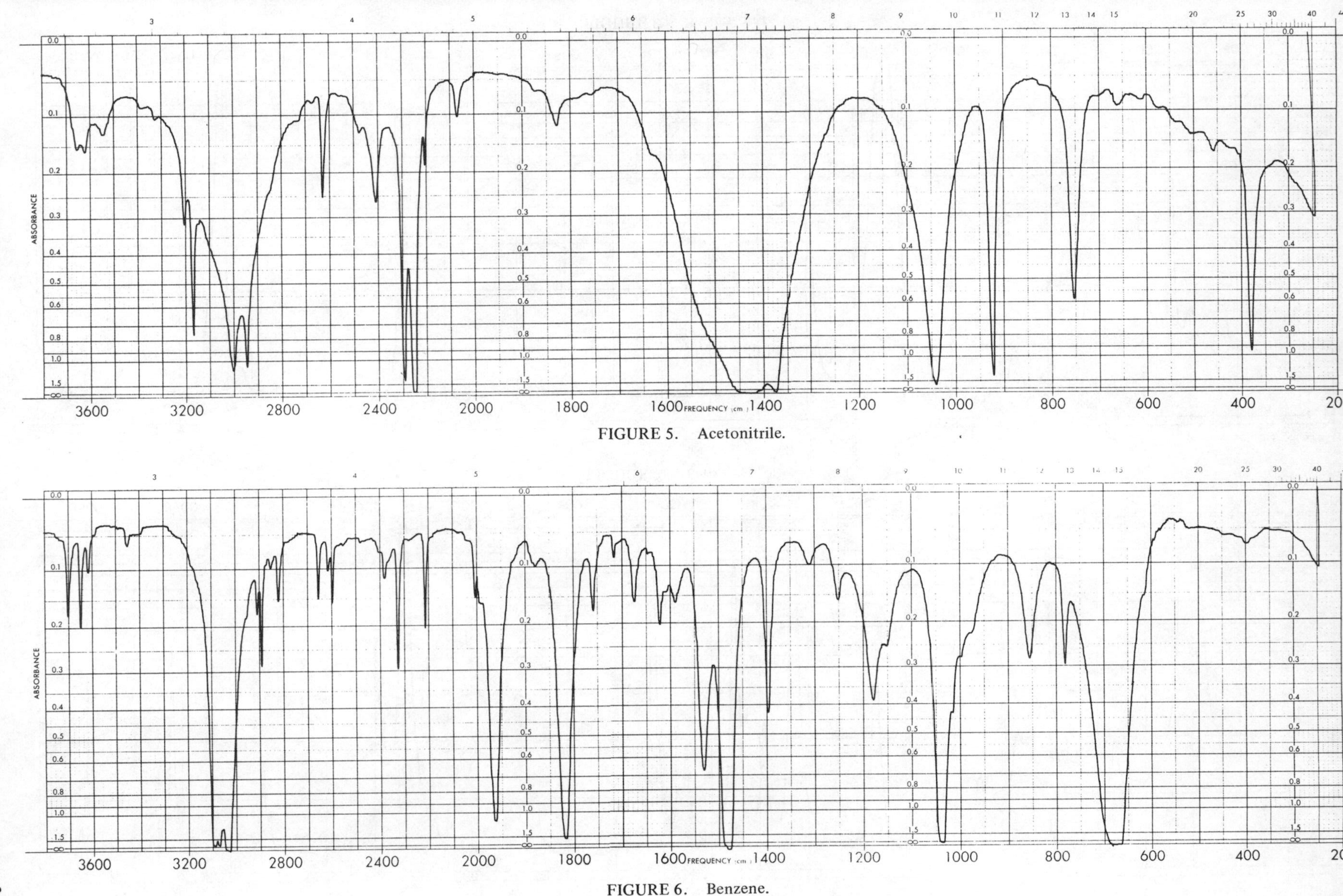

FIGURE 5. Acetonitrile.

FIGURE 6. Benzene.

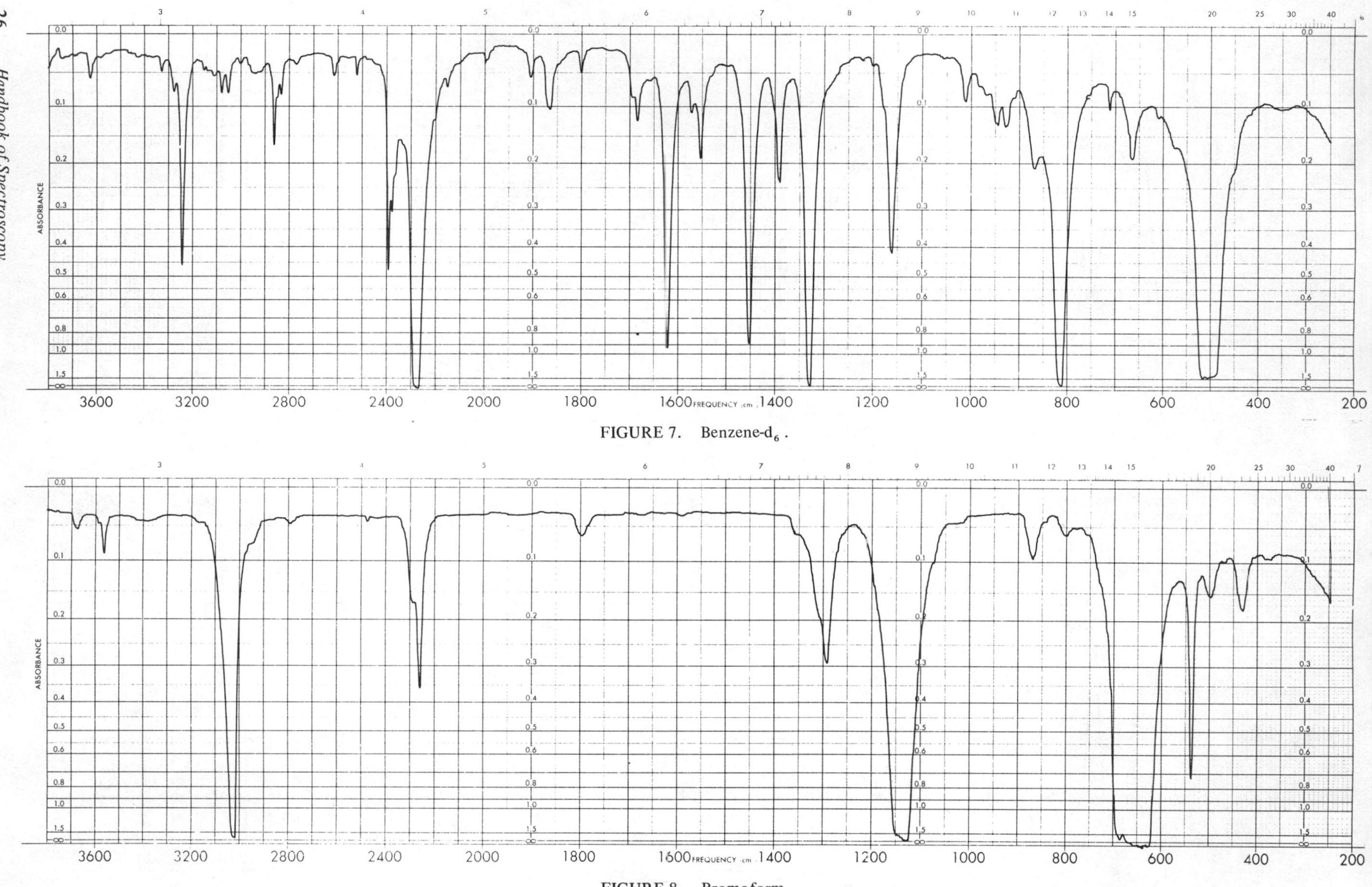

FIGURE 7. Benzene-d_6.

FIGURE 8. Bromoform.

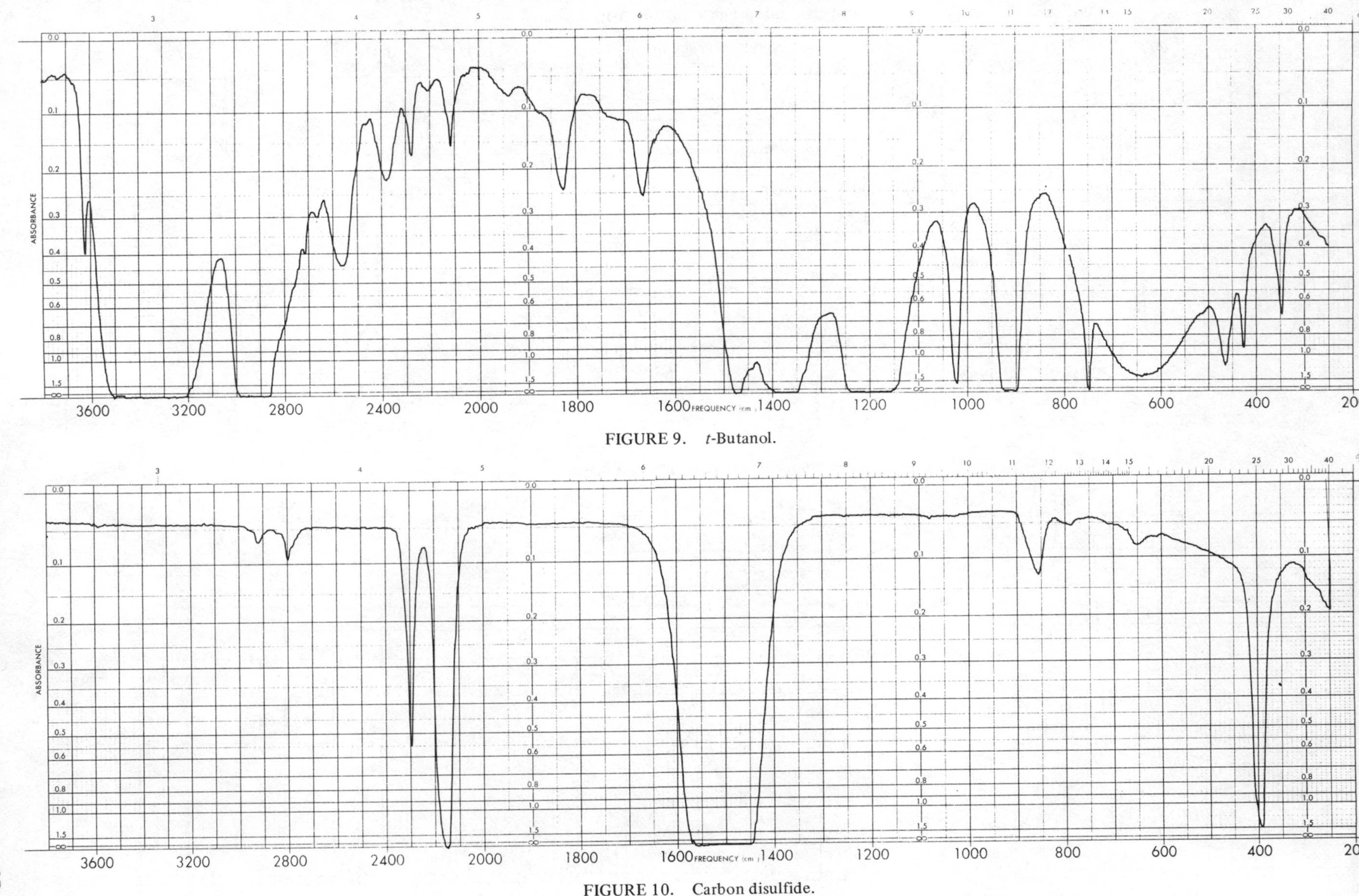

FIGURE 9. *t*-Butanol.

FIGURE 10. Carbon disulfide.

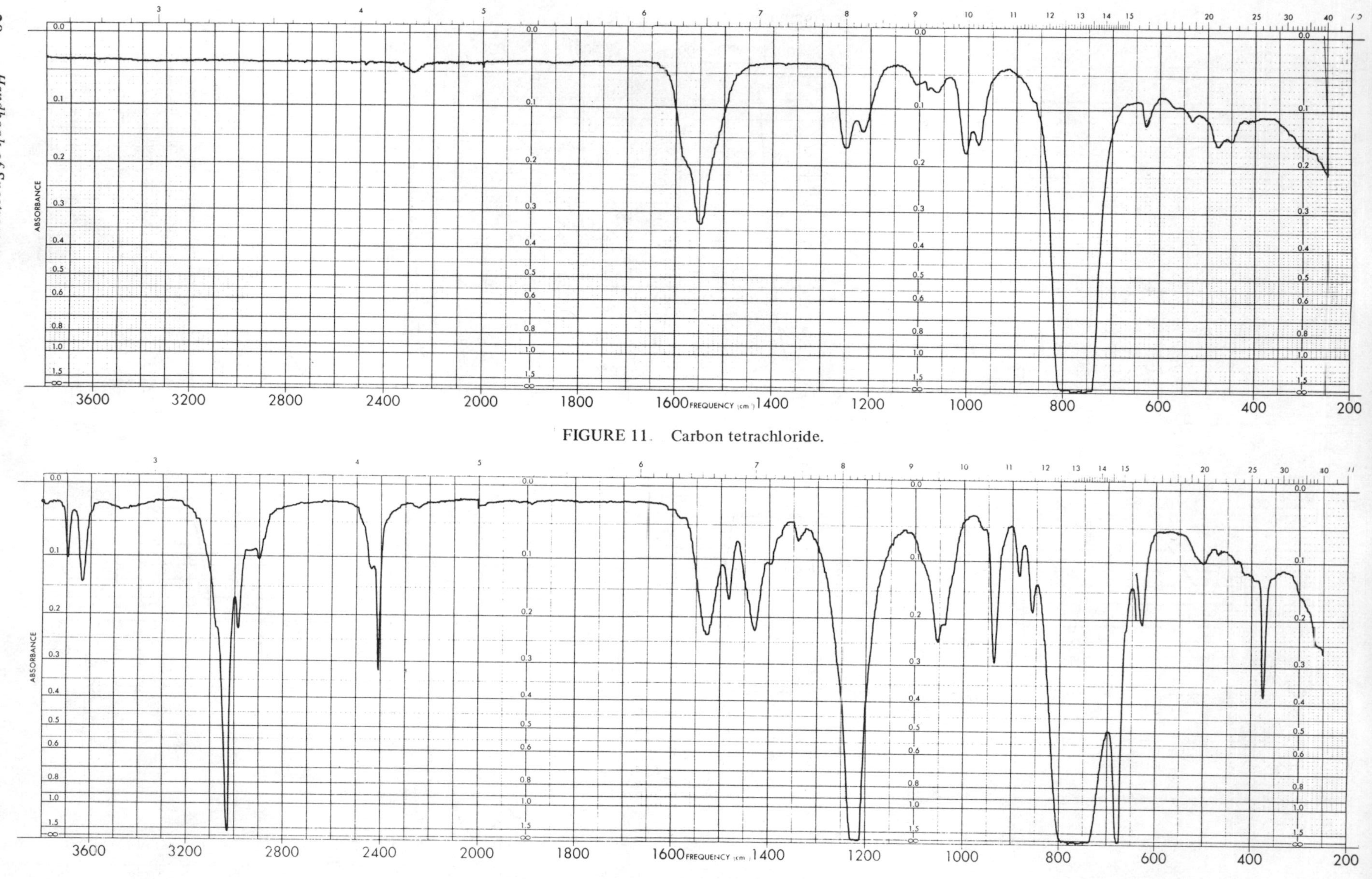

FIGURE 11. Carbon tetrachloride.

FIGURE 12. Chloroform.

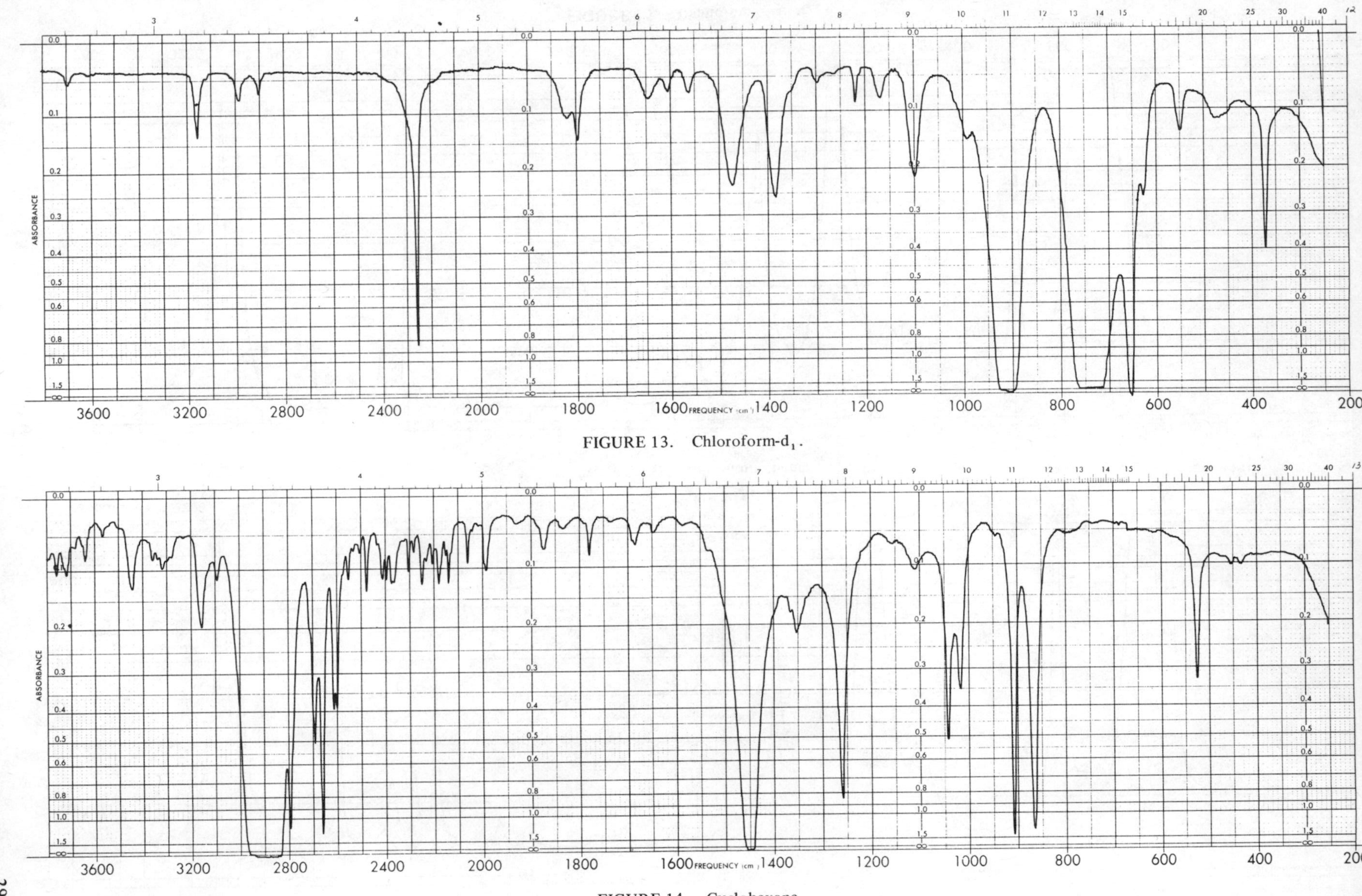

FIGURE 13. Chloroform-d_1.

FIGURE 14. Cyclohexane.

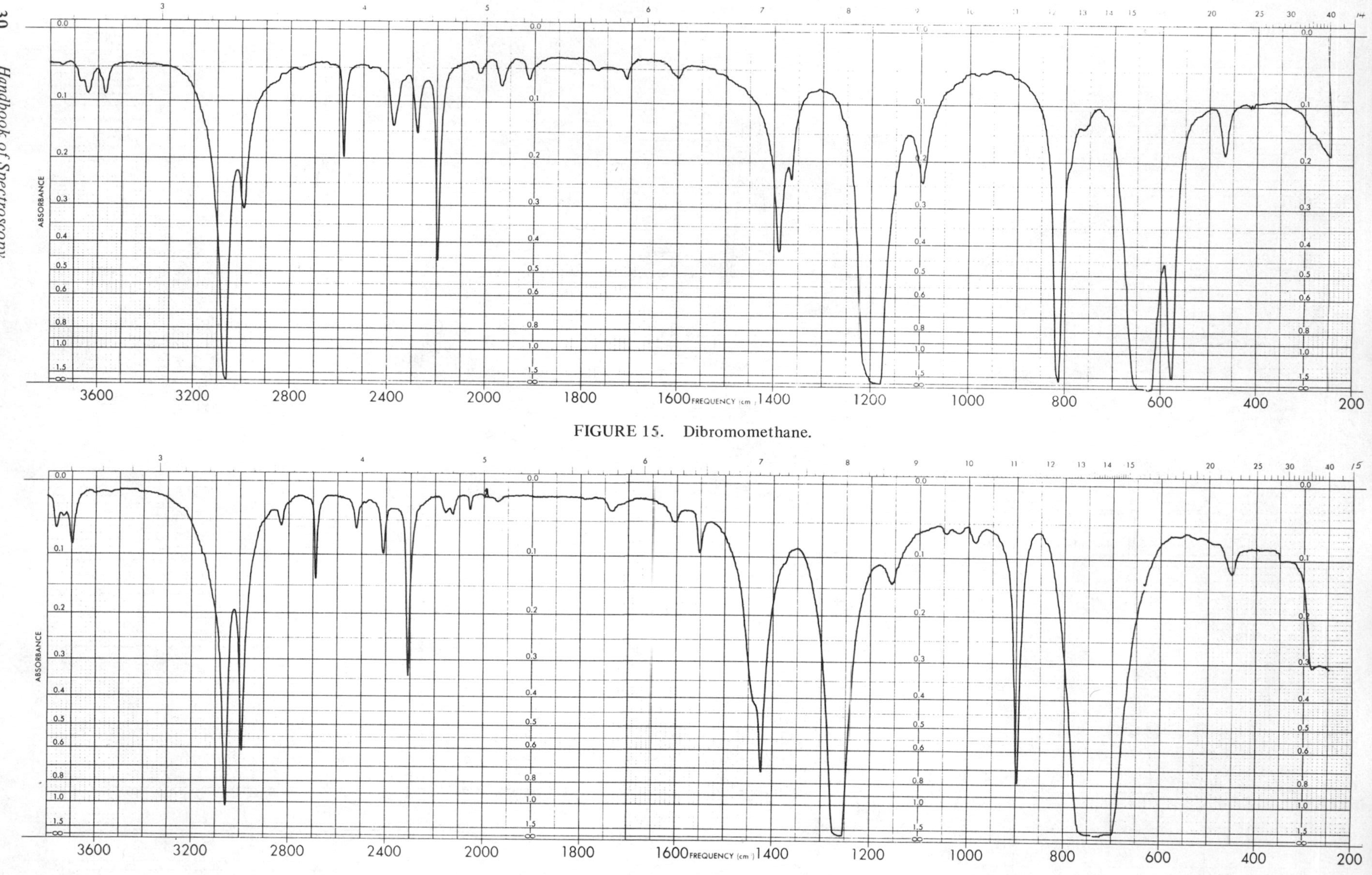

FIGURE 15. Dibromomethane.

FIGURE 16. Dichloromethane.

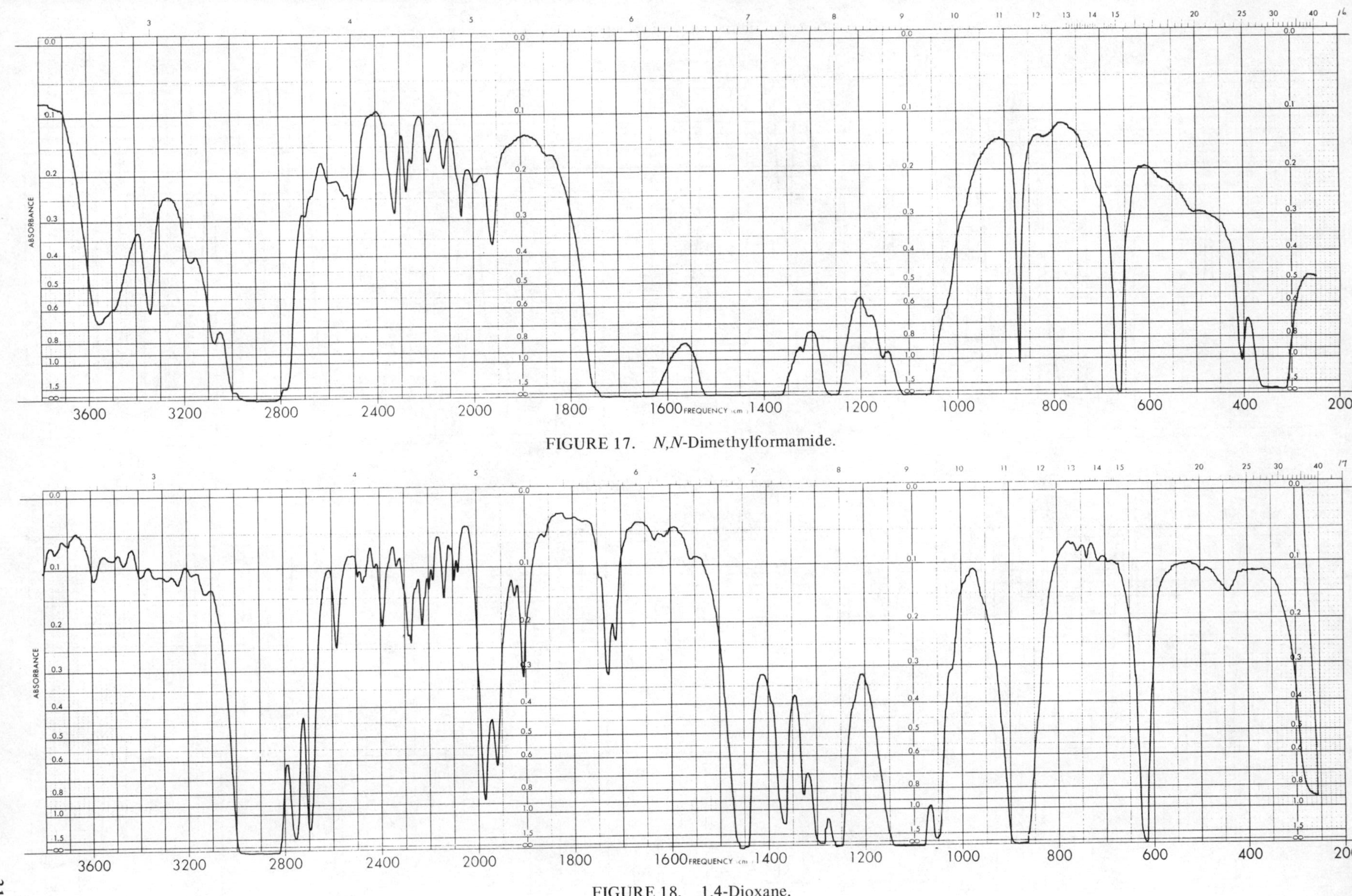

FIGURE 17. *N,N*-Dimethylformamide.

FIGURE 18. 1,4-Dioxane.

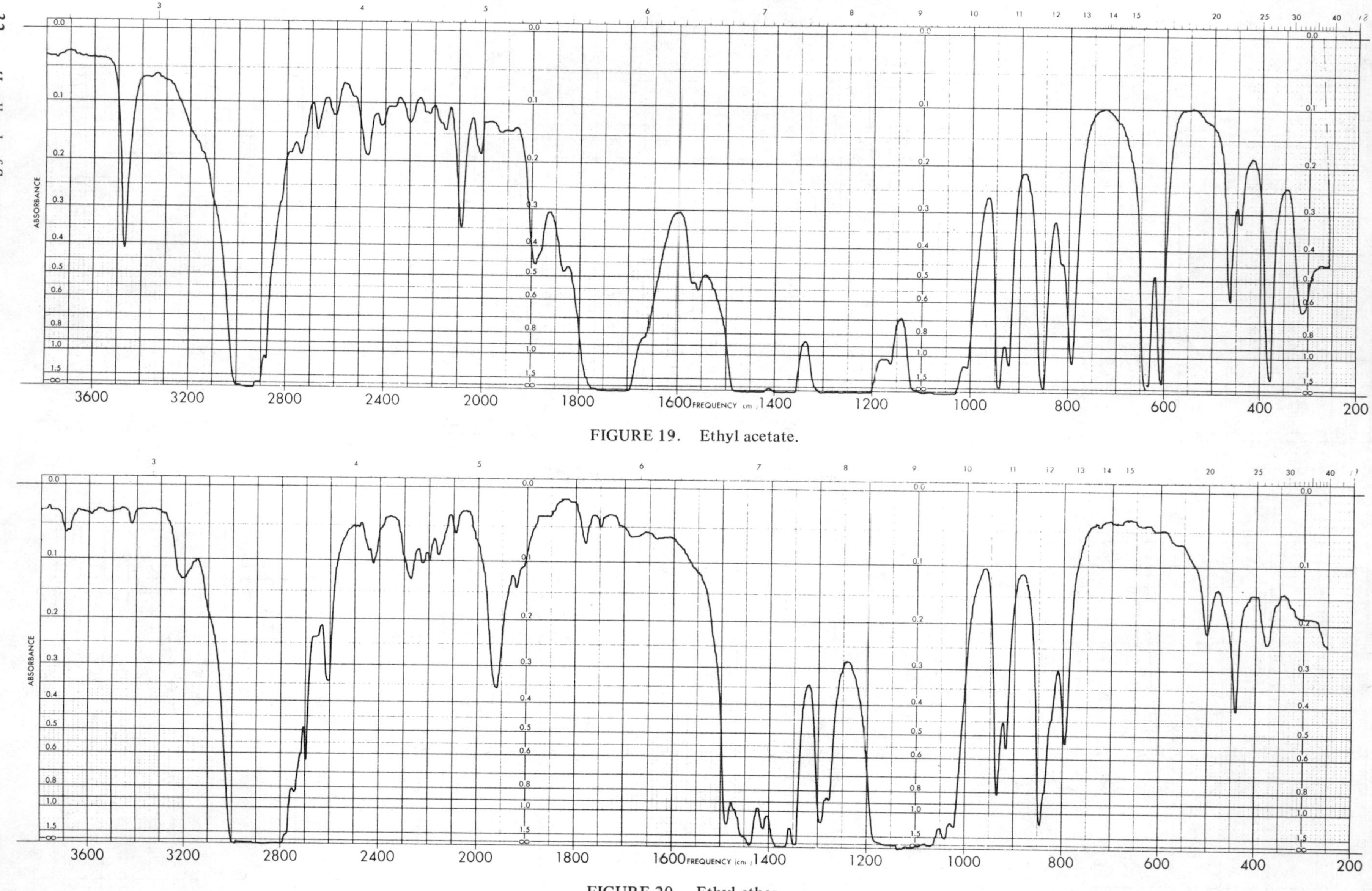

FIGURE 19. Ethyl acetate.

FIGURE 20. Ethyl ether.

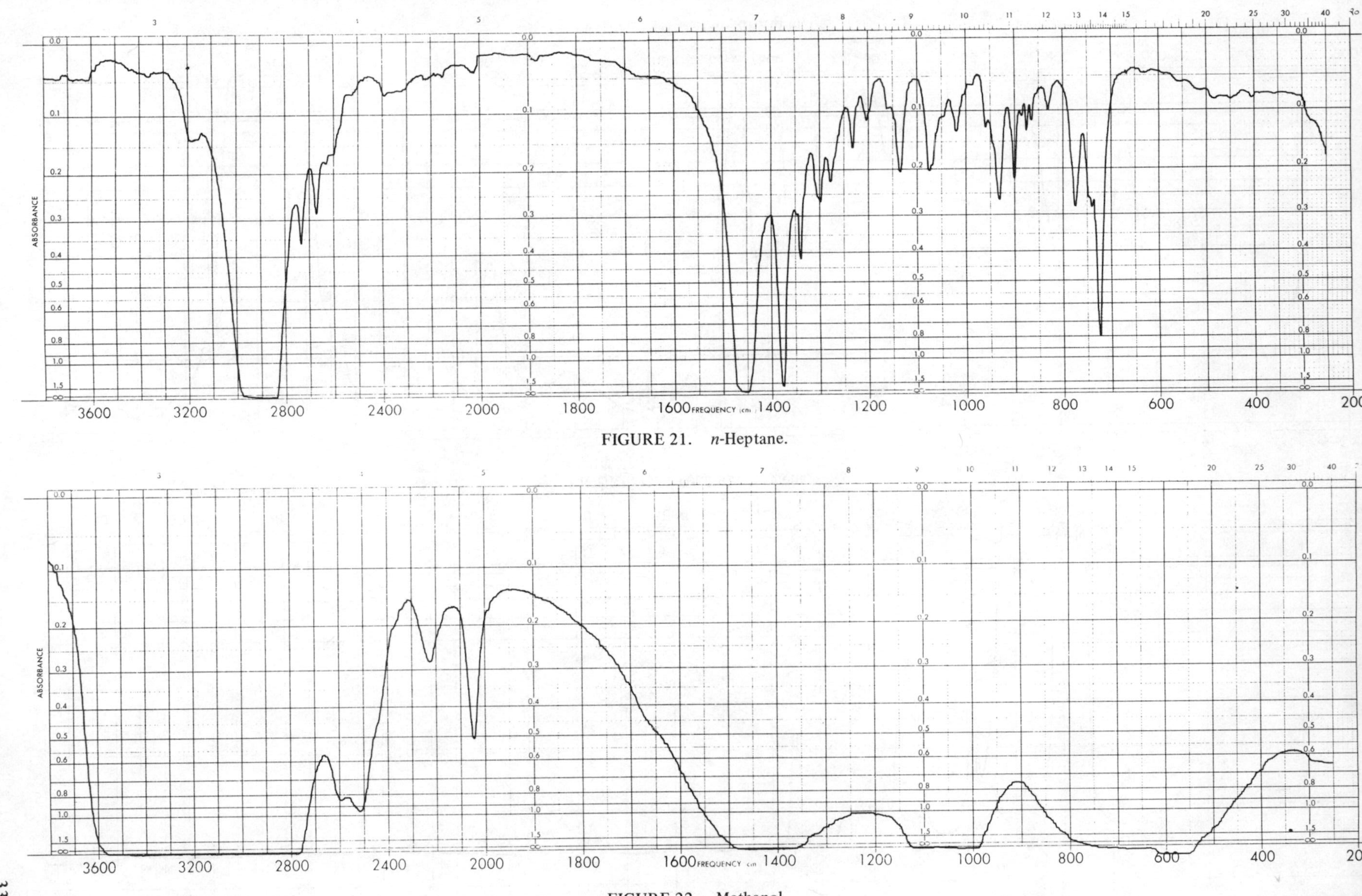

FIGURE 21. *n*-Heptane.

FIGURE 22. Methanol.

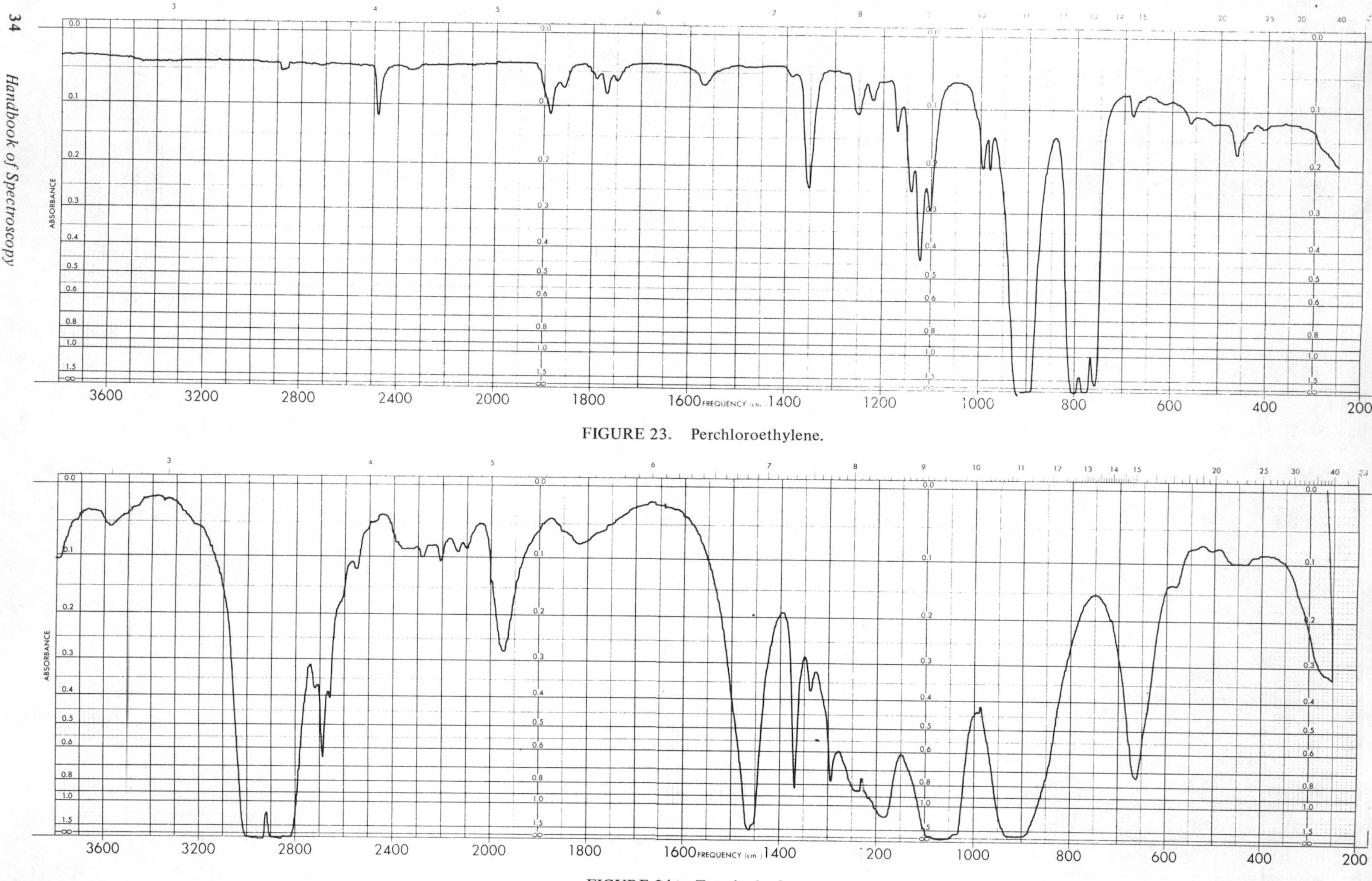

FIGURE 23. Perchloroethylene.

FIGURE 24. Tetrahydrofuran.

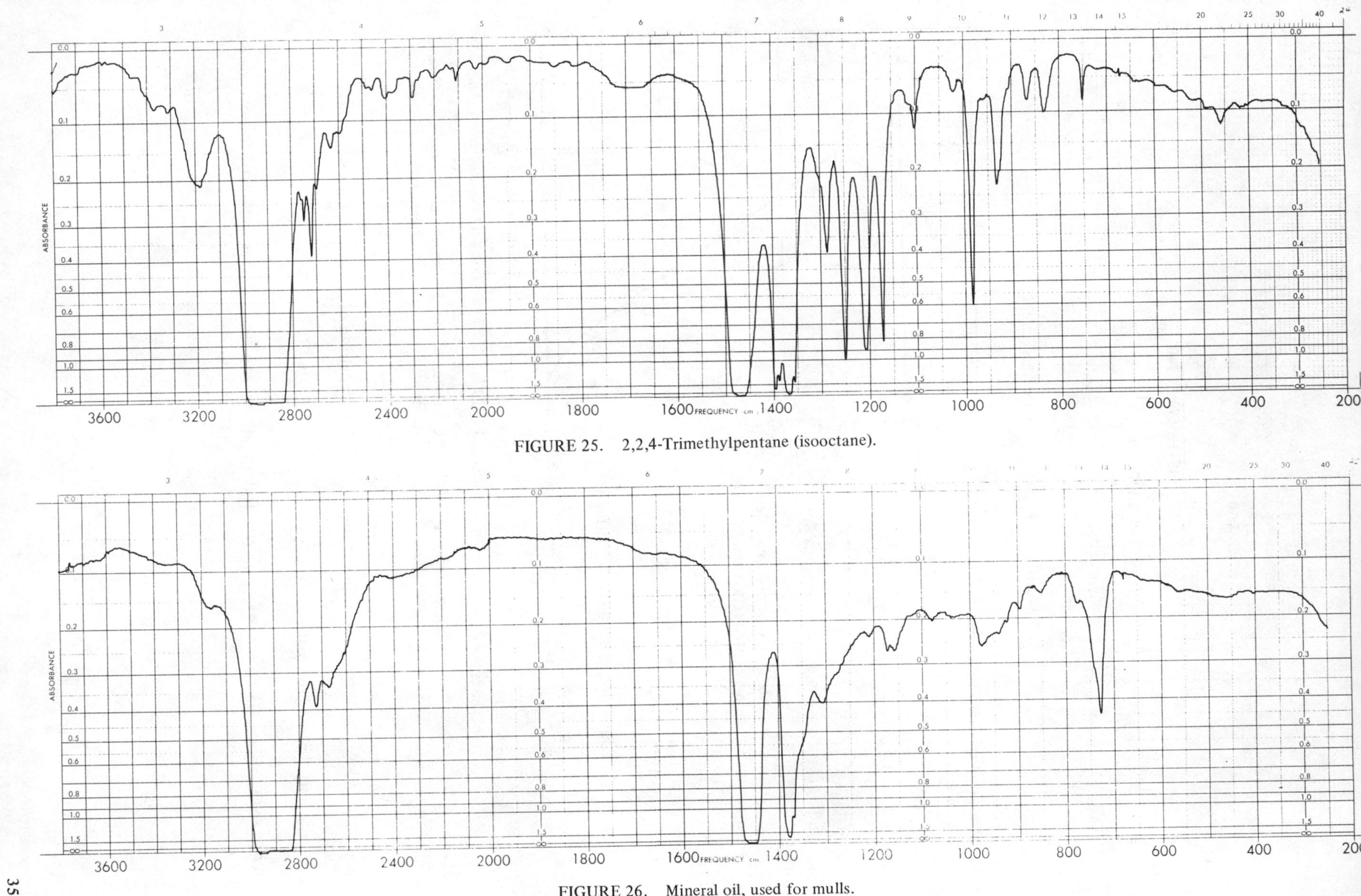

FIGURE 25. 2,2,4-Trimethylpentane (isooctane).

FIGURE 26. Mineral oil, used for mulls.

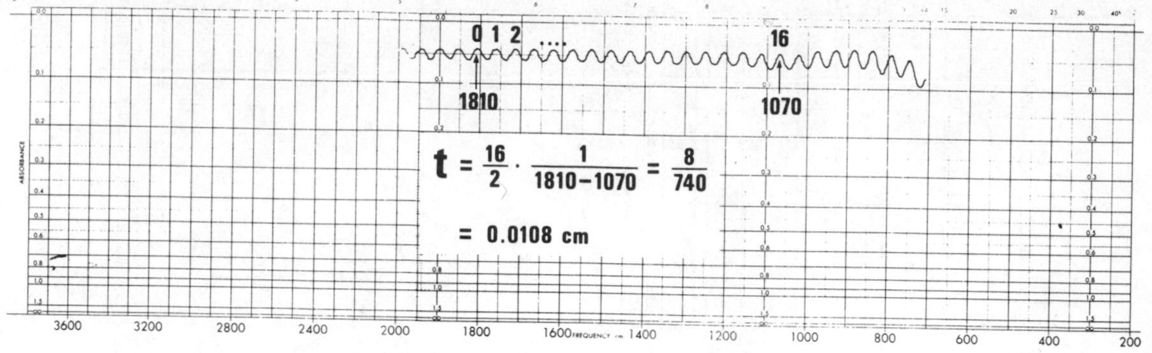

FIGURE 27. Example of cell thickness calculation.

1. Calculation of Cell Thickness

For an empty cell,

$$t(\text{cm}) = \frac{n}{2} \cdot \frac{1}{\nu_1 - \nu_2} \quad \text{or } t\,(\text{micrometers}) = \frac{n}{2} \cdot \frac{\lambda_1 \lambda_2}{\lambda_1 - \lambda_2} \cdot \qquad (1)$$

t = thickness
λ_1 and λ_2 = wavelength of two maxima in micrometers
ν_1 and ν_2 = wavenumber of two maxima in cm^{-1}
n = number of maxima counted (choose n between 10 and 20) (count λ_1 or ν_1 as zero)

REFERENCE: Smith, D. C. and Miller, E. C., *J. Opt. Soc. Am.*, 34, 130, 1944.

For a cell containing a material of refractive index μ:

$$t(\text{cm}) = \frac{n}{2} \cdot \frac{1}{\mu \cos \alpha(\nu_1 - \nu_2)}$$

α = angle of refraction of the radiation

REFERENCE: Strong, J., *Concepts of Classical Optics*, W. H. Freeman & Co., San Francisco, 1958, 234.

Note that cells filled with solvent or sample may give fringe patterns superimposed on the spectrum if the refractive indices of the cell contents and the window material do not match.

REFERENCE: White, J. U. and Ward, W. M., *Anal. Chem.*, 37, 268, 1965.

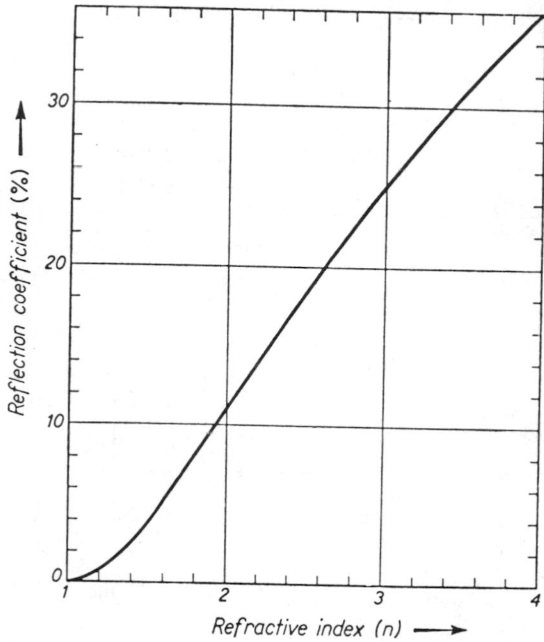

FIGURE 28. Reflection coefficient, $[(n - 1)/(n + 1)]^2$ as a function of n for an air-window interface. (From Conn, G. K. T. and Avery, D. G., *Infrared Methods*, Academic Press, New York, 1960. With permission.)

2. Calculation of Reflection Loss at an Interface

$$R = \frac{(n_2 - n_1)^2}{(n_2 + n_1)^2} \qquad (2)$$

n_1 and n_2 are refractive indices of the two media at the interface.

D. Internal Reflection Spectroscopy

N. J. Harrick, Harrick Scientific Corporation

1. Reflection of Light

If a surface is smooth, the reflection is called specular, i.e., mirrorlike, and obeys the simple law that the angle of incidence equals the angle of reflection as shown in Figure 29a for both external and internal reflection. Any light that passes into the second medium is refracted and obeys Snell's law:

$$n_1 \sin\Theta_1 = n_2 \sin\Theta_2 . \qquad (1)$$

a. Diffuse Reflection. Although diffuse reflection is a complicated phenomenon, it is important because in many practical cases reflection is diffuse. Interpretation of spectra is uncertain. There is no rigorous solution to a general diffuse reflectance case because the reflection is a combination of external specular reflection, internal reflection, transmission and scattering; it is dependent, therefore, on particle size, shape, refractive index, absorption coefficient, polarization, etc.

In spite of these difficulties, empirical methods have been developed to treat certain cases, and valuable information can be obtained where other methods cannot be employed.[11,17,18]

b. External (Specular) Reflection. When the light approaches an interface from an optically less dense to a more dense medium, the reflection is called external reflection, and its dependence on polarization and angle of incidence is as shown by the solid lines of Figure 30 [for the interface water (n = 1.33) – germanium (n = 4)]. The reflectivity

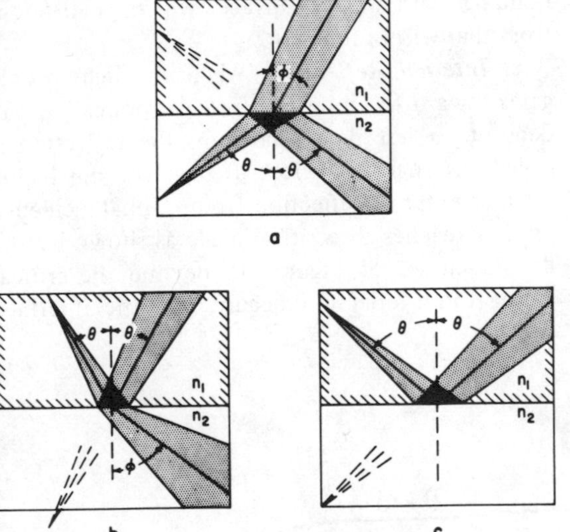

FIGURE 29. Reflection and refraction of a ray of light. (a) External reflection. (b) Internal reflection, $\theta < \theta_c$. (c) Total internal reflection, $\theta > \theta_c$ · θ_c is the critical angle.

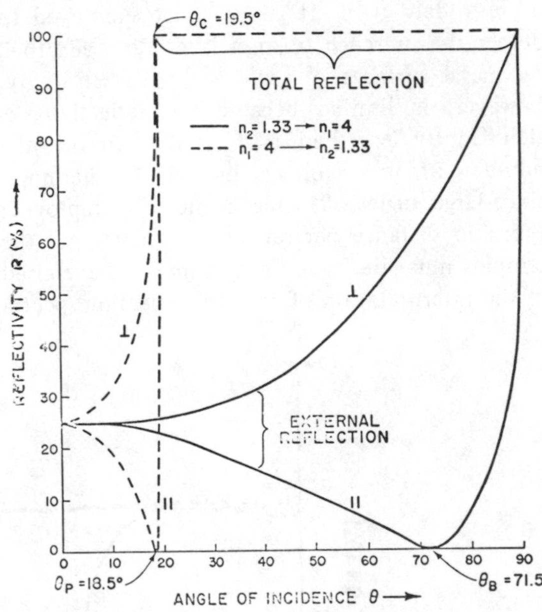

FIGURE 30. Reflectivity versus angle of incidence for an interface between media with indices n_1 = 4 and n_2 = 1.33 for light polarized perpendicular, $R_\perp$, and parallel, $R_\parallel$, to plane of incidence for external reflection (solid lines) and internal reflection (dashed lines). θ_c, θ_B, and θ_p are the critical, Brewster's and principal angles, respectively.

may be modified for parallel polarization by the presence of a thin film on the surface, especially near Brewster's angle. An example is shown in Figure 31 where a 500 Å SiO_2 film on the Al surface is undetectable near normal incidence but exhibits about 30% reflection loss at large angles of incidence. The reason the film is undetectable at normal incidence is that the incoming and reflected light waves interact to set up a standing wave with a node (zero electric field) at the reflecting surface for external reflection because of the high conductivity of the metal. Near Brewster's angle, more of the light propagates into the metal, and finite values of electric field are found at the surface.

External reflection spectroscopy is a nondestructive method where no sample contact is required, and the sample may even be far from the instrument. It has been highly neglected as a method of studying surfaces but is now being more widely used. It can even be employed to detect the presence of monolayer films adsorbed on metal surfaces.[5,6,12,13,15,16] Its sensitivity, however, is limited because the reflectivity is significantly less than 100%, and, therefore, the number of reflections is limited. Furthermore, since large angles of incidence must be employed, the skip distance per reflection is large, and the samples must be long. Caution must be exercised in the interpretation of external reflection spectra since the spectrum may be dispersionlike (e.g., reflection from a dielectric) or absorptionlike or some mixture of the two. Furthermore, because of the standing wave set up at the reflecting surface, contrast in the spectrum is dependent on wavelength, polarization, and angle of incidence and for thin films does not increase linearly with film thickness. For thick films on a metal surface, the spectrum can be regarded as double transmission since the light "propagates" through the film twice.

Another form of external specular reflection, called ellipsometry,[1,2] has the capability of studying one-hundredth monolayer films. Here it is not the change in reflectivity that is measured but the phase change of polarized light upon reflection. Ellipsometry has been widely employed in the study of clean surfaces. Information is obtained about the change in optical constants of the material resulting from the change in atomic bonding right at the surface, which is different from that within the bulk.[3]

c. Internal Reflection. When the light propagates toward the interface from an optically more dense to a less dense medium, the reflection is called internal reflection. It behaves much the same as external reflection from normal incidence until it reaches the critical angle as shown by the dashed curves of Figure 30. Beyond the critical angle, total reflection occurs, and the interface

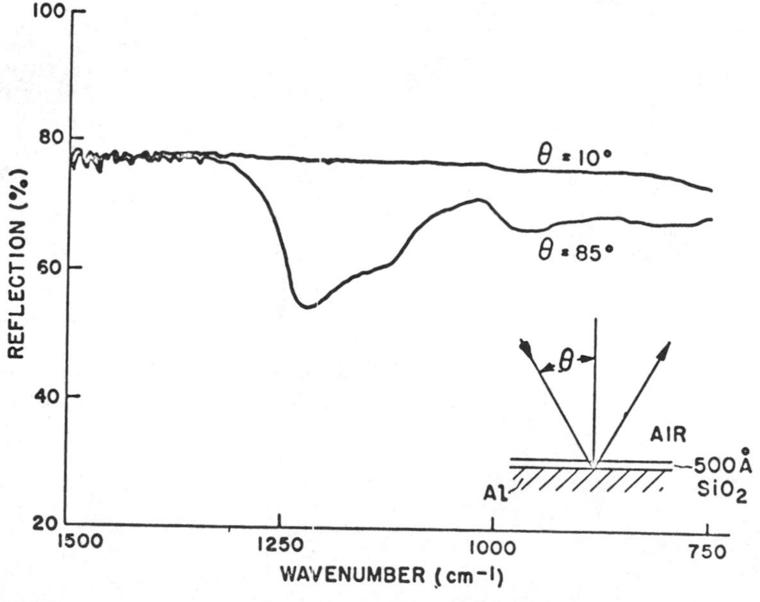

FIGURE 31. Spectra showing the power of specular external reflection near Brewster's angle for the study of thin films on metal surfaces. The SiO_2 film which is undetectable at 10° gives a signal at 85° of 30%.

then acts as a perfect mirror for nonabsorbing media. A metal, for example, is not a perfect mirror; e.g., if the reflectivity R = 95%, after 10 reflections the intensity of the light beam has dropped to $(.95)^{10}$ = 60%. For total internal reflection, on the other hand, the reflectivity is very near 100%. Light has been propagated through many thousands of internal reflections, and the transmission is limited only by the purity of the bulk.

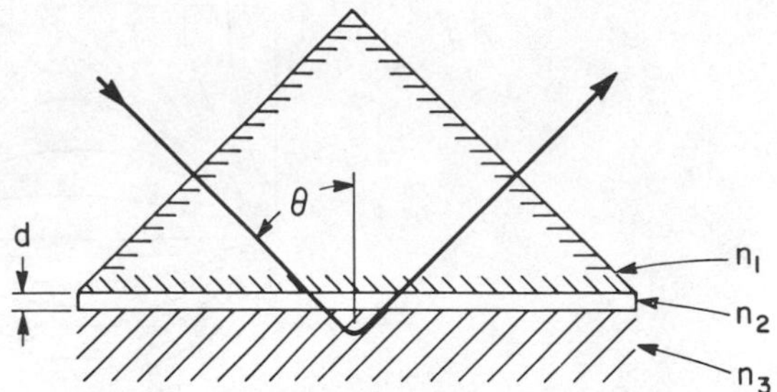

FIGURE 32. Schematic representation of path of ray of light for total internal reflection. The ray penetrates a fraction of a wavelength (d_p) beyond the reflecting interface. Medium 1 is the optically transparent internal reflection element; Medium 2 is the sample material; the surrounding Medium 3 is usually air.

2. Internal Reflection Spectroscopy (IRS)

Internal reflection spectroscopy* is a method of recording spectra by introducing light into an optically transparent medium at angles above the critical angle and measuring the intensity of the emerging radiation after it has suffered one or many internal reflections.

a. Evanescent Wave. It is at first puzzling that species outside of the surface of a transparent medium can be studied by means of a light beam that is reflected from the inside of the surface. The phenomenon of total internal reflection results from the fact that the electromagnetic field associated with the reflected light beam penetrates a certain distance beyond the reflecting interface. Figure 32 shows schematically the path of the light ray at the reflecting surface. Mathematically it can be shown that the incoming wave interacts with the reflected wave to form a standing wave perpendicular to the surface shown in Figure 33a, where the electric field perpendicular to the reflecting interface varies sinusoidally inside the reflecting medium and falls off exponentially beyond the reflecting interface. The (two-dimensional) field distribution near the reflecting interface is shown in Figure 33b. The depth of penetration of this field, given by the distance required for the field to fall to 1/e of its value at the surface, is given by

$$d_p = \frac{\lambda_1}{2\pi(\sin^2\Theta - n_{21}^{\ 2})^{1/2}}, \tag{2}$$

where λ_1 is λ/n_1 and $n_{21} = n_2/n_1$. Figure 34 gives a plot of d_p/λ_1 versus Θ for $n_1 > n_2$ where it will be noted that d_p becomes infinite at Θ_c and falls off to about one-tenth wavelength at grazing incidence.

This penetrating field (evanescent wave) is unusual since it has the frequency of the incoming

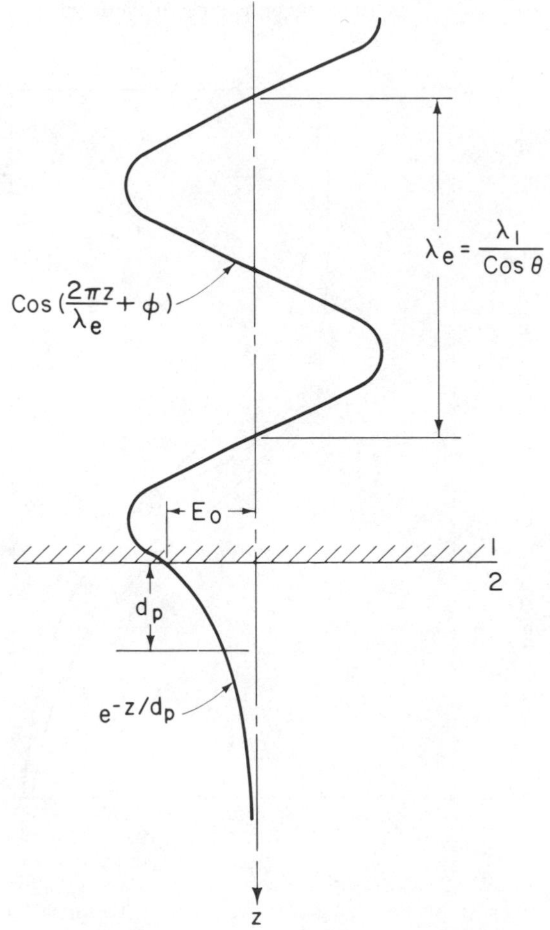

FIGURE 33a. Standing-wave amplitudes established near a totally reflecting interface. There is a sinusoidal dependence of the electric field amplitude on the distance from the surface in the denser Medium 1 and an exponentially decreasing amplitude in the rarer Medium 2. The E field may have a large value at the surface.

*Internal reflection spectroscopy is the nomenclature set for this method by ASTM (1966), although the method is also known as FTR, FMIR, ATR, and MATR.

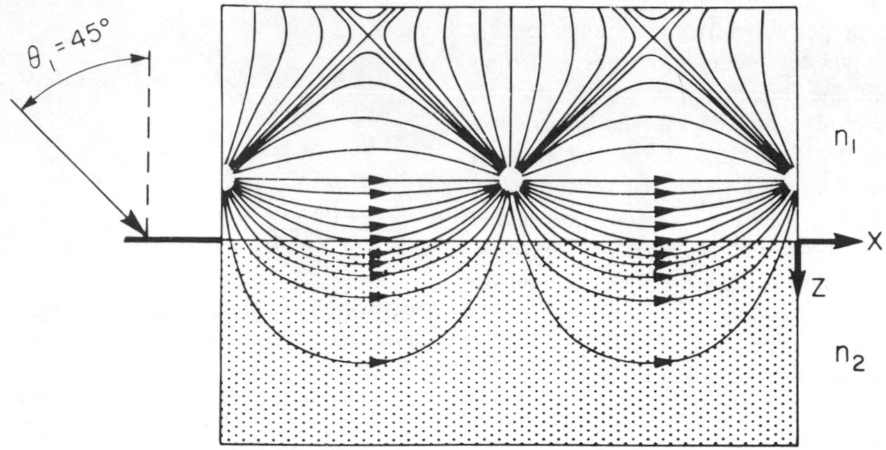

FIGURE 33b. Wave pattern near surface for total reflection. The density of the lines indicates the magnitude of the Poynting vector. The whole pattern is moving to the right in Medium 1.

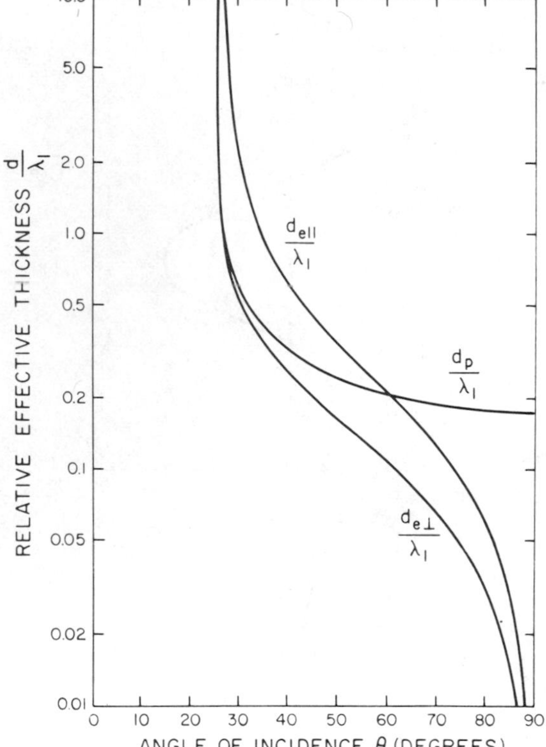

FIGURE 34. Relative penetration depth and effective thickness of the evanescent wave versus the angle of incidence for an interface whose refractive index ratio is n_{21} = 0.423. Near the critical angle, the effective thicknesses for both polarizations are greater than the penetration depth, and at large angles they are less.

wave, but its wavelength is infinite! Any medium brought to the proximity of a surface where this field is present can interact with it. In a recent experiment, it has been shown that materials not only can absorb evanescent waves but also can emit evanescent waves.[4]

For recording spectra it is only necessary to place the sample material on a suitable IRE (e.g., prism) as shown in Figure 35 and measure the reflectivity of the interface versus wavelength. Spectra very similar to those obtained in transmission can be recorded with little or no sample preparation.

b. Equivalent Path Length (EPL). For internal reflection several parameters can be changed that affect the character of the spectrum, including refractive index of the internal reflection element, angle of incidence, and polarization of the light. The strength of interaction of the standing wave with the absorber near the totally reflecting surface and its dependence on all of these parameters are expressed exactly by Fresnel's equations, which in most cases can be solved only with the aid of a computer. For most practical cases in which the absorption coefficient is not too high, the first order approximation gives the strength of interaction to a high degree of accuracy. Furthermore, these expressions are quite simple and give insight into the nature of the interaction, permitting one to select the parameters to optimize the interaction. These first order expressions for thick and thin films have been discussed in detail elsewhere[7] and will be only briefly reviewed here.

For transmission, neglecting reflection losses, the transmitted energy is related to the incident energy, absorption coefficient, and sample thickness as follows:

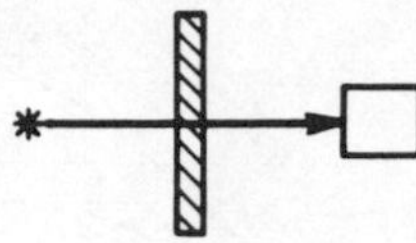

a. TRANSMISSION

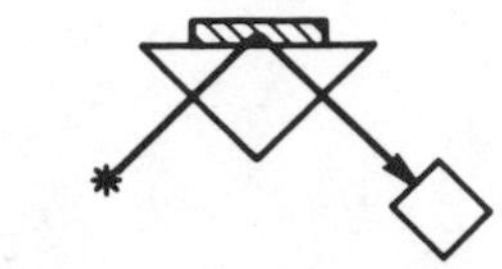

b. INTERNAL REFLECTION

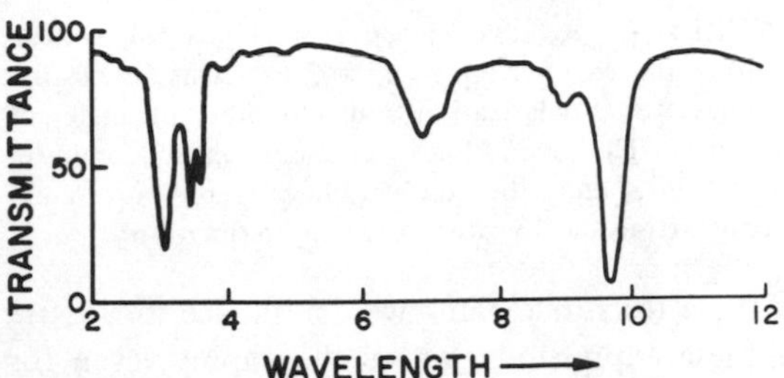

c. OPTICAL SPECTRUM

FIGURE 35. Comparison of conventional transmission and internal reflection spectroscopy. In the latter technique, the sample material absorbs energy via interaction with the evanescent wave. Spectra characteristic of the material are obtained via both techniques.

$$I = I_o e^{-\alpha d} \quad (3)$$

$$= I_o(1 - \alpha d) \text{ for } \alpha d << 1. \quad (4)$$

Similarly, for reflection

$$R = (1 - \alpha d_e), \quad (5)$$

where d_e is defined as the effective film thickness and is the film thickness required to give the same spectral contrast in transmission as is obtained in the reflection measurement. d_e may thus be considered as the equivalent path length. For multiple reflection EPL = Nd_e since

$$R^N = (1 - \alpha d_e)N \quad (6)$$

$$= 1 - N\alpha d_e \text{ for } \alpha d_e << 1. \quad (7)$$

As already pointed out, the exact expressions for d_e are complicated. For low absorptions and for thick or thin films, simple expressions can be derived for d_e which are valid for many applications.

For thick films or semi-infinite media*

$$\frac{d_{e\perp}}{\lambda_1} = \frac{n_{21} \cos\theta}{\pi(1 - n_{21}^2)(\sin^2\theta - n_{21}^2)^{1/2}} \quad (8)$$

$$\frac{d_{e\parallel}}{\lambda_1} = \frac{n_{21} \cos\theta(2 \sin^2\theta - n_{21}^2)}{\pi(1 - n_{21}^2)[(1 + n_{21}^2) \sin^2\theta - n_{21}](\sin^2\theta - n_{21}^2)^{1/2}}, \quad (9)$$

and for thin films (e.g., $d < \lambda$ at $\theta = 45°$)

$$d_{e\perp} = [4n_{21} d \cos\theta/(1 - n_{31}^2)], \quad (10)$$

$$d_{e\parallel} = \frac{4n_{21} d \cos\theta[(1 + n_{32}^4) \sin^2\theta - n_{31}^2]}{(1 - n_{31}^2)[(1 + n_{31}^2) \sin^2\theta - n_{31}^2]} \quad (11)$$

Variation of d_e with θ is shown in Figure 34 for thick films and in Figure 36 for thin films for a few selected interfaces.

These expressions show that even for isotropic media, EPL is dependent on polarization of light, and for quantitative measurements this fact must be taken into consideration since in most instruments the light is always partially polarized. For thick films d_e is finite even for samples of semi-infinite extent (except near the critical angle) and becomes zero at grazing incidence, even though the penetration depth is finite. For thin films d_e may be greater or less than the actual film thickness.

The above expressions for d_e can be decomposed into four parameters which determine the EPL. It should be noted that for thick films the penetration depth is only one of them. These parameters are:

1. Penetration depth, d_p, for thick films and film thickness, d, for thin films. For thick films spectral contrast increases sharply near $\theta = \theta_c$ and is wavelength independent.

2. Electric field strength. The electric field strength can readily be calculated and generally (except for E_x) decreases with increasing θ and becomes zero at grazing incidence. For this reason d_e is zero at grazing incidence, even though d_p has a finite value. The expressions for electric field

*There is an error in the sign of this equation in Reference 7, p. 43 – the second sign in the denominator of Equation 27 should be plus, not minus.

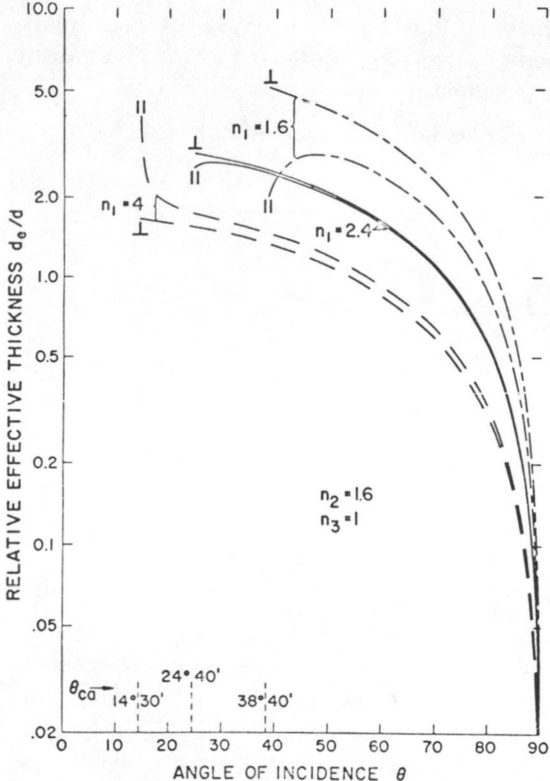

FIGURE 36. Relative effective thickness for a thin film of refractive index $n_2 = 1.6$ on internal reflection elements of various refractive indices, n_1. Here θ_{ca} is the critical angle of the crystal-air/interface.

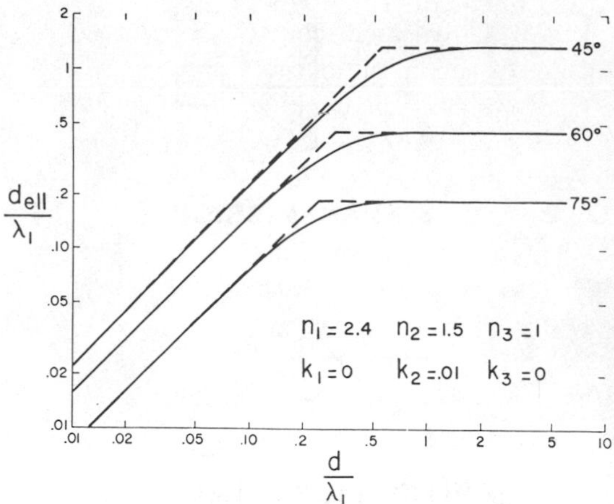

FIGURE 37. Relative effective thickness for a weak absorber placed on KRS-5 ($n_1 = 2.4$) versus actual film thickness for ||-polarization and a number of angles of incidence. The solid lines represent exact computer calculations, and the dashed lines represent values obtained from the low absorption approximation.

intensity at the surface are different for thick and thin films.

3. Sampling area. A simple factor that enters in these expressions is the sampling area which goes as $1/\cos\theta$.

4. Index matching. Another factor that controls spectral contrast is index matching. In general, the closer the refractive index of the internal reflection element is to that of the sample, the higher will be the spectral contrast, because both d_p and E increase.

The validity of the expressions for d_e for thin and thick films has been tested[9] by comparing them to exact computer calculations of Fresnel's equations for reflectivity at an interface where the refractive indices, extinction coefficients, and sample thickness were changed over a wide range. An example of these results is given in Figure 37, where it should be noted that except for a small range of film thickness between $d_e = 0.1\lambda_1$ to $0.5\lambda_1$, the expressions for d_e are valid. As a result of these tests, one can have confidence in the use of these expressions, where they apply, even for quantitative measurements.

Another parameter that can be varied for thin films is the refractive index (n_3) of the outside medium.[10] This is done by immersing the internal reflection element, usually in the form of a plate, into a medium of higher refractive index. The effect of immersion can readily be determined from the above equations for the effective thicknesses of a thin absorbing film on a totally reflecting surface. To maintain critical reflection, the refractive index of the outer medium can be increased only until it reaches the critical index for total reflection, viz., $n_{3_c} = n_1 \sin\theta_c$ or $n_3/n_1 = 0.707$ for $\theta = 45°$. In general, the effective thickness will increase as the refractive index of the surrounding medium is increased. The reason for this is that the electric field amplitudes tend to increase as the refractive index approaches the critical index. In certain cases, however, as n_3 is increased, d_e may remain unchanged or even decrease. The decrease occurs in cases where E_x plays a dominant role and decreases near θ_c as $\theta \to \theta_c$.

The variation of spectral contrast by immersion is quite practical for the visible spectral region where a wide range of optically transparent liquids are available and optical contact is thus readily achieved. For the infrared, on the other hand, there are a number of soft solid materials which, when pressed against the internal reflection plate, will give fairly good contact. These materials include selenium-sulfur mixtures where the refractive index can be varied between 2 to 3, AgCl (n = 2), AgBr (n = 2.2), and GaSe (n = 2.2).

Figure 38 shows the effect on spectral contrast resulting from pressing AgCl (N = 2) onto a Ge (n = 4) double sampling plate having about 35 reflections at 45° and coated with 100 Å film of Nylon 4. It should be noted that $d_{e\parallel}/d_{e\perp} = 1.2$, as predicted by theory. Also as predicted by the above equations, there is an increase in both $d_{e\parallel}$ and $d_{e\perp}$ when AgCl is pressed against the surface, and, furthermore, $d_{e\parallel}$ increases to a greater degree than does $d_{e\perp}$. The increase in d_e is not as large as theoretically predicted, which can be explained by the lack of intimate contact between the AgCl and the Ge.

The results further demonstrate the usefulness of the effective thickness expressions, which permit one to select the parameters to optimize sensitivity, make quantitative measurements, etc. With the wide choice of parameters, the unsuspecting worker may, however, reach inaccurate conclusions, which further emphasizes the need for such simple expressions for the EPL to give insight into the mechanism involved.

The dispersion in the refractive index affects the nature of the spectrum for thick films near $\theta = \theta_c$ and is fully covered elsewhere.[7] We only caution that "distorted" spectra where the absorption band is broadened on the long-wavelength side are obtained by working near the critical angle. Advantage can be taken of this change in character of the spectrum to determine optical constants.

3. Internal Reflection Elements (IREs)

a. Geometries. The heart of the internal reflection technique is the internal reflection element, for which a few geometries for fixed and variable angles of incidence are shown in Figure 39, where lengths range from a few mm to as much as 10 cm.

The simplest fixed angle IRE is the mini prism for one or two reflections, and the most commonly used IRE is the single-pass (SP) plate, which may be trapezoid (T) or parallelopiped (P). In the latter the light is introduced into an aperture on one end, propagates down the length via multiple reflections, and exits via an aperture at the other end. The skip distance, or distance between reflection for a given ray, is thickness (t) times $\tan\theta$, and the number of reflections is given by the length (1) divided by the skip distance, i.e., $N = l/t\tan\theta$. The double-pass (DP) and double-sampling (DS) geometries have entrance and exit apertures at the same end; thus, the light traverses the length twice. The free end makes them attractive for use in vacuum systems or dewars requiring only one window or as probes for dipping into liquids and powders to record their spectra. The double-pass plate has an aperture only half the size of the single-pass plate since the available aperture is split for the entrance and exit beams. In the double-sampling geometry, the entrance and exit beams use the same entire

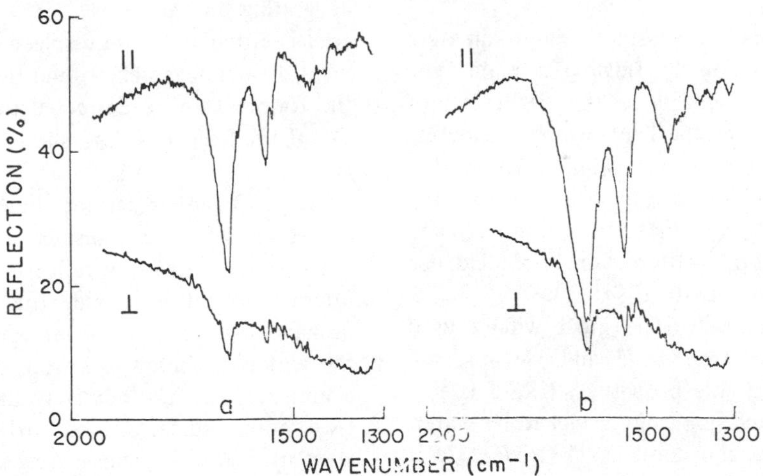

FIGURE 38. Spectra of 50 Å of Nylon 4 on Ge double sampling plate: (a) before and (b) after bringing AgCl in contact with nylon-covered Ge plate. Note increase in spectral contrast with greater increase for parallel polarization.

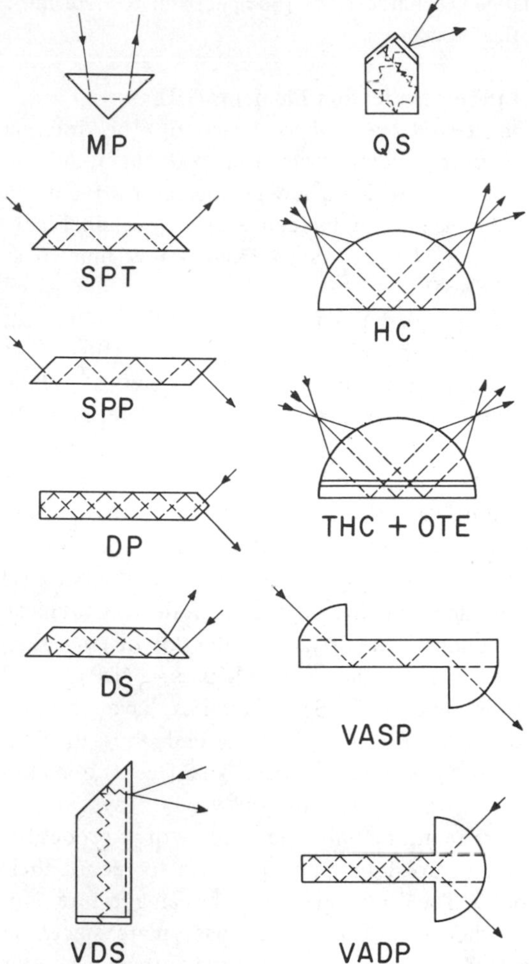

FIGURE 39. Geometries of internal reflection elements commonly used for internal reflection spectroscopy. Both fixed angle and variable angle elements are shown.

aperture, and, thus, the aperture is approximately the same as that for the single-pass plate. The other bevel is metallized so that light cannot escape. Separation of the light beams originating from reflection from the entrance aperture and the internal reflection mode is achieved by cocking the metallized bevel so that the return beam propagates at a slightly different angle of incidence and is refracted upon exiting.

b. Optical Materials. The most widely used materials for IRS are KRS-5 and Ge, both of which have undesirable properties. KRS-5 is soft and easily scratched, is readily attacked by water, acids, and alkalis, and contains Tl (toxic). Ge is brittle, has a limited transmission range because of lattice bands, and because of its high refractive index has high reflection losses. There is thus a constant search for new optical materials. For various applications a wide variety of optical materials have been employed to make internal reflection elements for wavelengths ranging from the UV to the far infrared. These materials include, in order of long wavelength cutoff, UV quartz, ZnO, UV sapphire, Si, MgO, CaF_2, As_2S_3, ZnS, Ge, Ge glass ($Ge_{35}Se_{50}As_{15}$), As_2Se_3, ZnSe, NaCl, KCl, KBr, AgCl, AgBr, CdTe, KRS-5, and Si. It will be noted that Si is listed twice because, although it has a sharp cutoff at 6.5 μ for internal reflection applications, it opens up again after 25 μ and is useful in the far infrared. The demands on the purity of the material are quite stringent since the path length in the material often exceeds 15 cm, and, therefore, weak absorption arising from impurities, free carriers, and weak lattice bands often undetectable in conventional transmission measurements through windows poses a severe problem for internal reflection spectroscopy.

Figure 40 shows the transmission curves for several IRS optical materials. Some of these materials, e.g., As_2Se_3, ZnSe, CdTe, have just recently become available in the required high optical quality to be used as IREs. These curves serve to emphasize a number of instrumental and optical material problems that become much more severe when hundreds of reflections and large-scale expansions are employed in the IRS mode.

The appearance of atmospheric bands may be due to instrument misalignment, but more likely it is due to beam displacement by the sample. TPMRA (described later) was employed for the IRS mode (except for CdTe). The discontinuities at grating interchanges (2000 and 630 cm^{-1}), caused either by beam displacement or by instrument slit opening greater than IRE aperture, can in the former case be corrected (usually by vertical tilt of the beam) as, e.g., shown by curves for Ge and Si.

Several points regarding these optical materials are of interest. The transmission level over useful range is determined by reflection losses.[7] For the internal reflection mode, the transmission will usually be lower because of weak absorptions in the material, energy loss from mirrors, imperfect alignment, etc. The relatively flat base line in the IRS mode indicates good surface polish of the element. Weak absorptions (e.g., lattice bands) are highly magnified in the IRS mode; e.g., Ge and Si, which are regarded as useful window materials out to 23 μm and 10 μm, respectively, cut off sharply

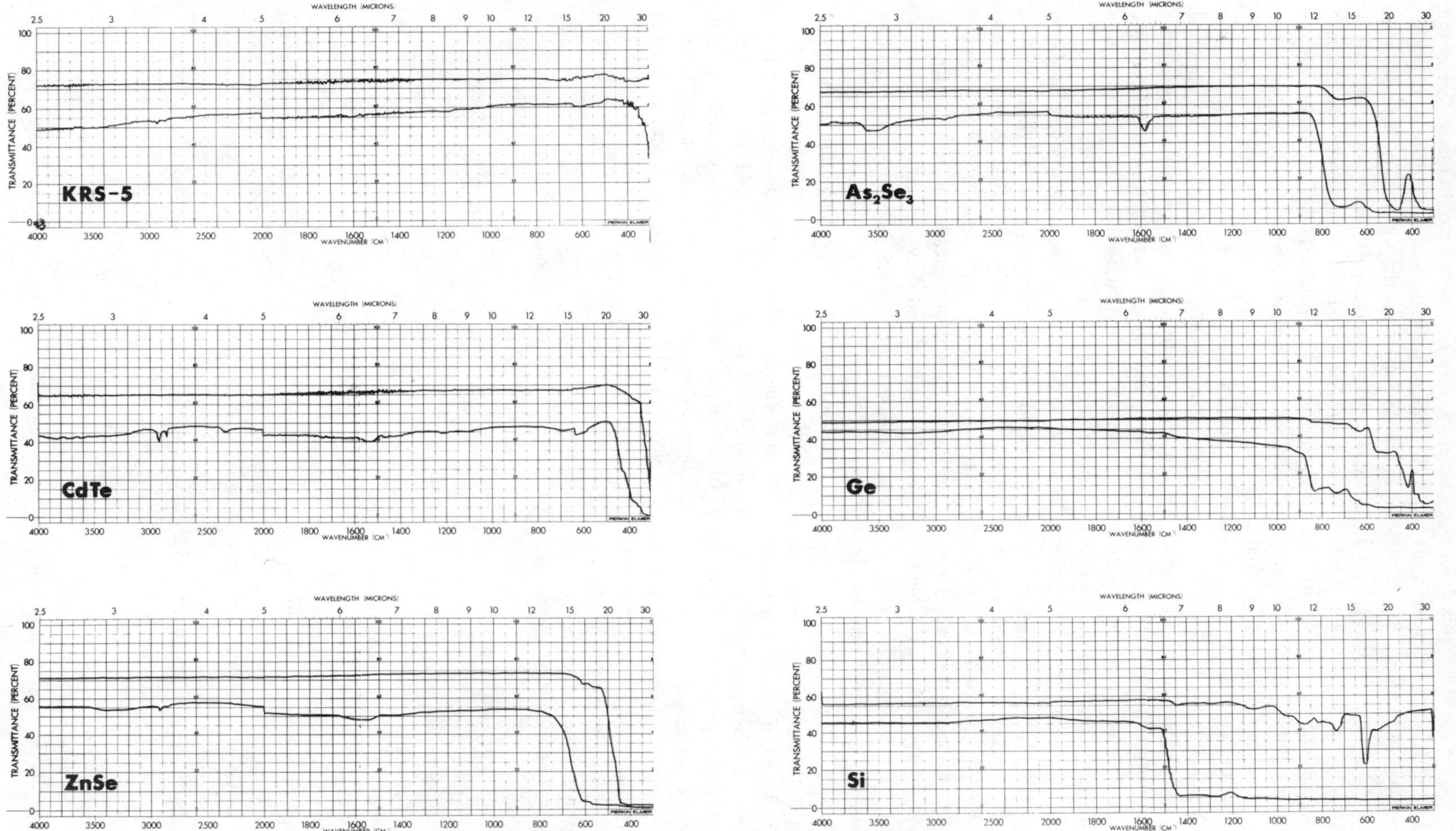

FIGURE 40. Transmission of a few optical materials as windows (t = 2mm except for Si, t = 1mm) and as internal reflection elements (t ~ 70mm, N = 25 in all cases except for Si, N = 50). Note the difference in long wavelength cutoff.

for internal reflection applications at 11.2 μm and 6.6 μm. The roll-off in Ge above 6.7 μ is due to free carrier absorption, which, according to Drude theory, increases as λ^2. Therefore, even the intrinsic-free carriers ($2 \times 10^{13}/cm^3$ at 20°C) decrease the transmission at the longer wavelengths. Furthermore, Ge can be used as optical window at temperatures above 250°C, while for internal reflection applications it cannot be used above 50°C because of the rapid increase in free carrier density with temperature.

The absorption bands seen in the IRS mode only may be from impurities either on the surface or in the bulk. It is possible to determine the location of the impurities by sending the radiation down the IRE first via the internal reflection mode and then down the length of the crystal parallel to the surface.[7] (Both modes of operation are possible with the HSPA described later.) For example, the bands appearing at 3.4 μm are due to surface contamination by hydrocarbons, while the bands in As_2Se_3 at 2.85 μm are due to bulk impurities. The former can be removed by appropriate cleaning.

A partial solution to the stringent requirements on optical material and cost of materials is to use microplates (with beam condensers). Some plates are now in use where the volume of material used is almost two orders of magnitude less than that used in plates most commonly employed and which still have the same number of reflections. Other advantages of microplates are that smaller samples can be employed, and, again, because of the smaller area, contact between IRE and sample is more readily achieved.

c. Cleaning. Careful surface preparation and cleanliness are imperative, especially in surface studies. Standard cleaning techniques often do not remove small traces of contamination which affect the surface properties and produce spurious absorption bands, especially when the techniques are capable of detecting sub-molecular films.

A small plasma cleaner has been found useful in removing organic contaminants. The instrument consists of an electrodeless gas discharge apparatus where the pressure in the vacuum chamber is adjusted (via a roughing pump) to about 0.1 torr, and the resulting gas discharge strips the substrate of contaminants in a few seconds. The resulting surface is both clean and sterile.

This method can be used for many materials such as sapphire, quartz, Si, and Ge, although through improper use, glass from the vacuum envelope may be sputtered onto the surface of the IRE. This method cannot be used for AgCl, AgBr, and KRS-5 because through photochemical reactions and reactions with residual O_2 and H_2O, films are produced on the surface which have strong absorption bands. Therefore, other cleaning methods must be developed.

4. Instrumentation

a. Attachments. Attachments for internal reflection spectroscopy are provided by a number of firms, and typical examples are described in a chapter on instrumentation for internal reflection spectroscopy (1967).[7]

The type of attachment employed is determined by the intended application, which in turn dictates the geometry of the IRE. A few attachments capable of employing all of the IREs shown in Figure 39 and of radically different designs are briefly discussed and show the capabilities that can be achieved for internal and external reflection measurements.

1. Twin-parallel Mirror Reflection Attachment (TPMRA). For routine use, an attachment using the twin-parallel mirror reflection principle based on an earlier proposal[7] (Figure 41a) has a number of attractive features. It employs SPP internal reflection plates (a version which takes SPT plates is also available, but the former is preferable) and

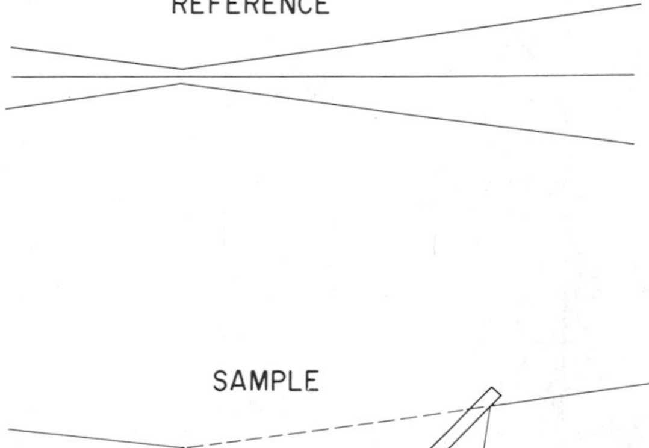

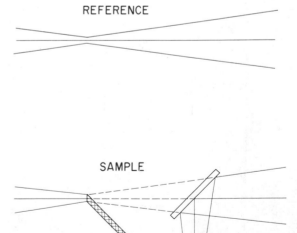

FIGURE 41a. The twin-parallel mirror reflection attachment (TPMRA) for internal reflection spectroscopy has attractive features, including ease of alignment, high efficiency, and no unbalance in the atmospheric bands.

takes advantage of the focus transfer phenomenon that occurs in internal reflection plates where the light beam is focused on and fills the entrance aperture and cannot expand while inside the plate. Thus, the beam is still in focus (concentrated) at the exit aperture, which acts as a new source image. Since the TPMRA requires only two plane mirrors, it is very efficient (especially for the UV, where the reflectivity of metals is lower than in the IR) and easy to align. Positive, well-defined change in angle of incidence is obtained by rotating the reflection plate about an axis coincident with the exit aperture. A most important feature not found in any other attachment is no unbalance in the atmospheric absorption bands when the attachment is placed in the instrument. While the light beam is inside the reflection plate, its path length in the atmosphere due to the evanescent wave is only a fraction of a millimeter. Thus, from Figure 41a it is evident that the path length of the light beam in the atmosphere is the same with the TPMRA in or out of the instrument, and there is thus no unbalance of the atmospheric bands. With this feature a unit for the reference beam is not necessary unless difference spectra are required.

The method of holding the internal reflection plate (by clamping along the bottom edge) leaves the sampling surface completely exposed and accessible and is convenient for cleaning the plate, which does not need to be touched. Pressure plates for pressing solid samples against the sampling surface may be bridge-type, which provide uniform pressure by means of a single thumb screw (or torque wrench), or alternately may be C-clamp pressure plates, which are open at the top and which allow some samples to be examined without cutting. Liquid sample holders consist of Teflon boat-type structures with the internal reflection plate placed in the middle. A boxlike accessory of rectangular cross section is employed for specular reflection.

2. Horizontal Single-pass Attachment (HSPA). With the horizontal single-pass attachment, the source image is rotated via an optical coupler so that the reflection plate can be operated with the sampling surface in a horizontal position and is the uppermost surface of the attachment. This arrangement permits recording of spectra in addition to the usual applications to the study of liquids or powders, without special sample holders.

b. Optical Goniometers. For many applications, commercially available spectrometers with well-designed attachments yield satisfactory performance. However, where complete flexibility and high sensitivity are required, advantage can be taken of recently developed instrumentation. Such systems can readily be assembled since good monochromators and electronic systems are available from a number of firms. The optical layout of such an instrument is shown in Figure 41b. The source optics are mounted on an arm which pivots at A at the rate of 2θ. The internal reflection elements for the sample and reference beams, as well as the beam chopper and recombiner, are mounted on a platform coupled to the 2θ arm, which also pivots about A but at θ rate, and the system remains in alignment for all angles of incidence. The beam splitter and recombiner are driven synchronously and must move together or farther apart symmetrically relative to AB at rate $\tan\theta$ as the angle of incidence is changed. Better than 0.01° mechanical accuracy can be obtained on both the θ and 2θ arms. With the ability to control the angle of incidence and the location of the beam focus relative to A, a high degree of flexibility is achieved. Such systems when used with suitable lock in amplifiers and optical beam splitters and recombiners operating at two frequencies can be employed to measure precisely either $\Delta I/I_0$ or I/I_0.

5. Sampling

An important feature of IRS is that particulate matter and rough surfaces do not cause light scattering, as observed in transmission measurements. Thus, powders, fabrics, paper, and similar materials are easily sampled. Thin films can be sampled without interference fringes superimposed on the spectrum. Adsorbed molecules and oxide films – even monomolecular films – can be studied. Sensitivity to small samples may be increased by spreading the sample thinly ($d<0.1\lambda$).[9]

Although ease of sampling preparation and handling is one of the advantages of IRS, caution must be exercised in the interpretation of spectral contrast and band intensity ratios because the nature of the contact may be unknown or the sample may not be placed on a portion of the IRE surface where the slit is imaged.

Parts of the surface of the IRE are or appear to be insensitive and thus give lower spectral contrast for samples narrower than a skip distance and

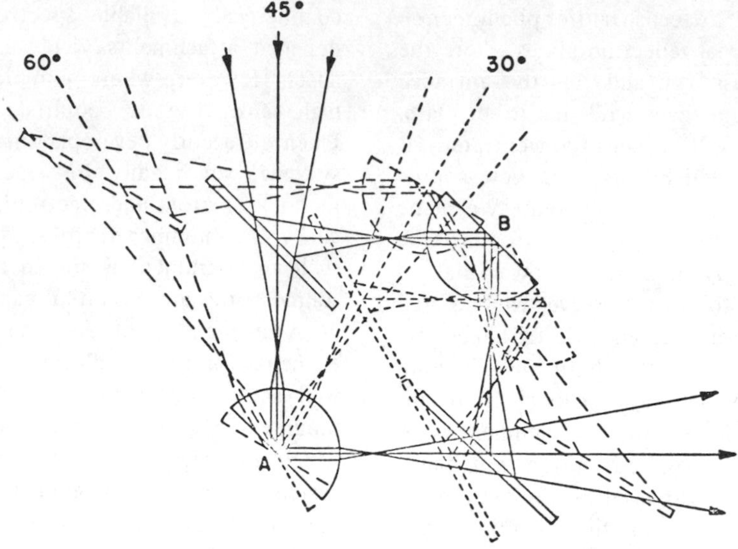

FIGURE 41b. Optical layout of double beam goniometer spectrometer for internal reflection, specular reflection, or transmission. Although it is shown here with a hemicylinder for single reflection, it may be used with multireflection variable angle double-pass plates. The angle of incidence can be changed continuously without misalignment.

placed at these regions. This is a real effect for $\theta>45°$ because the skip distance is such that the light does not see the entire sampling surface of the IRE.[7] For $\theta<45°$, there may appear to be insensitive areas, but this is an instrumental effect because often the slit width is less than the aperture of the IRE, and, therefore, light rays coming from certain portions of the sampling surface do not enter the spectrometer. Placing the sample on these regions is equivalent to placing the sample in a portion of the light beam that does not enter the instrument in transmission. Studies of these effects were made by Paralusz.[14]

The expressions for the equivalent path length show that for very thin films, band ratios are wavelength independent, while for thick films, band intensities are proportional to wavelength (as, e.g., shown in Figure 35). When contact is nonuniform, band ratios may have an even more complicated wavelength dependence;[7] and, in certain cases due to resonance phenomena, there is a large local enhancement with resulting band distortion.[8] Thus, for precise interpretation of band intensity ratios, the nature of the contact and film thickness must be known.

REFERENCES

1. **Archer, F. J.,** Determination of the properties of films on silicon by the method of ellipsometry, *J. Opt. Soc. Am.*, 52, 970, 1962.
2. **Beckmann, K. H. and Harrick, N. J.,** Internal reflection spectroscopy and ellipsometry for the study of thin films, *Proc. Electrochem. Soc.*, p. 123, May 1968.
3. **Bootsma, G. A. and Meyer, F.,** Measurement of adsorption on semiconductors by ellipsometry and other methods, *Surface Sci.*, 18, 123, 1969.
4. **Carniglia, C. K., Mandel, L., and Drexhage, K. H.,** Absorption and emission of evanescent photons, *J. Opt. Soc. Am.*, 62, 479, 1972.
5. **Drmaj, D. J. and Hayes, K. E.,** A practical application of infrared reflection to study of the gas-metal interface, *J. Catal.*, 19, 154, 1970.
6. **Francis, S. A. and Ellison, A. H.,** Infrared spectra of monolayers on metal mirrors, *J. Opt. Soc. Am.*, 49, 131, 1959.
7. **Harrick, N. J.,** *Internal Reflection Spectroscopy,* Interscience, New York, 1967. Also Russian translation, 1970.
8. **Harrick, N. J. and Turner, A. F.,** A thin film optical cavity to induce absorption or thermal emission, *Appl. Opt.*, 9, 2111, 1970.
9. **Harrick, N. J. and Carlson, A. I.,** Internal reflection spectroscopy: validity of effective thickness equations, *Appl. Opt.*, 10, 1, 1971.
10. **Harrick, N. J. and Beckmann, K. H.,** Internal reflection spectroscopy: study of surfaces and thin films, in *Characterization of Solid Surfaces,* Kane, P. F. and Larrabee, G. B., Eds., Plenum Press, New York, 1973.
11. **Kortüm, G.,** *Reflectance Spectroscopy,* Springer-Verlag, New York, 1969.
12. **McIntyre, J. D. E. and Aspnes, D. E.,** Differential reflection spectroscopy of very thin surface films, *Surface Sci.*, 24, 417, 1971.
13. **McIntyre, J. D. E.,** Specular reflection spectroscopy of the electrode-solution interphase, in *Advances in Electrochemistry and Electrochemical Engineering,* Vol. 9, Müller, R. H., Ed., Interscience, New York, 1972.
14. **Paralusz, C.,** Internal reflection spectroscopy applied to the analysis of adhesive tapes, *J. Colloid Interface Sci.*, in press, 1973.
15. **Poling, G. W.,** Infrared reflection studies of metal surfaces, *J. Colloid Interface Sci.*, 34, 365, 1970.
16. **Tompkins, H. G. and Greenler, R. G.,** Experimental development of reflection absorption spectroscopy; infrared spectra of carbon monoxide absorption on copper and copper oxide, *Surface Sci.*, 28, 194, 1971.
17. **Wendlandt, W. W. and Hecht, H. G.,** *Reflectance Spectroscopy,* Interscience, New York, 1966.
18. **Wendlandt, W. W.,** *Modern Aspects of Reflectance Spectroscopy,* Plenum Press, New York, 1968.

II. CALIBRATION: SECONDARY STANDARDS FOR WAVELENGTHS

POLYSTYRENE (SOLID FILM)[a]: 3300–600 cm^{-1}

Band No.	Wavenumber (vac.) (cm^{-1})
1	3027.1 ± 0.3
2	2924 ± 2
3	2850.7 ± 0.3
4	1944.0 ± 1
5	1871.0 ± 0.3
6	1801.6 ± 0.3
7	1601.4 ± 0.3
8	1583.1 ± 0.3
9	1181.4 ± 0.3
10	1154.3 ± 0.3
11	1069.1 ± 0.3
12	1028.0 ± 0.3
13	906.7 ± 0.3
14	698.9 ± 0.5

[a] Films from commercial sources of polystyrene frequently exhibit strong interference patterns; such films should be slightly bent or otherwise deformed before using for calibration purposes.

REFERENCE: IUPAC tables for the calibration of infra-red spectrometers, Butterworths, Washington, D.C., 1961. With permission.

CALIBRATION LINES, HG LAMP

Green Hg line @ 18,312.6

$$\nu = \frac{18{,}312.6}{N} - B$$

N = grating order
B = air-to-vacuum correction

N	
N = 5	3661.5 cm^{-1}
6	3051.3
7	2615.4
8	2288.5
9	2034.1
30	610.2
40	457.6
50	366.1
60	305.1
70	261.5

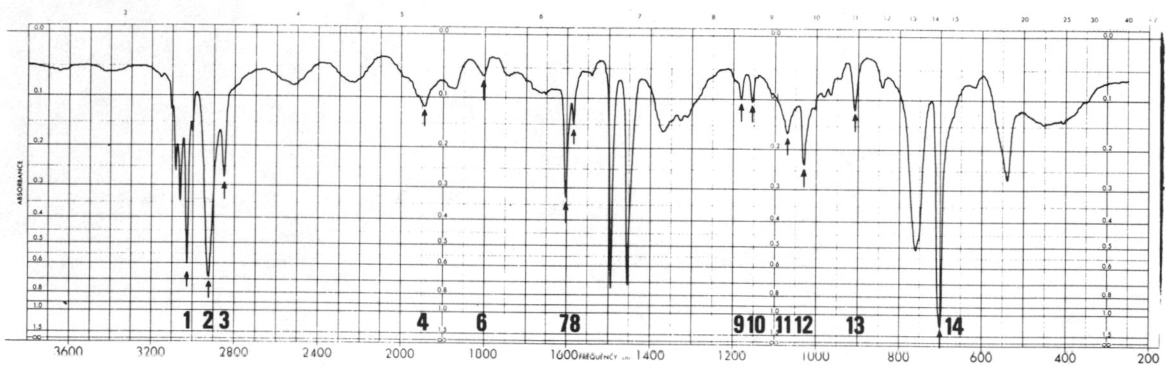

FIGURE 42. Spectrum of polystyrene film for calibration.

SPECTRUM

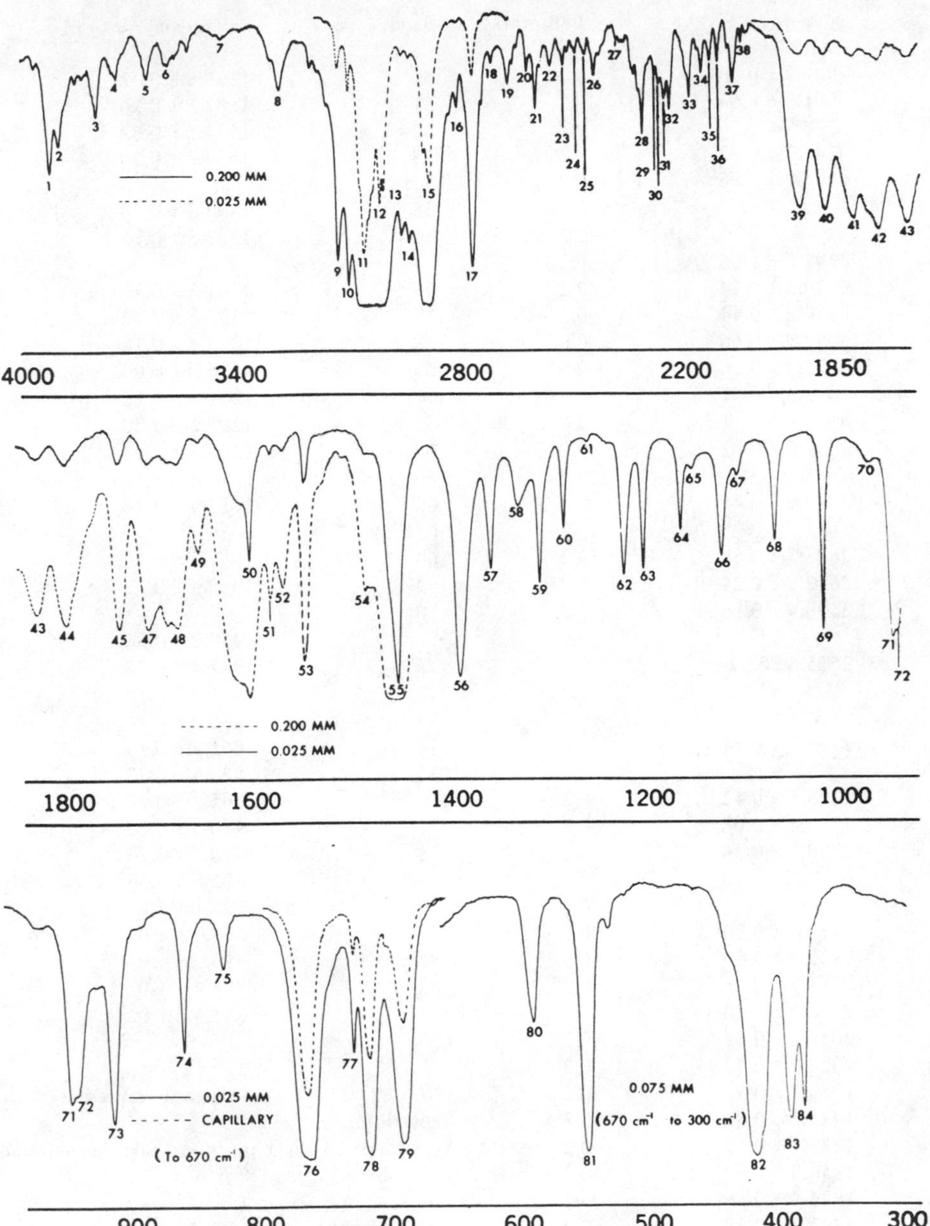

FIGURE 43. Spectrum of indene-camphor-cyclohexanone mixture for calibration. Segment A (4000 to 1500 cm^{-1}) run on Solution I, 0.2-mm cell; Segment B (1800 to 600 cm^{-1}) run on Solution I, 0.025-mm cell; Segment C (600 to 200 cm^{-1}) run on Solution II, 0.1-mm cell. Solution I: indene 98.4%, camphor 0.8%, cyclohexanone 0.8% by weight. Solution II: indene 33.3%, camphor 33.3%, cyclohexanone 33.3% by weight. (Courtesy of Perkin-Elmer Corporation.)

ABSORPTION MAXIMA RECOMMENDED FOR CALIBRATION PURPOSES

Band	ν(Vac)-cm^{-1}	Cell(mm)
1	3927.2 ± 0.56	0.2
2†	3901.6 ± 0.64	0.2
3 ‡	3798.9 ± 0.86	0.2
4 ‡	3745.2 ± 0.72	0.2
5 ‡	3660.6 ± 0.98	0.2
6		0.2
7		0.2
8 ‡	3297.8 ± 1.06	0.2
9†	3139.5 ± 0.44	0.2
10†	3110.2 ± 0.44	0.2
11 ‡	3068.9 ± 0.66	0.025
12†	3025.4 ± 0.26	0.025
13†	3015.3 ± 0.52	0.025
14†		0.025/0.2
15 ‡	2887.6 ± 0.82	0.025
16†		0.2
17	2770.9 ± 0.44	0.2
18†		0.2
19	2673.3 ± 0.56	0.2
20†	2622.3 ± 0.24	0.2
21	2598.4 ± 0.16	0.2
22		0.2
23	2525.5 ±0.32	0.2
24†		0.2
25†		0.2
26 ‡	2439.1 ± 0.24	0.2
27†		0.2
28	2305.1 ± 0.42	0.2
29†	2271.4 ± 0.08	0.2
30†	2258.7 ± 0.36	0.2
31		0.2
32		0.2
33	2172.8 ± 0.30	0.2
34	2135.8 ± 0.68	0.2
35	2113.2 ± 0.28	0.2
36	2090.2 ± 0.40	0.2
37 ‡	2049.1 ± 0.82	0.2
38†‡	2027.0 ± 0.42	0.2
39	1943.1 ± 0.52	0.2
40	1915.3 ± 0.30	0.2
41	1885.1 ± 0.42	0.2
42	1856.9 ± 0.52	0.2
43 ‡	1826.8 ± 0.56	0.2
44	1797.7 ± 0.50	0.2
45	1741.9 ± 0.50	0.2
46 ‡	1739.2 ± 0.78	0.2
47	1713.4 ± 0.66	0.2
48 ‡	1684.9 ± 1.14	0.2
49 ‡	1661.8 ± 0.64	0.2
50	1609.8 ± 0.42	0.025
51	1587.5 ± 0.26	0.2
52 ‡	1574.5 ± 0.62	0.2
53	1553.2 ± 0.20	0.2
54†		0.2
55 ‡	1457.3 ± 0.38	0.025
56 ‡	1393.5 ± 0.76	0.025
57	1361.1 ± 0.16	0.025
58 ‡	1332.8 ± 0.42	0.025
59	1312.4 ± 0.18	0.025
60	1288.0 ± 0.08	0.025
61†‡	1264.0 ± 0.12	0.025
63	1205.1 ± 0.20	0.025
64	1166.1 ± 0.08	0.025
65†		0.025
66	1122.4 ± 0.32	0.025
67†		0.025
68	1067.7 ± 0.30	0.025
69	1018.5 ± 0.32	0.025
70†		0.025
71	947.2 ± 0.36	0.025
72	942.4 ± 0.38	0.025
73	914.7 ± 0.16	0.025
73	914.7 ± 0.16	0.025
74	861.3 ± 0.14	0.025
75	830.5 ± 0.32	0.025
76	765.3 ± 0.22	0.012
77	730.3 ± 0.22	0.012
78	718.1 ± 0.24	0.012
79 ‡	692.6 ± 0.56	0.012
80 ‡	592.1 ± 0.5	0.025
81	551.3 ± 1.0	0.025
82	419.9 ± 1.0	0.025
83	393.4 ± 1.0	0.025
84	381.4 ± 1.0	0.025

NOTES: (1) Variation given represents twice standard deviation.

(2) Omitted band positions have been found unreliable for calibration.

† This band may not be resolved by the smaller types of prism spectrometers.

‡ Because of asymmetry, superposition on atmospheric water vapor or carbon dioxide bands, or for other reasons, these bands are less suited for accurate calibration.

III. SPECTROMETER OPERATION

A. The Coblentz Society Specifications for the Evaluation of Infrared Reference Spectra: Class II Spectra

(Revised to September 4th 1968)

Class II spectra are reference spectra obtained on the best currently available commercial infrared grating spectrophotometers, operated at maximum efficiency under conditions consistent with acceptable laboratory practice. The purity of the compounds should be rigidly specified with respect to the type and quantity of any impurity detectable in the spectroscopic measurements. The specifications for Class II spectra given in this report apply only to the absorption spectra of condensed phase systems, and it is not considered practical to write specifications for vapor phase spectra or for reflectance spectra at this time.

1. Spectrometer Operation

a. Resolution. The spectral slit width should not exceed 2 cm^{-1} through at least 80% of the wavenumber range, and at no place should it exceed 5 cm^{-1}. There are technical difficulties in measuring the spectral slit width, and its evaluation will be based on a spectrum of indene run under the same conditions as were used to produce the submitted spectrum (Appendix).

b. Wavenumber Accuracy. The abscissa as read from the chart should be accurate to ± 5 cm^{-1} at wavenumbers greater than 2000 cm^{-1} and to ± 3 cm^{-1} at wavenumbers less than 2000 cm^{-1}. Calibration corrections within these limits are to be encouraged and should be indicated on the chart.

Proof of the wavenumber accuracy will be an appended spectrum of indene run under the same conditions as the sample (Appendix). Fiduciary marks should be recorded on each chart at stated wavenumbers shortly after the beginning and near or at the end of each uninterruptedly scanned segment of the spectrum. These marks are required to guard against errors from paper shrinkage and from chart-spectrometer mismatch.

c. Noise Level. The noise level should not exceed 1% average peak-to-peak (or 0.25% rms). The evaluator's judgment is permissible.

d. Energy. The spectrophotometer should be purged with dry gas or evacuated to ensure that at least 50% of the source energy is available at all wavenumbers (except in the region of the 2350 cm^{-1} carbon dioxide absorption.)

If the control system of the spectrophotometer permits, it is desirable that adequate purging or evacuation be demonstrated by a single beam run or a run against a constant test signal, measured under the normal scanning conditions, with no sample in the beam.

e. Other Performance Criteria. (Established by reference to the indene spectrum. See Appendix.)

1. False radiation. Apparent stray radiation should be less than 2% at wavenumbers greater than 500 cm^{-1}.

2. Servo System. Any spectrum showing evidence of dead spots or of excessive overshoot should be rejected. The spectrometer time constant should be compatible with the scan rate (Appendix, Section b).

3. Photometric Accuracy. These spectra are not intended to have absolute quantitative significance, and, at present, it is not feasible to set specifications for photometric accuracy. Such a test might be added later, but for the time being it must suffice that the indene bands be in reasonable agreement in shape and relative intensity with an acceptable indene curve.

4. Temperature. It is to be assumed, unless stated otherwise, that the spectrum is run at the ambient temperature.

2. Presentation

a. Information to Appear on Chart. Both the structural and the molecular formulas of the compound should appear on the chart. It is also recommended that the compound name be included, and preferably this should conform with the nomenclature used by *Chemical Abstracts.* The make and model of the spectrophotometer should be recorded as well as the date on which the spectrum was obtained. All changes of gratings, filters, and cells should be specified, including the wavenumber at which they occur. No external mechanical attenuator is to be placed in the reference beam additional to the trimmer comb which is integral to some infrared spectrophotometers. The name and address of the laboratory contributing the spectrum will normally be given on the chart (see Section 3.a.).

The physical condition of the sample should be

stated (e.g., solution, pure liquid, Nujol mull, potassium bromide pellet matrix, etc.). For measurements on solutions, the solvent used in each region of the spectrum should be recorded. The concentration and nominal path length should be given both for solutions and pellets. The nominal path length of pure liquid samples should be indicated; a very thin layer may be described as a capillary film (see Section 3.b.1.c). In all cases the cell or support window material should be stated.

b. Spectral Range. The chart should cover 3800 cm^{-1} to 400 cm^{-1} without gaps; extensions above or below this range are acceptable. For such extended range spectra, the wavenumber accuracy, false radiation, atmospheric absorption, and spectral slit width should be stated and must be acceptable in the judgment of the evaluator.

c. Intensity. It is preferred that the intensity ordinate values be expressed in absorbance units and that the charts be plotted on paper having a logarithmic ordinate grid so that intensity in absorbance can be interpolated directly from linear transmittance measurements. Spectra plotted on a linear absorbance scale, or in linear transmittance presented on a linear percent transmission ordinate grid, are also acceptable.

Any band over 1.5 absorbance units should be reproduced on a less absorbing sample. A significant fraction of the useful bands should have absorbance greater than 0.2. At least one band in the spectrum should have absorbance exceeding 0.7. When multiple traces are required, their number should be kept to a minimum.

d. Wavenumber Readability. Sharp peaks should be readable to 5 cm^{-1} at wavenumbers greater than 2000 cm^{-1} and 2 cm^{-1} at wavenumbers less than 2000 cm^{-1}. Only spectra recorded with the abscissa linear in wavenumber are acceptable, but scale changes at designated abscissal positions are allowed.

e. Recording. Recording should be continuous with no gaps in wavenumber, but it is permissible for spectra to extend over more than one chart. Discontinuities in ordinate (absorbance), if present, should not exceed 0.01 absorbance unit. Hand retraced spectra are not acceptable.

f. Atmospheric Absorption. None should be detectable (note also Section 1.d).

3. Sample Identification

a. Compound Identity and Purity. Spectra should show no inconsistencies with the postulated structure; any spectrum exhibiting an obvious impurity band should be rejected. Some relaxation of this requirement may be permitted in the case of isotopically labeled substances in which complete exchange cannot reasonably be achieved. In such cases the bands associated with the minor isotopic species should be indicated on the chart.

Because the prime responsibility for the correctness of the structure lies with the laboratory contributing the spectrum, its name and address should be recorded on the chart. In exceptional cases spectra contributed anonymously may be published, but such spectra will be prominently labeled "Chemical Structure not Authenticated."

No spectrum should be published unless either (1) the evaluator is supplied with a reasonably detailed description of the preparation and purification history of the measured sample, together with other evidence for the correctness of the assigned chemical structure which is sufficient to satisfy an expert in the field or (2) two curves derived from samples obtained from independent sources are available; these spectra must be in reasonable agreement.

b. Sample Preparation

1. Liquid State

(a) For analytical purposes it is preferable that the sample be run in liquid solution, normally at concentrations in the range of 5 to 10% weight (g) per volume (ml). Solvent bands should be compensated, but not more than 75% of the energy should be removed from the beam by such compensation, and then only over a short region. Any solvent bands resulting from incomplete compensation should be clearly indicated on the chart. A suitable solvent combination is carbon tetrachloride in the range 3800 to 1335 cm^{-1} and carbon disulfide in the range 1350 to 430 cm^{-1}; both solvents should preferably be used at path lengths in the range 0.03 to 0.3 mm. Cases may arise that require the use of other solvents, and solubility limitations or other concentration dependent factors may necessitate the use of cells of longer path length. These conditions are acceptable, provided the requirement of a maximal 75% beam energy attenuation is maintained.

(b) For documentation purposes it is desirable that the spectrum of the pure liquid be recorded. Solution spectra and pure liquid spectra are to be regarded as complementary and not as substitutes for one another.

(c) Liquids not soluble in transparent solvents are to be run as capillary films (see Section 2.a).

2. Solid State

(a) Solution spectra in the most transparent solvents are preferred, provided the solvents and path lengths can be chosen to leave no significant gaps due to solvent obscuration (see 3.b.1.a).

(b) For insoluble compounds mulls are preferred to pressed pellets, unless it is established that the pellet gives an undistorted spectrum. Solid state spectra must meet the following criteria:

i. Isotropic materials. The background absorbance should be less than 0.20 near 3800 cm^{-1} and less than 0.10 near 2000 cm^{-1}. No gross abnormalities should be evident in the background. Compensation in the reference beam by a blank mull or pellet should be indicated, and in no case should it reduce the reference radiation intensity by more than 50%. The Christiansen effect should not be apparent, but minor distortions resulting from this effect may be permitted at the evaluator's discretion. Interference fringes should not be apparent. Pellets should exhibit no water absorption bands greater than 0.03 absorbance unit. Mulls should be made with perhalogenated oils (or equivalent) for the range 3800 to 1335 cm^{-1}, and the intensity of the overtone band near 2300 cm^{-1} should not exceed 0.02 absorbance unit. Nujol (or equivalent) should be used below 1335 cm^{-1}, and the intensity of the band near 720 cm^{-1} should not exceed 0.05 absorbance unit.

ii. Non-isotropic materials. Spectra of non-isotropic samples, such as single crystals or crystalline polymers, should also be accompanied by a record of the orientation of the sample with respect both to the radiation beam and to the grating rulings.

Amorphic and partially crystalline polymers of ill-defined molecular and conformational structure should not be included as pure materials.

4. Appendix. Spectrophotometer Performance Checks.

a. Wavenumber Calibration. For the range 3800 to 700 cm^{-1}, the wavenumber calibration should be checked on a sample of indene containing 0.8% (by weight) of cyclohexanone and 0.8% (by weight) of camphor. This solution, prepared from freshly distilled or sublimed materials, should be stored in sealed glass ampoules which are opened just before use. The spectrum is published in "Tables of Wavenumbers for the Calibration of Infrared Spectrometers" prepared by the Commission on Molecular Structure and Spectroscopy of I.U.P.A.C. (Butterworths, London, 1961, reprinted from *Pure and Applied Chemistry,* Vol. 1, 1961, 679-83. See also Jones, R. N. and Nadeau, A., *Spectrochim. Acta,* 20, 1175, 1964).

Below 700 cm^{-1} a solution prepared from equal parts (by weight) of indene, cyclohexanone, and camphor can be used pending the establishment of approved standards for this spectral range. (See Jones, R. N., Faure, P. K., and Zaharias, W., *Rev. Universelle Mines,* 15, 417, 1959).

Each set of spectra should be accompanied by a set of indene spectra run significantly close in time to the submitted spectra and measured at the same slit width, noise level, scanning speed, and time constant. A nominal cell thickness of 0.2 mm is recommended for the range 3800 to 1580 cm^{-1} and 0.03 mm for the range 1600 to 700 cm^{-1}. A cell thickness of 0.05 mm is recommended for the 1:1:1 mixture below 700 cm^{-1}.

Recommended calibration points (cm^{-1} in vacuo) are the absorption maxima shown in Table 1. Other secondary standards calibrated over the entire spectral range may also be accepted subject to their compatability with Sections b and c below.

b. Dynamic Error. The following dynamic error test is suitable for use with most spectrophotometers. The indene spectrum is rerun from 1350 to 850 cm^{-1} at one fourth of the scanning rate used for the reference spectra, with other operating conditions unchanged. The heights from the baseline of the bands at 1288.0, 1226.2, 1205.1, 1018.5, and 914.7 cm^{-1} are measured in absorbance units on both fast and slow scanned charts. The peak height ratios $A_{1288.0}/A_{1226.2}$, $A_{1205.1}/A_{1226.1}$, and $A_{1018.5}/A_{914.7}$ should not differ by more than ± 0.02 between the slow and the fast runs.

c. Spectral Slit Width. This quantity can be determined approximately in the neighborhood of 1200 cm^{-1} from the ratio $A_{1205.1}/A_{1226.2}$ computed in the dynamic error test, namely:

Ratio	Approximate Spectral Slit Width, cm^{-1}
0.80	4.0–5.0
0.85	3.0–3.5
0.90	2.0–2.5
0.95	1.0–1.5
0.97	<1.0

d. False Radiation. The indene spectrum should show total absorption at 3050.0, 1609.6, and 765.4 cm^{-1} if measured at the designated thicknesses. The test spectra at these wavenumbers, therefore, should match the spectrometer transmission zero within the allowed tolerances (see Section 1.e.1). A 0.4 mm layer of pure indene is totally absorbing at 392, 420, and 551 cm^{-1}, and this can be used to establish the false radiation below 600 cm^{-1}. The permissible amount of false radiation in this region of the spectrum is left to the discretion of the evaluator.

e. Check on I_o. Each set of spectra must be accompanied by an I_o check obtained by scanning the wavenumber range of the submitted spectra with no cell in either beam at the same slit width, noise level, scanning speed, and recorder time constant. The I_o trace should be nominally flat, i.e., lie between ± 0.01 nominal absorbance units (at the discretion of the evaluator).

f. Cell Blank Check. Each set of solution spectra must be accompanied by a trace obtained at the same slit width, noise level, scanning speed, and recorder time constant, with solvent in both cells. The same cells must be used as for the submitted spectra. No extraneous bands should appear, though it is recognized that solvent bands may not be completely compensated in the cell blank spectrum. The permissible degree of mismatch is left to the judgment of the evaluator.

g. Energy Check. See Section 1.d.

B. Class III Spectra

1. Spectrometer Operation

a. Resolution. The make and model of the spectrometer must be reported on the published chart, and the dispersing element must be identified (e.g., NaCl prism; grating). The resolution should be consistent with the operating specifications for the spectrometer. The minimum acceptable performance is that obtainable from a sodium chloride prism spectrometer in good operating condition.

b. Wavenumber Accuracy. Charts showing evidence of wavenumber calibration error in excess of ± 30 cm^{-1} at 3000 cm^{-1} or ± 5 cm^{-1} below 2000 cm^{-1} will be rejected. For spectra recorded on a linear wavelength scale, the permitted tolerance is ± 0.04 μm in all ranges

c. Noise Level. Charts exhibiting more than 2% average peak-to-peak noise should be rejected.

d. Energy. It is recommended that the spectrometer be purged with dry air to ensure that at least 50% of the source energy is available throughout the spectrum (except at the 2350 cm^{-1} CO_2 absorption).

e. Other Performance Criteria.

1. Charts exhibiting evidence of more than

TABLE 1

Absorption Maxima Recommended for Calibration Purposes:

Solution I

3927.2	3798.9	3660.6	3297.8	3139.5	2770.9	2598.4
2305.1	2090.2	1915.3	1797.7	1741.9	1713.4	1661.8
1587.5	1361.1	1312.4	1288.0	1226.2	1205.1	1122.4
1067.7	1018.5	914.7	830.5	730.3		

Solution II

692.6	592.1	551.7	490.2	393.1	381.6	301.4

Solution I (indene 98.4%, cyclohexanone 0.8%, camphor 0.8% [by weight]).

Solution II (indene 33.3%, cyclohexanone 33.3%, camphor 33.3% [by weight]).

5% stray radiation in any region of the spectrum, or excursions of any absorption band beyond the nominal zero transmission region, are not acceptable.

2. Charts exhibiting evidence of a dead servo system or of excessive overshoot will be rejected.

2. Presentation

a. Information to Appear on Chart. Both the structural and the molecular formulas of the compound must appear on the chart. It is also recommended that the compound name be included, and preferably this should conform with the nomenclature used by *Chemical Abstracts.* The make and model of the spectrophotometer must be recorded as well as the date on which the spectrum was obtained.

The physical condition of the sample must be stated (e.g., Nujol mull, solution, pure liquid, etc.). For measurements on solutions, the solvent used in each region of the spectrum must be recorded on the published chart. The path length and concentration should also be given, but spectra lacking this information may be accepted at the discretion of the evaluator. The path length of pure liquid samples and concentrations in pelleted disk spectra should be given if possible.

b. Spectral Range. The chart must cover 3700 to 700 cm^{-1}. Gaps caused by solvent interference or by obscuration from mulling agents may be permitted at the discretion of the evaluator, but must be designated as such on the published chart.

c. Intensity. It is anticipated that many spectra will be recorded on a linear transmittance ordinate grid, but spectra recorded on paper having a logarithmic ordinate grid are preferable, since this permits the direct interpolation of absorbance intervals.

The absorption bands must be strong enough to be useful in characterizing the material. Spectra are generally unacceptable if they show:

1. no bands more intense than 0.6 absorbance unit;
2. many bands exhibiting total absorption;
3. an average I_o less than 60 to 75% T.

d. Wavenumber Readability. Band peak positions must be readable on the published chart to ± 15 cm^{-1} at 3000 cm^{-1} and ± 2.5 cm^{-1} below 2000 cm^{-1}. Spectra recorded on a linear wavelength scale in microns are acceptable, but in selecting among alternative spectra for a given compound, preference should be given to the linear wavenumber presentation unless there are strong reasons to decide otherwise. The peak positions for linear wavelength charts must be readable to 0.02 μm.

e. Recording. It is preferred that the spectrum exhibit no gaps in wavenumber (evaluator's discretion).

Hand retraced spectra are undesirable, but if they are so designated on the published chart, they may be accepted at the discretion of the evaluator.

f. Atmospheric Absorption. Bands resulting from atmospheric absorption should ordinarily be no greater than 2% T. (Discretion of the evaluator.)

3. Sample Identification

a. Compound Identity and Purity

1. **Identity**. Spectra should not show any obvious inconsistencies with the postulated structure, but the consistency is not, by itself, acceptable as proof of the correctness of the postulated structure.

Purchase of a material from a reputable chemical supply house and preparation according to an accepted procedure are not, in themselves, acceptable as proof of structure. Additional physical and chemical evidence, sufficient to satisfy an expert in the field, should be supplied to the evaluator. Preferably this evidence should come from measurements on the same batch as was used for the infrared spectrum. The names and addresses of laboratories contributing spectra will normally appear on the published charts, and also literature references to the preparation of the compound, where such are available. Spectra may be published without the name and address of the supply laboratory, but such charts will be prominently labeled "Chemical Structure Not Authenticated."

The infrared spectrum itself may be acceptable as supporting proof of structure when it is in substantial agreement with the spectrum of another sample from an independent source.

2. **Purity**. The purity of the samples should be such that only bands of minor intensity due to impurities are present, and these bands should all be identified on the published chart. (The permitted intensity of the impurity band is at the discretion of the evaluator but should not normally exceed 10% of the absorbance of the

major band of established structural significance.) Not more than three impurity bands should appear. Allowance will be made for compounds that are readily hydrolyzed, oxidized, or isomerized. It should be noted that the presence of correctly identified impurity bands in the spectra of unstable materials is not necessarily a detriment, since one of the uses of the published spectra is for the detection and identification of such common impurities. It may be helpful to supply the evaluator with copies of spectra containing higher amounts of the designated impurities, where these are available, but such spectra should not be published. No spectrum containing known impurity bands should be published where acceptable curves of samples of higher purity are available. Cases may arise where it is desirable to publish spectra that fail to meet these criteria for proof of structure. If this is done, the published chart must be prominently marked "Chemical Structure Not Authenticated" (see also Section 3.a).

b. Sample Preparation

1. Liquid State

(a) Solution spectra should satisfy the requirement that the solvents and path lengths in different regions of the spectrum are selected to leave no significant gaps due to solvent obscuration (note also Section 2.c).

(b) Thin layers of the pure liquids are acceptable.

2. Solid State

(a) Solution spectra in the most transparent solvents are preferred, provided the solvents and path lengths leave no significant gaps due to solvent obscuration.

(b) For insoluble compounds mulls are preferred to pellets, unless it is known that the pellet gives an undistorted spectrum. Such solid state spectra must meet the following criteria:

There must be at least 25% nominal transmission at 3700 cm^{-1} and at least 40% nominal transmission at 2000 cm^{-1} in the absence of specific compound absorption. There must be no gross abnormalities or discontinuities. Spectra should not exhibit appreciable pseudo-structure attributable to interference fringes, and any such fringe patterns should be identified on the published chart. The Christiansen effect should not be great enough to distort the band contours significantly. In spectra of alkali halide pellets, the water absorption bands must not exceed 0.1 absorbance unit.

3. Tentative Recommendations for Gas and Vapor Spectra (Class III)

(a) For analytical purposes it is recommended that the following conditions be used:

The sample path length should be 5 to 10 cm and should be stated. A reference cell of the same path length, evacuated or filled with inert gas, may be used in the reference beam to reduce spurious atmospheric absorptions.

The pressure of the absorbing gas should be selected so as to display the significant features in the spectrum, while showing a minimum number of bands so strong that structure is lost (note also Section 2.c). For a cell path of 10 cm, a partial pressure of 20 to 50 mm of the absorbing species will often give an adequate spectrum, although considerable variation from the suggested pressure may sometimes be necessary. Very intense absorptions should be rescanned at lower pressure (by a factor of approximately 5), but the number of additional tracings should be kept to a minimum, and they should be placed on the chart in such a way that the recorder traces do not cross or otherwise interfere.

Bands containing closely spaced but resolved vibration-rotational structure should be presented on a second chart with an expanded abscissa scale. In this case it is desirable to attach a calibration spectrum indexed by fiducial wavenumber marks (preferably another gas; see "Tables of Wavenumbers" referenced in Appendix of Class II Spectra).

The pressure of the absorbing gas should be clearly indicated for each trace. A dry, inert diluent gas (N_2, A, He) should be used to bring the pressure of the system to 700 mm, and the total pressure as well as the identity of the inert gas should be stated. The approximate temperature of the system should also be given.

(b) For documentation purposes gas and vapor spectra may be recorded under a wide variety of conditions. Since the conditions chosen will reflect the purpose for which the spectrum is recorded, it is not considered feasible to recommend specific parameters. The following data should appear, however, as part of the record: pressure; temperature; path length; approximate resolution of the spectrometer; other gases present and their approximate partial pressure; and if a multi-reflection cell is used, the number of reflections.

(c) Users of gas and vapor spectra must recognize that such spectra are strictly qualitative, since the intensity of an absorption may depend strongly on the total pressure as well as on the partial pressure of the absorbing species. (Intensities may change by a factor of 5 or more upon pressurizing a gas from 0 to 1 atm with an inert diluent.) Furthermore, the intensities of different bands do not respond equally to pressurization.

On the other hand, the exact frequency of sharp spikes is likely to be important for qualitative analysis. Thus, it is especially important for gas and vapor spectra that wavenumber calibration accuracy be established and maintained.

B. Spectral Slit Width of a Grating Monochromator

(1) $$\Delta\nu = F(s)\frac{\nu\cos\theta}{na} + \frac{\nu^2 s}{mnf}\cos\theta$$

where θ = angle of diffraction and

(2) $$\sin\theta = \frac{mn}{2\nu}$$

F(s) = function of physical slit width
= 0.9 for extremely narrow slits
= 0.5 for normal slits

$\Delta\nu$ = spectral slit width in cm^{-1}

a = effective aperture of collimated beam

f = monochromator focal length

s = mechanical slit width in cm

m = grating order used

n = grating lines/cm

ν = frequency at which $\Delta\nu$ is determined

C. Relationship Between Noise (N), Slit Width (s), and Response Time (τ):

$$N \propto s^{-2}\,\tau^{-1/2}$$

Typical Relationships Between the Variables:

	N	s	τ	
a	1	1	1	(Normal conditions)
b	0.5	1.41	1	
c	0.5	1	4	
d	0.25	2	1	
e	4	0.5	1	
f	1	0.5	16	
g	2	0.5	4	

Example: To reduce noise by a factor of .5, either open the slit by a factor of $\sqrt{2}$ (line b) and reduce the gain, or increase the response time by a factor of 4 (line c).

REFERENCE: Potts, W. J., Jr. and Smith, A. L., *Appl. Opt.*, 6, 257, 1967.

ORDINATE EXPANSION BY A FACTOR X:

To reduce noise to normal level, open the slit by a factor of $\sqrt{x}$ (where x is the expansion factor) and reduce the gain by x.

D. Determination of Scan Speed from the Spectrometer Time Constant and the Half-band Width.

$$\text{Scan rate } (cm^{-1}/sec) = \frac{\Delta\nu_b}{k\theta}$$

where $\Delta\nu_b$ = half-width of band scanned

k = 10 for 1% dynamic error
= 6 for 5% dynamic error
= 4.5 for 10% dynamic error

θ = time constant; the time required for a critically damped system to reach 1/e or 63% of its steady-state value

$\tau \approx 4\theta$ approximately

E. The Ratio of the True to the Apparent Maximum Absorbance for Various Apparent Maximum Absorbances and Slit Widths of a Lorentzian Band

Apparent Absorbance	$s/\Delta\nu_{1/2}$ 0.00	0.05	0.10	0.15	0.20	0.25	0.30	0.35	0.40	0.45	0.50	0.55	0.60	0.65
2.0	1.00	1.00	1.01	1.02	1.03	1.04	1.06	1.09	1.13	1.18	1.24	1.32	1.44	1.61
1.8	1.00	1.01	1.01	1.02	1.03	1.04	1.06	1.09	1.13	1.18	1.24	1.32	1.44	1.59
1.6	1.00	1.01	1.01	1.02	1.03	1.04	1.06	1.09	1.13	1.18	1.24	1.32	1.43	1.58
1.4	1.00	1.01	1.01	1.02	1.03	1.04	1.06	1.09	1.13	1.18	1.24	1.32	1.43	1.57
1.2	1.00	1.01	1.01	1.02	1.03	1.04	1.06	1.09	1.13	1.17	1.24	1.31	1.42	1.56
1.0	1.00	1.01	1.01	1.02	1.03	1.04	1.06	1.09	1.13	1.17	1.24	1.31	1.42	1.55
0.8	1.00	1.01	1.01	1.02	1.03	1.04	1.06	1.09	1.13	1.17	1.24	1.31	1.41	1.54
0.6	1.00	1.01	1.01	1.02	1.03	1.04	1.06	1.09	1.13	1.17	1.24	1.31	1.41	1.53
0.4	1.00	1.01	1.01	1.02	1.03	1.04	1.06	1.09	1.13	1.17	1.23	1.30	1.40	1.53
0.2	1.00	1.01	1.01	1.02	1.03	1.04	1.06	1.09	1.13	1.17	1.23	1.30	1.40	1.52

REFERENCE: **Ramsey, D. A.,** *J. Am. Chem. Soc.,* 74, 72, 1952.

F. Theoretical Transmission of Mylar Beamsplitter Foils for Infrared Interferometers

Beamsplitter Thickness	Useful Range
3 μm	800–100 cm^{-1}
6	420–75
12	220–40
25	100–15
50	50–10
100	25–5
200	13–3

REFERENCE: **Bell, R. J.,** *Introductory Fourier Transform Spectroscopy,* Academic Press, New York, 1972.

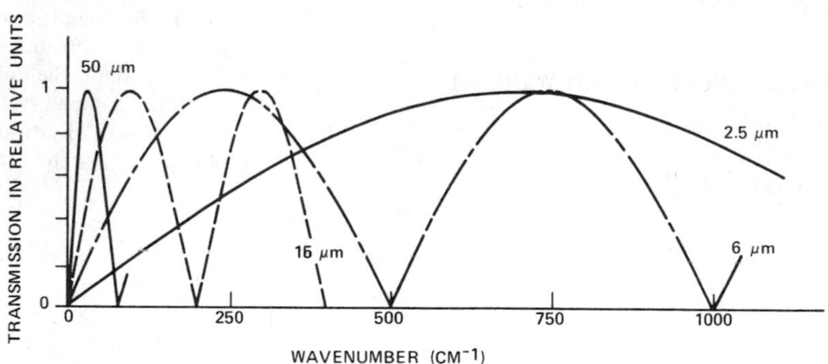

FIGURE 44. Theoretical transmittance of Mylar beamsplitter foils.

A. Common Spurious Absorption Bands and Their Origin

Approximate Frequency	Wavelength	Compound or Group	Origin
3700 cm^{-1}	2.70 μ	H_2O	Water in solvent
3650	2.74	H_2O	Water in some quartz windows
3450	2.9	H_2O	H-bonded water. Sometimes found in KBr disks
2350	4.26	CO_2	Atmospheric absorption
2330	4.3	CO_2	Dissolved gas from dry ice
2300 and 2150	4.35 and 4.65	CS_2	Leaky cells
1996	5.01	BO_2	Metaborate in the halide window
1400–2000	5–7	H_2O	Atmospheric absorption
1820	5.52	$COCl_2$	Decomposition product in purified $HCCl_3$
1755	5.7	Phthalic anhydride	Decomposition product of phthalate esters or resins
1700–1760	5.7–5.9	C=O	Bottle-cap liners leached by sample
1720	5.8	Phthalates	From plastic tubing
1640	6.1	H_2O	Entrained in sample, or water of crystallization
1520–1620	6.2–6.6	$\left(-C\begin{smallmatrix}\diagup O \\ \diagdown O\end{smallmatrix}\right)^-$	Reaction product of alkali halide windows or KBr pellet with organic acid
1520	6.6	CS_2	Leaky cells
1430	7.0	CO_3^{-2}	Contaminant in halide window
1360	7.38	NO_3^-	Contaminant in halide window
1270	7.9	$SiCH_3$	Silicone oil or grease
1110	9.0	?	Impurity in KBr for disks
1000–1110	9–10	SiOSi	Glass; silicones
980	10.2	K_2SO_4	From double decomposition of sulfates in KBr pellets
935	10.7	$(CH_2O)_X$	Deposit from gaseous formaldehyde
907	11.02	CCl_2F_2	Dissolved Freon 12
837	11.95	$NaNO_3$	(See 7.38 μ)
823	12.15	KNO_3	From double decomposition of nitrates in KBr pellets
794	12.6	CCl_4 vapor	Leaky cells
788	12.7	CCl_4 liquid	Incomplete drying of cell or contamination

Common Spurious Absorption Bands and Their Origins (continued)

Approximate Frequency	Wavelength	Compound or Group	Origin
720 and 730	13.7 and 13.9	Polyethylene	
728	13.75	Na_2SiF_6	SiF_4 + NaCl windows
667	14.98	CO_2	Atmosphere (beam imbalance)
	Any	Fringes	If refractive index difference between sample and windows high, or if a cell is partially empty, interference fringes may appear.

REFERENCE: Launer, P. C., *Perkin-Elmer Instrument News,* 13(3), 10, 1962.

B. Wavelength-to-wavenumber Conversion Tables and Refractive Index of Standard Air, 2–20 μm

Wavelength (μm)	ν vac. (cm^{-1})	Index (n – 1) x 10^9 for 15°C	Wavelength (μm)	ν vac. (cm^{-1})	Index (n – 1) x 10^9 for 15°C
2.00000	4998.636	272984	2.60000	3845.105	272826
.02	4949.144	976	.62	15.753	823
.04	4900.623	969	.64	3786.846	820
.06	4853.044	961	.66	58.373	816
.08	4806.380	955	.68	30.326	813
2.10000	4760.605	272948	2.70000	3702.694	272810
.12	4715.694	941	.72	3675.468	807
.14	4671.622	935	.74	48.640	804
.16	4628.367	929	.76	22.200	801
.18	4585.904	923	.78	3596.141	798
2.20000	4544.214	272917	2.80000	3570.455	272795
.22	4503.276	911	.82	45.132	792
.24	4463.068	905	.84	20.167	790
.26	4423.572	900	.86	3495.550	787
.28	4384.768	895	.88	71.275	784
2.30000	4346.640	272890	2.90000	3447.336	272782
.32	4309.169	885	.92	23.724	779
.34	4272.339	880	.94	00.433	777
.36	36.132	875	.96	3377.457	774
.38	00.535	870	.98	54.790	772
2.40000	4165.530	272866	3.00000	3332.424	272770
.42	4131.104	862	.02	10.355	767
.44	4097.243	857	.04	3288.577	765
.46	63.932	853	.06	67.083	763
.48	31.158	849	.08	45.868	761
2.50000	3998.909	272845	3.10000	3224.927	272759
.52	67.172	841	.12	04.254	757
.54	35.934	837	.14	3183.845	755
.56	05.185	834	.16	63.694	753
.58	3874.912	830	.18	43.797	751

Wavelength-to-wavenumber Conversion Tables and Refractive Index of Standard Air, 2–20 μm (continued)

Wavelength (μm)	$\nu_{vac.}$ (cm^{-1})	Index $(n - 1) \times 10^9$ for 15°C
3.20000	3124.148	272749
.22	04.743	747
.24	3085.578	745
.26	66.648	744
.28	47.949	742
3.30000	3029.477	272740
.32	11.227	738
.34	2993.196	737
.36	75.379	735
.38	57.773	734
3.40000	2940.375	272732
.42	23.179	730
.44	06.184	729
.46	2889.385	727
.48	72.780	726
3.50000	2856.364	272724
.52	40.135	723
.54	24.089	722
.56	08.223	720
.58	2792.535	719
3.60000	2777.021	272718
.62	61.678	716
.64	46.504	715
.66	31.496	714
.68	16.651	712
3.70000	2701.966	272711
.72	2687.439	710
.74	73.068	709
.76	58.849	708
.78	44.781	707
3.80000	2630.862	272705
.82	17.087	704
.84	03.457	703
.86	2589.967	702
.88	76.617	701
3.90000	2563.404	272700
.92	50.325	699
.94	37.379	698
.96	24.564	697
.98	11.878	696
4.00000	2499.319	272695
.025	83.795	694
.050	68.463	693
.075	53.319	692
.100	38.360	690
.125	23.582	689
.150	08.982	688
.175	2394.557	687
4.20000	2380.303	272686
.225	66.219	685
.250	52.300	684
.275	38.544	683
.300	24.947	682
.325	11.508	681
.350	2298.224	680
.375	85.091	679
4.40000	2272.108	272678
.425	59.271	677
.450	46.578	677
.475	34.028	676
.500	21.616	675
.525	09.342	674
.550	2197.203	673
.575	85.197	672
4.60000	2173.321	272672
.625	61.573	671
.650	49.951	670
.675	38.454	669
.700	27.080	669
.725	15.825	668
.750	04.689	667
.775	2093.670	666
4.80000	2082.765	272666
.825	71.974	665
.850	61.294	664
.875	50.723	664
.900	40.260	663
.925	29.903	662
.950	19.651	662
.975	09.502	661
5.00000	1999.455	272660
.05	79.658	659
.10	60.250	658
.15	41.218	657
.20	22.553	656
5.25000	1904.243	272655
.30	1886.278	654
.35	68.649	653
.40	51.347	652
.45	34.362	651
5.50000	1817.686	272650
.55	01.311	649
.60	1785.228	648
.65	69.429	647
.70	53.908	646

Wavelength-to-wavenumber Conversion Tables and Refractive Index of Standard Air, 2–20 μm (continued)

Wavelength (μm)	$\nu_{vac.}$ (cm^{-1})	Index (n – 1) x 10^9 for 15°C	Wavelength (μm)	$\nu_{vac.}$ (cm^{-1})	Index (n – 1) x 10^9 for 15°C
5.75000	1738.656	272645	8.00000	1249.659	272623
.80	23.668	645	.1	34.231	622
.85	08.936	644	.2	19.180	622
.90	1694.453	643	.3	04.491	621
.95	80.214	642	.4	1190.152	621
6.00000	1666.212	272642	8.50000	1176.150	272620
.05	52.442	641	.6	62.474	620
.10	38.897	640	.7	49.112	619
.15	25.573	640	.8	36.054	619
.20	12.464	639	.9	23.289	618
6.25000	1599.564	272638	9.00000	1110.808	272618
.30	86.869	638	.1	1098.602	618
.35	74.374	637	.2	86.660	617
.40	62.074	637	.3	74.976	617
.45	49.965	636	.4	63.540	616
6.50000	1538.042	272635	9.50000	1052.345	272616
.55	26.301	635	.6	41.383	616
.60	14.739	634	.7	30.647	615
.65	03.350	634	.8	20.130	615
.70	1492.131	633	.9	09.826	615
6.75000	1481.078	272633	10.0000	999.727	272614
.80	70.187	632	.1	89.829	614
.85	59.456	632	.2	80.125	614
.90	48.880	631	.3	70.609	614
.95	38.457	631	.4	61.276	613
7.00000	1428.182	272630	10.5000	52.121	272614
.05	18.053	630	.6	43.139	613
.10	08.067	629	.7	34.325	612
.15	1398.220	629	.8	25.674	612
.20	88.510	629	.9	17.181	612
7.25000	1378.934	272628	11.0000	908.843	272612
.30	69.490	628	.1	900.655	611
.35	60.173	627	.2	892.614	611
.40	50.983	627	.3	84.715	611
.45	41.916	627	.4	76.954	
7.50000	1332.970	272626	11.5000	869.328	272611
.55	24.142	626	.6	61.834	610
.60	15.431	626	.7	54.468	610
.65	06.833	625	.8	47.227	610
.70	1298.347	625	.9	40.107	610
7.75000	1289.971	272625	12.0000	833.106	272610
.80	81.702	624	.1	26.221	610
.85	73.538	624	.2	19.449	609
.90	65.478	624	.3	12.787	609
.95	57.519	623	.4	06.232	609

Wavelength-to-wavenumber Conversion Tables and Refractive Index of Standard Air, 2–20 μm (continued)

Wavelength (μm)	$\nu_{vac.}$ (cm^{-1})	Index (n – 1) x 10^9 for 15°C	Wavelength (μm)	$\nu_{vac.}$ (cm^{-1})	Index (n – 1) x 10^9 for 15°C
12.5000	799.782	272609	.2	17.116	605
.6	93.435	609	.4	09.590	605
.7	87.187	609	.6	02.245	605
.8	81.037	608	.8	595.076	604
.9	74.983	608			
13.0000	769.021	272608	17.0000	588.075	272604
.2	57.369	608	.2	81.237	604
.4	46.065	608	.4	74.556	604
.6	35.094	607	.6	68.027	604
.8	24.440	607	.8	61.645	604
14.0000	714.091	272607	18.0000	555.404	272604
.2	04.033	607	.2	49.301	604
.4	694.255	606	.4	43.330	604
.6	84.745	606	.6	37.488	603
.8	75.492	606	.8	31.770	603
15.0000	666.485	272606	19.0000	526.172	272603
.2	57.715	606	.2	20.691	603
.4	49.174	606	.4	15.323	603
.6	40.851	605	.6	10.065	603
.8	32.739	605	.8	04.913	603
16.0000	624.830	272605	20.0000	499.864	272603

REFERENCE: IUPAC Tables for the Calibration of Infrared Spectrometers, Butterworths, Washington, D.C., 1961. With permission.

C. Numbering of Fundamental Vibrational Frequencies in Molecules

Vibrations are grouped according to their symmetry species in the order

A (Symmetric with respect to symmetry axis)

- A′,A″
- A_g,A_u
- A_1,A_2
- etc.

B (Antisymmetric with respect to symmetry axis)

- B_1,B_2
- B_1',B_1''
- B_1g,B_1u
- etc.

E (Doubly degenerate)

F (Triply degenerate)

Frequencies are numbered consecutively, starting with the highest.

(Exception: for linear XY_2 and XYZ molecules, the perpendicular vibration is always ν_2.)

The species symbol is often added in parentheses, viz, $\nu_3(a_2)$; $\nu_5(b_1u)$.

REFERENCE: Herzberg, G., *Infrared and Raman Spectra of Polyatomic Molecules,* D. VanNostrand, New York, 1945. Report on notation for spectra of polyatomic molecules, *J. Chem. Phys.*, 23, 1997, 1955.

D. Form and Designation of Normal Vibrations for Common Groups

The diagrams shown below are intended to illustrate, in a qualitative way, the forms of some normal vibrations of common organic groups. Other groups of atoms having the same configuration will have similar vibrational modes, but the exact direction and amplitude of the displacements depend on the mass of the atoms and the force constants between atoms.

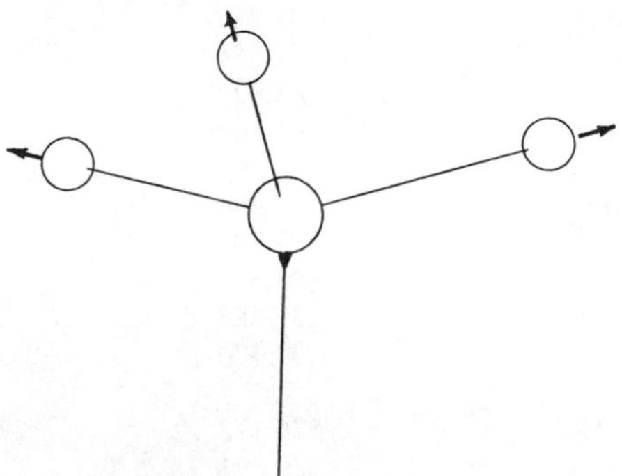

FIGURE 45. CH_3 Symmetric stretch.

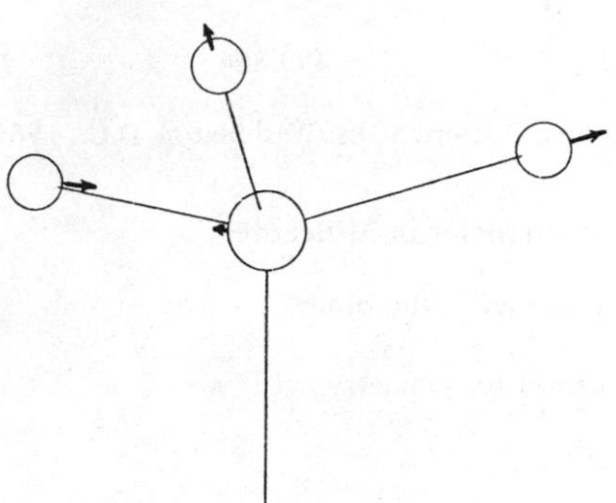

FIGURE 46. CH_3 Asymmetric stretch.

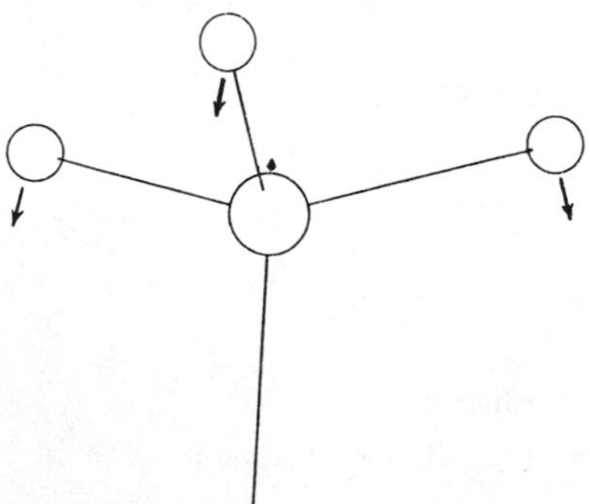

FIGURE 47. CH_3 Symmetric bend ("umbrella").

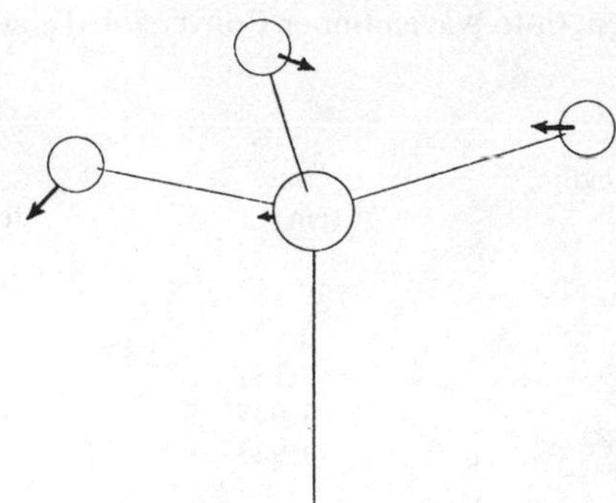

FIGURE 48. CH_3 Asymmetric bend.

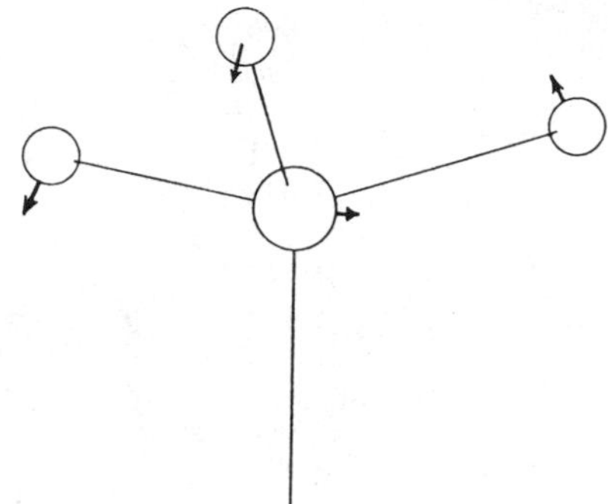

FIGURE 49. CH_3 Rocking.

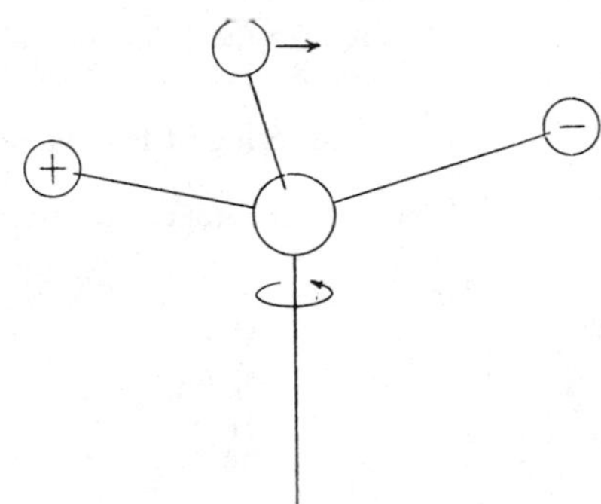

FIGURE 50. CH_3 Torsion.

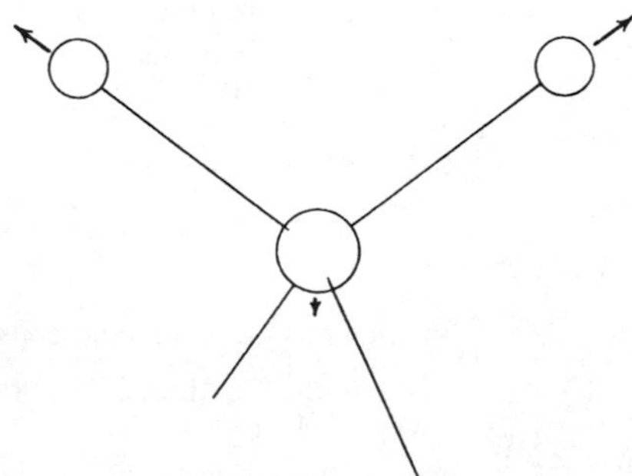

FIGURE 51. CH_2 Symmetric stretch.

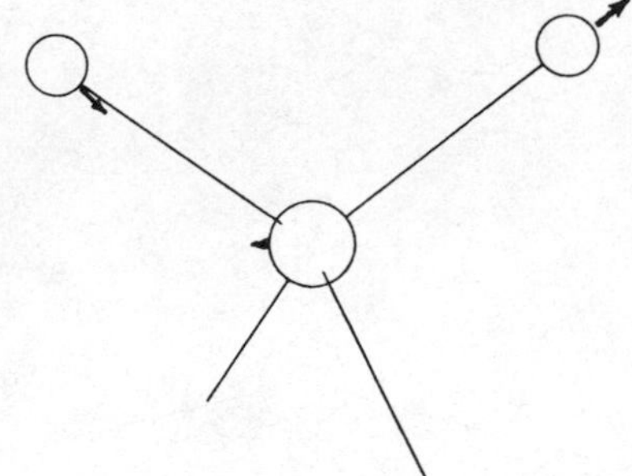

FIGURE 52. CH_2 Asymmetric stretch.

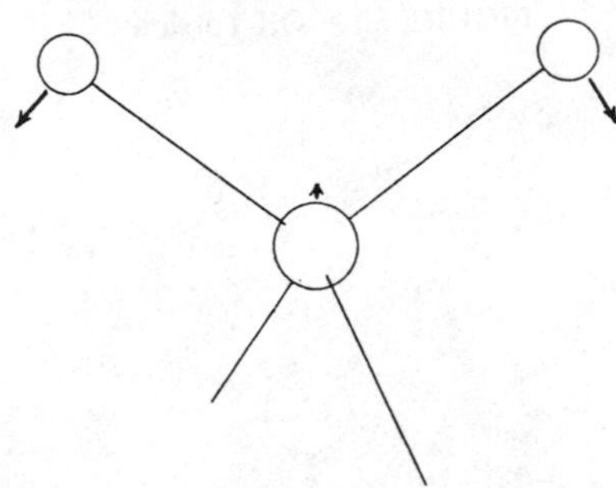

FIGURE 53. CH_2 Symmetric bend ("scissors").

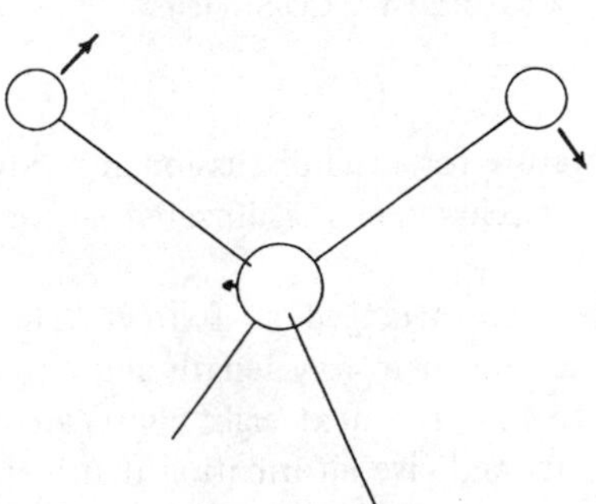

FIGURE 54. CH_2 Rock.

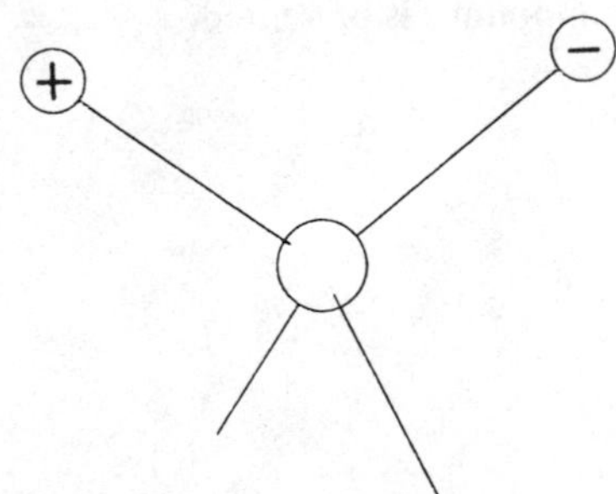

FIGURE 55. CH_2 Twist.

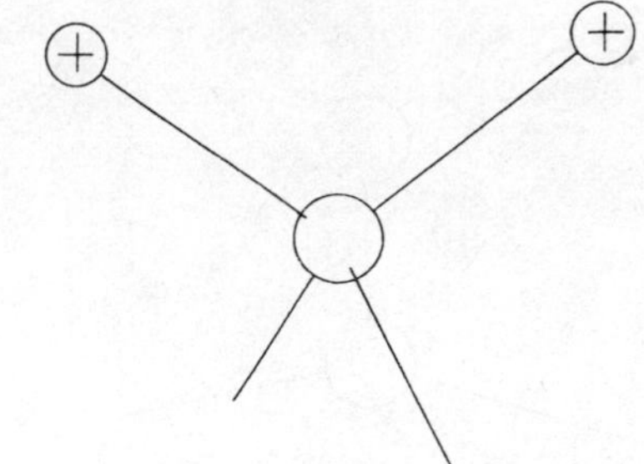

FIGURE 56. CH_2 Wag.

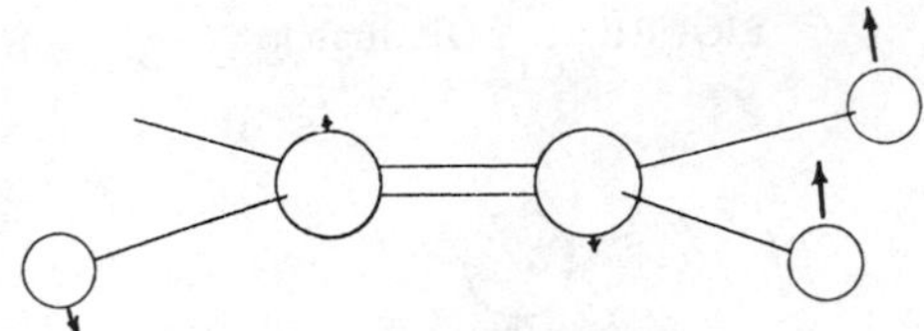

FIGURE 57. Vinyl CH_2 wag.

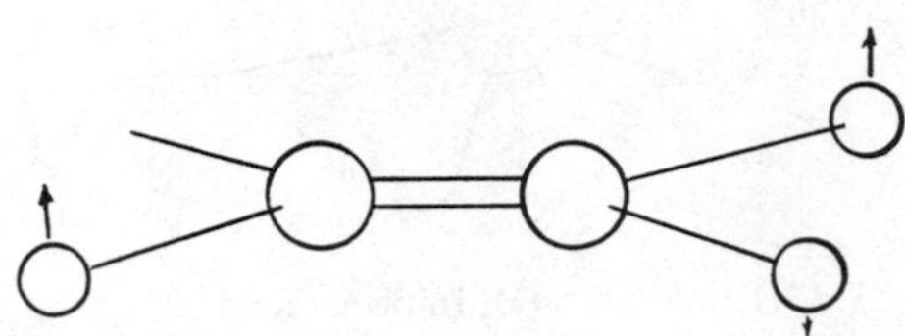

FIGURE 58. Vinyl C=C twist.

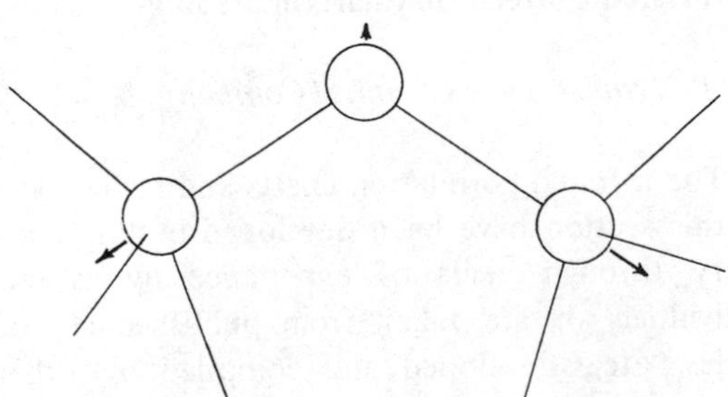

FIGURE 59. COC Symmetric stretch.

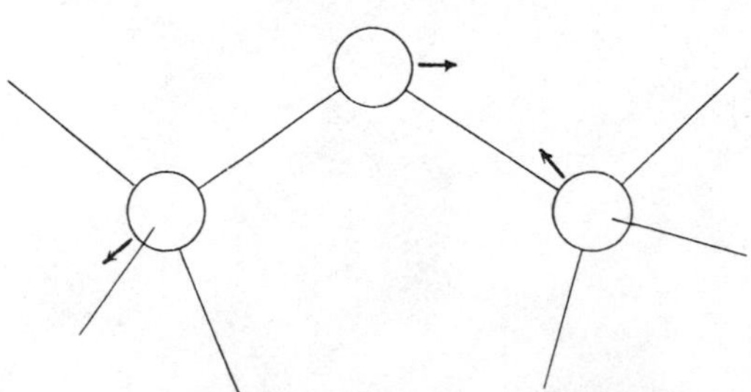

FIGURE 60. COC Asymmetric stretch.

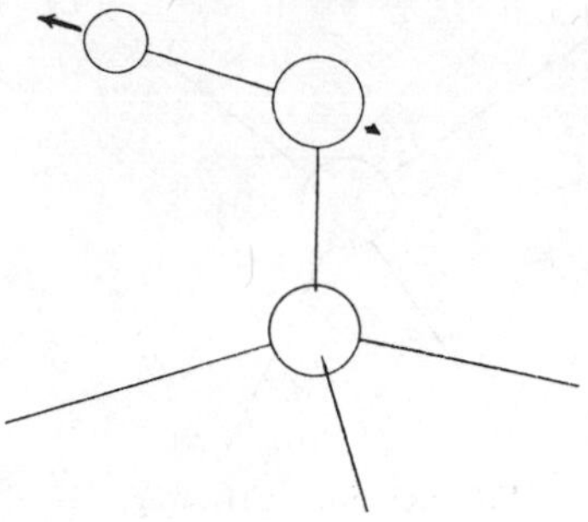

FIGURE 61. OH Stretch.

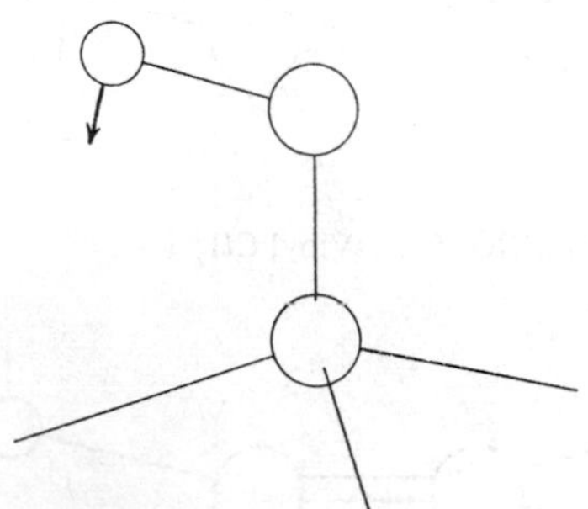

FIGURE 62. OH In-plane bend.

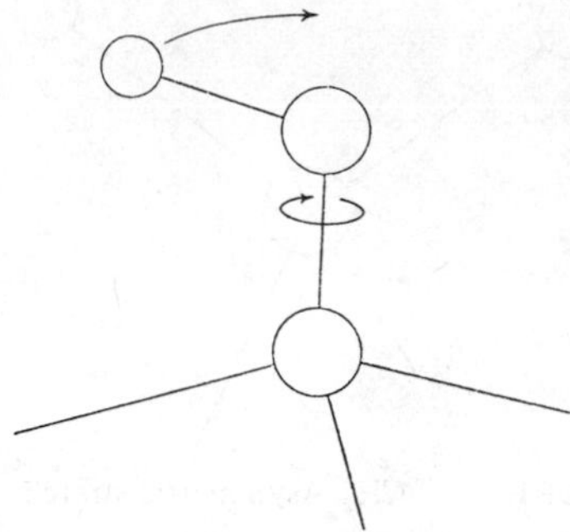

FIGURE 63. OH Torsion.

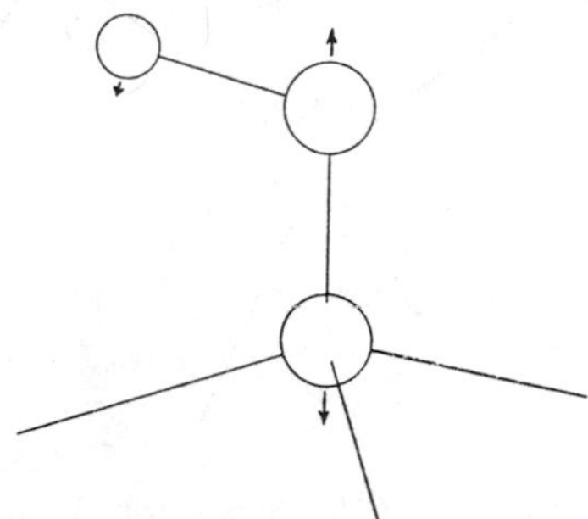

FIGURE 64. CO Stretch.

E. Infrared Correlation Charts and Tables

R. A. Nyquist, Dow Chemical Company

The infrared correlation charts and tables given in this section have been developed in our laboratory through years of experience by various individuals or are taken from published charts, tables, etc., developed and compiled by other spectroscopists throughout the world. Individuals who anticipate using these data should consult the original literature for a full discussion and explanation of these characteristic infrared absorption bands.

The charts are arranged as follows: The first four charts are linear in wavelength and cover the range 2 to 16 μm. The next eight charts are linear in wavenumber and give information that is similar but not identical to Charts 1 to 4. Correlations for the region 700 to 300 cm^{-1} are given on the following chart. Finally, a series of correlations for inorganic compounds is presented.

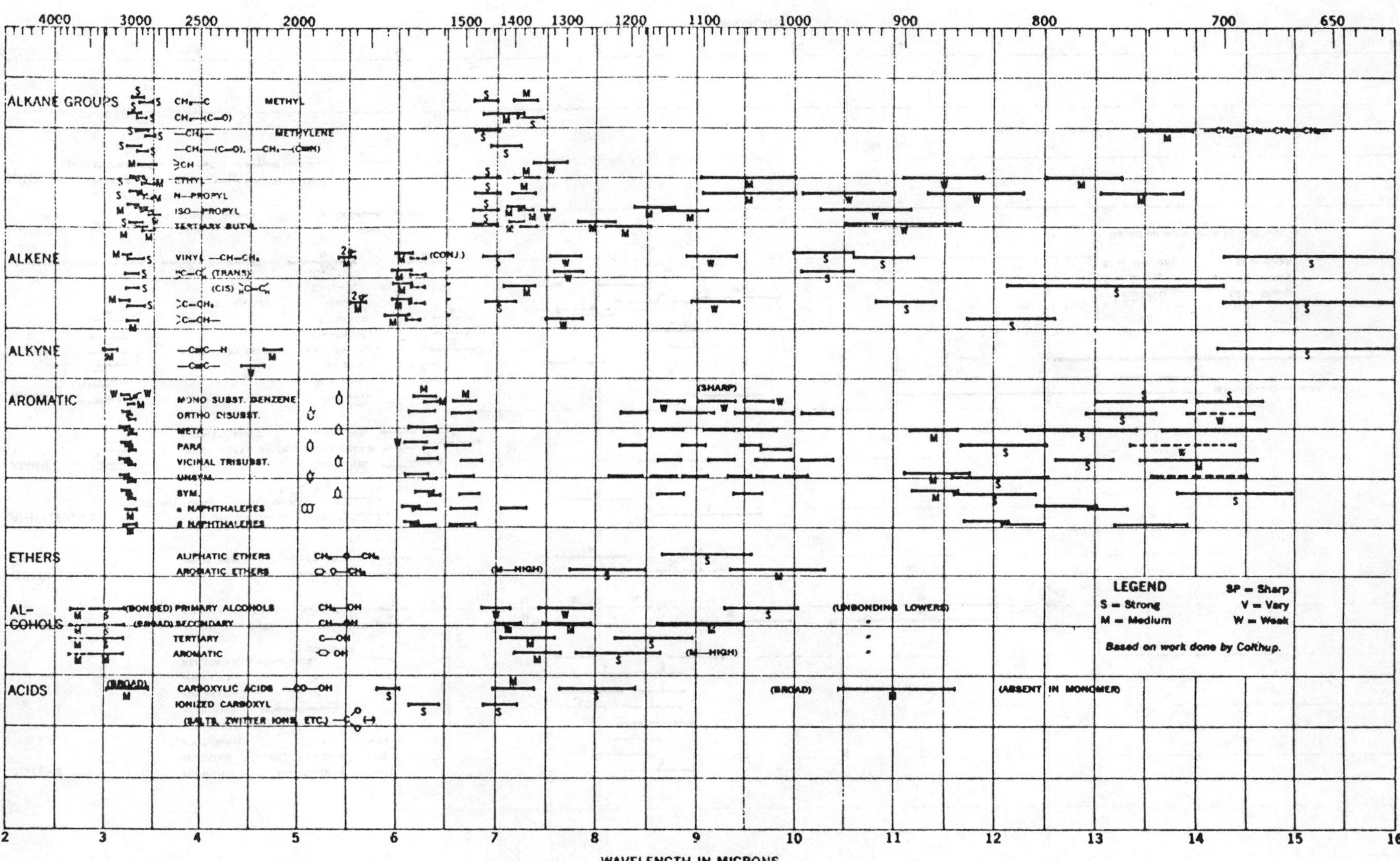

FIGURE 65, CHART 1. Infrared correlation chart. (Prepared from information supplied by Beckman Instruments.)

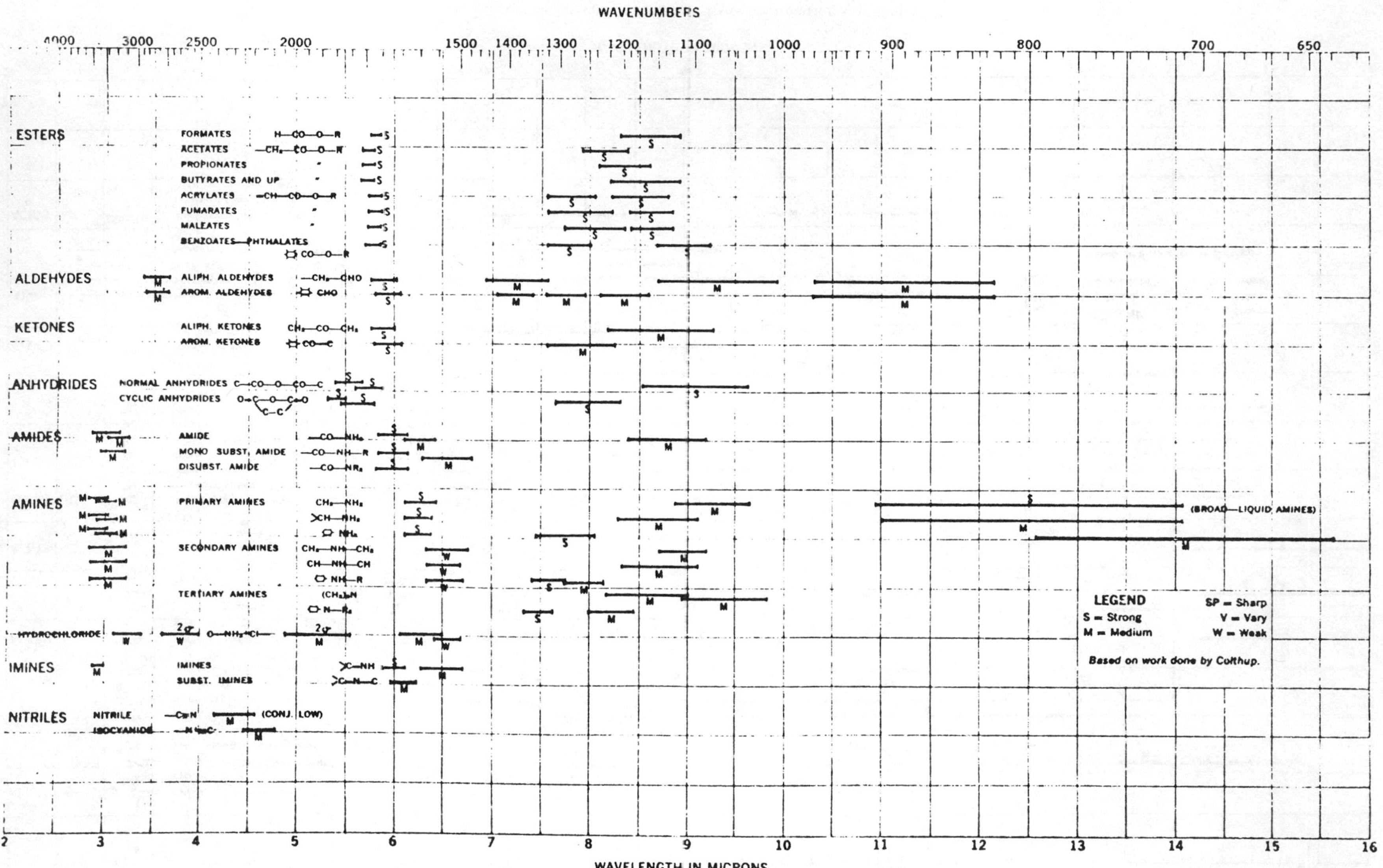

FIGURE 65, CHART 1 (continued).

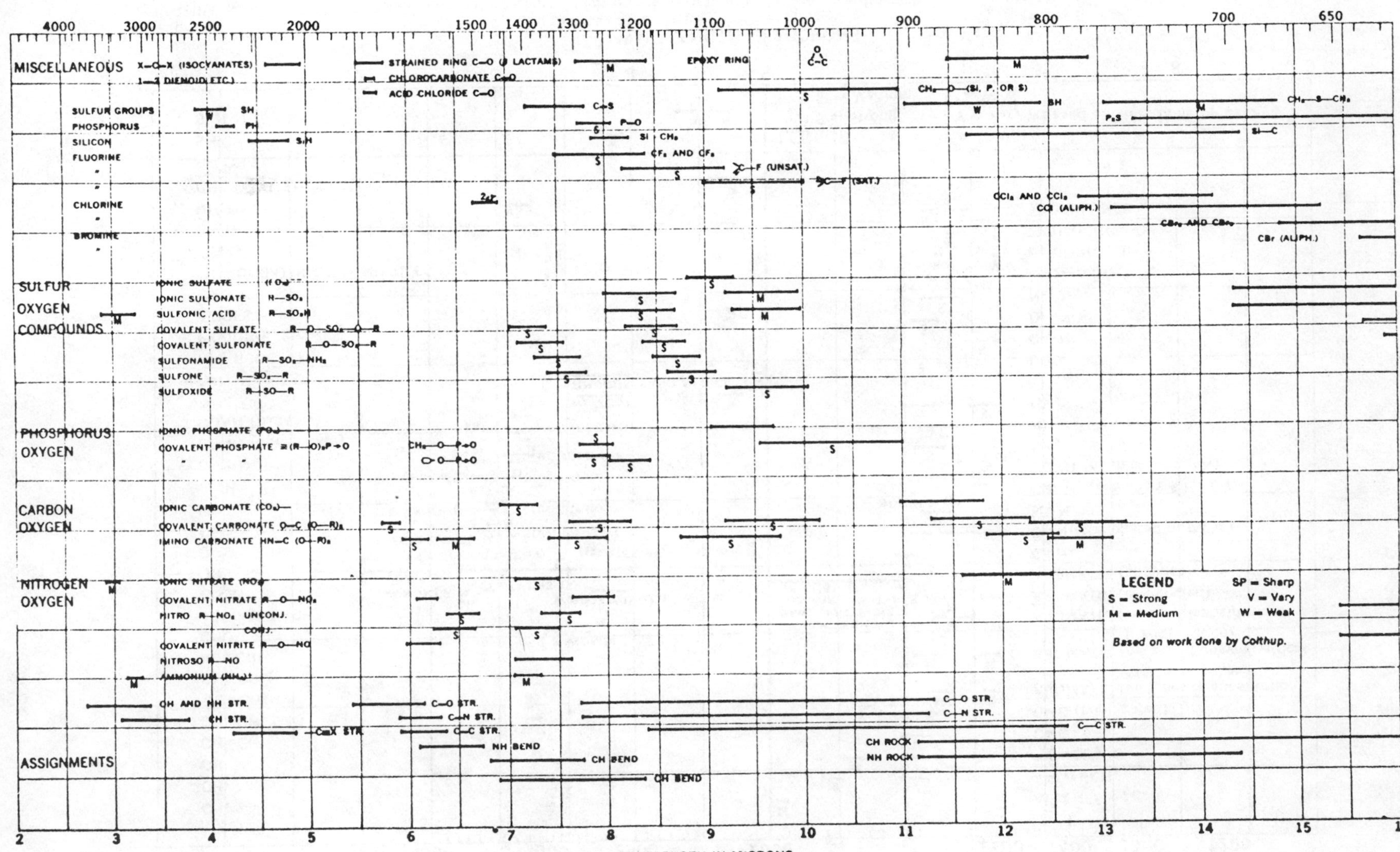

FIGURE 65, CHART 1 (continued).

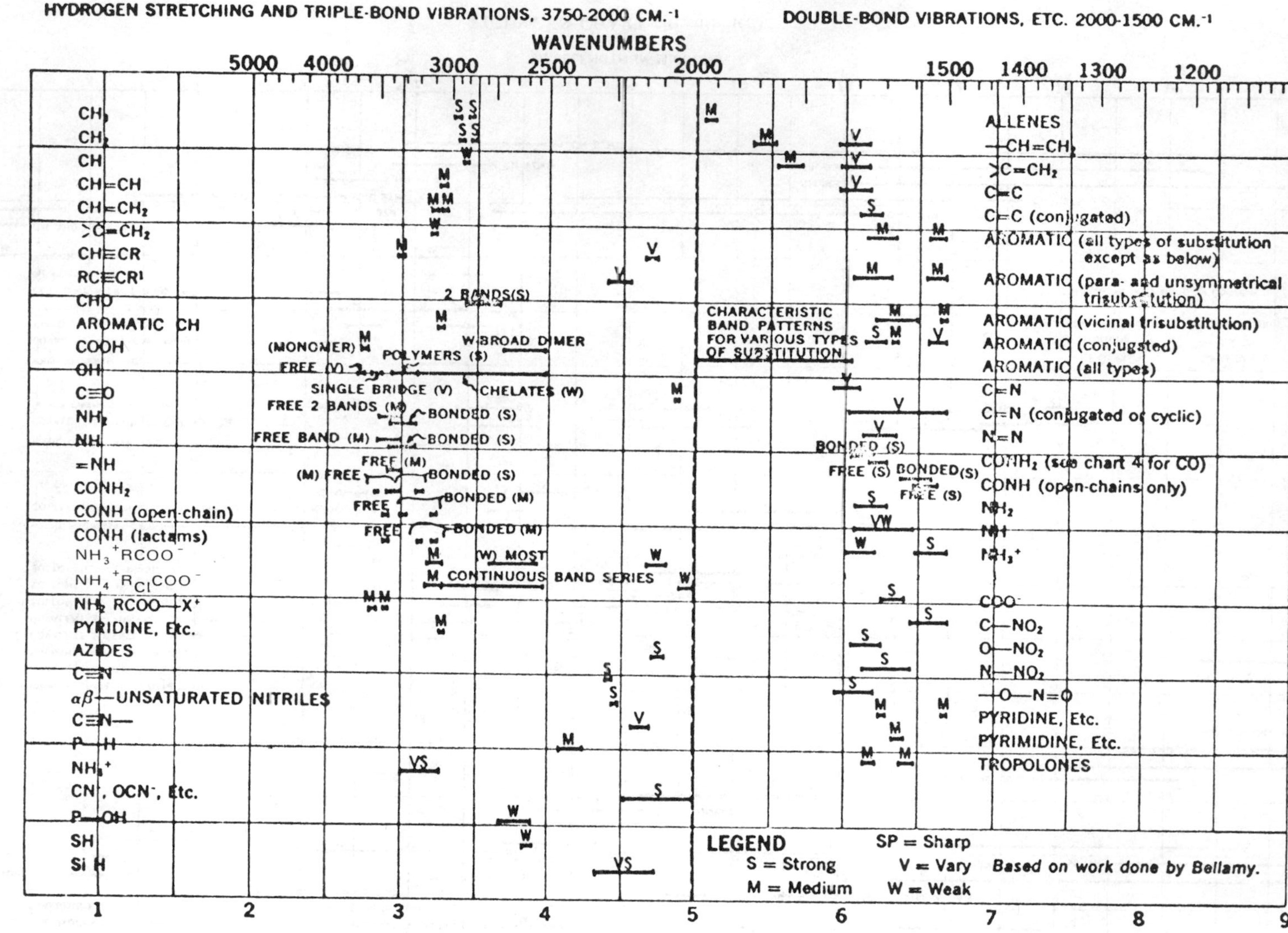

FIGURE 65, CHART 2. Infrared correlation chart which presents some information regarding structure, double-bond vibrations, hydrogen stretching, and triple-bond vibrations. (Prepared from information supplied by Beckman Instruments.)

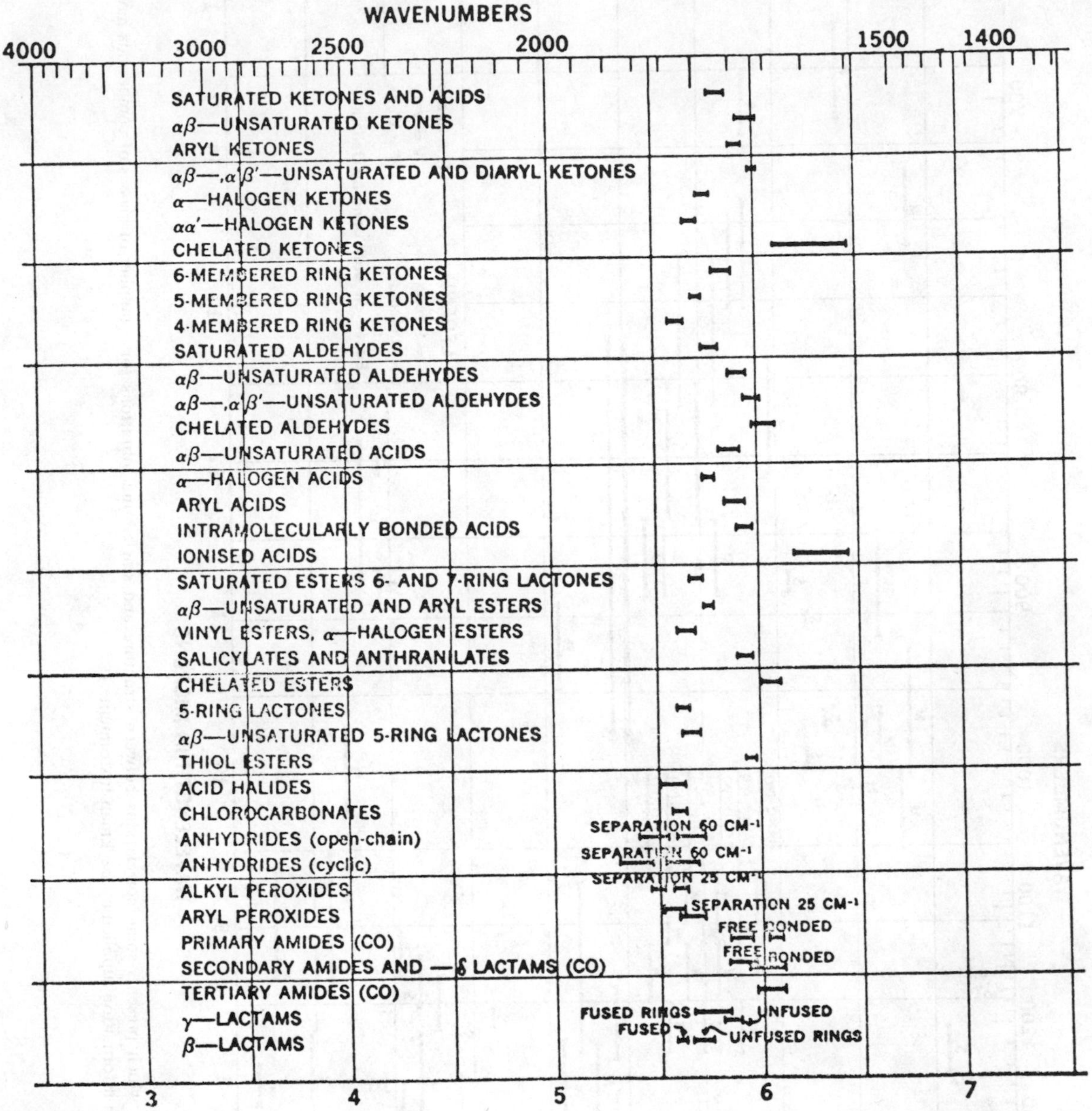

WAVENUMBERS

4000 3000 2500 2000 1500 1400

SATURATED KETONES AND ACIDS
αβ—UNSATURATED KETONES
ARYL KETONES
αβ—,α'β'—UNSATURATED AND DIARYL KETONES
α—HALOGEN KETONES
αα'—HALOGEN KETONES
CHELATED KETONES
6-MEMBERED RING KETONES
5-MEMBERED RING KETONES
4-MEMBERED RING KETONES
SATURATED ALDEHYDES
αβ—UNSATURATED ALDEHYDES
αβ—,α'β'—UNSATURATED ALDEHYDES
CHELATED ALDEHYDES
αβ—UNSATURATED ACIDS
α—HALOGEN ACIDS
ARYL ACIDS
INTRAMOLECULARLY BONDED ACIDS
IONISED ACIDS
SATURATED ESTERS 6- AND 7-RING LACTONES
αβ—UNSATURATED AND ARYL ESTERS
VINYL ESTERS, α—HALOGEN ESTERS
SALICYLATES AND ANTHRANILATES
CHELATED ESTERS
5-RING LACTONES
αβ—UNSATURATED 5-RING LACTONES
THIOL ESTERS
ACID HALIDES
CHLOROCARBONATES
ANHYDRIDES (open-chain) SEPARATION 60 CM⁻¹
ANHYDRIDES (cyclic) SEPARATION 60 CM⁻¹
ALKYL PEROXIDES SEPARATION 25 CM⁻¹
ARYL PEROXIDES SEPARATION 25 CM⁻¹
PRIMARY AMIDES (CO) FREE BONDED
SECONDARY AMIDES AND —δ LACTAMS (CO) FREE BONDED
TERTIARY AMIDES (CO)
γ—LACTAMS FUSED RINGS UNFUSED
β—LACTAMS FUSED UNFUSED RINGS

3 4 5 6 7

FIGURE 65, CHART 3. Infrared correlation chart which presents some correlations between structure and the carbonyl vibrations of some classes of organic compounds. In all cases the absorption bands are strong and fall within the range of 1900 to 1500 cm^{-1}. (Prepared from information supplied by Beckman Instruments.)

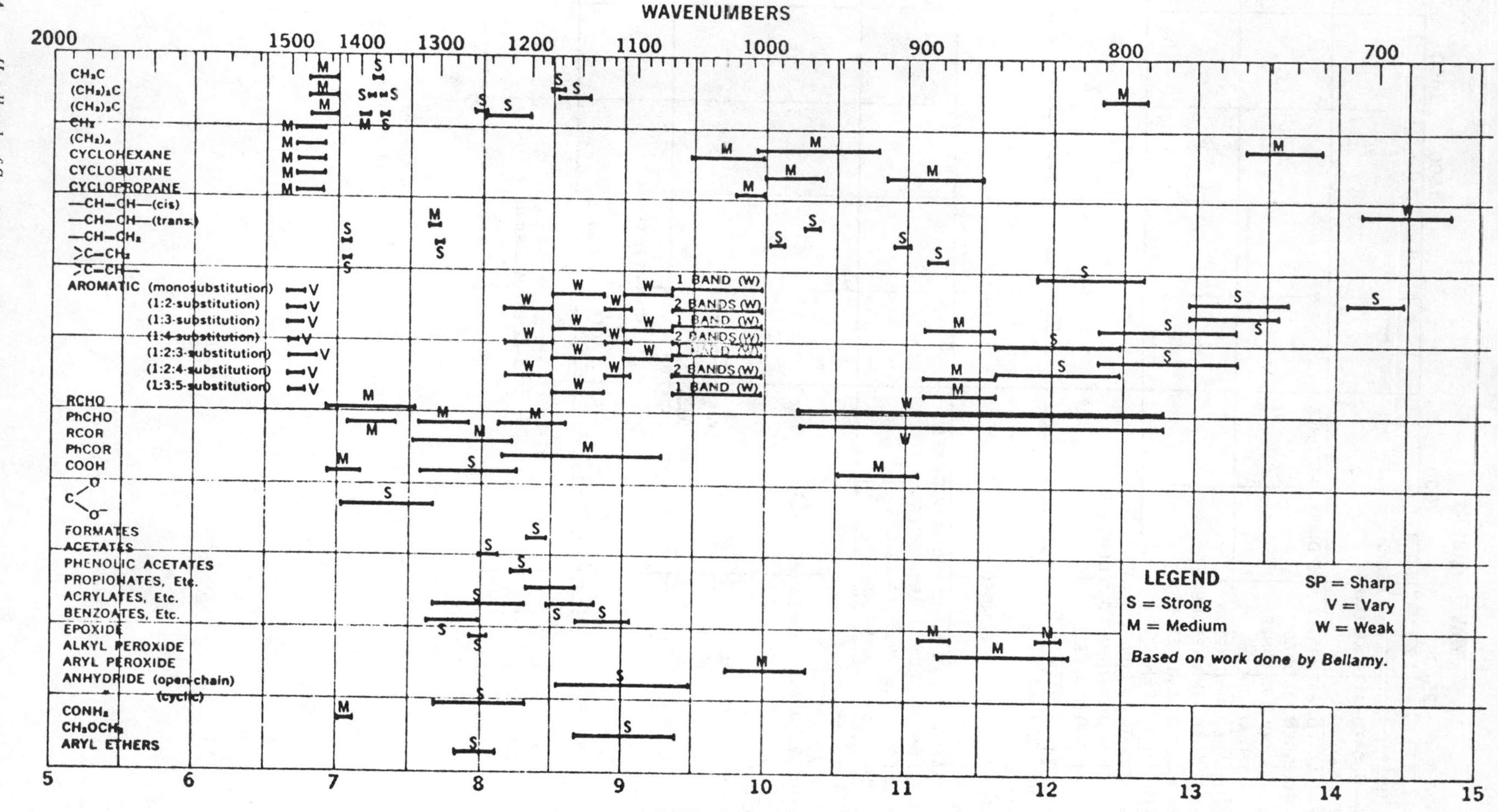

FIGURE 65, CHART 4. Infrared correlation chart which presents some correlations between structure and single-bond vibrations for a number of classes of compounds having absorption between 1500 to 650 cm^{-1}. (Prepared from information supplied by Beckman Instruments.)

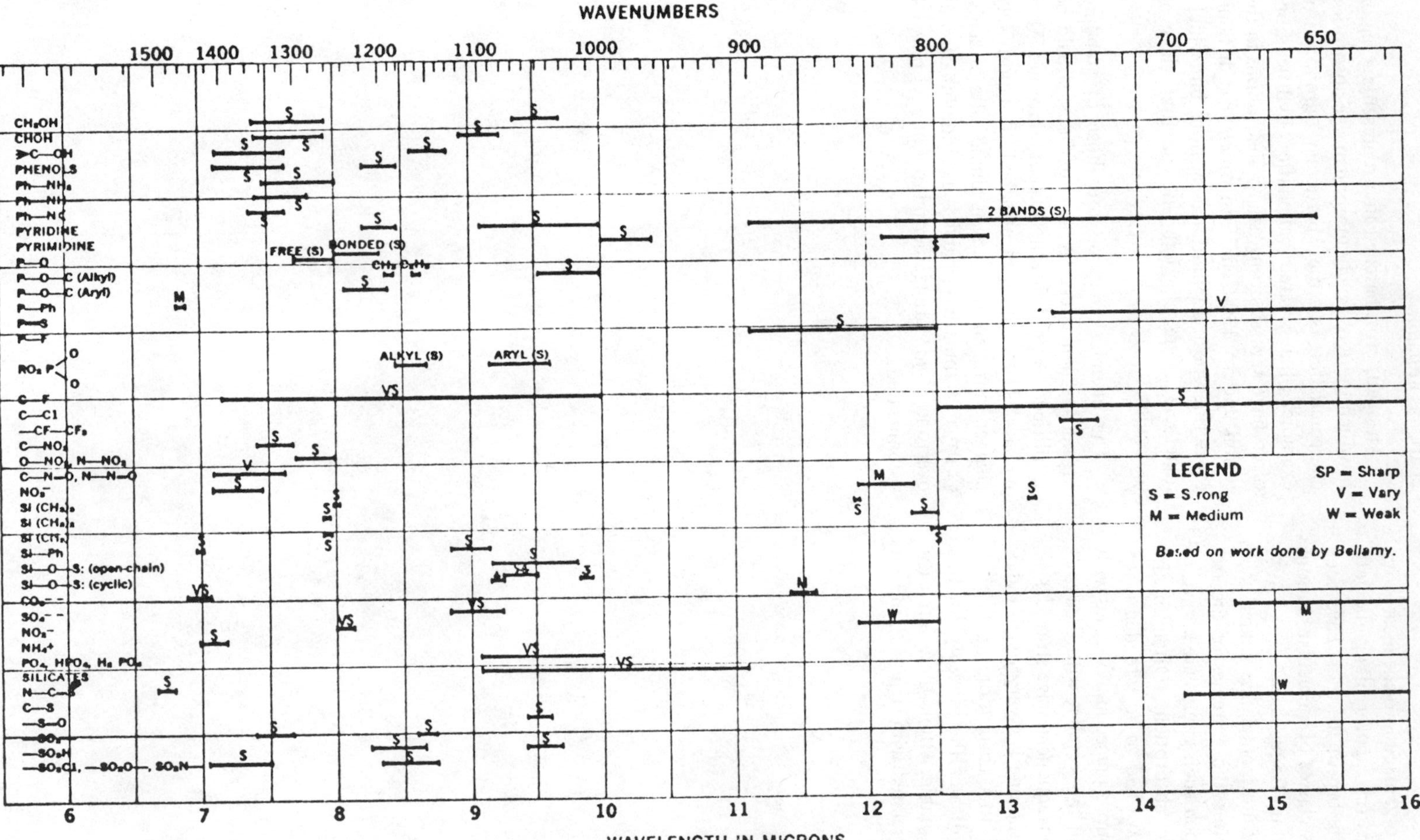

FIGURE 65, CHART 4 (continued).

Correlation Chart of Infrared Group Frequencies

Chart 5 has been organized into chemical group types whose designations appear along the left-hand edge. Across the top of the chart have been indicated the various classes of molecular motions which form usable group frequencies.

The short, heavy horizontal line under each group symbol indicates the extremes of the frequency region in which such groups are known to have a characteristic absorption. (Often in the past, such regions have had to be extended when such a particular group is placed in molecules with less familiar groups in the vicinity, with the result that its characteristic frequencies have strayed.)

The thickness of the line is a very rough index of the intensity of this absorption. A line of tapering thickness indicates the intensity for this group to be quite variable. Often these intensity variations can be correlated with structure, but no clever way to represent this on a limited-space chart was at hand.

An open, cross-hatched line represents a region in which there is usually more than one absorption characteristic of the particular group. For example, halogenated aliphatic hydrocarbons often have several strong, sharp absorptions in the region 950 to 1300 cm^{-1} to which it is difficult to ascribe specific vibrational motions but which, nonetheless, are characteristic of that class of molecules.

The chemical symbols are those of standard organic nomenclature. A few, perhaps, should be amplified: X = halogen, except fluorine; M = metal; N-H = hydrogen attached to a positively charged nitrogen atom as in amine salts of acids; (Σ) = a "summation" band – i.e., combination or overtone – *not* a fundamental; ϕ = phenyl ring; CJ = conjugated.

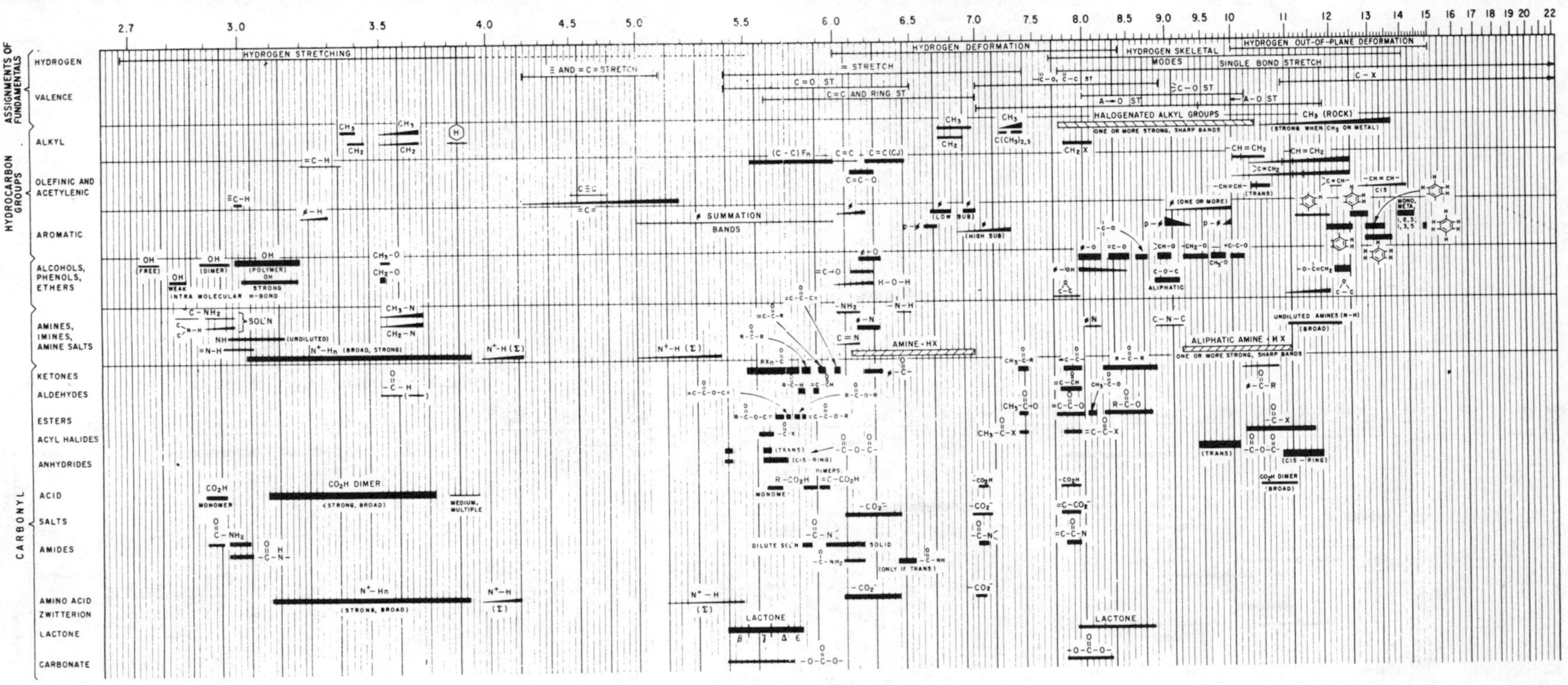

FIGURE 66, CHART 5.

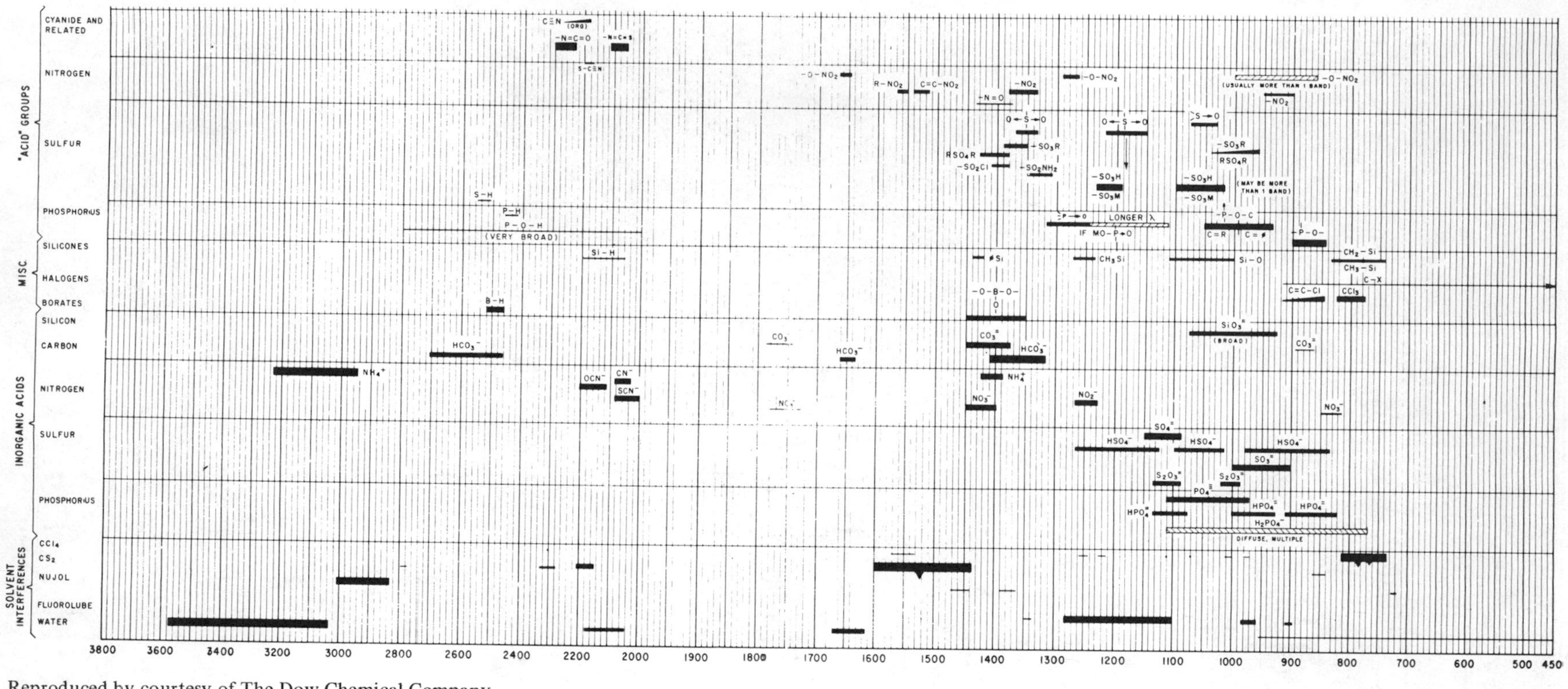

Reproduced by courtesy of The Dow Chemical Company.

FIGURE 66, CHART 5 (continued)

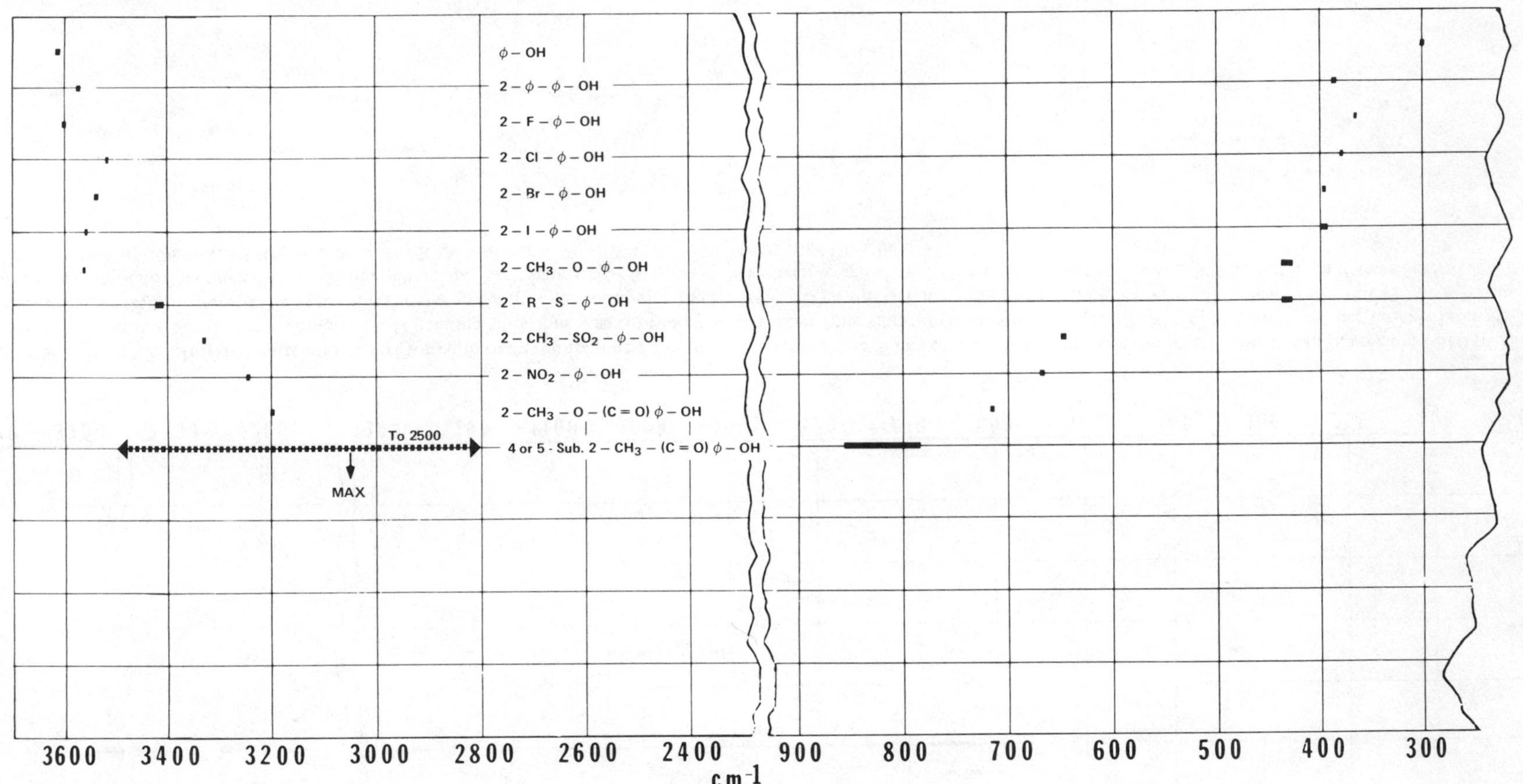

FIGURE 66, CHART 6. Infrared correlation chart for intramolecularly hydrogen bonded phenols. The 3600 to 2800 cm^{-1} band results from O-H stretching, and the 875 to 350 cm^{-1} band results from the O-H out-of-plane bending vibration. In phenols that are not intramolecularly hydrogen bonded, such as phenol, the lower frequency band is assigned to an O-H torsion vibration. The band intensities are strong for both vibrations. (REFERENCE: Nyquist, R. A., *Spectrochim. Acta.* 19, 1655, 1963.)

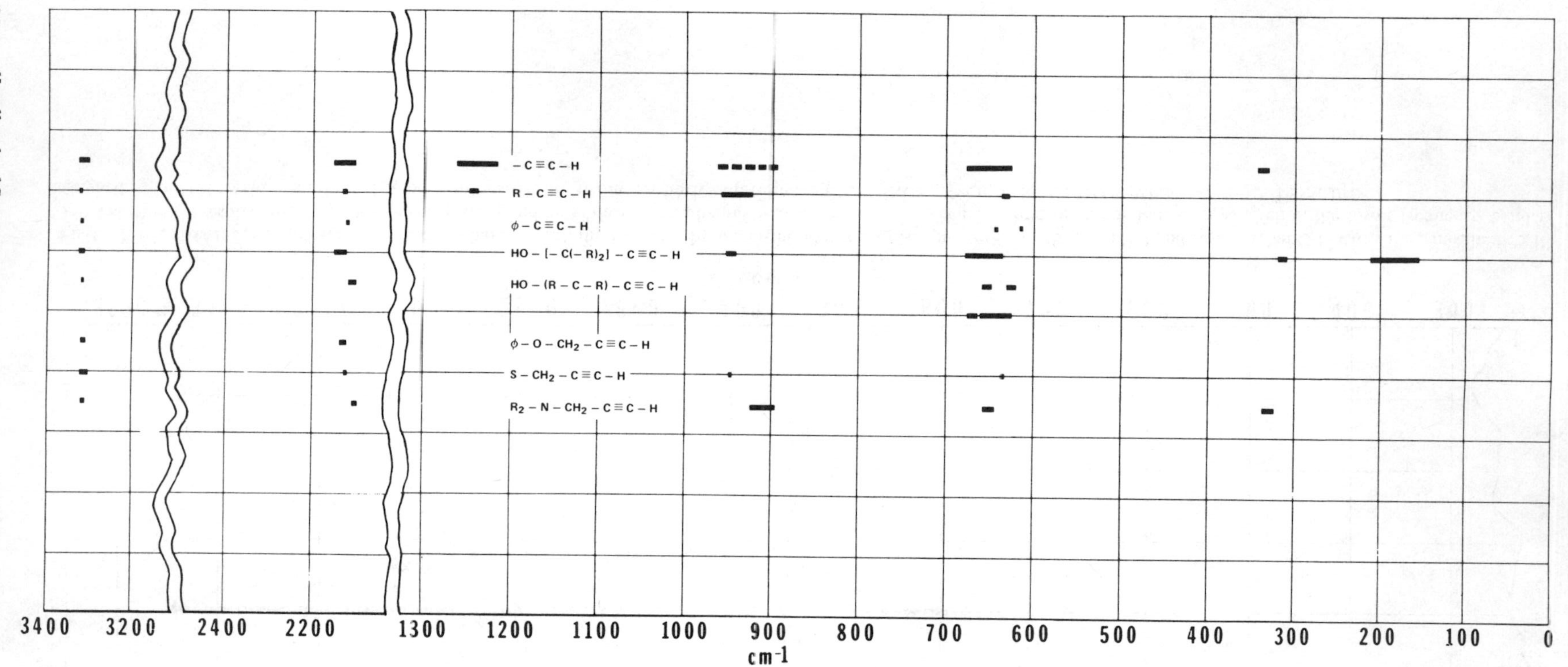

FIGURE 66, CHART 7. Infrared correlation chart for compounds containing a terminal acetylenic group. The acetylenic ≡C-H group exhibits strong bands in the regions 3310 to 3320 and 610 to 655 cm^{-1} from C-H stretching and C-H bending vibrations, respectively. The C≡C stretching vibration occurs in the region 2100 to 2150 cm^{-1} and has variable intensity. In most cases it is weak; however, the band becomes strong in compounds containing the H-C≡C-C=O group. Often a weak band will be observed in the region 1210 to 1275 cm^{-1}, due to the first overtone of the acetylenic C-H bending vibration. Weak bands near 900 cm^{-1} have been assigned to C-C stretching, and bands near 300 and 200 cm^{-1} have been assigned to skeletal bending vibrations. (REFERENCE: Nyquist, R. A. and Potts, W. J., *Spectrochim. Acta,* 16, 419, 1960.

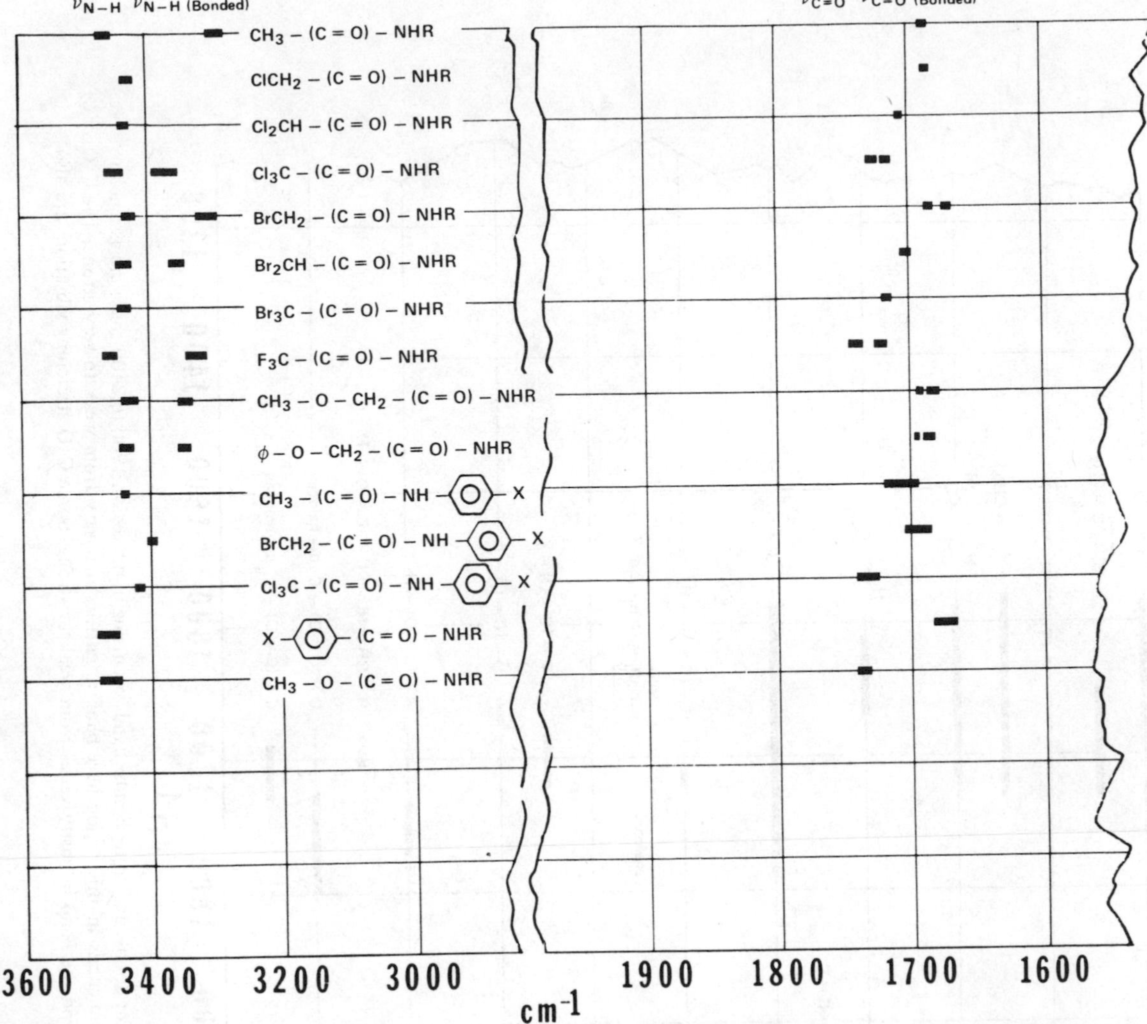

FIGURE 66, CHART 8. Infrared correlation chart for the N-H stretching and C=O stretching vibrations for secondary amides and carbamates. The lower frequency range in each series (if given) results from the hydrogen bonded species. (REFERENCES: Nyquist, R. A., *Spectrochim. Acta,* 19, 509, 1963. McLachlan, R. D. and Nyquist, R. A., *Spectrochim. Acta,* 19, 1595, 1963.)

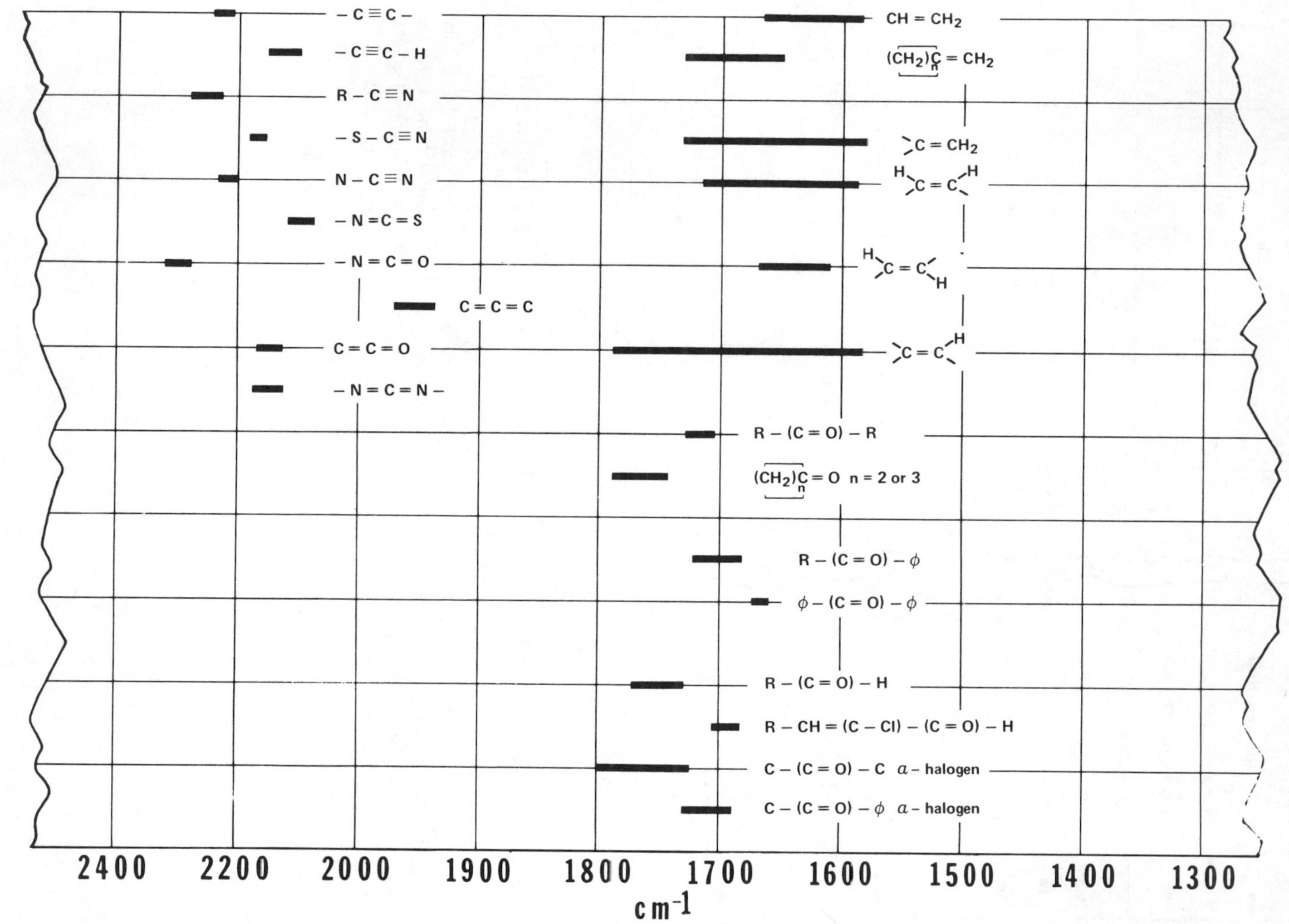

FIGURE 66, CHART 9. Infrared correlation chart for double and triple bonds. Bands occurring in the region 1900 to 2400 cm^{-1} are assigned to C≡C, C≡N, or asymmetric X=C=Y stretching. Fundamentals in this region have band intensities that vary from weak to very strong. The C=C stretching vibration occurs at 1570 to 1790 cm^{-1}, and the band intensity varies from weak to strong. Some C=O stretching vibrations are also included, and their band intensities are always strong.

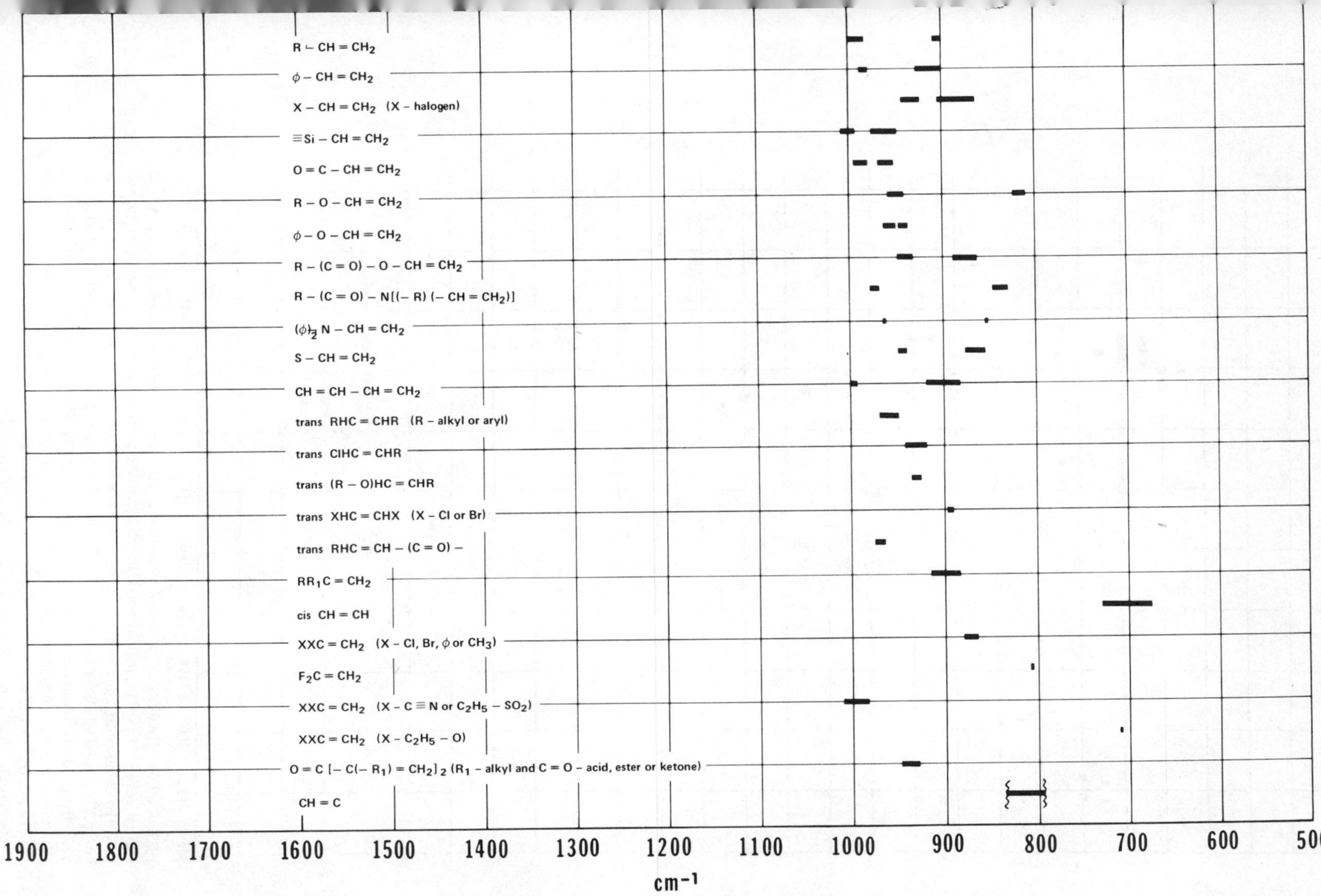

$R-CH=CH_2$
$\phi-CH=CH_2$
$X-CH=CH_2$ (X – halogen)
$\equiv Si-CH=CH_2$
$O=C-CH=CH_2$
$R-O-CH=CH_2$
$\phi-O-CH=CH_2$
$R-(C=O)-O-CH=CH_2$
$R-(C=O)-N[(-R)(-CH=CH_2)]$
$(\phi)_2N-CH=CH_2$
$S-CH=CH_2$
$CH=CH-CH=CH_2$
trans $RHC=CHR$ (R – alkyl or aryl)
trans $ClHC=CHR$
trans $(R-O)HC=CHR$
trans $XHC=CHX$ (X – Cl or Br)
trans $RHC=CH-(C=O)-$
$RR_1C=CH_2$
cis $CH=CH$
$XXC=CH_2$ (X – Cl, Br, ϕ or CH_3)
$F_2C=CH_2$
$XXC=CH_2$ (X – $C\equiv N$ or $C_2H_5-SO_2$)
$XXC=CH_2$ (X – C_2H_5-O)
$O=C[-C(-R_1)=CH_2]_2$ (R_1 – alkyl and C = O – acid, ester or ketone)
$CH=C$

1900 1800 1700 1600 1500 1400 1300 1200 1100 1000 900 800 700 600 500

cm^{-1}

FIGURE 66, CHART 10. Infrared correlation chart for the out-of-plane hydrogen vibrations for compounds containing olefinic groups. In compounds containing $-CH=CH_2$, the higher frequency band is assigned to the twisting vibration and the lower frequency band to the wagging vibration. Both of these bands are intense. (REFERENCE: Potts, W. J. and Nyquist, R. A., *Spectrochim. Acta*, 9, 679, 1959.)

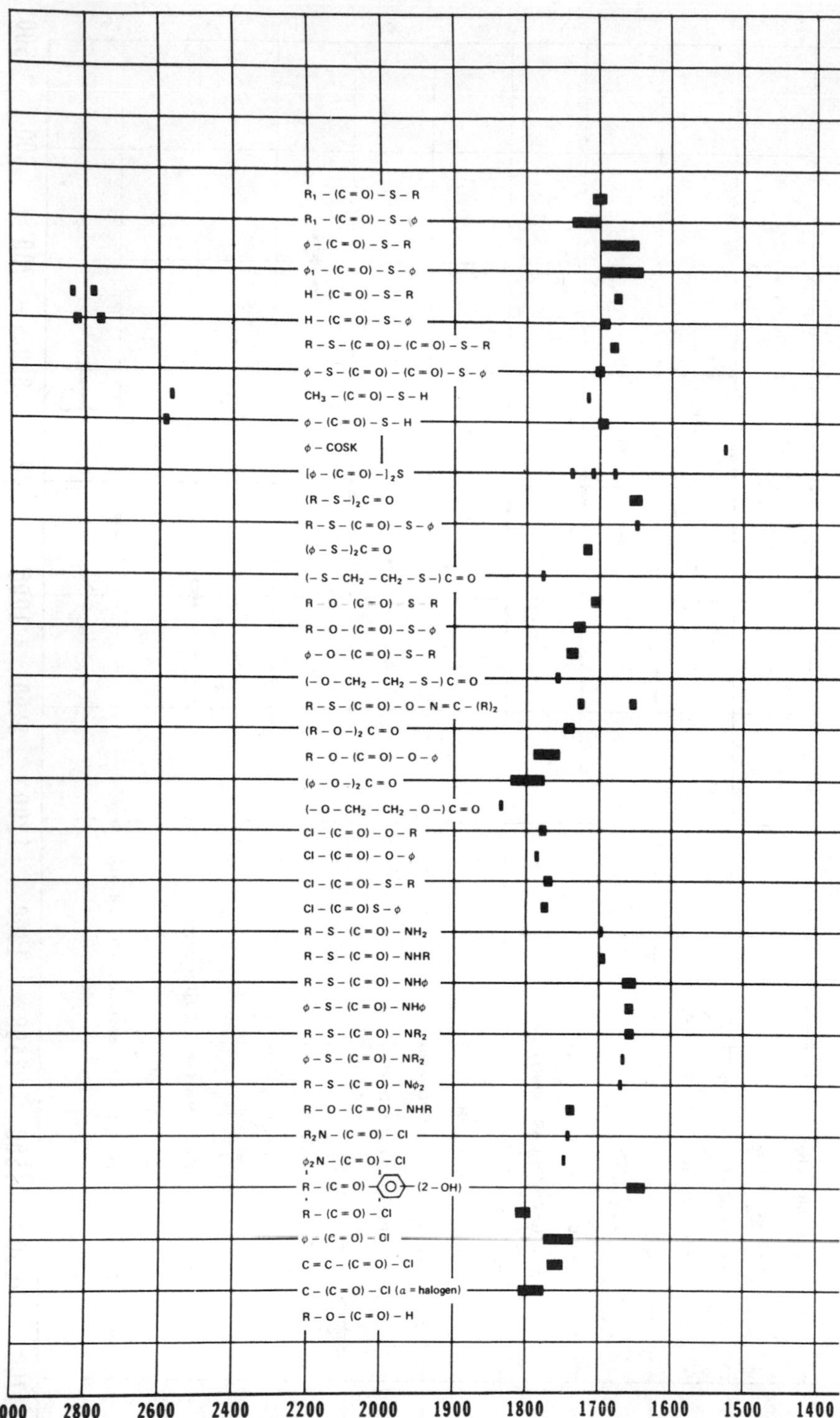

FIGURE 66, CHART 11. Infrared correlation chart for thiol esters, thiol carbonates, and related compounds. The pair of weak bands near 2800 cm^{-1} for thiol formates is assigned to C-H stretching and the first overtone of C-H bending, in Fermi resonance, for the O=C-H group. The weak-medium band near 2580 cm^{-1} for thiol acids is assigned to S-H stretching. The strong bands occurring in the region 1625 to 1825 cm^{-1} are assigned to C=O stretching vibrations. Bands occurring in the region 800 to 1300 cm^{-1} are assigned to X-C-Y stretching vibrations. (REFERENCES: Nyquist, R. A. and Potts, W. J., *Spectrochim. Acta,* 7, 514, 1959. Nyquist, R. A. and Potts, W. J., *Spectrochim. Acta,* 17, 679, 1961.)

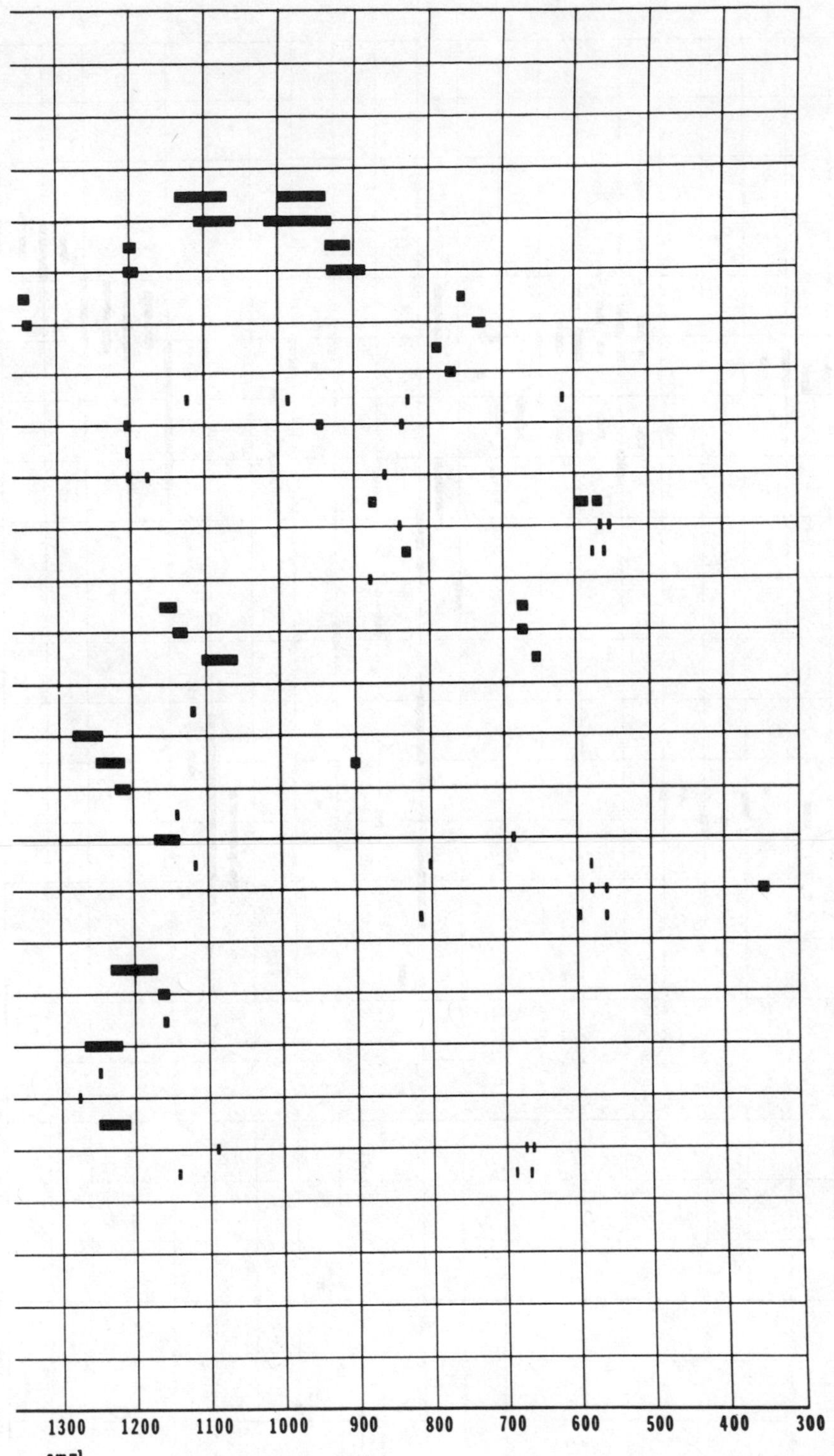

FIGURE 66, CHART 11 (continued)

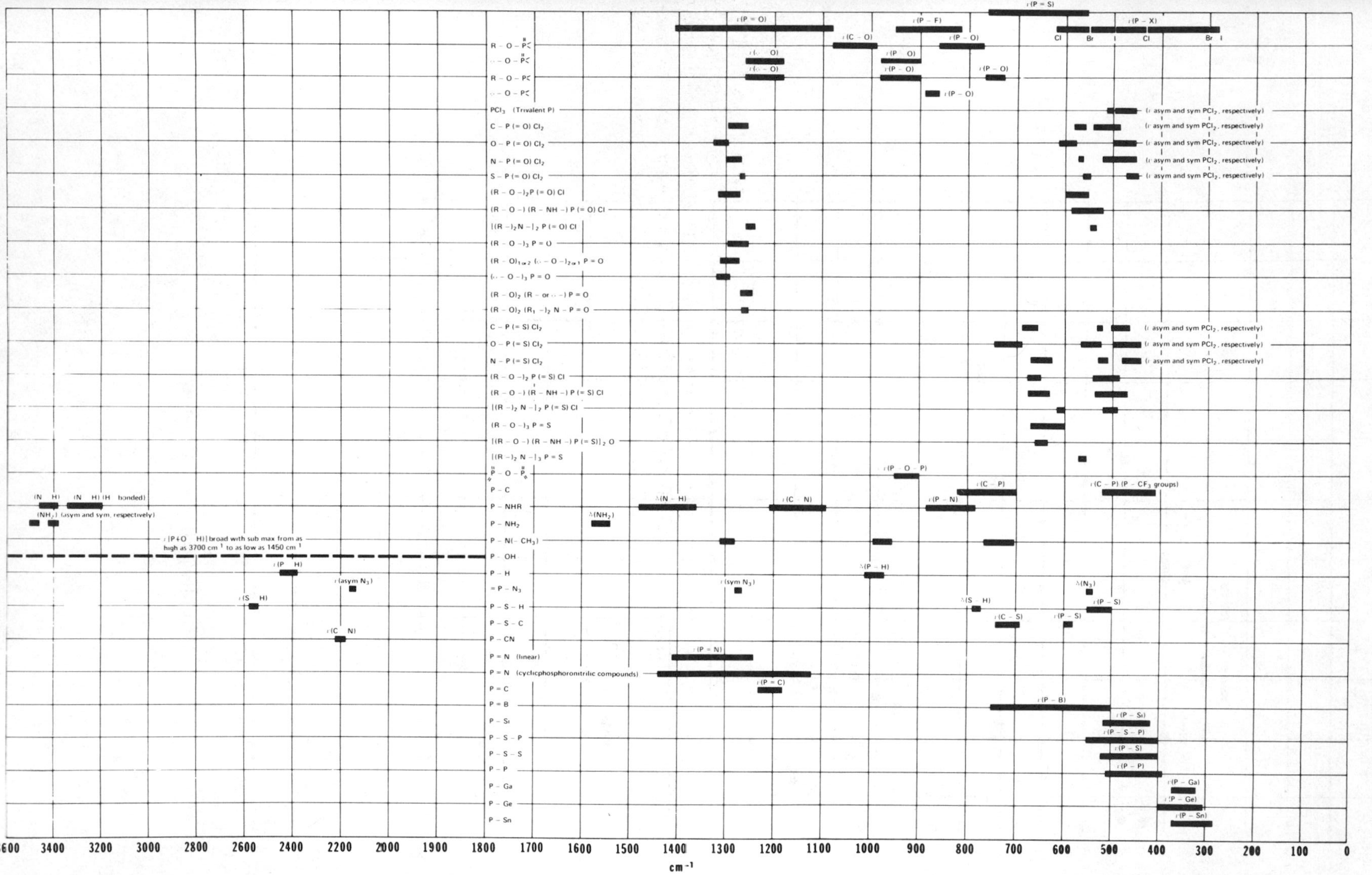

FIGURE 66, CHART 12. Infrared correlation chart for phosphorus compounds. In this chart, ν represents stretching, and δ represents bending. Individuals concerned with the identification of phosphorus compounds would do well to consult the reference and papers dealing with other methods of analysis, including Raman, nuclear magnetic resonance, mass spectrometry, and ultraviolet spectroscopy. (REFERENCE: Nyquist, R. A. and Potts, W. J., Vibrational spectroscopy of phosphorus compounds, in *Analytical Chemistry of Phosphorus and Its Compounds,* Halmann, M., Ed., Interscience, New York, 1972, 189.)

Chart of Characteristic Frequencies Between ~700 to 300 cm^{-1}

Freeman F. Bentley, Lee D. Smithson, and Adele L. Rozek

This chart summarizes the characteristic frequencies known to occur between approximately 700 to 300 cm^{-1}. Those who anticipate using this region of the spectrum should consult "Infrared Spectra and Characteristic Frequencies between ~700 to 300 cm^{-1}" by Interscience Publishers, a division of John Wiley and Sons, Inc. for a complete discussion of the characteristic frequencies summarized in this chart, a large collection of infrared spectra (700 to 300 cm^{-1}) of most of the common organic and inorganic compounds, and an extensive bibliography of references to infrared data below ~700 cm^{-1}.

In this chart the black horizontal bars indicate the range of the spectrum in which the characteristic frequencies have been observed to occur in the compounds investigated. The number of compounds investigated is given immediately to the right of the names or structures of the compounds. Obviously those characteristic frequency ranges based upon a limited number of compounds should be used with caution.

The letters above the bars indicate the relative intensities of the absorption bands. These intensities are based upon the strongest band in the spectra (700 to 300 cm^{-1}) of specific classes of compounds investigated, and they cannot be compared accurately with the intensities given for other classes.

When known, the specific vibration giving rise to the characteristic frequency is printed in abbreviated form immediately to the right of the bar indicating the frequency range except when lack of space prevents this. When there can be no ambiguity, this information may be printed other than to the right. In doubtful cases, arrows are used for clarification.

Naturally, the characteristic frequencies vary in their specificity and analytical value. The user is, therefore, cautioned to use this chart with some reserve. After reviewing this chart, the reader should be aware that there are many characteristic frequencies in the 700 to 300 cm^{-1} region. Used cautiously, this chart can be of considerable value in the elucidation of structures of unknown compounds.

It is important to emphasize that the region of the infrared between ~700 to 300 cm^{-1} should be used in conjunction with the more conventional 5000 to 700 cm^{-1} region. Much of the value of the 700 to 300 cm^{-1} region can only be realized after interpreting the spectrum between 5000 to 700 cm^{-1}.

The following symbols and abbreviations are used:

Symbol or Abbreviation	Definition
αCCC	In-plane bending of benzene ring
Antisym.	Antisymmetrical (Asymmetrical)
~	Approximately
β	In-plane bending of ring substituent bond
δ	In-plane bending
γ	Out-of-plane bending
i.p.	In-plane
m	Medium
ν	Stretching
ν_s	Symmetrical stretching
ν_{as}	Antisymmetrical stretching
o.p.	Out-of-plane
‖	Parallel
⊥	Perpendicular
ϕ	Phenyl
ϕCC	Out-of-plane bending of aromatic ring
r	Rocking
s	Strong
sh	Shoulder
Sym.	Symmetrical
v	Variable
w	Weak
"X" Sensitive	An aromatic vibrational mode whose frequency position is greatly dependent on the nature of the substituent.

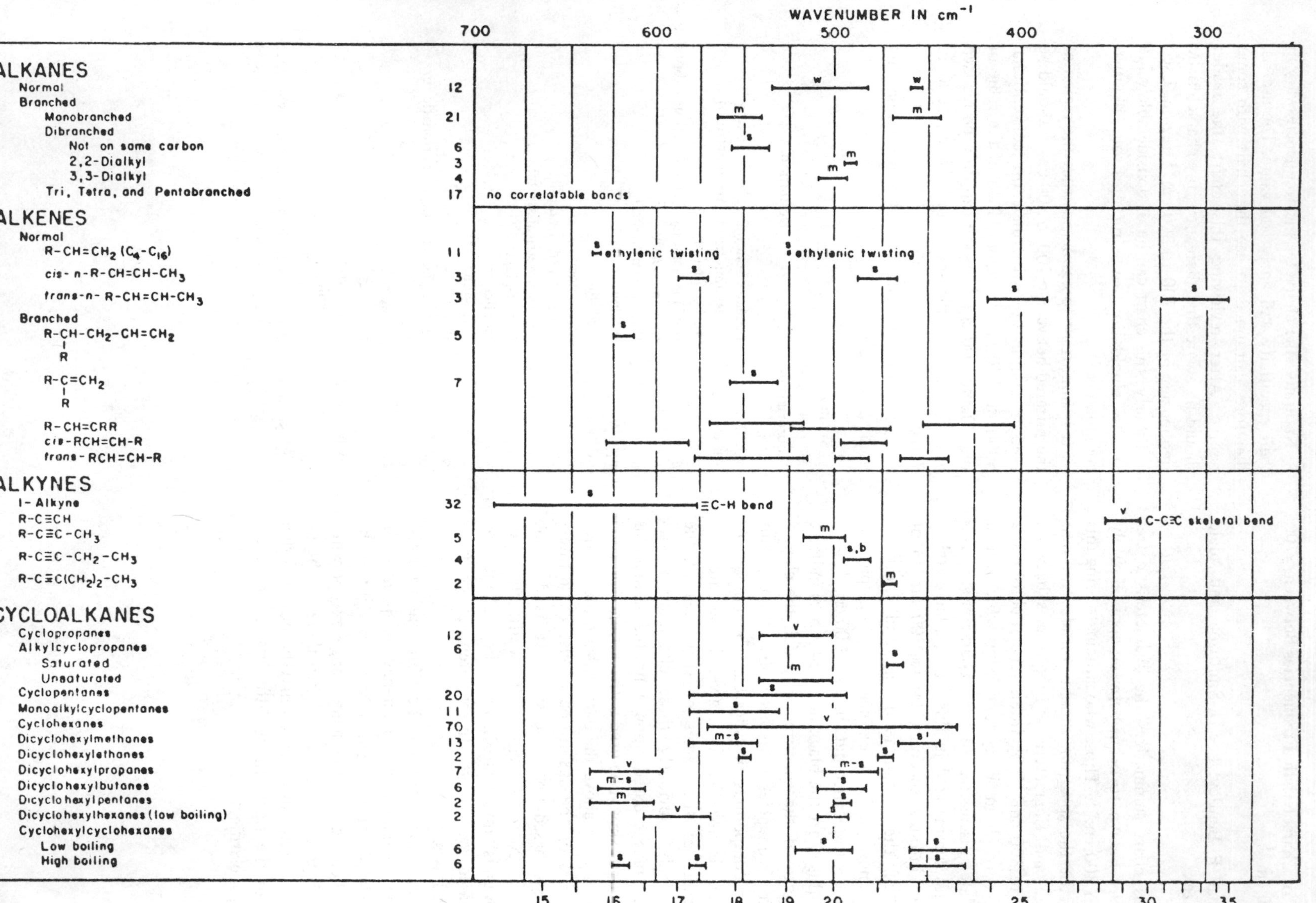

FIGURE 67, CHART 13. Chart of characteristic frequencies between ~700 to 300 cm^{-1}.

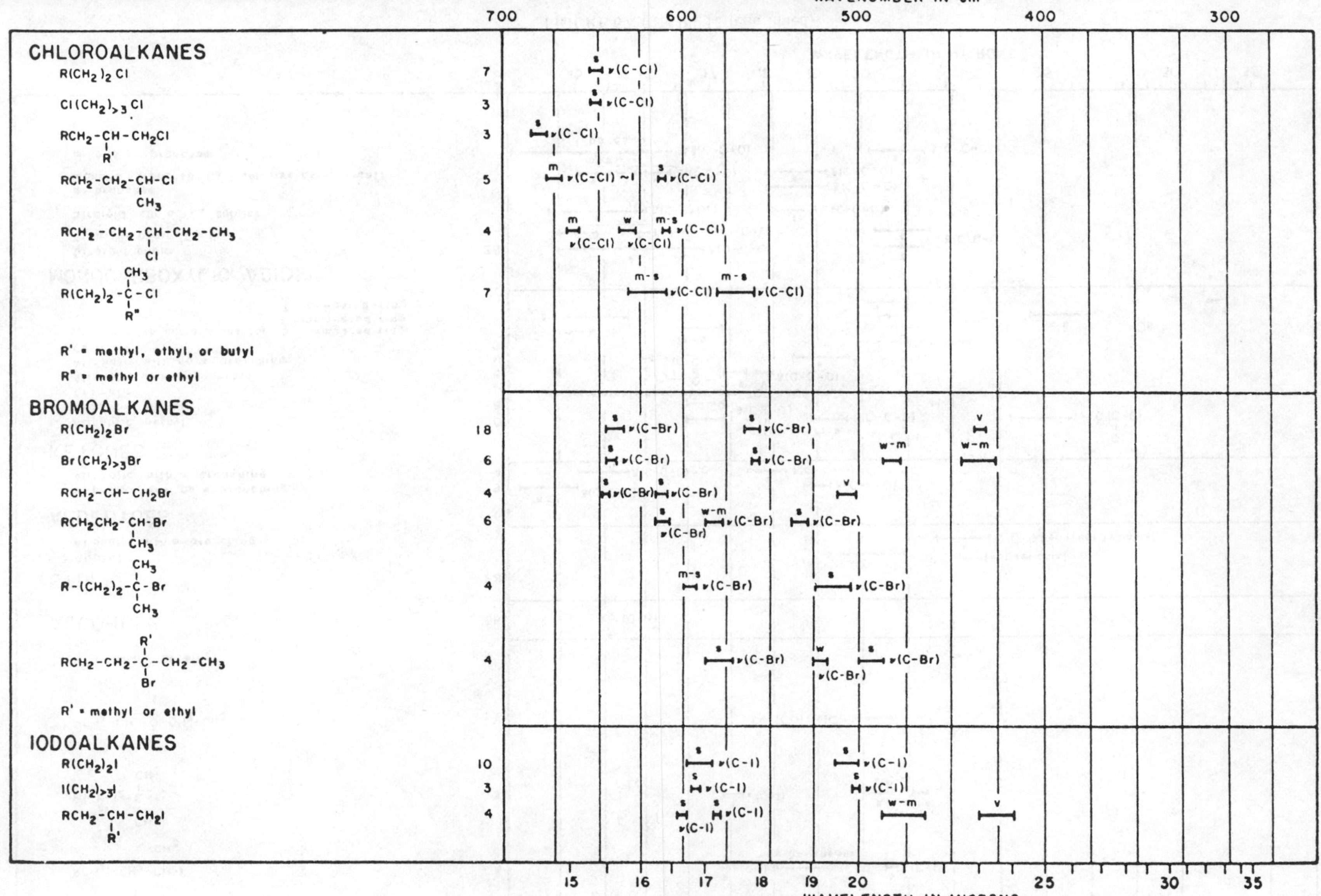

FIGURE 67, CHART 13 (continued).

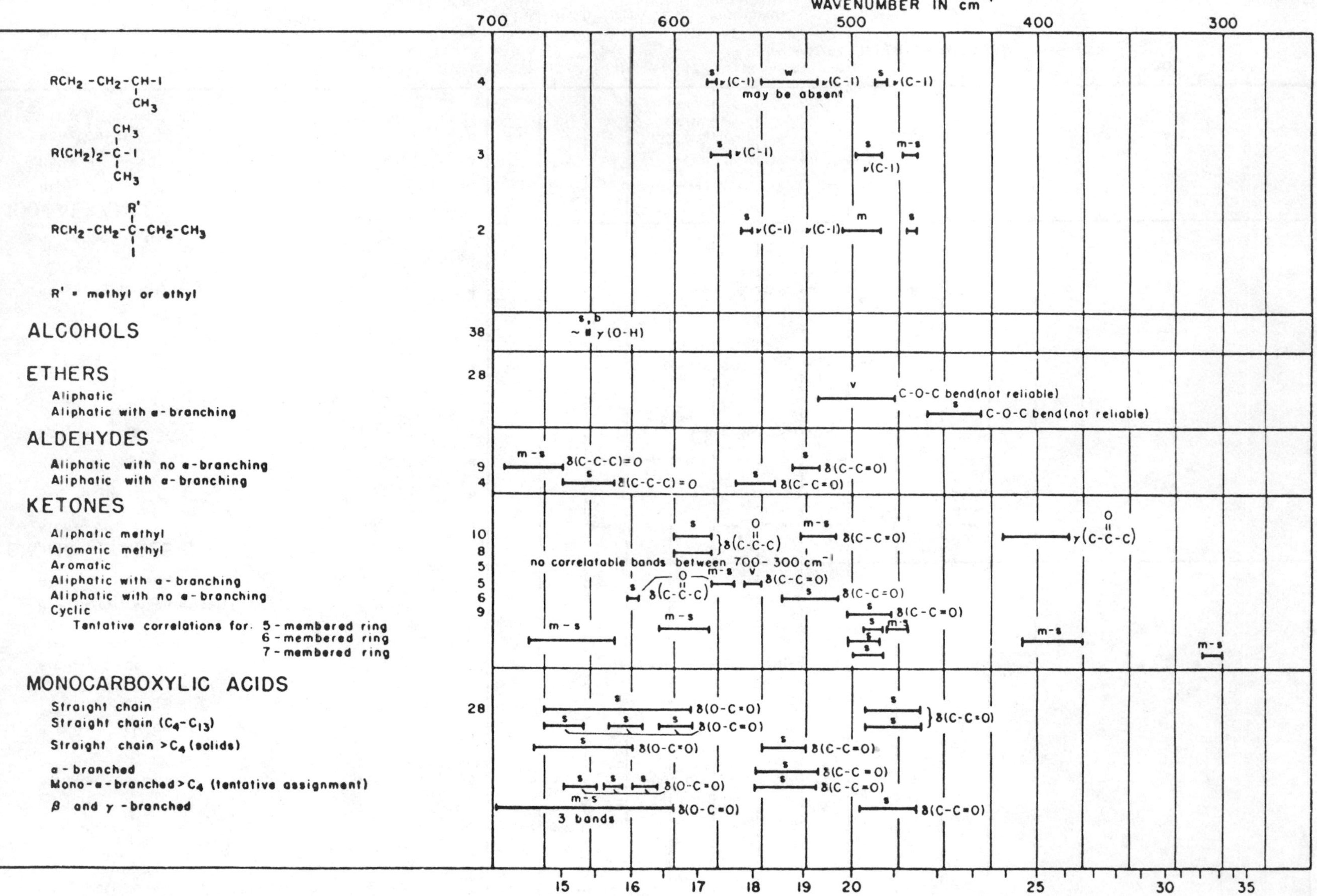

FIGURE 67, CHART 13 (continued).

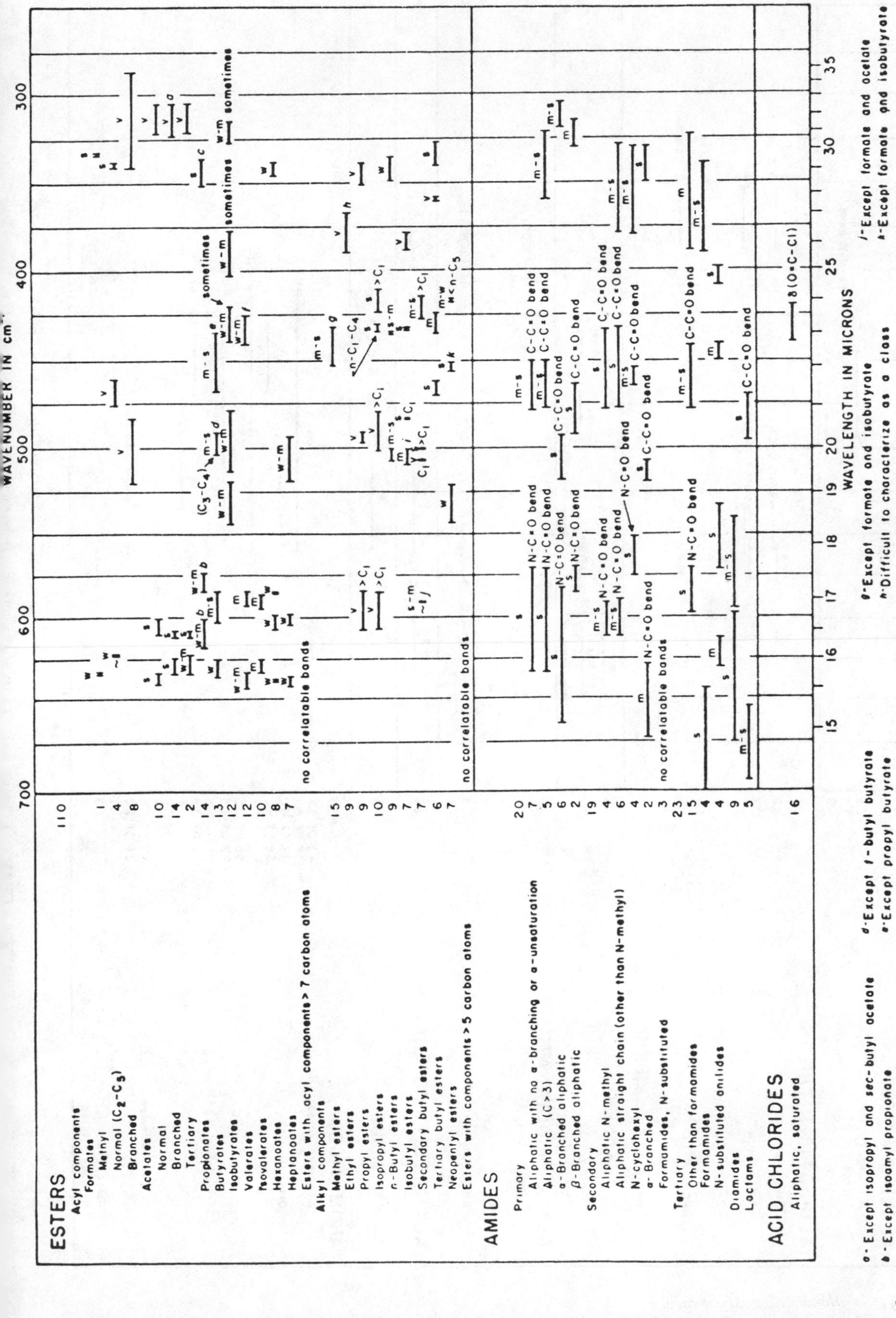

WAVENUMBER IN cm^{-1}

700 600 500 400 300

ESTERS	110
Acyl components	
Formates	
Methyl	1
Normal (C_2–C_5)	4
Branched	8
Acetates	
Normal	10
Branched	14
Tertiary	2
Propionates	14
Butyrates	13
Isobutyrates	12
Valerates	12
Isovalerates	10
Hexanoates	8
Heptanoates	7
Esters with acyl components > 7 carbon atoms	no correlatable bands
Alkyl components	
Methyl esters	15
Ethyl esters	9
Propyl esters	9
Isopropyl esters	10
n-Butyl esters	9
Isobutyl esters	7
Secondary butyl esters	7
Tertiary butyl esters	6
Neopentyl esters	7
Esters with components > 5 carbon atoms	no correlatable bands
AMIDES	
Primary	20
Aliphatic with no α-branching or α-unsaturation	7
Aliphatic (C > 3)	5
α-Branched aliphatic	6
β-Branched aliphatic	2
Secondary	19
Aliphatic N-methyl	4
Aliphatic straight chain (other than N-methyl)	6
N-cyclohexyl	4
α-Branched	2
Formamides, N-substituted	3 — no correlatable bands
Tertiary	23
Other than formamides	15
Formamides	4
N-substituted anilides	4
Diamides	9
Lactams	5
ACID CHLORIDES	
Aliphatic, saturated	16

15 16 17 18 19 20 25 30 35

WAVELENGTH IN MICRONS

a- Except isopropyl and sec-butyl acetate
b- Except isoamyl propionate
c- Except isopropyl and sec-butyl propionate
d- Except t-butyl butyrate
e- Except propyl butyrate
f- Except isopropyl and sec-butyl valerate
g- Except formate and isobutyrate
h- Difficult to characterize as a class
i- Except formate and isobutyrate
j- Except formate and acetate
k- Except formate and isobutyrate

FIGURE 67, CHART 13 (continued).

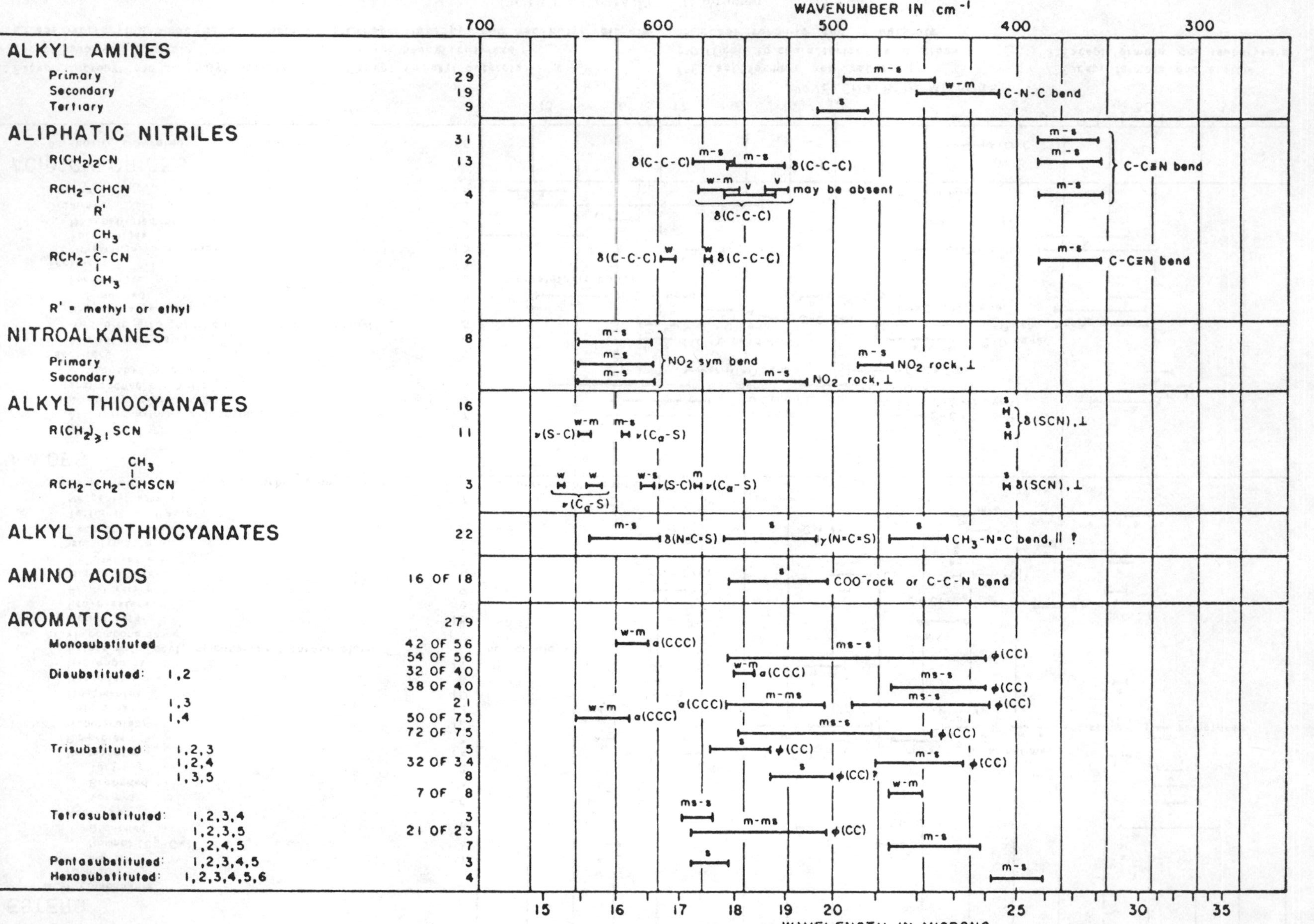

FIGURE 67. CHART 13 (continued). Chart of characteristic frequencies between ~700 to 300 cm⁻¹.

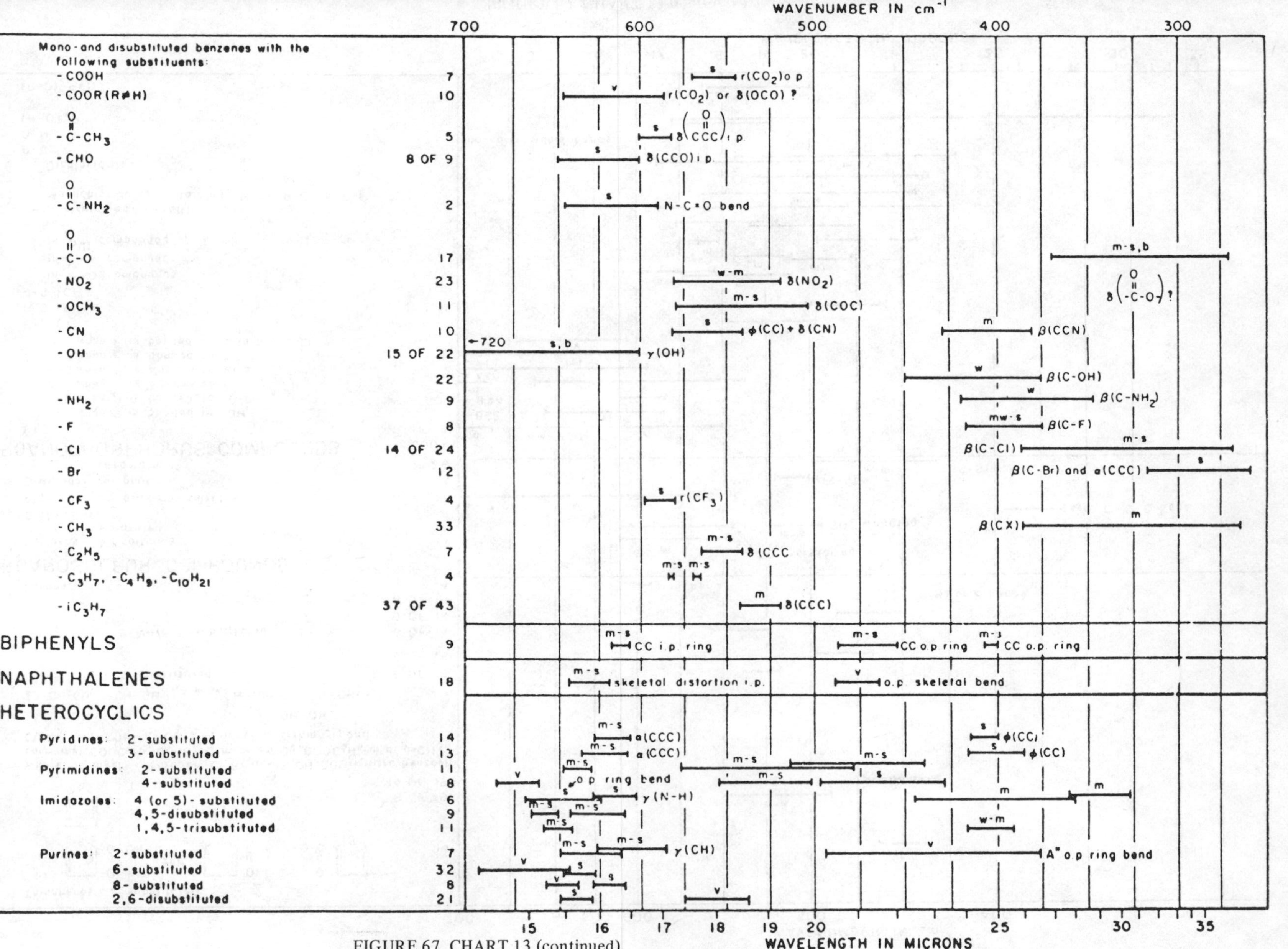

FIGURE 67, CHART 13 (continued).

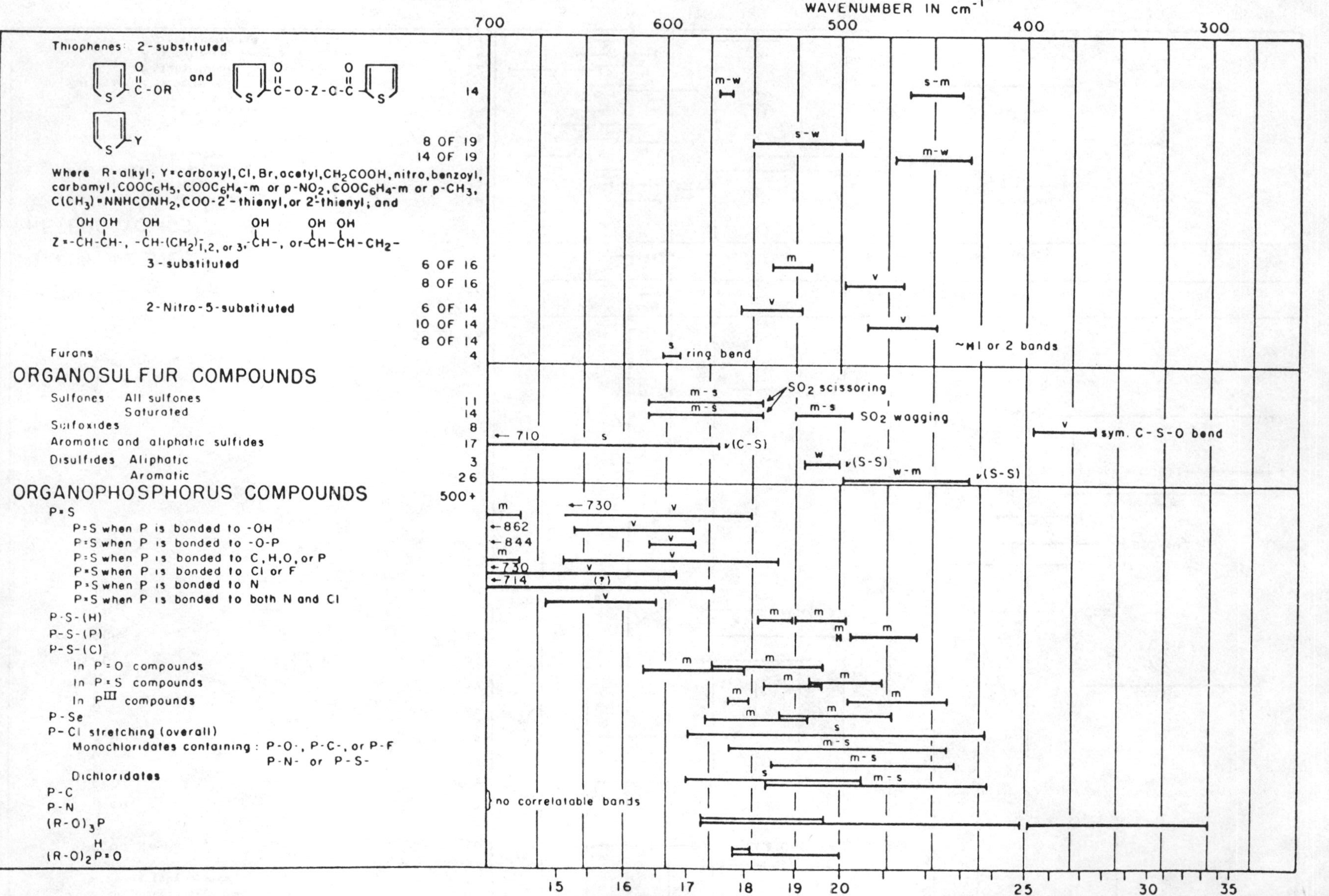

FIGURE 67, CHART 13 (continued).

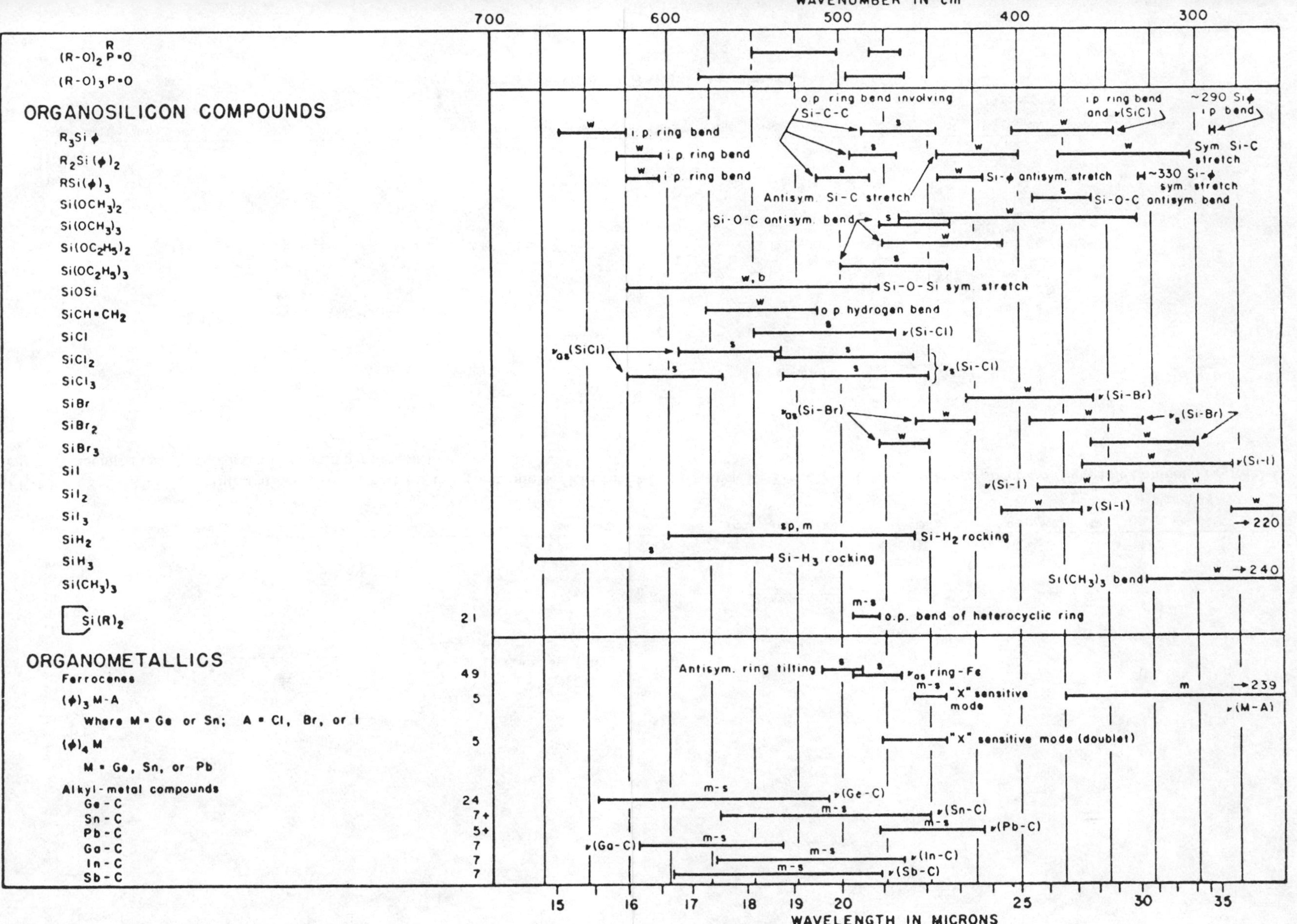

FIGURE 67, CHART 13 (continued).

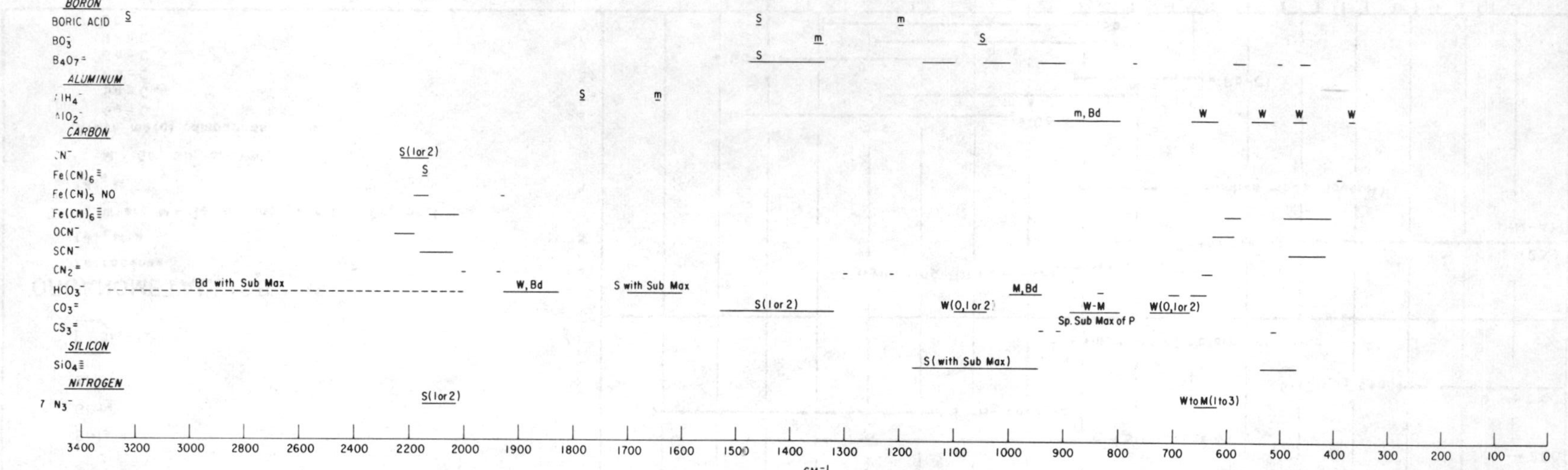

FIGURE 68, CHART 14. Infrared correlation chart for inorganic anions. (REFERENCE: Nyquist, R. A. and Kagel, R. O., *Infrared Spectra of Inorganic Compounds: 3800-45 cm*$^{-1}$, Academic Press, New York, 1971. With permission.)

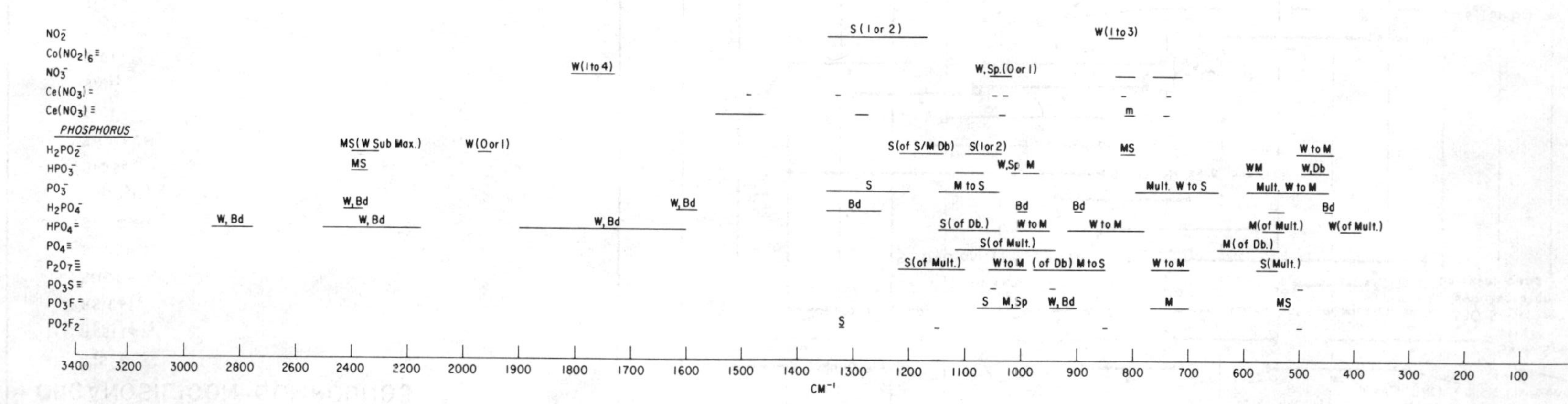

FIGURE 68, CHART 14 (continued).

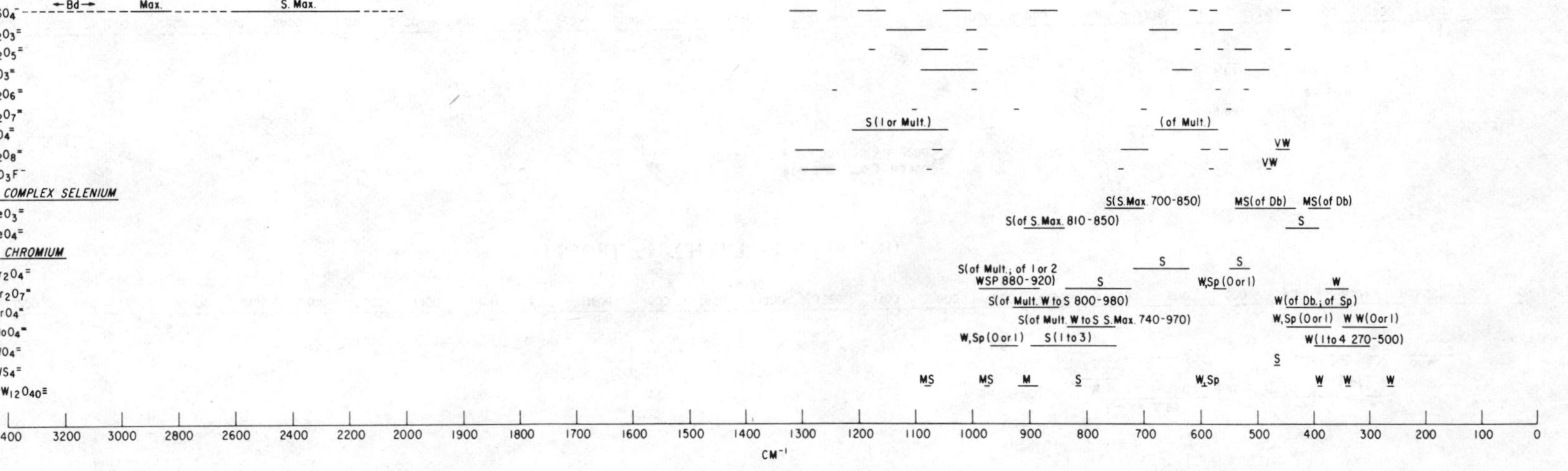

FIGURE 68, CHART 14 (continued).

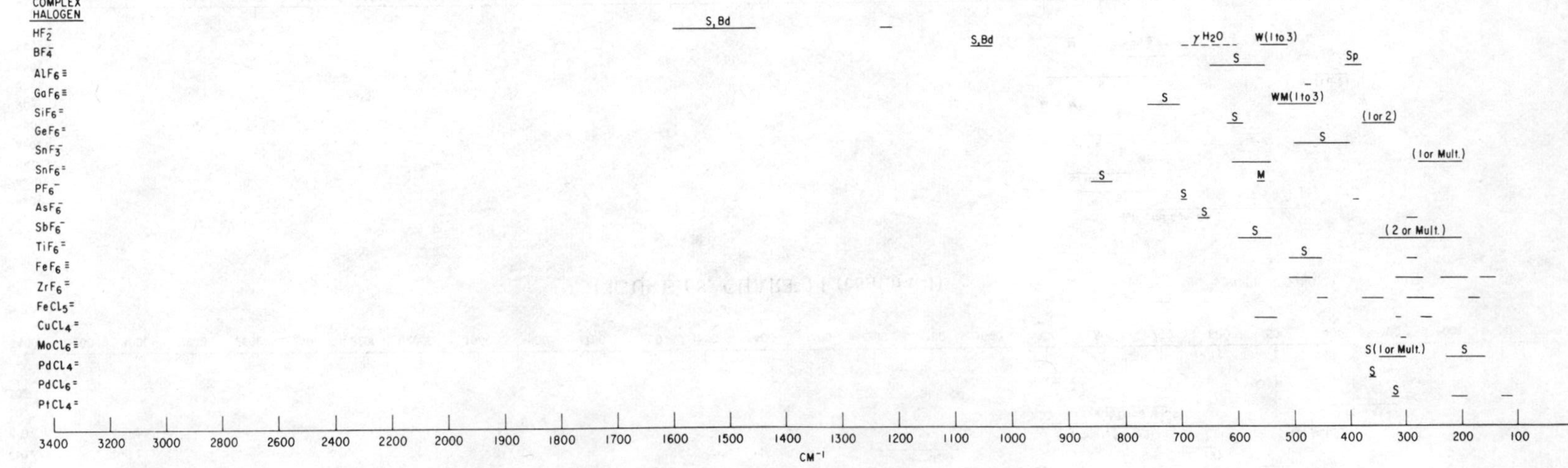

FIGURE 68, CHART 14 (continued).

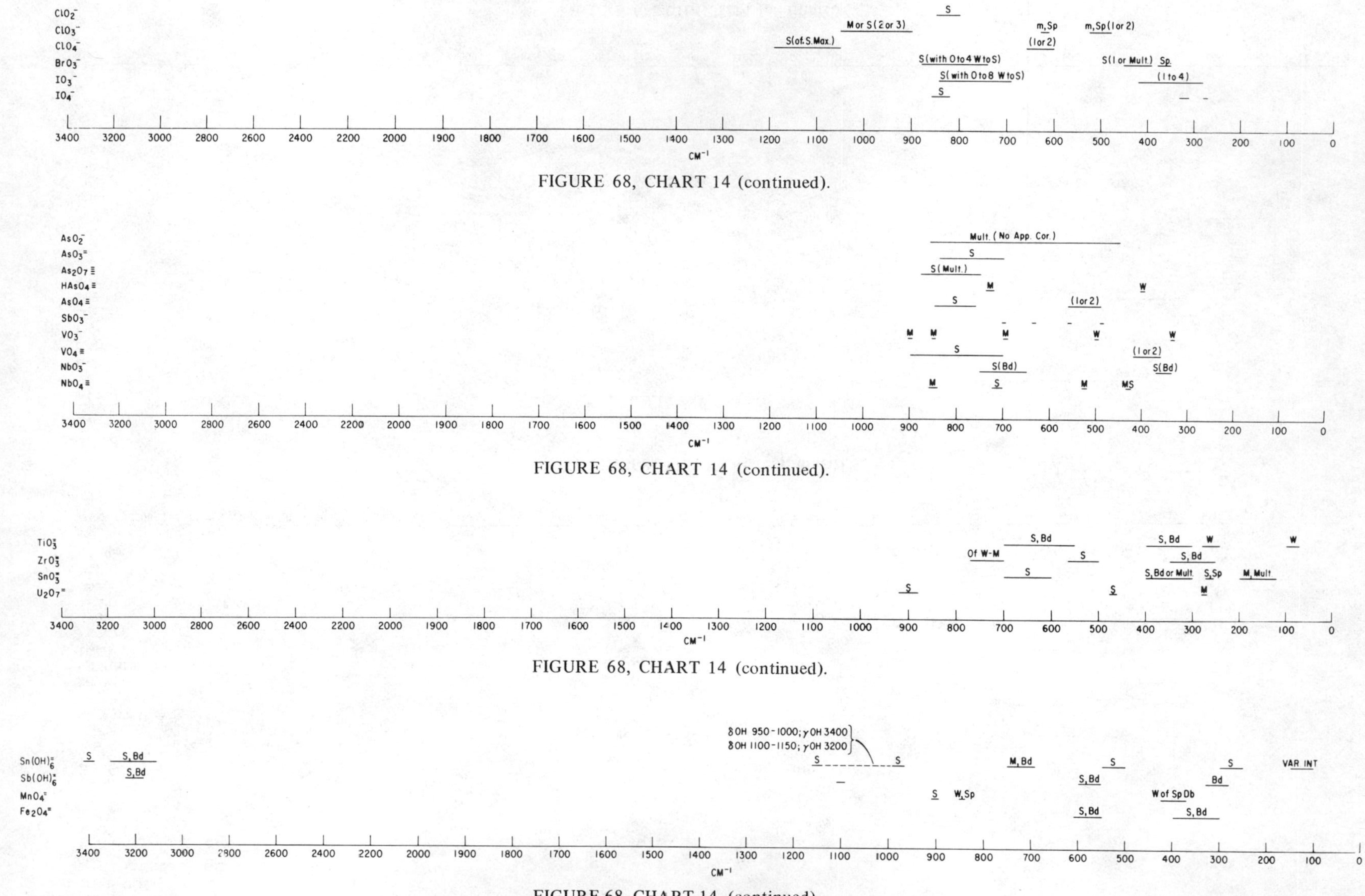

FIGURE 68, CHART 14 (continued).

FIGURE 68, CHART 14 (continued).

FIGURE 68, CHART 14 (continued).

FIGURE 68, CHART 14 (continued).

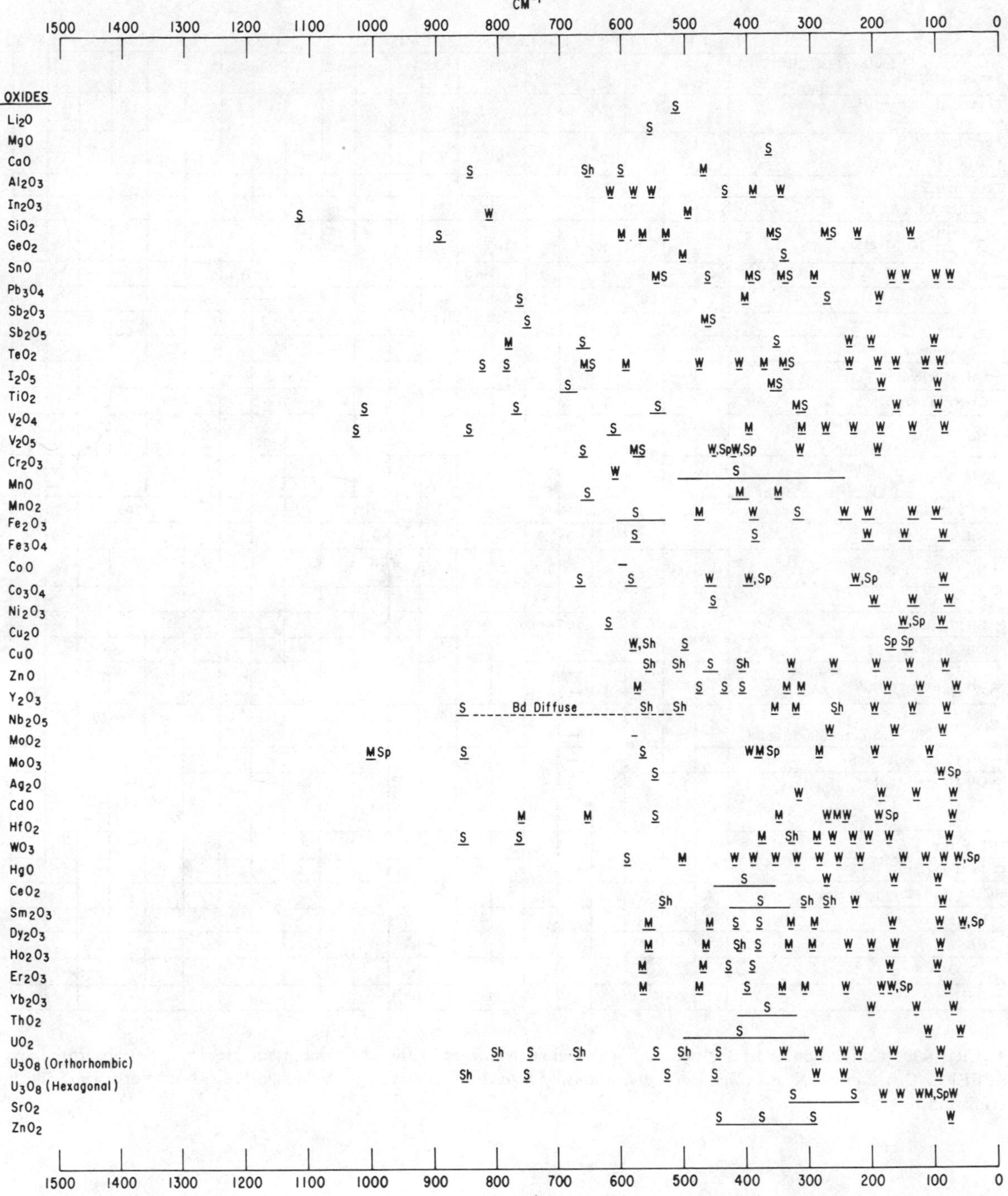

FIGURE 68, CHART 15. Infrared correlation chart for metal oxides. (REFERENCE: Nyquist, R. A. and Kagel, R. O., *Infrared Spectra of Inorganic Compounds: 3800-45 cm^{-1}*, Academic Press, New York, 1971. With permission.)

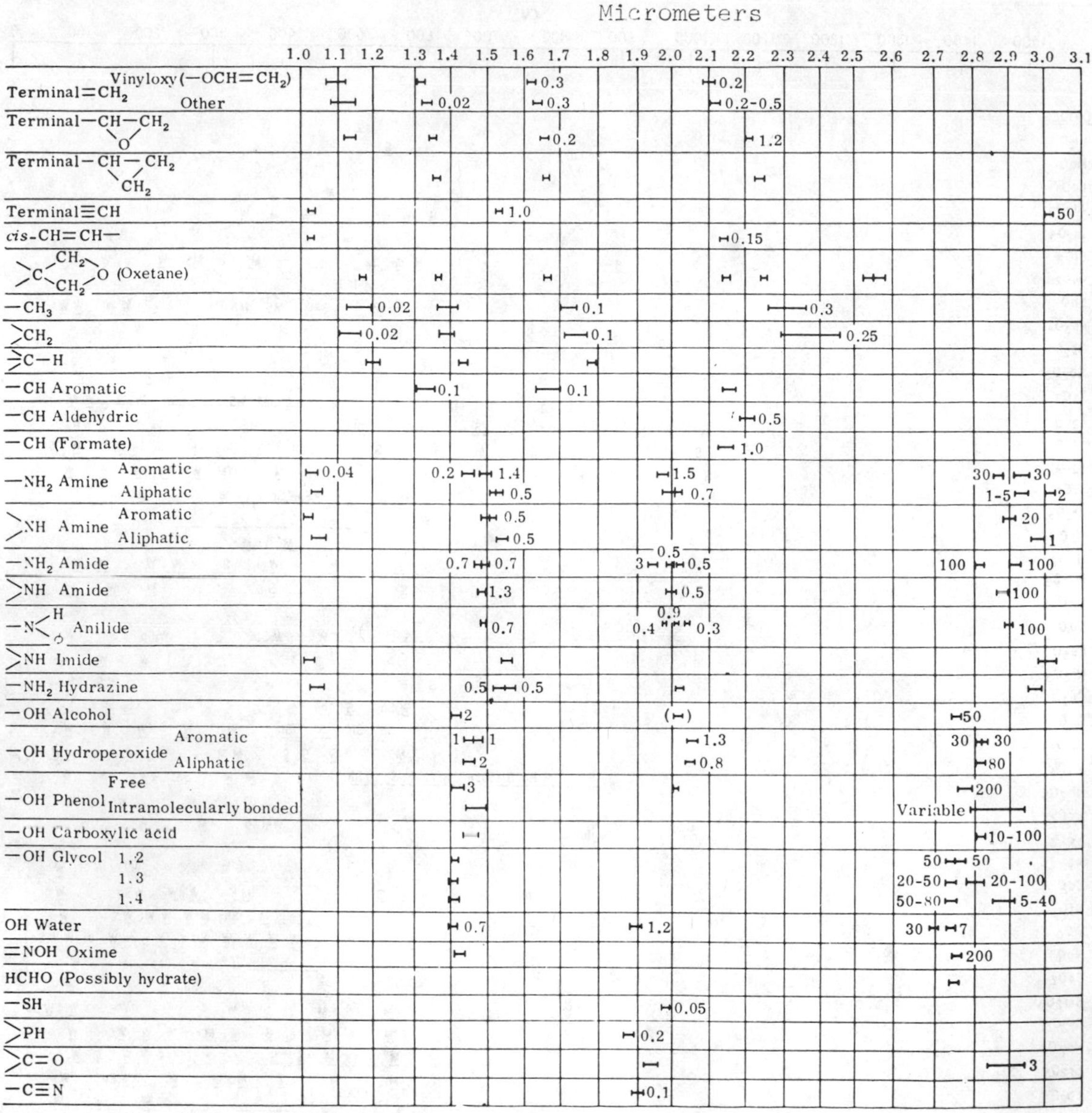

Micrometers

1.0 1.1 1.2 1.3 1.4 1.5 1.6 1.7 1.8 1.9 2.0 2.1 2.2 2.3 2.4 2.5 2.6 2.7 2.8 2.9 3.0 3.1

Group		Values printed in chart (left to right)
Terminal=CH_2	Vinyloxy (—OCH=CH_2)	0.3; 0.2
	Other	0.02; 0.3; 0.2-0.5
Terminal—CH—CH_2 (—O—)		0.2; 1.2
Terminal—CH—CH_2 (—CH_2—)		
Terminal≡CH		1.0; 50
cis-CH=CH—		0.15
>C<(CH_2)(CH_2)>O (Oxetane)		
—CH_3		0.02; 0.1; 0.3
>CH_2		0.02; 0.1; 0.25
≥C—H		
—CH Aromatic		0.1; 0.1
—CH Aldehydric		0.5
—CH (Formate)		1.0
—NH_2 Amine	Aromatic	0.04; 0.2; 1.4; 1.5; 30; 30
	Aliphatic	0.5; 0.7; 1-5; 2
>NH Amine	Aromatic	0.5; 20
	Aliphatic	0.5; 1
—NH_2 Amide		0.7; 0.7; 3; 0.5; 0.5; 100; 100
>NH Amide		1.3; 0.5; 100
—N<(H)(φ) Anilide		0.7; 0.4; 0.9; 0.3; 100
>NH Imide		
—NH_2 Hydrazine		0.5; 0.5
—OH Alcohol		2; (—); 50
—OH Hydroperoxide	Aromatic	1; 1; 1.3; 30; 30
	Aliphatic	2; 0.8; 80
—OH Phenol	Free	3; 200
	Intramolecularly bonded	Variable
—OH Carboxylic acid		10-100
—OH Glycol	1,2	50; 50
	1.3	20-50; 20-100
	1.4	50-80; 5-40
OH Water		0.7; 1.2; 30; 7
=NOH Oxime		200
HCHO (Possibly hydrate)		
—SH		0.05
>PH		0.2
>C=O		3
—C≡N		0.1

FIGURE 69. Correlation chart for near infrared region. Numbers in the chart represent average molar absorptivities. (REFERENCE: Rao, C. N. R., *Chemical Applications of Infrared Spectroscopy,* Academic Press, New York, 1963. With permission.)

V. QUANTITATIVE ANALYSIS

A. Absorption Laws

Bouguer's (Lambert's) Law:

$$-\frac{dI}{db} = aI$$

or

$$\ln\frac{I_o}{I} = ab$$

Beer's Law:

$$-\frac{dI}{dc} = aI$$

or

$$\ln\frac{I_o}{I} = ac\ ,$$

where a = absorptivity of pure sample
b = sample path length
I = intensity of transmitted radiation
I_o = intensity of incident radiation
c = concentration of sample

These laws are often combined into the *Bouguer-Beer (Beer-Lambert) Law:*

$$\log_{10}\frac{I_o}{I} = abc = \log_{10}\frac{1}{T} = \log_{10}\frac{100}{\%T} = A$$

where A = absorbance
$T = I/I_o$ = Transmittance of sample

B. Determination of Stray Radiation

Absorption Bands Suitable for Determination of Stray Radiation

Wavenumber Range	Wavelength Range	Substance[a]	Path (mm)
3620–3600	2.76–2.78	Phenol	20.0 (0.5 *M* soln.)
3335–3260	3.00–3.07	Phenylacetylene	0.5
3075–3045	3.25–3.28	Methylene chloride	1.0
2460–2380	4.07–4.20	Chloroform	10.0
1760–1675	5.68–5.97	Acetone	0.5
1590–1420	6.30–7.05	Carbon disulfide	1.0
1240–1190	8.07–8.42	Chloroform	1.0
1125–1120	8.90–8.93	Tetrachloroethylene	1.0
940–880	10.6–11.4	Tetrachloroethylene	1.0
800–740	12.5–13.5	Carbon tetrachloride	0.1
700–645	14.3–15.5	Benzene	0.5

[a]All measurements made on undiluted liquids except phenol.

Window Materials for Determination of Stray Radiation

Wavenumber Range	Wavelength Range	Substance	Thickness, mm.
2000–1000	5.0–10.0	SiO_2	7
1200–700	8.5–16.0	LiF	7
900–500	11.0–20.0	CaF_2	7
500–250	20.0–40.0	NaCl	14
300–250	33.0–40.0	KBr	14

REFERENCE: Kartha, B. V., quoted by Seshadri, K. S. and Jones, R. N., *Spectrochim. Acta,* 19, 1013, 1963.

C. To Minimize Errors in Quantitative Analysis:

1. Adjust the spectrometer for wide slits, low noise (Reference a).

2. Set zero accurately, allowing for stray radiation (a, b, also table below).

3. Use cell windows that match the refractive index of the solvent (c, d).

4. Use solutions as dilute as practical – 2% or less if possible (d).

5. Choose absorption bands as free as possible from interference and not subject to intensity changes from hydrogen bonding effects (a).

6. Adjust all thickness and concentrations such that band intensities lie between 20 and 60% T (.70 and .20 absorbance) (b and table below).

7. Scan slowly to minimize tracking errors (e).

REFERENCES

a. **Potts, W. J., Jr.,** *Chemical Infrared Spectroscopy. Vol. I. Techniques,* John Wiley & Sons, Inc., New York, 1963.

b. **Martin, A. E.,** *Trans. Faraday Soc.,* 47, 1182, 1951.

c. **White, J. U. and Ward, W. M.,** *Anal. Chem.,* 37, 268, 1965.

d. **Fujiyama, T., Herrin, J., and Crawford, B. L., Jr.,** *Appl. Spectroscopy,* 24, 9, 1970.

e. **Potts, W. J., Jr. and Smith, A. L.,** *Appl. Optics,* 6, 257, 1967.

D. Measurement of Absorbance

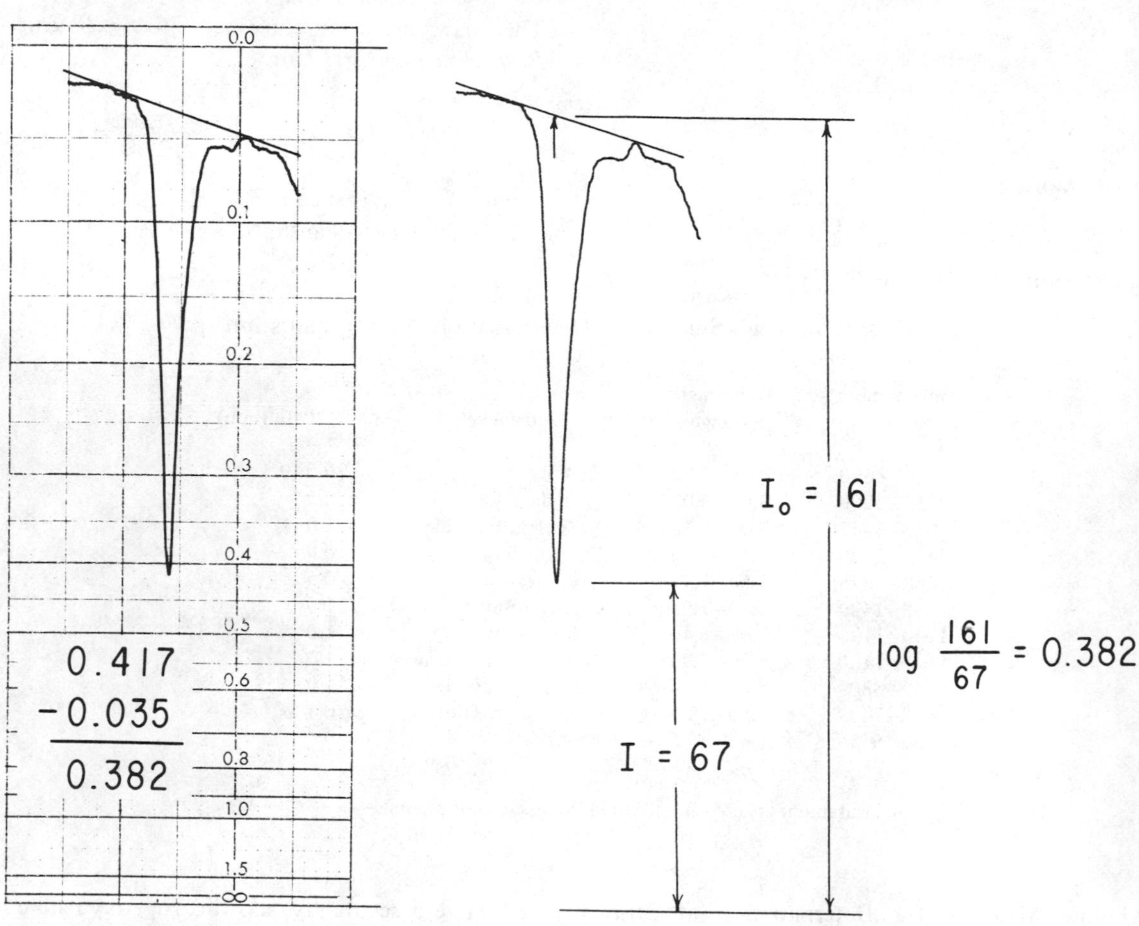

FIGURE 70. Measurement of absorbance using absorbance scale on the chart paper (left) and using a millimeter scale (right).

E. Possible Errors in Absorbance from Measurement Errors, Stray Light, Cell Inequality, and Non-linearity (Low Noise Case); Percentage Error in the Absorbance for Individual Errors of 1 Percent Deviation

	Percentage Transmittance Measured								
Type of Error	10	20	30	40	50	60	70	80	90
Measurement of I_o	0.43	0.62	0.83	1.09	1.44	1.96	2.80	4.48	9.49
Measurement of I	0.43	0.62	0.83	1.09	1.44	1.96	2.80	4.48	9.49
Stray light	4.14	2.56	1.98	1.67	1.47	1.33	1.22	1.13	1.07
Cell inequality	0.43	0.62	0.83	1.09	1.44	1.96	2.80	4.48	9.49
Non-linearity	1.56	1.99	2.33	2.62	2.88	3.14	3.36	3.58	3.80
Maximum total error	6.99	6.41	6.80	7.56	8.67	10.4	13.0	18.2	33.3

REFERENCE: Martin, A. E., *Trans. Faraday Soc.*, 47, 1182, 1951.

F. Ratio of the Apparent to the True Half-band Width for Various Apparent Maximum Absorbances and Slit Widths of a Band in the Form of a Lorentz Curve

	$s/\Delta\nu_{1/2}$													
Apparent Absorbance	0.00	0.05	0.10	0.15	0.20	0.25	0.30	0.35	0.40	0.45	0.50	0.55	0.60	0.65
2.0	1.00	1.00	1.01	1.02	1.03	1.04	1.06	1.09	1.13	1.17	1.22	1.28	1.36	1.51
1.8	1.00	1.00	1.01	1.02	1.03	1.05	1.07	1.10	1.14	1.18	1.23	1.29	1.38	1.53
1.6	1.00	1.00	1.01	1.02	1.03	1.05	1.07	1.10	1.14	1.18	1.24	1.31	1.40	1.55
1.4	1.00	1.00	1.01	1.02	1.03	1.05	1.08	1.11	1.15	1.19	1.25	1.33	1.43	1.58
1.2	1.00	1.00	1.01	1.02	1.03	1.05	1.08	1.11	1.15	1.20	1.27	1.35	1.45	1.60
1.0	1.00	1.00	1.01	1.02	1.03	1.05	1.08	1.12	1.16	1.21	1.28	1.37	1.48	1.63
0.8	1.00	1.00	1.01	1.02	1.03	1.06	1.09	1.12	1.16	1.22	1.30	1.39	1.51	1.66
0.6	1.00	1.00	1.01	1.02	1.04	1.06	1.09	1.13	1.17	1.23	1.31	1.41	1.54	1.70
0.4	1.00	1.00	1.01	1.02	1.04	1.06	1.09	1.13	1.18	1.24	1.32	1.43	1.57	1.75
0.2	1.00	1.00	1.01	1.02	1.04	1.07	1.10	1.14	1.19	1.25	1.34	1.46	1.60	1.80

REFERENCE: Ramsey, D. A., *J. Am. Chem. Soc.*, 74, 72, 1952.

Section B

Raman Spectroscopy

RAMAN SPECTROSCOPY

R. O. Kagel, Dow Chemical Company

I. INSTRUMENTATION

A. Sources

The recent resurgence of activity in chemical applications of Raman spectroscopy can be directly attributed to the advent of the laser as a source of exciting radiation. The laser is a stable, coherent, monochromatic source of high intensity radiation. These properties are ideal for excitation of the Raman radiation, which is a very inefficient process (1 Raman scattered photon per 10^7 to 10^8 incident photons).

The helium-neon, argon ion, krypton ion, and argon-krypton ion mixed gas lasers are most commonly used. The major wavelengths at which these lasers can be operated are listed in Table 1. The major lines of the argon ion laser are at 4,880 Å and 5,145 Å; they are at 5,682 Å and 6,471 Å for the krypton ion laser. The argon-krypton mixed gas laser can be operated at any of these wavelengths. Spurious lines or apparent Raman shifts which are due to plasma emission lines calculated for the argon ion laser are given in Table 2. The use of a spike filter to isolate a particular exciting line eliminates these spurious lines from the spectrum.

TABLE 1

Major Wavelengths for Some Common Gas Lasers[1]

Calibration Source	Wavelength (Å)	Frequency (cm^{-1}_{vac})
Helium-neon	6,328.1646	15,798.002
Argon ion	4,879.865	20,486.684
	5,145.27	19,429.91
	4,579.36	21,830.99
	4,657.95	21,462.66
	4,726.89	21,149.64
	4,764.88	20,981.02
	4,965.09	20,135.00
	5,017.17	19,926.00
Krypton ion	4,619.17	21,642.85
	4,680.45	21,359.49
	4,762.44	20,991.77
	4,825.18	20,718.83
	5,208.32	19,194.70
	5,308.68	18,831.83
	5,681.92	17,594.80
	6,471.00	15,449.29
	6,764.57	14,778.83

Courtesy of Heyden & Sons, Ltd., London.

B. Monochromators

Because the intensity of Raman scattered radiation is so low relative to Rayleigh scattered radiation, it is essential that stray light in the monochromator be minimized or, ideally, eliminated. This requires a monochromator system with very high discrimination. Almost all existing instrumentation utilizes a double monochromator system with a stray light rejection factor of 10^{-10} to 10^{-11} at 50 cm^{-1} from the exciting line. Where higher discrimination is necessary, triple monochromator systems are used. A typical stray light rejection factor for a triple monochromator system is 10^{-17} at 100 cm^{-1} from the exciting line. A typical stray light curve is shown in Figure 1.

C. Detector and Amplification

A S-20 response photomultiplier used in conjunction with D.C. amplification is standard in most commercial spectrometers. Amplification by photon counting is usually available as an option. Another option, thermoelectric cooling (−30°C), results in a subtstantial improvement in performance of the S-20 photomultiplier. A typical S-20 response curve is shown in Figure 2. Comparative data for the GaAs cathode tube are also given.

II. SPECTROMETER OPERATION

A. Monochromator Parameters

A useful relationship between slit width, scan speed, and time constant is given by

$$\mathrm{si} = \frac{\mathrm{sp}}{60} \cdot n\mathrm{t}, \qquad (1)$$

TABLE 2

Possible Spurious Lines due to Emission from the Laser Plasma when an Argon Ion Laser Is Being Used as the Raman Exciting Source[1]

Line	Frequency of Emission Line *in vacuo* (cm^{-1})	Wavelength in Standard Air (Å)	Peak Height	Apparent Raman Displacement of the Emission Lines in Wavenumbers (cm^{-1}) from the Laser Lines							
				4,579 Å	4,658 Å	4,727 Å	4,765 Å	4,880 Å	4,965 Å	5,017 Å	5,145 Å
1	21,995	4,545.2	350								
2	21,903	4,564.3	23								
3	21,831	4,579.4	380	0							
4	21,783	4,589.4	530	48							
5	21,739	4,598.7	15	92							
6	21,688	4,609.6	819	143							
7	21,557	4,637.6	74	274							
8	21,463	4,657.9	366	368	0						
9	21,150	4,726.8	500	681	313	0					
10	21,126	4,732.2	23	705	337	24					
11	21,108	4,736.2	800	723	355	42					
12	20,981	4,764.9	470	850	482	169	0				
13	20,803	4,805.7	1,150	1,028	660	347	178				
14	20,623	4,847.6	840	1,208	840	527	358				
15	20,547	4,865.5	40	1,284	916	603	434				
16	20,487	4,879.8	1,600	1,344	976	663	494	0			
17	20,450	4,888.6	90	1,381	1,013	700	531	37			
18	20,384	4,904.4	60	1,447	1,079	766	597	103			
19	20,267	4,932.8	460	1,564	1,196	883	714	220			
20	20,266	4,942.8	10	1,605	1,237	924	755	261			
21	20,135	4,965.1	530	1,696	1,328	1,015	846	352	0		
22	20,107	4,972.0	270	1,724	1,356	1,043	874	380	28		
23	19,959	5,008.9	830	1,872	1,504	1,191	1,022	528	176		
24	19,926	5,017.2	330	1,905	1,537	1,224	1,055	561	209	0	
25	19,750	5,061.9	790	2,081	1,713	1,400	1,231	737	385	176	
26	19,639	5,090.5	5	2,192	1,824	1,511	1,342	848	496	287	
27	19,444	5,141.5	27	2,387	2,019	1,706	1,537	1,043	691	482	
28	19,430	5,145.2	95	2,401	2,033	1,720	1,551	1,057	705	496	0
29	19,364	5,162.8	7	2,467	2,099	1,786	1,617	1,123	771	562	66
30	19,353	5,165.7	21	2,478	2,110	1,797	1,628	1,134	782	573	77
31	19,313	5,176.4	26	2,518	2,150	1,837	1,668	1,174	822	613	117
32	19,269	5,188.2	3	2,562	2,194	1,881	1,712	1,218	866	657	161
33	19,163	5,216.9	8	2,668	2,300	1,987	1,818	1,324	972	763	267
34	18,909	5,287.0	75	2,922	2,554	2,241	2,072	1,578	1,226	1,017	521
35	18,842	5,305.8	4	2,989	2,621	2,308	2,139	1,645	1,293	1,084	588
36	18,521	5,397.8	4	3,310	2,942	2,629	2,460	1,966	1,614	1,405	909
37	18,503	5,403.0	3	3,328	2,960	2,647	2,478	1,984	1,632	1,423	927
38	18,487	5,407.7	4	3,344	2,976	2,663	2,494	2,000	1,648	1,439	943
39	18,336	5,452.2	3	3,495	3,127	2,814	2,645	2,151	1,799	1,590	1,094
40	18,329	5,454.3	6	3,502	3,134	2,821	2,652	2,158	1,806	1,597	1,101
41	18,190	5,496.0	7	3,641	3,273	2,960	2,791	2,297	1,945	1,736	1,240
42	18,183	5,498.1	3	3,648	3,280	2,967	2,798	2,304	1,952	1,743	1,247
43	18,175	5,500.5	3	3,656	3,288	2,975	2,806	2,312	1,960	1,751	1,255
44	17,984	5,559.0	10	3,847	3,479	3,166	2,997	2,503	2,151	1,942	1,446
45	17,940	5,572.6	4	3,891	3,523	3,210	3,041	2,547	2,195	1,986	1,490

TABLE 2 (continued)

Possible Spurious Lines due to Emission from the Laser Plasma when an Argon Ion Laser Is Being Used as the Raman Exciting Source[1]

Line	Frequency of Emission Line *in vacuo* (cm^{-1})	Wavelength in Standard Air (Å)	Peak Height	Apparent Raman Displacement of the Emission Lines in Wavenumbers (cm^{-1}) from the Laser Lines							
				4,579 Å	4,658 Å	4,727 Å	4,765 Å	4,880 Å	4,965 Å	5,017 Å	5,145 Å
46	17,830	5,607.0	12	4,001	3,633	3,320	3,151	2,657	2,305	2,096	1,600
47	17,692	5,650.7	8	4,139	3,771	3,458	3,289	2,795	2,443	2,234	1,738
48	17,680	5,564.5	3	4,151	3,783	3,470	3,301	2,807	2,455	2,246	1,750
49	17,462	5,725.1	3	4,369	4,001	3,688	3,519	3,025	2,673	2,464	1,968
50	17,417	5,739.9	3	4,414	4,046	3,733	3,564	3,070	2,718	2,509	2,013
51	17,318	5,772.7	7	4,513	4,145	3,832	3,663	3,169	2,817	2,608	2,112
52	17,275	5,787.1	3	4,556	4,188	3,875	3,706	3,212	2,860	2,651	2,155
53	17,197	5,813.4	5	4,634	4,266	3,953	3,784	3,290	2,938	2,729	2,233
54	17,106	5,844.3	4	4,725	4,357	4,044	3,875	3,381	3,029	2,820	2,324
55	17,058	5,860.7	3	4,773	4,405	4,092	3,923	3,429	3,077	2,868	2,372
56	16,993	5,883.1	5	4,838	4,470	4,157	3,988	3,494	3,142	2,933	2,437
57	16,977	5,888.7	11	4,854	4,486	4,173	4,004	3,510	3,158	2,949	2,453
58	16,909	5,912.4	19	4,922	4,554	4,241	4,072	3,578	3,226	3,017	2,521
59	16,861	5,929.2	6	4,970	4,602	4,289	4,120	3,626	3,274	3,065	2,569
60	16,701	5,986.0	6	5,130	4,762	4,449	4,280	3,786	3,434	3,225	2,729
61	16,691	5,989.6	6	5,140	4,772	4,459	4,290	3,796	3,444	3,235	2,739
62	16,572	6,032.6	48	5,259	4,891	4,578	4,409	3,915	3,563	3,354	2,858
63	16,541	6,043.9	16	5,290	4,922	4,609	4,440	3,946	3,594	3,385	2,889
64	16,515	6,053.4	8	5,316	4,948	4,635	4,466	3,972	3,620	3,411	2,915
65	16,498	6,059.7	15	5,333	4,965	4,652	4,483	3,989	3,637	3,428	2,932
66	16,449	6,077.7	6	5,382	5,014	4,701	4,532	4,038	3,686	3,477	2,981
67	16,391	6,099.2	5	5,440	5,072	4,759	4,590	4,096	3,744	3,535	3,039
68	16,378	6,104.1	44	5,453	5,085	4,772	4,603	4,109	3,757	3,548	3,052
69	16,348	6,115.3	1,020	5,483	5,115	4,802	4,633	4,139	3,787	3,578	3,082
70	16,324	6,124.3	47	5,507	5,139	4,826	4,657	4,163	3,811	3,602	3,106
71	16,284	6,139.3	51	5,547	5,179	4,866	4,697	4,203	3,851	3,642	3,146
72	16,266	6,146.1	8	5,565	5,197	4,884	4,715	4,221	3,869	3,660	3,164
73	16,240	6,155.9	4	5,591	5,223	4,910	4,741	4,247	3,895	3,686	3,190
74	16,196	6,172.7	950	5,635	5,267	4,954	4,785	4,291	3,939	3,730	3,234
75	16,157	6,187.6	12	5,674	5,306	4,993	4,824	4,330	3,978	3,769	3,273
76	16,119	6,202.1	5	5,712	5,344	5,031	4,862	4,368	4,016	3,807	3,311
77	16,091	6,212.9	9	5,740	5,372	5,059	4,890	4,396	4,044	3,835	3,339
78	16,082	6,216.4	6	5,749	5,381	5,068	4,899	4,405	4,053	3,844	3,348
79	16,020	6,240.5	17	5,811	5,443	5,130	4,961	4,467	4,115	3,906	3,410
80	16,013	6,243.2	470	5,818	5,450	5,137	4,968	4,474	4,122	3,913	3,417
81	15,876	6,297.1	9	5,955	5,587	5,274	5,105	4,611	4,259	4,050	3,554
82	15,848	6,308.2	14	5,983	5,615	5,302	5,133	4,639	4,287	4,078	3,582
83	15,806	6,325.0	13	6,025	5,657	5,344	5,175	4,681	4,329	4,120	3,624
84	15,785	6,333.4	10	6,046	5,678	5,365	5,196	4,702	4,350	4,141	3,645
85	15,747	6,348.7	9	6,084	5,716	5,403	5,234	4,740	4,388	4,179	3,683
86	15,724	6,357.9	7	6,107	5,739	5,426	5,257	4,763	4,411	4,202	3,706
87	15,705	6,365.6	4	6,126	5,758	5,445	5,276	4,782	4,430	4,221	3,725
88	15,694	6,370.1	9	6,137	5,769	5,456	5,287	4,793	4,441	4,232	3,736
89	15,657	6,385.2	19	6,174	5,806	5,493	5,324	4,830	4,478	4,269	3,773

TABLE 2 (continued)

Possible Spurious Lines due to Emission from the Laser Plasma when an Argon Ion Laser Is Being Used as the Raman Exciting Source[1]

Line	Frequency of Emission Line *in vacuo* (cm^{-1})	Wavelength in Standard Air (Å)	Peak Height	Apparent Raman Displacement of the Emission Lines in Wavenumbers (cm^{-1}) from the Laser Lines: 4,579 Å	4,658 Å	4,727 Å	4,765 Å	4,880 Å	4,965 Å	5,017 Å	5,145 Å
90	15,634	6,394.5	7	6,197	5,829	5,516	5,347	4,853	4,501	4,292	3,796
91	15,628	6,397.0	8	6,203	5,835	5,522	5,353	4,859	4,507	4,298	3,802
92	15,621	6,399.9	104	6,210	5,842	5,529	5,360	4,866	4,514	4,305	3,809
93	15,611	6,404.0	7	6,220	5,852	5,539	5,370	4,876	4,524	4,315	3,819
94	15,598	6,409.3	5	6,233	5,865	5,552	5,383	4,889	4,537	4,328	3,832
95	15,579	6,417.1	79	6,252	5,884	5,571	5,402	4,908	4,556	4,347	3,851
96	15,563	6,423.7	5	6,268	5,900	5,587	5,418	4,924	4,572	4,363	3,867
97	15,543	6,432.0	3	6,288	5,920	5,607	5,438	4,944	4,592	4,383	3,887
98	15,528	6,438.2	19	6,303	5,935	5,622	5,453	4,959	4,607	4,398	3,902
99	15,517	6,442.8	14	6,314	5,946	5,633	5,464	4,970	4,618	4,409	3,913
100	15,513	6,444.4	11	6,318	5,950	5,637	5,468	4,974	4,622	4,413	3,917
101	15,453	6,469.4	8	6,378	6,010	5,697	5,528	5,034	4,682	4,473	3,997
102	15,444	6,473.2	6	6,387	6,019	5,706	5,537	5,043	4,691	4,482	3,986
103	15,437	6,476.2	5	6,394	6,026	5,713	5,544	5,050	4,698	4,489	3,993
104	15,419	6,483.7	480	6,412	6,044	5,731	5,562	5,068	4,716	4,507	4,011
105	15,378	6,501.0	56	6,453	6,085	5,772	5,603	5,109	4,757	4,548	4,052
106	15,358	6,509.5	10	6,473	6,105	5,792	5,623	5,129	4,777	4,568	4,072
107	15,289	6,538.8	65	6,542	6,174	5,861	5,692	5,198	4,846	4,637	4,141
108	15,231	6,563.7	15	6,600	6,232	5,919	5,750	5,256	4,904	4,695	4,199
109	15,153	6,597.5	3	6,678	6,310	5,997	5,828	5,334	4,982	4,773	4,277
110	15,135	6,605.4	28	6,696	6,328	6,015	5,846	5,352	5,000	4,791	4,295
111	15,113	6,615.0	19	6,718	6,350	6,037	5,868	5,374	5,022	4,813	4,317
112	15,098	6,621.6	24	6,733	6,365	6,052	5,883	5,389	5,037	4,828	4,332
113	15,059	6,638.7	2,800	6,772	6,404	6,091	5,922	5,428	5,076	4,867	4,371
114	15,047	6,644.0	5,700	6,784	6,416	6,103	5,934	5,440	5,088	4,879	4,383
115	14,996	6,666.6	37	6,835	6,467	6,154	5,985	5,491	5,139	4,930	4,434

Courtesy of Heyden & Sons, Ltd., London.

where sl = slit width in cm^{-1}
sp = speed in cm^{-1}/min
t = time constant in seconds
n = integer

Equation 1 relates the number of time constants required for a given scan speed to scan over a given spectral slit width. The spectral slit width is normally chosen so that it is less than the half-band width of a given band. For routine runs n is usually set equal to 2 cm^{-1}. The instrument is set up by adjusting the gain control to maximize a specific band or to set the strongest band at approximately 100-scale divisions at a given spectral slit width. The time constant is then adjusted to give the desired signal-to-noise ratio and the scan speed computed from Equation 1.

B. Spectrometer Calibration

Plasma emission lines can be used for crude spectrometer calibration. The neon emission spectrum provides a more precise means of calibration for both the 6,328 Å region of helium-neon and the 4,880 Å region of argon ion lasers. The neon emission spectra and tabulated frequencies

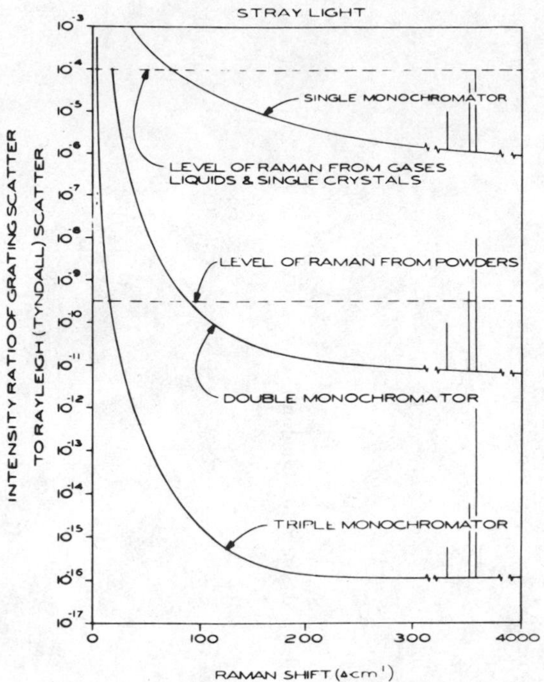

FIGURE 1. Scattered light, including ghosts appearing in a single, double, and triple monochromator.[2] (Reproduced by courtesy of Spex Industries, Metuchen, New Jersey.)

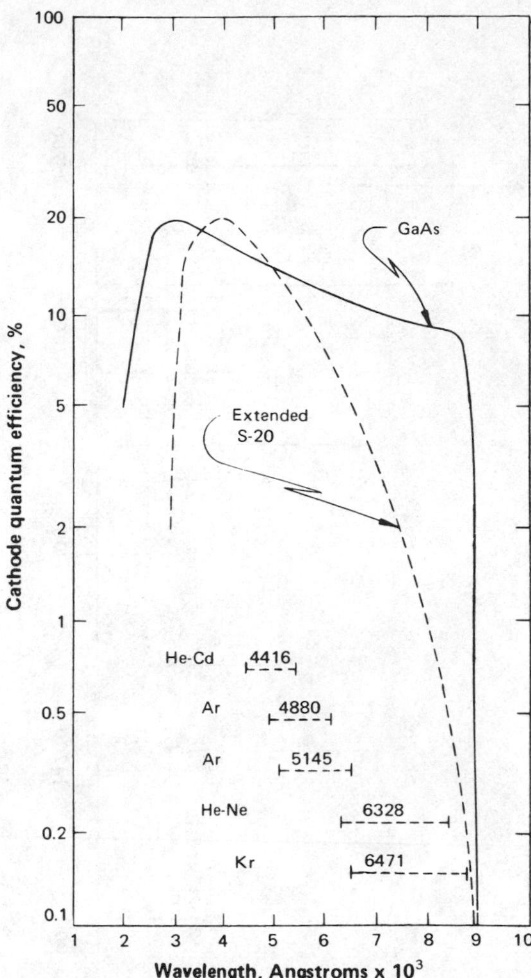

FIGURE 2. Response and cathode quantum efficiency curve for GaAs cathode tube and S-20 photomultiplier. (Reproduced by courtesy of Spex Industries, Metuchen, New Jersey.)

for these regions are shown in Figures 3 and 4 and Tables 3 and 4, respectively.

Hendra and Loader[3] have accurately measured the spectrum of indene (Figure 5) relative to the neon emission spectrum. Their results are tabulated in Table 5.

C. Resolution Check

The most common material used for checking the resolution of a Raman spectrometer is carbon tetrachloride. The 459 cm^{-1} band of carbon tetrachloride is a multiplet containing components due to both the symmetric $C\text{-}Cl^{35}$ and symmetric $C\text{-}Cl^{37}$ stretching vibrations. The chlorine isotopes give rise to the five bands listed in Table 6 and shown in Figure 6. The spectrum in Figure 6 should be reproducible if the instrument is properly aligned and operated at a resolution of less than 1 cm^{-1}.

D. Intensity Dependencies

The intensity of Raman scattered radiation is proportional to the fourth power of the frequency of the excitation line. For this reason it is more advantageous to use a higher frequency exciting line such as the 4,880 Å (20,487 cm^{-1}) line of argon ion than the 6,358 Å (15,728 cm^{-1}) line of helium-neon. The scattering efficiency increase is thus $\left(\frac{20,487}{15,728}\right)^4 = 2.8$. Unfortunately, the higher frequency excitation lines tend more to excite fluorescence than do the lower frequency lines, and one is often forced to compromise because of this.

The observed Raman intensity is dependent on monochromator throughput, phototube sensitivity, spectral slit width, and laser power as well as scattering efficiency. Some comparative data for

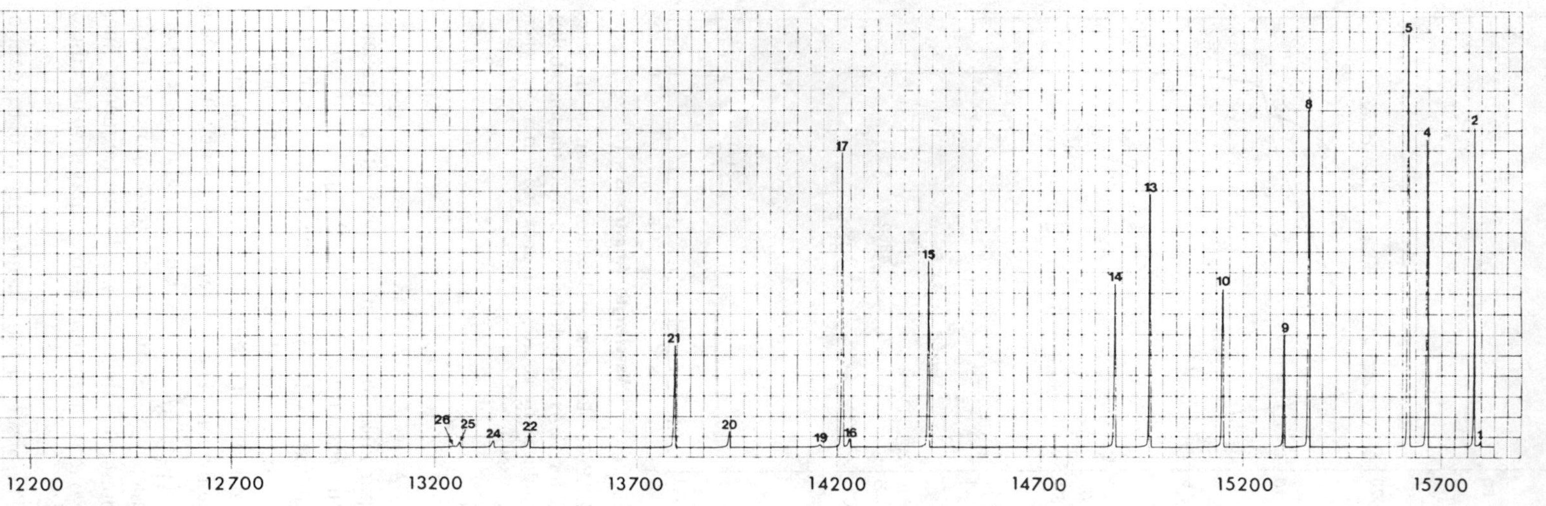

Light source: Neon lamp
Reference dynode: 3
Raman dynode: 4
Spectral slit width: 1 cm^{-1}
Scan speed: 250 cm^{-1}/min
Slit length: 10 cm
Sensitivity: 100
Single/Double slits: Single
Pen response: 0·1 sec

FIGURE 3. Neon emission spectrum.[1] (Reproduced by courtesy of Heyden and Sons, Ltd., London.)

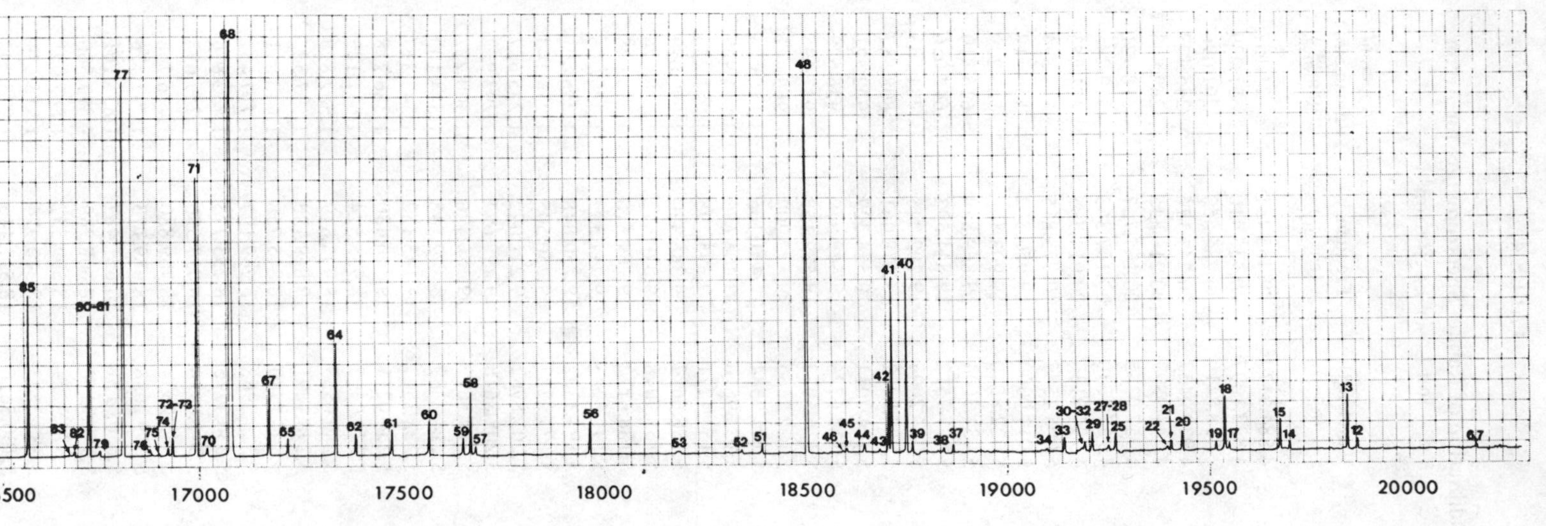

Light source: Neon lamp
Reference dynode: 3
Raman dynode: 4
Spectral slit width: 1 cm^{-1}
Scan speed: 250 cm^{-1}/min
Slit length: 10 cm
Sensitivity: 10
Single/Double slits: Single
Pen response: 0·1 sec

FIGURE 4. Neon emission spectra.[1] (Reproduced by courtesy of Heyden & Sons, Ltd., London.)

TABLE 3

Calibration of Laser Raman Spectrometers for Helium-neon Excitation[1]

Line	Wavelength (Å)	Frequency (cm^{-1}_{vac})	Apparent Raman Shift (cm^{-1}_{vac})
1	6,328.1646	15,798.002	0.000
2	6,334.4279	15,782.381	15.621
3	6,351.8618	15,739.064	58.938
4	6,382.9914	15,662.306	135.696
5	6,402.2460	15,615.202	182.800
6	6,421.7108	15,678.871	230.131
7	6,444.7118	15,512.310	285.692
8	6,506.5279	15,364.935	433.067
9	6,532.8824	15,302.951	495.051
10	6,598.9529	15,149.735	648.267
11	6,652.0925	15,028.714	769.288
12	6,666.8967	14,995.342	802.660
13	6,678.2764	14,969.790	828.212
14	6,717.0428	14,883.395	914.607
15	6,929.4672	14,427.144	1,370.858
16	7,024.0500	14,232.876	1,565.126
17	7,032.4128	14,215.950	1,582.052
18	7,051.2937	14,177.885	1,620.117
19	7,059.1079	14,162.191	1,635.811
20	7,173.9380	13,935.504	1,862.498
21	7,245.1665	13,798.503	1,999.499
22	7,438.8981	13,439.150	2,358.852
23	7,472.4383	13,378.828	2,419.174
24	7,488.8712	13,349.471	2,448.531
25	7,535.7739	13,266.384	2,531.618
26	7,544.0439	13,251.841	2,546.161
27	7,724.6281	12,942.045	2,855.957
28	7,839.0550	12,753.131	3,044.871
29	7,927.1172	12,611.457	3,186.545
30	7,936.9946	12,595.763	3,202.239
31	7,943.1805	12,585.954	3,212.048
32	8,082.4576	12,369.073	3,428.929
33	8,118.5495	12,314.085	3,483.917
34	8,128.9077	12,298.394	3,499.608
35	8,136.4061	12,287.060	3,510.942
36	8,248.6812	12,119.819	3,678.183
37	8,259.3795	12,104.120	3,693.882
38	8,266.0788	12,094.310	3,703.692
39	8,267.1166	12,092.792	3,705.210

Courtesy of Heyden & Sons, Ltd., London.

TABLE 4

Calibration of Raman Spectrometers for Argon Ion Laser Excitation[1]

Line	Wavelength (Å)	Frequency (cm^{-1}_{vac})	Apparent Raman Shift (cm^{-1}_{vac})
1	4,884.9170	29,465.461	21.187
2	4,892.1007	20,435.410	51.239
3	4,928.2410	20,285.553	201.096
4	4,939.0457	20,241.176	245.472
5	4,944.9899	20,216.845	269.803
6	4,957.0335	20,167.727	318.921
7	4,957.1230	20,167.363	319.285
8	4,994.9130	20,014.785	471.863
9	5,005.1587	19,973.815	512.834
10	5,011.0000	19,950.532	536.117
11	5,022.8640	19,903.409	583.239
12	5,031.3504	19,869.838	616.810
13	5,037.7512	19,844.593	642.056
14	5,074.2007	19,702.045	784.603
15	5,080.3852	19,678.061	808.587
16	5,104.7011	19,584.327	902.321
17	5,113.6724	19,549.970	936.679
18	5,116.5032	19,539.153	947.495
19	5,122.2565	19,517.207	969.441
20	5,144.9384	19,431.165	1,055.483
21	5,151.9610	19,404.679	1,081.969
22	5,154.4271	19,395.395	1,091.253
23	5,156.6672	19,386.970	1,099.679
24	5,158.9018	19,378.572	1,108.076
25	5,188.6122	19,267.610	1,219.038
26	5,191.3223	19,257.552	1,229.096
27	5,193.1302	19,250.848	1,235.801
28	5,193.2227	19,250.505	1,236.143
29	5,203.8962	19,211.022	1,275.627
30	5,208.8648	19,192.697	1,293.952
31	5,210.5672	19,186.426	1,300.222
32	5,214.3389	19,172.548	1,314.100
33	5,222.3517	19,143.132	1,343.517
34	5,234.0271	19,100.430	1,386.218
35	5,274.0393	18,955.524	1,531.125
36	5,280.0853	18,933.819	1,552.829
37	5,298.1891	19,869.123	1,617.525
38	5,304.7580	18,845.758	1,640.891
39	5,326.3968	18,769.197	1,717.452
40	5,330.7775	18,753.773	1,732.876
41	5,341.0938	18,717.550	1,769.098
42	5,343.2834	18,709.880	1,776.768
43	5,349.2038	18,689.173	1,797.476
44	5,360.0121	18,651.487	1,835.161
45	5,372.3110	18,608.789	1,877.860
46	5,374.9774	18,599.557	1,887.091
47	5,383.2503	18,570.974	1,915.674
48	5,400.5616	18,511.446	1,975.202
49	5,412.6493	18,470.106	2,016.542
50	5,418.5584	18,499.964	2,036.684
51	5,433.6513	18,398.717	2,087.932
52	5,448.5091	18,348.545	2,138.103
53	5,494.4158	18,195.242	2,291.407

TABLE 4 (continued)

Calibration of Raman Spectrometers for Argon Ion Laser Excitation[1]

Line	Wavelength (Å)	Frequency (cm^{-1}_{vac})	Apparent Raman Shift (cm^{-1}_{vac})
54	5,533.6788	18,066.143	2,420.506
55	5,538.6510	18,049.925	2,436.724
56	5,562.7662	17,971.677	2,514.971
57	5,652.5664	17,686.171	2,800.478
58	5,656.6588	17,673.375	2,813.273
59	5,662.5489	17,654.992	2,831.656
60	5,689.8163	17,570.385	2,916.264
61	5,719.2248	17,480.038	3,006.611
62	5,748.2985	17,391.628	3,095.020
63	5,760.5885	17,354.524	3,132.124
64	5,764.4188	17,342.993	3,143.656
65	5,804.4496	17,223.387	3,263.262
66	5,811.4066	17,202.768	3,283.880
67	5,820.1558	17,176.908	3,309.740
68	5,852.4878	17,082.016	3,404.633
69	5,868.4183	17,035.645	3,451.003
70	5,872.8275	17,022.855	3,463.793
71	5,881.8950	16,996.613	3,490.035
72	5,902.4623	16,937.388	3,549.260
73	5,902.7835	16,936.467	3,550.182
74	5,906.4294	16,926.012	3,560.636
75	5,913.6327	16,905.395	3,581.253
76	5,918.9068	16,890.332	3,596.317
77	5,944.8342	16,816.668	3,669.981
78	5,961.6228	16,769.311	3,717.338
79	5,965.4710	16,758.493	3,728.155
80	5,974.6273	16,732.811	3,753.838
81	5,975.5340	16,730.272	3,756.377
82	5,987.9074	16,695.701	3,790.948
83	5,991.6532	16,685.263	3,801.385
84	6,000.9275	16,659.477	3,827.172
85	6,029.9971	16,579.165	3,907.484
86	6,046.1348	16,534.914	3,951.735
87	6,064.5359	16,484.744	4,001.905

Courtesy of Heyden & Sons, Ltd., London.

He-Ne, Ar^+, and Kr^+ are summarized in Table 7. All values are normalized to unity at 6,328 Å, 80 mW of He-Ne. Column F indicates the Raman intensities for the major lines of Kr^+ and Ar^+ relative to He-Ne.

E. Depolarization Ratios

In addition to being monochromatic and coherent, laser radiation is also plane polarized. When a polarization analyzer is placed between the sample and the entrance slit of the monochromator, the intensity of Raman scattered radiation differs as the analyzer is rotated. When the analyzer is set to pass radiation that is polarized in the same direction as the source, the Raman scattered radiation will be more intense than when the analyzer is set to pass radiation polarized perpendicular to the direction of polarization of the source. The intensities of a Raman band observed in these two analyzer settings are referred to as $I_{\parallel}$ and $I_{\perp}$, respectively. The depolarization ratio, ρ, is defined as

$$\rho = \frac{I_{\perp}}{I_{\parallel}} \tag{2}$$

The maximum value of ρ for a plane polarized source is 0.75, and a band with a depolarization ration of ρ = 0.75 is said to be depolarized. Non-totally symmetric vibrations give Raman bands for which $\rho = 0.75$. Whenever $\rho < 0.75$, the band is said to be polarized. Totally symmetric vibrations give bands for which $\rho < 0.75$. The symmetry of a molecular vibration can be quickly determined from depolarization measurements, and these data are particularly useful in molecular structure determinations.

III. SAMPLING AND GEOMETRY

A. Conventional Solid and Liquid Phase Geometry

The conventional 90° sampling geometry is used in most spectrometers. The Raman scattered radiation is viewed at right angles to the direction of excitation. In this way only Rayleigh and Raman scattered radiation enters the monochromator and falls on the detector. Unscattered laser radiation, which is 10^3 to 10^4 times as intense as Rayleigh scattering and 10^7 to 10^8 times as intense as Raman scattering, does not reach the detector.

Pyrex® 1.5 mm O.D. melting point capillaries are the simplest cells. These are commonly used in the 90° configuration for liquids (neat or in solution) and solids. In the case of liquids, the beam is sometimes returned through the cell by an external mirror in order to gain sensitivity. Multipass cells have also been used. Cells should be thoroughly cleaned to remove dirt, fluorescing materials, etc., which might otherwise interfere with the Raman spectrum.

Some systems require other than 90° geometry.

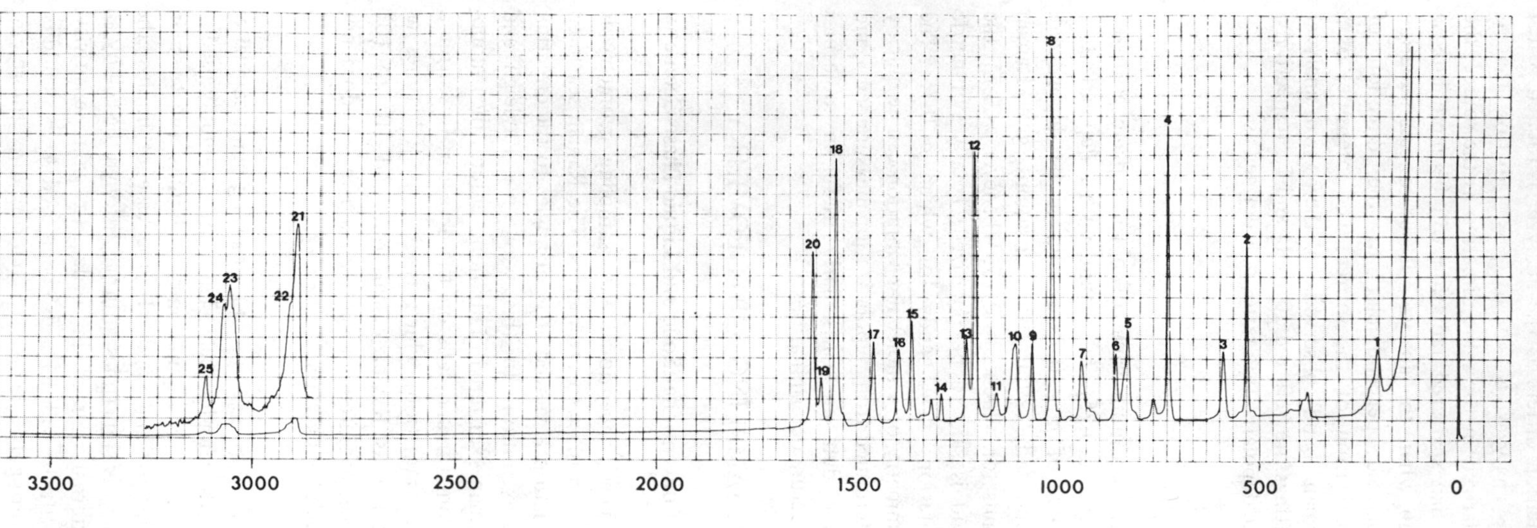

Compound: Indene
Phase: Liquid
Source: BDH
Purity: Reagent (vacuum distilled)
Sample cell: Sealed capillary
Reference dynode: 3
Raman dynode: 4
Spectral slit width: 4·6 cm^{-1}
Scan speed: 250 cm^{-1}/min
Slit length: 10 cm
Sensitivity: 40
Single/Double slits: Single
Pen response: 0·5 sec
Laser: He–Ne
Power: 40 mW

FIGURE 5. Indene calibration spectrum.[1] (Reproduced by courtesy of Heyden & Sons, Ltd., London.)

TABLE 5

Routine Calibration of the Laser Raman Spectrometer with Indene[3]

Line	Best (cm^{-1})	Source of Value[a]	Calibration Lines[b]
1	205.0 ± 2	N	
2	533.7 ± 0.5	N	←
3	593.0 ± 2	N	
4	730.1 ± 0.2	I	←
5	830.5 ± 0.2	I	
6	861.3 ± 0.2	I	
7	947.2 ± 0.3	I	
8	1,018.6 ± 0.2	I	←
9	1,067.9 ± 0.2	I	←
10	1,108.9 ± 1	N	
11	1,154.5 ± 0.5	I	
12	1,205.2 ± 0.2	I	←
13	1,226.2 ± 0.2	I	←
14	1,287.8 ± 0.2	I	
15	1,361.3 ± 0.4	I	←
16	1,393.2 ± 1	I	←
17	1,457.8 ± 0.5	I	←
18	1,553.3 ± 0.5	I	←
19	1,589.8 ± 1	N	
20	1,609.6 ± 0.2	I	←
21	2,892.2 ± 1	N	←
22	2,901.2 ± 1	N	←
23	3,054.7 ± 1	N	←
24	3,068.5 ± 2.5	I	←
25	3,112.7 ± 0.5	N	←

[a]I: IUPAC value for the position of the line obtained from interferometric measurements in the infrared.

N: Raman lines measured relative to the neon emission spectrum on the Cary 81 spectrometer.

[b]Those lines indicated with a horizontal arrow are recommended for calibration purposes.

Courtesy of Heyden & Sons, Ltd., London.

TABLE 6

Chlorine Isotope Bands[1]

Isotopic Modification	Percentage	Frequency Shift (cm^{-1})
$C^{37}Cl_4$	0.4	Not observed
$C^{35}Cl^{37}Cl_3$	4.7	452.0 ± 0.2
$C^{35}Cl_2{}^{37}Cl_2$	21.1	456.4 ± 0.2
$C^{35}Cl_3{}^{37}Cl$	42.2	459.4 ± 0.2
$C^{35}Cl_4$	31.6	462.4 ± 0.2

Courtesy of Heyden & Sons, Ltd., London.

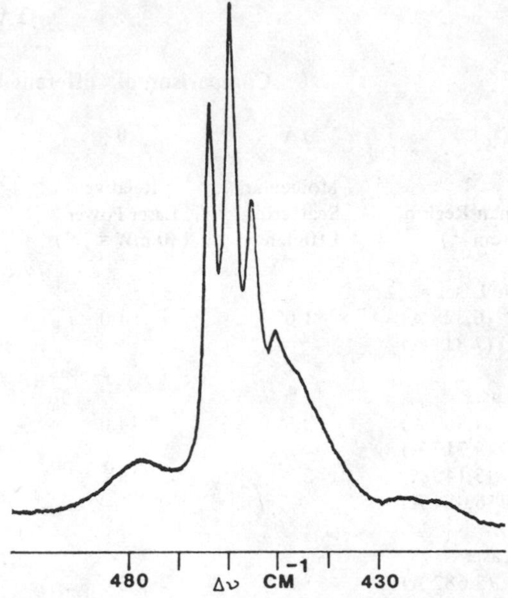

FIGURE 6. Multiplet structure of the carbon tetrachloride symmetric vibration [30% in cyclohexane; sample cell: capillary; spectral slit width: 0.8 cm^{-1}; scan speed: 1.5 cm^{-1}/min; laser: OIP He-Ne; power: 150 mW].[1] (Reproduced by courtesy of Heyden & Sons, Ltd., London.)

In some experimental setups, the beam is directed through the sample and onto the slit of the monochromator. This configuration is usually referred to as 0° geometry. In the 180° geometry, the beam is directed away from the slit. In both 0° and 180° geometries, one must take precautions to eliminate unscattered laser radiation by introducing an appropriate filter between the sample and slit, or phototube damage can result.

B. Special Geometries

Sample spinners are used in resonance Raman studies and for samples such as polymers or colored materials that normally decompose in the laser's beam.[5] The sample is prepared as a continous KBr disc pressed into a groove around the parameter of a wheel. The wheel is usually mounted at 45° to both the directions of incidence and the angle of view and spun at 1,800 to 6,000 r/min. In this way the sample does not decompose because of absorption (heating) of the laser radiation, and unscattered laser radiation does not enter the monochromator. Standard infrared KBr pellets or polymer films can also be mounted in the 45° configuration.

TABLE 7

Comparison of Different Laser Excitation Frequencies[4]

Raman Region (cm⁻¹)	A Molecular Scattering Efficiency	B Relative Laser Power (80 mW = 1.0)	C PM Quantum Efficiency[a]	D Grating Efficiency[b]	E Normalizing Factor for Equivalent Bandpass[c]	F[d] Raman Intensity
He-Ne Laser						
0 (6,328 Å)	1.0	1.0	1.0	1.0	1.0	1.0
3,000 (7,811 Å)			0.25	0.80	1.6	0.32
Ar^+ Laser						
0 (4,880 Å)	2.8	14.0	2.3	1.2	0.59	64.
3,000 (5,717 Å)			1.5	1.1	0.81	51.
0 (5,145 Å)	2.3	13.	2.2	1.2	0.65	51.
3,000 (6,084 Å)			1.2	1.1	0.91	36.
Kr^+ Laser						
0 (5,682 Å)	1.5	3.0	1.5	1.1	0.80	7.2
3,000 (6,850 Å)			0.73	1.0	1.1	3.6
0 (6,471 Å)	0.90	5.0	0.90	1.0	1.0	4.1
3,000 (8,030 Å)			0.17	0.75	1.7	1.0

[a]FW 130 photomultiplier
[b]5,000 Å blaze (average of two sets of gratings)
[c]Constant luminosity conditions
[d]A x B x C x D x E = F

Courtesy of Spex Industries, Metuchen, New Jersey.

Small single crystals are mounted on a goniometer in order to obtain orientation data.

C. Microsampling

A major advantage of the laser as a source of radiation is that it can be focused to a spot 10 to 50 μm in diameter. This focal volume is the minimum amount of sample necessary to produce a spectrum. Usable spectra of as little as 0.1 nl of benzyl alcohol have been obtained using 50-μm diameter capillaries.[6] Bulkin et al.[7] have devised a system based on small-diameter capillaries to trap, isolate, and obtain Raman spectra of gas chromatographic fractions.

Quite often the spectrum of a substance can be obtained without ever removing it from its original container (bottle, jar, ampule, etc.). In this case the container is usually mounted in the 90° or 45° configuration.

IV. INTERPRETATION

The Raman effect is particularly useful for characterizing vibrations centered in highly polarizable bonds (involving either hetero- or homo-atoms), whereas infrared excites vibrations centered in polarized bonds (involving hetero-atoms). In general, selection rules for the Raman effect are somewhat more liberal than those for infrared absorption. The well-known principle of mutual exclusion states that when a molecule contains a center of symmetry, those vibrations that are infrared active will not be Raman active and vice versa. Symmetric vibrations give rise to intense Raman bonds, while antisymmetric vibrations are generally weaker.

Table 8 summarizes characteristic Raman frequencies in the region 3,400 to 150 cm⁻¹.[8]

V. REPRESENTATIVE RAMAN SPECTRA

The following spectra were obtained as part of a round robin conducted by the Raman subcommittee of the Joint Committee on Atomic and Molecular Physical Data. The purpose of the round robin was to investigate a few well-known

TABLE 8

A Summary of Characteristic Raman Frequencies[8]

Frequency (cm^{-1})	Vibration	Compound
3,400–3,300	Bonded antisymmetric NH_2 stretch	Primary amines
3,380–3,340	Bonded OH stretch	Aliphatic alcohols
3,374	CH stretch	Acetylene (gas)
3,355–3,325	Bonded antisymmetric NH_2 stretch	Primary amides
3,350–3,300	Bonded NH stretch	Secondary amines
3,335–3,300	≡CH Stretch	Alkyl acetylenes
3,300–3,250	Bonded symmetric NH_2 stretch	Primary amines
3,310–3,290	Bonded NH stretch	Secondary amides
3,190–3,145	Bonded symmetric NH_2 stretch	Primary amides
3,175–3,154	Bonded NH stretch	Pyrazoles
3,103	Antisymmetric $=CH_2$ stretch	Ethylene (gas)
3,100–3,020	CH_2 Stretches	Cyclopropane
3,100–3,000	Aromatic CH stretch	Benzene derivatives
3,095–3,070	Antisymmetric $=CH_2$ stretch	$C=CH_2$ Derivatives
3,062	CH Stretch	Benzene
3,057	Aromatic CH stretch	Alkyl benzenes
3,040–3,000	CH Stretch	C=CHR Derivatives
3,026	Symmetric $=CH_2$ stretch	Ethylene (gas)
2,990–2,980	Symmetric $=CH_2$ stretch	$C=CH_2$ Derivatives
2,986–2,974	Symmetric NH_3^+ stretch	Alkyl ammonium chlorides (aq. soln)
2,969–2,965	Antisymmetric CH_3 stretch	*n*-Alkanes
2,929–2,912	Antisymmetric CH_2 stretch	*n*-Alkanes
2,884–2,883	Symmetric CH_3 stretch	*n*-Alkanes
2,861–2,849	Symmetric CH_2 stretch	*n*-Alkanes
2,850–2,700	CHO Group (2 bands)	Aliphatic aldehydes
2,590–2,560	SH Stretch	Thiols
2,316–2,233	C≡C Stretch (2 bands)	$R\text{-}C{\equiv}C\text{-}CH_3$
2,301–2,231	C≡C Stretch (2 bands)	R-C≡C-R′
2,300–2,250	Pseudoantisymmetric N=C=O stretch	Isocyanates
2,264–2,251	Symmetric C≡C-C≡C stretch	Alkyl diacetylenes
2,259	C≡N Stretch	Cyanamide
2,251–2,232	C≡N Stretch	Aliphatic nitriles
2,220–2,100	Pseudoantisymmetric N=C=S stretch (2 bands)	Alkyl isothiocyanates
2,220–2,000	C≡N Stretch	Dialkyl cyanamides
2,172	Symmetric C≡C-C≡C stretch	Diacetylene
2,161–2,134	$\overset{+}{N}{\equiv}\overset{-}{C}$ Stretch	Aliphatic isonitriles
2,160–2,100	C≡C Stretch	Alkyl acetylenes
2,156–2,140	C≡N Stretch	Alkyl thiocyanates
2,104	Antisymmetric N=N=N stretch	CH_3N_3
2,094	C≡N Stretch	HCN
2,049	Pseudoantisymmetric C=C=O stretch	Ketene
1,974	C≡C Stretch	Acetylene (gas)
1,964–1,958	Antisymmetric C=C=C stretch	Allenes
1,870–1,840	Symmetric C=O stretch	Saturated 5-membered ring cyclic anhydrides

TABLE 8 (continued)

A Summary of Characteristic Raman Frequencies[8]

Frequency (cm^{-1})	Vibration	Compound
1,820	Symmetric C=O stretch	Acetic anhydride
1,810–1,788	C=O Stretch	Acid halides
1,807	C=O Stretch	Phosgene
1,805–1,799	Symmetric C=O stretch	Noncyclic anhydrides
1,800	C=C Stretch	$F_2C=CF_2$ (gas)
1,795	C=O Stretch	Ethylene carbonate
1,792	C=C Stretch	$F_2C=CFCH_3$
1,782	C=O Stretch	Cyclobutanone
1,770–1,730	C=O Stretch	Halogenated aldehydes
1,744	C=O Stretch	Cyclopentanone
1,743–1,729	C=O Stretch	Cationic α-amino acids (aq. soln)
1,741–1,734	C=O Stretch	*O*-Alkyl acetates
1,740–1,720	C=O Stretch	Aliphatic aldehydes
1,739–1,714	C=C Stretch	$C=CF_2$ Derivatives
1,736	C=C Stretch	Methylene cyclopropane
1,734–1,727	C=O Stretch	*O*-Alkyl propionates
1,725–1,700	C=O Stretch	Aliphatic ketones
1,720–1,715	C=O Stretch	*O*-Alkyl formates
1,712–1,694	C=C Stretch	RCF=CFR
1,695	Nonconjugated C=O stretch	Uracil derivatives (aq. soln)
1,689–1,644	C=C Stretch	Monofluoroalkenes
1,687–1,651	C=C Stretch	Alkylidene cyclopentanes
1,686–1,636	Amide I band	Primary amides (solids)
1,680–1,665	C=C Stretch	Tetralkyl ethylenes
1,679	C=C Stretch	Methylene cyclobutane
1,678–1,664	C=C Stretch	Trialkyl ethylenes
1,676–1,665	C=C Stretch	*trans*-Dialkyl ethylenes
1,675	Symmetric C=O stretch (cyclic dimer)	Acetic acid
1,673–1,666	C=N Stretch	Aldimines
1,672	Symmetric C=O stretch (cyclic dimer)	Formic acid (aq. soln)
1,670–1,655	Conjugated C=O stretch	Uracil, cytosine, and guanine derivatives (aq. soln)
1,670–1,630	Amide I band	Tertiary amides
1,666–1,652	C=N Stretch	Ketoximes
1,665–1,650	C=N Stretch	Semicarbazones (solid)
1,663–1,636	Symmetric C=N stretch	Aldazines, ketazines
1,660–1,654	C=C Stretch	*cis*-Dialkyl ethylenes
1,660–1,650	Amide I band	Secondary amides
1,660–1,649	C=N Stretch	Aldoximes
1,660–1,610	C=N Stretch	Hydrazones (solid)
1,658–1,644	C=C Stretch	$R_2C=CH_2$
1,656	C=C Stretch	Cyclohexene, cycloheptene
1,654–1,649	Symmetric C=O stretch (cyclic dimer)	Carboxylic acids
1,652–1,642	C=N Stretch	Thiosemicarbazones (solid)

TABLE 8 (continued)

A Summary of Characteristic Raman Frequencies[8]

Frequency (cm^{-1})	Vibration	Compound
1,650–1,590	NH_2 Scissors	Primary amines (weak)
1,649–1,625	C=C Stretch	Allyl derivatives
1,648–1,640	N=O Stretch	Alkyl nitrites
1,648–1,638	C=C Stretch	H_2C=CHR
1,647	C=C Stretch	Cyclopropene
1,638	C=O Stretch	Ethylene dithiocarbonate
1,637	Symmetric C=C stretch	Isoprene
1,634–1,622	Antisymmetric NO_2 stretch	Alkyl nitrates
1,630–1,550	Ring stretches (doublet)	Benzene derivatives
1,623	C=C Stretch	Ethylene (gas)
1,620–1,540	Three or more coupled C=C stretches	Polyenes
1,616–1,571	C=C Stretch	Chloroalkenes
1,614	C=C Stretch	Cyclopentene
1,596–1,547	C=C Stretch	Bromoalkenes
1,581–1,465	C=C Stretch	Iodoalkenes
1,575	Symmetric C=C stretch	1,3-Cyclohexadiene
1,573	N=N Stretch	Azomethane (in soln)
1,566	C=C Stretch	Cyclobutene
1,560–1,550	Antisymmetric NO_2 stretch	Primary nitroalkanes
1,555–1,550	Antisymmetric NO_2 stretch	Secondary nitroalkanes
1,548	N=N Stretch	1-Pyrazoline
1,545–1,535	Antisymmetric NO_2 stretch	Tertiary nitroalkanes
1,515–1,490	Ring stretch	2-Furfuryl group
1,500	Symmetric C=Ċ stretch	Cyclopentadiene
1,480–1,470	OCH_3, OCH_2 Deformations	Aliphatic ethers
1,480–1,460	Ring stretch	2 Furfurylidene or 2-furoyl group
1,473–1,446	CH_3,CH_2 Deformations	*n*-Alkanes
1,466–1,465	CH_3 Deformation	*n*-Alkanes
1,450–1,400	Pseudoantisymmetric N=C=O stretch	Isocyanates
1,443–1,398	Ring stretch	2-Substituted thiophenes
1,442	N=N Stretch	Azobenzene
1,440–1,340	Symmetric CO_2^- stretch	Carboxylate ions (aq. soln)
1,415–1,400	Symmetric CO_2^- stretch	Dipolar and anionic α-amino acids (aq. soln)
1,415–1,385	Ring stretch	Anthracenes
1,395–1,380	Symmetric NO_2 stretch	Primary nitroalkanes
1,390–1,370	Ring stretch	Naphthalenes
1,385–1,368	CH_3 Symmetric deformation	*n*-Alkanes
1,375–1,360	Symmetric NO_2 stretch	Secondary nitroalkanes
1,355–1,345	Symmetric NO_2 stretch	Tertiary nitroalkanes
1,350–1,330	CH Deformation	Isopropyl group
1,320	Ring vibration	1,1-Dialkyl cyclopropanes
1,314–1,290	In-plane CH deformation	*trans*-Dialkyl ethylenes
1,310–1,250	Amide III band	Secondary amides
1,310–1,175	CH_2 Twist and rock	*n*-Alkanes

TABLE 8 (continued)

A Summary of Characteristic Raman Frequencies[8]

Frequency (cm^{-1})	Vibration	Compound
1,305–1,295	CH_2 In-phase twist	*n*-Alkanes
1,300–1,280	CC Bridge bond stretch	Biphenyls
1,282–1,275	Symmetric NO_2 stretch	Alkyl nitrates
1,280–1,240	Ring stretch	Epoxy derivatives
1,276	Symmetric N=N=N stretch	CH_3N_3
1,270–1,251	In-plane CH deformation	*cis*-Dialkyl ethylenes
1,266	Ring "breathing"	Ethylene oxide (oxirane)
1,230–1,200	Ring vibration	*para*-Disubstituted benzenes
1,220–1,200	Ring vibration	Mono- and 1,2-dialkyl cyclopropanes
1,212	Ring "breathing"	Ethylene imine (aziridine)
1,205	C_6H_5-C Vibration	Alkyl benzenes
1,196–1,188	Symmetric SO_2 stretch	Alkyl sulfates
1,188	Ring "breathing"	Cyclopropane
1,172–1,165	Symmetric SO_2 stretch	Alkyl sulfonates
1,150–950	CC Stretches	*n*-Alkanes
1,145–1,125	Symmetric SO_2 stretch	Dialkyl sulfones
1,144	Ring "breathing"	Pyrrole
1,140	Ring "breathing"	Furan
1,130–1,100	Symmetric C=C=C stretch (2 bands)	Allenes
1,130	Pseudosymmetric C=C=O stretch	Ketene
1,112	Ring "breathing"	Ethylene sulfide
1,111	NN Stretch	Hydrazine
1,070–1,040	S=O Stretch (1 or 2 bands)	Aliphatic sulfoxides
1,065	C=S Stretch	Ethylene trithiocarbonate
1,060–1,020	Ring vibration	*ortho*-Disubstituted benzenes
1,040–990	Ring vibration	Pyrazoles
1,030–1,015	In-plane CH deformation	Monosubstituted benzenes
1,030–1,010	Trigonal ring "breathing"	3-Substituted pyridines
1,030	Trigonal ring "breathing"	Pyridine
1,029	Ring "breathing"	Trimethylene oxide (oxetane)
1,026	Ring "breathing"	Trimethylene imine (azetidine)
1,010–990	Trigonal ring "breathing"	Mono-, meta-, and 1,3,5-substituted benzenes
1,001	Ring "breathing"	Cyclobutane
1,000–985	Trigonal ring "breathing"	2- and 4-Substituted pyridines
992	Ring "breathing"	Benzene
992	Ring "breathing"	Pyridine
939	Ring "breathing"	1,3-Dioxolane
933	Ring vibration	Alkyl cyclobutanes
930–830	Symmetric COC stretch	Aliphatic ethers
914	Ring "breathing"	Tetrahydrofuran

TABLE 8 (continued)

A Summary of Characteristic Raman Frequencies[8]

Frequency (cm^{-1})	Vibration	Compound
906	Symmetric CON stretch	Hydroxylamine
905–837	CC Skeletal stretch	*n*-Alkanes
900–890	Ring vibration	Alkyl cyclopentanes
900–850	Symmetric CNC stretch	Secondary amines
899	Ring "breathing"	Pyrrolidine
886	Ring "breathing"	Cyclopentane
877	OO Stretch	Hydrogen peroxide
851–840	Symmetric CON stretch	*O*-Alkyl hydroxylamines
836	Ring "breathing"	Piperazine
835–749	C_4 Skeletal stretch	Isopropyl group
834	Ring "breathing"	1,4-Dioxane
832	Ring "breathing"	Thiophene
832	Ring "breathing"	Morpholine
830–720	Ring vibration	*para*-Disubstituted benzenes
825–820	C_3O Symmetric skeletal stretch	Secondary alcohols
818	Ring "breathing"	Tetrahydropyran
815	Ring "breathing"	Piperidine
802	Ring "breathing"	Cyclohexane (chair form)
785–700	Ring vibration	Alkyl cyclohexanes
760–730	C_4O Symmetric skeletal stretch	Tertiary alcohols
750–650	C_5 Symmetric skeletal stretch	*tert*-Butyl group
740–585	CS Stretch (1 or more bands)	Alkyl sulfides
735–690	"C=S Stretch"	Thioamides, thioureas (solid)
733	Ring "breathing"	Cycloheptane
730–720	CCl Stretch, P_c conformation	Primary chloroalkanes
715–620	CS Stretch (1 or more bands)	Dialkyl disulfides
709	CCl Stretch	CH_3Cl
703	Ring "breathing"	Cyclooctane
703	Symmetric CCl_2 stretch	CH_2Cl_2
690–650	Pseudosymmetric N=C=S stretch	Alkyl isothiocyanates
688	Ring "breathing"	Tetrahydrothiophene
668	Symmetric CCl_3 stretch	$CHCl_3$
660–650	CCl Stretch, P_H conformation	Primary chloroalkanes
659	Symmetric CSC stretch	Pentamethylene sulfide
655–640	CBr Stretch, P_C conformation	Primary bromoalkanes
630–615	Ring deformation	Monosubstituted benzenes
615–605	CCl Stretch, S_{HH} conformation	Secondary chloroalkanes
610–590	CI Stretch, P_C conformation	Primary iodoalkanes
609	CBr Stretch	CH_3Br
577	Symmetric CBr_2 stretch	CH_2Br_2
570–560	CCl Stretch, T_{HHH} conformation	Tertiary chloroalkanes
565–560	CBr Stretch, P_H conformation	Primary bromoalkanes
540–535	CBr Stretch, S_{HH} conformation	Secondary bromoalkanes
539	Symmetric CBr_3 stretch	$CHBr_3$
525–510	SS Stretch	Dialkyl disulfides

TABLE 8 (continued)

A Summary of Characteristic Raman Frequencies[8]

Frequency (cm^{-1})	Vibration	Compound
523	CI Stretch	CH_3I
520–510	CBr Stretch, T_{HHH} conformation	Tertiary bromoalkanes
510–500	CI Stretch, P_H conformation	Primary iodoalkanes
510–480	SS Stretch	Dialkyl trisulfides
495–485	CI Stretch, S_{HH} conformation	Secondary iodoalkanes
495–485	CI Stretch, T_{HHH} conformation	Tertiary iodoalkanes
484–475	Skeletal deformation	Dialkyl diacetylenes
483	Symmetric CI_2 stretch	CH_2I_2
459	Symmetric CCl_4 stretch	CCl_4
437	Symmetric CI_3 stretch	CHI_3 (in soln)
425–150	"Chain expansion"	*n*-Alkanes
355–335	Skeletal deformation	Monoalkyl acetylenes
267	Symmetric CBr_4 stretch	CBr_4 (in soln)
200–160	Skeletal deformation	Aliphatic nitriles
178	Symmetric CI_4 stretch	CI_4 (solid)

Courtesy of John Wiley & Sons, New York.

compounds under varying instrumental conditions and using different excitation lines. The spectra were run on a Spex Ramalog System with a coherent Model 52MG argon-krypton laser. A complete set of toluene spectra run with 4,880 Å argon ion excitation at 5, 4, 3, 2, 1, and 0.25 cm^{-1} resolution (Figures 7 to 12) and a 1 cm^{-1} resolution spectrum run with 5,145 Å argon ion excitation (Figure 13) are included. Spectra of cyclohexane, cyclohexanone, and indene run with 4,880 Å argon ion excitation at 1 cm^{-1} resolution are also presented for comparison (Figures 14 to 16).

VI. THE DOCUMENTATION OF RAMAN SPECTRA

At the Second International Conference on Raman Spectroscopy held at Oxford, England in September 1970, a meeting was organized by the Subcommission on Infrared and Raman Spectroscopy of IUPAC to formulate draft recommendations for the presentation of Raman spectra intended for cataloging and documentation in permanent collections. A previous meeting was held during the First International Conference on Raman Spectroscopy at Ottawa, Canada in August 1969, and in the interim several informal discussions have also taken place at various spectroscopic conferences. These meetings have been attended by a large number of Raman spectroscopists concerned with the documentation of Raman spectral data.

At the Oxford conference the set of draft recommendations which follows in Sections A and B was approved; it has been submitted by the Commission on Molecular Structure and Spectroscopy to the Physical Chemistry Division of IUPAC for publication as a IUPAC information bulletin in the series "Appendices on Tentative Nomenclature, Symbols, Units and Standards."

A. Recommendation for the Presentation of Raman Spectra for Cataloging and Documentation in Permanent Data Collections

The use of optical lasers as exciting sources has led to increasing use of Raman spectrophotometry in chemical research, and it is desirable that Raman spectra intended for cataloging and documentation in permanent collections should be presented in a uniform manner. Commission I.5 (Molecular Structure and Spectroscopy) therefore proposes that the following recommendations be followed. These have been prepared after consulta-

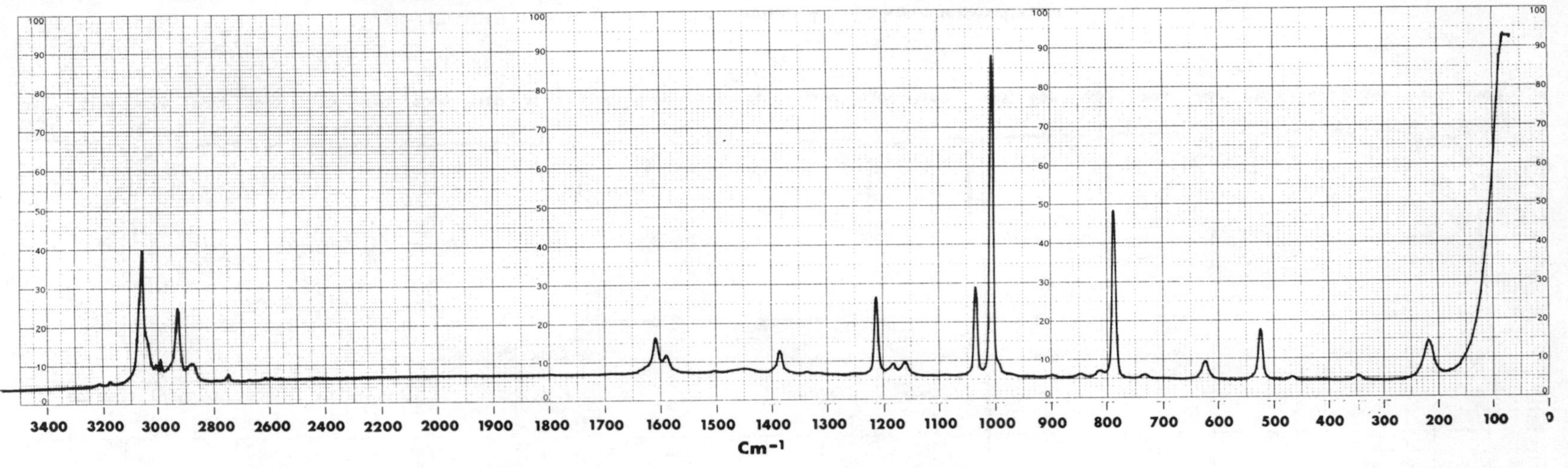

FIGURE 7. Toluene 5 cm^{-1} resolution; 4,880 Å argon ion excitation.

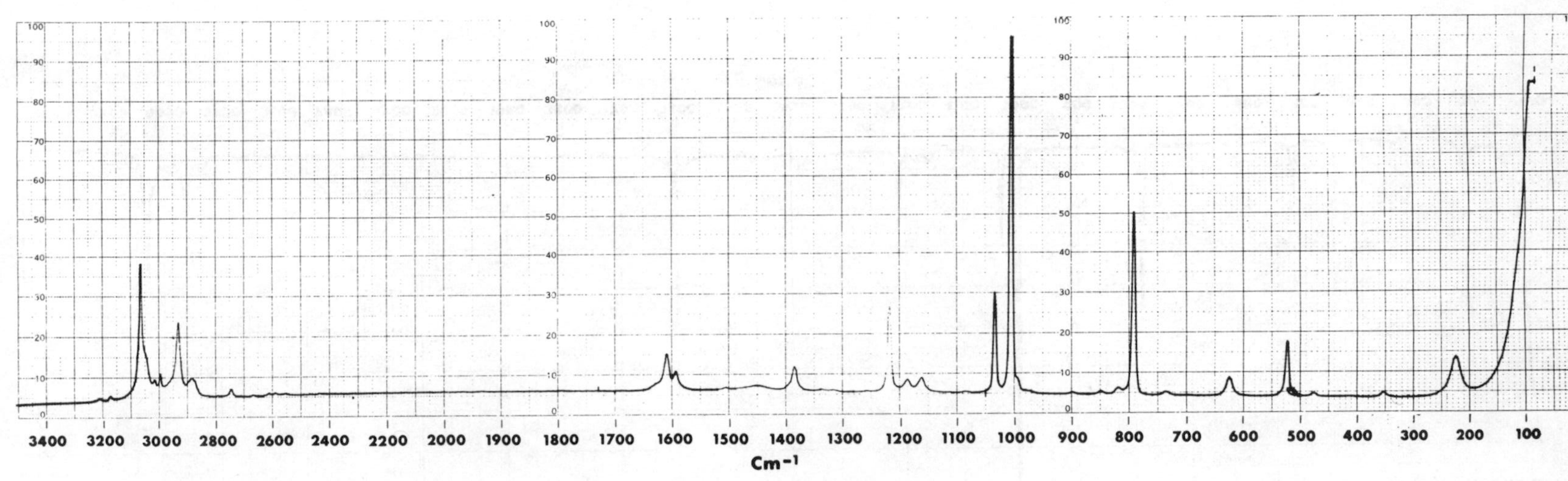

FIGURE 8. Toluene 4 cm^{-1} resolution; 4,880 Å argon ion excitation.

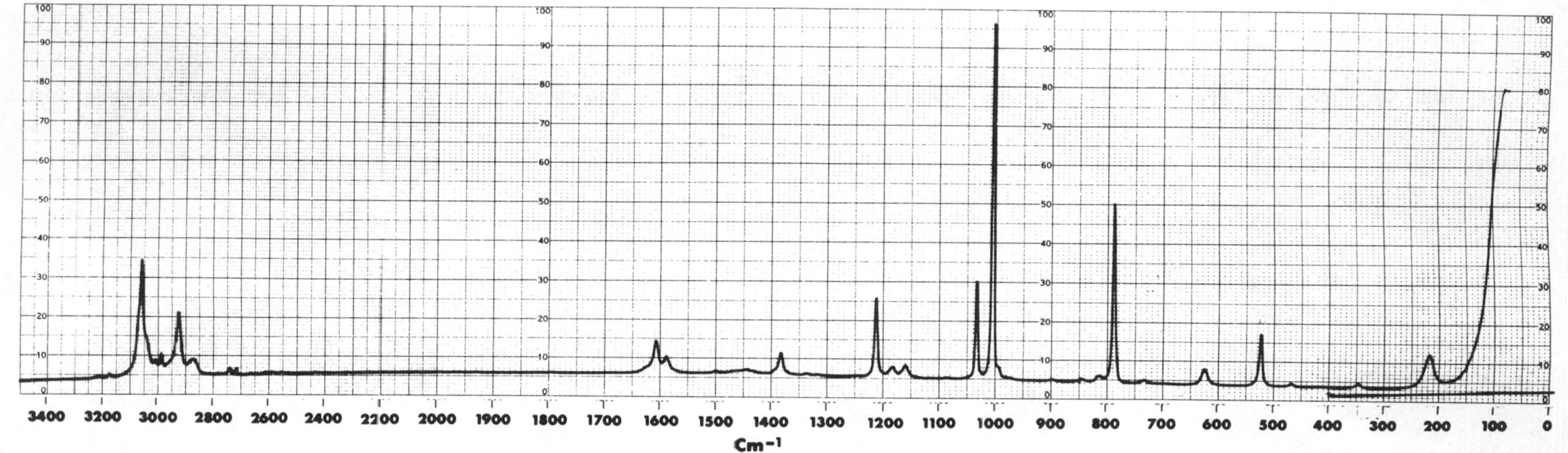

FIGURE 9. Toluene 3 cm^{-1} resolution; 4,880 Å argon ion excitation.

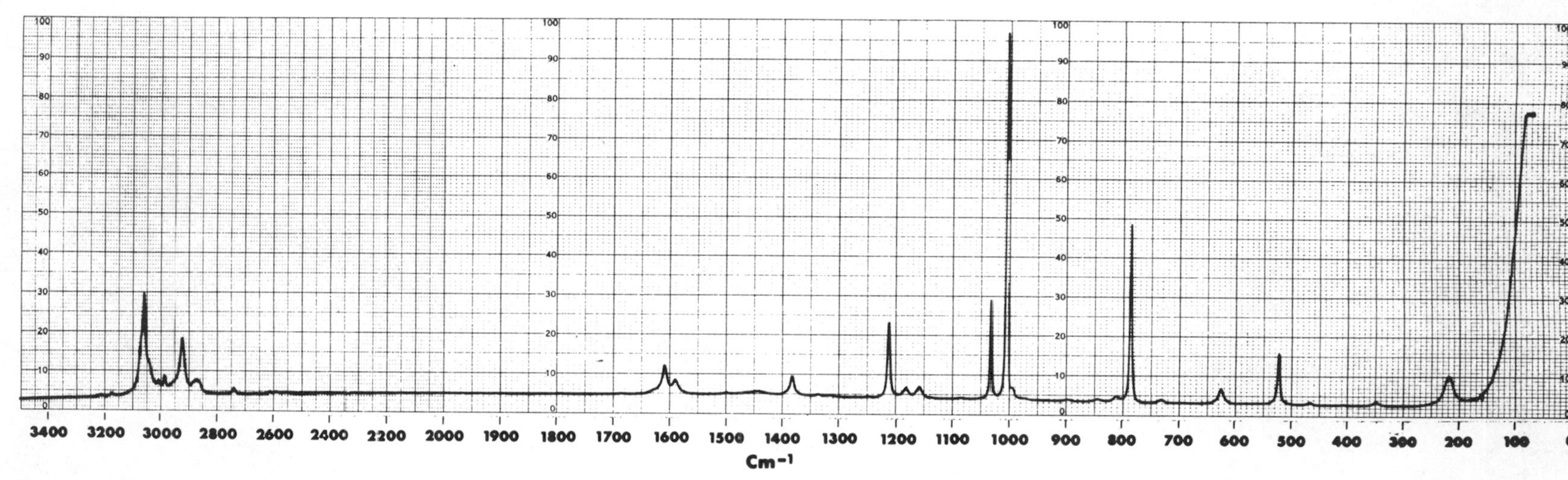

FIGURE 10. Toluene 2 cm^{-1} resolution; 4,880 Å argon ion excitation.

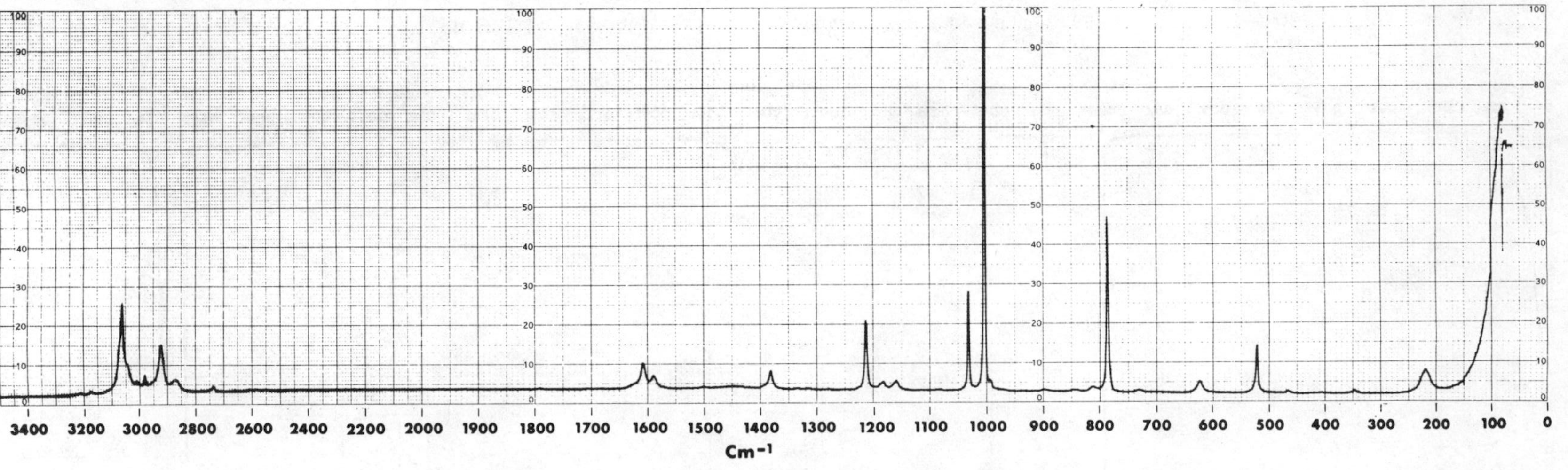

FIGURE 11. Toluene 1 cm^{-1} resolution; 4,880 Å argon ion excitation.

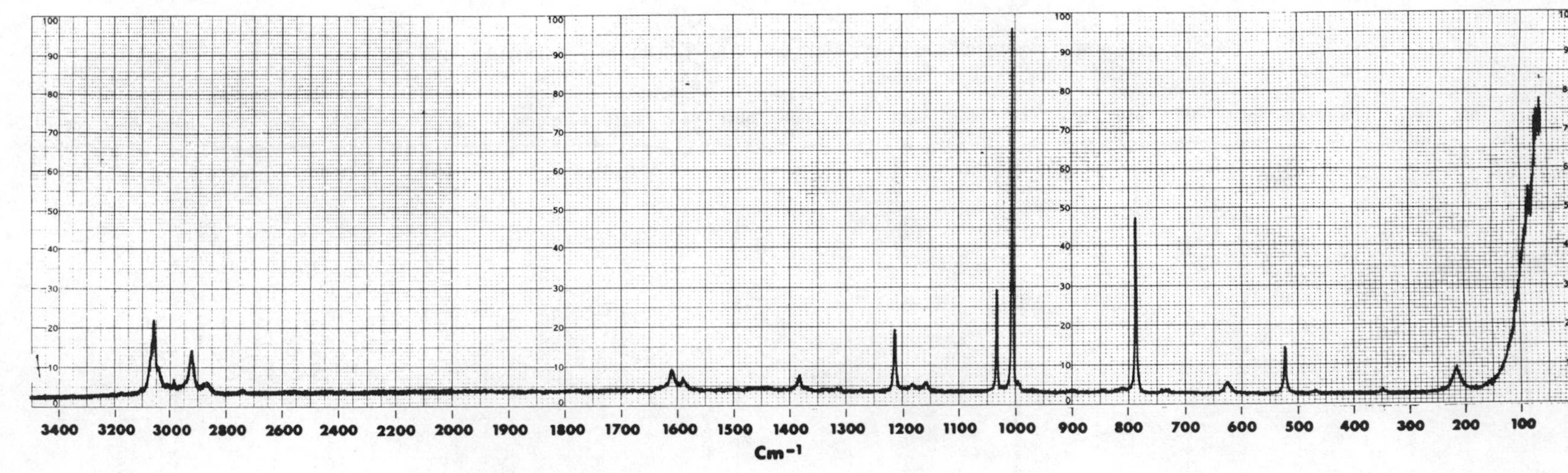

FIGURE 12. Toluene 0.25 cm^{-1} resolution; 4,880 Å argon ion excitation.

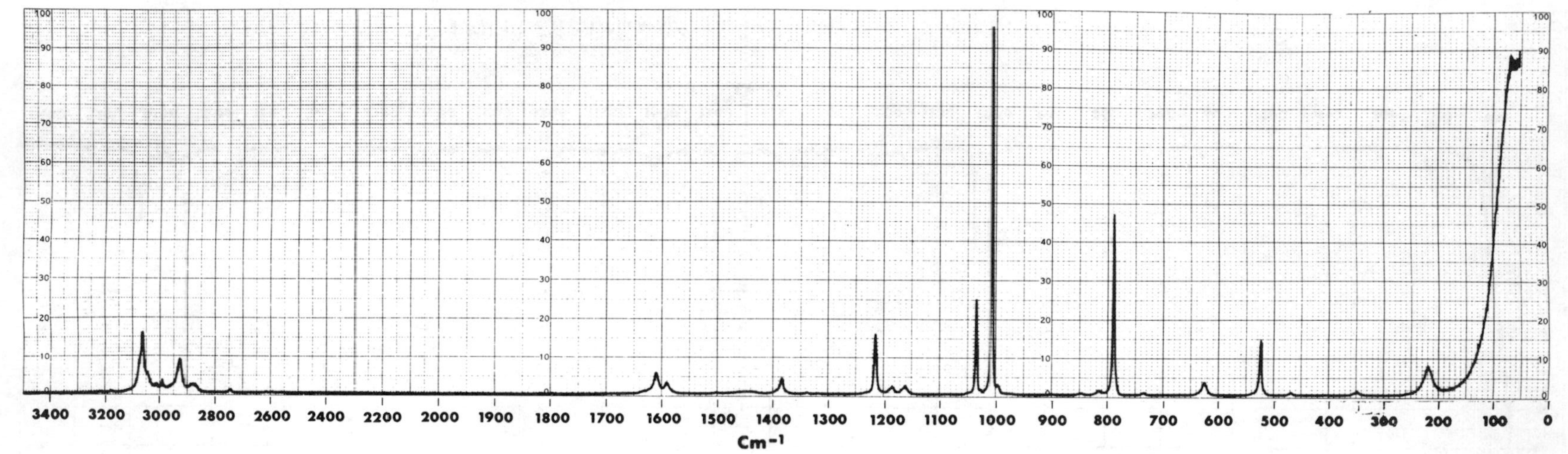

FIGURE 13. Toluene 1 cm^{-1} resolution; 5,145 Å argon ion excitation.

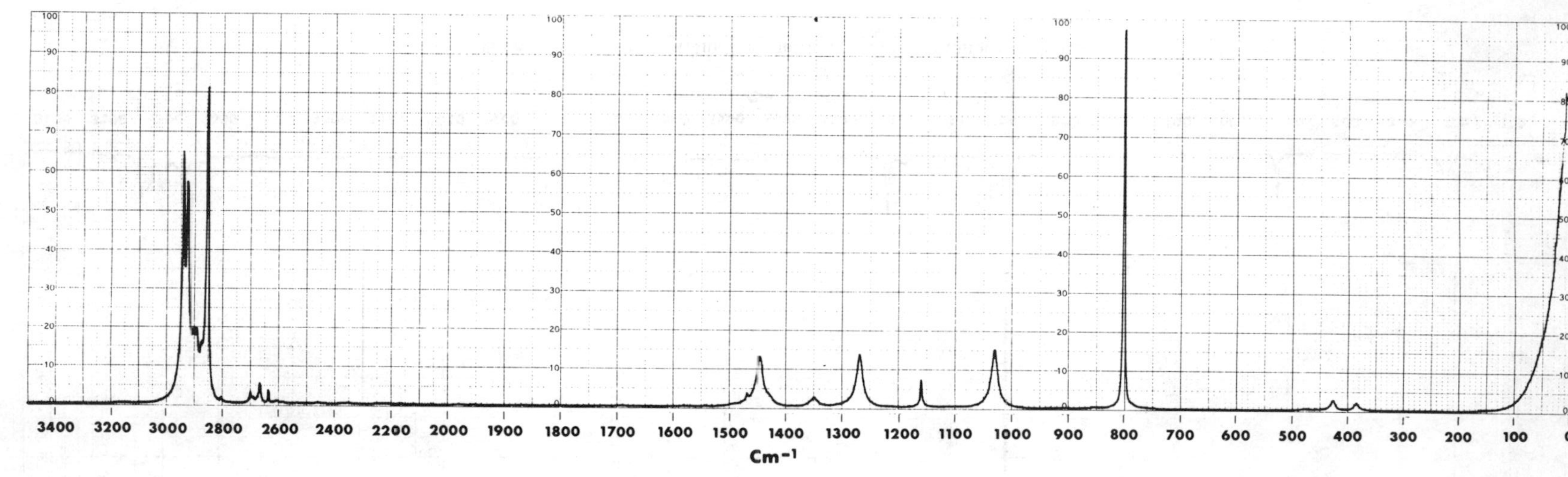

FIGURE 14. Cyclohexane 1 cm^{-1} resolution; 4,880 Å argon ion excitation.

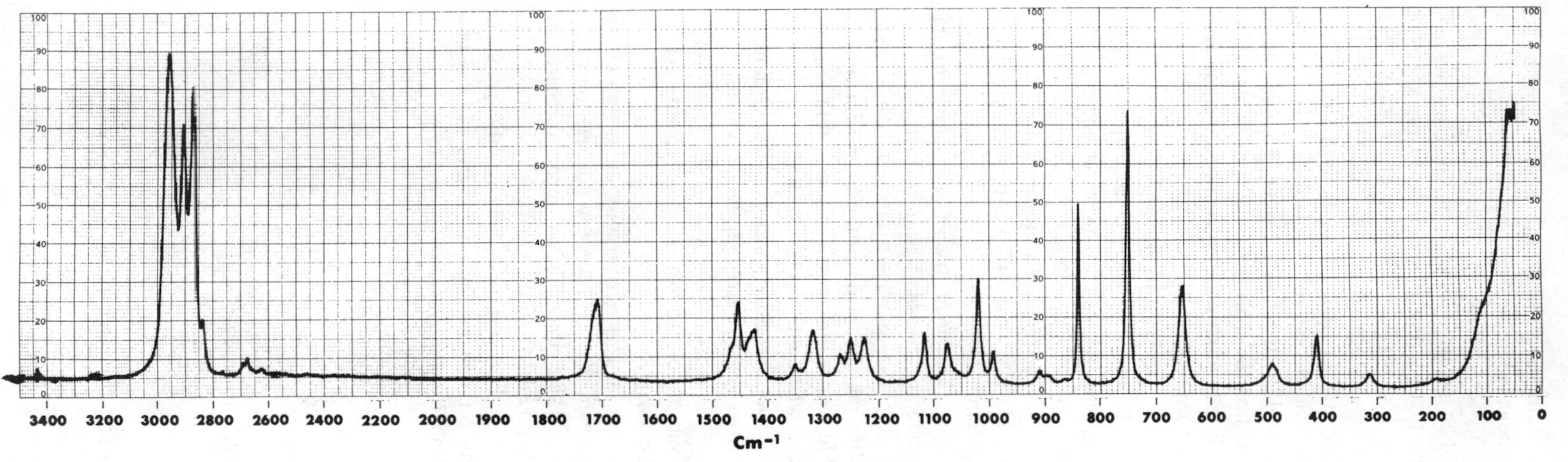

FIGURE 15. Cyclohexanone 1 cm^{-1} resolution; 4,880 Å argon ion excitation.

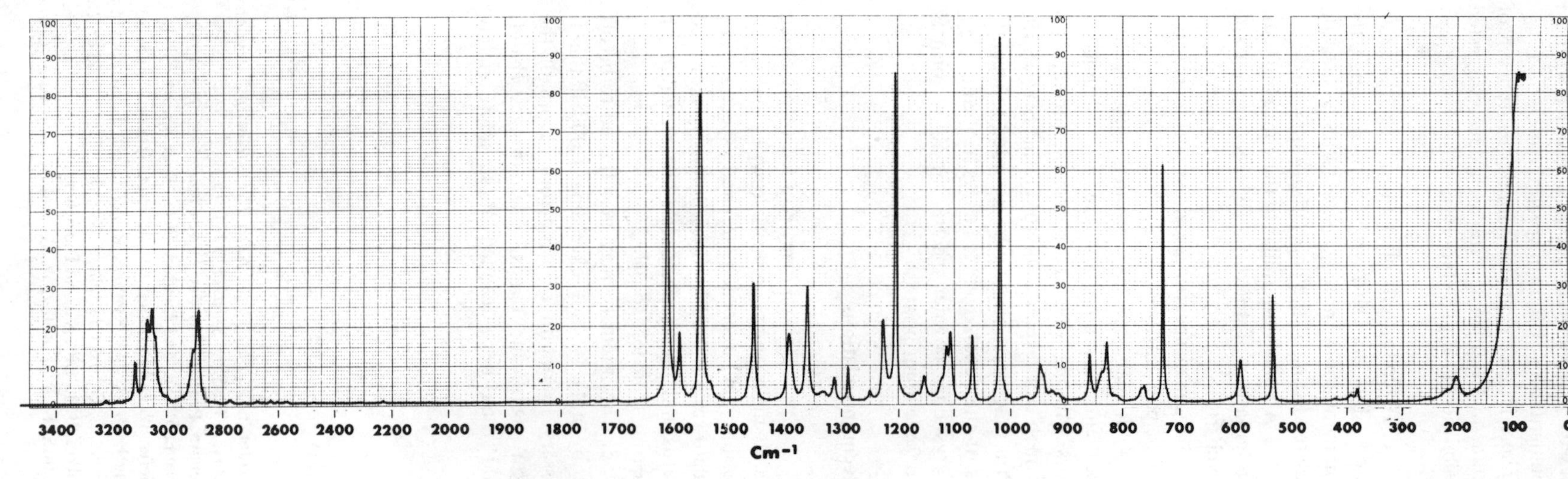

FIGURE 16. Indene 1 cm^{-1} resolution; 4,880 Å argon ion excitation.

tion with many spectroscopists concerned with the documentation of Raman spectral data.

There is agreement that various quality levels of documented Raman spectra are needed. Suggested possibilities for liquid state systems are

1. A collection of Raman spectra determined by standard methods meeting the recommendations noted below, with a separate tabulated listing of the depolarization factors.

2. A collection similar to the above but with a presentation of the infrared spectrum on the same chart.

3. Raman spectra presented with curves for different polarizations.

4. Raman spectra recorded digitally and subsequently computer corrected for instrumental factors. Among these correction factors are (a) photodetector response and (b) grating blaze. Such spectra may appropriately be recorded as separate plots of the depolarization factors $(\alpha')^2$ and $(\gamma')^2$. For crystalline powder spectra, the above formats 1 and 2 are appropriate.

B. Recommendations

1. Spectra should be recorded or presented so as to make them compatible with, and superimposible on, recorded infrared spectra. The ordinate scale should be linear intensity measured upwards and the abscissal scale linear $\Delta\tilde{\nu}$ (cm^{-1}), decreasing from left to right.

2. The intensity may be adjusted to be off scale by a factor not exceeding 1,000 if this is necessary to obtain a satisfactory record of the weaker significant bands. The strongest bands should then be rescanned at an appropriately reduced intensity, with the intensity reduction ratio indicated in the chart.

3. Corrections for instrumental response should be indicated. A minimal requirement would be the presentation of a standard lamp spectrum for all necessary polarization orientations. This may take the form of a curve or may be tabulated. If computer or digital readout is available, it is recommended that the standard lamp corrections be applied to the spectral data. This should be indicated on the chart.

4. The following operational parameters should be specified:

a. The spectral slit width (cm^{-1}).

b. The wavelength or wavenumber of the exciting radiation and the nominal power of this radiation at the laser source.

c. The spectral scanning rate.

d. The type of spectrometer and detecting system used.

e. The geometry of the sample excitation, including the polarization geometry.

f. The physical state of the sample, including as much quantitative information as possible concerning concentration, temperature, pressure, where such data are relevant.

5. Depolarization factors. The following alternatives are appropriate to liquid samples:

a. A list of ρ values for the spectrum of each substance, submitted as a separate set of tabulated data.

b. A graphical record of the spectrum measured in the two necessary polarization orientations. These may be on separate charts or superimposed.

c. For data recorded digitally, graphical records on one or separate charts of the two polarizability components $(\alpha')^2$ and $(\gamma')^2$.

REFERENCES

1. **Loader, E. J.,** *Basic Laser Raman Spectroscopy,* Heyden & Sons, Ltd., London, 1970.
2. **Scott, J. F.,** *Spex Speaker,* 17, 1, 1972.
3. **Hendra, P. J. and Loader, E. J.,** *Chem. Ind.,* 718, 1968.
4. **Freeman, S. K. and Landon, D. O.,** *Spex Speaker,* 8, 1, 1968.
5. **Kiefer, W. and Bernstein, H. J.,** *Appl. Spectrosc.,* 25, 500, 1971.
6. **Kagel, R. O. and Nyquist, R. A.,** Infrared and Raman spectroscopy, in *Handbook of Practical Spectroscopy,* Vol. 1, Brame, E. G. and Grasselli, J. G., Eds., Marcel Dekker, New York, in press.
7. **Bulkin, B. J., Dill, K., and Danneberg, J. J.,** *Anal. Chem.,* 43, 974, 1971.
8. **Dollish, F. R., Fateley, W. G., and Bentley, F. F.,** *Characteristic Raman Frequencies,* Interscience, New York, in press.

Section C

Ultraviolet Absorption Spectroscopy

ULTRAVIOLET ABSORPTION SPECTROSCOPY*

I. ULTRAVIOLET: SPECTRAL DATA INDEX

This index has been generated to enable one to identify a compound when an ultraviolet spectrum is the primary information available on the material. For specific aid in interpreting a spectrum, refer to the spectra-structure correlation charts in Section A, Part II, of the *CRC Atlas of Spectral Data and Physical Constants for Organic Compounds.*

The intensity (molar absorption coefficient) of the absorption bands is a characteristic feature, indicative of structure, in the ultraviolet spectra of materials. In this index, the UV data are sorted into groups on the basis of intensity of the strongest band present. In the first group are all the compounds whose strongest band has a molar absorption coefficient equal to or greater than 100,000. In the second group are those compounds whose strongest band has a molar absorption coefficient of 99,999 to 10,000, the third, 9,999 to 1,000, and the fourth, less than 1,000. A fifth group lists all the compounds with UV λ_{max} but no molar absorption coefficients given.

Within each group the compounds are listed in decreasing order by wavelength of the strongest band. Subsequent ordering is on the highest wavelength band, in order of decreasing wavelength, for all additional bands per compound. Each compound is listed only once in this index – in the intensity group of its strongest band. If there are two or more bands in the spectrum with intensities in the same group, the compound will be sorted by the strongest band only. For the fifth group of compounds, where no intensity data were available, the compounds are listed in decreasing order of the highest wavelength band, with all additional bands per compound included.

To determine if a compound is present, calculate the molar absorption coefficient of the strongest band in its UV spectrum. Go to the proper intensity range and find those entries that have the same intense band as the unknown. Eliminate unlikely candidates by comparing the positions of the remaining bands.

If the compound is not located by searching according to intensity of its strongest band, a check should also be made through the fifth group by longest wavelength band. It is possible that the reference curve or source may not have had a molar absorption coefficient listed for the strongest band.

*Taken from the *CRC Atlas of Spectral Data and Physical Constants for Organic Compounds,* Jeanette G. Grasselli, editor, 1973. (Published by CRC Press, Inc., 18901 Cranwood Parkway, Cleveland, Ohio.)

Strongest Band (ε)	Wavelengths (nm)	Compound
	ε Greater Than 99,999	
620(100000)	620 428 320	Methanol, bis(4(dimethylamino)phenyl)phenyl
608(147910)	608	Methanol, bis(4(dimethylamino)phenyl)
530(131830)	530	Erythrosin
520(125890)	520	Eosin
463(125890)	494 463 364 278	β-Carotene
458(123030)	488 458 436 340 277	α-Carotene
455(138040)	485 455 429	Taraxanthin
454(134890)	483 454 428	Violaxanthin
453(131830)	480 453 275	Zeaxanthin
440(100000)	460 440 355 280	Acridine, 3-amino
397(263030)	617 569 563 520 490 397	Porphin
310(251190)	575 310	Pentacene
304(158490)	395 385 351 338 304	1,2:7,8-Dibenzanthracene
300(158490)	395 385 373 300 290	1,2:5,6-Dibenzanthracene
293(147910)	371 293 255 216	Indanthrene
290(100000)	410 390 290	Anthracene, 9-amino
290(109650)	290	Coronene
288(134890)	392 384 365 305 288 280 247	1,2:6,7-Dibenzophenanthrene
286(134890)	374 349 321 286 275 265 248	1,2:3,4-Dibenzanthracene
278(100000)	358 342 330 318 278 264 258	1,2:7,8-Dibenzofluorene
274(371530)	274	Theobromine
272(100000)	345 330 272 228	Chrysene, 5,6-dimethyl
267(109650)	347 324 306 288 267	Isomycomycin
267(164000)	319 306 294 267 257	Chrysene
261(128820)	355 344 338 328 312 299 278 261 252	1,2:6,7-Dibenzofluorene
259(199530)	401 379 341 325 259 252	Anthracene, 9,10-dichloro
258(114820)	424 412 399 356 345 315 258 245	2,3:6,7-Dibenzophenanthrene
257(151360)	284 273 257 249	9,10-Benzophenanthrene
256(144540)	384 347 256	Anthracene, 9-phenyl
256(151360)	380 360 342 328 256	Phenanthrene, 2-chloro
256(151360)	380 342 256	Anthracene, 2-chloro
255(316230)	392 340 255	Anthracene, 9-chloro
255(158490)	382 364 347 255	Anthracene, 9-acetyl
255(280000)	347 331 316 255 249	Anthracene, 9-methyl
255(100000)	307 255 215	2,2-Binaphthyl
253(165960)	377 359 343 253	Anthracene, 1-methyl
251(125890)	382 362 344 337 313 299 251 249	Phenanthrene, 1-chloro
251(138040)	251	Hexa-*m*-phenylene
250(100000)	375 355 250	1-Anthracenecarboxylic acid
250(150000)	347 332 250 219 216 213	Anthracene, 9-nitro
248(125890)	350 248	Phenazine
238(13489000)	238	Carbamic acid, *N,N*-diphenyl-ethyl ester
235(125890)	330 324 316 298 291 287 282 235 228	Naphthalene, 1,2,5,6-tetramethyl
231(100000)	326 283 231	Naphthalene, 1,2,7-trimethyl
230(125890)	251 230	Rubicene
228(107000)	322 308 276 270 228	Naphthalene, 2,3,6-trimethyl
228(109650)	293 285 275 228	Naphthalene, 1,8-dimethyl
227(117490)	322 317 308 292 283 276 227	Naphthalene, 1,3-dimethyl
227(117490)	322 315 308 282 274 227	Naphthalene, 1,6-dimethyl
225(101000)	321 307 277 267 225	Naphthalene, 2-chloro
220(100000)	295 283 220	1,1-Binaphthyl
219(128000)	352 284 274 219	Naphthalene, picrate

Strongest Band (ε)	Wavelengths (nm)	Compound
	ε 99,999 to 50,000	
655(89125)	655	Methylene blue
645(79433)	645	Methane, di(1-naphthyl)
632(72443)	632 600 575 549	Phthalocyanine
602(54954)	602	Thionin, hydrochloride
600(66070)	600 440	Bromophenol blue
546(72443)	546	Rhodamine B
523(72443)	523	Erythrosin (dye)
521(57544)	521	Methyl red
519(81283)	519	Eosin, sodium salt decahydrate
500(50119)	500 350	Congo red
472(74132)	472	Methanol, di(4-tolyl)
450(79433)	500 450 370 325 240	Ethanol, 1,1-bis(4-chlorophenyl)
450(63096)	450 380 260	Azobenzene, 4-phenylamino
425(61660)	425 365	Auramine (dye)
424(61500)	448 424 314	Crocetin (*trans*)
420(58884)	420 265	Curcumin
403(58884)	403 340 298 254	Biacene
396(79200)	619 566 532 498 396	Hematoporphyrin
370(77625)	332 370 238	γ-Fagarine
362(63096)	362 335	5-Quinolinesulfonic acid, 8-hydroxy-7-iodo
345(79433)	370 345 270 230	Auramine, hydrochloride
336(57544)	336 260	Benzophenone, 2,2′-dihydroxy
320(87096)	430 320	5 β-Pregnane-3α,20α-diol
313(75858)	313	Cholanic acid
311(67200)	311 240	Ergotaminine
307(67607)	416 396 378 360 343 307 295	1,2:4,5-Dibenzopyrene
298(75858)	403 384 365 354 338 324 298 238	1,2:5,6-Dibenzanthracene,4′,4″-dihydroxy
297(79433)	384 364 345 297	1,2-Benzanthracene, 9,10-dihydro, 9,10-dimethyl
295(79433)	295 285 274 262	Cholanthrene
294(51286)	294 256	Benzoic acid, 3-hydroxy-4-methoxy
293(95500)	304 293 282 272 258	1,2-Benzanthracene, 7-methyl
290(50119)	290 255 240 220	2-Pyrrolecarboxaldehyde
289(74400)	327 314 302 289 278 268	1,2-Benzanthracene, 3-methyl
289(82600)	317 301 289 278 268 230	1,2-Benzanthracene, 8-methyl
289(50119)	289	Panthesin
288(79433)	384 372 340 325 300 288 277 266 255 224	1,2-Benz-9,10-anthraquinone
288(79600)	331 302 288 277 267 257	1,2-Benzanthracene, 6-methyl
288(50119)	315 288 278	1,2-Benzanthracene, 4′-hydroxy
288(95400)	302 288 277 267 257	1,2-Benzanthracene, 10-methyl
288(81283)	300 288 280 257 252	1,2-Benzanthracene, 4-methyl
288(63096)	288	Biphenyl, 4,4′-bis(methylamino)
287(79600)	315 301 287 279 269 256	1,2-Benzanthracene, 9-methyl
282(69800)	316 304 282 272 231 218	Chrysene, 3-methyl
282(73800)	315 298 282 272 230 218	Chrysene, 2-methyl
278(52481)	400 380 278 224	1,2-Benzophenazine
278(70795)	328 315 285 278 269 261	1,2-Benzanthracene, 5-methyl
278(97724)	278	Chloromycetin
277(66070)	318 298 277	1,5-Naphthalenedisulfonic acid
276(55500)	276 222 216	Cinnamic acid, ethyl ester (*trans*)
275(51286)	468 362 275 230	Phenazine, 2-amino
274(61660)	665 659 632 579 340 274	Azulene
274(50119)	274 263 253	2,4,6-Octatriene (*trans,trans,trans*)
273(83176)	335 297 273	Truxane
271(97724)	271	2,4-Hexadien-1-al
270(50119)	385 270	Azobenzene, 4-amino-3,5-dimethyl
268(60256)	279 268 259	9,11,13-Octadecatrienoic acid (*trans*)

Strongest Band (ε)	Wavelengths (nm)	Compound
266(58884)	368 304 266 218	Phenanthrene, 2-acetyl
265(63096)	460 290 265	Acridine, 3,6-diamino
265(50119)	370 265 240	Phenazine, 1-hydroxy
264(94500)	312 298 286 264 256	9-Fluorenone-2-carboxylic acid
263(50119)	425 348 263	Berberine
263(72443)	316 296 263	1,2-Benzofluorene
263(50119)	282 270 263 213	9,10-Anthraquinone, 1,7-dichloro
262(63096)	520 333 262	9,10-Anthraquinone-2,6-disulfonic acid
262(50119)	404 372 262 234	9-Anthracenecarboxaldehyde
262(83176)	380 304 262	9-Fluorenone, 2-bromo
262(52481)	360 262	9,10-Anthraquinone, 1,2-diamino
260(79435)	358 260 240	Acridine, 2-amino
260(63096)	350 260 240	Anthracene, 2-acetyl
260(50119)	345 260	Quinoline, 7-amino-8-hydroxy
260(59800)	332 315 260 218	Acridine, 9-amino
260(50119)	315 260	Xanthone, 1,7-dihydroxy-3-methoxy
258(68700)	318 300 288 279 258	Phenanthrene, 7-isopropyl-1-methyl
257(56234)	352 345 300 257 215	1,2-Cyclopentenophenanthrene
257(69300)	325 257 207	2,2′-Biquinolyl
255(79433)	351 334 294 278 255	1,2:5,6-Dibenzofluorene
255(50800)	324 274 255	Anthraquinone, 2-chloro-
255(52481)	255 251	2-Phenanthrenecarboxylic acid
255(50119)	255	9,10-Anthraquinone-2,7-disulfonic acid
254(75858)	355 299 254 211	9-Phenanthrenecarboxylic acid
254(60900)	318 254	Phenothiazine, 10-phenyl
253(59700)	294 253 214	Acridine, 9,10-dihydro 9-oxo
252(56300)	352 336 275 252 228	Phenanthrene, 2-hydroxy
252(64566)	350 296 274 252	Phenanthrene, 9-ethyl
252(75000)	294 282 276 252 210	Phenanthrene, 2-methyl
252(56600)	252	Benzene, 1,3,5-triphenyl
251(50119)	434 406 387 368 251	Perylene
251(50119)	375 251 240	Anthracene, 1-acetyl
251(57544)	300 275 251 232	1-Phenanthrenecarboxylic acid
250(64600)	291 250 211	Phenanthrene
249(50700)	286 249 212	Acetic acid, bromo-bromide
248(62200)	248 204	*m,m′*-Quaterphenyl
246(50300)	339 290 282 246 208	Naphthalene, 2-acetyl
246(50119)	309 246	Quinoline, 2,4-dimethyl-8-hydroxy
244(77625)	458 340 308 272 244	Bifluorenylidene
243(54954)	343 300 289 279 243 215	Naphthalene, 2-amino-1,4-dimethyl
243(53703)	339 331 323 296 283 273 265 252 243 237	Naphthalene, 2-ethenyl
242(73400)	377 366 355 342 325 312 274 263 254 242 232	Pyrene, 1-chloro-
242(51100)	330 315 282 273 242	Acetic acid, amide, *N*(2-naphthyl)
242(56234)	323 242	Quinoline, 5-hydroxy
242(62800)	318 309 253 242	Quinoline, 8-hydroxy, sulfate
241(52900)	326 291 241	Dibenzothiophene, 3,7-diamino
240(63096)	470 360 240	Azobenzene, 4-hydroxy-4′-methyl
240(85100)	334 318 305 294 272 261 251 240 231	Pyrene
240(79433)	327 315 280 240	Papaverine
240(63096)	315 240	Arsenobenzene
240(64000)	257 240	Anthracene, 1-amino
238(50100)	314 282 238	Papaveraldine
238(63096)	238	Thiophene, 2,5-dimethyl
237(77625)	342 273 237	1,6-Naphthalenedisulfonic acid
237(56234)	338 287 237	1,3-Naphthalenedisulfonic acid, 7-hydroxy
237(77625)	290 281 237	Toluene, 3-mercapto
236(61800)	334 279 270 236	2,3-Naphthalenedicarboxylic acid

Strongest Band (ε)	Wavelengths (nm)	Compound
236(60256)	329 309 236	Dictamnine
236(60256)	328 309 236	α-Dicyclopentadiene, 3,4,5,6,7,8,8a-heptachloro
235(66100)	363 296 284 274 235	1-Naphthoic acid, 2-hydroxy
235(50119)	351 335 316 235	2,7-Naphthalenedisulfonic acid, 4,5-dihydroxy
235(77500)	344 293 282 272 235	Naphthalene, 1,6-dibromo-2-hydroxy
234(52700)	357 339 286 274 234	Fluoranthene
233(52481)	340 233	Ethene, 1,2-di(1-naphthyl) (*trans*)
233(70795)	332 280 233	2-Naphthalenesulfonic acid, 6-hydroxy
233(87096)	323 308 266 233	2,7-Naphthalenedisulfonic acid
232(72443)	344 339 326 292 280 232 226	Naphthalene, 1,2,4-trimethyl
232(63096)	328 266 232	2-Naphthoic acid, 3-hydroxy
231(83100)	339 328 286 276 231	Naphthalene, 2-bromo-6-hydroxy
231(75800)	328 320 313 285 231	Naphthalene, 2,7-dihydroxy
231(95500)	325 289 231	Naphthalene, 1,2,5-trimethyl
231(97200)	305 239 231 226	2,4-Pentadienoic acid, 5-phenyl
230(50119)	338 320 260 250 230	Phenanthridine, 6-hydroxy
230(83176)	318 305 293 230	8,8′-Biquinolyl
229(83176)	355 327 282 229	Naphthalene, 1,2,6-trimethyl
229(61300)	322 309 280 229	Quinoline, 4,7-dichloro
229(74132)	322 301 280 251 229	Phenanthrene, 1,2,3,4-tetrahydro
229(53703)	302 229	Rescinnamine
228(74132)	321 314 306 290 280 274 228	Naphthalene, 7-isopropyl-1-methyl
228(50119)	305 228	Propynoic acid, 1-naphthyl
228(53703)	296 228	Naphthalene, 1-allyl
227(51286)	337 299 227	Naphthalene, 1-acetyl-2-hydroxy
227(72443)	321 290 227	Acenaphthanthracene
227(52481)	290 282 227	Carbazole, 1,2,3,4-tetrahydro
226(72600)	328 282 271 261 226	Naphthalene, 2-ethoxy
226(53600)	291 226	Benzene, 1,3,5-triacetyl
226(85114)	265 226	Naphthalene, 2-chloro-1-nitro
225(63096)	490 228 225	Fluorescein
225(52481)	338 259 225	Isoquinoline, 7-hydroxy
225(99600)	319 315 306 278 268 225	Naphthalene, 2,3-dimethyl
225(58300)	316 229 228 278 225	Naphthalene, 1-iodo
225(56234)	315 287 280 225	Thiocyanic acid, 1-naphthyl ester
225(56200)	304 294 284 225	Naphthalene, 1,4-dibromo
225(50119)	291 282 272 225	Corynantheine (β)
225(50119)	275 225	Yohimbine
225(50119)	270 230 225	1-Naphthaldehyde, 2-hydroxy
225(63096)	225	Acetophenone, 2-iodo
224(79433)	323 282 224	Naphthalene, 1-ethyl
224(61100)	287 224	Naphthalene, 1-phenyl
223(77400)	441 414 390 371 325 311 286 275 251 223	*peri*-Xanthenoxanthene
223(69183)	323 285 223	Naphthalene, 1,2,3,4-tetramethyl
223(75858)	321 223	2-Cyclooctenone (*cis*)
223(96900)	319 315 284 274 223	Naphthalene, 1-bromo
223(95500)	280 273 223	Benzoic acid, 2-fluoro
222(88100)	291 222	Urea, 1(1-naphthyl)
222(59200)	291 222	Urea, 1(2-naphthyl)
222(55900)	290 282 222	Butanoic acid, 4(3-indolyl)
222(64100)	287 282 222	Acetic acid, amide, *N*(1-naphthyl)
221(75858)	317 303 274 221	Naphthalene, 2-hydroxy,benzoate
221(52700)	290 221	Phthalic acid, monoamide, *N*(1-naphthyl)
220(63096)	319 280 268 220	Isoquinoline
220(51600)	293 268 264 257 220	Phthalic acid, imide, *N*-benzyl
220(53703)	284 257 220	Naphthalene, 1-chloro-2-nitro
218(85114)	364 288 262 218	1,1′-Azoxynaphthalene
218(66070)	331 247 218	Naphthalene, 6-amino-1-bromo

Strongest Band (ε)	Wavelengths (nm)	Compound
218(57544)	305 297 292 269 261 254 218	Phthalazine
218(58884)	271 218	Raunescine, hydrate
218(57544)	270 218	Isoraunescine
217(65700)	338 252 217	Amine, 1-naphthyl phenyl
217(63096)	320 307 270 217	Isoquinoline, 1-methyl
217(60256)	293 266 217	Pseudoreserpine
217(52481)	275 217	Benzoic acid, 3,4,5-trihydroxy-methyl ester
217(64566)	271 217	Deserpidine
216(57544)	381 310 264 216	1,2′-Azonaphthalene
216(51286)	346 289 263 216	2,2′-Azoxynaphthalene
216(54600)	302 216	Naphthalene, 1(dimethylamino)
215(50000)	319 288 282 255 215	Acetic acid, (1-naphthyloxy)
213(61600)	331 239 213	Naphthalene, 1-nitro
213(72900)	301 213	Benzene, nitro(pentachloro)
212(50000)	303 212	Biphenyl, 4,4′-diamino-3,3′-dimethoxy
212(52200)	280 272 250 212	Benzene, hexaethyl
211(57544)	313 291 211	α-Narcotine, hydrochloride
209(53400)	296 209	Benzene, 1-nitro-2,3,5,6-tetrachloro
208(57544)	277 208	Narceine, hydrochloride trihydrate
207(66070)	294 207	*p,p′*-Quaterphenyl
207(71400)	287 280 207	Benzene, 1,4-dimethyl-2,3,5,6-tetrachloro
204(72200)	293 286 204	Benzene, 1,3-dimethyl-5-hydroxy-2,4,6-trichloro
204(50800)	289 204	Brazilein
201(52481)	276 271 267 263 230 212 201	Biphenyl, 2,2′,4,4′-tetramethyl
190(60256)	267 220 190	Acetic acid, (2,4,6-trimethylphenyl)

ε 49,999 to 1,000

Strongest Band (ε)	Wavelengths (nm)	Compound
675(12023)	675	β-Toxicarol (*dl*)
660(3090)	660 480	Fluorene, 9-hydroxy
650(4677)	650	9,10-Anthraquinone, 2-amino-1-nitro
613(45709)	613	Bromocresol green
570(25119)	850 755 570 380	Dibenzanthrone
562(31623)	562 548 523 488	9,10-Anthraquinone, 1,4,5,8-tetrahydroxy
561(25119)	561	Resorufin
560(26925)	560	Eupittone
545(34674)	545 325	Azo, benzene 2-naphthalene, 4-dimethylamino
540(1000)	540 410 260	Methanol, tris(4-aminophenyl)
540(1259)	540	Methanol, (4-amino-3-methylphenyl)bis(4-aminophenyl)
524(7943)	560 543 524 488	Shikonine
522(34674)	522 275	Delphinidine, chloride
520(7943)	520 426 355	Resazurin
505(30903)	505 345	Sudan III
504(13804)	504 472 442 417	Naphthacene, 9,10,11-triphenyl
500(25119)	500 480 410	Azo, benzene 1-naphthalene, 2′-hydroxy-2-nitro
495(13489(	529 516 495 480	9,10-Anthraquinone, 1,4,5-trihydroxy
495(11482)	529 495 464 439	Rubrene
493(12589)	493 462 435 408	Naphthacene, 9,11-diphenyl
493(9550)	493 461 434	Naphthacene, 9,10-diphenyl
490(13183)	490 356 294	Azo, benzene 2-naphthalene, 1′-hydroxy
490(31623)	490	Fluorescin
489(41687)	489	Azobenzene, 4-hydroxy-3-methyl
485(1995)	485	Adrenochrome (*dl*)
480(6310)	550 480 465 400	Ecgonine hydrochloride (*l*)
480(6310)	550 480 465 400	1,4-Naphthoquinone, 2-ethyl-3,5,6,7,8-pentahydroxy
480(19953)	480 422 315	Azo, benzene 1-naphthalene, 2′-hydroxy
480(15100)	480 270	Aurin
480(6310)	480	1,4-Naphthoquinone, 2,5,8-trihydroxy
470(7943)	520 470 330	Anthraquinone, 1,4-dihydroxy
470(2512)	495 470 445 320 220	Isocarotene

Strongest Band (ϵ)	Wavelengths (nm)	Compound
469(7586)	469 308	9,10-Anthraquinone, 1-amino-2-bromo
460(15849)	650 460	Chlorophyll b
455(19953)	455 350 330 285	Azo, benzene 1-naphthalene, 4′-amino
450(15849)	450 340	Azo, benzene 1-naphthalene, 2′-amino
448(8318)	480 448	Bixin
444(7943)	444 424 343	Quinacrine, dihydrochloride (*dl*)
441(5495)	441 372 270	Auramine (base)
440(10000)	660 440	Chlorophyll a
437(46773)	437	Bilirubin
435(10000)	435	Ethanol, 1-phenyl-(*d*)
435(10000)	435	Ethanol, 1-phenyl-(*dl*)
435(10000)	435	Ethanol, 1-phenyl-(*l*)
431(39811)	431 404	Cyclopropenium, triphenyl, bromide
430(39811)	430 309 295 278	Hematein
430(6310)	430 280	Hydrazine, (2-nitrophenyl)
430(22387)	430	Ethane, 1,1-diphenyl
429(5012)	429 279	Aniline, *N*-methyl-2-nitro
429(31800)	429 275 238	Aniline, *N,N*-diethyl-4-nitroso
426(10000)	426 425 401 380 362	1,2:6,7-Dibenzanthracene
425(39811)	450 425 265	Methanol, tris(4-nitrophenyl)
422(19953)	422 288	Naphthalene, 1-hydroxy-2,4,5-trinitro
420(39811)	420 305 265	Methyl orange
420(33113)	420	Stilbene, 4-dimethylamino-4′-nitro (*trans*)
415(31623)	415 270	Aniline, 4-nitroso
414(19055)	611 575 414	Sulfide, diphenyl, 2-nitro
414(19953)	414	Methanol, bis(4-hydroxyphenyl)phenyl
413(16596)	600 413	Benzene, 1,3-dimethyl-2,4,6-trinitro
412(13489)	512 412	Yamogenin
412(8128)	485 412 305	Androsterone
410(15849)	470 410	Azo, benzene 1-naphthalene, 4′-hydroxy
409(6457)	409	Hydrazine, (2,6-dinitrophenyl)
406(20417)	406 259	Amine, diphenyl, 4-nitroso
405(33113)	485 405	Azobenzene, 4,4′-bis(dimethylamino)
405(22387)	425 405 360 348	1,4-Benzenedicarboxylic acid, dinitrile
405(25119)	405 285	Stilbene, 4-amino-4′-nitro (*trans*)
405(10000)	405	2-Butanol, 2-phenyl (*dl*)
404(8128)	404 345	Yuccagenin
404(7880)	404 291 234	Toluene, 4-amino-3-hydroxy
403(10233)	403	Stilbene, 4-dimethylamino-4′-nitro (*cis*)
402(22908)	402 358 200	Amine, diphenyl, 2,2′,4,4′-tetranitro
402(38019)	402 232	Amine, diphenyl, 4,4′-dinitro
400(15849)	400 331 250	Citrinin
400(12303)	400 310 257 219	Aniline, 2-methoxy-5-nitro
400(14454)	400 308 240	11,12-Benzofluoranthene
400(39811)	400 273	Diazoaminobenzene, 4,4′-dinitro
400(18621)	400 262	Fluorene, 7-amino-2-nitro
400(31623)	400 260	Chalcone, 4-amino
400(21379)	400 236	Aniline, *N,N*-diethyl-3-ethoxy
400(19953)	400	Benzene, 1,3-dihydroxy-2,4-dinitro
400(15849)	400	Benzene, 2,4-dihydroxy-1,3,5-trinitro
400(10965)	400	Naphthalene, 1-amino-2,4-dinitro
399(31623)	430 399 305	Azobenzene, 4,4′-diamino
397(20417)	397	Xylose, osazone
396(15849)	396 351	Hecogenin
395(3981)	395	Anthracene, 1-hydroxy
394(21878)	394 316 236	Aniline, *N,N*-diethyl-4-nitro
394(3162)	394	Tigogenin
393(12600)	393 264	Toluene, 5-amino-4-hydroxy-2-nitro
393(1585)	393	Benzenepentacarboxylic acid
391(24900)	391 261	Phenol, 5-amino-2-nitro

Strongest Band (ε)	Wavelengths (nm)	Compound
390(16900)	390 258	Amine, diphenyl, 4-nitro
389(28184)	480 389 303	Taurocholic acid
388(2239)	494 388	Polyporic acid
385(1585)	580 385	1,2-Benzoquinone
384(25200)	384 245	Azobenzene, 4-amino
384(17378)	384 230	Hydrazine, (4-nitrophenyl)
384(32359)	384	2-Naphthaldehyde
382(9772)	382	Benzene, 1-amino-2,3-dimethyl-4-nitro
382(1585)	382	Methane, tris(4-nitrophenyl)
380(15136)	380 276	Cholanic acid, 3α 6α dihydroxy
380(22387)	380 272	Cholanic acid, 3α 7α dihydroxy
380(32200)	380 262 208	1,4-Pentadien-3-one, 1,5-bis(3,4-methylenedioxyphenyl)
380(10000)	380	Aureomycin
380(14454)	380	Benzene, 2-amino-1,3-dimethyl-4-nitro
380(12023)	380	Benzene, 1,2-diamino-4-nitro
378(40738)	645 378	Biliverdin
377(10715)	377 329 275	Fluorene, 5-amino-2-nitro
376(26303)	376	Stilbene, 4-hydroxy-4′-nitro
375(25704)	375 318 278 243	Coumarin, 7-diethylamino-4-methyl
375(1622)	375	1,2-Benzoquinone, 3-methoxy
375(1000)	375	Hydrazine, (3-nitrophenyl)
374(13489)	374 233	Aniline, 3-chloro-4-nitro
374(13183)	374 233	Toluene, 5-amino-2-nitro
373(46773)	390 373 240	Fluorene, 9-cinnamylidene (*trans*)
373(20893)	373 301 256	Flavone, 3,3′,4′,5,7-pentahydroxy
373(15600)	373 248	Biphenyl, 4-amino-4′-nitro
373(25119)	373 248	Stilbene, 4-methoxy-4′-nitro (*trans*)
373(16596)	373	Naphthalene, 1-nitroso
370(12589)	370 317	Azobenzene, 2,2′-diethoxy
368(3715)	368	Phenol, 2,6-dibromo
367(4169)	387 367 352 335	Anthracene, 9,10-dinitro
367(9333)	367	Thiochrome
365(33885)	365 295 240	Hydantoin, 5-benzylidene-2-thio
364(25600)	364 264 216	3-Azobenzenecarboxylic acid, 4-hydroxy-4′-nitro
364(14700)	364	Aniline, 2-chloro-4-nitro
362(25119)	428 362	Azobenzene, 4,4′-diethoxy
360(1148)	360	Benzoic acid, 3-methyl-methyl ester
360(16596)	360	Methane, dinitro
360(37153)	360	2,4-Pentadienoic acid, 5-phenyl methyl ester
359(7586)	359 343 327	Cholanthrene, 20-methyl
358(19953)	380 358	2-Naphthalenesulfonic acid, 5,7-dinitro-8-hydroxy
358(31623)	358 270	Methane, di(4-tolyl)phenyl
358(5888)	358	Euparin
357(39811)	357 256 213	9,10-Anthraquinone, 1,4-dichloro
356(8128)	356 310	Indazole, 7-nitro
356(28184)	356 235	Stilbene, 4,4′-dinitro (*trans*)
355(21878)	355 295 238	Diazoaminobenzene, 4,4′-dimethyl
355(19953)	355 275	Diazoaminobenzene
355(17783)	355 256	Flavone, 3′,4′,5,7-tetrahydroxy
355(25119)	355 250	Azoxybenzene, 4-bromo
355(3311)	355	9,10-Anthraquinone-2-carboxylic acid
355(6310)	355	Biphenyl, 4,4′-dihydroxy-3,3′,5,5′-tetranitro
354(12589)	354 303 262	Coumarin, 6,7-dihydroxy
353(23988)	459 353 232	Equilin
353(15849)	430 353 317	Azobenzene, 2-methoxy
353(15849)	390 353	Benzene, 2-nitro-1,3,5-trihydroxy
352(17600)	352 230	Amine, diphenyl, 2,4-dinitro
352(15849)	352	Azobenzene, 4-hydroxy-2-methyl
351(28184)	351	Azobenzene, 3,5-dimethyl-4-hydroxy
350(4169)	350 315	Epiquinidine

Strongest Band (ε)	Wavelengths (nm)	Compound
350(12589)	350 299 255	Coumarin, 7-hydroxy-6-methoxy
350(13489)	350 281	Thiophene, 2-acetyl-3-hydroxy
350(38019)	350 270	Berberine, hydrochloride
350(23442)	350	Azobenzene, 2-amino-4′,5-dimethyl
350(6740)	350	Phenol, 2,4,6-trinitro
350(25119)	350	Stilbene, 4-nitro-(*trans*)
349(14300)	349 258 216	Hydrazine, (2,4-dinitrophenyl)
348(19953)	415 348 255	Azobenzene, 4-ethoxy
348(12303)	348 290	Coumarin, 6,7-dihydroxy-4-methyl
348(20000)	348 250 222	Formaldehyde, 2,4-dinitrophenylhydrazone
347(1585)	347 307 244	Methane, triiodo
347(23500)	347 235	Azobenzene, 4-hydroxy
347(23442)	347	Azobenzene, 4-acetamido
346(5129)	346 338 330 323 316	5,6-Benzoquinoline
346(39811)	346 250	1,3-Butadiene, 1,1,4,4-tetraphenyl
345(14125)	345	Benzene, 1,3-dihydroxy-2-nitro
345(18197)	345	Benzophenone, phenylhydrazone
345(31623)	345	Piperine
345(30903)	345	Stilbene, 4-dimethylamino (*trans*)
344(22800)	432 344 234	Azobenzene, 4-methoxy-
344(12303)	393 344	2,4,6-Cycloheptatrien-1-one, 2-hydroxy-4-isopropyl
344(26925)	344 260	2-Propen-1-one, 3(2-furyl)1-phenyl
344(19953)	344	Amine, 1,2′-dinaphthyl
343(37153)	358 343 328 288 276 232	Rutaecarpine
343(17200)	343 300 236	Benzaldehyde, phenylhydrazone
342(39811)	342 295 239	Benzil, osazone (anti)
342(32700)	342 260 211	Arginine flavianate (*l*)
342(23988)	342 245	1,3-Propanedione, 1,3-diphenyl(one enol form)
340(22400)	420 340 224 208	3-Azobenzenecarboxylic acid, 4-hydroxy
340(10000)	340 305	Fluorene, 9-nitro
340(20893)	340 296 239	Phthalide, 3-benzylidene-(*trans*)
340(15900)	340 251 227	Sulfide, diphenyl,4,4′-dinitro
340(4266)	340	Acetic acid, amide, *N*(1-nitro-2-naphthyl)
340(31623)	340	2,4-Pentadienoic acid, 5(3,4-methylenedioxyphenyl)
340(31623)	340	Urea, 1,3-di(4-nitrophenyl)
338(16218)	338	Amine, di-1-naphthyl
338(3715)	338	Benzaldehyde, 5-chloro-2-hydroxy
337(23988)	385 337	Hydrazine, (2,4,6-trinitrophenyl)
337(19953)	337 232	4,4′-Azobenzenedisulfonic acid, diamide
337(12000)	337 230	Pyridine, 4-mercapto
336(12000)	336 268 229	Aniline, 2-bromo-4,6-dinitro
336(1480)	336 257 225 210	Aniline, 2,4-dinitro
335(20893)	335 269	Flavone, 4′,5,7-trihydroxy
335(17378)	335 262	4,4′-Azoxybenzenedicarboxylic acid
335(12589)	335 258	Coumarin, 7,8-dihydroxy
335(43658)	335	Benzaldehyde, 4-hydroxy-azine
335(45709)	335	Biphenyl, 4,4′-bis(phenylamino)
335(12589)	335	Naphthalene, 2(benzylideneamino)
335(4467)	335	1-Naphthoic acid, 4-nitro
333(12589)	384 333 281	Anthraquinone, 2,6-diamino
333(23700)	333 238	Acetophenone, 4-dimethylamino
333(2512)	333	Cyclohexanol, 1-ethyl
332(23988)	395 332	Azobenzene, 3,5-dimethyl-2-hydroxy
332(37153)	332 286 276 256	Ethene, 1,2-di(2-naphthyl) (*trans*)
332(5012)	332	Quinine, hydrobromide
332(17783)	332	Uracil, 4-thio
331(15136)	447 331	Azobenzene, 3,3′-dimethyl (*trans*)
331(25704)	430 331 225	4,4′-Azobenzenedicarboxylic acid
331(7244)	396 331 233	5β-Pregnan-3α-ol-20-one
331(19953)	331 296 236	Echitamine

Strongest Band (ε)	Wavelengths (nm)	Compound
331(3236)	331 278	Quinine, hydrochloride hydrate
331(11749)	331 270	Sulfide, diphenyl,2,4-dinitro
331(4230)	331	Benzene, 1-*tert*-butyl-3,5-dimethyl-2,4,6-trinitro
331(35482)	331	1,4-Pentadien-3-one, 1,5-diphenyl
330(20800)	434 330 234	Azobenzene, 4,4′-dimethyl (*trans*)
330(30903)	410 330	Azobenzene, 2 -hydroxy-5-methyl
330(26925)	330 325 230	Pyrrole, 2,5-diphenyl
330(15849)	330 320 290 215	Echinopsine
330(15136)	330 224	Stilbene, 4,4′-dinitro (*cis*)
330(25000)	330	Azobenzene, 4-nitro
330(25119)	330	Cyclohexanone, 2,6-dibenzylidene
330(9550)	330	Phenol, 3-methoxy-4-nitro
330(18197)	330	Stilbene, 2,4-dichloro (*trans*)
330(5012)	330	Stilbene, 2,6-dinitro (*trans*)
329(6918)	424 329	Azobenzene, 3,3′-dimethyl (*cis*)
329(22908)	329 320 249	1,2-Benzocarbazole, 3,4-dihydro
329(4786)	329 272	Quinoline, 3-hydroxy
329(18000)	329 232	Fluorene, 2-nitro
328(7763)	328 253	Pyridoxamine, dihydrochloride
328(6310)	328 234	3-Pyridinecarboxylic acid, 2-hydroxy
328(19953)	328	Azobenzene, 4-bromo
328(39811)	328	Stilbene, 4,4′-diamino (*trans*)
326(25119)	342 326 293 237	Coumestrol, diacetate
326(15700)	326 255 246	Coumarin, 5,7-dimethoxy
326(3389)	326	Lithocholic acid
325(21878)	440 325	Azobenzene, 4-hydroxy acetate
325(18400)	325 291 238 217	Cinnamic acid, 2,4-dimethoxy (*cis*)
325(19055)	325 280 230	Stilbene, 2-methoxy (*trans*)
325(20600)	325 236	Acetophenone, 4-amino-α-chloro
325(12589)	325	1,4-Benzoquinone, 2,5-dichloro-3,6-dihydroxy
325(6310)	325	Thyroxine (*d*)
325(6310)	325	Thyroxine (*l*)
324(10000)	408 324	Aniline, 2,4,6-trinitro
324(35800)	340 324 226	Furan, 2,5-diphenyl
324(47863)	324 309	Ellagene
324(12589)	324 286 217	Cinnamic acid, 2,4-dihydroxy (*trans*)
324(12589)	324 267 235	Azoxybenzene, 3,3′-dimethoxy
324(8460)	324 256	Barbituric acid, 5-benzylidene
324(14600)	324 254 216	Coumarin, 7-hydroxy
324(7244)	324 254	Vitamin B_6
324(25704)	324 241	Benzothiazoline, 3-methyl-2-thioxo
324(28184)	324	Stilbene, 4-amino (*trans*)
323(6918)	496 428 323 239	5β-Pregnane-3α,20β-diol
323(14791)	323 290	Coumarin, 7-methoxy
323(3548)	323 283	Quinoline, 3-chloro
323(14454)	323 260 231	Azoxybenzene (*cis*)
323(8060)	323 249	Quinoline, 5,7-dibromo-8-hydroxy
323(23442)	323 234	3-Buten-2-one, 4(4-hydroxyphenyl)
323(18197)	323	Azobenzene, 2-hydroxy
323(26303)	323	4-Azobenzenecarboxylic acid
323(7943)	323	Benzene, 1,2-dimethoxy-4-nitro
323(7943)	323	Benzene, 2,4-dimethoxy-1-nitro
323(11221)	323	Benzene, 1,3-dimethyl-2-hydroxy-5-nitro
323(1585)	323	1,3-Cyclopentadiene, hexachloro
323(13804)	323	Visnadin
322(10900)	339 333 322 311 275 265	Acenaphthylene
322(15100)	322 293 241 218	Cinnamic acid, 3-hydroxy-4-methoxy (*trans*)
322(15849)	322 286 244 217	Cinnamic acid, 2,4-dimethoxy (*trans*)
322(10000)	322 267	Stilbene, 4-nitro (*cis*)
322(11221)	322 241	Coumarin, 3-hydroxy

Strongest Band (ε)	Wavelengths (nm)	Compound
322(18621)	322 234	3-Buten-2-one, 4(4-methoxyphenyl)
322(17378)	322 231	Benzoxazole, 2(2-hydroxyphenyl)
322(15849)	322	Benzoic acid, 4-hydrazino
322(1413)	322	Samidin
322(35482)	322	4-Stilbenecarboxylic acid, nitrile (*trans*)
321(6607)	480 410 321	Ergostanol
321(19953)	321	Benzoic acid, amide, *N*(4-nitrophenyl)
321(19953)	321	Benzoic acid, 4-nitro, amide, *N*-phenyl
320(10471)	402 320	Aniline, 2,3,4,6-tetranitro
320(15849)	320 261	Azoxybenzene, 3,3′-dimethyl (*trans*)
320(12023)	320 250	Coumarin, 5,7-dihydroxy-4-methyl
320(15849)	320 240 225	Cinnamic acid, 3,5-dimethoxy-4-hydroxy (*trans*)
320(3162)	320	Chlorpromazine
320(38019)	320	2,4-Pentadienal, 5-phenyl
320(13489)	320	Stilbene, 4-dimethylamino (*cis*)
320(9772)	320	Toluene, 2-hydroxy-4-nitro
319(8913)	469 419 319 238	Ergosterol, 5,6-dihydro
319(6780)	319 283	Hydroquinonephthalein
319(3631)	319 279	Quinoline, 7-chloro
319(4169)	319 277	Quinoline, 2-bromo
319(36308)	319 234	3,5-Hexadien-2-one, 6-phenyl
319(12589)	319	Skimmin
318(8128)	390 318	Pyridoxal, hydrochloride
318(14454)	378 318	Cholic acid
318(4571)	318 282	Quinoline, 2-chloro
318(23988)	318	Benzene, 1-mercapto-4-nitro
318(7244)	318	Ergotamine
318(15136)	318	Glycocholic acid
318(15136)	318	Pyrimidine, 2-amino-5-nitro
318(7080)	318	Quinoline, 6-methyl
317(24000)	317 231	1-Penten-3-one, 1(4-methoxyphenyl)
317(11482)	317	Propenoic acid, 3(1-naphthyl) (*trans*)
316(19055)	332 316	$\Delta^{3,5,7,22}$-Ergostatetraene
316(14125)	325 316 258	Benzene, 1,2-dichloro-4,5-dihydroxy
316(23442)	316 304 230	Stilbene, 4-hydroxy (*trans*)
316(22908)	316 236	3-Buten-2-one, 4(2-furyl)
316(20500)	316 233	Acetophenone, 4-amino
316(29000)	316	1,4-Benzoquinone, dioxime
316(12589)	316	1-Naphthoic acid, 4-hydroxy
316(6761)	316	Quinoline, 3-methyl
315(12023)	750 315 293 227	Benzene, 1-bromo-4-nitroso
315(25119)	740 315 231	Pyocyanine
315(8128)	315 225	Furan, 2-nitro
315(8128)	315 225	2-Furancarboxylic acid, allyl ester
315(30199)	315 210	Chalcone, 4-nitro
315(6607)	315	Iodogorgoic acid (*dl*)
315(3236)	315	Phenol, 4-amino-2,6-dibromo
315(5754)	315	Quinoline, 5-methyl
315(5754)	315	Quinoline, 8-methyl
314(7413)	314 308 298	Cinchotine
314(23988)	314 285 275 228 222	2-Stilbazole (*trans*)
314(3981)	314 248	Purine, 2-amino-9-methyl
314(28184)	314 247	Chalcone, 3,3′-dinitro
314(6520)	314 238	1,4-Benzoquinone, tetrahydroxy
314(9050)	314 237	Benzene, hexahydroxy
314(20800)	314 233	1-Pentanone, 1(4-aminophenyl)
314(18200)	314 228	Azobenzene (*trans*)
314(10000)	314	Barbituric acid, 5-nitro
313(12023)	750 313 288 226	Benzene, 1-chloro-4-nitroso
313(14791)	424 313 258 222	Azobenzene, 2-amino

Strongest Band (ε)	Wavelengths (nm)	Compound
313(7763)	313 256	Ricinine
313(30199)	313 239	1,3-Butadiene, 1,4-diphenyl (*cis,cis*)
313(3162)	313	Apocodeine
313(25119)	313	2-Stilbenecarboxylic acid, nitrile (*trans*)
312(11749)	326 312 262	Quinoxaline, 2,3-dihydroxy
312(21200)	312	Disulfide, diphenyl, 4,4′-dinitro
312(8350)	312	Ergocristine
312(9333)	312	Isolysergic acid (*d*)
312(10300)	312	Oxalic acid, dithiono diamide
312(26303)	312	Propenal, 3(2-furyl)
312(8128)	312	Pteridine, 2-amino-4-hydroxy
311(29512)	322 311 226	Stilbene, 4-methoxy (*trans*)
311(11000)	311 228	Phenol, 4-nitro-
310(31623)	600 310 260	5,5′-Indigotindisulfonic acid, sodium salt
310(6457)	328 310	1-Naphthoic acid, 5-nitro
310(6761)	310 234	Benzene, 1,4-dimethyl-2-hydroxy-5-nitro
310(14125)	310 233	Furan, 2,4-dioxo(tetrahydro)
310(16300)	310 227	Styrene, β-nitro(*trans*)
310(1995)	310	Violuric acid
309(4898)	309 291	α-Narcotine (*l*)
309(5012)	309 290	α-Narcotine (*dl*)
309(10471)	309 279	Benzaldehyde, 4-hydroxy-3-methoxy
309(22908)	309 237	Carbazole, 1-oxo-1,2,3,4-tetrahydro
309(14125)	309 236	1,3-Butanedione, 1(3-pyridyl)
309(7943)	309 234	Cytisine, (*l*), *N*-methyl
308(7244)	351 308	1-Naphthoic acid, 3-nitro
308(12589)	335 308 245	Phenanthrene, 1-hydroxy
308(10965)	308 270 237	2,4-Pyrroledicarboxylic acid, 5-formyl-3-methyl, diethyl ester
308(17400)	308 247 230	1,3-Butanedione, 1-phenyl
308(25704)	308 227	Benzoic acid, 4(dimethylamino)
308(21600)	308 226	Chalcone (*trans*)
308(12900)	308 222	4-Hexenoic acid, 2-acetyl-5-hydroxy-3-oxo-lactone
308(8913)	308	1,4-Dithiine, 2,5-diphenyl
308(9333)	308	Fumaric acid, dihydroxy
308(31623)	308	Stilbene, 4-bromo-(*trans*)
307(28840)	325 307 300 228	Stilbene, 4,4′-dihydroxy (*trans*)
307(10471)	307 291 283 276 223	Propene, 2-nitro-1-phenyl
307(6918)	307	Propenoic acid, 3(1-naphthyl) (*cis*)
306(10471)	400 306	Benzene, 1-nitro-4-triazo
306(28184)	330 306	Benzaldehyde, 3-hydroxy azine
306(31700)	324 306 227 206	Stilbene, 4,4′-dimethoxy
306(22000)	306 297 225 210	Cinnamic acid, 4-methoxy (*trans*)
306(6918)	306 262	Indazole, 4-amino
306(10000)	306 235	Cytisine (*l*)
305(7413)	471 305	9,10-Anthraquinone, 1-amino-3-bromo
305(33885)	315 305	Stilbene, 4,4′-dichloro (*trans*)
305(3162)	305 250	Julolidine, 1,6-dioxo
305(10600)	305 227	Benzene, 1-methoxy-4-nitro
305(14700)	305 222	Biphenyl, 4-nitro
305(28184)	305 220	Stilbene, 3,4′,5-trihydroxy
305(5012)	305	Benzene, 1,4-dichloro-2,5-dihydroxy
305(5012)	305	Benzene, 1,4-dihydroxy-2,3,5,6-tetrachloro
305(25900)	305	Biphenyl, 4,4′-dinitro
305(9333)	305	1-Naphthoic acid, 4-bromo-
305(7943)	305	1-Naphthoic acid, 5-bromo-
304(33885)	376 358 329 315 304 287	Picene
304(28840)	304 228	4-Stilbazole (*trans*)
304(3162)	304	Anthranil
304(6026)	304	Bufotalin
303(9333)	505 303	Javanicin

Strongest Band (ε)	Wavelengths (nm)	Compound
303(4898)	303	Benzene, 5-amino-1,3-dibromo-2-methoxy
303(6761)	303	Eucarvone
303(7080)	303	1-Naphthoic acid, 5-chloro
303(30199)	303	Oxazole
302(44668)	383 302 292	1,2-Benzanthracene-10-carboxaldehyde
302(12600)	302 266	Acetic acid, amide, *N*(2,4-dinitrophenyl)
302(23500)	302 240	Benzimidazole, 2-phenyl
302(21600)	302 228 222 204	Malonic acid, benzylidene monomethyl ester mononitrile (*trans*)
302(24547)	302 222	Benzothiazole, 2-phenylamino
302(15488)	302 164	Ether, diethenyl
302(6330)	302	Azoxybenzene, 2,2′-dimethoxy
302(1318)	302	Benzene, 1-bromo-3-nitro
302(11500)	302	Ether, diphenyl, 4-nitro
302(23442)	302	Propenoic acid, 3(2-furyl), methyl ester
302(4467)	302	Scilliroside
301(15849)	461 301	Azobenzene, 3-amino
301(34674)	369 338 301 256	3,4-Benzofluoranthene
301(12882)	301 246	2,2′-Bithiophene
301(25100)	301 225	Lophine
301(22900)	301 224	Benzoic acid, 4(methylamino)
301(21379)	301 218	Ether, diphenyl, 4,4′-dinitro
301(12023)	301	5-Pyrazolone, 1-methyl-3-phenyl
301(14454)	301	Styrene, 4-nitro
300(25119)	490 300 283	Thioindigo
300(7943)	380 300 267	Pteridine
300(6310)	330 300	Isoquinoline, 1-amino
300(5623)	327 319 312 305 300 290	Naphthalene, 1-hydroxy-4-methyl
300(15849)	313 300 290 250	Acenaphthene, 5-bromo
300(33885)	313 300 229	Stilbene, 4-chloro (*trans*)
300(7763)	300 290	Fluorene, 9-methyl
300(4467)	300 268	Benzene, 1,3-dinitroso
300(17783)	300 264	Sulfoxide, diphenyl, 4,4′-diamino
300(6026)	300 262 251	Phthalic acid, hydrazide
300(1349)	300 237	2-Propanol, 2-methyl
300(22908)	300 230	Propenoic acid, 3(2-furyl) (*cis*)
300(7943)	300	Benzoic acid, 2-hydroxy, pentyl ester
300(3162)	300	Chlorpromazine, hydrochloride
300(21000)	300	Cinnamic acid, 4-nitro (*trans*)
300(21878)	300	Cinnamic acid, 4-nitro, ethyl ester (*trans*)
300(20893)	300	Cinnamic acid, 4-nitro, methyl ester (*trans*)
300(7080)	300	Naphthalene, 1-triazo
300(5012)	300	Pyridine, 2(methylamino)
300(26925)	300	Stilbene, 3-chloro (*trans*)
299(8129)	313 299	1-Naphthoic acid, 8-iodo
299(21300)	299 252	Benzaldehyde, azine
299(10233)	299 250	Uric acid, 9-methyl
299(5012)	299 243	Sorbose (*l*)
299(1230)	299	Gitogenin
299(22387)	299	2-Stilbenecarboxylic acid (*trans*)
298(18197)	497 298	Testosterone, 17-methyl
298(15849)	360 298	Croconic acid
298(12882)	337 298 232	Benzene, 1,3-dihydroxy-4-nitro
298(10233)	298 250	Coumarin, 5-hydroxy
298(15300)	298 228	Phenol, 4-nitroso
298(26700)	298 223	Benzoic acid, 4-amino, 2-diethylaminoethyl ester hydrochloride
298(31400)	298 221	Benzil, 4,4′-dimethoxy
298(19055)	298	Cinnamic acid, 3,4,5-trimethoxy (*trans*)
298(7763)	298	Methazonic acid
298(5370)	298	1-Naphthoic acid, 4-chloro
298(26303)	298	Stilbene, 2-chloro (*trans*)

Strongest Band (ϵ)	Wavelengths (nm)	Compound
298(3802)	298	γ-Tocopherol
298(3467)	298	δ-Tocopherol
298(2138)	298	Toluene, 4-amino-3-bromo
297(28840)	310 297 285 227 220	Aniline, 2,4,5-tribromo
297(28840)	310 297 256	Isothiocyanic acid, 4(dimethylamino)phenyl ester
297(19953)	297	Amine, triphenyl
297(3720)	297	Benzene, 2-chloro-1,4-dihydroxy
297(1585)	297	Benzoic acid, 3-acetamido
297(21878)	297	Naphthalene, 1-mercapto
297(25119)	297	Stilbene, 3-amino (*trans*)
297(23988)	297	Stilbene, 3-methoxy (*trans*)
296(3631)	306 296 254	Indazole, 5-chloro
296(16218)	296 291	Benzaldehyde, 4-amino
296(2550)	296 289	Phenol, 2,4,6-trichloro
296(4750)	296 257	3-Pyridinecarboxylic acid, 6-hydroxy
296(19953)	296 253	Rhodanine, 5-ethyl
296(20000)	296 227	Ethene, triphenyl
296(25119)	296	Stilbene, 2-bromo (*trans*)
296(28184)	296	Stilbene, 3-bromo (*trans*)
296(3715)	296	β-Tocopherol
295(43652)	438 349 295 258 222	9,10-Anthraquinone, 1,2,3,5,6,7-hexahydroxy
295(25119)	415 295	4-Azobenzenesulfonic acid, 4′-chloro
295(33113)	395 305 295 285 277	Fulvene, 6-ethenyl (*trans*)
295(28840)	307 295 228	Stilbene, 2,2′-diamino (*trans*)
295(10471)	295 268	Reserpine
295(10000)	295 255	Coumarin, 8-hydroxy
295(25704)	295 252	Flavone
295(12589)	295 250 230 220	Rhodanine, 3-phenyl
295(8750)	295 235	Uracil, 5-nitro
295(10715)	295 228	β-Ionone
295(11221)	295 226	β-Irone
295(10600)	295 212	Isatin
295(3510)	295	Acetic acid, (2,5-dihydroxyphenyl)
295(1445)	295	Benzene, 1,4-dimethyl-2,3-dinitro
295(1514)	295	Benzene, 2,5-dimethyl-1,3-dinitro
295(19055)	295	Benzophenone, 4,4′-dihydroxy
295(19953)	295	Cinnamaldehyde, 4-nitro
295(15849)	295	Heptane, 3,5-dimethyl
295(7586)	295	β (-)-Hydrastine
295(27543)	295	Stilbene, 3-methyl (*trans*)
295(2512)	295	Toluene, 4-hydroxy-2,3,5,6-tetrachloro
294(27400)	333 294	Fluorene, 2,7-diamino
294(20417)	330 294 215	Benzaldehyde, 2,4-dimethoxy-6-hydroxy
294(11482)	294 264	Thiophene, 2-acetyl-5-methyl
294(5370)	294 259	Indazole, 1-methyl
294(23988)	294 228	Propenoic acid, 3,3-dichloro
294(20417)	294 225 222 204	Cinnamaldehyde, α-bromo (*cis*)
293(4467)	330 324 316 310 303 297 293 285	Naphthalene, 1-hydroxy-2-methyl
293(5012)	317 293	Quinoline, 5-bromo
293(6026)	293 282	1-Naphthoic acid, 2-chloro
293(12303)	293 268	Thiophene, 2-acetyl-5-bromo
293(20417)	293 259	Hydrazine, tetraphenyl
293(4786)	293 233	Lycorine (*l*)
293(23988)	293 232	Stilbene, 2,2′-dibromo (*trans*)
293(3890)	293	Benzene, 1,4-dihydroxy-2-isopropyl-5-methyl
293(5540)	293	Biphenyl, 2,2′-diamino
293(8128)	293	Biphenyl, 2,2′-dihydroxy-5,5′-dimethyl
293(14125)	293	Ether, diphenyl, 2,2′-dinitro
293(10471)	293	Junipic acid

Strongest Band (ε)	Wavelengths (nm)	Compound
293(25119)	293	Stilbene, 4-fluoro (*trans*)
293(27543)	293	3-Stilbenecarboxylic acid, nitrile (*trans*)
293(1738)	293	Toluene, 2-amino-4-bromo
292(4571)	317 292	Quinoline, 5-chloro
292(4467)	315 292	Quinoline, 8-chloro
292(7763)	303 292 283	1-Naphthoic acid, 8-bromo
292(2850)	299 292	Phenol, 2,4,5-trichloro
292(5495)	292 283	Indole, 1,3-dimethyl
292(11221)	292 265	Thiophene, 2-acetyl-5-chloro
292(20893)	292 262	Sulfamethylthiazole
292(17378)	292 250	Flavanone, 3′,4′,5,7-tetrahydroxy
292(13804)	292 225	Cinnamaldehyde, β-bromo (*cis*)
292(18100)	292 223	Benzoic acid, 4-amino-3-methyl
292(25000)	292 223	Benzophenone, 4,4′-dimethoxy
292(26500)	292 219	Benzaldehyde, 2-hydroxy, azine
292(5200)	292 211	2-Furancarboxylic acid, 5-nitro
292(1072)	292	Anilinediacetic acid
292(2512)	292	Benzaldehyde, 2-acetamido
292(4920)	292	Hematoxylin
292(3467)	292	α-Tocopherol
292(7720)	292	Vitamin B_6 hydrochloride
291(12589)	403 291	1,4-Benzoquinone, 2-chloro, oxime
291(19953)	345 291	Carbamic acid, dithio
291(23442)	325 291	Griseofulvin
291(5012)	315 291	Quinoline, 8-bromo
291(30903)	291 282	β-Ionone, semicarbazone
291(10000)	291 242	Rheadin
291(1202)	291 224	3-Hexanol, 3-ethyl
291(2040)	291	1,2,4,5-Benzenetetracarboxylic acid
291(5012)	291	Maleic acid, dihydroxy
291(4366)	291	Podophyllotoxin
291(16218)	291	Thiophene, 2-methyl-5-phenyl
291(4169)	291	Vomicine
290(34674)	500 372 365 290 240	Phenazine, 1-amino
290(12882)	429 353 290	Naphthalene, 1-amino-6-nitro
290(7080)	313 290 280	1-Naphthoic acid, 8-chloro
290(5428)	300 290 254	Indazole, 3-chloro
290(19499)	299 290 218	4H-Thiin-4-one
290(1906)	290 280	Phenol, 2,3,5-trichloro
290(3802)	290 255	Indazole, 3-methyl
290(16218)	290 252 224	Benzophenone, 4-methoxy
290(39811)	290 248	Cinnamic acid, 2-nitro (*trans*)
290(10000)	290 245	Amine, diphenyl methyl
290(3981)	290 240	Erythramine
290(7943)	290 235	Rubiginol
290(10965)	290 235	Uric acid
290(7943)	290 228	Pyridine, 2-iodo
290(26925)	290 215	Chalcone, 3-nitro
290(8913)	290	Cyclohexanone, 2-acetyl
290(8913)	290	Pentanoic acid, 2,4-dioxo
290(4780)	290	Picropodophyllin
290(10000)	290	Protopine
290(25119)	290	Pseudoionone
290(10715)	290	Pyrrole, 2-phenyl
290(7413)	290	Stilbene, 2,4-dichloro (*cis*)
289(14300)	322 289 243	Benzophenone, 2,4-dihydroxy
289(4898)	316 289	Quinoline, 4-chloro
289(3090)	289 283	Coumaran
289(1950)	289 280	Phenol, 2,3,6-trichloro

Strongest Band (ε)	Wavelengths (nm)	Compound
289(18200)	289 219	Benzoic acid, 4-amino
289(4677)	289 216	2-Pyrone
289(3388)	289	Benzene, 1,4-dihydroxy-2-isopropyl
289(15849)	289	Ketone, 2-furyl phenyl
289(12900)	269 289	Benzoic acid, amidine, hydrochloride
288(12589)	395 288	Stilbene, 4-amino-4′-nitro (*cis*)
288(9333)	337 288	Indazole, 6-nitro
288(5540)	320 314 306 300 288	Acenaphthene
288(4677)	299 288 256	Indazole, 4-chloro
288(2580)	288 279 271	Aniline, 2-phenoxy
288(7244)	288 274	Benzimidazole, 2-methyl
288(25200)	288 259 230	Sulfathiazole, phthalyl
288(17500)	288 245	Azulene, 1,4-dimethyl-7-isopropyl
288(12882)	288 243	Carbothialdine
288(22600)	288 233 226 221 210	Cinnamaldehyde, oxime (*syn*)
288(12023)	288 223	Benzoic acid, 4-amino-2-methyl
288(17378)	288 220	Benzoic acid, 4-hydroxy, amide
288(10965)	288	Acetic acid, amide, *N*-methyl-*N*(4-nitrophenyl)
288(10233)	288	Amine, diphenyl, 4-hydroxy
288(2188)	288	Benzene, 1-amino-2-propyl
288(2754)	288	Benzene, 1,2,4-trihydroxy
288(6761)	288	Canadine (*d*)
288(6761)	288	Canadine (*l*)
288(9772)	288	Corycavine
288(20300)	288	Flavanone, 4′-methoxy-3′,5,7-trihydroxy
288(9772)	288	2,2′-Nicotyrine (solid)
288(9772)	288	2,2′-Nicotyrine (liquid)
288(9772)	288	3,2′-Nicotyrine
288(19055)	288	Propanoic acid, 2-oxo-3-phenyl
287(7080)	443 332 287	Dunnione
287(30903)	414 287 245	Anthraquinone, 1,2,3-trihydroxy
287(7943)	396 287	Azo, benzene methane
287(1140)	295 287	Benzoic acid, 3,5-dichloro
287(2138)	287 283 278	Phenol, 2,3,4,5-tetramethyl
287(6480)	287 281 277 246	Benzimidazole, 5,6-dimethyl
287(1380)	287 260	Benzene, 2-chloro-1,3-dimethyl-5-hydroxy
287(10471)	287 245	Pyrrole, 2-acetyl-1-methyl
287(11400)	287 225	Benzene, 1,2-dichloro-4-nitro
287(1205)	287	Arsine, bis(trifluoromethyl)iodo
287(3162)	287	Benzene, 1,2-dihydroxy-4,5-dimethyl
287(1905)	287	Benzene, 1,2-dihydroxy-3,4,5,6-tetrachloro
287(20893)	287	Chalcone, 2′-nitro
287(15849)	287	Disulfide, 1,1′-dinaphthyl
287(6310)	287	Stilbene, α,β-dichloro (*cis*)
286(38905)	368 350 305 286	Azulene, 1,5-dimethyl-8-isopropyl
286(12600)	364 286	1,4-Benzoquinone, tetrachloro
286(39811)	344 286	Benzoic acid, pentamethyl
286(8128)	320 286	Junipal
286(16596)	286 240	Stilbene, 2-amino (*trans*)
286(12882)	286 233	Urea, 9-methyl
286(16200)	286 227 207	Acetophenone, 2,4,6-trihydroxy
286(19900)	286 225 221	1-Penten-3-one, 1-phenyl
286(3388)	286	Benzene, 1,5-dihydroxy-2,4-dimethyl
286(1450)	286	Benzoic acid, 2-iodo
286(1698)	286	Codeine, dihydro (*d*)
286(5754)	286	Corybulbine (*d*)
286(5888)	286	3,4-Pyridinedicarboxylic acid, 2,6-dimethyl
286(6310)	286	Toluene, 2-nitroso
285(1995)	603 285	Indirubin
285(8710)	363 285	Pyridine, 2-mercapto

Strongest Band (ε)	Wavelengths (nm)	Compound
285(5888)	358 285	Benzene, 1,4-dimethyl-2-hydroxy-3-nitro
285(12589)	335 285	3-Buten-2-one, 4(2-hydoxyphenyl)
285(7660)	320 315 297 285	Naphthalene, 1,5-dimethyl
285(21100)	285 257 205	Sulfathiazole, succinyl
285(35482)	285 257	Sulfone,diphenyl, 4,4′-diacetamido
285(23900)	285 225 220 207	3-Buten-2-one, 4-phenyl (*trans*)
285(1585)	285	Benzene, 1,2-dimercapto
285(19953)	285	Benzoic acid, 4-amino, amide
285(18197)	285	Biphenyl, 4-amino-4′-hydroxy
285(24400)	285	Butanoic acid, 4-phenylphenacyl ester
285(5970)	285	Canadine (*dl*)
285(5754)	285	Glycine
285(6166)	285	Naphthalene, 1,3,6,8-tetramethyl
285(1950)	285	Phenol, 2-amino-4-chloro-5-nitro
285(3236)	285	Vasicine (*dl*)
284(14100)	377 284	1,4-Benzoquinone, 2,6-dimethoxy
284(28840)	336 284	9-Fluorenone, 2-nitro
284(2693)	284 276	Chroman
284(1150)	284 247	Benzoic acid, 4-hydroxy, nitrile
284(21878)	284 220	Stilbene, α-chloro (*trans*)
284(2290)	284	Benzene, 1-chloro-2,4-dihydroxy
284(2290)	284	Benzene, 1-chloro-3,5-dihydroxy
284(1030)	284	Benzene, 1,4-dinitro-2,3,5,6-tetramethyl
284(22908)	284	$\Delta^{4,6}$-Cholestadien-3-one
284(26303)	284	$\Delta^{4,6,22}$-Ergostatrienone
284(23500)	284	Propanoic acid, 4-phenylphenacyl ester
283(3386)	404 283	Toluene, 3-amino-2-nitro
283(8318)	366 283	Benzene, 1,5-dimethyl-2-hydroxy-3-nitro
283(9333)	357 283	Benzene, 1,2-dimethyl-4-hydroxy-5-nitro
283(37153)	323 283 274 237	1,3-Indandione, 2(3-methylbutoxy)
283(7490)	320 315 310 291 283 273	Naphthalene, 1-chloro
283(5012)	314 283	Quinoline, 4-methyl-8-nitro
283(10715)	313 283	Coumarin, 7-methyl
283(7943)	312 290 283 273	Methane, (1-naphthyl)phenyl
283(2188)	307 283 278	Benzene, 1,3-di-*tert*-butyl-5-ethyl-2-hydroxy
283(1880)	283 276	Phenol, 3-bromo
283(25700)	283 221	Benzoic acid, 4-phenylphenacyl ester
283(33885)	283	Acetic acid, amide, *N*(4-acetylphenyl)
283(2138)	283	Benzene, 1,4-dihydroxy-2,3,5,6-tetramethyl
283(1698)	283	Hydrocotarnine, hemihydrate
283(6310)	283	Isocorybulbine
283(7943)	283	1-Naphthalenesulfonic acid, 4-amino
283(23442)	283	Naringin
283(10000)	283	4-Pyrone-2-carboxylic acid, 5,6-dihydro-6,6-dimethyl, butyl ester
283(14125)	283	Testosterone, 4,5-dihydro-17-methyl
283(1778)	283	Thebainone A
283(3020)	283	Toluene, 2,4-dihydroxy
283(6960)	283	6-Uracilcarboxylic acid, monohydrate
282(45709)	806 282 237 215	Benzene, 1-nitro-4-nitroso
282(7080)	340 282	4-Dibenzothiophenecarboxylic acid
282(33600)	323 282 228 207	Sanguinarine
282(13100)	306 282 271	Coumarin, 4-hydroxy-3(1-phenyl-3-oxobutyl)
282(13800)	282 235	2,2′-Bipyridyl
282(17400)	282 217 213 207	Benzene, 1,3,5-trimethyl
282(43500)	282 215	Cinnamic acid, *p*-phenylphenacyl ester (*trans*)
282(5012)	282	Acetic acid, (3-indolyl)
282(9120)	282	Bebeerine (*d*)
282(1995)	282	Benzene, 1,2-dihydroxy-3,5-dimethyl
282(2239)	282	Benzene, 1,5-dihydroxy-3,4-dimethyl
282(9550)	282	Cinnamic acid, α-methyl-4-nitro

Strongest Band (ε)	Wavelengths (nm)	Compound
282(5754)	282	Corydaline (*d*)
282(5754)	282	Corydaline (*dl*)
282(5754)	282	Corydaline (*meso, d*)
282(5754)	282	Corydaline (*meso, dl*)
282(5754)	282	Corydaline (*meso, l*)
282(21878)	282	Formic acid, amidine, *N,N'*-diphenyl
282(18200)	282	Hippuric acid, *p*-amino
282(2818)	282	1-Propanol, 3(4-hydroxy-3-methoxyphenyl)
282(5754)	282	Toluene, 3-nitroso
281(11749)	310 281 244	Coumarin, 8-methyl
281(5495)	308 281	1-Naphthoic acid, 8-nitro
281(1820)	289 281	Glycerol, 1(4-chlorophenyl) ether
281(25704)	281 242	2-Pyrazoline, 1-phenyl
281(11749)	281 220	Uracil, 3,6-dimethyl
281(17800)	281	Amine, diphenyl, 3-hydroxy
281(1660)	281	Benzene, 2-*tert*-butyl-1-hydroxy-4-methyl
281(1585)	281	Benzene, hydroxy(pentamethyl)
281(22100)	281	Biphenyl, 4-acetyl
281(2188)	281	Estriol
281(24700)	281	Furfural, 5-methyl
281(10965)	281	Oxyacanthine
281(1585)	281	Phenol, pentamethyl
280(15849)	510 370 280	3-Isophenothiazin-3-one
280(5495)	395 280	Benzene, 1,4-dihydroxy-2-nitro
280(15136)	370 280	1,2-Naphthoquinone, 6-hydroxy
280(6310)	343 280	Benzoic acid, 2-hydrazino
280(13800)	327 280 217	Quinoline, 8-hydroxy-5-nitroso
280(42300)	320 307 280 277 221 205	Chrysene, 1-methyl
280(13804)	310 280 232	Benzaldehyde, 2,4-dihydroxy
280(22387)	306 280 233	1,3-Butadiene, 1-phenyl (*trans*)
280(12023)	290 280 251	Benzaldehyde, 3-methyl
280(6918)	288 280	Apomorphine
280(15849)	280 240	Oxazole, 2,4-diphenyl
280(7586)	280 226	Benzimidazole, 2-hydroxy
280(19100)	280 225	Cinnamic acid, 2,3-dimethoxy (*trans*)
280(39811)	280 215	Mimosine (*l*)
280(37300)	280 213 203	Cinnamic acid, anhydride (*trans*)
280(1698)	280	Benzene, 1-hydroxy-2,3,4,6-tetramethyl
280(2720)	280	Benzene, 1-hydroxy-2,4,5-trimethyl
280(1585)	280	Benzenesulfonic acid, 2-nitro, chloride
280(3840)	280	Catechin *(cis,d)*
280(19953)	280	Cinnamaldehyde, α-methyl
280(21878)	280	Dicoumarol
280(4130)	280	Epicatechin (*l*)
280(2344)	280	Estrone
280(2042)	280	8-Isoestradiol
280(2720)	280	Phenol, 2,4,5-trimethyl
280(4571)	280	3,4-Pyridinedicarboxylic acid, 2,6-dimethyl
280(10471)	280	Stilbene, 2-methoxy (*cis*)
280(27543)	280	Tachysterol
280(25119)	280	*p*-Terphenyl
280(6310)	280	Tryptophan (*d*)
279(22908)	392 324 279	Quinoline, 4-amino-6-nitro
279(32000)	339 318 279 208	9-Fluorenone, 2,4,7-trinitro
279(39811)	334 279 240	Jacareubin
279(3389)	323 279	Quinoline, 3-bromo
279(6026)	320 279	4,5-Benzindane
279(8913)	294 279	Lumisterol
279(1570)	287 279 226	Acetic acid, (4-chlorophenoxy)
279(3236)	285 279 275	Benzene, 1-fluoro-4-methoxy

Strongest Band (ϵ)	Wavelengths (nm)	Compound
279(1585)	279 274 271	Benzene, 1,2-dimethyl-3-methoxy
279(1000)	279 270 262	3-Toluenesulfonic acid, amide
279(7080)	279 267	Benzene, 1-chloro-4-triazo
279(14800)	279 225	Furfural, 5-hydroxymethyl
279(18197)	279 221 213	Cinnamic acid, 2,4,6-trimethyl (*cis*)
279(1380)	279	Acetic acid, (4-bromophenoxy)
279(1549)	279	Benzene, 1,3-dihydroxy-2,4-dimethyl
279(3162)	279	Benzoic acid, 2-phenylhydrazide
279(1047)	279	Benzoic acid, 2-methyl, ethyl ester
279(3631)	279	Epicatechin, (*dl*)
279(5248)	279	Indole, 3(2-aminoethyl)
279(16218)	279	Sulfide, di(dimethylthiocarbamyl)
279(6607)	279	Uracil, 3-methyl
278(12589)	362 278	1,4-Benzoquinone, trichloro
278(13800)	356 278 249	Cinnamic acid, 2,5-dihydroxy (*trans*)
278(3981)	330 278	1-Naphthalenesulfonic acid, 7-hydroxy
278(28184)	312 278	Benzophenone, 2,2′,4,4′-tetramethoxy
278(19953)	309 278 231	Acetophenone, 4-hydroxy-2-methoxy
278(30300)	296 286 278 271 263	Ethyne, diphenyl
278(39811)	289 278 270	2,4,6-Octatriene, 2,6-dimethyl (4-*trans*, 6-*trans*)
278(2560)	285 278	Phenol, 2,6-dichloro
278(12882)	281 278	Stilbene, 4-methyl (*cis*)
278(1549)	278 273	Benzene, 1,2-dimethyl-3-hydroxy
278(1400)	278 269 262	Benzoic acid, 2-benzyl
278(2270)	278 244	Benzene, 1,5-dimethyl-3-hydroxy-2-nitro
278(17100)	278 215	Cinnamic acid, α-acetamido (*trans*)
278(1000)	278	Benzene, 1,2-diacetamido
278(6310)	278	Biphenyl, 2,2′-dimethoxy
278(4467)	278	Methane, (2-hydroxyphenyl) (4-hydroxyphenyl)
278(23988)	278	Naphthalene, 1-hydroxy-6-nitro
278(1000)	278	Narceine
278(1413)	278	Succinic acid, anhydride
278(10233)	278	Sulfoxide, diphenyl, 4-amino
277(15849)	352 277	Naphthalene, 6-amino-1-nitro
277(3000)	288 277 270	Aniline, 3-phenoxy
277(2510)	285 277	Benzene, 1-iodo-3-methoxy
277(3311)	283 280 277	Phenol, 2,3-dichloro
277(2291)	279 277	4-Flavanol
277(13804)	277 235	Glucose phenylhydrazone (*d*, β)
277(21700)	277 224 218 206	Cinnamic acid, 4-chloro (*trans*)
277(1995)	277 207	Acetic acid, 2-methoxyphenyl ester
277(9772)	277	Benzene, 2-methoxy-1,3,5-triiodo
277(2042)	277	Benzoic acid, 2-hydroxy, methyl ester, benzoate
277(1047)	277	Benzoic acid, 3-isopropyl
277(3162)	277	Hexanoic acid, 3,5-dioxo
277(19953)	277	Patulin
277(2670)	277	Phenol, 2-bromo
277(1820)	277	Phenol, 3-iodo
277(10471)	277	Pyridine, 2-phenyl
277(3270)	277	2,4-Pyridinedicarboxylic acid
277(15849)	277	Styrene, 4-amino
277(21379)	277	Sulfoxide, diphenyl, 4-amino-4′-nitro
277(15849)	277	Uracil, 6-methyl-4-thio
277(18621)	277	Urocanic acid
276(46773)	361 312 292 276 268	Phenanthrene, 2-nitro
276(17500)	333 325 318 296 284 276	Phenanthrene, 3-methyl
276(12589)	330 276	Benzoic acid, 3-hydrazino
276(13804)	324 276 215	Isocyanic acid, 4-nitrophenyl ester
276(26303)	324 276	Flavone, 5,6,7-trihydroxy
276(3631)	319 276	Quinoline, 6-chloro

Strongest Band (ε)	Wavelengths (nm)	Compound
276(3388)	283 276 269	Benzene, 1-iodo-2-methoxy
276(18700)	276 233	Hydantoin, 1-acetyl-2-thio
276(19499)	276 210	Chalcone, 2-nitro
276(2200)	276	Benzene, 1-benzyl-2-hydroxy
276(1810)	276	Benzene, 1,4-dimethyl-2-hydroxy
276(2320)	276	Benzene, 2-hydroxy-1-isopropyl-4-methyl
276(1585)	276	Benzoic acid, 3-tolyl ester
276(10965)	276	$\Delta^{2,4}$-Cholestadiene
276(1259)	276	Phthalic acid, dibenzyl ester
276(19499)	276	2-Pyrrolecarboxylic acid, 3,5-dimethyl, ethyl ester
276(10715)	276	Stilbene, 4-chloro (*cis*)
276(9120)	276	Toluene, α-hydroxy-4-nitro
275(10000)	800 330 275	Benzaldehyde, 4-nitroso
275(16596)	427 347 275	Naphthalene, 7-amino-1-nitro
275(1660)	359 345 275 251	Benzene, 1,2-dimethyl-4-hydroxy-3-nitro
275(46773)	345 332 275	Naphthalene, octachloro
275(15849)	330 275	Pelargonidin, chloride
275(10965)	315 275	Coumarin, 5-methyl
275(15849)	313 275	Chromone
275(17783)	293 275	Indazole, 2-methyl
275(1510)	281 275	Toluene, 3,5-dihydroxy
275(2570)	280 275	Benzene, 1,5-di-*tert*-butyl-2-hydroxy-3-methyl
275(2512)	275 260	Benzene, 1-allyl-2-hydroxy
275(9910)	275 252	2-Thiophenecarboxylic acid, 5-methyl
275(21200)	275 251	Benzene, 1,2-dihydroxy-3-methyl
275(21200)	275 251	Toluene, 2,3-dihydroxy
275(10200)	275 247	Antipyrine, *p*-bromo
275(18900)	275 231 217	Cinnamic acid, 3-methoxy (*trans*)
275(10000)	275 228	Benzoic acid, 3,5-dimethoxy-4-hydroxy
275(22500)	275 222 216 205	Cinnamic acid, methyl ester (*trans*)
275(15800)	275 214	Uracil, 6-propyl-2-thio
275(2010)	275	Acetic acid, (3-hydroxyphenyl)
275(16596)	275	Barbituric acid, 5-hydroxy
275(2370)	275	Benzene, 1,2-dihydroxy-4-isopropyl
275(19953)	275	Benzoic acid, 4-amino, nitrile
275(10000)	275	Benzoic acid, 3,4,5-trihydroxy, ethyl ester
275(19953)	275	Biphenyl, 3,4′-dinitro
275(18197)	275	2-Butenoic acid, 3-amino, ethyl ester (*trans*)
275(26400)	275	Methane, bis(2,4-dinitrophenyl)
275(8913)	275	Pyrazine, 2,6-dimethyl
275(1097)	275	2,4,5-Pyridinetricarboxylic acid
275(15849)	275	2,4-Pyrroledicarboxylic acid, 3,5-dimethyl-1-ethyl, diethyl ester
275(6310)	275	Quinoline, 4-methoxy
275(2512)	275	Semicarbazide, 1,4-diphenyl
275(1413)	275	Tyrosine (*d*)
275(1413)	275	Tyrosine (*dl*)
275(1413)	275	Tyrosine (*l*)
274(33885)	349 302 274	Anthraquinone, 2,6-dihydroxy
274(16100)	348 274 240 217	Cinnamic acid, 2,5-dimethoxy (*trans*)
274(16400)	321 274 225 212	Cinnamic acid, 2-methoxy (*cis*)
274(16400)	321 274 225 212	Cinnamic acid, 2-methoxy (*trans*)
274(8511)	314 274	Heptanoic acid, anhydride
274(16596)	306 274	Apomorphine, hydrochloride
274(15849)	298 274	Amine, diphenyl, 2-hydroxy
274(1740)	281 274	Benzene, 2-chloro-1,3-dihydroxy
274(2818)	280 274 269	Benzene, 1,3-diethoxy
274(1130)	279 274	Benzene, 1,3-dihydroxy-2-methyl
274(1130)	279 274	Toluene, 2,6-dihydroxy
274(21400)	274 215	Benzene, 1-ethyl-4-nitro
274(11700)	274 215	Toluene, 4-nitro

Strongest Band (ε)	Wavelengths (nm)	Compound
274(2042)	274	Acetic acid, (2-bromophenoxy)
274(2360)	274	Acetic acid, (2-hydroxyphenyl)
274(2230)	274	Hydrazine, (3-tolyl)
274(10000)	274	Stilbene, 3-methoxy (*cis*)
274(19953)	274	Stilbene, 2-nitro (*trans*)
274(14800)	274	2,3-Thiazoline, 2-mercapto
274(16218)	274	Vicine
273(2270)	376 360 280 273	Acetic acid, (3-hydroxyphenoxy)
273(3311)	372 273	Benzene, 1,4-dimethoxy-2-nitro
273(15849)	320 273 235	Flavone, 3,4′,5,7-tetrahydroxy
273(3802)	320 273	Quinoline, 6-bromo
273(33885)	315 297 273	α-Toxicarol (*l*)
273(11200)	311 273	Coumarin
273(1000)	292 273 260	Indan, 2-methyl
273(42658)	285 273 265	2,4,6-Octatriene, 2,6-dimethyl (4-*trans*,6-*cis*)
273(2420)	279 273	Benzene, 1-hydroxy-2-methoxy-4-propenyl (*cis*)acetate
273(2420)	279 273	Eugenol, acetate
273(17378)	273 265	Flavone, 2′,3,4′,5,7-pentahydroxy
273(5012)	273 260	Indan, 1-methyl
273(7080)	273 245	Guanine
273(15488)	273 217 206	Cinnamic acid, α-bromo (*trans*)
273(1778)	273	Benzene, 1-ethyl-3-hydroxy
273(1905)	273	Benzene, isopropoxy
273(12882)	273	Benzoic acid, amidine, *N,N′*-diphenyl
273(1995)	273	Benzoic acid, 2-tolyl ester
273(11482)	273	Benzoic acid, 3,4,5-trihydroxy
273(25119)	273	Cinnamic acid, amide (*trans*)
273(16596)	273	Cinnamic acid, nitrile (*cis*)
273(7244)	273	Prontosil
273(12589)	273	Propenoic acid, 3,3-diphenyl
273(4677)	273	2-Propen-1-ol
273(10233)	273	Pyridine, 3,4-dihydroxy
273(3162)	273	Pyridine, 2,3,6-trimethyl
272(27543)	374 272 228	Azulene, 4,8-dimethyl-2-isopropyl
272(21379)	348 272	Xanthoxyletin
272(4898)	326 311 272	Acetic acid, (2-naphthyloxy)
272(7586)	281 272	Benzene, 1,3-dihydroxy-2,5-dimethyl
272(1862)	280 272 260	2-Toluenesulfonic acid, 2-tolyl ester
272(1862)	280 272	2-Toluenesulfonic acid, 3-tolyl ester
272(1862)	280 272	2-Toluenesulfonic acid, 4-tolyl ester
272(1738)	278 272 260	Toluene, 2-ethoxy
272(1840)	272 268	Toluene, 2,4,5-trihydroxy triacetate
272(1230)	272 266 260	Indan
272(39500)	272 222 216 211	Cinnamic acid, nitrile (*trans*)
272(15136)	272 220	Cinnamic acid, 2-carboxy (*trans*)
272(19500)	272 219	2-Coumaronecarboxylic acid, 3-methyl
272(16596)	272 218	Benzoic acid, 4-mercapto
272(9670)	272 207	Urea, 1-acetyl-2-thio
272(6761)	272	Amine, ethyl *N*-nitrosophenyl
272(6310)	272	Aniline, *N*-ethyl-*N*-nitroso
272(8510)	272	Caffeine
272(11482)	272	2-Furancarboxylic acid, 5-methyl, methyl ester
272(6800)	272	2,4-Pentanedione
272(6761)	272	Pyrazine, 2,3-dimethyl
272(1000)	272	1,3,5-Triazine
271(5754)	354 271	Benzene, 1-mercapto-2-nitro
271(4366)	322 271	Isoquinoline, 4-methyl
271(21379)	315 304 271	Fluorene, 2-hydroxy
271(46773)	281 271 261	9,11,13-Octadecatrienoic acid (*cis*)
271(1660)	277 271 265	Propanoic acid, 2-methyl-2-phenoxy

Strongest Band (ε)	Wavelengths (nm)	Compound
271(1549)	276 271	Benzene, 1,3-dimethyl-2-hydroxy
271(3548)	276 271	Benzene, 1-hydroxy-2-isopropyl
271(17783)	271 266	Hydantoin, 3,5-diphenyl-2-thio
271(15900)	271 222 211	Cinnamic acid, 2-chloro (*trans*)
271(2089)	271	Acetic acid, amide, *N*(3-aminophenyl)
271(7230)	271	Acetic acid, 4-nitrophenyl ester
271(13489)	271	Benzaldehyde, 4-iodo
271(7413)	271	Benzene, 1,3-dimethyl-5-nitro
271(2908)	271	Benzenesulfonic acid, 4(4-aminophenylsulfonamido), amide
271(5710)	271	1,4-Benzoquinone, 2,5-dichloro
271(5330)	271	Coniferyl alcohol
271(20893)	271	Disulfide, 2,2′-dibenzothiazyl
271(1950)	271	Ethanol, 2-phenyl
271(21878)	271	3,5-Heptadien-2-one
271(7943)	271	2-Stilbenecarboxylic acid, nitrile (*cis*)
271(13200)	271	2,5-Thiophenedicarboxylic acid
271(11600)	271	Toluene, α-bromo-4-nitro
271(1000)	271	Toluene, α,2-dihydroxy-glucoside
270(7943)	520 270	1,4-Naphthoquinone, 5,8-dihydroxy
270(23442)	390 270	1,4-Naphthoquinone, 6-hydroxy
270(11749)	380 270	Pteridine, 2-amino-4,6-dihydroxy
270(15849)	365 270 245	Isopimpinellin
270(14700)	348 270 243	Benzoic acid, 3-hydroxy-4-nitro
270(14000)	337 270 252 247	1,4-Naphthoquinone, 2-chloro
270(16596)	328 270 263	Vitamin K_1
270(7943)	328 270	Isoquinoline, 1-hydroxy
270(28840)	316 270	Flavone, 5,7-dihydroxy
270(14791)	316 270 232	Acetophenone, 2,4-dihydroxy
270(10000)	315 270	1-Propanone, 1(2-furyl)
270(3981)	280 270 260	Pyridine, 2,5-dimethyl
270(16100)	270 217	Acetophenone, 4-methoxy
270(10300)	270 215	Benzene, 1-chloro-4-nitro
270(1259)	270	α-Alanine, *N*-alanyl (*l*)
270(3715)	270	Alloxantin
270(8320)	270	1,4-Benzoquinone, 2,6-dichloro
270(10000)	270	Chelidonic acid, diethyl ester
270(19953)	270	Cinnamic acid, 3-chloro (*trans*)
270(15849)	270	Furfural oxime, *(anti)*
270(15849)	270	2-Propanone, 1(4-methoxyphenyl)
270(19953)	270	Propenoic acid, 3(4-nitrophenyl)2-phenyl (*cis*)
270(12589)	270	Semicarbazide, 1,4-diphenyl-3-thio
270(11221)	270	Stilbene, 2-chloro (*cis*)
270(10000)	270	Stilbene, α,β-dichloro (*trans*)
270(18621)	270	Sulfone, diphenyl, 4-amino
270(9840)	270	Theophylline
270(12882)	270	2-Thiazolidinethione
270(10400)	270	Toluene, 2-bromo-4-nitro
270(13000)	270	Toluene, α,α-dibromo-4-nitro
269(4074)	320 269	Quinoline, 7-bromo
269(5980)	313 269	2,3-Pyrazinedicarboxylic acid
269(39811)	308 269	Propenoic acid, 3(2-naphthyl) (*trans*)
269(22900)	269	Benzoic acid, 4-acetamido
269(18621)	269	2-Butene-1,4-dione, 1,4-diphenyl (*trans*)
269(7413)	269	2,3-Decalindione (*trans*)
269(3030)	269	3,4-Pyridinedicarboxylic acid
269(9333)	269	Thymidine
268(20893)	440 330 268	1,4-Naphthoquinone, 2,3-dihydroxy
268(33113)	406 268	Biquinone, 3,3′-dihydroxy-5,5′-dimethyl
268(4780)	317 310 303 268	Naphthalene, 2-fluoro
268(16218)	315 268 257	5,8,11,14-Eicosatetraenoic acid

Strongest Band (ε)	Wavelengths (nm)	Compound
268(41500)	310 298 268 210	9-Fluorenone, 2-amino
268(19953)	300 268	Isocorydine
268(15849)	268 262	2,5-Cyclohexadien-1-one, hexachloro
268(20417)	268 221 215 210	Cinnamic acid (*trans*)
268(19953)	268 210	Biphenyl, 4,4′-dihydroxy
268(21700)	268	Benzenearsonic acid, 4-amino
268(17783)	268	Cinnamic acid, α-chloro, methyl ester (*trans*)
268(6607)	268	Naphthalene, 1,2-dihydro-3-methyl
268(4571)	268	Quinoline, 5,6,7,8-tetrahydro
268(10233)	268	Stilbene, 2-bromo (*cis*)
268(12589)	268	Toluene, 2,4-dinitro-6-hydroxy
268(9772)	268	Uracil, 1-methyl
267(32359)	447 373 267	Riboflavin
267(19953)	417 317 267	Ketone, benzyl phenyl, α-diazo
267(15849)	297 267	Phenanthrene, 9,10-dihydro
267(1259)	273 267	Benzenesulfonic acid, fluoride
267(38019)	267 260	Pyridine, 2(hydroxymethyl)
267(15849)	267 222	Benzoic acid, amide, *N*-phenyl
267(15849)	267	Benzaldehyde, hydrazone
267(9550)	267	Cinnamic acid (*cis*) (2nd form)
267(7413)	267	α-Elaterin
267(16982)	267	Imidazole, 2-mercapto-1-methyl
267(4367)	267	Pyridine, 2,6-dimethyl
267(4074)	267	β-Sitosterol
267(11482)	267	Toluene, 2,5-dinitro
267(20417)	267	Urea, 1,1,3,3-tetraphenyl
266(25200)	425 266	Biphenyl, 4-amino-3-nitro
266(20400)	397 309 295 266	Naphthalene, 1-hydroxy-2-nitro
266(21878)	348 266	Xanthyletin
266(14125)	315 266	Thiophene, 2,5-diiodo
266(29400)	303 292 266	9,9′-Bifluorenyl
266(19953)	301 290 266	Fluorene
266(17378)	293 266	2-Coumaronecarboxylic acid
266(1862)	280 271 266	Benzene, 1-fluoro-4-iodo
266(2200)	273 266	Phosphoric acid, tris(3,4-dimethylphenyl) ester
266(21200)	266 259	1,4-Benzoquinone, tetramethyl
266(15488)	266 245	Urea, 1-phenyl-2-thio
266(2818)	266	Acetic acid, amide, *N*(2-aminophenyl)
266(14454)	266	Benzene, 1,4-dinitro
266(9772)	266	Cinnamic acid (*cis*) (3rd form)
266(2630)	266	1,2-Cyclohexanedione
266(5012)	266	Pyridine, hydrochloride
266(3631)	266	Pyridine, 2,3-dimethyl
265(15849)	750 390 320 265	Benzene, 1-nitro-3-nitroso
265(18197)	367 282 265	Amine, diphenyl, 3-nitro
265(29512)	335 265	1,2-Naphthoquinone, 7-hydroxy
265(12589)	310 265	Benzaldehyde, 3,4-methylenedioxy, oxime
265(15849)	305 292 265	Fluorene, 9-phenyl
265(6310)	305 265	Benzaldehyde, 2-hydroxy, oxime
265(13489)	295 265	Benzoic acid, 2-hydroxy, amide, *N*-phenyl
265(1259)	285 265	Disulfide, dibenzyl
265(3981)	272 265	3-Pyridinecarboxylic acid, 1-methyl
265(2512)	270 265	Pyridine, 2,4-dimethyl
265(7244)	265 234	Urea, 1,3-diethyl-2-thio
265(11000)	265 210	Acetic acid, thiono, amide
265(17378)	265	Benzaldehyde, 4-methoxy, oxime
265(10600)	265	Benzaldehyde, 4-nitro
265(10233)	265	Benzene, 1-bromo-2,4-dinitro
265(5012)	265	Benzenesulfinic acid, 2-nitro

Strongest Band (ϵ)	Wavelengths (nm)	Compound
265(19953)	265	Biphenyl, 4,4′-dihydroxy-3,3′-dimethyl
265(15849)	265	Biphenyl, 2,4′-dinitro
265(26303)	265	4-Biphenylcarboxylic acid, nitrile
265(18621)	265	Calciferol
265(3162)	265	Disulfide, dimethyl, 1,1,1′,1′-tetraphenyl
265(15136)	265	Ethene, tetracyano
265(16982)	265	Furfural oxime *(syn)*
265(40200)	265	2,5-Heptadien-4-one-2,6-dimethyl
265(3981)	265	Pyridine, 2,3,4-trimethyl
265(31623)	265	Stilbene, α,β-dinitro (*cis*)
265(6918)	265	α-Terpinene
265(12589)	265	2-Thiophenecarboxaldehyde,oxime *(syn)*
265(10700)	265	Toluene, α-chloro-2-nitro
265(7230)	265	Toluene, 5-chloro-2-nitro
265(7943)	265	Uracil, 5-methyl
264(19055)	430 300 282 264	Frangulin A
264(13804)	429 312 264	1,4-Benzoquinone, 2-methyl
264(16596)	420 264 255	Amine, diphenyl, 2,2′-dinitro
264(24100)	311 264 220	Amine, di(2-pyridyl)
264(16218)	304 264 288	Benzene, 1,4-diamino-2,3,5,6-tetramethyl
264(16218)	304 264 228	Benzene, 1,4-bis(dimethylamino)
264(10000)	299 264	2-Stilbenecarboxylic acid (*cis*)
264(13804)	295 264 240	Aniline, 4-methylthio
264(3440)	270 264	Pyridine, 2-bromo
264(1180)	269 264	Benzene, 1,2,4-trihydroxy triacetate
264(16982)	264 222	Hydantoin, 2-thio
264(11221)	264	Benzenesulfinic acid, 4-nitro
264(9310)	264	Benzenesulfonic acid, 4-nitro
264(21379)	264	Benzoic acid, 4-bromo, chloride
264(23100)	264	Biphenyl, 4,4′-dimethoxy
264(1023)	264	Disiloxane, 1,3-diphenyl-1,1,3,3-tetramethyl
264(10900)	264	Furfural, 5-nitro, semicarbazone
264(14454)	264	Guanidine, 1-nitro
264(30199)	264	α-Ionone, semicarbazone (*dl*)
264(5890)	264	2-Pyridinesulfonic acid
264(7700)	264	Toluene, 3-nitro
263(33885)	416 338 263	Quinoxaline, 5-hydroxy
263(32400)	344 263	Benzene, 1,4-dibenzoyl
263(31623)	325 263	Isoflavone, 4′,5,7-trihydroxy
263(29800)	307 263	Anthracene, 9,10-dihydro-9-oxo
263(14600)	306 263	Chalcone, 3,4-methylenedioxy
263(25119)	305 263	Cinnamic acid, 3-nitro (*trans*)
263(1122)	271 263	Ethane, 1,1,2,2-tetraphenyl
263(1080)	270 263	Phosphoric acid, tri(3-tolyl)ester
263(13400)	263 217 212	β-Styrenesulfonic acid, chloride (*trans*)
263(11221)	263	Benzenediazonium chloride
263(3981)	263	3-Chromene
263(19500)	263	Ergothioneine
263(13804)	263	2,3-Furandicarboxylic acid
263(15849)	263	2,5-Furandicarboxylic acid
263(5248)	263	Mannosaccharic acid, γ,γ′-dilactone (*d*)
263(3311)	263	α-Phellandrene (*d*)
263(8128)	263	1-Propanone, 2,2-dimethyl-1-phenyl
263(7080)	263	Pyridine, 2-ethyl
263(3981)	263	4-Pyridinecarboxylic acid, hydrazide
262(15488)	503 314 262	Indophenin
262(15488)	503 314 262	Indophenol
262(31623)	365 262	Flavone, 2′,3,3′,5,7-pentahydroxy
262(46773)	335 296 266 262	Phenanthrene, 3-nitro

Strongest Band (ε)	Wavelengths (nm)	Compound
262(15136)	319 262 251 242 233 225	Benzaldehyde,imine, *N*(3-tolyl)
262(19953)	319 262	Benzoic acid, amide, *N*(3-nitrophenyl)
262(15849)	310 262	Sulfapyridine
262(6457)	308 262	Benzene, 1-iodo-3-nitro
262(5012)	294 285 262 257	Indazole, 6-methyl
262(6310)	290 262	Benzaldehyde, pentachloro
262(15849)	280 262	Thiocyanic acid, 4-aminophenyl ester
262(1288)	273 262	Methane, tetraphenyl
262(3802)	268 262	Pyridine, 2-isopropyl
262(15849)	262	Acetophenone, 4-iodo
262(3388)	262	Anatabine (*l*)
262(3430)	262	Benzenesulfonic acid, 4-amino, amide
262(24700)	262	Benzophenone, 4,4′-dichloro
262(13300)	262	Biphenyl, 4-amino-2′-nitro
262(9772)	262	$\Delta^{5,7}$-Cholestadien-3β-ol
262(14454)	262	Cinnamic acid, α-chloro (*cis*)
262(22908)	262	Cinnamic acid, α-fluoro
262(2951)	262	Nicotine (*d*)
262(2951)	262	Nicotine (*l*)
262(2951)	262	Nornicotine (*l*)
262(13000)	262	Phenol, 6-bromo-2,4-dinitro
262(11482)	262	Propenoic acid, 3(2-nitrophenyl)-2-phenyl (*trans*)
262(3981)	262	Pyridine, 2-propyl
262(3548)	262	2-Pyridinecarboxylic acid, ethyl ester
262(12023)	262	2-Pyrrolecarboxylic acid
262(25119)	262	Stilbene, α,β-dinitro (*trans*)
262(7210)	262	Toluene, α-hydroxy-3-nitro
262(6310)	262	Urea, 1,3-diphenyl-1-methyl
262(15300)	262	Urea, 2-thio-1(4-tolyl)
262(10000)	262	Uridine
262(10471)	262	Uridylic acid
261(12303)	325 261 244 235 226	Benzaldehyde,imine, *N*(2-tolyl)
261(10965)	320 261	Benzoic acid, 2-amino-4-hydroxy
261(7413)	318 261	Isocoumarin
261(14125)	312 298 261	Acetophenone, 4-nitro
261(6420)	311 267 261 255	Pyrazine
261(2130)	297 261 255	Anabasine (*l*)
261(41687)	272 261 252	1,3,5-Hexatriene, 2,5-dimethyl
261(1730)	271 264 261 257 250	Benzene, bromo
261(22300)	261 244	Sulfadiazine
261(15200)	261 236	Aniline, *N*-benzylidene
261(14791)	261 203	Imidazole, 4-phenyl
261(15800)	261	Acetophenone, α,4-dibromo
261(16900)	261	Benzene, 1-iodo-4-methoxy
261(5500)	261	Benzenearsonic acid, 2-nitro
261(20500)	261	Benzoic acid, 4-hydroxyphenyl ester
261(18100)	261	Biphenyl, 4-hydroxy
261(20893)	261	Biphenyl, 4-methoxy
261(3467)	261	1,3,5-Cycloheptatriene
261(16982)	261	2-Furancarboxylic acid, 5-chloro, methyl ester
261(18700)	261	Sulfide, diphenyl 4-nitro
260(28000)	389 349 333 260	Naphthalene, 1-hydroxy-2-nitroso
260(39811)	375 295 260	2-Naphthaldehyde, 1-hydroxy
260(25119)	370 260	Benzophenone, 3(dimethylamino)
260(30902)	360 260	Acridine, 9-phenyl
260(19953)	350 330 300 270 260	1,2-Naphthoquinone, dioxime
260(15849)	350 260	Stilbene, 4-methoxy-4′-nitro (*cis*)
260(5012)	346 304 260	Benzaldehyde, 2,4,6-trichloro
260(8710)	335 285 260	Thiophene, 3-nitro

Strongest Band (ϵ)	Wavelengths (nm)	Compound
260(15849)	335 260	Benzophenone, 4-methyl
260(34000)	335 260	4-Quinolinecarboxylic acid, 2-phenyl
260(6166)	313 260	Benzene, 1-methoxy-3-nitro
260(19499)	310 260	Aniline, 4-bromo-*N,N*-dimethyl
260(5012)	310 260	Styrene, 3-amino
260(12023)	305 267 260	Isosafrole (*trans*)
260(1220)	304 293 260	Propanoic acid, 3,3,3-triphenyl
260(1390)	304 260	Aniline, *N,N*-diethyl
260(10965)	269 260 259 248	Cyclopentane, phenyl
260(16982)	260 241	Sulfamethazine
260(22387)	260 237	Sulfone, diphenyl,4,4′-dimethoxy
260(11221)	260 230	3,3′-Bithiophene
260(4800)	260	Benzene, 2,4-dichloro-1-nitro
260(3880)	260	Benzene, 1-nitro-2,3,4-trichloro
260(3981)	260	Benzenesulfenic acid, 2,4-dinitro, chloride
260(6310)	260	Benzoic acid, 3-nitro, amide
260(6026)	260	Borine, trimethyl
260(18197)	260	2-Butene-1,4-dione, 1,4-diphenyl (*cis*)
260(1660)	260	Coniferin
260(11749)	260	Guanylic acid
260(5012)	260	Humulon
260(6310)	260	Naphthalene, 1,2-dihydro-4-methyl
260(14125)	260	2,4-Pentadienoic acid, 4-hydroxy, lactone
260(10000)	260	Phosphine, triphenyl
260(19953)	260	2-Propen-1-ol, 3(4-hydroxyphenyl)
260(2512)	260	3-Pyridinecarboxylic acid, methyl ester
260(18621)	260	Pyrrolidine, 1-phenyl
260(10471)	260	Stilbene, 4-fluoro (*cis*)
260(12882)	260	Stilbene, 2-nitro (*cis*)
260(15849)	260	Styrene, β,β-dichloro
260(6918)	260	Thiazole, 2-amino-5-methyl
260(5800)	260	Toluene, α-hydroxy-2-nitro
259(11600)	373 308 259 224	Phenol, 2-amino-4-nitro
259(32359)	368 259	Folic acid
259(13300)	305 259	Aniline, *N,N*-dibutyl
259(16900)	305 259	Aniline, *N,N*-dipropyl
259(7080)	298 259	Indazole, 7-amino
259(8710)	293 259	Benzoic acid, 3,4-dihydroxy
259(18621)	289 259	Benzene, 1-hydroxy-4(1-propenyl)
259(12589)	278 268 259	Thiophthene (solid)
259(1288)	266 259 254	Benzene, fluoro
259(2990)	265 259 253 241	2-Pyridinecarboxaldehyde
259(2700)	265 259	4-Pyridinecarboxaldehyde
259(12023)	259 221	Barbituric acid, 1-methyl
259(7520)	259 218	Phthalide, 6-nitro
259(14800)	259	Acetic acid, amide, *N*(4-aminophenyl)
259(5710)	259	Acetic acid, (2-nitrophenyl)
259(7943)	259	Amine, di-3-tolyl
259(7180)	259	Benzene, nitro
259(20500)	259	Benzil
259(10000)	259	Benzoic acid, 4-nitro, ethyl ester
259(25704)	259	Biphenyl, 4-iodo
259(10000)	259	1,3-Cyclohexadiene
259(4898)	259	1,3-Cyclohexadiene, 5-methyl (*dl*)
259(3162)	259	Pyridine, 4-benzyl
258(24500)	500 331 258	1,3-Cyclopentadienone, tetraphenyl
258(14400)	424 258 218	Amine, diphenyl, 2-nitro
258(39811)	420 323 258	9,10-Anthraquinone, 2-nitro
258(39811)	400 322 258	9,10-Anthraquinone, 1,5-dinitro
258(38019)	382 364 329 258	2,4,6-Cycloheptatrien-1-one, 3-bromo-2-hydroxy

Strongest Band (ε)	Wavelengths (nm)	Compound
258(25119)	352 306 258	Naphthalene, 2-nitro
258(19953)	350 258	Quercitrin
258(34674)	330 258	Fluorene, 9(4-bromobenzylidene)
258(35482)	330 258	Fluorene, 9(4-methylbenzylidene)
258(41687)	312 298 258	Fluorene, 9(2-methylbenzylidene)
258(19055)	295 258	Propene, 1,1-dichloro-3-phenyl
258(23442)	293 258	Fluorene, 9-amino
258(13804)	292 258	Benzene, 1-hydroxy-2-methoxy-4-propenyl (*cis*)
258(24547)	290 258	Pyridine, 4(dimethylamino)
258(19055)	282 258	Sulfide, diphenyl,4,4′-dibromo
258(6166)	279 258	Indazole, 6-amino
258(43658)	268 258 247	1,3,5-Hexatriene (*trans*)
258(1200)	264 258 253	Ethanol, 1,1,2-triphenyl
258(12000)	258	Benzoic acid, 4-nitro, methyl ester
258(19953)	258	Benzophenone, 2-nitro
258(22387)	258	Cinnamic acid, α-methyl-3-nitro
258(15136)	258	Propynoic acid, phenyl, ethyl ester
258(1995)	258	Pyridine, 4-chloro
258(5012)	258	Pyridine, 3,4-dimethyl
258(3631)	258	1,3,5-Triazine, 2,4-diamino
257(10471)	384 365 257	Anthracene, 1-chloro
257(10000)	335 257	Toluene, 3-hydroxy-2,4,6-trinitro
257(35482)	334 325 257	Quinoline, 4-hydroxy-2-phenyl
257(16218)	329 282 257	Thiophene, 3-benzoyl
257(40738)	328 257	9,10-Anthraquinone-1-sulfonic acid
257(16218)	313 257	Chalcone, α-nitro
257(14791)	308 257	Aniline, 4-chloro-*N*,*N*-dimethyl
257(6166)	307 257	Benzene, 1,3-dichloro-5-nitro
257(5012)	294 257	1,2,3,4-Benzenetetracarboxylic acid
257(10000)	275 257	Selenide, di(4-tolyl)
257(16596)	257 253	1-Propanone, 1,3,3-triphenyl
257(38100)	257 241	Thianthrene
257(18700)	257 208	Benzoic acid, 4-ethoxy, ethyl ester
257(14454)	257 206	Cinnamic acid, α-bromo (*cis*)
257(7943)	257	Acetic acid, 3-nitrophenyl ester
257(7763)	257	Benzene, (ethylthio)
257(22387)	257	Benzenesulfonic acid, 4-amino, amide, *N*-acetyl
257(12600)	257	Benzoic acid, 4-nitro, nitrile
257(20100)	257	Benzophenone, 4-chloro
257(8128)	257	Cinnamic acid, β-chloro (*cis*)
257(16596)	257	1,3-Cyclohexanedione, 5,5-dimethyl
257(26303)	257	Formaldomedone
257(12589)	257	2-Furancarboxylic acid, 5-methyl
257(5496)	257	Thiazole, 2-amino-4-methyl
257(19953)	257	Urea, 1(4-aminobenzenesulfonyl)-2-thio
256(15849)	450 292 256	9,10-Anthraquinone, 1,3,8-trihydroxy
256(36308)	400 256 234	1,2-Benz-3,4-anthraquinone
256(32359)	332 307 256	Carbazole, 3-nitro-9-nitroso
256(46800)	302 293 256 247 225	9-Fluorenone, oxime
256(16982)	294 256	Disulfide, diphenyl, 4,4′-diamino
256(14454)	289 256	Benzene, 1,2-dimethoxy-4-propenyl-(*cis*)
256(11400)	288 256	Anthracene, 1,8,9-trihydroxy
256(7763)	267 256 228	Biphenyl, 2,2′-dimethyl
256(22387)	266 256 247	1,3,5-Hexatriene (*cis*)
256(1995)	262 256 252	Pyridine, 4-isopropyl
256(19953)	256 310	Glucose phenylosazone (*d*)
256(18700)	256 206	Cinnamic acid, α-methyl (*cis*)
256(10300)	256	Acetaldehyde, 2-oxo-2-phenyl, 1-oxime
256(5623)	256	Acetic acid, 2-nitrophenyl ester
256(2470)	256	Benzoic acid, 4-hydroxy, butyl ester

Strongest Band (ε)	Wavelengths (nm)	Compound
256(16400)	256	Benzoic acid, 4-hydroxy, ethyl ester
256(17100)	256	Benzoic acid, 4-hydroxy, propyl ester
256(10000)	256	Ethane, 1,2-bis(phenylthio)
256(19953)	256	Semicarbazide, 4-phenyl-3-thio
256(14454)	256	Toluene, α,α-dichloro-4-nitro
256(36308)	256	Urea, 1,3-di(2-naphthyl)-2-thio
256(36308)	256	Urea, 1,3-diphenyl
256(16982)	256	Urea, 1,1,3,3-tetramethyl-2-thio
255(33113)	362 255	Sulfaquinoxaline
255(19953)	355 310 270 255	Isobergaptene
255(10000)	350 255	Benzoic acid, 3-nitro, hydrazide
255(10471)	350 255	Reductic acid
255(25119)	340 298 255	Peucedanin
255(12023)	337 327 255	Acetophenone, α,α-dibromo
255(39811)	335 322 288 255	Disulfide, 2,2′-dinaphthyl
255(37153)	325 255	9,10-Anthraquinone, 1-nitro
255(10000)	315 255	Benzophenone, 3-methoxy
255(6166)	315 255	Ether, diphenyl, 2-nitro
255(44200)	298 255 219	Thioxanthone
255(12589)	290 280 255	Strychnine
255(13489)	289 255	Biphenyl, 2,2′,4,4′-tetrahydroxy
255(6310)	288 255	Gelsemine hydrochloride (*d*)
255(9333)	275 255 235	Selenide, diphenyl
255(12303)	274 272 263 255	4-Toluenesulfonic acid, propyl ester
255(1995)	265 255	Pyridine, 3,5-dimethyl-2-ethyl
255(1995)	265 255	Pyridine, 4-ethyl
255(6310)	262 255 250	Pyridine, sulfate
255(19200)	255 207	Benzoic acid, 4-methoxy, methyl ester
255(8440)	255	Acetophenone, 3,4-dimethyl
255(5220)	255	Acetophenone, 2-nitro
255(14454)	255	5-Adenylic acid
255(13183)	255	Amine, 3,4-ditolyl, hydrochloride
255(31623)	255	9,10-Anthraquinone-1,5-disulfonic acid
255(21300)	255	Benzaldehyde, 4-methyl
255(19953)	255	Benzenesulfonic acid, 4-acetamido, amide
255(7120)	255	Benzoic acid, 3-methyl-4-nitro
255(18621)	255	Benzoic acid, 4-phenoxy
255(12023)	255	Biphenyl, 3,3′-dihydroxy
255(21600)	255	Biphenyl, 4,4′-dimethyl
255(15488)	255	Biuret, thio
255(15488)	255	1,3-Cyclobutanedione, 2-methyl
255(6310)	255	Ethanol, 1-cyclohexyl
255(10965)	255	Phenol, 4-mercapto
255(14000)	255	Propynoic acid, phenyl
255(8128)	255	Semicarbazide, 2-phenyl-3-thio
255(12882)	255	Stibine, triphenyl
255(10715)	255	Strychnine, sulfate
255(6026)	255	5-Thiazolecarboxylic acid, 4-methyl
255(6330)	255	2,3-Thiazoline, 2-amino
254(35800)	352 339 254 246 220	2-Naphthoic acid, l-hydroxy
254(46600)	336 254	Ellagic acid, dihydrate
254(15400)	324 254 210	Benzaldehyde, 4-hydroxy-3-nitro
254(12882)	303 254	Aniline, 3-bromo-*N*,*N*-dimethyl
254(11900)	290 254	Benzoic acid, 3-chloro-4-hydroxy
254(12589)	287 279 254	Strychnine, hydrochloride
254(9333)	282 254	Oxindole, l-amino
254(6026)	281 274 254	Benzimidazole, l-methyl
254(22908)	254	Acetic acid, amide, *N*(4-iodophenyl)
254(9270)	254	Acetic acid, oxo(phenyl), methyl ester

Strongest Band (ε)	Wavelengths (nm)	Compound
254(18300)	254	Acetophenone, 4-bromo
254(7943)	254	Ascorbic acid (*d*)
254(22000)	254	Benzene, 1,2-dibenzoyl
254(7800)	254	Benzene, 1-fluoro-3-nitro
254(9550)	254	Benzene, methylthio
254(17800)	254	Benzoic acid, 4-ethoxy
254(15100)	254	Benzoic acid, 4-hydroxy
254(19953)	254	Benzoic acid, 4-methoxy, ethyl ester
254(12303)	254	Butanal, 2-benzylidene
254(14125)	254	Cinnamic acid, β-chloro, methyl ester (*trans*)
254(9120)	254	2,3-Furandicarboxylic acid, dimethyl ester
254(15849)	254	Pyrimidine, 4(methylamino)
254(16596)	254	Styrene, β-chloro (*trans*)
254(6810)	254	Sulfide, benzyl phenyl
254(5610)	254	Toluene, 2,3-dinitro
254(4330)	254	Toluene, 2-nitro
253(2512)	511 253	1,2,4,5-Tetrazine
253(19499)	426 317 253	1,4-Benzoquinone, 2,6-dimethyl
253(42658)	415 333 270 266 253	9,10-Phenanthroquinone, 1-chloro
253(16100)	344 329 253 221 218	9-Anthracenecarboxylic acid
253(25119)	340 253	1,2-Naphthoquinone, 3-methyl
253(14454)	329 253	Benzene, 1-amino-4-methylamino
253(12700)	310 253	Physostigmine
253(13183)	298 253	Toluene, 3(dimethylamino)
253(10000)	294 253 228	Tetralin, 1,4-dioxo
253(11200)	294 253 221	1,4-Benzoquinone, 2,5-di-*tert*-butyl
253(10233)	293 253	Benzene, 1,3-dihydroxy-2,4-dinitroso
253(10000)	291 253	Benzene, l-bromo-4-triazo
253(14454)	285 253	Phthalic acid, 3,4-dimethoxy
253(6060)	253 210	Toluene, 2-chloro-6-nitro
253(10700)	253	Benzene, 1-amino-4-dimethylamino
253(7763)	253	Benzenearsonic acid, 3-nitro
253(16500)	253	Benzoic acid, 4-methoxy
253(13000)	253	Guanosine
253(10000)	253	Piperidine, 1-phenyl
253(14791)	253	1-Propanone, 2,3-dibromo-1,3-diphenyl (threo)
253(13804)	253	1-Propanone, 2,3-dibromo-1,3-diphenyl (erythro)
253(1906)	253	Propene, 1-chloro-1-phenyl
253(3020)	253	Propene, 1-chloro-3-phenyl
253(20417)	253	Propene, 3-chloro-1-phenyl (*trans*)
253(31623)	253	Quinoline, 3-phenyl
253(43658)	253	Quinoline, 6-phenyl
253(19499)	253	Styrene, 4-chloro
253(4467)	253	Thiazole, 2,4-dimethyl
253(6457)	253	Verbenone (*d*)
252(28839)	402 327 266 252	Anthraquinone, 1-hydroxy
252(23988)	382 331 278 252	Lapachol
252(7943)	380 334 252	Xanthone, 1,8-dihydroxy
252(21700)	376 356 338 296 252	Anthracene, 2-methyl
252(42700)	356 340 276 252 224	Phenanthrene, 3-hydroxy
252(17378)	350 338 291 252	Benzophenone, 3,3′-dibromo
252(25119)	345 252	1,2-Naphthoquinone, 4-methyl
252(12023)	344 252	Chalcone, 2-methoxy
252(28500)	335 252	Quinoline, 8-amino-2-methyl
252(15849)	332 282 252	Benzophenone, 2-methyl
252(31623)	332 275 252	Dibenzothiophene, 2-nitro, dioxide
252(18600)	331 252	Benzophenone
252(31623)	330 303 276 252	Cyanamide, phenyl
252(39811)	325 252	Quinoline, 2-phenyl
252(45709)	318 275 252	Benzene, 1,5-diacetyl-2,4-dihydroxy

Strongest Band (ϵ)	Wavelengths (nm)	Compound
252(40738)	314 252 210	Phenanthrene, 3-acetyl
252(4571)	305 293 252	Indazole, 5-methyl
252(11200)	303 252	Benzaldehyde, 2,5-dimethyl
252(44000)	297 287 252 216 210	Styrene, 3-chloro
252(5248)	296 286 259 252	Indazole, 7-methyl
252(5248)	292 252	Oxindole, 3-hydroxy
252(9333)	291 284 252	Indene, 3-methyl
252(23200)	291 252 217	Isatin, 3-oxime
252(8710)	286 278 252	Benzothiazoline, 3-methyl-2-imino
252(25119)	283 279 252	Piperazine, 1,4-diphenyl
252(20893)	282 252	Hydrolapachol
252(7413)	280 252	Gelsemine (*d*)
252(13700)	274 252	Sulfide, 4,4′-ditolyl
252(1259)	265 258 252	Acetic acid, hydroxy(phenyl) (*dl*)
252(16700)	264 258 252 247	Acetic acid, phenyl, amide
252(18621)	252	Acetic acid, amide, *N*(4-bromophenyl)
252(12300)	252	Acetophenone, 4-methyl
252(4400)	252	Benzaldehyde, 2-nitro
252(3236)	252	Benzene, 1-chloro-2-nitro
252(9120)	252	Benzene, 1-isopropyl-4-nitro
252(3060)	252	Benzenesulfonic acid, 4-amino
252(25704)	252	Benzil, dioxime *(syn)*
252(16500)	252	Benzoic acid, 4-iodo
252(17800)	252	Biphenyl, 4-methyl
252(23700)	252	Dithizone
252(13400)	252	Formic acid, amide, *N*-phenyl
252(13489)	252	2-Furancarboxylic acid, methyl ester
251(16596)	350 339 326 290 251	Benzophenone, 3,3′-dichloro
251(17300)	316 251 211	Acetophenone, 4-methoxy-3-nitro
251(7943)	305 295 251	Indene, 7-hydroxy
251(11600)	298 251	Aniline, *N,N*-dimethyl
251(11600)	293 251 220	1,4-Benzoquinone, 2,5-dimethyl
251(14125)	291 282 251	Acetophenone, 2,4-dimethyl
251(45600)	290 280 251 227	2-Naphthoic acid, 3-amino
251(4074)	290 251	Pyrrole, 2-acetyl
251(17783)	251 284 293	1-Butene, 1-phenyl (*cis*)
251(13489)	251 220	2-Furancarboxylic acid, ethyl ester
251(18000)	251 214	Furfurin
251(16982)	251	Acetic acid, amide, *N*-acetyl-*N*-(4-chlorophenyl)
251(7740)	251	1,4-Benzoquinone, 2-bromo-6-methyl
251(16218)	251	1-Butene, 1-phenyl (*trans*)
251(13700)	251	5-Pyrazolone-3-carboxylic acid, 1-phenyl
251(12589)	251	Quinoline, 2-oxo-1,2,3,4-tetrahydro
251(13183)	251	3-Thiophenecarboxaldehyde
251(13600)	251	Urea, 1,3-di(2-tolyl)-2-thio
250(25119)	490 458 435 250	9,10-Anthraquinone, 1,8-diamino
250(12589)	460 369 280 250	1,4-Benzoquinone, phenyl
250(28840)	390 304 250	Naphthalene, 2-acetyl-3-hydroxy
250(31623)	385 250	5,6-Chrysoquinone
250(20000)	376 355 338 322 309 296 250 220 218	Anthracene
250(31623)	375 308 250	Alstonine
250(5012)	360 250	Benzoic acid, 2-amino-5-hydroxy
250(10471)	354 338 287 253 250	Benzophenone, 2,2′-dichloro
250(6166)	343 287 250	Quinoxaline, 2-hydroxy
250(10700)	341 250	Malonic acid, ethoxymethylene dinitrile
250(39811)	340 290 250	Khellin
250(27543)	340 250	Quinoline, 8-amino
250(45500)	334 324 250	Quinoline, 5,7-dichloro-8-hydroxy
250(5012)	323 250	Benzoic acid, 3-amino, methyl ester

Strongest Band (ϵ)	Wavelengths (nm)	Compound
250(6310)	320 250	Benzoic acid, 3-amino, nitrile
250(43100)	312 250 221 209	Phenanthrene, 9-amino (a form)
250(48978)	311 281 250	Papaverine, hydrochloride
250(6310)	310 250	2-Propanone, 1(3-methoxyphenyl)
250(4930)	309 250	Benzoic acid, 3,5-dihydroxy
250(14900)	309 250	Dibenzoic acid, 2,2′-dithio
250(1000)	307 250	1,4-Dioxine
250(19953)	307 250	Hydrastinine
250(26925)	303 250	Isoflavone, 4′,7-dihydroxy
250(15849)	300 250	Hydrazine, 1,2-di(3-tolyl)
250(25119)	300 250	Propynal, 1-phenyl
250(7080)	300 250	Quinoline, 1,2,3,4-tetrahydro
250(12023)	297 286 250 223	Benzene, 1-hydroxy-2(1-propenyl) (*trans*)
250(5495)	296 284 250	Benzothiazole
250(8511)	293 250	Styrene, 3-methoxy
250(17378)	292 283 250	3-Butenoic acid, 4-phenyl
250(17100)	291 282 250 215	2-Propen-1-ol, 3-phenyl, acetate (*trans*)
250(12589)	280 250	Benzoic acid, 4-hydroxy-3-methyl
250(19953)	280 250	Cinnamaldehyde, 2-nitro
250(11482)	275 250 232	Sulfide, diphenyl,3-methyl
250(12303)	274 250 230	Sulfide, diphenyl,4-methyl
250(11400)	273 250 230	Sulfide, diphenyl
250(4677)	255 250 244 238 232	Thiophene, 3,4-dichloro
250(10100)	250 222	Acetophenone, 4-chloro
250(2020)	250	Aniline, *N,N*-dimethyl-3-nitro
250(2188)	250	Benzene, 2-nitro-1,3,5-trimethyl
250(16596)	250	Benzene, propenyl (*trans*)
250(10233)	250	Benzil, monooxime (α)
250(10233)	250	Benzil, monooxime (β)
250(7080)	250	1,2-Benzo-1-cyclooctene-3-one
250(5012)	250	Benzoic acid, 2-nitro, amide
250(12023)	250	Cyclohexene, 1-phenyl
250(17783)	250	α-Elemene (*d*)
250(6310)	250	Ethane, 1,2-dibromo-1,2-diphenyl (*meso*)
250(5012)	250	Formimidic acid, *N*-phenyl, ethyl ester
250(30600)	250	Hydrobenzamide
250(5120)	250	Methane, dichloro(diphenyl)
250(27543)	250	Phenanthrene, 4-amino
250(15136)	250	Pseudojervine
250(6607)	250	Pseudothiohydantoin
250(3311)	250	Pyrimidine, 5-methyl
250(5012)	250	Succinic acid, 2,3-diacetyl, diethyl ester (diketo form)
250(3467)	250	Thiazole, 4-methyl
250(8320)	250	Thiophene, 2,5-dibromo
249(31623)	345 310 249	Quinine, hydrochloride
249(31623)	345 310 249	Strychnine, nitrate
249(21500)	332 275 249 243	1,4-Naphthoquinone, 2-hydroxy
249(22387)	300 249	Xanthotoxin
249(12000)	296 249	Aniline, *N-sec*-butyl
249(2693)	295 255 249 245	Pyrimidine, 2-methyl
249(7943)	290 249	Ajmaline
249(4550)	280 249	Benzaldehyde, 2-methyl
249(2970)	279 249	Benzene, 1,3-dimethyl-4-hydroxy-2-nitro
249(1202)	275 249	Isothiocyanic acid, cyclohexyl ester
249(16596)	249 238	Propyne, 1-phenyl
249(17783)	249	Acetic acid, amide, *N*(4-chlorophenyl)
249(3000)	249	Acetophenone, 2,4,6-trimethyl
249(11000)	249	Hypoxanthine
249(13489)	249	Inosine

Strongest Band (ϵ)	Wavelengths (nm)	Compound
249(7763)	249	Pentanoic acid, 2-methyl (*l*)
249(16982)	249	α-Progesterone
249(15849)	249	Propanoic acid, 2-hydroxy, amide, *N*(4-ethoxyphenyl)
249(9300)	249	1-Propanone, 2-bromo-1-phenyl
249(40000)	249	1-Propanone, 1(4-chlorophenyl)
249(40738)	249	Thiazole, 5(2-hydroxyethyl)-4-methyl
248(25119)	520 440 280 248	3-Iosphenothiazin-3-one, 7-hydroxy
248(10965)	438 296 248	Azobenzene, 4,4′-dimethyl (*cis*)
248(25119)	435 248	9,10-Anthraquinone, 1,2-dihydroxy
248(12589)	424 321 248	1,4-Benzoquinone, 2-chloro
248(21878)	348 265 248	Rhizopterin
248(10471)	343 248	1,4-Benzoquinone, 2-methoxy
248(48600)	342 299 276 248 210	Phenanthrene, 9-hydroxy
248(16982)	338 325 287 278 248	Quinoline, 4-hydroxy-3-methyl
248(19499)	337 324 288 248	Quinoline, 2,3-dimethyl-4-hydroxy
248(12200)	335 292 248	1,4-Benzoquinone, 2,3-dimethyl
248(8318)	316 287 248	α-Benzosuberone
248(33700)	297 248 214	Naphthalene, 1,2-diamino
248(7943)	296 248	1,2,4-Benzenetricarboxylic acid
248(11000)	295 248	Aniline, *N*-isopropyl
248(17300)	290 280 248	Indene
248(15849)	290 248	Biphenyl, 4,4′-diamino-2,2′-dimethyl
248(11482)	290 248	1-Tetralone
248(23442)	284 257 248	Quinoline, 7-nitro
248(9333)	283 276 248	Benzofuran, 3-methyl
248(7943)	278 256 248	Benzene, triazo
248(25900)	277 248 226	Sulfone, diphenyl,4,4′-dichloro
248(12882)	274 248	Sulfide, 2,2′-ditolyl
248(12023)	272 248 232	Sulfide, diphenyl,2-methyl
248(1738)	270 248	Isothiocyanic acid, butyl ester
248(8710)	248 235	Propene, 1,1-diphenyl
248(14900)	248	Acetic acid, amide, *N*(4-methoxyphenyl)
248(13183)	248	Arsine, triphenyl
248(15488)	248	Benzene, 1-amino-3-mercapto
248(13804)	248	Benzenesulfonic acid, 4(4-aminophenylsulfonamido), amide
248(9550)	248	Benzoic acid, 3-chloro, amide
248(26100)	248	Biphenyl, 3-nitro
248(19953)	248	1,3-Butadiene, 1,2,3,4-tetrachloro (solid)
248(14454)	248	Butanoic acid, 3-oxo amide, *N*(4-tolyl)
248(15849)	248	Corticosterone
248(1318)	248	Isothiocyanic acid, benzyl ester
248(12900)	248	1,4-Naphthoquinone, 5-hydroxy
248(6310)	248	Toluene, 2(dimethylamino)
248(12023)	248	Toluene, 3,5-dinitro
248(11221)	227 292 248	Benzoic acid, 2,4-dihydroxy
247(12589)	370 247	Jervine
247(13804)	329 317 285 247	Quinoline, 4-hydroxy-2-methyl
247(10965)	316 247	Phenol, 4(dimethylamino)
247(1300)	309 247 242	Pyridazine
247(36900)	305 247	9,10-Anthraquinone, 1-amino-2-methyl
247(15300)	299 247	Benzoic acid, 2,5-diiodo
247(16200)	296 247	Toluene, 2-amino-5-iodo
247(12400)	295 247	Amine, benzyl phenyl
247(10400)	295 247	Aniline, *N*-butyl
247(9772)	291 247	2-Butenoic acid, 2-phenyl (*cis*)
247(15849)	288 247	Benzaldehyde, oxime *(anti)*
247(7080)	279 271 247	Benzimidazole, 4-methyl
247(25119)	276 247	Urea, 1(4-bromophenyl)
247(12400)	266 247	2-Thiophenecarboxylic acid, ethyl ester
247(13489)	247	Acetic acid, diazo, ethyl ester

Strongest Band (ε)	Wavelengths (nm)	Compound
247(4560)	247	Apoatropine, hydrochloride
247(4169)	247	Benzene, 1-isopropyl-2-nitro
247(16596)	247	Benzoic acid, 2-benzoyl, methyl ester
247(19300)	247	Biphenyl
247(25119)	247	Biphenyl, 3,3′-dichloro
247(12300)	247	2-Furancarboxylic acid
247(5623)	247	Phenanthrene, 1,2,3,4,11,12-hexahydro
247(5500)	247	Pyridine, 4-amino-2,6-dimethyl
247(8380)	247	2-Thiophenecarboxylic acid
247(4786)	229 247	Benzoic acid, 3,5-dimethoxy, amide
246(12589)	429 273 246	Aniline, *N,N*-dimethyl-2-nitro
246(26916)	415 284 246	9,10-Anthraquinone, 1,3-dihydroxy
246(42658)	354 285 246	Quinoline, 7-amino
246(19953)	354 246	Benzoic acid, amide, *N*(2-nitrophenyl)
246(19953)	354 246	Benzoic acid, 2-nitro, amide, *N*-phenyl
246(39811)	327 287 246	1-Naphthoic acid, 2-phenyl
246(8511)	315 246	Benzene, 1,4-diamino
246(7080)	309 246	Phenol, 3,4,5-tribromo
246(13183)	302 246	Toluene, 4(methylamino)
246(12589)	301 292 252 246	Benzaldehyde, 2-bromo
246(12589)	301 292 252 246	Benzaldehyde, 2-iodo
246(10000)	300 246	Aniline, *N,N*-dimethyl
246(2291)	298 246	Styrene, 2-methyl
246(7410)	291 282 246	Xanthene
246(15849)	289 278 246	Benzaldehyde, imine, *N*-ethyl
246(5560)	287 246	Biphenyl, 2-hydroxy
246(14125)	286 278 246	Acetic acid, amide, *N*(3-bromophenyl)
246(9610)	284 246	Biphenyl, 2-methoxy
246(8080)	281 246	Acetophenone, 2,4-dichloro
246(12589)	276 246	Pyridine, 3-phenyl
246(10000)	246	Aniline, *N,N*-diethyl-2-nitro
246(27300)	246	Benzene, 1-bromo-4-mercapto
246(16200)	246	Biphenyl, 3,3′-difluoro
246(6330)	246	Cyclohexanone, 2-butylidene
246(5623)	246	Propenoic acid, 2-phenyl
246(15849)	246	Pyridine, 4-amino
246(15849)	246	4-Pyrone
245(10000)	360 315 285 245	Benzophenone, 2-methoxy
245(40738)	355 285 245	Quinoline, 6-amino
245(3981)	350 245	Benzoic acid, 2-nitro, hydrazide
245(6310)	345 245	Benzene, 1,2-dihydroxy-4-nitro
245(31623)	340 325 315 245	Quinoxaline, 2,3-dichloro
245(19953)	335 245	Benzophenone, 3-amino
245(7943)	331 245	Pulegone
245(31900)	329 245	Quinoline, 5-bromo-8-hydroxy
245(7943)	326 279 245	Cotarnine
245(6310)	325 245	Benzoic acid, 2-amino, nitrile
245(3162)	320 245	Visnagin
245(19953)	318 245	Benzene, 1-nitro-3-triazo
245(15136)	310 280 245	Benzophenone, 2,4-dimethoxy
245(10900)	305 245	Aniline, 2,4-dichloro
245(12882)	301 245	1,3-Decalindione (*cis*)
245(10965)	300 245	Glycine, *N*(3-tolyl)
245(8511)	300 245	Pereirine
245(10000)	299 245	Conquinamine
245(10000)	299 245	Quinamine
245(7943)	298 245	Benzene, 1-amino-3-dimethylamino
245(10715)	295 245	Aniline, 4-chloro-*N*-methyl
245(12700)	294 283 277 245	Styrene, 4-fluoro

Strongest Band (ε)	Wavelengths (nm)	Compound
245(10233)	294 245	Acetic acid, (3-hydroxyphenyl), nitrile
245(11221)	291 285 245	Acetophenone, 3-methyl
245(6500)	291 245	Benzaldehyde, 3-bromo
245(13804)	290 278 245	Amine, benzylidene ethyl
245(10000)	290 245	2-Tetralone
245(10233)	288 245	Benzofuran, 5-methyl
245(10000)	285 278 245	Benzofuran
245(9910)	285 245	1,3-Benzenedicarboxylic acid, 4-bromo
245(19953)	285 245	Hydrazine, 1,2-di(2-tolyl)
245(5495)	283 277 245	Benzimidazole, 5-methyl
245(16596)	281 275 245	Benzimidazole, 1-phenyl
245(14125)	281 245	Ketone, phenyl 4′-piperidyl, 1′-methyl
245(11749)	280 245	Acetic acid, amide, *N*(3-methoxyphenyl)
245(13183)	280 245	Lobeline (*l*)
245(12882)	280 245	Propanoic acid, 3-oxo-3-phenyl, nitrile
245(10100)	261 245	1,3,6,8-Nonatetraen-5-one, 1,9-diphenyl
245(8913)	256 245	Benzaldehyde, 3-amino
245(19953)	245 233	Sulfone, 3,4′-ditolyl
245(14200)	245	Acetic acid, mercapto, amide, *N*-phenyl
245(10965)	245	Acetic acid, trifluoro, amide, *N*-phenyl
245(15136)	245	Amine, benzylidene methyl
245(7943)	245	Ascorbic acid (*dl*)
245(15136)	245	Benzaldehyde, imine, *N*-methyl
245(25119)	245	Benzoic acid, amide, *N*-benzoyl
245(13600)	245	Benzoic acid, 2-benzoyl
245(18197)	245	Benzoic acid, 4-bromo, methyl ester
245(14500)	245	Biphenyl, 4,4′-difluoro
245(11749)	245	2-Biphenylcarboxylic acid
245(15849)	245	Guanidine, 1-phenyl
245(10000)	245	1-Propanone, 1-phenyl,oxime
245(10000)	245	Pyrazole, 5-amino-3-methyl-l-phenyl
245(4786)	245	3-Pyrrolecarboxylic acid
244(18621)	372 266 244	Sulfide, methyl 2-nitrophenyl
244(12589)	362 244 241	Fulvene
244(29512)	350 244	Colchiceine
244(3162)	346 331 244	Ethene, 1,2-diiodo (*cis*)
244(26925)	331 320 244	β-Fagarine
244(15849)	304 244	Indazole, 5-nitro
244(3311)	302 290 244	Paraisobutyraldehyde
244(30199)	300 244	Biphenyl, 3,3′-dinitro
244(10471)	295 244	1,3-Decalindione (*trans*)
244(12589)	294 244	Toluene, 2(methylamino)
244(14454)	292 286 244	1-Indanone
244(7244)	291 244	Toluene, 2(ethylamino)
244(3162)	286 244	Morphine, 3-ethyl ether, hydrochloride dihydrate
244(11000)	286 244	1-Propanone, 1(3 tolyl)
244(13800)	282 244	Acetic acid, amide, *N*(3-tolyl)
244(10715)	282 244	Benzofuran, 7-methyl
244(14454)	281 268 244	Butanoic acid, 2,4-diphenyl-4-oxo, nitrile
244(24547)	280 244	Stilbene (*trans*)
244(7943)	253 245 244	Benzaldehyde, 3-iodo
244(41687)	244 234	Fluorene, 9,9-dichloro
244(18197)	244	Acetic acid, phenyl, amide, *N*-phenyl
244(17378)	244	Benzoic acid, 4-bromo, ethyl ester
244(8710)	244	2-Butene, 2-phenyl (*trans*)
244(2540)	244	Cyclohexanone, 2-ethylidene
244(14600)	244	Formic acid, amide, *N*-4-tolyl
244(3389)	244	Pyrimidine, 4-methyl
244(8913)	244	Urea, 1,3-dimethyl-1,3-diphenyl
243(10471)	433 281 243	Azobenzene (*cis*)

Strongest Band (ϵ)	Wavelengths (nm)	Compound
243(25119)	345 243	2-Quinolinecarboxylic acid, 4,8-dihydroxy
243(25119)	345 243	2-Quinolinecarboxylic acid, 4-hydroxy
243(49000)	337 285 278 243 214	Naphthalene, 2,3-diamino
243(21200)	325 243	Acetic acid, amide, *N*(4-chloro-3-nitrophenyl)
243(41600)	304 243	Quinoline, 8-hydroxy-2-methyl
243(10400)	296 243	Toluene, 2-amino-5-bromo
243(28184)	295 243	Quinoline, 3-nitro
243(12589)	290 282 243	Benzoic acid, 2,4-dimethyl
243(7160)	290 243	Benzaldehyde, 3-chloro
243(16218)	289 243	Urea, 1(4-methoxyphenyl)
243(9333)	285 243	Thiophene, 2-iodo
243(15300)	282 243	Benzene, 1,2-diethoxy
243(12589)	282 243	Disulfide, bis(dimethylthiocarbamyl)
243(2360)	280 243 238	Pyrimidine
243(12589)	280 243	Benzenesulfonic acid, 3-acetamido, amide
243(10965)	277 243	Benzene, isopropenyl
243(10200)	267 243 220	Antipyrine (α-form)
243(10200)	267 243 220	Antipyrine (β-form)
243(9700)	243	Acetic acid, amide, *N*(2-ethoxyphenyl)
243(11400)	243	Acetophenone, 2-methoxy
243(2512)	243	Alloxan
243(12300)	243	Azobenzene, 4,4′-dihydroxy
243(6340)	243	Benzaldehyde, 4-diethylamino
243(12023)	243	2-Butene, 2-phenyl (*cis*)
243(15136)	243	Coprostenone
243(12303)	243	2,4-Furandicarboxylic acid, dimethyl ester
243(15136)	243	Hexanoic acid, amide, *N*-phenyl
243(10800)	243	Isatoic acid, anhydride
243(14791)	243	Octadecanoic acid, anhydride
243(14454)	243	Propanoic acid, amide, *N*-phenyl
243(9772)	243	Pyridine, 4-bromo
243(13183)	243	Pyridine, 4-ethenyl
243(27900)	243	1,3,5-Triazine, 2,4-diamino-6-phenyl
242(22387)	426 304 242	Isatin, 1-methyl
242(17800)	420 304 248 242 213	Isatin, 7-methyl
242(25119)	397 337 242	2,4,6-Cycloheptatrien-1-one, 2-amino
242(39811)	383 332 318 242	10,11-Benzofluoranthene
242(22387)	370 282 242	Coumarin, 6-amino
242(39811)	361 242	Acetophenone, 3-dimethylamino
242(12589)	353 278 242	3-Terpinolenone
242(30199)	350 242	Quinoline, 3-amino (unstable form)
242(11500)	342 242	Phenol, 2-benzylideneamino
242(31623)	340 307 242	Naphthalene, 1-amino-3-hydroxy
242(47863)	329 290 242	Dibenzothiophene, 2,8-dibromo
242(22387)	326 270 242	Acetic acid, amide, *N*(3-nitrophenyl)
242(19499)	315 270 242	Disulfide, di-4-tolyl
242(10000)	315 242	Eseroline (*dl*)
242(10000)	315 242	Eseroline (*l*)
242(1660)	311 280 272 242	Fluorene, 9-hydroxy-9-phenyl
242(13300)	296 242	Toluene, 2-amino-5-chloro
242(18197)	290 242	Urea, 1(4-ethoxyphenyl)
242(44100)	283 242	Pyrene, 1-amino
242(13400)	280 242	Propanoic acid, 2-methyl, amide, *N*-phenyl
242(26500)	279 242	1,3,5-Triazine, hexahydro-1,3,5-triphenyl
242(8128)	275 242	Benzoic acid, 4-hydroxy-2-methyl
242(6310)	242 218	Maleic acid, dichloro
242(1023)	242	Acetic acid, amide, *N*-acetyl-*N*-phenyl
242(11900)	242	Acetophenone, 4-fluoro
242(8318)	242	Acetophenone, 2-methyl
242(1000)	242	Amine, tributyl

Strongest Band (ε)	Wavelengths (nm)	Compound
242(8913)	242	Benzoic acid, 2-chloro, chloride
242(38905)	242	Benzoic acid, 4-methyl, anhydride
242(25119)	242	Biphenyl, 3-acetamido
242(15600)	242	Butanoic acid, amide, *N*-phenyl
242(15488)	242	Corticosterone, 17-hydroxy
242(14454)	242	2-Cyclohexen-1-one, 2,3-dimethyl
242(14125)	242	Ergosterone
242(12303)	242	18 α-Glycyrrhetinic acid
242(13100)	242	2,4-Hexadiene, 2,5-dimethyl
242(24547)	242	2,4-Pentadienoic acid
242(10000)	242	Semicarbazide, 2-phenyl
242(10000)	242	Stilbene, α,β-dimethyl (*trans*)
242(12882)	242	Succinic acid, monoamide, *N*-phenyl
242(11482)	242	Urea, 1,1-diphenyl
241(10471)	354 241	Toluene, 3,5-dinitro-4-hydroxy
241(8710)	335 270 241	Phenol, seleno
241(21900)	325 275 241 218	Acetophenone, 3-amino-4-methoxy
241(28840)	323 312 241	1-Naphthalenesulfonic acid, 5-hydroxy
241(9772)	318 241	Eremophilone
241(13800)	313 278 241	1-Propanone, 2-methyl-1-phenyl
241(21379)	312 241	Ergocristinine
241(20893)	312 241	Ergosinine
241(19953)	311 241	Ergine
241(12400)	308 241	Benzoic acid, 2-hydroxy, phenyl ester
241(16300)	303 241	4-Cholesten-3-one
241(14125)	287 278 247 241	Benzaldehyde
241(17500)	286 241	1,4-Benzenedicarboxylic acid
241(9333)	283 241	Hydrazine, phenyl
241(16218)	280 241	Disulfide, di-3-tolyl
241(13489)	280 241	Urea, 1(3-ethoxyphenyl)
241(10500)	278 241	1-Dodecanone, 1-phenyl
241(14200)	277 241	1-Hexanone, 1-phenyl
241(16982)	250 241	2-Propyn-1-ol, 3-phenyl
241(3631)	241 238	Ascaridole
241(23442)	241 234	Abietic acid
241(7260)	241 233 220	Abietic acid, methyl ester
241(15800)	241	Biguanide, 1(2-tolyl)
241(11221)	241	1,3-Butadiene, 2-phenyl
241(2570)	241	Cyanuric acid, trichloride
241(28300)	241	Disulfide, diphenyl, 3,3′-dinitro
241(15488)	241	Dodecanoic acid, amide, *N*-phenyl
241(18621)	241	2,4-Pentadienoic acid, nitrile (*trans*)
241(2010)	241	Pentanedioic acid, 3-oxo, diethyl ester
241(16982)	241	Testosterone
241(8318)	241	3-Thiophenecarboxylic acid
241(12023)	241	Toluene, 4-amino-α-hydroxy
240(20417)	515 468 405 330 283 240	4-Pregnene-11β,17α,20β,21-tetrol-3-one
240(23800)	445 297 240	9,10-Anthraquinone, 2-amino
240(25119)	415 340 240	1,2-Naphthoquinone
240(23442)	388 240	1,4-Benzoquinone, 2,5-diphenyl
240(12589)	380 270 240	Benzaldehyde, 2-dimethylamino
240(39811)	365 290 240	2-Naphthoic acid, 3-hydroxy, methyl ester
240(39811)	360 240	Quinoline, 8-methoxy
240(7943)	350 290 280 240	Luminol
240(19055)	346 300 275 240	4,7,11-Docosatrien-18-ynoic acid
240(44668)	345 282 240	Naphthalene, 2(dimethylamino)
240(27500)	336 324 300 240	Harmine
240(16596)	330 240	Selenanthrene
240(17378)	329 265 240	Diselenide, diphenyl
240(16218)	325 280 240	Disulfide, di-2-tolyl

Strongest Band (ε)	Wavelengths (nm)	Compound
240(7763)	320 240	Benzoic acid, 4-amino-3-methyl, nitrile
240(23988)	316 240	Styrene, 3-nitro
240(20417)	313 240	Ergocryptinine
240(20417)	312 240	Ergocryptine
240(21379)	312 240	Ergosine
240(6310)	310 240	Benzoic acid, 3-amino, amide
240(5623)	307 240	Benzoic acid, 2-hydroxy-6-methyl
240(16982)	300 270 240	Disulfide, diphenyl
240(1906)	300 260 240	Methane, nitrotribromo
240(25100)	300 240	Physostigmine, 2-hydroxybenzoate
240(9550)	293 287 240	Acetophenone, 3-bromo
240(6457)	293 240	Benzene, 1-amino-2-dimethylamino
240(7080)	293 240	Benzene, 1,3-diamino
240(7820)	292 240	Toluene, 2-amino-4-chloro
240(9120)	291 240	1,2,4,5-Benzenetetracarboxylic acid, tetramethyl ester
240(7943)	290 240	Coumalic acid
240(6310)	290 240	Toluene, 2-amino-α-hydroxy
240(10000)	288 240	Acetic acid, 2-aminophenyl, nitrile
240(8128)	288 240	1,2,3,4-Benzenetetracarboxylic acid, tetramethyl ester
240(19953)	287 240	Hydantoin, 1-benzoyl-2-thio
240(12589)	286 272 240	6-Tetralincarboxylic acid
240(10000)	286 240	Acetophenone, 3-chloro
240(20300)	285 240	1,4-Benzenedicarboxylic acid, dimethyl ester
240(13300)	285 240	Benzoic acid, 3,4-dimethyl
240(18197)	281 240	Urea, 1(4-tolyl)
240(28184)	280 240	Stilbene, 2-amino (*cis*)
240(7150)	279 240	Acetophenone
240(1470)	278 240	1-Propanone, 1-phenyl
240(17783)	277 240	Urea, 1(3-tolyl)
240(1995)	275 240	Urea, 1-ethyl-3-phenyl
240(10965)	270 240	Borine, triphenyl
240(10000)	268 240	Santonin
240(12023)	266 240	Acetophenone, α-iodo
240(41687)	255 240	Sulfide, diethenyl
240(12700)	240	Acetic acid, (2,4-dinitrophenyl)
240(1820)	240	Acetic acid, mercapto
240(6918)	240	Amine, di-2-tolyl
240(12882)	240	Barbituric acid, 5-ethyl-5(2-pentyl)
240(12600)	240	Benzoic acid, 2-formyl
240(14900)	240	4,4′-Bipyridyl
240(21379)	240	Boric acid, diphenyl
240(1514)	240	Butanoic acid, 3-oxo, methyl ester
240(10000)	240	2-Butyne, 1,4-diiodo
240(5012)	240	Carbamic acid, *N*-isopropyl-*N*-nitro, ethyl ester
240(15849)	240	Desoxycorticosterone
240(23442)	240	Disulfide, diphenyl, 2,2′-dinitro
240(10471)	240	2,4-Furandicarboxylic acid
240(16300)	240	Hippuric acid, *p*-bromo
240(14454)	240	Paludrine
240(12882)	240	1-Pentanone, 1-phenyl
240(12589)	240	4-Pregnene-17α,20β,21-triol-3-one
240(1585)	240	1-Propanethiol
240(3162)	240	5-Pyrazolone, 3-methyl
240(3981)	240	Thiazole
240(1445)	240	1,3,5-Trithiane
239(11800)	312 239	Ergocornine
239(23800)	309 239	Ethene, tetraphenyl
239(8318)	289 239	Chelidonine (*d*)
239(4898)	288 239	Benzoic acid, 2,3,5-trimethyl
239(10715)	288 239	Pyrrole, 1-acetyl

Strongest Band (ε)	Wavelengths (nm)	Compound
239(12882)	287 278 239	Ketone, cyclobutyl phenyl
239(10200)	282 276 239	Toluene, 4-mercapto
239(24547)	281 239	Thiophenetetracarboxylic acid, tetranitrile
239(11749)	275 239	Biphenyl, 2,4′-dimethyl
239(18700)	239	Benzene, 1-bromo-4-iodo
239(10233)	239	Benzoic acid, 3,4,5-trimethyl
239(16218)	239	Butanoic acid, 3-oxo, ethyl ester (enol form)
239(2693)	239	Carbamic acid, *N-tert*-butyl-*N*-nitro, ethyl ester
239(6310)	239	Carbamic acid, *N*-nitro-*N*-propyl, ethyl ester
239(16300)	239	Sulfoxide, 4,4′-ditolyl
239(12303)	239	Toluene, 2,3,4-trinitro
238(12589)	540 238	Benzene, 1,4-dihydroxy-2-nitro
238(42658)	325 311 285 238	Quinoline, 2,6,8-trimethyl
238(20417)	310 238 223	Lysergic acid
238(22500)	310 238	Thiophene, tetraphenyl
238(10700)	306 238	Benzoic acid, 2-hydroxy, benzyl ester
238(8990)	306 238	Benzoic acid, 2-hydroxy, butyl ester
238(9840)	306 238	Benzoic acid, 2-hydroxy, methyl ester
238(8420)	306 238	Benzoic acid, 2-hydroxy, 3-methylbutyl ester
238(13800)	305 238	Benzoic acid, 2-hydroxy, ethyl ester
238(14791)	304 238	Methapyrilene (base)
238(20700)	298 288 238	Indole, 1-acetyl
238(46900)	293 282 238	9,10-Naphthacenequinone
238(18000)	291 282 246 238	1,4-Benzenedicarboxylic acid, mononitrile
238(12500)	290 281 273 238	Benzoic acid, 3,4-dichloro
238(7763)	290 238	Aniline, 3-bromo
238(25119)	290 238	Erythraline
238(6457)	287 238	Benzene, 2-amino-1-isopropyl-4-methyl
238(16200)	286 278 238	Isocyanic acid, 3-chlorophenyl ester
238(5012)	286 238	Codeine, hydrochloride
238(11482)	278 238	Pyridine, 3-ethenyl
238(33113)	277 238	Benzoic acid, anhydride
238(14125)	275 238	2,3′-Bipyridyl
238(9550)	271 238	Biphenyl, 2,3′-dimethyl
238(10233)	238 231	Benzene, 1-chloro-3-iodo
238(5495)	238	Acetic acid, amide, *N*-ethyl-*N*-phenyl
238(11200)	238	Benzaldehyde, 2,4-dinitro
238(3890)	238	Benzene, 2,4-dinitro-1,3,5-trimethyl
238(12300)	238	Benzoic acid, 4-formyl
238(14100)	238	Benzoic acid, 4-propyl
238(1698)	238	Bullvalene
238(4467)	238	2-Butenoic acid, 2-bromo (*cis*)
238(6761)	238	Carbamic acid, *N*-butyl-*N*-nitro, butyl ester
238(15136)	238	Cortisone
238(4169)	238	1,3-Cyclopentadiene
238(25119)	238	β-Erythroidine
238(13300)	238	Formic acid, amide, *N,N*-diphenyl
238(2512)	238	3-Furancarboxylic acid, methyl ester
238(22387)	238	Rhamnetin
238(18100)	238	Semicarbazide, 4-phenyl
238(12303)	238	Thiocyanic acid, 4-chlorophenyl ester
238(5623)	238	Thiophene, 3,4-dimethyl
238(14125)	238	Urea, 1-benzyl-2-thio
237(19600)	396 289 237	Phenol, 2-amino-4,6-dinitro
237(41687)	346 296 289 262 237	Dibenzothiophene, 2-amino
237(19600)	339 237	Benzoic acid, 4-hydroxy-3-nitro
237(38019)	328 294 237	2-Naphthalenesulfonic acid, 1-hydroxy
237(28184)	311 237	5-Acenaphthenecarboxylic acid
237(19953)	310 268 237	Naphthalene, 2,3-dichloro-1,4-dihydroxy
237(11200)	305 237	Benzoic acid, 2-hydroxy, methyl ester

Strongest Band (ε)	Wavelengths (nm)	Compound
237(8318)	292 237	Aniline, 2-iodo
237(11800)	291 237 229 215	Phthalic acid, imide, *N*(hydroxymethyl)
237(42600)	289 237 206	2-Quinolinecarboxylic acid
237(6026)	287 237	Benzoic acid, 2,3,4-trimethyl
237(7763)	286 237	Benzene, 1-amino-2-*tert*-butyl
237(7413)	286 237	Benzoic acid, 2,4,5-trimethyl
237(10100)	284 237	Aniline, 3-fluoro
237(24300)	280 237	Benzoic acid, 4-amino-3,5-diiodo
237(15200)	280 237	Benzoic acid, 4-chloro
237(8913)	278 237	Glucose phenylhydrazone (*d*,α)
237(16300)	274 269 237	Urea, 1-phenyl
237(8300)	237 222	Benzene, 1,4-bis(bromomethyl)
237(9180)	237	Benzoic acid, 4-*tert*-butyl
237(19499)	237	Biphenyl, 4-acetamido
237(10000)	237	Biphenyl, 2-methyl
237(5623)	237	Carbamic acid, *N*-ethyl-*N*-nitro-, ethyl ester
237(15136)	237	Cortisone, 21-acetate
237(5012)	237	5β-Pregnane-3,20-dione
237(7943)	237	Propyne, 3-cyclohexyl
237(6761)	237	Thiophene, 2,3,5-trimethyl
236(14125)	393 284 236	Aniline, 2-methoxy-6-nitro
236(24500)	388 236	Benzophenone, 2-amino-5-chloro
236(33885)	351 338 289 236	Yobyrine
236(34900)	334 280 236	Cinchonidine, sulfate
236(34900)	334 280 236	Quinidine sulfate (*d*)
236(40400)	333 236 217 205	Quinoline, 2-amino
236(16596)	323 280 236	Benzophenone, 3,3′,4,4′-tetrahydroxy
236(35400)	321 314 307 276 236	Quinoline, 2,6-dimethyl
236(22387)	321 236	Quinoxaline, 6-amino
236(22387)	321 236	Quinoxaline, 6-chloro
236(10800)	301 236	Fluorene, 2-bromo
236(7300)	300 236	Benzoic acid, 2-hydroxy, hydrazide
236(8190)	296 236	Aniline, 2,4-dimethoxy
236(39811)	295 270 236 220	Naphthalene, 2-benzyl-1-hydroxy
236(25119)	292 275 236	Naphthalene, 2-iodo
236(7120)	290 236	Toluene, 3-amino-4-methoxy
236(10300)	289 236	Benzene, 1-amino-4-ethyl
236(6607)	289 236	Benzene, 1,2-diamino
236(7586)	287 279 271 236	Toluene, 2-mercapto
236(12882)	287 236	Semicarbazide, 1(4-tolyl)
236(7413)	286 236	Aniline, 2-methoxy
236(8900)	286 236	Toluene, 3-amino
236(4169)	285 236	Safrole
236(4898)	282 236	Acetophenone, 2-bromo
236(19000)	281 275 269 262 236	Benzoic acid, 4-chloro, nitrile
236(13500)	280 236	Benzoic acid, 4-methyl
236(6310)	279 236	Benzene, hydroxylamino
236(16982)	274 236	Carbamic acid, *N*-phenyl-, isopropyl ester
236(19953)	272 236	Pyrimidine, 4-amino
236(10471)	270 236	Urea, 1(2-tolyl)
236(13400)	267 236	Pyrimidine, 4-amino-6-methyl
236(8511)	264 236	Imidazole, 1-phenyl
236(5012)	236	Benzene, 1(bromomethyl)-4-methyl
236(17400)	236	Benzene, 1-chloro-4-iodo
236(10000)	236	Benzenesulfonic acid, 3-nitro, chloride
236(3020)	236	Butanoic acid, 3-oxo amide, *N*(2-tolyl)
236(12589)	236	2-Cyclohexen-1-one, 3,6-dimethyl
236(3162)	236	Glutathione
235(15136)	375 287 235	Toluene, 3-amino-5-nitro
235(25119)	372 352 320 235	2,4,6-Cycloheptatrien-1-one, 2-hydroxy-4-methyl

Strongest Band (ϵ)	Wavelengths (nm)	Compound
235(28840)	363 350 319 235	2,4,6-Cycloheptatrien-1-one, 2-methoxy
235(15849)	360 285 235	Emetine, (*l*)
235(14000)	348 235	Toluene, 2-amino-6-nitro
235(39811)	338 260 235	Fluorene, 9-benzhydrylidene
235(15849)	325 235	Propanoic acid, 3-oxo-3-phenyl, amide, *N*-phenyl
235(8511)	318 235	Carvone, (*d*)
235(8511)	318 235	Carvone, (*dl*)
235(8511)	318 235	Carvone, (*l*)
235(27400)	316 235	1,4,5,8-Naphthalenetetracarboxylic acid
235(39700)	315 235	Quinolinium, *N*-ethyl, iodide
235(9120)	311 235	Azoxybenzene, 2,2′-dimethyl (*trans*)
235(2512)	311 235	Phthalic acid, 3-hydroxy
235(19953)	310 235	Idene, 2,3-diphenyl
235(19953)	302 235	Benzimidazole, 6-nitro
235(7120)	302 235	Benzoic acid, 2-hydroxy, amide
235(9333)	300 235	Aniline, 4-methoxy
235(15849)	300 235	Biphenyl, 2,4′-diamino
235(8511)	295 235	Echitamine, hydrochloride
235(6310)	294 235	Benzenesulfonic acid, 2-amino
235(9220)	291 284 235	Benzoic acid, 3,5-dimethyl
235(8511)	289 235	Aniline, 2-bromo
235(9333)	288 235	Sesamin
235(16596)	287 273 235	Isocyanic acid, 4-chlorophenyl ester
235(6310)	286 278 272 235	Phthalic acid, dichloride
235(4180)	286 235	Toluene, α-hydroxy-3,4-methylenedioxy
235(25119)	285 235	Erysodine
235(6026)	285 235	5-Tetralincarboxylic acid
235(12200)	284 276 268 235	Isocyanic acid, 2-chlorophenyl ester
235(22908)	282 235	Naphthalene, 1,2,3,4-tetrahydroxy
235(8770)	281 273 235	Carbamic acid, *N*-phenyl-, ethyl ester
235(37900)	281 235	Ergosterol
235(15849)	280 275 235	Ethane, 2(2-chlorophenyl)-2(4-chlorophenyl)-1,1,1-trichloro
235(10000)	280 235	Hydrazine, 1,1-dimethyl
235(10000)	280 235	Hydrazine, 1-isobutyl-1-phenyl
235(3981)	280 235	Phenol, 4-mercapto
235(12589)	277 235	Ethane, 2,2-di-4-tolyl-1,1,1-trichloro
235(14700)	276 235	Amine, diphenyl, 2-amino
235(10000)	276 235	Pyridine, 3-acetyl
235(3236)	270 235	Benzoic acid, 2,4,6-trimethyl
235(10300)	266 235	Pyridoin
235(18621)	244 235 228 193	$\Delta^{3,5}$-Cholestadiene
235(9772)	235 229	Propene, 1-nitro
235(6310)	235	Acetic acid, bromo (phenyl)-, nitrile
235(11482)	235	Benzene, 1-bromo-3-iodo
235(15488)	235	Benzene, 1,2,4-trinitro
235(7943)	235	Creatinine
235(12589)	235	2-Cyclohexen-1-one, 5-isopropyl-3-methyl
235(9550)	235	2-Cyclohexen-1-one, 2-methyl
235(12589)	235	2-Cyclohexen-1-one, 3-methyl
235(11800)	235	Isophorone
235(13804)	235	Jasmone
235(16596)	235	1,3,7-Octatriene, 3,7-dimethyl
235(6670)	235	Thiophene, 2-bromo
235(6310)	235	Thiophene, 2,4-dimethyl
235(3981)	235	Thiophene, 3-ethyl
235(5623)	235	Thiophene, 3-methyl
235(14125)	235	Toluene, 2,4,5-trinitro
234(23200)	415 234	Aniline, 4-chloro-2-nitro
234(31300)	331 234	Perimidine
234(31623)	320 300 234	1-Naphthalenesulfonic acid, 4-hydroxy

Strongest Band (ε)	Wavelengths (nm)	Compound
234(30199)	317 309 297 250 234	Quinoxaline, 2-methyl
234(25119)	316 284 234	Benzophenone, 3,3′,4,4′-tetramethoxy
234(17378)	309 234	Benzene, 1,4-dibromo-2-nitro
234(7770)	301 234	Phenol, 4-amino
234(39811)	299 234	Naphthalene, 1-amino-3-methyl
234(6230)	297 234	Benzoic acid, 3-hydroxy
234(6607)	294 234	Benzoic acid, 2-methoxy, methyl ester
234(7770)	288 234	Benzene, 2-amino-1,3,5-trimethyl
234(15000)	287 234	Aniline, phosphate
234(8570)	285 234	Aniline, sulphate (neutral)
234(10000)	285 234	Cryptopine
234(11800)	281 234	Hydrazine, 1-acetyl-2-phenyl
234(11400)	280 272 234	3,5-Pyridinedicarboxylic acid, 2,6-dimethyl, diethyl ester
234(19900)	277 270 262 245 234	Benzene, ethynyl
234(6310)	274 234	Thiazole, 2-methyl
234(14125)	273 266 234	Sulfone, phenyl(2-tolyl)
234(3467)	272 266 261 234	Phosphine, phenyl
234(7586)	234	Acetic acid, amide, *N*(2-bromophenyl)
234(10500)	234	Acetic acid, amide, *N*,*N*-diphenyl
234(24500)	234	Benzoic acid, 2,3,5-triiodo
234(5495)	234	2-Butenoic acid, 2-phenyl (*trans*)
234(16218)	234	Carvone, oxime (α,*d*)
234(5248)	234	β-Ionol
234(15136)	234	Piperitone (*d*)
234(15136)	234	Piperitone (*dl*)
234(15136)	234	Piperitone (*l*)
234(3802)	234	Thiophene, 2-methyl
234(7586)	234	Thiophene, 2-propyl
234(5012)	234	Thiophene, 3-propyl
233(12882)	374 233	Toluene, 3-amino-4-nitro
233(12000)	371 233	Aniline, 3-nitro
233(10471)	356 290 233	Aniline, 3-methoxy-2-nitro
233(5012)	350 233	Amine, diethyl *N*-nitroso
233(38019)	340 293 280 273 233	Pyrrocoline
233(46773)	337 326 263 255 233	Isoquinoline, 7-methoxy
233(45900)	335 322 292 256 233	Carbazole
233(36308)	322 275 233	3-Quinolinecarboxylic acid
233(19055)	320 233	Quinoline, 4-amino
233(31623)	312 233	Quinoline, hydrochloride
233(31623)	300 233	Quinoline, 8-phenyl
233(8740)	297 233	Toluene, 2-amino-5-methoxy
233(7490)	283 233	Benzene, 2-amino-1,3-dimethyl
233(15300)	283 233	Phenol, 4-iodo
233(30200)	282 233	Usnic acid (*d*)
233(30200)	282 233	Usnic acid (*dl*)
233(14454)	280 273 233	Sulfone, 2,2′-ditolyl
233(12303)	274 233	Cocaine hydrochloride (*dl*)
233(12303)	274 233	Cocaine hydrochloride (*l*)
233(20900)	233	Benzaldehyde, 3-nitro
233(18500)	233	Benzene, 1,3-dinitro
233(29300)	233	Benzoic acid, 3,4,5-triiodo
233(16982)	233	Glyoxal, dioxime
233(2344)	233	Maleic acid, methyl dimethyl ester
233(3236)	233	10, 12-Octadecadienoic acid (*trans, trans*)
233(5888)	233	Thiophene, 2,3-dimethyl
233(9670)	233	Toluene, 2,6-dinitro
232(9040)	440 312 232	Azobenzene, 2,2′-dimethyl
232(11749)	439 232	4-Azobenzenesulfonic acid
232(13183)	409 285 232	1,4-Naphthoquinone, 3,5-dihydroxy-2-methyl
232(37600)	387 354 282 242 232	Pyrene, 1-acetyl

Strongest Band (ε)	Wavelengths (nm)	Compound
232(16596)	382 275 232	Aniline, 6-chloro-2-nitro
232(31623)	375 315 232	Quinolinium, *N*-methyl, chloride
232(19953)	375 232	3,5-Pyridinedicarboxylic acid, 1,4-dihydro-2,6-dimethyl, diethyl ester
232(14125)	361 290 232	Pyridine, 3-mercapto
232(16400)	344 232	Acetic acid, amide, *N*(2-nitro-4-tolyl)
232(25119)	315 305 232	Quinoxaline
232(21379)	312 280 232	Piperoin
232(12023)	312 279 232	Adrenalone
232(8913)	294 232	Benzoic acid, 2-methoxy, nitrile
232(8300)	289 232	Benzoic acid, 2-methoxy, amide
232(31623)	282 232	Acetic acid, 1-naphthyl ester
232(10000)	280 232	Semicarbazide, 1(2-tolyl)
232(14700)	279 272 267 259 232	Benzoic acid, 4-methyl, nitrile
232(6310)	275 232	9,12-Octadecadienoic acid (*cis, cis*)
232(9640)	267 232	Biphenyl, 2,2′-difluoro
232(20893)	248 232	Benzophenone, 3-nitro
232(20900)	232	Aniline, 4-methoxy-2-nitro
232(15100)	232	Benzene, 2,4-dinitro-1-fluoro
232(36301)	232	Benzene, 1,3,5-triiodo
232(25119)	232	Benzoic acid, 3-nitro, chloride
232(19500)	232	1,4-Benzoquinone, monoimine, *N*-chloro
232(2291)	232	3-Furancarboxylic acid
232(15849)	232	α-Ionone (*dl*)
232(6026)	232	9,12-Octadecadienoic acid, methyl ester
232(4074)	232	Thiophene, 3-bromo
231(19953)	448 285 259 231	Aniline, 4-methoxy-3-nitro
231(28184)	363 306 280 231	Carbazole, 3-nitro
231(7080)	346 231	Amine, dimethyl *N*-nitroso
231(17500)	338 231	Acetic acid, amide, *N*(2-nitrophenyl)
231(47500)	334 231	Naphthalene, 1,8-diamino
231(28600)	332 279 231 208	Hydroquinidine
231(44000)	329 231	Naphthalene, 1,5-diamino
231(19499)	322 231	Helvolic acid
231(14100)	314 273 231 205	Benzaldehyde, 2,4-dimethoxy
231(16600)	312 272 231	Benzaldehyde, 3,4-methylenedioxy
231(39811)	310 274 231	Acetophenone, 3-hydroxy-4-methoxy
231(15600)	308 277 231	Benzaldehyde, 3-ethoxy-4-hydroxy
231(8913)	294 231	Benzoic acid, 2-hydroxy, nitrile
231(7710)	294 231	Benzoic acid, 3-hydroxy, nitrile
231(9820)	294 231	Pyridine, 2-amino-3-methyl
231(15849)	282 231	Laudanosine (*d*)
231(15849)	280 231	Sarpagine
231(12000)	279 256 247 235 231	Benzoic acid, 4-formyl, nitrile
231(10200)	278 231	Benzoic acid, 3-methyl
231(7943)	276 270 231	Benzoxazole
231(17100)	271 231	Benzoic acid, 4-tolyl ester
231(5370)	265 260 231	3-Pyridinecarboxaldehyde
231(14125)	231	Acetaldehyde, 2-oxo-2-phenyl, dioxime
231(9550)	231	Biguanide
231(12589)	231	Biphenyl, 2-acetamido
231(9772)	231	1-Cholesten-3-one
231(13183)	231	1-Cyclohexene-1-carboxaldehyde
231(3090)	231	Cysteine (*l*)
231(4366)	231	1-Decanethiol
231(20893)	231	Propanal, 2-oxo, dioxime
230(41687)	440 255 230	9,10-Anthraquinone-2-carboxylic acid, 4,5-dihydroxy
230(33885)	336 280 230	Quinidine
230(18621)	331 230	Benzoic acid, 2-amino-3-hydroxy
230(19953)	330 262 230	Benzoic acid, 3-nitro, azide

Strongest Band (ϵ)	Wavelengths (nm)	Compound
230(12589)	316 230	Styrene, 2-amino
230(23700)	309 265 230	Benzoic acid, 3-amino-4-hydroxy, methyl ester
230(19953)	307 276 230	Acetophenone, 3,4-dihydroxy
230(22908)	301 230	4-Stilbenecarboxylic acid, nitrile (*cis*)
230(6761)	293 230	Benzoic acid, 3-methoxy, chloride
230(15849)	292 282 230	Cinchonamine
230(6100)	290 230	Aniline, 4-fluoro
230(7080)	286 230	Morphine, hydrochloride trihydrate
230(8318)	284 230	Benzoic acid, 3-chloro
230(13489)	284 230	α-Conidendrin
230(13183)	283 274 230	Isocyanic acid, 4-tolyl ester
230(12200)	281 274 230	Choline, *O*-benzoyl-,chloride
230(6310)	281 230	Morphine, *O,O*-diacetyl
230(2700)	281 230	Uracil, 5-hydroxy
230(7080)	280 274 230	Benzoic acid, amide, *N*-methyl
230(1470)	280 272 267 263 257 230	Benzoic acid, benzyl ester
230(6310)	280 230	Toluene, α,4-dihydroxy-3-methoxy
230(6560)	279 230	Acetic acid, (3,4-dimethoxyphenyl)
230(19953)	275 270 238 230	Ethane, 2,2-bis(4-methoxyphenyl)1,1,1-trichloro
230(14125)	273 230	Delphinine
230(6310)	266 230	Sinomenine
230(2512)	263 230	Maleic acid, methyl diethyl ester
230(19953)	257 230	Benzene, 1,2-diethenyl
230(17378)	250 230	Naphthalene, 1-chloro-4-nitro
230(25119)	245 230	Sulfide, ethenyl methyl
230(5930)	230	Acetic acid, amide, *N*(2-tolyl)
230(13804)	230	Amine, methyl *N*-nitro
230(7586)	230	Ammeline
230(14500)	230	Benzoic acid, 2,6-dinitro
230(14454)	230	Cholesterol, benzoate
230(20893)	230	Cyclohexene, 1-ethenyl
230(22908)	230	Isogeraniolene
230(3162)	230	9-Octadecenoic acid, methyl ester (*cis*)
230(1000)	230	Oxysparteine
230(15849)	230	Phytadiene (*d*)
230(11100)	230	Toluene, 4-bromo-α-chloro
230(8128)	230	Uracil, 5,6-dihydro
229(26000)	438 318 229	Aniline, 4-chloro-2,6-dinitro
229(13000)	435 315 244 235 229	Hydrazine, 1,2-diphenyl
229(19200)	418 279 229	Toluene, 4-amino-3-nitro
229(22700)	340 262 229	Benzoic acid, 3(dimethylamino)
229(43900)	323 308 263 229	1,10-Phenanthroline
229(31623)	315 255 229	Aniline, 2,4,6-triiodo
229(17300)	307 273 229	Benzaldehyde, 3,4-dimethoxy
229(28200)	306 280 273 229	Benzoic acid, isobutyl ester
229(6190)	305 229 226	Benzoic acid, 5-amino-2-hydroxy
229(4571)	303 229	Pyridine, 1,2-dihydro-1-methyl-2-oxo
229(38019)	299 229	Reserpinine
229(19400)	291 229	Ethene, 1-bromo-1,2,2-triphenyl
229(25200)	288 281 229	Benzene, 1-chloro-4-ethoxy
229(10100)	287 278 235 229	Benzoic acid, 2-chloro, nitrile
229(13400)	286 278 269 229	Ether, diphenyl, 4,4′-dimethyl
229(15849)	281 274 229	Cocaine (*d*)
229(15849)	281 274 229	Cocaine (*dl*)
229(15849)	281 274 229	Cocaine (*l*)
229(12900)	281 273 229	Benzoic acid, allyl ester
229(3500)	281 273 229	1,2-Ethanediol, dibenzoate
229(9550)	281 273 229	Isocyanic acid, 3-tolyl ester
229(11600)	280 229	Benzene, 2,4-dimethyl-1-iodo
229(8460)	278 229	Benzoic acid, 2-methyl

Strongest Band (ε)	Wavelengths (nm)	Compound
229(19700)	276 268 265 257 229	Benzenesulfonic acid, 4-chloro, 4-chlorophenyl ester
229(10400)	270 263 229	Benzoic acid, 4-fluoro
229(9120)	268 229	Benzoic acid, amidine
229(14125)	229	2,3-Octanedione, dioxime
228(12303)	399 228	Indazole, 4-nitro
228(43658)	357 228	Ninhydrin
228(22908)	351 320 228	2,4,6-Cycloheptatrien-1-one, 2-hydroxy
228(15849)	338 296 228	Coumarin, 6,7,8-trimethoxy
228(14125)	338 280 228	Lupulone
228(22387)	322 307 297 236 228	Cyclobutene, 1,2-diphenyl
228(48978)	320 275 228	1-Naphthalenesulfonic acid
228(21379)	319 280 274 228	Sulfone, diphenyl 2-amino
228(36308)	314 302 228	Biphenyl, 3,3′-diamino
228(13804)	311 228	2-Pentenal, 2-methyl
228(22700)	306 263 228	Benzoic acid, 3-amino-4-hydroxy
228(30199)	304 288 276 228	Isothiocyanic acid, 4-chlorophenyl ester
228(16218)	304 273 228	Acetophenone, 3,4-dimethoxy
228(38019)	304 228	Isoreserpiline
228(11200)	288 281 228	Benzene, 1-bromo-4-ethoxy
228(19953)	288 228	Ethene, 1-chloro-1,2,2-triphenyl
228(10471)	287 271 228	Benzoic acid, 3-chloro, nitrile
228(15488)	282 273 266 228	Benzene, 1,4-dibromo
228(8280)	282 228	Toluene, 2-chloro-5-hydroxy
228(25600)	281 273 228	Ether, diethyl, 2,2′-dibenzoyloxy
228(12023)	280 273 228	Benzoic acid, 2-ethoxyethyl
228(12600)	280 273 228	Benzoic acid, ethyl ester
228(11221)	280 273 228	Benzoic acid, hexyl ester
228(10233)	280 273 228	Benzoic acid, isopropyl ester
228(10233)	280 273 228	Isocyanic acid, 2-tolyl ester
228(11000)	280 272 228	Benzoic acid, methyl ester
228(12400)	280 272 228	Benzoic acid, 3-methylbutyl ester
228(8470)	280 272 228	Benzoic acid, 2-acetyl
228(11900)	279 272 228	Benzoic acid
228(12200)	279 272 228	Benzoic acid, butyl ester
228(8620)	276 228	Acetic acid, (2-carboxyphenyl)
228(12023)	275 268 228	Biphenyl, 2,2′-dibromo
228(13489)	275 264 228	4-Toluenesulfonic acid, 2-tolyl ester
228(17700)	273 263 256 228	Benzenearsonic acid, 4-chloro
228(13500)	272 267 263 257 228	Benzoic acid, 1-phenylethyl ester
228(10000)	272 258 228	Ether, diphenyl, 3,3′-dimethyl
228(7763)	228 219	1-Buten-3-yne
228(6710)	228	Acetic acid, amide, *N*(2,4-dimethylphenyl)
228(19700)	228	Benzoic acid, 3,5-dinitro
228(10700)	228	2,3-Butanedione, monooxime
228(7586)	228	2-Butenoic acid, 2-bromo (*trans*)
228(7080)	228	2-Butenoic acid, 2-chloro (*cis*)
228(15800)	228	Pentanoic acid, 2-oxo
228(15300)	228	2-Propanone, 2,4-dinitrophenylhydrazone
228(9030)	228	Propenoic acid, 2,3-dichloro
227(26900)	395 255 227	Aniline, 3,5-dinitro
227(23800)	370 257 227	Kynurenine (*l*)
227(46773)	344 329 247 227	Benzanthrene
227(32359)	331 274 227	Quinoline, 6-hydroxy
227(10715)	328 288 227	Isoquinoline, 1-chloro
227(39811)	325 256 227	Fluorene, 9-benzylidine
227(7760)	321 307 288 277 227	Naphthalene, 2-bromo
227(44668)	314 299 227	Quinoline, 4-acetamido
227(11400)	303 227	Benzene, 1-iodo-2-nitro
227(25704)	296 227	2-Indolecarboxylic acid, 3-methyl
227(36308)	295 227	Quinoline, 4-phenyl

Strongest Band (ε)	Wavelengths (nm)	Compound
227(7030)	295 227	Uracil, 5-amino
227(20900)	292 227	Benzoic acid, 4-chloro-3-nitro
227(11200)	288 281 227	Benzene, 1-chloro-4-methoxy
227(12000)	287 279 231 227 221	1,3-Benzenedicarboxylic acid, dinitrile
227(19953)	286 227	Stilbene, 4-methoxy (*cis*)
227(11000)	284 276 227	Benzoic acid, 2-methyl, nitrile
227(5623)	283 277 227	Benzene, 1,3-di-*tert*-butyl-2-hydroxy-5-methyl
227(11000)	283 275 227	Benzoic acid, 3-methyl, nitrile
227(8128)	281 227	Capsaicin
227(7080)	280 227	Morphine, *o,o*-diacetyl hydrochloride monohydrate
227(7410)	280 227	Toluene, 3,4-dimethoxy
227(26900)	279 227	Propane, 2,2-bis(4-hydroxyphenyl)
227(8850)	274 227	Hydrazine, phenyl, hydrochloride
227(17378)	272 227	Benzophenone, 2,3,4-trihydroxy
227(19953)	270 227	Propene, 1,1,2,3-tetraphenyl
227(6530)	249 227	Benzene, hexabromo
227(7943)	227	2-Butenoic acid, 2,3-dichloro-4-oxo
227(25704)	227	2,4-Heptadiene
226(27900)	437 297 288 256 226	Benzothiophene
226(5480)	314 301 278 226	Cinchonidine
226(5480)	314 301 278 226	Cinchonine
226(26900)	303 226	Benzoic acid, 4-chloro-2-nitro, nitrile
226(25119)	297 226	Phthalic acid, 3-nitro, imide
226(10200)	290 226	Benzene, 1,4-diethoxy
226(8570)	285 276 226	Saccharin
226(6166)	285 226	Salsoline
226(12100)	282 226	Phenol, 4-bromo
226(10400)	280 275 226	Toluene, α-hydroxy-4-methoxy
226(10900)	279 226	Benzene, 1-benzyl-4-hydroxy
226(10965)	277 270 256 226	Benzene, isocyano
226(10965)	277 263 226	Isocyanic acid, phenyl ester
226(13100)	273 226	Benzoxazole, 2-hydroxy
226(9333)	270 226	Thiocyanic acid, phenyl ester
226(11700)	250 226	Benzene, iodo
226(23300)	226	Acetophenone, 3-nitro
226(12600)	226	Benzaldehyde, 2,6-dinitro
226(19953)	226	Biphenyl, 2-iodo
226(21379)	226	1,3-Butadiene, 2,3-dimethyl
226(43658)	226	2-Butenoic acid, 3-chloro (*cis*)
226(12700)	226	Hippuric acid
226(10471)	226	Penicillic acid
226(23400)	226	Phthalic acid, imide, *N*-phenyl
225(37153)	437 418 287 253 225	9,10-Anthraquinone, 1,5-dihydroxy
225(25119)	405 300 225	Julolidine
225(20300)	343 268 225	1,3-Benzenedicarboxylic acid, 5-amino, dimethyl ester
225(19953)	338 250 225	Benzoic acid, 2-amino, ethyl ester
225(34200)	334 321 225	1,3-Indandione, 2-phenyl
225(19953)	325 315 225	Quinoline, 4-hydroxy
225(2818)	316 225	2-Butyn-1-al
225(10000)	315 225	1-Propanone, 1-(4-tolyl)
225(32600)	313 265 225	Cytosine, 5-methyl
225(19953)	303 232 225	2,4,6-Cycloheptatrien-1-one
225(6310)	300 225	Benzene, 1,4-dihydroxy-2,3-dimethyl
225(10000)	299 265 252 225	3-Hexanone, 6-dimethylamino-4,4-diphenyl-5-methyl (*l*)
225(19953)	297 225	Benzothiazole, 2-phenyl
225(26925)	295 269 225	Reserpic acid
225(5180)	294 225	Benzene, 1,4-dihydroxy
225(19953)	291 225	2-Naphthoic acid, 3,4-dihydro
225(19953)	290 255 225	Biphenyl, 2,3′-dinitro

Strongest Band (ϵ)	Wavelengths (nm)	Compound
225(4250)	289 282 225	Phenol, 2,5-dichloro
225(9670)	289 225	Benzene, 1,4-dimethoxy
225(15849)	285 225	Thebaine
225(14900)	284 225	Toluene, 2-amino-3-nitro
225(6940)	283 277 225 218	Benzene, 2,4-di-*tert*-butyl-1-hydroxy
225(9640)	283 277 225	Acetic acid, (4-methoxyphenyl)
225(15849)	283 225	Laudanine
225(8913)	280 273 268 235 225	Benzeneboronic acid
225(47863)	280 225	Ajmalicine
225(12023)	280 225	Benzoic acid, 3-methyl-4-nitro, nitrile
225(7943)	278 225	Acetic acid, (4-hydroxyphenyl)
225(8270)	278 225	Benzene, 1(2-aminopropyl)-4-hydroxy (*l*)
225(11700)	275 225	Benzene, 1,2-dimethoxy
225(19953)	274 271 225	Ether, ethenyl phenyl
225(6910)	274 267 261 225	Toluene, α,α,α-trichloro
225(4366)	274 225	3,3′-Bipyridyl
225(7960)	274 225	Phthalic acid, dibutyl ester
225(9400)	274 225	Phthalic acid, dicyclohexyl ester
225(8310)	274 225	Phthalic acid, diethyl ester
225(12600)	273 267 262 256 225	4-Toluenesulfonic acid, 2-chloroethyl ester
225(19000)	272 266 261 256 225	4-Toluenesulfonic acid, butyl ester
225(17378)	270 225	Benzoic acid, amidine, *N,N*-diphenyl
225(17378)	270 225	Benzoic acid, amidine, *N,N*-diphenyl hydrochloride
225(15849)	270 225	Mescaline
225(11000)	268 225	Benzoic acid, amide
225(35300)	252 225	Sulfide, 2,2′-dinaphthyl
225(39811)	225 283	Acenaphthene, 5-amino-4-nitro
225(5360)	225	Benzene, (1-bromoethyl) (*dl*)
225(17700)	225	Benzothiazole, 2-mercapto-6-nitro
225(8230)	225	2-Cyclohexen-1-one
225(10000)	225	2-Cyclohexen-1-one, 5-methyl (*dl*)
225(21379)	225	3,5-Hexadien-2-ol
225(5623)	225	Malonic acid, ethylidene, diethyl ester
225(19953)	225	Myrcene
225(12700)	225	Phthalic acid, diphenyl ester
225(3311)	225	Propene, 2-nitro
225(7060)	225	Toluene, α-bromo
225(22908)	225	Toluene, 2,4,6-trinitro
224(29512)	438 340 286 224	Naphthalene, 1-amino-7-nitro
224(45000)	428 282 251 224	Anthraquinone, 1,8-dihydroxy
224(34674)	403 301 260 224	Carbazole, 1-nitro
224(1778)	383 356 334 224	Nitrous acid, pentyl ester
224(10800)	369 331 287 224	Naphthalene, 2-hydroxy-1-nitro
224(14500)	362 275 224	Phenol, 2,4-dibromo-6-nitro
224(16400)	357 255 224	Acetophenone, 2-hydroxy-5-methoxy
224(14000)	334 297 249 224	Esculin
224(25704)	307 251 224	Lappaconitine
224(3162)	307 224	1,4-Dioxene
224(24547)	295 250 224	Acetophenone, 3-iodo
224(20893)	290 224	4-Pyrone-2-carboxylic acid, 5-hydroxy
224(9110)	284 277 224	Benzene, 1-methoxy-4-propyl
224(7080)	281 274 224	Toluene, α,α,α,2-tetrachloro
224(8220)	280 273 224	Phenol, pentachloro
224(12800)	280 272 264 224	Benzene, 1,4-dichloro
224(8080)	279 271 264 224	Benzene, 1,2,3-trichloro
224(8240)	278 224	Phenol, 4(2-aminopropyl)
224(8190)	278 224	Propanoic acid, 3(4-hydroxyphenyl)
224(8840)	276 224	Benzene, 1-chloro-2-iodo
224(7460)	276 224	Hordenine, sulfate dihydrate
224(8770)	274 224	Phthalic acid, anhydride

Strongest Band (ε)	Wavelengths (nm)	Compound
224(8760)	274 224	Phthalic acid, diisobutyl ester
224(10300)	273 268 262 257 224	4-Toluenesulfonic acid, amide
224(14300)	273 224	Benzaldehyde, 4-hydroxy-3-methoxy-2-nitro
224(13183)	272 265 260 224	Phosphinic acid, diphenyl
224(15849)	271 224	Benzoic acid, 2-methoxyphenyl ester
224(12000)	270 263 257 224	Benzoic acid, 4-fluoro, nitrile
224(21379)	230 224 218	1,3-Butadiene, 2-methyl
224(7870)	224	Acetic acid, amide, *N*-methyl-*N*-phenyl
224(16600)	224	Amine, diphenyl, 2,4-dinitro-4′-hydroxy
224(22800)	224	Aniline, *N*-methyl-*N*,2,4,6-tetranitro
224(11482)	224	Ether, 2-furyl phenyl
224(10965)	224	4-Hexen-3-one, 2-methyl
224(22908)	224	1,3-Pentadiene
224(4786)	224	1-Pyrrolecarboxylic acid
223(1413)	384 356 333 223	Nitrous acid, butyl ester
223(42900)	346 280 223	7,8-Benzoflavone
223(32359)	325 268 223	Quinoline, 6-methoxy
223(16800)	318 311 304 275 223	Naphthalene, 2-methyl
223(19300)	314 223	Phthalic acid, imide, *N*(4-nitrophenyl)
223(21600)	299 288 278 223	Benzothiazole, 2(methylthio)
223(32359)	290 281 223	Indole, 3-methyl
223(9780)	289 223	Phenol, 2,4-dibromo
223(7570)	286 223	Arbutin
223(9772)	279 223	Benzoic acid, 2,3,6-trimethyl
223(7090)	278 223	Benzene, 1-ethyl-4-hydroxy
223(8130)	277 223	Benzene, 1-hydroxy-4(2-methyl-2-butyl)
223(20600)	276 223	Stilbene (*cis*)
223(12589)	274 223	1-Naphthoic acid, 3,4-dihydro
223(19953)	271 223	Stilbene, α-chloro (*cis*)
223(11221)	262 223	4-Toluenesulfinic acid
223(13400	223	Acetaldehyde, 2,4-dinitrophenylhydrazone (stable form)
223(16600)	223	Benzil, dioxime *(anti)*
223(14125)	223	1,3-Butadiene, 2-chloro
223(12882)	223	3-Hexen-2-one (*trans*)
223(7943)	223	Hydantoin
223(4160)	223	Pyrazole, 4-bromo-3,5-dimethyl
222(23442)	335 300 253 222	Isocyanic acid, 3-nitrophenyl ester
222(23988)	321 272 222	Coumarin, 6-chloro
222(31623)	320 240 222	Dibenzothiophene, 3-nitro
222(19953)	318 257 222	Benzoic acid, 4,5-dimethoxy-2-hydroxy
222(16982)	316 259 222	Isocyanic acid, 2-nitrophenyl ester
222(38019)	310 288 251 222	Dibenzofuran, 2-bromo
222(17000)	301 222	Benzoic acid, 2-hydroxy-5-nitro
222(17000)	301 222	Benzoic acid, 2-hydroxy-5-nitroso
222(26303)	295 284 270 222	Indole, 5-methyl
222(13804)	285 222	Benzoic acid, 2-phenoxy
222(10600)	277 263 230 222	Benzoic acid, nitrile
222(8110)	277 222	Benzene, 1,2-dipropoxy
222(6310)	277 222	3-Toluenesulfonic acid
222(19200)	270 222	Cinnamic acid, 3-bromo (*trans*)
222(41700)	270 222	Toluene, pentabromo
222(7080)	238 222	γ-Pyran
222(14125)	222	Ammelide
222(21800)	222	Benzaldehyde, 2,4,6-trinitro
222(10471)	222	2-Butenoic acid, 2-chloro (*trans*)
222(12303)	222	3-Hepten-2-one (*trans*)
222(4240)	222	Pyrazole, 3,4-dimethyl
222(10000)	222	2-Toluenesulfonic acid
222(1288)	222	Urea, 1-acetyl
221(1698)	397 382 353 221	Nitrous acid, *tert*-butyl ester

Strongest Band (ε)	Wavelengths (nm)	Compound
221(19055)	349 265 221	Benzene, 4-chloro-1-methoxy-2-nitro
221(15849)	343 275 267 254 221	Ethane, 1,2-di-4-tolyl
221(25704)	342 221	Disulfide, diphenyl, 2,2′-diamino
221(39811)	336 304 275 221	4,7-Phenanthroline
221(10600)	311 304 301 297 286 283 275 266 258 221	Naphthalene
221(25800)	309 299 264 256 221	Betulinic acid
221(42300)	306 221	Propanoic acid, 3(2-nitrophenyl)2-oxo
221(25704)	305 252 221	Benzoic acid, 2-acetamido
221(29512)	293 282 276 221	Indole, 1-methyl
221(35900)	292 221	1-Naphthoic acid
221(33100)	291 281 221	Propanoic acid, β(3-indolyl)
221(36000)	289 281 273 221	Tryptophan, *N*-acetyl (*dl*)
221(6580)	287 229 221	Phenol, 2,4-dichloro
221(8290)	287 221	Chelidonic acid
221(10700)	280 273 265 225 221	Benzene, 1,3,5-trichloro
221(27543)	273 221	2,4-Pyrroledicarboxylic acid, 3,5-dimethyl, diethyl ester
221(32600)	267 221	Benzothiazole, 2-amino-6-ethoxy
221(28300)	221	1,3-Benzenedicarboxylic acid, 5-nitro, dimethyl ester
221(19953)	221	2-Butenoic acid, 3-chloro (*trans*)
221(9550)	221	2-Butenoic acid, 2,3-dimethyl
221(6607)	221	Furan, 2-methoxy
221(4677)	221	Pyrazole, 1,3-dimethyl
220(5012)	430 283 255 220	9,10-Anthraquinone, 1,8-dihydroxy-3-hydroxymethyl
220(7943)	320 263 220	Thiophene, 2-hydroxy
220(12589)	310 220	Benzene, 1,4-dinitro-2-methoxy
220(5770)	304 268 220	Quinazoline
220(18200)	304 220	Benzene, 1,4-dichloro-2-nitro
220(21000)	299 264 220 208	Benzoic acid, 2,4,6-trihydroxy
220(25600)	298 220	Aniline, 3-mercapto
220(28600)	296 289 220	Iodogorgoic acid (*l*)
220(23500)	296 261 220	Benzoic acid, 3,4-methylenedioxy
220(23988)	294 258 220	Metameconin
220(25119)	290 258 220	Benzoic acid, 3-phenoxy
220(38800)	289 280 273 220	Tryptophan (*l*)
220(9340)	286 277 269 227 220	Benzene, 1,2,4-trichloro
220(35482)	285 220	Cannabinol
220(14791)	285 220	2-Stilbazole (*cis*)
220(7130)	283 276 220	Phenol, 3-chloro
220(21878)	280 220	Benzoic acid, 4-amino-3,5-dichloro
220(7943)	280 220	Pyridine, 3,5-dihydroxy
220(12023)	278 271 266 220	Ether, diphenyl, 2,2′-dimethyl
220(6400)	278 271 220	Benzene, ethoxy
220(13183)	278 220	Gitoxigenin
220(7244)	278 220	Phenol, 3,5-dichloro
220(7740)	277 271 220	Ethanol, 2-phenoxy
220(8090)	277 271 220	Glycerol, 1-phenyl ether
220(7950)	277 270 265 220	Propanoic acid, 3-phenoxy
220(18000)	277 270 220	Ethane, 1,2-diphenoxy
220(11000)	277 269 263 220	Toluene, 4-chloro
220(10600)	277 269 261 220	Toluene, 4-bromo
220(6530)	276 271 220	Toluene, α-hydroxy-2-methoxy
220(7943)	276 258 220	Cyclopropane, phenyl
220(18621)	275 220	Oxazole, 4,5-diphenyl
220(10500)	267 220	3,5-Pyridinedicarboxylic acid
220(18300)	264 220	Pyrimidine, 4,5-diamino
220(18197)	263 220	Arsinic acid, diphenyl
220(10965)	260 220	Benzeneseleninic acid
220(33113)	256 220	Aspidospermine
220(25500)	251 220	1,3-Benzenedicarboxylic acid, 5-nitro

Strongest Band (ε)	Wavelengths (nm)	Compound
220(18300)	249 220	1,3-Butadiene, hexachloro
220(18800)	220 215	Ethene, tetrabromo
220(1660)	220	2-Butenoic acid, 4-hydroxy, lactone
220(6310)	220	3-Buten-2-one, 3-methyl
220(7586)	220	Cyclohexane, 1,2-dimethylene
220(16218)	220	Digitoxigenin
220(19953)	220	Digitoxin
220(13489)	220	Digoxigenin
220(7943)	220	Furan, 2,5-dimethyl
220(13183)	220	2-Pentenoic acid, 2-methyl (*trans*)
220(7943)	220	Pyridine, 4-methoxy
220(38019)	220	Urea, *S*-methyl-2-thio
219(38019)	372 290 273 266 219	Azo, benzene 1-naphthalene
219(18000)	340 263 219	Benzaldehyde, 2-hydroxy-3-methoxy
219(19000)	338 259 219	Harmaline
219(26600)	337 248 219	Benzoic acid, 2-amino, isobutyl ester
219(23400)	336 219	Benzoic acid, 3,5-diamino
219(30199)	328 287 277 265 219	Azo, benzene 2-naphthalene
219(41687)	325 296 282 255 235 219	Benzene, 1,3-diacetyl
219(35600)	319 266 219	Dibenzothiophene, 3-nitro, monoxide
219(25800)	317 219	Benzoic acid, 3-amino
219(17100)	315 253 219	Benzaldehyde, 4-hydroxy
219(38905)	313 219	Purine, 2-amino-6-methyl
219(21600)	310 252 219	Benzaldehyde, 3-methoxy
219(36400)	302 253 219	1,3-Benzenedicarboxylic acid, 4-hydroxy
219(35482)	300 290 254 219	Dibenzofuran, 3-bromo
219(32800)	299 254 219	Benzenearsonic acid, 3-amino-4-hydroxy
219(25119)	291 219	2-Indolecarboxylic acid
219(24800)	288 257 219	Benzoic acid, 5-chloro-2-hydroxy
219(6770)	284 278 223 219	Benzene, 2,4-dimethyl-1-methoxy
219(6810)	284 277 219	Benzene, 1,2-dimethyl-4-methoxy
219(7250)	282 275 219	Benzene, (2-chloroethoxy)
219(6900)	281 275 219	Benzene, 1,4-dimethyl-2-methoxy
219(7244)	279 272 219	Benzene, 1-chloro-3-methoxy
219(13183)	272 265 259 219	Sulfone, benzyl phenyl
219(1097)	219	Acetic acid, amidine
219(21100)	219	Benzoic acid, 2,4,6-trinitro
219(6607)	219	Hydantoin, 5,5-dimethyl
219(8913)	219	3-Penten-1-yne, 3-methyl
219(39811)	219	Phthalic acid, imide, *N*-ethyl
219(5495)	219	Pyrrole, 2,3,4,5-tetramethyl
218(20300)	384 261 218	Pyridine, 2-amino-3-nitro
218(27900)	337 247 218	Benzoic acid, 2-amino, methyl ester
218(32100)	334 243 218	Benzoic acid, 2-amino-3-methyl
218(19953)	321 265 218	Acetophenone, 3,5-dihydroxy
218(37700)	320 235 218	Benzoic acid, 2-hydroxy-5-iodo
218(28840)	314 261 238 218	Dibenzofuran, 2-amino
218(14500)	301 218	2-Butenal (*trans*)
218(23100)	292 282 251 218	Benzothiazole, 2-methyl
218(7943)	290 238 218	Pyridine, 3-iodo
218(9333)	282 274 229 218	Phenol, 2-iodo
218(8318)	281 274 266 218	Benzene, 1-bromo-2-methoxy
218(3740)	281 273 266 218	Toluene, 2,4-dichloro
218(8060)	281 273 266 218	Toluene, 3,4-dichloro
218(8511)	280 273 267 218	Benzene, 1-bromo-3-methoxy
218(10471)	280 218	Phenol, 3,5-dibromo
218(4360)	279 218 210	Benzene, 1-ethoxy-4-fluoro
218(7060)	276 269 264 218	Acetic acid, phenoxy
218(6050)	276 218	Phenol, 2-methoxy
218(7120)	275 269 218	Benzene, 1-ethoxy-2-fluoro

Strongest Band (ε)	Wavelengths (nm)	Compound
218(7350)	275 269 218	Benzene, 1-fluoro-2-methoxy
218(6310)	275 224 218	Ecgonine (*dl*)
218(7980)	273 267 264 259 218	Benzene, 1,4-diethyl
218(8511)	272 265 259 218	Benzenesulfonic acid, propyl ester
218(9180)	271 264 258 253 218	Benzenesulfonic acid, amide
218(6230)	270 218	Benzene, 1,2-dimethyl-4-hydroxy
218(10000)	270 218	Stilbene, α,β-dimethyl (*cis*)
218(6761)	266 260 254 218	Toluene, 4-butoxy
218(5370)	260 218	Benzene, (1-chloroethyl) (*dl*)
218(9772)	245 218	Benzenesulfinic acid
218(5248)	243 218	Imidazole, 1-acetyl
218(1000)	218	Acetic acid, amide, *N,N*-dimethyl
218(7430)	218	Barbituric acid, 5,5-diethyl-1-methyl
218(10233)	218	1-Cyclohexene-1-carboxylic acid
218(19499)	218	Guanidine, 1-ureido
218(4677)	218	Pyrrole, 2,4-dimethyl
218(1950)	218	Urea, 1,1,3,3-tetramethyl
217(16800)	401 380 360 342 258 221 217	Anthracene, 9,10-dibromo
217(44100)	384 278 217	Quinoline, 2-mercapto
217(13183)	354 278 217	Phenol, 2-chloro-6-nitro
217(28400)	335 247 217	Benzoic acid, 2-amino
217(14600)	325 289 234 217	Cinnamic acid, 3,4-methylenedioxy (*trans*)
217(38019)	324 311 285 277 217	5,5′-Biquinolyl (*dl*)
217(16200)	317 249 217	Benzoic acid, 2,6-dihydroxy
217(27543)	313 302 261 237 217	Dibenzofuran, 3-amino
217(33100)	313 300 281 217	Quinoline, 8-nitro
217(10400)	310 231 217	Phenol, 2-chloro-4-nitro
217(19500)	309 250 217	Acetophenone, 3-hydroxy
217(20500)	305 246 217	Acetophenone, 3-methoxy
217(39400)	300 295 279 250 217	Dibenzofuran
217(32300)	293 255 217	Benzoic acid, 3,5-dichloro-4-hydroxy
217(22900)	290 259 217	Benzoic acid, 4-hydroxy-3-methoxy
217(22400)	290 258 217	Benzoic acid, 3,4-dimethoxy
217(17378)	288 217	Sarmentogenin
217(1259)	280 275 217	Cannabidiol
217(8390)	280 274 217	Acetic acid, (2-isopropyl-5-methylphenoxy)
217(6590)	279 272 217	Toluene, 3-methoxy
217(7510)	275 217	Benzene, 2-hydroxy-4-isopropyl-1-methyl
217(24800)	273 217	Benzoic acid, 2,4-dimethoxy-6-hydroxy
217(7080)	271 264 258 253 217	Sulfone, methyl phenyl
217(10000)	270 263 256 250 217	Benzene, 1,4-di-*tert*-butyl
217(39811)	270 217	Aconic acid
217(12700)	269 217	4-Pyrone, 5-hydroxy-2(hydroxymethyl)
217(6970)	265 259 254 217	Toluene, α-chloro
217(7690)	264 217	2-Pyridinecarboxylic acid
217(7410)	264 217	2-Pyridinecarboxylic acid, amide
217(8610)	262 217	3-Pyridinecarboxylic acid
217(8790)	262 217	3-Pyridinecarboxylic acid, ethyl ester
217(8230)	259 253 217	Benzenesulfonic acid, 4-fluoro, amide
217(26200)	255 217	Benzoic acid, 3-nitro, methyl ester
217(13804)	217	Acetic acid, 1-cyclohexenyl-, nitrile
217(24400)	217	Benzoic acid, 3-iodo
217(20893)	217	1,3-Butadiene
217(13489)	217	2-Hexenoic acid, 2-methyl (*trans*)
217(17900)	217	Phthalic acid, 3-nitro
217(2951)	217	2-Propanone, azine
217(4366)	217	Pyrazole, 1,5-dimethyl
217(4571)	217	1,2,4-Triazole
216(34100)	332 287 257 249 216	Benzothiazole, 2(2-hydroxyphenyl)
216(44400)	321 240 216	Acenaphthene, 5-amino

Strongest Band (ε)	Wavelengths (nm)	Compound
216(30199)	297 262 216	Benzoic acid, 2,6-dihydroxy-4-methyl
216(30500)	291 237 229 216	Phthalic acid, imide
216(16000)	291 237 216	Acetophenone, 2,3,4-trihydroxy
216(2920)	290 257 216	Benzoic acid, 2,4-dichloro, chloride
216(36800)	288 278 272 216	Gramine
216(8020)	278 271 216	Glycerol, 1(2-tolyl) ether
216(6270)	278 271 216	Toluene, 2-methoxy
216(12800)	278 270 263 256 250 216	Benzene, 1,3-dichloro
216(9120)	278 269 216	Ionene
216(5129)	277 271 216	Benzene, 1-*tert*-butyl-2-hydroxy
216(7110)	274 216	Benzene, 1-butyl-2-hydroxy
216(6500)	274 216	Benzene, 1-*sec*-butyl-2-hydroxy
216(10100)	269 262 256 216	Benzenearsonic acid
216(15600)	269 216	Benzoic acid, 2-chloro-5-nitro
216(7080)	265 216	Benzenephosphinic acid
216(7490)	264 216	2,3-Pyridinedicarboxylic acid
216(12400)	262 216	Toluene, 3,4-dinitro
216(9333)	234 216	Arsine oxide, phenyl
216(5623)	216	Biuret
216(9333)	216	2-Butenoic acid, 2-methyl (*cis*)
216(9772)	216	Furan, 2-bromo
216(5623)	216	Pilocarpine
216(10965	216	Propenal, 2-methyl
216(16982)	216	Strophanthidin
215(14300)	337 267 235 215	Toluene, 4-hydroxy-2-nitro
215(25900)	330 318 251 244 215	Quinoline, 7-chloro-4-hydroxy
215(12000)	326 266 239 215	Toluene, 2-hydroxy-6-nitro
215(1778)	325 238 215	Geraniol
215(1995)	325 235 215	Farnesol (*trans, trans*)
215(5495)	320 215	1-Penten-3-one
215(20417)	309 231 215	Benzaldehyde, 3,5-dimethoxy-4-hydroxy
215(20893)	306 215	3-Indazolinone
215(24900)	298 260 215	Benzoic acid, 2,4-dihydroxy-6-methyl
215(33700)	295 243 215	Aniline, 3-iodo
215(7943)	290 260 215	Carbamic acid, *N*-nitro-, ethyl ester
215(25119)	284 215	6-Uracilcarboxylic acid
215(7080)	278 271 265 215	Benzene, 1-bromo-4-fluoro
215(8150)	278 269 265 215	Benzene, 4-chloro-1,2-dimethyl
215(5495)	277 271 263 215 209	Benzene, 1-chloro-4-fluoro
215(9120)	274 262 238 215	Sulfoxide, ethyl (4-tolyl) (*d*)
215(6460)	274 215	Toluene, α,2-dihydroxy
215(24900)	273 237 215	Phthalic acid, diamide
215(6600)	273 215	Benzene, 1-*tert*-butyl-3-hydroxy
215(6880)	269 263 215	Benzene, 1,4-dihydroxy, diacetate
215(9840)	262 258 215	3-Pyridinecarboxylic acid, amide
215(22387)	255 215	Benzoic acid, 3-nitro
215(1259)	215	Creatine
215(6026)	215	Episarsapogenin
215(4677)	215	Imidazole, 4-methyl
215(1000)	215	Sulfide, dimethyl, hexafluoro
214(31800)	320 252 214	Flavone, 3-hydroxy
214(30700)	319 251 214	Flavanone
214(21600)	319 250 214	Chromanone
214(33000)	298 268 214	1,8-Naphthalenedicarboxylic acid, 3-nitro anhydride
214(16100)	298 226 214	Acetophenone, 3,5-dimethoxy-4-hydroxy
214 (13800)	293 252 214	Benzene, 1,4-dinitro-2-ethoxy
214(13800)	293 252 214	Benzene, 2,4-dinitro-1-ethoxy
214(32500)	292 284 214	Benzoic acid, 3-acetyl
214(17600)	286 232 214	Benzaldehyde, 5-bromo-4-hydroxy-3-methoxy
214(10900)	277 214	4-Pyrone, 3-hydroxy-2-methyl

Strongest Band (ε)	Wavelengths (nm)	Compound
214(6600)	276 270 214	Acetic acid, 2-tolyloxy
214(6030)	273 214	Toluene, 2-hydroxy
214(10000)	272 266 260 214 210	Benzene, 1-chloro-2-fluoro
214(15849)	268 284 261 258 253 248 238 214	Butane, 2,3-diphenyl (*meso*)
214(14400)	260 214	Phenol, 2-chloro-4,6-dinitro
214(15500)	260 214	Toluene, α-bromo-3-nitro
214(13900)	255 214	Toluene, α-bromo-2-nitro
214(1259)	237 214	Thiophene, 2-methyltetrahydro
214(10715)	214	Arecoline
214(10233)	214	Cyanuric acid, dihydrate
214(6761)	214	Propenoic acid, 2-methyl, butyl ester
214(9120)	214	Pyrazole-3-carboxylic acid
214(5129)	214	Sparteine (*d*)
213(18000)	323 250 213	1-Propanone, 1(2-hydroxyphenyl)
213(32359)	319 213	1,3-Benzenedicarboxylic acid, 2-hydroxy
213(34600)	312 248 213	Aniline, 2,4,5-trichloro
213(25119)	308 213	Meconin
213(10400)	305 237 213	Meconic acid
213(14000)	290 252 213	Benzene, 2,4-dinitro-1-methoxy
213(8870)	274 266 260 213	Acetic acid, (3-chlorophenyl)
213(5560)	274 265 260 213	Toluene, 3-chloro
213(22500)	268 227 213	Benzoic acid 2,3,4 -trihydroxy
213(17600)	264 213	Benzaldehyde, 2,4,6-trimethyl
213(14500)	259 213	Phthalic acid, 4-nitro, anhydride
213(12303)	213	2-Butenoic acid, 2-methyl (*trans*)
213(15849)	213	2-Octadecenoic acid (*cis*)
213(15849)	213	2-Octadecenoic acid (*trans*)
213(1585)	213	Piperidine, 1-methyl
213(2512)	213	Sulfide, diisopropyl
213(1000)	213	Sulfide, methyl propyl
212(5012)	382 335 212	Propynal
212(25600)	370 261 212	Naphthalene, 2-hydroxy-1-nitroso
212(22100)	350 307 212	Sulfide, diphenyl, 2,2′4,4′-tetranitro
212(43500)	329 212	Isoquinoline, 5-nitro
212(46600)	320 306 293 231 212	Naphthalene, 1-methoxy
212(31400)	318 244 212	Benzophenone, 4(dimethylamino)
212(39300)	313 273 212	5,6-Benzoflavone
212(31623)	305 250 212	Aniline, 3,5-dibromo
212 (19953)	300 269 212	Indole, 2-amino
212(25119)	286 236 212	Codeine
212(17500)	286 233 212	Benzaldehyde, 5-chloro-4-hydroxy-3-methoxy
212(25704)	284 212	Codeine, phosphate
212(6310)	274 267 261 212	*ar*-Curcumene
212(9390)	273 265 212	Toluene, 2-chloro
212(9060)	272 220 215 212	4-Pyridinecarboxylic acid, nitrile
212(27700)	271 263 217 212	Benzene, 1,4-diisopropyl
212(20417)	266 229 224 212	Cinnamic acid, 2-bromo (*trans*)
212(38000)	264 212	Urea, 1(2-napthyl)-2-thio
212(14100)	263 212	Benzene, 1-fluoro-4-nitro
212(14454)	250 212	2-Butenoic acid, methyl ester (*trans*)
212(1000)	240 212	Sulfide, ethyl methyl
212(1259)	212	Butane, 1,2-dibromo
212(3230)	212	Hydantoin, 1-methyl
212(1097)	212	Phytol (*dl*)
212(7763)	212	Pyrrole, 2,5-dimethyl
211(15300)	351 248 211	Aniline, 2,6-dibromo-4-nitro
211(43800)	329 315 304 237 211	Napththalene, 1-hydroxy-4-chloro
211(37400)	302 211	Aniline, 2,5-dibromo
211(25100)	295 287 250 211	Acetophenone, 3,4-dichloro

Strongest Band (ε)	Wavelengths (nm)	Compound
211(41500)	289 282 211	Benzene, 2-methoxy-1,3,5-tribromo
211(26800)	274 267 265 211	Phosphoric acid, tris(2,5-dimethylphenyl) ester
211(6350)	274 267 211	Pyridine, 5-ethyl-2-methyl
211(20417)	272 211	Cinnamic acid, 2,4,6-trimethyl (*trans*)
211(8680)	271 263 256 211	Benzene, 1,2-diethyl
211(7070)	271 211	4-Pyridinecarboxylic acid
211(8970)	270 263 257 211	Benzene, 1,3-diisopropyl
211(25100)	252 211	Benzoic acid, 3-amino-5-nitro
211(6310)	211	Histidine (*l*)
211(5770)	211	Histidine, monohydrochloride monohydrate (*l*)
211(14300)	211	Imidazole, 1-methyl
211(3981)	211	Isoxazole
210(44668)	336 244 210	Dibenzofuran, 1-nitro
210(25200)	305 258 210	Aniline, 3-chloro-*N,N*-dimethyl
210(7943)	300 260 219 210	Phthalaldehyde
210(38700)	299 210	1,4-Benzenedicarboxylic acid, 2,5-dichloro
210(30199)	297 239 210	Benzenesulfonic acid, 3-amino, amide
210(39200)	296 287 210	1,3-Benzenedicarboxylic acid, 5-methyl
210(19500)	294 284 251 216 210	Styrene, 4-methyl
210(25119)	287 236 210	Morphine
210(4169)	285 279 210	Phenol, 4-fluoro
210(33700)	285 277 244 210	Acetic acid, amide, *N*(3-chlorophenyl)
210(39811)	284 210	β-Codeine
210(12023)	270 210	Benzenesulfonic acid, chloride
210(15700)	269 212 210	1,2-Ethanedione, 1,2-di(2-furyl)
210(11400)	259 210	Benzoic acid, 4-hydroxy, methyl ester
210(20893)	256 210	Cinnamic acid, 2-chloro (*cis*)
210(1778)	229 210	Sulfide, diethyl
210(12589)	210	2-Butenoic acid, ethyl ester (*trans*)
210(6457)	210	3-Buten-2-one
210(3340)	210	Furazan, 3,4-dimethyl
210(13804)	210	Maleic acid
210(4366)	210	α-Pinene (*dl*)
210(3740)	210	Pyrazole
210(7943)	210	Toluene, α-isocyano
210(4366)	210	1,2,3-Triazole
209(31700)	310 244 209	Aniline, 2,4,6-trichloro
209(24400)	302 264 209	Brucine
209(23800)	299 259 209	Phenol, 3(diethylamino)
209(31200)	299 236 209	Benzoic acid, 3-hydroxy, methyl ester
209(29400)	298 237 209	Benzoic acid, 3-hydroxy, ethyl ester
209(13000)	274 209	Benzene, 1-nitro-2,4,5-trimethyl
209(18100)	270 264 217 209	Carbonic acid, di-4-tolyl ester
209(9010)	269 262 209	Acetic acid, 2-tolyl, nitrile
209(12500)	268 261 259 254 209	Benzene, pentyl
209(7244)	264 258 209	Toluene, α-hydroxylamino
209(19800)	258 209	Benzaldehyde, 2,4-dimethyl
209(30000)	255 209	2-Stilbenecarboxylic acid, 4-nitro, nitrile (*trans*)
209(5248)	209	5-Cholestene, 3 β-bromo
209(6730)	209	Pyrrole
209(3467)	209	Zymosterol
208(31900)	330 234 208	Naphthalene, 1,5-dinitro
208(19100)	322 208	Isatin, 5-nitro
208(46400)	318 311 305 231 208	Quinoline, 2,7-dimethyl
208(46900)	306 283 252 228 208	1,9-Benzanthr-10-one
208(40900)	297 234 208	Benzoic acid, 3-sulfo
208(13100)	291 252 208	Benzene, 1-bromo-2-nitro
208(26900)	290 254 208	Benzoic acid, 2,4-dimethoxy
208(28500)	289 280 208	Benzene, 1,2-bis(dibromomethyl)
208(17100)	289 208	Benzene, 2-chloro-1,3-dinitro

Strongest Band (ε)	Wavelengths (nm)	Compound
208(39811)	288 280 225 208	1,3-Benzenedicarboxylic acid
208(25119)	284 235 208	Morphine, *N*-oxide
208(36308)	274 267 230 208	Biphenyl, 2,2′-dichloro
208(7520)	270 261 255 208	Benzene, ethyl
208(25119)	270 261 208	Ethane, 1,1,2-triphenyl
208(7210)	268 262 257 251 208	Amygdalin
208(6310)	262 208	3-Pyridinesulfonic acid
208(20200)	251 208	Benzoic acid, 2,5-dinitro
208(28200)	208	Benzoic acid, 3,5-dinitro, furfuryl ester
208(28500)	208	Benzoic acid, 3,5-dinitro, isobutyl ester
208(26900)	208	Benzoic acid, 3,5-dinitro, isopropyl ester
208(27800)	208	Benzoic acid, 3,5-dinitro, pentyl ester
208(21600)	208	Benzoic acid, 3,5-dinitro, propyl ester
208(4467)	208	Cyclohexene, 1-bromo
208(1413)	208	Cyclohexene, 1-methyl
208(11221)	208	α-Ergostenol
208(7943)	208	Furan
208(1585)	208	Methionine (*l*)
208(5248)	208	β-Pinene, (*d*)
208(5248)	208	β-Pinene, (*l*)
208(6918)	208	Propenoic acid, ethyl ester
208(8511)	208	Propenoic acid, 2-methyl, ethyl ester
208(13804)	208	Pyrrole, 1-benzyl
208(5770)	208	1,2,4-Triazole, 3,5-diamino
207(22200)	317 247 214 207	Benzoic acid, 2,3 -dihydroxy
207(34100)	308 240 207	Benzoic acid, 2-hydroxy-3-methyl
207(28840)	303 236 207	Benzoic acid, 2-hydroxy
207(39600)	295 286 280 248 217 207	Ether, diphenyl
207(20400)	291 258 207	Styrene, 4-methoxy
207(35900)	288 239 207	Benzene, 1-amino-3,5-dimethyl
207(18300)	286 233 207	Benzaldehyde, 2-amino
207(38600)	284 242 207	Biphenyl, 2,2′-dihydroxy
207(42300)	283 242 207	Acetic acid, amide, *N*(2-hydroxyphenyl)
207(21500)	283 241 207	Benzoxazole, 2-methyl
207(48600)	281 241 207	Benzimidazole, 2-amino
207(7586)	269 262 207	Toluene, 3-fluoro
207(15849)	260 207	Cinnamic acid, β-chloro (*trans*)
207(18500)	259 207	Adenosine
207(24700)	257 207	Ethane, 1,2-bis(2-nitrophenyl)
207(45709)	253 210 207	Biphenyl, 3,4′-dimethyl
207(12200)	251 207	Benzene, 1,3-dimethyl-2-nitro
207(1349)	247 207	1,3-Dithiolane
207(6607)	207	α-Amyrin
207(6607)	207	β-Amyrin
207(4677)	207	Caryophyllin
207(3311)	207	5-Cholestene, 3 β-chloro
207(6457)	207	Coprostenol
207(14400)	207	Fumaric acid
207(3389)	207	3-Hexen-1-al (*trans*)
207(5180)	207	Imidazole
207(8070)	207	Maleic acid, dimethyl, anhydride
207(2512)	207	2-Pentene, 2,4,4-trimethyl
207(11221)	207	Propenal
206(9890)	319 231 206	Toluene, 2-hydroxy-5-nitro
206(31200)	312 237 206	Benzoic acid, 2-hydroxy-5-methyl
206(26303)	306 246 206	Benzenesulfonic acid, 2-amino, amide
206(46773)	298 244 206	Benzoic acid, 3-hydroxy-4-methyl
206(47900)	297 289 206	Acetic acid, (2,4,5-trichlorophenoxy)
206(17900)	289 244 226 206	1,3-Benzenedicarboxaldehyde

Strongest Band (ε)	Wavelengths (nm)	Compound
206(32700)	282 237 206	Tetralin, 5-amino
206(7244)	273 264 206	Toluene, 4-fluoro
206(7943)	268 262 206	Toluene, 2-fluoro
206(6310)	262 206	4-Pyridinesulfonic acid
206(15849)	256 220 206	2-Butenoic acid, 3-phenyl (*trans*)
206(15849)	248 206	2-Butenoic acid, 3-phenyl (*cis*)
206(1318)	206 270	Cyclopropane, acetyl
206(6310)	206	2-Butynoic acid
206(5495)	206	Camphene (*d*)
206(3389)	206	Cholesterol
206(8540)	206	1-Cyclohexene-1,2-dicarboxylic acid, anhydride
206(2512)	206	Lupeol
206(9730)	206	Maleic acid, methyl, anhydride
205(34200)	384 205	Amine, diphenyl, 2,2′,4,4′,6,6′-hexanitro
205(15800)	360 205	Aniline, 2-bromo-4-nitro
205(17500)	352 248 205	Pyridine, picrate
205(29500)	334 241 205	Isoquinoline, 5-amino
205(42000)	318 304 279 229 205	Quinoline, 7-methyl
205(18700)	292 252 205	Benzaldehyde, oxime (*syn*)
205(20900)	275 205	Ethane, 1,2-bis (4-nitrophenyl)
205(49200)	268 205	Benzoic acid, amide, *N,N*-diphenyl
205(19953)	267 230 205	Cinnamic acid, β-bromo (*cis*)
205(8430)	263 257 251 247 205	Benzene, (1-aminoethyl) (*dl*)
205(9500)	263 257 251 246 205	Amine, benzyl ethyl
205(15849)	263 205	Cinnamic acid, β-bromo (*trans*)
205(42658)	254 205	Biphenyl, 3,4-dimethyl
205(29100)	240 205	Stilbene, 2,4-dinitro (*trans*)
205(7586)	240 205	Succinic acid, methylene, dimethyl ester
205(9380)	239 205	Semicarbazide, 4-methyl-3-thio
205(2041)	230 220 214 205	Bicyclo [2,2,1] hepta-2,5-diene
205(1905)	205	Arginine (*dl*)
205(1905)	205	Arginine (*l*)
205(26700)	205	Benzenehexacarboxylic acid
205(15849)	205	2-Butenoic acid (*trans*)
205(5623)	205	2-Cholestene
205(1778)	205	1,2-Cyclopropanedicarboxylic acid, 3-methylene (*trans*)
205(3311)	205	5-Pregnen-3β-ol-20-one
205(2884)	205	2-Pyrrolidone, 1-methyl
205(5495)	205	Stigmasterol
204(37500)	318 248 204	Flavone, 3,3′,4′,7-tetrahydroxy
204(10715)	307 204	Phenol, 3,4,5-trichloro
204(42100)	299 236 204	Benzohydroxamic acid, 2-hydroxy
204(29200)	291 234 204	Indan, 5-amino
204(39200)	288 281 225 204	Benzoic acid, 3-bromo
204(14500)	279 204	Benzene, 1,2-dimethyl-4-nitro
204(2089)	252 204	Disulfide, dibutyl
204(40500)	249 204	Biphenyl, 3-methyl
204(41687)	237 204	Biphenyl, 2,3-dimethyl
204(11482)	204	2-Butenoic acid (*cis*)
204(1000)	204	4-Piperidinecarboxylic acid, 1-methyl, methyl ester
203(18900)	203 242	Amine, diphenyl, 2,2′,4,4′-tetrabromo
203(6166)	203	Propenoic acid, nitrile
202(33600)	281 245 202	Urea, 1(4-chlorophenyl)
202(31200)	275 202	Biphenyl, 3-amino-4-hydroxy
202(2089)	252 202	Disulfide, diethyl
201(27700)	322 277 237 201	Uranin
201(18621)	201	Phosphine, trimethyl
200(10471)	200	Benzene, 1,3-dimethyl-5-ethyl
200(2754)	200	1-Butene, 2-methyl
200(9120)	200	1,5,9-Cyclododecatriene (*cis,cis,cis*)

Strongest Band (ε)	Wavelengths (nm)	Compound
198(9333)	210 198	1,4,7-Cyclononatriene (*cis,cis,cis*)
198(13183)	198	2-Butene, 2,3-dimethyl
198(3162)	198	Piperidine
197(8710)	197 162	Formic acid, amide, *N,N*-dimethyl
197(7763)	197	Cholesterol, acetate
196(5012)	196	Amine, triethyl
196(8511)	196	β-Ergostenol
196(8318)	196	γ-Ergostenol
196(5012)	196	Piperazine
195(1413)	225 195	Ethanethiol
195(1413)	225 195	Ethanethiol, sodium salt
195(3802)	195	γ-Pyran, 2,3-dihydro
194(2951)	222 194	Amine, diethyl
193(8128)	193	5-Cholestene
192(6310)	192	Cyclohexene, 1-chloro
192(8913)	192	Epicholesterol
192(10000)	192	2-Pentene, 2-methyl
191(3890)	227 191 161	Amine, trimethyl
191(3236)	222 191	Amine, dimethyl
191(3236)	215 191	Methane, amino
190(5012)	190	2-Propanone, oxime
189(7943)	194 189 184	1-Pentene, 2-methyl
189(7943)	189	9-Octadecenoic acid (*trans*)
189(9550)	189	Phosphine, dimethyl
188(39811)	255 216 188	Aniline, 2-bromo-*N,N*-dimethyl
188(12589)	200 192 188 184 159	Propene, 2-methyl
187(10000)	198 187 169	1-Butene, 2,3-dimethyl
187(7943)	195 187 172	1-Butene, 2-ethyl
186(39811)	256 211 186	Aniline, 2-chloro-*N,N*-dimethyl
186(12589)	186	Triglycine
185(1995)	223 185	1-Octyne
185(6310)	185	9-Octadecenoic acid (*cis*)
185(8128)	185	3-Octene, (*trans*)
184(10000)	199 187 184 179	2-Pentene, 3-methyl (*cis*)
183(13489)	183	Cyclopentene
183(12882)	183	2-Octene (*trans*)
181(14125)	201 181 158	2-Pentene (*trans*)
181(25119)	181 177	1,2-Pentadiene
180(12589)	186 180 175	2-Pentene, 3-methyl (*trans*)
180(12589)	186 180	2-Pentene, 4-methyl (*trans*)
180(6310)	180	1,3-Dioxane
180(6310)	180	1,4-Dioxane
179(12589)	201 179 170	2-Hexene (*trans*)
179(14791)	179	3-Hexene (*cis*)
179(14125)	179	2-Octene (*cis*)
178(10000)	196 178	2-Octyne
178(15849)	194 186 178	2-Hexene (*cis*)
178(19953)	186 178	1,2-Butadiene
178(10000)	178 173	1-Pentene, 4-methyl
178(16982)	178	1,4-Pentadiene
177(1585)	213 177	Ethane, amino
177(18197)	205 185 177 167	2-Pentene (*cis*)
177(15849)	204 197 177	2-Pentene, 4-methyl (*cis*)
177(12589)	202 187 177 163	2-Butene (*trans*)
177(16596)	187 181 177	1-Pentene
177(15849)	186 183 177	1-Pentene, 3-methyl
177(25119)	177	1,5-Hexadiene
177(12589)	177	1-Octene
175(19953)	200 196 175 160	2-Butene (*cis*)
175(15849)	187 175 162	1-Butene

Strongest Band (ϵ)	Wavelengths (nm)	Compound
175(1995)	187 175	γ-Pyran, tetrahydro
175(10000)	175	Cyclobutene
175(7080)	175	Propanoic acid, amide
174(2754)	188 184 174 171 167	Propane, 1,3-epoxy
174(12589)	188 174	1-Butene; 3,3-dimethyl
172(4467)	172	1-Butyne
171(19953)	202 194 180 171	2,3-Pentadiene
171(2512)	196 171	Pyrrolidine
171(3981)	188 171	Ether, diethyl
169(3802)	171 169	Ethane, 1,2-epoxy
163(3981)	184 163	Ether, dimethyl
162(8710)	174 166 162	Ethene
156(23442)	175 156	Formaldehyde

ϵ Less Than 1,000

Strongest Band (ϵ)	Wavelengths (nm)	Compound
750(47)	750	Benzene, 1-nitro-2-nitroso
750(45)	750	Benzene, nitroso
745(46)	745	Toluene, 4-nitroso
708(23)	708 692	Ethane, nitrosopentafluoro
700(20)	700 680	Methane, nitrosotrifluoro
686(22)	686	Propane, heptafluoro-1-nitroso
595(166)	595	Benzophenone, thio
580(10)	584 580 576 565	Acetic acid, oxo
560(59)	560	Malvidine, chloride
535(603)	535	Tyramine
510(5)	510	Murexide
504(474)	504	Aphanin
474(200)	474	9,10-Anthraquinone, 1-amino-4-nitro
468(32)	468 279 269	Camphorquinone (*l*)
451(891)	451	*p,p'*-Azobiphênyl
445(562)	445	Azobenzene, 3-methoxy
442(13)	442	Acetic acid, chloro, amide
435(3)	435 408 380	Methane, diazo
432(759)	432 411	1,2,3-Propenetricarboxylic acid (*trans*)
411(603)	411 389	1,2,3-Propenetricarboxylic acid (*cis*)
405(794)	405	Epiandrosterone
394(45)	394	Laureline
380(63)	380	Azobenzene, 2-hydroxy, benzoate
380(79)	380	Berbamine
375(302)	386 375 365	Benzene, 1-chloro-3,5-dimethyl
366(110)	377 366 354	Piperidine, 1-nitroso
360(759)	378 369 360	Benzene, 1-bromo-1,4-dimethyl
359(50)	387 359 327	Nitrous acid, isopropyl ester
358(871)	375 370 358	Benzene, 1-chloro-2,4-dimethyl
357(81)	387 357	Nitrous acid, hexyl ester
357(83)	384 357	Nitrous acid, decyl ester
357(83)	384 357	Nitrous acid, octyl ester
356(85)	383 356 315	Nitrous acid, heptyl ester
355(76)	382 368 355 343 333 323	Nitrous acid, isobutyl ester
354(562)	354	Benzoic acid, 4-methyl, methyl ester
350(17)	350	Cyclohexanecarboxylic acid, 1,1-azobis, dinitrile
345(20)	345	Azomethane (*trans*)
345(200)	345	Benzene, 2-nitro-1,3,5-trichloro
341(126)	341	Pentanoic acid, nitrile
340(631)	340	Benzene, 2-chloro-1,3,5-trinitro
338(8)	338 255	Cotarnine, chloride
333(54)	333	Isothiocyanic acid, acetyl
333(151)	333	α-Lipoic acid (*d*)
330(10)	330	Ketene

Strongest Band (ε)	Wavelengths (nm)	Compound
330(33)	330	β-Vetivone
328(14)	371 328 303	Malonic acid, oxo, dinitrate
328(166)	328	α-Vetivone
324(12)	324	Methanesulfenic acid, trichloro, chloride
323(76)	323	Camphor, 3,3-dibromo (*d*)
320(25)	369 351 340 330 320 316 306	Oxalic acid, dichloride
320(501)	335 320	Benzophenone, 3,3′-dinitro
320(24)	320	Benzoic acid, 3-hydroxyphenyl ester
312(30)	312	Butanoic acid, 3,3-dimethyl-2-oxo
312(89)	312	Camphor, 3-bromo (*d*,α′)
312(50)	312	Carvenone (*dl*)
310(41)	310	3-Penten-2-one (*trans*)
307(67)	307	Butanal, 2-bromo
306(56)	306	Camphor, 3-chloro (*d*,α′)
306(832)	306	Cyclooctatetraenecarboxylic acid
306(10)	306	2-Indanone
305(52)	305	Camphor, 3-chloro (*d*,α)
303(28)	303	Butanoic acid, 3-methyl-2-oxo
302(614)	302	2,4-Piperidinedione, 3,3-diethyl
301(7)	301	Amine, dibutyl
301(7)	301	Amine, diisopropyl
301(35)	301	Ketone, dicyclohexyl
300(6)	300	Glycine, *N*-leucyl (*dl*)
300(42)	300	2-Propanone, 1,3-dichloro
300(200)	300	Tetraphenylene
296(295)	296 285 274	Pyrocalciferol
296(8)	296	Amine, diallyl
295(162)	295	Acetic acid, 4-aminophenyl, nitrile
295(21)	295	Butanal, 2-methyl (*dl*)
295(56)	295	3,6-Cholestanedione
295(50)	295	Eremophilone, 8,9-epoxy
295(457)	295	3-Heptanone, 6-dimethylamino-4,4-diphenyl (*l*)
295(13)	295	Octanal
294(47)	365 294	3,4-Hexanedione, 2,2,5,5-tetramethyl
294(30)	294	Camphor, 5-bromo (*exo*)
294(24)	294	Cyclohexanone, 2-chloro
294(1)	294	Glyceraldehyde (*d*)
294(1)	294	Glyceraldehyde (*dl*)
294(1)	294	Glyceraldehyde (*l*)
294(63)	294	2-Propanone, 1,1-dichloro
294(219)	294	2-Propanone, 1,3-diphenyl
293(19)	293	Cyclohexanone, 2-isopropyl
293(245)	293	1,2-Dithiane
293(5)	293	Erythratine
293(28)	293	Hexadecanal
293(20)	293	Menthone (*l*)
292(32)	292	Glucose pentaacetate (d, α)
292(31)	292	2-Propanone, 1-chloro
291(209)	301 291	Benzene, hexachloro
291(126)	291	Veratrine
290(17)	290	Acetaldehyde
290(38)	290	Acetaldehyde, trichloro
290(794)	290	Adrenaline (*d*)
290(30)	290	Camphor (*d*)
290(562)	290	Cyclooctatetraene, bromo
290(229)	290	Galactose (*d*)
290(154)	290	Propanal, 2-methyl
290(8)	290	Protoveratrine B
289(36)	289	Camphor (*dl*)
289(59)	289	Camphor, 8-bromo (*d*)

Strongest Band (ϵ)	Wavelengths (nm)	Compound
289(20)	289	3-Pentanone, 2,2,4-trimethyl
289(20)	289	3-Pinanone (*trans, d*)
288(363)	298 288	Benzene, pentachloro
288(27)	288	3-Camphorsulfonic acid, methyl ester (*d*)
288(22)	288	Cyclopentanone, 3-methyl (*d*)
288(22)	288	Cyclopentanone, 3-methyl (*dl*)
288(22)	288	Fenchone (*dl*)
288(229)	288	2-Propanone, 1,1-diphenyl
288(724)	274 288	Benzoic acid, 3,4,5-trichloro
287(35)	287	1,6-Cyclodecanedione
286(813)	286 269 232	Benzoic acid, 2,5-dimethyl
286(29)	286	3-Hexanone, 2,2-dimethyl
286(28)	286	3-Pentanone, 2,4-dimethyl
285(25)	285	Acetic acid, triazo
285(35)	285	10-Camphorsulfonic acid (*d*)
285(100)	285	5-Cholesten-3-one
285(20)	285	Cycloheptanone
285(21)	285	Fenchone (*l*)
285(25)	285	Naphthalene, 5,8-dioxo-1,4,5,8,9,10-hexahydro-1,4-methylene
285(8)	285	Sulfoxide, diallyl
284(16)	284	Cyclohexanone, 2-methyl (*dl*)
284(27)	284	2-Heptanone, 1-chloro
284(26)	284	3-Pentanone, 2,2-dimethyl
283(813)	294 283 273	Ether, 1-naphthyl phenyl
283(13)	283 225	Butanal
283(550)	283	Benzoic acid, 2,3,6-trichloro
283(79)	283	Butanoic acid, anhydride
283(27)	283	Carvomenthone (*d*)
283(15)	283	Cyclodecanone
283(27)	283	3-Hexanone, 2-methyl
282(479)	282	Butanoic acid, amide
282(417)	282	2-Butanone, 3,3-dimethyl
282(21)	282	Cyclopentadecanone
282(16)	282	Glucose (*d*)(equilibrium mixture)
282(25)	282	4-Heptanone, 2-methyl
282(25)	282	2-Pentanone, 3-methyl (*dl*)
282(8)	282	Propanal
282(36)	282	Propane, heptafluoro-1-nitro
281(316)	291 281 274	Benzene, 1,2,3,5-tetrachloro
281(28)	281	Ethane, nitropentafluoro
281(26)	281	Pentanoic acid, 5-oxo-5-phenyl
281(26)	281	3-Pentanone, 2-methyl
281(159)	281	Propanoic acid, amide, *N*-propionyl
280(20)	420 405 375 280	1,2-Cycloheptanedione
280(126)	340 280	Hypochlorous acid, *tert*-butyl ester
280(575)	304 293 280	Malonic acid, dichloride
280(27)	280 276	Cyclohexanone
280(35)	280	Acetaldehyde, chloro
280(259)	280	Benzene, 1,3-dimethyl-2,3,5,6-tetrachloro
280(240)	280	Benzene, 1,2-dimethyl-3,4,5,6-tetrachloro
280(788)	280	Benzoic acid, 2-chloro
280(21)	280	2-Butanone, 3-methyl
280(126)	280	α-Caryophyllene
280(50)	280	Cevagenine
280(72)	280	3-Cholestanone
280(25)	280	Cyclohexane, nitro
280(16)	280	Cyclononanone
280(316)	280	Cyclooctatetraene, chloro
280(316)	280	Cyclooctatetraene, methyl
280(58)	280	Ethane, 1,1-dinitro

Strongest Band (ϵ)	Wavelengths (nm)	Compound
280(0.04)	280	Glucoside, α-methyl (*d*)
280(24)	280	4-Heptanone
280(25)	280	3-Hexanone, 5-methyl
280(23)	280	4-Octanone
280(58)	280	Propane, 1,1-dinitro
280(8)	280	Sulfurous acid, dimethyl ester
280(240)	280	Toluene, 2,3,4,5,6-pentachloro
280(40)	280	Toluene, 3,4,5-trihydroxy
279(829)	293 279 271	Benzoic acid, 3-formyl, nitrile
279 (25)	279	Butane, 2-nitro (*dl*)
279(19)	279	Cyclohexanone, 2-hydroxy
279(23)	279	Cyclopentane, acetyl
279(0.38)	279	β-Fructose (*d*)
278(0.2)	357 278	Semicarbazide, hydrochloride
278(570)	287 278 270 263	Benzene, 2-bromo-1,4-dichloro
278(741)	278 264	Ether, 2-naphthyl phenyl
278(15)	278	Cyclobutanone
278(7)	278	Gluconic acid, nitrile (*d*)
278(49)	278	6-Hendecanone
278(242)	278	1,6-Hexanedione, 1,6-diphenyl
278(22)	278	3-Hexanone
278(11)	278	Methane, nitrotrifluoro
278(29)	278	5-Nonanone
278(24)	278	2-Pentanone, 4-hydroxy
278(52)	278	Propane, 2,2-dinitro
277(20)	319 313 308 277	Piperazine, 2,5-dimethyl (*cis*)
277(40)	277	Butane, 1,4-dinitro
277(31)	277	Cyclopentane, nitro
277(62)	277	Methane, nitrotrichloro
276(501)	276 267	Benzene, 1,4-dimethyl-2-ethyl
276(501)	276 267	Benzene, 2,4-dimethyl-1-ethyl
276(19)	276	2-Butanone, 1-hydroxy
276(19)	276	2-Butanone, 4-hydroxy
276(4)	276	Germine
276(45)	276	Hexane, 1,6-dinitro
276(20)	276	2-Hexanone
276(26)	276	Pentane, 1-nitro
276(38)	276	2-Propanol, 1-nitro
276(708)	276	Toluene, α,α-dibromo
275(501)	278 275 269	Benzene, 1,2,3,5-tetramethyl
275(501)	275 266	Benzene, 1,2-dimethyl-4-ethyl
275(871)	275 266	Benzene, 1-fluoro-2,4,6-trimethyl
275(32)	275	16-Hentriacontanone
275(28)	275	Hexane, 1-nitro
275(49)	275	Pentane, 1,5 dinitro
275(31)	275	1-Propanol, 2-nitro
274(794)	286 274 266 259	Tetralin
274(200)	284 274 268	Aniline, 2,4,5-tribromo
274(891)	274 271	Benzene, 1,3,5-trihydroxy-2,4,6-trimethyl
274(501)	274 268 259	Benzene, 1-methyl-4-propyl
274(501)	274 266	2-Tetralincarboxylic acid (*dl*)
274(0.002)	274	Acetic acid, nitrile
274(269)	274	Benzoic acid, 2,4,6-trichloro
274(17)	274	2-Butanone
273(55)	280 273	Nerolidol (*dl*)
273(363)	273	Benzoic acid, 2,6-dichloro
273(407)	273	2-Naphthoic acid, 1,4-dihydro
273(40)	273	Propane, 1,3-dinitro
273(10)	273	Sulfone, ethenyl methyl
272(251)	272 269	Benzene, 1-ethyl-3-methyl

Strongest Band (ε)	Wavelengths (nm)	Compound
272(251)	272 268 265 259	Benzene, 1-methyl-3-propyl
272(25)	272	Butane, 1-nitro
272(45)	272	2-Butanol, 1-nitro
272(25)	272	Sulfide, trimethylene
271(339)	278 271	Toluene, α,2-dichloro
270(8)	342 322 270	Phthalic acid, tetraiodo, anhydride
270(302)	278 274 270	Benzene, hexamethyl
270(589)	278 270 264 257	Benzene, 1,3-dibromo
270(288)	278 270 263 257	Benzene, 1,2-dibromo
270(8)	270	Acetaldehyde, diethyl acetal
270(158)	270	Acetic acid, nitro, ethyl ester
270(20)	270	Benzene, pentamethyl
270(724)	270	Benzoic acid, 2,6-dimethyl
270(28)	270	Ethanol, 2-nitro
270(0.06)	270	Glycerol
270(277)	270	Indan, 4-hydroxy
270(316)	270	Neocarvomenthol (*l*)
270(17)	270	Nitric acid, *sec*-butyl ester (*dl*)
270(15)	270	Nitric acid, octyl ester
270(50)	270	Octadecanoic acid, 9,10-dioxo
270(25)	270	Pentanoic acid, 4-oxo
270(0.20)	270	Propanoic acid, 2-hydroxy, nitrile
270(22)	270	2-Propanone, 1,3-dihydroxy
269(501)	269	Benzene, 1,3,5-trihydroxy
269(629)	269	Benzene, 1,3,5-trihydroxy, triacetate
269(62)	269	Ethene, nitro
269(47)	269	2-Propanone, 1-hydroxy
268(47)	425 268	4,5-Octanedione
268(240)	274 268 262	Benzene, 1-bromo-3,5-dimethyl
268(912)	274 268	Biphenyl, 2,2′,4,4′,6,6′-hexamethyl
268(457)	272 268 264	Benzene, 1-ethyl-4-methyl
268(224)	268	Benzene, 2-chloro-1,3,5-trimethyl
268(100)	268	Malonic acid, methyl, diethyl ester
268(427)	268	Piperidine, 3-methyl (*dl*)
268(427)	268	Piperidine, 3-methyl (*l*)
268(398)	268	2-Propanone, 1-iodo
268(631)	268	Veratramine
267(303)	274 267 260	Toluene, 3-bromo
267(200)	267 261	Benzene, 1,2-bis(hydroxymethyl)
267(398)	267 260	Sulfone, ethyl(4-tolyl)
267(309)	267	Acetic acid, 4-tolyl, nitrile
267(661)	267	Benzene, 1,2,3-trimethoxy
267(406)	267	Benzoic acid, 2-bromo, amide
267(3)	267	Malonic acid, dinitrile
266(305)	287 273 266 259	Toluene, 2-bromo
266(275)	277 272 266	Benzene, 1-chloro-2,6-dimethyl
266(631)	275 266 261	Methane, phenyl(4-tolyl)
266(214)	273 266	Acetic acid, (2-chlorophenyl), nitrile
266(200)	266 259	Butanoic acid, phenyl ester
266(234)	266	Acetic acid, (4-bromophenyl), nitrile
266(15)	266	Nitric acid, ethyl ester
266(527)	266	Phenol, 3,5-dimethoxy
266(263)	266	Toluene, 4-chloro-α-hydroxy
265(446)	271 265	Acetic acid, 4-tolyl ester
265(759)	265	Benzene, 1,3-dihydroxy-5-methoxy
265(479)	265	Benzene, 1,3,5-trimethoxy
265(10)	265	9-Octadecynoic acid
265(126)	265	Succinic acid, methylene, diethyl ester
265(178)	265	Succinic acid, oxo, diethyl ester
264(282)	272 264 258 251 245	Benzene, chloro

Strongest Band (ε)	Wavelengths (nm)	Compound
264(251)	271 268 264 257	Benzene, 1-isopropyl-3-methyl
264(251)	271 264	Benzene, 1-ethyl-2-methyl
264(224)	270 264 258	Benzene, 1,3,5-triethyl
263(251)	275 263	Methanol, (2-tolyl)
263(246)	271 268 263 257	Benzene, 1,2-diisopropyl
263(159)	271 263	Benzene, 1-methyl-2-propyl
263(251)	270 267 263 257	Benzene, 1-isopropyl-2-methyl
263(316)	263	Acetic acid, amide, *N*-methyl-*N*(2-tolyl)
263(295)	263	Butanoic acid, 3-oxo, ethyl ester (keto form)
263(1)	263	Propanoic acid, 2-hydroxy-2-methyl, nitrile
262(969)	274 269 265 262 260	Benzene, 1,4-dibenzyl
262(794)	273 262	Succinic acid, imide, *N*-phenyl
262(933)	272 262	Benzoic acid, 2,6-dibromo
262(254)	270 262	Benzene, 1,2-dimethyl
262(316)	269 262 260	Butanoic acid, 3-phenyl (*dl*)
262(501)	269 262	Pentane, 1,1-diphenyl
262(204)	268 265 262 249	Benzene, propyl
262(414)	268 265 256 251	Ammonium, benzyl trimethyl, bromide
262(235)	268 262 256	Benzene, 1,3,5-triisopropyl
262(501)	268 262 254	Pentane, 1,5-diphenyl
262(707)	268 262	Phosphoric acid, tris (3,5-dimethylphenyl) ester
262(257)	267 262 256 251	Benzene-1,4-diacetic acid
262(240)	266 262	Acetaldehyde, semicarbazone
262(200)	262	1-Butene, 4-phenyl
262(794)	262	Ethane, 1,1,1-triphenyl
262(18)	262	Guanidine, hydrochloride
262(239)	262	Vitamin B_1
261(295)	284 261 239	Toluene, α,α-difluoro
261(374)	269 261	Benzene, 1,2,3-trimethyl
261(501)	268 265 261 259 253 248	Butane, 1,4-diphenyl
261(238)	268 264 261 260 255 254	Toluene
261(206)	268 264 261 259 255 253 248 243	1-Propanol, 3-phenyl
261(620)	268 261	Carbonic acid, di-3-tolyl ester
261(183)	267 264 261 253	Benzene, *sec*-butyl (*dl*)
261(2)	261 255 243	Fluorophosphoric acid, diisopropyl ester
261(288)	261	Ethanol, 2,2-diphenyl
261(4)	261	Phosphorous acid, triisopropyl ester
261(371)	261	Pyridine, pentachloro
261(224)	261	Succinic acid, benzyl (*dl*)
260(10)	330 260	Protoverine
260(32)	310 260	Hypochlorous acid, ethyl ester
260(501)	300 260	2-Butanone, 3,3-diphenyl
260(13)	290 260	Protoveratrine
260(501)	269 260	Methane, diphenyl
260(398)	268 260	Ethane, 2,2-diphenyl-1,1,1-trichloro
260(89)	260	Acetic acid, amide, *N*-acetyl
260(159)	260	Butanoic acid, 4-phenyl, amide
260(43)	260	Ethane, nitro
260(50)	260	9,12,15-Octadecatrienoic acid, ethyl ester (*cis, cis, cis*)
260(200)	260	Phenylalanine, *N*-acetyl ($d,^{+}$)
260(200)	260	Phenylalanine, *N*-acetyl (*dl*)
260(200)	260	Phenylalanine, *N*-acetyl (*l*,–)
260(1)	260	Phosphorous acid, triethyl ester
260(112)	260	Succinic acid, phenyl (*d*)
260(115)	260	Succinic acid, phenyl (*dl*)
260(115)	260	Succinic acid, phenyl (*l*)
259(631)	341 259	Butane, 1,1-diphenyl
259(319)	269 265 263 259 253	Sulfone, dibenzyl

Strongest Band (ε)	Wavelengths (nm)	Compound
259(240)	268 265 259 254 248 243	Benzene, (3-bromopropyl)
259(221)	268 264 261 259	Benzene, isobutyl
259(489)	268 264 259 253	Ethane, 1,2-diphenyl
259(208)	268 264 259 253	α-Toluenesulfonic acid, amide
259(283)	268 261 259 253	Benzene, allyl
259(615)	267 259	Phosphoric acid, tris (2,6-dimethylphenyl) ester
259(434)	265 259 253	Propanoic acid, 2,2-diphenyl
259(398)	264 259 252	Atropine, sulfate
259(822)	259 253	Methane, chloro(triphenyl)
259(398)	259	Butane, 1,2-diphenyl
259(589)	259	Butane, 2-iodo (*dl*)
258(471)	269 261 258 253 242	Propanoic acid, 3,3-diphenyl
258(401)	268 264 258 253 248	Butanoic acid, 4-phenyl, nitrile
258(246)	267 264 260 258 253 247 242 237	Cyclohexanol, 2-phenyl (*cis, dl*)
258(244)	267 264 258 252 247	Pentanoic acid, 4-phenyl
258(196)	267 264 258 252 247	Propanoic acid, 3-phenyl, nitrile
258(417)	267 258	Butanoic acid, 4-phenyl
258(200)	266 258 252	Ephedrine (*l*)
258(520)	264 258 253 242	Methanol, diphenyl
258(192)	264 258 252 248	1,3-Dioxane, 4-methyl-4-phenyl
258(289)	264 258 252 247	Acetic acid, phenyl, methyl ester
258(397)	264 258 252 247	Acetic acid, phenyl, 2-phenylethyl ester
258(209)	264 258 252 247	Butanoic acid, 2-phenyl, amide
258(617)	264 258 252	Acetic acid, diphenyl(hydorxy)
258(198)	264 258 252	Butanoic acid, 2-phenyl
258(200)	264 258 252	Hyoscyamine (*l*)
258(755)	264 258	Barbituric acid, 5-ethyl-1-methyl-5-phenyl
258(380)	263 258 253	1,2-Ethanediol, 1,2-diphenyl (*d*)
258(398)	263 258 253	1,2-Ethanediol, 1,2-diphenyl (*l*)
258(398)	263 258 253	1,2-Ethanediol, 1,2-diphenyl (*meso*)
258(427)	263 258 252	Lobelanidine
258(219)	258	Acetic acid, amide, *N*-benzyl
258(0.50)	258	Acetic acid, ethenyl ester
258(316)	258	Cyclopentanecarboxylic acid, 2-oxo, ethyl ester
258(159)	258	Succinic acid, phenyl, anhydride (*d*)
258(32)	258	Thiirane
257(209)	267 263 261 257 251 247	Butanoic acid, benzyl ester
257(240)	267 263 260 257 241	Cyclohexanol, 4-phenyl (*cis*)
257(214)	267 263 257 252 248	2-Butanol, 2-phenyl (+)
257(214)	267 263 257 252	Acetic acid, benzyl ester
257(178)	267 257 242	Phenylalanine (*d*)
257(178)	267 257 242	Phenylalanine (*dl*)
257(178)	267 257 242	Phenylalanine (*l*)
257(734)	264 257	Hydantoin, 5,5-diphenyl
257(340)	264 257	Urea, 1(phenylacetyl)
257(213)	263 261 257 251	Toluene, α-amino, hydrochloride
257(239)	263 257 252 246	Glycine, *N*-benzyl, ethyl ester
257(631)	263 257 251	Phosphorous acid, trimethyl ester
257(200)	263 257 250	Ephedrine, hydrochloride (*d*)
257(200)	263 257 250	Ephedrine, hydrochloride (*dl*)
257(631)	260 257	Cyclopentane, iodo
256(132)	259 256 244	Aniline, sulfate (acid)
256(316)	256	Disulfide, dimethyl
255(794)	370 345 325 255 245	Irene
255(398)	290 255 235	Pentanedioic acid, 3(2(3,5-dimethyl-2-oxocyclohexyl)2-hydroxyethyl), imide
255(132)	263 255 250	Acetic acid, hydroxy(phenyl), nitrile (*l*,–)
255(457)	258 255	Propane, 1-chloro-3-iodo
255(200)	255	Ammonium, phenyl trimethyl, chloride

Strongest Band (ε)	Wavelengths (nm)	Compound
255(159)	255	Butanoic acid, 2-methyl (*dl*)
255(490)	255	Propane, 1-iodo
254(276)	264 258 254 248	Ammonium, phenyl trimethyl, bromide
254(151)	260 254 248 243	Aniline, hydrochloride
254(195)	260 254 248	Aniline, *N-tert*-butyl
254(219)	260 254 248	Aniline, *N*-isobutyl
254(501)	254	Butane, 1-iodo
252(813)	291 288 252	Acetaldehyde, phenyl
252(233)	267 263 257 252	Toluene, α-hydroxy
252(385)	264 258 252 247	Benzene, (2-bromoethyl)
251(379)	272 251 240	Methanol, (3-tolyl)
251(832)	257 251 248 242	2-Propen-1-ol, 1-phenyl
251(389)	251	Disulfide, dibutyl, 3,3′-dimethyl
251(10)	251	Disulfide, dibutyl (β-form)
250(251)	380 250	Ketene, diethyl acetal
250(447)	323 250	β-Cadinene (*l*)
250(204)	289 264 250 244	Toluene, α-fluoro
250(126)	250	Cyclohexanol, 1-phenyl
250(316)	250	Cystine (*l*)
250(372)	250	Cystine (*meso*)
250(501)	250	Disulfide, dipropyl
250(501)	250	Maleic acid, diethyl ester
250(63)	250	Oxalic acid
250(427)	250	Trisulfide, diethyl
249(98)	249	Styrene, 3-fluoro
248(631)	380 248	Azobenzene, 3-hydroxy
248(251)	282 248	Aniline, *N,N*-dimethyl-*N*-oxide
248(20)	248	Cyclohexanone, 2,4-dimethyl (*trans,d*)
248(69)	248	Styrene, 2-bromo
248(69)	248	Styrene, 3-bromo
248(661)	248	Urea, 1-allyl-2-thio
245(229)	245	Disulfide, diisopropyl
244(912)	244	Butanoic acid, 3-oxo, isopropyl ester
243(38)	272 243	Linalool (*d*)
243(347)	257 243 233	Butadiyne, 1,4-bis(1-hydroxycyclohexyl)
243(398)	243	Homocystine (*l*)
242(60)	242	1-Hexanol, 1-phenyl
242(337)	242	1-Indanone, 2-nitro
241(229)	296 241	Uric acid, 3-methyl
241(424)	263 257 246 241	Propanal, 2-phenyl
240(126)	240	Acetic acid, thiolo
240(200)	240	Methane, bromotrichloro
240(50)	240	Thiophene, tetrahydro
239(832)	269 260 239	Toluene, 4-amino, hydrochloride
238(98)	294 238	Uric acid, 7-methyl
238(813)	238	1,3,5-Trithiane, 2,4,6-trimethyl (α-form)
237(2)	263 237	1-Heptene
237(13)	237	Geraniol, tetrahydro (*dl*)
237(32)	237	9-Octadecenoic acid, ethyl ester (*cis*)
237(12)	237	1-Octanol, 3,7-dimethyl (*d*)
237(12)	237	1-Octanol, 3,7-dimethyl (*l*)
236(25)	287 236	Menthone (*d*)
236(331)	250 236 219	2,4-Hexadiyne
236(389)	249 236 227	1,3-Pentadiyne
235(85)	290 235	Citronellal (*d*)
235(85)	290 235	Citronellal (*dl*)
235(85)	290 235	Citronellal (*l*)
235(731)	269 265 262 258 252 235	Benzenesulfonic acid
235(692)	235	Acetaldehyde, diethyl mercaptal
235(288)	235	Disulfide, dimethyl, hexafluoro

Strongest Band (ε)	Wavelengths (nm)	Compound
235(50)	235	Malonic acid, diethyl ester
233(126)	270 233	9,12 -Octadecadienoic acid, ethyl ester
233(287)	233	4-Heptanone, 2,6-dimethyl
233(126)	233	9,12,15-Octadecatrienoic acid (*cis,cis,cis*)
233(18)	233	1-Pentene, 4-chloro
230(40)	280 230	Emetine, hydrochloride (*l*)
230(408)	255 242 230 218	4,6-Decadiyne-3,8-diol, 3,8-dimethyl
230(138)	230	Cyclohexanethiol
230(159)	230	1-Pentanethiol
230(159)	230	Sulfide, pentamethylene
229(55)	263 229	Phosphoric acid, trimethyl ester
229(141)	229	Methanethiol
228(363)	253 239 228	3,5-Octadiyne
228(159)	228	1-Butanethiol
228(135)	228	2-Butanethiol (*d*)
228(219)	228	Malonic acid
228(159)	228	1-Propanethiol, 2-methyl
227(724)	227	Methane, dibromodifluoro
227(100)	227	2-Pentanethiol
226(182)	285 226	3-Cyclohexen-1-one, 4-methyl
226(159)	226	2-Propanethiol, 2-methyl
226(129)	226	Trimethadione
225(347)	292 225	1,4-Dithiane
225(48)	225	Acetic acid, anhydride
225(200)	225	1-Butanethiol, 3-methyl
225(100)	225	3-Butenoic acid, ethyl ester
225(159)	225	1-Heptanethiol
225(159)	225	1-Hexadecanethiol
225(398)	225	Oxalic acid, diethyl ester
224(513)	273 224	Acetic acid, iodo
224(32)	270 224	1,4-Cyclohexadiene
224(224)	252 247 224	Butadiyne
224(501)	252 224	Succinic acid, imide, *N*-methyl
224(126)	224	1-Hexanethiol
223(159)	223	2-Hexanethiol
223(100)	223	2,6-Octadiene, 2,6-dimethyl
222(79)	293 222	Decanal
222(794)	241 231 222	1-Butene, 1-bromo (*trans*)
220(200)	250 220	Δ^3-Carene (*l*)
220(257)	250 220	Limonene (*d*)
220(257)	250 220	Limonene (*dl*)
220(251)	250 220	Limonene (*l*)
220(0.2)	250 220	*p*-Menthane, (*cis*)
220(468)	241 231 220	1-Butene, 1-bromo (*cis*)
220(102)	220	Acetic acid, chloride
220(100)	220	β-Asparagine (*dl*)
220(100)	220	Glutamine (*l*,+)
220(126)	220	Octadecanoic acid, 9,10-dihydroxy
218(115)	241 228 218	Propynoic acid, nitrile
218(50)	218	Acetic acid, chloro (α)
218(79)	218	Glycine, ethyl ester
218(251)	218	Glycine, *N*-alanyl (*dl*)
218(283)	218	Indan, 5-hydroxy
217(316)	217	β-Asparagine (*l*)
217(25)	217	α-Dicyclopentadiene (*endo* form)
217(13)	217	Methanephosphonic acid, dimethyl ester
217(794)	217	Thiophene, 3-methyltetrahydro
216(309)	216	Sulfide, ethyl propyl
215(178)	260 215	α-Terpineol (*dl*)
215(398)	215	α-Alanine, *N*-acetyl (*dl*)

Strongest Band (ε)	Wavelengths (nm)	Compound
215(501)	215	Glutamic acid, *N*-acetyl (*l*)
215(251)	215	Glycine, *N*-acetyl
215(631)	215	Leucine, *N*-acetyl (*dl*)
215(676)	215	Propenoic acid, 2-methyl, nitrile
215(912)	215	Sulfide, isopropyl methyl
214(234)	333 214	Methanesulfenic acid, trifluoro, chloride
214(83)	214	Acetic acid, ethoxy, ethyl ester
212(940)	273 266 259 212	Benzene, 1-chloro-2-ethyl
212(631)	212	Butane, 1,4-dibromo
212(955)	212	Citronellol (*d*)
212(955)	212	Citronellol (*dl*)
212(955)	212	Citronellol (*l*)
212(254)	212	Histidine (*dl*)
212(71)	212	Tetradecanoic acid, methyl ester
211(269)	211	Jaconecic acid
210(708)	210	2-Butene, 2-bromo (*cis*)
210(126)	210	Glycine, amide
210(50)	210	Hexadecanoic acid
210(100)	210	Hexanedioic acid, diethyl ester
210(49)	210	Octadecanoic acid
210(71)	210	Tetradecanoic acid
209(72)	209	Acetic acid, ethyl ester
209(43)	209	Butanoic acid, 4-hydroxy, lactone
208(63)	270 208	Butanoic acid
208(32)	208	Acetic acid
208(7)	208	Cyclopropanecarboxylic acid, nitrile
208(40)	208	Malonic acid, mononitrile
208(33)	208	Methane, bromotrifluoro
208(100)	208	Succinic acid
207(447)	207	Cyclohexene
207(66)	207	Leucine (*dl*)
206(100)	206	Glutamic acid, (*l*,+)
206(813)	206	1-Pentene, 2,4,4-trimethyl
205(162)	205	Acetic acid, amide
205(5)	205	α-Alanine (*dl*)
205(851)	205	2-Butene, 2-methyl
205(45)	205	Formic acid
205(158)	205	Formic acid, amide
205(282)	205	Guanidine, thiocyanate
205(398)	205	Tetracyclo [$2.2.1.0^{2,6}.0^{3,5}$] heptane
204(182)	204	Methane, bromo
195(316)	195	1-Butene, 3-methyl
193(45)	193	Propanal, 2,2-dimethyl
183(151)	183	Methanol
183(240)	183	1-Propanol
181(324)	181	Ethanol
181(617)	181	2-Propanol
178(251)	215 178	1-Pentanol
175(316)	175	2-Octanol (*dl*)
174(316)	211 174	2-Butanol (*dl*)

No ε Given

Wavelengths (nm)	Compound
641 552 502 453	Benzene, 1-bromo-2,4,6-trinitro
600	Thymol blue
575 550	Hematin
570	Methanol, bis(4-aminophenyl)phenyl
547 507 473	Lycoxanthin
537 502 476 323	Echinochrome, 3,6,7-trimethyl ether

Strongest Band (ε)	Wavelengths (nm)	Compound
	533 494 461	Rubixanthin
	530 355	1,1′-Azonaphthalene, 4-amino
	530	Glucose, 2-amino (*d,β*)
	497	β-Citraurin
	492 475	Fucoxanthin
	491 460 435 410	γ-Carotene
	477	Methanol, (4-aminophenyl)diphenyl
	470 405	Tomatidine
	470	Carbazone, 1,5-diphenyl
	467	Azo, benzene 1-naphthalene, 4′-hydroxy-2′-nitro
	458	Biphenyl, 4,4′-dichloro
	447	Azo, benzene 1-naphthalene, 4′-hydroxy-3-nitro
	420	Glycogen
	399	Isothebaine (*d*)
	355 335 242 217	1,3,5-Hexatriene, 1,6-diphenyl
	354 242	Azoxybenzene, 4,4′-dimethoxy
	353 237	Azobenzene, 2-hydroxy-4-methyl
	350 342 334 327 301 289 278 256	Phenanthrene, 9-bromo
	350 245	Aniline, 2,6-dichloro-4-nitro
	350 225	Pyridine, 2(dimethylamino)
	349 297 252	Phenanthrene, 4-methyl
	348 339 250 212	Acridine
	347 298	3,4-Benzopyrene
	346 258 207	Quinoline, 8-amino-6-methoxy
	345 337 334 291 287 280 269 259 237	Naphthalene, 2-amino
	345 330 293 261 235	Carbazole, 9-ethyl
	345 272	Phenol, 2-nitro
	345 264 232	7,8-Benzoquinoline
	344 256 225	Anthracene, 1,3-dimethyl
	342 256	Anthraquinone, 1,5-dichloro
	342 247	Coumestrol
	342 237	Furfural, phenylhydrazone
	342 219	Pyridine, 2-amino-5-nitro
	341 335 327 320 313 247 212	Phenanthridine
	341 326 311 256 226	Anthracene, 2,3-dimethyl
	341 300 288 277	1,2-Benzanthracene
	341 241	Chalcone, 4-methoxy
	340 326 298 287 242 218	Naphthalene, 1,7-dihydroxy
	340 311 299 289 274 269 259 299 212	9-Phenanthrenecarboxylic acid, nitrile
	340 291 282 246 238	Naphthalene, 1-acetyl
	340 281 235	Equilenin (*d*)
	340 281 235	Equilenin (*dl*)
	340 281 235	Equilenin (*l*)
	340 251	Phthalic acid, tetrabromo, anhydride
	340 242	Benzaldehyde, 4-dimethylamino
	340	Aniline, 2-mercapto
	340	Benzene, 1-amino-2-mercapto
	340	Phenol, 2,6-dinitro
	339 315 311 280 242	1-Naphthalenesulfonic acid, 6-amino
	339 293 270 263 251	Anthracene, 9,10-dihydro
	339 234	Anthraquinone, 1,8-dichloro
	338 326 231	1,8-Naphthalenedicarboxylic acid
	338 303 246	Naphthalene, 1-amino-7-hydroxy
	337 279 252 246	1,4-Naphthoquinone, 2,3-dichloro
	336 288 283 259 237 205	Xanthone
	336 288 283 258 238	Xanthene, 9-hydroxy
	336 287 235 214	Naphthalene, 1,3-dihydroxy

Strongest Band (ϵ)	Wavelengths (nm)	Compound
	336 260	Anthracene, 2-amino
	336 251 221	Benzaldehyde, 5-bromo-2-hydroxy
	335 321 307 267 231 227	1,7-Phenanthroline
	335 293 251	Rhodanine
	335 258	Pyridine, 4-benzoyl
	335 256	Benzoic acid, 4-benzoyl
	335 248	Naphthalene, 1-amino-4-bromo
	335 237 213	Benzoic acid, 2,5-dihydroxy
	334 320 291 281 241 214	Naphthalene, 2-mercapto
	334 292 280 269 229	Naphthalene, 1-bromo-2-hydroxy
	334 253 209	Anthraquinone, 1-chloro
	333 324 321 262 251	Naphthalene, 2-amino-1-nitro
	333 324 321 261 250	Naphthalene, 1-amino-4-nitro
	333 264 229	Quinoline, 6-methoxy-8-nitro
	333 263	2,2′-Azonaphthalene
	333 258	Quinoline, 5-chloro-8-hydroxy-7-iodo
	333 247	Naphthalene, 1-amino-4-chloro
	333 244	Benzophenone, 4-amino
	333 230	Cinnamic acid, 4-amino (*trans*)
	333 230	Citral a
	333 230	Citral b
	333 321 298 286 243 223	Naphthalene, 1,6-dihydroxy
	332 320 278 231	Quinine
	332 318 289 279 270 230	2-Naphthoic acid
	332 250 245	1,4-Naphthoquinone
	330 322 315 309 281 271 234	2-Naphthoic acid, nitrile
	330 321 238 217	Quinoline, 4-amino-2-methyl
	330 316 298 225	Naphthalene, 1,5-dihydroxy
	330 313 301 277	Naphthalene, 2,6-dichloro
	330 268 229	Phenol, 3-nitro
	330	Benzoic acid, 3,5-dinitro-2-hydroxy
	329 324 319 308 296	Naphthalene, 1,8-dichloro
	329 318 284 273 263 225	Naphthalene, 2-hydroxy
	329 278 270 245 229	Quinoline, 1,2-dihydro-1-methyl-2-oxo
	329 265	1,4-Naphthoquinone, 2-amino
	329 233	Pyridine, 2,5-dihydroxy
	329 226	Benzoic acid, 2-hydroxy-3-nitro
	328 318 243	Naphthalene, 1-amino
	328 275 268 229	Quinoline, 2-hydroxy
	328 274	Azobenzene, 2,5-dihydroxy
	328 270 262 245	1,4-Naphthoquinone, 2,3-dimethyl
	328 264 253 249 244	1,4-Naphthoquinone, 2-methyl
	328 259	Benzaldehyde, 2-hydroxy
	328 255	Barbituric acid
	328 225	Purine, 6-mercapto
	327 311 281 270 260	Naphthalene, 2,7-dichloro
	327 280 275	Toluene, 2,4-dimethoxy
	327 271 261 229	Ether, benzyl 2-naphthyl
	327 255	Anthraquinone, 2-methyl
	327 250 221	Benzoic acid, 3,4-diamino
	327	2-Hexen-4-one
	326 320 296 273 267	Naphthalene, 1,7-dichloro
	326 319 312 277 272	Naphthalene, 1,3-dichloro
	326 312 283 272	Naphthalene, 2,3-dichloro
	325 318 311 304 291 280 272 229	Naphthalene, 2,3-dihydroxy
	325 317 288 276	Naphthalene, 1,6-dichloro
	325 316 284 273	Naphthalene, 1,2-dichloro
	325 315 308 283 281 275 228	Naphthalene, 1,7-dimethyl
	325 275 267 229	Quinoline, 2-hydroxy-4-methyl

Strongest Band (ε)	Wavelengths (nm)	Compound
	325 238 206	Benzothiazole, 2-mercapto
	324 320 292 280	Naphthalene, 1,5-dichloro
	324 311 288 277 219	Isoquinoline, 4-bromo
	324 297 235 218	Cinnamic acid, 3,4-dihydroxy (*trans*)
	324 230	Furan, tetraphenyl
	323 318 308 265 218	Isoquinoline, 3-methyl
	323 309 295 233	Naphthalene, 1-hydroxy
	323 255 232	Dibenzothiophene
	323 230	Acetic acid, amide, *N*(2,3-dinitrophenyl)
	322 315 308 270 263 257	Pyridine, 2-benzyl
	322 313 307 292 284 275 228	Naphthalene, 1,2-dimethyl
	322 260 239 232	Azoxybenzene (*trans*)
	322 220	Coumarin, 7-ethoxy-4-methyl
	322	Coumarin, 7-hydroxy-4-methyl
	321 305 292 256 247	9-Fluorenone
	321 258 211 209	Benzene, 1-methoxy-2-nitro
	321 248	Azobenzene, 2,2′-dihydroxy
	321 231	3-Biphenylcarboxylic acid, 2-hydroxy
	321	Dibenzofuran, 3-nitro
	320 314 308 303 277 270	Pyrazine, 2,5-dimethyl
	320 312 305 274 265 227	2-Naphthalenesulfonic acid
	320 275 215 202	Coumarin, 6-methyl
	320 269 207	Pyrazinecarboxylic acid, amide
	320 235 218	Cinnamic acid, 4-hydroxy-3-methoxy (*trans*)
	320 230	4-Azobenzenesulfonic acid, chloride
	319	1,3-Butadiene, 1,4-diphenyl (*trans,trans*)
	318 315 286 275 266 223	Acetic acid, 2-naphthyl ester
	318 311 305 276 224	Naphthalene, 2-ethyl
	318 290 226	Isocyanic acid, 1-naphthyl ester
	318 254	Phenothiazine
	318 248	Benzoic acid, 3-amino-2,4,6-tribromo
	318 243	Quinoline, 8-hydroxy
	317 313 302 287 279 269 242	Naphthalene, 1-amino, hydrochloride
	317 305 240	5-Quinolinesulfonic acid, 8-hydroxy
	317 303 278 233 229	Quinoline, 2-chloro-4-methyl
	317 250 221	Aniline, 2,6-dinitro
	317 240	2-Buten-1-one, 1,3-diphenyl
	317	Carbon disulfide
	316 310 302 296 289 272 266 258	Isoquinoline, 1,2,3,4-tetrahydro
	316 309 303 297 290 274 233 229 226 207	Quinoline, 2-methyl
	315 303 276 228 210	Quinoline, 2,4-dimethyl
	315 278 263 217	Amine, di-2-naphthyl
	315 253	Benzaldehyde, 3-hydroxy
	315 246	Benzenearsonic acid, 2-amino
	314 292 281 271 224	Propanoic acid, 3(1-naphthyl)
	314 280 270 217	3,4-Benzophenanthrene
	314 261	Pyrrole, 2,3,4,5-tetraphenyl
	314 236	Quinoxaline, 2,3-dimethyl
	314 231	Naphthalene, 1,8-dinitro
	314 220	Benzoic acid, 2-mercapto
	313 306 300 294 288 277 231 226 205	Quinoline
	313 300 290 281 244 229	Styrene, 2-chloro
	313 300 276 269 222	Quinoline, 4-methyl
	313 280 224	Acetic acid, (1-naphthyl), amide
	313 280 223	Acetic acid, (1-naphthyl)
	313 253	Azobenzene, 4-dimethylamino
	313 251	Aniline, 2,4,6-tribromo

Strongest Band (ε)	Wavelengths (nm)	Compound
	313 241 222	Naphthalene, 1-diethylamino
	313 239	Phenol, 4-amino-2,6-dichloro
	313 227	Sulfone, diphenyl,3,3′-diamino
	313 223	Acetic acid, amide, *N*(4-nitrophenyl)
	313 211	Histidine, dihydrochloride (*dl*)
	312 301 225 219	Acenaphthenequinone
	312 290 286 279 270	Methanol, (1-naphthyl)
	312 280 231	Benzaldehyde, 3,4-dihydroxy
	312 243	Pyridine, 2-amino-5-bromo
	312 242 223 211	1-Naphthaldehyde
	312	Benzoic acid, 5-bromo-2-hydroxy
	312	Pentanedioic acid, 2-oxo
	311 270 212	Coumarin, 4-methyl
	311 234	Pyridine, 5-amino-2-butoxy
	310 297 279 249 241	Phthalazine, 1,2-dihydro-1-oxo
	310 271	Acetic acid, 3-hydroxyphenyl ester
	310 242 217	Quinazoline, 2,4-dioxo-1,2,3,4-tetrahydro
	310 241	Quinoline, 8-hydroxy-4-methyl
	310	Methane, bis(3-carboxy-4-hydroxyphenyl)
	310	Pyridazine, 3,6-dioxo-1,2,3,6-tetrahydro
	309 244	Pyridine, 2,3-diamino (one form)
	309 244	Pyridine, 2,3-diamino (one form)
	309 240 207	Indole, 2-phenyl
	309 227	Furfural, 5-nitro
	308 299 293 224	Cinnamic acid, 4-hydroxy (*trans*)
	308 295 292 284 265 256	Naphthalene, 2-acetyl-1-hydroxy
	308 284 222	Anthracene, 1,2,3,4,5,6,7,8-octahydro
	308 247	Benzaldehyde, 2-methoxy
	308 244	Pyridine, 2-amino-5-chloro
	308 244	Pyridine, 2,6-diamino
	308 244	Quinoline, 8-hydroxy-3-methyl
	308 241	Benzoic acid, 2-hydroxy-4-methyl
	308 5810	Thiophene, 2-nitro
	307 275 229	Benzaldehyde, 4-ethoxy-3-methoxy
	307 254	Benzoic acid, 5-bromo-2,4-dihydroxy
	307 227	Benzene, 1-ethoxy-4-nitro
	307 218	Phenol, 2,6-dichloro-4-nitro
	306 244	9,10-Anthraquinone, 1-amino
	306 226 202	Oxazole, 2,4,5-triphenyl
	305 275 229 207	Acetophenone, 4-hydroxy-3-methoxy
	305 272 266	Pyrazine, 2-methyl
	305 261 223	Benzene, 1-nitro-2,4,5-trichloro
	305 260 225	Equilin, α-dihydro
	305 245	Quinoline, 2,3-dimethyl-8-hydroxy
	305 234	Benzoic acid, 2-hydroxy-5-sulfo
	304 294 216	Toluene, α, α,2,3,4,5,6-heptachloro
	304 254	Toluene, 2-chloro-4-nitro
	304 253	Toluene, 4(dimethylamino)
	304 238	Aniline, 4-ethoxy
	303 274 244 207	Anthracene, 1,2,10-trihydroxy
	303 266 240	Benzoic acid, 3-hydroxy, amide, *N*-phenyl
	303 249	Benzoic acid, 2,6-dimethoxy, nitrile
	303 247	Benzene, 4-chloro-1,2-diamino
	303 241	Dibenzothiophene, 2-nitro
	303 221	1,3-Benzenedicarboxylic acid, 5-amino
	303 217	Maleic acid, imide, *N*-ethyl
	303	Benzoic acid, 4-amino-2-hydroxy
	302 290 278	1,3,5,7-Octatetraene
	302 241 203	Pyridine, 3-amino
	302 233 205	Biphenyl, 3-amino

Strongest Band (ϵ)	Wavelengths (nm)	Compound
	302 233 205	Propenoic acid, 3(2-furyl), ethyl ester
	302 220 205	Oxazole, 2,5-diphenyl
	300 290 250	1,2,3,4-Tetrazolium, 2,3,5-triphenyl,chloride
	300 250 213	Aniline, 3,5-dichloro
	300 227 218	Benzaldehyde, 2,5-dihydroxy
	300	Biphenyl, 2-amino
	300	Cyclopentanone
	300	Phenol, 2,6-dibromo-4-nitro
	299 289 250	Pyridine, 3-ethyl-4-methyl
	299 253	Amine, benzyl ethyl phenyl
	299 250	Amine, dibenzyl phenyl
	299	Benzene, 2-bromo-1,4-dihydroxy
	298 297 295	Phosgene
	298 289 266 259 221	Propanoic acid, 3,3-dichloro-2-hydroxy-2-methyl
	298 289 266 259 221	Propanoic acid, 3(3,5-diiodo-4-hydroxyphenyl)2-phenyl
	298 250	Toluene, 4-chloro-2-nitro
	298 250	Toluene, 4-chloro-3-nitro
	298 227	Pyridine, 2-hydroxy
	298	Phthalic acid, tetrachloro, anhydride
	297 289 284 279 258 251	Indazole
	297 289	Phenol, 2,4,6-tribromo
	297 245	Aniline, 4-bromo
	297	Toluene, 3,4-diamino
	297	Toluene, 3-hydroxy-2,4,6-tribromo
	296 287 254 216 205	Styrene, 4-bromo
	296 260	Sulfone, diphenyl,4,4′-diamino
	296 255	Benzene, 1,4-dimethyl-2-nitro
	296 249	Aniline, 4-iodo
	296 243	Aniline, 4-chloro
	296 241	Aniline, 2,5-dichloro
	296 241	Aniline, 2,6-dichloro
	296 237	Toluene, 4-amino-2-chloro
	296 237	Toluene, 4-amino-3-chloro
	296 234	Pyridine, 2-amino
	296 227	Pyrimidine, 2-amino
	296	Benzoic acid, 2,3,4,5-tetrachloro
	295 286 230	Acetic acid, (2,4-dichlorophenoxy)
	295 285 258 208	Styrene, β-bromo (*trans*)
	295 285 249	Styrene, 3-methyl
	295 256	Benzene, 1,4-diacetyl
	295 247	Toluene, 3(ethylamino)
	295 246	Aniline, *N*-ethyl
	295 239	Aniline, 3,4-dimethoxy
	295 238	Toluene, 3-amino-α,α,α-trifluoro
	295 235 208	Aniline, 2,5-dimethoxy
	295 233	Benzoic acid, 3-hydroxy, amide
	295 232	Benzene, 1,2,4,5-tetrachloro
	295 226	Benzaldehyde, 4-hydroxy-5-iodo-3-methoxy
	295 220	Benzoic acid, 4-amino, 2-diethylaminoethyl ester
	295	Benzoic acid, 2,3,5-trichloro
	294 291 288 237	Toluene, 4-amino
	294 275 265	Naphthacene
	294 254	Benzene, 1,4-di-*tert*-butyl-2,5-dihydroxy
	294 249 203	Ethane, 1,2-bis(phenylamino)
	294 246	Benzaldehyde, 2-chloro
	294 243	Aniline, 4-chloro-2-methoxy
	294 243	Aniline, 5-chloro-2-methoxy
	294 242	Aniline, 3-chloro
	294 242	Quinhydrone
	294 228	Phenol, 4-ethoxy

Strongest Band (ε)	Wavelengths (nm)	Compound
	294	Toluene, 2,4-diamino
	294	Uric acid, 3,7,9-trimethyl
	293 286 254 217	Benzoic acid, 3,4-dimethoxy, nitrile
	293 285 264 208	Fluorene, 1-hydroxy
	293 272 265 241	Aniline, 3-chloro, hydrochloride
	293 261 222	Benzothiazole, 2-amino
	293 258	Amine, diethyl, 2,2′-diphenyl
	293 249 228	Benzophenone, 4-hydroxy
	293 245	Aniline, *N*-methyl
	293 243	Benzoic acid, 3-chloro-, chloride
	293 241 233 218	Phthalic acid, imide, *N*(3-bromopropyl)
	293 240 232 219	Phthalic acid, imide, *N*(2-bromoethyl)
	293 240	Aniline, 2,3-dichloro
	293 238 217	Phthalic acid, imide, *N*(bromomethyl)
	293 238	Benzene, 4-amino-1,2-dimethyl
	293 233	Benzoic acid, 2-ethoxy, amide
	293 233	Benzoic acid, 4-ethoxy, amide
	293 232	Benzoic acid, 2-methoxy
	293 220	Benzoic acid, 4-amino, butyl ester
	293 208	Sulfone, diphenyl,2,2′-dihydroxy
	292 286 209	Tyrosine, 3,5-dibromo (*l*)
	292 286	Toluene, 5-chloro-2-hydroxy
	292 256 216	Benzaldehyde, 2,4-dichloro
	292 241 232	Phthalic acid, imide, *N*(2-hydroxyethyl)
	292 241	1,4-Benzenedicarboxylic acid, 2-bromo
	292 236 222 202	Phenoxanthin
	292 227	Pyrimidine, 2-amino-4-methyl
	292 225	Phenol, 4-methoxy
	292	Benzene, 1,4-dihydroxy-3-methyl
	292	Benzene, 2,4-dimethyl-1-hydroxy
	292	3-Heptanone, 6-dimethylamino-4,4-diphenyl, hydrochloride (*dl*)
	292	Toluene, 2,5-dihydroxy
	291 285 222	Toluene, 3,5-dichloro-2-hydroxy
	291 283 270 249	Xanthene, 9-phenyl
	291 282 251	2-Propen-1-ol, 3-phenyl (*trans*)
	291 282 243 237 233	Phthalic acid, dinitrile
	291 256	Benzoic acid, 3,4-dichloro, chloride
	291 240 207	1,4-Benzenedicarboxylic acid, 2-chloro
	291 237	Benzene, 1-amino-4-*tert*-butyl
	291 236	Pyridine, 2-amino-4-methyl
	291 219	Cyclohexane, 4-methyl
	291	Benzoic acid, 4-amino, methyl ester
	291	Dehydrocholic acid
	290 283 260 225	Indole, 2-methyl
	290 283 245 212	Acetic acid, amide, *N*(3-hydroxyphenyl)
	290 281 273 221	Tryptophan, *N*-acetyl (*l*)
	290 280 274 220	Tryptophan (*dl*)
	290 251	Phenol, 3(dimethylamino)
	290 251	Quinoline, 6-nitro
	290 243	Ethanol, 2-phenylamino
	290 241 207	Toluene, 2-amino-6-chloro
	290 237	Rotenone
	290 236	Aniline, 2-chloro (α)
	290 236	Aniline, 2-chloro (β)
	290 233	Benzoic acid, 2,4,5-trichloro
	290 231	Aniline, 4-fluoro-2-methyl
	290 228	Pyrimidine, 2-amino-4,6-dihydroxy
	290 224	Succinic acid, imide, *N*-iodo
	290 222	Cyclooctanone
	290 221	Benzoic acid, amide, *N*(1-naphthyl)

Strongest Band (ε)	Wavelengths (nm)	Compound
	290	2,3-Butanedione
	290	Phenol, 4-benzyloxy
	289 282 218	Toluene, 3-bromo-4-hydroxy
	289 281 272 246	Styrene
	289 281 238 232	Benzoic acid, 2-bromo, nitrile
	289 280	1,3-Benzenedicarboxylic acid, diethyl ester
	289 261	Sulfathiazole
	289 257 212	Benzoic acid, 3,4-dimethoxy, amide
	289 254	Phenol, 2,4-dinitro
	289 251 228	Toluene, 4-amino-2-nitro
	289 240	Glycine, *N*-phenyl, nitrile
	289 228	Pyrimidine, 2-amino-4,6-dimethyl
	289 226	Benzoic acid, 2,5-dichloro
	289 222	Naphthalene, 1-chloro-8-nitro
	289 218	Benzoic acid, 4-amino, ethyl ester
	289	Acetic acid, (2,4,6-trichlorophenoxy)
	289	Propane, 1-chloro-1-nitro
	289	Uric acid, 1,3,7-trimethyl
	288 281 272 236	Ether, diphenyl, 4,4′-dibromo
	288 280 273 229 224	Benzoic acid, 3-bromo, nitrile
	288 280	1,3-Benzenedicarboxylic acid, dimethyl ester
	288 278 270 235	Ether, diphenyl, 4-bromo
	288 272 265 259 247 240 220	Toluene, α,α-dichloro
	288 252 215	Biphenyl, 3,3′-dimethoxy
	288 240	Acetic acid, 4-aminophenyl
	288 238	Aniline, 2-ethoxy
	288 237	Benzene, 2-amino-1,4-dimethyl
	288 237	Benzoic acid, 2,3,4-trichloro
	288 207	Sulfone, diphenyl, 2,2′-dimethoxy
	288	Benzene, 2-methoxy-1,3,5-trichloro
	288	Fluorene, 2-acetamido
	287 279 266 261 214	Indole
	287 257 249 208	Quinoline, 5-nitro
	287 235	Aniline
	287 235	Benzene, 1-amino-2,4-dimethyl
	287	Folinic acid (*d*)
	287	Phenol, 3-amino
	287	Phenol, 4-bromo-2-chloro
	287	Toluene, 2,4-dichloro-5-hydroxy
	286 279 224	Toluene, 4-ethoxy
	286 252	Piperazine, 1-phenyl
	286 249 226	Toluene, 2-amino-4-nitro
	286 236	Benzene, 1-amino-2,3-dimethyl
	286 235	Aniline, 2-*sec*-butyl
	286 204	1,4-Benzoquinone, 2,5-dihydroxy
	286	Amine, diphenyl, 4-amino
	286	Fluorene, 2-amino
	285 278 227	Acetic acid, (4-chloro-2-methylphenoxy)
	285 248	Morpholine, 4-phenyl
	285 242	1,4-Benzenedicarboxylic acid, diethyl ester
	285 236	2-Pyrrolecarboxylic acid, 4-acetyl-3,5-dimethyl, ethyl ester
	285 235	Benzene, 1-amino-2-ethyl
	285 235	Benzene, 1-amino-2-isopropyl
	285 233	Phenol, 2-amino
	285 233	Toluene, 2-amino
	285	Aniline, 3-methoxy
	285	Morphine, sulfate pentahydrate
	285	Phenol, 3,4-dichloro
	284 278	Toluene, 4-methoxy

Strongest Band (ϵ)	Wavelengths (nm)	Compound
	284 277 275	Phenol, 2-*tert*-butyl-4-methyl
	284 277 225	Benzoic acid, 3-fluoro
	284 266 258	Toluene, 2-amino, hydrochloride
	284 255	Ketone, phenyl 2-thienyl
	284 255	Thiophene, 2-benzoyl
	284 241	Benzophenone, 2,2′,4,4′-tetrahydroxy
	284 228	Phenol, 4-chloro
	284	Biphenyl, 4,4′-diamino
	284	2,2′-Biphenyldicarboxylic acid
	284	1,4-Cyclohexanedione
	283 276 269	Toluene, α,α,α,3-tetrachloro
	283 276 226	Acetic acid, (4-methoxyphenyl), nitrile
	283 275 218	Acetic acid, (2-chlorophenoxy)
	283 275	Benzoic acid, 2-iodoso
	283 274 265 230	2-Propanone, 1-phenyl
	283 259	2-Thiophenecarboxaldehyde
	283 244 207	Formic acid, amide, *N*-3-tolyl
	283 236	2-Pentanone, 4-methyl
	283 218	Benzene, 1-chloro-2-methoxy
	283	Aniline, 4-phenoxy
	283	Barbituric acid, 2-thio
	283	3-Octanone
	283	Thymolphthalein
	283	Toluene, 3,4-dihydroxy
	283	Uracil
	282 279 274	Benzene, 1-hydroxy-2,3,5,6-tetramethyl
	282 276 203	Benzene, 1,3-dimethyl-5-hydroxy
	282 276	Phenol, 2-ethoxy
	282 275 229	Benzenesulfonic acid, 3-amino-4-hydroxy
	282 275	Phenol, 3-ethoxy
	282 275	Toluene, 3-chloro-2-hydroxy
	282 274 229	Toluene, α-chloro-4-methoxy
	282 270 263 240	Benzoic acid, 4-bromo, nitrile
	282 259	1-Butanone, 3-methyl-1-phenyl
	282 246	Methantheline, bromide
	282 241	Benzoic acid, 4-bromo
	282 233	Semicarbazide, 1-phenyl
	282 230	Benzoic acid, phenyl ester
	282	Amine, diphenyl
	282	Benzene, 1,2,3,4-tetrachloro
	282	1,3,5-Benzenetricarboxylic acid
	282	Biphenyl, 4,4′-diamino-3,3′-dimethyl
	282	Ethane, 1-chloro-1-nitro
	282	3-Heptanone
	281 278 270 261 228	Naphthalene, 2,6-dihydroxy
	281 273	Phenol, 2-chloro
	281 245	Benzene, 1-chloro-4-mercapto
	281 244 207	Acetic acid, amide, *N*(2-methoxyphenyl)
	281 241	Benzoic acid, chloride
	281 238	2-Pentanone, 4-hydroxy-4-methyl
	281 235 204	Formic acid, amide, *N*-2-tolyl
	281 228	Benzoin, 4,4′-dimethoxy
	281 222	1-Naphthoic acid, amide
	281	Benzene, 1-bromo-2,4,5-trimethyl
	281	Benzene, 4-cyclohexyl-1,3-dihydroxy
	281	Benzene, 2,4-dihydroxy-1-ethyl
	281	Benzene, 2,4-dihydroxy-1-hexyl
	281	Benzene, 1,3-dimethyl-5-methoxy
	281	Benzoic acid, 2-bromo
	281	Cinnamaldehyde (*trans*)

Strongest Band (ε)	Wavelengths (nm)	Compound
	281	Propane, 2-chloro-2-nitro
	281	2-Tridecanone
	280 276 271	Phenol, 2,4,6-trimethyl
	280 275	Phenol, 3-methoxy
	280 272 266	Benzenearsonic acid, 3-chloro
	280 272 265 227	Ketone, benzyl phenyl
	280 255 245 208	Fluorene, 9-bromo
	280 248 205	Hydrazine, 1-methyl-1-phenyl
	280 237	Benzene, mercapto
	280 230	Benzene, 1-allyl-3,4-dimethoxy
	280 225 219 207	Cinnamic acid, benzyl ester (*trans*)
	280 219	Phenol, 2-isopropyl-4-methyl
	280 218	Pyridine, 3-hydroxy
	280 214	Pyrrole, 1-methyl
	280	Benzaldehyde, 3,4-dichloro
	280	Benzene, 2-hydroxy-1,3,5-tri-*tert*-butyl
	280	Benzene, 2-hydroxy-1,3,5-trimethyl
	280	Benzoic acid, 4-methoxy, chloride
	280	Noradrenaline (*l*)
	280	2-Pentanone
	280	Propane, 1-nitro
	279 274 271	Toluene, 2,4,6-trihydroxy
	279 274 216	Benzene, 1-hydroxy-3-propyl
	279 273 220	Acetic acid, (2-methoxyphenyl)
	279 272 226	Phthalide
	279 271	Benzene, 4-bromo-1,2-dimethyl
	279 271	Phosphorous acid, tri(2-tolyl) ester
	279 269 263	Acetic acid, 3-tolyl ester
	279 268	Isothiocyanic acid, phenyl ester
	279 241	1-Butanone, 1-phenyl
	279 238	Benzenearsonic acid, 4-hydroxy
	279 236	Benzoic acid, 2,4-dichloro
	279 228	Methane, bis(4-hydroxyphenyl)
	279 226	Benzoic acid, 2-amino, butyl ester
	279 223	Benzene, 1-butyl-4-hydroxy
	279	Benzene, 1-isopropyl-4-methyl
	279	2-Hendecanone
	279	2-Nonadecanone
	279	Toluene, 4-hydroxy
	278 273	Toluene, 3-hydroxy
	278 272 269	Benzene, 1,2,3,4-tetramethyl
	278 272 265 243	Benzimidazole
	278 271 216	Acetic acid, 3-tolyloxy
	278 270 263 256	Benzene, 1-bromo-2-chloro
	278 269 264 215	Benzene, 2-chloro-1,4-dimethyl
	278 269 260 229	Toluene, 3-iodo
	278 234	Pyridine, 2-ethenyl
	278 223	Hordenine, sulfate
	278 221	Benzene, 1-cyclohexyl-4-hydroxy
	278 220	Benzene, 1-hydroxy-4-isopropyl
	278	Benzene, 1,2,4,5-tetramethyl
	278	Benzene, 1,3,5-tribromo
	278	1,2,3-Benzenetricarboxylic acid
	278	Benzoic acid, 4-amino, amide, *N*(2-diethylaminoethyl), hydrochloride
	278	Biphenyl, 4-amino
	278	3-Pentanone
	278	Propane, 2-methyl-2-nitro
	278	Propane, 2-nitro
	278	1,3-Propanediol, 2-ethyl-2-nitro
	278	1,3-Propanediol, 2-methyl-2-nitro

Strongest Band (ε)	Wavelengths (nm)	Compound
	278	1-Propanol, 2-methyl-2-nitro
	278	Toluene, 2-amino-5-hydroxy
	277 270 264	Phenol
	277 270 219	Butanoic acid, 2-phenoxy
	277 268 236 212	Naphthalene, 2-amino-, hydrochloride
	277 267	Benzene, 1,2,4-trimethyl
	277 234	2-Toluenesulfonic acid, chloride
	277 232	Aniline, 2-nitro
	277 226	Toluene, α,4-dihydroxy
	277 223 217 206	Cinnamic acid, allyl ester
	277 214	Uracil, 6-methyl-2-thio
	277	1-Butanol, 2-nitro
	277	Galacturonic acid (*d*)
	277	Methane, nitro
	276 270 264	Acetic acid, phenyl ester
	276 268 258 233 228	Toluene, 2-iodo
	276 233 215	Cinnamic acid, 3-hydroxy (*trans*)
	276 229	Benzoic acid, 3-methyl, amide
	276 229	Phenolphthalein
	276 220	Benzene, 1-*sec*-butyl-4-hydroxy
	276 217	Furoin
	276 214	Benzene, 1-bromo-4-nitro
	276	Succinic acid, imide
	276	Tannic acid
	275 268 262 213	Pyridine, 3-bromo
	275 268	2-Toluenesulfonic acid, amide
	275 267 207	Pyridine, 3,5-dimethyl
	275 266	1,3-Cyclooctadiene, (*cis,cis*)
	275 258 253	1,2,3-Benzotriazole
	275 257	Thiophene, 2-acetyl
	275 240	Butanoic acid, 4 oxo-4-phenyl
	275 235	Peroxide, dibenzoyl
	275 229	Anthraquinone, 1,5-diamino
	275 225	Benzoic acid, 2-hydroxy, acetate
	275 225	Benzoic acid, 4-methoxy, nitrile
	275 225	Glycerol, 1(2-methoxyphenyl) ether
	275 220	Acetophenone, 4-hydroxy
	275 218	2,3-Pyrazinedicarboxylic acid, 5-methyl
	275 216	Toluene, α,3-dihydroxy
	275 212	Benzene, 1,4-dimethyl
	275	Benzene, 1,3-dihydroxy
	275	Benzoic acid, 3,4,5-trihydroxy, propyl ester
	275	Cinnamic acid, isopropyl ester (*trans*)
	275	Cytidylic acid b
	274 268 263 256 228	Tolbutamide
	274 267 261	Pyridine, 3-chloro
	274 267 242	Sulfone, diphenyl,4-chloro
	274 266 262 259	Toluene, 2,6-dichloro
	274 230	Benzaldehyde, 3-hydroxy-4-methoxy
	274 228	4-Toluenesulfonic acid, amide, *N,N*-dichloro
	274 224	Phthalic acid, dimethyl ester
	274 222	Benzoic acid, 3,5-diiodo-2-hydroxy
	274 216	Maleic acid, imide
	274	Cyclooctatetraene
	274	Quinine, sulfate dihydrate
	274	Urea, 1,3-diphenyl-2-thio
	273 277 268 261 256 226	Toluene, α,4-dichloro
	273 267 265 261 257 225	4-Toluenesulfonic acid, methyl ester
	273 267 260 237	Sulfone, diphenyl
	273 266	Coumarin, 3,4-dihydro

Strongest Band (ϵ)	Wavelengths (nm)	Compound
	273 241	2,4′-Bipyridyl
	273 232	Sulfoxide, diphenyl
	273 218	1-Propanone, 1(4-hydroxyphenyl)
	273	Aniline, *N,N*-dimethyl-4-nitroso
	273	Benzaldehyde, 4-methoxy
	273	Benzene, 1-bromo-4-chloro
	273	Benzene, 1,3-dimethoxy
	273	Cinnamic acid, 2-hydroxy (*trans*)
	273	Coumarin, 3-methyl
	273	4-Pyridinecarboxylic acid, ethyl ester
	273	4-Pyridinecarboxylic acid, methyl ester
	272 266 263 260 258 252	Benzene, 1,4-difluoro
	272 266 261 255	4-Toluenesulfonic acid, isopropyl ester
	272 265 260 219 216	2-Pyridinecarboxylic acid, nitrile
	272 265 259 254 223	Phosphine, triphenyl, oxide
	272 262	4-Toluenesulfonic acid, amide, *N*-methyl-*N*-nitroso
	272 244	Anthraquinone, 1-methylamino
	272 212	Uracil, 2-thio
	272	Benzene, 1-cyclohexyl-2-hydroxy
	272	Cinnamic acid, (*cis*) (1st form)
	272	Cytidine
	272	Phthalic acid
	272	Styracin
	271 266 260 255 223	4-Toluenesulfonic acid, ethyl ester
	271 265 253 248	Acetic acid, diphenyl
	271 262 218	Benzene, 1,4-dihydroxy-2,5-dimethyl
	271 227 220	Furfural
	271 225	2,5-Pyridinedicarboxylic acid
	271 221	Amine, 2-naphthyl phenyl
	271 221	Ether, allyl phenyl
	271 220	Phenol, 4(methylamino)-, sulfate
	271	Benzene, *sec*-butoxy
	271	Benzene, 1,3-di-*tert*-butyl-2-hydroxy
	271	Benzene, methoxy
	271	2-Butanone, 3-hydroxy (*dl*)
	270 266 260 253 220	Sulfoxide, dibenzyl
	270 264 258 225 216	3-Pyridinecarboxylic acid, nitrile
	270 264	Benzene, 2-bromo-1,3-dimethyl
	270 263 257 208	Pyridine, 2-chloro
	270 263 256	Methane, triphenyl
	270 250	Benzene, 1,2-dihydroxy-3-methoxy
	270 244 239	Anthraquinone, 2-hydroxy
	270 235	Antipyrine, *p*-dimethylamino
	270 233	Thiophene, 2-amino
	270 220	2,5-Hexanedione
	270 219	Benzene, 1-chloro-3-ethoxy
	270	Acetic acid, (4-nitrophenyl)
	270	Methanol, (2-furyl)
	270	2-Propanone
	269 264	2,6-Pyridinedicarboxylic acid
	269 263	Toluene, α-mercapto
	269 262 257	Pyridine, 3-methyl
	269 262 209	Phosphoric acid, tri(4-tolyl) ester
	269 220	Benzene, 1,2-dichloro
	269	Benzoic acid, 2-methyl, amide
	269	α-Tocopherolquinone
	268 265 258 253 247 243 210	2-Propanol, 2-phenyl
	268 264 261 258 253 247 242 208	Propanal, 3-phenyl
	268 264 258 252	Malonic acid, ethyl(phenyl), diethyl ester

Strongest Band (ϵ)	Wavelengths (nm)	Compound
	268 264 258 252	Propanoic acid, 3,3-diphenyl-3-hydroxy
	268 261 259 209	2-Butanone, 4-phenyl
	268 261 256	Pyridine, 2-methyl
	268 260 254 248 243	Benzene
	268 236	Pyrimidine, 4-amino-2,6-dimethyl
	268 231	Ethane, 1,1-bis(4-chlorophenyl)2,2-dichloro
	268 228	Pyridine, 2-acetyl
	268	Benzene, 2-bromo-1,3,5-trimethyl
	268	Isopomiferin
	267 264 258 252 247	Acetic acid, phenyl, amide, *N*-methyl
	267 263 261 257 251 247 206	Formic acid, benzyl ester
	267 263 260 258 252 247 242	Propane, 1-chloro-3-phenyl
	267 263 260 257 252 247	Propanoic acid, 3-phenyl
	267 263 257 251	Propenoic acid, benzyl ester
	267 261	Benzene, 1,2-dihydroxy,diacetate
	267 257	Benzene, *tert*-butyl
	267 235	Cytosine
	267	1,1′-Azonaphthalene
	267	Benzene, 1,2,3-trihydroxy
	267	Sulfamerazine
	266 262 260 257 251	Succinic acid, dibenzyl ester
	266 260	Sulfide, dibenzyl
	266 259 253 249	Toluene, α,α,α-trifluoro
	266 236	Ethane, 2,2-bis(4-chlorophenyl)1,1,1-trichloro
	266 222	Naphthalene, 2-methyl-1-nitro
	266	Carbamic acid, 4-benzylphenyl ester
	266	2-Furancarboxylic acid, chloride
	266	Homatropine, hydrochloride
	265 258 252	Toluene, α(dimethylamino)
	265 236	Isatin, 1-acetyl
	265 217	Benzenesulfonic acid, ethyl ester
	265 217	Benzenesulfonic acid, methyl ester
	265	Benzene, 5-*tert*-butyl-1,3-dinitro-4-methoxy-2-methyl
	265	Benzene, 1,3-dimethyl
	265	Benzenephosphonic acid
	265	Purine
	265	Sulfuric acid, dimethyl ester
	264 258 253	Methane, bromo (diphenyl)
	264 258 252 247	Acetic acid, diphenyl, nitrile
	264 257	Acetic acid, phenyl, isobutyl ester
	264 227	Benzene, 1,4-bis(chloromethyl)
	264 223	Benzothiazole, 2-amino-6-methyl
	264 208	Pyridine, 2,4,6-trimethyl
	264 203	Uracil, 1,3-dimethyl
	264	Benzene, 1,3-diethyl
	264	Benzene, 1,3-dimethyl-2-methoxy
	264	Benzenesulfonic acid, sodium salt
	264	Benzophenone, 4,4′-dimethyl
	264	1,4-Naphthoquinone, 2-hydroxy-3-phenyl
	264	Phenol, 4-chloro-2-nitro
	264	Phosphorous acid, triphenyl ester
	264	Sulfide, diphenyl,4,4′-diamino
	263 257 252	Pseudoephedrine (*dl*)
	263 257 251	Propanoic acid, 2-hydroxy-2-phenyl,hemihydrate (*dl*)
	263 256 206	Hydantoin, 5-ethyl-5-phenyl (*dl*)
	263 239	Benzene, 1-bromo-2-iodo
	263 215	Toluene, 3,5-dinitro-2-hydroxy
	263 211	Pyridine, *N*-oxide
	263	Acetic acid, 4-tolyl
	263	Benzene, iodoxy

Strongest Band (ε)	Wavelengths (nm)	Compound
	263	Benzoic acid, 4-nitro, hydrazide
	263	Brucine sulfate, heptahydrate
	263	Cinnamic acid, α-ethyl (*cis*)
	262 255	Pyridine, 4-methyl
	262 225	4-Toluenesulfonic acid, amide, *N*-methyl
	262 209	Benzoic acid, 2-chloro-4-nitro
	262	Amine, diphenyl *N*-nitroso
	262	Benzoic acid, 4-hydroxy-3-methoxy, ethyl ester
	262	Benzophenone, 2,2′,4,4′-tetramethyl
	262	2-Butanol, 2-methyl-4-phenyl
	262	Phenol, 2-amino-5-nitro
	261 256 250	Pyridine
	261 256 228	Pyridine, 3-ethyl
	261	Acetic acid, (4-nitrophenyl), nitrile
	261	Benzene, butyl
	261	Benzene, (1,2-epoxyethyl)
	261	Benzenesulfonic acid, hydrate
	261	Benzophenone, 4-bromo
	261	Carbonic acid, di-2-tolyl ester
	260 254 203	3-Pyridinecarboxylic acid, amide, *N,N*-diethyl
	260 239	2-Butanone, 1-phenyl
	260 230	Benzene, 1-iodo-4-nitro
	260 222	4-Quinolinecarboxylic acid, 6-methoxy
	260 211	Benzoic acid, 3,4,5-trimethoxy
	260	Benzene, 1-hydroxy-2-methoxy-4-propenyl (*trans*)
	260	Benzoic acid, 4-nitro, amide
	260	Biphenyl, 3-bromo-4-hydroxy
	260	Biphenyl, 4,4′-dibromo
	260	Biphenyl, 2,2′-dinitro
	260	Toluene, α-chloro-4-nitro
	259 254	1,2-Ethanediol, tetraphenyl
	259 254	Methane, amino(diphenyl)
	259 253	Thiocyanic acid, benzyl ester
	259 216	Acenaphthene, 5-nitro
	259	Acetophenone, α-bromo-4-chloro
	259	Benzene, (2-aminoethyl)
	259	Benzene, cyclohexyl
	259	Benzene, 1-methoxy-4-propenyl (*trans*)
	259	Benzoic acid, 2-amino-5-iodo
	259	Benzoic acid, 3-nitro, amide, *N*-phenyl
	259	Benzophenone, 2-hydroxy
	259	1-Indenone, 2,3-diphenyl
	259	Uracil, 6-methyl
	258 236	Sulfone, diphenyl 4,4′-dihydroxy
	258 209	Benzenesulfonic acid, 3-nitro
	258 207	Benzene, 1,2-dimethyl-3-nitro
	258	Acetic acid, phenyl
	258	Atropine
	258	Benzene, isopropyl
	258	Benzoic acid, 4(benzylsulfonamido)
	258	Ephedrine (*dl*)
	258	Ether, dibenzyl
	257 206	Benzene, 1-chloro-3-nitro
	257	Barbituric acid, 5-ethyl-5-phenyl
	257	Benzene, 1-bromo-4-methoxy
	257	Benzenearsonic acid, 4-ureido
	257	Benzoic acid, 2(4-chlorobenzoyl)
	257	2-Furancarboxylic acid, 5-bromo
	257	Pyridine, 4-hydroxy
	256 232 228	Toluene, 4-iodo

Strongest Band (ϵ)	Wavelengths (nm)	Compound
	256 226	Acetophenone, 2-amino
	256 205	Benzene, 1-ethyl-2-nitro
	256	Aniline, 4-mercapto
	256	Benzene, 1-amino-4-mercapto
	256	Benzoic acid, 4-chloro, chloride
	256	Benzophenone, 2,4′-dichloro
	256	Leucomethylene blue
	256	Nicotine (*dl*)
	256	Pyridine, 4-phenyl
	256	Thiazole, 2-amino
	255 226	Acetophenone, 2,5-dihydroxy
	255	Benzaldehyde, 4-isopropyl
	255	Biphenyl, 4-bromo
	255	4-Pentenoic acid, 2-acetyl, ethyl ester
	254 218	Phenol, 2,5-dinitro
	254 205	Biphenyl, 4-benzyl
	254	Benzaldehyde, 4-chloro
	254	1,4-Benzenedicarboxaldehyde
	254	Benzophenone, 3-methyl
	254	1,3-Cyclohexanedione
	254	Propene, 1,1,3,3-tetraphenyl
	253 216	Benzoic acid, 3-nitro, nitrile
	253	Amine, tribenzyl
	253	Pyrrole, 1-phenyl
	252 243	1,3-Butadiene, 1,1-dichloro
	252 233	Sulfone, diphenyl, 4,4′-dibromo
	252	Acetaldehyde, diphenyl
	252	Amine, dibenzyl
	252	Antipyrine, 4-amino
	252	Antipyrine, *o*-amino
	252	Benzophenone, oxime
	252	Benzophenone, 2,2′-dimethyl
	252	Biphenyl, 4-chloro
	252	Quinoline, 5-amino
	251 204	Benzenesulfinic acid, 4-acetamido
	250	Acetic acid, amide, *N*(2-chlorophenyl)
	250	Biphenyl, 3-hydroxy
	250	Ethene, 1,1-diphenyl
	250	Ketone, benzyl phenyl, α-chloro
	250	Urea, 2-thio-1(2-tolyl)
	249	Acetophenone, α-bromo
	249	Phenothiazine, 10(2-dimethylaminopropyl), hydrochloride
	249	Toluene, 3-nitro-α,α,α-trifluoro
	248 213	Benzoic acid, 2-amino, amide
	248	Acetic acid, amide, *N*(4-hydroxyphenyl)
	248	Anthraquinone, 1,4-diamino
	248	1,2-Ethanediol, 1,2-diphenyl (*dl*)
	248	Toluene, α-amino
	247 211	4-Pyrone, 2,6-dimethyl
	247 208	Aniline, 2,6-dibromo
	247	Aniline, 3,4-dichloro
	247	Ascorbic acid (*l*)
	247	Benzoin (*dl*)
	247	Benzoin acetate (*dl*)
	247	Butanoic acid, 3-oxo, amide, *N*(2-chlorophenyl)
	247	Sulfoxide, diphenyl, 4,4′-dibromo
	246	Benzaldehyde, 4-bromo
	245	Acetophenone, 2-chloro
	245	Benzophenone, 4,4′-bis(dimethylamino)
	245	Malonic acid, diamide, *N*,*N*′-diphenyl

Strongest Band (ε)	Wavelengths (nm)	Compound
	245	*m*-Terphenyl
	245	Urea, 1,3-diethyl-1,3-diphenyl
	244	Butanoic acid, 3-oxo amide, *N*-phenyl
	244	Colchicine (*l*)
	244	Isothiocyanic acid, ethyl ester
	244	Thiocyanic acid, butyl ester
	243	Benzenesulfonic acid, 3-amino
	243	1,4-Benzoquinone
	243	Butanoic acid, 3-oxo, ethyl ester
	243	5-Pyrazolone, 3-methyl-1-phenyl
	243	Thiophene, 2,5-dichloro
	242	Acetophenone, oxime
	242	Barbituric acid, 5-ethyl-5(3-methylbutyl)
	242	Guanidine, 1,3-diphenyl
	242	Propenoic acid, butyl ester
	241	Acetic acid, amide, *N*-phenyl
	241	Biphenyl, 2-chloro
	241	Propene, 2-phenyl
	241	Urea, 2-thio
	240	Cinnamic acid, α,β-dibromo (*cis*)
	240	Urea, 1-methyl-2-thio
	239	4-Azobenzenesulfonic acid, 4′-hydroxy
	239	2-Imidazolidinethione
	239	Stilbene, α,β-diethyl-4,4′-dihydroxy (*trans*)
	239	Testosterone, 17-ethynyl
	238 206	Benzene, 1-chloro-2,4-dinitro
	238	Acetic acid, amide, *N*-butyl-*N*-phenyl
	238	Benzoic acid, 2-hydroxy, isobutyl ester
	238	Benzoic acid, 4-methyl, ethyl ester
	238	Eleutherin
	238	Toluene, α, 4-dibromo
	237 233	Thiophene
	237	Benzoic acid, 2,4-dinitro
	237	2-Butenoic acid, 4-oxo-4-phenyl
	237	1,2-Cyclohexanedione, dioxime
	237	3-Penten-2-one, 4-methyl
	236	1,3-Butadiene, 1-methoxy
	235	Adenosterone
	235	Benzoic acid, 4-methyl, amide
	235	Thiophene, 2-chloro
	235	Toluene, 2-acetamido-5-bromo
	234	Acetic acid, amide, *N*(methoxy-2-nitrophenyl)
	234	Aniline, *N*-formyl-*N*-methyl
	234	Benzophenone, 2-amino
	234	2-Cyclohexen-1-one, 3,5-dimethyl
	234	Phenol, 4-amino-2-nitro
	234	Thiophene, 2-ethyl
	234	Toluene, 2,4-dinitro
	233	Benzene, 1,3-dihydroxy, dibenzoate
	232	3,5-Pyridinedicarboxylic acid, 1,4-dihydro-2,4,6-trimethyl, diethyl ester
	232	*o*-Terphenyl
	232	Urea, 1-benzoyl
	227 31400	*o,o′*-Quaterphenyl
	231	Aniline, *N,N*-dimethyl-4-nitro
	231	Biphenyl, 2-nitro
	231	Hydrazine, 1,2-dibenzoyl
	230	2-Butanone, 3,4-dibromo-4-phenyl
	230	Propene, 3-chloro
	229 205	Phthalic acid, 4-nitro, imide

Strongest Band (ε)	Wavelengths (nm)	Compound
	229	Aniline, *N*-methyl-4-nitro
	228	Acetic acid, (4-bromophenyl)-α-hydroxy (*dl*)
	228	Aniline, 4-nitro
	228	Benzoic acid, 3,5-dinitro, ethyl ester
	228	Methane, tetrabromo
	227	Aniline, 2,3-dinitro
	227	2,3-Butanedione, dioxime
	227	Malonic acid, benzoylamino, diethyl ester
	225	Acetic acid, amide, *N*(2-aminoethyl), hydrochloride
	225	Benzene, 1,4-diiodo
	225	3-Biphenylcarboxylic acid
	225	Lycopene
	225	Toluene, 2-amino-5-nitro
	225	4-Toluenesulfonic acid, amide, *N*(4-tolyl)
	224	Benzohydroxamic acid
	224	Benzoic acid, hydrazide
	224	Methane, tribromo
	223	Benzene, α,β-dibromoethyl
	223	Benzene, 1,3,5-trinitro
	223	Isopulegol (*d*)
	223	Phthalic acid, 3,6-dihydroxy, imide
	222	Benzoic acid, 4-methyl-3-nitro
	221	4-Toluenesulfonic acid
	220 276	Benzene, 1-*tert*-butyl-4-hydroxy
	219	Cyanogen
	218	Benzoic acid, 4-chloro-2-nitro
	218	Benzoic acid, 3,4-dinitro
	218	Δ-2-Imidazoline, 2-methyl
	218	Methane, chloro(diphenyl)
	215	Benzene, 1,2-dichloro-3-nitro
	214	Benzoic acid, 2-nitro
	214	Pyrazole, 3-methyl
	213	Fumaric acid, diethyl ester
	212	Furan, 2-methyl
	211	Histamine, dihydrochloride
	210	Benzene, 1-nitro-2-triazo
	209	Guanidine
	197	1-Octanol
	196 193 177	3-Nonanone
	196 192 188 176	2-Hexanone, 5-methyl
	191	Butanal, 3-methyl
	185	Hexanal
	184 182 178	Pentanal
	175	Cholestane

Section D

Electron Spin Resonance

ELECTRON SPIN RESONANCE

Charles P. Poole, Jr., University of South Carolina, and
Horacio A. Farach, University of South Carolina

I. INTRODUCTION

This electron spin resonance (ESR) chapter contains physical constants and conversion factors which pertain to magnetic resonance, instrumentation, data, discussions of spin hamiltonians and related theoretical concepts, tabulations of data on transition ions and free radicals, information on relaxation and double resonance, and a treatment of lineshapes. Some sections present a summary of equations and related graphs, while others contain extensive lists of data. In all cases, it has been necessary to be highly selective in the choice of what to include because the available information is so extensive.

In some sections such as those on instrumentation, theory, and lineshapes, it has been possible to assemble information that is particularly basic and inherently appropriate for handbook purposes. In other sections such as those on transition ions, free radicals, and relaxation, the specific data on particular systems are so extensive that it seemed more appropriate to include tabulations of typical data. These should be useful for those seeking general comparisons and trends between individual systems.

Many of the tables contain general references to the source of each particular tabulation and particular references to the sources of individual data. These may be consulted for further details. Many of the figures are from standard texts. At the end of this chapter there is a general bibliography to books and reviews of electron spin resonance. The books are numbered sequentially by B-1, B-2, B-3, etc., and the reviews by R-1, R-2, R-3, etc., and they are referred to by these numbers in the text. Individual articles generally appear as footnotes to tables.

II. PHYSICAL CONSTANTS AND CONVERSION FACTORS

TABLE 2-1

Recommended Consistent Values of the Fundamental Constants*

Quantity	Symbol	Value	Uncertainty (ppm)
Permeability of vacuum	μ_0	$4\pi \times 10^{-7}$ H m^{-1}	
		$= 12.5663706144 \times 10^{-7}$ H m^{-1}	
Speed of light in vacuum	c	299792458(1.2) m s^{-1}	0.004
Permittivity of vacuum	$\epsilon_0 = (\mu_0 c^2)^{-1}$	$8.85418782(7) \times 10^{-12}$ F m^{-1}	0.008
Fine structure constant,	α	0.0072973506(60)	0.82
$\mu_0 ce^2/2h$	α^{-1}	137.03604(11)	0.82
Elementary charge	e	$1.6021892(46) \times 10^{-19}$ C	2.9
Planck constant	h	$6.626176(36) \times 10^{-34}$ J Hz^{-1}	5.4
	$\hbar = h/2\pi$	$1.0545887(57) \times 10^{-34}$ J s	5.4
Avogadro constant	N_A	$6.022045(31) \times 10^{23}$ mol^{-1}	5.1
Atomic mass units	$u = (10^{-3}$ kg mol$^{-1})/N_A$	$1.6605655(86) \times 10^{-27}$ kg	5.1
Electron rest mass	m_e	$0.9109534(47) \times 10^{-30}$ kg	5.1
		$5.4858026(21) \times 10^{-4}$ u	0.38
Muon rest mass	m_μ	$1.883566(11) \times 10^{-28}$ kg	5.6
		0.11342920(26) u	2.3
Proton rest mass	m_p	$1.6726485(86) \times 10^{-27}$ kg	5.1
		1.007276471(11) u	0.011
Neutron rest mass	m_n	$1.6749543(86) \times 10^{-27}$ kg	5.1
		1.008665012(37) u	0.037
Ratio, proton mass to electron mass	m_p/m_e	1836.15152(70)	0.38
Ratio, muon mass to electron mass	m_μ/m_e	206.76865(47)	2.3
Specific electron charge	e/m_e	$1.7588047(49) \times 10^{11}$ C kg^{-1}	2.8
Proton gyromagnetic ratio	$\gamma_p = \gamma_p' [1 + \sigma (H_2O)]$	$2.6751987(75) \times 10^8$ s^{-1} T^{-1}	2.8
Diamagnetic shielding factor, spherical H_2O sample	$1 + \sigma(H_2O)$	1.000025637(67)	0.067
Proton gyromagnetic ratio (uncorrected)	γ'_p	$2.6751301(75) \times 10^8$ s^{-1} T^{-1}	2.8
	$\gamma'_p/2\pi$	42.57602(12) MHz T^{-1}	2.8
Proton moment in nuclear magnetons (uncorrected)	μ'_p/μ_N	2.7927740(11)	0.38
Boltzmann constant	$k = R/N_4$	$1.380662(44) \times 10^{-23}$ J K^{-1}	32
Electron gyromagnetic ratio	$\gamma_e = g_e\mu_\beta/\hbar$	1.7608443×10^{11} s^{-1} T^{-1}	–
	$\gamma_e/2\pi$	2.8024708×10^4 MHz T^{-1}	–
Free electron g-factor	$\frac{1}{2}g_e = \mu_e/\mu_B$	1.0011596567(35)	0.0035
	$g_e = 2\mu_e/\mu_B$	2.0023193134(70)	0.0035
Muon g-factor	$\frac{1}{2} g_\mu$	1.00116616(31)	0.31
Proton moment in nuclear magnetons	μ_p/μ_N	2.7928456(11)	0.38
Bohr magneton	$\beta = \mu_B = e\hbar/2m_e$	$9.274078(36) \times 10^{-24}$ J T^{-1}	3.9
Nuclear magneton	$\beta_N = \mu_N = e\hbar/2m_p$	$5.050824(20) \times 10^{-27}$ J T^{-1}	3.9
Electron magnetic moment	μ_e	$9.284832(36) \times 10^{-24}$ J T^{-1}	3.9
Proton magnetic moment	μ_p	$1.4106171(55) \times 10^{-26}$ J T^{-1}	3.9
Proton magnetic moment in Bohr magnetons	μ_p/μ_B	$1.521032209(16) \times 10^{-3}$	0.011
Ratio, electron to proton magnetic moments	μ_e/μ_p	658.2106880(66)	0.010
Ratio, muon moment to proton moment	μ_μ/μ_p	3.1833402(72)	2.3
Muon magnetic moment	μ_μ	$4.490474(18) \times 10^{-26}$ J T^{-1}	3.9
Pi	π	3.1415926535	–

* From Cohen, E. R., *Res. Devel.*, 25(3), 32, 1974. With permission.

TABLE 2-2

Conversion Factors[B-61]

1. Magnetic field, H (gauss), to electron resonant frequency, ν_{el} (MHz) and ν_{el} (cm^{-1}) corresponding to g relative to free electron value g_e

$$\nu_{el}\,(\text{MHz}) = \frac{g_e\beta H}{h}\left(\frac{g}{g_e}\right) = 2.8024709\left(\frac{g}{g_e}\right)H\,(\text{gauss})$$

$$H\,(\text{gauss}) = 0.3568280\,\frac{g_e}{g}\,\nu_{el}\,(\text{MHz})$$

$$\nu_{el}\,(\text{MHz}) = c \times 10^{-6}\,\nu_{el}\,(\text{cm}^{-1}) = 2.99792458 \times 10^{4}\,\nu_{el}\,(\text{cm}^{-1})$$

$$\nu_{el}\,(\text{cm}^{-1}) = 0.3335641 \times 10^{-4}\,\nu_{el}\,(\text{MHz})$$

2. Magnetic field, H (gauss), to proton (uncorrected) resonant frequency, ν_p' (MHz)

$$\nu_p' = 4.257602 \times 10^{-3}\,H$$

$$H = 234.8740\,\nu_p'$$

3. Ratio of proton (uncorrected) to electron resonant frequency since $\gamma_p'\hbar = g_p'\beta$

$$\nu_p'/\nu_{el} = \frac{\gamma_p'\hbar}{g\beta} = 1.5192314 \times 10^{-3}\,\frac{g_e}{g}$$

4. Calculation of g-factors

$$g = \frac{h\nu_{el}}{\beta H} = 0.71448353\,\frac{\nu_{el}\,(\text{MHz})}{H\,(\text{G})}$$

$$= \frac{\gamma_p'\hbar\,\nu_{el}}{\beta\ \nu_p} = 3.0419864 \times 10^{-3}\,\frac{\nu_{el}}{\nu_p'}$$

5. Hyperfine couplings and hyperfine splittings

$$A\,(\text{MHz}) = 2.802471\left(\frac{g}{g_e}\right)A\,(\text{gauss})$$

$$A\,(\text{gauss}) = 0.3568280\left(\frac{g_e}{g}\right)A\,(\text{MHz})$$

$$A\,(\text{cm}^{-1}) = 0.3335641 \times 10^{-4}\,A\,(\text{MHz})$$

TABLE 2-3

Energy Conversion Factors[B-44]

The energy in a unit at the left is multiplied by the appropriate factor in the table to convert it to the energy unit given at the top of the corresponding column. For example, 1 electron volt (eV) is equal to 8066.03 cm^{-1} and corresponds to a temperature of 1.16049 × 10^{4} °K.

	cal/mol	**cm^{-1}**	**erg**
cal/mol	1.0	0.3497551	0.6947806 × 10^{-16}
cm^{-1}	2.859144	1.0	1.986478 × 10^{-16}
erg	1.439303 × 10^{16}	0.5034036 × 10^{16}	1.0
eV	2.306036 × 10^{4}	0.8065478 × 10^{4}	1.602189 × 10^{-12}
°K	1.987191	0.6950302	1.380662 × 10^{-16}
sec^{-1}	0.9537077 × 10^{-10}	0.3335641 × 10^{-10}	0.6626176 × 10^{-26}

	eV	**°K**	**sec^{-1}**
cal/mol	0.4336445 × 10^{-4}	0.5032228	1.048539 × 10^{10}
cm^{-1}	1.239852 × 10^{-4}	1.438786	2.997925 × 10^{10}
erg	0.6241460 × 10^{12}	0.7242902 × 10^{16}	1.509166 × 10^{26}
eV	1.0	1.160450 × 10^{4}	2.417970 × 10^{14}
°K	0.8617349 × 10^{-4}	1.0	2.083648 × 10^{10}
sec^{-1}	0.413570 × 10^{-14}	0.4799275 × 10^{-10}	1.0

TABLE 2-4

Nuclear Spins, Abundances, Moments and Hyperfine Couplings for Some Common Magnetic Nuclei† (see B-61)

Nucleus	Spin	% Natural Abundance	Magnetogyric Ratio‡ (rad G^{-1} x 10^{-4})	Anisotropic Hyperfine Coupling B, MHz §	Isotropic Hyperfine Coupling A_o, MHz ¶	Quadrupole Moment* x 10^{-24} cm^2
^{1}H	1/2	99.985	2.67510	–	1,420.0	0.0
^{2}H	1	0.015	0.41064	–	218.0	0.00273
^{6}Li	1	7.42	0.39366	–	152.0*	0.00069
^{7}Li	3/2	92.58	1.03964	–	402.0* (291.0 calc)	−0.03
^{9}Be	3/2	100.0	−0.37594		−358.0	0.052
^{10}B	3	19.58	0.28748	17.8	672.0	0.074
^{11}B	3/2	80.42	0.85828	53.1	2,020.0	0.0355
^{13}C	1/2	1.108	0.67263	90.8	3,110.0	0.0
^{14}N	1	99.63	0.19324	47.8	1,540.0	0.071
^{15}N	1/2	0.37	−0.27107	−67.1	−2,160.0	0.0
^{17}O	5/2	0.037	−0.36266	−144.0	−4,628.0	−0.026
^{19}F	1/2	100.0	2.51665	1,515.0	47,910.0	0.0
^{23}Na	3/2	100.0	0.70760	–	886.0*	0.15
^{25}Mg	5/2	10.13	−0.16370	–	–	–
^{27}Al	5/2	100.0	0.69706	59	2,746.0	0.149
^{29}Si	1/2	4.70	−0.53141	−86.6	−3,381.0	0.0
^{31}P	1/2	100.0	1.08290	287.0	10,178.0	0.0
^{33}S	3/2	0.76	0.20517	78.0	2,715.0	−0.064
^{35}Cl	3/2	75.53	0.26212	137.0	4,664.0	−0.0789
^{37}Cl	3/2	24.47	0.21818	117.0	3,880.0	−0.0621
^{39}K	3/2	93.10	0.12484	–	231.0*	0.11
^{43}Ca	7/2	0.145	−0.17999	–	–	
^{45}Sc	7/2	100.0	0.64989	–	1,833.0	−0.22
^{47}Ti	5/2	7.28	−0.15079	–	−492.0	0.0
^{49}Ti	7/2	5.51	−0.15083	–	−492.0	0.0
^{51}V	7/2	99.76	0.70323	–	2,613.0	−0.04
^{53}Cr	3/2	9.55	−0.15120	–	−630.0	–
^{55}Mn	5/2	100.0	0.65980	–	3,063.0	0.55
^{57}Fe	1/2	2.19	0.08644	–	450.0	0.0
^{59}Co	7/2	100.0	0.63171	–	3,666.0	0.40
^{61}Ni	3/2	1.19	−0.23905	–	1,512.0	–
^{63}Cu	3/2	69.09	0.70904	–	4,952.0	−0.16
^{65}Cu	3/2	30.91	0.75958	–	5,305.0	−0.15
^{67}Zn	5/2	4.11	0.16731	–	1,251.0	0.15
^{75}As	3/2	100.0	0.45816	255.0	9,582.0	0.3
^{77}Se	1/2	7.58	0.51008	376.0	13,468.0	0.0
^{79}Br	3/2	50.54	0.67021	646.0	21,738.0	0.33
^{81}Br	3/2	49.46	0.72245	696.0	23,432.0	0.28
^{83}Kr	9/2	11.55	−0.10293	–	–	0.15
^{85}Rb	5/2	72.15	0.25829	–	1,012.0*	0.27
^{87}Rb	3/2	27.85	0.87533	–	3,417.0*	0.13
^{95}Mo	5/2	15.72	0.17428	–	−3,528.0	0.12
^{97}Mo	5/2	9.46	−0.17796	–	−3,601.0	1.1
^{107}Ag	1/2	51.82	−0.10825	–	−3,520.0	0.0
^{109}Ag	1/2	48.18	−0.12445	–	−4,044.0	0.0
^{127}I	5/2	100.0	0.53522	–	–	−0.69
^{129}Xe	1/2	26.44	−0.73995	1,052.0	33,030.0	0.0
^{131}Xe	3/2	21.18	0.21935	–	–	−0.12
^{133}Cs	7/2	100.0	0.35089	–	2,298.0*	−0.003
^{207}Pb	1/2	22.6	0.55968	–	–	0.0

TABLE 2-4 (Continued)

†Compiled from data in the following references:

a. **Morton, J. R., Rowlands, J. R., and Whiffen, D. H.,** *National Physical Laboratory Bulletin.* No. BPR 13, 1962.
b. **Weast, R. C., Ed.,** *Handbook of Chemistry and Physics,* 50th ed., The Chemical Rubber Co., Cleveland, 1969, E75.
c. **Morton, J. R.,** *Chem. Rev.,* 64, 453, 1964.
d. **Whiffen, D. H.,** *J. Chim. Phys.,* 61, 1589, 1964.
e. **Goodman, B. A. and Raynor, J. B.,** *J. Inorg. Nucl. Chem.,* 32, 3406, 1970.

‡The magnetic moment (erg G^{-1}) can be obtained from the magnetogyric ratio by using the relation

$$\mu_n = hI\gamma_n.$$

§The anisotropic hyperfine couplings are tabulated as

$$B = 2/5\ h^{-1}\ g_n\beta_n g\beta\langle r^{-3}\rangle,$$

where $\langle r^{-3}\rangle$ is computed for a valence *p* electron from self-consistent-field wave functions. The couplings are such that the principal values of the traceless tensor are, respectively, −1, −1, and +2 times the number quoted.

¶The isotropic hyperfine couplings are tabulated as

$$A_o = \frac{8\pi}{3} h^{-1}\ g_n\beta_n g\beta|\psi_s(0)|^2,$$

where $\psi_s(0)$ is the value of the valence-shell, self-consistent-field S wave function at the nucleus of the neutral atom. Values indicated with an asterisk are the experimental atomic hyperfine couplings as measured using the atomic-beam technique. (See Kusch, P. and Taub, H., *Phys. Rev.,* 75, 1477, 1949.)

*Quadrupole moment data were obtained from Becker, E.D., *High Resolution NMR,* Academic Press, New York, 1969.

III. INSTRUMENTATION

A. Block Diagram of Superheterodyne Spectrometer

Figure 3-1 shows the block diagram of a superheterodyne ESR spectrometer which is somewhat more complex than the usual homodyne spectrometer type. Standard instrumentation treatises may be consulted for a description of the various components and a comparison of spectrometer types.

B. Sensitivity

The minimum detectable ESR absorption signal is equivalent to the minimum detectable susceptibility χ''_{min}. For a typical ESR spectrometer, it has the form

$$\chi''_{min} = \frac{1}{Q\eta}\left[\frac{F_k - 1 + (t + F_{amp} - 1)L}{P}(kT_d\Delta f)\right]^{\frac{1}{2}} \tag{3-1}$$

where

t = $G_dF_d = F_d/L$

F_k = klystron or generator noise figure ($F_k \geqslant 1$)

F_{amp} = preamplifier noise figure ($F_{amp} \geqslant 1$)

t = the so-called detector noise temperature (It is not a temperature but a gain-noise factor.)

G_d = conversion gain of detector

L = detector insertion loss (reciprocal of conversion gain)

F_d = detector noise figure ($F_d \geqslant 1$)

k = Boltzmann's constant

T_d = actual temperature of detector

Δf = bandwidth in Hz

Q = quality factor of resonant cavity

η = filling factor of resonant cavity

P = microwave power incident on cavity.

The filling factor η of a resonant cavity characterizes its effectiveness in concentrating the radiofrequency magnetic field H_1 at the sample

$$\eta = \frac{\int_{sample} H_1^2\,dV}{\int_{cavity} H_1^2\,dV} = \frac{V_s\,\langle H_1^2\rangle_s}{V_c\,\langle H_1^2\rangle_c} \tag{3-2}$$

where V_s and V_c are the sample and cavity volumes, respectively, and $\langle H_1{}^2\rangle$ denotes the average value of H_1. For a rectangular, TE_{012} mode resonance cavity of length d, height a, and width b with a small sample at its center,

$$\eta = \frac{V_s}{V_c}\;\frac{4}{1 + (d/2a)^2} \tag{3-3}$$

independent of the cavity's narrowest dimension b. For a typical cavity, $d \approx 2a \approx 4b$, to give

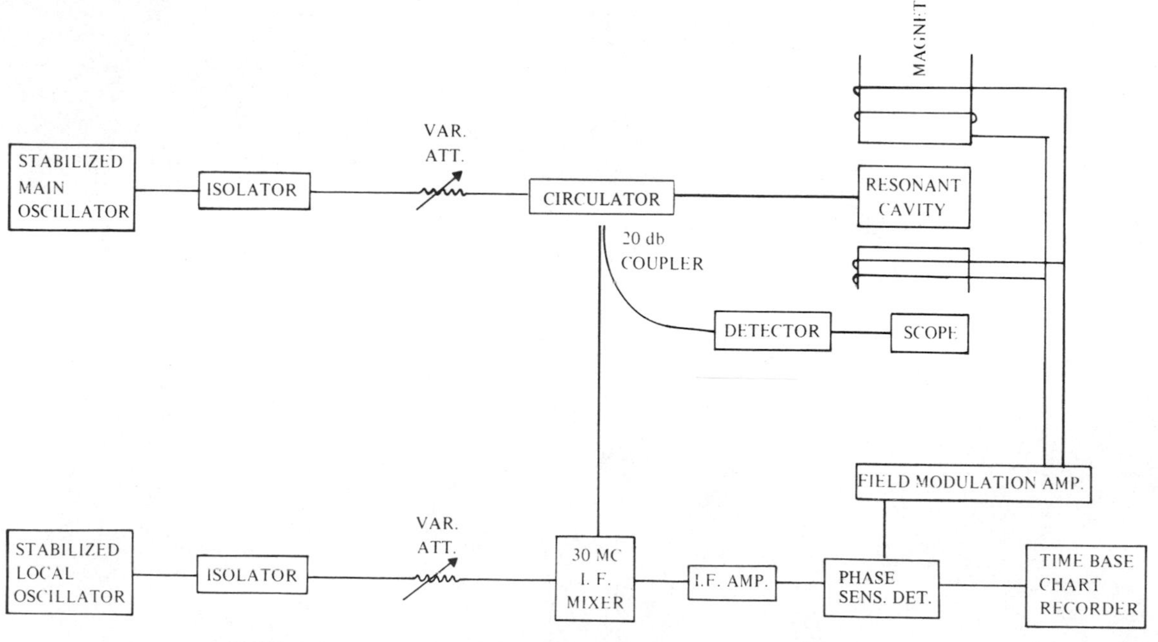

FIGURE 3-1. Block diagram of a typical superheterodyne spectrometer.

$$\eta \approx 2V_s \backslash V_c \tag{3-4}$$

corresponding to an average squared magnetic field at the sample equal to twice that in the overall cavity. For a flat cell or ESR sample tube oriented as shown in Figure 3-2, the filling factor is

$$\eta = V_s \backslash V_c \tag{3-5}$$

For a cylindrical TE_{011} resonant cavity of length d and radius a with a small sample located in the center, the filling factor is

$$\eta = \frac{12.33}{1 + (0.82\ a/d)^2} \frac{V_s}{V_c} \tag{3-6}$$

For a cylindrical sample of radius $r \ll a$ located along the axis of such a cavity (e.g., filling a sample tube), the filling factor is

$$\eta = \frac{6.16}{1 + (0.82\ a/d)^2} \frac{V_s}{V_c} \tag{3-7}$$

The coefficients 6.16 and 12.33 arise from Bessel functions.

The minimum detectable number of spins N_{min} for first derivative lines in the absence of saturation and overmodulation is given by

$$N_{min} \approx \frac{V_s K T_s D_m \Lambda}{Q \eta g^2 \omega_o S(S+1)} \left(\frac{\Delta H_{pp}}{H_o}\right)\left(\frac{\Delta H_{pp}}{H_{mod}}\right) \left[\frac{F_K - 1 + (t + F_{amp} - 1)L}{P}(T_d \Delta f)\right]^{\frac{1}{2}} \tag{3-8}$$

where

K = constant
V_s = sample volume
T_s = sample temperature
D_m = multiplicity factor
Λ = lineshape factor (3.63 for Lorentzian and 1.03 for Gaussian lines)
ΔH_{pp} = peak-to-peak linewidth
H_o = $\omega_o/\gamma = \omega_o \hbar/g\beta$ is the applied magnetic field strength
H_{mod} = modulation field amplitude
g = g-factor
β = Bohr magneton ($e\hbar/2\,mc$)
S = spin

The derivation of this expression assumes the high temperature approximation $kT_S \gg g\beta H$ and the

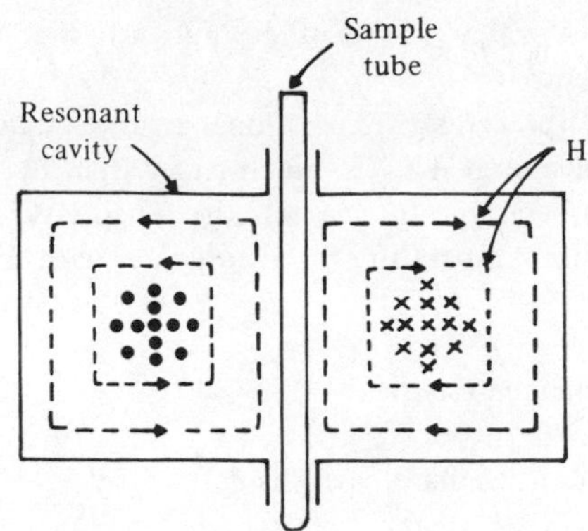

FIGURE 3-2. ESR sample tube (or flat cell) in TE_{102} rectangular resonant cavity of length d and height a.[B-42]

validity of the Curie law for the static susceptibility

$$\chi_o = \frac{N_{spin}\, g^2 \beta^2 S(S+1)}{3kT_S} \tag{3-9}$$

For a resolved multiplet with the strongest line of amplitude y_m', the multiplicity factor arises from a sum over the line amplitudes y_i'

$$D_m = \frac{1}{y_m'} \sum y_i' \tag{3-10}$$

For five lines of intensity ratio 1 : 4 : 6 : 4 : 1, one has, for example,

$$D_6 = \frac{1 + 4 + 6 + 4 + 1}{6} = \frac{8}{3} \ . \tag{3-11}$$

With overlapping lines the situation is more complex.

The number of spins in the sample is equal to the minimum detectable number of spins times the signal-to-noise ratio:

$$N_{spins} = N_{min}\ (\text{Signal-to-Noise Ratio}) \ . \tag{3-12}$$

When two samples, A and B, are compared with the same spectrometer, filling factor, Q, temperature, power level, and modulation amplitude, one has

$$\frac{N^A_{spin}}{N^B_{spin}} = \left(\frac{D^A_m}{D^B_m}\right)\left(\frac{g^B}{g^A}\right)^2 \left(\frac{S^B(S^B+1)}{S^A(S^A+1)}\right)\left(\frac{\Delta H^A_{pp}}{\Delta H^B_{pp}}\right)^2 \left(\frac{\Lambda^A}{\Lambda^B}\right)\left(\frac{y'^A_m}{y'^B_m}\right) \tag{3-13}$$

where $y_m'^A/y_m'^B$ is the ratio of the signal amplitudes.

The preceding expressions assume that the thermal energy kT_S is much larger than the ESR Zeeman energy. In general, the sensitivity varies with the temperature in accordance with Figure 3-3.

C. Resonance Cavities

The Q of a resonant cavity is defined by

$$Q = \frac{2\pi \text{ (stored energy)}}{\text{energy dissipated per cycle}} = 2\pi \frac{U_S}{U_{Dw}}$$

$$= \frac{\omega_o}{\Delta\omega} \tag{3-14}$$

where ω_o is the resonance frequency and $\Delta\omega$ is the width of the cavity mode. The stored energy is given by

$$U_S = \frac{1}{2}\varepsilon' \int |E_m|^2 \, dV = \frac{1}{2}\mu \int |H_m|^2 \, dV \quad . \tag{3-15}$$

The energy dissipated in the cavity walls per cycle is given by

$$U_{Dw} = \frac{\pi R_S}{\omega_o} \int |H_{tm}|^2 \, dA \tag{3-16}$$

where the skin effect resistance (or surface resistivity) R_S and skin depth (depth of penetration) δ are

$$R_S = \sqrt{\omega\mu/2\sigma} \tag{3-17}$$

$$\delta = \sqrt{2/\omega\mu\sigma} \tag{3-18}$$

$$R_s\sigma\delta = 1 \quad . \tag{3-19}$$

Several representative values are given in Table 3-1, and the frequency dependences of R_s and δ are shown in Figure 3-4.

The energy U_ϵ dissipated in a dielectric of volume V_s in a cavity of volume V_c is given by

$$U_\varepsilon = \frac{1}{2} \int \varepsilon''|E_m|^2 \, dV = \frac{1}{2}\varepsilon'' V_s \langle E_m^2 \rangle_s \tag{3-20}$$

where the imaginary part of the dielectric constant ϵ'' is constant in the expression on the extreme right. The dielectric constant ϵ has real and imaginary parts

$$\varepsilon = \varepsilon' - j\varepsilon''$$

$$= \varepsilon' (1 - j \tan \delta) \tag{3-21}$$

where the former contributes to the stored energy and the latter to the losses.

For the rectangular TE_{102} mode in a cavity of dimensions a, b, d,

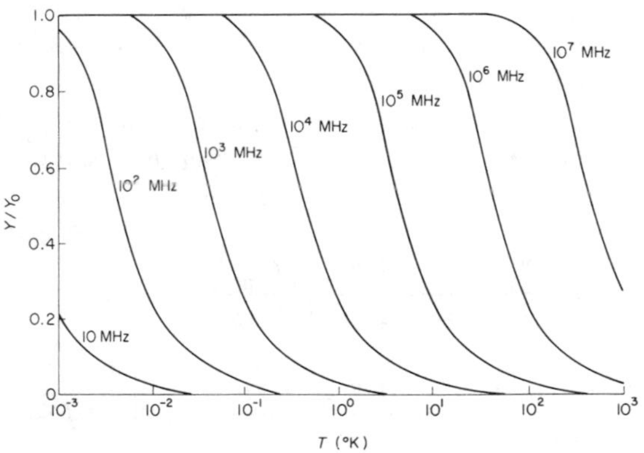

FIGURE 3-3. Temperature dependence of the ESR amplitude Y relative to its value Y_o at T = 0 for several microwave frequencies.[B-42]

TABLE 3-1

Electrical Properties of Several Metals, Where f Is in the Units Hz[B-47]

Metal	Conductivity σ mho/meter	Skin Depth δ meters	Surface Resistivity R_s ohms
Silver	6.17×10^7	$0.0642/\sqrt{f}$	$2.52 \times 10^{-7} \sqrt{f}$
Copper	5.80×10^7	$0.0660/\sqrt{f}$	$2.61 \times 10^{-7} \sqrt{f}$
Aluminum	3.72×10^7	$0.0826/\sqrt{f}$	$3.26 \times 10^{-7} \sqrt{f}$
Typical brass	1.57×10^7	$0.127\ /\sqrt{f}$	$5.01 \times 10^{-7} \sqrt{f}$
Typical solder	0.71×10^7	$0.185\ /\sqrt{f}$	$7.73 \times 10^{-7} \sqrt{f}$

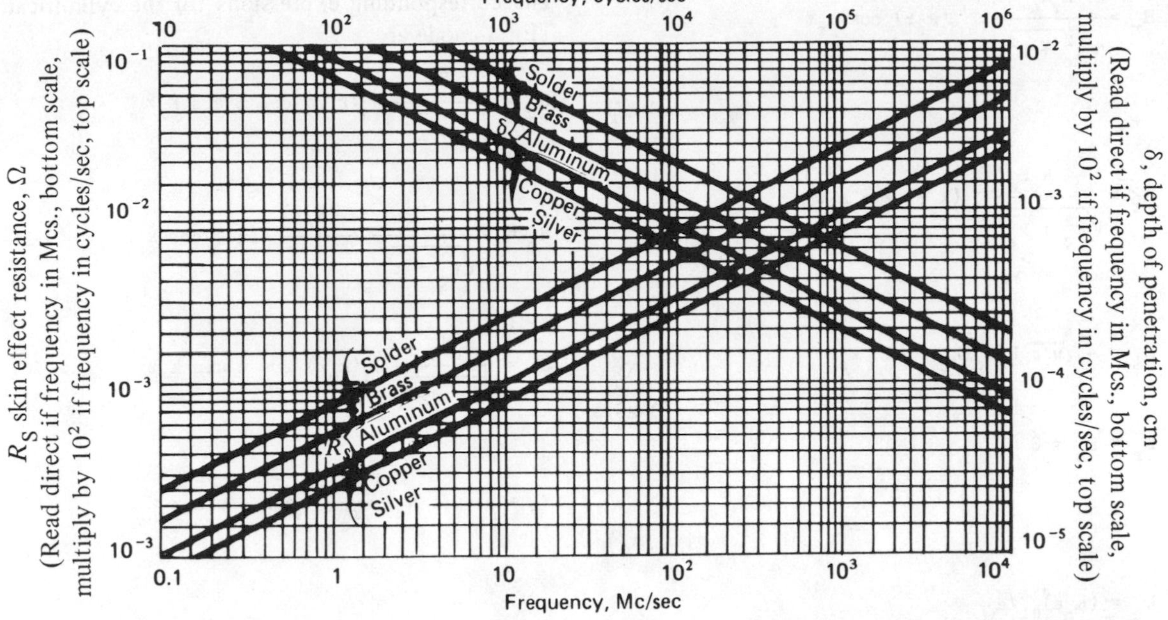

FIGURE 3-4. Skin effect quantities for plane conductors.[B-47]

$$H_x = \frac{H_o}{\sqrt{1 + (d/2a)^2}} \sin \frac{\pi x}{a} \cos \frac{2\pi z}{d} \qquad (3\text{-}22)$$

$$H_y = 0$$

$$H_z = \frac{-H_o}{\sqrt{1 + (2a/d)^2}} \cos \frac{\pi x}{a} \sin \frac{2\pi z}{d} \qquad (3\text{-}23)$$

$$E_x = E_z = 0$$

$$E_y = j\sqrt{\mu/\varepsilon}\, H_o \sin \frac{\pi x}{a} \sin \frac{2\pi z}{d} \qquad (3\text{-}24)$$

$$Z = \sqrt{(\mu/\varepsilon)\,[1 + (d/2a)^2]} \qquad (3\text{-}25)$$

$$Q = \frac{\lambda}{\delta} \frac{4b\,[a^2 + (\frac{1}{2}\,d)^2]^{3/2}}{d^3(a + 2b) + 4a^3(d + 2b)} \qquad (3\text{-}26)$$

Figure 3-5 shows the mode configuration, and Figure 3-6 shows the rf surface current distribution for this mode. The latter is useful for making slots in cavities since such slots should be cut along lines of current flow. For the cylindrical TE_{011} mode in a cavity of radius a and length d, one has

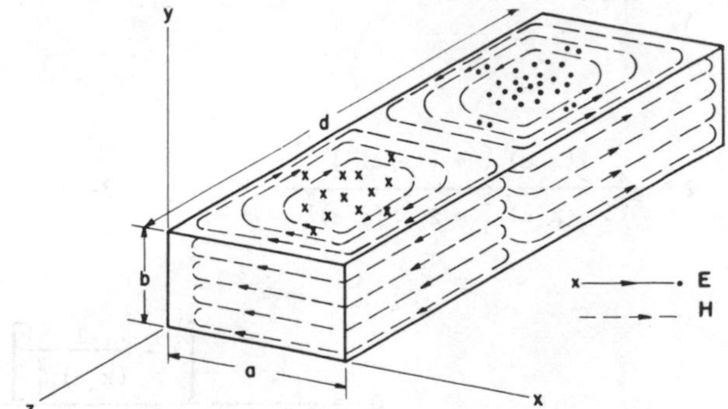

FIGURE 3-5. Electromagnetic field configurations in a TE_{102} mode rectangular resonant cavity of dimensions a, b, and d.[B-42]

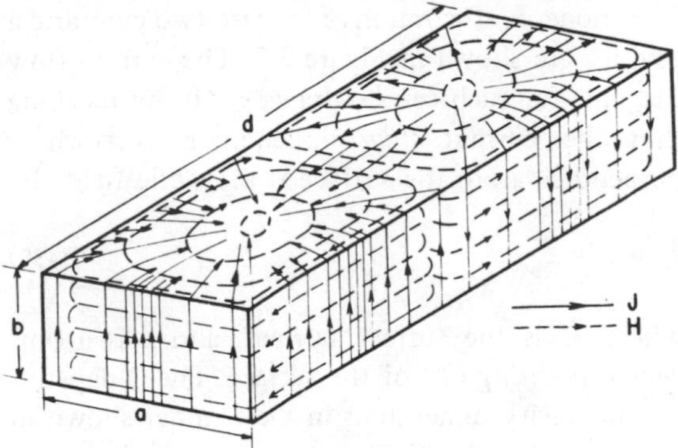

FIGURE 3-6. Current distribution J in a TE_{102} mode rectangular resonant cavity with dimensions a, b, and d.[B-42]

$$H_r = \frac{k_z H_o}{\sqrt{k_c^2 + k_z^2}} J_o'(k_c r) \cos k_z z$$

$$H_\phi = 0 \qquad (3\text{-}27)$$

$$H_z = \frac{k_c H_o}{\sqrt{k_c^2 + k_z^2}} J_o(k_c r) \sin k_z z$$

$$E_\phi = -\sqrt{\mu/\varepsilon}\, H_o J_o'(k_c r) \sin k_z z$$

$$E_r = E_z = 0 \qquad (3\text{-}28)$$

$$k_c = (k_c a)'_{01}/a$$

$$k_z = \pi/d \qquad (3\text{-}29)$$

$$Q = \frac{\lambda}{2\pi\delta} \frac{[(k_c a)'^2_{01} + (\pi a/d)^2]^{2/3}}{(k_c a)'^2_{01} + 2\pi^2 (a/d)^3} \qquad (3\text{-}30)$$

The corresponding expressions for the cylindrical TE_{111} mode are

$$H_r = \frac{k_z H_o}{\sqrt{k_c^2 + k_z^2}} J_1'(k_c r) \cos\phi \cos k_z z$$

$$H_\phi = -\frac{k_z H_o}{\sqrt{k_c^2 + k_z^2}} \frac{J_1(k_c r)}{k_c r} \sin\phi \cos k_z z \qquad (3\text{-}31)$$

$$H_z = \frac{k_c H_o}{\sqrt{k_c^2 + k_z^2}} J_1(k_c r) \cos\phi \sin k_z z$$

$$E_r = -\sqrt{\mu/\varepsilon}\, H_o \frac{J_1(k_c r)}{k_c r} \sin\phi \sin k_z z$$

$$E_\phi = -\sqrt{\mu/\varepsilon}\, H_o J_1'(k_c r) \cos\phi \sin k_z z \qquad (3\text{-}32)$$

$$E_z = 0$$

$$k_c = (k_c a)_{11}/a$$

$$k_z = \pi/d \qquad (3\text{-}33)$$

$$Q = \frac{\lambda}{2\pi\delta} \frac{\left[1 - \frac{1}{(k_c a)'^2_{11}}\right]\left[(k_c a)'^2_{11} + \left(\frac{\pi a}{d}\right)^2\right]^{2/3}}{(k_c a)'^2_{11} + 2\pi^2 (a/d)^3 + (1 - 2a/d)\left[\frac{\pi a}{d(k_c a)'_{11}}\right]^2} \qquad (3\text{-}34)$$

The mode configurations for these two cylindrical cavities are shown in Figure 3-7. The current flow diagram for each can be drawn easily by recalling that the current flow direction is everywhere perpendicular to the surface rf magnetic field $\vec{H}_t$:

$$\vec{J}_t = \hat{n} \times \vec{H}_t \qquad (3\text{-}35)$$

where $\vec{J}_t$ is the surface current, and $\hat{n}$ is a unit vector pointing out of the surface. The Q depends on the cavity dimensions in the manner shown in Figures 3-8 and 3-9. Resonant cavities should be designed with the use of Figure 3-10 by selecting an operating region which avoids mode degeneracies.

It is frequently desirable to insert dielectric materials into resonant cavities, and Table 3-2 lists dielectric constants and loss tangents for several representative materials, where $\tan\delta = \epsilon''/\epsilon'$.

D. Waveguides and Generators

Table 3-3 lists the characteristics of various waveguides and couplings, and Figure 3-11 compares the noise figures of several types of microwave generators.

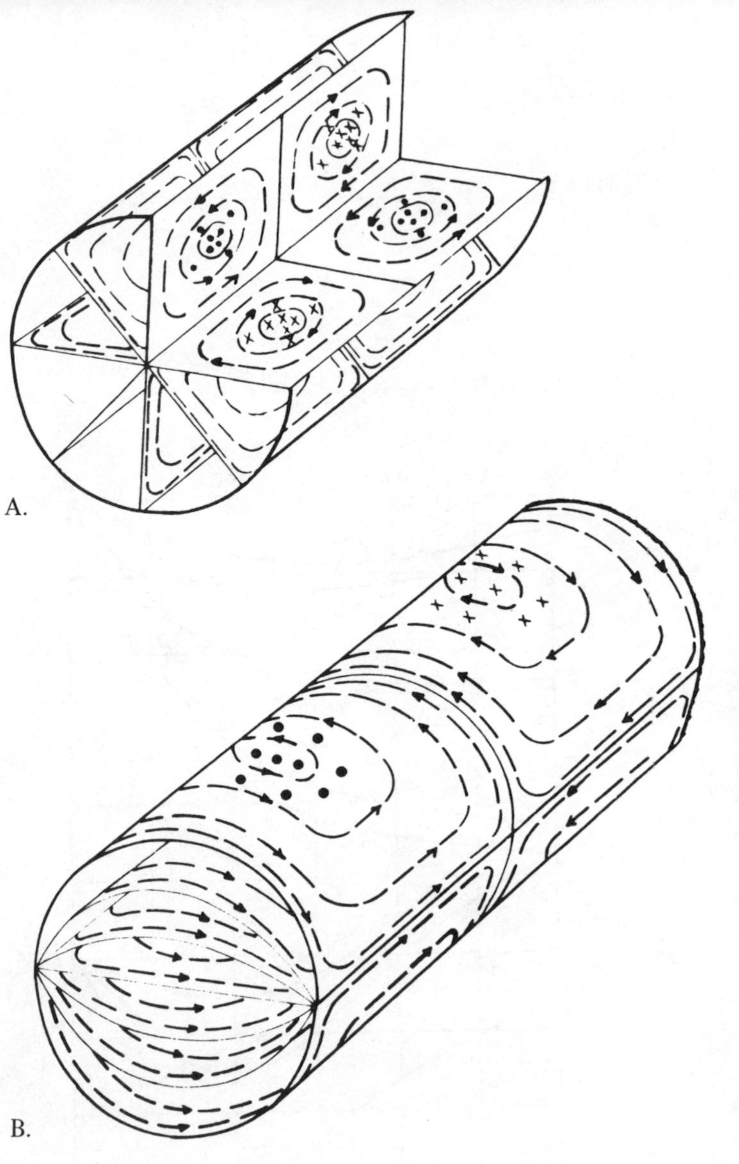

FIGURE 3-7. Diagrammatic sketch of the TE_{012} (A) and TE_{112} (B) cylindrical resonant cavity modes. (Adapted from B-42 and B-48.)

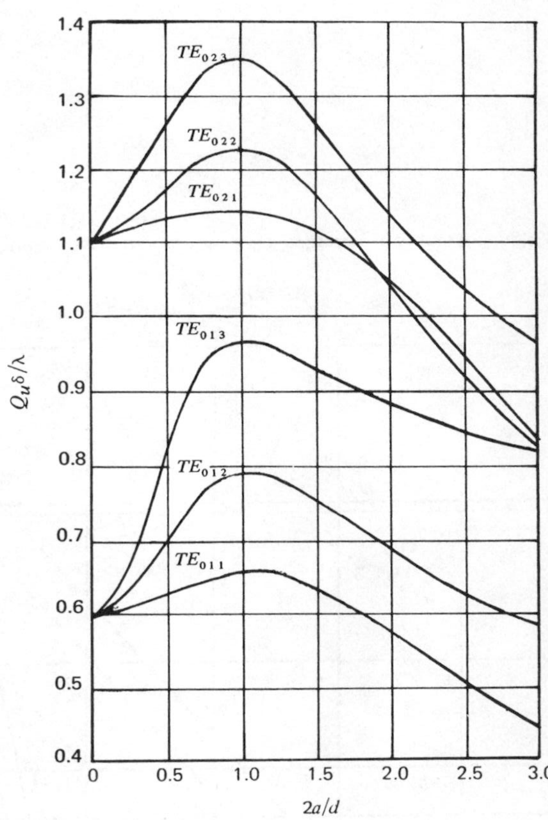

FIGURE 3-8. $Q_u\ \delta/\lambda$ vs. 2a/d for several TE_{onp} modes in a right circular cylinder[B-45, Vol. II]

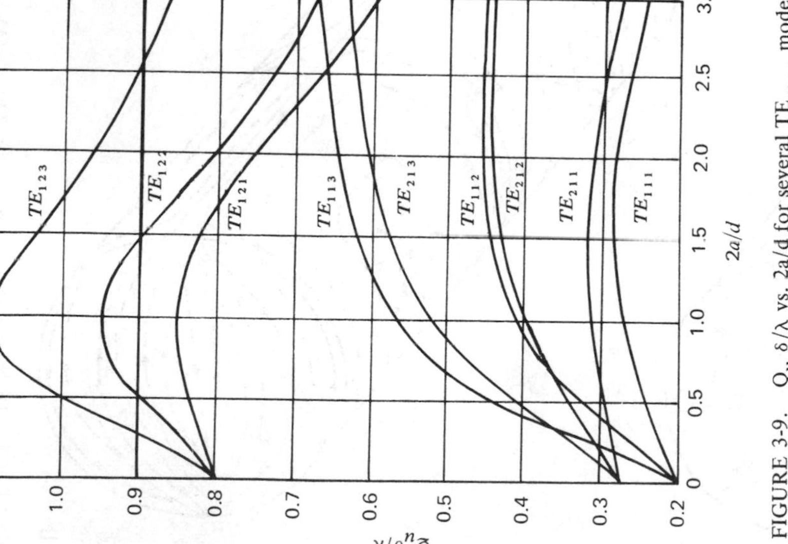

FIGURE 3-9. Q_u δ/λ vs. 2a/d for several TE_{mnp} modes in a right circular cylinder.[B-45,Vol. II]

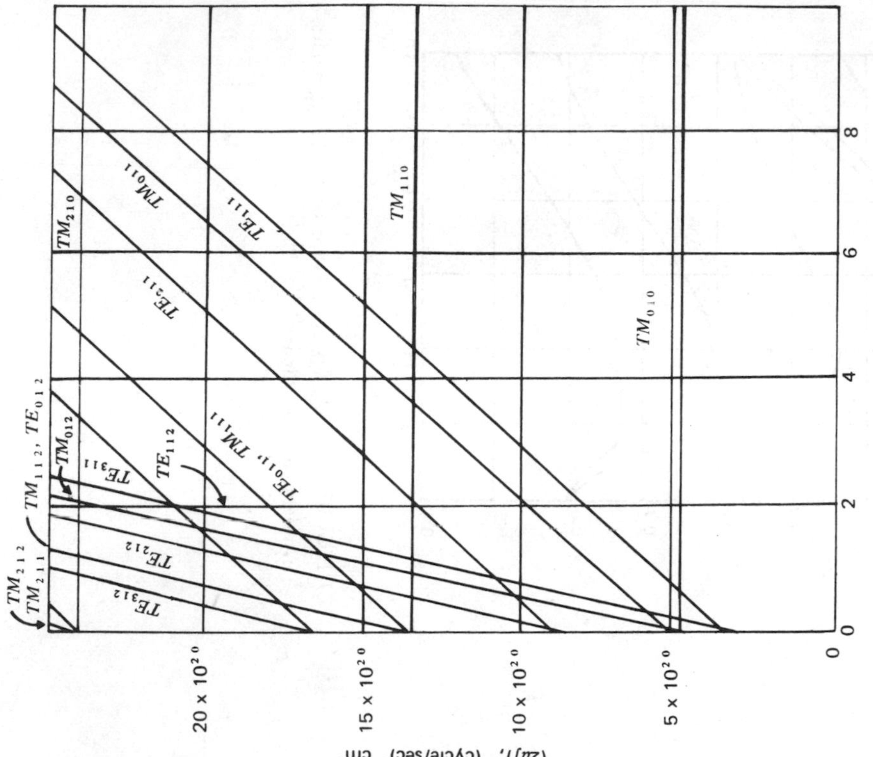

FIGURE 3-10. Mode chart for right circular cylinder of radius a, length d, and resonant frequency f.[B-45,Vol. II]

TABLE 3-2

Dielectric Properties of Materials Sometimes Encountered Inside Cavities[B-3,B-55]

(All values of tan δ have been multiplied by 10^4)

Material	Temperature °C		Frequency cps: 10^6	10^8	3×10^9	10^{10}	2.5×10^{10}
Fused quartz	25	ϵ'/ϵ_0	3.78	3.78	3.78	3.78	3.78
		tan δ	2.0	1.0	0.6	1.0	2.5
Pyrex®	25	ϵ'/ϵ_0	4.84	4.84	4.82	4.80	4.65
		tan δ	36.0	30.0	54.0	98.0	90.0
Polyethylene	24	ϵ'/ϵ_0	2.25	2.25	2.25	2.25	2.24
		tan δ	<4.0		3.0	4.0	6.7
Polytetrafluoro-ethylene (Teflon®)	22	ϵ'/ϵ_0	2.1	2.1	2.1	2.08	2.08
		tan δ	<2.0	<2.0	1.5	3.7	6.0
Polystyrene	25	ϵ'/ϵ_0	2.56	2.55	2.55	2.54	2.54
		tan δ	0.7	<1.0	3.3	4.3	12.0
Epoxy	25	ϵ'/ϵ_0	3.62–4.4	3.35–3.7	3.09–3.2	3.01–3.1	
		tan δ	190.0–770.0	340.0–1,300.0	270.0–460.0	220.0–390.0	
Nylon 610	25	ϵ'/ϵ_0	3.14	3.0	2.84		2.73
		tan δ	218.0	200.0	117.0		105.0
Lucite	23	ϵ'/ϵ_0	2.63	2.58	2.58	2.57	2.57
		tan δ	145.0	67.0	51.3	49.0	32.0
Water, conductivity	25	ϵ'/ϵ_0	78.2	78.0	76.7	55.0	34.0
		tan δ	400.0	50.0	1,570.0	5,400.0	2,650.0
Water, 0.5 molal solution of NaCl	25	ϵ'/ϵ_0			69.0	51.0	
		tan δ			39,000.0	6,300.0	
Apiezon wax "W"	22	ϵ'/ϵ_0	2.63		2.62		
		tan δ	25.0		16.0		
Ceresin wax (white)	25	ϵ'/ϵ_0	2.3	2.3	2.25	2.24	
		tan δ	4.0	4.0	4.6	6.5	
Silicone oil DC500	22	ϵ'/ϵ_0	2.26		2.20	2.19	2.13
		tan δ	<3.0		14.5	30.0	60.0
Pliobond M-190-C	24	ϵ'/ϵ_0	6.3	4.0	3.76		
		tan δ	2,000.0	1,000.0	740.0		
LiF	25	ϵ'/ϵ_0	9.00			9.00	
		tan δ	<2.0			1.8	
KBr	25	ϵ'/ϵ_0	4.90			4.90	
		tan δ	<2.0			2.3	
Liquid helium	−269	ϵ'/ϵ_0	1.025	1.025	1.025		

TABLE 3-3

Standard Rectangular Waveguides and Couplings[B-42,B-45]

RMA Designation	Waveguide Army-Navy Type No.	OD, in. (1 in. = 2.54 cm)	Wall in	Wavelength Band cm	Wavelength for P_{max} and Loss cm	P_{max} MW	Loss for Copper dB/m	Choke Coupling	Flange Coupling	Design Wavelength cm	Bandwidth for VSWR <1.05, %
WR 284	RG-48/U	3.0 x 1.5	0.080	7.3–13.0	10.0	10.5	0.020	UG-54/U	UG-53/U	10.7	± 15.0
		ID 2.75 x 0.375	0.049	7.0–12.6	10.0	2.77	0.058	UG-200/U	UG-214/U	9.0	± 15.0
WR 187	RG-49/U	2.0 x 1.0	0.064	4.8–8.5	6.5	4.86	0.031	UG-148/U	UG-149/U		
WR 137	RG-50/U	1.5 x 0.75	0.064	3.6–6.3	5.0	2.29	0.063				
WR 112	RG-51/U	1.25 x 0.625	0.064	2.9–5.1	3.2	1.77	0.072	UG-52/U	UG-51/U	3.20	
WR 90	RG-52/U	1.0 x 0.5	0.050	2.3–4.1	3.2	0.99	0.117	UG-40/U	UG-39/U	3.20	± 6.0
WR 42	RG-53/U	0.5 x 0.25	0.040	1.07–1.9	1.25	0.223	0.346	UG-117/U	UG-116/U	1.25	> ± 2.0
WR 34		0.42 x 0.25	0.040	0.9–1.4							
WR 28	RG-96/U	0.36 x 0.22	0.040	0.75–1.1			0.56	UG-600/U	UG-599/U		
WR 22		0.304 x 0.192	0.040	0.6–0.9							
WR 19		0.268 x 0.174	0.040	0.5–0.75							
WR 15		0.228 x 0.154	0.040	0.4–0.6							
WR 12		0.202 x 0.141	0.040	0.33–0.5							
WR 10		0.180 x 0.130	0.040	0.27–0.4							

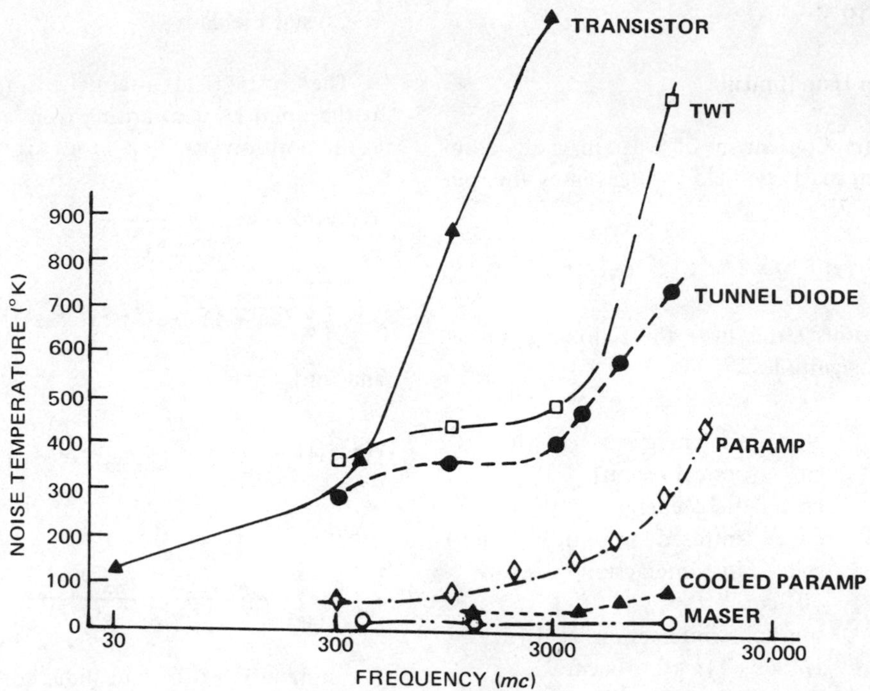

FIGURE 3-11. State of the art of low-noise amplifiers showing the noise temperature as a function of the frequency. (From Eastman, R. S. and Miller, R. A., Jr.; see B-3).

IV. THEORY

A. The Spin Hamiltonian

The interaction energy of a paramagnetic atom in a constant magnetic field H_o is given by the spin hamiltonian $\mathcal{H}$:

$$\mathcal{H} = \mathcal{H}_{elect} + \mathcal{H}_{cf} + \mathcal{H}_{LS} + \mathcal{H}_{SS} + \mathcal{H}_{Zee} + \mathcal{H}_{hfs} + \mathcal{H}_{Q} + \mathcal{H}_{N}, \tag{4-1}$$

and the various terms have the following typical forms and magnitudes:

$\mathcal{H}_{elect}$ = electronic energy $\approx 10^4$ to 10^5 cm^{-1} (optical region)

$\mathcal{H}_{cf}$ = crystal field energy $\approx 10^3$ to 10^4 cm^{-1} (infrared or optical region)

$\mathcal{H}_{LS}$ = spin orbit interaction = $\lambda L \cdot S \approx 10^2\ cm^{-1}$

$\mathcal{H}_{SS}$ = spin-spin interaction = $D(S_z^2 - 1/3S(S+1)) \approx 0$ to 1 cm^{-1}

$\mathcal{H}_{Zee}$ = Zeeman energy = $\beta\vec{H}\cdot(\vec{L} + 2\vec{S}) = \beta(g_xH_xS_x + g_yH_yS_y + g_zH_zS_z) \approx 0$ to 1 cm^{-1}

$\mathcal{H}_{hfs}$ = hyperfine structure = $(A_xS_xI_x + A_yS_yI_y + A_zS_zI_z) \approx 0$ to 10^{-2} cm^{-1}

$\mathcal{H}_{Q}$ = quadrupole energy = $\{3eQ/[4I(2I-1)]\} \times (\partial^2V/\partial z^2)\,[I_z^2 - 1/3I(I+1)] \approx 0$ to 10^{-2} cm^{-1}

$\mathcal{H}_{N}$ = nuclear spin energy = $\gamma\beta_N\vec{H}\cdot\vec{I} \approx 0$ to 10^{-3} cm^{-1}

Several of the symbols in these eight equations are defined as follows:

λ = spin orbit coupling constant

S_z, L_z = z component (along $\vec{H}_o$) of the spin and orbital angular momenta, respectively

D = axial zero field splitting constant

β = Bohr magneton

g_z = z component of g-factor

A_z = z component of hyperfine coupling constant A

I_z = z component of nuclear spin I

e = electronic charge

Q = nuclear electric quadrupole moment

V = crystalline electric field potential

γ = nuclear gyromagnetic ratio

β_N = nuclear magneton

B. Crystal Fields

The crystal field potential energy of an electron at the point $(r, \theta\ \phi)$ arising from a charge $q_j = eZ_j$ at the position (R_j, θ_j, ϕ_j) for $r<R_j$ is given by

$$V(r,\theta,\phi) = eq_j \sum_{n=0}^{\infty} \frac{r^n}{R_j^{(n+1)}} \left[\sum_{\alpha} \frac{4\pi}{(2n+1)} Z_{n\alpha}(\theta_j,\phi_j)\, Z_{n\alpha}(\theta,\phi)\right], \tag{4-2}$$

and for k charges

$$V(r,\theta,\phi) = \sum_{n=0}^{\infty} \sum_{\alpha} r^n \gamma_{n\alpha} Z_{n\alpha}(\theta,\phi), \tag{4-3}$$

where

$$\gamma_{n\alpha} = \sum_{j=1}^{k} \frac{4\pi e}{(2n+1)}\, q_j \frac{Z_{n\alpha}(\theta_j,\phi_j)}{R_j^{(n+1)}}. \tag{4-4}$$

The summation over α includes both $Z_{n\alpha}^c$ and $Z_{n\alpha}^s$ forms of the tesseral harmonics which are listed in Table 4-1 and are related to the spherical harmonics by

$$Z_{n0} = Y_n^0 \qquad m = 0$$

$$\left.\begin{aligned} Z_{nm}^c &= (1/\sqrt{2})\,[Y_n^{-m} + (-1)^m Y_n^m] \\ Z_{nm}^s &= (i/\sqrt{2})\,[Y_n^{-m} - (-1)^m Y_n^m] \end{aligned}\right\} \quad m > 0, \tag{4-5}$$

The potentials for several common charge configurations are given in Table 4-2 with the tesseral harmonics written out explicitly in terms of spherical harmonics. These potentials may also be expressed in Cartesian coordinates in the manner of Table 4-3, with the explicit coefficients for C_4 and D_6 given in Table 4-4 for the cubic, octahedral, and tetrahedral cases.

The charge distribution for several electrons i gives rise to the crystal field hamiltonian

$$\mathcal{H}_{CF} = \sum_i V(r_i\theta_i\phi_i) = \sum_{nm} B_n^m O_n^m \tag{4-6}$$

where the operator equivalents O_n^m are listed on Table 4-5 and the coefficients B_n^m depend on the symmetry, ligand charge distribution, and electron configuration. The crystal field energy splitting is given in terms of these coefficients in Figure 4-1 to 4-4. Other notations in common use are

TABLE 4-1

Some of the More Commonly Occurring Tesseral Harmonics Expressed in Cartesian Coordinates[R-48]

$Z_{20} = 1/4(\frac{5}{\pi})^{1/2}[(3z^2 - r^2)/r^2]$

$Z^c_{22} = 1/4(\frac{15}{\pi})^{1/2}[(x^2 - y^2)/r^2]$

$Z_{40} = 3/16(\frac{1}{\pi^{1/2}})[(35z^4 - 30z^2r^2 + 3r^4)/r^4]$

$Z^c_{42} = 3/8(\frac{5}{\pi})^{1/2}[(7z^2 - r^2)(x^2 - y^2)/r^4]$

$Z^c_{43} = 3/8(\frac{70}{\pi})^{1/2}[z(x^3 - 3xy^2)/r^4]$

$Z^s_{43} = 3/8(\frac{70}{\pi})^{1/2}[z(3x^2y - y^3)/r^4]$

$Z^c_{44} = 3/16(\frac{35}{\pi})^{1/2}[(x^4 - 6x^2y^2 + y^4)/r^4]$

$Z^s_{44} = 3/16(\frac{35}{\pi})^{1/2}[4(x^3y - y^3x)/r^4]$

$Z_{60} = 1/32(\frac{13}{\pi})^{1/2}[(231z^6 - 315z^4r^2 + 105z^2r^4 - 5r^6)/r^6]$

$Z^c_{62} = 1/64(\frac{2{,}730}{\pi})^{1/2}[(16z^4 - 16(x^2 + y^2)z^2 + (x^2 + y^2)^2)(x^2 - y^2)/r^6]$

$Z^c_{63} = 1/32(\frac{2{,}730}{\pi})^{1/2}[(11z^3 - 3zr^2)(x^3 - 3xy^2)/r^6]$

$Z^c_{64} = 21/32(\frac{13}{7\pi})^{1/2}[(11z^2 - r^2)(x^4 - 6x^2y^2 + y^4)/r^6]$

$Z^c_{66} = 231/64(\frac{26}{231\pi})^{1/2}[(x^6 - 15x^4y^2 + 15x^2y^4 - y^6)/r^6]$

$$b_2^0 = 3B_2^0 = D \qquad b_6^6 = 1260B_6^6$$

$$b_2^2 = 3B_2^2 = 3E \qquad b_4^m = 60B_4^m$$

$$b_4^0 = 60B_4^0 = \frac{1}{3}F \qquad b_6^m = 1260B_6^m \tag{4-7}$$

$$b_6^0 = 1260B_6^0$$

and, especially for cubic,fields,

$$b_4^0 = 60B_4^0 = \frac{1}{2}a = \frac{1}{4}c$$

$$b_6^0 = 1260B_6^0 = \frac{1}{4}d \quad . \tag{4-8}$$

The cubic irreducible representations have two common nomenclatures as follows:

Singlet A_1 Γ_1		
Singlet A_2 Γ_2		
Doublet E Γ_3	Integral J	
Triplet T_1 Γ_4		
Triplet T_2 Γ_5		
Doublet E′ Γ_6		
Doublet E″ Γ_7	Half-integral J	
Quartet U Γ_8		

Additional information is contained in Tables 4-6 to 4-8.

C. Spin Orbit Interaction

The spin orbit hamiltonian is

$$\mathcal{H}_{so} = \lambda L \cdot S = \frac{1}{2}\lambda[J(J+1) - L(L+1) - S(S+1)] \; . \tag{4-9}$$

Its influence on free-ion atomic states is illustrated in Figure 4-5. The spin orbit coupling constant λ is sometimes expressed in terms of the positive definite parameter ζ:

$$\lambda = \pm \zeta/2S \tag{4-10}$$

where the positive sign refers to a shell that is less than half filled, and the negative sign refers to a shell which is more than half filled. The spin orbit coupling constant for d-electrons in neutral atoms varies in the manner illustrated in Figure 4-6. Coupling constants in the solid state are smaller by 30% or 40% than their free-ion counterparts.

D. Zero Field Splittings

For spin S>1/2 and lower than cubic symmetry, the zero field D-term hamiltonian is present:

$$\mathcal{H}_D = \vec{S} \cdot \overleftrightarrow{D} \cdot \vec{S} = \sum_{i,j} S_i S_j D_{ij} \tag{4-11}$$

which is analogous to the quadrupole hamiltonian. The $\overleftrightarrow{D}$ tensor is symmetric and may be considered traceless since a nontraceless tensor would add a

TABLE 4-2

Potential Functions for Various Crystalline Symmetries[B-33]

Sixfold cubic coordination

$V = D_4 [7/2Y_4{}^0 + 1/4(70)^{1/2}(Y_4{}^4 + Y_4{}^{-4})] + D_6 [3/4Y_6{}^0 - 3/8(14)^{1/2}(Y_6{}^4 + Y_6{}^{-4})].$

Fourfold cubic coordination-tetrahedron

$V = -D_4 [14/9Y_4{}^0 + 1/9(70)^{1/2}(Y_4{}^4 + Y_4{}^{-4})] + D_6 [8/9Y_6{}^0 - 4/9(14)^{1/2}(Y_6{}^4 + Y_6{}^{-4})].$

Eightfold cubic coordination

$V = -D_4 [28/9Y_4{}^0 + 2/9(70)^{1/2}(Y_4{}^4 + Y_4^{-4})] + D_6 [16/9Y_6{}^0 - 8/9(14)^{1/2}(Y_6{}^4 + Y_6{}^{-4})].$

Sixfold trigonal coordination

$V = C_2 [3(3 \cos^2 \theta_i - 1)Y_2{}^0] + C_3 [-3/2(5)^{1/2} \sin^3 \theta_i(Y_3{}^3 + Y_3{}^{-3})] + C_4 [3/4(35 \cos^4 \theta_i$
$-30 \cos^2 \theta_i + 3)Y_4{}^0] + C_6 [3/8(231 \cos^6 \theta_i - 315 \cos^4 \theta_i + 105 \cos^2 \theta_i - 5)Y_6{}^0$
$+ 3/16(231)^{1/2}(1 - \cos^2 \theta_i)^3 Y_6{}^6 + Y_6{}^{-6})].$

Ninefold trigonal coordination

$V = C_2 [9/2(2 \cos^2 \theta_i - 1)Y_2{}^0] + C_3 [3/4(5)^{1/2}(1 - 2 \sin^3 \theta_i)(Y_3{}^3 + Y_3{}^{-3})]$
$C_4 [3/8(70 \cos^4 \theta_i - 60 \cos^2 \theta_i + 9)Y_4{}^0] +$
$C_6 [3/16(462 \cos^6 \theta_i - 630 \cos^4 \theta_i + 210 \cos^2 \theta_i - 45)Y_6{}^0 + 3/32(231)^{1/2}$
$(1 + 2 \sin^6 \theta_i)(Y_6{}^6 + Y_6{}^{-6})].$

Sixfold tetragonal coordination

$V = C_2 [2(1/a_1{}^3 - 1/a_2{}^3)Y_2{}^0] + C_4 [1/2(4/a_1{}^5 + 3/a_2{}^5)Y_4{}^0$
$+ (1/4a_2^5)(70)^{1/2}(Y_4{}^4 + Y_4{}^{-4})] + \ldots$

Eightfold tetragonal coordination

$V = C_2 [4(3 \cos^2 \theta_i - 1)Y_2{}^0] + C_4 [(35 \cos^4 \theta_i - 30 \cos^2 \theta_i + 3)Y_4{}^0$
$+ 1/2(70)^{1/2}(1 - \cos^2 \theta_i)^2(Y_4{}^4 + Y_4{}^{-4})] + \ldots$

Sixfold orthorhombic coordination

$V = C_2 [(2/a_1{}^3 - 1/a_2{}^3 - 1/a_3{}^3)Y_2{}^0 + 1/2(6)^{1/2}(1/a_2{}^3 - 1/a_3{}^3)(Y_2{}^2 + Y_2{}^{-2})] +$
$C_4 [1/4(8/a_1{}^5 + 3/a_2{}^5 + 3/a_3{}^5)Y_4{}^0 - 1/4(10)^{1/2}(1/a_2{}^5 - 1/a_3{}^5)(Y_4{}^2 + Y_4{}^{-2})$
$+ 1/8(70)^{1/2}(1/a_2{}^5 + 1/a_3{}^5)(Y_4{}^4 + Y_4{}^{-4})] + \ldots$

Eightfold orthorhombic coordination

$V = C_2 [4(3 \cos \theta_i - 1)Y_2{}^0 + 2(6)^{1/2} \sin^2 \theta_i \cos 2\varphi_i(Y_2{}^2 + Y_2^{-2})] +$
$C_4 [(35 \cos^4 \theta_i - 30 \cos^2 \theta_i + 3)Y_4{}^0 - (10)^{1/2} \sin^2 \theta_i\ (7 \cos^2 \theta_i - 1)$
$\cos 2\varphi_i(Y_4{}^2 + Y_4{}^{-2}) + 1/2(70)^{1/2} \sin^4 \theta_i \cos 4\varphi_i(Y_4{}^4 + Y_4{}^{-4})] + \ldots$

Assuming point charges, the constants C_i and D_i are given by**

$D_4 = Z_i e^2 r^4 / a_i{}^5 (4\pi/9)^{1/2}$
$D_6 = Z_i e^2 r^6 / a_i{}^7 (4\pi/13)^{1/2}$
$C_2 = Z_i e^2 r^2 / a_i{}^3 (4\pi/5)^{1/2}$
$C_3 = Z_i e^2 r^3 / a_i{}^3 (4\pi/7)^{1/2}$
$C_4 = Z_i e^2 r^4 / a_i{}^5 (4\pi/9)^{1/2}$
$C_6 = Z_i e^2 r^6 / a_i{}^7 (4\pi/13)^{1/2}$

*If the crystal has no center of symmetry, the matrix elements within a configuration involving the odd terms are still zero. However, such a potential may admix different configurations.
**For several cases these constants should be used with the factor $a_i{}^n$ omitted.

TABLE 4-3

Potential Functions in Cartesian Coordinates[B-33]

$$V_{cubic} = C_4(x^4 + y^4 + z^4 - 3/5r^4) + D_6[(x^6 + y^6 + z^6) + 15/4(x^2y^4 + x^4y^2 + x^2z^4 + x^4z^2 + y^2z^4 + y^4z^2) - 15/14r^6]$$

$$V_{axial} = A_2{}^0(x^2 + y^2 - 2z^2) + A_4{}^0(35z^4 - 30r^2z^2 + 3r^4) + A_4{}^4(x^4 - 6x^2y^2 + y^4) + A_6{}^0(231z^6 - 315r^2z^4 + 105r^4z^2 - 5r^6) + A_6{}^6(x^6 - 15x^4y^2 + 15x^2y^4 - y^6)$$

$$V_{rhombic} = Ax^2 + By^2 + Cz^2 + \text{higher terms}$$

$$V_{3v} = V_{axial} + A_4{}^3z(x^3 - 3xy^2) + A_6{}^3(11z^3 - 3zr^2)(x^3 - 3xy^2)$$

TABLE 4-4

Coefficients C_4 and D_6 of Table 4-3 for Three Coordinations[R-48]

	C_4	D_6
Eightfold coordination	$-\frac{70Ze^2}{9d^6}$	$-\frac{224Ze^2}{9d^7}$
Sixfold coordination	$+\frac{35Ze^2}{4d^5}$	$-\frac{21Ze^2}{2d^7}$
Fourfold coordination	$-\frac{35Ze^2}{9d^5}$	$-\frac{112Ze^2}{9d^7}$

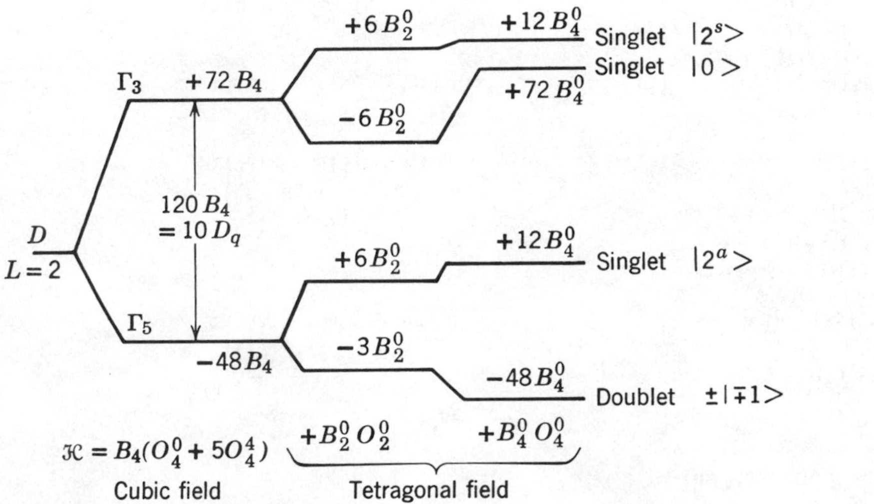

FIGURE 4-1. Splitting of a $3d^9$, D state in cubic (left) and tetragonal (center) crystalline electric fields. The wave functions are shown on the right in terms of $|M_L\rangle$ and the symmetric and antisymmetric combinations of $|\pm 2\rangle$. (Adapted from B-2.)

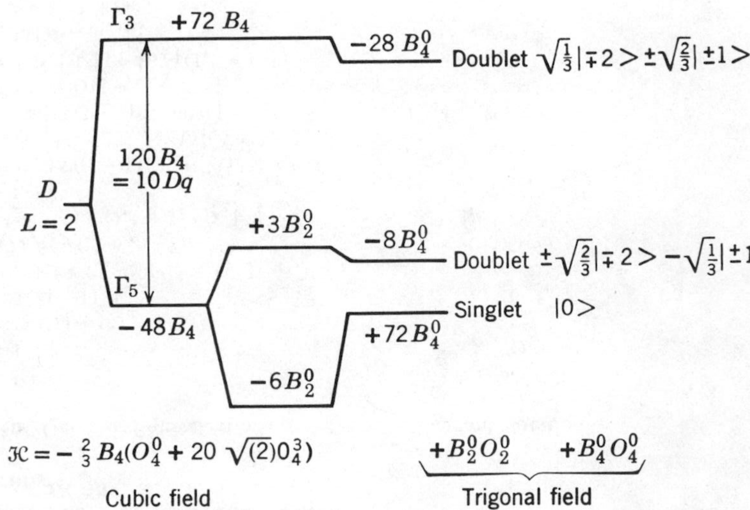

FIGURE 4-2. Splitting of a $3d^9$, D state in cubic (left) and trigonal (center) crystalline electric fields, using the notation of Figure 4-1. (Adapted from B-2.)

TABLE 4-5

List of Operator Equivalents to Some Commonly Occurring Functions Within a Manifold of Given J, the Summation Being Over the Coordinates of the Magnetic Electrons[a] R-48

$\Sigma f_{n\alpha}$	Stevens' Operator Equivalent	Standard Notation
$\Sigma(3z^2 - r^2)$	$\equiv \alpha_J\langle r^2\rangle[3J_z^2 - J(J+1)]$	$= \alpha_J\langle r^2\rangle O_2^0$
$\Sigma(x^2 - y^2)$	$\equiv \alpha_J\langle r^2\rangle \frac{1}{2}[J_+^2 + J_-^2]$	$= \alpha_J\langle r^2\rangle O_2^2$
$\Sigma(35z^4 - 30r^2z^2 + 3r^4)$	$\equiv \beta_J\langle r^4\rangle[35J_z^4 - 30J(J+1)J_z^2 + 25J_z^2 - 6J(J+1) + 3J^2(J+1)^2]$	$= \beta_J\langle r^4\rangle O_4^0$
$\Sigma(7z^2 - r^2)(x^2 - y^2)$	$\equiv \beta_J\langle r^4\rangle \frac{1}{4}[(7J_z^2 - J(J+1) - 5)(J_+^2 + J_-^2) + (J_+^2 + J_-^2)(7J_z^2 - J(J+1) - 5)]$	$= \beta_J\langle r^4\rangle O_4^2$
$\Sigma z(x^3 - 3xy^2)$	$\equiv \beta_J\langle r^4\rangle \frac{1}{4}[J_z(J_+^3 + J_-^3) + (J_+^3 + J_-^3)J_z]$	$= \beta_J\langle r^4\rangle O_4^3$
$\Sigma(x^4 - 6x^2y^2 + y^4)$	$\equiv \beta_J\langle r^4\rangle \frac{1}{2}[J_+^4 + J_-^4]$	$= \beta_J\langle r^4\rangle O_4^4$
$\Sigma(231z^6 - 315z^4r^2 + 105z^2r^4 - 5r^6)$	$\equiv \gamma_J\langle r^6\rangle[231J_z^6 - 315J(J+1)J_z^4 + 735J_z^4 + 105J^2(J+1)^2J_z^2 - 525J(J+1)J_z^2 + 294J_z^2 - 5J^3(J+1)^3 + 40J^2(J+1)^2 - 60J(J+1)]$	$= \gamma_J\langle r^6\rangle O_6^0$
$\Sigma[16z^4 - 16(x^2+y^2)z^2 + (x^2+y^2)^2](x^2 - y^2)$	$\equiv \gamma_J\langle r^6\rangle \frac{1}{4}[[33J_z^4 - (18J(J+1) + 123)J_z^2 + J^2(J+1)^2 + 10J(J+1) + 102](J_+^2 + J_-^2) + (J_+^2 + J_-^2)[33J_z^4 - \text{etc.}]]$	$= \gamma_J\langle r^6\rangle O_6^2$
$\Sigma(11z^3 - 3zr^2)(x^3 - 3xy^2)$	$\equiv \gamma_J\langle r^6\rangle \frac{1}{4}[(11J_z^3 - 3J(J+1)J_z - 59J_z) \times (J_+^3 + J_-^3) + (J_+^3 + J_-^3)(11J_z^3 - 3J(J+1)J_z - 59J_z)]$	$= \gamma_J\langle r^6\rangle O_6^3$
$\Sigma(11z^2 - r^2)(x^4 - 6x^2y^2 + y^4)$	$\equiv \gamma_J\langle r^6\rangle \frac{1}{4}[(11J_z^2 - J(J+1) - 38)(J_+^4 + J_-^4) + (J_+^4 + J_-^4)(11J_z^2 - J(J+1) - 38)]$	$= \gamma_J\langle r^6\rangle O_6^4$
$\Sigma(x^6 - 15x^4y^2 + 15x^2y^4 - y^6)$	$\equiv \gamma_J\langle r^6\rangle \frac{1}{2}[J_+^6 + J_-^6]$	$= \gamma_J\langle r^6\rangle O_6^6$

[a] After Bleaney, B. and Stevens, K. W. H., *Rept. Progr. Phys.*, 16, 108, 1953; Stevens, K. W. H., *Proc. Phys. Soc. (Lond.)*, A65, 209, 1952; Baker, J. M., Bleaney, B., and Hayes, W., *Proc. Roy. Soc.*, A247, 141, 1958; Elliott, R. J. and Stevens, K. W. H., *Proc. Roy. Soc.*, A218, 553, 1953; Judd, B. R., *Proc. Roy. Soc.*, A227, 552, 1955; Jones, D. A., Baker, J. M., and Pope, D. F. D., *Proc. Phys. Soc. (Lond.)*, 74, 249, 1959.

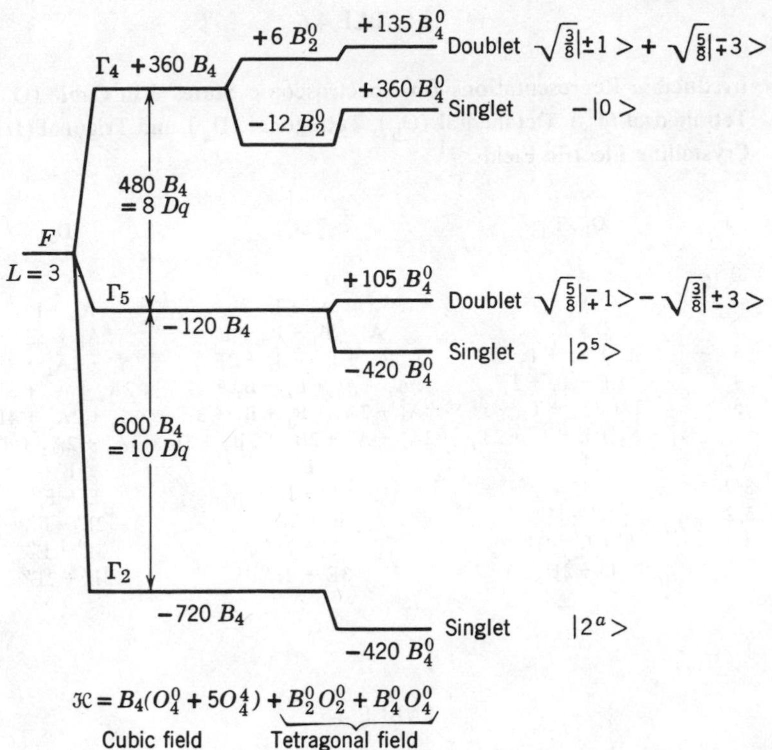

FIGURE 4-3. Splitting of an F state in cubic (left) and tetragonal (center) crystalline electric fields, using the notation of Figure 4-1.[B-2]

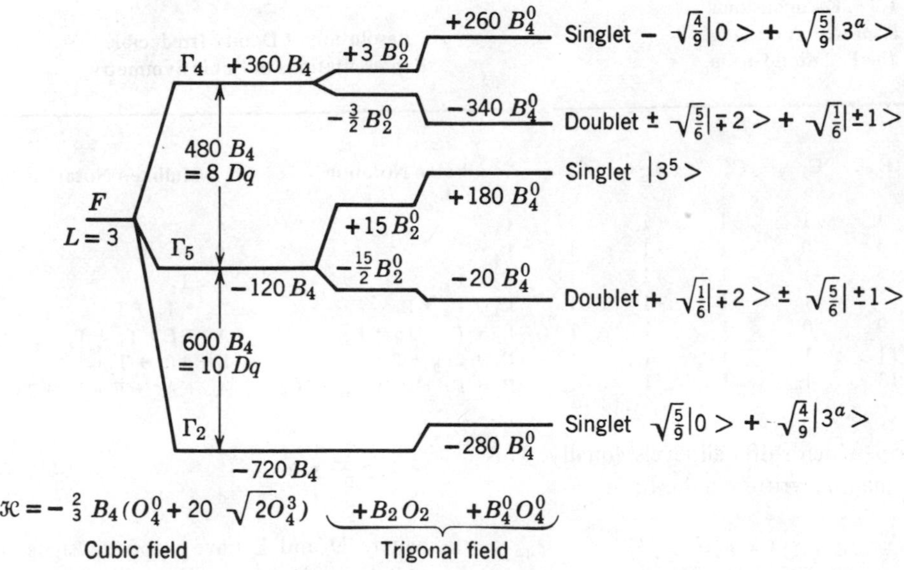

FIGURE 4-4. Splitting of an F state in cubic (left) and trigonal (center) crystalline electric fields, using the notation of Figure 4-1.[B-2]

TABLE 4-6

Irreducible Representations for Spectroscopic States J in Cubic (O_h), Tetrahedral (T_d), Octahedral (O_h), Tetragonal (D_4), and Trigonal (D_3) Crystalline Electric Fields[B-44]

J	O_h, T_d	D_4	D_3
0	A_1	A_1	A_1
1	T_1	$A_2 + E$	$A_2 + E$
2	$E + T_2$	$A_1 + B_1 + B_2 + E$	$A_1 + 2E$
3	$A_2 + T_1 + T_2$	$A_2 + B_1 + B_2 + 2E$	$A_1 + 2A_2 + 2E$
4	$A_1 + E + T_1 + T_2$	$2A_1 + A_2 + B_1 + B_2 + 2E$	$2A_1 + A_2 + 3E$
5	$E + 2T_1 + T_2$	$A_1 + 2A_2 + B_1 + B_2 + 3E$	$A_1 + 2A_2 + 4E$
6	$A_1 + A_2 + E + T_1 + 2T_2$	$2A_1 + A_2 + 2B_1 + 2B_2 + 3E$	$3A_1 + 2A_2 + 4E$
1/2	E'	E'	E'
3/2	U	$E' + E''$	$E' + E''$
5/2	$E'' + U$	$E' + 2E''$	$2E' + E''$
7/2	$E' + E'' + U$	$2E' + 2E''$	$3E' + E''$
9/2	$E' + 2U$	$3E' + 2E''$	$3E' + 2E''$

TABLE 4-7

Characters of the Cubic Group[B-33]

	Character of Classes of Cubic Symmetry in the (2l + 1)-dimensional Representation D′ of the Rotation Group						Resolution of D′ into Irreducible Representations of Cubic Symmetry		
	l	E	C_3	C_2^z	C_2	C_4	Bethe Notation	Mulliken Notation	Number of Terms
S	0	1	1	1	1	1	Γ_1	A_1	1
P	1	3	0	−1	−1	1	Γ_4	T_1	1
D	2	5	−1	1	1	−1	$\Gamma_3 + \Gamma_5$	$E + T_2$	2
F	3	7	1	−1	−1	−1	$\Gamma_2 + \Gamma_4 + \Gamma_5$	$A_2 + T_1 + T_2$	3
G	4	9	0	1	1	1	$\Gamma_1 + \Gamma_3 + \Gamma_4 + \Gamma_5$	$A_1 + E + T_1 + T_2$	4
H	5	11	−1	−1	−1	1	$\Gamma_3 + 2\Gamma_4 + \Gamma_5$	$E + 2T_1 + T_2$	4
I	6	13	1	1	1	−1	$\Gamma_1 + \Gamma_2 + \Gamma_3 + \Gamma_4 + 2\Gamma_5$	$A_1 + A_2 + E + T_1 + 2T_2$	6

constant term which shifts all levels equally. This hamiltonian may be written in the form

$$\mathcal{H}_D = D[S_z^2 = \frac{1}{3} S(S + 1)] + E(S_x^2 - S_y^2) \quad . \qquad (4\text{-}12)$$

If the principal axes are selected so that

$$|D_{zz}| \geq |D_{xx}| \geq |D_{yy}| \qquad (4\text{-}13)$$

then one has

$$-1 \leq \frac{3E}{D} \leq 0 \qquad (4\text{-}14)$$

where D and E have opposite signs and for axial symmetry E = 0.

For triplet states of two electron systems with dipolar coupling where

$$\vec{S}\cdot\vec{\vec{D}}_{dip}\cdot\vec{S} = g^2\beta^2 \left[\frac{\vec{S}_1\cdot\vec{S}_2}{r^3} - \frac{3(\vec{S}_1\cdot\vec{r})(\vec{S}_2\cdot\vec{r})}{r^5}\right] \qquad (4\text{-}15)$$

TABLE 4-8

Degeneracies of States for Various Crystalline Symmetries[B-33]

System	Degeneracy	J = 0	1	2	3	4	5	Degeneracy	J = 1/2	3/2	5/2	7/2	9/2	11/2
Cubic (O, O_h, T_d)	1	1	0	0	1	1	0	2	1	0	1	2	1	2
	2	0	0	1	0	1	1	4	0	1	1	1	2	2
	3	0	1	1	2	2	3							
Tetragonal ($D_{2h}, C_{4h}, D_4, D_{4h}$)	1	1	1	3	3	5	5							
	2	0	1	1	2	2	3							
Hexagonal (D_{3h}, D_6, D_{6h})	1	1	1	1	3	3	3							
	2	0	1	2	2	3	4							
Tetragonal, Hexagonal, Trigonal, Rhombic, Triclinic, Monoclinic and all others								2	1	2	3	4	5	6
Trigonal (C_{3v}, D_{3d}, D_3)	1	1	1	1	3	3	3							
	2	0	1	2	2	3	4							
Rhombic (C_{2v}, D_{3d}, D_3); Triclinic (C_1, C_i); Monoclinic (C_3, C_2, C_{2h}) and all others	1	1	3	5	7	9	11							

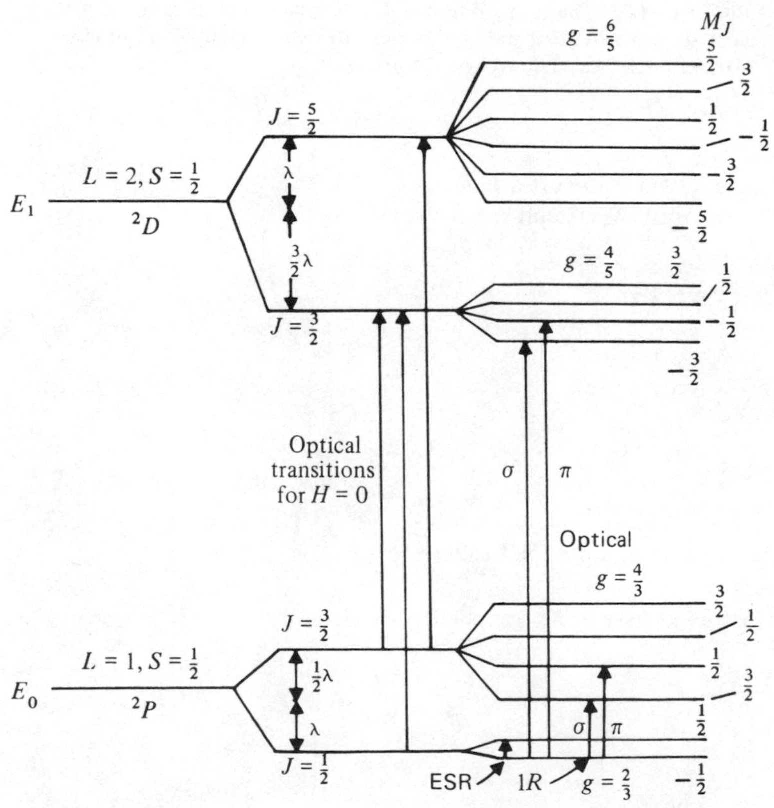

FIGURE 4-5. Energy level diagram for a lower ^2P and an upper ^2D state (left), with spin-orbit coupling added (center) and with a magnetic field added (right). The levels are labeled with their quantum numbers. Several optical, two infrared, and one ESR transition are indicated. The Zeeman spacings are exaggerated.[B-44]

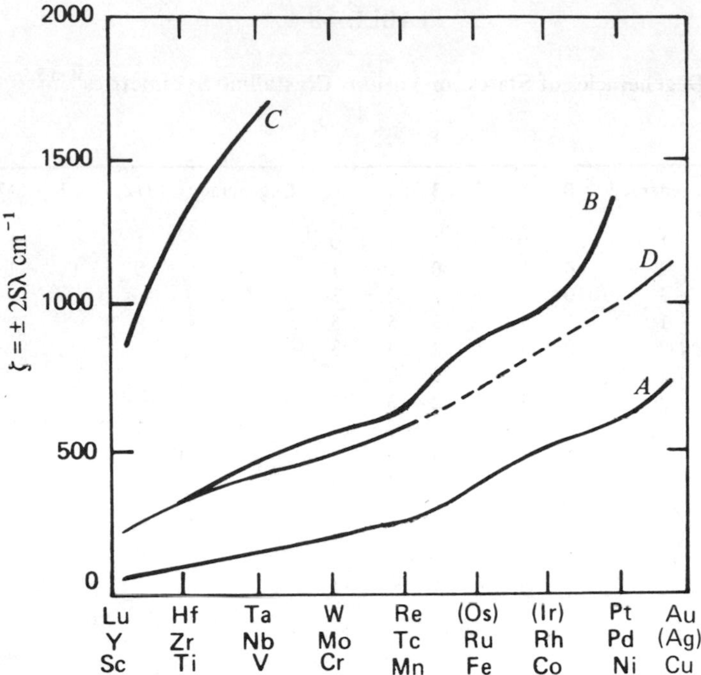

FIGURE 4-6. The spin-orbit coupling constant ζ for d-electrons in neutral atoms: (A) first transition series, (B) second series, (C) third series, (D) third series scaled down by a factor of 4.[B-23]

one has a principal axes system where off-diagonal terms vanish (e.g., $\langle xy/r^5 \rangle = 0$). As a result

$$\frac{1}{2} g^2\beta^2 \left\langle \frac{r^2 - 3x^2}{r^5} \right\rangle = -\frac{1}{3} D + E$$

$$\frac{1}{2} g^2\beta^2 \left\langle \frac{r^2 - 3y^2}{r^5} \right\rangle = -\frac{1}{3} D - E$$

$$\frac{1}{2} g^2\beta^2 \left\langle \frac{r^2 - 3z^2}{r^5} \right\rangle = \frac{2}{3} D \quad . \tag{4-16}$$

These expressions are important for triplet states of organic molecules.

The $\vec{S}\cdot\vec{\vec{D}}\cdot\vec{S}$ matrices have the explicit forms[B-44]

$$\vec{S}\cdot\vec{\vec{D}}\cdot\vec{S} = \begin{pmatrix} 0 & 0 \\ 0 & 0 \end{pmatrix} \qquad (S = \tfrac{1}{2})$$

$$= \begin{pmatrix} \frac{1}{3}D & 0 & E \\ 0 & -\frac{2}{3}D & 0 \\ E & 0 & \frac{1}{3}D \end{pmatrix} \qquad (S = 1)$$

$$= \begin{pmatrix} D & 0 & \sqrt{3}E & 0 \\ 0 & -D & 0 & \sqrt{3}E \\ \sqrt{3}E & 0 & -D & 0 \\ 0 & \sqrt{3}E & 0 & D \end{pmatrix} \qquad (S = \tfrac{3}{2})$$

$$= \begin{pmatrix} 2D & 0 & \sqrt{6}E & 0 & 0 \\ 0 & -D & 0 & 3E & 0 \\ \sqrt{6}E & 0 & -2D & 0 & \sqrt{6}E \\ 0 & 3E & 0 & -D & 0 \\ 0 & 0 & \sqrt{6}E & 0 & 2D \end{pmatrix} \qquad (S = 2)$$

$$= \begin{pmatrix} \frac{10}{3}D & 0 & \sqrt{10}E & 0 & 0 & 0 \\ 0 & -\frac{2}{3}D & 0 & 3\sqrt{2}E & 0 & 0 \\ \sqrt{10}E & 0 & -\frac{8}{3}D & 0 & 3\sqrt{2}E & 0 \\ 0 & 3\sqrt{2}E & 0 & -\frac{8}{3}D & 0 & \sqrt{10}E \\ 0 & 0 & 3\sqrt{2}E & 0 & -\frac{2}{3}D & 0 \\ 0 & 0 & 0 & \sqrt{10}E & 0 & \frac{10}{3}D \end{pmatrix} \qquad (S = \tfrac{5}{2})$$

(4-17)

For a spin S = 1 in the presence of a magnetic field, the zero field energies are identical with the corresponding quadrupolar energies listed below by making the identification

$$I_i \to S_i, Q_{ij} \to D_{ij}, \quad \frac{3}{2}A \to D, \quad \frac{1}{2}\eta A \to -E,$$

$$g_N\beta_N \to -g\beta . \tag{4-18}$$

For spin $S > 3/2$ there are two additional zero field terms, H_a and H_F, to add to the spin hamiltonian.

$$H_a = \frac{1}{6}a\left[S_\xi^4 + S_\eta^4 + S_\zeta^4 - \frac{1}{5}S(S+1)\right.$$
$$\left.\times (3S^2 + 3S - 1)\right]$$

$$H_F = \frac{F}{180}\left[35S_z^4 + 5[5 - 6S(S+1)]S_z^2\right.$$
$$\left.+ 3S(S+1)[S(S+1) - 2]\right] \tag{4-19}$$

where the a-term can occur even in cubic symmetry, and the F-term arises for axial distortion. For tetragonal distortion the xyz axes coincide with $\xi\eta\zeta$; for trigonal distortion they do not.

Some zero field data are given in Table 4-9.

E. Anisotropic Hyperfine Interactions and Forbidden Transitions

The energy levels for a system with S = I = 1/2, isotropic electronic and nuclear g-factors, and an anisotropic hyperfine interaction $\vec{S}\cdot\vec{\vec{T}}\cdot\vec{I}$ are given by

$$\left.\begin{aligned} E_1 &= \frac{1}{2}g\beta H + \frac{1}{4}T\sqrt{1 + A_-} \\ E_2 &= \frac{1}{2}g\beta H - \frac{1}{4}T\sqrt{1 + A_-} \end{aligned}\right] \quad (m_s = 1/2) \tag{4-20}$$

$$\left.\begin{aligned} E_3 &= -\frac{1}{2}g\beta H + \frac{1}{4}T\sqrt{1 + A_+} \\ E_4 &= -\frac{1}{2}g\beta H - \frac{1}{4}T\sqrt{1 + A_+} \end{aligned}\right] \quad (m_s = -1/2) \tag{4-21}$$

where the levels are listed in the order of decreasing energy, using the notation

$$T = \sqrt{T_{xz}^2 + T_{yz}^2 + T_{zz}^2}$$

$$A_\pm = \frac{2N}{T^2}\left(\frac{1}{2}N \pm T_{zz}\right) \tag{4-22}$$

$$N = 2g_N\beta_N H \quad .$$

The following expressions are valid:

$$\begin{aligned} T^2 &= T_i^2 + T_o^2 - N^2 \\ |T_{zz}| &= \frac{T_iT_o}{N} \end{aligned} \tag{4-23}$$

and it is always true that

$$\begin{aligned} T_i &\le N \le T_o \\ T_i &\le T \le T_o \end{aligned} \tag{4-24}$$

where T_o and T_i are defined in Figure 4-7. The outer lines separated by T_o are stronger for $T > N$, and the inner lines separated by T_i are stronger for $T < N$. Their respective intensities I_o and I_i are

$$I_o = \frac{T_o^2 - N^2}{T_o^2 - T_i^2} \qquad I_i = \frac{N^2 - T_i^2}{T_o^2 - T_i^2} \tag{4-25}$$

with the normalization condition

$$I_o + I_i = 1 \quad . \tag{4-26}$$

These expressions are easily generalized to larger numbers of spins.

Hyperfine coupling constants T obtained during the sample rotation about an angle θ in a plane perpendicular to the applied magnetic field direction for the case of an isotropic g-factor satisfy the equations

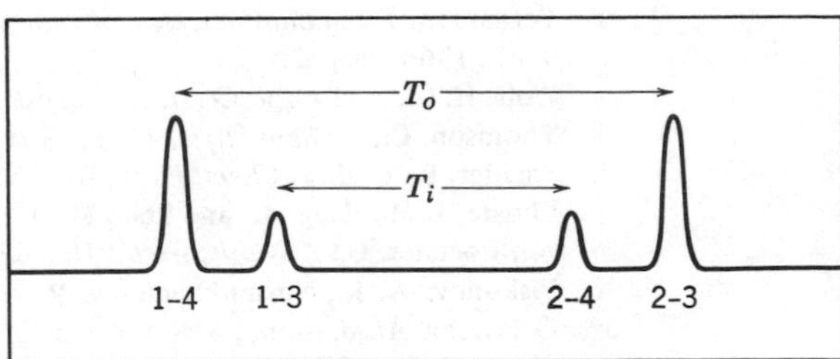

FIGURE 4-7. The spectrum for S = 1/2, I = 1/2, showing the two strong (1-4, 2-3) and two weak (1-3, 2-4) transitions for $|T| > |N|$.[B-44]

TABLE 4-9

Zero Field Parameters in cm^{-1} of Organic Molecules, where $D^* = [D^2 + 3E^2]^{1/2}$R-25

Molecule	Host	D	D*	E	Ref.
Benzene		+0.1581		−0.0065	a,b,c
Naphthalene in	Durene	+0.1003		−0.0137	a,b,c,e
Naphthalene in	Biphenyl	±0.0992		∓0.01545	a,f,g
Naphthalene in	Glass		0.1030		h
Naphthalene in	Lucite		0.1063		i
Naphthalene-d_8 in	Durene	±0.10134		∓0.01393	a
Anthracene in	Anthracene-d_{10}	+0.0688		−0.0081	j
Anthracene in	Biphenyl	+0.07156		−0.0084	e
Phenanthrene in	Biphenyl	±0.1201		∓0.0269	a
Phenanthrene in	Glass	±0.1203		∓0.0269	a,b,f,g
1-Methylphenanthrene in	Lucite		0.1288		k
Chrysene in	Heptane		0.103		a
Pyrene in	Glass		0.0929		k,l
Coronene in	Glass		0.0971		b,l,m,n
Coronene in	Lucite		0.0983		k
Biphenyl in	Lucite		0.1111		k
Fluorene in	Glass		0.1096		k,l,o
Azulene ion			0.0674		p
Quinoline in	Durene	±0.1030		∓0.0162	c
Pyrimidine in	Benzene	±0.1724		∓0.0154	q
Acridine in	Diphenyl	+0.0736		−0.0087	r
Carbazole in	Glass	±0.1022		∓0.0066	l
Aniline in	EPA		0.1317		l
Guanine			0.141		s
Adenine			0.121		s
Orotic acid			0.22		t

REFERENCES:

a. **Hutchison, C. A.**, et al., *J. Chem. Phys.*, 29, 952, 1958; 34, 908, 1961; 37, 447, 1962; 40, 3717, 1964; 41, 3717, 1964; *Proc. 10th Colloq. Spectroc. Int.*, Lippincott, E. R. and Margoshes, M., Eds., Spartan Book Co., Washington, D.C., 1963, 681.
b. **de Groot, M. S.**, et al., *Mol. Phys.*, 2, 333, 1959; 3, 190, 1960; 6, 545, 1963; 13, 583, 1967; 16, 45, 1969; *Physica*, 29, 1128, 1963.
c. **Vincent, J. S.**, et al., *J. Chem. Phys.*, 54, 2237, 1971; *Chem. Phys. Lett.*, 8, 37, 1971; *J. Chem. Phys.*, 42, 865, 1965.
d. **Hornig, A. W. and Hyde, J. S.**, *Mol. Phys.*, 6, 33, 1963.
e. **Grivet, J. P.**, et al., *Chem. Phys. Lett.*, 4, 104, 1969; *Mol. Phys.*, 21, 999, 1971.
f. **Brinen, J. S. and Orloff, M. K.**, *J. Chem. Phys.*, 45, 4747, 1966.
g. **Kwiram, A. L.**, et al., *Chem. Phys. Lett.*, 20, 491, 1968; *J. Chem. Phys.*, 49, 4714, 1968.
h. **Varsanyi, F., Wood, D. L., and Schawlow, A. L.**, *Phys. Rev. Lett.*, 3, 544, 1959.
i. **Teegarden, K.**, in *Luminescence of Inorganic Solids*, Goldberg, P., Ed., Academic Press, New York, 1966, chap. 2.
j. **Wolf, H. C.**, et al., *Mol. Cryst. Liq. Cryst.*, 10, 359, 1970; *Phys. Stat. Sol.*, 23, 633, 1967.
k. **Thomson, C.**, *J. Chem Phys.*, 41, 1, 1964.
l. **Smaller, B.**, et al., *J. Chem. Phys.*, 37, 1578, 1962; 42, 2608, 1965.
m. **Lhoste, J. M., Haug, A., and Ptak, M.**, *J. Chem. Phys.*, 44, 654, 1966.
n. **von Foerster, G.**, *Z. Naturforsch.*, 18a, 620, 1963.
o. **Piskunov, A. K., Nurmukhametov, R. N., Shigorin, D. N., Muromtsev, V. I., and Ozerova, G. A.**, *Izv. Akad. Nauk., SSR Ser. Fiz.*, 27(5), 636, 1963.
p. **Blears, D. J. and Danyluk, S. S.**, *J. Am. Chem. Soc.*, 88, 3162, 1966.
q. **Burland, D. M. and Schmidt, J.**, *Mol. Phys.*, 22, 19, 1971.
r. **Grivet, J. P.**, *Chem. Phys. Lett.*, 11, 267, 1971.
s. **Shulman, R. G. and Rahn, R. O.**, *J. Chem. Phys.*, 45, 2940, 1966.
t. **Haug, A. and Douzou, P.**, *Z. Naturforsch.*, 206, 509, 1965.

$$T^2 = P\cos^2\theta + Q\sin^2\theta - 2R\sin\theta\cos\theta$$

$$= \frac{1}{2}(P + Q) + \frac{1}{2}(P - Q)\cos 2\theta - R\sin 2\theta \qquad (4\text{-}27)$$

where clockwise rotations are assumed. For counterclockwise rotations the sign of R is changed.

Using the initial positions defined in Figure 4-8 and clockwise rotations one finds that $P_1 = Q_2$, $P_2 = Q_3$, $P_3 = Q_1$, and the T^2 matrix is

$$T^2 = \begin{bmatrix} [P_2 = Q_3] & R_3 & R_2 \\ R_3 & [P_3 = Q_1] & R_1 \\ R_2 & R_1 & [P_1 = Q_2] \end{bmatrix} . \qquad (4\text{-}28)$$

This matrix may be diagonalized to give the squares of the principal values of the hyperfine coupling constant T^2 and the direction cosines relative to the initial crystal directions. Usually the satellite lines are too weak to observe, and one approximates $T_o \sim T$ in using Equation 4-27.

Angular rotation data for the g-factor also satisfy the PQR equations. When both g and T are significantly anisotropic, the situation is more complex, and other texts should be consulted.[B-44, R-30]

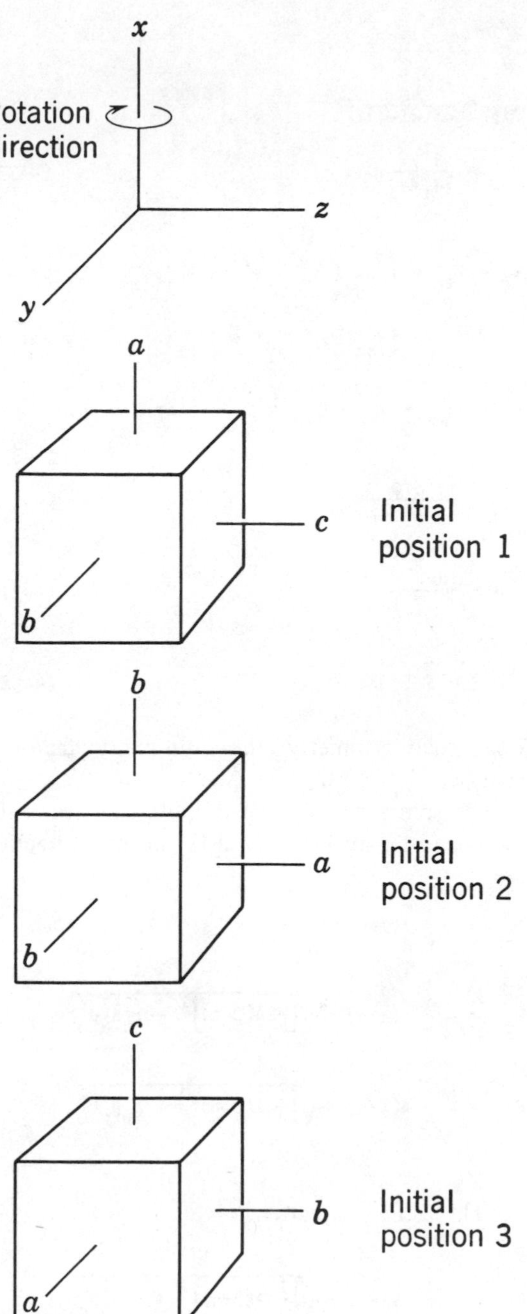

FIGURE 4-8. Initial crystal orientations for the three planes of rotation in the laboratory coordinate system.[B-44]

F. Quadrupole Interaction

The quadrupole hamiltonian

$$\mathcal{H}_Q = \vec{I} \cdot \overleftrightarrow{Q} \cdot \vec{I} = \sum_{ij} I_i I_j Q_{ij} \qquad (4\text{-}29)$$

which may exist for nuclear spins $I > 1/2$ has a symmetric and traceless quadrupole energy tensor:

$$Q = \begin{bmatrix} Q_{xx} & Q_{xy} & Q_{xz} \\ Q_{yx} & Q_{yy} & Q_{yz} \\ Q_{zx} & Q_{zy} & Q_{zz} \end{bmatrix} \qquad (4\text{-}30)$$

$$Q_{ij} = Q_{ji}$$

$$Q_{xx} + Q_{yy} + Q_{zz} = 0 \quad . \qquad (4\text{-}31)$$

In the principal axis system, the off-diagonal elements vanish, and the hamiltonian assumes the form

$$\mathcal{H}_Q = \frac{1}{2} A \left[3I_z^2 - I(I+1) + \eta(I_x^2 - I_y^2)\right] \qquad (4\text{-}32)$$

where

$$Q_{ij} = \frac{eQ}{2I(2I-1)} V_{ij}$$

$$V_{ij} = \frac{\partial^2 V}{\partial x_i \partial x_j} \quad (4\text{-}33)$$

$$eq = V_{zz} = \int \rho_{(r)}(3z^2 - r^2)d\tau = \int \rho_{(r)} r^2 (3\cos^2\theta - 1)d\tau$$

$$|V_{zz}| > |V_{yy}| > |V_{xx}| \quad (4\text{-}34)$$

$$\nabla^2 V = V_{xx} + V_{yy} + V_{zz} = 0 \quad \text{(Laplace eq.)} \quad (4\text{-}35)$$

$$A = \frac{e^2 q Q}{2I(2I-1)} \quad (4\text{-}36)$$

$$\eta = \frac{V_{xx} - V_{yy}}{V_{zz}} \quad (4\text{-}37)$$

$$0 \leq \eta \leq 1 \quad . \quad (4\text{-}38)$$

For axial symmetry the asymmetry factor η vanishes.

For spin I = 1 the quadrupole energies in the presence of a magnetic field H_o in the x direction are

$$E_1 = \frac{1}{2} A(1+\eta)$$

$$E_o = -\frac{1}{4} A(1+\eta) - \sqrt{\left[\frac{1}{4} A(3-\eta)\right]^2 + g_N^2 \beta_N^2 H_o^2}$$

$$E_{-1} = -\frac{1}{4} A(1+\eta) + \sqrt{\left[\frac{1}{4} A(3-\eta)\right]^2 + g_N^2 \beta_N^2 H_o^2} \quad (4\text{-}39)$$

For H_o in the y direction

$$E_1 = -\frac{1}{4} (1-\eta) + \sqrt{\left[\frac{1}{4} A(3+\eta)\right]^2 + g_N^2 \beta_N^2 H_o^2}$$

$$E_o = -\frac{1}{4} A(1-\eta) - \sqrt{\left[\frac{1}{4} A(3+\eta)\right]^2 + g_N^2 \beta_N^2 H_o^2}$$

$$E_{-1} = \frac{1}{2} A(1-\eta) \quad (4\text{-}40)$$

For H_o in the z direction

$$E_1 = \frac{1}{2} A + \sqrt{\frac{1}{4} A^2 \eta^2 + g_N^2 \beta_N^2 H_o^2}$$

$$E_o = -A$$

$$E_{-1} = \frac{1}{2} A - \sqrt{\frac{1}{4} A^2 \eta^2 + g_N^2 \beta_N^2 H_o^2} \quad . \quad (4\text{-}41)$$

In zero field ($H_o = 0$), then I = 1 levels become

$$E_{\pm 1} = \frac{1}{2} A(1 \pm \eta)$$

$$E_o = -A \quad . \quad (4\text{-}42)$$

For I = 3/2 the zero field levels are

$$E_{\pm 1/2} = -\frac{3A}{2}\sqrt{1 + \frac{1}{3}\eta^2}$$

$$E_{\pm 3/2} = +\frac{3A}{2}\sqrt{1 + \frac{1}{3}\eta^2} \quad . \quad (4\text{-}43)$$

For I > 3/2 the level formulae become complicated. With axial symmetry ($\eta = 0$) one always has

$$E_m = \frac{1}{2} A \left[3m^2 - I(I+1)\right] \quad . \quad (4\text{-}44)$$

In irreducible tensor form, the quadrupole moment operator is given by

$$Q_2^0 = \frac{eQ}{2I(2I-1)} (3I_z^2 - I^2)$$

$$Q_2^{\pm 1} = \frac{eQ\sqrt{6}}{4I(2I-1)} \left[I_z(I_x \pm iI_y) + (I_x \pm iI_y)I_z\right]$$

$$Q_2^{\pm 2} = \frac{eQ\sqrt{6}}{4I(2I-1)} (I_x \pm iI_y)^2 \quad . \quad (4\text{-}45)$$

G. Matrix Representation

Using the properties of angular momentum,

$$J_z |m\rangle = m |m\rangle$$

$$J^{\pm} |m\rangle = \sqrt{(J \mp m)(J \pm m + 1)} \, |m \pm 1\rangle$$

$$J^2 |m\rangle = J(J+1) |m\rangle \quad (4\text{-}46)$$

one can construct a mnemomic triangle with the property that one half of the coefficients in each row provide the coefficients in the matrices for J_x and J_y.[B-33]

$$\begin{array}{ll}
J = \frac{1}{2} & \sqrt{1} \\
J = 1 & \sqrt{2}\ \sqrt{2} \\
J = \frac{3}{2} & \sqrt{3}\ \sqrt{2\cdot 2}\ \sqrt{3} \\
J = 2 & \sqrt{4}\ \sqrt{3\cdot 2}\ \sqrt{2\cdot 3}\ \sqrt{4} \\
J = \frac{5}{2} & \sqrt{5}\ \sqrt{4\cdot 2}\ \sqrt{3\cdot 3}\ \sqrt{2\cdot 4}\ \sqrt{5} \\
J = 3 & \sqrt{6}\ \sqrt{5\cdot 2}\ \sqrt{4\cdot 3}\ \sqrt{3\cdot 4}\ \sqrt{2\cdot 5}\ \sqrt{6} \\
J = \frac{7}{2} & \sqrt{7}\ \sqrt{6\cdot 2}\ \sqrt{5\cdot 3}\ \sqrt{4\cdot 4}\ \sqrt{3\cdot 5}\ \sqrt{2\cdot 6}\ \sqrt{7}
\end{array} \qquad (4\text{-}47)$$

The row for a general spin J is

$$\sqrt{(2J)\cdot(1)}\ \sqrt{(2J-1)\cdot(2)}\ \sqrt{(2J-2)\cdot(3)}$$

$$\sqrt{(2J-3)\cdot(4)}\ \ldots\ \sqrt{(1)\cdot(2J)}$$

The various matrices for J = 1/2, 1, and 3/2 have the following explicit forms, where J may be any orbital, spin, or total angular momentum:[B-44]

$$\text{unit matrix} \rightarrow \begin{pmatrix} 1 & 0 \\ 0 & 1 \end{pmatrix} \rightarrow \begin{pmatrix} 1 & 0 & 0 \\ 0 & 1 & 0 \\ 0 & 0 & 1 \end{pmatrix} \rightarrow \begin{pmatrix} 1 & 0 & 0 & 0 \\ 0 & 1 & 0 & 0 \\ 0 & 0 & 1 & 0 \\ 0 & 0 & 0 & 1 \end{pmatrix}$$

$$\vec{J}_x \rightarrow \frac{1}{2}\begin{pmatrix} 0 & 1 \\ 1 & 0 \end{pmatrix} \rightarrow \frac{1}{2}\begin{pmatrix} 0 & \sqrt{2} & 0 \\ \sqrt{2} & 0 & \sqrt{2} \\ 0 & \sqrt{2} & 0 \end{pmatrix} \rightarrow \frac{1}{2}\begin{pmatrix} 0 & \sqrt{3} & 0 & 0 \\ \sqrt{3} & 0 & 2 & 0 \\ 0 & 2 & 0 & \sqrt{3} \\ 0 & 0 & \sqrt{3} & 0 \end{pmatrix}$$

$$\vec{J}_y \rightarrow \frac{1}{2}\begin{pmatrix} 0 & -i \\ i & 0 \end{pmatrix} \rightarrow \frac{1}{2}\begin{pmatrix} 0 & -i\sqrt{2} & 0 \\ i\sqrt{2} & 0 & -i\sqrt{2} \\ 0 & i\sqrt{2} & 0 \end{pmatrix} \rightarrow \frac{1}{2}\begin{pmatrix} 0 & -\sqrt{3}i & 0 & 0 \\ \sqrt{3}i & 0 & -2i & 0 \\ 0 & 2i & 0 & -\sqrt{3}i \\ 0 & 0 & \sqrt{3}i & 0 \end{pmatrix}$$

$$\vec{J}_z \rightarrow \frac{1}{2}\begin{pmatrix} 1 & 0 \\ 0 & -1 \end{pmatrix} \rightarrow \begin{pmatrix} 1 & 0 & 0 \\ 0 & 0 & 0 \\ 0 & 0 & -1 \end{pmatrix} \rightarrow \frac{1}{2}\begin{pmatrix} 3 & 0 & 0 & 0 \\ 0 & 1 & 0 & 0 \\ 0 & 0 & -1 & 0 \\ 0 & 0 & 0 & -3 \end{pmatrix}$$

$$\vec{J}^2 \rightarrow \frac{3}{4}\begin{pmatrix} 1 & 0 \\ 0 & 1 \end{pmatrix} \rightarrow 2\begin{pmatrix} 1 & 0 & 0 \\ 0 & 1 & 0 \\ 0 & 0 & 1 \end{pmatrix} \rightarrow \frac{15}{4}\begin{pmatrix} 1 & 0 & 0 & 0 \\ 0 & 1 & 0 & 0 \\ 0 & 0 & 1 & 0 \\ 0 & 0 & 0 & 1 \end{pmatrix}$$

$$\vec{J}^+ \rightarrow \begin{pmatrix} 0 & 1 \\ 0 & 0 \end{pmatrix} \rightarrow \begin{pmatrix} 0 & \sqrt{2} & 0 \\ 0 & 0 & \sqrt{2} \\ 0 & 0 & 0 \end{pmatrix} \rightarrow \begin{pmatrix} 0 & \sqrt{3} & 0 & 0 \\ 0 & 0 & 2 & 0 \\ 0 & 0 & 0 & \sqrt{3} \\ 0 & 0 & 0 & 0 \end{pmatrix}$$

$$\vec{J}^- \rightarrow \begin{pmatrix} 0 & 0 \\ 1 & 0 \end{pmatrix} \rightarrow \begin{pmatrix} 0 & 0 & 0 \\ \sqrt{2} & 0 & 0 \\ 0 & \sqrt{2} & 0 \end{pmatrix} \rightarrow \begin{pmatrix} 0 & 0 & 0 & 0 \\ \sqrt{3} & 0 & 0 & 0 \\ 0 & 2 & 0 & 0 \\ 0 & 0 & \sqrt{3} & 0 \end{pmatrix}$$

(4-48)

One may define the addition:

$$\begin{pmatrix} A & B \\ C & D \end{pmatrix} + \begin{pmatrix} a & b \\ c & d \end{pmatrix} = \begin{pmatrix} A + a & B + b \\ C + c & D + d \end{pmatrix} \tag{4-49}$$

multiplication:

$$\begin{pmatrix} A & B \\ C & D \end{pmatrix} \begin{pmatrix} a & b \\ c & d \end{pmatrix} = \begin{pmatrix} Aa + Bc & Ab + Bd \\ Ca + Dc & Cb + Dd \end{pmatrix} \tag{4-50}$$

and direct product expansion:

$$\begin{pmatrix} A & B \\ C & D \end{pmatrix} \times \begin{pmatrix} a & b \\ c & d \end{pmatrix} = \begin{pmatrix} Aa & Ab & Ba & Bb \\ Ac & Ad & Bc & Bd \\ Ca & Cb & Da & Db \\ Cc & Cd & Dc & Dd \end{pmatrix} \tag{4-51}$$

of square matrices. The first two operations are defined for matrices of the same order, n x n, and produce a matrix of that same order. The direct product expansion, on the other hand, forms an (mn) x (mn) matrix from an m x m and an n x n matrix. Column vectors may be added:

$$\begin{pmatrix} A \\ B \end{pmatrix} + \begin{pmatrix} a \\ b \end{pmatrix} = \begin{pmatrix} A + a \\ B + b \end{pmatrix} \tag{4-52}$$

and expanded as direct products:

$$\begin{pmatrix} A \\ B \end{pmatrix} \times \begin{pmatrix} a \\ b \end{pmatrix} = \begin{pmatrix} Aa \\ Ab \\ Ba \\ Bb \end{pmatrix} \tag{4-53}$$

A square matrix times a column vector gives another column vector, and similarly for the reciprocal operator:

$$\begin{pmatrix} A & B \\ C & D \end{pmatrix} \begin{pmatrix} a \\ b \end{pmatrix} = \begin{pmatrix} Aa + Bb \\ Ca + Db \end{pmatrix}$$

$$(a^* \quad b^*) \begin{pmatrix} A & B \\ C & D \end{pmatrix} = (Aa^* + Cb^* \quad Ba^* + Db^*) \tag{4-54}$$

and the simple scalar product is

$$(a^* \quad b^*) \begin{pmatrix} A \\ B \end{pmatrix} = Aa^* + Bb^* \tag{4-55}$$

These operations are easily generalized to higher dimensions.

V. TRANSITION IONS

A. Introduction

Table 5-1 gives the electronic configurations of the neutral ions in various transition groups. The s- and p-electrons outside the d- and f-shells are valence electrons which are not present in the ions that are studied in solids. Table 5-2 lists the characteristics of various host crystals for such ions. Table 5-3 presents some properties of actinide ions.

TABLE 5-1

Electronic Configuration of the Transition Groups[B-33]

Iron group			Palladium group		
Atomic No.	Element	Ground state	Atomic No.	Element	Ground state
21	Sc	(Ar)$3d4s^2$	39	Y	(Kr) $4d5s^2$
22	Ti	$3d^2 4s^2$	40	Zr	$4d^2 5s^2$
23	V	$3d^3 4s^2$	41	Nb	$4d^4 5s$
24	Cr	$3d^5 4s$	42	Mo	$4d^5 5s$
25	Mn	$3d^5 4s^2$	43	Tc	$4d^5 5s^2$
26	Fe	$3d^6 4s^2$	44	Ru	$4d^7 5s$
27	Co	$3d^7 4s^2$	45	Rh	$4d^8 5s$
28	Ni	$3d^8 4s^2$	46	Pd	$4d^{10}$
29	Cu	$3d^{10} 4s$	47	Ag	$4d^{10} 5s$
30	Zn	$3d^{10} 4s^2$	48	Cd	$4d^{10} 5s^2$
Rare earth group			**Platinum group**		
57	La	(Xe) $5d6s^2$	71	Lu	(La) $5d6s^2$
58	Ce	$4f^2 6s^2$	72	Hf	$5d^2 6s^2$
59	Pr	$4f^3 6s^2$	73	Ta	$5d^3 6s^2$
60	Nd	$4f^4 6s^2$	74	W	$5d^4 6s^2$
61	Pm	$4f^5 6s^2$	75	Re	$5d^5 6s^2$
62	Sm	$4f^6 6s^2$	76	Os	$5d^6 6s^2$
63	Eu	$4f^7 6s^2$	77	Ir	$5d^7 6s^2$
64	Gd	$4f^7 5d6s^2$	78	Pt	$5d^9 6s$
65	Tb	$4f^8 5d6s^2$	79	Au	$5d^{10} 6s$
66	Dy	$4f^{10} 6s^2$	80	Hg	$5d^{10} 6s^2$
67	Ho	$4f^{11} 6s^2$			
68	Er	$4f^{12} 6s^2$			
69	Tm	$4f^{13} 6s^2$			
70	Yb	$4f^{14} 6s^2$			

Actinide group		
89	Ac	(Rn) $6d7s^2$
90	Th	$6d^2 7s^2$
91	Pa	$5f^2 6d7s^2$
92	U	$5f^3 6d7s^2$
93	Np	$5f^4 6d7s^2$
94	Pu	$5f^6 7s^2$
95	Am	$5f^7 7s^2$
96	Cm	$5f^7 6d7s^2$
97	Bk	$5f^8 6d7s^2$
98	Cf	$5f^{10} 7s^2$
99	Es	$5f^{11} 7s^2$
100	Fm	$5f^{12} 7s^2$

TABLE 5-2

Host Crystals for Transition Ions[B-3,B-33,R-16]

Crystal	Formula	Examples of Ions	Symmetry	Transition Ion Group
Tutton salts	$M_2^{1+}M^{2+}(S^*O_4)_2 \cdot 6H_2O$	M^{1+} = K, Rb, NH_4; M^{2+} = Mg, Zn; S* = S, Se	Octahedral	Iron group
Alums	$M^{1+}M^{3+}(S^*O_4)_2 \cdot 12H_2O$	M^{3+} = Al or any trivalent ion of 3d group	Octahedral	Iron group
Double nitrates	$M_3^{2+}M_2^{3+}(NO_3)_{12} \cdot 24H_2O$	M^{2+} = Mg or any divalent 3d group ion; M^{3+} = Bi or 4f group ion	Octahedral	Iron group Rare earth group
Fluosilicates	$M^{2+}SiF_6 \cdot 6H_2O$	M^{2+} = Zn or any divalent ion of the 3d group	Trigonal	Iron group
Bromates	$M^{2+}(BrO_3)_2 \cdot 6H_2O$	M^{2+} = Zn or any divalent ion of the 3d group	Cubic	Iron group
Sulfates	$M^{2+}SO_4 \cdot 7H_2O$	M^{2+} = Zn or any divalent ion of the 3d group	Orthorhombic	Iron group
Complex cyanides	$K_3M^{3+}(CN)_6$	M^{3+} = Cr, Mn, Fe, or Co	Orthorhombic	Iron group
Complex cyanides	$K_4M^{2+}(CN)_6 \cdot 3H_2O$	M^{2+} = V, Mn, or Fe	Tetragonal	Iron group
Complex halides	$M_2^{1+}M^{4+}X_6$	M^{4+} = Ir, Pt; X = Cl, Br	Cubic	Platinum group
	$Na_2M^{4+}X_6 \cdot 6H_2O$	M^{4+} = Ir, Pt; X = Cl, Br	Triclinic	Platinum group
Ethyl sulfates	$M^{3+}(C_2H_5SO_4)_3 \cdot 9H_2O$	M^{3+} = trivalent rare earth ion	Hexagonal	Rare earth group
Uranyl-type rubidium nitrate	$M^{4+}O_2Rb(NO_3)_3$	M^{4+} = U, Np, Pu, etc.	Hexagonal	Actinide group

TABLE 5-3

Magnetic Properties of the Ground States of Actinide Ions[B-61]

Number of magnetic electrons	0	1	2	3	4	5	6	7
Representative ions	UO_2^{++}	NpO_2^{++}	PuO_2^{++}	AmO_2^{++}				
			Pa^{3+}	U^{3+}	Np^{3+}	Pu^{3+}	Am^{3+}	Cm^{3+}
	Th^{4+}	Pa^{4+}	U^{4+}	Np^{4+}	Pu^{4+}	Am^{4+}		
		U^{5+}	Np^{5+}	Pu^{5+}				
		Np^{6+}	Pu^{6+}	Am^{6+}				
Ground state		${}^2F_{5/2}$	${}^3H_4$	${}^4I_{9/2}$	${}^5I_4$	${}^6H_{5/2}$	${}^7F_0$	${}^8S_{7/2}$

B. First Transition Series Ions

This section consists mainly of tables. Tables 5-4 and 5-5 summarize the properties of the most important first transition series valence states. Tables 5-6 to 5-19 list the characteristic ESR data on many transition metal ions in various host lattices.

In the following Tables 5-6 to 5-19, we list the values of the g-factor, of the hyperfine structure constants A and B, and the crystal field parameters b_n^m for transition group ions in the systems

1. Magnesium oxide MgO
2. Calcium oxide CaO
3. Strontium oxide SrO
4. Zinc oxide ZnO
5. Aluminum oxide Al_2O_3
6. Titanium oxide TiO_2
7. Perovskite ABO_3
8. Spinel AB_2O_4
9. Garnet $A_3B_5O_{12}$

The tables list in each crystal host the individual ion, the frequency band, and the temperature at which the parameters were measured. The frequency bands are called X-band for frequencies near 9 GHz, K_μ near 16 GHz, K near 24 GHz, and Q-band near 35 GHz. The temperatures are listed in degrees Kelvin. Room temperature has been uniformly designated as 290° K.

The errors of measurement are indicated in parentheses; i.e., 2.01 ± 0.02 is abbreviated as 2.01(2) and g = 2.0017 ± 0.0012 as 2.0017(12). The g-factor without subscript means that the g-factor is isotropic within the limits of error.

The values of A, B, and b_n^m are given in units of 10^{-4} cm^{-1}, except where explicitly indicated otherwise. We have used the crystal field parameters b_n^m and also the conventional D, E, a, and F. The conversion from the b_n^m to the usual nomenclature is given in Equations 4-7 and 4-8. A difficulty arises when b_4^0 is used for two different types of measurements – for example, for crystals which have cubic and trigonal symmetry. The conventional way is to designate the fourth-order cubic component as a and the fourth-order trigonal component as F. We have listed these as $(b_4^0)_c$ and b_4^0, where $(b_4^0)_c = a/2$ and $b_4^0 = F/3$, so that $(a - F) = 2(b_4^0)_c - 3b_4^0$.

We have not included measurements on powdered samples, except when these contain significant information not available from measurements on single crystals. The references are listed separately for each individual table.

C. Rare-earth Ions

Table 5-20 presents the spectroscopic and nuclear properties of rare-earth ions, and Tables 5-21 and 5-22 list representative ESR results in chlorides and ethyl sulfates, respectively.

TABLE 5-4

Ground States, Quantum Numbers, and Degeneracies† in Various Fields of Ions of the Iron Group[B-61]

Configuration	d^1	d^2	d^3	d^4	d^5	d^6	d^7	d^8	d^9
	^2D	^3F	^4F	^5D	^6S	^5D	^4F	^3F	^2D
Examples	Sc^{++}	Ti^{++}	Ti^{+}		Cr^{+}		Fe^{+}	Co^{+}	Ni^{+}
	Ti^{3+}	V^{3+}	V^{++}	Cr^{++}	Mn^{++}	Fe^{++}	Co^{++}	Ni^{++}	Cu^{++}
	VO^{++}	Cr^{4+}	Cr^{3+}	Mn^{3+}	Fe^{3+}				
	Cr^{5+}		Mn^{4+}				Ni^{3+}		
S	1/2	1	3/2	2	5/2	2	3/2	1	1/2
L	2	3	3	2	0	2	3	3	2
J (free ion)	3/2	2	3/2	0	5/2	4	9/2	4	5/2
$\lambda(cm^{-1})$	154 (Ti^{3+})	104 (V^{3+})	56 (V^{++})	58 (Cr^{++})		−103	−178	−325	−829
(Free ion)‡	248 (V^{4+})		91 (Cr^{3+})	88 (Mn^{3+})		(Fe^{++})	(Co^{++})	(Ni^{++})	(Cu^{++})
Orbital degeneracy in fields of various symmetries†									
Free ion	(5)	(7)	(7)	(5)	(1)	(5)	(7)	(7)	(5)
Octahedral	(2), (3)	(1), 2 (3)	(1), 2 (3)	(2), (3)	(1)	(2), (3)	(1), 2 (3)	(1), 2 (3)	(2), (3)
Trigonal	(1), 2 (2)	3 (1), 2 (2)	3 (1), 2 (2)	(1), 2 (2)	(1)	1, 2 (2)	3 (1), 2 (2)	3 (1), 2 (2)	(1), 2 (2)
Tetragonal	3 (1), (2)	3 (1), 2 (2)	3 (1), 2 (2)	3 (1), (2)	(1)	3 (1), 2	3 (1), 2 (2)	3 (1), 2 (2)	3 (1), 2
Rhombic	5 (1)	7 (1)	7 (1)	5 (1)	(1)	5 (1)	7 (1)	7 (1)	5 (1)
Spin degeneracy in fields of various symmetries for a single orbital level									
Free ion	(2)	(3)	(4)	(5)	(6)	(5)	(4)	(3)	(2)
Octahedral	(2)	(3)	(4)	(2), (3)	(2), (4)	(2), (3)	(4)	(3)	(2)
Trigonal	(2)	(1), (2)	2 (2)	(1), 2 (2)	3 (2)	(1), 2 (2)	(2),(2)	(1), (2)	(2)
Tetragonal	(2)	(1), (2)	2 (2)	3 (1), (2)	3 (2)	3 (1), (2)	2 (2)	(1), (2)	(2)
Rhombic	(2)	(3) (1)	2 (2)	5 (1)	3 (2)	5 (1)	2 (2)	(3) (1)	(2)

After Gordy, W., Smith, W. V., and Trambarulo, R. F., *Microwave Spectroscopy*, John Wiley & Sons, Inc., New York, 1963, 225.

† *a(b)* means that there are *a* sets of states of *b*-fold degeneracy; when *a* is one, it is omitted.

‡ Some authors have used Griffith's spin-orbit coupling parameter ζ in place of λ. For one *d*-electron, $\lambda = \zeta$. However, if more than one *d*-electron is present, $\lambda = \pm\zeta/2S$. The positive sign applies to ions with less than a half-filled shell and the negative sign to ions with more than a half-filled shell (See Griffith, J. S., *The Theory of Transition Metal Ions*, Cambridge University Press, 1961, 111.)

TABLE 5-5

Comparison of Spin-orbit Coupling of Gaseous Ions (λ_0) and That in Crystals (λ)[B-33]

	Complex	λ_0 cm^{-1}	λ cm^{-1}	Ref.
$d^2 V^{3+}$	Alum	104.0	64.0	
$d^3 Cr^{3+}$	MgO	91.0	63.0	a
	Alum		57.0	b
$d^3 V^{2+}$	MgO	55.0	34.0	c
	Tutton salts		44.0	d
$d^7 Co^{2+}$	MgO	−178.0	−151.0	e
$d^8 Ni^{2+}$	MgO	−324.0	−250.0	f
	Tutton salts		−270.0	g
	Magnetic measurement		−250.0	g
$d^9 Cu^{2+}$	Tutton salts	−829.0	−695.0	h

REFERENCES

a. Low, W., *Phys. Rev.,* 105, 801, 1957.
b. Bleaney, B., Bogle, G. S., Cooke, A. H., Duffus, R. J., O'Brien, M. C. M., and Stevens, K. W. H., *Proc. Phys. Soc.,* A68, 57, 1955.
c. Low, W., *Phys. Rev.,* 101, 1827, 1956.
d. Bleaney, B., Ingram, D. J. E., and Scovil, H. E. D., *Proc. Phys. Soc.,* A64, 601, 1951.
e. Low, W., *Phys. Rev.,* 108, 256, 1958.
f. Low, W., *Bull. Am. Phys. Soc.,* 1(2), 398, 1956; *Phys. Rev.,* 109, 247, 1958.
g. Griffiths, J. H. E. and Owen, J., *Proc. Roy. Soc.,* A213, 459, 1952.
h. Abragam, A. and Pryce, H. M. L., *Proc. Phys. Soc.,* A63, 409, 1950.

TABLE 5-6

ESR Data for Transition Group Ions in Magnesium Oxide (MgO)[R-58]

Ion	Frequency Band	Temperature (°K)		g	A	1/2 a $(b_4{}^0)_c$	D $b_2{}^0$	Remarks	Ref.
V^{2+}	X	290		1.9803 (5)	74.24 (2)				a, b
	X	290		1.9800(5)	−75.1(1)				c
Cr^{3+}	K_μ	290, 77		1.9800 (5)	16.0 (3)			A third pattern arises from ions with axes of symmetry in the face diagonal [110] type direction	a, d
	X	290		1.9797	16.0				e, f
	X			$g_\parallel = g_\perp = 1.9782$			819.4		
Mn^{2+}	K	290		2.0016 (1)	−81.2 (5)	9.33 (15)			
	K	70		2.0015 (1)	−81.3 (5)	9.33 (15)			g
	X	290		2.0014 (5)	−81.0 (2)	9.33 (15)			
	X	290		1.9942 (5)	70.8			"Anomalous spectrum," probably Mn^{4+}	h
	X	290		2.0010	−81.1	9.50			e
Fe^{3+}	K	77		2.0037 (7)	10.1 (2)	102.5 (5)			a, i, j
	X	290		2.0037 (7)	11.4				h
	X	290		2.0030		101.9			e
Fe^{2+}	K, X	4.2	Measurement of g-factor on double quantum transition	3.4277 (1)					
	K	4.2		6.83 (1)				(a) Broad line (b) Narrow asymmetric line (c) Asymmetric line, opposite phase	
Fe^{1+}	K	20		4.15 (1)					h, l
Co^{2+}	K_μ	20, 4.2		4.2785 (1)	97.79 (20) 96.85 (20)				m, n o

TABLE 5-6 (Continued)

Ion	Frequency Band	Temperature (°K)	g	A	1/2 a $(b_4{}^0)_c$	D $b_2{}^0$	Remarks	Ref.
Co^{1+}	X	77	2.1728 (5)	54.0 (2)				h, l, p
Ni^{2+}	X	290	2.225 (5)					b, q, r
	X	70	2.227 (2)					b, q, r
	X	4.2	2.234 (2)					b, q, r
	X	77	2.2145 (5)	8.3(4)			Double quantum transition	l, s
Ni^{1+}	X	77	2.1693 (5)					h, l
Cu^{2+}	X	77	2.190 (2)	19.0 (1)			Line with anomaly below 1.2° K, evidence for anisotropy	h
Ru^{+1}	X	77	2.1697				Identification uncertain	h
Rh^0	X	77	2.1708				Identification uncertain	h
Pd^{1+}	X	77	2.1698				Identification uncertain	h
Er^{3+}	X	20	$g_{100} = 4.62, g_{110} = 3.86, g_{111} = 3.6$					
	Q	20	$g_{100} = 11.84, g_{110} = 12.13$				$-1/2 \rightarrow +1/2$	
	Q	20	$g_{100} = 3.576, g_{110} = 12.13, g_{111} = 4.29$				$-3/2 \rightarrow +3/2$	
	Q	20	$g_{100} = 3.625, g_{110} = 12.13, g_{111} = 4.29$				$-1/2 \rightarrow -3/2$	

REFERENCES:

a. **Low, W.,** *Ann. N.Y. Acad. Sci.,* 72, 69, 1958.
b. **Low, W.,** *Phys. Rev.,* 101, 1827, 1956.
c. **Van Wieringen, J. S. and Rensen, J. G.,** *Proc. 1st Int. Conf. Paramagnetic Resonance, Jerusalem, 1962,* Vol. 1, Academic Press, New York, 1963, 105.
d **Low, W.,** *Phys. Rev.,* 105, 801, 1957.

TABLE 5-6 (Continued)

e. **Walsh, W. M., Jr.,** *Phys. Rev.,* 122, 762, 1961.
f. **Wertz, J. E. and Auzins, P.,** *Phys. Rev.,* 106, 484, 1957.
g. **Low, W.,** *Phys. Rev.,* 105, 793, 1957.
h. **Auzins, P., Orton, J. W., and Wertz, J. E.,** *Proc. 1st Int. Conf. Paramagnetic Resonance, Jerusalem, 1962,* Vol. 1, Academic Press, New York, 1963, 90.
i. **Low, W.,** *Proc. Phys. Soc., (Lond.),* B69, 1169, 1956.
j. **Rosenvasser, E. S. and Feher, G.,** *Bull. Am. Phys. Soc.,* 6(2), 116, 1961.
k. **Low, W. and Weger, M.,** *Phys. Rev.,* 118, 1130, 1960.
l. **Orton, J. W., Auzins, P., Griffiths, J. H. E., and Wertz, J. E.,** *Proc. Phys. Soc. (Lond.),* 78, 554, 1961.
m. **Low, W.,** *Phys. Rev.,* 109, 256, 1958.
n. **Bleaney, B. and Hayes, W.,** *Proc. Phys. Soc. (Lond.)* B70, 626, 1957.
o. **Fry, D. J. I. and Llewellyn, P. M.,** *Proc. Roy. Soc.,* A266, 84, 1962.
p. **Orton, J. W., Auzins, P., and Wertz, J. E.,** *Phys. Rev.,* 119, 1691, 1960.
q. **Low, W.,** *Phys. Rev.,* 109, 247, 1958.
r. **Low, W.,** *Bull. Am. Phys. Soc.,* 1(2), 398, 1956.
s. **Orton, J. W., Auzins, P., and Wertz, J. E.,** *Phys. Rev. Lett.,* 4, 128, 1960.
t. **Descamps, D. and D'Aubigne, Y. Merle,** *Phys. Lett.,* 8, 5, 1964.

TABLE 5-7

ESR Data for Iron Group Elements in Calcium Oxide (CaO)[R-58]

Ion	Frequency Band	Temperature (°K)	g_{isot}	A	(1/2)a $(b_4{}^0)_c$	Remarks	Ref.
V^{2+}	X	290	1.9683(5)	76.04(5)			a, b
		77	1.9683(5)	76.15(5)			
		20	1.9683(5)	76.22(5)			
Cr^{3+}	X	290, 77	1.9732 (5)	17.0 (1)			a, b
Mn^{2+}	X	290	2.0009 (5)	80.8 (2)	2.95 (15)	A and a are of opposite signs	c
		290	2.0011 (5)	80.7 (1)			a, b
		77	2.0011 (5)	81.6 (1)			
		20	2.0011 (5)	−81.7 (1)	+3.0 (2)		
		77	2.0015 (5)	81.4		Powder spectrum probably	d
		77	1.9931 (5)	72.8		Mn^{4+}	
Fe^{3+}	X	77	2.0052 (5)		31.9 (2)		c
		77	2.0059 (6)		+32.2 (2)		
		20	2.0059 (6)	10.5 (5)	+32.6 (2)		a
Fe^{2+}	X	4.2, 2	3.30			Broad line,	e
		2	3.298(3)			Narrow double quantum	
			6.58			Symmetric	
						$\Delta M = \pm 2$ transition	
Fe^{1+}	X	4.2, 2	4.1579 (6)	33.9 (2)			f
Co^{2+}	X	20	4.372 (2)	132.2 (2)			a, b
		20, 4.2	4.3747 (2)	131.5 (1)			f
Ni^{2+}	X	20, 4.4	2.327 (1)			Double quantum transition	a, g
Ni^{1+}	X	77	2.2814 (6)			g-factor slightly temperature dependent; below 65° K, 3 sets of lines of tetragonal symmetry	i
			$g_{\parallel} = 2.0672(6)$, $g_{\perp} = 2.3828(6)$				
Cu^{2+}	X	77	2.2201 (6)	$A^{63} = 21.6$ (3)		Both g and A are strongly temperature dependent; below 1.2° K, 3 sets of tetragonal lines with $g_{\parallel} < g_{\perp}$; in addition, there are many weak lines at $T < 2°$ K	g
		4.2	2.2223 (10)	$A^{63} = 29.1$ (8)			

Note: All lines show angular anisotropy with the minimum along the [111] axis.

For references, see Table 5-8.

TABLE 5-8

ESR Data for Rare-earth Ions in Calcium Oxide (CaO)[R-58]

Ion	Frequency Band	Temperature (°K)	g	A	1/3 F $b_4^{\,0}$	1/4 d $b_6^{\,0}$	Remarks	Ref.
Eu^{2+}	X	77	1.9941 (5)	A^{151} = 30.1 (2) A^{153} = 13.4 (2)	28.8			a, b
		290	1.9914 (10)	A^{151} = 29.63 (10) A^{153} = 13.05 (20)	24.0 (5)	−1.6 (5)		h
		77	1.9917 (10)	A^{151} = 30.09 (10)	25.1 (1)	−2.1 (5)		
		4.2	1.9918 (10)	A^{151} = 30.16 (10) A^{153} = 13.46 (10)	25.7 (5)	−15 (5)		
Gd^{3+}	X	290, 4.2	1.9922(5)		−12.2 (1)	1.2 (1)		a, b
	X	290	1.9913 (5)		−11.6 (1)	−1.15 (10)		h
		77	1.9908 (5)		12.1 (1)	−1.16 (10)		h
		4.2	1.9925 (10)		12.2 (1)	−1.19 (1)		h
Dy^{3+}	X	20	6.60 (5) $g_{\parallel}$ = 3.09(2), $g_{\perp} \sim 15$					
Er^{3+}	X	20, 4.2	g_{100} = 4.84(1), g_{110} = 3.85(1), g_{111} = 3.50(1) $g_{\parallel}$ = 4.730(5) $g_{\perp}$ = 7.86(1)				3 sets with tetragonal axes along cubic axes; in addition, a broad line $g_{100} < 1.5$	i
Yb^{3+}	X	20	2.585 (3)	A^{171} = 698 (6)				i

REFERENCES:

a. **Low, W. and Rubins, R. S.,** *Proc. 1st Int. Conf. Paramagnetic Resonance, Jerusalem, 1962,* Vol. 1, Academic Press, New York, 1963, 79.
b. **Low, W. and Rubins, R. S.,** *Phys. Lett.*, 1, 316, 1962.
c. **Shuskus, A. J.,** *Phys. Rev.*, 127, 1529, 1962.
d. **Auzins, P., Orton, J. W., and Wertz, J. E.,** *Proc. 1st Int. Conf. Paramagnetic Resonance, Jerusalem, 1962,* Vol. 1, Academic Press, New York, 1963, 90.
e. **Shuskus, A. J.,** *J. Chem. Phys.*, 40, 1602, 1964.
f. **Low, W. and Suss, J. T.,** *Bull. Am. Phys. Soc., [2]*, 9, 36, 1964.
g. **Low, W. and Suss, J. T.,** *Phys. Lett.*, 7, 310, 1963.
h. **Shuskus, A. J.,** *Phys. Rev.*, 127, 2022, 1962.
i. **Low, W. and Rubins, R. S.,** *Phys. Rev.*, 131, 2527, 1963.

TABLE 5-9

Paramagnetic Resonance Data for Transition Elements in Strontium Oxide (SrO)[R-58]

Ion	Frequency Band	Temperature (°K)	g_i	A	1/3 F $b_4^{\,0}$	Remarks	References
Cr^{3+}	X	77	1.9520 (5)				a
	X, K_μ	77	1.9683 (6)				b
		20	1.9683 (6)	17.2 (5)			
		4.2	1.9686 (5)	17.3 (4)			
Mn^{2+}	X	290	2.0012 (5)	−78.7 (2)	2.15 (4)		c
			2.0014 (5)	−80.2 (2)			a
	K_μ	81	2.0010 (6)	−80.0 (2)			b
		77	2.0012 (6)	−80.2 (2)	<0.5		b
		20	2.0010 (6)	−80.7 (2)	<0.5		
		4.2	2.0008 (5)	−80.9 (2)	<0.25		
Ni^{3+}	K_μ	4.2	$g_{\parallel} = 4.36(1)$, $g_{\perp} = 4.647(5)$			Assignment doubtful	b
Eu^{2+}	K	1.6–77	1.991 (1)	$\lvert A^{151}\rvert = 29.9$			d
				$\lvert A^{153}\rvert = 13.2$			
	K_μ		1.991 (1)	$\lvert A^{151}\rvert = 30.1$	<0.5		b
				$\lvert A^{153}\rvert = 13.3$			
Gd^{3+}	K_μ	290	1.991 (1)		5.9 (3)		b
		70	1.991 (1)		6.5 (3)		
		4.2	1.989 (1)		5.8 (5)		
Yb^{3+}	K_μ	4.2	2.578 (5)				e

Note: There exists line width anisotropy for all lines. The narrowest line width is along the [111] direction and the widest along [100] direction.

REFERENCES

a **Auzins, P., Orton, J.W., and Wertz, J.E.,** *Proc. 1st Int. Conf. Paramagnetic Resonance, Jerusalem, 1962,* Vol. 1, Academic Press, New York, 1963, 90.

b **Low, W. and Suss, J.T.,** *Phys. Lett.,* 11, 115, 1964.

c **Holroyd, L.V. and Kolopus, J.L.,** *Phys. Stat. Sol.,* 3, No. 12, K456, 1963.

d **Calhoun, B.A. and Overmeyer, J.,** *J. Appl. Phys.,* 35, 989, (Atlantic City Conf.).

e **Low, W.,** unpublished results, 1964.

TABLE 5-10

ESR Data for Transition Group Ions in Zinc Oxide (ZnO)[R-58]

Ion	Frequency Band	Temperature (°K)	$g_{\parallel}$	g_i	$g_{\perp}$	A	B	D b^o_2	1/2 a $(b^o_4)_c$	(a – F) $[2(b^o_4)_c - 3b^o_4]$	Remarks	Ref.
V^{2+}	X	1.3	1.977 (1)		~2	46.7						a
Mn^{2+}	K	77		2.0016 (6)			–76.0 (4)	–216.9 (22)	–1.0 (25)			b
	X	300		2.0012 (2)			74.1 (5)	236.2 (4)		5.23 (5)	Sign of D = sign of A = –sign of $(b^o_4)_c$	c
Fe^{3+}	X	290		2.0060(5)			9.02(2)	–593.7(10)	19.95(2.5)	4.0 ± 5.0	Sign of D = sign of A = –sign of $(b^o_4)_c$	d
Co^{2+}	X	1.3	2.243 (1)		2.2791 (2)	16.11 (5)	3.0 (3)	2.75 (15)				a
Ni^{3+}	X	4.2 1.3	2.1426 (5)		4.3179 (1)							e
Cu^{2+}	X, K	1.2	0.74 (2) 0.7383 (3)	1.50 (2) 1.5237 (3)		219.0 (14) 198.0 (3)	235.0 (3) 224.0 (1)					f, g, h

REFERENCES:

a **Estle, T.L. and deWit, M.,** *Bull. Am. Phys. Soc.*, 6(2), 445, 1961.
b **Dorain, P.B.,** *Phys. Rev.*, 112, 1058, 1958.
c **Schneider, J. and Sircar, S.R.,** *Z. Naturforsch,* 17a, 570, 1962.
d **Walsh, W.M., Jr. and Rupp, L.W., Jr.,** *Phys. Rev.*, 126, 952, 1962.
e **Holton, W.C., Schneider, J., and Estle, T.L.,** *Phys. Rev.*, 133, A1638, 1964.
f **Kamimura, H. and Yariv, A.,** *Bull. Am. Phys. Soc.*, 8(2), 23, 1963.
g **Dietz, R.E., Kamimura, H., Sturge, M.D., and Yariv, A.,** *Phys. Rev.*, 132, 1559, 1963.
h **deWit, M. and Estle, T.L.,** *Bull. Am. Phys. Soc.*, 8(2), 24, 1963.

TABLE 5-11

ESR Data For Transition Group Ions in Corundum (Al_2O_3)[R-58]

Ion	Frequency Band	Temperature (°K)	g	$g_{\|\|}$	$g_{\perp}$	A
Ti^{3+}	X	4.2		1.067(1)	≪0.1	
V^{4+}	X	300		1.97	1.97	|1.32|
Cr^{4+}	X	4.2		1.90 (2)		
V^{2+}	X	300		1.991	1.991	−73.538 (8)
Cr^{3+}	X	4.2		1.984	1.984	16.2 (3)
	X	300		2.003 (6)	2.002	
Mn^{4+}	17	4.2	1.993			−69.608 (8)
	K	1.6–295		1.9937 (7)	1.9937 (7)	|70.0|(5)
Mn^{2+}	X	300		2.0017 (10)	2.0001 (2)	−79.6 (5)
Fe^{3+}	25–40	290			2.003 (1)	
	X	4.2			2.003 (1)	
	X	77			2.003 (1)	
	X	299			2.003 (1)	
Co^{2+}	X	4.2		2.292 (1)	4.947 (3)	32.4 (1)
	Q			2.808 (3)	4.855 (5)	20.8 (5)
	X	1.6		2.316 (5)	4.98 (1)	33.8
Ni^{3+}	K	290–50			2.146	
Ni^{2+}	X	290–4.2		2.1957 (13)	2.1859 (13)	
	X	290		2.196 (4)	2.187 (4)	
Cu^{3+}	K	1.4		2.0784 (5)	2.0772 (5)	Cu^{63} = −64.316 (13) Cu^{65} = −68.893 (13)
Ru^{3+}	K	20		<0.06	2.430	
Gd^{3+}	K	290	1.9912 (5)			
Pt^{+}(3 + 6)	K	79			2.220 (1)	
		4.2		2.011 (6)	2.328 (4)	

TABLE 5-11 (Continued)

ESR Data for Transition Group Ions in Corundum (Al_2O_3)$^{R-58}$

B	D b^O_2 $10^{-4}cm^{-1}$	1/2a b^O_4	Remarks	Ref.
				a
|1.32|				b
	<0.15 (in cm^{-1})			e
−74.267(30)	−1,601.2(3)			f
16.2	−1,907.8(10)			g
	1,930.0(10)			h
−70.480 (33)	−1,956.0 (3)			f
|70.0| (5)	−1,957.0 (1)			i
−78.8	194.2 (10)			j
	|1,684.0 (3)|	|131.0 (10)|	$2b^O_4 - 3b^O_4$ = 334.0 (2)	k
	1,719.0 (1)	|112.0 (2)|	+339.0 (2)	l
	1,716.0 (1)	|118.0 (2)|	+337.0 (2)	l
	1,679.0 (1)	|120.5 (10)|	+329.0 (2)	l
97.2 (5)			Two inequivalent sites	m, n
151.0 (11)			Additional splittings at 4.2° K	m, n
97.4	13,760.0 at 300° K 13,287.0 at T 0° K			o
	13,850.0 (20)			p
−60.03 (2)				q
−64.305 (17)				r
	−1,883.8 (5)			s
	1,032.9 (20)	26.0 (10)	b^O_6 = 1.0 (5)	s
			b_4^3 = 18.3 (10)	p
			$b_6^3 \leqslant 1.0$	t
			b^6_6 = 5.0 (5)	p

REFERENCES:

a Kornienko, L.S. and Prokhorov, A.M., *Soviet Phys. JETP (English Transl.),* 11, 1189, 1960.
b Lambe, J. and Kikuchi, C., *Phys. Rev.,* 118, 71, 1960.
c Zverev, G.M. and Prokhorov, A.M., *Soviet Phys. JETP (English Transl.),* 7, 707, 1958; 11, 330, 1960.
d Foner, S. and Low, W., *Phys. Rev.,* 120, 1585, 1960.
e Hoskins, R.H. and Soffer, B.H., *Phys. Rev.,* 133, A490, 1964.
f Laurance, N. and Lambe, J., *Phys. Rev.,* 132, 1029, 1963.
g Terhune, R.W., Lambe, J., Kikuchi, C., and Baker, J., *Phys. Rev.,* 123, 1265, 1961.
h Geusic, J.E., *Phys. Rev.,* 102, 1252, 1956.
i Geschwind, S., Kisliuk, P., Klein, M.P., Remeika, J.P., and Wood, D.L., *Phys. Rev.,* 126, 1684, 1962.
j Low, W. and Suss, J.T., *Phys. Rev.,* 119, 132, 1960.

TABLE 5-11 (Continued)

k **Kornienko, L.S. and Prokhorov, A.M.,** *Soviet Phys. JETP (English Transl.),* 6, 620, 1958.
l **Bogle, G.S. and Symmons, H.F.,** *Proc. Phys. Soc. (Lond.),* 73, 531, 1959.
m **Zverev, G.M. and Prokhorov, A.M.,** *Soviet Phys. JETP (Eng. Transl.),* 9, 451, 1959.
n **Zverev, G.M. and Prokhorov, A.M.,** *Soviet Phys. JETP (Eng. Transl.),* 12, 41, 1961.
o **Geusie, J.E.,** *Bull. Am. Phys. Soc.,* 4(2), 261, 1959.
p **Geschwind, S. and Remeika, J.P.,** *J. Appl. Phys.,* 33, 370, 1962.
q **Marshall, S.A., Kikuehi, T.T., and Reinberg, A.R.,** *Phys. Rev.,* 125, 453, 1962.
r **Marshall, S.A. and Reinberg, A.R.,** *J. Appl. Phys.,* 31, 336S, 1960.
s **Blumberg, W.E., Eisinger, J., and Geschwind, S.,** *Phys. Rev.,* 130, 900, 1963.
t **Geschwind, S. and Remeika, J.P.,** *Phys. Rev.,* 122, 757, 1961.

TABLE 5-12

ESR Data for Transition Group Ions in Titanium Dioxide (TiO_2)[R-58]

α is the angle between one of the magnetic axes in the plane perpendicular to the c axis and the [110] direction. The A^{Ti} are the hyperfine constants for the superhyperfine interaction with the Ti^{47} and Ti^{49} nuclei.

Ion	Frequency Band	Temperature (°K)	α	$g_{\bar{1}10}$	g_{110}	g_c	A_{110}	$A_{\bar{1}10}$
Ti^{3+}	X	4.2	19°	1.974	1.977	1.941		
	Not given	4.2	0°	1.975	1.978	1.953		
V^{4+}	X + K	4.2 and 78	0°	1.915	1.956 (5)	1.912 (5)	31.0_5	142.0
	X	77	0°	1.913 (1)	1.955 (1)	1.912 (1)	30.9 (3)	141.5 (7)
Cr^{3+}	X + K	4.2 and 350	0°	1.97 (1)	1.97 (1)	1.97 (1)		
Mn^{4+}	X	4.2 and 300	0°	1.9909 (5)	1.995 (5)	1.9898 (5)	72.3 (1)	70.3 (2)
Mn^{3+}	2–70 kMc/sec	4.2 and 77	0°	2.00 (2)	2.00 (2)	1.99(1)	|84.5|(20)	|52.8|(5)
Fe^{3+}	X	1.4 and 78	0°	2.000 (5)	2.000 (5)	2.000 (5)		
Co^{2+}	X	4.2	0°	5.88 (2)	2.19 (05)	3.75 (1)	150.0 (2)	(–)40.0 (2)
	X	4.2	0°	5.860 (1)	2.090 (1)	3.725 (2)	142.8 (6)	39.1 (4)
Ni^{3+}	X + K	4.2 and 78	0°	2.272 (3)	2.050 (3)	2.237 (3)		
Ni^{3+}	X + K	4.2 and 290	9.1(± 0.3)°	2.084 (3)	2.254 (3)	2.085 (3)		
Ni^{2+}	X + K	4.2	5.4°	2.1 (5)	2.2 (5)	2.1 (5)		
Cu^{2+}	?	4.2 and 77	0°	2.105	2.344	2.093	–19.0	–88.0
Nb^{4+}	X	4.2 and 25	0°	1.973	1.981	1.948	8.04	1.75
Mo^{5+}	X	4.2 and 77	0°	1.8117 (10)	1.9125 (10)	1.7884 (10)	2.474 (25)	65.85 (15)
Ce^{3+}	?	4.2		4.397 (4)	2.06_9	3.86_6		
Gd^{3+}	X	295	0°			1.993		
	X	77				1.9941		
		1.8				1.9986		
Er^{3+}	Not given	4.2	0°	<0.1	<0.1	15.1	495.0	
Ta^{4+}	X	1.4 and 10	?	1.979	1.979	1.945	<2.5	<2.5
W^{5+}	Not given	63	0°	1.5945	1.4731	1.4463	92.0	40.5

TABLE 5-12 (Continued)

α is the angle between one of the magnetic axes in the plane perpendicular to the c axis and the [110] direction. The A^{Ti} are the hyperfine constants for the superhyperfine interaction with the Ti^{47} and Ti^{49} nuclei.

Ion	Ac	D $(10^{-4} cm^{-1})$ b_2^0	3E b_2^2	1/3F b_4^0	Remarks	Ref.
					Other spectra have been observed, but these are not understood	a
						b
Ti^{3+}	43.0				$A_{110}^{Ti} = A_{1\bar{1}0}^{Ti} = 1.86$; $A_c^{Ti} = 2.23$	c, q
	441.0 (3)					d
V^{4+}	16.7	−6,800.0 (50)	−6,800.0 (50)			b, e, f
	15.0 (2)					
Cr^{3+}	72.7 (2)	4,000.0	3,900.0		$A_{110}^{Ti} < 0.47$; $A_{1\bar{1}0}^{Ti} < 0.47$; $A_c^{Ti} = 0.93$	g, q
Mn^{4+}						
Mn^{3+}	|80.6| (10)	−34,000.0 (± 3%)	3,480.0 (± 1%)	650.0 (± 14%)		b, h
Fe^{3+}		6,780.0 (± 0.5%)	2,210.0 (5%)	183.0 (± 20%)	$F = -170.0$ (± 60%)$(10^{-4} cm^{-1})$	i
Co^{2+}	26.0 (1)					j
	25.0 (3)					k
Ni^{3+}						l
Ni^{3+}					Interstitial, light generated	l
		−83,000.0 (± 2%)	1,370.0 (± 5%)			l
Ni^{2+}	−29.0					b, l
Cu^{2+}	2.1					b, m
Nb^{4+}	30.5 (2)					n
Mo^{5+}						m
Ce^{3+}		143.2		+20.5	$b_4^2 = -2.4$	o
Gd^{3+}		120.9	+22.8	+20.2	$b_4^4 = -182.0$	
		107.8		+21.5	$b_6^0 \doteq -1.0$	
					$b_6^4 \doteq -30.0$	b
Er^{3+}	~2.7				$b_6^2 \doteq b_6^6 \doteq +4.8$	m
Ta^{4+}	63.9				Superhyperfine lines also observed: $A^{Ti} = 2.5$; $A_{110}^{Ti} = 3.0$; $A_c^{Ti} = 4.0$	p
W^{5+}						

TABLE 5-12 (Continued)

REFERENCES:

a **Chester, P.F.,** *J. Appl. Phys.,* 32, Suppl., 2233, 1961.
b **Gerritsen, H.J.,** *Proc. 1st Int. Conf. Paramagnetic Resonance. Jerusalem, 1962,* Vol. 1, Academic Press, New York, 1963.
c **Gerritsen, H.J. and Lewis, H.R.,** *Phys. Rev.,* 119, 1010, 1960.
d **Zverev, G.M. and Prokhorov, A.M.,** *Soviet Phys. JETP (English Transl.),* 12, 160, 1960.
e **Gerritsen, H.J., Harrison, S.E., Lewis, H.R., and Wittke, J.P.,** *Phys. Rev. Lett.,* 2, 153, 1959; Gerritsen, H.J., Harrison, S.E., and Lewis, H.R., *J. Appl. Phys.,* 31, 1566, 1960.
f **Sierro, I., Müller, K.A., and Lacroix, R.,** *Arch. Sci. (Geneva),* 12, 122, 1959.
g **Andersen, H.G.,** *Phys. Rev.,* 120, 1606, 1960; *J. Chem. Phys.,* 35, 1090, 1961.
h **Gerritsen, H.J. and Sabisky, E.S.,** *Phys. Rev.,* 132, 1507, 1963.
i **Carter, D.L. and Okaya, A.,** *Phys. Rev.,* 118, 1485, 1960.
j **Yamaka, E. and Barnes, R.G.,** *Phys. Rev.,* 125, 1568, 1962.
k **Zverev, G.M. and Prokhorov, A.M.,** *Soviet Phys. JETP (English Transl.),* 16, 303, 1963; *Proc. 1st Int. Conf. Paramagnetic Resonance, Jerusalem, 1962,* Vol. 1, Academic Press, New York, 1963, 13.
l **Gerritsen, H.J. and Sabisky, E.S.,** *Phys. Rev.,* 125, 1853, 1962.
m **Chester, P.F.,** *J. Appl. Phys.,* 32, 866, 1961.
n **Kyi, Ru-Tao,** *Phys. Rev.,* 128, 151, 1962.
o **Yamaka, E.,** *J. Phys. Soc. Jap.,* 18, 1557, 1963.
p **Chang, T.,** *Bull. Am. Phys. Soc.,* 9(2), 568, 1964.
q **Yamaka, E. and Barnes, R.G.,** *Phys. Rev.,* 135, A144, 1964.

TABLE 5–13

ESR Data for Perovskite-Type Materials–Data fro $BaTiO_3$ and $SrTiO_3$ [R-58]

Host Material	Ion	Frequency Band	Temperature (°K)	g	$g_{\parallel}$	$g_{\perp}$	A	D b_2^0	1/3 F b_4^0	Ref.
$BaTiO_3$	Fe^{3+}	X	425		2.003(1)				17.0(2)(1)	a,b
			300					930.0	51.0 ± (10)	
$SrTiO_3$	Fe^{3+}	X	300	2.004(1)					96.14	c
		X	300	2.004(1)					98.8(50)	
			80	2.004(1)				7.7(3)		c
			77	2.004(1)				7.3(3)	110.0(6)	d
			4.2	2.004(1)				16.1(7)	112.8(10)	d
			1.9	2.004(1)				17.9(10)	115.0(5)	d
		X	295		2.0054(7)	5.993(1)				e
		Kμ	295		2.0054(7)	5.961(1)				
	Mn^{4+}	X	295	1.994(1)			75.0(1)			f
	Cr^{3+}	X	295	1.978(7)			15.8(1)			g
			80							

Host Material	Ion	Frequency Band	Temperature (°K)	g	$g_{\parallel}$	$g_{\perp}$	A	B	Ref.
$SrTiO_3$ (continued)									h
	Ni^{2+}(A)	X	80	2.204(1)					
	Ni^{3+}(B)	X	203	2.180(2)					
			80		2.172(1)	2.184(1)			
			20		2.136(1)	2.202(1)			h
			4.2		2.110(2)	2.213(2)			
	Ni^{1+}(C)	X	203, 80, 20		2.029(1)	2.352(1)			h
	Ni^{1+}(D)	X	77		2.375(2)	2.084(2)			i
	Ce^{3+}	X	4.2		3.005(5)	1.118(3)			h
	Nd^{3+}	X	4.2		2.609(3)	2.472(3)			h,j
		K_μ	2		2.61(1)	2.470(5)			j
		Q	2		2.62(1)	2.740(5)			
	Yb^{3+}	K_μ	50		2.18(1)	2.720(5)			
		K_μ	2		2.11(1)	2.780(5)			
		Q	77			2.67(1)			j
			65		2.25(1)	2.70(1)			
			50		2.170(5)	2.720(5)			
			2		2.10(1)	2.785(5)	A_{171} 530.0 (20)	B_{171} 720.0(5)	
								B_{175} 11.0(5)	

For references, see Table 5-15.

TABLE 5-14

ESR Data for Perovskite-Type Materials—S State Ions[R-58]

Host Material	Ion	Frequency Band	Temperature (°K)	g	D b_2^0	1/3 F b_4^0	1/4 d b_6^0	b_4^4	b_6^4	b_6^6	Ref.
$BaTiO_3$	Gd^{3+}	K_μ	425	1.995(3)		≅6	≅0				k
		K_μ	300	1.995(3)	−293.6(1)	4.0(1)	1.6(1)	−2.0(1)	≅0		
$SrTiO_3$	Gd^{3+}	K_μ	300	1.992(2)		−5.7(2)	0.5(3)				k
			77	1.992(2)	−233.6(5)	−4.8(5)	−0.25(5)	−2.5(3)	0.1(5)		
			4.2	1.992(2)	−362.5(5)	−3.24(50)	1.4(5)	−4.2(5)	−0.69(50)		
	Eu^{2}	K_μ	300	1.990(1)		105.9(2)	1.1(2)	1.1 ± 2			j
			2	1.990(1)	−10.0(4)	106.6(2)	6.7(2)	6.7 ± 2			
$LaAlO_3$	Gd^{3+}	X	689	1.991	67.0(10)						
			575	1.991	150.5(10)	5.60(3)	0.9(2)				
			505	1.9910	208.3(10)	5.80(3)	1.0(2)				
			415	1.9910(5)	307.0(10)	5.99(3)	1.0(2)				
			358	1.9915(5)	337.0(10)	6.13(3)	1.0(2)			9.9(12)	
			293	1.9908(5)	371.2(10)	6.17(3)	1.0(2)			7.6(12)	
			273	1.9911(5)	383.8	6.23(3)	0.9(2)			9.4(12)	1
			203	1.9904(5)	426.7	6.42(3)	0.9(2)			7.2	
			80	1.9911(5)	479 2	6.42(3)	0.9(2)			10.2	
			20	1.9909(5)	+490.7	+6.46(3)	+0.9(2)			+8.0	

For references, see Table 5-15.

TABLE 5-15

ESR Data for Perovskite-Type Materials–Data for $PbTiO_3$ $KTaO_3$, $LaAlO_3$, $KMgF_3$ R-58

Host Material	Ion	Temperature (°K)	g	D b_2^0	1/3 F b_4^0	A	A′	B′	Ref.
$PbTiO_3$	Fe^{3+}	290	$g_{\parallel} = 2.009(5)$						m
			$g_{\perp} = 5.97(2)$						
$KTaO_3$		4.2	1.99 ± 0.01		172.5				n
		4.2	$g_{\parallel} = 1.99$						n
			$g_{\perp} = 6.0$						
$LaAlO_3$	Cr^{3+}	291	1.9825(5)	450.0(1)		19.0(3)			o
		273	1.9825(5)	475.5(10)					
		80	1.9825(5)	587.0(6)					
		20		600.0(2)					
$KMgF_3$	V^{2+}	77	1.9720(2)			86.2(2)	7.1(2)	2.0(2)	p
	Cr^{3+}	77	1.9733(2)				9.4(2)	2.3(2)	
	Cr^{1+}	77	2.0005(5)		2.25(100)		23.0(5)	17.5(5)	
	Mn^{2+}	300	2.0015(5)		3.25(25)	91.0(5)	23.9(5)	18.0(5)	
	Fe^{3+}	77	2.0031(2)		25.75(3)		36.0(5)	18.0(5)	
	Ni^{2+}	20, 77	2.2797(4)						l
	Co^{2+}	4.2	4.28						

REFERENCES:

a. **Hornig, A. W., Rempel, R. C., and Weaver, H. E.,** *J. Phys. Chem. Solids,* 10, 1, 1959.
b. **Shaltiel, D.,** Ph.D. thesis, Haifa Institute of Technology, 1966.
c. **Müller, K. A.,** *Helv. Phys. Acta,* B1, Suppl., 173, 1959.
d. **Dobrov, W. I., Vieth, R. F., and Browne, M. E.,** *Phys. Rev.,* 115, 79, 1959.
e. **Kirkpatrick, E. S., Müller, K. A., and Rubins, R. S.,** *Phys. Rev.,* 135A, 86, 1964.
f. **Müller, K. A.,** *Phys. Rev. Lett.,* 2, 341, 1959.
g. **Müller, K. A.,** 7eme Colloque Ampère Genève, *Arch. Sci. (Geneva),* 11, 150, 1958.
h. **Rubins R. S. and Low, W.,** *Proc. 1st Int. Conf. Paramagnetic Resonance, Jerusalem, 1962,* Vol. 1, Academic Press, New York, 1963, 59.
i. **Müller, K. A. and Rubins, R. S.,** to be published.
j. **Rimai, L. and de Mars, G. A.,** *Proc. 1st Int. Conf. Paramagnetic Resonance, Jerusalem, 1962,* Vol. 1, Academic Press, New York, 1963, 51.
k. **Rimai, L. and de Mars, G. A.,** *Phys. Rev.,* 127, 702, 1962.
l. **Low, W. and Zusman, A.,** *Phys. Rev.,* 130, 145, 1963.
m. **Gainon, D. A.,** *Phys. Rev.,* A134, 1300, 1964.
n. **Wemple, W.,** Ph.D. thesis, M. I. T., 1963.
o. **Kiro, D., Low, W., and Zusman, A.,** *Proc. 1st Int. Conf. Paramagnetic Resonance, Jerusalem, 1962,* Vol. 1, Academic Press, New York, 1963, 44.
p. **Hall, T. P. P., Hayes, W., Stevenson, R. W. H., and Wilkens, J.,** *J. Chem. Phys.,* 38, 1977, 1963.

TABLE 5-16

ESR Data for Transition Group Ions in Spinels (AB_2O_4)[R-58]

Host Lattice	Ion	Site	Frequency Band	Temperature (°K)	g	A	b_2^0	$(b_4^0)_c$	$\lvert 2(b_4^0)_c - 3b_4^0 \rvert$	Remarks	Ref.
$MgAl_2O_4$	Cr^{3+}	B	X	290	$g_\parallel = 1.986(1)$		−0.92				a,b,c,d
			K,Q		$g_\perp = 1.989(2)$						d
$ZnAl_2O_4$		B	X	290			−0.93				d
$MgAl_2O_4$	Mn^{2+}	A	X	290	2.0015(3)	75.4(6)					e
$ZnAl_2O_4$		A	X	290	2.0002(1)	74.9(5)					
$MgAl_2O_4$	Fe^{3+}	B	X	290	2.001(7)		|0.247|(1)	|0.024|(2)	0.046(2)	If $(b_4^0)_c$ and b_2^0 are of opposite sign	f
$Li_{0.5}Al_{2.5}O_4$ Ordered	Fe^{3+}	A	K	290	2.006(2)		|0.104|	~|0.01|	0.0166		g,h,i,
Dissordered		B	K	290			0.13			A rhombic component is present as well	
$Li_{0.5}Ga_{2.5}O_4$		A	K	290	2.008(3)		|0.080|				g,h,i
$Li_{0.5}Al_{2.5}O_4$	Mn^{2+}	B?	K	290	2.0023(1)	77.2(1)					j

REFERENCES:

a. **Stahl-Brade, R. and Low, W.,** *Phys. Rev.*, 116, 561, 1959.
b. **Atsarkin, V. A.,** *Soviet Phys. JETP (English Transl.)*, 16, 593, 1963.
c. **Overmeyer, J.,** private communication, 1964.
d. **Brun, E., Hofner, S., Loelinger, H., and Waldner, F.,** *Helv. Phys. Acta,* 33, 966, 1960.
e. **Waldner, F.,** *Helv. Phys. Acta,* 35, 756, 1962.
f. **Brun, E., Loelinger, H., and Waldner, F.,** *Arch. Sci. (Geneva),* 14, 167, 1961.
g. **Folen, V. J.,** *J. Appl. Phys.,* 33, 1084, 1962.
h. **Folen, V. J.,** *Proc. 1st Int. Conf. Paramagnetic Resonance, Jerusalem, 1962,* Vol. 1, Academic Press, New York, 1963, 68.
i. **Folen, V. J.,** *J. Appl. Phys.,* 31, 166S, 1960.
j. **Kelly, R. H., Folen, V. J., Hass, M., Schreiner, W. N., and Beard, W. G.,** *Phys. Rev.,* 124, 80, 1961.

TABLE 5-17

ESR Data for Iron Group Ions in Garnets ($A_3B_5O_{12}$) R-58

Host Material	Ion	Frequency Band	Temperature (°K)	g	D b_2^0	1/2 a $(b_4^0)_c$	F $3b_4^0$	Remarks	Ref.
YGaG	Cr^{3+}	K	290	$g_{\parallel}$ = 1.9767(2)	$g_{\perp}$ = 1.9757(2)				a
		Q	300	1.98	3,500.0				b
			77	1.98	3,490.0				
YAlG		Q	300	1.98	2,550.0				
				1.98	2,620.0				
YGaG	Fe^{3+}	K	295	2.003(1)	−1,295.0(3)	+93.0(2)	26.0(4)	Octahedral(a) site	c
			4.2	2.003(1)	−1,320.0(4)	+95.0(3)	34.0(7)		
			295	2.0047(5)	−885.0(5)	31.0(2)	37.0(4)	Tetrahedral(d) site	
			4.2	2.0047(5)	−880.0(6)	31.0(2)	38.0(5)		

REFERENCES:

a. **Geschwind, S. and Nielsen, J. W.,** *Bull. Am. Phys. Soc.*, 5(2), 252, 1960.
b. **Carson, J. W. and White, R. L.,** *J. Appl. Phys.*, 32, 1787, 1961.
c. **Geschwind, S.,** *Phys. Rev.*, 121, 363, 1961.

TABLE 5-18

ESR Data for Rare-earth Ions in Garnets ($A_3B_5O_{12}$) R-58

All measurements at X-band and 4.2° K except Yb^{3+}, which was measured at 20° K.

Host Material	Ion	g_x	g_y	g_z	Ref.
LuGaG	Nd^{3+}	2.083(7)	1.323(7)	3.550(7)	d
YGaG		2.027(8)	1.251(8)	3.667(8)	d
LuAlG		1.789(5)	1.237(6)	3.834(5)	d
YAlG		1.733(2)	1.179(2)	3.915(26)	d
LuGaG	Dy^{3+}	13.45(10)	0.57(10)	3.41(3)	d
YGaG		11.07(20)	1.07(14)	7.85(10)	d
LuAlG		2.29(3)	0.91(5)	16.6(3)	d
YAlG		0.73(15)	0.40(20)	18.2(4)	e
LuGaG	Er^{3+}	3.183(15)	3.183(15)	12.62(10)	d
YGaG		4.69(3)	4.03(2)	10.73(5)	d
LuAlG		6.93(2)	4.12(3)	8.43(4)	d
YAlG		7.75(9)	3.71(2)	7.35(8)	d
LuGaG	Yb^{3+}	3.653(13)	3.559(13)	2.994(11)	d
YGaG		3.73(2)	3.60(2)	2.85(2)	f,g
LuAlG		3.842(5)	3.738(7)	2.594(4)	d
YAlG		3.87(1)	3.78(1)	2.47(1)	d

REFERENCES:

d. **Wolf, W. P., Bell, M., Hutchins, M. T., Leask, M. J. M., and Wyatt, A. F. G.,** *J. Phys. Soc. Jap.,* 17(Suppl. B1), 443, 1962.

e. **Bleaney, B.,** *Tech. Rept.,* AFCRL 63-192, 1963.

f. **Carson, J. W. and White, R. L.,** *J. Appl. Phys.,* 31, 53S, 1960.

g. **Boakes, D., Garton, G., Ryan, D., and Wolf, W. P.,** *Proc. Phys. Soc. (Lond.),* 74, 663, 1959.

TABLE 5-19

ESR Data for Gd^{3+} In Garnets ($A_3B_5O_{12}$) R-58

Host	YGaG	LuGaG	LuGaG	LuAlG	YGaG	YGaG	YAlG	YAlG
Temperature (°K)	300.0	300.0	4.2	300.0	300.0	4.2	300.0	4.2
g	1.991	1.99	1.99	1.989	1.992(3)	1.992(3)	1.990(3)	1.990(3)
b_2^0	+440.7	+275.0	+279.0	+571.5	441.3(5)	448.0(5)	777.7(5)	776.4(5)
b_2^2	+216.1	+228.0	+238.0	+115.4	−269.7(5)	−283.8(5)	−85.1(5)	−96.9(5)
b_4^0	−43.2	−44.9	−47.2	−50.2	−42.2(5)	−45.2(5)	−46.9(5)	−48.6(5)
b_4^2	+0.3							
b_4^4	+36.1	+39.2	+43.3	+40.4	21.1(5)	22.1(5)	23.2(5)	23.5(5)
b_6^0	+0.3				+0.6(5)	+4.15(5)	+3.77(5)	4.62(5)
b_6^2	+0.04							
b_6^4	−0.7				0.1(5)	1.28(5)	2.43(5)	4.29(5)
b_6^6	+3.9							
K_1/ion	−611.0	−658.0	−715.0	−699.0	189.5	205.5	211.8	222.2
K_2/ion	−23.0	−20.0	−21.0	−25.0	11.2	11.8	15.1	16.0
Ref.	h	h	h	h	i	i	i	i

REFERENCES:

h. **Overmeyer, J., Giess, E. A., Freiser, M. J., and Calhoun, B. A.,** *Proc. 1st Int. Conf. Paramagnetic Resonance, Jerusalem, 1962,* Vol. 1, Academic Press, New York, 1963, 224.

i. **Rimai, L. and de Mars, G. A.,** *J. Appl. Phys.,* 33, 1254S, 1962.

TABLE 5-20

Spectroscopic and Nuclear Properties of Rare-earth Ions B-33

Trivalent Ion	Ground State of Free Ion	Spin-orbit Coupling in cm^{-1}	$<r^{-3}>$ in $(A°)^{-3}$	Isotope	Nuclear Spin	Nuclear Magnetic Moment	Larmor Frequency MHZ at 10^4 Gauss	Quadrupole Moment Q $X 10^{-24}$ cm^2
^{58}Ce	$^2F_{5/2}$	640.0	32.5					
^{59}Pr	$^3H_4$	800.0	37.0	141	5/2	3.92	11.95	$-5.4 X 10^{-2}$
^{60}Nd	$^4I_{9/2}$	900.0	42.0	143	7/2	−1.03	2.24	<1.2
				145	7/2	0.64	1.4	<1.2
^{61}Pm	$^5I_4$	(1,070.0)	47.0					
^{62}Sm	$^6H_{3/2}$	1,200.0	51.0	147	7/2	−0.83	1.8	0.72
				149	7/2	−0.68	1.5	0.72
^{63}Eu	$^7F_0$	1,410.0	57.0	151	5/2	3.4	10.0	~1.2
				153	5/2	1.5	4.6	~2.5
^{64}Gd	$^8S_{7/2}$	1,540.0	62.0	155	3/2	−0.24	1.2	1.1
				157	3/2	−0.32	1.6	1.0
^{65}Tb	$^7F_6$	1,770.0	68.0	159	3/2	1.52	7.72	
^{66}Dy	$^6H_{15/2}$	1,860.0	74.0	161	5/2	0.38	1.2	
				163	5/2	0.53	1.6	
^{67}Ho	$^5I_8$	2,000.0	80.0	165	7/2	3.29	7.17	2.0
^{68}Er	$^4I_{15/2}$	2,350.0	86.0	167	7/2	0.48	1.04	~10.0
^{69}Tm	$^3H_6$	2,660.0	92.0	169	1/2	−0.20	3.05	
^{70}Yb	$^2F_1$	2,940.0	98.0	171	1/2	0.43	6.6	
				173	5/2	−0.6	1.8	3.9

TABLE 5-21

Paramagnetic Resonance Results on Several Rare-earth Chlorides B-33

Trivalent Ions	$g_{\parallel}$	$g_{\perp}$	A cm^{-1} X 10^4	B cm^{-1} X 10^4	Δ cm^{-1}	Calculated Values: Corrected for Z $g_{\parallel}$	Corrected for Z $g_{\perp}$	Uncorrected for Z $g_{\parallel}$	Uncorrected for Z $g_{\perp}$
Ce	4.0366 ±0.0015	0.17 ±0.08				4.22	0.133	4.14	0.2
^{141}Pr	1.035 ±0.005	0.1 ±0.15	502.0 ± 3.0	–	0.02	0.997·	0.0	0.997	0.0
^{143}Nd	3.996	1.763	425.0 ± 2.0	167 ± 1		4.09	1.86	4.06	1.88
^{145}Nd	±0.001	±0.001	264.0 ± 2.0	104 ± 1					
^{147}Sm	0.5841	0.6127	60.7 ± 0.2	245 ± 1		0.498	0.745	0.518	0.599
^{149}Sm	+0.0003	±0.0006	49.9 ± 0.2	202 ± 1					
^{155}Gd	1.991	1.991	3.8 ± 0.2						
^{157}Gd	±0.001	±0.001	5.0 ± 0.2						
^{159}Tb	17.78 ±0.01	<0.1	2,120.0 ± 30.0	–	0.201	18.0	0.0	17.9	0.0
^{165}Ho	16.01 ±0.018	~0.0	3,510.0 ± 70.0	–		16.8	0.0	15.2	0.0
^{167}Er	1.989 ±0.001	8.757 ±0.002	66.4 ± 0.3	304 ± 2		1.78	8.9	2.48	8.76

TABLE 5-22

Paramagnetic Results on Ethyl Sulfates[a] B-33

Crystal Field Parameters in 10^{-4} cm^{-1}

Trivalent Ions	$g_{\parallel}$	$g_{\perp}$	$\frac{Bg_{\parallel}}{Ag_{\perp}}$	$A_2^0 \overline{r^2}$	$A_4^0 \overline{r^4}$	$A_6^0 \overline{r^6}$	$A_6^6 \overline{r^6}$	Ground State
Ce	0.955	2.185		−15.0 ± 10.0	−40.0 ± 12.0	−92.0 ± 2.0	1,150.0 ± 30.0	±1/2 and ±5/2
	3.725	0.2						
Pr	1.525			−50.0	−100.0	−48.0	660.0	$\cos\theta\| \pm 4\rangle + \sin\theta\| \mp 2\rangle$
Nd	3.535	2.072	0.892	−15.0	−35.0	−60.0	640.0	$\cos\theta\| \pm 7/2\rangle + \sin\theta\| \mp 5/2\rangle$
Sm	0.596	0.604	4.2	0.0	−30.0	−54.0	590.0	$\cos\theta\|5/2, \pm 1/2\rangle \pm \sin\theta\|7/2 \pm 1/2\rangle$
Eu^{2+}	1.991	1.991						
Gd	1.991	1.991						$^8S_{7/2}$
Tb[c]	17.72	<0.3		37.0	−20.0	−20.0	220.0	$\cos\theta\| \pm 6\rangle + \sin\theta\|0\rangle$
Ho[b,c]	15.36			0.0	−18.0	−22.0	170.0	$a\| \pm 7\rangle + b\| \pm 1\rangle + c\| \mp 5\rangle$
Er	1.47	8.85	1.0	0.0	−40.0	−30.0	330.0	$\cos\theta\| \pm 7/2\rangle + \sin\theta\| \mp 5/2\rangle$

[a] From Elliott, R. J. and Stevens, K. W. H., *Proc. Roy. Soc.*, A219, 387, 1953.
[b] Compare Baker, J. M. and Bleaney, B., *Proc. Phys. Soc.*, A68, 1090, 1955.
[c] Compare Baker, J. M. and Bleaney, B., *Proc. Roy. Soc.*, A245, 156, 1958.

TABLE 5-23

Transition Metal Ions in Liquid Solutions at X-band (~ 9 GHz)

State	Ion	Compound	Solvent	T, °K	g	A, 10^{-4} cm^{-1}	Ref.
$3d^1$	Ti^{+3}	$TiCl_3 6H_2O$	C_2H_5OH	room, 77	$g_{\parallel} = 2.0$ $g_{\perp} = 1.9$	–	a
$3d^1$	V^{+4}	$VOSO_4$	H_2O	room	1.961	190.0	b
$3d^1$	Cr^{+5}	$K_3[CrO_8]$	H_2O	room	1.973	–	c
$3d^3$	Cr^{+3}	$Cr(C10_4)_3$	$HClO_4$	room	2.0	–	d
$3d^5$	Mn^{+2}	$MnCl_2$	H_2O	room	2.0	89.3	e, f, g
$3d^5$	Fe^{+3}	$FeCl_3$	acetone	room	2.016	–	h
$3d^6$	Fe^{+2}	$[K_3Fe(CN)_5NO]$	H_2O	room	2.026	–	i
$3d^7$	Co^{+2}	α[Co pc]	H_2SO_4	77	$g_{\parallel} = 2.029$ $g_{\perp} = 2.546$	A = 85.0 B = 96.0	j, k, 1
$3d^9$	Cu^{+2}	$CuCl_2$	H_2O	room	2.182	–	m
$3d^9$	Cu^{+2}	$CuBr_2$	CH_3OH	77	$g_{\parallel} = 2.39$ $g_{\perp} = 2.07$	A = 118.5 B = 67.8	n
$4d^1$	Mo^{+5}	$MoOCl_3$	$CHCl_3$	room	1.947	48.2	o
$4d^9$	Ag^{+2}	$AgSO_4$	H_2O	room	2.133	–	p
$4d^9$	Ag^{+2}	$AgSO_4$	H_2O	77	$g_{\parallel} = 2.265$ $g_{\perp} = 2.065$	A = 51.0 B = 30.5	p
$5d^1$	W^{+5}	WCl_5	HCl	room	1.745	183.0	q

REFERENCES:

a. **Avvakumov, V. I., Garifyanov, N. S., and Semenova, E. I.,** *Zh. Eksperim i Teor. Fiz.*, 39; 1215, 1960.
b. **Wuethrich, K.,** *Helv. Chim. Acta,* 48, 779, 1965.
c. **Garifyanov, N. S.,** *Dokl. Akad. Nauk SSSR,* 155, 385, 1964.
d. **Sancier, K. M. and Mills, J. S.,** *J. Phys. Chem.*, 67, 1438, 1964.
e. **Garifyanov, N.S. and Kozyrev, B. M.,** *Dokl. Akad. Nauk SSSR,* 98, 929, 1954.
f. **Garifyanov, N. S.,** *Dokl. Akad. Nauk SSSR,* 109, 725, 1956.
g. **McGarvey, B. R.,** *J. Phys. Chem.*, 61, 1232, 1957.
h. **Golding, R. M. and Orgel, L. E.,** *J. Chem. Soc.*, p.363, 1962.
i. **Raynor, J. B.,** *Nature,* 201, 1216, 1964.
j. **Assour, J. M.,** *J. Am. Chem. Soc.*, 87, 4701, 1965.
k. **Aasa, R. and Vänngård, T.,** *Z. Naturforsch.*, 19a, 1425, 1964.
l. **Vänngård, T. and Aasa, R.,** Parmagnetic resonance, *Proc. 1st Int. Conf., Jerusalem, 1962,* 2, 509, 1963.
m. **Fujiwara, S. and Hayashi, H.,** *J. Chem. Phys.*, 43, 23, 1965.
n. **Garifyanov, N. S. and Usacheva, N. F.,** *Ph. Fiz. Khim.*, 38, 1367, 1964.
o. **Garifyanov, N. S., Kucheryavenko, N. S., and Fedotov, V. N.,** *Dokl. Akad. Nauk SSSR,* 150, 802, 1963.
p. **McMillan, J. A. and Smaller, B.,** *J. Chem. Phys.*, 35, 1698, 1961.
q. **Garifyanov, N. S. and Fedotov, V. N.,** *Fiz. Tverd. Tela,* 4, 3537, 1962.

VI. FREE RADICALS, CENTERS, SEMICONDUCTORS, CONDUCTION ELECTRONS AND IRRADIATION

A. Introduction

There is considerable overlap in the topics enumerated in this section heading. Nevertheless, each will be treated in turn.

B. Free Radicals

This section tabulates representative data for inorganic radicals, organic radicals, and organic radical ions in Tables 6-1 to 6-5. The third table of this group gives the proportionality constant Q~22.5 gauss from McConnell's relation

$$A_H = Q\rho$$

between the unpaired electron density ρ and the hyperfine coupling constant A_H of a C–H bond in an organic radical or radical ion. Tables 6-4 and 6-5 give g-factor and linewidth data for α,α,′-diphenyl-β-picrylhydrazyl (DPPH).

C. Centers

This section consists of tables of representative ESR data on centers in insulators, semiconductors, and conductors. (Tables 6-6 to 6-13.)

TABLE 6-1

g-Tensors and Hyperfine Coupling Constants (MHz) of Inorganic Radicals[a] B-14

Radical	g_{xx}	g_{yy}	g_{zz}	Nucleus	a	t'_1	t'_2	t'_3	Notes
N_2^-	1.984	2.001	2.001	N^{14}	± 13	∓ 2	∓ 2	± 5	KN_3
F_2^-	2.0230	2.0230	2.0031	F^{19}	± 883	∓718	∓ 718	±1,437	LiF
OH	2.008	2.008	2.013	H^1	± 116	∓ 17	∓ 17	± 34	H_2O
XeF	2.1264	2.1264	1.9740	F^{19}	±1,230	∓704	∓ 704	±1,407	XeF_4
				Xe^{129}	±1,605	∓381	∓ 381	± 763	
CO_2^-	2.0032	1.9975	2.0014	C^{13}	+ 468	− 32	− 46	+ 78	$NaHCO_2$
NO_2	2.006178	1.991015	2.00199	N^{14}	+ 146.53	− 18.73	− 19.77	+ 38.50	Microwave spectrum
ClO_2	2.0036	2.0183	2.0088	Cl^{35}	+ 42	+162	− 86	− 76	$KClO_4$
F_3^{--}	–	–	–	F^{19}	+1,455	−740	+1,691	− 951	LiF
				$2F^{19}$	+ 561	−337	+ 499	− 163	
CO_3^-	2.0086	2.0184	2.0066	C^{13}	− 31	+ 3	+ 3	− 7	$KHCO_3$
SO_3^-	2.004	2.004	2.004	S^{33}	+ 353	− 37	− 39	+ 75	$NH_3^+SO_3^-$
ClO_3^-	2.008	2.008	2.007	Cl^{35}	+ 358	− 35	− 35	+ 71	$NH_4^+ClO_4^-$
HPO_2^-	2.0019	2.0035	2.0037	P^{31}	+1,385	+314	− 157	− 157	$NH_4^+H_2PO_2^-$
				H^1	+ 230	− 3	+ 8	− 6	

[a]For diatomic radicals, the z axis is parallel to the bond. For XO_2, z bisects the bond angle and x is perpendicular to the molecular plane. For XO_3, z is the vertical symmetry axis. HPO_2^-, SO_3^-, and ClO_3^- are pyramidal.

TABLE 6-2

Hyperfine Characteristics of Typical Ions and Radicals in the Liquid Phase[B-3]

Paramagnetic Species	Method of Production	Solvent	Number of Lines	Linewidth mG	Hf coupling coefficients, G Aα	Aβ	Aγ	Ref.
Benzene anion	Reduction with K	DME	7	700	3.715			a
Naphthalene anion	Reduction with K	DME	25	150	4.84	1.83		a
Diphenyl anion	Reduction with K	THF	45	150	5.30	0.43	2.65	a
Pyrazine anion	Electrochemical	Acetonitrile	25	200	7.18(N)**	2.63		a
Phenazine anion	Electrochemical	Acetonitrile	77	125	5.15(N)	1.80	1.54	a
1,3-Bisdipheny-leneallyl		CS_2	>400	30	13.2	1.92, 0.48, 0.36***	1.86	b
Wursters blue			>240	150	7.02(N)	6.74	1.98	b
Methyl radical	Irradiation e^-	Liquid methane	4	290	23.04			c
Ethyl radical	Irradiation e^-	Liquid ethane	12	Between 130 and 310	22.38	26.87		c
Propyl radical	Irradiation e^-	Liquid propane	9	Between 130 and 310	22.1	33.2		c
Cyclopentyl radical	Irradiation e^-	Liquid cyclopentane	10	Between 130 and 310	21.48	35.16		c
Cyclohexyl radical	Irradiation e^-	Liquid cyclohexane	6	Between 130 and 310	21.0	46.0		c
Cycloheptyl radical	Irradiation e^-	Liquid cycloheptane	10	Between 130 and 310	21.79	24.69		c
Cyclooctyl radical	Irradiation e^-	Cyclooctane, 195°K	11	6,000	21.0			c
	Irradiation e^-	Benzene* 233°K	12		48.0	23.0–36.0		c

*Benzene irradiated at 193°K and annealed to 233°K to increase resolution.
**Splitting due to interaction with nitrogen nucleus.
***Five coupling coefficients were observed in this radical.

REFERENCES:

a. **Henning, J. C. M.,** *J. Chem. Phys.*, 44, 2139, 1966.
b. **Hausser, K. H.,** *Proc. 10th Colloquium Spectroscopicum Internationale, University of Maryland, 1962,* Spartan Books, Washington, D.C., 1963.
c. **Fessenden, R. W. and Schuler, R. H.,** *J. Chem. Phys.*, 39, 2147, 1963.

TABLE 6-3

Hyperfine Splittings and Spin Distributions in some Cyclic Polyene Radicals C_nH_n [B-14]

Radical	Spin Density p_π	Hyperfine Splitting a_H	Effective Value of Q
CH_3	1	−23.04	−23.04
C_5H_5	1/5	− 5.98	−29.9
$C_6H_6^-$	1/6	− 3.75	−22.5
C_7H_7	1/7	− 3.91	−27.4
$C_8H_8^-$	1/8	− 3.21	−25.7

TABLE 6-4

Variation in g Values for DPPH at Room Temperature[B-3]

Sample	g Value	Ref.
Single crystal	2.0035–2.0041	R-91
Single crystal	2.0028–2.0038	B-28
Single crystal	2.0030–2.0040	B-4
Polycrystalline	2.0036 ± 0.0003	B-28
Polycrystalline	2.0036	B-42

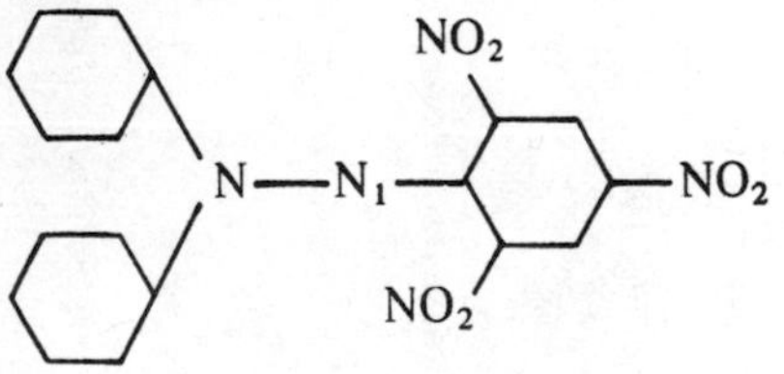

FIGURE 6-1. DPPH (α,α′-diphenyl-β-picrylhydrazyl).

TABLE 6-5

Linewidth in DPPH Samples Crystallized from Various Solvents[B-4]

	ΔH, G		
	v = 300 MHz		v = 9400 MHz
Solvent	295°K	90°K	295°K
Benzene	6.8	4.6	4.7
Toluene	2.9	2.6	2.6
Xylene (mixture)	2.5	2.2	2.3
Pyridine	5.3	5.0	5.0
Bromoform	2.2	2.5	2.5
Carbon tetrachloride	1.9	2.7	2.3
Chloroform	1.7	2.1	2.0
Carbon disulfide	1.3	1.3	1.5

TABLE 6-6

Representative Deep Impurity Centers in Semiconductor Host Crystals[B-3]

Host	Impurity	Nuclear Spin	Hf Lines Reported	A 10^{-4} cm^{-1}	g	Splitting G	Temperature °K	H_o ∥ to	Ref.
Si	$^{51}V^{2+}$	7/2	8	−42.10	1.9892	45.3	1.3		a
Si	$^{53}Cr^{+}$	3/2	4	+10.67	1.9978	11.4	20.4		a
Si	$^{55}Mn^{-}$	5/2	6	−71.28	2.0104	76.0	20.4		a
Si	$^{55}Mn^{2+}$	5/2		−53.47	2.0066				a
Si	$^{55}Mn^{0}$	5/2		12.8	2.0063				a
Si	$^{57}Fe^{0}$	1/2	1	6.98	2.0699				a
Si	$^{32}S^{+}$	1/2	1						
Si	$^{33}S^{+}$	3/2	4	104±0.2	2.0054 ±0.0002	114.0			b
Si	$^{105}Pd^{-}$	5/2		12.2	1.9190		<20.0	[$\bar{1}$10]	c
				6.0	2.0544			[001]	
				~36.0	1.9715			[110]	
Si	$^{195}Pt^{-}$	1/2		184.2	1.4266		<12.0	[$\bar{1}$10] or [$\bar{1}$10]	c
				127.0	2.0789			[001]	
				147.0	1.3867			[110] or [I10]	
Si	^{195}Pt	1/2		156.0	2.021		<20.0	∥ to [111]	c
				62.0	2.126			⊥ to [111]	
Ge	^{61}Ni	3/2	4	A_1 = 10.3	g_1 = 2.1128				d
				A_2 ⩽ 1.6	g_2 = 2.0294				
				A_3 = 12.2	g_3 = 2.0176				
SiC	^{11}B	3/2	4	A_1 = 1.7	$g_{\parallel}$ = 2.0020		21.0	Site I	e
				A_2 = 1.3	$g_{\perp}$ = 2.0068				
SiC	^{11}B	3/2	4	2.1	$g_{\parallel}$ = 2.0056		21.0	Site II	e
					$g_{\perp}$ = 2.003				
SiC	^{11}B	3/2	4	1.7	$g_{\parallel}$ = 2.0062	~1.8	21.0	Site III	e
					$g_{\perp}$ = 2.005				
SiC	^{14}N	1	3	11.08	$g_{\parallel}$ = 2.0036	12.0	20.4		e
					$g_{\perp}$ = 2.0030				
				11.20	$g_{\parallel}$ = 2.0040				
					$g_{\perp}$ = 2.0026				
C (diamond)	^{14}N	1	3		2.0024 ±0.0005	33.6			f

REFERENCES:

a. Woodbury, H. H. and Ludwig, G. W., *Phys. Rev.*, 117, 102, 1960.
b. Ludwig, G. W., *Phys. Rev.*, 137, A1520, 1965.
c. Woodbury, H. H. and Ludwig, G. W., *Phys. Rev.*, 126, 466, 1962.
d. Ludwig, G. W. and Woodbury, H. H., *Phys. Rev.*, 113, 1014, 1959.
e. Woodbury, H. H. and Ludwig, G. W., *Phys. Rev.*, 124, 1083, 1961.
f. Smith, W. V., Sorokin, P. P., Gelles, I. L., and Lasher, G. J., *Phys. Rev.*, 115, 1546, 1959.

TABLE 6-7

Examples of Spin Centers and ESR Parameters Studied in Semiconductors[B-3]

Host Crystal	Donor or Acceptor: Element	Donor or Acceptor: Concentration	Spin center or impurity: Treatment	Spin center or impurity: Studied	Spin center or impurity: Concentration per cm^3	Temperature °K	Observed Parameters	Mode	Ref.
Silicon	P	$10^{15}-10^{16}$	Strained, irradiated (e)	Si-A center	$\sim10^{18}$	20 and 77	g, hfs, τ	Dispersion	a
Silicon	Sb, P, As	10^{16}	Strained	Donors		1.25	Δg, Ts	Dispersion	b
Silicon	P	$10^{15}-10^{16}$	Strained, irradiated (e)	Si-E center		4.2–155	hfs, g, τ	Dispersion and ENDOR	a
Silicon	B, Al, Ga, I		Strained, irradiated (e)	Si-G6 Si-G7		40–110	hfs, g, τ	Dispersion	a
Silicon	B, P	$\sim2 \times 10^{16}$ (B) $\sim2 \times 10^{15}$ to 5×10^{16} (P)	Irradiated (e)	Si-G6 formerly Si-A	$\sim10^{15}$	20.4	hfs, g	Dispersion	a
Silicon	B, P	$\sim10^{16}$	Transition metals diffused in at 1,250°C	$V^{2+}Cr^{+}Mn^{-}$ $Mn^{2+}Fe^{0}$	$10^{15}-10^{16}$	1.3 and 20.4	hfs, g	ENDOR	c
Silicon			Metals diffused in at 1,300°C	Pd and Pt	$1-4 \times 10^{16}$	Up to 20	hfs, g	ENDOR	c
Silicon	P, As, Sb	5×10^{16} – 6×10^{18}	Strained		4.2		hfs, g	Dispersion	d,e
Silicon	P	3×10^{6} – 10^{17}			12 to 4		hfs, τ		b
Silicon	^{121}Sb, ^{123}Sb	5×10^{6}			1.2		hfs, g	ENDOR	b
Silicon	B, As	10^{15} As, residual B	Neutron irradiated, $10^{18}-10^{19}$ n/cm^2	N(II, III) IX, (I, I′) (V, VI), (VII, VIII)	300, 77, 4.2		hfs, g	Absorption	f
Silicon	P	6×10^{16} and 8×10^{16}			1.3		hfs	ENDOR	d
Germanium	P, As	8×10^{14} – 5×10^{15}			1.3		hfs, ΔH, g		b
SiC				S, N, B, Ni	$5 \times 10^{17}-10^{18}$	78	g, ΔH, hfs		g
SiC				B N	5×10^{17} 3×10^{16}	14 and 20.4	hfs, g	ENDOR	c c

TABLE 6-7 (Continued)

REFERENCES:

a. **Watkins, G. D. and Corbett, J. W.,** *Phys. Rev.,* 121, 1001, 1961; 134, A1359, 1964; 138, A555, 1965.
b. **Feher, G.,** et al., *Phys. Rev.,* 100, 1784, 1955; 109, 1172, 1958; 114, 1219, 1245, 1959; 124, 1068, 1961; *Phys. Rev. Lett.,* 3, 25, 1959.
c. **Woodbury, H. H. and Ludwig, G. W.,** *Phys. Rev.,* 124, 1083, 1961; 126, 466, 1962; Solid State Physics, Vol. 13, Academic Press, New York, 1962, 223.
d. **Jerome, D. and Winter, J. M.,** *Phys. Rev.,* 134, A1001, 1964.
e. **Fletcher, R. C.,** et al., *Phys. Rev.,* 94, 1392, 1954; 95, 844, 1954.
f. **Jung, W. and Newell, G. S.,** *Phys. Rev.,* 132, 648, 1963.
g. **Willenbrock, F. K. and Bloembergen, N.,** *Phys. Rev.,* 91, 1281, 1953.

TABLE 6-8

Parameters of Typical Donor-impurity Atoms in Silicon at 1.25°K[B-31]

Donor Impurity	Ionization Energy (eV)	g−gC.E.† (x10⁴)	Nuclear Spin I	a (MHz)	$\|\Psi(o)\|^2$ ($\times 10^{24}$ cm^{-3}) Experiment	Theory	Width of Hyperfine Components (gauss)
Sb^{121}	0.043	−1.7 ± 1	5/2	186.802 ± 0.005	1.18		2.3
Sb^{123}	0.043		7/2	101.516 ± 0.004	1.18		
P^{31}	0.045	−2.5 ± 1	1/2	117.53 ± 0.02	0.43	0.4	2.5
As^{75}	0.054	−3.8 ± 1	3/2	198.366 ± 0.02	1.73		2.9
As^{76}	0.054			198.35 ± 0.02	1.73		
Bi^{209}	0.071	+15.0 ± 1	9/2	1,475.5 ± 0.1	14.0		4.5

† $g_{C.E.}$ (conduction electrons) = 1.99875 + 0.00010.
g_c (free electrons) = 2.00229 ± 0.000026.

TABLE 6-9

Representative Results on Shallow Donor Centers in Germanium[B-31]

Donor Impurity	Optical Ionization Energy (eV)	g_0	$g_{\parallel}$	$g_{\perp}$	(ΔH) Ge^{73} (gauss)	Total h.f.s. (gauss)	$\lvert\Psi(o)\rvert^2$ ($\times 10^{24}$ cm^{-3})	Valley-orbit Splitting E_{13} (eV)	Wave Function Spread a_o* (Å) Experiment	Wave Function Spread a_o* (Å) Theory	Energy of Triplet State below Conduction Band (eV)
Phosphorus	0.0125	1.5631 ±0.0002	0.83 ±0.05	1.93 ±0.02	10.0 ± 1	21 ± 1	0.17	0.0029	31.8	38.5	0.0096
Arsenic	0.0145	1.5700 ±0.0002	0.87 ±0.04	1.92 ±0.02	11.0 ± 1	107 ± 3	0.69	0.0042	29.8	36.8	0.0103
Bismuth	0.0123	1.5671 ±0.0004			10.0 ± 1	944 ± 5	2.15	0.0028	31.8	39.0	0.0095
Theoretical Value		1.70	0.98	2.07							0.0092

TABLE 6-10

Representative Experimental Results for Localized Centers in Group III-V Compounds[B-31]

Impurity	Temperature (°K)	g	δg	Cubic Field Splitting Parameter a (x10^4 cm^{-1})	Line Width ΔH (gauss)	Hyperfine Interaction Constant A (gauss)
Iron in gallium arsenide	1.3	2.0462 ∓0.0006	+0.044	+339.7 ± 0.3	54.0 ± 2	10.0 approx.
	77	2.0453 ±0.0008	+0.043	+342.2 ± 0.5		
	77	2.0424 ±0.0004	+0.040	+330.0 ± 2		
	77	2.05	+0.05	+330.0 approx.	51.6	
Iron in indium arsenide	1.3	2.035 ±0.0002	+0.033	+421.0 ± 1	125.0 ± 3[100] 132.0 ± 3[111]	
Iron in gallium phosphide	10	2.025	+0.023	+390.0		
Manganese in gallium arsenide	77	2.004	+0.002	3.3	56.0 approx.	56.0 approx.
Nickel in gallium arsenide	1.3	2.106 ±0.008	+0.104			

TABLE 6-11

ESR Characteristics of Typical Color Centers[B-3]

Crystal	Color Centers per cm^3	Temperature °K	g Value	ΔH, G	T_1,* sec	Number of Resolved hf Lines	Hf Splitting G	Ref.
LiF		294	1.999 ± 0.001	65.0				a
LiF**		296	2.002 ± 0.001	110.0				a
LiF**		1.3	2.0005 ± 0.0006					b
LiF**			2.008 ± 0.001	77.0				B-4
				160.0				
LiF**			1.999	65.0				c
LiCl	~10^{18}	1.3	1.9980 ± 0.0008	57.2	9.2			b
NaF			2.0021 ± 0.0001					B-4
NaF		1.3	2.0011 ± 0.0008	220.0		19	37.7	b
NaCl		77	1.987	162.0				c
NaCl	~10^{18}	1.3		142.0	<3.0			b
NaBr	>5 x 10^{17}	1.3	1.994 ± 0.005		43.0			b
KCl	5 x 10^{16}	1.3	1.9955 ± 0.0014	49.5	216.0			b
KCl	2 x 10^{17}	1.3	1.9955 ± 0.0014	49.5	72.0			b
KCl	10^{18}	1.3	1.9955 ± 0.0014	49.5	<3.0			b
KCl			1.996 ± 0.001	45.0				d
KCl	8 x 10^{16}	2			~450.0			e
KBr	>10^{18}	1.3	1.986 ± 0.01		<1.0			b
KBr		77	1.980	146.0				c
KI			1.971 ± 0.001	200.0				B-4
^{6}LiH		78	2.004 ± 0.001	14.3				f
^{7}LiH		78		30.6				f
^{7}LiD		78		28.5				f
^{6}LiD				10.1				f

*Relaxation time by rapid passage inversion-recovery methods.
**Produced by proton bombardment.

REFERENCES:

a. **Jen, C. K. and Lord, N. W.,** *Phys. Rev.,* 96, 1150, 1954.
b. **Holton, W. C. and Blum, H.,** *Phys. Rev.,* 125, 89, 1962.
c. **Portis, A. M.,** *Phys. Rev.,* 91, 1071, 1953.
d. **Moran, P. R., Christensen, S. H., and Silsbee, R. H.,** *Phys. Rev.,* 124, 442, 1961.
e. **Ovenall, D. W. and Whiffen, D. H.,** *Mol. Phys.,* 4, 135, 1961.
f. **Lewis, W. B. and Pretzel, F. E.,** *J. Phys. Chem. Solids,* 19, 139, 1961.

TABLE 6-12

Values for Typical F-Centers and F_2-Centers in Powders[B-3]

Powder	g (F-center)	g (F_2-center)
MgO	2.0023	2.0008
CaO	2.0001	1.9995
SrO	1.9846	1.982
BaO	1.936	
MgS	2.0062	2.0038
CaS	2.0033	
SrS	2.0036	2.0023
BaS	1.9641	
MgSe	2.0035	1.9981
CaSe	2.003	
SrSe	2.003	1.990
BaSe	1.967	

TABLE 6-13

Shift in g-Factors for Conduction Electrons in Several Metals[B-3]

Metal	Sample Case	Preparation Technique	Method*	$\Delta g \times 10^{-4}$ Experimental	$\Delta g \times 10^{-4}$ Calculated a	Frequency kMHz	Ref.
Li	Thin	Evaporated Li–NH_3 and dispersed Li in mineral oil	ν and H	0.02 ± 0.02 0.02 ± 0.02	–	9.5	b
Na	Thick	Bulk metal	DPPH	–8 ± 2	–7	9.5	c
Na	Thin	Decomposed sodium azide	ν and H	–6 ± 2	–7	9.1	d
K	Thin	Irradiated KN_3	ν and H	–41 ± 5	14–25	9.1	e
Cs	Thin	Cs–NH_3	DPPH	~700	100–300	0.3	f
Be	–	–	DPPH	+9 ± 1	–	9.5	c

*v and H = independent measurements of v and H; DPPH = by comparison to DPPH.

REFERENCES:

a. **Bienstock, A. and Brooks, H.,** *Phys. Rev.,* 136, A784, 1964.
b. **Pressley, R. J. and Berk, H. L.,** *Bull. Am. Phys. Soc.,* 8, 345, 1963.
c. **Feher, G. and Kip, A. F.,** *Phys. Rev.,* 98, 337, 1955.
d. **King, G. J., Miller, B. S., Carlson, F. F., and McMillan, R. C.,** *J. Chem. Phys.,* 32, 940, 1960.
e. **McMillan, R. C.,** *J. Phys. Chem. Solids,* 25, 773, 1964.
f. **Levy, R. A.,** *Phys. Rev.,* 102, 31, 1956.

D. Irradiation

This section consists of tables of characteristic properties of irradiation sources, typical compounds studied by irradiation, and results found with some low temperature chars. (Tables 6-14 to 6-17).

TABLE 6-14

Typical Energies per Photon or per Particle of Several Types of Irradiation Sources[B-42]

Radiation	Energy kcal/mol	Energy eV	Typical Source
γ-rays	10^7–10^9	10^6–10^8	^{60}Co
X-rays	10^5–10^6	40–40,000	X-ray tube
Ultraviolet	70–350	3.2–15	Arc lamp
Visible	35–70	1.6–3.2	Incandescent lamp
Infrared	1–35	0.04–1.6	Incandescent lamp
Electrons	~3 x 10^7	~1 x 10^6	Van de Graaff
Protons	~5 x 10^8	~2 x 10^7	Cyclotron
Thermal neutrons	~0.6	~0.025	Nuclear reactor
Fast neutrons	~10^8	~4 x 10^6	Nuclear reactor
α-particles	~5 x 10^8	~2 x 10^7	Cyclotron

TABLE 6-15

Typical Energies Associated with Several Molecular and Lattice Characteristics[B-42]

System	Energy kcal/mol	Energy eV	Comments
Bonding energy per nucleon in nucleus	2 x 10^8	8 x 10^6	Nuclear excited states are in this energy range
Activation energy of diffusion in ionic lattice	20	1	
Lattice energy of ionic solid	~200	~8	Approximate energy to completely remove atom from ionic lattice
F center energy in alkali halide lattice	50–100	2–4	From optical spectra
Covalent bond energy	50–100	2–4	Organic compounds
Activation energy of thermal conductivity	20–70	1–3	Intrinsic } Alkali halide lattice defects
	7–20	0.3–0.9	Extrinsic } Alkali halide lattice defects
Electronic transitions of organic molecules	50–150	2–6	
Characteristic group vibrational frequencies	1–10	0.04–0.4	Vibrational frequencies of organic chemical groups
Lattice vibrations of ionic solid	0.25	10^{-2}	
Rotations of diatomic molecules	10^{-3}–10^{-2}	10^{-4}–10^{-3}	Region of microwave spectroscopy

TABLE 6-16

Typical Irradiation Conditions[B-3]

Material	Source	Dose Rate	Total Dose	Temperature °K	Ref.
H_2O, D_2O, H_2S, HF, HCl, H_2, CH_4, NaH, LiH, CD_4 in N_2	^{60}Co	4,000 R/min	10^6 R	4.2	a
Sodium formate	Spent fuel elements, approx. 1 MeV	Not given	10^6–5 x 10^6 rads	300	b
$Na_2HPO_3 5H_2O$	^{60}Co	1,900 curies	6.5 x 10^6 rads	77	c
Acetonitrile	^{60}Co	26.8 x 10^{19} eV/g-hr	1, 2, 4, 6 hr	78	B-3
	^{60}Co, 2,000 curies	3 x 10^6 rads/hr		195	B-3
Nylon	^{60}Co, 2,000 curies	6 x 10^5 rads/hr	10^7 rads	77	d
Polyethylene	2 MeV electrons	3 x 10^3–3 x 10^6 rads/s	Simultaneous IRR and EPR measurements	123–423	e
Saturated hydrocarbons, alcohol, aromatic compounds	2 MeV electrons	2 x 10^4–10^6 rads/s	2 x 10^6–10^8 rads		f
Aqueous solutions of sulfur compounds	220 kV x-rays	4,000 R/min	4.15 x 10^5 R	77	B-3
Amino acids	14.3 MeV electrons 15 MeV electron linear accelerator	130,000 rads/s	10^6–2 x 10^8 rads		g
Alkyl halides	^{60}Co, 1,750 curies	7 x 10^{17} eV/ml-min	10^{20} eV/ml	77	h
H_2SO_4, $HClO_4$, H_3PO_4	^{60}Co, 1,000 curies	3,000 R/min	Very rough, ~10^7 R	77	i
2,2-Polystyrene, 2,3-polyethylene, 2,4-polytetrafluoroethylene.	200 kV x-rays	2,000 R/min 8,000 R/min	10^7 R	300, 77	j
CH_4, H_2, D_2, N_2 in Xe, A, Ne, H_2	^{60} Co, 2,000 curies	0.68 x 10^6 R/hr	2–60 x 10^6 R	4.2	k
T_2O + alcohols	Tritium		4 x 10^{19} eV/ml	77	l
Alcohols, ethers, aromatic esters, ketones	2 MeV electrons 2 MeV x-rays 50 kV x-rays	~0.1 W	180 W sec	77 4.2	m

REFERENCES:

a. **Rexroad, H. M. and Gordy, W.,** *Phys. Rev.*, 125, 242, 1962.
b. **Ovenall, D. W. and Whiffen, D. H.,** *Mol. Phys.*, 4, 135, 1961.
c. **Atkins, P. W., Keen, N., and Symons, M. C. R.,** *J. Chem. Soc.*, p. 250, 1963.
d. **Graves, C. T. and Ormerod, M. G.,** *Polymer*, 4, 81, 1963.
e. **Molin, Y. N. et al.,** *Pribory Tekh. Eksp.*, 6, 73, 1960.
f. **Voevodskii, V. V. and Molin, Y. N.,** *Radiat. Res.*, 17, 366, 1962.
g. **Rotblat, J. and Simmons, J. A.,** *Phys. Med. Biol.*, 7, 489, 1963.
h. **Ayscough, P. B. and Thomson, C.,** *Trans Faraday Soc.*, 58, 1477, 1962.
i. **Livingston, R., Zeldes, H., and Taylor, E. H.,** *Disc. Faraday Soc.*, 19, 166, 1955.
j. **Schneider, E. E.,** *Disc. Faraday Soc.*, 19, 158, 1955.
k. **Wall, L. A., Brown, D. W., and Florin, R. E.,** *J. Phys. Chem.*, 63, 1762, 1959.
l. **Kroh, J. and Spinks, J. W. T.,** *J. Chem. Phys.*, 35, 760, 1961.
m. **Alger, R. S., Anderson, T. H., and Webb, L. A.,** *J. Chem. Phys.*, 30, 695, 1959.

TABLE 6-17

Production and Characteristics of Radicals in some Low-Temperature Chars[B-3]

Material Charred	g Value	ΔH, G	Temperature for Peak Radical Production, °C	Ref.
Glucose and other sugars	2.0020 ± 0.0003	8.0 ± 2	550	a
Deposits from luminous flames	2.0020 ± 0.0003	8.0 ± 2	550	a
Natural or artificial cellulose	2.0020 ± 0.0003	8.0 ± 2	550	a
Anthracene and glycerine	2.0020 ± 0.0003	8.0 ± 2	550	a
Vegetable root and other complex natural organic materials	2.0020 ± 0.0003	8.0 ± 2	550	a
Charcoals formed below 600°C	2.0020 ± 0.0003	8.0 ± 2	550	a
Coals and coal derivatives formed below 600°C	2.0020 ± 0.0003	8.0 ± 2	550	a
Charcoals from pinewood and cocoanut				b
Saccharose and glucose				b
Pitches from crude oil distillation				b
Naphthalene	2.0024 ± 0.0003	1.0	670	c
Anthracene	2.0024 ± 0.0030	1.5	640	c
Decalin	2.0024 ± 0.0003	1.5	600	c
Secondary butyl alcohol	2.0024 ± 0.0003	0.5	670	c
Anthracite coal*				b
Fossilized plants*	2.002			d
Peats*	2.002			d
Lignites*	2.002			d
Coals*	2.002			d
Carbonized coals	2.0030 ± 0.0003	7.0 ± 1	550	e
Donetz coal*	2.007 ± 0.001			f

*Radicals exist in these natural materials without heat treatment.

REFERENCES:

a. **Bennett, J. E., Ingram, D. J. E., and Tapley, J. G.,** *J. Chem. Phys.,* 23, 215, 1955.
b. **Uebersfeld, J., Étienne, A., and Combrisson, J.,** *Nature,* 174, 614, 1954.
c. **Mangiaracina, R. and Mrozowski, S.,** *Proc. 5th Carbon. Conf.,* 2, 1963.
d. **Duchesne, J., Depireux, J., and van der Kaa, J. M.,** *Geochim. Cosmochim. Acta,* 23, 209, 1961.
e. **Ingram, D. J. E. et al.,** *Nature,* 174, 797, 1954.
f. **Vescial, F., Van der Ven, N. S., and Schumacher, R. T.,** *Phys. Rev.,* 134, A1286, 1964.

VII. RELAXATION

A. Introduction

This section begins with a discussion of the ordinary and modified Bloch equations followed by subsections on exchange and motional effects. Then a brief summary of relaxation in solids is followed by summaries of saturation and pulse methods for measuring relaxation times.

B. Bloch Equations

The Bloch equations

$$\frac{d\vec{M}}{dt} = \gamma\vec{M}\times\vec{H} - \frac{M_x\hat{i} + M_y\hat{j}}{T_2} - \frac{M_z - M_o}{T_1}\hat{k} \quad (7\text{-}1)$$

have the solutions

$$\chi' = \frac{\frac{1}{2}\chi_o T_2^2\omega_o(\omega - \omega_o)}{1 + (\omega - \omega_o)^2T_2^2 + H_1^2\gamma^2T_1^2T_2} \quad (7\text{-}2)$$

$$\chi'' = \frac{\frac{1}{2}\chi_o T_2\omega_o}{1 + (\omega - \omega_o)^2T_2^2 + H_1^2\gamma^2T_1T_2} \quad (7\text{-}3)$$

where

$$\chi_o = M_o/H_o$$

$$\omega_o = \gamma H_o \quad (7\text{-}4)$$

$$\chi = \chi' - j\chi''$$

$$T_2 = \frac{2}{\Delta\omega_{\frac{1}{2}}} = \frac{2}{\gamma\Delta H_{\frac{1}{2}}} .$$

C. Modified Bloch Equations

For two spins (½, ½), several coupled or modified Bloch equations have been proposed (B-1, B-43). Using the notation

$$\gamma_A H = \omega_o + \tfrac{1}{2}\delta\omega, \qquad \gamma_B H = \omega_o - \tfrac{1}{2}\delta\omega \quad (7\text{-}5)$$

$$h_o = H_o - (\omega/\gamma), \qquad \gamma = \tfrac{1}{2}(\gamma_A + \gamma_B) \quad (7\text{-}6)$$

the modified Bloch equations assume the form

$$dM_x/dt = M_y(\gamma h_o + \delta\omega) - M_x/T_2$$

$$dM_y/dt = M_z\gamma H_1 - M_x(\gamma h_o + \delta\omega) - M_y/T_2 \quad (7\text{-}7)$$

$$dM_z/dt = - M_y\gamma H_1 - (M_z - M_o)/T_1$$

Gutowsky, McCall, and Slichter defined

$$G_\pm = M_x \pm iM_y \quad (7\text{-}8)$$

and derived the expression

$$\langle G\rangle_{av} = \langle G_+\rangle_{av} + \langle G_-\rangle_{av}$$

$$= \frac{\gamma H_1M_o\tau\{2 + [1/T_2 + i(\omega-\omega_o)]\tau\}}{[1/\tau+i(\omega-\omega_o + \frac{1}{2}\delta\omega)][1/\tau+i(\omega-\omega_o - \frac{1}{2}\delta\omega)]-1} \quad (7\text{-}9)$$

When the lifetime τ is very large, we have

$$\langle G\rangle_{av} = \tfrac{1}{2}\gamma H_1M_o\left\{\frac{1}{1/T_2+i(\gamma h_o+\frac{1}{2}\delta\omega)} + \frac{1}{1/T_2+i(\gamma h_o-\frac{1}{2}\delta\omega)}\right\} \quad (7\text{-}10)$$

which corresponds to two lines separated by the frequency interval $\delta\omega$. If τ is very small, then Equation 7-9 reduces to

$$\langle G\rangle_{av} = \frac{-\gamma H_1M_o}{1/T_2 + i\gamma h_o} \quad (7\text{-}11)$$

which represents a single line with double the intensity of each of the other two.

Anderson derived the following expression:

$$\chi''(\omega) = 2\chi_o\omega_o\left[\frac{2\omega_{ex} + \omega(x^2-1)^{-\frac{1}{2}}}{(\omega+\omega_{ex}(x^2-1)^{-\frac{1}{2}})^2 + \omega_{ex}^2} + \frac{2\omega_{ex} - \omega(x^2-1)^{-\frac{1}{2}}}{(\omega-\omega_{ex}(x^2-1)^{\frac{1}{2}})^2 + \omega_{ex}^2}\right] \quad (7\text{-}12)$$

where ω_{ex} is the exchange frequency and $x = \delta\omega/2\omega_{ex}$.

Gutowsky and Holm derived an equation with the lifetimes $\tau_\pm$ and populations $p_\pm$ of the two states,

$$M = \frac{i\gamma H_1M_o[(\tau_++\tau_-) + \tau_+\tau_-(\alpha_+p_-+\alpha_-p_+)]}{(1+\alpha_+\tau_+)(1+\alpha_-\tau_-) - 1} \quad (7\text{-}13)$$

where

$$\alpha_\pm = \frac{1}{T_2} - i(\omega - \omega_o \pm \tfrac{1}{2}\delta\omega) \quad . \quad (7\text{-}14)$$

McConnell derived the expression

$$G = \frac{-i\gamma H_1M_o\tau\{2 \pm [1/T_2 - i(\omega-\omega_o)]\tau\}}{\tau^2(1+\alpha_+\tau)(1+\alpha_-\tau) - 1} \quad (7\text{-}15)$$

which is identical with Equation 7-13 for two sites having equal populations ($p_\pm = ½$) and equal lifetimes ($\tau_+ = \tau_- = \tau$).

Sack derived the expression

$$\chi(\omega) \approx \frac{2p\chi_o\omega_o\delta\omega^2}{(\omega-\omega_o + \tfrac{1}{2}\delta\omega)^2(\omega-\omega_o - \tfrac{1}{2}\delta\omega)^2 + 4p^2(\omega-\omega_o)^2} \qquad (7\text{-}16)$$

where p is the transition probability.

D. Exchange

For spin 1/2 the Anderson exchange theory gives the eigenvalues λ:

$$\lambda = i\Delta\omega + P \qquad (7\text{-}17)$$

$$= i\omega_e + \omega_o \pm\sqrt{\tfrac{1}{4}A^2 - \omega_e^2} \qquad (7\text{-}18)$$

where the real part P is the line position and the imaginary part $\Delta\omega$ is the width, ω_o is the Larmor frequency, ω_e is the exchange frequency, and A is the hyperfine interaction frequency (or chemical shift in NMR studies). For $½A > \omega_e$ one has

$$\Delta\omega = \omega_e \qquad (7\text{-}19)$$

$$P \approx \omega_o \pm [\tfrac{1}{2}A - (\omega_e^2/A)] \qquad (7\text{-}20)$$

and for $½A < \omega_e$ one has

$$\Delta\omega \approx A^2/8\omega_e \qquad (7\text{-}21)$$

$$P = \omega_o \quad . \qquad (7\text{-}22)$$

Figures 7-1 to 7-3 illustrate these results. The analytical lineshape is

$$Y(\omega-\omega_o) = \frac{2\omega_e A^2}{(\omega-\omega_o)^4 + 2(\omega-\omega_o)^2(2\omega_e^2 - \tfrac{1}{4}A^2) + (\tfrac{1}{2}A)^4} \qquad (7\text{-}23)$$

with the limiting cases

$$Y(\omega-\omega_o) \approx \frac{2\omega_e}{(\omega-\omega_o \pm \tfrac{1}{2}A)^2 + \omega_e^2} \qquad \omega_e << \tfrac{1}{2}A \qquad (7\text{-}24)$$

which corresponds to Lorentzian lines at $\omega = \omega_o \pm A$, and

$$Y(\omega-\omega_o) = \frac{A^2/2\omega_e}{(\omega-\omega_o)^2 + (A^2/8\omega_e)^2} \qquad \omega_e >> \tfrac{1}{2}A \qquad (7\text{-}25)$$

which is a singlet of width $A^2/8\,\omega_e$.

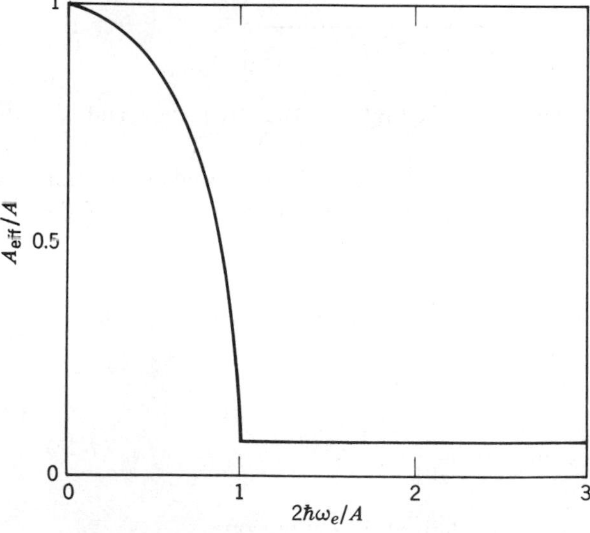

FIGURE 7-1. Variation of the effective hyperfine splitting A_{eff} on the exchange frequency ω_e. Both the abscissa and ordinate are normalized relative to the true hyperfine coupling constant A.[R-2, B-44]

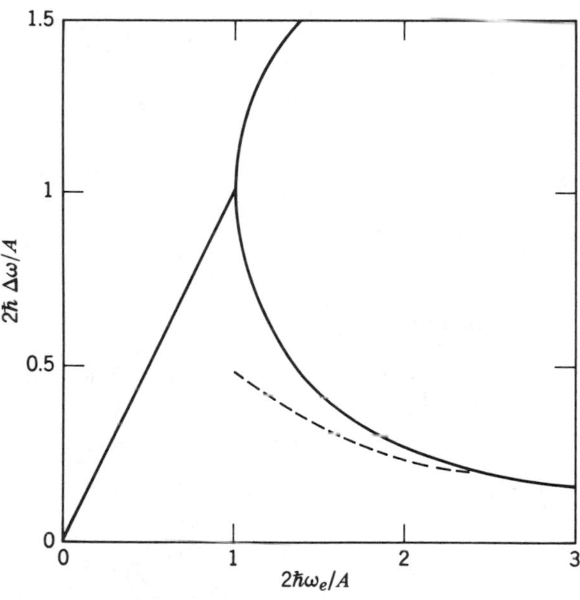

FIGURE 7-2. Dependence of the linewidth $\Delta\omega$ on the exchange frequency ω_e for the case of zero intrinsic linewidth ($\Delta\omega_o = 0$). Both the ordinate and the abscissa are normalized relative to the true hyperfine coupling constant A. The dotted line corresponds to the asymptotic exchange narrowing formula (Equation 7-21).[R-2, B-44]

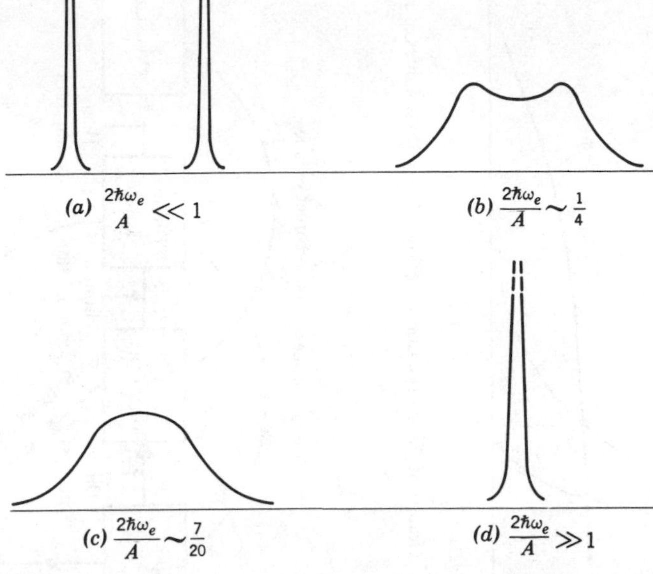

FIGURE 7-3. Hyperfine doublet (A) in the absence of exchange, (B) with weak exchange, (C) with moderate exchange, and (D) with strong exchange.[R-2, B-44]

E. Motional Effects on Relaxation

When relaxation is associated with motion characterized by a correlation time τ_c, the spin lattice and spin-spin relaxation times are given by expressions of the type[B-14,B-43]

$$\frac{1}{T_1} = A\left[\frac{\tau_c}{1 + \omega_o^2\tau_c^2}\right] \qquad \frac{1}{T_2} = B\tau_c + C\left[\frac{\tau_c}{1 + \omega_o^2\tau_c^2}\right] \tag{7-26}$$

and sometimes additional terms such as $4D\tau_c/(1 + 4\omega_o^2\tau_c^2)$ are also present. Rapid motion ($\omega_o\tau_c \ll 1$) renders $T_1 \sim T_2$, and slow motion ($\omega_o\tau_c \gg$) renders $T_1 \gg T_2$, as shown in Figure 7-4. The correlation function $\tau_c/(1 + \omega_o^2\tau_c^2)$ is shown in Figure 7-5 for three values of τ_c. The constants A, B, and C depend on the interaction which averages out the particular rigid lattice relaxation mechanism.

F. Relaxation in Solids

Spin systems relax via various paths of the type shown in Figure 7-6. Tables 7-1 and 7-2 give general data on temperature and field dependences of relaxation times. Some typical experimental data are given in Tables 7-3 and 7-4.

G. Saturation Method of Measuring Relaxation Times

For a Lorentzian shaped homogeneous line, the spin-spin relaxation time T_2 may be estimated from the linewidth

$$T_2 = \frac{2}{\gamma\Delta H^0_{1/2}} = \frac{2}{\sqrt{3}\gamma\Delta H^0_{pp}} \tag{7-27}$$

and T_1 may be deduced from a saturation curve

$$T_1 = \left(\frac{\sqrt{3}\Delta H^0_{pp}}{2\gamma}\right)\left(\frac{(1/S - 1)}{H_1^2}\right) \tag{7-28}$$

where the saturation factor S

$$\frac{1}{S} = 1 + \gamma^2 H_1^2 T_1 T_2 \tag{7-29}$$

may be expressed in terms of the half amplitude or peak-to-peak linewidth relative to its value below saturation, or the absorption amplitude y_m, or its first derivative counterpart, y'_m relative to their values below saturation as follows:

$$\left.\begin{aligned} \frac{1}{S} &= \left(\frac{\Delta H_{1/2}}{\lim_{H_1 \to 0} (\Delta H_{1/2})}\right)^2 \\ \frac{1}{S} &= \frac{\lim_{H_1 \to 0} (y_m/H_1)}{y_m/H_1} \end{aligned}\right\} \quad \text{Absorption Lineshape} \tag{7-30}$$

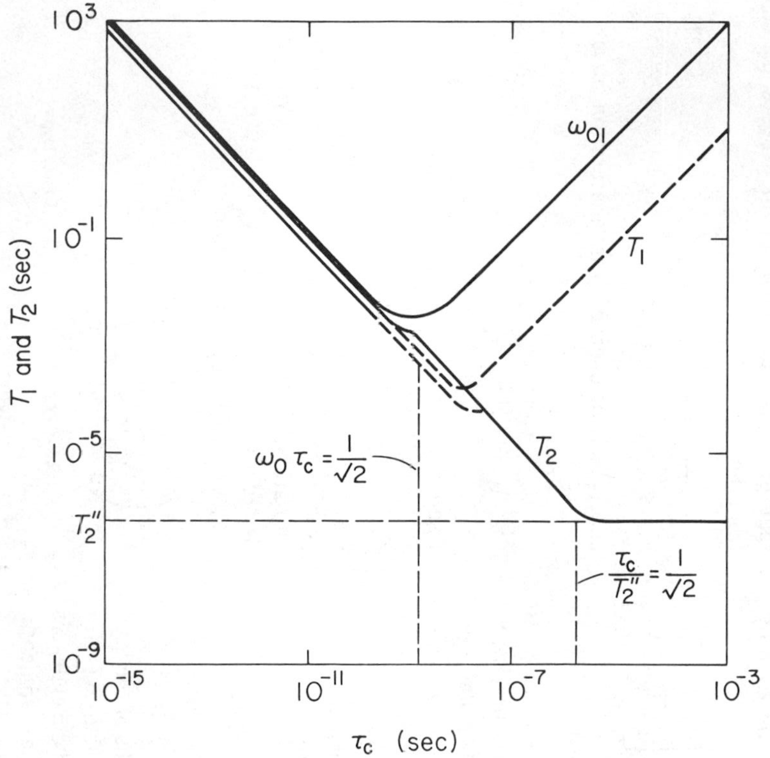

FIGURE 7-4. Dependence of the relaxation times T_1 and T_2 on the correlation time τ_c.[R-14]

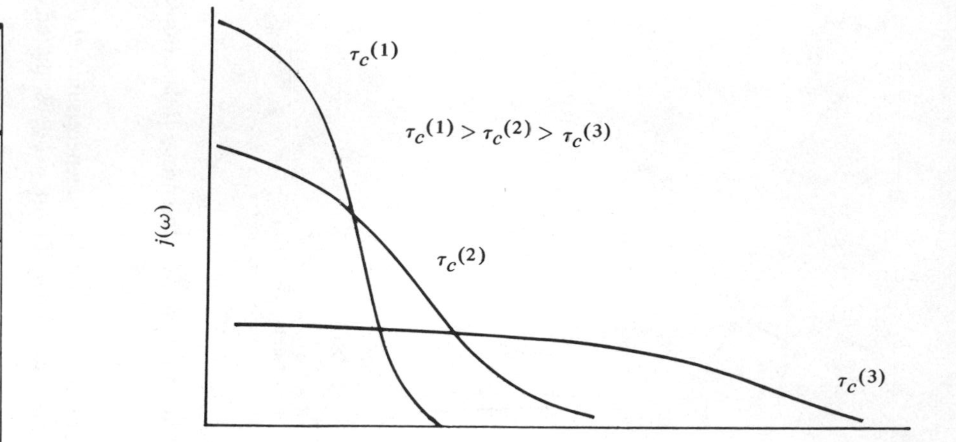

FIGURE 7-5. Graphs of the correlation function[B-41] for three values of τ_c.

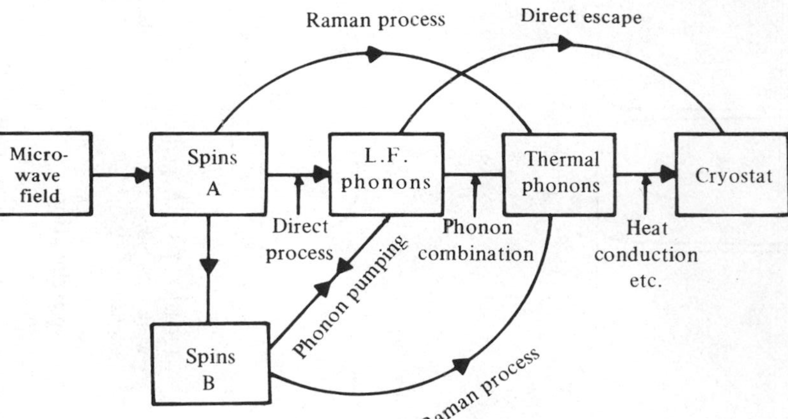

FIGURE 7-6. Relaxation processes for resonant spins A that absorb microwave energy and pass it on via spins B, low-frequency (LF) phonons, and thermal phonons to the heat bath cryostat. (From Bowers, K. D. and Mims, W. B., *Phys. Rev.*, 115, 285, 1959. With permission.)

TABLE 7-1

Typical Temperature and Field Dependence Formulas for the Spin-lattice Relaxation Time T_1 [a] [B-43]

Spin System	Crystal Field and Debye Energies	Two Phonon or Raman Process Relaxation $(1/T_1)$	One Phonon or Direct Process Relaxation $(1/T_1)$
Kramers' salt	$k\,\Theta_D > E_{cf}$	$a\exp(-E_{cf}/kT) + bT^9$	aH^4T
Kramers' salt	$k\,\Theta_D < E_{cf}$	$\begin{cases} bT^9 \\ bH^2T^7 \end{cases}$	aH^4T
Non-Kramers' salt	$k\,\Theta_D > E_{cf}$	$a\exp(-E_{cf}/kT) + bT^7$	$a\coth(E_{cf}/2kT)$
Non-Kramers' salt	$k\,\Theta_D < E_{cf}$	bT^7	$a\coth(E_{cf}/2kT)$

[a]Values given at the conditions such as temperature wherein each process is dominant (typically 3°K for direct and 60°K for Raman processes in rare-earth salts). The symbol E_{cf} denotes the crystal field energy splitting. The parameters a and b differ fro the various formulas.

TABLE 7-2

Characteristics of Relaxation Times in Solids and Liquids[B-10]

Relaxation Time	Interaction	Identifying Feature
Solids		
T_1	Direct, spin-phonon	
	(1) Waller, modulation of dipolar interaction	$T_1 \sim H_0^{-1}T^{-1}$
	(2) modulation of spin-orbit interaction	$T_1 \sim H_0^{-4}T^{-1}$
	Raman, spin-two phonons	
	(1) Waller, modulation of dipolar interaction	$T_1 \sim T^{-7}, \theta_D >> T$
	(2) modulation of spin-orbit interaction	$T_1 \sim T^{-9}, \theta_D >> T$ T_1 independent of T for $\theta_D \leqslant T$
	Cross-relaxation, overlapping spin-packet – spin-packet	T_1 depends on H_0
	Spin-diffusion, spin-packet to rapidly relaxing impurity of defect site	T_1 depends on H_0 and T
T_2	Spin-spin dipolar interaction depends on xy components of dipolar interaction	T_2 independent of H_0 and T
Liquids		
$T_1 = T_2$	Electron spin exchange	T_1, T_2 independent of H_0 and T to a first approximation, viscosity effect
	Dipolar: electron spin, electron spin	Same as above
	Dipolar: electron spin, nuclear spin	Same as above

TABLE 7-3

Examples of Relaxation Time Measurements of Alkali Halide Crystals[B-3]

Salt	Measuring Technique	Spectrometer Type	F-center Concentration per cm³	Temperature °K	T_1, sec	H_0, G	Ref.
LiF	Rapid passage	TS1-K	~3.4 x 10^{18}	300.0	1.5 x 10^{-4}	~10^4	a
LiF	Rapid passage	TS1-K		4.0	2.6 x 10^{-3}	~10^4	a
LiCl	Rapid passage	Similar to RH1-X	~10^{18}	1.3	9.2	3,500	b
NaCl	Rapid passage	Similar to RH1-X	~10^{18}	1.3	<3.0	3,500	b
NaBr	Rapid passage	Similar to RH1-X	>5 x 10^{17}	1.3	43.0	3,500	b
KCl	Rapid passage	Similar to RH1-X	5 x 10^{16}	1.3	216.0	3,500	b
KCl	Rapid passage	Similar to RH1-X	2 x 10^{17}	1.3	72.0	3,500	b
KCl	Rapid passage	Similar to RH1-X	10^{18}	1.3	<3.0	3,500	b
KCl	Saturation-recovery	RS1-X	8 x 10^{16}	2.0	450.0	3,500	c
KBr	Rapid passage	Similar to RH1-X	>10^{18}	1.3	<1.0	3,500	b

REFERENCES:

a. **Hyde, J. S.,** *Phys. Rev.*, 119, 1483, 1960.
b. **Holton, W. C. and Blum, H.,** *Phys. Rev.*, 125, 89, 1962.
c. **Ohlsen, W. D. and Holcomb, D. F.,** *Phys. Rev.*, 126, 1953, 1962.

$$\frac{1}{S} = \left(\frac{\Delta H_{pp}}{\lim_{H_1 \to 0} \Delta H_{pp}}\right)^2 \qquad \frac{1}{S} = \left(\frac{\lim_{H_1 \to 0} (y_m'/H_1)}{y_m'/H_1}\right)^{2/3} \quad \text{First Derivative Lineshape} \tag{7-31}$$

Figures 7-7A and 7-7B show the linewidth ΔH_{pp} and first derivatives amplitude y_m' plotted against the square root of the power, and y_m' is seen to be linear with H_1 or $\sqrt{P}$ below saturation. The peak of this curve occurs at $S = 2/3$ to give

$$T_1 = 1.97 \times 10^{-7}\, \Delta H^0_{pp}/g(2H_1)^2 \tag{7-32}$$

Figures 7-8A and 7-8B show the linear section of $1/S$ versus H_1^2 for the first derivative linewidth and amplitude function. The slope of the straight line on each plot gives T_1:

$$T_1 = (\text{slope})/\gamma^2 T_2 \tag{7-33}$$

One may also compare power levels at which an unknown and standard sample experiences a drop in the ratio y_m'/H_1 to half of its value below saturation.

H. PulseTechniques and Spin Echos

The classic Figure 7-9 of Carr and Purcell shows the formation of an echo by pulses which rotate the magnetization vector in the rotating coordinate system. The requirement for a single pulse of width t_w is

$$\frac{2\pi}{\omega_o} < t_w < T_m \tag{7-34}$$

where ω_o is the Larmor or resonant frequency, and T_m depends on the spin-spin relaxation time T_2 and the contribution from magnetic field inhomogeneities $T_2{}^*$ in the following manner:

$$\frac{1}{T_m} = \frac{1}{T_2} + \frac{1}{T_2^*} \quad . \tag{7-35}$$

The transverse magnetization components M_x and M_y decay exponentially as $\exp(-t/T_m)$ after a single pulse, and the echos after a 90° pulse ($\gamma H_1 t_w = \pi/2$) followed by successive 180° pulses ($\gamma H_1 t_w = \pi$) decrease in amplitude as $\exp(-t/T_2)$, as shown in Figures 7-10 and 7-11. The magnitude of M_z shown in Figure 7-12 after a single 180° pulse returns to equilibrium with the time constant T_1.

$$M_z(t) = M_o(1 - 2e^{-t/T_1}) \quad . \tag{7-36}$$

This figure also applies to an adiabatic fast passage wherein for liquids one requires

$$\frac{1}{T_2} \ll \frac{1}{H_1}\left|\frac{dH_o}{dt}\right| \ll |\gamma H_1| \quad . \tag{7-37}$$

TABLE 7-4

Typical Values of Spin Lattice Relaxation Times of Rare Earth Ions in Single Crystals[B-30]

Salt	Ref.	Direct T_{1d}^{-1} (sec^{-1})	Orbach T_{1O}^{-1} (sec^{-1})	Raman T_{1R}^{-1} (sec^{-1})
1% Nd in LaMN $z \perp H$	Meas. (a,b,c)	1.7T	$6.3 \times 10^{9} \exp(-47.6/T)$	
H = 2.48 koe	Theor. (a)	2.6T	$2.2 \times 10^{10} \exp(-47.6/T)$	$7.8 \times 10^{-4} T^{9}$
1% Pr in LaMN $z \parallel H$	Meas. (a,b)	$>10^{3} T$	$4.6 \times 10^{10} \exp(-54.6/T)$	$2.35T^{7}$
H = 6.8 koe	Theor. (a)	$3 \times 10^{5} T$	$4 \times 10^{10} \exp(-54.6/T)$	$2.2T^{7}$
Sm MN $z \perp H$	Meas. (a)	>10T		$5 \times 10^{-2} T^{9}$
H = 17.3 koe	Theor. (a)	120T		$4.6 \times 10^{-2} T^{9}$
DyES	Meas. (d)	4.2T	$1.1 \times 10^{7} \exp(-23/T)$	
$<z, H = 45^\circ$				
H = 1.1 koe	Theor. (e)	6.2T	$1.2 \times 10^{7} \exp(-23/T)$	$1.3 \times 10^{-5} T^{9}$
0.05% Sm in LaMN	Meas. (a)	8T		$4 \times 10^{-3} T^{9}$
$z \parallel H$				
H = 9.04 koe	Theor. (a)	80T		$2.5 \times 10^{-2} T^{9}$
1% Ce in LaES $\perp H$	Meas. (a)		$2.2 \times 10^{6} \exp(-5.6/T)$	
H = 3.08 koe	Theor. (a)		$6.9 \times 10^{7} \exp(-5.7/T)$	
1% Nd in LaES $z \perp H$	Meas. (a)	1.7T		$3.6 \times 10^{-4} T^{9}$
H = 3.24 koe	Theor. (a)	1.4T		$1.3 \times 10^{-4} T^{9}$
0.2% Ce in LaMN $z \perp H$	Meas. (f,c,g,h)	>80T	$2.7 \times 10^{9} \exp(-34/T)$	
H = 3.75 koe	Theor. (f,c)	6T	$3.5 \times 10^{2} \exp(-34/T)$	

REFERENCES:

a. Scott, P. L. and Jeffries, C. D., *Phys. Rev.*, 127, 32, 1962.
b. Cowen, J. A., Kaplan, D. E., and Browne, M. E., *J. Phys. Soc. Jap.*, 17 (Suppl. B-I), 472, 1962.
c. Ruby, R. H., Benoit, H., and Jeffries, C. D., *Phys. Rev.*, 127, 51, 1962.
d. Cooke, A. H., Finn, C. B. P., Mangum, B. W., and Orbach, R. L., *J. Phys. Soc. Jap.*, 17 (Suppl. B-1), 462, 1962.
e. Orbach, R., *Proc. Roy. Soc. (Lond.)*, A264, 458, 485, 1961.
f. Finn, C. B. P., Orbach, R., and Wolf, W. P., *Proc. Phys. Soc. (Lond.)*, 77, 261, 1961.
g. Cowen, J. A. and Kaplan, D. E., *Phys. Rev.*, 124, 1098, 1961.
h. Leifson, O. S. and Jeffries, C. D., *Phys. Rev.*, 122, 1781, 1961.

For solids the following less restrictive condition is sufficient:

$$\frac{1}{T_1} \ll \frac{1}{H_1}\left|\frac{dH_o}{dt}\right| \ll |\gamma H_1| \approx \frac{1}{T_2} \qquad (7\text{-}38)$$

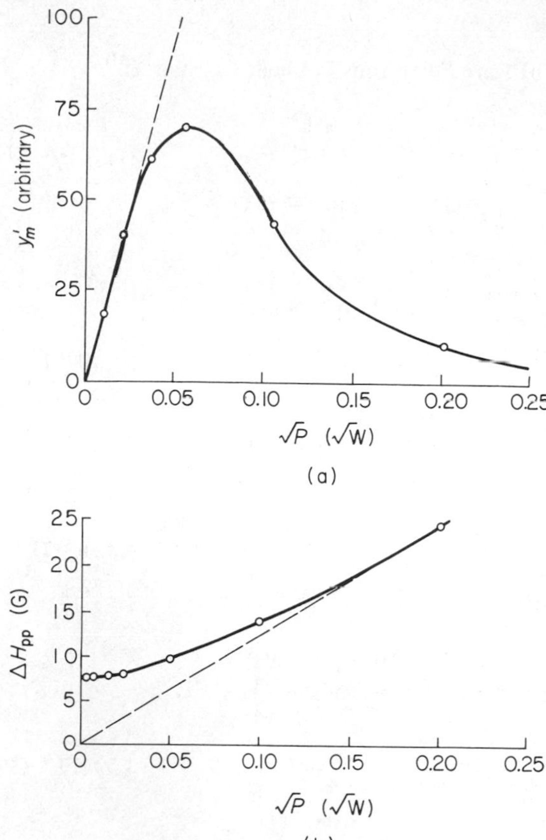

FIGURE 7-7. (A) Peak-to-peak amplitude y_m' plotted as a function of the square root of the microwave power P. The dotted line is an extrapolation of the linear dependence at low powers. (B) Peak-to-peak linewidth ΔH_{pp} plotted as a function of the square root of the microwave power P. The dotted line gives the linear asymptotic behavior at very high powers.[B-42]

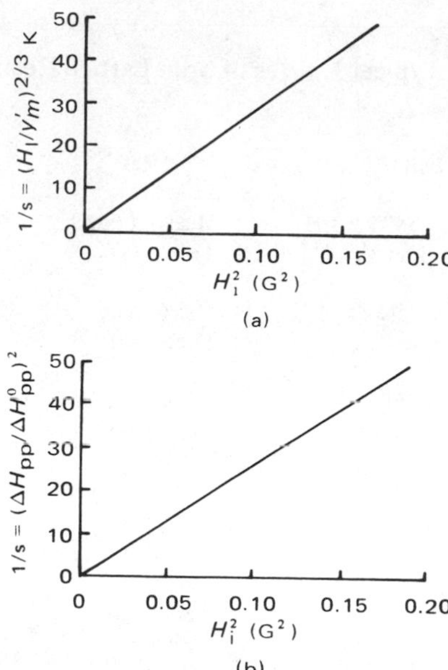

FIGURE 7-8. (A) The normalized quantity $(y_m'/H_1)^{-2/3}$ depends linearly on the square of the microwave field strength H_1^2, as shown. The slope of the line is $\gamma^2 T_1 T_2$, and $1/s = 1$ when $H_1 = 0$. (B) The linear dependence of $(\Delta H_{pp})^2$ normalized relative to the value below saturation depends linearly on H_1^2, as shown. The slope of the line is $\gamma^2 T_1 T_2$, and $1/s = 1$ when $H_1 = 0$. The values of K and ΔH°_{pp} correspond to those used to plot Figure 7-7.[B-42]

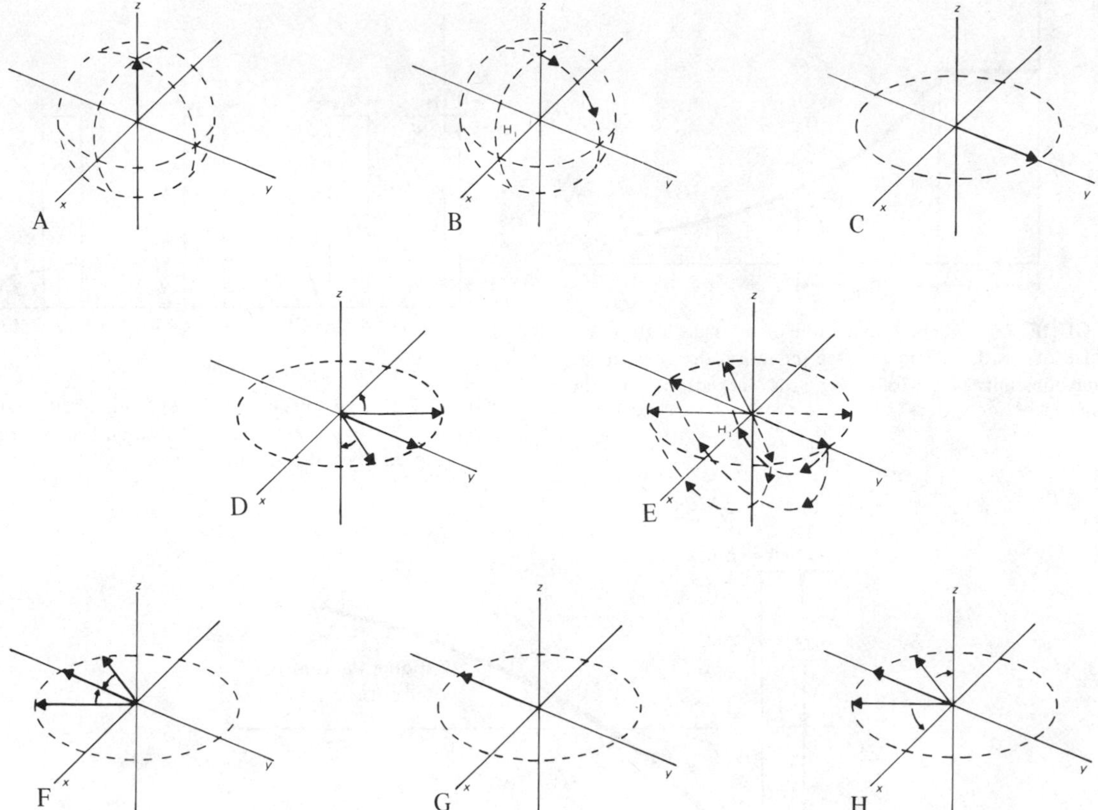

FIGURE 7-9. The formation of an echo. Initially the net magnetic moment vector is in its equilibrium position (A) parallel to the direction of the strong external field. The rf field H_1 is then applied. As viewed from the rotating frame of reference, the net magnetic moment appears (B) to rotate quickly about H_1. At the end of a 90° pulse, the net magnetic moment is in the equatorial plane (C). During the relatively long period of time following the removal of H_1, the incremental moment vectors begin to fan out slowly (D). This is caused by the variations in H_1 over the sample. At time $t = \tau$, the rf field H_1 is again applied. Again the moments (E) are rotated quickly about the direction of H_1. This time H_1 is applied just long enough to satisfy the 180° pulse condition. This implies that at the end of the pulse all the incremental moment vectors begin to recluster slowly (F). Because of the inverted relative positions following the 180° pulse and because each incremental vector continues to precess with its former frequency, the incremental vectors will be perfectly reclustered (G) at $t = 2\tau$. Thus, maximum signal is induced in the pickup coil at $t = 2\tau$. This maximum signal, or echo, then begins to decay as the incremental vectors again fan out (H). (From Carr, H. Y. and Purcell, E. M., *Phys. Rev.*, 94, 630, 1954. With permission.)

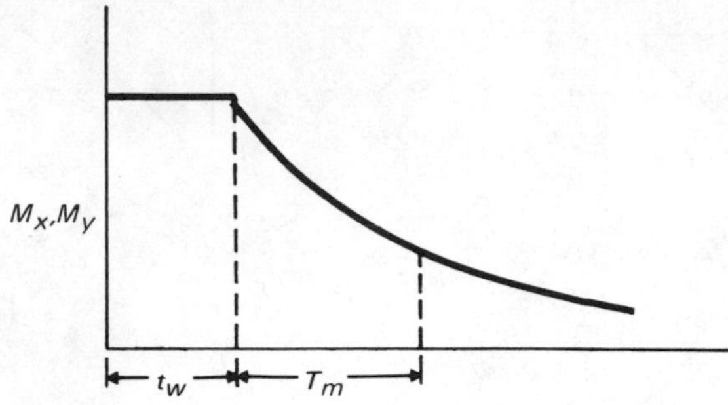

FIGURE 7-10. The application of a single high-power pulse of width t_w and the free induction decay with the time-constant T_m following the cessation of the pulse.[B-43]

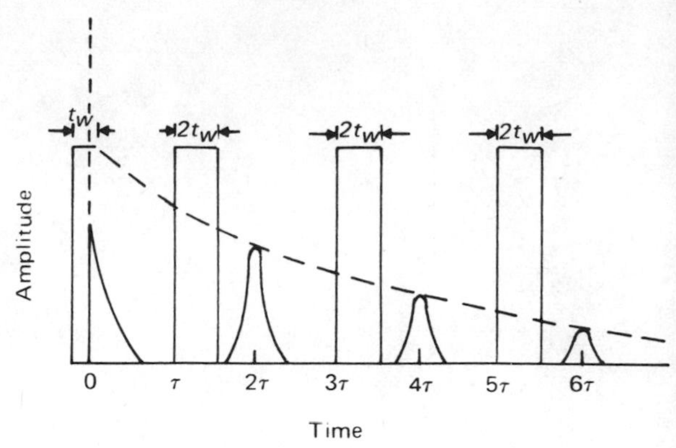

FIGURE 7-11. Application of a 90° pulse followed by successive 180° pulses, and the resultant exponential decay (dotted line) of the echos.[B-43]

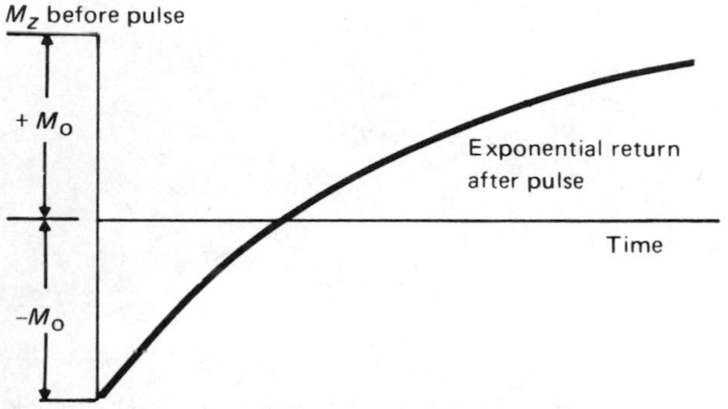

FIGURE 7-12. Return of M_z to its equilibrium value M_o after a 180° pulse which inverts it to the value $-M_o$. The same decay occurs after an adiabatic fast passage.[B-43]

VIII. LINESHAPES

A. Lorentzian and Gaussian Lineshapes

The two most common lineshapes are Lorentzian and Gaussian with the following analytical forms for the absorption $Y_{(H)}$, absorption first derivative $Y'_{(H)}$, absorption second derivative $Y''_{(H)}$, dispersion $d_{(H)}$, and dispersion first derivative $d'_{(H)}$. The Lorentzian expressions are

$$Y_{(H)} = \frac{Y_m}{1 + [(H-H_o)/\frac{1}{2}\Delta H_{\frac{1}{2}}]^2} \tag{8-1}$$

$$Y'_{(H)} = \frac{16\, Y'_m \dfrac{H-H_o}{\frac{1}{2}\Delta H_{pp}}}{\left[3+\left(\dfrac{H-H_o}{\frac{1}{2}\Delta H_{pp}}\right)^2\right]^2} \tag{8-2}$$

$$Y''_{(H)} = (27y''_m)\frac{\left[1-\left(\dfrac{H-H_o}{\frac{1}{2}\Delta H_{pp}}\right)^2\right]}{\left[3+\left(\dfrac{H-H_o}{\frac{1}{2}\Delta H_{pp}}\right)^2\right]^3} \tag{8-3}$$

$$d_{(H)} = \frac{2\left(\dfrac{H-H_o}{\frac{1}{2}\Delta H_{\frac{1}{2}}}\right)}{1+\left(\dfrac{H-H_o}{\frac{1}{2}\Delta H_{\frac{1}{2}}}\right)^2} \tag{8-4}$$

$$d'_{(H)} = \frac{9-3\left(\dfrac{H-H_o}{\frac{1}{2}\Delta H_{pp}}\right)^2}{\left[3+\left(\dfrac{H-H_o}{\frac{1}{2}\Delta H_{pp}}\right)^2\right]^2} \tag{8-5}$$

The corresponding Gaussian expressions are

$$Y_{(H)} = y_m \exp\left[-\left(\frac{H-H_o}{\frac{1}{2}\Delta H_{\frac{1}{2}}}\right)^2 \ln 2\right] \tag{8-6}$$

$$Y'_{(H)} = y'_m\left(\frac{H-H_o}{\frac{1}{2}\Delta H_{pp}}\right)\exp\left\{-\frac{1}{2}\left[\left(\frac{H-H_o}{\frac{1}{2}\Delta H_{pp}}\right)^2-1\right]\right\} \tag{8-7}$$

$$Y''_{(H)} = y''_m\left[\left(\frac{H-H_o}{\frac{1}{2}\Delta H_{pp}}\right)^2-1\right]\exp\left[-\frac{1}{2}\left(\frac{H-H_o}{\frac{1}{2}\Delta H_{pp}}\right)^2\right] \tag{8-8}$$

Tables 8-1 to 8-6 and Figures 8-1 to 8-3 give data and comparisons between these two lineshapes. Table 8-1 lists values of zeroth (i.e., the area A), second, and fourth moments (n = 2, 4, respectively) defined by

$$A = \int_{-\infty}^{\infty} Y dH = -\int_{-\infty}^{\infty}(H-H_o)Y'dH \tag{8-9}$$

$$H^n = \int_{-\infty}^{\infty}(H-H_o)^n Y dH = -\frac{1}{n+1}\int (H-H_o)^{n+1}Y'dH. \tag{8-10}$$

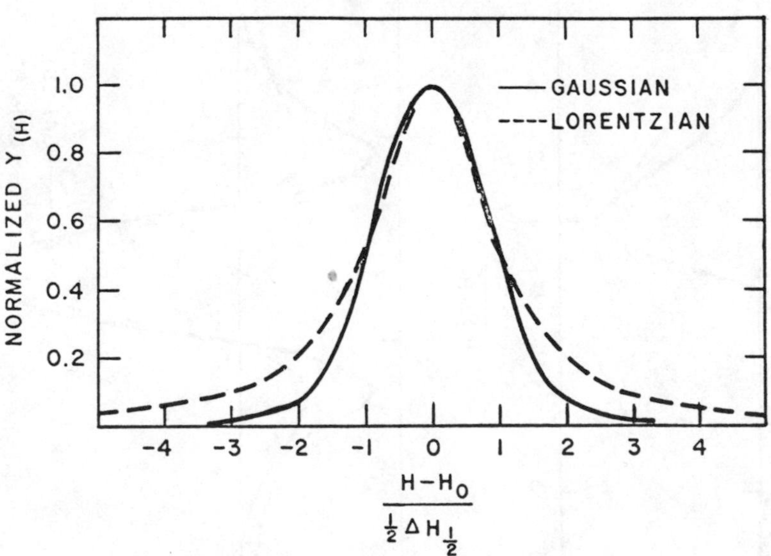

FIGURE 8-1A

FIGURE 8-1. (A) Lorentzian and Gaussian absorption curves with the same half amplitude linewidth. (B) Lorentzian and Gaussian absorption first derivative curves with the same peak-to-peak linewidth. (C) Lorentzian and Gaussian absorption second derivative curves with the same peak-to-peak linewidth.[B-42]

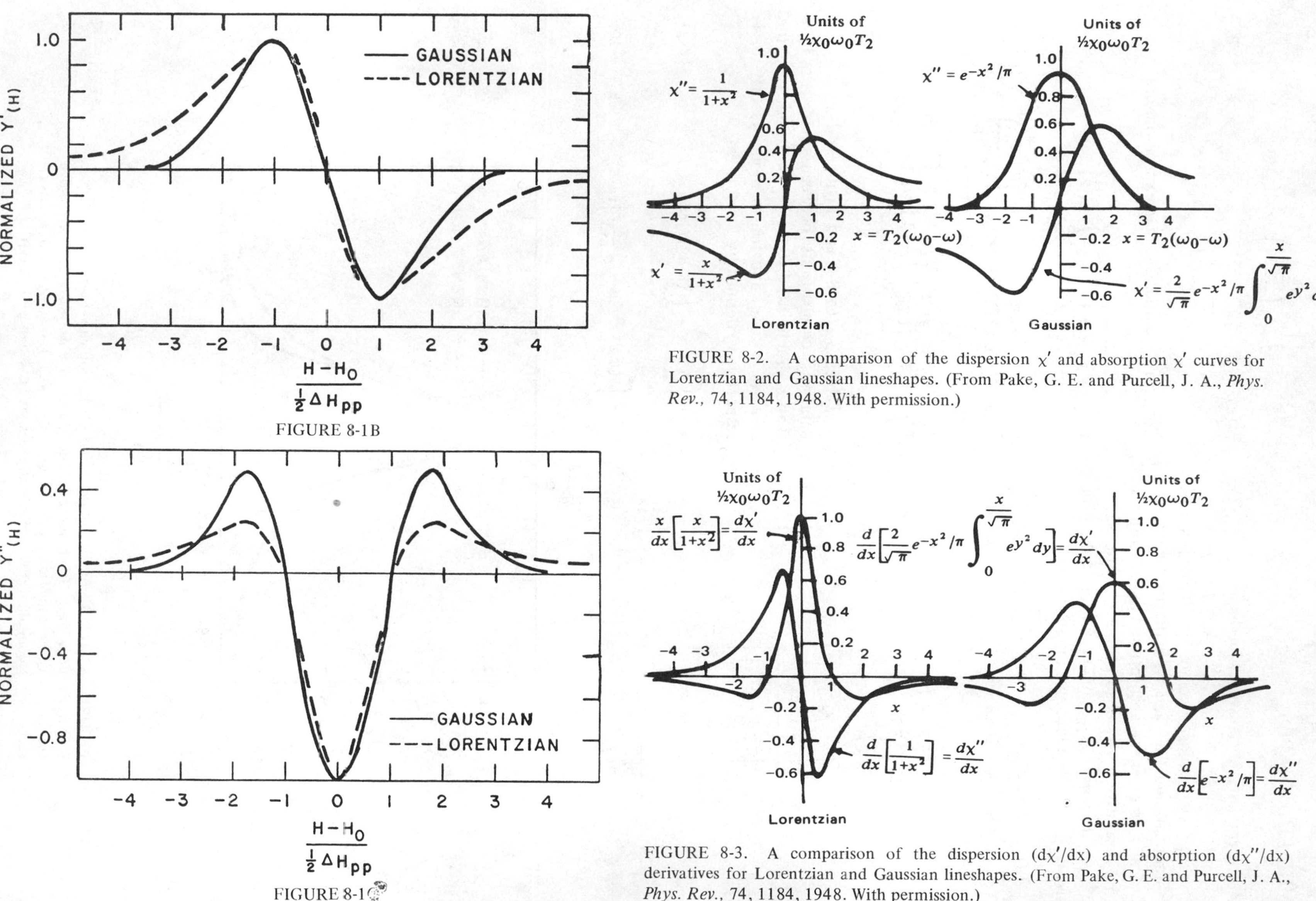

FIGURE 8-1B

FIGURE 8-1C

FIGURE 8-2. A comparison of the dispersion χ' and absorption χ' curves for Lorentzian and Gaussian lineshapes. (From Pake, G. E. and Purcell, J. A., *Phys. Rev.*, 74, 1184, 1948. With permission.)

FIGURE 8-3. A comparison of the dispersion $(d\chi'/dx)$ and absorption $(d\chi''/dx)$ derivatives for Lorentzian and Gaussian lineshapes. (From Pake, G. E. and Purcell, J. A., *Phys. Rev.*, 74, 1184, 1948. With permission.)

TABLE 8-1

Comparison of Gaussian and Lorentzian Lineshapes[B-42]

Parameter	Gaussian Shape	Lorentzian Shape
$\Delta H_{1/2}/\Delta H_{pp}$	$(2 \ln 2)^{1/2} = 1.1774$	$3^{1/2} = 1.7321$
$y_m/(y_m'\Delta H_{pp})$	$e^{1/2}/2 = 0.8244$	$4/3 = 1.3333$
$y_m/(y_m''\Delta H_{pp}^2)$	$1/4 = 0.2500$	$3/8 = 0.3750$
$A/(y_m \Delta H_{1/2})$	$(1/2)(\pi/\ln 2)^{1/2} = 1.0645$	$\pi/2 = 1.5708$
$A/(y_m'\Delta H_{pp}^2)$	$(1/2)(\pi e/2)^{1/2} = 1.0332$	$2\pi/3^{1/2} = 3.6276$
$\langle H^2\rangle/(\Delta H_{1/2})^2$	$1/(8 \ln 2) = 0.1803$	∞
$\langle H^4\rangle/(\Delta H_{1/2})^4$	$3/[64(\ln 2)^2] = 0.0976$	∞
$\langle H^2\rangle/(\Delta H_{pp})^2$	$1/4 = 0.2500$	∞
$\langle H^4\rangle/(\Delta H_{pp})^4$	$3/16 = 0.1875$	∞
y_1''/y_2''	$(1/2)e^{3/2} = 2.2408$	$64^{1/3} = 4.0$
$H_1''/\Delta H_{pp}$	0.626	0.567
$H_2''/\Delta H_{pp}$	$3^{1/2} = 1.7321$	$3^{1/2} = 1.7321$
$H_3''/\Delta H_{pp}$	2.52	$81^{1/4} = 3.0$
$d'(0)/d'(3^{1/2}) = A/B$	$7/2 = 3.50$	$2^3 = 8.0$

For solid DPPH, $A/[y_m'(\Delta H_{pp})^2] = 2.2$

$e = 2.718282$ $\quad$ $\left.\begin{matrix}\ln 2\\ \log_e 2\end{matrix}\right\} = 0.693147$

$\pi = 3.141593$

$2^{1/2} = 1.414214$ $\quad$ $\pi^{1/2} = 1.772454$

$3^{1/2} = 1.732051$ $\quad$ $(\ln 2)^{1/2} = 0.832555$

$e^{1/2} = 1.648721$

TABLE 8-2

Amplitudes of Gaussian and Lorentzian Absorption Lineshapes at Multiples of ½ΔH½ from the Center[B-42]

$\left(\frac{H - H_0}{\frac{1}{2}\Delta H_{1/2}}\right)$	Amplitude Y(H) Gaussian	Amplitude Y(H) Lorentzian[a]
0.0	1.0000	1.0000
0.5	0.8409	0.8000
1.0	0.5000	0.5000
1.5	0.2101	0.3077
2.0	0.0626	0.2000
3.0	0.00195	0.1000
4.0	1.5×10^{-5}	0.0588
5.0	–	0.0384
6.0	–	0.0270
7.0	–	0.0200
8.0	–	0.0154
9.0	–	0.0122
10.0	–	0.0099

TABLE 8-3

Amplitudes of Gaussian and Lorentzian Absorption First Derivative Lineshapes at Multiples of ½ΔHpp from the Center[B-42]

$\left(\frac{H - H_0}{\frac{1}{2}\Delta H_{pp}}\right)$	Amplitude Y′(H) Gaussian	Amplitude Y′(H) Lorentzian[a]
0.0	0.0000	0.0000
0.5	0.7275	0.7574
1.0	1.0000	1.0000
1.5	0.8029	0.8701
2.0	0.4461	0.6531
3.0	0.0549	0.3333
4.0	0.0022	0.1773
5.0	3×10^{-5}	0.1020
6.0	1.5×10^{-7}	0.0631
7.0	–	0.0414
8.0	–	0.0285
9.0	–	0.0204
10.0	–	0.0151

[a]When $|H - H_0| > 10\Delta H_{pp}$, we may set $Y'(H) \sim 16 y_m'[(H - H_0)/\frac{1}{2}\Delta H_{pp}]^{-3}$ for the Lorentzian shape.

TABLE 8-4

Amplitudes of Gaussian and Lorentzian Absorption Second Derivative Lineshapes at Multiples of $\frac{1}{2}\Delta H_{pp}$ from the Center[B-42]

$\left(\frac{H - H_o}{\frac{1}{2}\Delta H_{pp}}\right)$	Amplitude $Y''(H)^a$ Gaussian	Lorentzian[b]
0.0	−1.0000	−1.0000
0.5	−0.6619	−0.5899
1.0	0.0000	0.0000
1.5	0.4058	0.2332
$3^{\frac{1}{2}}$	0.4463	0.2500
2.0	0.4060	0.2362
3.0	0.0889	0.1250
4.0	0.0050	0.0590
5.0	10^{-4}	0.0295
6.0	–	0.0159
7.0	–	0.0092
8.0	–	0.0057
9.0	–	0.0036
10.0	–	0.0025

[a]The maximum amplitude occurs at $(H - H_o)/\frac{1}{2}\Delta H_{pp} = 3^{\frac{1}{2}}$ for both lineshapes. It has the value $2e^{-3/2} = 0.44626$ for the Gaussian shape and ¼ for the Lorentzian shape.

[b]When $|H - H_o| > 10\Delta H_{pp}$, we may use the approximation $Y''(H) \sim 27y_m''[(H - H_o)/\frac{1}{2}\Delta H_{pp}]^{-4}$ for Lorentzian lines.

For a symmetric lineshape such as Lorentzian and Gaussian, all odd moments vanish, the area is

$$A = \begin{cases} 1.0645\ y_m\Delta H_{\frac{1}{2}} = 1.0332\ y'_m\Delta H_{pp}^2 & \text{Gaussian} \\ 1.5708\ y_m\Delta H_{\frac{1}{2}} = 3.6276\ y'_m\Delta H_{pp}^2 & \text{Lorentzian} \end{cases} \tag{8-11}$$

and the even moments are

$$\langle H^n\rangle_{n\ \text{even}} = \begin{cases} (n-1)!!(\frac{1}{2}\Delta H_{pp})^n & \text{Gaussian} \\ \infty & \text{Lorentzian} \end{cases} \tag{8-12}$$

where $(n - 1)!! = (n - 1)(n - 3) \ldots\ldots.(5)(3)(1)$.

The Voight lineshape is a convolution of Lorentzian and Gaussian shapes with the respective widths ${}^L\Delta H_{\frac{1}{2}}$ and ${}^G\Delta H_{\frac{1}{2}}$.[B-42]

TABLE 8-5

Amplitudes of Lorentzian Dispersion Lineshape at Multiples of $\frac{1}{2}\Delta H_{\frac{1}{2}}$ from the Center[B-42]

$\left(\frac{H - H_o}{\frac{1}{2}\Delta H_{\frac{1}{2}}}\right)$	Amplitude, d^a
0.0	0.0000
0.5	0.8000
1.0	1.0000
1.5	0.9231
2.0	0.8000
3.0	0.6000
4.0	0.4706
5.0	0.3846
6.0	0.3243
7.0	0.2800
8.0	0.2462
9.0	0.2195
10.0	0.1980

[a]When $|H - H_o|/\frac{1}{2}\Delta H_{\frac{1}{2}}$ exceeds 10, we may use the approximation $d \sim \Delta H_{\frac{1}{2}}/(H - H_o)$.

TABLE 8-6

Amplitudes of Lorentzian Dispersion First Derivative Lineshape at Multiples of $\frac{1}{2}\Delta H_{pp}$ from the Center[B-42]

$\frac{H - H_o}{\frac{1}{2}\Delta H_{pp}}$	Amplitude, d'^a
0.0	−1.0000
0.5	−0.7811
1.0	−0.3750
1.5	−0.0816
$3^{\frac{1}{2}}$	0.0000
2.0	0.0612
3.0	0.1250
4.0	0.1080
5.0	0.0842
6.0	0.0651
7.0	0.0510
8.0	0.0408
9.0	0.0332
10.0	0.0274

[a]$d' \sim 3[(H - H_o)/\frac{1}{2}\Delta H_{pp}]^{-2}$ when $|H - H_o| > 10\Delta H_{pp}$.

$$Y_{(H)} = \frac{(\ln 2)^{\frac{1}{2}}}{\pi}\left(\frac{{}^L\Delta H_{\frac{1}{2}}}{{}^G\Delta H_{\frac{1}{2}}}\right)\int_{\infty}^{\infty}\frac{e^{-x^2}\,dx}{\left(\frac{{}^L\Delta H_{\frac{1}{2}}}{{}^G\Delta H_{\frac{1}{2}}}\right)^2\ln 2 + \left(2(\ln 2)^{\frac{1}{2}}\frac{H-H_o}{\Delta H_{\frac{1}{2}}} - x\right)^2} \tag{8-13}$$

Dysonian lineshapes obtained from conduction electrons in metals depend on the time T_D that it takes for an electron to traverse the skin depth δ, the time T_T that it takes an electron to traverse the sample, and the relaxation times T_1 and T_2. Often they are very anisotropic.[B-42]

In terms of the spin lattice relaxation time T_2 for homogeneous lines, one has

$$\Delta\omega_{1/2} = \gamma\Delta H_{1/2} = \frac{2}{T_2} \qquad \text{Lorentzian} \tag{8-14}$$

$$\Delta\omega_{1/2} = \gamma\Delta H_{1/2} = \frac{2\sqrt{\pi \cdot \ln 2}}{T_2} \qquad \text{Gaussian .} \tag{8-15}$$

The above lineshapes $Y_{(H)}$ were normalized to unit amplitude. Lineshapes $g_{(\omega)}$ normalized to unit area are

$$g_{(\omega)} = \begin{cases} \dfrac{T_2/\pi}{1 + (\omega-\omega_o)^2 T_2^2} & \text{Lorentzian} \\[2ex] \dfrac{T_2}{\pi} \exp[-(\omega-\omega_o)^2 (T_2^2/\pi)] & \text{Gaussian .} \end{cases} \tag{8-16}$$

B. Cutoff Lorentzian Lineshape

A cutoff Lorenzian lineshape is identical to a Lorentzian shape in the range

$$-a \le (H-H_o) \le a \tag{8-17}$$

and zero outside this range. Such a lineshape has finite even moments and zero odd moments.

$$A = y_m \Delta H_{1/2} \left[\frac{\pi}{2} - \cot^{-1}(2a/\Delta H_{1/2})\right] \tag{8-18}$$

$$\langle H^2 \rangle = \frac{(\tfrac{1}{2}\Delta H_{1/2})^2 \left[\dfrac{2a}{\Delta H_{1/2}} - \dfrac{\pi}{2} + \cot^{-1}\left(\dfrac{2a}{\Delta H_{1/2}}\right)\right]}{\left[\dfrac{\pi}{2} - \cot^{-1}(2a/\Delta H_{1/2})\right]} \tag{8-19}$$

For the limit $2a >> \Delta H_{1/2}$, one has

$$A \sim y_m \Delta H_{1/2} \left(\frac{\pi}{2} - \frac{\Delta H_{1/2}}{2a}\right) \tag{8-20}$$

$$\langle H^2 \rangle \sim a\Delta H_{1/2}/\pi \tag{8-21}$$

$$H^4 \sim a^3 \Delta H_{1/2}/3\pi \tag{8-22}$$

C. Zero Field Powder Pattern Lineshape

A D-term zero field powder pattern lineshape for $S = 3/2$ is shown in Figure 8-4.

D. Dipolar Lineshapes

The generalized spin-spin interaction between the spins $\mathcal{H}_{ij}$ contains dipolar $(g_i g_j \beta^2/r^3_{ij})$, pseudodipolar (B_{ij}), and exchange (A_{ij}) terms, and it has the explicit form

$$\mathcal{H}_{sp-sp} = A + B + C + D + E + F \tag{8-23}$$

with

$$A = \sum_{j>i} \left[A_{ij} + \left(\frac{g_i g_j \beta^2}{r_{ij}^3} + B_{ij}\right)(1 - 3\cos^2\theta_{ij})\right] S_{zi} S_{zj}$$

$$B = \frac{1}{2}\left[\sum_{i>j} A_{ij} - \frac{1}{2}\left(\frac{g_i g_j \beta^2}{r_{ij}^3} + B_{ij}\right)(1 - 3\cos^2\theta_{ij})\right] \times (S_{+i}S_{-j} + S_{-i}S_{+j})$$

$$C = -\frac{3}{2}\sum_{j>i}\left(\frac{g_i g_j \beta^2}{r_{ij}^3} + B_{ij}\right)\sin\theta_{ij}\cos\theta_{ij} \times \exp(-i\phi_{ij})(S_{+i}S_{zj} + S_{zi}S_{+j})$$

$$D = -\frac{3}{2}\sum_{j>i}\left(\frac{g_i g_j \beta^2}{r_{ij}^3} + B_{ij}\right)\sin\theta_{ij}\cos\theta_{ij} \times \exp(i\phi_{ij})(S_{-i}S_{zj} + S_{zi}S_{-j})$$

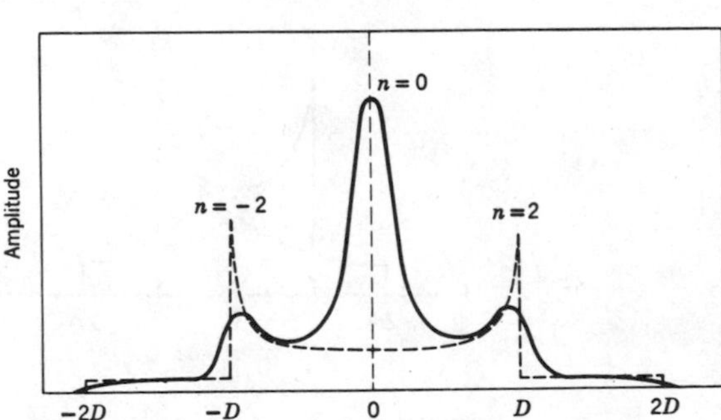

FIGURE 8-4. Powder pattern ESR lineshape arising from the zero field D-term with S = 3/2. The same lineshape arises in NMR for quadrupolar broadening with I = 3/2.[B-44]

$$E = -\frac{3}{4}\sum_{j>i}\left(\frac{g_i g_j \beta^2}{r_{ij}^3} + B_{ij}\right) \sin^2\theta_{ij}\exp(-2i\phi_{ij})\, S_{+i}S_{+j}$$

$$F = -\frac{3}{4}\sum_{j>i}\left(\frac{g_i g_j \beta^2}{r_{ij}^3} + B_{ij}\right) \sin^2\theta_{ij}\exp(2i\phi_{ij})\, S_{-i}S_{-j} \quad (8\text{-}24)$$

where θ_{ij} and ϕ_{ij} are the polar angles of the radius vector connecting ions i and j with respect to the z axis. When the pseudodipolar and exchange terms vanish, the spin-spin interaction reduces to the dipole-dipole interaction $\mathcal{H}_{dd}$*

The powder pattern lineshape for two spin ½ magnetic moments is given in Figure 8-5.

E. Anisotropic g-Factor and Hyperfine Tensors

Powder pattern lineshapes for completely anisotropic and axially symmetric g-factors are shown on Figures 8-6 and 8-7.

If hyperfine structure is present and the hyperfine and g-factor tensors have the same symmetry axis, then each hyperfine component has the powder pattern shown in Figure 8-8.

F. Inhomogeneous Lines

An inhomogeneously broadened line is a superposition of many individual resonant lines as shown in Figure 8-9. For such a line, the relative spectrometer absorption signal which is proportional to $\chi''H_1$ is given by

$$Y_m = \frac{z}{\sqrt{1+z^2}}\, e^{(a^2z^2)}\, \frac{\{1 - \phi(a[1+z^2]^{\frac{1}{2}})\}}{[1-\phi(a)]} \quad (8\text{-}25)$$

where

$$a = \left(\frac{3}{2}\right)^{\frac{1}{2}} \Delta\omega_{Lpp}/\Delta\omega_{Gpp} = 1.225\, \Delta\omega_{Lpp}/\Delta\omega_{Gpp} \quad (8\text{-}26)$$

It is convenient to define $H_{1/2}$ as the value of the microwave field H_1, which makes $\gamma^2 H_1{}^2 T_1 T_2 = 1$

$$H_{\frac{1}{2}} = 1/\gamma(T_1T_2)^{\frac{1}{2}} \quad (8\text{-}27)$$

and in terms of this notation one has

$$z = H_1/H_{\frac{1}{2}} \quad (8\text{-}28)$$

Figure 8-10 shows the saturation behavior for various ratios of a.

To compare these curves to experimental data it is convenient to define H_L and H_U as the points below and above the maximum where Y_m is half of its maximum value, as shown in Figure 8-11. The ratio H_U/H_L is plotted on Figure 8-12 and may be employed for deducing the ratio a. For the completely inhomogeneous case, a = 0 and $H_U = \infty$, while for the completely homogeneous case, a is infinite.

The curves in Figure 8-10 may be used to determine $H_{1/2}$ once a is known. On Figure 8-11 the point A, which is the intersection of the extrapolated low power slope (dashed) and the horizontal tangent to the top Y_{max} of the saturation curve, gives an approximate value of $H_{1/2}$ for all amounts of saturation. It may be considered as a first approximation to $H_{1/2}$. For a = 0 the $H_{1/2}$ found by this method is correct; for the completely homogeneous case it is a factor of two too small. For the homogeneous case, Y_{max} comes at

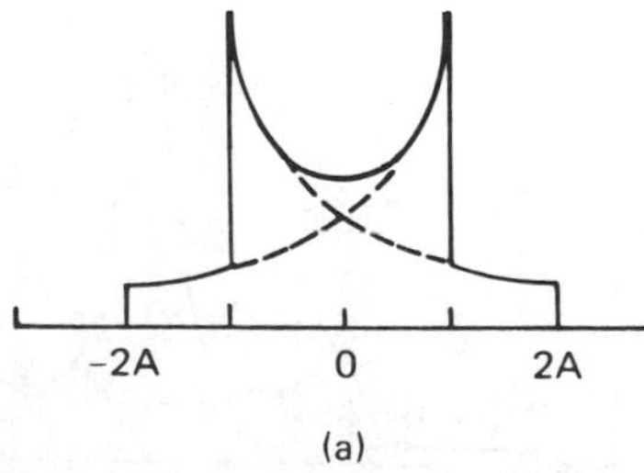

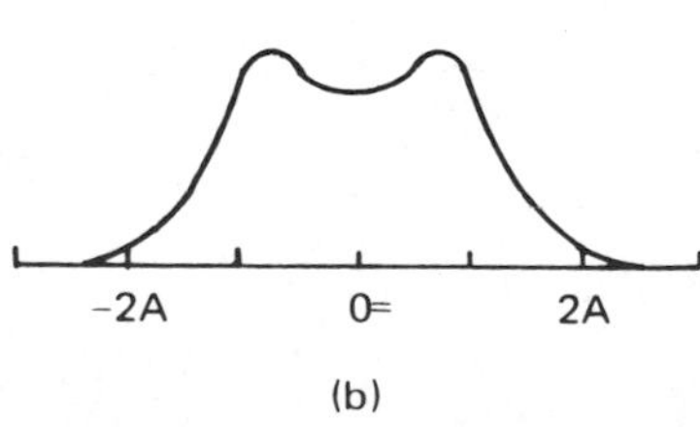

FIGURE 8-5. Powder pattern lineshape from two-spin one-half magnetic moments interacting via the dipole-dipole coupling where A = $3\mu/2r^3$. The lineshape (A) for infinitely narrow component lines reduces to (B) when other broadening mechanisms are present. (From Pake, G. E., *J. Chem. Phys.*, 16, 327, 1948. With permission.)

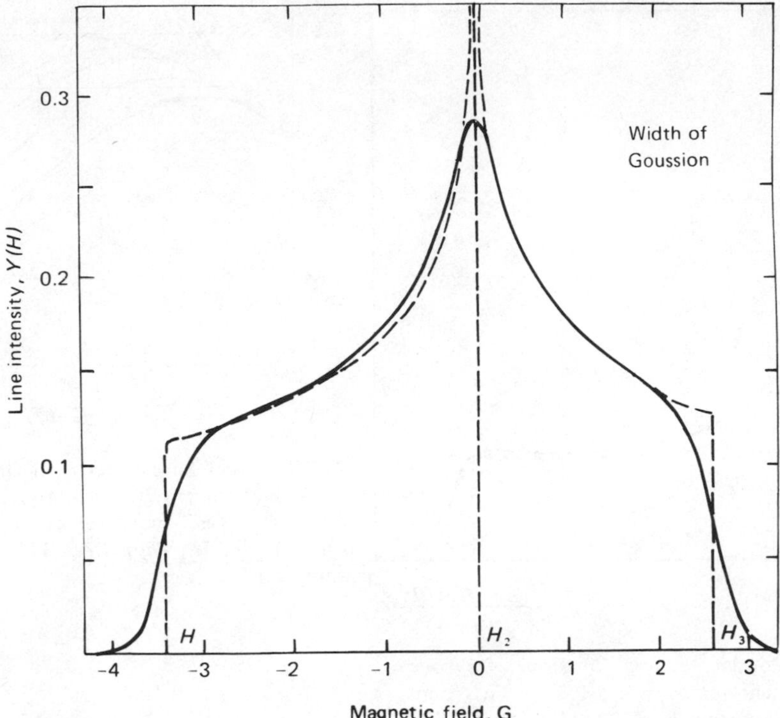

FIGURE 8-6. Calculated powder pattern lineshape for carbazyl (k-band, H_2 = 8230 G) assuming both zero (dashed line) and nonzero (solid line) component linewidths.[B-42]

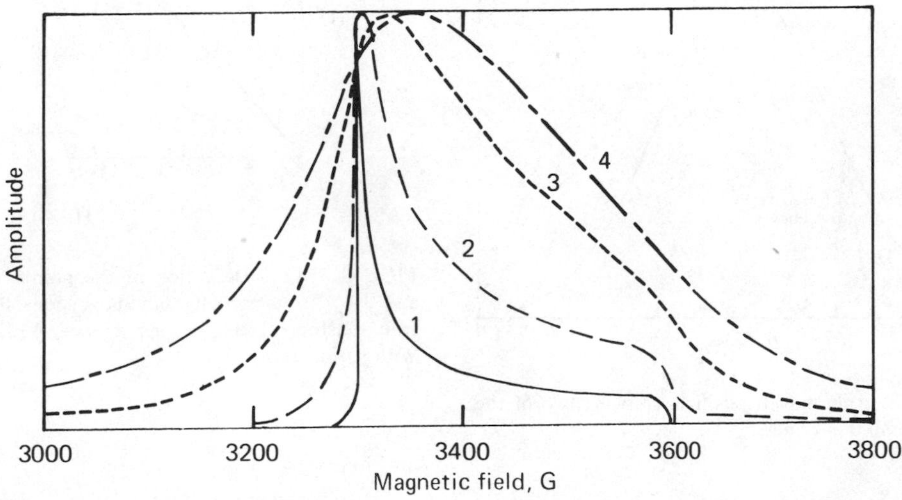

FIGURE 8-7. The effect of increasing the component linewidth on the calculated spectrum for an axially symmetric powder pattern. Lorentzian linewidths: (1) 1 G, (2) 10 G, (3) 50 G, (4) 100 G. (From Ibers, J. A. and Swalen, J. D., *Phys. Rev.*, 127, 1914, 1962. With permission.)

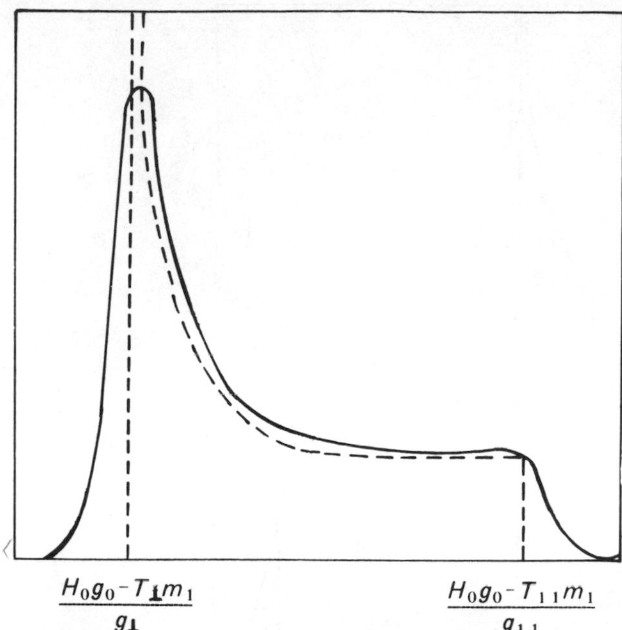

FIGURE 8-8. Powder pattern lineshape for one hyperfine component m_I when $g_o\beta H_o \gg T_{\|}, T_\perp$. (From O'Reilly, D. E., *J. Chem. Phys.*, 29, 1188, 1958. With permission.)

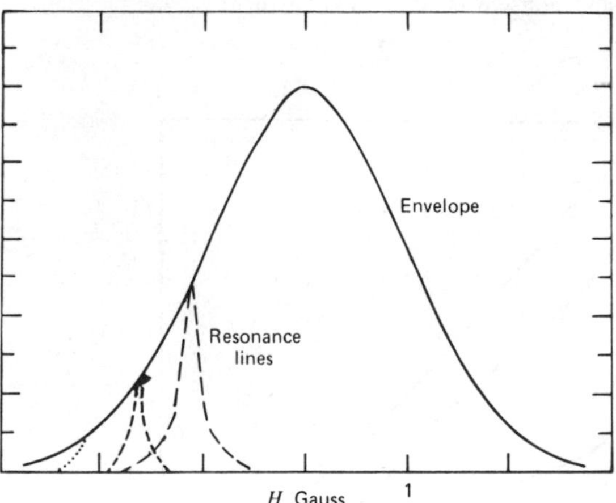

FIGURE 8-9. Inhomogeneous line, showing two of the individual component lines.[B-43]

the point $H_1 = H_{1/2}$. The foregoing method provides us with the product T_1T_2 since by definition

$$T_1T_2 = 1/(\gamma H_{1/2})^2 \quad . \tag{8-29}$$

The value of T_2 is determined from the Lorentzian spin packet width

$$T_2 = 2/(\sqrt{3}\,\Delta\omega_{Lpp}) \tag{8-30}$$

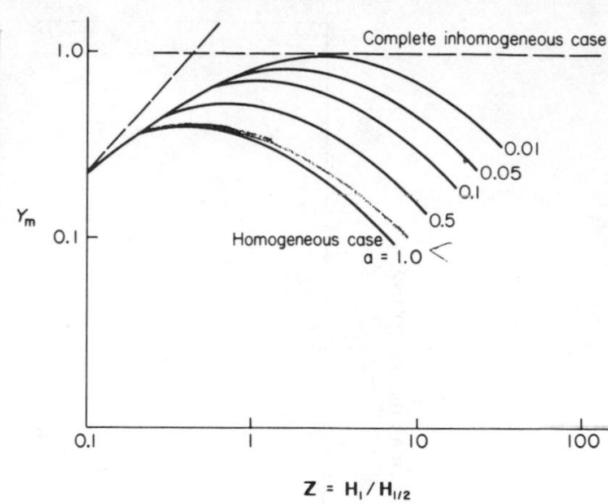

FIGURE 8-10. Spectrometer absorption signal Y_m versus reduced microwave field $H_1H_{1/2}$, where $H_{1/2} = 1/\gamma(T_1T_2)^{1/2}$ for various values of a. (Adapted from Castner, T. G., Jr., *Phys. Rev.*, 115, 1506, 1959. With permission.)

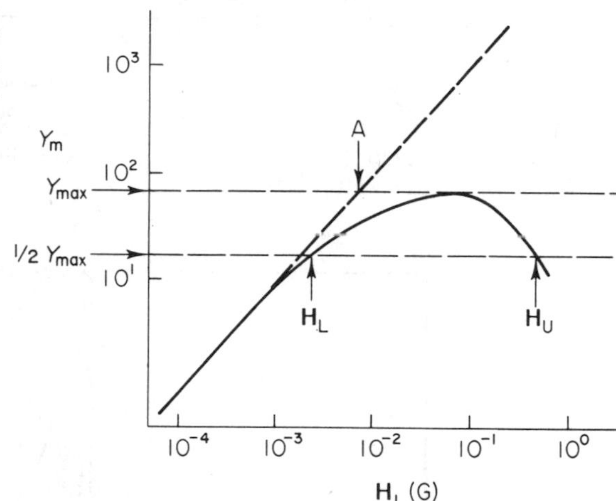

FIGURE 8-11. Definition of the points Y_{max}, A, H_L, and H_U for a partially inhomogeneous line. (Adapted from Castner, T. G., Jr., *Phys. Rev.*, 115, 1506, 1959. With permission.)

and hence

$$T_1 = \sqrt{3}\,\Delta\omega_{Lpp}/2(\gamma H_1)^2 \quad . \tag{8-31}$$

Figure 8-12 is useful for a < 1 since the curve becomes asymptotic at higher values of a. Castner employed this technique to measure spin-lattice relaxation times of F-centers in the range $2 \times 10^{-7} < T_1 < 10^{-4}$ where $T_1 = T_2$. For shorter relaxation times ($T_1 < 10^{-8}$ s when $T_1 = T_2$), he employed the expression

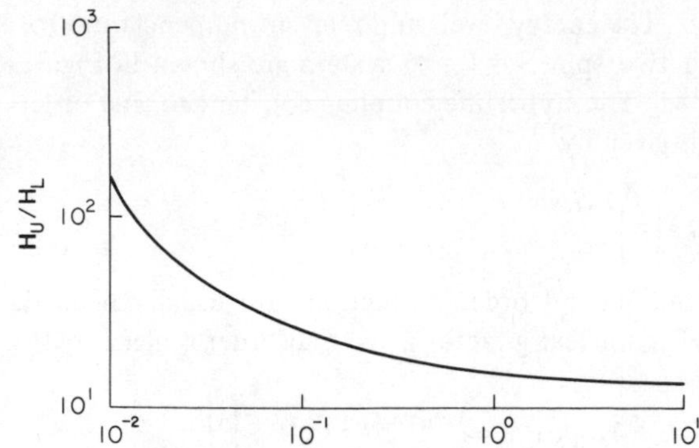

FIGURE 8-12. Dependence of the ratio H_U/H_L defined in Figure 8-11 on the parameter a = $\sqrt{2/3}\ \Delta H_{Lpp}/\Delta H_{Gpp}$. (Adapted from Castner, T. G., Jr., *Phys. Rev.*, 115, 1506, 1959. With permission.)

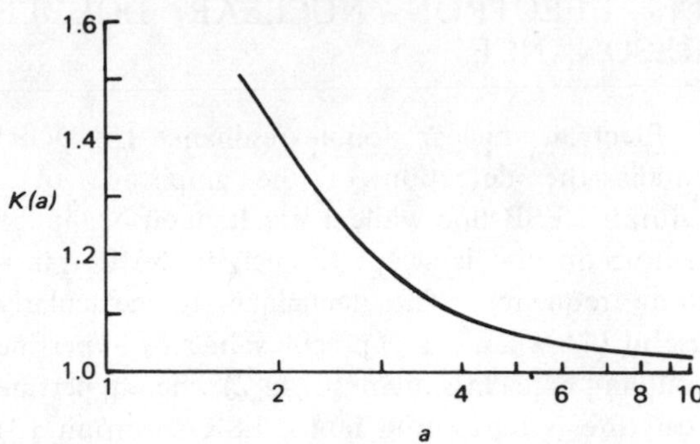

FIGURE 8-13. Dependence of the correction factor K(a) of Equation 8-32 on the parameter a. (Adapted from Castner, T. G., Jr., *Phys. Rev.*, 130, 58, 1963. With permission.)

$$T_2 = (2/\sqrt{3}\ \gamma\Delta H_{envpp})K(a) \qquad (8\text{-}32)$$

where ΔH_{envpp} is the experimentally observed peak-to-peak full linewidth corresponding to the envelope lineshape, and K(a) is plotted in Figure 8-13.

These two techniques were not convenient to use at longer spin-lattice relaxation times.

IX. ELECTRON NUCLEAR DOUBLE RESONANCE

Electron nuclear double resonance (ENDOR) entails the detection of the amplitude of a saturated ESR line while a simultaneously applied radiofrequency is swept through an NMR transition frequency. The technique is particularly useful (1) when more precise values of hyperfine coupling constants are desired, (2) when hyperfine structure is unresolved in the ESR spectrum, (3) when the identity of a nuclear spin is to be established by determining the nuclear g-factor, and (4) for measuring nuclear quadrupole coupling constants.

The energy levels and relevant nomenclature for a two spin S = I = ½ system are shown in Figure 9-1. The hyperfine coupling constant to first order is given by

$$|A| = \begin{cases} \nu_{n1} + \nu_{n2} & \nu_o < \tfrac{1}{2}|A| \\ \nu_{n1} - \nu_{n2} & \nu_o > \tfrac{1}{2}|A|, \end{cases} \qquad (9\text{-}1)$$

but second order corrections are usually needed. The nuclear g-factor g_n to first order is given by

$$2\nu_o = 2g_N\beta_N H/h = \begin{cases} \nu_{n1} - \nu_{n2} & \nu_o < |A| \\ \nu_{n1} + \nu_{n2} & \nu_o > |A|, \end{cases} \qquad (9\text{-}2)$$

and again second order corrections may be indicated.

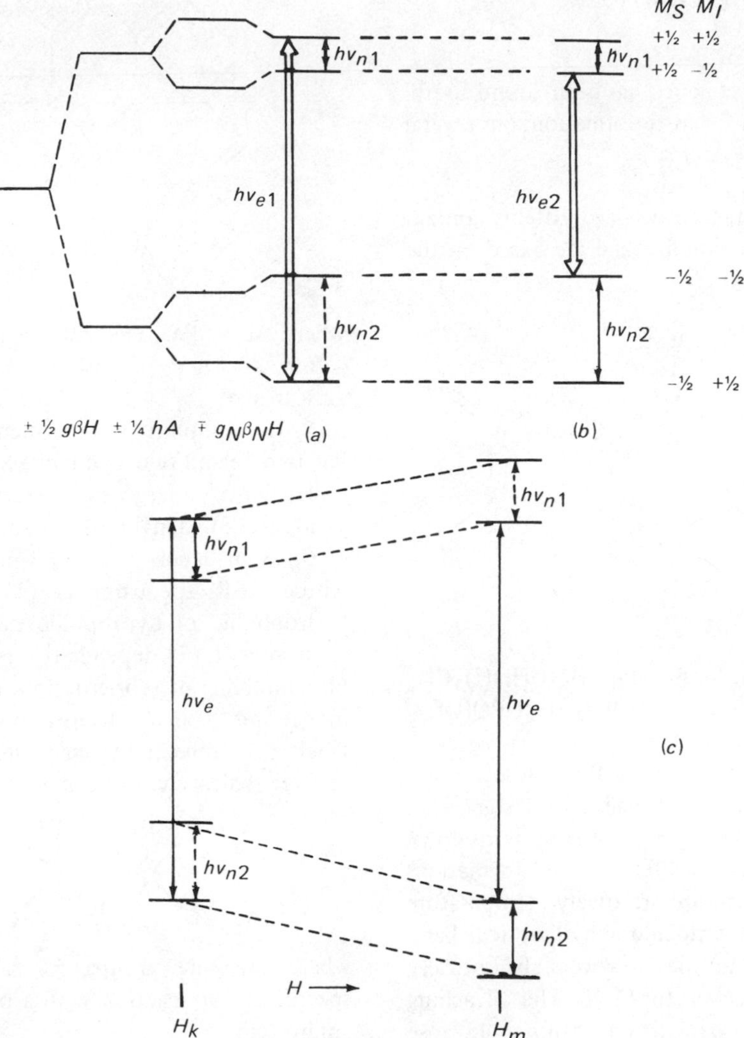

FIGURE 9-1. Energy levels of a system with S = 1/2 and I = 1/2 in a constant magnetic field. The usual ESR transitions corresponding to the selection rules $\Delta M_S = \pm 1$, $\Delta M_I = 0$ are shown with wide arrows to symbolize the application of higher than usual microwave power. The transitions at the frequencies ν_{nl} and ν_{n2} correspond to the selection rule $\Delta M_S = 0$, $\Delta M_I = \pm 1$. The solid lines represent nuclear transitions which will give rise to ENDOR lines if there is only one cross-relaxation process represented by T_x. The dotted transitions will also result in ENDOR lines if a second cross-relaxation process is operative. (A) Microwave saturation of the transition $M_I = +1/2.(h\gamma_{el})$. (B) Microwave saturation of the transition $M_I = -1/2.$ $(h\nu_{e2})$. (C) Energy levels at constant microwave frequency. For the simplest assumptions about relaxation paths in steady-state ENDOR, the partially saturated transition at the field H_k will be enhanced by simultaneous irradiation with high rf power at the frequency ν_{nl}. The line at the field H_m will be enhanced if the second frequency is ν_{n2}. In some systems, precisely this behavior is observed; however, more typically, enhancement of either line will occur both at ν_{nl} and at ν_{n2}. Since one observes the enhancement as the rf field is scanned, the recorder traces out "ENDOR lines."[B-61]

X. BIOLOGICAL APPLICATIONS

Electron spin resonance has been found useful for obtaining significant information on several types of biological systems.

1. Substrate free radicals.
2. Flavins and metal free flavoproteins contain one or more flavin subunits and are based on the isoalloxazine moiety

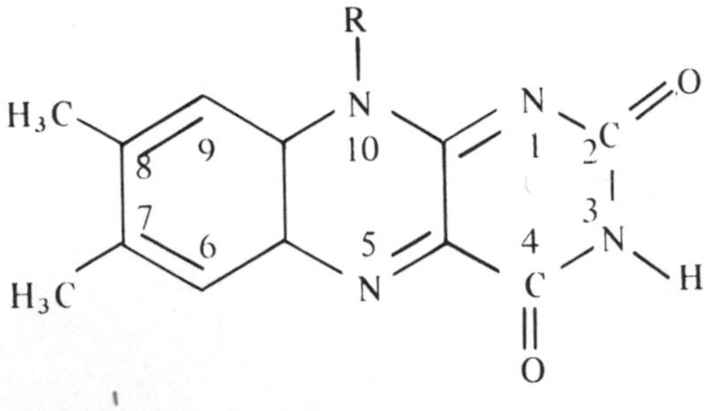

where R is CH_3 in lumiflavin, $CH_2(CHOH)_3CH_2OH$ in riboflavin and $CH_2(CHOH)_3CH_2OPO(OH)_2$ in flavin mononucleotide.

3. Photosynthesis involves free radical intermediates. Light induced reversible ESR signals are produced in photosensitive bacteria systems down to 4°K with millisecond lifetimes, and formations and decay kinetics are relatively temperature insensitive. The bacteriochlorophyll optical band centered at ~870 nm may be reversibly optically bleached in vivo down to 1° K. The bleaching occurs in less than 1 μs with a quantum yield close to one.
4. Heme proteins contain the porphyrin ring

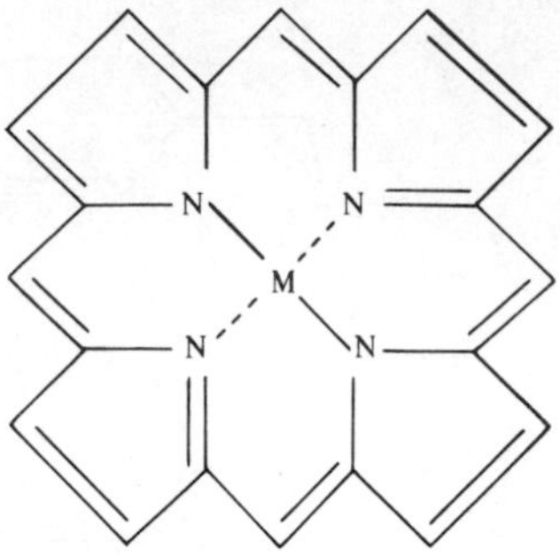

where M is Fe. The zero field D-term is large (often 20 cm^{-1} to 30 cm^{-1}), and g is often anisotropic.

5. Iron sulphur protein such as putidaredoxin has two Fe and two acid labile S atoms per protein molecule. It undergoes one-electron reduction and yields an ESR signal in the reduced state.
6. Spin labels are free radical substituents whose ESR spectrum is (1) sensitive to the hydrophobic or hydrophilic nature of the local environment, (2) dependent on the rate of molecular tumbling or reorientation, and (3) lacking an interfering "blank" absorption. A variety of spin labels is commercially available. Many are nitroxide free radicals with the general formula

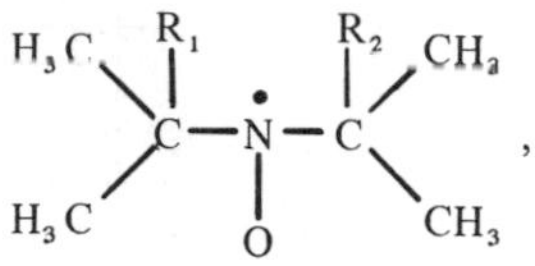

where the side groups R_1 and R_2 provide a specificity for reaction with a particular group or amino acid.

Table 10-1 gives typical irradiation conditions for several biological materials.

TABLE 10-1

Typical Irradiation Conditions for Biological Materials[B-3]

Material	Radiation	Rate	Total Dose	Temperature °K	Atmosphere	Ref.
Seeds						
Agrostis stolonifere (barley)	x-rays		$0.8–3 \times 10^5$ rads	193	Air	a
Dry *Agrostis stolonifere*, 4.5% H_2O	185 KV x-rays	800 R/min	1.5×10^5 rads	293	N_2	b
Proteins and Nucleic acids						
Gelatine	100–150 KV x-rays	1,000–20,000 R/min	$10^6–10^7$ rads	77–300	Vacuum	B-3
Human serum albumin	100–150 KV x-rays	1,000–20,000 R/min	$10^6–10^7$ rads	77–300	Vacuum	B-3
Pepsin	100–150 KV x-rays	1,000–20,000 R/min	$10^6–10^7$ rads	77–300	Vacuum	B-3
Casein	100–150 KV x-rays	1,000–20,000 R/min	$10^6–10^7$ rads	77–300	Vacuum	B-3
Thiogel	100–150 KV x-rays	1,000–20,000 R/min	$10^6–10^7$ rads	77–300	Vacuum	B-3
Hemoglobin	100–150 KV x-rays	1,000–20,000 R/min	$10^6–10^7$ rads	77–300	Vacuum	B-3
Deoxyribonucleic acid	100–150 KV x-rays	1,000–20,000 R/min	$10^6–10^7$ rads	77–300	Vacuum	B-3
(DNA)	^{60}Co	7×10^5 rads/hr	10^7 rads	77	Vacuum	c
Ribonucleic acid	100–150 KV x-rays	1,000–20,000 R/min	$10^6–10^7$ rads	77–300	Vacuum	B-3
DNA from salmon sperm	^{60}Co	7×10^5 rads/hr	10^7 rads	77	Vacuum	
	^{60}Co	6×10^6 rads/hr	to 5×10^7 rads	77	Vacuum	d
DNA from herring sperm	^{60}Co	2.7×10^4 R/hr	$0.8–6 \times 10^7$ R	Room	Various atmospheres	B-3
		5.6×10^5 R/hr				
Silk, chicken feather quill	^{60}Co		$\sim 5 \times 10^6$ R	77		e
Rat-tail tendon, fish fin bone						f
Bird leg bone, porcupine quill, etc.						f

REFERENCES:

a. **Ehrenberg, A., Ehrenberg, L., and Lofroth, G.,** *Abhandl. Deut. Akad. Wiss. Berlin Kl. Med.*, 1, 229, 1961.
b. **Sparrman, B., Ehrenberg, L., and Ehrenberg, A.,** *Acta Chem. Scand.*, 13, 199, 1959.
c. **Alexander, P., Lett, J. T., and Ormerod, M. G.,** *Biochim. Biophys. Acta*, 51, 207, 1961.
d. **Ormerod, M. G. and Alexander, P.,** *Rad. Res.*, 18, 495, 1963.
e. **Patten, F. and Gordy, W.,** *Proc. Natl. Acad. Sci.*, U.S., 46, 1137, 1960.
f. **Gordy, W. and Shields, K.,** *Compte Rend. Colloq. Brussels*, April 1961; *Proc. Natl. Acad. Sci.*, 46, 1124, 1960.

ACKNOWLEDGMENTS

Acknowledgment is made to the following authors, editors, and publishers whose material has been used in this chapter of the *Handbook of Spectroscopy,* for which permission has been received.

Jeffries, C. D., Low, W., Offenbacher, E. L., and Hutchings, M. T., Academic Press, New York: Tables 4-1, 4-2, 4-3, 4-4, 4-5, 4-7, 4-8, 5-1, 5-5, 5-6, 5-7, 5-8, 5-9, 5-10, 5-12, 5-13, 5-14, 5-15, 5-16, 5-17, 5-18, 5-19, 5-20, 5-21, 5-22, 6-4, 7-1; Figures 6-1, 7-10, 7-11, 7-12, 8-9.

Bersohn, M. and Baird, J. C., W. A. Benjamin, New York: Table 7-2; Figure 7-5.

Griffith, J. S., *The Theory of Transition Metal Ions,* Cambridge University Press, New York: Figure 4-6.

Abragam, A. and Bleaney, B., Clarendon Press, Oxford: Figures 4-1, 4-2, 4-3, 4-4.

Harper & Row Publishers, Inc., New York: Tables 6-1, 6-3.

Jeffries, C. D., Interscience, New York: Tables 2-3, 3-1, 3-2, 3-3, 4-6, 5-2, 6-2, 6-6, 6-7, 6-11, 6-12, 6-13, 6-14, 6-15, 6-16, 6-17, 7-3, 7-4, 8-1, 8-2, 8-3, 8-4, 8-5, 8-6, 10-1; Figures 3-1, 3-2, 3-3, 3-4, 3-5, 3-6, 3-11, 4-5, 4-7, 4-8, 7-1, 7-2, 7-3, 7-7, 7-8, 8-1, 8-4, 8-6.

Wertz, J. E. and Bolton, J. R., McGraw-Hill Book Company, New York: Tables 2-2, 2-4, 5-3, 5-4; Figures 3-7, 3-8, 3-9, 3-10, 9-1.

Lancaster, G., Plenum Publishing Corp., New York: Tables 6-8, 6-9, 6-10.

Carr, H. Y., Bowers, K. D., Mims, W. B., Castner, T. G., Jr., Pake, G. E., Purcell, E. M., Taylor, B. N., Parker, W. H., and Langenberg, D. N., American Institute of Physics, New York: Tables 2-1, 2-2, 8-9; Figures 7-4, 7-5, 7-6, 7-9, 8-2, 8-3, 8-5, 8-7, 8-8, 8-10, 8-11, 8-12, 8-13, 9-1.

The authors wish to thank R. Chappell, C. O. Clark, S. I. Jon, K. T. and M. E. Poole, P. Pai, J. S. Shaffer, and C. Smith for their help in checking the manuscript.

REFERENCES

B-1. **Abragam, A.,** *The Principles of Nuclear Magnetism,* Clarendon Press, Oxford, 1961.

B-2. **Abragam, A. and Bleaney, B.,** *Electron Paramagnetic Resonance of Transition Ions,* Clarendon Press, Oxford, 1970.

B-3. **Alger, R. S.,** *Electron Paramagnetic Resonance, Techniques and Applications,* Interscience, New York, 1968.

B-4. **Al'tshuler, S. A. and Kozyrev, B. M.,** *Electron Paramagnetic Resonance,* transl. *Scripta Technica,* Poole, C. P., Jr., Ed., Academic Press, New York, 1964.

B-5. **Assenheim, H. M.,** *Introduction to Electron Spin Resonance,* Plenum Press, New York, 1967.

B-6. **Atkins, P. W. and Symons, M. C. R.,** *The Structure of Inorganic Radicals,* Elsevier, New York, 1967.

B-7. **Ayscough, P. B.,** *Electron Paramagnetic Resonance in Chemistry,* Barnes & Noble, New York, 1967.

B-8. **Bass, A. M. and Broida, H. P.,** Eds., *Formation and Trapping of Free Radicals,* Academic Press, New York, 1960.

B-9. **Benedek, G. B.,** *Magnetic Resonance at High Pressure,* Interscience, New York, 1963.

B-10. **Bersohn, M. and Baird, J. C.,** *An Introduction to Electron Paramagnetic Resonance,* W. A. Benjamin, New York, 1966.

B-11. **Bielski, B. H. and Gebicki, J. M.,** *Atlas of Electron Spin Resonance Spectra,* Academic Press, New York, 1967.

B-12. **Blumenfeld, L. A., Voevodskii, V. V. and Semenov, A. G.,** *Applications of ESR in Chemistry,* Acad. Nauk, SSSR, Sibirsk. Otd., 1962.

B-13. **Buchacheko, A. L.,** *Stable Radicals,* Consultants Bureau, New York, 1965.

B-14. **Carrington, A. and McLachlan, A. D.,** *Introduction to Magnetic Resonance (with Applications to Chemistry and Chemical Physics),* Harper & Row, New York, 1967.

B-15. **Caspers, W. J.,** *Theory of Spin Relaxation,* Interscience, New York, 1964.

B-16. **Coogan, C. K. et al.,** Eds., *International Symposium on Electron and Nuclear Magnetic Resonance, Melbourne, 1969,* Plenum Press, New York, 1970.

B-16a. **Denison, A. B.**, Magnetic resonance involving the optically excited state, *Magnetic Resonance Rev.*, 2, 1, 1973.

B-17. **Dixon, W. T.**, *Theory and Interpretation of Magnetic Resonance Spectra*, Plenum Press, New York, 1972.

B-18. **Ehrenberg, A., Malmström, B. G., and Vänngärd, T.**, Eds., *Magnetic Resonance in Biological Systems*, Pergamon Press, New York, 1967.

B-19. **Emsley, J. W., Feeney, J., and Sutcliffe, L. H.**, *High Resolution Nuclear Magnetic Resonance Spectroscopy*, Vol. 1, Pergamon Press, New York, 1965; Vol. 2, 1966.

B-20. **Feher, G.**, *Electron Paramagnetic Resonance with Applications to Selected Problems in Biology*, Gordon and Breach, New York, 1970.

B-21. **Gerson, F.**, *High Resolution Electron Spin Resonance Spectroscopy*, John Wiley & Sons, New York, 1970.

B-22. **Geschwind, S.**, *Electron Paramagnetic Resonance*, Plenum Press, New York, 1972.

B-23. **Griffith, J. S.**, *The Theory of Transition Metal Ions*, Cambridge University Press, 1961.

B-24. **Hecht, H. G.**, *Magnetic Resonance Spectroscopy*, John Wiley & Sons, New York, 1967.

B-25. **Hedvig, P. and Mohes, B.**, *Electron Spin Resonance Spectra*, Akademiai Kiado, Bucharest.

B-26. **Hershenson, H. M.**, *Nuclear Magnetic Resonance and Electron Spin Resonance Spectra*, Academic Press, New York, 1965.

B-27. **Ingram, D. J. E.**, *Spectroscopy at Radio and Microwave Frequencies*, Butterworths, London, 1955.

B-28. **Ingram, D. J. E.**, *Free Radicals As Studied by Electron Spin Resonance*, Butterworths, London, 1958.

B-29. **Ingram, D. J. E.**, *Biological and Biochemical Applications of Electron Spin Resonance*, Plenum Press, New York, 1969.

B-30. **Jeffries, C. D.**, *Dynamic Nuclear Orientation*, Interscience, New York, 1963.

B-31. **Lancaster, G.**, *Electron Spin Resonance in Semiconductors*, Plenum Press, New York, 1967.

B-32. **Lebedev, Ya. S. et al.**, *Atlas of ESR Spectra*, Vol. 1, Consultants Bureau, New York, 1963; Vol. 2, 1964.

B-33. **Low, William**, *Paramagnetic Resonance in Solids*, Academic Press, New York, 1960.

B-34. **Low, W., Ed.**, *Paramagnetic Resonance, Proc. Jerusalem Conf. 1962*, Vols. 1 and 2, Academic Press, New York, 1963.

B-35. **Manenkov, A. A. and Orbach, R.**, *Spin Lattice Relaxation in Ionic Solids*, Harper & Row, New York, 1966, (a reprint collection).

B-36. **McLachlan, A. D.**, *Electron Spin Resonance*, Harper & Row, New York, 1969.

B-37. **McMillan, J. A.**, *Electron Paramagnetism*, Reinhold, New York, 1968.

B-38. **Memory, J. D.**, *Quantum Theory of Magnetic Resonance Parameters*, McGraw-Hill, New York, 1968.

B-39. Michigan State University, Electron spin resonance spectroscopy, Symposium, 1966, *J. Phys. Chem.*, 71(1), 1967.

B-40. **Minkoff, G. J.**, *Frozen Free Radicals*, Interscience, New York, 1960.

B-41. **Pake, G. E.**, *Paramagnetic Resonance*, W. A. Benjamin, New York, 1962.

B-42. **Poole, C. P., Jr.**, *Electron Spin Resonance, A Comprehensive Treatise on Experimental Techniques*, Interscience, New York, 1967.

B-43. **Poole, C. P., Jr. and Farach, H. A.**, *Relaxation in Magnetic Resonance*, Academic Press, New York, 1971.

B-44. **Poole, C. P., Jr. and Farach, H. A.**, *Theory of Magnetic Resonance*, Interscience, New York, 1972.

B-45. *Radiation Laboratory Series*, Vols. 1-28, McGraw-Hill, New York, 1947-53.

B-46. **Rado, G. T. and Suhl, H., Eds.**, *Magnetism*, 5 vols., Academic Press, New York, 1963-66.

B-47. **Ramo, S., Whinnery, J. R., and Van Duzer, T.**, *Fields and Waves in Communication Electronics*, John Wiley & Sons, New York, 1965.

B-48. **Reintjes, J. F. and Coate, G. T.**, *Principles of Radar*, 3rd ed., The Technology Press, MIT, and McGraw-Hill, New York, 1952.

B-49. **Schoffa, G.**, *Elektronen Spin Resonanz in der Biologie*, G. Braun, Karlsruhe, 1964.

B-50. **Schumacher, R. T.**, *Introduction to Magnetic Resonance*, W. A. Benjamin, New York, 1970.

B-51. **Slichter, C. P.**, *Principles of Magnetic Resonance*, Harper & Row, New York, 1963.

B-52. **Squires, T. L.**, *An Introduction to Electron Spin Resonance*, Academic Press, New York, 1964.

B-53. **Standley, K. J. and Vaughan, R. A.**, *Electron Spin Relaxation Phenomena in Solids*, Plenum Press, New York, 1970.

B-54. **Swartz, H. M., Bolton, J. R., and Borg, D.**, *Biological Applications of Electron Spin Resonance*, John Wiley & Sons, New York, 1972.

B-55. *Tables of Dielectric Materials*, Vol. 4, Tech. Rep. 57, Lab for Insulation Res., MIT, 1953.

B-56. **Talpe, J.**, *Theory of Experiments in Paramagnetic Resonance*, Pergamon Press, New York, 1971.

B-57. **ter Haar, D.**, *Fluctuation, Relaxation and Resonance in Magnetic Systems*, Oliver & Boyd, London, 1962.

B-58. **Ursu, I.**, *La Resonance Paramagnetique Electronique*, Dunod, Paris, 1968.

B-59. *Varian Workshop on Nuclear Magnetic Resonance and Electron Paramagnetic Resonance*, Pergamon Press, New York, 1960.

B-60. **Vonsovskii, S. V., Ed.**, *Ferromagnetic Resonance*, U.S. Dept. Commerce, Washington, 1964.

B-61. **Wertz, J. E. and Bolton, J. R.**, *Electron Spin Resonance*, McGraw-Hill, New York, 1972.

B-62. **Wilmshurst, T. H.**, *Electron Spin Resonance Spectrometers*, Plenum Press, New York, 1968.

B-63. **Winter, J.**, *Magnetic Resonance in Metals*, Oxford University Press, 1971.

B-64. **Wyard, S. J.,** *Solid State Biophysics,* McGraw-Hill, New York, 1969.
B-65. **Yen, Teh Fu, Ed.,** *Electron Spin Resonance of Metal Complexes,* Proceedings of Symposium in Cleveland, Ohio, March 1968, Plenum Press, New York, 1969.

R-1. **Al'tshuler, S. A., Kochelaev, B. I., and Leushin, A. M.,** Paramagnetic absorption of sound, *Sov. Phys. Usp.,* 4, 880, 1962.
R-2. **Anderson, P. W.,** A mathematical model for the narrowing of spectral lines by exchange of motion, *J. Phys. Soc. Jap.,* 9, 316, 1954.
R-3. **Anderson, P. W.,** Theory of magnetic exchange interactions, *Solid State Phys.,* 14, 99, 1963.
R-4. **Anderson, R. S.,** Methods of experimental physics, in *Electron Spin Resonance,* Vol. 3, Williams, D., Ed., Academic Press, New York, 1962, 441.
R-5. Applications of ESR in chemical reactions, *Proc. Roy. Soc.,* 302A, 287, 1968.
R-6. **Artman, J. O.,** Electron paramagnetic resonance of transiton metal and rare earth ions in solids, *Magnetic Resonance Rev.,* 1, 169, 1972.
R-7. **Assenheim, H. M.,** The interpretation of spectra in electron spin resonance investigations, *Res. Dev.,* 22, 22, June 1963.
R-8. **Atherton, N. M., Parker, K. J., and Steiner, H.,** Electron spin resonance, *Annu. Rep. Phys. Chem.,* 63, 62, 1966.
R-9. **Bagguley, D. M. S. and Owen, J.,** Microwave properties of solids, *Rep. Progr. Phys.,* 20, 304, 1957.
R-10. **Barry, T. I.,** Exploring the role of impurities in non-metallic materials by electron paramagnetic resonance, *J. Mater. Sci.,* 4, 485, 1969.
R-11. **Berthet, G.,** Paramagnetic electron resonance, *Cah. Phys.,* 67, 6, 1956.
R-12. **Bleaney, B. and Stevens, K. W. H.,** Paramagnetic resonance, *Rep. Progr. Phys.,* 16, 108, 1953.
R-13. **Blinder, S. M.,** Atomic hyperfine couplings, *Adv. Quant. Chem.,* 2, 47, 1965.
R-14. **Bloembergen, N., Purcell, E. M., and Pound, R. V.,** Relaxation effects in nuclear magnetic resonance absorption, *Phys. Rev.,* 73, 679, 1948.
R-15. **Bolton, J. R.,** Electron spin resonance in solution, *Magnetic Resonance Rev.,* 1, 195, 1972.
R-16. **Bowers, K. D. and Owen, J.,** Paramagnetic resonance II, *Rep. Progr. Phys.,* 18, 304, 1955.
R-17. **Bowers, K. W.,** Electron spin resonance of radical ions, *Adv. Magnetic Resonance,* 1, 317, 1965.
R-18. **Carrington, A.,** Electron spin resonance spectra of aromatic radicals and radical ions, *Q. Rev.,* 17, 67, 1963.
R-19. **Cauguis, G.,** Radicaux libres, resonance paramagnetique electronique et electrochimie organique, *Bull. Chim. Soc. France,* P-1618, 1968.
R-20. **Che, M., Vedrime, J., and Naccache, C.,** Le facteur g de l'électron, *J. Chim. Phys.,* 66, 579, 1969.
R-21. **Colburn, C. B.,** Free radicals in inorganic chemistry (142nd ACS Meeting), *Adv. Chem. Ser. 36,* ACS, Washington, 1962.
R-22. **Cook, R. J. and Whiffen, D. H.,** Electron spin resonance and its applications, *Phys. Med. Biol.,* 7, 277, 1962.
R-23. **Dalton, L. R.,** Double resonance, *Magnetic Resonance Rev.,* 1, 301, 1972.
R-24. **Damon, R. W.,** Ferromagnetic resonance at high power, in *Magnetism,* Vol. 1, Rado, G. T. and Suhl, H., Eds., Academic Press, New York, 1963, 552.
R-25. **Denison, A. B.,** Magnetic Resonance involving the optically excited state, *Magnetic Resonance Rev.,* 2, 1, 1973.
R-26. **Dwek, R. A., Richards, R. E., and Taylor, D.,** Electron nuclear double resonance in liquids, *Annu. Rev. NMR Spectrosc.,* 2, 293, 1969.
R-27. **Eargle, D. H., Jr.,** Electron paramagnetic resonance, *Anal. Chem.,* 40, 303R, 1968.
R-28. **Erbei, A., Ed.,** *Résonances Magnétiques,* Masson, Paris, 1969.
R-29. **Ernst, R. R.,** Sensitivity enhancement in magnetic resonance, *Adv. Magnetic Resonance,* 2, 1, 1966.
R-30. **Farach, H. A. and Poole, C. P., Jr.,** Solving the spin hamiltonian for the electron spin resonance of irradiated organic single crystals, *Adv. Magnetic Resonance,* 5, 229, 1971.
R-31. **Farach, H. A. and Poole, C. P.,** Guide to the magnetic resonance literature, *Magnetic Resonance Rev.,* 1, 3, 1972.
R-32. **Feher, G.,** Review of electron spin resonance experiments in semiconductors, in *Paramagnetic Resonance,* Vol. 2, Academic Press, New York, 1963, 715.
R-33. **Fischer, H.,** *Magnetic Properties of Free Radicals, Ions, Group 2, Vol. 1,* Springer-Verlag, Berlin, 1965, 1.
R-34. **Foner, S.,** Antiferromagnetic and ferromagnetic resonance, in *Magnetism,* Vol. 1, Rado, G. T. and Suhl, H., Eds., Academic Press, New York, 1963, 384.
R-35. **Fraenkel, G. K.,** Paramagnetic resonance absorption, in *Technique of Organic Chemistry,* Vol. 1, Weissberger, A., Ed., Interscience, New York, 1960, 2801.
R-36. **Gerson, F.,** Theorie und Experiment in der ESR Spektroskopie aromatischer Radikal-ionen, *Chimia,* 22, 293, 1968.
R-37. **Geske, D. H.,** Conformational analysis, *Progr. Phys. Org. Chem.,* 4, 125, 1967.
R-38. **Gorter, C. J.,** Applications of electron spin resonance, *Mem. Acad. R. Med. Belg. C1. Sci.,* 33, 9, 1961.
R-39. **Hall, G. G. and Amos, A. T.,** Spin distribution in π-radicals, *Adv. Atom. Mol. Phys.,* 1, 1, 1965.
R-40. **Hamilton, E. J., Jr. and Fischer, H.,** Electron spin resonance of free radicals and centers in solids, *Magnetic Resonance Rev.,* 1, 351, 1972.
R-41. **Hausser, K. H.,** Elektronen- und Kernresonanz als Methode der Molekülforschung, *Angew. Chem. [Engl.],* 68, 729, 1956.

R-42. **Hecht, H. G.**, ESR spectra, in *Molecular Properties*, Henderson, D., Ed., *Physical Chemistry*, Vol. 4, Eyring, H., Jost, W., and Henderson, D., Eds., Academic Press, New York, 1970.

R-43. **Herring, C.**, Direct exchange between well separated atoms, in *Magnetism*, Vol. 2B, Rado, G. T. and Suhl, H., Eds., Academic Press, New York, 1966, 2.

R-44. **Honerjäger, R.**, Paramagnetic resonance, *Fortschr. Chem. Forsch.*, 3, 722, 1958.

R-45. **Horsfield, A.**, ESR applied to organic chemistry, *Annu. Rep.*, 64, 257, 1966.

R-46. **Hudson, A. and Luckhurst, G. R.**, The electron resonance line shapes of radicals in solution, *Chem. Rev.*, 69, 191, 1969.

R-47. **Hudson, A. and Root, K. D. J.**, Halogen hyperfine interactions, *Adv. Magnetic Resonance*, 5, 1, 1971.

R-48. **Hutchings, M. T.**, Point charge calculation of energy levels of magnetic ions in crystalline electric fields, *Solid State Phys.*, 16, 227, 1964.

R-49. **Jarrett, H. S.**, Electron spin resonance spectroscopy in molecular solids, *Solid State Phys.*, 14, 215, 1963.

R-50. **Jeener, J.**, Thermodynamics of spin systems in solids, *Adv. Magnetic Resonance* 3, 205, 1968.

R-51. **Kastler, A.**, The methods of paramagnetic resonance, *Cah. Phys.*, 65, 1, 1956.

R-52. **Kevin, L.**, Free radical study by electron paramagnetic resonance, *Meth. Free Radical Chem.*, 1, 1, 1969.

R-53. **König, E.**, Electron paramagnetic resonance, Landolt-Bornstein, Group 2, Vol. 2, Springer-Verlag, Berlin, 1966.

R-54. **König, E.**, EPR in *Physical Methods in Advanced Inorganic Chemistry*, Hill, H. A. and Day, P., Eds., John Wiley & Sons, New York, 1968, 266.

R-55. **Kuska, H. A.**, ESR of coordination compounds, in *Spectroscopy in Inorganic Chemistry*, Rao, C. N. R. and Ferraro, J. R., Eds., Academic Press, New York, Vol. 2, 1971.

R-56. Electron spin resonance, *Lab. Sci.*, November 1964.

R-57. **Lax, B. and Mavroides, J. G.**, Cyclotron resonance, *Solid State Phys.*, 11, 261, 1960.

R-58. **Low, W. and Offenbacher, E. L.**, Electron Spin Resonance of Magnetic Ions in Complex Oxides, *Solid State Phys.*, 17, 135, 1965.

R-59. **Ludwig, G. W. and Woodbury, H. H.**, Electron spin resonance in semiconductors, *Solid State Phys.*, 13, 223, 1962.

R-60. **McMillan, J. A.**, Notes on electron paramagnetic resonance spectroscopy, *Argonne Natl. Lab. Rep.*, 1970.

R-61. **McWeeny, R.**, On the origin of spin hamiltonian parameters, *J. Chem. Phys.*, 42, 1717, 1965.

R-62. **Maire, J. C.**, La résonance paramagnétique électronique appliquée à l'étude des radicaux libres, *Bull. Soc. Chim. France*, 26, 1702, 1959.

R-63. **Mieher, R. L.**, Double resonance, *Magnetic Resonance Rev.*, 1, 225, 1972.

R-64. **Morton, J. R.**, Electron spin resonance spectra of oriented radicals, *Chem. Rev.*, 64, 453, 1964.

R-65. **O'Reilly, D. E.**, Magnetic resonance techniques in catalytic research, *Adv. Catal.*, 12, 31, 1960.

R-66. **O'Reilly, D. E. and Anderson, J. H.**, Magnetic properties, in *Physics and Chemistry of the Organic Solid State*, Vol. 2, Fox, D. E. et al., Eds., John Wiley & Sons, New York, 1965.

R-67. **Orton, J. W.**, Paramagnetic resonance data, *Rep. Progr. Phys.*, 22, 204, 1959.

R-68. **Orton, J. W.**, Application of paramagnetic resonance to non-destructive testing, in *Progress in Non-Destructive Testing*, Vol. 2, Heywood, London, 1960, 223.

R-69. **Pippard, A. B.**, Metallic conduction at high frequencies and low temperatures, *Adv. Electron. Phys.*, 6, 11, 1954.

R-70. **Poole, C. P., Jr. and MacIver, D. S.**, The physical-chemical properties of chromia-alumina catalysts, *Adv. Catal.*, 17, 223, 1967.

R-71. **Praddaude, H. C.**, Resonance phenomena in metals and semiconductors, *Magnetic Resonance Rev.*, 1, 261, 1972.

R-72. **Robertson, R. E.**, Electron paramagnetic resonance of the organometallics, in *Determination of Organic Structures by Physical Methods*, Vol. 2, Nachod, F. C. and Phillips, W. D., Eds., Academic Press, New York, 1962, 617.

R-73. **Root, K. D. J.**, ESR spectra of inorganic radicals and radical ions, in *Spectroscopy in Inorganic Chemistry*, Vol. 1, Rao, C. N. R. and Ferraro, J. R., Eds., Academic Press, New York, 1970.

R-74. **Rozantsev, E. G.**, Paramagnetic derivatives of oxides of nitrogen, *Usp. Khim.*, 35, 415, 1966.

R-75. **Sales, K. D.**, Theory of isotropic hyperfine splitting constants for organic free radicals, *Adv. Free Radical Chem.*, 3, 139, 1969.

R-76. **Shlyapintokh, V. Ya.**, Free radicals and chemiluminescence, *Usp. Khim.*, 35, 684, 1966.

R-77. **Schneider, F.**, Instruments and measuring techniques in electron spin resonance spectroscopy I and II, *Z. Instr.*, 71, 315, 1963; 72, 11, 1964.

R-78. **Schoffa, G.**, Use of electron spin resonance in biochemistry, *Chimia (Aarau)*, 20, 165, 1966.

R-79. **Semenov, A. G.**, Electron paramagnetic resonance spectrometers, *Prib. Tekh. Ekxp.*, 5, 5 (transl. p. 875), 1962.

R-80. **Smart, J. S.**, Evaluation of exchange interactions from experimental data, in *Magnetism*, Vol. 3, Rado, G. T. and Suhl, H., Eds., Academic Press, New York, 1963, 63.

R-81. **Smaller, B.**, ESR studies of biological interest, *Adv. Biol. Med. Phys.*, 9, 225, 1963.

R-82. **Stapleton, H. J.**, Electron spin lattice relaxation, *Magnetic Resonance Rev.*, 1, 65, 1972.

R-83. **Stevens, K. W. H.**, Theory of paramagnetic relaxation, *Rep. Progr. Phys.*, 30, 189, 1967.

R-84. **Stevens, K. W. H.**, Spin hamiltonians, in *Magnetism*, Vol. 1, Rado, G. T. and Suhl, H., Eds., Academic Press, New York, 1963, 1.

R-85. **Sturge, M. D.**, Jahn-Teller effects in solids, *Solid State Phys.*, 20, 91, 1967.
R-86. **Sullivan, P. D.**, Electron spin resonance in solution, *Magnetic Resonance Rev.*, 2, 35, 1973.
R-87. **Sullivan, P. D. and Bolton, J. R.**, The alternating linewidth effect, *Adv. Magnetic Resonance*, 4, 39, 1970.
R-88. **Symons, M. C. R.**, Electron spin resonance, *Adv. Phys. Org. Chem.*, 1, 284, 1963.
R-89. **Symons, M. C. R.**, The identification of organic free radicals by ESR, *Annu. Rep. Chem. Soc.*, 59, 45, 1962.
R-90. **Townsend, J.**, Magnetic resonance, in *Methods of Experimental Physics*, Vol. 2, Bleuler, E. and Haxby, R. O., Eds., Academic Press, New York, 1964.
R-91. **Wertz, J. E.**, Nuclear and electronic spin magnetic resonance, *Chem. Rev.*, 55, 829, 1955.
R-92. **Yafet, Y.**, g-Factors and spin lattice relaxation of conduction electrons, *Solid State Phys.*, 14, 1, 1963.

Section E

Mass Spectral Tabulations

MASS SPECTRAL TABULATIONS

Francis W. Karasek, University of Waterloo

I. INTRODUCTION

When a molecule is bombarded by 70 eV electrons at pressures of 10^{-5} torr, it fragments into a group of characteristic positive ions. A spectrum of these ions is produced in a mass spectrometer by accelerating the ions into a magnetic field where their motion toward a detector follows the equation: $m/e = H^2 r^2/2V$, where m is the mass of the ion of charge e, H is the magnetic field strength, r is the radius of curvature of the motion of the ions in the magnetic field, and V is the accelerating voltage of the ion. A mass spectrum is generally tabulated as ionic masses in descending order of intensity. The most intense ion peak is known as the base peak, and the relative abundances of all the other peaks are normalized to it. Tabulations used for identification of an unknown compound by spectral matching usually contain only the eight most intense ion peaks. The molecular weight ion may or may not appear in these eight, since some compounds produce no stable molecular ion.

The tabulations presented here list compounds from each of 16 classes of organic compounds; each list consists of 15 compounds except for the drug list, which contains 25. Each group of compounds within a class is listed in order of increasing molecular weight. On the first line of each set of spectral data appears the name of the compound followed by the molecular formula. Below the name is listed the molecular weight. To the right of these data are the mass values of the eight most abundant ions arranged in order of decreasing intensity. Below each of these mass values appears its relative abundance, normalized to the most abundant ion at a value of 1,000.

Identification of a compound is achieved by a match of its mass spectrum with references such as tabulated here. A match consists of observing the same ions in roughly the same order of intensities. An exact match is not always to be expected since these mass spectral patterns are dependent upon the type of mass spectrometer used and the temperature of ionization. The mass spectra for these selected compounds were extracted from published indices containing as many as 17,000 mass spectra. The reader is referred to these collections for more extensive information:

1. Cornu, A. and Massot, R., Compilation of Mass Spectral Data, Heyden and Son, London, Vol. I, 1966; 1st Suppl., 1967; 2nd Suppl., 1971.
2. Eight Peak Index of Mass Spectra, Mass Spectrometry Data Centre, Vols. I and II, AWRE.
3. Mass Spectra of Drugs, collection compiled by the MIT Mass Spectrometry Laboratory in cooperation with Committee VI of the American Society for Mass Spectrometry.

These tabulated reference spectra were obtained with mass spectrometers that separate unit masses up to about 1,000 a.m.u. However, there is a fractional divergence between the actual mass of an element and the nearest whole number as indicated in Table 1. This difference can be used to distinguish between compounds such as CO, N_2, and C_2H_4 that appear at the same nominal unit mass of 28 but differ by a few parts per thousand in actual mass. In more complicated molecules, the empirical formula of the molecule can be obtained by determining its exact mass. High resolution mass spectrometers, capable of separating masses that differ by 1 part in 50,000, are commonly used for positive identification of ionic masses from complicated molecules as well as simple ones. Because of their complexity the high resolution mass spectra have not been tabulated in reference tables, and one usually refers to lengthy tabulations of empirical formulae versus exact masses to determine an unknown.

TABLE 1

Mass Spectral Tabulations

Species	Mass	Species	Mass
^{1}H	1.007825	$^{12}CH_4$	16.031298
^{12}C	12.000000	$^{14}NH_3$	17.026547
^{14}N	14.003074	$^{12}C^{16}O$	27.994914
^{16}O	15.994914	$^{14}N_2$	28.006148
^{19}F	18.998402	$^{12}C_2H_4$	28.031298

Name	Formula	Ion Mass and Relative Intensity							
Acids									
Acetic acid	$C_2H_4O_2$	43	45	60	29	42	28	44	41
M = 60		1,000	936	577	156	145	56	49	45
Propionic acid	$C_3H_6O_2$	28	29	74	27	45	73	57	26
M = 74		1,000	836	785	617	557	484	301	211
Butyric acid	$C_4H_8O_2$	60	27	73	42	41	43	29	45
M = 88		1,000	409	268	253	242	221	205	194
Oxalic acid	$C_2H_2O_4$	44	18	17	28	45	16	46	36
M = 90		1,000	584	132	108	43	43	41	17
Valeric acid	$C_5H_{10}O_2$	60	43	41	87	45	27	74	39
M = 102		1,000	349	264	207	186	125	117	101
Isovaleric acid	$C_5H_{10}O_2$	60	43	41	27	45	29	39	74
M = 102		1,000	606	538	332	307	273	243	240
Malonic acid	$C_3H_4O_4$	44	45	43	60	15	28	42	16
M = 104		1,000	384	370	333	95	73	63	39
Caproic acid	$C_6H_{12}O_2$	60	73	27	41	43	29	45	39
M = 116		1,000	416	360	328	265	260	198	156
Succinic acid	$C_4H_6O_4$	18	28	26	56	27	14	29	25
M = 118		1,000	781	204	178	156	57	41	39
Adipic acid	$C_6H_{10}O_4$	55	28	41	100	27	45	42	43
M = 146		1,000	690	550	460	386	367	346	336
Pimelic acid	$C_7H_{12}O_4$	55	83	60	114	101	41	45	73
M = 160		1,000	752	742	706	587	389	359	358
Capric acid	$C_{10}H_{20}O_2$	73	60	129	57	43	71	41	55
M = 172		1,000	905	569	401	390	382	323	314
Lauric acid	$C_{12}H_{24}O_2$	73	60	41	43	57	55	129	71
M = 200		1,000	929	419	586	477	408	340	296
Palmitic acid	$C_{16}H_{32}O_2$	73	71	83	129	256	98	85	97
M - 256		1,000	335	246	234	220	208	202	166
Stearic acid	$C_{18}H_{32}O_2$	43	57	41	55	71	73	128	60
M = 284		1,000	920	587	567	507	468	434	440
Alcohols									
Ethanol	C_2H_6O	31	45	27	29	46	43	15	26
M = 46		1,000	439	197	192	189	81	76	63
n-Propanol	C_3H_8O	31	29	59	27	42	28	60	41
M = 60		1,000	171	152	137	134	109	105	102
Isopropanol	C_3H_8O	45	43	27	41	29	39	28	31
M = 60		1,000	192	103	72	60	57	52	45
n-Butyl alcohol	$C_4H_{10}O$	56	41	31	43	27	42	44	29
M = 74		1,000	696	694	648	341	318	295	248
tert-Butyl alcohol	$C_4H_{10}O$	59	31	41	43	15	29	57	27
M = 74		1,000	277	183	121	100	98	87	72

TABLE 1 (Continued)

Name	Formula	Ion Mass and Relative Intensity							
2-Butanol	$C_4H_{10}O$	45	27	31	59	29	43	41	44
M = 74		1,000	219	216	200	180	126	115	83
n-Amyl alcohol	$C_5H_{12}O$	42	55	41	70	29	31	43	57
M = 88		1,000	737	605	561	494	448	302	294
3-Pentanol	$C_5H_{12}O$	59	31	27	29	41	43	58	57
M = 88		1,000	555	240	229	229	89	79	79
2-Methyl-2-butanol	$C_5H_{12}O$	59	55	45	73	43	41	31	29
M = 88		1,000	859	572	517	433	331	288	250
3-Methyl-1-butanol	$C_5H_{12}O$	41	29	57	31	56	55	27	70
M = 88		1,000	981	828	715	657	600	594	552
Cyclohexanol	$C_6H_{12}O$	57	67	82	41	39	54	29	44
M = 100		1,000	680	528	448	446	340	300	246
1-Hexanol	$C_6H_{14}O$	56	43	55	31	41	42	27	29
M = 102		1,000	760	570	570	570	530	520	430
1-Heptanol	$C_7H_{16}O$	70	56	55	43	41	69	42	57
M = 116		1,000	890	670	640	590	530	440	260
1-Octanol	$C_8H_{18}O$	56	55	41	70	43	69	84	42
M = 130		1,000	820	690	670	660	630	550	510
1-Nonanol	$C_9H_{20}O$	56	41	55	43	70	69	29	31
M = 144		1,000	950	940	900	680	610	570	510

Aldehydes

Name	Formula	Ion Mass and Relative Intensity							
Acetaldehyde	C_2H_4O	29	44	43	42	28	41	26	27
M = 44		1,000	883	500	149	90	64	55	35
Propanal	C_3H_6O	29	58	28	27	57	18	41	39
M = 58		1,000	830	820	570	260	80	70	60
Butanal	C_4H_8O	44	43	72	41	27	29	57	39
M = 72		1,000	790	730	600	590	540	260	230
2-Methylpropanal	C_4H_8O	43	41	72	27	29	39	42	28
M = 72		1,000	660	530	390	230	160	80	80
Pentanal	$C_5H_{10}O$	44	29	41	58	43	57	27	42
M = 86		1,000	460	440	380	290	290	250	160
2-Methylbutanal	$C_5H_{10}O$	57	29	41	58	27	39	86	43
M = 86		1,000	850	780	630	260	160	150	100
2,2-Dimethylpropanal	$C_5H_{10}O$	57	41	29	86	43	39	27	55
M = 86		1,000	827	394	339	183	168	108	66
Hexanal	$C_6H_{12}O$	44	43	56	41	57	29	27	72
M = 100		1,000	860	860	740	650	400	360	330
Heptanal	$C_7H_{14}O$	44	43	41	70	29	42	55	27
M = 114		1,000	917	809	701	681	581	548	546
2,4-Dimethylpentanal	$C_7H_{14}O$	43	58	41	27	29	39	55	28
M = 114		1,000	757	304	159	157	132	67	65
Octanal	$C_8H_{16}O$	43	41	44	57	56	84	55	29
M = 128		1,000	790	770	740	680	670	590	470
Nonanal	$C_9H_{18}O$	57	41	43	56	44	55	98	70
M = 142		1,000	700	680	630	560	500	400	360
Decanal	$C_{10}H_{20}O$	57	43	41	55	44	70	82	71
M = 156		1,000	950	770	650	560	550	520	500
Hendecanal	$C_{11}H_{22}O$	43	57	41	55	82	44	56	29
M = 170		1,000	910	750	690	570	490	490	470
Dodecanal	$C_{12}H_{24}O$	57	43	41	55	82	68	56	69
M = 184		1,000	900	690	660	610	470	430	430

Alkanes

Name	Formula	Ion Mass and Relative Intensity							
Butane	C_4H_{10}	43	29	27	28	41	39	58	42
M = 58		1,000	442	371	326	378	125	123	122

TABLE 1 (Continued)

Name	Formula	Ion Mass and Relative Intensity							
Cyclopentane	C_5H_{10}	42	70	41	55	39	27	40	29
M = 70		1,000	295	293	288	215	146	72	46
Pentane	C_5H_{12}	43	42	41	27	29	39	57	72
M = 72		1,000	579	405	346	244	142	126	88
Isopentane	C_5H_{12}	43	42	41	57	29	27	39	56
M = 72		1,000	860	673	540	457	422	215	168
Neopentane	C_5H_{12}	57	41	29	27	39	15	58	56
M = 72		1,000	415	385	157	132	64	45	43
Cyclohexane	C_6H_{12}	56	84	41	55	42	27	39	69
M = 84		1,000	705	676	341	310	297	280	220
Hexane	C_6H_{14}	57	43	41	29	27	56	42	39
M = 86		1,000	815	740	631	531	443	404	241
2,3-Dimethylbutane	C_6H_{14}	43	42	41	27	39	71	29	15
M = 86		1,000	867	312	254	165	155	98	82
Ethylcyclopentane	C_7H_{14}	69	41	68	55	70	42	56	27
M = 98		1,000	938	728	561	547	521	520	413
Decahydronaphthalene	$C_{10}H_{18}$	138	67	96	81	82	68	95	41
M = 138		1,000	930	900	780	730	620	580	500
Decane	$C_{10}H_{22}$	43	57	41	29	71	27	85	56
M = 142		1,000	818	434	380	300	280	213	171
Hexadecane	$C_{16}H_{34}$	57	43	71	41	85	55	56	42
M = 226		1,000	977	568	493	351	222	152	134
2-Methylpentadecane	$C_{16}H_{34}$	43	57	41	71	85	55	42	56
M = 226		1,000	738	482	385	254	220	172	159
n-Eicosane	$C_{20}H_{42}$	57	43	71	85	41	29	55	56
M = 282		1,000	910	670	480	420	280	270	150
Triacontane	$C_{30}H_{62}$	57	422	71	43	85	55	69	423
M = 422		1,000	820	820	780	720	340	300	270

Alkenes

Name	Formula	Ion Mass and Relative Intensity							
cis-2-Butene	C_4H_8	41	56	39	55	28	27	29	53
M = 56		1,000	571	314	259	247	219	136	83
1-Butene	C_4H_8	41	56	39	27	28	55	29	26
M = 56		1,000	390	370	319	286	179	131	102
cis-2-Pentene	C_5H_{10}	55	42	70	39	41	29	27	53
M = 70		1,000	427	347	289	270	252	207	78
1-Pentene	C_5H_{10}	42	55	41	39	27	70	29	40
M = 70		1,000	579	450	346	323	317	270	86
3-Methyl-1-butene	C_5H_{10}	55	27	42	70	39	29	41	53
M = 70		1,000	290	268	262	256	256	208	81
2-Methyl-2-butene	C_5H_{10}	55	70	41	39	42	27	29	53
M = 70		1,000	357	354	312	305	261	236	97
Cyclohexene	C_6H_{10}	67	54	39	41	82	27	53	81
M = 82		1,000	800	413	404	380	287	132	108
1-Hexene	C_6H_{12}	41	56	42	27	43	55	39	84
M = 84		1,000	860	751	684	597	594	494	282
2-Ethyl-1-butene	C_6H_{12}	41	69	55	27	84	39	29	42
M = 84		1,000	889	749	509	409	393	341	316
1-Heptene	C_7H_{14}	41	56	29	55	42	27	39	70
M = 98		1,000	870	710	600	530	510	450	370
1-Octene	C_8H_{16}	43	41	55	56	42	70	29	27
M = 112		1,000	910	760	650	640	610	580	570
1-Nonene	C_9H_{18}	43	41	56	55	29	27	42	39
M = 126		1,000	820	780	650	480	460	390	370
1-Decene	$C_{10}H_{20}$	41	43	56	55	29	70	57	27
M = 140		1,000	809	809	764	611	590	555	462

TABLE 1 (Continued)

Name	Formula	Ion Mass and Relative Intensity							
1-Tridecene	$C_{13}H_{26}$	41	43	55	57	56	69	70	83
M = 182		1,000	840	690	490	460	410	400	370
1-Tetradecene	$C_{14}H_{28}$	41	43	55	57	56	69	83	70
M = 196		1,000	948	772	627	528	518	483	454

Amides

Name	Formula	Ion Mass and Relative Intensity							
Acetamide	C_2H_5ON	44	59	43	15	42	28	41	40
M = 59		1,000	929	746	477	381	346	198	119
Propionamide	C_3H_7ON	44	29	73	27	28	57	26	72
M = 73		1,000	339	313	237	210	140	89	84
N,N-Dimethylformamide	C_3H_7ON	44	73	42	28	15	30	29	18
M = 73		1,000	861	466	397	386	309	234	163
Butyramide	C_4H_9ON	59	44	41	43	27	29	28	72
M = 87		1,000	941	437	400	274	176	172	162
N,N-Dimethylacetamide	C_4H_9ON	44	43	15	87	42	45	30	72
M = 87		1,000	479	379	321	232	182	119	115
N,N-Diethylformamide	$C_5H_{11}ON$	30	58	101	28	29	27	44	86
M = 101		1,000	825	600	558	526	435	403	254
N-Methylformanilide	C_8H_9ON	105	135	77	51	28	93	106	79
M = 135		1,000	498	475	359	324	272	271	264
N-Isobutylisobutyramide	$C_8H_{17}ON$	71	43	57	72	28	44	29	27
M = 143		1,000	940	400	290	230	210	200	190
N-n-Octylformamide	$C_9H_{19}ON$	30	58	59	41	46	29	27	43
M = 157		1,000	920	780	410	390	330	280	250
Nonanamide	$C_9H_{19}ON$	59	72	43	44	41	55	86	29
M = 157		1,000	270	130	130	90	60	60	50
N,N-Diethylcaproamide	$C_{10}H_{21}ON$	58	115	60	100	42	72	73	128
M = 171		1,000	710	490	470	410	350	300	300
Undecanamide	$C_{11}H_{23}ON$	59	72	43	41	44	86	55	60
M = 185		1,000	310	120	90	80	70	50	50
Lauramide	$C_{12}H_{25}ON$	59	72	28	43	41	57	44	55
M = 199		1,000	340	250	220	180	130	120	110
N-n-Heptylcaproamide	$C_{13}H_{27}ON$	30	43	73	44	99	57	41	29
M = 213		1,000	970	450	450	450	440	440	360
N-Methyllauramide	$C_{13}H_{27}ON$	58	41	43	42	29	44	55	85
M = 213		1,000	40	30	20	20	20	20	20

Amines

Name	Formula	Ion Mass and Relative Intensity							
Trimethylamine	C_3H_9N	58	42	59	15	30	28	43	41
M = 59		1,000	463	387	337	176	133	97	80
n-Propylamine	C_3H_9N	30	28	27	59	42	26	29	39
M = 59		1,000	214	92	91	38	37	35	31
Isopropylamine	C_3H_9N	44	18	42	15	28	41	27	43
M = 59		1,000	215	154	136	111	105	84	68
n-Butylamine	$C_4H_{11}N$	30	73	28	41	27	18	44	42
M = 73		1,000	100	50	30	30	30	20	20
Piperidine	$C_5H_{11}N$	84	85	57	56	44	42	43	41
M = 85		1,000	526	520	509	401	346	288	227
N-Methylpyrrolidine	$C_5H_{11}N$	42	84	57	85	15	28	27	41
M = 85		1,000	764	743	400	287	211	203	189
n-Amylamine	$C_5H_{13}N$	30	87	41	28	45	42	27	56
M = 87		1,000	80	40	40	30	30	30	20
N-Methylpiperidine	$C_6H_{13}N$	98	99	42	41	70	58	71	84
M = 99		1,000	382	162	171	134	61	56	55

TABLE 1 (Continued)

Name	Formula	Ion Mass and Relative Intensity							
Cyclohexylamine	$C_6H_{13}N$	56	43	28	30	99	27	42	41
M = 99		1,000	274	139	137	97	91	65	63
Triethylamine	$C_6H_{15}N$	86	30	27	58	29	28	42	101
M = 101		1,000	339	269	262	233	221	184	157
n-Hexylamine	$C_6H_{15}N$	30	27	28	29	41	39	18	43
M = 101		1,000	70	58	47	46	33	32	30
2,3-Dimethylpiperidine	$C_7H_{15}N$	98	42	56	28	43	41	27	44
M = 113		1,000	688	594	544	514	434	398	365
n-Heptylamine	$C_7H_{17}N$	30	44	41	45	27	29	43	55
M = 115		1,000	70	60	50	40	40	40	40
n-Octylamine	$C_8H_{19}N$	30	27	41	28	29	45	39	43
M = 129		1,000	70	70	60	60	40	30	30
n-Decylamine	$C_{10}H_{23}N$	30	41	29	27	43	28	18	45
M = 157		1,000	110	80	80	80	70	70	50

Aromatic Hydrocarbons

Name	Formula								
Toluene	C_7H_8	91	92	39	65	51	63	90	50
M = 92		1,000	756	187	131	96	87	80	60
Ethylbenzene	C_8H_{10}	91	106	51	39	65	77	92	78
M = 106		1,000	306	131	97	81	78	75	69
1,2-Dimethylbenzene	C_8H_{10}	91	106	105	39	51	77	27	65
M = 106		1,000	598	241	162	153	132	96	79
1,3-Dimethylbenzene	C_8H_{10}	91	106	105	39	51	77	27	52
M = 106		1,000	627	282	186	154	132	101	81
1,4-Dimethylbenzene	C_8H_{10}	91	106	105	51	39	77	27	92
M = 106		1,000	615	296	159	157	135	113	75
1,2,3-Trimethylbenzene	C_9H_{12}	105	120	39	119	77	27	51	91
M = 120		1,000	533	144	126	120	104	97	89
n-Propylbenzene	C_9H_{12}	91	120	92	65	78	39	51	105
M = 120		1,000	240	111	87	60	52	43	39
1-Methyl-2-ethylbenzene	C_9H_{12}	105	120	91	106	77	79	39	103
M = 120		1,000	293	94	90	88	75	57	57
n-Butylbenzene	$C_{10}H_{14}$	91	92	134	27	65	39	105	51
M = 134		1,000	550	245	115	105	105	85	74
sec-Butylbenzene	$C_{10}H_{14}$	105	134	91	77	27	106	51	79
M = 134		1,000	180	135	103	93	86	72	71
n-Pentylbenzene	$C_{11}H_{16}$	91	92	148	39	65	41	105	51
M = 148		1,000	580	210	130	120	110	90	70
n-Hexylbenzene	$C_{12}H_{18}$	91	92	162	105	43	65	27	78
M = 162		1,000	760	240	100	100	70	70	60
n-Heptylbenzene	$C_{13}H_{20}$	91	92	43	176	41	65	105	29
M = 176		1,000	960	300	180	140	110	110	100
n-Octylbenzene	$C_{14}H_{22}$	92	91	57	41	190	42	105	39
M = 190		1,000	980	210	200	180	170	110	110
n-Decylbenzene	$C_{16}H_{26}$	92	91	43	41	218	57	105	39
M = 218		1,000	810	230	210	140	90	90	80

Drugs

Name	Formula								
4-(ω-Aminoethyl)-1,3-	$C_5H_9N_3$	82	81	44	54	55	83	94	41
diazole (histamine)		1,000	343	162	141	111	81	51	40
M = 111									
1-Phenyl-2-propylamine	$C_9H_{13}N$	44	91	45	65	42	43	41	51
(amphetamine)		1,000	81	61	51	40	30	20	20
M = 135									
Nicotine	$C_{10}H_{14}N_2$	84	42	133	162	161	51	119	65
M = 162		1,000	273	263	131	101	81	71	71

TABLE 1 (Continued)

Name	Formula	Ion Mass and Relative Intensity							
Acetyl salicylic acid (aspirin)	$C_9H_8O_4$	120	138	43	92	64	65	63	42
M = 180		1,000	596	485	343	101	91	81	61
5,5-Diethylbarbituric acid	$C_8H_{12}N_2O_3$	156	141	98	155	55	112	41	83
(barbital)		1,000	899	202	202	182	182	162	111
M = 184									
Caffeine	$C_8H_{10}N_4O_2$	194	109	55	67	82	15	18	42
M = 194		1,000	596	374	222	172	141	111	101
5-Ethyl-5-isoamylbarbituric	$C_{11}H_{18}N_2O_3$	156	141	157	41	55	43	142	197
acid (amytal)		1,000	677	293	162	152	121	121	101
M = 226									
Pentobarbital	$C_{11}H_{18}N_2O_3$	156	141	43	41	157	55	69	71
M = 226		1,000	707	323	222	202	131	101	101
Ethylphenylbarbituric acid	$C_{12}H_{12}N_2O_3$	204	63	146	232	117	143	174	89
(phenobarbital)		1,000	343	343	283	222	182	182	172
M = 232									
p-Aminobenzoate (procaine)	$C_{13}H_{20}N_2O_2$	86	99	120	58	87	65	92	71
M = 236		1,000	242	162	71	71	61	61	51
Secobarbital	$C_{12}H_{18}N_2O_3$	41	168	167	43	39	55	97	124
M = 238		1,000	798	727	687	566	414	343	293
Phencyclidine	$C_{17}H_{25}N$	200	91	243	84	242	186	166	201
M = 243		1,000	485	263	253	232	212	182	172
Meperidine	$C_{15}H_{21}NO_2$	71	70	42	28	57	43	172	25
M = 247		1,000	545	495	465	333	313	293	222
Diphenylhydantoin	$C_{15}H_{12}N_2O_2$	180	77	104	209	223	252	51	181
M = 252		1,000	566	566	566	444	333	273	253
Diazepam (valium)	$C_{16}H_{13}ClN_2O$	256	283	255	284	257	258	285	165
M = 284		1,000	758	606	596	485	384	343	313
Morphine	$C_{17}H_{19}NO_3$	285	162	42	28	44	31	215	70
M = 285		1,000	636	586	556	384	343	343	283
Librium (chlordiazepoxide)	$C_{16}H_{14}ClN_3O$	282	283	284	299	285	77	56	41
M = 299		1,000	717	434	343	232	222	192	182
Cocaine	$C_{17}H_{21}NO_4$	82	28	182	83	77	42	94	105
M = 303		1,000	455	444	323	313	293	263	253
6-Dimethylamino-4,4-diphenyl-	$C_{21}H_{27}NO$	72	28	165	42	180	178	179	91
3-heptanone (methadone)		1,000	309	104	78	72	70	69	67
M = 309									
Chlorpromazine	$C_{17}H_{19}ClN_2S$	58	86	318	85	272	320	42	232
M = 318		1,000	263	232	121	91	81	61	51
LSD (lysergide)	$C_{20}H_{25}N_3O$	323	221	181	222	223	207	324	72
M = 323		1,000	646	414	364	323	293	222	212
Darvon metabolite-1	$C_{21}H_{27}NO_2$	44	220	100	57	205	91	129	221
M = 325		1,000	929	626	424	354	263	202	202
Darvon (propoxyphene)	$C_{22}H_{29}NO_2$	58	57	59	29	49	91	42	105
M = 339		1,000	40	40	40	40	30	10	10
Chlorophenothane (D.D.T.)	$C_{14}H_9Cl_5$	235	237	165	212	246	75	176	36
M = 352		1,000	657	404	232	162	152	152	152
Heroin	$C_{21}H_{23}NO_5$	327	369	268	43	310	215	42	204
M = 369		1,000	657	545	495	475	303	283	253

Esters

Name	Formula	Ion Mass and Relative Intensity							
Methyl formate	$C_2H_4O_2$	31	29	32	60	28	30	18	44
M = 60		1,000	631	340	279	71	69	23	15
Methyl acetate	$C_3H_6O_2$	43	15	74	28	42	59	29	32
M = 74		1,000	209	193	171	87	70	47	40
Ethyl formate	$C_3H_6O_2$	31	28	29	27	45	26	43	74
M = 74		1,000	727	658	432	287	126	75	71

TABLE 1 (Continued)

Name	Formula	Ion Mass and Relative Intensity							
Methyl propionate	$C_4H_8O_2$	29	57	27	59	88	28	26	31
M = 88		1,000	752	367	246	213	158	114	72
Ethyl acetate	$C_4H_8O_2$	43	29	45	27	61	42	70	28
M = 88		1,000	255	135	131	99	59	47	41
Ethyl propionate	$C_5H_{10}O_2$	57	29	27	102	75	28	45	74
M = 102		1,000	836	174	169	147	142	128	121
Propyl acetate	$C_5H_{10}O_2$	43	61	31	27	42	73	29	41
M = 102		1,000	191	178	148	112	93	88	85
Isopropyl acetate	$C_5H_{10}O_2$	43	45	27	61	41	42	39	59
M = 102		1,000	319	140	119	113	86	73	68
n-Amyl acetate	$C_7H_{14}O_2$	43	70	42	55	27	15	41	61
M = 130		1,000	304	208	184	162	156	152	151
Isoamyl acetate	$C_7H_{14}O_2$	43	70	55	15	41	27	42	29
M = 130		1,000	358	269	166	146	146	122	120
Cyclohexyl acetate	$C_8H_{14}O_2$	43	82	67	57	54	55	41	83
M = 142		1,000	932	574	202	191	166	150	110
Methyl caprate	$C_{11}H_{22}O_2$	74	87	43	41	55	143	75	59
M = 186		1,000	405	231	146	145	133	96	88
Methyl laurate	$C_{13}H_{26}O_2$	74	87	43	41	29	55	15	27
M = 214		1,000	543	393	362	292	254	198	185
Methyl myristate	$C_{15}H_{30}O_2$	74	87	43	57	41	29	42	55
M = 242		1,000	582	433	417	406	319	303	270
Methyl palmitate	$C_{17}H_{34}O_2$	74	87	43	41	55	57	75	29
M = 270		1,000	664	379	242	238	160	157	139

Ethers

Name	Formula	Ion Mass and Relative Intensity							
Tetrahydrofuran	C_4H_8O	42	41	27	72	71	39	43	29
M = 72		1,000	517	326	292	267	246	222	219
Diethyl ether	$C_4H_{10}O$	31	59	29	45	27	43	41	28
M = 74		1,000	530	410	390	170	70	60	50
Methyl *n*-propyl ether	$C_4H_{10}O$	45	41	29	27	43	15	73	42
M = 74		1,000	80	80	60	40	30	20	20
Methyl isopropyl ether	$C_4H_{10}O$	59	29	43	15	31	27	41	42
M = 74		1,000	330	290	250	180	180	170	90
Tetrahydropyran	$C_5H_{10}O$	41	28	56	85	45	27	29	86
M = 86		1,000	594	588	567	558	507	506	499
2-Methyl tetrahydrofuran	$C_5H_{10}O$	71	43	41	42	27	29	39	45
M = 86		1,000	974	709	583	478	351	313	259
Methyl *n*-butyl ether	$C_5H_{12}O$	45	56	41	29	27	59	57	31
M = 88		1,000	200	80	70	50	30	20	20
Methyl *tert*-butyl ether	$C_5H_{12}O$	73	57	41	43	29	27	45	55
M = 88		1,000	250	200	130	120	50	50	40
Ethyl isopropyl ether	$C_5H_{12}O$	45	43	73	27	29	15	41	59
M = 88		1,000	320	280	170	170	100	90	60
1,4-Dioxane	$C_4H_8O_2$	28	29	88	58	31	15	30	43
M = 88		1,000	371	306	240	174	168	132	114
Tetramethyl ethylene oxide	$C_6H_{12}O$	59	43	58	41	42	39	31	57
M = 100		1,000	652	642	486	239	198	179	137
4-Methyl-1,3-dioxone	$C_5H_{10}O_2$	43	55	72	102	31	45	29	42
M = 102		1,000	636	548	516	453	367	339	330
Ethyl *n*-butyl ether	$C_6H_{14}O$	59	31	29	57	41	56	27	73
M = 102		1,000	610	250	230	210	200	110	80
Isopropyl ether	$C_6H_{14}O$	45	43	87	59	41	27	39	69
M = 102		1,000	390	240	110	110	60	40	40
n-Propyl ether	$C_6H_{14}O$	43	73	41	102	27	31	57	42
M = 102		1,000	230	190	110	110	80	70	60

TABLE 1 (Continued)

Name	Formula	Ion Mass and Relative Intensity							
Halogen Compounds									
Methyl chloride	CH_3Cl	50	15	49	47	48	35	36	
M = 50		1,000	210	90	60	30	20	7	
n-Propyl chloride	C_3H_7Cl	43	27	63	79	41	42	62	64
M = 78		1,000	300	280	250	190	50	30	20
Methylene chloride	CH_2Cl_2	49	84	86	51	47	35	48	88
M = 84		1,000	577	362	301	178	121	87	57
n-Butyl chloride	C_4H_9Cl	56	41	43	27	29	28	57	55
M = 92		1,000	520	310	250	160	140	70	70
Methyl bromide	CH_3Br	15	94	96	79	81	95	93	14
M = 94		1,000	915	802	142	138	128	111	100
Chloroform	$CHCl_3$	83	85	47	35	48	49	87	37
M = 118		1,000	640	371	201	163	119	102	62
1-Bromopropane	C_3H_7Br	43	41	27	122	124	39	42	57
M = 122		1,000	350	280	220	220	100	70	60
1,4-Dichlorobutane	$C_4H_8Cl_2$	55	27	41	90	54	62	28	49
M = 126		1,000	424	414	212	188	183	178	139
1-Bromobutane	C_4H_9Br	57	41	29	27	56	136	138	28
M = 136		1,000	490	340	200	130	130	130	90
Methyl iodide	CH_3I	142	127	141	15	139	140	128	
M = 142		1,000	380	140	130	50	40	30	
1-Bromopentane	$C_5H_{11}Br$	71	43	41	42	55	27	29	39
M = 150		1,000	990	360	280	260	190	190	130
Carbon tetrachloride	CCl_4	117	119	121	82	84	47	35	49
M = 152		1,000	974	317	194	127	127	64	43
Methylene bromide	CH_2Br_2	174	93	95	172	176	91	79	81
M = 172		1,000	724	620	519	487	93	89	89
Bromoform	$CHBr_3$	173	171	175	93	91	79	81	92
M = 250		1,000	501	490	222	218	175	171	127
Methylene iodide	CH_2I_2	268	141	127	254	140	139	134	63
M = 268		1,000	680	390	120	70	60	20	10
Ketones									
Acetone	C_3H_6O	43	58	27	42	26	29	39	38
M = 58		1,000	271	80	70	58	43	38	23
Methyl ethyl ketone	C_4H_8O	43	29	72	27	57	42	26	28
M = 72		1,000	245	170	157	61	52	50	29
2-Pentanone	$C_5H_{10}O$	43	57	86	29	27	58	71	41
M = 86		1,000	262	252	157	103	92	92	82
Cyclohexanone	$C_6H_{10}O$	55	42	41	27	98	39	69	70
M = 98		1,000	845	342	333	314	268	260	200
3-Methylcyclopentanone	$C_6H_{10}O$	42	55	69	98	41	56	28	27
M = 98		1,000	967	859	674	663	647	577	503
2-Hexanone	$C_6H_{12}O$	43	58	29	27	41	57	39	100
M = 100		1,000	422	209	151	143	136	72	64
3-Methyl-2-pentanone	$C_6H_{12}O$	43	29	57	41	72	27	56	39
M = 100		1,000	337	274	262	171	148	90	77
3-Methylcyclohexanone	$C_7H_{12}O$	69	41	55	46	42	112	39	27
M = 112		1,000	910	456	450	420	269	222	178
Di-*n*-propyl ketone	$C_7H_{14}O$	43	71	41	39	42	114	70	29
M = 114		1,000	676	352	218	122	121	91	66
2,4-Dimethyl-3-pentanone	$C_7H_{14}O$	43	71	27	41	39	114	42	28
M = 114		1,000	275	215	186	114	59	58	55
2-Octanone	$C_8H_{16}O$	43	58	41	59	71	128	57	42
M = 128		1,000	690	120	110	110	40	30	30

TABLE 1 (Continued)

Name	Formula	Ion Mass and Relative Intensity							
2-Nonanone	$C_9H_{18}O$	43	58	41	27	57	59	71	29
M = 142		1,000	860	200	180	180	180	180	160
2-Decanone	$C_{10}H_{20}O$	58	43	59	71	57	41	156	55
M = 156		1,000	600	330	290	150	100	100	90
2-Undecanone	$C_{11}H_{22}O$	57	43	58	71	41	29	56	54
M = 170		1,000	820	320	300	180	110	100	80
2-Tridecanone	$C_{13}H_{26}O$	43	58	59	41	71	29	27	55
M = 198		1,000	920	330	300	290	210	160	150

Nitriles

Name	Formula	Ion Mass and Relative Intensity							
Acetonitrile	C_2H_3N	41	40	39	15	28	26	27	29
M = 41		1,000	540	180	8	3	2	1	1
Propionitrile	C_3H_5N	28	54	55	26	27	53	15	40
M = 55		1,000	780	150	150	130	8	4	4
Valeronitrile	C_5H_9N	41	43	54	27	55	28	39	29
M = 83		1,000	990	590	320	220	180	150	140
Isovaleronitrile	C_5H_9N	43	41	27	39	68	29	40	28
M = 83		1,000	610	180	140	70	50	40	40
Capronitrile	$C_6H_{11}N$	41	54	55	29	68	57	27	43
M = 97		1,000	890	490	340	340	320	270	240
Isocapronitrile	$C_6H_{11}N$	55	41	43	54	57	82	27	29
M = 97		1,000	350	340	240	240	140	130	120
2-Methylpentanonitrile	$C_6H_{11}N$	55	41	43	27	39	57	54	29
M = 97		1,000	520	457	389	290	272	255	219
Heptanonitrile	$C_7H_{13}N$	41	82	43	83	54	55	27	29
M = 111		1,000	950	630	580	560	510	300	280
3-Methylhexanonitrile	$C_7H_{13}N$	55	41	57	68	29	54	96	27
M = 111		1,000	530	490	470	320	230	210	190
Nonanonitrile	$C_9H_{17}N$	41	96	82	69	54	83	43	55
M = 139		1,000	880	850	780	760	680	670	610
Caprinitrile	$C_{10}H_{19}N$	41	96	110	82	97	43	83	69
M = 153		1,000	920	880	870	830	830	750	730
Undecanonitrile	$C_{11}H_{21}N$	41	43	97	96	110	82	55	57
M = 167		1,000	960	910	790	750	720	710	690
Lauronitrile	$C_{12}H_{23}N$	97	43	41	110	96	57	82	124
M = 181		1,000	820	800	780	760	650	570	550
Hexadecanonitrile	$C_{16}H_{31}N$	97	57	43	110	41	96	124	55
M = 237		1,000	970	930	800	730	650	570	550
Heptadecanonitrile	$C_{17}H_{33}N$	57	43	97	41	110	83	70	69
M = 251		1,000	920	840	680	540	480	440	440

Phenols

Name	Formula	Ion Mass and Relative Intensity							
Phenol	C_6H_6O	94	66	39	65	40	95	38	55
M = 94		1,000	276	275	223	132	109	102	84
o-Cresol	C_7H_8O	108	107	79	77	39	51	90	50
M = 108		1,000	890	523	464	420	323	288	245
m-Cresol	C_7H_8O	108	107	79	39	77	27	51	53
M = 108		1,000	942	353	320	315	289	185	172
p-Cresol	C_7H_8O	107	108	77	79	51	39	53	44
M = 108		1,000	750	302	258	142	133	124	112
Catechol	$C_6H_6O_2$	110	64	63	52	53	81	39	51
M = 110		1,000	389	215	150	150	142	123	105
Resorcinol	$C_6H_6O_2$	110	82	81	69	53	55	111	39
M = 110		1,000	115	113	85	76	73	70	65

TABLE 1 (Continued)

Name	Formula	Ion Mass and Relative Intensity							
Hydroquinone	$C_6H_6O_2$	110	53	81	55	39	54	82	51
M = 110		1,000	268	225	221	169	132	94	72
p-Ethylphenol	$C_8H_{10}O$	107	122	77	39	27	51	108	53
M = 122		1,000	290	166	134	99	78	78	60
m-Ethylphenol	$C_8H_{10}O$	107	122	77	108	39	121	91	51
M = 122		1,000	398	149	78	56	47	40	37
o-Ethyphenol	$C_8H_{10}O$	107	122	77	79	108	39	51	103
M = 122		1,000	395	181	86	78	57	52	42
2,6-Dimethylphenol	$C_8H_{10}O$	122	107	121	77	39	91	51	79
M = 122		1,000	826	380	320	304	228	204	192
2,4-Dimethylphenol	$C_8H_{10}O$	122	107	121	39	77	51	91	79
M = 122		1,000	896	552	275	275	188	185	136
p-Isopropylphenol	$C_9H_{12}O$	121	136	77	103	91	122	39	65
M = 136		1,000	299	129	120	104	91	49	45
2,4,6-Trimethylphenol	$C_9H_{12}O$	121	136	135	39	91	77	51	41
M = 136		1,000	941	405	308	259	174	143	126
p-*tert*-Butylphenol	$C_{10}H_{14}O$	135	107	41	150	39	28	95	77
M = 150		1,000	271	245	203	202	182	170	129
Substituted Aromatics									
Pyridine	C_5H_5N	79	52	51	50	26	39	78	53
M = 79		1,000	758	399	305	206	118	117	90
Aniline	C_6H_7N	93	66	65	39	92	46	28	38
M = 93		1,000	334	183	178	106	88	80	75
Cyanobenzene	C_7H_5N	103	76	50	51	75	104	39	52
M = 103		1,000	325	172	96	75	74	67	57
Benzaldehyde	C_7H_6O	77	106	105	51	50	78	52	39
M = 106		1,000	909	892	579	344	196	146	111
o-Toluidine	C_7H_9N	106	107	77	79	39	53	52	51
M = 107		1,000	830	170	125	123	96	96	94
Acetophenone	C_8H_8O	105	77	51	120	43	50	78	28
M = 120		1,000	826	305	247	177	128	89	55
Benzoic acid	$C_7H_6O_2$	105	122	77	51	50	39	38	74
M = 122		1,000	775	752	455	295	114	103	99
Ethyl phenyl ether	$C_8H_{10}O$	94	122	39	66	27	65	51	77
M = 122		1,000	350	191	169	122	117	95	92
2-Phenylethanol	$C_8H_{10}O$	91	92	122	65	63	80	77	78
M = 122		1,000	501	246	177	76	61	60	44
Benzyl chloride	C_7H_7Cl	91	126	2	39	65	63	92	128
M = 126		1,000	230	153	128	118	99	91	74
Phenylacetic acid	$C_8H_8O_2$	91	136	92	65	39	63	51	137
M = 136		1,000	341	167	117	58	41	32	31
Benzoyl chloride	C_7H_5ClO	105	77	51	50	52	106	74	37
M = 140		1,000	674	377	260	107	92	79	78
Ethyl benzoate	$C_9H_{10}O_2$	105	122	77	150	51	106	50	29
M = 150		1,000	330	330	250	110	90	40	30
Diphenyl ether	$C_{12}H_{10}O$	170	51	77	141	39	142	169	50
M = 170		1,000	556	526	203	294	203	176	146
Benzophenone	$C_{13}H_{10}O$	105	182	77	51	106	183	181	76
M = 182		1,000	540	444	127	77	77	64	35

Section F

Nuclear Magnetic Resonance

NUCLEAR MAGNETIC RESONANCE

Norman S. Bhacca, Louisiana State University

Chemical shift and spin-spin coupling are the two most important features of nuclear magnetic resonance (NMR) spectroscopy. This section deals with tabulations of these two important parameters as they occur in proton magnetic resonance (PMR) spectroscopy along with very brief descriptions of the nmr phenomena and the two terms.

NMR is a technique for measuring the interaction between an atomic nucleus and a magnetic field. This magnetic interaction is ordinarily affected by the number and arrangement of the surrounding electrons and therefore provides molecular structural information. Only nuclei possessing angular momentum have magnetic dipole moments and are suitable for nmr experiments. When a sample solution is placed in magnetic field H_o, the stationary states for spin ½ nuclei correspond to alignment either parallel or antiparallel to H_o, i.e., two energy levels. According to the Boltzman distribution the probability of occupation of the two levels by nuclei is not equal. The lower state (all nuclear spins parallel to H_o) has a slightly greater probability of being occupied by nuclei. The distribution of nuclei among the energy states is altered from that predicted by the Boltzman distribution (an nmr phenomenon occurs) when the sample solution is irradiated by electro-magnetic radiation at a radiofrequency ν which is exactly equal to the Larmor frequency of the nuclei under observation:

$$\nu = \frac{\gamma}{2\pi} H_o \qquad 1$$

where γ = magnetogyric ratio

Thus by slowly changing H_o while ν (usually in the radio-frequency region) is held constant, or changing ν while H_o is held constant, causes different nuclei in different electronic environment to successively satisfy the resonance condition in Equation 1. If the energy absorbed by the sample is continuously monitored, a series of peaks will be observed corresponding to first one and then the other class of nuclei. The device for sweeping H_o or ν and monitoring the result is called an NMR spectrometer. The frequencies of resonances in an NMR spectrum reflect the electronic environment at the nuclei and are proportional to H_o. The difference between resonance frequencies is termed chemical shift and is linearly proportional to H_o. Since NMR spectra may be obtained at various magnetic field strengths, chemical shifts are almost universally reported in a field-independent scale that is defined as

$$\text{ppm } (\delta) = \frac{\nu_{sample} - \nu_{reference}}{\text{spectrometer frequency}} \times 10^6$$

Tetramethylsilane (TMS) and sodium 2,2-dimethyl-2-silapentane-5-sulfonate (DDS) are employed as internal reference compounds for nonaqueous and aqueous media, respectively. The frequency position of TMS or DDS resonance is defined as exactly 0.0 ppm. The numbers on the dimensionless (shift) scale down field from TMS or DDS are designed as positive.

Chemical shift of a specific nucleus *A* depends upon the field H_A experienced at the nucleus and is given by the expression $H_A = H_o(1-\sigma_A)$; where σ_A is the total magnetic screening arising from the orbital currents induced by external magnetic field H_o. The screen factor σ_A may be arbitrarily subdivided into five contributions as follows:

$$\sigma_A = \sigma_d^{AA'} + \sigma_p^{AA'} + \Sigma\sigma_{A \neq B}^{AB} + \sigma^{A,\,ring} + \sigma^{solvent}$$

The local diamagnetic contribution ($\sigma_d^{AA'}$) arises from induced, *local isotropic* circulation of electrons (A′) about nucleus *A*, and causes increased shielding (upfield shift) of the signal. The local paramagnetic term ($\sigma_p^{AA'}$) arises from induced *local anisotropic* circulation of electrons (*A*′) about the *A* nucleus; the resultant effect may be an increase or a decrease in the nuclear shielding depending upon the geometry of the molecule in question. Both these terms depend upon the electronic cloud generated by substituents directly bonded to atom A. Unlike the $\sigma_d^{AA'}$ factor which is due to the circulation of electrons in spherically symmetrical orbitals, the $\sigma_p^{AA'}$ contribution has its origin in the electronic circulation induced by the mixing of a symmetrically occupied ground state with only slightly more energetic, nonspherical orbitals centered about the nucleus under observation. Since the hydrogen atom does not contain any low-lying electronic states that could mix with the ground state orbital 1 s, and the excitation energy required for the interaction of higher energy orbitals with the ground state in this atom is too large to be observed during nmr experimental conditions, the $\sigma_p^{AA'}$ term in pmr is very small. This paramagnetic term accounts for the increasing range of chemical shifts as the atomic number is increased from ^1H (10 to 20 ppm) through ^{13}C(~350 ppm) to ^{59}(~20,000 ppm). The distant anisotropic effects σ^{AB} arising from circulation of electrons around neighboring atoms are small (1 to 2 ppm). The term $\sigma^{A,\,ring}$ represents the screening effect due to "ring currents" that cannot be localized on any atom and is observed in the range of 3 to 15 ppm. Thus pmr chemical shifts are mainly attributed to the local diamagnetic $\sigma_d^{AA'}$ and distant anisotropic $\sigma_{A \neq B}^{AB}$ and because of the small shift range, pmr spectra of molecules having protons of similar chemical and stereochemical environments often result in overlapping, undecipherable pmr signals. In many instances, this difficulty is overcome by employing a variety of techniques such as (a) change of solvents, (b) use of higher-field NMR, (c) Lanthanide shift reagents.

Spin-spin coupling – Although direct magnetic dipole-dipole coupling between interacting nuclei averages out to zero because of rapid molecular motion, an indirect spin-spin interaction caused by the polarization of the surrounding electrons remains and is generally observed as spin-spin splittings in an nmr spectrum. The number of lines and their intensities present in the resonance of a spin-spin coupled nucleus depend upon the number of neighboring magnetic nuclei. The spacing between the lines is characteristic of the nature and/or number of intervening chemical bonds and the geometrical relationship between the coupled nuclei. In the simplest cases, it is the separation in frequency between adjacent component bands of a spin-spin multiplet, but in more complex cases, it must be determined by detailed calculations. It is independent of the strength of the applied magnetic field. The only recommended unit for J is Hertz (Hz).

I. AROMATIC COMPOUNDS

TABLE 1[1–3]

Monosubstituted Benzenes

Benzene $\delta = 7.27$ $J_{23} = 7.56$ $J_{26} = 1.38$ $J_{25} = 0.68$

($\delta = 7.27 \pm$ values in the table)

Substituent	o	m	p	J_{23}	J_{34}	J_{26}	J_{35}	J_{24}	J_{25}
NHMe	−0.8	−0.3	−0.6	8.17	7.31	2.54	1.70	1.07	0.46
NH_2	−0.55	−0.15	−0.55	8.02	7.33	2.46	1.65	1.12	0.49
NMe_2	−0.5	−0.2	−0.5	8.42	7.31	2.71	1.83	1.01	0.48
OH	−0.45	−0.1	−0.40						
OR	−0.45	−0.1	−0.40	8.33	7.37	2.73	1.71	1.07	0.32
OCOR	−0.20	+0.10	−0.20	8.19	7.45	2.51	1.71	1.13	0.49
Me	−0.15	−0.10	−0.10						
CH_2X*	−0.0–0.1	−0.0–0.1	−0.0–0.1						
Cl	+0.10	0.00	0.00	8.05	7.46	2.27	1.70	1.17	0.44
Br	+0.10	0.0	0.0	8.01	7.42	2.12	1.76	1.18	0.44
SR	+0.1	−0.1	−0.2						
$CHCl_2$	+0.15	+0.15	+0.15						
C=C	+0.2	+0.2	+0.2						
CF_3	+0.25	+0.25	+0.25						
I	+0.3	−0.2	−0.1	7.92	7.47	1.90	1.74	1.16	0.44
CN	+0.3	+0.3	+0.3	7.79	7.68	1.76	1.30	1.28	0.63
NHCOR	+0.4	−0.2	−0.3						
NH_3^+	+0.4	+0.2	+0.2						
$CONH_2$	+0.5	+0.2	+0.2						
CHO	+0.65	+0.25	+0.10						
COR	+0.70	+0.25	+0.10	7.82–7.87	7.38–7.47	1.90–1.92	1.34–1.36	1.28–1.30	0.58–0.63
CCl_3	+0.8	+0.2	+0.2	8.13	7.45	2.39	1.44	1.14	0.53
COOH(R)	+0.80	+0.25	+0.20						
COCl	+0.9	+0.2	+0.3	7.97	7.49	1.96	1.40	1.27	0.58

TABLE 1 (continued)

Substituent	o	m	p	J_{23}	J_{34}	J_{26}	J_{35}	J_{24}	J_{25}
NO_2	+0.85	+0.10	+0.55	8.35	7.46	2.46	1.47	1.17	0.48
$OCH_2CH=CH_2$				8.32	7.38	2.74	1.78	1.08	0.49
SC_6H_5				7.84	7.44	2.01	1.50	1.22	0.56
SO_3CH_3				7.95	7.56	2.05	1.36	1.24	0.56
SO_2Cl				8.09	7.53	2.20	1.34	1.16	0.54
$COOCH_3$	+0.73	+0.16	+0.16	7.88	7.52	1.85	1.33	1.31	0.61 (7)
$COOCH(CH_3)_2$				7.84	7.47	1.83	1.34	1.34	0.61

*X = R, OH, NH_2, or Cl.

TABLE 2[4]

ortho-Disubstituted Benzenes

Solvent: CCl_4

X	Y	δ_3	δ_4	δ_5	δ_6	J_{34}	J_{45}	J_{56}	J_{35}	J_{46}	J_{36}	Ref.
Cl	OCH_3	6.81	7.10	6.80	7.26	7.99	7.30	7.74	1.19	1.62	0.31	
Br	OCH_3	6.87	7.15	6.73	7.44	8.31	7.63	7.80	1.54	1.63	0.19	
I	OCH_3	6.71	7.20	6.61	7.69	8.05	7.17	7.55	1.38	1.62	0.29	
OCH_3	OCH_3	6.75	6.75	6.75	6.75							
Cl	NO_2	7.82	7.41	7.49	7.54	8.23	7.13	7.67	1.17	1.41	0.78	
Br	NO_2	7.78	7.44	7.40	7.71	7.86	7.53	8.27	1.66	1.22	0.19	
I	NO_2	7.80	7.36	7.29	7.99	7.90	7.20	7.71	1.35	1.45	0.28	
NO_2	NO_2	7.97	7.87	7.87	7.97							
Cl	CN	7.64	7.38	7.53	7.50	7.52	7.58	8.08	1.48	0.95	0.46	
Br	CN	7.63	7.43	7.45	7.67	7.78	7.44	7.84	1.33	1.59	0.43	
CN	CN	7.81	7.75	7.75	7.81							
NO_2	OCH_3	7.06	7.46	6.96	7.70	8.54	7.91	7.85	1.21	1.76	0.27	
Cl	Cl	7.37	7.12	7.12	7.37							4a
Br	Br	7.55	7.19	7.19	7.55							4a
I	I	7.81	6.96	6.96	7.81							4a
Cl	Br	7.53	7.01	7.14	7.38							4a
Cl	I	7.79	6.84	7.21	7.37							4a
Br	I	7.78	6.88	7.10	7.55							4a

TABLE 3[5]

ortho-Disubstituted Benzenes

Solvent: TMS

1	2	J_{34}	J_{35}	J_{36}	J_{45}	J_{46}	J_{56}
Cl	Cl	8.06	1.54	0.31	7.48	1.54	8.06
Br	Br	8.00	1.52	0.30	7.48	1.52	8.00
I	I	7.92	1.56	0.30	7.35	1.56	7.92
OMe	NO_2	8.06	1.75	0.31	7.41	1.16	8.52
Br	Cl	8.02	1.61	0.30	7.46	1.49	8.06
Br	I	7.97	1.58	0.28	7.38	1.49	8.00
Cl	I	7.96	1.55	0.30	7.40	1.53	8.01
OMe	Br	7.83	1.61	0.25	7.42	1.42	8.25

TABLE 4

meta-Disubstituted Benzenes

δ[1]

To obtain δ, add the value in Table 4 to 7.27

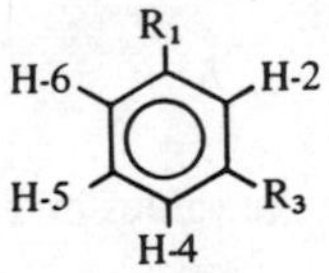

H-2, H-4, H-5, and H-6 can be computed by application of the following relationships and use of the table below

$$H\text{-}2 = A_{R_1} + A_{R_3} \qquad H\text{-}5 = B_{R_1} + B_{R_3}$$
$$H\text{-}4 = A_{R_3} + C_{R_1} \qquad H\text{-}6 = A_{R_1} + C_{R_3}$$

Substituent R	A	B	C
NH_2	−0.77	−0.27	−0.67
OMe	−0.48	−0.11	−0.41
Me	−0.18	−0.11	−0.16
Cl	0.00	−0.07	−0.16
Br	+0.16	−0.13	−0.07
I	+0.36	−0.27	−0.07
NO_2	+0.96	+0.16	+0.29
CHO	+0.54	+0.20	+0.2
$COCH_3$	+0.64	+0.09	+0.1
COCl	+0.83	+0.16	+0.2
CN	+0.27	+0.10	+0.1

TABLE 5

meta-Substituted Benzenes

(J)

Coupling Constants in Hz[5]

meta Compounds Substituent Position 1	3	2,4	2,5	2,6	4,5	4,6	5,6
Cl	Cl	1.97	0.36	1.97	8.10	0.89	8.10
Br	Br	1.85	0.29	1.85	8.03	0.95	8.03
I	I	1.62	0.28	1.62	7.93	0.99	7.93
Br	Cl	1.96	0.36	1.87	8.06	0.95	8.06
Br	I	1.60	0.25	1.88	7.93	0.96	8.05
Cl	I	1.62	0.30	2.04	7.94	0.96	8.06
NO_2	Cl	2.09	0.40	2.06	8.04	0.99	8.26

TABLE 6

para-Disubstituted Benzenes

δ[1]

To obtain δ, add the values in Table 7 to 7.27

R_4 \ R_1	NH_2	OMe	Me	Cl	Br	I	NO_2	CHO	$COCH_3$	COCl	CN
NH_2	−0.96	−0.66	−0.43	−0.27	−0.12	+0.07	+0.63	+0.21	+0.37	+0.56	0.00
OMe	−0.84	−0.55	−0.28	−0.11	+0.05	+0.24	+0.83	+0.41	+0.53	+0.72	+0.16
Me	−0.84	−0.55	−0.28	−0.11	+0.05	+0.24	+0.83	+0.41	+0.53	+0.72	+0.16
Cl	−0.81	−0.52	−0.24	−0.07	+0.09	+0.29	+0.88	+0.46	+0.58	+0.76	+0.20
Br	−0.86	−0.57	−0.30	0.13	+0.02	+0.22	+0.79	+0.38	+0.51	+0.70	+0.14
I	−0.95	−0.65	−0.42	−0.27	−0.11	+0.07	+0.64	+0.22	+0.37	+0.56	0.00
NO_2	−0.66	−0.37	−0.04	+0.16	+0.32	+0.53	+1.14	+0.73	+0.80	+0.99	+0.43
CHO	−0.63	−0.35	−0.01	+0.20	+0.36	+0.58	+1.19	+0.77	+0.84	+1.03	+0.47
$COCH_3$	−0.70	−0.42	−0.10	+0.09	+0.25	+0.46	+1.06	+0.65	+0.73	+0.92	+0.36
COCl	−0.66	−0.37	−0.04	+0.16	+0.32	+0.53	+1.14	+0.73	+0.80	+0.99	+0.43
CN	−0.70	−0.41	−0.09	+0.10	+0.26	+0.47	+1.08	+0.66	+0.74	+0.93	+0.37

TABLE 7

J^6

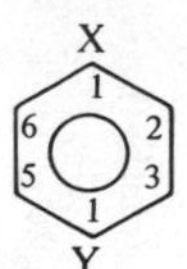

X	Y	J_{23}	J_{25}	J_{26}	J_{35}	Solvent	Ref.
Cl	Br	8.4	0.4	2.5	2.5	C_6H_{12}	
Br	I	8.6	0.3	2.5	2.2	C_6H_{12}	
Br	NO_2	8.9	0.4	2.6	2.2	C_6H_{12}	
Cl	I	8.4	0.4	2.4	2.4	C_6H_{12}	
Cl	NO_2	8.7	0.3	2.8	2.2	C_6H_{12}	
NH_2	Br	8.5	0.3	2.9	2.3	C_6H_{12}	
NH_2	Cl	8.6	0.4	2.8	2.5	C_6H_{12}	
NH_2	F	9.0	0.0			neat	8
NH_2	I	8.5	0.3	2.9	2.2	C_6H_{12}	
NH_2	NO_2	9.0	0.3	2.6	2.3	C_6H_{12}	
CN	Cl	8.4	0.4	2.1	2.1	C_6H_{12}	
COCl	Cl	8.5	0.5	2.3	2.3	C_6H_{12}	
CHO	Cl	8.3	0.4	2.1	2.1	C_6H_{12}	
CH_3	Br	8.1	0.6	2.3	2.3	C_6H_{12}	
OCH_3	Br	8.7	0.3	3.1	2.5	C_6H_{12}	
CH_3	Cl	8.4	0.4			C_6H_{12}	
OCH_3	Cl	8.8	0.3	3.1	2.5	C_6H_{12}	
CH_3	I	7.9	0.6	2.4	2.0	C_6H_{12}	
OCH_3	I	8.9	0.4	3.0	2.4	C_6H_{12}	
CH_3	NO_2	8.5	0.4	2.3	2.1	C_6H_{12}	
OCH_3	NO_2	9.0	0.3	2.7	2.7	C_6H_{12}	
NH_2	OCH_3	8.5	0.5	2.8	2.8	C_6H_{12}	
$COCH_3$	Cl	8.4	0.5	2.2	2.2	C_6H_{12}	
COCl	OCH_3	8.9	0.3	2.7	2.4	C_6H_{12}	
CN	CH_3	8.4				CCl_4	7
CN	OCH_3	8.8	0.4	2.2	2.7	C_6H_{12}	
CHO	OCH_3	8.6	0.4	2.5	2.1	C_6H_{12}	
CH_3	OCH_3	8.3	0.4			C_6H_{12}	
$COCH_3$	OCH_3	8.7	0.4	2.6	2.3	C_6H_{12}	
Cl	Cl	8.55	0.39	2.58	2.58	TMS	5
Br	Br	8.41	0.46	2.38	2.38	TMS	5
I	I	8.26	0.33	2.21	2.21	TMS	5

TABLE 8

Substituted Benzenes in General

Contributions to δ by Various Substituents on the Benzene Ring (Add the Values in Table 9 to 7.26)[9]

R	o	m	p
CH_3	+0.17	+0.13	+0.17
	+0.15	+0.10	+0.10
	+0.20	+0.13	+0.20
	+0.10	+0.10	+0.10
	+0.16	+0.09	+0.17
$HC(CH_3)_2$	0.00	0.00	0.00
C≡	−0.02	+0.09	+0.18
OCH_3	+0.45	+0.10	+0.40
	+0.42	+0.10	+0.33
	+0.23	+0.23	+0.23
CH_2Cl	0.00	0.00	0.00
Br	−0.10	0.00	0.00
	−0.22	+0.11	0.06

TABLE 9

Biphenyls

Compound	δ	J	Ref.
Biphenyl	7.4		10
4,4′-Difluoro biphenyl	$\delta_2 = 7.37$ $\delta_3 = 7.04$	$J_{23} = 8.7$	7
4,4′-Dichloro biphenyl	$\delta_2 = \delta_3 = 7.38$		7

TABLE 10

Bridged Biphenyls[11]

X	δ (aromatic)	δ (methylene)
O	7.47	4.34
NCH_3	7.40	3.35
C=O	7.38	3.52
S	7.32	3.35, 3.44 (two broad peaks)

X	δ (aromatic)	δ (methylene)	δ (methyl)	J_{AB}
O	7.29	4.00, 4.39	2.20	11.0
NCH_3	7.22	3.02, 3.35	2.19	12.1
CH_2	7.20	1.67, 2.58	2.14	complex
C=O	7.23	3.32, 3.53	2.20	15.2
S	7.19	3.25	2.08	

X	Y	δ (aromatic)	δ (methylene)	J_{AB}
O	O	7.52	4.18, 4.55	11.5
NCH_3	NCH_3	7.38	3.21, 3.54	12.5
CH_2	CH_2	7.20	1.9-2.8	complex
C=O	C=O	7.30	3.57 (unresolved at 100 Mc)	
S	S	7.29	3.29, 3.38	12.7
O	S	7.38	4.10, 4.47	11.5
			3.34, 3.53	12.7

TABLE 11

cis-Stilbenes[12]

	δ_a	δ_b	δ_c	δ_d	J_{ab}	J_{ba}	J_{cd}	J_{dc}	δ_e	δ_f	J_{ex}	J_{fe}
4-OCH_3	6.76	7.19	6.50	6.50	8.9	8.9						
3-NH_2				6.53			12.4	~12.3				
4-F	6.84	6.93	6.56		8.8	8.7	~12.5	~12.5				
3-OCH_3				6.59			12.5	12.5				
4-Cl			6.52	6.62			12.3	12.3				
3-Cl			6.52	6.65			12.3	12.3				
4-CN	7.49	7.33	6.57	6.77	8.4	8.5	12.3	12.3				
4-NO_2	8.06	7.36	6.60	6.81	8.7	9.2	12.1	12.2				
4-$N(CH_3)_2$, 4′NO_2	6.56	7.11	6.62	6.42	9.0	9.1	12.2	12.2	7.45	8.08	8.9	9.0
4-OCH_3, 4′-NO_2	6.78	7.14	6.63	6.51	8.8	9.0	12.3	12.2	7.39	8.08	9.0	8.9
4-Cl, 4′-NO_2	7.12	7.22	6.74	6.64	8.8	8.7	12.2	12.5	7.35	8.09	8.9	8.8

TABLE 12

trans-Stilbenes[13]

	δ_a	δ_b	δ_c	δ_d	J_{ab}	J_{ba}	J_{cd}	J_{dc}
4-$N(CH_3)_2$	6.71	7.41	7.04	6.91	8.9	8.9	16.5	16.5
4-NH_2	6.67	7.36	7.02	6.92	8.6	8.6	16.4	16.4
4-OH	6.81	7.40	7.04	6.97	8.7	8.6	16.5	16.5
4-OCH_3	6.89	7.43	7.06	6.98	8.7	8.7	16.5	16.5
4-Cl			7.07				16.7	16.7
4-F			7.07				16.6	16.6
4-Br	7.36	7.48	7.04	7.08	8.7	8.7	16.5	16.5
4-CN			7.09	7.22			16.5	16.5
4-NO_2	8.23	7.63	7.15	7.28	8.9	8.9	16.5	16.5
4-$N(CH_3)_2$, 4′-NO_2	6.71	7.44	7.20		8.8	8.7	~16.0	
4-NH_2, 4′-NO_2	6.69	7.38	7.18		8.4	8.5	16.2	
4-OH, 4′-NO_2	6.85	7.42	7.21		8.9	8.9	16.1	
4-OCH_3, 4′-NO_2	6.93	7.49	7.22		8.6	8.6	16.2	
4-Cl, 4′-NO_2	7.38	7.46	7.22		8.7	8.7	16.1	
4-NO_2, 4′-NO_2	8.25	7.67	7.30					

TABLE 13

Naphthalenes

Compound	δ_1	δ_2	δ_3	δ_4	δ_5	δ_6	J_{12}	J_{13}	J_{14}	J_{23}	Ref.
Naphthalene	7.66	7.30					8.5	1.4	0.7	7.5	14
2-Methyl naphthalene	7.48		7.20	7.48	7.55	7.39					7

Both in CCl_4.

TABLE 14A

1,4-Disubstituted Naphthalenes[14]

R_1	R_2	δ_2	δ_3	δ_5	δ_6	δ_7	δ_8	J_{23}	J_{56}	J_{57}	J_{58}	J_{67}	J_{68}	J_{78}		Ref.
OCH_3	OCH_3	6.70	6.70	8.19	7.45	7.45	8.19		8.3	1.4	0.3	6.6	1.4	8.3		15, 16
NO_2	NO_2	8.41	8.41	8.27	7.95	7.95	8.27		8.9	1.0	0.0	5.6	1.0	8.9		17
Cl	Cl	7.39	7.39	8.23	7.57	7.57	8.23		8.3	1.5	0.3	6.3	1.5	8.3		15
Cl	NH_2	7.29	6.57	7.71	7.41	7.52	8.11	8.0	8.4	0.7	0.6	6.9	1.2	8.6	δNH_2 = 3.97	15
Br	CH_3	7.44	7.01	7.85	7.45	7.59	8.22	7.8	8.6	1.1	1.1	7.5	2.0	8.0	δCH_3 = 3.52	15
NO_2	OCH_3	8.31	6.71	8.29	7.52	7.67	8.72	8.7	8.3	1.3	1.0	6.9	1.0	8.0	δCH_3 = 4.00	15
F	F	6.94	6.94	7.99	7.48	7.48	7.99		8.1	1.5	1.0	6.9	1.5	8.1	$J_{2,F}$ = 6.9; $J_{5,F}$ = 1.1	15

All of the above in $CDCl_3$, 10%, except the dinitro, which was in DMA.

TABLE 14B

1,4-di-X-Naphthalenes[14a]

Solvent:	Cyclohexane			Acetone			Acetonitrile		
X	δ_2	δ_5	δ_6	δ_2	δ_5	δ_6	δ_2	δ_5	δ_6
CH_3	7.12	7.92	7.42	7.20	7.97	7.51	7.20	7.97	7.51
Cl	7.39	8.27	7.55	7.75	8.26	7.60	7.54	8.23	7.71
Br	7.56	8.24	7.56	7.77	8.29	7.77	7.69	8.20	7.72
OH	6.84	8.18	7.30						
NO_2	8.23	8.39	7.83	8.37	8.39	7.97	8.14	8.28	7.84

TABLE 15

2,3-Disubstituted Naphthalenes[14]

R_2	R_3	δ_1	δ_4	δ_5	δ_6	δ_7	δ_8	J_{14}	J_{56}	J_{57}	J_{58}	J_{67}	J_{68}	J_{78}		Ref.
CH_3	CH_3	7.50	7.50	7.64	7.31	7.31	7.64		8.0	1.4	0.4	6.3	1.4	8.0	δCH_3 = 2.49	15
Cl	Cl	7.87	7.87	7.65	7.43	7.43	7.65		8.0	1.8	0.5	7.7	1.8	7.7		15
Br	Br	8.07	8.07	7.45	7.45	7.45	7.65		7.9	1.7	0.5	7.7	1.7	7.7		15
NO_2	NO_2	7.88	7.88	8.32	7.90	7.90	8.32		8.3	1.2	0.0	6.2	1.2	8.3		17
Cl	Br	7.90	8.08	7.67	7.46	7.46	7.67	0.0	8.3	1.4	0.5	7.1	1.4	8.3		15
Cl	I	7.29	8.39	7.68	7.48	7.48	7.68	0.0	8.1	1.5	0.4	7.2	1.5	8.1		15

All in $CDCl_3$, 10%, except the dinitro, which was in DMA.

TABLE 16

2,6-Disubstituted Naphthalenes[14]

$R_2 = R_6$	δ_1	δ_3	δ_4	J_{13}	J_{14}	J_{34}		Ref.
$C(CH_3)_3$	7.73	7.52	7.75	1.7		8.7	$\delta_{CH_3} = 1.41$	18
C_6H_{13} (n)	7.53	7.26	7.66	1.5		8.1	$\delta_{phCH_2} = 2.73$ $\delta_{CH_3} = 0.88$ $J_{phCH_2,CH_2} = 7.2$	18
C_8H_{17} (n)	7.54	7.28	7.65	1.8		8.6	$\delta_{phCH_2} = 2.73$ $\delta_{CH_3} = 0.87$ $J_{phCH_2,CH_2} = 7.3$	18
$C_{10}H_{21}$ (n)	7.54	7.26	7.65	1.5		8.4	$\delta_{phCH_2} = 2.73$ $\delta_{CH_3} = 0.88$ $J_{phCH_2,CH_2} = 7.1$	18
$C_{12}H_{25}$ (n)	7.53	7.26	7.65	1.6		8.3	$\delta_{phCH_2} = 2.73$ $\delta_{CH_3} = 0.88$ $J_{phCH_2,CH_2} = 6.9$	18
1,1,3,3-tetra-methylbutyl	7.71	7.51	7.71	1.5		8.8	$\delta_{CH_2} = 1.83$ $\delta_{CH_3} = 0.74, 1.45$	18
OCH_3 (a)	7.07	7.11	7.60	2.5	0.6	8.9	$\delta_{CH_3} = 3.82$	15
COCl (b)	8.80	8.36	8.12	1.3	0.3	8.6		15
$COOCH_3$ (a)	8.58	8.08	7.94	1.5	0.3	8.6	$\delta_{CH_3} = 3.97$	15

All in $CDCl_3$ except (a) $CDCl_3$, 10%, (b) DMA, 10%.

TABLE 17

1,8-Disubstituted Naphthalenes[14]

R_1	R_8	δ_2	δ_3	δ_4	δ_5	δ_6	δ_7	J_{23}	J_{24}	J_{34}	J_{56}	J_{57}	J_{67}		Ref.
Cl	Cl	7.53	7.25	7.64	7.64	7.25	7.53	7.6	1.1	8.6	8.6	1.1	8.6		15
NO_2	NO_2 (c)	8.40	7.90	8.63	8.63	7.90	8.40	8.2	1.0	7.8	7.8	1.0	8.2		17
Cl	Br	7.59	7.22	7.75	7.61	7.31	7.88	7.1	1.1	8.6	7.8	1.2	7.5		15
Cl	NH_2	7.30	7.14	7.57	7.22	7.11	6.62	7.2	1.5	8.4	8.0	1.7	6.2	δ_{NH_2} = 5.0	15
Cl	NO_2	7.62	7.44	7.79	7.66	7.47	7.94	7.1	0.6	8.3	8.0	1.3	7.5		15
(structure: H_2C, O, O; positions 2, 3, 4)		8.30	7.73	8.22	8.22	7.73	8.30	7.2	1.2	8.0	8.0	1.2	7.2	δ_{CH_2} = 5.58	15

All in $CDCl_3$, 10%, except (c) DMA and (d) 10% DMSO-d_6.

TABLE 18

Polysubstituted Naphthalenes[19] δ

Di-*t*-butyl-2,7	H_1	H_3	H_4	H_5	H_6	H_8		*t*-Bu	
Hydrocarbon	7.82	7.50	7.76	7.76	7.50	7.82			
1-Nitro	–	7.68	7.95	7.98	7.68	7.37	1.32		1.43
4-Nitro	8.29	8.29		8.28	7.75	8.06	1.41		1.43
1,5-Dinitro		8.07	8.44		8.54	7.65	1.44		1.49
4,5-Dinitro	8.62	8.45			8.45	8.62		1.50	
1,4,5-Trinitro		8.77			8.78	7.71	1.45		1.54
1-Amino		7.00	7.29	7.60	7.38	8.04	1.38		1.47
1-Chloro		7.70	7.93	7.97	7.88	8.48	1.41		1.58
4-Chloro	8.12	7.82		8.20	7.82	8.02		1.39	
1,4-Dichloro		7.84		8.25	7.95	8.51	1.40		1.57
1,4,8-Trichloro		7.69		7.98	7.71			1.61	
4-Bromo	7.97	7.97		8.07	7.70	7.90		1.39	
1,4-Dibromo		7.92		8.10	7.79	8.51	1.42		1.61
1,4-Dicarboxylic		8.34		8.89	7.73	7.89	1.35		1.55
1-Cyano-4-carboxylic		8.25		8.87	7.88	8.25	1.44		1.66
1-Cyano-4-methoxycarbonyl		8.25		8.74	7.90	8.25	1.45		1.65
4-Sulfonamide	8.26	8.08		8.65	7.62	7.98		1.41	
4-Sulfonate of cyclohexyl	8.30	8.23		8.44	7.70	8.07	1.40		1.43
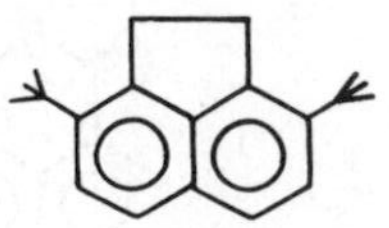		7.43	7.43	7.43	7.43			1.42	
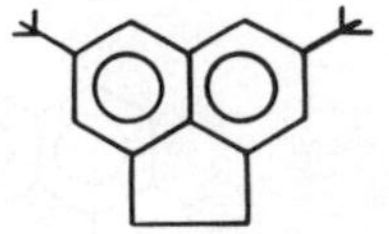	7.54	7.35			7.35	7.54		1.38	
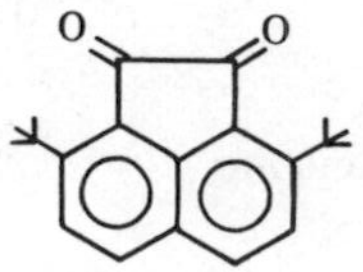		7.80	8.28	8.28	7.80			1.56	

TABLE 18 (continued)

Di-*t*-butyl-2,7	H_1	H_3	H_4	H_5	H_6	H_8	*t*-Bu
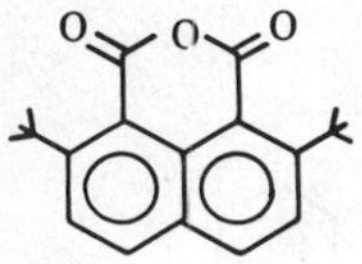		7.98	8.35	8.35	7.98		1.62
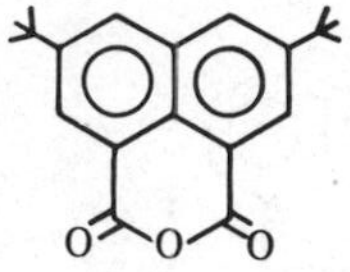 (a)	8.55	8.02			8.02	8.55	1.47
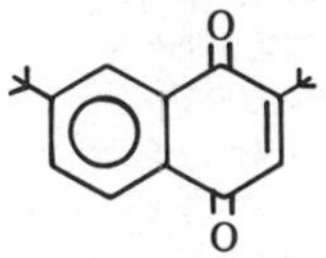		6.75		7.94	7.68	8.10	1.38
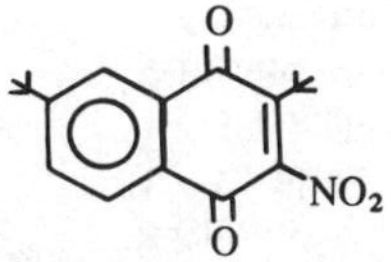				8.15	7.97		1.37–1.43

All in dimethylacetamide, except (a) $CDCl_3$.

TABLE 19

Polynuclear Aromatic Hydrocarbons[20]

Compound	δ_1	δ_2	δ_3	δ_4	δ_5	δ_9	Other	J	Ref.
Anthracene	7.91	7.39				8.31		J_{12} 8.3; J_{23} 6.5	21, 22
Phenanthrene	8.12	7.82	7.88	8.93		7.71		J_{12} 8.0–9.0; J_{23} 6.9–7.3; J_{34} 8.0–8.5; J_{13} 0.9–1.6; J_{24} 1.2–1.8; J_{14} 0.3–0.7	21–24
Pyrene		7.99	8.16	8.06				J_{12} 8–8.4; J_{45} 9.2–9.5	21, 22, 24a
Chrysene	← 7.5–7.9		→	8.7			δ_{11} 8.65 δ_{12} 7.95		22, 24b
Triphenylene	8.56	7.61							21, 22, 24c

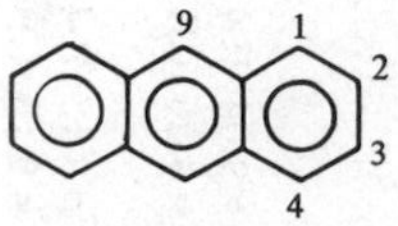

Anthracene

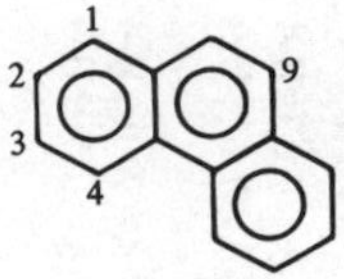

Phenanthrene

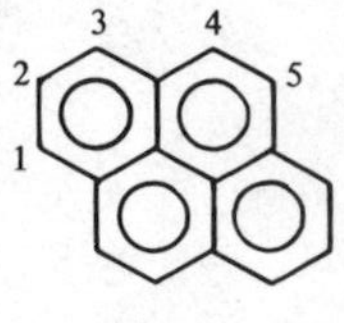

Pyrene

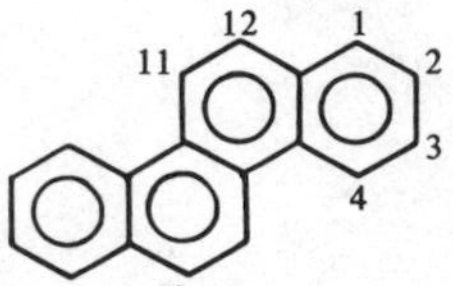

Chrysene

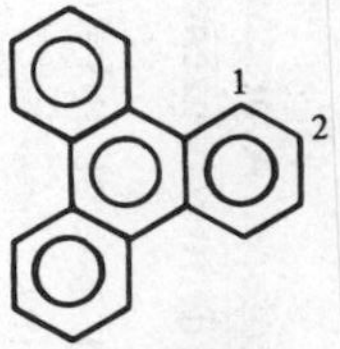

Triphenylene

TABLE 20

Polynuclear Aromatics.[25] Solvents: C, deuterochloroform; A, arsenic trichloride; N, nitromethane; T, carbon tetrachloride; D, diethyl ether; B, deuterobenzene; S, trifluoroacetic acid

Compound	Solvent	Data
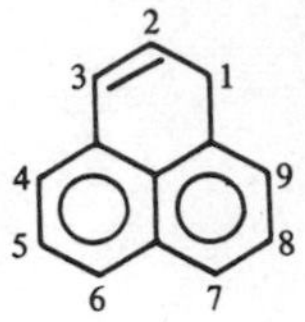	C	H-1 = 3.91; H-2 = 5.88; H-3 = 6.49; H-4 = 7.08; H-5 = 7.23; H-6 = 7.45; H-7 = 7.42; H-8 = 7.16; H-9 = 6.87
	T	H-1 = 3.88; H-2 = 5.83; H-3 = 6.43; H-4 = 7.02; H-5 = 7.17; H-6 = 7.39; H-7 = 7.36; H-8 = 7.09; H-9 = 6.80
	B	H-1 = 3.65; H-2 = 5.66; H-3 = 6.41; H-4 = 6.88; H-5 = 7.13; H-6 = 7.38; H-7 = 7.35; H-8 = 7.07; H-9 = 6.77
	C[a]	$J_{1,2}$ = 4.0; $J_{1,3}$ = 2.1; $J_{1,4}$ = 1.6; $J_{1,6}$ = 1.1; $J_{1,7}$ = 0.7; $J_{1,9}$ = 1.2; $J_{2,3}$ = 9.6; $J_{4,5}$ = 7.0; $J_{4,6}$ = 1.6; $J_{5,6}$ = 7.8; $J_{7,8}$ = 8.2; $J_{7,9}$ = 1.3; $J_{8,9}$ = 6.8
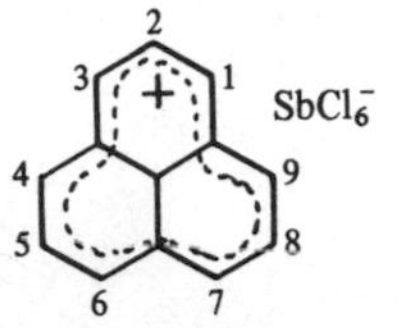 $SbCl_6^-$	A	H-1 = H-3 = H-4 = H-6 = H-7 = H-9 = 9.30; H-2 = H-5 = H-8 = 8.48; J_{ortho} = 7.2
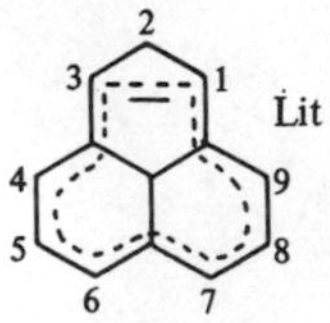 Li^+	D	H-1 = H-3 = H-4 = H-6 = H-7 = H-9 = 5.17; H-2 = H-5 = H-8 = 5.91 (Ref. 26)
	D	J_{ortho} = 7.5
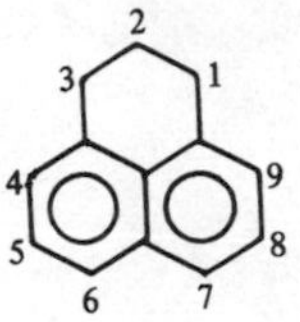	C	H-1 = H-3 = 3.01; H-2 = 1.97; H-4 = H-9 = 7.12; H-5 = H-8 = 7.28; H-6 = H-7 = 7.59
	B	H-1 = H-3 = 2.76; H-2 = 1.70; H-4 = H-9 = 7.00; H-5 = H-8 = 7.20; H-7 = 7.53
	C[b]	$J_{1,9}$ ~ 1.0; $J_{1,7}$ ~ 0.7; $J_{4,5}$ = 6.8; $J_{4,6}$ = 1.4; $J_{5,6}$ = 8.0
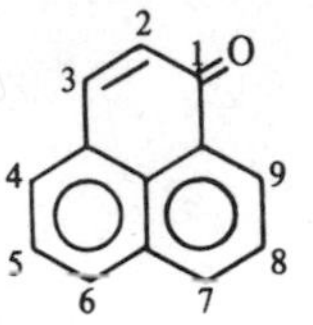	C	H-2 = 6.66; H-3 = 7.63; H-4 = 7.63; H-5 = 7.48; H-6 = 7.91; H-7 = 8.08; H-8 = 7.67; H-9 = 8.52
	B	H-2 = 6.63; H-3 = 7.06; H-4 ~ 7.1; H-5 = 7.05; H-6 = 7.43; H-7 = 7.55; H-8 = 7.19; H-9 = 8.62
	C[b]	$J_{2,3}$ = 9.6; $J_{4,5}$ = 7.5; $J_{7,8}$ = 8.0; $J_{8,9}$ = 7.2
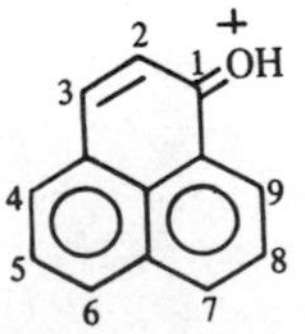	S	H-2 = 7.76; H-3 = 8.88; H-4 = 8.78; H-5 = 8.20; H-6 = 8.86; H-7 = 9.01; H-8 = 8.30; H-9 = 9.46
	S	$J_{2,3}$ = 9.0; $J_{4,5}$ = 7.6; $J_{4,6}$ = 1.4; $J_{5,6}$ = 7.6; $J_{7,8}$ = 7.8; $J_{8,9}$ = 7.7
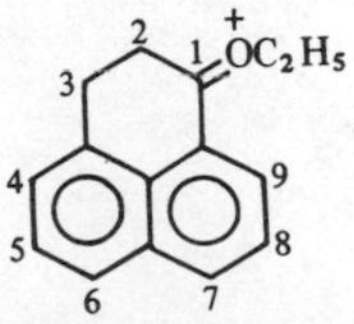	N	H-2 = 7.81; H-3 = 9.04; H-4, H-6 = 8.57–8.60; H-5 = 8.14; H-7 = 8.96; H-8 = 8.21; H-9 = 9.26 (CH_2 = 4.96; CH_3 = 1.78)
	S	H-2 = 7.88; H-3 = 9.15; H-4, H-6 = 8.90–8.95; H-5 = 8.24; H-7 = 9.07; H-8 = 8.34; H-9 = 9.15 (CH_2 = 4.99; CH_3 = 1.84)

TABLE 20 (continued)

Compound	Solvent	Data
	N	$J_{2,3}$ = 9.2; $J_{4,5}$ = 7.7; $J_{4,6}$ = 1.3; $J_{5,6}$ = 7.7; $J_{7,8}$ = 7.8; $J_{7,9}$ = 1.2; $J_{8,9}$ = 7.8
	S	$J_{2,3}$ = 9.3; $J_{4,5}$ = 7.5; $J_{4,6}$ = 1.2; $J_{5,6}$ = 7.5; $J_{7,8}$ = 7.8; $J_{7,9}$ = 1.2; $J_{8,9}$ = 7.9
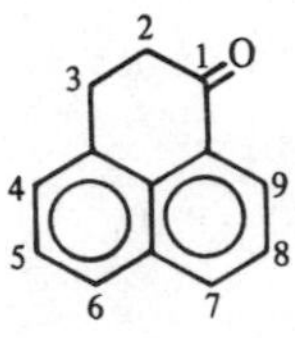	C	H-2 = 2.81; H-3 = 3.22; H-4 = 7.25; H-5 = 7.32; H-6 = 7.62; H-7 = 7.90; H-8 = 7.41; H-9 = 8.08
	B	H-2 = 2.57; H-3 = 2.84; H-4 = 6.98; H-5 = 7.17; H-6 = 7.46; H-7 = 7.66; H-8 = 7.20; H-9 = 8.22
	S	H-2 = 2.77; H-3 = 3.07; H-4 = 7.20; H-5 = 7.29; H-6 = 7.51; H-7 = 7.85; H-8 = 7.29; H-9 = 7.93
	C	$J_{7,8}$ = 8.2; $J_{7,9}$ = 1.3; $J_{8,9}$ = 7.1
	B	$J_{3,4}$ = 1.2; $J_{3,6}$ = 0.9; $J_{4,5}$ = 6.9; $J_{5,6}$ = 7.9; $J_{7,8}$ = 8.0; $J_{7,9}$ = 1.3; $J_{8,9}$ = 7.1
	S	$J_{3,4}$ ~ 1.0; $J_{3,6}$ ~ 0.6; $J_{7,8}$ = 8.3; $J_{7,9}$ = 1.1; $J_{8,9}$ = 7.4
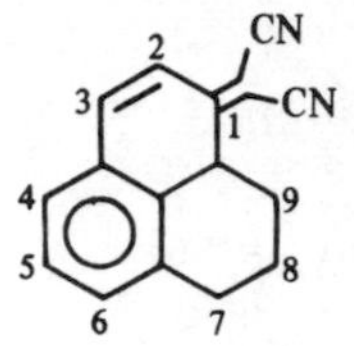	C	H-2 = 7.50; H-3 = 7.50; H-4 = 7.77; H-5 = 7.64; H-6 = 8.02; H-7 = 8.23; H-8 = 7.78; H-9 = 9.39
	S	H-2 = 7.36; H-3 = 7.65; H-4 = 7.90; H-5 = 7.74; H-6 = 8.13; H-7 = 8.32; H-8 = 7.78; H-9 = 9.23
	C	$J_{4,5}$ = 7.0; $J_{4,6}$ = 1.5; $J_{7,8}$ = 8.0; $J_{7,9}$ = 1.0; $J_{8,9}$ = 7.8
	S	$J_{2,3}$ = 9.6; $J_{4,5}$ = 7.3; $J_{4,6}$ = 1.3; $J_{5,6}$ = 7.8; $J_{7,8}$ = 8.0; $J_{7,9}$ < 1; $J_{8,9}$ = 8.0
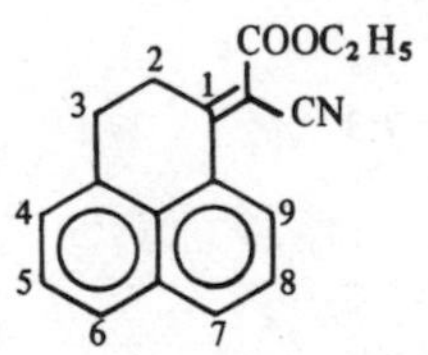	C	H-2 = 8.46; H-3 = 7.30; H-4 = 7.59; H-5 = 7.52; H-6 = 7.88; H-7 = 8.06; H-8 = 7.67; H-9 = 9.35
	S	H-2 = 8.26; H-3 = 7.47; H-6 = 7.98; H-7 = 8.16; H-8 ~ 7.7; H-9 = 9.11
	C	$J_{2,3}$ = 10.0; $J_{4,5}$ = 7.0; $J_{4,6}$ = 1.0; $J_{5,6}$ = 8.0; $J_{7,8}$ = 8.0; $J_{7,9}$ ~ 1; $J_{8,9}$ = 7.8
	S	$J_{2,3}$ = 9.6; $J_{8,9}$ = 8.0
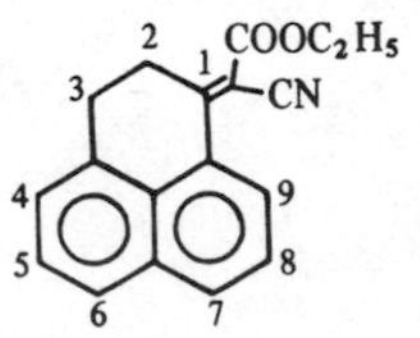	C	H-2 = 3.47; H-3 = 3.20; H-4 = 7.28; H-5 = 7.38; H-6 = 7.68; H-7 = 7.92; H-8 = 7.47; H-9 = 8.20
	S	H-2 = 3.50; H-3 = 3.31; H-4 = 7.34; H-5 = 7.43; H-6 = 7.72; H-7 = 8.01; H-8 = 7.50; H-9 = 8.17
	C	$J_{3,4}$ ~ 1.0; $J_{3,6}$ < 1.0; $J_{4,5}$ = 7.3; $J_{4,6}$ = 1.2; $J_{5,6}$ = 8.1; $J_{7,8}$ = 8.2; $J_{7,9}$ = 1.2; $J_{8,9}$ = 7.4
	S	$J_{3,4}$ ~ 1.0; $J_{3,6}$ < 1.0; $J_{4,5}$ = 7.0; $J_{5,6}$ = 8.0; $J_{7,8}$ = 8.2; $J_{7,9}$ = 1.0; $J_{8,9}$ = 7.3
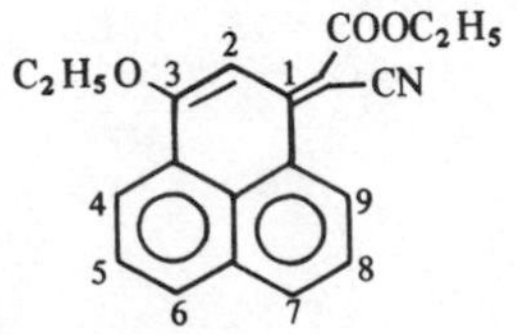	C	H-2 = 8.22; H-4 = 8.14; H-5 = 7.55; H-6 = 7.94; H-7 = 8.02; H-8 = 7.62; H-9 = 9.40
	C	$J_{4,5}$ = 7.4; $J_{4,6}$ = 1.0; $J_{5,6}$ = 8.0; $J_{7,8}$ = 8.0; $J_{7,9}$ < 1; $J_{8,9}$ = 7.8

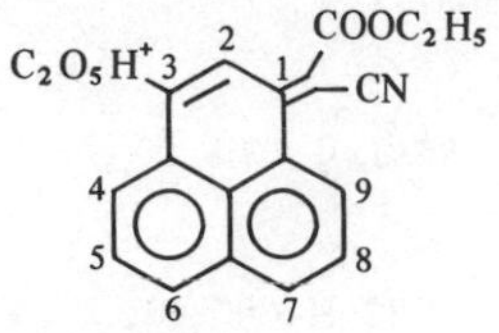	S	H-2 = 8.12; H-4 = 9.00; H-5 = 8.27; H-6 = 9.19; H-7 = 9.11; H-8 = 8.34; H-9 = 9.53
	S	$J_{4,5}$ = 8.0; $J_{4,6}$ ~ 1.0; $J_{5,6}$ = 8.0; $J_{7,9}$ = 1.2; $J_{8,9}$ = 8.0
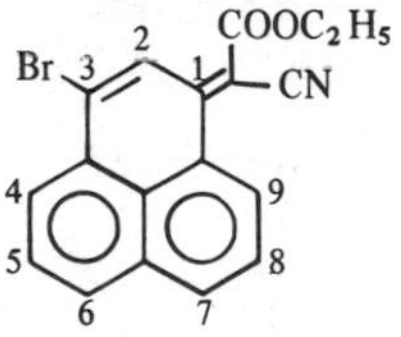	C	H-2 = 8.95; H-4 = 8.06; H-5 = 7.57; H-6 = 7.92; H-7 = 8.06; H-8 = 7.67; H-9 = 9.30
	S	H-2 = 8.66; H-4 ~ 8.1; H-5 = 7.58; H-6 = 7.95; H-7 = 8.10; H-8 = 7.62; H-9 = 9.05
	C	$J_{4,5}$ = 7.2; $J_{4,6}$ ~ 1.0; $J_{5,6}$ = 8.0; $J_{7,8}$ = 7.8; $J_{7,9}$ = 1.0; $J_{8,9}$ = 7.8
	S	$J_{4,5}$ ~ 7.5; $J_{5,6}$ = 8.0; $J_{7,8}$ ~ 8.0; $J_{8,9}$ = 7.8
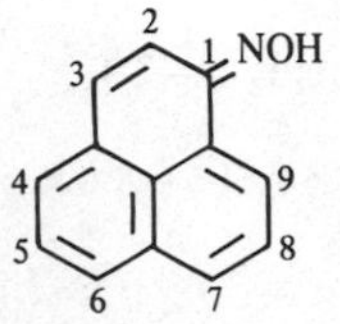	C	H-2 = 7.09; H-3 = 7.36; H-4 ~ 7.4; H-5 ~ 7.35; H-6 = 7.70; H-7 = 7.82; H-8 = 7.51; H-9 = 8.32
	S	H-2 = 7.67; H-3 = 8.18; H-4 = 8.15; H-5 = 7.86; H-6 = 8.32; H-7 = 8.53; H-8 = 7.96; H-9 = 8.71
	C	$J_{2,3}$ = 10.0; $J_{7,8}$ = 8.0; $J_{7,9}$ = 1.0; $J_{8,9}$ = 7.5
	S	$J_{2,3}$ = 9.5; $J_{4,5}$ = 7.2; $J_{4,6}$ = 1.0; $J_{5,6}$ = 8.1; $J_{7,8}$ = 7.6; $J_{7,9}$ = 0.7; $J_{8,9}$ = 7.6
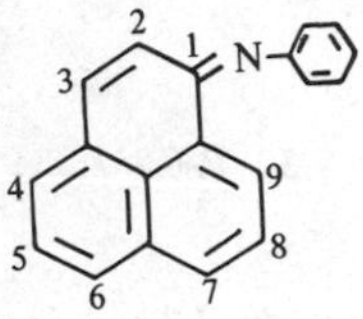	C	H-2 = 6.63; H-3 = 7.09; H-4 ~ 7.35; H-5 ~ 7.35; H-6 = 7.75; H-7 = 7.91; H-8 = 7.60; H-9 = 8.72
	S	H-2 = 7.41; H-3 = 8.34; H-4 = 8.35; H-5 = 7.98; H-6 = 8.53; H-7 = 8.76; H-8 = 8.18; H-9 = 9.19
	C	$J_{2,3}$ = 10.0; $J_{7,8}$ = 8.0; $J_{7,9}$ = 1.3; $J_{8,9}$ = 7.3
	S	$J_{2,3}$ = 9.5; $J_{4,5}$ = 8.1; $J_{4,6}$ = 1.0; $J_{5,6}$ = 7.4; $J_{7,8}$ = 8.0; $J_{7,9}$ = 1.0; $J_{8,9}$ = 7.8

[a]The variations of the corresponding coupling constants in CCl_4 or C_6D_6 are not greater than ±0.1 Hz.
[b]The variations of the corresponding coupling constants in C_6D_6 are not greater than ±0.1 Hz.

TABLE 21

Partially Hydrogenated Polynuclear Hydrocarbons[27]

R_1	δ_1	δ_3	δ_4	δ_{OCH_3}	δ_{CH_3}
H	6.57	6.63	6.96	3.73	
CH_3	6.62	6.72	7.12	3.76	1.26
C_2H_5	6.62	6.70	7.11	3.76	0.95
$CH(CH_3)_2$	6.61	6.69	7.13	3.77	0.93, 0.82

R_1	R_2	R_3	B/C	δ_1	δ_3	δ_4	δ_{OCH_3}	Other Protons
H_2	O	H	*trans*	6.63	6.72	7.23	3.77	
O	H_2	H	*trans*	6.64	6.73	7.22	3.77	
$(CH_3)_2$	H_2	CH_3	*trans*	6.58	6.68	7.16	3.74	4bCH_3 1.20 8CH_3 1.04, 0.92
H_2	O	H	*cis*	6.64	6.73	7.12	3.76	
O	H_2	H	*cis*	6.62	6.71	7.06	3.76	
$(CH_3)_2$	H_2	CH_3	*cis*	6.56	6.65	7.14	3.74	4bCH_3 1.13 8βCH_3 0.92 8αCH_3 0.38

TABLE 22

Fluorenes[14]

R_2	R_4	R_5	R_7	R_8	δ_1	δ_2	δ_3	δ_4	Other δ	J
H	H	H	H	H	7.55	7.28	7.38	7.84	δ_{CH_3} 3.87	J_{12} 7.17 J_{13} 1.64 J_{14} 0.19 J_{23} 6.51 J_{24} 1.56 J_{34} 7.52
NH_2	H	H	H	H	7.01		6.84	7.42	δ_{NH_2} 5.5	J_{13} 2.17 J_{14} 0.21 J_{34} 7.99
NO_2	H	H	H	H	8.41		8.17	7.98		J_{12} 1.89 J_{14} 0.0 J_{34} 7.93
NH_2	H	H	NH_2	H	6.87		6.72	7.18	δ_{NH_2} 5.04	J_{13} 2.09 J_{14} 0.13 J_{34} 7.94
NH_2	H	H	H	NO_2	6.88		6.80	7.49	δ_5 7.59; δ_6 8.28; δ_8 7.98; δ_{NH_2} 4.3	J_{13} 2.00 J_{14} 0.03 J_{34} 7.89 J_{56} 7.52 J_{58} 0.00 J_{68} 1.71
NO_2	NO_2	H	NO_2	H	8.58		8.99		δ_5 8.14; δ_6 8.56; δ_8 8.39	J_{13} 2.08 J_{56} 8.60 J_{58} 0.37 J_{68} 2.24
NO_2	NO_2	NO_2	NO_2	H	8.75		8.94			J_{13} 2.05

TABLE 23

Naphthoquinones[28]

Substituent		Chemical Shift of R_i, δ							
R_2	R_3	H	OH	OCH_3	$OCOCH_3$	$COCH_3$	CH_3	CH_2CH_3	CH_2CH_3
H	H	6.97							
OH	H	6.37	s.n.o.[a]						
OCH_3	H	6.17		3.89					
$OCOCH_3$	H	6.76			2.38				
$COCH_3$	H	7.06				2.56			
OH	$COCH_3$		s.n.o.			2.77			
						2.85			
CH_2CH_3	H	6.79[b]						2.63[c,d]	1.21[e]
OH	CH_2CH_3		7.32					2.61[c]	1.11[e]
OCH_3	CH_2CH_3			4.12				2.61[c]	1.10[e]
$OCOCH_3$	CH_2CH_3				2.40			2.56[c]	1.11[e]
OH	OCH_3		6.92	4.23					
$OCOCH_3$	$OCOCH_3$				2.42				
CH_3	H	6.79[f]					2.13[g]		
OH	CH_3		7.35				2.10		
$OCOCH_3$	CH_3				2.42		2.10		

[a]Signal not observed.
[b]Triplet, J = 1.7 cps.
[c]Quartet, J = 7.5 cps.
[d]Each line of the quartet is doubled, J = 1.7 cps.
[e] Triplet, J = 7.5 cps.
[f]Quartet, J = 1.7 cps.
[g]Doublet, J = 1.7 cps.

Substituent		Chemical Shift of R_i, δ			Chemical Shift of Ring Proton, δ			
R_5	R_8	H	OCH_3	$OCOCH_3$	C-2	C-3	C-6	C-7
OCH_3	H	7.75	3.99		6.87	6.87	7.28	7.67
$OCOCH_3$	H	8.07		2.46	6.85 or 6.93[a]	6.85 or 6.93[a]	7.39	7.77
OCH_3	OCH_3		3.93		6.75	6.75	7.31	7.31
$OCOCH_3$	$OCOCH_3$			2.45	6.80	6.80	7.40	7.40

[a]Doublet, J = 10 cps.

TABLE 23 (continued)

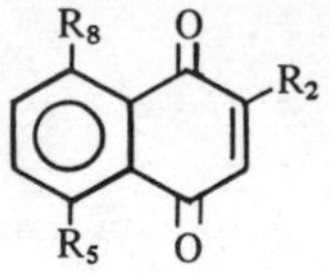

Substituent			Chemical Shift of R_2, δ			Chemical Shift of Ring Proton, δ		
R_2	R_5	R_8	OH	OCH_3	$OCOCH_3$	C-3	C-6	C-7
OH	OCH_3	OCH_3	s.n.o.[a]	3.95 (5)[b] 4.00 (8)		6.23	7.40[c]	7.30[c]
$OCOCH_3$	$OCOCH_3$	$OCOCH_3$			2.36 (2) 2.45 (5, 8)	6.62	7.38[d]	7.38[d]

[a]Signal not observed.
[b]Number in parentheses refers to position i of substituent R_i.
[c]Assignments are based on NMR data of naphthopurpurin where the C-2 hydroxyl causes a larger paramagnetic shift of the C-6 proton.
[d]Unresolved singlet.

TABLE 24

Naphthazarins[29]

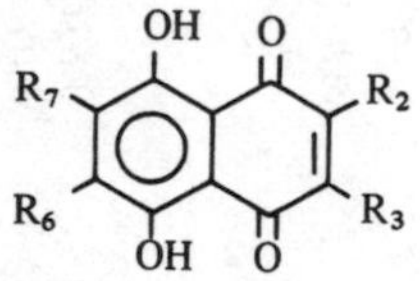

Substituents			Chemical Shift of R_i[e]						Chemical Shift of Peri Hydroxyl	
R_3	R_6	R_7	H	OH	OMe	Ac	CH_2CH_3	CH_2CH_3	C-5	C-8
Et	H	OMe	6.58	s.n.o.[a]	3.96		2.63[b]	1.14[c]	13.33	
Et	OMe	OMe		s.n.o.	4.13 (6)[d] 4.07 (7)		2.60[b]	1.13[c]	13.48	12.15
OMe	OMe	Et			4.17 (3) 4.08 (6)					
OMe	Et	OMe			4.20 (3) 4.04 (7)		2.75[b]	1.16[c]		
OMe	Et	OH			4.20		2.68[b]	1.16[c]		
OMe	OH	Et			4.13					
Ac	OMe	OMe		14.28	4.18 (6) 4.07 (7)	2.83			12.75 or 12.90	12.75 or 12.90
OMe	Ac	OMe		s.n.o.	4.20 (3) 4.04 (7)	2.51			12.68	12.00
Ac	OMe	OH[d]			4.24	2.83				
H	OMe	OMe	6.45	s.n.o.	4.15 (6) 4.04 (7)					
OMe	OH	H[d]	6.60		4.13					
OMe	H	OH[d]			4.25					

[a]Signal not observed.
[b]Quartet, J = 7.5 c/s.
[c]Triplet, J = 7.5 c/s.
[d]Insufficient material or solubility difficulties prevented observance of the entire spectrum.
[e]The number in parentheses refers to the position of R_i.

See also Reference 28.

TABLE 25

Juglones[28,29]

Substituents				Chemical Shift of R_i, δ					Chemical Shift of δ		
R_2	R_3	R_6	R_7	H	OH	OCH_3	$OCOCH_3$	CH_2CH_3	CH_2CH_3	C-5OH	C-8H
H	H	H	H	6.97(2, 3)[a] 7.6 (7) 7.25(6)						11.93	7.7
OH	H	H	H	6.28(3)	s.n.o.[b]					12.31	
H	OH	H	H	6.33(2)	s.n.o.					11.06	
OCH_3	H	H	H	6.09(3)		3.89				12.23	
H	OCH_3	H	H	6.15(2)		3.90				11.70	
H	OCH_3	H	OCH_3	6.08(2)		3.91(3,7)[d]				11.97	7.08[c]
H	CH_2CH_3	H	$OCOCH_3$	6.60(6)[c] 6.75(2)[e] 6.99(6)[c]			2.32	2.62[f]	1.20[g]	12.16	7.32[c]
OCH_3	OCH_3	H	OCH_3	6.61[c]		3.87(7) 4.07 4.11				12.09	7.17[c]
OCH_3	OCH_3	H	OH	6.63[c]	s.n.o.	4.07 4.11				12.04	7.16[c]
OCH_3	OCH_3	CH_2CH_3	OH		s.n.o.	4.03 4.08		2.72[f]	1.11[g]	12.36	7.13

Substituents				Chemical Shift of R_i[b]					Chemical Shift of δ	
R_2	R_3	R_6	R_7	H	OH	OMe	CH_2CH_3	CH_2CH_3	C-5OH	C-8H
H	OH	H	OMe	6.27(2) 6.60(6)	s.n.o.[c]	3.91			11.28	7.08[c]
OMe	Et	H	OH[h]	–	–	4.10	–	–	–	–
OH	H	Et	OMe[h]	6.21(3)	–	3.98	–	1.12[g]	12.57	–
OMe	H	Et	OH[h]	–	–	3.90	–	–	–	–

TABLE 25 (continued)

Substituents				Chemical Shift of R[b]				Chemical Shift of δ		
R_2	R_3	R_6	R_7	H	OH	OMe	CH_2CH_3	CH_2CH_3	C-5OH	C-8H
OMe	OH	H	OMe	6.58	6.90[i]	4.15(2) 3.90(7)			11.31	7.23
OMe	OH	Et	OH			4.14				
OH	OME	Et	OH			4.17				
OH	OH	Et	OMe			3.97	–	–	–	–
OMe	OH	Et	OMe		s.n.o.	4.14(2) 3.96(7)	2.67[f]	1.11[g]	11.38	7.24
OH	Et	OMe	OMe		s.n.o.	4.01(6 or 7) 3.97(6 or 7)	2.59[f]	1.13[g]	12.68	7.33
Et	OH	OMe	OMe		s.n.o.	4.01(6 or 7) 3.97(6 or 7)	2.57[f]	1.11[g]	11.18	7.32
OMe	Et	OMe	OMe[h]			4.12(2) 4.00(6, 7)	2.58[f]	1.12[g]	12.48	7.23
Et	OMe	OMe	OMe[h]			4.11(3) 4.01(6 or 7) 3.99(6 or 7)	–	1.13[g]	–	–
OMe	Et	OH	OMe		–	4.13(2) 4.01(7)	–	–	–	–
OH	Et	OH	OMe[h]		–	4.01	–	1.12[g]	–	–
OMe	OMe	OMe	OMe		–	4.08(2, 3) 3.98(6 or 7) 3.97(6 or 7)			–	–

[a] Numbers in parentheses refer to position i of substituent R_i.
[b] Signal not observed.
[c] Doublet, J = 2.5 cps.
[d] Unresolved, but slightly broadened singlet.
[e] Triplet, J = 1.7 cps.
[f] Quartet, J = 7.5 cps.
[g] Triplet, J = 7.5 cps.
[h] Insufficient material or solubility difficulties prevented observance of the entire spectrum.
[i] Broad band.

TABLE 26

Cyclohept [f] Indenes[30]

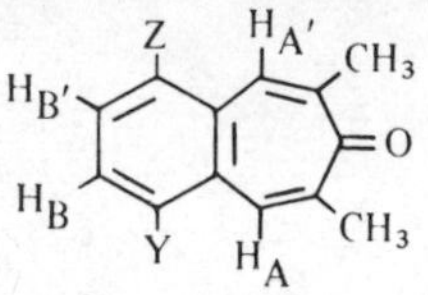

Y	Z	H_B' and H_B[c] ($CDCl_3$)	H_A and H_A' ($CDCl_3$)	H_A and H_A' (F_3CCO_2H)	H_B' and H_B[c] (F_3CCO_2H)
H	H	7.20	7.20	9.35	8.30–8.80
H	NH_2	6.85–7.50	7.67, 7.83	–	–
H	NHAc	–	–	8.98, 9.11	8.05–8.45
H	OCH_3	6.60–7.15	7.22, 7.95	–	–
H	Br	7.00–7.65	7.15, 7.86	9.00, 9.57	7.80–8.55
H	OH	–	–	9.22, 10.10	7.75–8.50
NO_2	NHAc	–	–	7.80–8.30	7.80–8.30
NO_2	NH_2	–	–	8.00–8.30	8.00–8.30
Br	Br	–	–	8.62	7.71
H	NAc_2	7.30–7.80	7.30–7.80	8.35, 8.52	7.85–8.35
H	NO_2	–	–	7.80–8.40	7.80–8.40
H	NH_3^+	–	–	7.80–8.40	7.80–8.40

When Y = H, the signal appears with that of H_B and H_B'.

TABLE 27

Fulvenes[31] in CCl_4

Compound	δ CH_3 (CH_2)	δ Ring[a]	δ Phenyl[b]	Ref.
Fulvene	5.78	6.11, 6.44		20
Dimethylfulvene	2.13	6.30		
Dibenzylfulvene	3.66	6.52	7.15	
Diphenylfulvene		6.30	7.28	

[a] Taken from the center of the band where splitting occurs, except for fulvene.
[b] Taken from the strongest peak, where splitting occurs.

TABLE 28[a]

Pyrroles[14,32]

R_2	R_3	R_4	R_5	δ_2	δ_3	δ_4	δ_5	Other δ	J
H	H	H	H	6.68	6.12			δ_{NH}9.25	J_{23}2.6; J_{24}1.3; J_{25}2.1; J_{34}3.7; J_{2NH}2.6; J_{3NH}2.3
									J_{34} J_{35} J_{45}
CH_3	H	H	H		5.75	5.96	6.52	δ_{CH_3}2.24	3.40 1.50 2.45
CN[b]	H	H	H		6.88	6.28	7.13		3.74 1.45 2.62 (other J: J_{3NH}2.25; J_{4NH}2.42; J_{5NH}2.70)
CHO	H	H	H		6.93	6.26	7.13	δ_{CHO}9.47	3.80 1.40 2.40 (Other J: J_{4NH}2.4; J_{5NH}1.15)
$COCH_3$	H	H	H		6.90	6.19	7.02		3.75 1.35 2.40 (Other J: J_{3NH}2.50; J_{4NH}2.4; J_{5NH}3.00)
COOH[c,d]	H	H	H		6.78	6.07	6.61		3.6 1.6 2.5
H	$COOCH_3$	H	H	7.44		6.57	6.76		J_{24}1.40; J_{25}1.95; J_{45}2.80
CH_3	CH_3	H	H			0.62	1.17	δ_{NH}3.08; δ_{CH_3} −3.25 and −3.30	J_{45}=J_{4NH}=J_{5NH}=2.6
CH_3	$COOCH_3$	H	H			6.44	6.50		J_{45}3.10
CH_3[e]	H	CH_3	H		0.62		1.05	δ_{NH}1.65; δ_{CH_3} −3.02 and −3.15	
CH_3[e]	H	H	CH_3		0.62	0.62		δ_{NH}2.00; δ_{CH_3} −3.08	J_{3NH}2.7
CHO	H	H	CH_3		6.93	5.99		δ_{CHO}9.30; δ_{CH_3}2.28	J_{34}3.75; J_{3CH_3}0.45; J_{4CH_3}0.65
H	CH_3	$COOC_2H_5$	H	6.47			7.30	δ_{CH_3}2.24	J_{25}2.20; J_{2CH_3}1.00; J_{5NH}3.05
CH_3	SCN	SCN	CH_3					δ_{CH_3}2.30	

[a] Solvent: dioxane/water unless otherwise noted.
[b] Solvent: acetone/water.
[c] Solvent: aq NaOH.
[d] Reference 33.
[e] Solvent: water.

TABLE 29[14]

N-Substituted Pyrroles

R_1	R_2	R_5	Solvent	δ_3	δ_4	δ_5	δ_{CH_3}	δ_{NCH_3}	J_{34}	J_{35}	J_{45}	Ref.
CH_3	COOH	H	$CDCl_3$	7.13	6.18	6.87			4.07	1.94	2.33	34
CH_3	CH_3	CH_3	Cyclohexane	5.59	5.59		2.01	3.05				35

TABLE 30[14]

2-Substituted Furans

R	Solvent	Ref.	δ_3	δ_4	δ_5	J_{34}	J_{35}	J_{45}	
CH_3	TMS	42-46	5.83	6.12	7.15	3.4	1.0	1.9	$\delta_{GH_3} = 2.17$ $J_{3,CH_3} = -1.1$ $J_{4,CH_3} = 0.4$ $J_{5,CH_3} = -0.35$
CH_2OH	10% Acetone	43, 44	6.29	6.37	7.48	3.17	0.84	1.90	
CH_2SH	–	44	6.17	6.29	7.37	3.25	0.73	1.91	$\delta_{CH_2} = 3.66; \delta_{SH} = 1.98$ $J_{3,CH_2} = 0.79$ $J_{CH_2,SH} = 7.4$
CH_2NH_2	10% Acetone	44, 47	6.20	6.34	7.43	3.18	0.76	1.94	$J_{3,CH_2} = 0.84$
OCH_3	Cyclohexane	45	4.96	6.07	6.70	3.15	1.15	2.15	
SCH_3	Cyclohexane	45	6.18	6.24	7.29	3.20	0.85	1.95	
CN	Cyclohexane	45	6.86	6.36	7.38	3.55	0.70	1.75	
$COCH_3$	Cyclohexane	45, 47	6.96	6.33	7.33	3.45	0.75	1.70	
CHO	5% Cyclohexane	44	7.03	6.42	7.49	3.55	0.80	1.70	$J_{4,CHO} = 0.45$ $J_{5,CHO} = 0.45$
$COCF_3$	10% Acetone	44	7.642	6.80	8.02	3.70	0.76	1.70	
COOH	10% Acetone	44, 47, 48	7.24	6.63	7.79	3.51	0.86	1.73	
$COOCH_3$	Cyclohexane	45	6.98	6.30	7.34	3.40	0.85	1.70	
$COOC_2H_5$	10% Acetone	44, 49	7.22	6.63	7.80	3.47	0.91	1.76	
COCl	–	44	7.52	6.70	7.88	3.79	0.79	1.70	
Br	Cyclohexane	45	6.15	6.21	7.25	3.25	0.80	2.10	
I	Cyclohexane	45	6.42	6.17	7.37	3.25	0.95	1.95	
NO_2	10% Acetone	44	7.51	6.85	7.89	3.66	0.98	1.92	
SCN	Cyclohexane	45	6.70	6.36	7.48	3.40	0.85	1.95	
CH=CH–COOH	10% Acetone	44	6.85	6.59	7.70	3.44		1.84	
CH=CH–CHO	10% Acetone	44, 50	7.00	6.65	7.80	3.41	0.75	1.81	$J_{5,=CH(\alpha)} = 0.38$
$COCH_2CH_2OCOCH_3$	10% Acetone	44	7.40	6.70	7.87	3.60	0.82	1.72	
$CH=C(CN)_2$	Acetone+CCl_4, 1:3	46	7.43	6.80	7.98	3.75	0.70	1.65	$\delta_{=CH} = 7.88$ $J_{3,=CH} = -0.40$ $J_{4,=CH} = +0.40$ $J_{5,=CH} = +0.50$
$CH=NC_6H_5$	CCl_4, 10%	46	6.91	6.41	7.48	3.50	0.80	1.75	$\delta_{=CH} = 8.18$ $J_{3,=CH} = -0.35$ $J_{4,=CH} = +0.40$ $J_{5,=CH} = +0.20$
$CH=CHCOCH_3$	CCl_4		6.58	6.42	7.44	3.5	0.5	1.8	
–COCH=CH–	CCl_4		7.17	6.50	7.54	3.5	0.8	1.7	
			6.64	6.43	7.45	3.4		1.8	

TABLE 31[14]

3-Substituted Furans

R	Solvent	Ref.	δ_2	δ_4	δ_5	J_{24}	J_{25}	J_{45}	
CH_3	Cyclohexane	45, 46	7.03	6.06	7.14	0.85	1.55	1.75	J_{2,CH_3} =−0.95 J_{4,CH_3} =−0.45 J_{5,CH_3} =0.40
OCH_3	Cyclohexane 4.5%	45	6.92	6.02	7.01	1.00	1.65	1.90	
SCH_3	Cyclohexane	45	7.20	6.25	7.23	0.80	1.50	1.85	
CN	Cyclohexane	45	7.83	6.52	7.36	0.75	1.55	1.95	
$COCH_3$	Cyclohexane	45	7.84	6.66	7.26	0.75	1.40	1.80	
CHO	Cyclohexane 4.5%	45	7.86	6.67	7.31	0.80	1.45	1.90	$J_{2,CHO}$ =0.40 $J_{5,CHO}$ =0.75
$COOCH_3$	Cyclohexane	45	7.83	6.63	7.24	0.70	1.55	1.85	
I	Cyclohexane	45	7.25	6.34	7.16	0.70	1.50	1.90	
SCN	Cyclohexane	45	7.57	6.49	7.41	0.85	$J_{25} + J_{45}$ = 3.55		
HgCl	Dioxane sat.	51	7.33	6.40	7.67	0.6	1.3	1.7	$J_{2,Hg}$ =48.4 $J_{4,Hg}$ =74.9 $J_{5,Hg}$ =27.9
COOH	Acetone 10%	44	8.27	6.84	7.74	0.8	1.5	1.8	

TABLE 32[14]

2,3-Disubstituted Furans

R_2	R_3	Solvent	Ref.	δ_4	δ_5	J_{45}	
CH_3	COOH	Acetone	44	6.74	7.49	1.94	
COOH	COOH	Acetone	44	7.09	7.99	1.83	
Br	CH_3	CCl_4	52	6.24	7.32	2.0	δ_{CH_3} =2.00
Br	CH_2 Br	CCl_4	52	6.36	7.31	2.1	δ_{CH_2} =4.14
$COOCH_3$	CH_3	CCl_4	52	6.28	7.37	1.9	δ_{CH_3} =2.28; δ_{OCH_3} =3.78
$COOCH_3$	CH_2Br	CCl_4	52	6.55	7.46	2.1	δ_{CH_2} =4.65; δ_{OCH_3} =3.85
$COOCH_3$	CH_2CN	CCl_4	52	6.72	7.66	2.1	δ_{CH_2} =4.01; δ_{OCH_3} =3.92
CHO	CH_3	CCl_4		6.38	7.50	1.6	δ_{CHO} =9.71; δ_{CH_3} =2.36; $J_{4,CHO}$ =0.4; J_{4,CH_3} =$J_{5,CHO}$ =J_{5,CH_3} =0.5
$COCH_3$	OH	CCl_4	53	6.23	7.23	2.0	δ_{OH} =8.95; δ_{CH_3} =2.35
$COCH_3$	OCH_3	CCl_4	53	6.25	7.28	2.0	δ_{CH_3} =2.28; δ_{OCH_3} =3.88

TABLE 33[14]

2,4-Disubstituted Furans

R_2	R_4	Solvent	δ_3	δ_5	J_{35}	
CHO	CH_3	CCl_4	7.01	7.42	0.9	δ_{CHO} =9.53; δ_{CH_3} =2.09 J_{3,CH_3} =0.5; $J_{5,CHO}$ =1.1; $J_{5,CHO}$ =0.5
CN	CH_3	CCl_4	6.86	7.29	0.8	ν_{CH_3} =2.08; J_{3,CH_3} =0.4; J_{5,CH_3} =1.1

TABLE 34[14]

2,5-Disubstituted Furans

R_2	R_5	Solvent	Ref.	δ_3	δ_4	J_{34}	
CH_3	CH_3	TMS	44, 54	5.69	5.69	–	$\delta CH_3 = 2.14$; $J_3,CH_3 = 0.3, 0.4$; $J_4,CH_3 = 0.3, 0.4$
$COOCH_3$	CH_2Br	CCl_4, 10%	49	7.05	6.46	3.5	$\delta CH_2 = 4.47$; $J_3,CH_2 = 0.4$; $J_4,CH_2 = 0.5$
$COOC_2H_5$	CH_3	CCl_4, 10%	49	6.95	6.04	3.3	$\delta CH_3 = 2.37$; $J_3,CH_3 = 0.5$; $J_4,CH_3 = 0.9$
$COOC_2H_5$	Br	CCl_4, 10%	49	7.06	6.41	3.4	
$COOC_2H_5$	Cl	CCl_4, 10%	49	7.09	6.27	3.4	
$COOC_2H_5$	CH_2Cl	CCl_4, 10%	49	7.04	6.44	3.5	$\delta CH_2 = 4.56$; $J_3,CH_2 = 0.3$; $J_4,CH_2 = 0.5$
CHO	CH_2Cl	–	43, 44	7.42	6.77	3.67	
CHO	CH_3	CCl_4		7.05	6.17	3.4	$\delta CHO = 9.45$; $\delta CH_3 = 2.38$; $J_3,CH_3 = 0.4$; $J_4,CH_3 = 0.9$; $J_4,CHO = 0.3$
CH=CHCHO	$CH_2C{\equiv}CH$	CCl_4		6.63	6.33	3.5	$J_4,CH_2 = 1.2$

TABLE 35A[14,44]

3,4-Disubstituted Furans

R_3	R_4	Solvent	δ_2	δ_5	J_{25}	
COOH	CH_3	Acetone	8.09	7.37	1.6	$J_5,CH_3 = 1.4$

TABLE 35B

Miscellaneous Furans[41]

Compound	Hydrogens 2	3	4	5	$-CH_3$	$-CH_2-$	$-OCH_3$	Coupling Constant, $J_{4,5}$
Furan	7.38	6.30	6.30	7.38				
2-Bromofuran		6.28	6.33	7.37				
2,5-Dibromofuran		6.25	6.25					
3-Methylfuran	7.11		6.13	7.23	2.02			
2-Bromo-3-methylfuran			6.24	7.32	2.00			2.0
2,5-Dibromo-3-methylfuran			6.20		1.96			
2-Bromo-3-bromomethylfuran			6.36	7.31		4.14		2.1
2,5-Dibromo-3-bromomethylfuran			6.32			4.09		
2,4,5-Tribromo-3-methylfuran					2.08			
Methyl 3-methyl-2-furoate			6.28	7.37	2.28		3.78	1.9
Methyl 3-methyl-2-furoate ($DCCl_3$)			6.33	7.40	2.35		3.88	
Methyl 3-bromomethyl-2-furoate			6.55	7.46		4.65	3.85	2.1
Methyl 3-bromomethyl-2-furoate ($DCCl_3$)			6.61	7.51		4.69	3.90	
Methyl 3-cyanomethyl-2-furoate ($DCCl_3$)			6.72	7.66		4.01	3.92	2.1

TABLE 36[14]

Unsubstituted Thiophenes

R	Solvent	δ_2	δ_3	J_{23}	J_{24}	J_{25}	J_{34}	Ref.
Thiophene	CS_2	7.18	6.99	4.90	1.04	2.84	3.50	55-59

2-Substituted Thiophenes

R	Solvent	δ_3	δ_4	δ_5	J_{34}	J_{35}	J_{45}		Ref.
CH_3	TMS	6.63	6.75	6.91	3.46	1.16	5.20	$\delta_{CH_3}=2.41$ $J_{3,CH_3}=1.00$ $J_{4,CH_3}=0.24$ $J_{3,C^{13}}=163.56$ $J_{4,C^{13}}=165.50$ $J_{5,C^{13}}-184.92$ $J_{CH_3,C^{13}}=128.26$	60
OCH_3	Cyclohexane	6.11	6.59	6.41	3.7	1.8	5.2		61
Br	TMS	6.93	6.73	7.05	3.62	1.39	5.63		33, 55, 62
$COCH_3$	Cyclohexane	7.64	7.09	7.64	3.7	–	5.1		61
CHO	Cyclohexane	7.99	7.14	7.79	3.7	–	5.0		61
COOH	TMS	7.76	7.04	7.60	3.5	1.2	4.9		33, 47, 61
SO_2CH_3	Acetone	7.99	7.16	7.99	3.9	–	4.7		61
NO_2	Cyclohexane	7.88	7.11	7.59	3.8	1.5	5.4		47, 61
CL	TMS	6.79	6.74	6.92	3.71	1.48	5.60	$J_{3,C^{13}}=171.54$ $J_{4,C^{13}}=169.77$ $J_{5,C^{13}}=188.26$	55
I	TMS	7.13	6.66	7.18	3.56	1.25	5.41	$J_{3,C^{13}}=172.22$ $J_{4,C^{13}}=169.44$ $J_{5,C^{13}}=187.50$	55

TABLE 37[14]

3-Substituted Thiophenes

R	Solvent	Ref.	δ_3	δ_4	δ_5	J_{34}	J_{35}	J_{45}	
CH_3	TMS	60, 61	6.75	6.77	7.05	1.28	2.94	4.88	δ_{CH_3}=2.21 J_{2,CH_3}=1.06 J_{4,CH_3}=0.40 J_{5,CH_3}=0.35 $J_{3,C^{13}}$=182.36 $J_{4,C^{13}}$=164.48 $J_{5,C^{13}}$=184.92 $J_{CH_3,C^{13}}$=217.10
OCH_3	Cyclohexane	61	6.06	6.66	6.94	1.6	3.1	5.0	
SCH_3	Cyclohexane	61	6.86	6.86	7.14	–	2.8	5.2	
Br	Dioxane	33, 62	7.35	7.04	7.37	1.2	3.2	5.2	
$COCH_3$	Cyclohexane	61	8.34	7.74	7.54	1.4	2.7	5.1	
CHO	Cyclohexane	61	8.16	7.59	7.59	1.5	2.4	–	
COOH	Acetone	61	8.19	7.44	7.44			–	
SO_2CH_3	Acetone	61	8.16	7.44	7.66	1.4	2.8	4.9	

TABLE 38

2,3-Disubstituted Thiophenes[63]

Proton Chemical Shifts, $\delta_{H(5)}$ and $\delta_{H(4)}$, and Ring Coupling Constants, J_{45}, of 2,3-Carbonyl Chelated Hydroxy Thiophenes and Their Corresponding *t*-Butyl Ethers in Solutions of CCl_4

	R	H_5	H_4	J_{45}
3-OR, 2-$COCH_3$ (S)	*t*-Bu	7.38	6.87	5.5
	H	7.34	6.70	5.3
3-OR, 2-COOEt (S)	*t*-Bu	7.25	6.73	5.3
	H	7.27	6.67	5.3
3-COMe, 2-OR (S)	*t*-Bu	6.51	7.09	6.2
	H	6.25	6.65	6.7
3-COOEt, 2-OR (S)	*t*-Bu	6.55	7.10	6.1
	H	6.24	6.85	6.0

TABLE 39A

Monosubstituted Pyridines[64]

2-H, 8.5; 3-H, 6.99; 4–H, 7.36

$J_{2,3}$,5.5; $J_{3,4}$, 7.5; $J_{2,4}$, 1.9; $J_{3,5}$, 1.6; $J_{2,6}$, 0.4; $J_{2,5}$, 0.9 c/s

(Unsubstituted Pyridines)

Substituent	Position δ_2	δ_3	δ_4	δ_5	δ_6	Other Attached Groups	δ
2CH=CH_2		7.27	7.55	7.08	8.52		
2-CH_2CONH$_2$		7.25	7.65	7.17		–CH_2 –	3.72
4-SCH_2 CH_2 CH_3	8.38	7.10		7.10	8.38		
2-CH_2 Ph			7.54		8.56	–CH_2 –	4.18
N-methyl-2-pyridone					7.31	N–Me	3.51
3-OH	8.08				8.29		
2-NH_2				6.64	8.09		
3-CONH_2	9.04		8.16	7.38	8.75		
3-Me, N-oxide	8.10					Me	2.33
(D_2O) 1-N-Ph, 3-CON$\overset{+}{H}_3$ Ī	9.37		8.97	8.29	9.12	–CH_2	4.74
5-Me, 2-CH_2 OEt		7.32	7.32		8.27	–CH_3	

TABLE 39B

2,3-Disubstituted Pyridines[14]

R_2	R_3	Solvent	Ref.	δ_4	δ_5	δ_6	J_{45}	J_{46}	J_{56}	
CH_3	CH_3	–	75	0.29	0.00	1.38	7.35	1.3	5.0	
CH_3	COOC_2 H_5	DMSO, 30%	65	8.31	7.43	8.75	7.9	1.8	4.9	δ_{CH_2}=4.42; δ_{CH_3}=2.71 1.37; J_{CH_2, CH_3}=7.2
CH_3	COCH_3	DMSO, 30%	65	8.32	7.45	8.69	7.9	1.7	4.8	
CH_3	CN	DMSO, 30%	65	8.18	7.38	8.78	8.2	1.5	4.9	
CH_3	OH	DMSO, 30%	65	7.39	7.28	8.06	6.8	0.8	4.6	δ_{CH}=8.7; δ_{CH_3}=2.47
OH	CH_3	DMSO, 30%	65	7.41	6.20	7.41	6.7	0.0	6.7	δ_{OH}=12; δ_{CH_3}=2.05; J_{4, CH_3}=0.5
OH	NO_2	DMSO, 30%	65	8.58	6.48	8.03	7.5	1.7	6.6	δ_{OH}=12.9
NH_2	NH_2	DMSO, 30%	65	6.96	6.56	7.58	7.5	1.7	4.9	δ_{NH_2}=5.22
NH_2	CH_3	DMSO, 30%	65, 66	7.28	6.54	7.99	7.4	1.7	4.8	δ_{NH_2}=5.91; δ_{CH_3}=2.09; J_{4, CH_3}=0.7
Cl	Cl	DMSO, 30%	65	8.22	7.61	8.57	7.3	1.7	4.8	
Cl	NH_2	DMSO, 30%	65	7.38	7.15	7.90	7.9	1.9	4.4	δ_{NH_2}=5.44

TABLE 40

2,4-Disubstituted Pyridines[14,65]

	Solvent	δ_3	δ_5	δ_6	δ_{CH_3}	J_{35}	J_{36}	J_{56}
R_2=R_4=CH_3	DMSO, 30%	7.11	7.07	8.43	2.46, 2.27	<0.5	1.4	5.6
R_2=CH_3, R_4=COON_a	D_2O	2.40	2.46	3.26	–2.66	<0.5	1.0	4.6

TABLE 41

2,5-Disubstituted Pyridines[14,65]

(All in 30% DMSO)

R_2	R_5	δ_3	δ_4	δ_6	J_{34}	J_{36}	J_{46}	
CH_3	C_2H_5	7.17	7.57	8.41	8.1	0.7	2.4	δ_{CH_3} = 1.16, 2.47; J_{CH_2,CH_3} = 7.5
CH_3	$CH = CH_2$	7.24	7.87	8.76	8.1	0.5	2.0	δ_{CH_3} = 2.55
CH_3	OH	7.15	7.23	8.23	8.7	0.6	2.3	δ_{CH} = 8.8; δ_{CH_3} = 2.50
OH	COOH	6.53	7.98	8.22	9.7	<0.3	2.6	δ_{CH} = 11.5; δ_{COOH} = 11.5
OC_4H_9	NO_2	7.07	8.59	9.18	9.1	<0.3	2.8	δ_{OCH_2} = 4.46; $\delta_{CH_2CH_2}$ = 1.63; δ_{CH_3} = 98; J_{OCH_2,CH_2} = 6.2; J_{CH_2,CH_3} = 6.0
NH_2	Cl	6.63	7.49	8.05	9.0	<0.3	2.5	δ_{NH_2} = 6.20
Cl	Cl	7.68	8.13	8.70	9.0	<0.3	3.0	
Br	Br	7.71	8.08	8.63	8.3	<0.3	2.5	

TABLE 42

Symmetrical 2,6-Disubstituted Pyridines[14]

$R_2 = R_6$	S	Ref.	δ_1	δ_4	J_{34}	
D	–	76	0.00	0.37	7.7	
CH_3	DMSO, 30%	65, 75	7.04	7.59	8.2	δ_{CH_3} = 2.44
CN	DMSO, 30%	65	8.49	8.52	~8	
OH	DMSO, 30%	65	6.35	8.03	8.4	δ_{OH} = 11.4
NH_2	DMSO, 30%	65	5.90	7.22	7.8	δ_{NH_2} = 5.54
$CSNH_2$	DMSO, 30%	65	8.93	8.29	7.8	δ_{NH_2} = 10.6

TABLE 43

Unsymmetrical 2,6-Disubstituted Pyridines[14,65]

(All in 30% DMSO)

R_2	R_6	δ_3	δ_4	δ_5	J_{34}	J_{35}	J_{45}	
CH_3	CH_2OH	7.65	7.81	7.16	8.1	0.7	7.8	δ_{OH} = 5.73; δ_{CH_3} = 4.74
CH_3	CH_2NH_2	7.31	7.68	7.13	7.3	1.0	7.8	δ_{CH_2} = 3.89; δ_{NH_2} = 2.0
CH_3	CH_2NHCH_3	7.36	7.66	7.12	7.4	0.9	7.9	δ_{CH_2} = 3.77; δ_{CH_3} = 2.47; δ_{NH} = 2.37
CH_3	CH=NOH	7.80	7.73	7.35	8.1	0.6	8.3	δ_{OH} = 12.00; $\delta_{=CH}$ = 8.29; δ_{CH_3} = 2.58
CH_3	CN	7.76	7.95	8.09	8.0	1.2	7.8	δ_{CH_3} = 2.63
CH_3	$COCH_3$	7.56	7.87	7.95	7.5	1.3	7.4	
CH_3	CHO	7.65	7.92	8.07	7.7	1.5	7.6	δ_{CHO} = 10.15
CH_3	COOH	7.82	8.13	8.27	~8	~1	~8	δ_{COOH} = 6.19; δ_{CH_3} = 2.75
CH_3	$COOC_4H_9$	7.60	7.90	8.05	~8	~1	~8	δ_{OCH_2} = 4.39; $\delta_{CH_2CH_3}$ = 1.65; δ_{CH_3} = 0.95
CH_3	$CSNH_2$	7.61	8.01	8.61	7.9	1.4	7.7	δ_{NH_2} = 10.3; δ_{CH_3} = 2.66

TABLE 44

3,5-Disubstituted Pyridines

R_3	R_5	Solvent	Ref.	δ_2	δ_4	J_{24}	
Cl	Cl	DMSO, 30 wt %	65	8.71	8.23	1.4	
CN	CN	DMSO, 30 wt %	65	9.30	8.95	2.0	
$COOCH_3$	$COOCH_3$	CCl_4, 10 wt %		9.24	8.69	2.0	δ_{OCH_3} = 4.63

TABLE 45

Trisubstituted Pyridines[14]

R_2	R_3	R_6	δ_4	δ_5	J_{45}	
CH_3	$COCH_3$	CH_3	8.17	7.24	8.4	$J_{5,CH_3} = 0.5$
CH_3	COOH	CH_3	8.26	7.27	8.1	$\delta_{COOH} = 11.30$ $\delta_{CH_3} = 2.47$
						$J_{5,CH_3} = 0.5$
CH_3	$COCH_3$	C_6H_5	8.36	8.15	8.4	$\delta_{COCH_3} = 2.65$
CH_3	COOH	C_6H_5	8.53	8.18	8.8	$\delta_{COOH} = 12.03$ $\delta_{CH_3} = 3.14$
CH_3	$COCH_3$	OH	8.03	6.32	9.7	$\delta_{OH} = 12.2$ $\delta_{COCH_3} = 2.61$

$R_2 = CH_3$, $R_4 = R_6 = CHO$
$\delta_3 = 7.82$ $\delta_5 = 7.93$ $\delta_{CHO} = 9.22, 9.70$
$\delta_{CH_3} = 2.46$ $J_{35} < 0.5$

$R_2 = R_4 = CH_3$, $R_6 = COOH$
$\delta_3 = 7.36$ $\delta_5 = 7.87$ $\delta_{COOH} = 10.44$
$\delta_{CH_3} = 2.40$ $J_{35} < 0.5$

TABLE 46

Pyridazine, Pyrazine, and Pyrimidine[77]

(All in $CDCl_3$)

Parameter	Pyridazine	Pyrazine	Pyrimidine
δ_2		8.63	9.26
δ_3	9.24	8.63	
δ_4	7.54		9.78
δ_5	7.54	8.63	7.36
δ_6	9.24	8.63	9.78
$J_{2,3}$		1.8	
$J_{2,4}$			~0
$J_{2,5}$		1.8	1.5
$J_{2,6}$		~0.5	~0
$J_{3,4}$	4.9		
$J_{3,5}$	2.0	~0.5	
$J_{3,6}$	3.5	1.8	
$J_{4,5}$	8.4		5.0
$J_{4,6}$	2.0		2.5
$J_{5,6}$	4.9	1.8	5.0
$JC^{13}-H_2$		183	206
$JC^{13}-H_3$	181.5	183	
$JC^{13}-H_4$	168.5		181.8
$JC^{13}-H_5$	168.5	183	168
$JC^{13}-H_6$	181.5	183	181.8

TABLE 47

Quinoline and Related Compounds[64]

7.95
5 4
6 3 7.24
7 2 8.84
8 1 N

ABX Group

$J_{3,4} = 7.3$; $J_{2,3} = 5.0$

$J_{7,8} \sim 7$

Substituent	2	3	4	8	5	7	CH_3
2,4-ME_2		7.14					2-Me,2.70,4-Me,2.66
2,6-Me_2		7.21	7.90	7.90			2,2.72;6, 2.50
6-OCH_3	8.71	7.28	7.97	7.97	7.00	7.35	$-OCH_2$,3.87
8-Me	8.72	7.12	7.82				3.77
5,7-Me_2	8.62	7.05	7.91	7.95			2.35,2.43
5,7-Cl_2	8.82	7.34	8.39	7.57			

Coupling constants for 5,7-Me_2 : $J_{2,3}$ 3.9, $J_{3,4}$ 8.6, $J_{2,4}$ 1.7, $J_{4,8}$ 0.8 c/s

$J_{2,3} = 6.0$

2,3-Me_2 5,8-OH_2 7.03 (6,7)

2,3-Me_2 , 2.72

TABLE 48

Borazoles[14,78]

(All in Cyclohexane)

Borazole ($R_1 = R_2 = H$)

$\delta_{NH} = 5.49$ $\quad J_{H,N^{14}} = 56$

$\delta_{BH} = 4.51$ $\quad J_{H,B^{11}} = 138$

Substituted borazoles

1. $R_1 = H, R_2 = Cl$
   $\delta_{NH} = 5.37$
2. $R_1 = CH_3, R_2 = Cl$
   $\delta_{NCH_3} = 3.11$
3. $R_1 = C_2H_5, R_2 = Cl$
   $\delta_{NCH_2} = 3.64$ $J_{NCH_2,CH_3} = 8$
   $\delta_{CH_3} = 1.06$
4. $R_1 = CH_3, R_2 = H$
   $\delta_{NCH_3} = 4.49$ $J_{H,B} = 125$
   $\delta_{NCH_3} = 3.04$
5. $R_1 = R_2 = CH_3$
   $\delta_{NCH_3} = 3.02$
   $\delta_{BCH_3} = 0.44$
6. $R_1 = C_2H_3, R_2 = CH_3$
   $\delta_{NCH_2} = 3.42$ $J_{NCH_2,CH_3} = 7.2$
   $\delta_{CH_3} = 1.04$
   $\delta_{BCH_3} = 0.51$
7. $R_1 = CH_3, R_2 = C_2H_5$
   $\delta_{NCH_3} = 2.94$ $J_{CH_3,N} = 3.0$
   $\delta_{BCH_2} = 0.99$
   $\delta_{BCH_3} = 0.99$
8. $R_1 = R_2 = C_2H_5$
   $\delta_{NCH_3} = 3.61$ $J_{NCH,CH_3} = 8.1$
   $\delta_{CH_3} = 1.04$
   $\delta_{BCH_2} = 0.92$
   $\delta_{BCH_3} = 0.92$
9. $R_1 = C_6H_5, R_2 = CH_3$
   $\delta_{BCH_3} = 0.16$
   $\delta_{ph} = 7.19$
10. $R_1 = C_6H_5, R_2 - C_2H_5$
    $\delta_{BCH_2} = 0.41$
    $\delta_{ph} = 7.19$

TABLE 49A
Benzo Compounds[14]

Compound	Solvent	δ_1	δ_2	δ_3	δ_4	J_{12}	J_{13}	J_{14}	J_{23}	J_{24}	J_{34}	J_{37}	Ref.
Benzofuran	CCl_4	7.49	7.13	7.19	7.42	7.89	1.23	0.80	7.27	0.92	8.43		78a, 78b
Dibenzofuran	CCl_4	7.84	7.23	7.35	7.48	7.6	1.3	0.6	7.3	0.9	8.5		78a
Indole	$CDCl_3$	7.10	6.74	6.41									78d
Carbazole	Acetone	8.08	7.16	7.36	7.49	7.80	1.18	0.67	7.17	0.89	8.21		78a
Phenazine	$CDCl_3$	8.16	7.74	7.74	8.16	9.0	1.3	0.0	5.3	1.3	9.0		78c

TABLE 49B
Indoles

(Structure: indole ring with positions numbered 2, 3, 4, 5, 6, 7 and N–H at 1)

1	2	3	4	5	6	7	δ_2	δ_3	δ_{aryl}	Other δ	J_{12}	J_{13}	J_{23}	J_{37}	Ref.
H	H	H	H	H	H	H	6.68	6.38	6.90		2.4	2.1	3.3	0.7	37, 38
H	CH_3	H	H	H	H	H		6.13	7.08	δ_{CH_3} 2.20					37
H	H	CH_3	H	H	H	H	6.80		7.18	δ_{CH_3} 2.30					
H	H	H	CH_3	H	H	H	6.65	6.40			2.4	2.1	3.3	0.8	38
H	H	H	H	CH_3	H	H	6.58	6.24			2.4	2.0	3.2	0.6	38
H	H	H	H	H	CH_3	H	6.67	6.34			2.4	2.1	3.3	1.0	38
H	H	H	H	H	H	CH_3	6.67	6.31			2.3	2.15	3.3		38
CH_3	H	H	H	H	H	H	6.82	6.48	7.17	δ_{NCH_3} 3.37					37
CH_3	φ	H	H	H	H	H		6.53	7.17	δ_{NCH_3} 3.57					37
H	H	φ	H	H	H	H	7.03		7.17						37
H	CO_2Et	H	H	H	H	H		7.20							39
H	H	CO_2Et	H	H	H	H	8.12								39
H	H	$COCH_3$	H	H	H	H	8.34								39
H	H	CO_2H	H	H	H	H	8.18								39
H	CO_2H	H	H	H	H	H		7.20							39
H	H	Br	H	H	H	H	7.04								39
H	CH_3	H	H	CH_3	H	H		6.10		δ_{2CH_3} 2.28, δ_{5CH_3} 2.40					39
H	CH_3	H	H	Cl	H	H		6.10		δ_{4H} 7.44, δ_{6H} 7.02, δ_{7H} 7.02					39

TABLE 49C

Benzofurans and Benzothiophenes[38]

Benzofurans	2	3	J_{23}	J_{37}
2-Me¶				1.0
3-Me‖				
4-ME	7.66	6.72	2.15	0.8
5-Me	7.51	6.59	2.2	0.8
6-Me	7.47	6.62	2.2	1.0
7-Me	7.55	6.67	2.2	

Benzothiophenes	2	3	J_{23}	J_{37}
2-Me¶		6.88		0.9
3-Me‖	6.70			

¶ $J_{2\text{-Me},3\text{-H}} = 1.2$ c/s

‖ $J_{2\text{-H},3\text{-ME}} = 1.2$ c/s

1-Phenylpyrazole and Its Derivatives

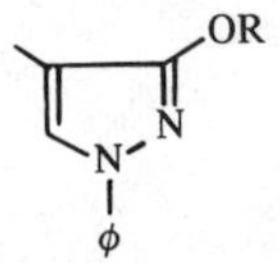

OR	δ_4H	($J_{4,5}$, cps)	δ_5H	Solvent
OH, −0.24	5.59	(3.0)	8.25	DMSO
$OCOCH_3$, 7.69	6.36	(2.7)	7.84	$CDCl_3$
OCH_3, 6.05	5.86	(2.5)	7.67	$CDCl_3$
OCH_2, 5.22; = CH_2, 4.62; CH, 3.63	5.92	(2.9)	7.69	$CDCl_3$

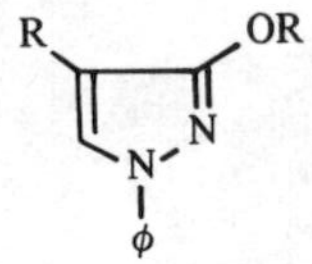

R	δ_5H	δ_{OH}	Solvent
CH_3, 8.08	7.99	9.75	DMSO
NO_2	9.36	12.11	DMSO
NH_2, 4.46	7.49	5.54	DMSO
Br	9.53	10.99	DMSO
Cl	9.55	11.01	DMSO
$C_6H_5N = N$, 2.50–2.90	9.40	9.72	$CDCl_3$
$CH_2NC_5H_{10}$	9.12	5.60	DMSO
CH_2, 6.35;			Pyridine
NC_5H_{10}, 8.50, 7.52 CH_3, 8.04; CH, 6.23;	6.97	11.62	$CDCl_3$.
C_6H_{11}, 8.00–8.50 CH_2 6.71; = CH_2, 4.83; CH, 4.00	7.45	11.11	$CDCl_3$

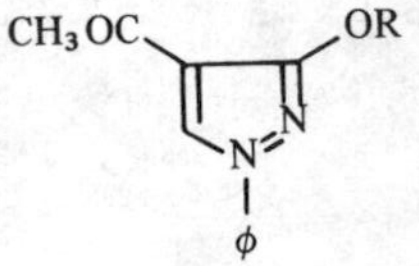

R	δ_{OR}	δ_{COCH_5}	δ_5H	Solvent
H	11.11	2.43	8.88	DMSO
CH	4.08	2.48	8.23	CDCl

In all spectra, the phenyl protons appear as a multiplet, 7.20 – 7.90 .

TABLE 50

Monomethyl-Indoles, -Benzofurans, and -Benzothiophenes[38]

Solvent: CCl_4

Indoles	δ_2	δ_3	$J_{1,2}$	$J_{1,3}$	$J_{2,3}$	$J_{3,7}$
Unsubstituted	†6.52	†6.29	2.4	2.1	3.3	0.7
4-Me	6.65	6.40	2.4	2.1	3.3	0.8
5-Me	6.58	6.24	2.4	2.0	3.2	0.6
6-Me	6.67	6.34	ca. 2.4	2.1	3.3	1.0
7-Me	6.67	6.31	2.3	2.15	3.3	
Benzofurans						
2-Me¶		6.25				1.0
3-Me‖	‡					
4-Me-	7.66	6.72			2.15	0.8
5-Me	7.51	6.59			2.2	0.8
6-Me	7.47	6.62			2.2	1.0
7-Me	7.55	6.67				
Benzothiophenes						
2-Me¶		6.88				0.9
3-Me‖	6.90					

†These multiplet signals were appropriately collapsed by irradiation at a point 75 c/s to low field of their mean position. Hence, δ_{NH} = ca. 7.65. We are indebted to Dr. D. W. Turner for this decoupling result. ‡Not identifiable because of overlap with the aromatic band. ¶J_2-Me, 3-H = 1.2 c/s. ‖J_2-II,3-Me = 1.2 c/s.

II. ALKANES

TABLE 51A

Methyl Groups CH_3-R[10]

δ	Group
0.88–1.05	$-CH_2CH_2R'$
0.90–1.13	$-CH_2CH(R')(R'')$
0.83–1.24	$-CH_2C(R')(R'')(R''')$
1.48–1.83	$-CH_2X$ X = halogen
1.05–1.23	$-CH_2C(=O)R'$
0.97–1.23	$-CH_2-C(R')(R'')$
0.97–1.13	$-CH_2-N(R')(R'')$
1.20–1.47	$-CH_2OR'$
1.25–1.40	$-CH_2OC(=O)R'$
1.22–1.25	$-CH(CH_3)-\phi$
0.90–0.95	$-C(R')(R'')H$
1.20–1.52	$-CH_2SR'$
1.25–1.30	$-CH_2\phi$
0.82–0.93	$-CH(CH_3)-CH_2R$
0.82–1.02	$-CH(CH_3)-CH(R')(R'')$
0.75–0.97	$-CH(CH_3)-C(R')(R'')(R''')$
1.10–1.22	$-CH(CH_3)-C(=O)-R'$
0.72–1.02	$-C(CH_3)_2-CH_2R'$
1.30–1.43	$-C(CH_3)_2-\phi$

R′,‴ = alkyl, but not methyl

TABLE 51A (continued)

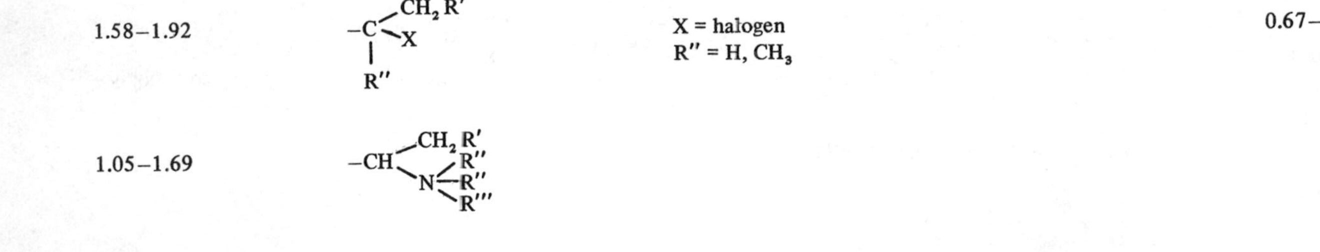

2.12–2.40	–C(φ)=C(R″)–C(R‴)R′		3.02–(3.90)	–N(φ)C =
2.25–2.57	–N(R′)R″	R′, R″ = alkyl	3.33–3.47 3.67–4.40	–O–R′ R′ = alkyl –O–Ar Ar = nonphenyl aromatic (e.g., heterocyclic)
2.83–3.07	–N(R″)C(=O)R′	R″ = alkyl	3.67–3.87 3.62–3.96	–OC(=O)R′ –OC(=O)–C(=R″)R′
2.87–3.05	–N(φ)R′	R′ = alkyl	2.08–2.12	–S–R′
3.20–(4.00)	–N(φ)C(=O)R′	*Cyclic or noncyclic; cyclic only: 3.83–(4.00)		
1.53–2.78 –4.23–2.97	–φ –Ar (b)			
0.82–1.29	–C(H)(R′) (cyclic)			–C(CH₃)R′ (cyclic)
1.58–1.92	–C(R″)(X)CH₂R′	X = halogen R″ = H, CH_3	0.67–1.27	
1.05–1.69	–CH(CH₂R′)(R″)N(R″)R‴			

TABLE 51A (continued)

δ	Group	δ	Group
1.12–1.44		1.12–1.75	$-C(CH_3)(CH_2R')-N(R'')(R''')$
	$-CH(CH_2R')(OR'')$	1.60–2.18	$-C(CH_3)=C(R'')-C(R''')=R'$
2.12–2.17	$-C(=O)-CH_2-R''$	1.60–2.11	$-C(H)=C(R'')-C(R''')=R'$
2.13–2.35	$-C(=O)-CH(R')(R'')$		
1.88–2.68	$-C(=O)-C(R')=C(R'')(R'')$	1.61–2.27	$-C(C(=O)R')=C(R'')-C(R''')=R''''$
1.87–2.50	$-C(=O)-N(R')(R'')(R''')$	1.92–2.40	$-C(N\ (\text{or } O^-))=C(R'')-C(R'')=R'$
2.47–2.59	$-C(=O)-\phi$	2.07–2.37	Same, but cyclic only
1.92–2.25	$-C(=O)-OR'$ (R′, not ϕ)		
2.06–(2.58)	$-C(=O)O\phi$		

(a) R′, R″, etc. may be any group, unless otherwise specified. ϕ = phenyl skeleton (but not heterocyclic aromatic). (b) The value −4.23 corresponds to the situation in which the methyl group is constrained to a position directly over the aromatic ring.

TABLE 51B

Alkanes

δ for the α-Protons[1]

X	CH_3X	$R'CH_2X$	$R'R''CHX$
–R	0.10	1.25	1.50
$-CH^b$ ⟋ $CH_2{}^a$ ⟍ O	1.32	a2.4, 2.7	b3.0
=, R =, =end-of-chain position			
R	1.70	1.95	2.6
=-=-= etc.			
–C≡C	1.80	2.5	
mid-chain position			
=-=-= etc.	1.95	2.2	
=N–	2.0		
–CO·OR	2.00	2.10	
$-CO\cdot NH_2$, $-CO\cdot NR_2$	2.02	2.05	
–CO·OH	2.07	2.34	2.57
–CO·R	2.10	2.40	2.48
–CN	2.00	2.48	
–I	2.16	3.15	4.20
–Br	2.65	3.34	4.10
–Cl	3.02	3.44	4.02
–SH, –SR	2.10	2.40	
$-NH_2$, $-NR_2$	2.15	2.50	2.87
–CHO	2.17	2.2	2.4
–Ph	2.34	2.62	2.87
–NH·CO·R, –NR·CO·R	2.9	3.3	3.5
–Cl	3.02	3.44	4.02
–SH, –SR	2.10	2.40	
$-NH_2$, $-NR_2$	2.15	2.50	2.87
–CHO	2.17	2.2	2.4
–Ph	2.34	2.62	2.87
–NH·CO·R, –NR·CO·R	2.9	3.3	3.5
–OR	3.30	3.36	3.80
–OH	3.38	3.56	3.85
$-\overset{+}{N}H_3$	3.33	3.40	
–O·CO·R	3.65	4.15	5.01
–OPh	3.73	3.90	4.0
–O·CO·Ph	3.90	4.23	5.12
$-O\cdot COCF_3$	4.10	4.43	
NO_2	4.33	4.40	4.60
–F	4.26	4.35	

*If R′ and X form part of a 3-membered ring, –1.05;
If R′ and X form part of a 5-membered ring, +0.25;
If R′ and X form part of a 6-membered ring, +0.20;
If R′ and X form part of a 7-membered ring, +0.30;
except for a CH_2 next to C=O, when the sign is changed.

TABLE 52

Alkanes Effect of β-Substituents[1]

Relative to 0.9δ (CH_3), 1.25δ (CH_2), and 1.5δ (CH)

The effect of a β-substituent can be predicted by adding its shielding constant to the relevant δ value for a methyl, methylene, or methine group. Thus, for CH_3–C–C=C, δCH_3 = 0.9 + 0.1 = 1.0.

X	CH_3–C–X	CH_2–C–X	CH–C–X
–C=C	+0.1	±0.05	
–CO·OH, –CO·OR	+0.25		
–CN		+0.4	
–CO·NH_2	+0.23		
–CO·R, –CHO	+0.2		
–SH, –SR	+0.45	+0.3	
–NH_2, –NR_2	+0.1	+0.05	
–I	+1.0	+0.5	+0.4
–Ph	+0.35	+0.3	
Br	+0.8	+0.6	+0.25
–NH·CO·R	+0.1		
–Cl	+0.6	+0.4	+0.02
–OH, –OR	+0.27	+0.1	
–O·CO·R	+0.37		
–O·Ph		+0.35	
–F		+0.2	
–NO_2	+0.67	+0.8	

C–Y shifts 0 to +0.15 δ where Y is any common function (–OH, –CO, –N, halogen, etc.).

TABLE 53

Methane and Halomethanes

	δ	Ref.	Solvent		δ	Ref.	Solvent
CH_4	0.22	7, 80	CCl_4				
CH_3F	4.26	7, 81	CCl_4	$CHClBr_2$	7.20	79	CCl_4
CH_3Cl	3.05	7, 81	CCl_4				
CH_3Br	2.68	7, 81	CCl_4				
CH_3I	2.16	79	CCl_4	CH_2ClBr	5.16	79	CCl_4
				CH_2ClI	4.99	79	CCl_4
CH_2Cl_3	5.33	79	CCl_4	$CHBrCl_2$	7.25	7, 82	Cyclohexane
CH_2Br_2	4.94	79	CCl_4	$CHBr_2Cl$	7.06	7, 82	CCl_4
CH_2I_2	3.90	79	CCl_4				
$CHCl_3$	7.25	79	CCl_4				
$CHBr_3$	6.82	79	CCl_4				
CHI_3	4.93	7, 82	Cyclohexanes				

TABLE 54

Methyl Attached to Aromatic Rings[83]

Ring System	Methyl Substituent	δ, ppm
Benzene	1	2.37
	1,2	2.25
	1,3	2.30
	1,4	2.28
	1,3,5	2.25
	1,2,4,5	2.15
	1,2,3,4,5	2.13, 2.18
	1,2,3,4,5,6	2.17
Naphthalene	1	2.68
	2	2.50
	1,2	2.47, 2.57
	1,5	2.70
	1,6	2.50, 2.63
	2,3	2.40
	2,3,6	2.38, 2.47
Phenanthrene	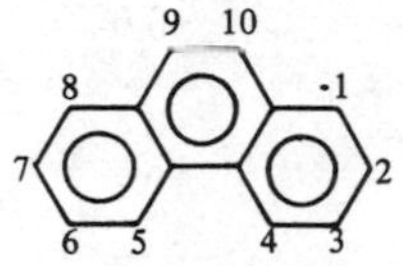 1	2.73
	2	2.53
	3	2.62
	9	2.72[a]
Anthracene	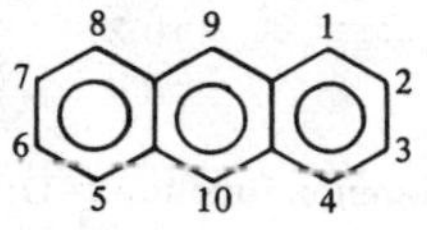 2	2.55
	9	3.05
	9,10	3.05
Pyrene	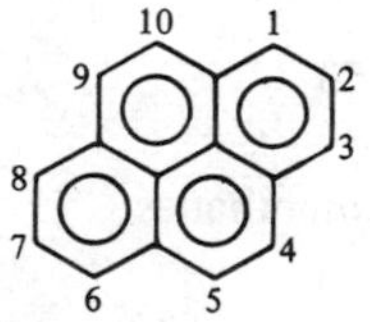 1	2.93
	2	2.80
	4	2.87
Coronene	1	3.30[b]

[a]Data of Reference 84.
[b]Measured in CS_2 with reference to toluene.

TABLE 55[85]

Toluene Methyls

Toluenes	δ_{CH_3} ortho	meta	para
Chloro	2.36	2.32	2.30
Bromo	2.40	2.33	2.26
Iodo	2.39	2.29	2.29
Cyano	2.51	2.42	2.42
Nitro	2.45	2.47	2.58
Methoxy	2.18	2.30	2.27

The toluene methyl group appeared at δ2.34 under the conditions employed here.

TABLE 56

Tertiary Butyl Groups[86]

Compound	δCMe_3	Compound	δCMe_3
t-Butylcyclohexane	0.852	$Me_3C-NH_2BH_3$	1.300
$Me_3C-CH_2CHMe_2$	0.86[a]	p-$Me_3C-C_6H_4Br$	1.302[h]
Me_3C-CMe_3	0.870[b]	m-$(Me_3C)_2-C_6H_4$	1.31[j]
Me_3C-H	0.905	p-$(Me_3C)_2C_6H_4$	1.31[j]
Me_3C-CH_3	0.927[b]	$Me_3C-C_6H_5$	1.320
4-t-Butylcyclohexanone	0.928	4-t-Butylpyridine	1.323
$Me_3C-CH{=}CH_2$	1.00[c, d]	Me_3CF	1.337
Me_3C-NH_2	1.102	1,3,5-$(Me_3C)_3C_6H_3$	1.34[j]
$Me_3C-OC_2H_5$	1.135	p-$Me_3C-C_6H_4-CO_2CH_3$	1.340[h]
Me_3C-OCH_3	1.137	$Me_3C-NHCHO$	1.352
$Me_3C-CONH_2$	1.165	p-$Me_3C-C_6H_4CO_2H_3$	1.355
$Me_3C-O_2-CMe_3$	1.177	m-$Me_3C-C_6H_4CO_2CH_3$	1.362[h]
Me_3C-O_2H	1.19[a]	p-$Me_3C-C_6H_4NO_2$	1.368[h]
$Me_3C-C{\equiv}CH$	1.20[e]	$(Me_3C-)_2S$	1.39[f, g]
Me_3C-OH	1.200	$Me_3C-O_2CCH_3$	1.405
Me_3C-CO_2H	1.225	2,6-(Me_3C-)-4-$CH_3C_6H_2OH$	1.408
Me_3COCMe_3	1.248[b]	Me_3C-SH	1.417
$Me_3C-SC_6H_5$	1.263	$(Me_3C-)_2SO_2$	1.44[f, g]
p-$Me_3C-C_6H_4OH$	1.270	Me_3C-NC	1.440[i]
Me_3C-SCH_3	1.27[f, g]	5-Me_3C-2,4,6-$(NO_2)_3C_6Me_2$	1.467
$Me_3C-SS-CMe_3$	1.280	$Me_3C-O_2CCH{=}CH_2$	1.458
p-$Me_3C-C_6H_4OCH_3$	1.282[h]	1,2,4,5-$(Me_3C)_4C_6H_2$	1.48[j]
3,5-$(Me_3C-)_2C_6H_3OH$	1.283	1,2,4,-$(Me_3C)_3-C_6H_3$	1.52[j, l]
3-Me_3C-5-$CH_3C_6H_3CH_3$	1.287	1,2,4-$(Me_3C)_3-C_6H_3$	1.43[j, m]
p-$Me_3C-C_6H_4CH_3$	1.287	o-$(Me_3C)_2-C_6H_4$	1.54[j]
p-$Me_3C-C_6H_4SH$	1.287	Me_3C-NO_2	1.59[n, o]
m-$Me_3C-C_6H_4OH$	1.288	Me_3C-Cl	1.592
1,2,4-$(Me_3C-)_3C_6H_3$	1.29[j, k]	Me_3C-Br	1.778
p-$Me_3C-C_6H_4CH_2CH_3$	1.295[h]	Me_3C-I	1.940

[a]Ref. 87. [b]Ref. 88. [c]30%v. in CCl_4. [d]Ref. 89. [e]Ref. 90. [f]0.5*M* in CCl_4. [g]Ref. 91. [h]Ref. 92. [i]Ref. 93. [j]Ref. 94. [k]Position 4. Position 1. [m]Position 2. [n]10% in CCl_4. [o]Ref. 95.

TABLE 57

Alkene-carbonyl Compounds[135]

Compound[a]	cis- β-CH_3	trans- β-CH_3	cis- β-CH_2	trans- β-CH_2
	Chemical shift, δ			
CMe_2=CHCOMe	2.11	1.83	–	–
CMe_2=CHCOEt	2.09	1.85	–	–
CEtMe=CHCOEt	–	1.85	2.54	–
CMeEt=CHCOEt	2.11	–	–	2.14
CMe_2=CHCOPr	2.05	1.82	–	–
CMePr=CHCOMe	2.05	–	–	2.05
CMePr=CHCOPr	2.07	–	–	2.08
CPrMe=CHCOPr	–	1.84	2.54	–
CMe_2=CEtCOMe	1.74	1.74	–	–
CPrMe=CEtCOMe	–	1.70	2.14	–
CMePr=CEtCOMe	1.70	–	–	2.14
CMe_2=CMeCOEt	1.74	1.74	–	–
CEt_2=CMeCOEt	–	–	2.10	2.08
CEt_2=CMeCOi–Pr	–	–	2.04	1.95
CMe_2–CMeCOMe	1.82	1.72	–	–
CEtMe=CMeCOMe	–	1.72	2.25	–
CMeEt=CMeCOMe	1.81	–	–	2.11
CHEt=CMeCOEt	–	–	2.24	–
CHMe=CMeCOMe	–	1.72	–	–

[a]The first alky group (or hydrogen) listed is *cis* to the carbonyl group.

TABLE 58

Methyl and Halomethyl Silanes, Germanes, and Stannanes[96]

Compound	δ[a]	Compound	δ[b]	Compound	δ[c]
Me_4Si	0.00	Me_4Ge	–0.14	Me_4Sn	0.07
Me_3SiCl	1.42	Me_3GeCl	0.64	Me_3SnCl	0.67
Me_2SiCl_2	1.80	Me_2GeCl_2	1.30	Me_2SnCl_2	1.17
$MeSiCl_3$	1.14	$MeGeCl_3$	1.83	$MeSnCl_3$	1.65

[a]From Ref. 88.
[b]From Ref. 97.
[c]From Ref. 88.

TABLE 59

Disubstituted Methylenes[1]

Shielding Constants for Disubstituted Methylenes
Shoolery's Rules

δ Values are obtained by adding the sum of the shielding constants to 0.23.
Example: For $PhCH_2Br$, $\delta CH_2 = 0.23 + 2.33 + 1.85 = 4.41$.

X or Y	Shielding Constants	X or Y	Shielding Constants
–Br	2.33	–C=C	1.32
–Cl	2.53	–C≡C	1.44
–I	1.82	–Ph	1.85
$-NR_2$	1.57	$-CF_3$	1.14
–OH	2.56	–C≡N	1.70
–OR	2.36	–RC=O	1.70
–OC(=O)R	3.13	–C(OR)=O	1.55
–OPh	3.23		
–SR	1.64		
$-CH_3$ and aliphatic CH_2	0.47	$-C(NR_2)=O$	1.59

The shielding constants fail to reproduce δ values of methylene groups in cyclic systems.

TABLE 60

Ethane Derivatives[97a]

CH_3-CH_2-X (Ref. 98)		$X-CH_2-CH_2-Y$ (Ref. 99)			$X-CH_AH_B-Y$ Refs. 100, 101)		
$J(CH_3,CH_2)$	X	$J(CH_2,CH_2)$	X	Y	J_{AB}	X	Y
8.90	Li	6.83	Cl	Cl	– 5.5	Br	Br
8.0	H	5.83	Cl	OH	– 6.2	Cl	Br
7.23	Cl	6.80	CH_3CO	CO_2Me	– 7.5	Cl	Cl
6.97	OEt	5.3	OMe	OMe	–14.5	CN	Br
					– 7.3	OR	OR

See also Reference 102.

TABLE 61

Geminal Coupling Constants Across an sp^3 Hybridized Carbon Atom[20]

Compound	Coupling Constants (Hz)	Ref.
CH_4	−12.4 ± 0.6	103, 104
$(CH_3)_4Si$	−14.15 ± 0.08	105
CH_3F	− 9.6	104
CH_3OH	−10.8	104
CH_3Cl	−10.8	104
CH_3I	− 9.2	104
CH_2Br_2	− 5.5	106
CH_2Cl_2	− 7.5	106
$CH_2(CN)_2$	−20.3	107
$PhCH_2CN$	−18.5	107
CH_3CN	−16.9	107
$CH_3-CO-CH_3$	−14.9	107
CH_3-COOH	−14.5	107
$ArCH_3$	−13.8 to −14.8	108
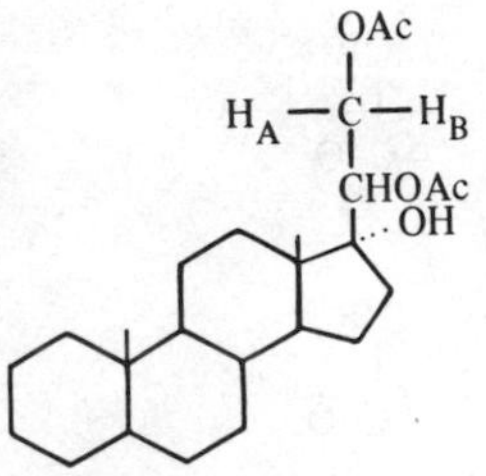 OAc; H_A-C-H_B; CHOAc; ...OH (steroid)	J_{AB} = −12	109
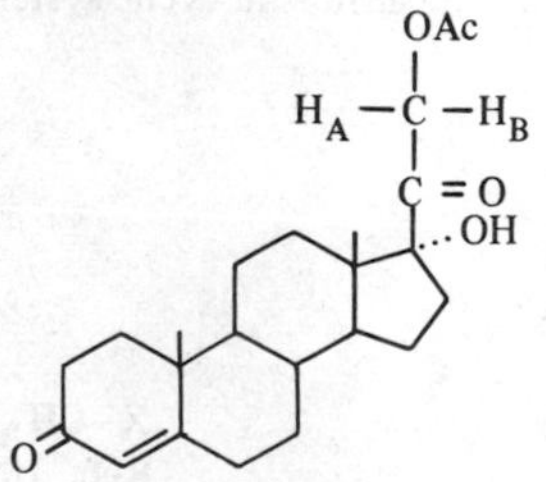 OAc; H_A-C-H_B; C=O; ...OH (steroid, O=)	J_{AB} = −17.6	109
$CH_3CH(OCH_AH_BCH_3)_2$	J_{AB} = − 9.4	110

See also References 111 and 112.

TABLE 62

Alcohols[113]

Chemical Shifts of Methyl Groups

Alcohol	Methyl Group[a]	Number of C–C Bonds Between Methyl Carbon and R_2CHOH Carbon	δ Alcohol	δ 3,5-Dinitrobenzoate
2-Octanol	α	1	1.11	1.42
2-Decanol	α	1	1.11	1.43
2-Dodecanol	α	1	1.12	1.43
3-Octanol	α	2	0.91	1.00
3-Decanol	α	2	0.91	1.00
3-Dodecanol	α	2	0.91	1.00
4-Octanol	α	3	0.92	0.98
4-Decanol	α	3	0.93	0.98
4-Dodecanol	α	3	0.92	0.98
4-Octanol	ω	4	0.92	0.93
5-Decanol	α	4	0.93	0.93
5-Dodecanol	α	4	0.93	0.93
3-Octanol	ω	5	0.90	0.90
5-Decanol	ω	5	0.91	0.90
6-Dodecanol	α	5	0.89	0.90
4-Decanol	ω	6	0.89	0.89
6-Dodecanol	ω	6	0.89	0.88
3-Decanol	ω	7	0.88	0.87
5-Dodecanol	ω	7	0.89	0.87
4-Dodecanol	ω	8	0.89	0.87
3-Dodecanol	ω	9	0.88	0.87
2-Octanol	ω	6	0.89	0.89
2-Decanol	ω	8	0.89	0.88
2-Dodecanol	ω	10	0.89	0.87

[a]The methyl group in the number 1 position according to conventional naming rules is labeled (α). The methyl group at the opposite end of the chain is labeled (ω).

TABLE 63

Amines[114]

Compound	J_{NH-CH}
N-methylaniline	5.21
Dimethylamine	6.11
Diethylamine	~6.8

TABLE 64

Alkyl-metal Compounds[96]

Chemical Shifts of Ethyl Groups Bonded to Metal Atoms

Metal	Periodic Group	$\delta(CH_3)$ Range	$\delta(CH_2)$ Range
Li	I	1.0–2.0	–0.5 to –1.0
Mg	II	1.0–2.0	–0.5 to –1.0
Al, Ga, Tl	III	0.5–2.0	–0.5 to 2.7
Si, Ge, Sn, Pb	IV	1.0–2.0	0.0 to 2.0
Se, Te	VI	1.0–2.0	2.0 to 3.0
Zn, Cd, Hg		1.0–2.0	0.5 to 2.5

Chemical Shifts of Methyl Groups Bonded to Metal Atoms

Metal	Periodic Group	δ Range
Li	I	–1.3 to –1.5
Be, Mg	II	–1.0 to –1.5
Al, Ga, In, Tl	III	–0.5 to 0.6
Si, Ge, Sn, Pb	IV	0.0 to 1.0
As, Sb, Bi	V	0.3 to 0.6
Se, Te	VI	2.0
Zn, Cd		–1.0 to 0.0
Hg		0.0 to 1.0
Pt, Rh, Ir		0.0 to 1.5

TABLE 65[1,115]

Calculations for Monosubstituted Ethylenes
δ Values for Protons Attached to Double Bonds

R_{cis}, H / R_{trans}, R_{gem}

$$\delta = 5.28 + \sum_i Zi$$

Substituent R		Zi for gem	Zi for cis	Zi for trans
–Alkyl		+0.44	–0.26	–0.29
–Alkyl ring		+0.71	–0.33	–0.30
$-CH_2O-CH_2I$		+0.67	–0.02	–0.07
$-CH_2S$		+0.53	–0.15	–0.15
$-CH_2Cl, -CH_2Br$		+0.72	+0.12	+0.07
$-CH_2N$		+0.66	–0.05	–0.23
–C≡C		+0.50	+0.35	+0.10
–C≡N		+0.23	+0.78	+0.58
–C=C		+0.98	–0.04	–0.21
–C=C further conjugated		+1.26	+0.08	–0.01
–C=O		+1.10	+1.13	+0.81
–C=O further conjugated		+1.06	+1.01	+0.95
–COOH		+1.00	+1.35	+0.74
–COOH further conjugated		+0.69	+0.97	+0.39
–COOR		+0.84	+1.15	+0.56
–COOR further conjugated		+0.68	+1.02	+0.33
–C(=O)H		+1.03	+0.97	+1.21
=C(=O)N		+1.37	+0.93	+0.35
–C(=O)Cl		+1.10	+0.41	+0.99
–OR,R=aliph		+1.18	–1.06	–1.28
–OR,R=conjugated		+1.14	–0.65	–1.05
–OCOR		+2.09	–0.40	–0.67
–Aromat		+1.35	+0.37	–0.10
–Cl		+1.00	+0.19	+0.03
–Br		1.04	+0.40	+0.55
–NR(R)	R=aliph	+0.69	–1.19	–1.31
–NR(R)	R=conjugated	+2.30	–0.73	–0.81
–SR		+1.00	–0.24	–0.04
$-SO_2$		+1.58	+1.15	+0.95

TABLE 66[14]

Monosubstituted Ethylenes

$(H_a)(H_b)C{=}C(H_c)(R)$

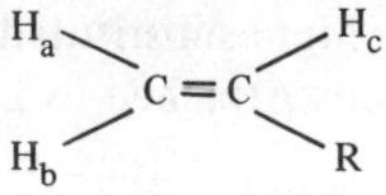

R	δa	δb	δc	Solvent		Ref.
Alkyl	4.87–8	4.94–7	5.72–8	CCl_4	Alkyl = CH_3,CH_3CH_2 $CH_3CH_2CH_2CH_2$	116
CH_2X	5.05–.17	5.23–9	5.89–6.04	CCl_4	X = F,Cl,Br,I,OH	117, 118
CH_2COCH_3	4.98	5.03	5.80	$CDCl_3$		118
OR′	3.94	4.15–6	6.42–7	$CDCl_3$	R′ = C_4H_9 (n) or C_4H_9 (i)	118, 119
OCOR′	4.51–6	4.84–8	7.27–30	$CDCl_3$	R′ = CH_3,C_4H_9 (n), $CH(CH_3)(C_2H_5)$	118, 120,
					C_7H_{15} (n),$C_{15}H_{31}$,(n) C_7H_{15} (n),$C_{15}H_{31}$ (n)	121
 C_6H_5 (benzene ring)	5.20	5.72	6.72	$CDCl_3$		118, 122
$COCH_3$	5.90	6.27	6.30			123, 124
F	4.03	4.37	6.17	CCl_4		118, 125, 126
Cl	5.39	5.48	6.26	CCl_4		118, 121, 122, 126, 127
Br	5.97	5.84	6.44	$CDCl_3$		118, 120, 122, 126, 128, 129
I	6.23	6.57	6.53	–		126
CN	6.07	6.20	5.73	CCl_4		118, 122, 130-134

TABLE 67[97a]

Monosubstituted Ethylenes
Coupling Constants

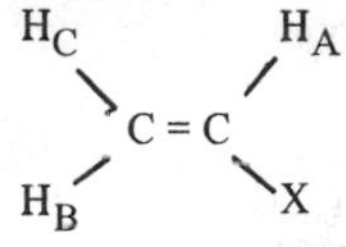

$(H_C)(H_B)C{=}C(H_A)(X)$

J_{AB}	J_{AC}	X
23.9	19.3	Li
19.1	11.6	H
17.2	10.4	CO_2H
14.3	7.0	OMe
13.9	6.3	OAc
12.7	4.7	F

(Ref. 20, 98, 136-139)

$H_A{-}XC{=}CY{-}H_B$

J_{trans}	J_{cis}	X	Y
16.8	10	H	Me
15.5	11.4	Me	CO_2Me
14.4	11.0	Ph	SPh
13.1	7.2	Cl	CH_2Cl
12.1	5.3	Cl	Cl
9.5	2.0	F	F

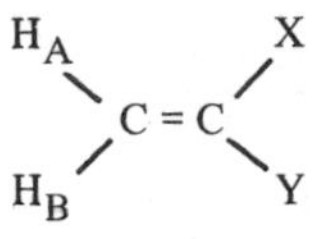

$(H_A)(H_B)C{=}C(X)(Y)$

J_{AB}	X	Y
+7.1	H	Li
+2.5	H	H
+1.3	H	CO_2H
0	H	NR_2
−1.3	H	Cl
−4.6	F	F

(Ref. 98, 137, 140, 141)

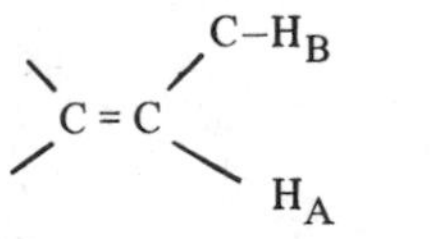

$C{=}C(C{-}H_B)(H_A)$

J_{AB} *gauche*	J_{AB} *trans*
1.8–37	9.6–13.4

(Ref. 142)

TABLE 68

Olefinic Methylene Groups[143]

Compound		J(Hz)	Ref.
$H_2C{=}O$		+41	111,144
$H_2C{=}N{-}R$	R=CMe_3	+16.5	111, 145
	R=$NH{\cdot}C_6H_3(NO_2)_2$	+11.6	145
	R=OH	+ 8	145
$H_2C{=}CHR$	R=MgBr	+ 7.4	146
	R=Li	+ 7.1	147
	R=H	+ 2.3	148
	R=Me	+ 2.1	116
	R=CH_2Ph	+ 1.9	117
	R=Ph	+ 1.3	149
	R=CH_2Cl	+ 1.3	117
	R=CH_2CN	+ 0.8	150
	R=SMe	– 0.3	119
	R=Cl	– 1.4	151, 152
	R=Br	– 1.8	152

TABLE 69[20,138,140]

Average Values of Coupling Constants in Vinyl Compound CH_2=CHX (in Hz)

X	J_{gem}	J_{cis}	J_{trans}
–F	-3.2	46.5	12.75
–Cl	-1.4	7.3	14.6
–Br	-1.8	7.1	15.2
–OR	-1.9	6.7	14.2
–OAr	-1.5	6.5	13.7
–OCOR	-1.4	6.3	13.9
–Phosphate	-2.3	5.8	13.2
$-NO_2$	-2.0	7.6	15.0
$-NR_2$	0.0	9.4	16.1
–COOR	1.7	10.2	17.2
–CN	1.3	11.3	18.2
–COR	1.8	11.0	18.0
–R	1.6	10.3	17.3
–Ar	1.3	11.0	18.0
–Py	1.1	10.8	17.5
–Sulphone	-0.6	9.9	16.6
–Sn	2.8	14.1	20.3
–As	1.7	11.6	19.1
–Sb	2.0	12.6	19.5
–Pb	2.0	12.1	19.6
–Hg	3.5	13.1	21.0
–Al	6.3	15.3	21.4
–Li	7.1	19.3	23.9

Vicinal Coupling Constants in Disubstituted Olefins X–CH=CH–Y

X	Y	J_{cis}(Hz)	J_{trans}(Hz)
F	F	-2.0	9.5
F	Br	3.5	11.10
Cl	OEt	6.0	–
Cl	Cl	5.3	12.1
F	Me	4.5	11.1
OCOMe	C_5H_{11}	7.0	12.5
Br	Br	4.7	11.8
OR	R	6.2–6.7	12.0–12.6
OMe	C≡CH	6.8	–
Ph	SPh	11.0	14.4
Cl	CH_2Cl	7.2	13.1
Ph	SCH_2Ph	11.6	15.5
Ph	COOH	12.3	15.8
Ph	CN	–	17.1
COOEt	COOEt	11.9	15.5
COOMe	Me	11.4	15.5
Me	CN	11.0	16.0
H	H	11.7	19.0

See also References 112 and 155.

TABLE 70

Dienes

1,3-Butadiene and 1,3-Pentadiene[14]

1,3-Butadiene — **Solvent: Cyclohexane**

δ_{1a} = 5.06	$J_{1a,1b}$ = 1.75	$J_{1b,2}$ = 17.05
δ_{1b} = 5.16	$J_{1a,2}$ = 10.17	$J_{1a,3}$ = −0.83
δ_{2} = 6.27	$J_{1a,3}$ = −0.86	$J_{1b,4b}$ = 0.69
	$J_{1a,4a}$ = 1.30	J_{23} = 10.41
	$J_{1a,4b}$ = 0.60	

a⟩C = C 3 4 b
b⟋ 1 2 C = C⟨a

R_{1b} = CH_3 (1,3-Pentadiene) — **Solvent: 50% CCl_4**

δ_{1a} = 5.41	$J_{1a,2}$ = 11.0	$J_{3,4b}$ = 16.6
δ_{2} = 5.92		
δ_{3} = 6.58	J_{23} = 10.5	J_{1a,CH_3} = 6.8
δ_{4a} = 4.99		J_{2,CH_3} = 1.5
δ_{4b} = 5.07		J_{1a,CH_3} ≈ 0.6(?)
δ_{CH_3} = 1.70	$J_{3,4a}$ = 10.5	

TABLE 71

2-Substituted 1,3-Butadienes[14]

R_2	Solvent	Ref.	δ_{1a}	δ_{1b}	δ_3	δ_{4a}	δ_{4b}	$J_{1a,1b}$	$J_{1a,3}$
CH_3	CCl_4, 50 vol %	157	4.87	4.87	6.35	4.94	5.05		
$C(CH_3)_3$	Cyclohexene	156	4.75	4.97	6.35	4.94	5.31	1.70	(±) 0.40
OCH_3	Cyclohexane	156	4.07	4.04	6.05	5.02	5.49	−1.90†	0.00
Cl	Xylene, 50%	158	5.20	5.07	6.18	5.09	5.59	−1.07	0.18
F	Xylene, 50%	158	4.59	4.32	6.06	5.12	5.52	−2.74	0.10

R_2	$J_{1a,4a}$	$J_{1a,4b}$	$J_{1b,3}$	$J_{1b,4a}$	$J_{1b,4a}$	$J_{1b,4b}$	$J_{3,4b}$	$J_{4a,4b}$	
CH_3		≈0.6			0.6	10.5	17.4	1.5	δCH_3 = 1.79; J_{1a,CH_3} = 1.2; J_{1b,CH_3} = 1.2
$C(CH_3)_3$	0.00	0.00	(±) 0.40	0.00	0.00	10.80	17.00	2.30	δ_{CH_3} = 1.08
OCH_3	1.50	0.51	0.0	0.57	0.51	10.82	17.27	1.87	δ_{CH_3} = 3.60
Cl	1.42	0.61	−0.60	0.72	0.67	10.51	16.54	0.95	
F	1.49	0.62	−0.19	0.73	0.70	11.15	17.32	1.24	trans J_{3F} = 47.93; cis J_{3F} = 15.76; $J_{4a,F}$ = 1.19; $J_{4b,F}$ = 0.41

†Value assumed.

TABLE 72

Monosubstituted Cyclopropanes

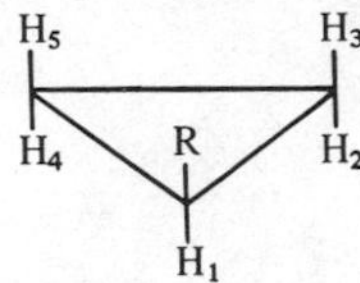

R	δ_1	δ_2	δ_3	J_{12}	J_{24}	J_{35}	J_{13}	J_{25}	J_{23}	Solvent	Ref.
H	0.22									a	180
				8.97			5.58		4.34	a	181
F	4.321	0.270	0.691	5.89	10.80	12.01	2.39	7.70	–6.69	b	182
Br	2.84	1.00	0.88	7.3	10.3	10.0	3.9	6.6	–5.9	a	182a
I	2.93	0.48	0.83	7.51	9.78	9.98	4.37	6.65	–5.93	a	182b
OH	3.353	0.341	0.587	6.19	10.27	10.88	2.94	6.84	–5.43	c	182
COOH	1.58	0.97	1.06							d	182a
				8.0	10.5	11.0	4.6	7.5	–4.3	a	182a
Li	–2.528	0.434	–0.124	11.8	3.0	3.0	9.5	1.5	–0.5	e	182, 183
	2.55	0.91	1.13	8.4	19.1	10.2	3.7	4.0	–7.8	f	184
	2.53	0.86	1.10	9.2	11.2	19.6	5.4	2.3	–8.4	f	184

[a]Neat
[b]Benzene + $CFCl_3$
[c]Benzene
[d]CCl_4
[e]Hexane + THF
[f]Deuteroacetone

TABLE 73

1,1-Disubstituted Cyclopropanes

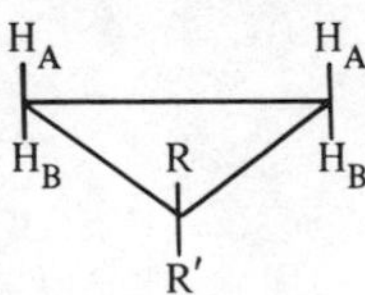

R	R′	δ_A	δ_B	J_{cis}	J_{trans}	J_{gem}	Solvent	Ref.
CH_3	CH_3	0.2		9.2	5.4	–4.5	b	185
Cl	Cl	1.47		11.2	8.0	–6.0	b	185
C_6H_5	Br	0.88[c]	1.17[c]	10.5	7.0	–5.9	a	185
C_6H_5	COOH	1.24	1.65	9.6	6.9	–4.0	d	169, 185

[a]Neat
[b]Benzene
[c]Assignments may be reversed
[d]$CHCl_3$

TABLE 74

1,2-Disubstituted Cyclopropanes

(a) cis

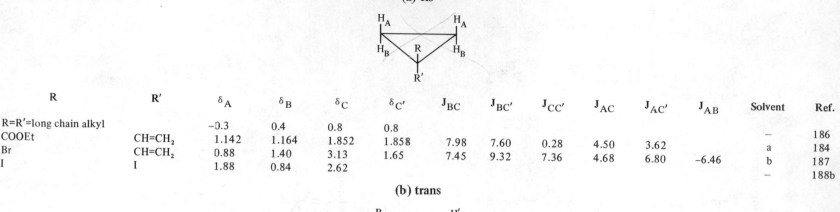

R	R′	δ_A	δ_B	δ_C	$\delta_{C'}$	J_{BC}	$J_{BC'}$	$J_{CC'}$	J_{AC}	$J_{AC'}$	J_{AB}	Solvent	Ref.
R=R′=long chain alkyl		−0.3	0.4	0.8	0.8							—	186
COOEt	$CH=CH_2$	1.142	1.164	1.852	1.858	7.98	7.60	0.28	4.50	3.62		a	184
Br	$CH=CH_2$	0.88	1.40	3.13	1.65	7.45	9.32	7.36	4.68	6.80	−6.46	b	187
I	I	1.88	0.84	2.62								—	188b

(b) trans

R	R′	δ_A	δ_B	δ_C	$\delta_{C'}$	$J_{AC'}$	J_{BC}	J_{AC}	J_{BC}	$J_{CC'}$	J_{AB}	Solvent	Ref.
COCl	COCl	1.82		2.83		9.1		5.9				a	188
$COOCH_3$	$COOCH_3$	1.33		2.03		8.8		6.6				a	188
CN	CN	1.58		2.06		10.2		5.5				b	188
CH_2I	CH_2I	0.79		1.20								a	188
COOEt	C_6H_5	1.110	1.445	1.794	2.388	7.58	8.36	3.8	4.54	4.34	−7.93	a	184
CN	C_6H_5	1.252	1.343	1.506	2.430	9.36	7.03	3.69	5.85	5.77	−5.81	a	184
BR	$CH=CH_2$	1.21	1.10	2.73	1.82	9.52	7.58	4.36	6.44	3.40	−6.44	b	187
$-C_6H_4-CH_3$	COOH	1.30	1.48	2.44	1.84							c	188a
$-C_6H_4-NO_2$	COOH	1.47	1.59	2.58	2.05							c	188a
Br	Br	1.47		3.10			6.5					—	188b
I	I	1.35		2.73								—	188b

[a] CCl_4
[b] $CHCl_3$
[c] Deuteroacetone

TABLE 75

1,1,2-Trisubstituted Cyclopropanes

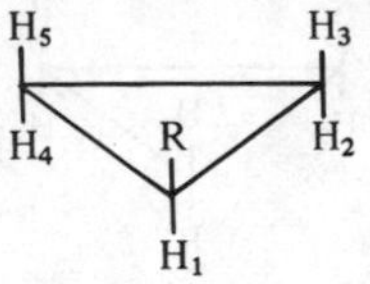

R	R′	R″	δ_A	δ_B	δ_X	J_{AX}	J_{BX}	J_{AB}	Solvent	Ref.
Cl	Cl	Br	2.08	1.58	3.45	9.4	6.6	−8.6	a	189
Cl	Cl	$SiMe_3$	1.43	1.12	0.58	12.6	9.6	−4.9	a	189
Cl	Cl	OMe	1.67	1.51	3.62	7.9	5.28	−8.38	b	189a
CH_3	CH_3	CH_3	0.41	−0.17	0.45	8.0	3.76	−4.6	c	189b
CH_3	CH_3	Cl	0.38	0.52	2.60	7.39	4.11	−5.98	c	189b, c
CH_3	CH_3	COOH	0.79	0.98	1.38	8.0	5.6	−4.3	b	189b, 185
Br	Br	$CH{=}CH_2$	1.93	1.52	2.26	10.20	7.53	−7.47	c	187
Br	Br	C_6H_5	2.00	1.88	2.84	8.85	8.50	−7.49	b	34
$COOCH_3$	CH_3	$COOCH_3$	1.55	1.15	1.92	6.3	8.6	−4.7	b	185
CH_3	$COOCH_3$	$COOCH_3$	1.20	1.48	2.22	6.6	8.8	−4.2	b	185
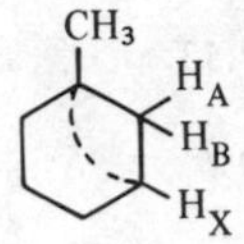			0.30	0.15					e	189b
						3.62	7.98	−4.82	c	189b
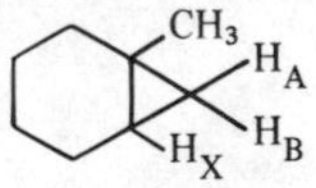			0.18	0.05		8.52	5.58	−3.97	e	189b
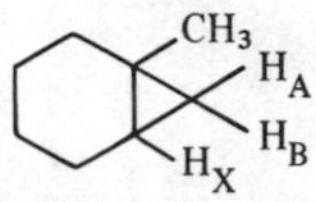			0.46	0.16	0.51	8.09	3.41	−3.27	c	189b

[a]CS_2
[b]Neat
[c]Benzene
[d]$CHCl_3$
[e]CCl_4

TABLE 76

1,2,3-Trisubstituted Cyclopropanes

R_1	R_2	R_3	δ_1	δ_2	δ_3	J_{12}	J_{13}	J_{23}	Solvent	Ref.
$-\langle O\rangle-OCH_3$	$COOCH_3$	$COOCH_3$	3.1	2.27	2.27	~7	~7		a	189d
$COOCH_2$	$-\langle O\rangle-OCH_3$	$COOCH_3$	~2.8	~2.8	~2.8				a	189d
$-\langle O\rangle$ OCH_3	$COOCH_3$	$COOCH_3$	3.16	2.38	2.38	~7	~7		a	189d
COPh	COPh	$-CO-\langle O\rangle-CH_3$	4.20	3.73	3.73	5.6	5.6		a	190
COPh	COPh	$-CO-\langle O\rangle-NO_2$	4.191	3.693	3.869	5.72	5.60	9.22	a	190
COPh	COPh	$-CO-\langle O\rangle-Br$	4.29	3.772	3.661	5.71	5.67	9.53	a	190
COPh	COPh	$-COCMe_3$	4.023	3.571	3.362	5.8	5.4	9.7	a	190
COPh	COCOOEt	COCOOEt	3.76	2.70	2.70	5.6	5.6		a	190

[a]$CHCl_3$

TABLE 77

1,1,2,2-Tetrasubstituted Cyclopropanes

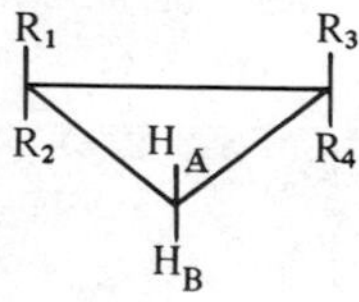

R_1	R_2	R_3	R_4	δ_A	δ_B	J_{AB}	Solvent	Ref.
CH_3	CN	Cl	$COOCH_3$	0.89	2.09	−7.02	a	191
CH_3	CN	COOMe	Cl	1.45	1.64	−7.06	a	191
COOH	Cl	CH_3	COOH	1.80	2.11	−6.44	b	191
Cl	COOH	CH_3	COOH	1.21	2.27	−6.39	b	191
Cl	$COOCH_3$	CH_3	$COOCH_3$	0.99	2.23	−6.52	a	191
		CH_3, H_A, OCH_3, H_B		0.53	−0.46	−4.50	c	189b
		OH, CH_3, H_B, H_A, CH_3		0.66	−0.06	−4.65	c	189b

[a]Benzene
[b]Acetone + benzene
[c]CCl_4

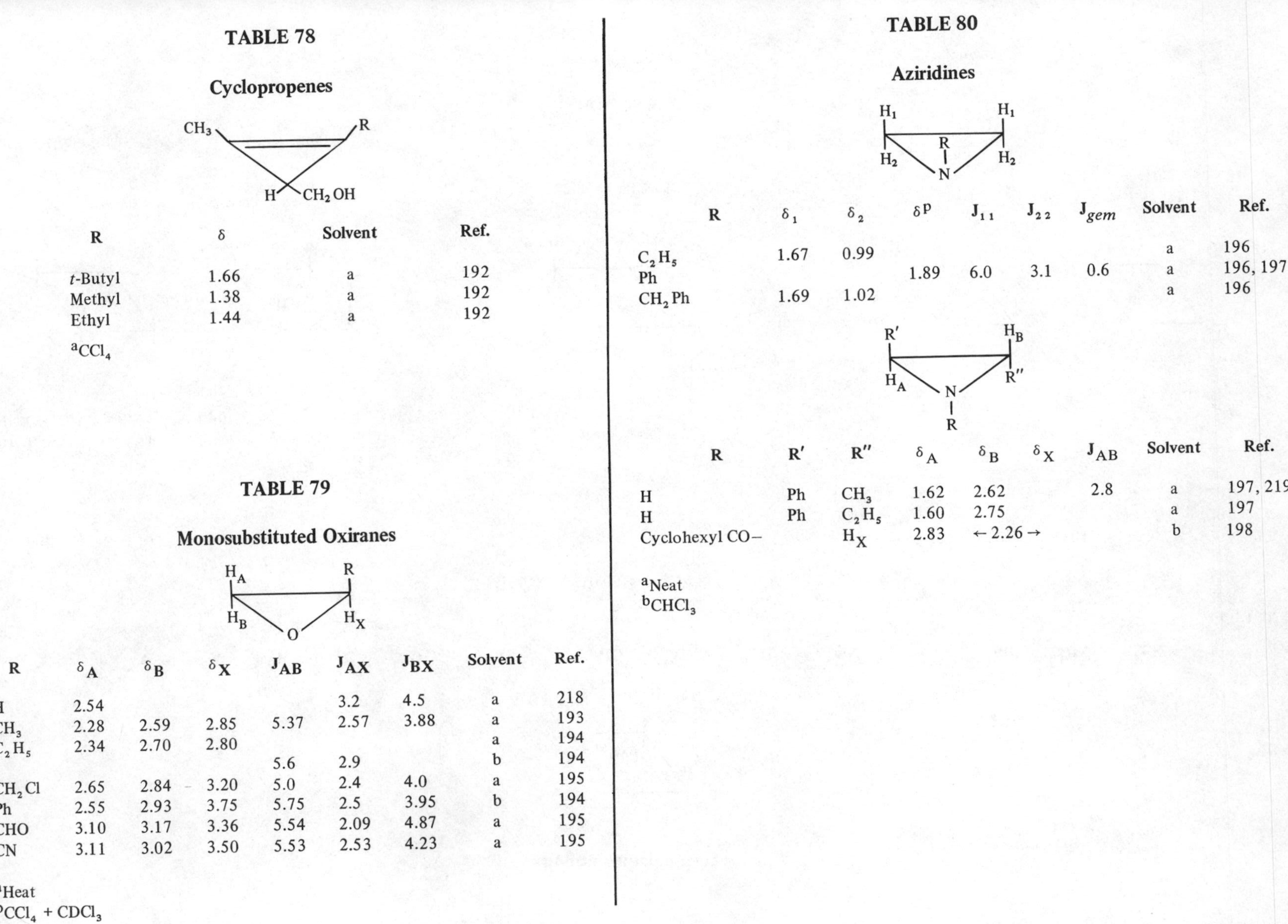

TABLE 78

Cyclopropenes

R	δ	Solvent	Ref.
t-Butyl	1.66	a	192
Methyl	1.38	a	192
Ethyl	1.44	a	192

[a]CCl_4

TABLE 79

Monosubstituted Oxiranes

R	δ_A	δ_B	δ_X	J_{AB}	J_{AX}	J_{BX}	Solvent	Ref.
H	2.54				3.2	4.5	a	218
CH_3	2.28	2.59	2.85	5.37	2.57	3.88	a	193
C_2H_5	2.34	2.70	2.80				a	194
				5.6	2.9		b	194
CH_2Cl	2.65	2.84	3.20	5.0	2.4	4.0	a	195
Ph	2.55	2.93	3.75	5.75	2.5	3.95	b	194
CHO	3.10	3.17	3.36	5.54	2.09	4.87	a	195
CN	3.11	3.02	3.50	5.53	2.53	4.23	a	195

[a]Heat
[b]CCl_4 + $CDCl_3$

TABLE 80

Aziridines

R	δ_1	δ_2	δP	J_{11}	J_{22}	J_{gem}	Solvent	Ref.
C_2H_5	1.67	0.99					a	196
Ph			1.89	6.0	3.1	0.6	a	196, 197
CH_2Ph	1.69	1.02					a	196

R	R′	R″	δ_A	δ_B	δ_X	J_{AB}	Solvent	Ref.
H	Ph	CH_3	1.62	2.62		2.8	a	197, 219
H	Ph	C_2H_5	1.60	2.75			a	197
Cyclohexyl CO–		H_X	2.83	← 2.26 →			b	198

[a]Neat
[b]$CHCl_3$

TABLE 81

Four-membered Rings

X	δ_X	δ_A	δ_B	δ_C	δ_D	J_{AB}	J_{AC}	J_{AD}	J_{CD}	$J_{AA'}$	$J_{AB'}$	$J_{BB'}$	J_{DX}	J_{CX}	Ref.
CH_2		1.96				−11 to −15									143, 180, 205
C=O		3.03		1.96		−17.54	10.03	6.34	−11.06	4.17	−2.99				180, 199
$C{=}CH_2$		2.7		1.92											10
CH_XOH	4.15									−0.01	−0.93	5.16	0.01	−1.07	200, 200a
O						−9.5				0.20	0.14				201, 202
S										1.20	−0.20				201
N						−6.5									203
+NR						−3.0									204
CH_XBr	4.51														7
CH_XCH_2OH	2.15	1.90		1.90											7

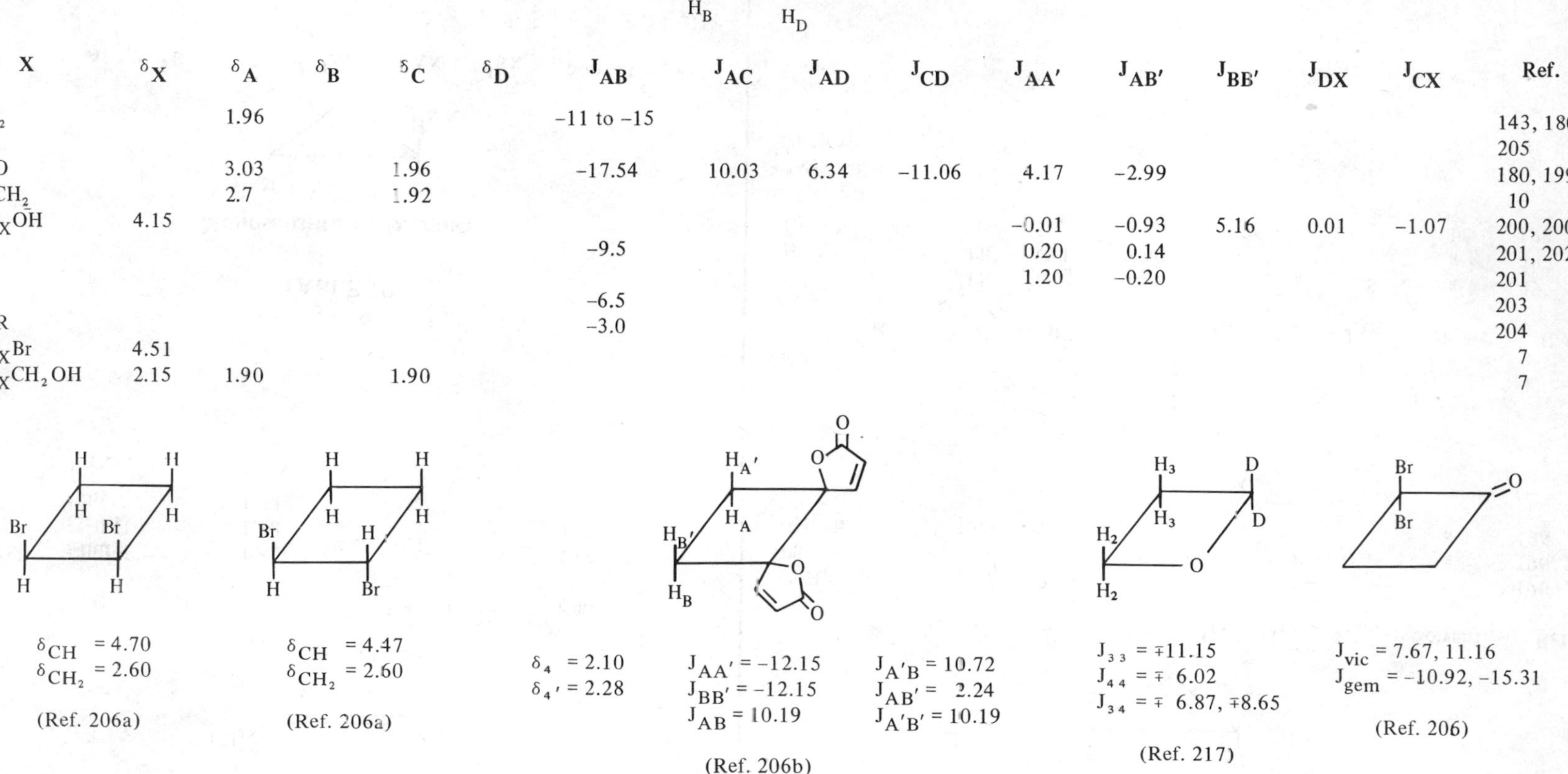

δ_{CH} = 4.70
δ_{CH_2} = 2.60

(Ref. 206a)

δ_{CH} = 4.47
δ_{CH_2} = 2.60

(Ref. 206a)

δ_4 = 2.10
$\delta_{4'}$ = 2.28

$J_{AA'}$ = −12.15
$J_{BB'}$ = −12.15
J_{AB} = 10.19

$J_{A'B}$ = 10.72
$J_{AB'}$ = 2.24
$J_{A'B'}$ = 10.19

(Ref. 206b)

J_{33} = ∓11.15
J_{44} = ∓ 6.02
J_{34} = ∓ 6.87, ∓8.65

(Ref. 217)

J_{vic} = 7.67, 11.16
J_{gem} = −10.92, −15.31

(Ref. 206)

TABLE 81 (continued)

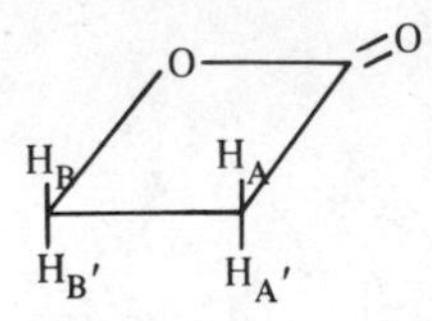

J_{AB} = 6.93 $J_{AB'}$ = 4.61
$J_{AA'}$ = −16.40 $J_{BB'}$ = −5.00

(Ref. 207)

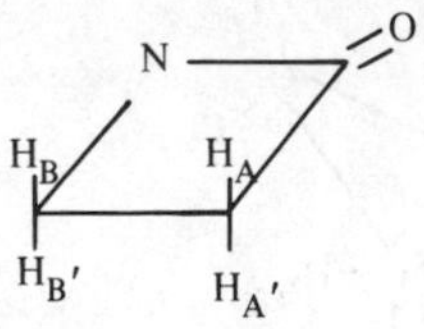

$J_{AA'}$ = −14.2 to −15.0
$J_{BB'}$ = −5.5 to −5.6

(Ref. 209)

δ_X = 3.70

(Ref. 208)

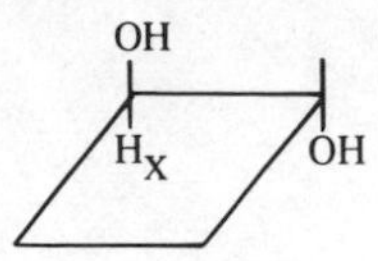

δ_X = 3.50

(Ref. 208)

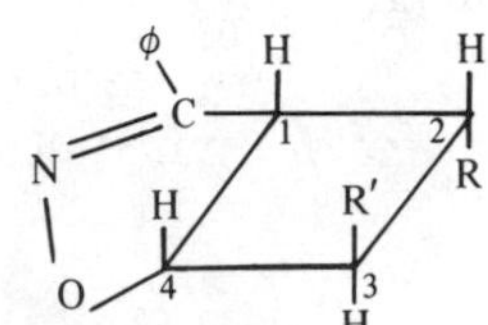

R	R′	$^4J_{1,3}$ *trans*	$^4J_{2,4}$ *cis*
Cl	Cl	−1.49	1.23
Br	Br	−1.38	1.21
Cl	OH	−1.55	1.42

(Ref. 210)

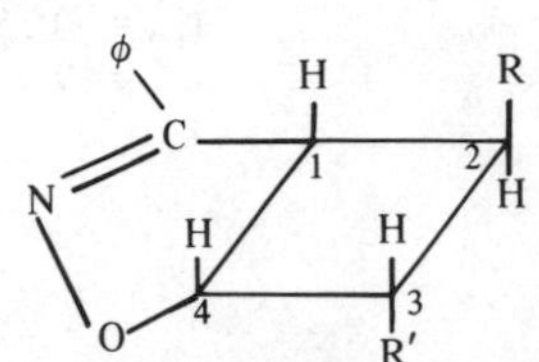

R	R′	$^4J_{2,4}$ *trans*	$^4J_{1,3}$ *cis*
Cl	Cl	−0.91	2.42
Br	Br	−0.61	2.48

(Ref. 210)

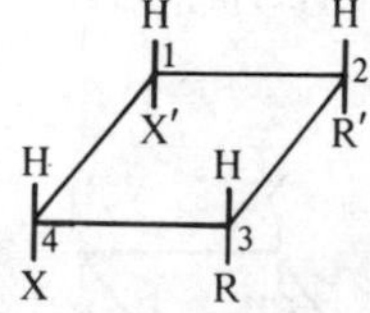

X	X′	R	R′	$^4J_{1,3}$ *cis*	$^4J_{2,4}$ *cis*	Ref.
Cl	Cl	COOH	COOH	1.3	1.3	210a
Cl	Cl	COOCH	COOCH	1.4	1.4	210a
Br	Br	COOCH	COOCH	1.2	1.2	210a
Cl	Cl	CO–O–CO		1.5	1.5	210a
COONa	O–PhONa	COONa	O–PhONa	0.6	0.6	210b

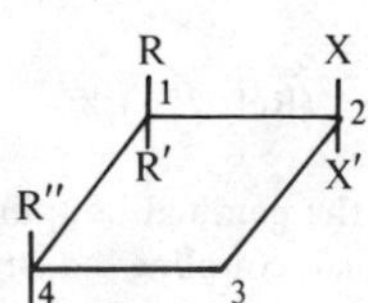

R	R′	X	X′	R″	$J_{3,3'}$	$J_{4,4'}$	J_{34}	J_{trans}	Ref.
CN	Cl	Cl	CN	H	−13.1	−13.1	9.4	4.5, 9.3	211
Br	$COOCH_3$	$COOCH_3$	Br	H	−12.0	−12.0	6.2	8.4, 10.0	211
CN	CN	CN	CN	OCH_3	−14		(J_{vic} = 7.8, 9.2)		213
$COOCH_3$	Cl	$COOCH_3$	Cl	$CH{=}CH_2$	−12.96		11.38	9.52	214
Cl	COOH	Cl	COOH	$CH{=}CH_2$	−11.97		10.75	7.68	214
Cl	$COOCH_3$	Cl	$COOCH_3$	$CH{=}CH_2$	−11.66		10.81	7.93	214

TABLE 81 (continued)

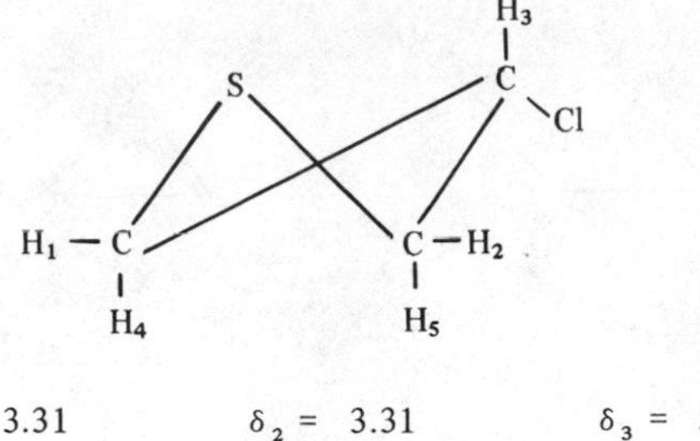

$\delta_1 = 3.31$	$\delta_2 = 3.31$	$\delta_3 = 5.13$
$\delta_4 = 3.66$	$\delta_5 = 3.66$	
$J_{12} = 3.116$	$J_{13} = 7.670$	$J_{14} = 8.633$
$J_{15} = -0.751$	$J_{23} = 7.670$	$J_{24} = -0.751$
$J_{34} = 9.343$	$J_{45} = -0.482$	

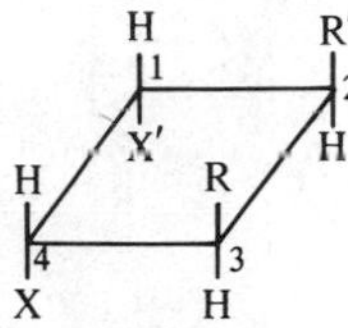

X	X'	R	R'	$^4J_{1,3}$ *trans*	$^4J_{2,4}$ *trans*	Ref.
Cl	Cl	COOH	COOH	-1.4	-1.4	210a
Cl	Cl	CH_2OH	CH_2OH	-1.5	-1.5	210c
COONa	O–PhONa	COONa	O–PhONa	-1.1	-1.1	210b

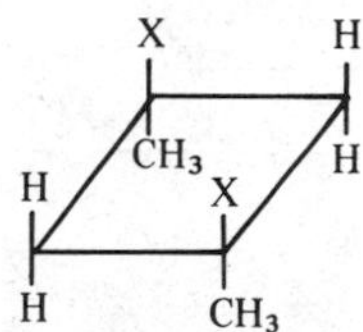

X	Isomer	δ_{CH_3}	δ_{CH_2}
Br	*cis*	1.88	3.19
Br	*trans*	2.13	3.21
Cl	*cis*	1.69	2.96
Cl	*trans*	1.86	2.88

(Ref. 221)

For the cis isomers, the geminal coupling constants were ~13 c/s. The diagonal coupling constants were in the order of 2 c/s or smaller.

TABLE 81 (continued)

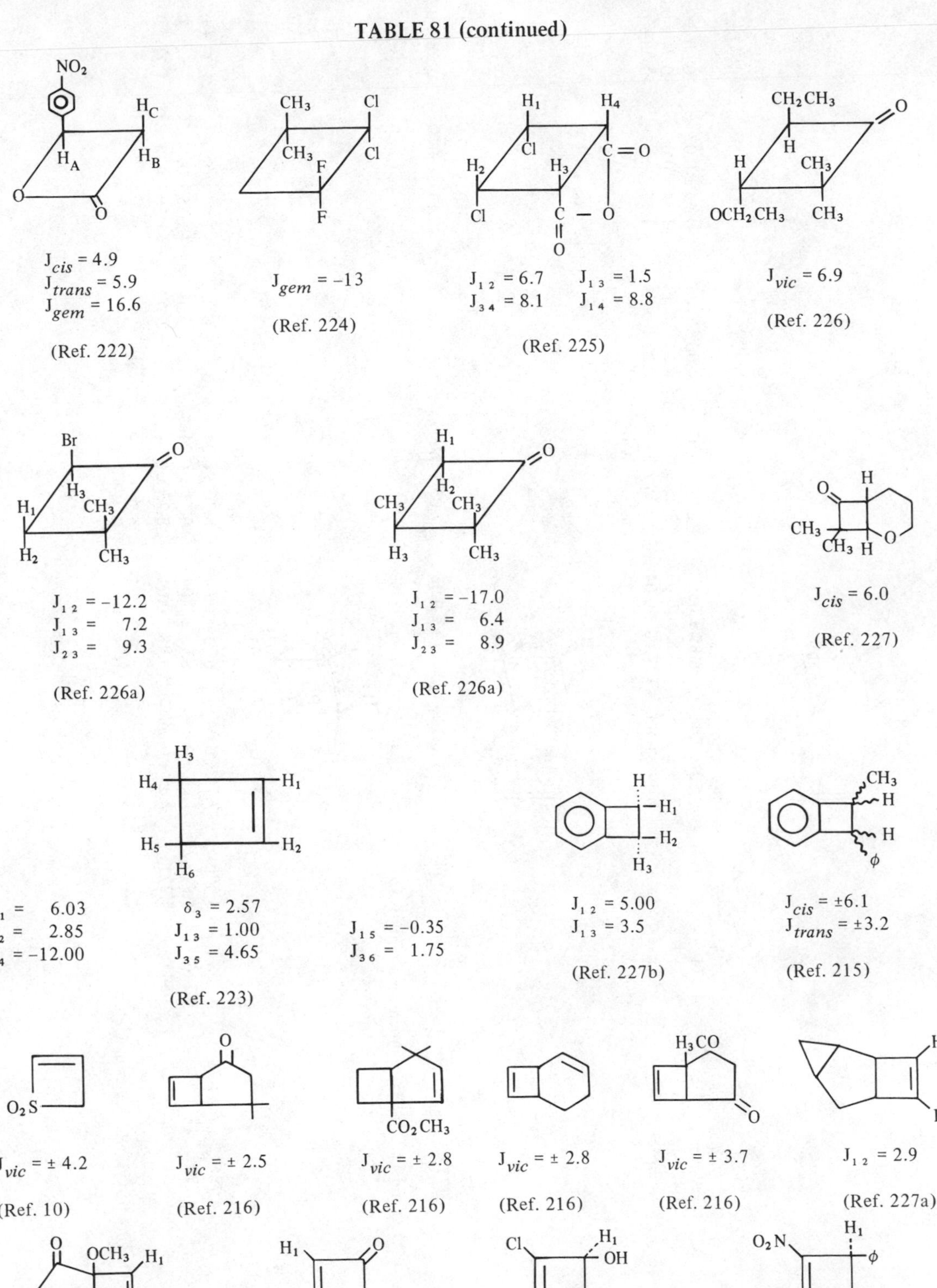

$J_{12} = 4.0$
$J_{23} < 0.2$

(Ref. 227c)

$J_{12} = 0.44$

(Ref. 227d)

$J_{12} = 1.6$
$J_{13} = 4.1$

(Ref. 227d)

$J_{12} = 2.0$
$J_{13} = 6.0$

(Ref. 227e)

TABLE 81 (continued)

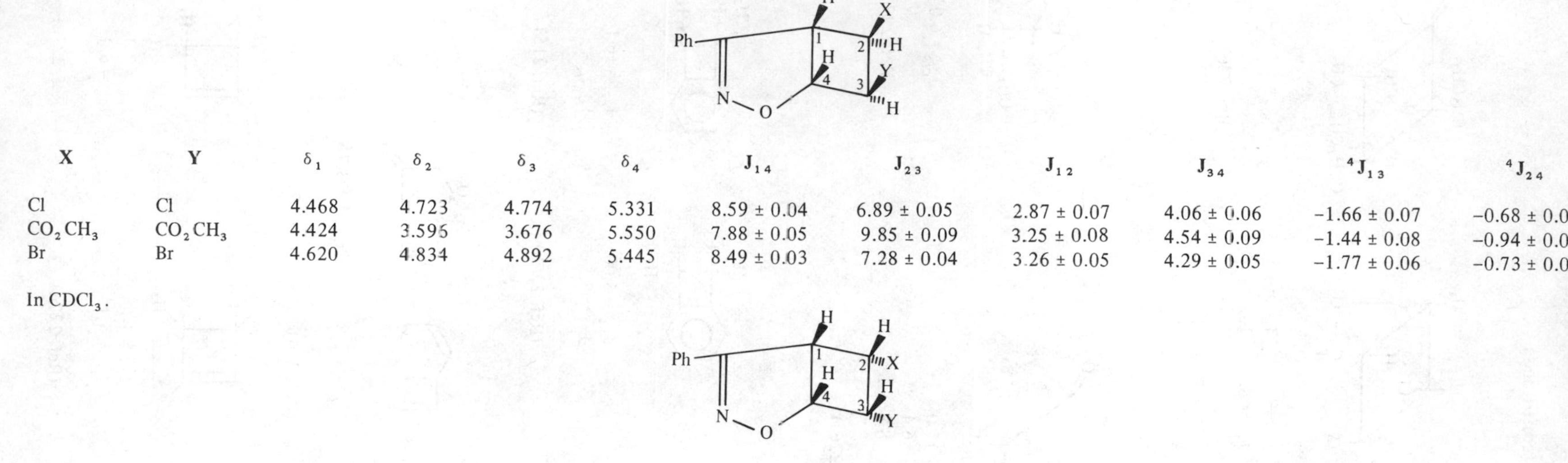

X	Y	δ_1	δ_2	δ_3	δ_4	J_{14}	J_{23}	J_{12}	J_{34}	$^4J_{13}$	$^4J_{24}$
Cl	Cl	4.468	4.723	4.774	5.331	8.59 ± 0.04	6.89 ± 0.05	2.87 ± 0.07	4.06 ± 0.06	−1.66 ± 0.07	−0.68 ± 0.07
CO_2CH_3	CO_2CH_3	4.424	3.595	3.676	5.550	7.88 ± 0.05	9.85 ± 0.09	3.25 ± 0.08	4.54 ± 0.09	−1.44 ± 0.08	−0.94 ± 0.09
Br	Br	4.620	4.834	4.892	5.445	8.49 ± 0.03	7.28 ± 0.04	3.26 ± 0.05	4.29 ± 0.05	−1.77 ± 0.06	−0.73 ± 0.05

In $CDCl_3$.

X	Y	δ_1	δ_2	δ_3	δ_4	J_{14}	J_{23}	J_{12}	J_{34}	$^4J_{13}$	$^4J_{24}$
Cl	Cl	5.3778	5.029	5.396	5.244	7.64 ± 0.12	6.79 ± 0.06	7.05 ± 0.06	5.12 ± 0.10	2.13 ± 0.04	2.98 ± 0.04

In acetone-d_6. Except for $^4J_{13}$ and $^4J_{24}$, the assignments are tentative.

X	Y	δ_1	δ_2	δ_3	δ_4	J_{14}	J_{23}	J_{12}	J_{34}	$^4J_{13}$	$^4J_{24}$
Cl	Cl	4.786	4.596	4.398	5.090	7.75 ± 0.04	6.71 ± 0.04	8.30 ± 0.04	3.68 ± 0.03	−1.49 ± 0.04	1.23 ± 0.04
Cl	OH	4.774	4.570	4.246	4.972	7.66 ± 0.04	6.18 ± 0.04	8.11 ± 0.04	3.35 ± 0.04	−1.55 ± 0.04	1.42 ± 0.04
Br	Br	4.851	4.728	4.544	5.271	7.65 ± 0.04	6.98 ± 0.04	8.25 ± 0.04	3.57 ± 0.03	−1.38 ± 0.05	1.21 ± 0.04

In $CDCl_3$, except the chlorohydroxyl, which was in acetone-d_6.

TABLE 81 (continued)

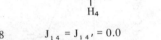

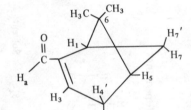

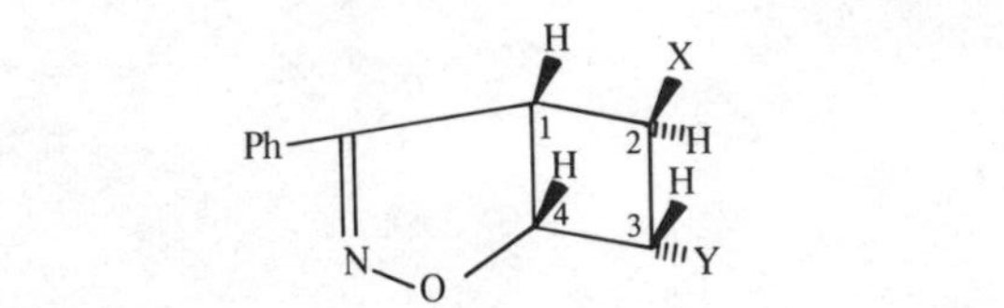
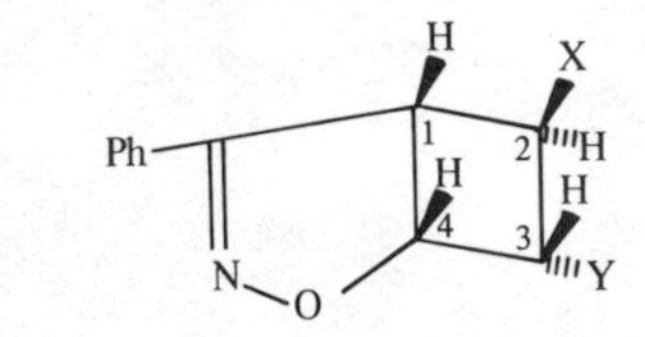

X	Y										
Cl	Cl	4.305	4.354	4.710	5.489	7.67 ± 0.10	5.05 ± 0.07	3.93 ± 0.05	6.00 ± 0.05	2.42 ± 0.07	−0.91 ± 0.05
Br	Br	4.488	4.476	4.922	5.465	7.51 ± 0.13	5.47 ± 0.10	4.01 ± 0.08	6.10 ± 0.07	2.48 ± 0.10	−0.61 ± 0.13

In $CDCl^3$

J_{12} = 2.8
J_{24} = 2.8
J_{13} = 1.5

(Ref. 228)

J_{14} = ~7 J_{23} = ~2
J_{45} = ~0 J_{56} = ~0

(Ref. 229)

J_{13} = 1.488 $J_{14} = J_{14'}$ = 0.0 J_{15} = 5.779
J_{17} = 0.038 $J_{17'}$ = 5.394 J_{34} = 3.012
$J_{34'}$ = 3.048 J_{35} = 1.505 $J_{37} = J_{37'}$ = 0.0

$J_{44'}$ = 0.060 J_{45} = 2.771 $J_{47} = J_{47'}$ = 0.0
$J_{4'5}$ = 3.066 $J_{4'7} = J_{4'7'}$ = 0.0 J_{57} = 0.110
$J_{57'}$ = 5.747 $J_{77'}$ = 9.049

A positive value for all vicinal and a negative value for all geminal coupling constants were assumed.

J = 0

(Ref. 230)

J_{AB} = −3.1

(Ref. 232)

$J_{A'B'}$ = −5.4 to −8.4 (Ref. 230)
If R = $H_{B'}$ $J_{AA'}$ = 6.7; J_{AB} = −5.4 (Ref. 231)
$J_{B'C}$ = 2.6 to 3.3 (Ref. 231)
$J_{CD} = J_{CE}$ = 0.5 to 1.0 (Ref. 231)

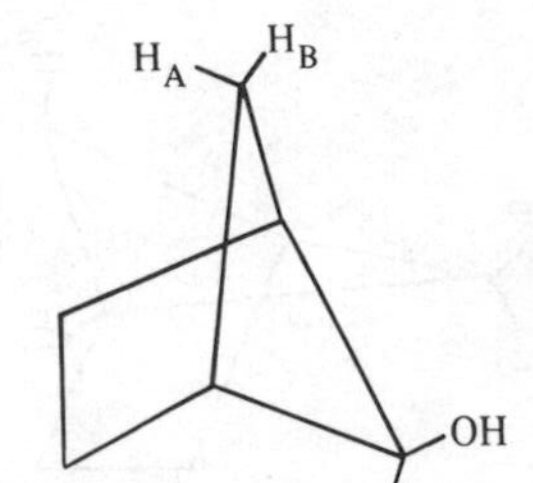

$J_{AA'}$ = 6.8 J_{AB} = −6.8
δ_B = 2.59

(Ref. 231)

See also Ref. 233

TABLE 81 (continued)

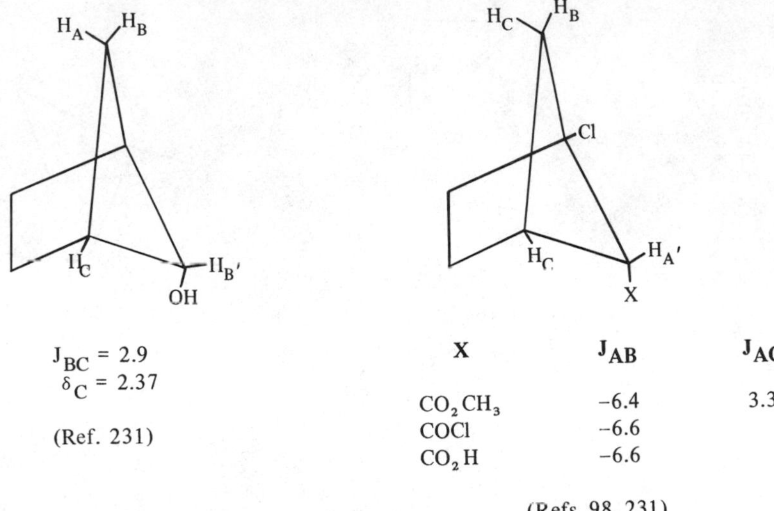

J_{BC} = 2.9
δ_C = 2.37

(Ref. 231)

X	J_{AB}	J_{AC}
CO_2CH_3	−6.4	3.3
COCl	−6.6	
CO_2H	−6.6	

(Refs. 98, 231)

TABLE 82

Monosubstituted Cyclopentanes

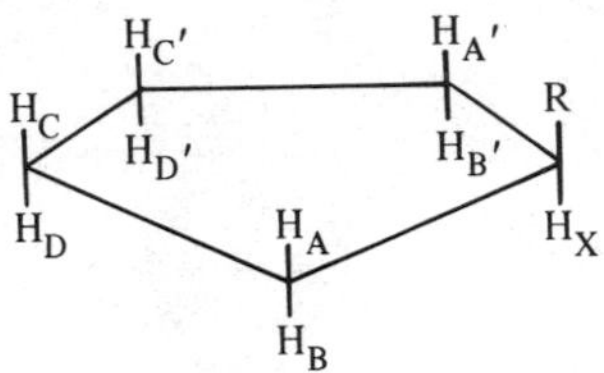

R	δ_X	δ_A	δ_B	δ_C	Solvent	Ref.
H	1.51				a	180
OH	4.18				a	235
NH_2	3.25				a	235
$NHCH_3$	2.98				b	236
$N(CO)_2C_6H_4$	4.70				a	235
Cl	4.36	~1.86		~1.86	c	116
Br	4.37	1.95		1.95	a	7, 116, 235
I	4.36	~1.91		~1.91	c	116

[a] CCl_4
[b] $CDCl_3$
[c] Cyclohexane

TABLE 83

Polysubstituted Cyclopentanes

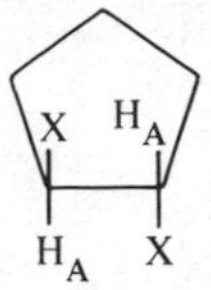

X	δ_A	Ref.
ϕ	1.2	236a
Cl	4.30	236c
Br	4.58	236c

In CCl_4

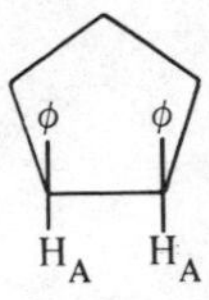

$\delta_A = 0.9$

In CCl_4

(Ref. 236a)

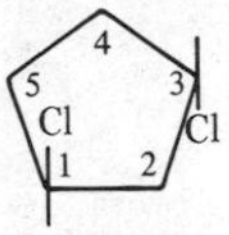

$\delta_2 = 2.43$

In CCl_4

(Ref. 236b)

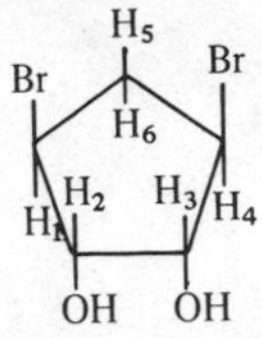

$\delta_1 = 4.14$ $\delta_2 = 4.37$
$\delta_5 = 2.34$ $\delta_6 = 3.22$
$J_{56} = 14.9–15.0$ $J_{16} = 7.6$
$J_{15} = 6.1$ $J_{12} = 4.5$

(Ref. 237)

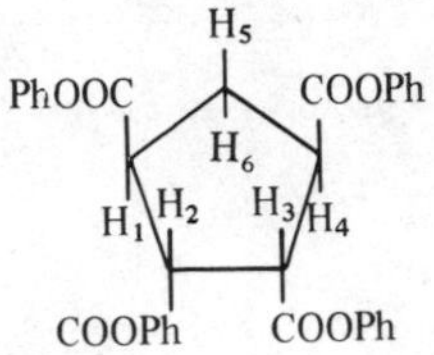

$\delta_1 = 5.72$ $\delta_2 = 6.03$
$\delta_5 = 2.12$ $\delta_6 = 3.30$
$J_{56} = 15.6$ $J_{16} = 7.6$
$J_{15} = 2.8$ $J_{12} = 4.7$

(Ref. 237)

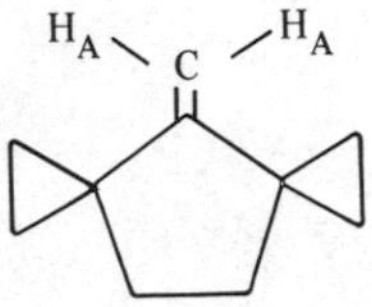

$\delta_A = 3.88$

(Ref. 237a)

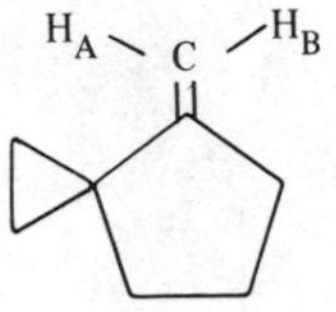

$\delta_A = 4.16$ $\delta_B = 4.46$

(Ref. 237b)

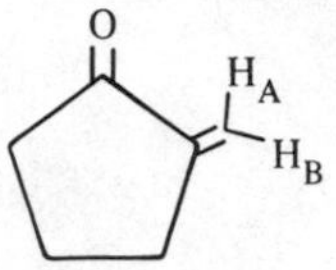

$\delta_A = 5.72$ $\delta_B = 5.04$

(Ref. 237c)

TABLE 84

Cyclopentene and Related Compounds

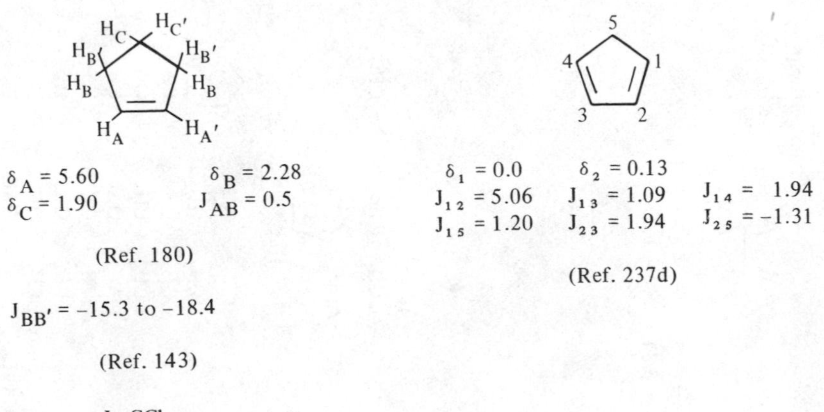

$\delta_A = 5.60$ $\delta_B = 2.28$
$\delta_C = 1.90$ $J_{AB} = 0.5$

(Ref. 180)

$J_{BB'} = -15.3$ to -18.4

(Ref. 143)

In CCl_4

$\delta_1 = 0.0$ $\delta_2 = 0.13$
$J_{12} = 5.06$ $J_{13} = 1.09$ $J_{14} = 1.94$
$J_{15} = 1.20$ $J_{23} = 1.94$ $J_{25} = -1.31$

(Ref. 237d)

TABLE 84 (continued)

$\delta_1 = 6.28$ $\delta_3 = 6.45$ $J_{12} = 2.80$
$J_{13} = 3.84$ $J_{14} = 1.89$ $J_{34} = 2.16$

(Ref. 237e)

$J_{AB} = 8.65$ $J_{AB'} = 3.49$

(Ref. 237f)

Q	R	X	Y	δ_2	δ_3	δ_4	δ_5	J_{45} *trans*	J_{45} *cis*	J_{34}	J_{24}	J_{55} (*gem*)	J_{23}	Solvent	Ref.
H	H	H	H	3.93	3.19										20
H	OCH_3	H	CH_3	5.28		2.60	2.80							a	238
CH_3	OCH_3	O O					2.45							a	238
CH_3	OCH_3	H	H O O			2.81								a	238
H	OCH_3	OAc	CH_3	5.37		5.86	2.77							a	238
H	OCH_3	CH_3	OAc	5.28		3.17	5.31							a	238
H	OAc	OAc	CH_3	6.37		5.97								b	238
H	OCH_3	CH_2CH_3	H	1.73		2.58	1.92, 2.40								238
H	OCH_3	CH_3	H	5.25		2.88	2.38							a	238
CH_3	OCH_3	OH	H			4.64	2.28, 2.96	2.6	6.8			−19.8		a	238a
$(CH_2)_6COOCH_3$	H	OAc	H		7.1	5.65	2.79		6.1	2.6	−1.2	−18.4		a	238a
$(CH_2)_6COOCH_3$	H	OH	H		7.18	4.92	2.29, 2.79	2.3	5.7			−18.5		a	238a
H	H	OBz	H	6.28	7.58	5.98	2.38, 2.83	2.3	6.6	2.7	−1.3	−19	5.7	b	238a
H	H	Br	H	6.17	7.62	5.15	2.56, 2.92	1.8	6.4	2.6, 3.0	−1.2, ±1.3			c	238a

[a] $CDCl_3$
[b] CCl_4
[c] CS_2

TABLE 84 (continued)

Q	R	X	Y	δ_2	δ_3	δ_4	δ_5	Solvent	Ref.
H	OCH_3	OAc	CH_3	5.37		5.43	2.41	a	238
H	OAc	OAc	CH_3	6.37		5.54		b	238
H	OCH_3	CH_3	OAc	5.30		2.80	4.87	a	238
H	OAc	CH_3	OAc	6.30			4.83	b	238

[a]$CDCl_3$
[b]CCl_4

X	Y	δ_1	δ_2	δ_3	$\delta_{4\alpha}$	$\delta_{4\beta}$	δ_5	$J_{4\alpha 4\beta}$	$J_{34\beta}$	$J_{34\alpha}$	J_{15}	$J_{14\alpha}$	$J_{14\beta}$	Solvent	Ref.
OH	OH	5.88	5.88	4.66	1.51	2.66	4.66	–14.7	7.3	3.6	1.0	0.5		a	238a
OBz	OBz	6.28	6.28	5.88	2.07	3.10	5.88	–15.0	7.5	4.0	0.8			a	238a
Br	Br	6.13	6.13	5.06	2.72	3.08	5.06	–16.5	6.5	1.8	1.0			b	238a

[a]$CDCl_3$
[b]CCl_4

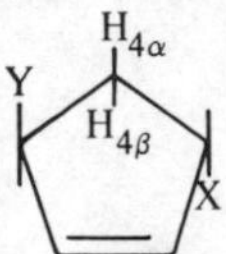

X	Y	δ_1	δ_2	δ_3	$\delta_{4\alpha}$	$\delta_{4\beta}$	δ_5	J_{15}	Solvent	Ref.
OH	OH	5.73	5.73	4.71	1.78	1.78	4.71	0.6	a	238a
OBz	OBz	6.34	6.34	6.17	2.53	2.53	6.17	0.8	b	238a

[a]DMSO-d_6
[b]$CDCl_3$

TABLE 85

Heterocyclic, Nonaromatic, Five-membered Rings

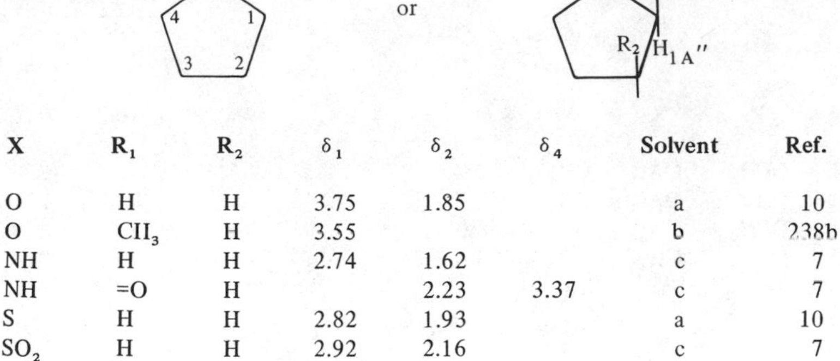

X	R_1	R_2	δ_1	δ_2	δ_4	Solvent	Ref.
O	H	H	3.75	1.85		a	10
O	CH_3	H	3.55			b	238b
NH	H	H	2.74	1.62		c	7
NH	=O	H		2.23	3.37	c	7
S	H	H	2.82	1.93		a	10
SO_2	H	H	2.92	2.16		c	7

[a]$CDCl_3$
[b]Benzene
[c]CCl_4

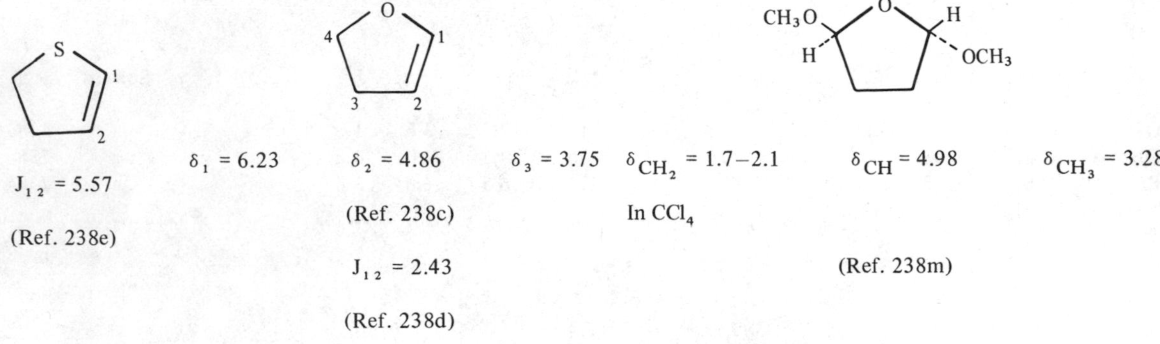

$J_{12} = 5.57$

(Ref. 238e)

$\delta_1 = 6.23$ $\delta_2 = 4.86$ $\delta_3 = 3.75$

(Ref. 238c)

$J_{12} = 2.43$

(Ref. 238d)

$\delta_{CH_2} = 1.7–2.1$ $\delta_{CH} = 4.98$ $\delta_{CH_3} = 3.28$

In CCl_4

(Ref. 238m)

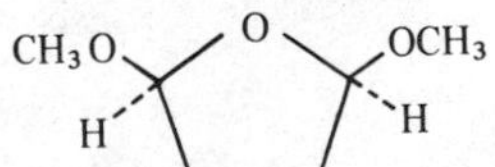

$\delta_{CH_2} = 1.91$ $\delta_{CH} = 4.95$ $\delta_{CH_3} = 3.31$

In CCl_4

(Ref. 238m)

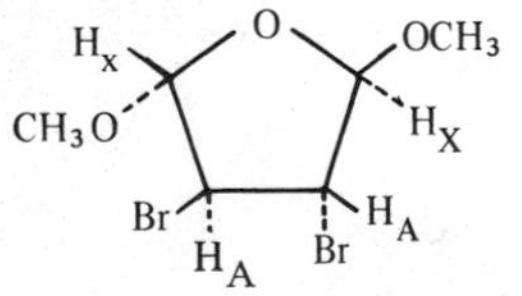

$\delta_A = 4.10$ $\delta_X = 5.20$ $\delta_{CH_3} = 3.47$

(Ref. 238g)

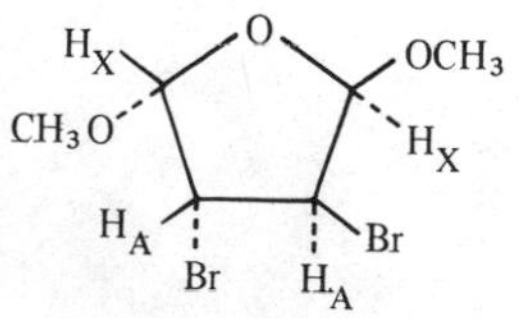

$\delta_A = 4.36$ $\delta_X = 5.16$ $\delta_{CH_3} = 3.44$

(Ref. 238g)

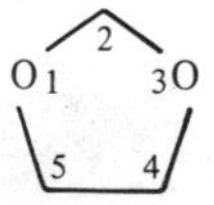

$\delta_2 = 4.57$ $\delta_4 = 3.57$

(Ref. 238n)

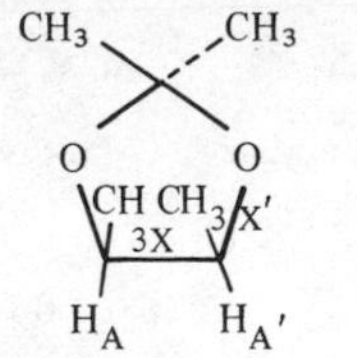

CH_3 CH_3 / O O / CH CH_{3X} X′ / H_A $H_{A'}$

δ: Methyl (position 2) 1.33, 1.22
Methyl (H_X) 1.05
Methine (H_A) 4.15

(Ref. 238o)

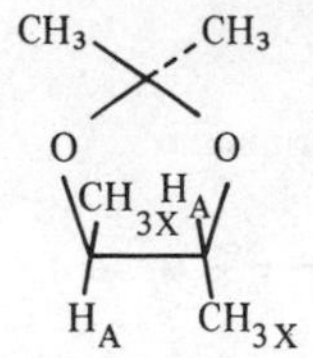

CH_3 CH_3 / O O / CH_{3X} H_A / H_A CH_{3X}

δ: Methyl (position 2) 1.28, 1.28
Methyl (H_X) 1.15
Methine (H_A) 3.38

(Ref. 238o)

Compound	δ_2	δ_3	δ_4	δ_5	Ref.
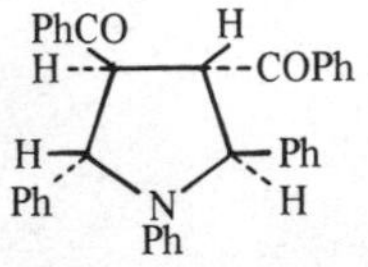 PhCO, H / H, COPh / H, Ph / Ph, H / N Ph	5.70	4.69	4.73	5.60	238h
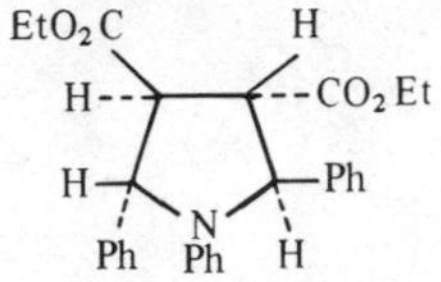 EtO_2C, H / H, CO_2Et / H, Ph / Ph, N Ph, H	5.78	3.57	3.57	5.78	238h
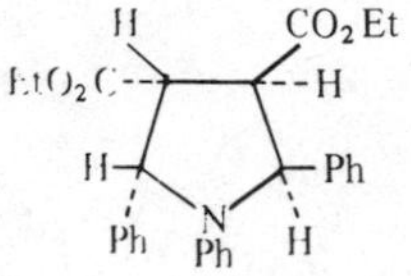 H, CO_2Et / EtO_2C, H / H, Ph / Ph, N Ph, H	5.62	3.69	3.69	5.90	238h

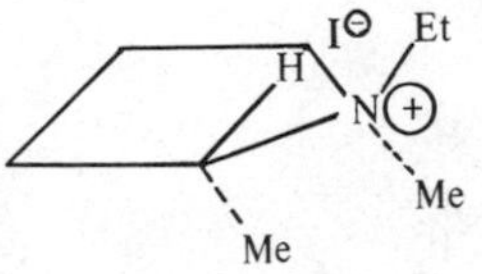

$I^{\ominus}$ Et / H N⊕ / Me / Me

$\delta_{N-Me} = 2.98$

(Ref. 238i)

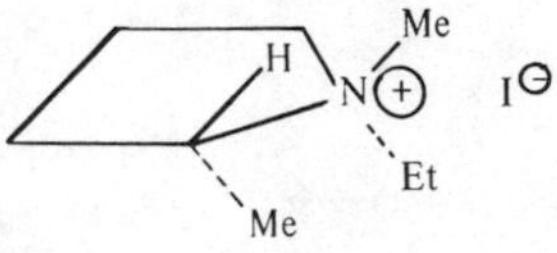

Me / H N⊕ $I^{\ominus}$ / Et / Me

$\delta_{N-Me} = 3.28$

(Ref. 238i)

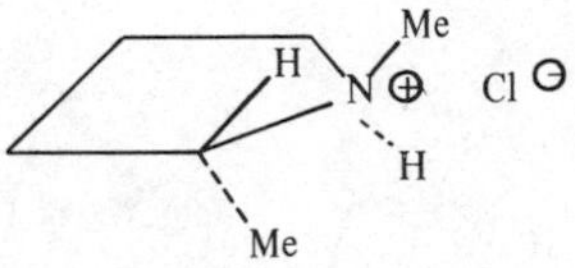

Me / H N⊕ $Cl^{\ominus}$ / H / Me

$\delta_{N-Me} = 3.03$

(Ref. 238i)

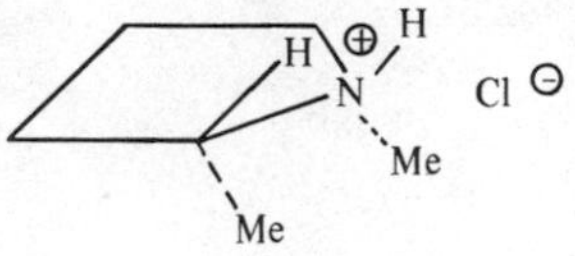

H ⊕ H / N $Cl^{\ominus}$ / Me / Me

$\delta_{N-Me} = 2.73$

(Ref. 238i)

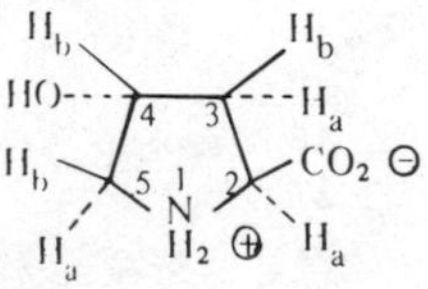

H_b H_b / HO 4 3 H_a / H_b 5 1 2 $CO_2^{\ominus}$ / H_a $NH_2^{\oplus}$ H_a

δ

$H_2a = 4.17$ $H_4b = 4.48$
$H_3a = 2.30$ $H_5a = 3.17$
$H_3b = 1.95$ $H_5b = 3.31$
H_4a –

(Ref. 238j)

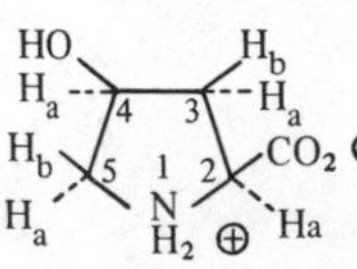

HO H_b / H_a 4 3 H_a / H_b 5 1 2 $CO_2^{\ominus}$ / H_a $NH_2^{\oplus}$ Ha

δ

$H_2a = 4.04$ H_4b –
$H_3a = 2.31$ $H_5a = 3.19$
$H_3b = 2.05$ $H_5b = 3.25$
$H_4a = 4.40$

(Ref. 238j)

TABLE 85 (continued)

Formula	Stereochemistry	Chemical Shifts Methyl	Chemical Shifts H_2
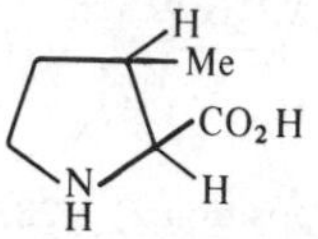 3-Me-pyrrolidine-2-CO_2H (N–H)	*cis*	1.00	4.08
	cis	–	–
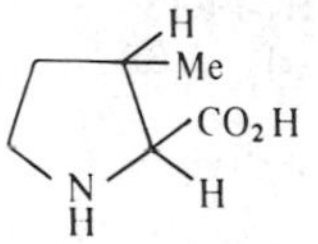 3-Me-pyrrolidine-2-CO_2H (N–H)	*trans*	1.22	3.32
	trans	–	–
3-Me-pyrrolidine-2-CO_2H (N–Tos)	*cis*	–	–
	trans	–	–
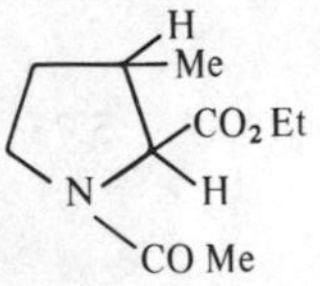 3-Me-pyrrolidine-2-CO_2Et (N–CO Me)	*cis*	1.05	4.41
	trans	1.18	3.96
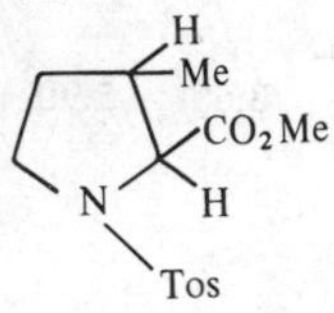 3-Me-pyrrolidine-2-CO_2Me (N–Tos)	*cis*	0.86	4.17
	trans	0.86	–

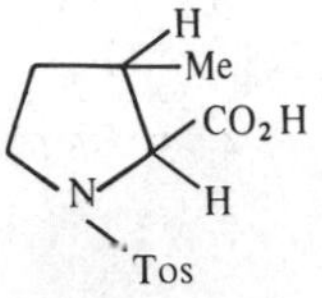

(Ref. 238k)

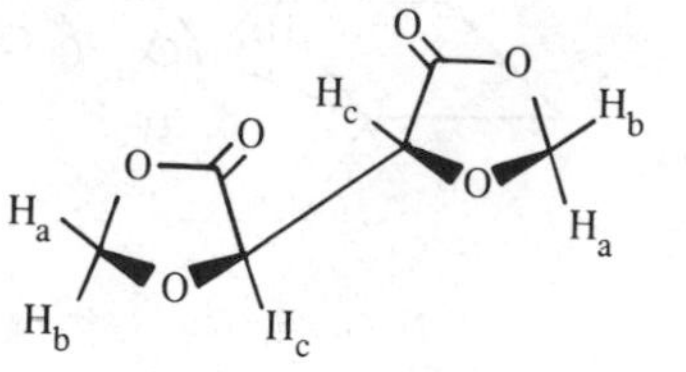

(I) 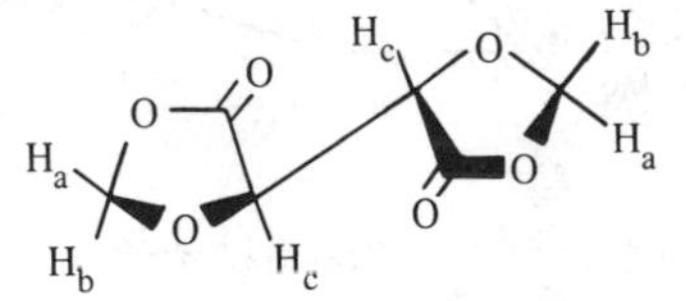 (II)

			δ_a	δ_b	δ_c
(I)	(+)-	CCl_4	4.46	4.48	5.46
		$CDCl_3$	4.35	4.41	5.27
		C_6H_6	5.32	5.52	6.02
	ASIS[5]	$\Delta^{C_6H_6}_{CCl_4}$ (ppm)	+0.86	+1.04	+0.56
(II)	*meso-*	CCl_4	4.45	4.49	5.42
		$CDCl_3$	4.40	4.44	5.29
		C_6H_6	5.20	5.52	6.07
	ASIS	$\Delta^{C_6H_6}_{CCl_4}$ (ppm)	+0.75	+1.03	+0.55

(Ref. 238f)

TABLE 85 (continued)

$\delta_2 = 5.05$

(Ref. 2381)

$\delta_2 = 5.07$

(Ref. 2381)

Hydrogen Chemical Shifts of Some Symmetrically Substituted 1,3-Dioxolane[208]

	δ(ppm)
meso-4,5-Dimethyl dioxolane	4.7, 4.99
d,l-4,5-Dimethyl dioxolane	4.85
meso-4,5-Dipropenyl dioxolane	5.06, 4.80
d,l-4,5-Dipropenyl dioxolane	4.92
meso-4,5-Divinyl dioxolane	4.15, 4.83
d,l-4,5-Divinyl dioxolane	4.99

Chemical Shifts of the Methine Hydrogen of Some Symmetrically Substituted 1,3-Glycols and 1,3-Dioxolane

	δ(ppm)
meso-3,4-Dihydroxy-1,5-hexadiene	4.06
d,l-3,4-Dihydroxy-1,5-hexadiene	3.80
meso-4,5-Dihydroxy-2,6-octadiene	4.00
d,l-4,5-Dihydroxy-2,6-octadiene	3.80
meso-4,5-Dimethyl dioxolane	3.99
d,l-4,5-Dimethyl dioxolane	3.40
*meso*4,5-Dipropenyl dioxolane	4.25
d,l-4,5-Dipropenyl dioxolane	3.82
meso-4,5-Divinyl dioxolane	4.40
d,l-4,5-Divinyl dioxolane	3.92

TABLE 86

Bridged Five-membered Rings

X	Y	Z	δ_1	δ_{6ex}	δ_{5en}	δ_4	δ_{3ex}	δ_{3en}	δ_{2ex}	δ_{7a}	δ_{7b}	δ_8	J_{43exo}	J_{2exo4}
I	C=O	H	3.22	5.12	3.92	2.70	2.06	1.52	2.54	2.32	1.82		10.5	~5
Br	C=O	H	3.25	4.94	3.87	2.65	2.11	1.75	2.52	2.28	1.74			
AcO	C=O	H	3.20	4.49	4.55	2.50	2.03	1.72	2.55	1.99	1.62			
TsO	C=O	H	3.13	4.48	4.25	2.49	1.96	1.57	2.40	1.98	1.57			
I	C=O	CH_3	2.78	5.07	3.85	2.66	1.52	1.94	1.17(CH_3)	2.36	1.88			
Br	C=O	CH_3	2.80	4.85	3.79	2.59	1.59	1.81	1.16(CH_3)	2.29	1.76			
TsO	CH_2	H	2.52	4.05	4.09	2.24	1.79	1.90	2.24	1.85	1.47	3.47, 3.53		
AcO	CH_2	H	2.62	4.06	4.32	2.22	1.83	1.10	2.30	1.90	1.52	3.66, 3.81		

TABLE 86 (continued)

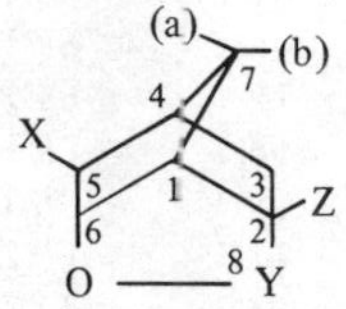

In CDCl
(ref. 392)

X	Y	Z	$J_{2exo6exo}$	$J_{6exo5endo}$	J_{7a4}	J_{3exo4}	J_{3endo4}	J_{7b4}	$J_{3exo3endo}$	J_{7a7b}	J_{8a8b}	J_{16exo}	J_{12exo}	J_{5endo4}
I	C=O	H			1.8	3.6	0.5	1.5	13.4	11.2		5.4	5.0	0.5
Br	C=O	H	~5	0.3	1.4	3.8	0.8	1.5	13.2	11.4		5.0	4.9	0.5
AcO	C=O	H				3.8			13.0	11.0		4.6	4.6	0.8
TsO	C=O	H				4.0			13.4	11.0		4.8	5.0	1.1
I	C=O	CH_3			1.6	4.7	0.7	1.6	13.5	11.1		5.1		1.0
Br	C=O	CH_3			1.6	4.1	0.8	1.3	13.5	11.1		5.0		0.6
TsO	CH_2	H				4.7			13.0	10.6	8.2			
AcO	CH_2	H			1.7			1.4	13.2	10.6	8.2	5.2	4.0	1.1

X	Y	Z	$J_{3endo2exo}$	$J_{3exo2exo}$	J_{7a1}	J_{7b1}	J_{8a2exo}	J_{6exo4}	J_{3exo1}	$J_{7b5endo}$	$J_{7a3endo}$	J_{26exo}	J_{24}	J_{14}
I	C=O	H	3.0	10.2	1.6	0.6		1.0	0.5	2.6	1.3	1.2	0.6	1.4
Br	C=O	H	2.0	10.6	1.4	1.5		1.0	0.3	2.4	2.0	1.0		1.6
AcO	C=O	H		10.5	1.5	1.6		1.2	0.3	1.7		1.2		1.2
TsO	C=O	H		10.3	1.8	1.8		1.1		1.7		1.1		1.0
I	C=O	CH_3			1.4	1.6			0.8	2.1	2.1			1.4
Br	C=O	CH_3			1.4	1.3		1.0		2.1	1.9			1.4
TsO	CH_2	H	2.6	10.8			3.6				2.2			
AcO	CH_2	H	2.2	10.0	1.7	1.4	3.6			1.8	2.2	1.0		

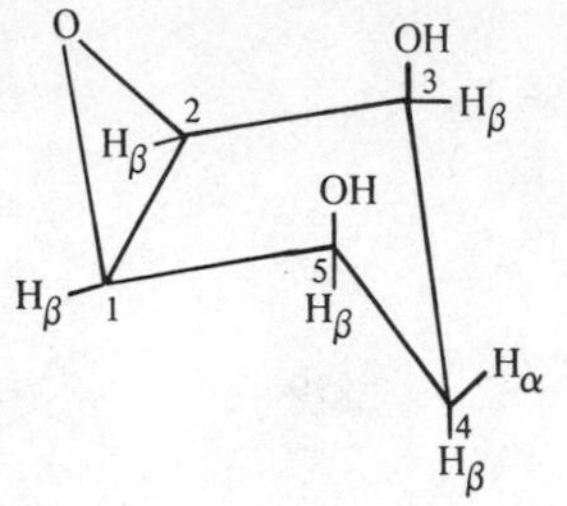

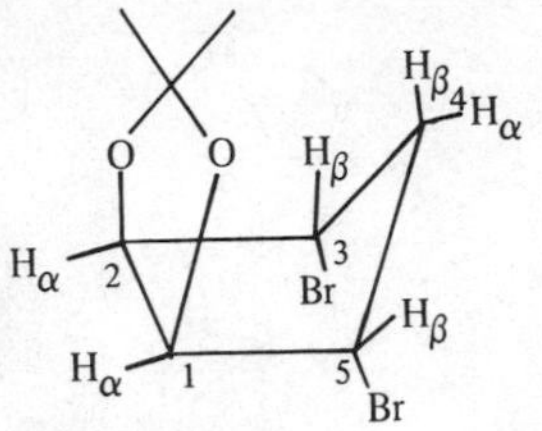

TABLE 86 (continued)

δ_1 = 3.33 δ_3 = 3.91 $\delta_{4\alpha}$ = 1.13
$\delta_{4\beta}$ = 1.86 $J_{4\alpha 4\beta}$ = −12.0 $J_{3\beta 4\beta}$ = 7.5
$J_{3\beta 4\alpha}$ = 8.8 J_{15} = 0.5 $J_{14\beta}$ = 0.5

In DMSO-d_6.

(Ref. 238a)

δ_1 = 5.01 δ_3 = 4.27 $\delta_{4\alpha}$ = 2.46
$\delta_{4\beta}$ = 3.12 $J_{4\alpha 4\beta}$ = −16.1 $J_{3\beta 4\beta}$ = 6.2
$J_{3\beta 4\alpha}$ = 3.2 J_{15} = 0.8 $J_{14\alpha}$ = 0.9

In $CDCl_3$.

(Ref. 238a)

TABLE 87

CH_2 Couplings in Five-membered Rings

Ring System	−J	Ref.
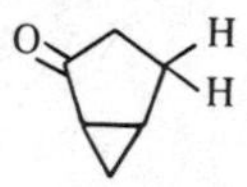 (bicyclic cyclopropane-fused cyclopentanone, O, H, H)	8.4	179
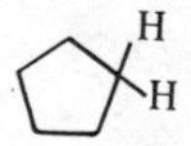 (cyclopentane, H, H)	11.0 to 11.9 (18 examples) 12.0 to 12.9 (28 examples) 13.0 to 13.9 (24 examples) 10.7 14.0 (2 examples) 14.5 15.0 17.0	179
X = C or O 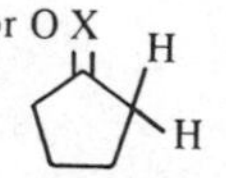 (X, H, H)	16.0 17.3, 17.4, 17.4, 17.6 18.0, 19.4, 18.0, 19.5 20.0 (3 examples)	179
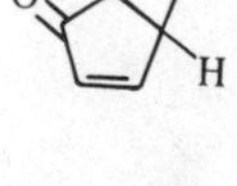 (cyclopentenone, O, H, H)	17.0 to 18.8	143
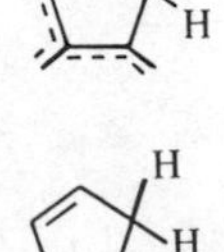 (H, H)	17.5 to 18.8	143
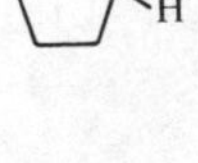 (cyclopentene, H, H)	15.3 to 18.4	143

TABLE 87 (continued)

Ring System	–J	Ref.
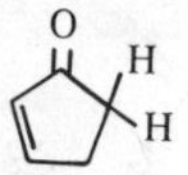	18.5 19.0 (3 examples) 19.2	179
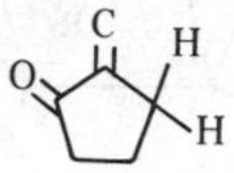	15.0 15.2 15.5 (4 examples)	179
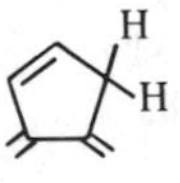	21.0	179
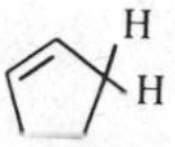	15.0, 15.0 15.9 16.0 (3 examples) 16.2 17.0 (5 examples) 17.2, 17.6, 17.8 18.0 (4 examples)	179
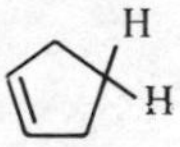	16.4 12.5, 12.6	179
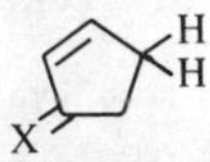 X = O or N	17.0 18.5, 18.6 19.0	179
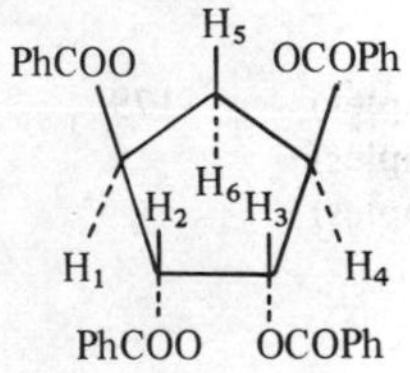	15.6 (J_{56})	237
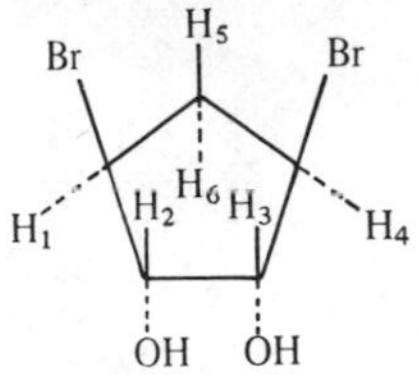	14.9 to 15.0 (J_{56})	237
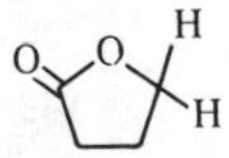	8.8 to 10.5	143
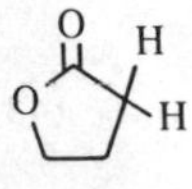	17.0 to 18.9	143
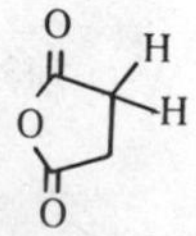	18.2 to 19.8	143

TABLE 87 (continued)

Ring System		–J	Ref.
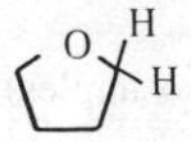 tetrahydrofuran (O, CH_2 H/H)		6, 6.7, 6.9 7.0 to 8.0 (12 examples) 8.1 to 9.0 (12 examples) 9.5 10.0 to 10.5 (6 examples) 11.3	238p
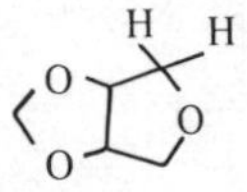 dioxolane-fused tetrahydrofuran (H, H)		11.8, 11.8	238p
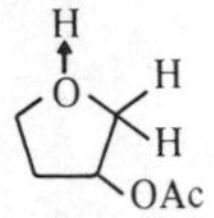 protonated tetrahydrofuran (H→O, H/H, OAc)		11.0	238p
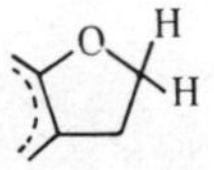 dihydrofuran (O, H/H)		8.0, 8.5	238p
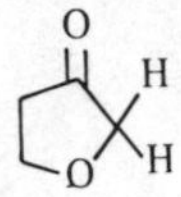 tetrahydrofuran-3-one (O, H/H)		17.0	143
succinic anhydride (H, H, H, X)	–X		
	–OH	±18.2	
	–Cl	±19.1	
	–Br	±19.8	
cyclopentene-1,3-dione (O, O, H/H)		21.5	
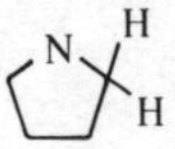 pyrrolidine (N, H/H)		8.6, 9.5, 9.5, 9.6, 9.75 10.0 (5 examples) 10.2, 10.5, 11.0 15.0	238p
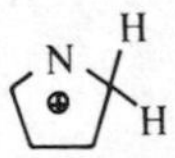 pyrrolidinium (N⊕, H/H)		11.50	238p
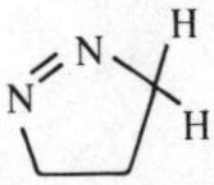 1-pyrazoline (N=N, H/H)		16.8 to 19.6 (6 examples)	238p
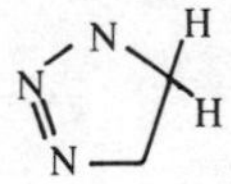 triazoline (N, N=N, H/H)		9.65	238p

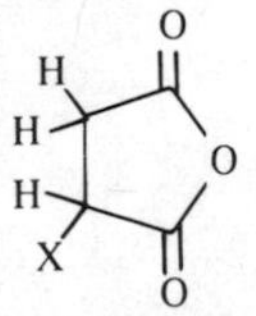

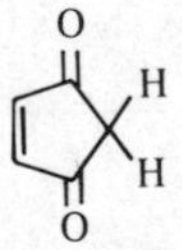

TABLE 87 (continued)

Ring System	–J	Ref.
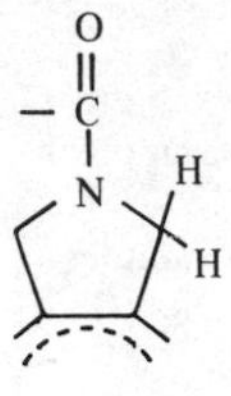 N-acyl pyrrolidine (–C(=O)–N, ring CH₂: H, H)	12.1 to 12.7 (4 examples)	238p
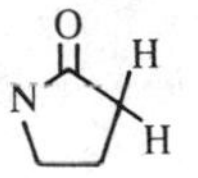 2-pyrrolidinone (O, N; CH₂: H, H)	17.7	238p
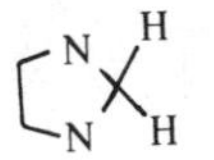 imidazolidine (N, N; CH₂: H, H)	3.4 to 7.0	143
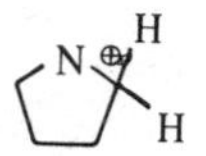 pyrrolidinium (N⊕; CH₂: H, H)	11.50	238p
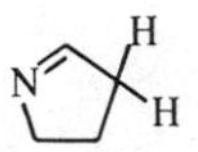 1-pyrroline (N=; CH₂: H, H)	15.5	143
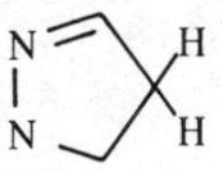 2-pyrazoline (N=, N; CH₂: H, H)	17.5 to 18.8	143
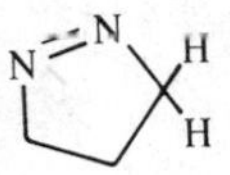 1-pyrazoline (N=N; CH₂: H, H)	16.5 to 19.6	143
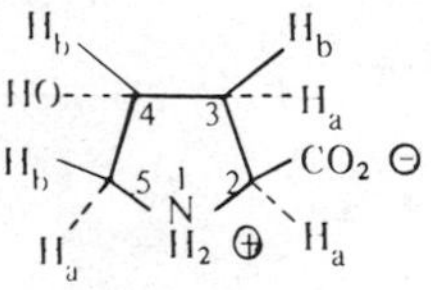 H_b, HO, H_b, H_a, H_a, CO_2 ⊖, H_b, H_a, H_2 ⊕, 1–5	14.06 (3a3b) 12.69 (5a5b)	238j
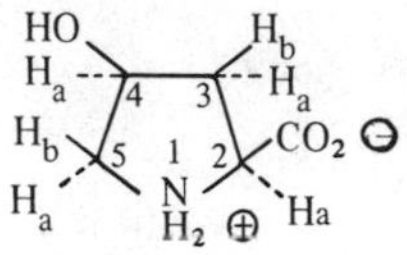 HO, H_a, H_b, H_a, CO_2 ⊖, H_b, H_a, Ha, H_2 ⊕, 1–5	14.23 (3a3b) 12.5 (5a5b)	238j
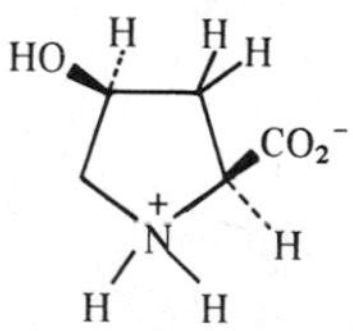 HO, H, H, H, CO_2^-, H, $\overset{+}{N}$, H, H	±14.23	238j
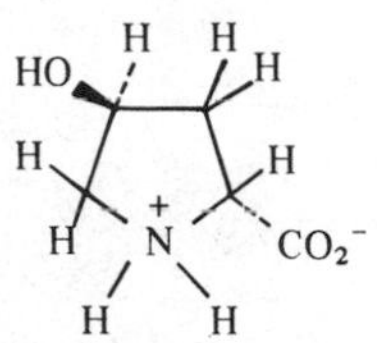 HO, H, H, H, H, H, H, $\overset{+}{N}$, CO_2^-, H, H	±14.06	238j

TABLE 87 (continued)

Ring System	–J	Ref.
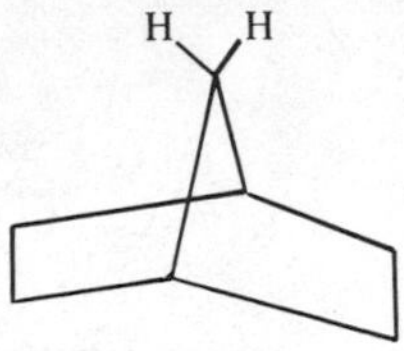	9.0, 9.8 10.0 (2 examples) 11.2 (2 examples)	179
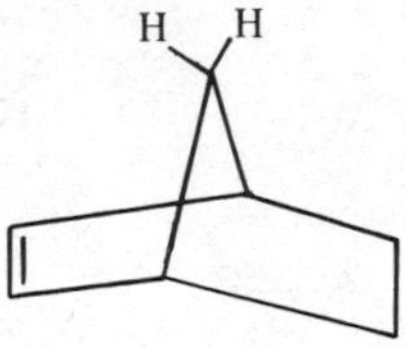	7.5 8.0 to 8.9 (12 examples) 9.0 (8 examples) 10.2 10.5 (5 examples) 11.0 (7 examples) 12.0 (3 examples)	179
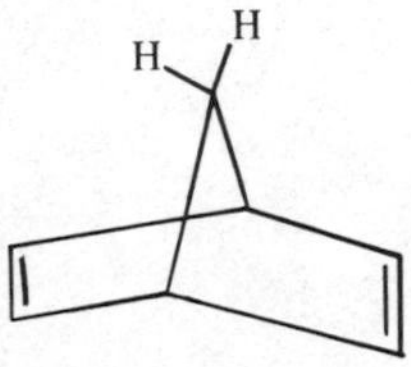	ca. 6.5 ca. 5.0 to 6.0 6.9 to 7.1 (7 examples)	179
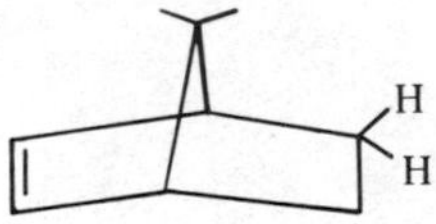	10.6 (2 examples) 11.6 11.8 (2 examples) 12.0 to 12.9 (18 examples) 13.0 to 13.8 (18 examples) 14.0	179
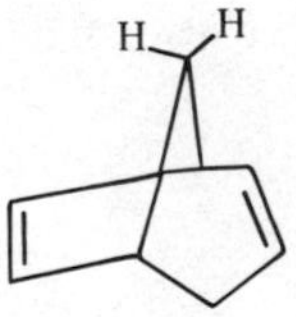	9.0 9.5 to 10.5 (4 examples)	179
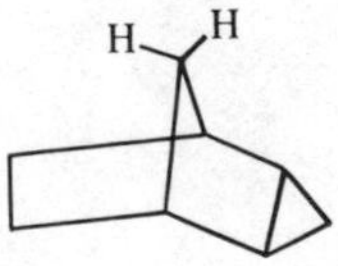	10.0	179
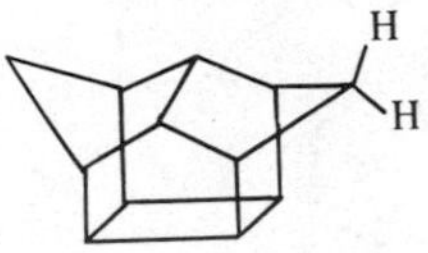	10.0, 10.5 11.0 (2 examples) 11.5 (3 examples) 12.5	179
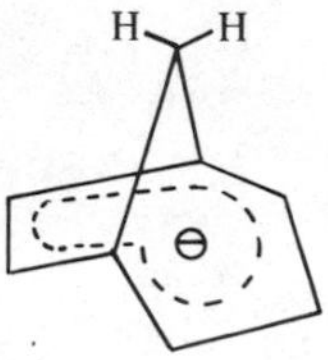	8.0	179

TABLE 87 (continued)

Ring System	–J	Ref.
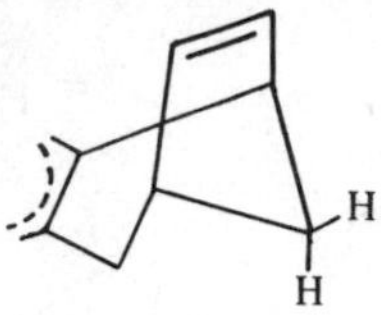 [structure: H, H]	10.0, 10.3	179
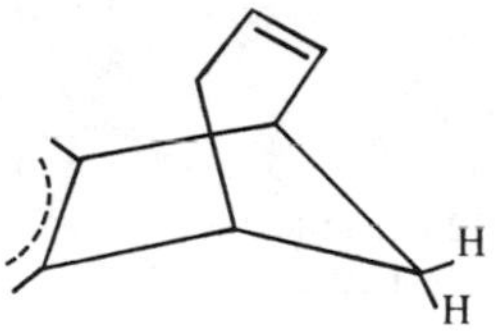 [structure: H, H]	10.0, 10.1	179
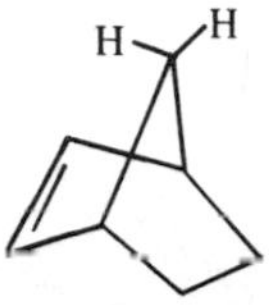 [structure: H, H]	8.0 to 12.0	143
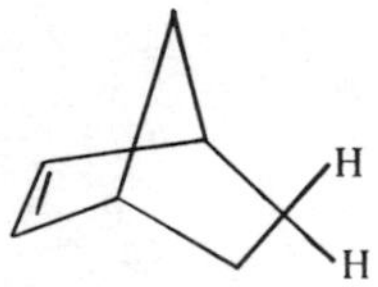 [structure: H, H]	10.4 to 13.2	143
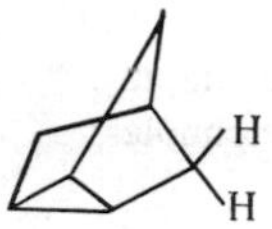 [structure: H, H]	10.5 to 11.5	143
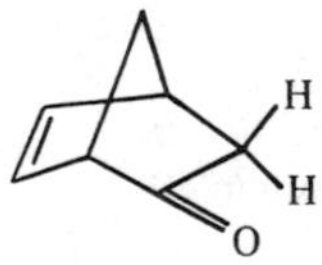 [structure: H, H, O]	16.2 to 16.4	143
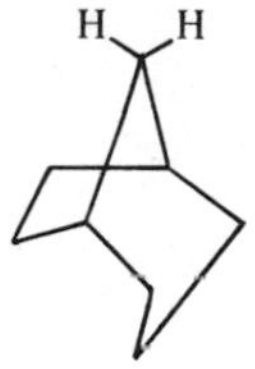 [structure: H, H]	10.0 to 12.0	143
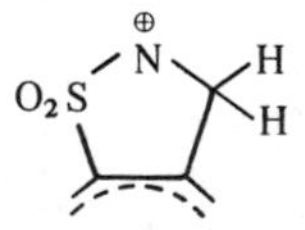 [structure: O_2S, $N^{\oplus}$, H, H]	15.0	238p
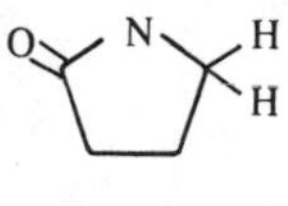 [structure: O, N, H, H]	15.0	238p
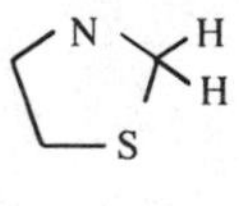 [structure: N, S, H, H]	6.0 (4 examples) 6.25, 8.5, 9.0, 9.0	238p

TABLE 87 (continued)

Ring System	–J	Ref.
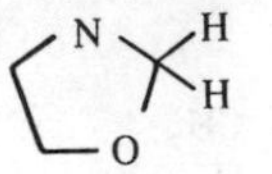	0.7 to 5.0 (9 examples)	238p
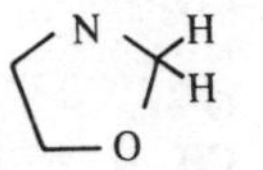	3.4 to 3.8 (5 examples) 4.0 to 4.8 (11 examples) 5.7, 5.9, 6.5 8.0, 10.0	238p
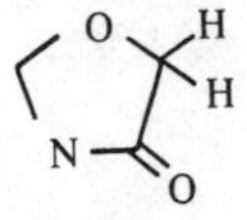	13.0	238p
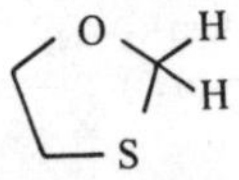	5.2, 5.2	238p
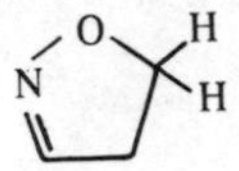	8.1, 9.8, 9.4	238p
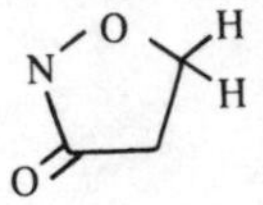	8.5, 8.6	238p
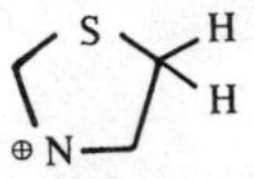	13.8	238p
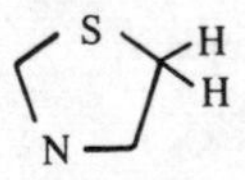	11.5, 12.0	238p
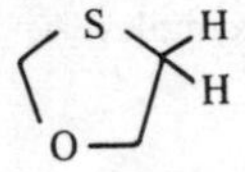	9.0 to 11.24 (13 examples)	238p
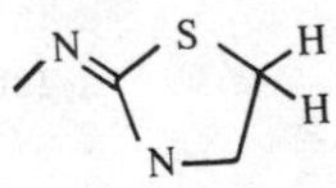	11.5, 11.9, 12.0 (2 examples)	238p
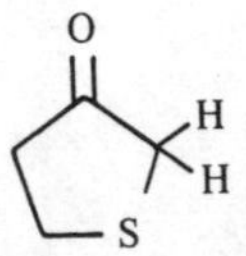	15.5	143
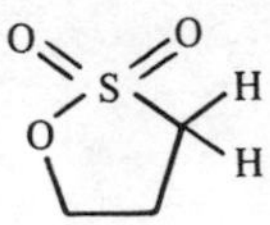	14.0	143
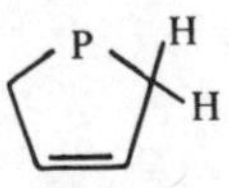	Ca. 15.5	238p

TABLE 87 (continued)

Ring System	–J	X	Y	Ref.
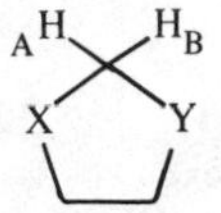	8	O	CH_2	238q, r
	O	O	O	
	9.5	N	CH_2	
	3.5	N	N	
	2.5	N	O	
	10	S	CH_2	
	9.7	S	S	
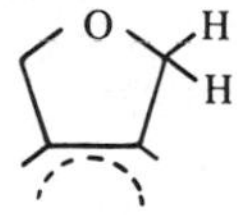	14.0			238p
	8.8 9.0 to 9.9 (6 examples) 10.0 to 12.0 (15 examples)			238p
	17.0 to 18.8			143
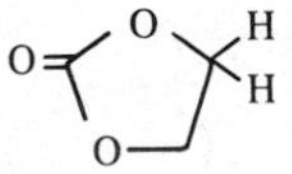	8.64			238p
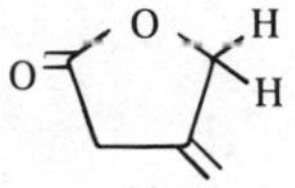	13.0 (4 examples)			143
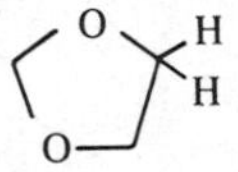	7.0 to 9.0 (28 examples)			238p
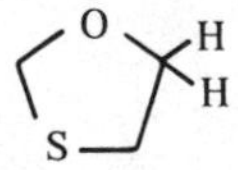	8.57 to 9.79 (11 examples)			238p
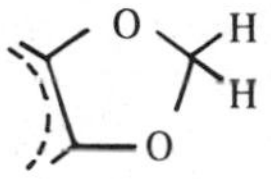	1.0			238p
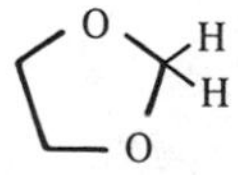	Ca. 1 (2 examples)			238p
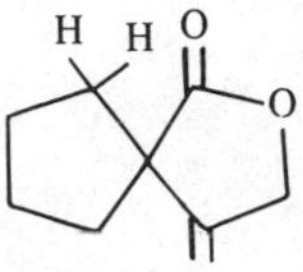	14.0 (3 examples)			179

TABLE 87 (continued)

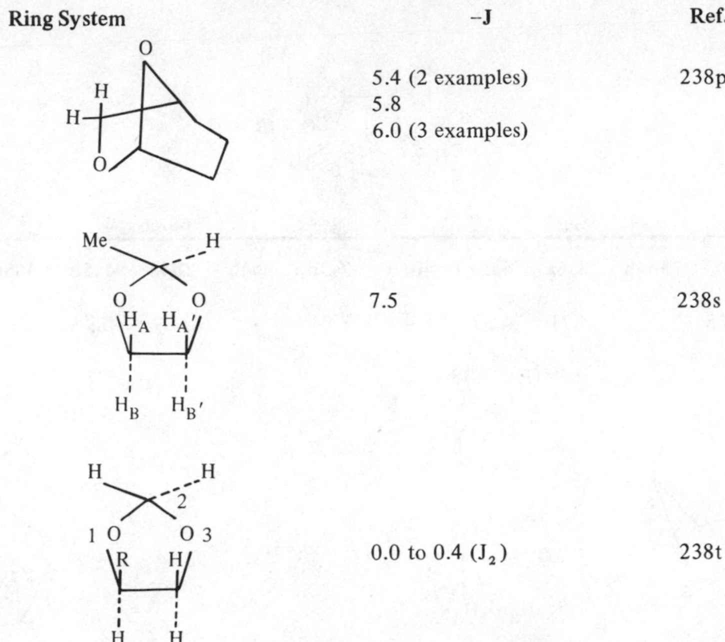

Ring System	$-J$	Ref.
	5.4 (2 examples)	238p
	5.8	
	6.0 (3 examples)	
	7.5	238s
	0.0 to 0.4 (J_2)	238t

(R is Me, Ph, CH_2Cl, and $CH_2OCONHPh$.)

TABLE 88

Vicinal Coupling in Five-membered Rings

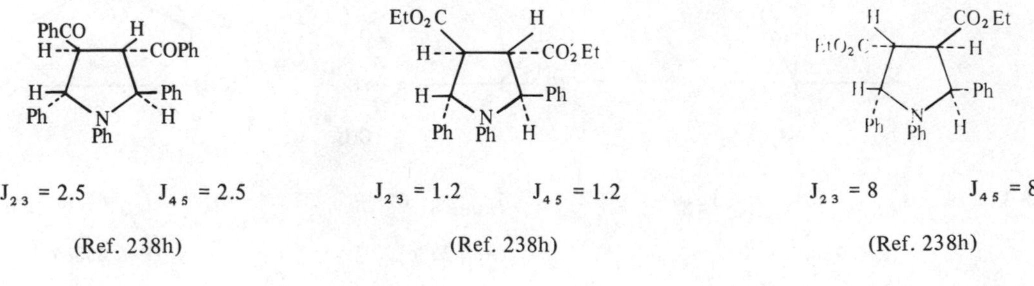

$J_{23} = 2.5$ $J_{45} = 2.5$ (Ref. 238h)

$J_{23} = 1.2$ $J_{45} = 1.2$ (Ref. 238h)

$J_{23} = 8$ $J_{45} = 8$ (Ref. 238h)

J_{cis}					J_{trans}				
2a3a	3b4b	3a4a	4a5a	4b5b	2a3b	3a4b	3b4a	4a5b	4a5a
7.66	4.31	–	–	4.09	10.44	1.41	–	–	1.22

(Ref. 238j)

TABLE 88 (continued)

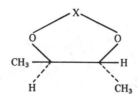

J_{cis}					J_{trans}				
2a3a	3b4b	3a4a	4a5a	4b5b	2a3b	3a4b	3b4a	4a5b	4a5a
10.48	–	4.71	4.57	–	3.84	–	2.09	0.94	–

(Ref. 238j)

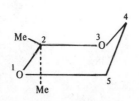

$J_{4,5} = 6.3$

(Ref. 238u)

$J_{AA'} = J_{BB'} = J_{cis} = 7.1$ c/s
$J_{AB'} = J_{A'B} = J_{trans} = 6.0$ c/s

(Ref. 238s)

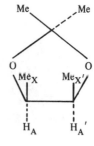

$J_{AA'} = 5.85$ $J_{AX} = 6.30$ $J_{AX'} = -0.25$

(Ref. 238o)

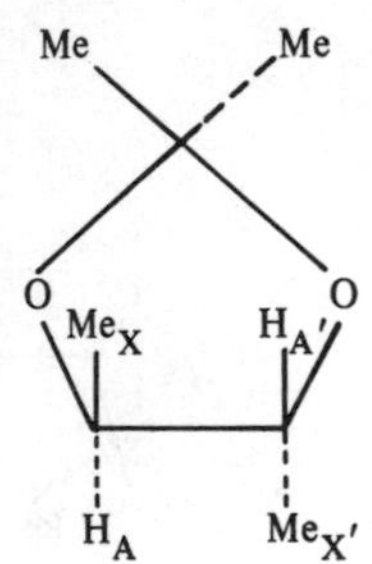

$J_{AA'} = 8.35$ $J_{AX} = 5.90$ $J_{AX'} = -0.15$

(Ref. 238o)

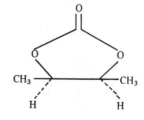

$J_{trans} = 6.62$

(Ref. 238o)

$J_{cis} = 7.35$

(Ref. 238o)

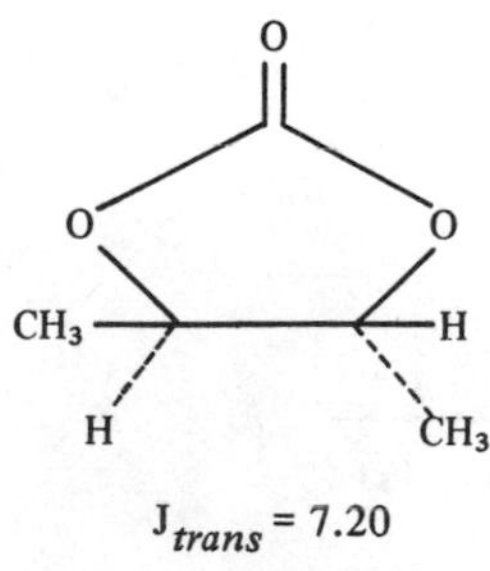

$J_{trans} = 7.20$

(Ref. 238o)

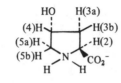

$J_{2,3a} = 7.66$ $J_{3b,4} = 4.31$
$J_{2,3b} = 10.44$ $J_{4,5a} = 1.22$
$J_{3a,4} = 1.41$ $J_{4,5b} = 4.09$

(Ref. 238j)

$J_{2,3a} = +10.48$ $J_{3b,4} = +2.09$
$J_{2,3b} = +3.84$ $J_{4,5a} = +4.57$
$J_{3a,4} = +4.71$ $J_{4,5b} = +0.94$

(Ref. 238j)

TABLE 88 (continued)

Formula	Stereochemistry	Coupling Constant $J_{H_2H_3}$
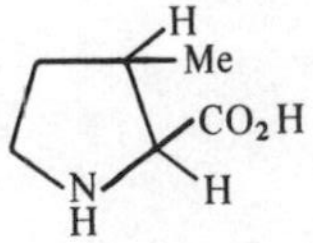 H, Me, CO_2H, H, N–H	*cis*	7.2
	cis	7.8
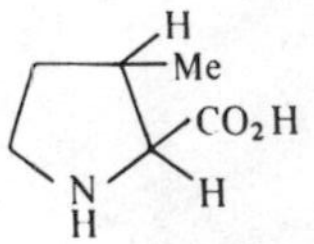 H, Me, CO_2H, H, N–H	*trans*	7.7
	trans	7.8
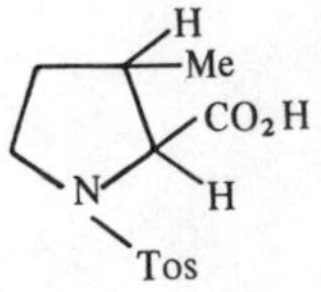 H, Me, CO_2H, H, N–Tos	*cis*	7.2
	trans	4.6
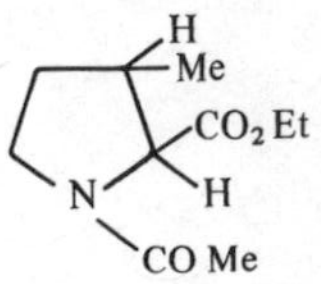 H, Me, CO_2Et, H, N–CO Me	*cis*	7.9
	trans	5.1
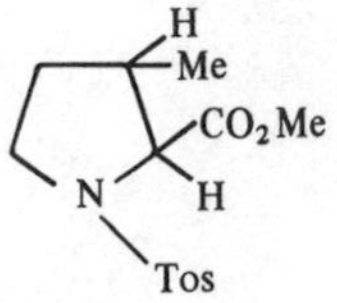 H, Me, CO_2Me, H, N–Tos	*cis*	8.0
	trans	–

(Ref. 238k)

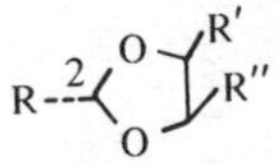

R--2, O, O, R′, R″

Coupling Constants (cps) between H(2) and the Isopropyl Methine Proton

Dioxolane				
R	R′	R″	J(*cis* or *syn*)	J(*trans* or *anti*)
i-Pr	Me	H	4.4	4.5
i-Pr	Me	Me	4.4	5.0
i-Pr	*i*-Pr	*i*-Pr	6.9	5.7
i-Pr	*t*-Bu	*t*-Bu	7.5	6.2
			Change: 3.1	Change: 1.7

(Ref. 208)

Coupling Constants (cps) in Substituted 1,3-Dioxolanes

Compound	$J^{cis}_{H(4)H(5)}$	$J^{trans}_{H(4)H(5')}$	$J^{gem}_{H(\delta)H(5')}$
cis-2,4-Ph_2	7.04	6.93	−7.72
trans-2,4-Ph_2	6.39	7.51	−8.14
cis-2,4-Me_2	6.6	7.2	−7.3
trans-2,4-Me_2			
cis-2-*t*-Bu-4-Me	6.50	6.98	−7.18
trans-2-*t*-Bu-4-Me			
cis-2,4-*t*-Bu_2	6.8	5.8	−7.0
cis-2-Me-4-*t*-Bu			
trans-2-Me-4-*t*-Bu	7.0	7.1	−8.7
syn-2-Ph-4,5-Me_2	5.8		
anti-2-Ph-4,5-Me_2	5.8		
syn-2,4,5-*t*-Bu_3	7.9		
anti-2,4,5-*t*-Bu_3	5.2		

(Ref. 208)

TABLE 88 (continued)

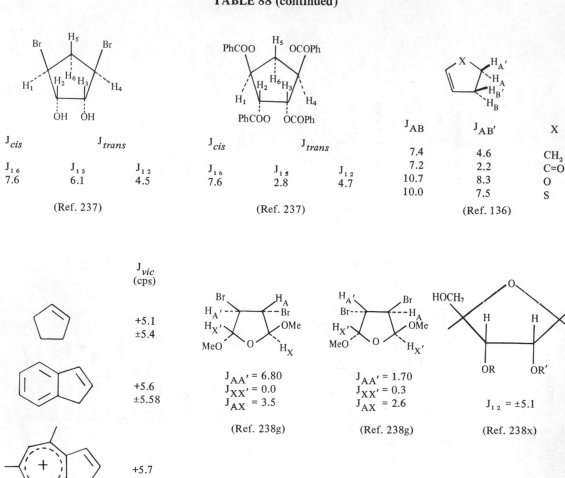

J_{cis}	J_{trans}	
J_{16}	J_{15}	J_{12}
7.6	6.1	4.5

(Ref. 237)

J_{cis}	J_{trans}	
J_{16}	J_{15}	J_{12}
7.6	2.8	4.7

(Ref. 237)

J_{AB}	$J_{AB'}$	X
7.4	4.6	CH_2
7.2	2.2	C=O
10.7	8.3	O
10.0	7.5	S

(Ref. 136)

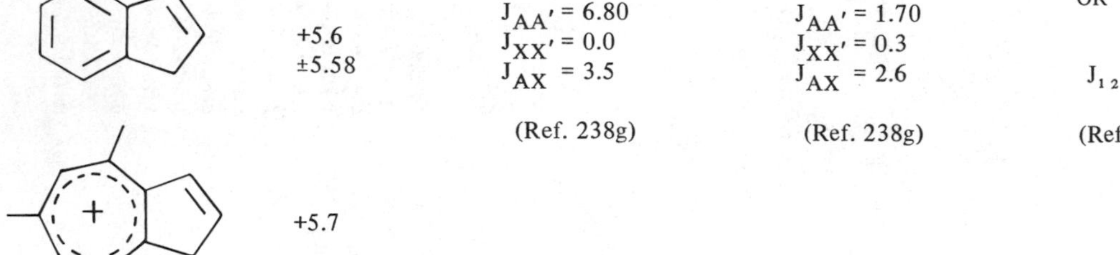

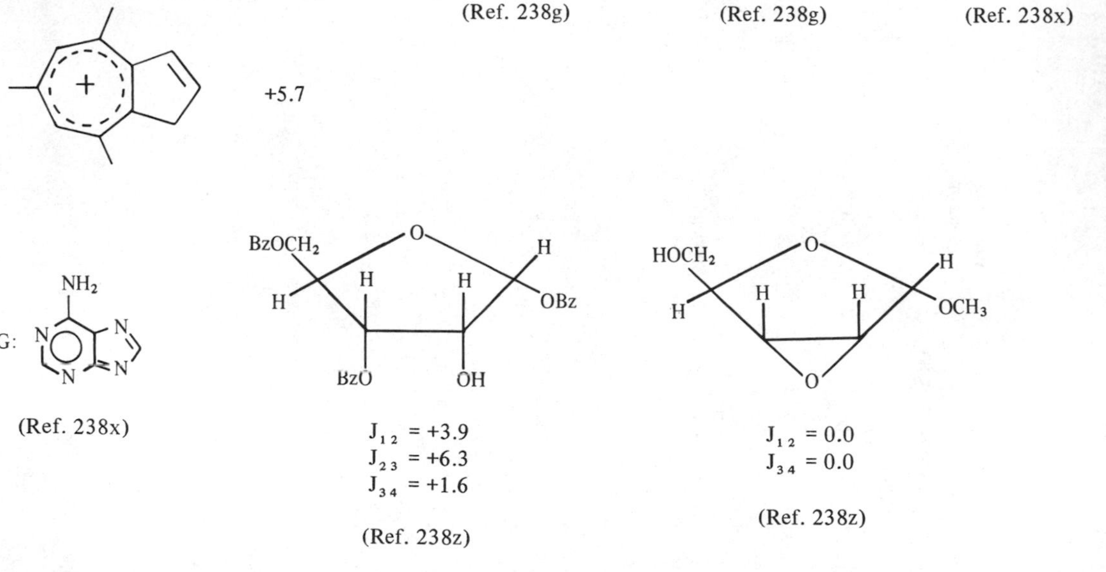

TABLE 88 (continued)

Compound	J_{vic} (cps)	Ref.
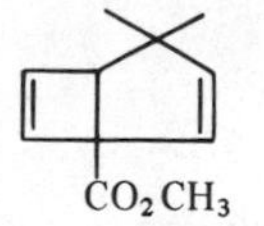	±6.0	238v
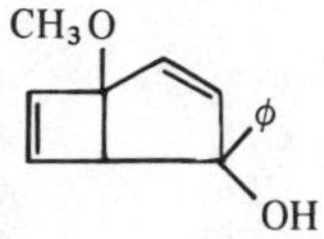	±5.6	238v
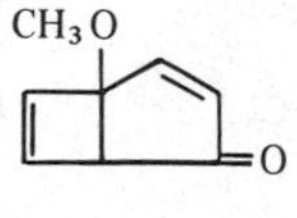	±6.0	238v
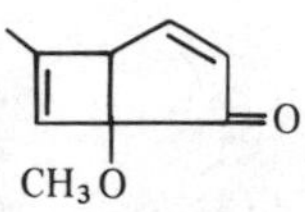	±6.3	238v
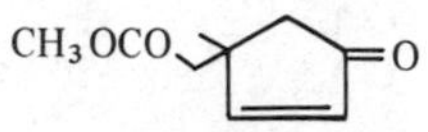	±6.0	238v
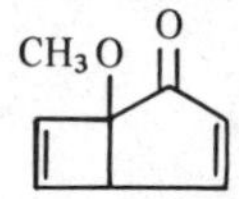	±6.0	238v
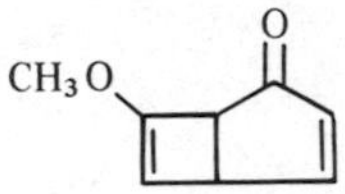	±7.0	238v
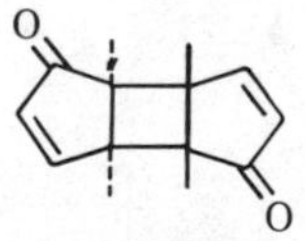	±5.9	238v
	±5.8	238w

R	J_{23}	J_{34}
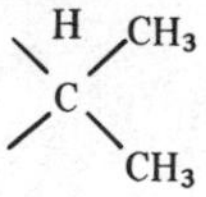	±5.5	<0.5
	±5.5	<0.5

G	R	R	J_{12}
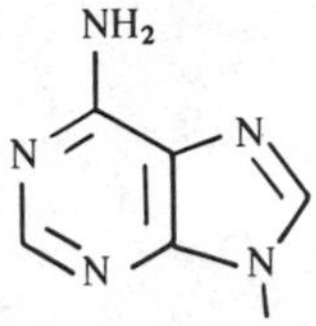	H	H	±5.2
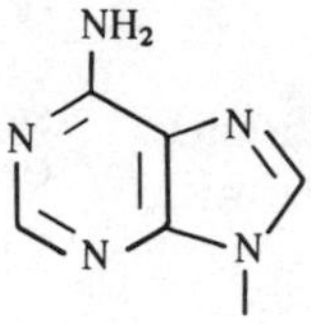	Ac	Ac	±4.7
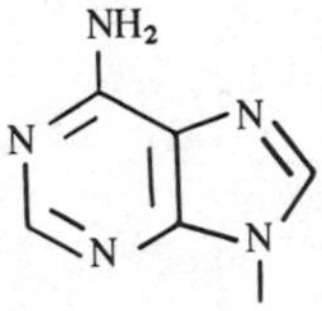	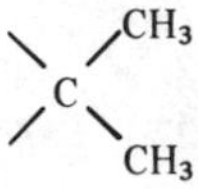	H	±2.9

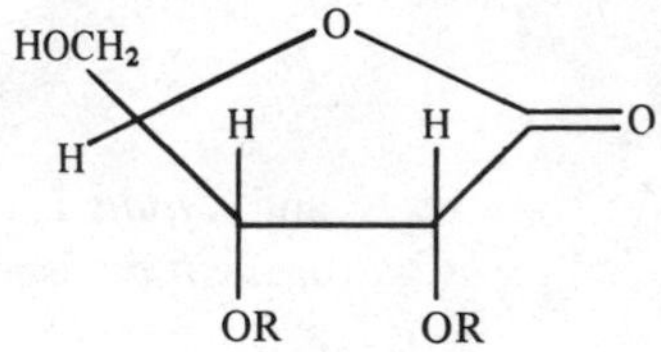

(Ref. 238y)

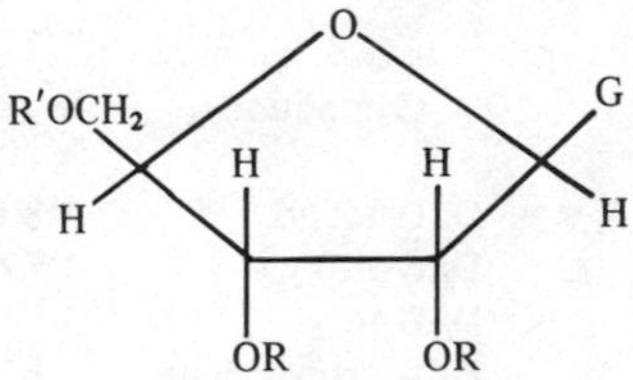

(Ref. 238x)

TABLE 89

Cyclohexane and Flexible Monosubstituted Cyclohexanes

Cyclohexane:	Ref.
δ = 1.34 at 30°C in CS_2	
δ_{ax} = 1.12 at −75°C in CS_2	417
δ_{eq} = 1.6 at −75°C in CS_2	417
1,1,2,2,4,4,5,5-Octadeuterocyclohexane:	
δ = 1.39 at 35°C in CS_2	396
δ_{ax} = 1.13 at −95°C in CS_2	396
δ_{eq} = 1.60 at −95°C in CS_2	396
J_{gem} = −12.6 at −95°C in CS_2	396

TABLE 91

Cyclohexanols[426]

δ of the carbinol proton: δ_{ax} is for the isomer with an axial OH, and δ_{eg} is for the isomer with an equatorial OH

Compound	δ_{ax}	δ_{eg}
4-*t*-Butyl	3.37	3.93
3-*t*-Butyl	3.43	4.07
2-*t*-Butyl	3.40	4.19
Menthol	3.27	
Neomenthol		4.02
2,6-Dimethyl	2.42	3.47
4-Methyl	3.38	3.88

TABLE 90

Monosubstituted Cyclohexanes

(structure: cyclohexane with X and H at C-1)

X	δ_1	Solvent	Ref.
CH_3	1.37	CCl_4	418
CO_2Et	1.68	CCl_4	419
CO_2H	2.30	$CDCl_3$	420
C_6H_5	2.50	$CDCl_3$	420
NH_2	2.55	CCl_4	421
OH	3.50	CCl_4	423
Cl	3.87	CS_2	422
Br	4.07	CCl_4	420
F	4.45	CS_2	424
NO_2	4.28	$CDCl_3$	425
$N(CO)_2C_6H_4$	4.04	$CDCl_3$	420
OCH_3	3.05	CCl_4	419
$OSO_2C_6H_4CH_3$ (p)	4.18	CCl_4	419
SC_6H_5	3.98	CCl_4	419
OAc	4.65	CCl_4	430

TABLE 92

cis- and *trans*-1,4,4-Trideuterio-Disubstituted-1,2-Cyclohexanes,[427] e.g., for the *trans* Isomers:

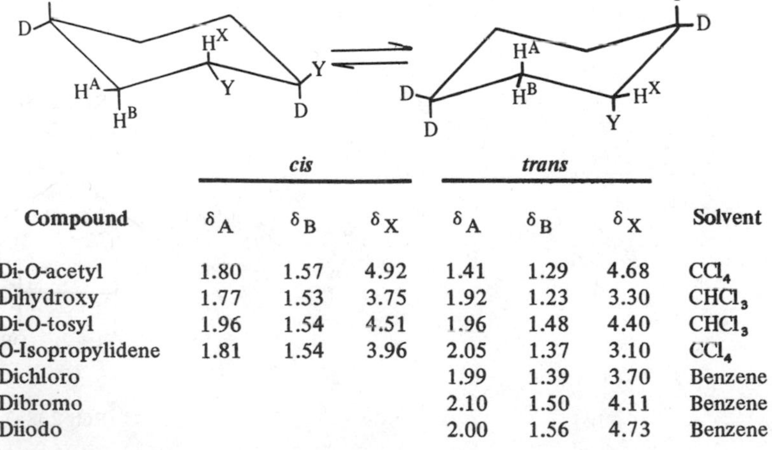

Compound	*cis* δ_A	*cis* δ_B	*cis* δ_X	*trans* δ_A	*trans* δ_B	*trans* δ_X	Solvent
Di-O-acetyl	1.80	1.57	4.92	1.41	1.29	4.68	CCl_4
Dihydroxy	1.77	1.53	3.75	1.92	1.23	3.30	$CHCl_3$
Di-O-tosyl	1.96	1.54	4.51	1.96	1.48	4.40	$CHCl_3$
O-Isopropylidene	1.81	1.54	3.96	2.05	1.37	3.10	CCl_4
Dichloro				1.99	1.39	3.70	Benzene
Dibromo				2.10	1.50	4.11	Benzene
Diiodo				2.00	1.56	4.73	Benzene

TABLE 93

1,3,5-Trimethylcyclohexane in CCl_4[428]

cis,cis-isomer　　*trans,cis*-isomer

Isomer	δ_A	δ_B	δ_C	δ_E	δ_F	δ_G	δ_{CH_3}	J_{AB}	J_{AC}	J_{ACH_3}	J_{AE}	J_{BC}	J_{EF}	J_{EG}	J_{FG}	J_{GCH_3}
cis,cis	1.40	1.64	0.47				0.86	3	11	6.3		13				
trans,cis	1.52	1.52	0.47	1.01	1.52	2.00	0.83 (e), 0.97 (a)		12.0	6.2	12.5	13.5	12.5	4.7	2.3	7.2

TABLE 94

4-*t*-Butyl-3,3,5(Axial)-Trideuterocyclohexanol in $CDCl_3$[429]

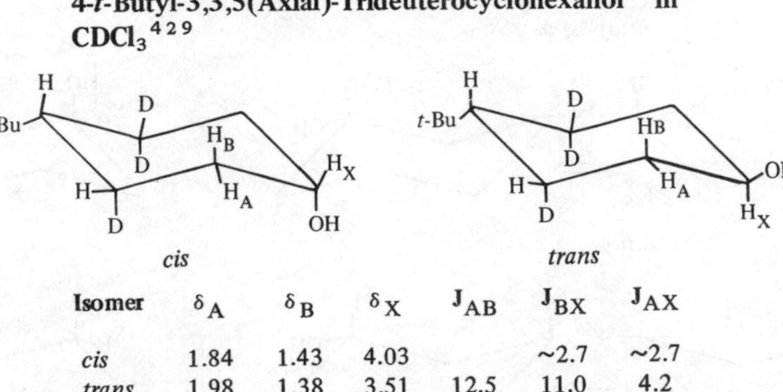

Isomer	δ_A	δ_B	δ_X	J_{AB}	J_{BX}	J_{AX}
cis	1.84	1.43	4.03		~2.7	~2.7
trans	1.98	1.38	3.51	12.5	11.0	4.2

TABLE 95

2,5-Dialkylcyclohexanols[433]

Conformation *e* ⇌ Conformation *a*

Menthol-form

Iso-form

Conformation *e* ⇌ Conformation *a*

Neo-form

Neo-iso-form

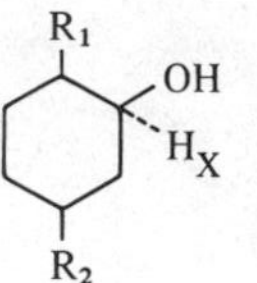

R_1	R_2	Form	δ_X	J_{aa}	J_{ea}	J_{ae}	J_{ee}
CH_3	CH_3	menthol	3.08				
$(CH_3)_2CH$	CH_3	menthol	3.38	9.4	4.2		
CH_3	$(CH_3)_2CH$	menthol	2.98				
$(CH_3)_3C$	CH_3	menthol	3.50	9.4	4.2		
CH_3	CH_3	*iso*	3.73				
$(CH_3)_2CH$	CH_3	*iso*	3.75	6.7	5.1		
CH_3	$(CH_3)_2CH$	*iso*	3.50				
$(CH_3)_3C$	CH_3	*iso*	3.80	7.6	5.2		
CH_3	CH_3	*neo*	3.47	(not split)			
$(CH_3)_2CH$	CH_3	*neo*	4.05	(not split)			
CH_3	$(CH_3)_2CH$	*neo*	3.83			3.0	2.0
$(CH_3)_3C$	CH_3	*neo*	4.15	(not split)			
CH_3	CH_3	*neo-iso*	3.70	10.5	4.5		
$(CH_3)_2CH$	CH_3	*neo-iso*	3.95				
CH_3	$(CH_3)_2CH$	*neo-iso*	3.65	10.0	4.6		
$(CH_3)_3C$	CH_3	*neo-iso*	4.23			3.6	2.2

TABLE 96A

δ_α for Acetoxycyclohexanes in CCl_4 [430,431]

	δ_α
Cyclohexyl acetate	4.65
cis-4-*t*-Butylcyclohexyl acetate	4.91
trans-4-*t*-Butylcyclohexyl acetate	4.51
trans-4-Methylcyclohexyl acetate	4.54
cis-3-Methylcyclohexyl acetate	4.59
trans-2-Methylcyclohexyl acetate	4.34

TABLE 96B

δ_{CH_3} for Acetoxycyclohexanes in OAc [432]

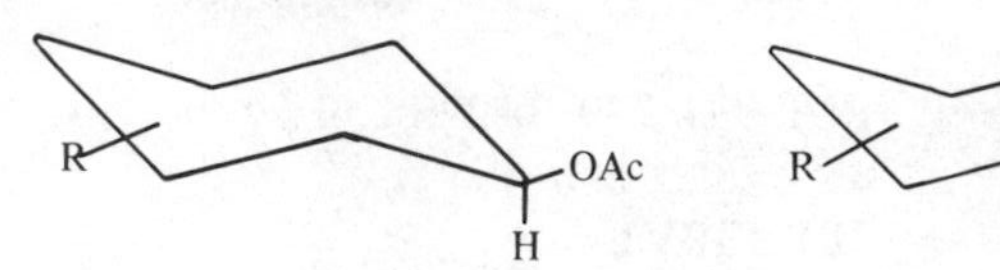

$\delta = 1.97–2.12$

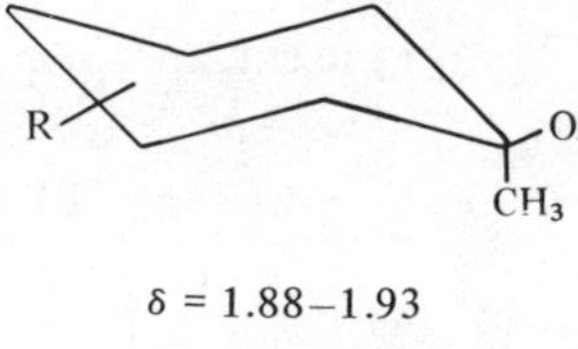

$\delta = 1.88–1.93$

R H OAc

$\delta = 2.10–2.20$

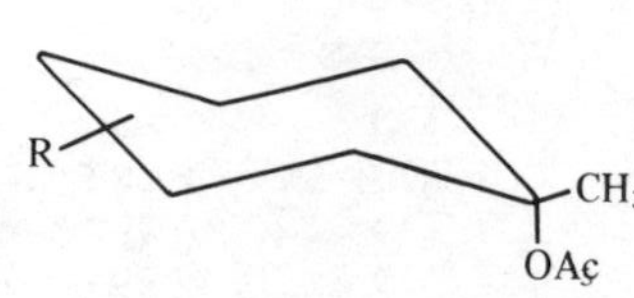

$\delta = 1.96–2.07$

TABLE 97A

3,3,5,5-Tetramethylcyclohexylamine in $CDCl_3$ [400]

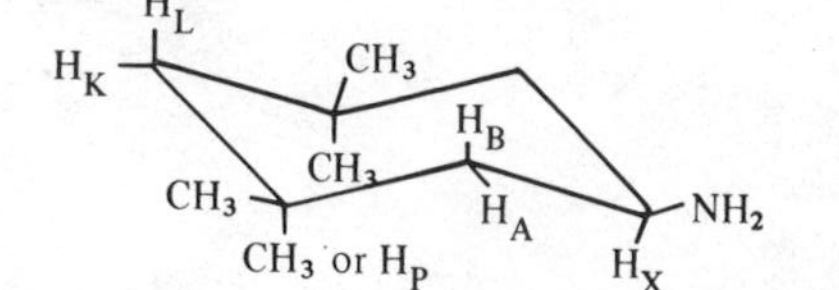

$\delta_{CH_3(ax)} = 0.98$ $\quad \delta_A = 1.56$ $\quad \delta_B = 0.79$ $\quad \delta_K = 1.19$

$\delta_{CH_3(eq)} = 0.88$ $\quad \delta_L = 0.99$ $\quad \delta_X = 2.91$ $\quad J_{AB} = \sim 11.5$

$J_{AX} = 3.65$ $\quad J_{BX} = 11.50$ $\quad J_{KL} = 13.8$ $\quad J_{KA} = 1.8$

TABLE 97B

cis-3,3,5-Trimethylcyclohexylamine in $CDCl_3$ [400]

See above table for figure

$\delta_{3CH_3(ax)} = \sim 0.9$ $\quad \delta_A = 1.98$ $\quad \delta_B = 0.54$ $\quad \delta_C = 1.50$

$\delta_{3CH_3(eq)} = \sim 0.9$ $\quad \delta_D = 0.69$ $\quad \delta_K = 1.30$ $\quad \delta_L = 0.90$

$\delta_{5CH_3} = \sim 0.97$ $\quad \delta_X = 2.78$ $\quad J_{AB} = \sim 11.8$ $\quad J_{CD} = \sim 12.4$

$J_{CX} = 3.9$ $\quad J_{AX} = 3.9$ $\quad J_{DX} = 11.4$ $\quad J_{BX} = 11.4$

$J_{KL} = \sim 13.0$ $\quad J_{LP} = \sim 10.5$ $\quad J_{BP} = \sim 11.5$

TABLE 98

δ_α for Nitrocyclohexanes

Compound	δ_α	Solvent	Ref.
Nitrocyclohexane	4.38	Neat	434
4-Methylnitrocyclohexane	4.47	$CDCl_3$	435
trans-4-*t*-Butylmethylnitrocyclohexane	4.32	$CDCl_3$	434
cis-4-*t*-Butylmethylnitrocyclohexane	4.51	$CDCl_3$	434

TABLE 99

δ_α for Bromocyclohexanes

Compound	δ_α	Solvent	Ref.
trans-4-*t*-Butylbromocyclohexane	3.81	Neat	436
cis-4-*t*-Butylbromocyclohexane	4.62	Neat	436
trans-2-Methylbromocyclohexane	3.68	CCl_4	437
cis-2-Methylbromocyclohexane	4.35	CCl_4	437
cis-3-Methylbromocyclohexane	3.87	CCl_4	437
trans-3-Methylbromocyclohexane	4.50	CCl_4	437

TABLE 100

Substituted 5,5-Dimethyl-2-Cyclohexenones in $CDCl_3$[437a]

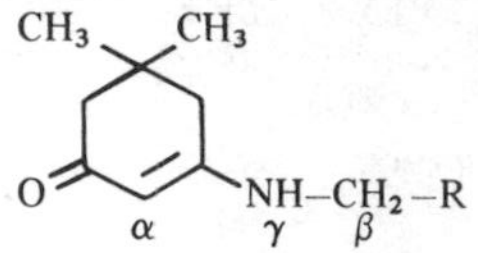

R	δ_{CH_3}	δ_α	δ_β	δ_γ	$\delta_{ring\ CH_2}$
C_6H_5	1.04	5.08	4.20	5.9	2.10, 2.23
CF_3	1.08	5.23	3.71		2.19, 2.26

TABLE 101

δ_2 in 2-Substituted Tetrahydropyrans in CCl_4

Substituent	δ_2	Ref.
Cl	6.17	438
Br	6.62	438
OCH_3	4.45	439
OAc	5.88	439

TABLE 102

2,3-Disubstituted Tetrahydropyrans in $CDCl_3$

R_2	R_3	Isomer	δ_2	J_{23}	Ref.
OH	OH	*cis*	4.95	2.5	440
$O(CH_2)_2Cl$	OH	*cis*	4.69	3.2	440
OCH_3	OH	*cis*	4.57	3.2	441
OH	OH	*trans*	4.47	6.5	440
$O(CH_2)_2Cl$	OH	*trans*	4.29	5.0	440
OCH_3	OH	*trans*	4.20	5.2	441

TABLE 103

Coupling Constants for Alkyl-substituted 1,3-Dioxanes in a Range of Solvents[420]

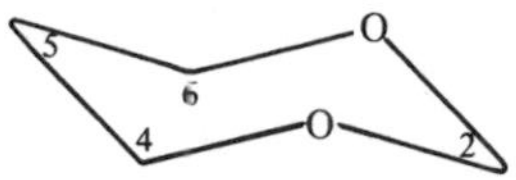

gem	*cis*	*trans*
$J_{2e2a} = -6.0$ to -6.2	$J_{4e5a} = 4.4$ to 7.0	$J_{4e5e} = 0.6$ to 1.9
$J_{4e4a} = -10.9$ to -11.5	$J_{4a5e} = 2.6$ to 3.3	$J_{4a5a} = 10.1$ to 12.1
$J_{5e5a} = -12.6$ to -13.2		

TABLE 104

Substituted 1,3-Dioxanes (Equatorial Substituents)

Substituent	Position	δ_2	δ_{4e}	δ_{4a}	δ_{5e}	δ_{5a}	Solvent	Ref.
t-Butyl	2	3.95			1.20	1.91	CS_2	444
$C_6H_4OCH_3$ (p)	2	5.20			1.19	1.97	CS_2	444
$C_6H_4OCH_3$ (m)	2	5.70			1.20	2.03	CS_2	444
Piperonyl	2	5.18			1.19	1.98	CS_2	444
t-Butyl	5		3.97	3.40	(1.64)		CS_2	444

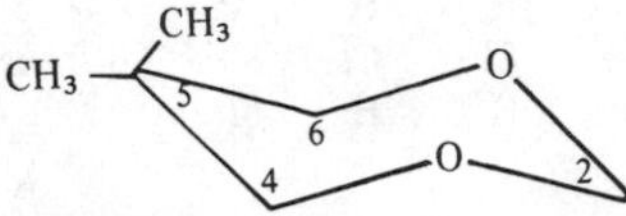

At −89.5°C in CD_3COCD_3 (Ref. 420)

δ_{CH_3} = 1.16, 0.74 δ_{4e} = 3.62 δ_{4a} = 3.45

δ_{2e} = 5.04 δ_{2a} = 4.56

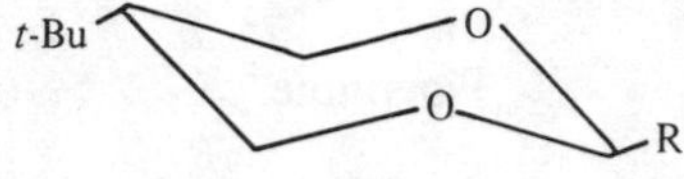

In CCl_4 (Ref. 445)

R	δ_2	J_{4e5a}	J_{4a5a}
Me	4.40	5.6	10.6
Et	4.20	4.4	11.2
i-Pr	4.03	4.5	11.3
t-Bu	3.86	4.7	12.1

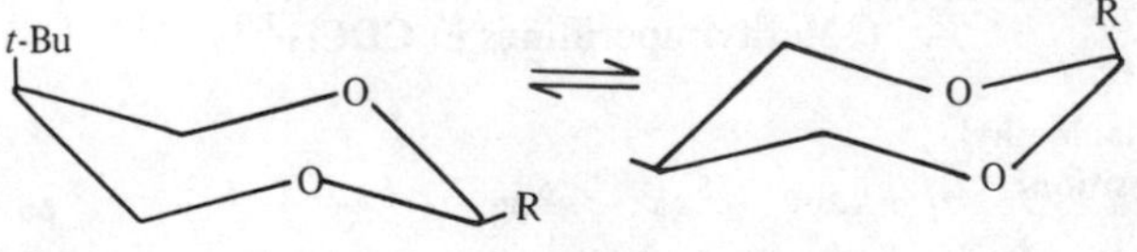

R	δ_2	J_{4e5a}	J_{4a5e}
Me	4.56	1.3	4.0
Et	4.37	1.1	3.9
i-Pr	4.14	1.1	4.0
t-Bu	3.99	1.1	3.9

TABLE 105

1,4-Dioxanes[446]

Substituents in Position 2	3	5	6	Configuration	δ_2	δ_5
H	H	H	H		3.71	
ϕ	ϕ	H	H	*trans*	4.78	4.42
ϕ	ϕ	H	H	*cis*	5.12	3.86
Cl	Cl	H	H	*trans*	5.95	4.05
Cl	Cl	H	H	*cis*	5.70	3.99
Cl	Cl	Cl	Cl	(*cis*-2,6-*trans*-2,3)	6.11	
CH_3COO	CH_3COO	H	H	*trans*	5.76	3.91
					4.65	3.79

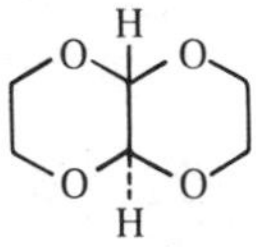

TABLE 106

Piperidine

In CCl_4, δ_2 = 2.69, δ_3 = 1.50, δ_{NH} = 1.3 to 2, depending on concentration (dilution causes the sharp singlet to shift to high field) (Ref. 420).

For 3,3,5,5-tetradeuteropiperidine, see Ref. 442.

TABLE 107

C-Methylpiperidines in $CDCl_3$[10]

Equatorial Methyl in Position:	δ_{2e}	δ_{2a}	δ_{3a}	δ_{4a}	δ_{6e}	δ_{6a}	δ_{CH_3}
2		2.57			3.10		1.05
3	3.00	2.21	1.55		3.00	2.52	0.82
4	3.09	2.60		1.53	3.09	2.60	0.91

TABLE 108

N-Acylpiperidines in CCl_4[443]

N-Substituent	δ_2
CHO	3.35
$COCH_3$	3.40
$CSCH_3$	3.75
$CSCH_2Ph$	3.55

TABLE 109

Six-membered Rings, Geminal Coupling

Compound	Position	$-J_{gem}$	Ref.
Cyclohexane		11.6–15.0	143
Cyclohexanone	α	12.0–16.0	143
1,1,2,2,4,4,5,5-Octa-deuterocyclohexane		12.6	396
Cyclohexene	α	17.0–19.0	143
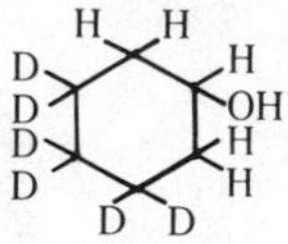		12.2	393
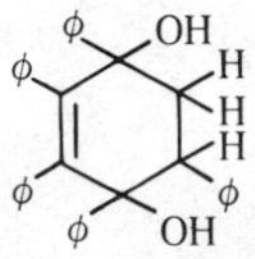		14.0	394
		16.0	143
		17.0–19.0	179
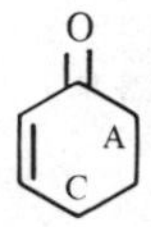	A	16.0–20.0	143
	C	17.0–19.7	143
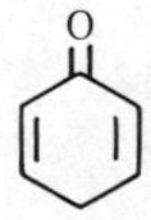		10.4	143a
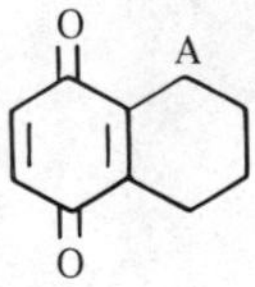	A	19.0	179
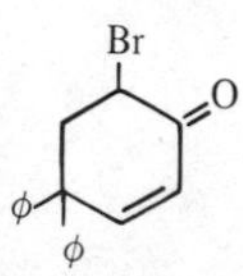		9.8	143a
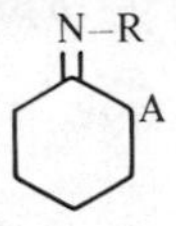	A	13.8–15.9	179
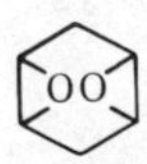		17.0	179

TABLE 109 (continued)

Compound	Position	$-J_{gem}$	Ref.
 (structure)	A	15.5	179
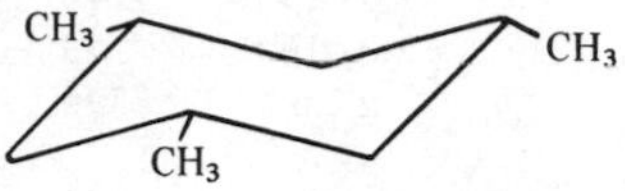 (structure; CH_3, CH_3, CH_3)		13.0	397
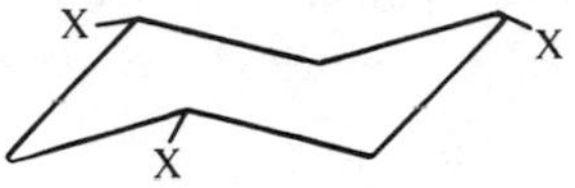 (structure; X, X, X)		12.5	398
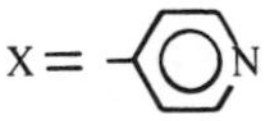 X = (4-pyridyl)	A B	11.5 13.8	400
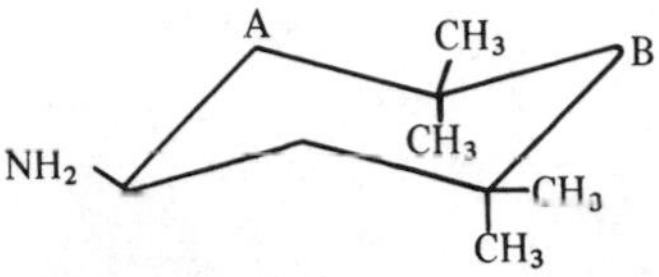 (structure; NH_2, CH_3, CH_3, CH_3, CH_3, A, B)	A	11.9	427
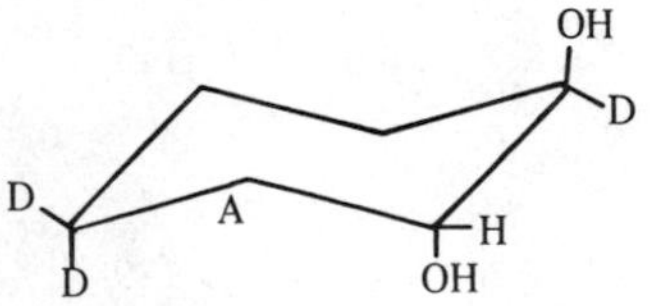 (structure; OH, D, D, D, H, OH, A)	A	10.0	427
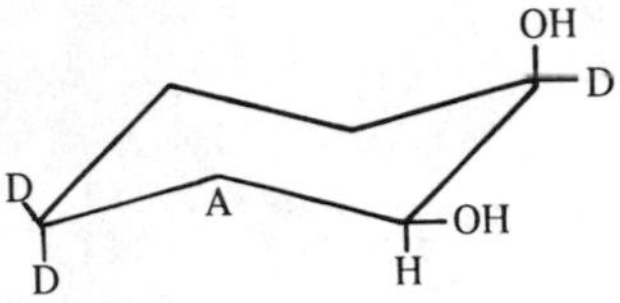 (structure; OH, D, D, D, OH, H, A)	A B	12.5 13.5	397 397
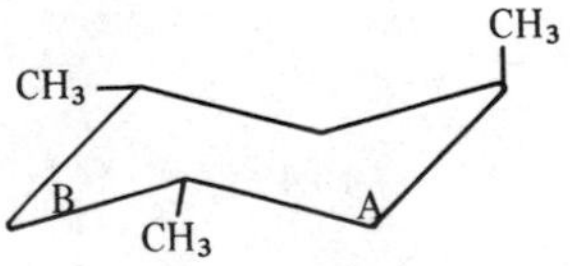 (structure; CH_3, CH_3, CH_3, A, B)		12.5	399
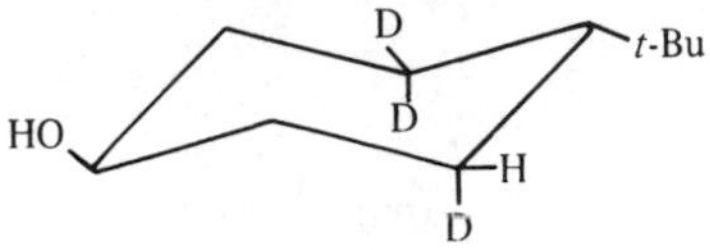 (structure; HO, D, D, t-Bu, H, D) *trans*-1,4,4-Trideutero-1,2-dichlorocyclohexane		12.0	401
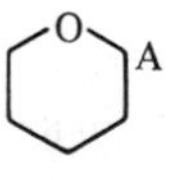 (structure; O, A)	A	8.0–14.0	238p
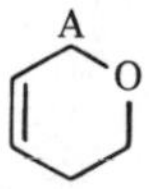 (structure; A, O)	A	13.0–16.6	238p
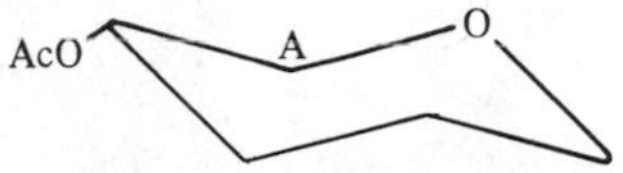 (structure; AcO, A, O)	A	10.7–12.0	238p

TABLE 109 (continued)

Compound	Position	$-J_{gem}$	Ref.
(OAc-substituted tetrahydropyran, chair)	A	11.8–12.9	238p
(2-phenylchroman-4-one, ϕ, H, H, H)		17.1	395
(1,3-dioxane, A)	A	5.8–6.3	143
(δ-valerolactone, A, D)	A	16.0–20.0	143
	D	11.0–13.4	143
(5,6-dihydro-2-pyranone, D)	D	10.0–12.0	238p
(dihydrothiopyran, A)	A	12.6–13.0	238p
(thiane 1,1-dioxide, A)	A	13.8, 14.5	238p
(1,3-oxathiane, A)	A	11.1	238p
(thiane, A)	A	13.4–15.0	143
(1,3-dithiane, A)	A	14.0	238p
(1,2-oxathiane 2,2-dioxide, A)	A	13.9	143
(1,3-oxathiane 3-oxide, A)	A	11.0	238p
(piperidine, A)	A	11.0–14.0	143
(piperidinium, A)	A	13.0	238p

TABLE 109 (continued)

Compound	Position	$-J_{gem}$	Ref.
	A	16.4–18.0	143
	E	11.0	238p
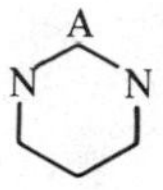	A	8.0–11.2	143
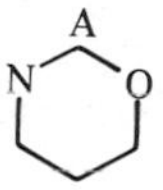	A	8.0–10.0	143
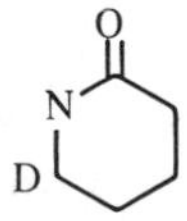	D	12.5, 13.0	238p
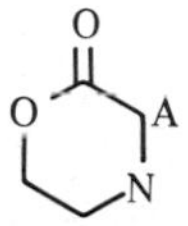	A	17.0–18.0	238p
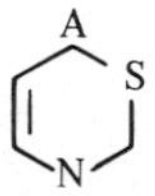	A	18.5, 19.0	238p
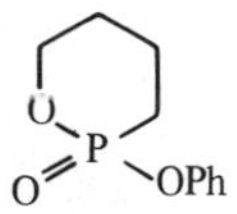		15.6	179
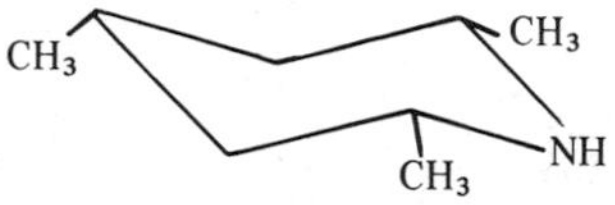		~11.0	402

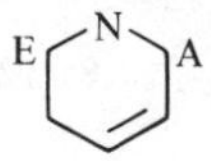

TABLE 110

Vinyl Coupling Constants in Large Rings[448]

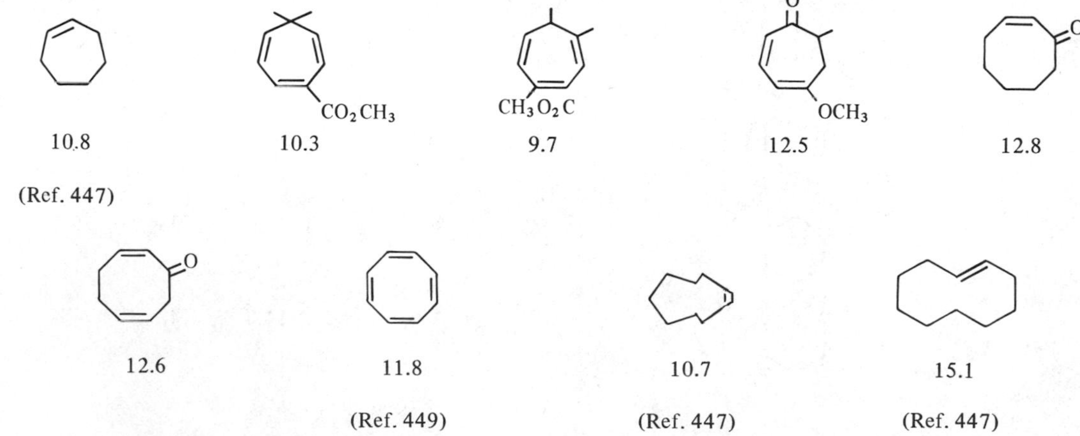

TABLE 111

Miscellaneous Six-membered Heterocyclic Rings

			Ref.
N-Methylmorpholine	δ_{ae} = ~0.49 for N–CH		450
	δ_{ae} = ~0.22 for O–CH		450
N,N'-Dimethylpiperazine	δ_{ae} = 0.63		450
Thiane 1-oxide (pentamethylene sulfoxide)	δ_{α} = 0.87, 0.48; $J_{gem\alpha}$ = 11.7, 13.7;	δ_{γ} = 0.40, 0.34 $J_{gem\gamma}$ = 14.0, 14.3	451

TABLE 112

Pentapyranoses

Compound	δ_1	δ_2	δ_3	δ_4	δ_{5a}	δ_{5e}	J_{12}
α-Xylose[a]	5.26	3.63					3.1
β-Xylose[a]	4.65	3.26	3.49	3.58	3.36	4.00	7.4
α-D-Xylotetraacetate[b]							3.5
β-D-Xylotetraacetate[b]							6.9
Peracetylated-β-D-xylo-1-thioaldopyranose[c]	5.38	5.00	5.22	4.92	3.53	4.16	8.1
α-Lyxose[a]	5.08	3.90					4.2
β-Lyxose[a]	4.94	4.04			3.32	4.09	1.5
α-D-Lyxotetraacetate[b]							2.9
β-D-Lyxotetraacetate[b]							2.0
α-Arabinose[a]	4.60	3.58	3.75	4.04			7.2
β-Arabinose[a]	5.34	3.93	3.93	4.07			2.7
α-D-Arabinotetraacetate[b]							6.3
β-D-Arabinotetraacetate[b]							2.7
Peracetylated-α-L-arabino-1-thioaldopyranose[c]	5.35	5.19	5.11	5.26	3.47	3.96	7.0
α-Ribose[a]	4.91	3.85					2.1
β-Ribose[a]	4.99	3.60	4.13	3.79			6.4
α-D-Ribotetraacetate[b]							3.7
Peracetylated-β-D-ribo-1-thioaldopyranose[c]	5.62	5.06	5.49	5.07	3.83	3.98	7.7
β-D-Ribotetraacetate[b]							4.8
2,3,4-Tri-O-benzoyl-β-D-ribopyranosyl fluoride[c]	5.88		5.59–5.90		4.31[d]	4.31[d]	1.5
2,3,4-Tri-O-benzoyl-β-D-ribopyranosyl chloride[c]	6.34	5.70	6.03	~5.7	4.38[d]	4.38[d]	1.7
2,3,4-Tri-O-benzoyl-β-D-ribopyranosyl bromide[c]	6.75	5.84	6.18	~5.81	4.43[d]	4.43[d]	1.2
2,3,4-Tri-O-benzoyl-β-D-ribopyranosyl iodide[c]	7.06	5.77	6.12	~5.75	4.18[d]	4.18[d]	~1.0
2,3,4-Tri-O-benzoyl-β-D-ribopyranosyl methoxide[c]	4.96	5.51	5.79	~5.56	4.09[d]	4.09[d]	2.5
2,3,4-Tri-O-benzoyl-β-D-ribopyranosyl benzyl ether[c]	5.20	5.59	5.86	~5.6	4.17[d]	4.17[d]	2.4
2,3,4-Tri-O-benzoyl-α-D-ribopyranosyl fluoride[c]	5.81	5.28	6.16	5.44	4.19[d]	4.19[d]	3.3
2,3,4-Tri-O-benzoyl-α-D-ribopyranosyl chloride[c]	6.33	5.46	6.16	5.42	4.20[d]	4.20[d]	4.4
2,3,4-Tri-O-benzoyl-α-D-ribopyranosyl bromide[c]	6.53	5.47	6.25	5.52	4.27[d]	4.27[d]	4.4

TABLE 112 (continued)

Compound	δ_1	δ_2	δ_3	δ_4	δ_{5a}	δ_{5e}	J_{12}
α-D-Ribopyranose tetrabenzoate[c]	6.60	5.66	6.20	5.52	4.22[d]	4.22[d]	3.7
β-D-Ribopyranose tetrabenzoate[c]	6.63	5.74	6.04	~5.72	4.30[d]	4.30[d]	3.5
2,3,4-Tri-O-benzoyl-β-D-ribopyranosyl cyanide[c]	5.04	5.66	6.10	~5.56	4.22[d]	4.22[d]	6.7
					A D		
Methyl-2,3-anhydro-β-D-ribopyranoside[e]	4.84	3.56	3.20		←3.6–4.0→		0
Methyl-2,3-anhydro-β-L-ribopyranoside[e]	4.85	3.52	3.17		←3.55–3.95→		0

[a]In D_2O.
[b]In CD_3COCD_3.
[c]In $CDCl_3$.
[d]Axial and equatorial protons not differentiated.
[e]In ethanol-free chloroform.
[f]In CH_3CN.

TABLE 112 (continued)

Compound	J_{23}	J_{34}	J_{45a}	J_{45e}	J_{5a5e}	Other	Ref.
α-Xylose[a]							259
β-Xylose[a]	~8.5	~8.5	~10	4.3	10.4		259
α-D-Xylotetraacetate[b]			11.0[d]	5.4[d]	11.2		260
β-D-Xylotetraacetate[b]			8.6[d]	4.7[d]	11.8		260
Peracetylated-β-D-xylo-1-thioaldopyranose[c]	7.5	7.5	8.3	4.7	11.8		261
α-Lyxose[a]							259
β-Lyxose[a]	3			~5	~10		259
α-D-Lyxotetraacetate[b]			8.6[d]	4.3[d]	11.6		260
β-D-Lyxotetraacetate[b]			5.3[d]	3.1[d]	12.4		260
α-Arabinose[a]	9.9	3.6					259
β-Arabinose[a]		3.4					259
α-D-Arabinotetraacetate[b]			3.5[d]	1.8[d]	13.0		260
β-D-Arabinotetraacetate[b]			1.8[d]	1.2[d]	13.2		260
Peracetylated-α-L-arabino-1-thioaldopyranose[c]	8.0	3.3	2.3	4.7	12.5		261
α-Ribose[a]							259
β-Ribose[a]	3.1	~3	~10				259
α-D-Ribotetraacetate[b]			9.1[d]	4.6[d]	11.2		260
Peracetylated-β-D-ribo-1-thioaldopyranose[c]	3.0	3.0	7.5	4.7	11.8		261
β-D-Ribotetraacetate[b]			3.3[d]	5.8[d]	12.4	J_{13} = 0.1; J_{15e} = 0.2; J_{15a} = 0.1; J_{14} = 0.1; J_{24} = 0.8; J_{35e} = 0.45	260, 263
2,3,4-Tri-O-benzoyl-β-D-ribopyranosyl fluoride[c]			1.9	1.35	13.5		264
2,3,4-Tri-O-benzoyl-β-D-ribopyranosyl chloride[c]	3.9	3.9	1.9	1.7	14.0		264
2,3,4-Tri-O-benzoyl-β-D-ribopyranosyl bromide[c]	3.9	3.9	1.5	1.4	13.8		264
2,3,4-Tri-O-benzoyl-β-D-ribopyranosyl iodide[c]	4.0	4.0	1.6	1.5	13.4		264
2,3,4-Tri-O-benzoyl-β-D-ribopyranosyl methoxide[c]	3.8	3.8	2.1	2.8	13.0		264
2,3,4-Tri-O-benzoyl-β-D-ribopyranosyl benzyl ether[c]	3.8	3.8	2.5	2.95	13.25		264
2,3,4-Tri-O-benzoyl-α-D-ribopyranosyl fluoride[c]	3.3	2.9	10.75	5.3	10.9		264
2,3,4-Tri-O-benzoyl-α-D-ribopyranosyl chloride[c]	3.3	3.3	10.7	5.1	10.9		264
2,3,4-Tri-O-benzoyl-α-D-ribopyranosyl bromide[c]	~3.0	3.1	10.65	5.6	10.8		264

TABLE 112 (continued)

Compound	J_{23}	J_{34}	J_{45a}	J_{45e}	J_{5a5e}	Other	Ref.
α-D-Ribopyranose tetrabenzoate[c]	3.4	3.2	9.3	4.6	10.9		264
β-D-Ribopyranose tetrabenzoate[c]	3.6	3.6	2.5	3.9	12.95		264
2,3,4-Tri-O-benzoyl-β-D-ribopyranosyl cyanide[c]	3.2	3.2	6.6	4.3	12.4		264
Methyl-2,3-anhydro-β-D-ribopyranoside[e]	4	0					265
Methyl-2,3-anhydro-β-L-ribopyranoside[e]	3.8	0					265

TABLE 113

Pentafuranoses

Compound	δ_1	δ_2	δ_3	δ_4		δ_5
1,2,3,5-Tetra-O-benzoyl-β-D-xylofuranose[a]	6.72	5.87	6.01	5.13		4.73
1-O-Acetyl-2,3,5-tri-O-benzoyl-β-D-xylofuranose[a]	6.45	5.70	5.93	5.03		4.68
2,3,5-Tri-O-acetyl-β-D-xylofuranosyl fluoride[a]	5.63	5.18	5.34	4.70		4.20, 4.29
1,2,3,5-Tetra-O-benzoyl-α-D-xylofuranose[a]	6.98	5.98	6.27	5.12		4.65
1-O-Acetyl-2,3,5-tri-O-benzoyl-α-D-xylofuranose[a]	6.74	5.83	6.15	5.02		4.60
1,3,5-Tri-O-benzoyl-2-O-methylsulfonyl-α-D-xylofuranose[a]	6.83	5.63	6.05	5.03		4.57
1,3,5-Tri-O-benzoyl-α-D-xylofuranose[a]	6.67	4.78	5.78	5.00		4.53
1,2,3,5-Tetra-O-benzoyl-β-D-lyxofuranose[a]	6.90	5.80	6.28	4.97		4.78
1,2,3,5-Tetra-O-benzoyl-α-D-lyxofuranose[a]	6.82	6.02	6.25	5.08		4.75
1,2,3,5-Tetra-O-benzoyl-β-D-arabinofuranose[a]	6.93	5.97	6.23		←4.77→	
1,3,5-Tri-O-benzoyl-3-O-acetyl-β-D-arabinofuranose[a]	6.77	5.73	6.00		←4.70→	
1,3,5-Tri-O-benzoyl-3-O-methylsulfonyl-β-D-arabinofuranose[a]	6.77	5.58	6.00		←4.72→	
1,3,5-Tri-O-benzoyl-β-D-arabinofuranose[a]	6.62	4.75	5.72		←4.65→	
1,2,3,5-Tetra-O-benzoyl-α-D-arabinofuranose[a]	6.80	5.88	5.73		←4.85→	
1-O-Methyl-2,3,5-tri-O-benzoyl-α-D-arabinofuranose[a]	5.25	5.48	5.62		←4.67→	
2,3,5-Tri-O-benzoyl-α-D-arabinosyl fluoride[a]	5.99	5.65	5.57	4.85		4.69, 4.80
1,2,3,5-Tetra-O-benzoyl-α-D-ribofuranose[a]	6.98	5.77	5.97	4.95		4.75
1,3,5-Tri-O-benzoyl-2-O-acetyl-α-D-ribofuranose[a]	6.83	5.58	5.85	4.88		4.72
1,3,5-Tri-O-benzoyl-2-O-methylsulfonyl-α-D-ribofuranose[a]	6.85	5.47	5.82	4.87		4.68
1,3,5-Tri-O-benzoyl-α-D-ribofuranose[a]	6.70	~4.70	5.62		←~4.70→	
1,2,3,5-Tetra-O-benzoyl-β-D-ribofuranose[a]	6.72	6.05	6.05		←5.00–5.42→	
1,3,5-Tri-O-benzoyl-2-O-acetyl-β-D-ribofuranose[a]	6.55	5.80	5.93		←4.93–4.35→	
1-0-Acetyl-2,3,5-tri-O-benzoyl-β-D-ribofuranose[a]	6.47	5.82	5.97		←4.95–4.35→	
1,2-Di-O-acetyl-3,5,-di-O-benzoyl-β-D-ribofuranose[a]	6.30	5.58	5.82		←4.63→	
1,3,5-Tri-O-benzoyl-2-O-methylsulfonyl-β-D-ribofuranose[a]	6.60	5.55	5.83		←4.67→	
1,3,5-Tri-O-benzoyl-β-D-ribofuranose[a]	6.47		5.63			
2,3,5-Tri-O-benzoyl-β-D-ribofuranosyl fluoride[a]	5.96	5.46	5.57	4.90		4.57, 4.74
2,3,5-Tri-O-benzoyl-α-D-ribofuranosyl fluoride[a]	6.14	5.47	5.84	4.90		4.59, 4.77
2-O-Acetyl-3,5-di-O-benzoyl-β-D-ribofuranosyl fluoride[a]	5.79	5.76	5.62	4.77		4.52, 4.71
2,5-Di-O-benzoyl-3-O-acetyl-β-D-ribofuranosyl fluoride[c]	5.95	5.70	5.62	4.74		4.42, 4.68
2,3-Di-O-benzoyl-5-O-acetyl-β-D-ribofuranosyl fluoride[c]	6.04	5.81	5.75	4.82		4.25, 4.61

[a]In $CDCl_3$.
[b]In CH_3CN.
[c]In CD_3COCD_3.

TABLE 113 (continued)

Pentafuranoses

Compound	J_{12}	J_{23}	J_{34}	J_{45}	J_{55}	Ref.
1,2,3,5-Tetra-O-benzoyl-β-D-xylofuranose[a]						266
1-O-Acetyl-2,3,5-tri-O-benzoyl-β-D-xylofuranose[a]	<0.5	1.8	5.2			266
2,3,5-Tri-O-acetyl-β-D-xylofuranosyl fluoride[a]	1.0	<0.5	5.5	5.3, 7.1	11.4	267
1,2,3,5-Tetra-O-benzoyl-α-D-xylofuranose[a]						266
1-O-Acetyl-2,3,5-tri-O-benzoyl-α-D-xylofuranose[a]						266
1,3,5-Tri-O-benzoyl-2-O-methylsulfonyl-α-D-xylofuranose[a]	4.4	6.4	6.8			266
1,3,5-Tri-O-benzoyl-β-D-xylofuranose[a]						266
1,2,3,5-Tetra-O-benzoyl-β-D-lyxofuranose[a]	4.6	5.5	4.3			266
1,2,3,5-Tetra-O-benzoyl-α-D-lyxofuranose[a]	1.5	5.2	5.4			266
1,2,3,5-Tetra-O-benzoyl-β-D-arabinofuranose[a]						266
1,3,5-Tri-O-benzoyl-3-O-acetyl-β-D-arabinofuranose [a]						
1,3,5-Tri-O-benzoyl-3-O-methylsulfonyl-β-D-arabinofuranose[a]	4.5	7.2	5.1			266
1,3,5-Tri-O-benzoyl-β-D-arabinofuranose[a]						266
1,2,3,5-Tetra-O-benzoyl-α-D-arabinofuranose[a]						266
1-O-Methyl-2,3,5-tri-O-benzoyl-α-D-arabinofuranose[b]	<0.5	1.6	4.9			266
2,3,5-Tri-O-benzoyl-α-D-arabininosyl fluoride[a]	<0.5	1.0	3.5	3.0, 6.5	12.1	267
1,2,3,5-Tetra-O-benzoyl-α-D-ribofuranose[a]						266
1,3,5-Tri-O-benzoyl-2-O-acetyl-α-D-ribofuranose[a]						
1,3,5-Tri-O-benzoyl-2-O-methylsulfonyl-α-D-ribofuranose[a]	4.3	6.5	2.3			266
1,3,5-Tri-O-benzoyl-α-D-ribofuranose[a]						266
1,2,3,5-Tetra-O-benzoyl-β-D-ribofuranose[a]						266
1,3,5-Tri-O-benzoyl-2-O-acetyl-β-D-ribofuranose[a]						266
1-O-Acetyl-2,3,5-tri-O-benzoyl-β-D-ribofuranose[a]						266
1,2-Di-O-acetyl-3,5-di-O-benzoyl-β-D-ribofuranose[a]						266
1,3,5-Tri-O-benzoyl-2-O-methylsulfonyl-β-D-ribofuranose[a]	<0.5	4.6	7.0			266
1,3,5-Tri-O-benzoyl-β-D-ribofuranose[a]	<0.5	1.8	5.2			266
2,3,5-Tri-O-benzoyl-β-D-ribofuranosyl fluoride[a]	<0.5	4.9	6.2	3.9, 5.2	11.9	267
2,3,5-Tri-O-benzoyl-α-D-ribofuranosyl fluoride[a]	3.5	6.9	2.5	3.2, 3.8	12.3	267
2-O-Acetyl-3,5-di-O-benzoyl-β-D-ribofuranosyl fluoride[a]	<0.5	4.7	6.7	3.8, 5.6	12.5	267
2,5-Di-O-benzoyl-3-O-acetyl-β-D-ribofuranosyl fluoride[c]	<0.5	5.0	5.0	4.5, 5.4	12.4	267
2,3-Di-O-benzoyl-5-O-acetyl-β-D-ribofuranosyl fluoride[c]	<0.5	4.9	4.9	3.6, 5.3	12.1	267

TABLE 114

Noncyclic Pentoses[268]

2,3,4,5-Tetra-O-acetylpentose dimethyl acetals in $CDCl_3$

Compound	J_{12}	J_{23}	J_{34}	J_{45}	$J_{45'}$	$J_{55'}$
ribo	6.5	3.9	5.5	2.5	6.3	12.2
arabino	6.7	2.6	8.3	2.9	5.1	12.3
xylo	5.5	4.7	5.4	4.3	5.9	12.0
lyxo	5.6	6.5	3.3	4.4	6.3	11.6

TABLE 115

Noncyclic Pentoses[262]

2,3,4,5-Tetra-O-acetylpentose diethyl dithioacetals in $CDCl_3$

Compound	δ_1	δ_2	δ_3	δ_4	δ_5	$\delta_{5'}$	J_{12}	J_{23}	J_{34}	J_{45}	$J_{45'}$	$\|J_{55'}\|$
ribo	3.99	5.33	5.63	5.38	4.45	4.11	6.2	5.7	3.6	3.1	7.7	12.0
arabino	3.91	5.30	5.72	5.13	4.30	4.02	8.3	2.8	7.9	2.9	6.0	12.3
xylo	3.98	5.35	5.74	5.38	4.33	4.01	5.2	5.9	4.2	4.3	6.6	11.8
lyxo	3.89	5.35	5.65	5.39	4.27	3.90	4.2	7.9	2.0	4.9	7.6	11.5

TABLE 116

Hexapyranoses

Compound	δ_1	δ_2	δ_3	δ_4	δ_5	δ_6	J_{12}	J_{23}	J_{34}	J_{45}	J_{56}	$J_{56'}$	$J_{66'}$	Ref.
α-D-Glucose[a]	5.28													269
β-D-Glucose[a]	4.70													269
2-Amino-2-deoxy-α-D-glucose hydrochloride[a]	5.46													269
2-Amino-2-deoxy-β-D-glucose hydrochloride[a]	4.97													269
2-Acetamido-2-deoxy-α-D-glucose[a]	5.18													269
2-Acetamido-2-deoxy-β-D-glucose[a]	4.70													269
Methyl 4-acetamido-4-deoxy-2,3,6-tri-O-acetyl-β-L-glucopyranoside[b]	4.45	4.95	5.22	4.20	3.78	4.28								270
Methyl 3-acetamido-3-deoxy-2,4,6-tri-O-acetyl-α-D-glucopyranoside[b]	4.17	←	4.9	→	4.00	4.22								270
Methyl 2-acetamido-2-deoxy-3,4,6-tri-O-acetyl-α-D-glucopyranoside[b]	4.75	4.30	5.25	5.08	3.93	4.20								270
Methyl 2-acetamido-2-deoxy-3,4,6-tri-O-acetyl-β-D-glucopyranoside[b]	4.65	3.92	5.33	5.08	3.75	4.25								270
Methyl 4-acetamido-4-deoxy-2,3,6-tri-O-acetyl-α-L-glucopyranoside[b]	5.02	5.20	5.37	~4.27	3.96	4.27								270
Methyl 4-acetamido-4-deoxy-2,3,6-tri-O-acetyl-α-D-glucopyranoside[b]	~5.00	~5.00	5.30	~4.18	3.90	4.22								270
4-Acetamido-4-deoxy-1,2,3,6-tetra-O-acetyl-β-L-glucopyranose[b]	5.73	~5.23	~5.23	~4.25	3.77	4.23								270
Methyl 4,6-O-benzylidene-α-D-glucopyranoside[c]	5.05	(	3.64–4.64			)	3.5							271
Methyl 4,6-O-benzylidene-α-D-glucopyranoside-d_2 [d]	4.65	(	3.21–4.28			)	3.6							271
Methyl 2,3-di-O-acetyl-4,6-O-benzylidene-α-D-glucopyranoside[c]	5.14	5.23	5.97	(	3.66–4.52	)	3.6	9.8	~8.5					271
Methyl 2,3-di-O-benzoyl-4,6-O-benzylidene-α-D-glucopyranoside[e]	5.28	5.48	6.29	(	3.40–4.54	)	3.6	9.5	9.0					271
Methyl 3-O-benzoyl-4,6-O-benzylidene-2-O-toluene-*p*-sulphonyl-α-D-glucopyranoside[b]	5.04	4.68	5.83	(	3.53–4.45	)	3.7	9.6	9.5					271
Methyl 4,6-O-benzylidene-2,3-di-O-toluene-*p*-sulphonyl-α-D-glucopyranoside[c]	5.23	4.92	5.52	(	3.43–4.50	)	3.6	9.4	9.0					271
Methyl 2-O-acetyl-4,6,-O-nitrobenzylidene-α-D-glucopyranoside-3-nitrate[b]	5.06	4.90	5.72	(	3.59–4.50	)	3.7	9.6	9.5					271
Methyl 4,6-O-benzylidene-2,3-di-O-methyl-α-D-glucopyranoside[b]	4.82	(	3.14–4.38			)	3.6							271
Methyl 2-acetamido-3-O-acetyl-4,6-O-benzylidene-2-deoxy-α-D-glucopyranoside[b]	4.73	4.38	5.34	(	3.52–4.17	)	3.5	~9.2	~9.2					271
Barium methyl α-D-glucopyranoside 2,3-disulphate[a]	5.15	4.34	4.5	(	3.5–4.0	)	3.5	10.0						272

TABLE 116 (continued)

Compound	δ_1	δ_2	δ_3	δ_4	δ_5	δ_6	J_{12}	J_{23}	J_{34}	J_{45}	J_{56}	$J_{56'}$	$J_{66'}$	Ref.
Sodium 4,6-O-benzylidene-α-D-glucopyranoside 2,3-disulphate[a]	5.34	4.58	4.8	(	3.6–4.4	)	3.5	10.0						272
Barium methyl α-D-glucopyranoside 4,6-disulphate[a]	4.83	3.70	(	3.8–4.6		)	3.25	9.25						272
Barium 2,3-di-O-benzyl-α-D-glucopyranoside 4,6-disulphate[a]		3.62					3.5	10.0						272
1-Thio-β-D-glucopyranose pentaacetate[f]	5.38	5.03	5.37	5.06	~4.02	4.05, 4.26	10.6	9.5	9.5	10.1	5.4		13.2	261
α-D-Glucopyranose pentaacetate[g]	6.12	4.86	5.17	4.89	3.92	3.83, 4.15	3.6	10	9.3	9.3	4.7	2.3	12.2	273
1-O-Methyl-2,3,4,6-tetra-O-acetyl-α-D-glucopyranose[g]	4.86	4.74	5.29	4.92	3.88	3.97, 4.17	3.7	9.2	9.3	9.3	4.7	2.3	12.2	273
β-D-Glucopyranose pentaacetate[g]	5.63	(	4.90–5.20	)	3.94	4.09, 4.28	8.0	10.2		9.5	4.6	2.0	12.5	273
1-O-Methyl-2,3,4,6-tetra-O-acetyl-β-D-glucopyranose[g]	4.35	(	4.72–5.10	)	3.55	4.02, 4.22	7.5				4.7	2.5	12.5	273
1,3,4,6-Tetra-O-acetyl-2-(N-acetylacetamido)-2-deoxy-β-D-glucopyranose[b]	6.60	3.90	5.92	5.13	3.9		8.3	10.3	9.0	10.2	4.7	2.0		274
1,3,4,6-Tetra-O-acetyl-2-(N-acetylacetamido)-2-deoxy-α-D-glucopyranose[b]	6.25	4.66	6.11	5.10	4.1		3.5	10.3	9.0	9.0				274
1,3,4,6-Tetra-O-acetyl-2-(N-acetylbenzamido)-2-deoxy-β-D-glucopyranose[b]	6.55	4.23	5.91	5.07	3.9		8.5	10.0	9.0	10.0	4.5	1.9		274
1,3,4,5-Tetra-O-acetyl-2-(N-acetylbenzamido)-2-deoxy-α-D-glucopyranose[b]	6.40	5.12	6.02	5.10	4.2		3.5	11.0	9.0	9.0				274
2-Acetamido-1,3,4,6-tetra-O-acetyl-β-D-glucopyranose[b]	5.77	4.44	~5.2	~5.1	~3.9		8.8							274
2-Acetamido-1,3,4,6-tetra-O-acetyl-2-deoxy-α-D-glucopyranose[b]	6.20	4.46	~5.2	~5.2	4.0		3.5							274
α-D-Galactose[a]	5.29													269
β-D-Galactose[a]	4.63													269
2-Acetamido-2-deoxy-α-D-galactose[a]	5.28													269
2-Acetamido-2-deoxy-β-D-galactose[a]	4.69													269
2-Amino-2-deoxy-α-D-galactose hydrochloride[a]	5.48													269
2-Amino-2-deoxy-β-D-galactose hydrochloride[a]	4.89													269
1-Thio-β-D-galactopyranose pentaacetate[h]	5.45	5.67	5.27	5.50	3.72	4.03, 4.17	10.0	9.4	3.4	1.2	6.7	6.0	11.2	261
Barium methyl α-D-galactopyranoside 2,3-disulphate[a]	5.17	4.55	4.55	4.38	(3.6–4.0	)								272
Barium methyl β-D-galactopyranoside 2,3-disulphate[a]	(	4.3–4.6		)	3.74	3.74								272
Barium methyl 4,6-O-benzylidene-α-D-galactopyranoside 2,3-disulphate[a]	5.33	4.8	4.8	4.8	3.95	4.24								272
Barium methyl 4,6-O-benzylidene-β-D-galactopyranoside 2,3-disulphate[a]	(	4.7 multiplet		)	3.80	4.26								272
Barium methyl α-D-galactopyranoside 2,6-disulphate[a]	5.14	4.55	~3.85	(	4.0–4.2	)	3.5	10.0						272
Barium benzyl β-D-galactopyranoside 2,6-disulphate[a]	4.60	4.40	3.84	4.07	3.93	4.24	7.75	9.25	3.0	0.5	6.25			272
Barium methyl α-D-galactopyranoside 4-sulphate	4.88	(3.6–4.2)		4.73	(3.6–4.2)									272
Barium methyl β-D-galactopyranoside 4-sulphate	4.37						7.0							272
Barium benzyl β-D-galactopyranoside 4-sulphate	4.52	(3.6–4.0)		4.78	(3.6–4.0)		7.0							272
α-D-Mannose[a]	5.20													269

TABLE 116 (continued)

Compound	δ_1	δ_2	δ_3	δ_4	δ_5	δ_6	J_{12}	J_{23}	J_{34}	J_{45}	J_{56}	$J_{56'}$	$J_{66'}$	Ref.
β-D-Mannose[a]	4.92													269
2-Acetamido-2-deoxy-α-D-mannose[a]	5.11													269
2-Acetamido-2-deoxy-β-D-mannose[a]	5.01													269
2-Amino-2-deoxy-α-D-mannose hydrochloride[a]	5.40													275
2-Amino-2-deoxy-β-D-mannose hydrochloride[a]	5.22													275
Methyl 4,6-O-benzylidene-α-D-mannopyranoside[b]	4.65	(3.67–4.35)					0.6							271
Methyl 2,3-di-O-acetyl-4,6-O-benzylidene-α-D-mannopyranoside[b]	4.66	(5.30–5.53)		(3.79–4.37)			1.2							271
Methyl 2,3-di-O-benzoyl-4,6-O-benzylidene-α-D-mannopyranoside[b]	4.91	(5.74–6.03)		(3.42–4.63)			0.9	3.6						271
Methyl 4,6-O-benzylidene-2,3-di-O-toluene-*p*-mannopyranoside[c]	5.17	5.38	5.15	(3.67–4.47)			1.7	3.3	9.4					271
Methyl 4,6-O-benzylidene-2,3-di-O-nitrobenzene-*p*-sulphonyl-α-D-mannopyranoside[b]	5.08	4.97	4.76	(3.60–4.30)			1.6	3.3	9.3					271
Methyl 2,3-acetylepimino-4,6-O-benzylidene-2,3-dideoxy-α-D-mannopyranoside[i]	4.87	3.07	2.75	4.26	3.70	3.67	0	6.5	0	7.5				265
Methyl 4,6-O-benzylidene-2,3-dideoxy-2,3-epimino-α-D-mannopyranoside[i]	4.79	2.6	2.3	4.2	3.62	3.58	0	6.5	0					265
Methyl 2,3-anhydro-4,6-O-benzylidene-α-D-mannopyranoside[i]	4.86	3.44	3.12	4.23	3.75	3.64	0	4.0	0	5				265
Methyl 3-acetamido-3-deoxy-2,4,6-tri-O-acetyl-α-D-mannopyranoside[b]	4.77	5.08	4.42	4.92	3.93	4.22								270
Methyl 3-acetamido-3,6-dideoxy-2,4-di-O-acetyl-α-D-mannopyranoside[b]	4.65	4.95	(4.67–4.83)		3.96									270
α-D-Mannopyranose pentaacetate[g]	5.81	(5.07–5.23)			3.94	4.20, 3.97	1.8				4.8	2.5	12.5	273
1-O-Methyl-2,3,4,6-tetra-O-acetyl-α-D-mannopyranose[g]	4.60	(5.00–5.30)			3.85	4.16, 4.01	1.6			9.2	5.2	2.7	12.1	273
β-D-Mannopyranose pentaacetate[g]	5.75	5.33	5.07	5.12	3.70	4.22, 4.04	1.4	3.2	9.5	9.3	5.0	2.5	12.2	273
1-O-Methyl-2,3,4,6-tetra-O-acetyl-β-D-mannopyranose[g]							1.2	3.4	10	10	5.0	2.7	12.5	273
Methyl 3-acetamido-4,6-O-benzylidene-3-deoxy-α-D-allopyranoside[b]	4.68	3.30–4.43	4.86	(3.30–4.43)			3.3							271
Methyl 3-acetamido-4,6-O-benzylidene-3-deoxy-α-D-allopyranoside-d_2[c]	4.99	3.60–4.66	5.43	(3.60–4.66)			3.4	3.9	3.9					271
Methyl 3-acetamido-2-O-acetyl-4,6-O-3-deoxy-α-D-allopyranoside-d[c]	5.02	5.23	5.49	(3.59–4.51)			3.3	4.0	4.0					271
Methyl 3-acetamido-2-O-acetyl-4,6-O-benzylidene-3-deoxy-α-D-allopyranoside[c]	5.04	5.27	5.54	(3.63–4.53)			3.5	4.4	4.2					271
β-D-Allopyranose pentaacetate[b]	6.05	5.02	5.75	~5.05	4.26		8.6	2.9	2.9					264
Methyl 2,3-acetylepimino-4,6-O-benzylidene-2,3-dideoxy-α-D-allopyroanoside[i]	4.90	3.1	3.0	4.2	(3.55–4.05)		4.5	6.0	4.5	10.5				265

TABLE 116 (continued)

Compound	δ_1	δ_2	δ_3	δ_4	δ_5	δ_6	J_{12}	J_{23}	J_{34}	J_{45}	J_{56}	$J_{56'}$	$J_{66'}$	Ref.
Methyl 4,6-O-benzylidene-2,3-dideoxy-2,3-epimino-α-D-allopyranoside[i]	4.86			4.2	(3.55–4.0)		3.5[j]		5	8				265
Methyl 2,3-anhydro-4,6-O-benzylidene-α-D-allopyranoside[i]	4.88	(3.35–3.60)		4.3	(3.60–4.07)		2.5[j]	4.5[j]	4.5[j]	10				265
Methyl 4,6-O-benzylidene-2,3-dideoxy-2,3-epithio-α-D-allopyranoside	5.12	(3.37–3.57)		(	3.6–4.4)	4.24	4.2[j]	7.2						265
Methyl 4,6-O-benzylidene-α-D-altropyranoside[b]	4.68	(		3.79–4.49		)	<0.8							271
Methyl 4,6-O-benzylidene-α-D-altropyranoside-d_2 [d]	4.62	(		3.73–4.43		)	~0.8							271
Methyl 2,3-di-O-acetyl-4,6-O-benzylidene-α-D-altropyranoside[b]	4.59	5.03	5.24	(	3.55–4.46	)	0.9	2.9	2.9					271
Methyl 2,3-di-O-benzoyl-4,6-O-benzylidene-α-D-altropyranoside[b]	4.82	5.45	5.75	(	3.71–4.72	)	0.8	3.1						271
Methyl 4,6-O-benzylidene-2-O-methyl-α-D-altropyranoside[b]	4.69	3.46	(	3.57–4.42		)	1.0	3.0						271
Methyl 4,6-O-benzylidene-3-O-methyl-α-D-altropyranoside[b]	4.53	(		3.61–4.44		)	<0.8							271
Methyl 4,6-O-benzylidene-2,3-di-O-methyl-α-D-altropyranoside	4.78	3.62	3.85	(	3.74–4.62	)	0.8	2.8	2.8					271
Methyl 2-amino-4,6-O-benzylidene-2-deoxy-α-D-altropyranoside[b]	4.51	3.24	(	3.52–4.44		)	0.8	2.5						271
Methyl 3-amino-4,6-O-benzylidene-3-deoxy-α-D-altropyranoside[d]	4.67	3.70–4.44	3.28	(	3.70–4.44	)	~0.9							271
Methyl 3-acetamido-4,6-O-benzylidene-3-deoxy-α-D-altropyranoside[b]	4.65	3.62–4.35	4.72	(	3.62–4.35	)								271
Methyl 3-acetamido-2-O-acetyl-4,6-O-benzylidene-3-deoxy-α-D-altropyranoside[c]	4.88	5.38	5.11	(	3.66–4.56	)	1.0	2.7						271
Methyl 3-benzamido-4,6-O-benzylidene-3-deoxy-α-D-altropyranoside[b]	4.73	3.64–4.50	5.14	(	3.64–4.50	)								271
Methyl 4,6-O-benzylidene-3-deoxy-3-(2,4-dinitrophenylamino)-α-D-altropyranoside[b]	4.76	(	3.83–4.60			)								271
Methyl 2-O-acetyl-4,6-O-benzylidene-3-deoxy-3-(2,4-dinitrophenylamino)-α-D-altropyranoside[b]	4.82	5.10	(	3.70–4.60		)	1.1	2.5						271
Methyl 4,6-O-benzylidene-3-deoxy-3-(2,4-dinitrophenylamino)-2-O-methyl-α-D-altropyranoside[c]	5.02	3.77	(	3.87–4.86		)	0.9	2.5						271
α-D-Idopyranose pentaacetate[f]	5.98	4.81	5.01	4.91	4.53	4.15	2.1	3.6	3.5	2.1	6.0			276

[a] In D_2O.
[b] In $CDCl_3$.
[c] In pyridine.
[d] In $CDCl_3 + D_2O$.
[e] In $CDCl_3$ – pyridine, 1:1 v/v.
[f] In acetone-d_6.
[g] In CCl_4.
[h] In C_6D_6.
[i] In ethanol-free chloroform.
[j] Benzene used as solvent to measure coupling constants.

TABLE 117

Norbornane and Related Compounds

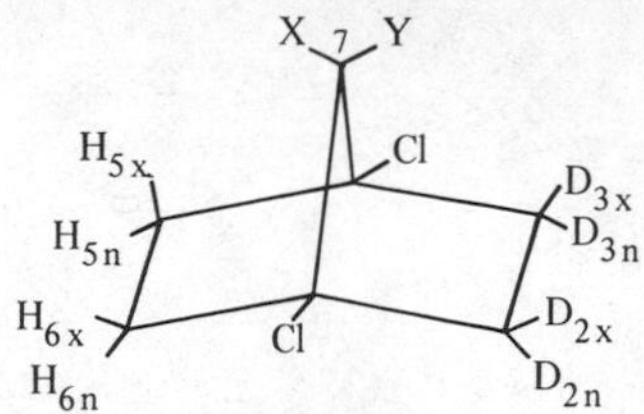

In pyridine
(Ref. 403)

X	Y	δ_{5n}	δ_{5x}	δ_{7s}	δ_{7a}	J_{5n6n}	J_{5n5x}	J_{5n6x}	J_{5x7s}	J_{5n7s}	J_{5x6x}
OCH_3	OCH_3	1.537	2.174			9.82	−11.78	4.46			12.71
OAc	H	1.541	2.142	5.362		9.15	−12.15	4.16	0.40	1.16	12.85
Cl	Cl	1.431	2.001			9.97	−12.31	4.47			12.50
H	H	1.543	1.790	1.889	1.889	9.15	−12.09	4.74		−2.19	13.20

TABLE 118

Norbornene and Related Compounds

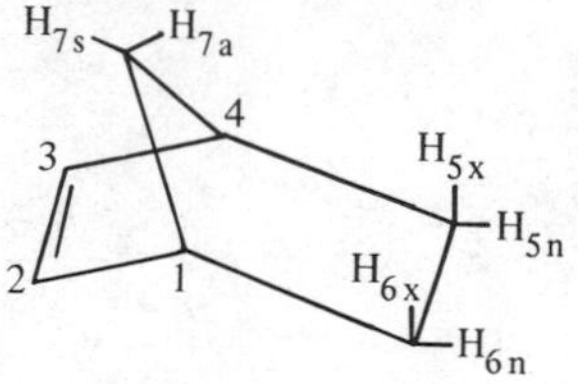

In CCl_4

(Ref. 404)

$\delta_2 = 5.93$
$\delta_1 = 2.82$
$\delta_{5x} = 1.59$
$\delta_{5n} = 0.96$
$\delta_{7s} = 1.33$
$\delta_{7a} = 1.06$
$J_{17a} = 1.5$

$J_{17s} = 1.8$
$J_{5n7s} = 2.2$ (Ref. 405)
$J_{27a} = \sim 0.5$
$J_{7s7a} = 7.7$
$J_{12} = 2.0$ (Ref. 406)
$J_{23} = 6.0$ (Ref. 407)
$J_{13} = 1.2$ (Ref. 407)

$J_{16n} = 0$
$J_{16x} = 3.5$
$J_{14} = 0$ (Ref. 408)
$J_{5n6n} = 4.4–5.6$ (Ref. 409)
$J_{5x6x} = 8.0–9.1$ (Ref. 409)
$J_{5n6x} = 4.4$ (Ref. 405)
$J_{5n5x} = 10.6$ (Ref. 405)

TABLE 118 (continued)

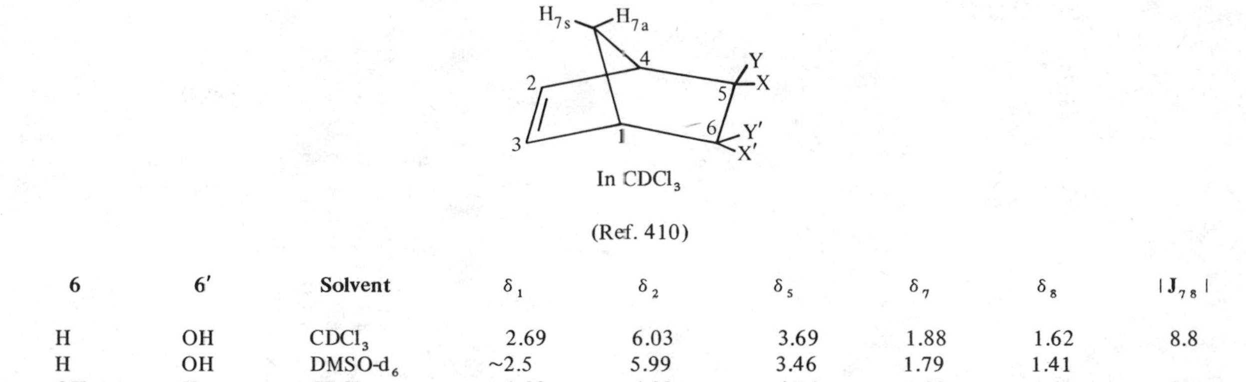

In $CDCl_3$

(Ref. 410)

5	5′	6	6′	Solvent	δ_1	δ_2	δ_5	δ_7	δ_8	$\lvert J_{78} \rvert$	$\lvert J_{68} \rvert$	$\lvert J_{18} \rvert$
OH	H	H	OH	$CDCl_3$	2.69	6.03	3.69	1.88	1.62	8.8	1.7	1.7
OH	H	H	OH	DMSO-d_6	~2.5	5.99	3.46	1.79	1.41			
H	OH	OH	H	$CDCl_3$	2.99	6.23	4.14	1.20	1.49	9.4	0.0	2.0
H	OH	OH	H	DMSO-d_6	2.81	6.06	~4.0	1.11	1.24			
OAc	H	H	OAc	$CDCl_3$	2.82	6.16	4.73	2.03	1.72	9.2	1.8	1.5
H	OAc	OAc	H	$CDCl_3$	3.12	6.20	5.22	1.36	1.58	9.9	0.0	2.1

5	5′	6	6′	Solvent	$\lvert J_{17} \rvert$	$\lvert J_{27} \rvert$	$\lvert J_{14} \rvert$	$\lvert J_{23} \rvert$	$\lvert J_{12} \rvert$	$\lvert J_{13} \rvert$	$\lvert J_{56} \rvert$	$\lvert J_{16} \rvert$	$\lvert J_{15} \rvert$
OH	H	H	OH	$CDCl_3$	1.5	~0.5	1.6[a]	6.0[a]	2.6[b]	1.1[b]		0.0	0.0
OH	H	H	OH	DMSO-d_6									
H	OH	OH	H	$CDCl_3$	1.5	~0.5	1.1, 1.2[c, d]	6.0	2.5[b]		7.6[d]	3.7[e]	0.1–0.2[e]
H	OH	OH	H	DMSO-d_6									
OAc	H	H	OAc	$CDCl_3$	1.6	~0.6						0.0	0.0
H	OAc	OAc	H	$CDCl_3$	1.5	~0.5	1.4				7.4	4.0[f]	0.2[f]

[a] J_{14} and J_{23} have the same sign. It was assumed that $|J_{23}| > |J_{14}|$.
[b] J_{12} and J_{13} have the same sign. It was assumed that $|J_{12}| > |J_{13}|$.
[c] Values from calculations of two separate AA′-XX′ subspectra.
[d] J_{56} and J_{14} are of the same sign. It was assumed that $|J_{56}| > |J_{14}|$.
[e] J_{15} and J_{16} appear to have the same sign. It was assumed that $|J_{16}| > |J_{15}|$.
[f] J_{15} and J_{16} appear to be of different sign. It was assumed that $|J_{16}| > |J_{15}|$.

TABLE 119

Norbornadiene and Related Compounds

Compound	δ_1	δ_2	δ_5	δ_{7s}	δ_{7a}	J_{12}	J_{13}	J_{17}	J_{15}	J_{16}	J_{14}	J_{23}	J_{27}	J_{57}	Solvent	Ref.
Norbornadiene	3.47	6.65		1.95		2.70	0.95	1.5				5.05			CCl_4	408, 411
Benzonorbornadiene	3.87	6.77		2.33	2.20										$CDCl_3$	412
Quadricyclene	1.47			2.02											$CDCl_3$	412
7-Chloronorbornadiene	3.62	6.78	6.64	4.22				1.66						0.7	$CDCl_3$	413
7-Norbornadienyl fluoroborate	5.27	7.58	6.26	3.48		6.1	1.5	2.8	1.8	1.8	0.5	4.6	2.7		SO_2	414

V. LONG-RANGE COUPLING CONSTANTS

TABLE 120

Aromatic Systems

(Reference 97b was the basic source of most of the data in Tables 112 to 126.)

J_{ortho} = 6.0–9.5
J_{meta} = 1.2–3.3
J_{para} = 0.1–1.5

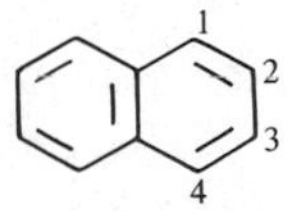

1, 2, 3, 4

J_{12} = 8.3–9.1
J_{23} = 6.1–6.9
J_{13} = 1.2–1.6
J_{14} = *ca.* 1

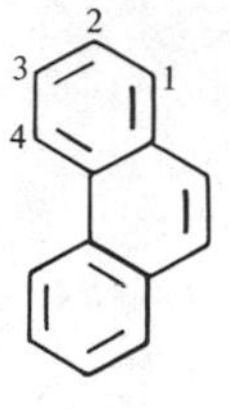

2, 3, 1, 4

J_{12} = 8.0–9.0
J_{23} = 6.9–7.3
J_{34} = 8.0–8.5
J_{13} = 0.9–1.6
J_{24} = 1.2–1.8
J_{14} = 0.3–0.7

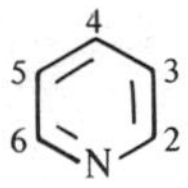

4, 5, 3, 6, N, 2

J_{23} = 4.0–6.0
J_{34} = 6.9–9.1
J_{24} = 0–2.7
J_{35} = 0.5–1.8
J_{26} = 0–0.6
J_{25} = 0–2.3

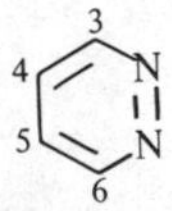

3, 4, N, N, 5, 6

J_{34} = 5.1
J_{45} = 8.0–9.6
J_{35} = 1.8
J_{36} = 3.5

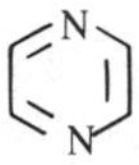

N, N

J_{23} = 1.8–3
J_{26} = 0 to –0.5
J_{25} = 1.3–1.8

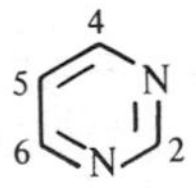

4, 5, N, 6, N, 2

J_{45} = 4–6
J_{46} = 2.5
J_{24} = 0–1
J_{25} = 1–2

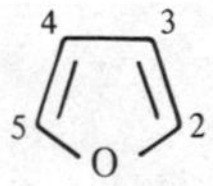

4, 3, 5, 2, O

J_{23} = 1.3–2.0
J_{34} = 3.1–3.8
J_{24} = 0.4–1
J_{25} = 1–2

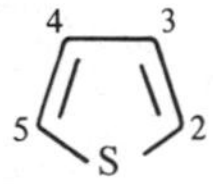

4, 3, 5, 2, S

J_{23} = 4.9–6.2
J_{34} = 3.4–5.0
J_{24} = 1.2–1.7
J_{25} = 3.2–3.7

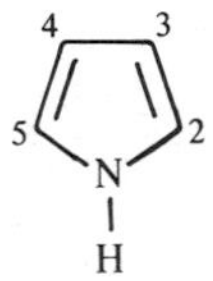

4, 3, 5, 2, N, H

J_{12} = 1
J_{13} = 2
J_{23} = 2.6
J_{34} = 3.4
J_{24} = 1.1
J_{25} = 2.2

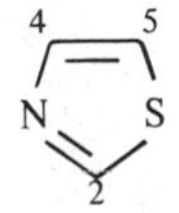

4, 5, N, S, 2

J_{45} = 3.2
J_{24} = <0.5
J_{25} = 1.9

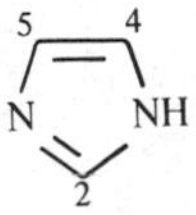

5, 4, N, NH, 2

J_{45} = 1.6
J_{24} and J_{25} = 0.8–1.5

H, M, H

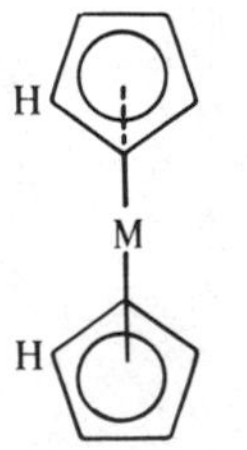

J_{ortho} = 2.3–3.1
J_{meta} = 1.0–1.6

(Refs. 20, 98, 227)

TABLE 121

Benzylic Coupling Constants, J, in Derivatives of Benzene and Polycyclic Hydrocarbons[321]

Compound	$J^{ortho}_{CH_3,H}$	$J^{para}_{CH_3,H}$	Ref.
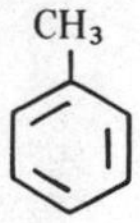 CH_3	−0.746 ± 0.026	−0.619 ± 0.016	322
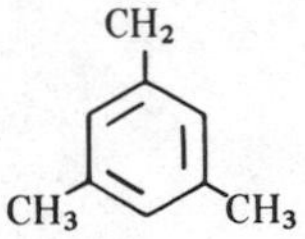 CH_2, CH_3, CH_3	−0.62 ± 0.02	−0.62 ± 0.02	323
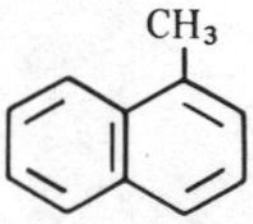 CH_3	−0.7 ($J_{CH_3,H(2)}$)		324
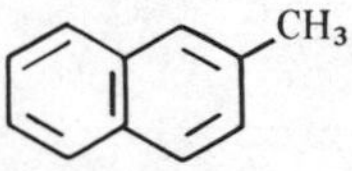 CH_3	−0.7 ($J_{CH_3,H(1)}$)		
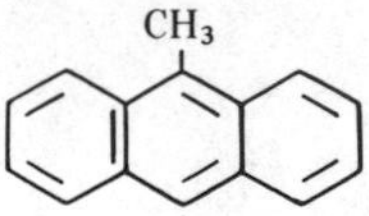 CH_3		−0.75	325
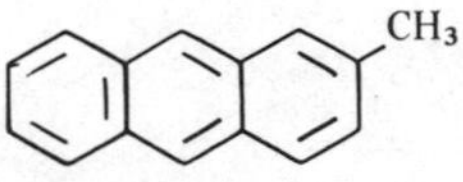 CH_3	−0.8		324
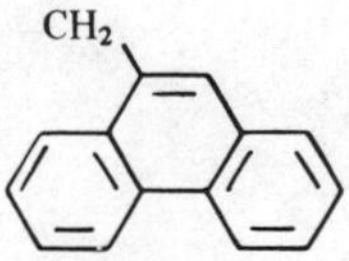 CH_2	−1.1 ± 0.1		323, 326, 327
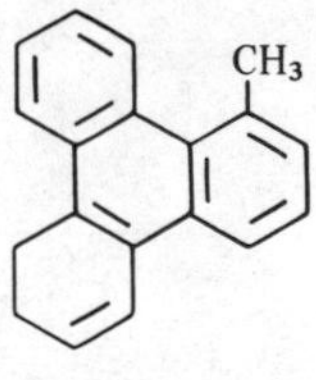 CH_3	−0.5		325
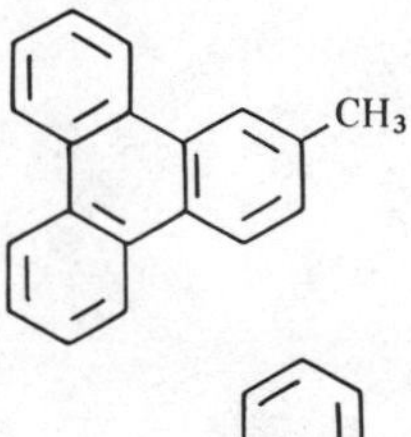 CH_3	−0.5 ($J_{CH_3,H(3)}$)		325
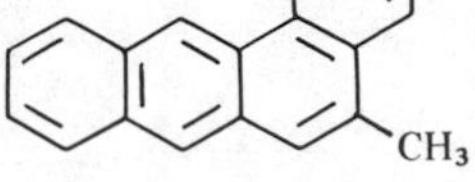 CH_3	−1.2		328

TABLE 121 (continued)

Compound	$J^{ortho}_{CH_3,H}$	$J^{para}_{CH_3,H}$	Ref.
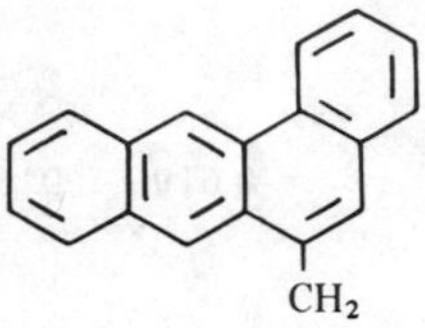 CH_2	−1.2		
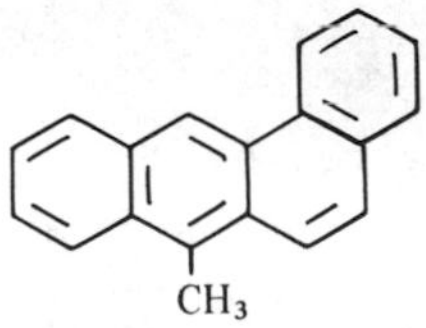 CH_3		−0.7	325
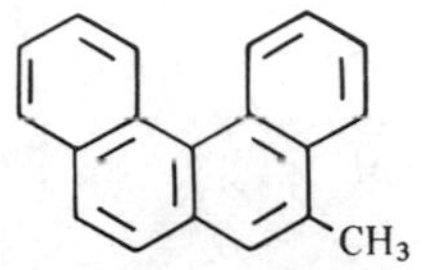 CH_3	−0.8		328
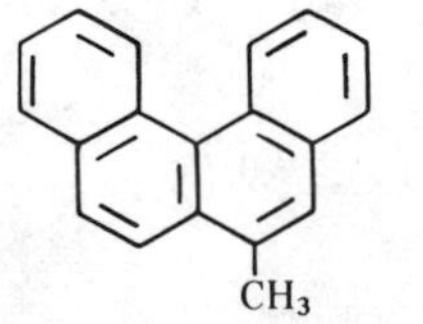 CH_3	−1.0		
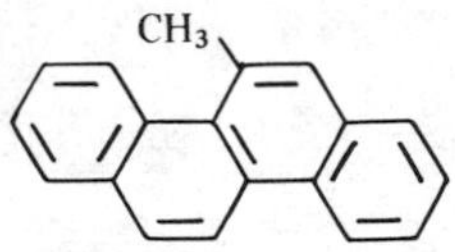 CH_3	−1		329
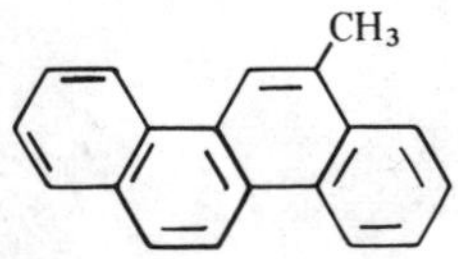 CH_3	−1		
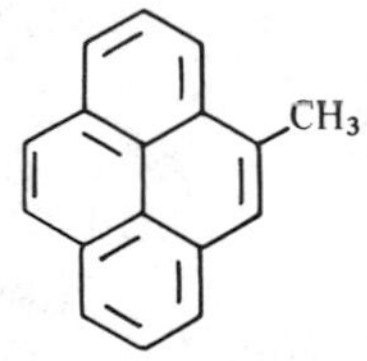 CH_3	−1.3 (−1.2 in 4,9-dimethyl derivative)		327
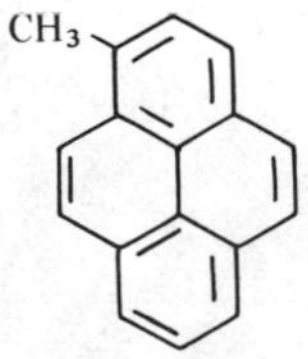 CH_3	−0.6		325

TABLE 121 (continued)

Compound	$J^{ortho}_{CH_3,H}$	$J^{para}_{CH_3,H}$	Ref.
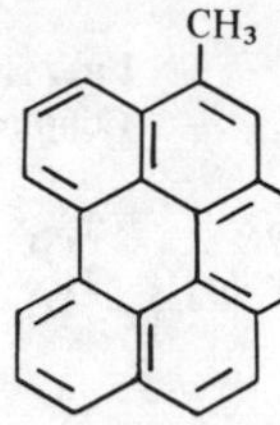 CH_3	−1.1 (−1.0 in 3,10-dimethyl derivative)		330
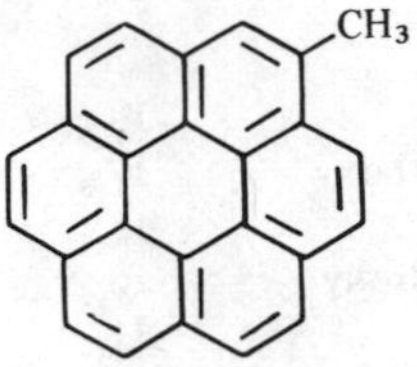 CH_3	−0.9		327
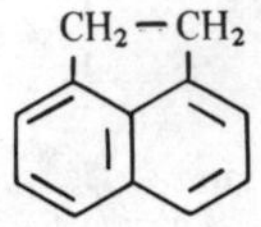 CH_2-CH_2	−0.9	−0.3	331
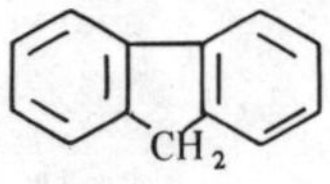 CH_2	−0.6		325
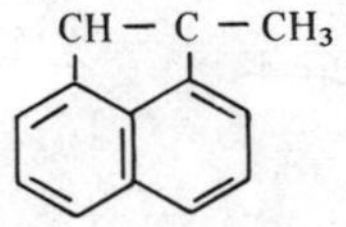 $CH-C-CH_3$	−1.5		332

TABLE 122

Inter-ring Couplings in Derivatives of Polynuclear Hydrocarbons[321]

System	Derivative	Inter-ring Coupling		Magnitude (c/s)	Ref.
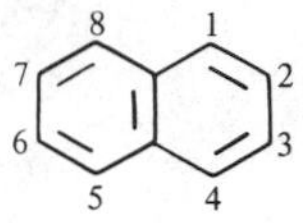 Naphthalene	Methylnitro; dinitro	$J_{4,5}$	*peri*	≅0.5	333
	1-Chloro-2-hydroxy	$J_{4,5}$	*peri*	0.4	
		$J_{4,8}$	*epi*	0.8	
	1-Chloro-2-methoxy	$J_{4,5}$	*peri*	0.4	
		$J_{4,8}$	*epi*	0.8	
	1-Bromo-2-hydroxy	$J_{4,5}$	*peri*	0.5	
		$J_{4,8}$	*epi*	0.9	
	1-Bromo-2-amino	$J_{4,5}$	*peri*	0.3	
		$J_{4,8}$	*epi*	0.7	
	1-Nitro-2-amino	$J_{4,5}$	*peri*	0.2	
		$J_{4,8}$	*cpi*	0.6	
	1-Bromo-2-acetylamino	$J_{4,5}$	*peri*	0.2	
		$J_{4,8}$	*epi*	0.6	
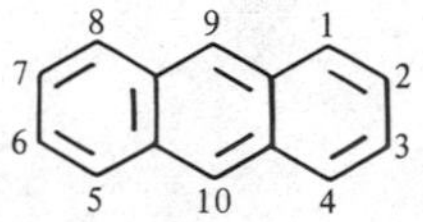 Anthracene	Unspecified	$J_{4,10}$	*peri*	0.4	334
	9-Substituted	$J_{1,10}$	*epi*	0.8	334
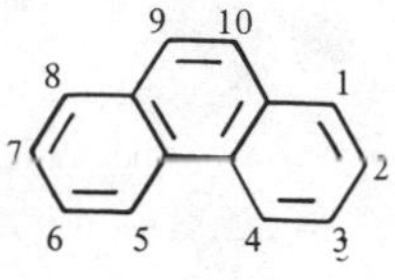 Phenanthrene	1-Hydroxy	$J_{4,10}$	*epi*	0.7	335
	1-Methoxy	$J_{4,10}$	*epi*	0.6	335
	1,2,3,4-Tetrahydro-4-oxachrysene	$J_{4,10}$	*epi*	0.7	335
	9,10-Dibromo	$J_{4,5}$	*bay*	0.3	326
	9,10-Dimethyl	$J_{4,5}$	*bay*	0.3	326
	9,10-Diethyl	$J_{4,5}$	*bay*	0.3	326
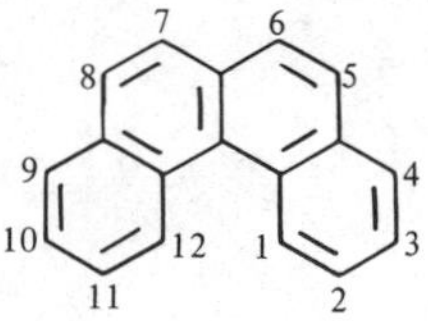	9-*t*-Butyl	$J_{4,5}$	*bay*	0.4	326
	9-*t*-Pentyl	$J_{4,5}$	*bay*	0.4	326
Benzo[*c*]phenanthrene	4-Methoxy	$J_{1,5}$	*epi*	0.8	335
		$J_{1,8}$		0.8	
	4-Amino	$J_{1,5}$	*epi*	1.0	335
		$J_{1,8}$		1.0	

TABLE 123

Coupling Across Four Single Bonds

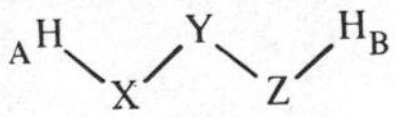

$_AH$–X–Y–Z–H_B

X, Y, Z = sp^3 carbon, sp^2 carbon

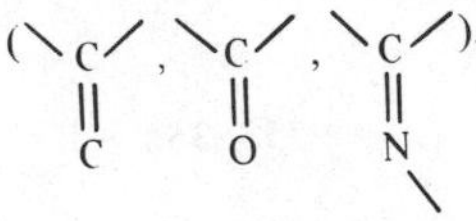

(C=C, C=O, C=N), O, N, and S

J_{AB} (common range) = +1 to +3 Hz

(Refs. 20, 280–282)

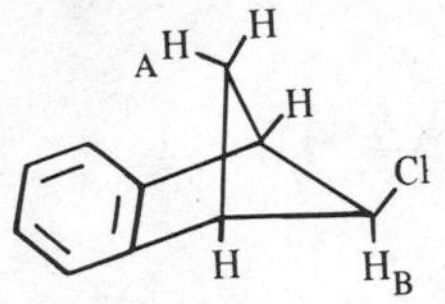

J_{AB} = +7.4 Hz

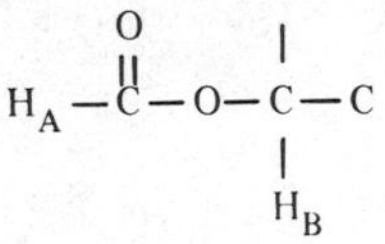

H_A—C(=O)—O—C—C(H_B)

J_{AB} = −0.8 to −1.0

(Refs. 20, 296)

$_AH$, CH_3 (B), H, H (X), O

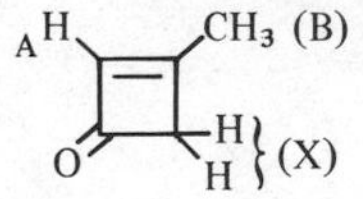

J_{BX} = 1.25, J_{AB} = 1.48, J_{AX} = 0.63 Hz

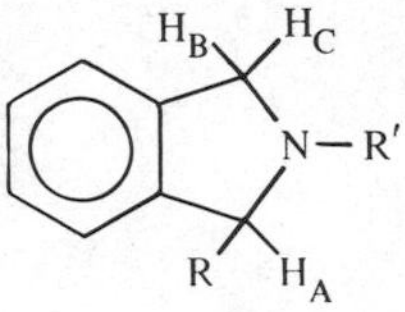

H_B, H_C, N—R′, R, H_A

$J_{AB} \neq J_{AC}$ = 1 to 3

(Refs. 20, 297)

Molecule	$^4J_{HH'}$, Hz	Ref.
Bicyclo[2.2.1]heptanes		
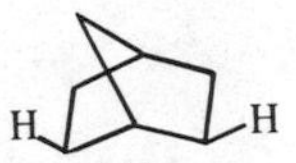	1,0–1.2 1.0–1.4 1.35–1.8	343, 344 345 346
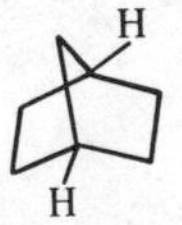	1.0–1.6	344
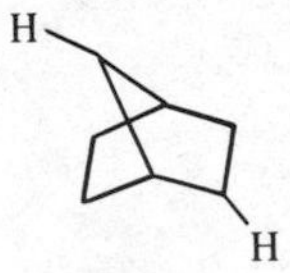	3–4 1.7–2.6	347 344
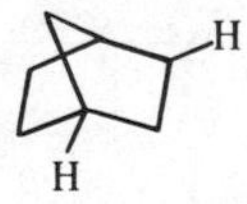	1.0	348
Bicyclo[2.2.1]heptenes		
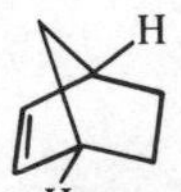	0–1.0	349
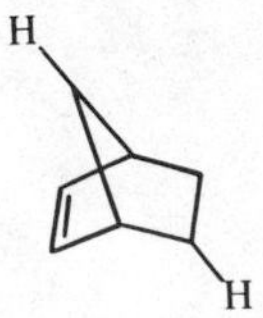	2.0–3.1	349, 350

TABLE 123 (continued)

Molecule	$^4J_{HH'}$,Hz	Ref.
Bicyclo[3.1.1]heptenes	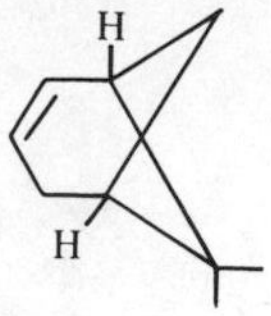 5.8–6.4	351, 352
Bicyclo[2.1.1]hexanes	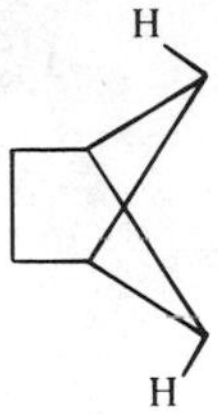 6.7–8.1	353, 354
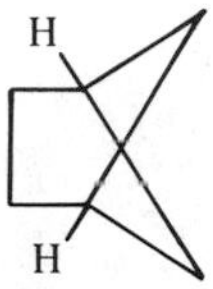	8	355
Bicyclo[1.1.1]pentane	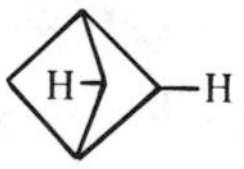 10	279
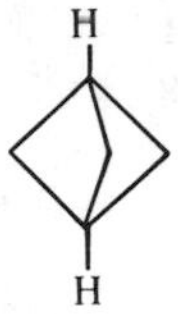	18	279
Tricyclo[1.1.1.$0^{4,5}$]pentanone	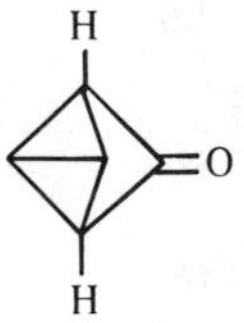 14	356
Bicyclo[1.1.0]butane	 10	279

cis-4-Phenyl-6-methyl-m-dioxane
$J_{2e4a} = 0.5$

(Ref. 285)

α-D-Idopyranose pentaacetate
$J_{13} = 1.0$, $J_{24} = 0.9$

(Ref. 276)

TABLE 123 (continued)

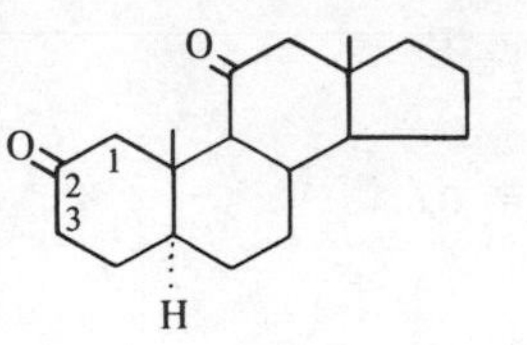

$J_{1e3e} = 2.0$

(Ref. 212)

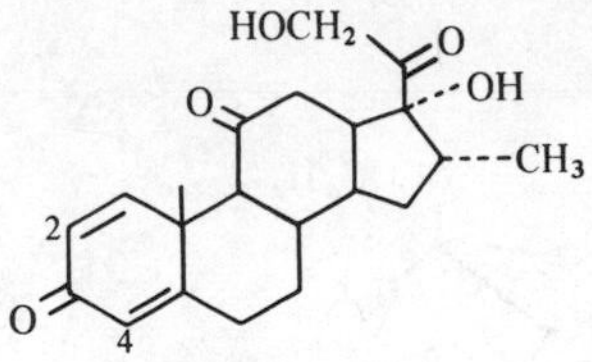

$J_{24} = 2.0$

(Ref. 212)

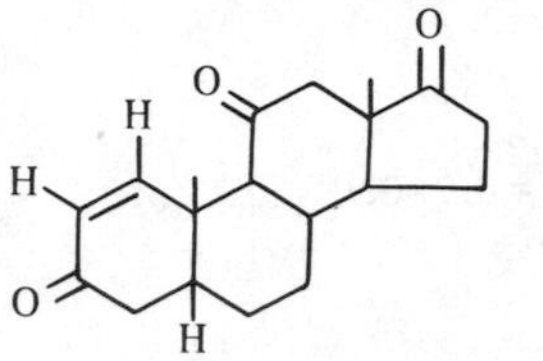

$J_{H_2H_4} = 1.5$ Hz

(Ref. 357)

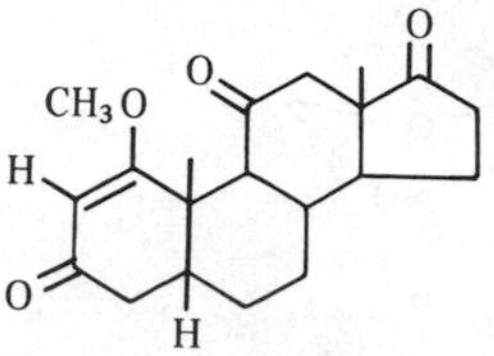

$J_{H_2H_4} = 1.5$ Hz

(Ref. 357)

	X	$^4J_{HH'}$,[a] Hz	Ref.
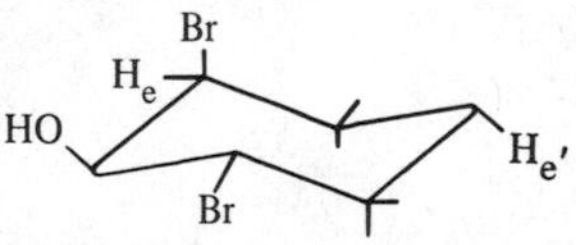	–	ee′ = 1.7	343
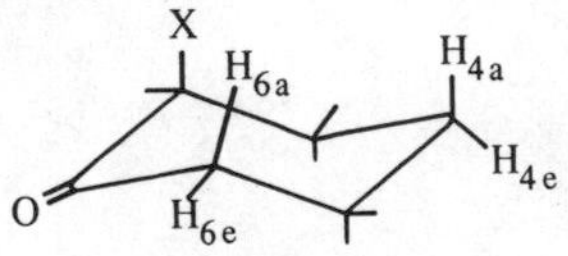	Cl Br	4e6e = 1.55 4e6e = 1.25 2e4a = 0.70 4a6a = 0.9	358
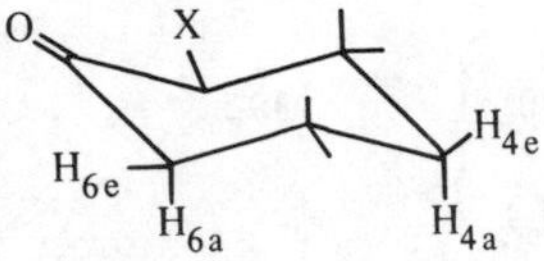	Cl Br	4a6a = 2.25 4a6e = 0.6 4a6a = 1.3	358
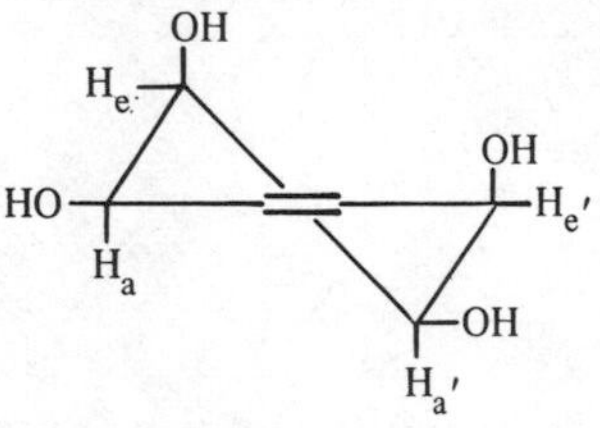	–	ee′ = 2.1 aa′ = –0.3	359
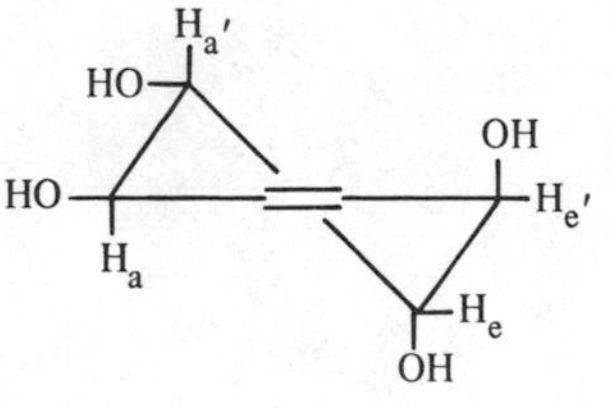	–	ea = +0.4 e′a′ = –0.8	359

TABLE 123 (continued)

	X	$^4J_{HH'}$,[a] Hz	Ref.
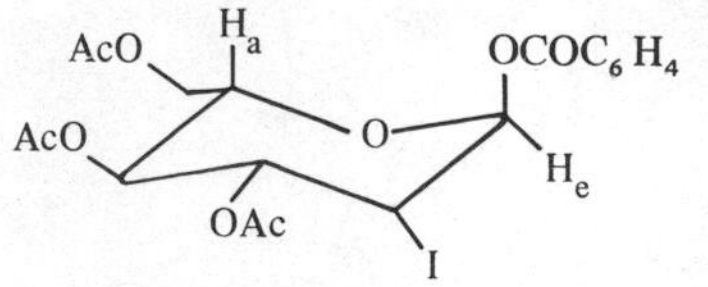	–	ae = –0.65	360
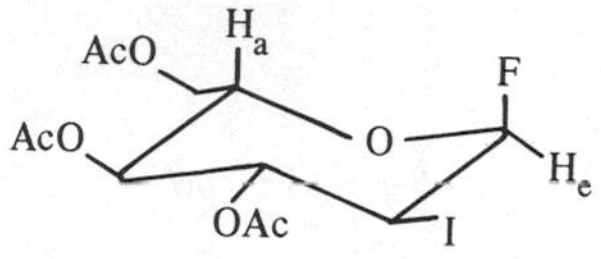	–	ae = –0.4	360
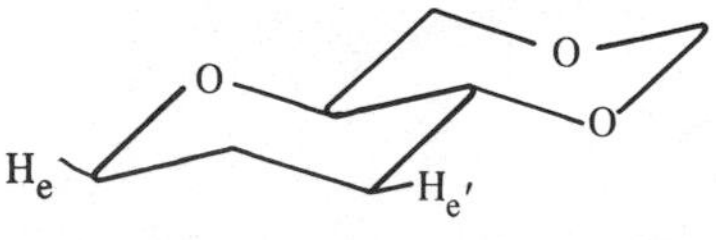	–	ee′ = 0.5–0.9	271
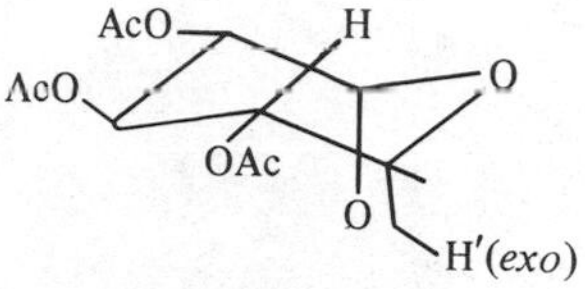	–	$J_{HH'(exo)}$ = +1.2 ($\phi \cong 180°$, $\phi' \cong 150°$)	360
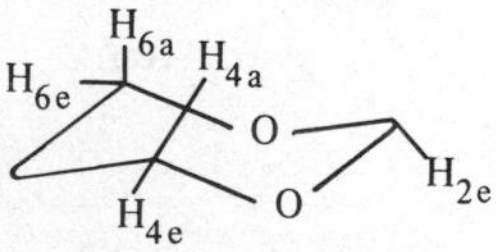	–	2e4e = 1.5, 1.0 2e6a = 0.4–0.5	379, 380
		4e6e = 2.50 4a6a = 0.3–0.4	379
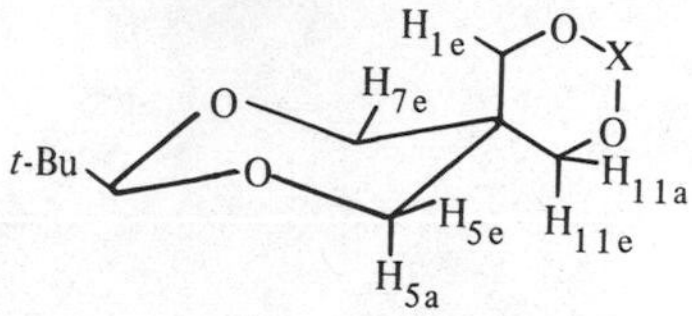	> C-*t*-Bu	1e5e = 2.5 7e11e = 2.5 5a11a = 1.90	381
	> S = O	1e5e = 2.70 7e11e = 2.25 5a11a = 1.85	381
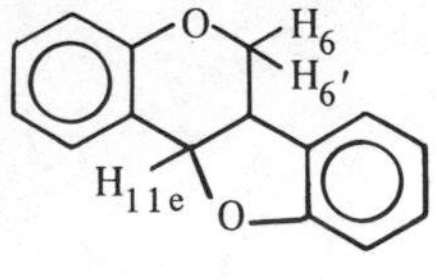	–	6,11e = +0.5–0.7 ($\phi \cong 120°$, $\phi' \cong 180°$) 6′11e = –0.7–0.9 ($\phi \cong 120°$, $\phi' \cong 60°$)	382
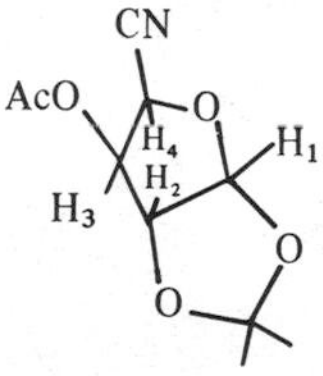	–	1,3 = –0.6 1,4 = –0.4 2,4 = –0.4	383
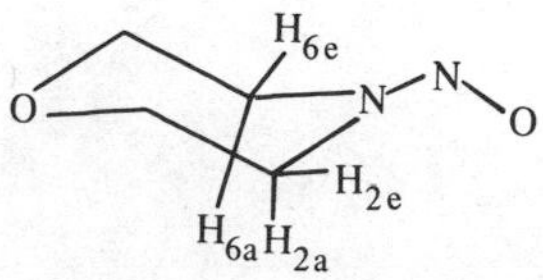	–	2e6e = 1.4 2a6a = 1.0	384
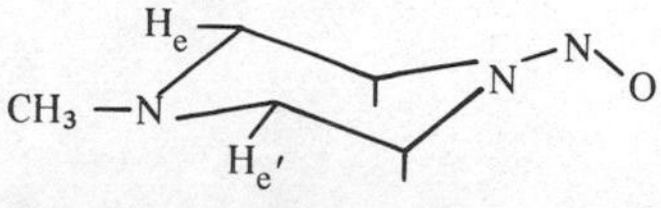	–	ee′ = 2.2	384

[a] Unless specified, signs were not determined.

TABLE 124

Coupling Across One Double and Three Single Bonds

H–X=Y–Z–H

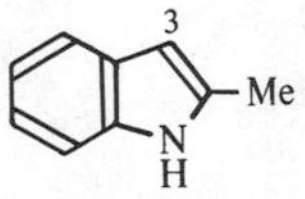

$J_{CH_3-H_3}$ = 1.0 c/s (Ref. 296)	$J_{CH_3-H_2}$ = 1.1 c/s (Ref. 296)	J_{AB} = –(?) 3.28 Hz (Ref. 278)	$J_{CH_3-H_3}$ = 0.6 c/s (Ref. 338)
$J_{CH_3-H_5}$ = 2.0 c/s (Ref. 339)	J_{CH_3-CH} = 1.5 (Ref. 315)	J_{CH_3-CH} = 1.5 (Ref. 316)	J_{CH_3-CH} = 1.6 (Ref. 318)

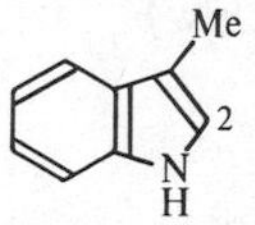

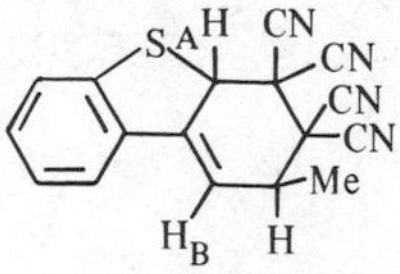

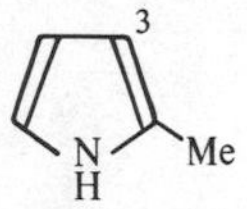

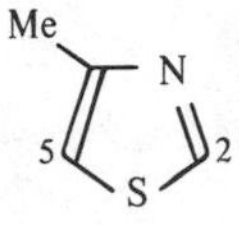

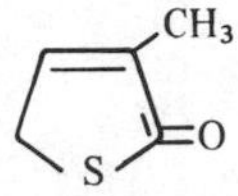

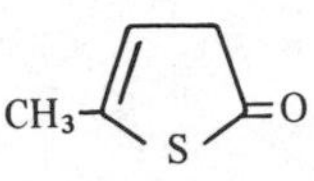

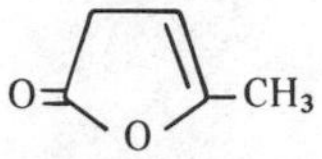

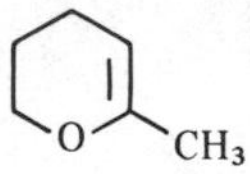

J_{CH_3-CH} = 1.1 (Ref. 318)	J_{CH_3-4} = 1.5 (Ref. 318)	J_{CH_3-2} = 1.9 (Refs. 318, 320)	J_{CH_3-3} = 0.9–1.1 (Refs. 336, 337)	J_{CH_2-3} = 0.79 (Ref. 336)

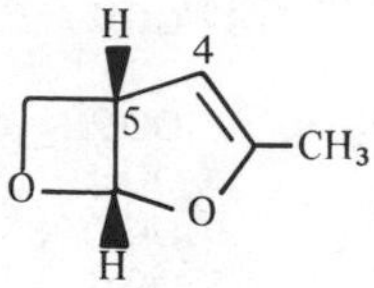

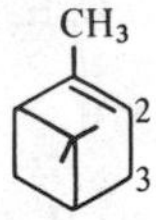

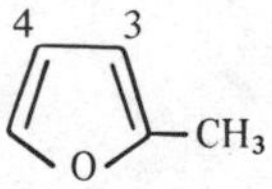

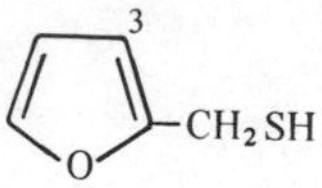

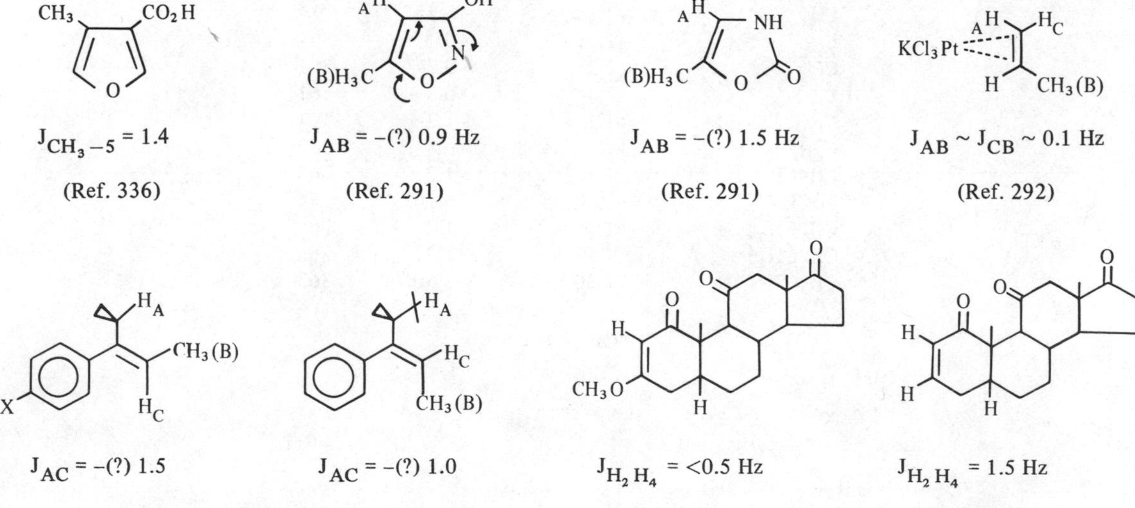

J_{CH_3-5} = 1.4 (Ref. 336)	J_{AB} = –(?) 0.9 Hz (Ref. 291)	J_{AB} = –(?) 1.5 Hz (Ref. 291)	$J_{AB} \sim J_{CB} \sim$ 0.1 Hz (Ref. 292)
J_{AC} = –(?) 1.5	J_{AC} = –(?) 1.0	$J_{H_2H_4}$ = <0.5 Hz (Ref. 357)	$J_{H_2H_4}$ = 1.5 Hz (Ref. 357)

X = H, F, CH_3, OCH_3

(Ref. 295)

(Ref. 302 and those below)

TABLE 124 (continued)

$R_2(R_3)C=C(CH_2R_1)(R_4)$

(Ref. 302 and those below)

J^{cis}, c/s	J^{trans}, c/s	R_1	R_2	R_3	R_4	Ref.
−1.7	−1.3	H	H	H	H	
−1.7	−1.3	CH_3	H	H	H	
−1.9	−1.3	CH_3	H	H	H	303
−1.5	−1.2	C_3H_7	H	H	H	
−1.8	–	H	H	C_6H_5	H	304
−1.2	–	H	H	CH_3	H	
–	−1.2	H	CH_3	H	H	
~0.4	–	Cl	H	Cl	Cl	305
−0.5	–	Cl	H	Cl	H	305
−1.2	–	Cl	H	Cl	H	306
–	−0.9	Cl	Cl	H	H	305
–	−1.2	Cl	Cl	H	H	306
−1.8	−1.7	NH_2	H	H	H	303
−1.6	–	H	H	CHO	H	
1.2	–	H	H	COOH	H	307
1.6	–	H	H	COOH	COOH	308
–	1.6	H	COOH	H	COOH	308
–	1.4	H	C_6H_5	H	H	309
1.2	–	H	H	CH_3	$COOCH_3$	310
1.3	–	H	H	CH_3	COOH	310
–	1.4	H	CH_3	H	$COOCH_3$	310
–	1.4	H	CH_3	H	COOH	310
–	0.8	Cl	Cl	H	Cl	305

$CH_2=C(X)(CH_3)$

X	$J_{CH_3-H_{cis}}$	$J_{CH_3-H_{trans}}$	Ref.
CH_3	−1.25	−1.25	14
F	−1.0	−0.4	361
Cl	−1.3	−0.7	361
Br	−1.4	−0.8	361
CN	−1.7	−1.2	134
C_6H_5	−1.5	−0.8	362
$CH=CH_2$	−1.2	−1.2	363
C≡CH	−1.60	−1.10	364
CH_2CH_3	−1.7	−1.2	365
CH_2CH_2F	−1.63	−1.27	366
$CH_2CH=CH_2$	−1.30	−1.50	363

$J_{CH_3-H_A}$

$X(H_A)C=C(CH_3)(H)$	$H_A(X)C=C(CH_3)(H)$	X	Ref.
−1.8	−1.6	F	361
−1.7	−1.7	Cl	361
−1.8	−1.6	Br	361
−1.5	−1.4	CN	134

TABLE 125

Transoid and Cisoid Allylic Coupling Constants in Rigid, Cyclic Molecules

Molecule	Dihedral Angle, ϕ deg	$^4J_{HH'}$,[a] Hz	Ref.
	A. Transoid		
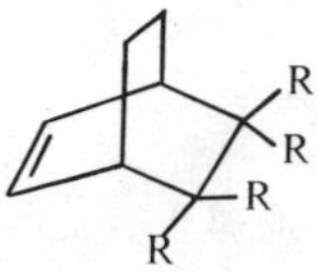 (R,R,R,R-substituted bicyclo[2.2.2]octene)	180	+1.3	367
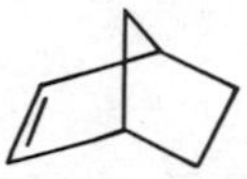 (norbornene)	160	+0.5	368
 (norbornadiene)	160	+0.95	368
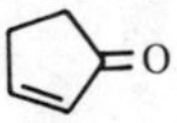 (cyclopent-2-enone)	120	2.2	367
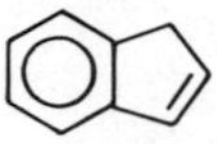 (indene)	120	−1.98	369
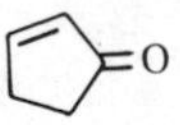 (cyclopent-3-enone)	120	−2.1	370
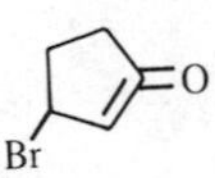 (4-bromocyclopent-2-enone) Br	120	1.3	367
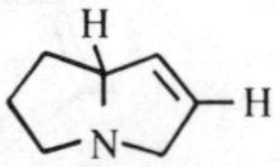 (H, N, H-substituted pyrrolizidine)	120	−1.6	371
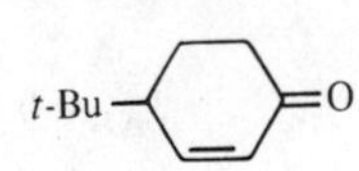 t-Bu (4-t-butylcyclohexenone) =O	100	2.3	367
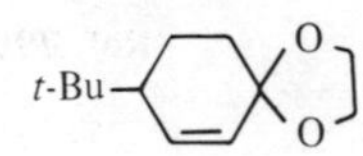 t-Bu (ketal, O, O)	100	2.1	367
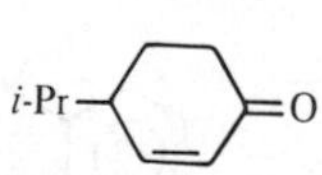 i-Pr (cyclohexenone) =O	100	2.1	367
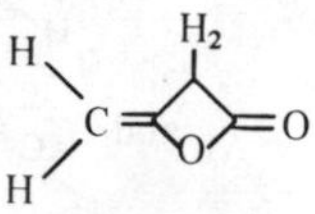 H_2C=(oxetanone, H_2, O, =O)	60	−1.94	300
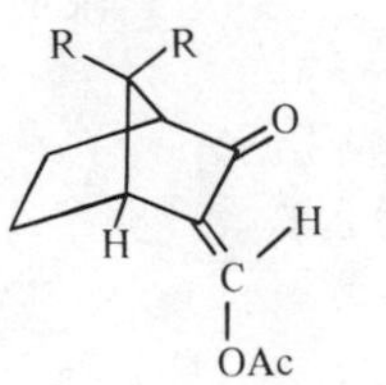 R, R, O, H, H, C, OAc (bicyclic ketone)	20	0.7–0.8	367
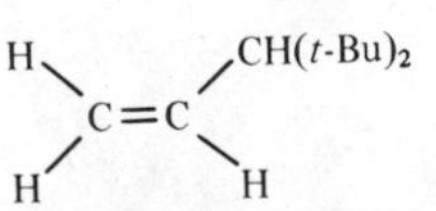 $H_2C{=}CH{-}CH(t\text{-Bu})_2$	0	−0.1	367, 372

TABLE 125 (continued)

Molecule	Dihedral Angle, ϕ deg	$^4J_{HH'}$,[a] Hz	Ref.
	0	0.4	373
	B. Cisoid		
	60	1.6–2.0	373
	60	–1.36	300
	0	–0.63	367, 372

[a]Signs are undetermined unless specified.

TABLE 126

Coupling Across Five Single Bonds

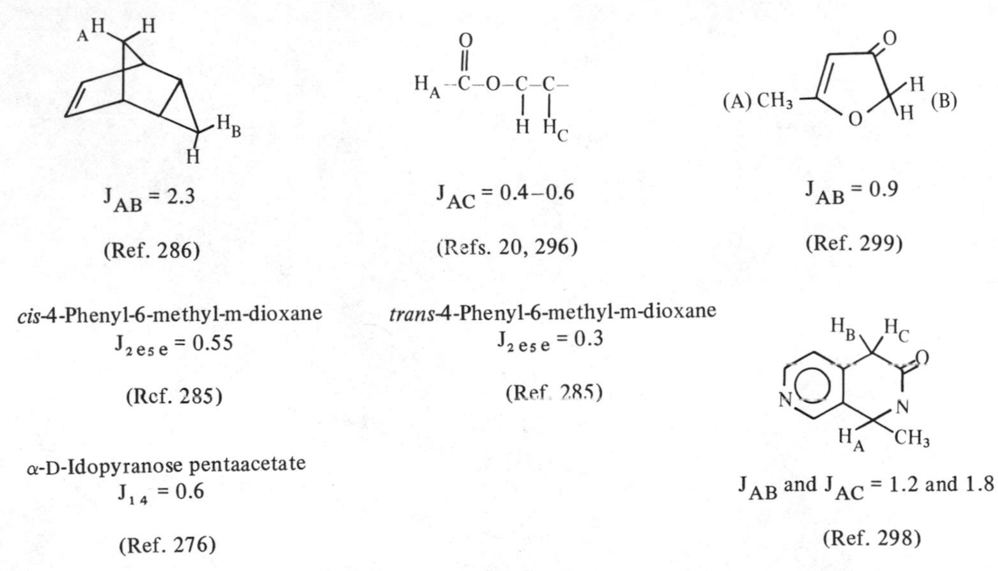

TABLE 127

Coupling Across One Double and Four Single Bonds, Allylic

H–X=Y–Z–Q–H

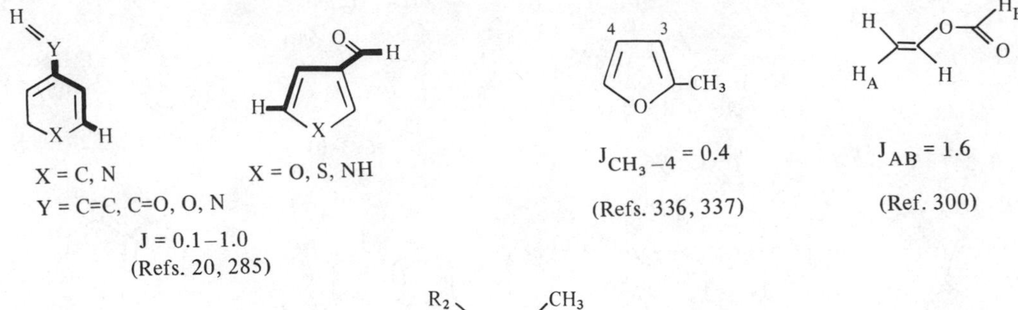

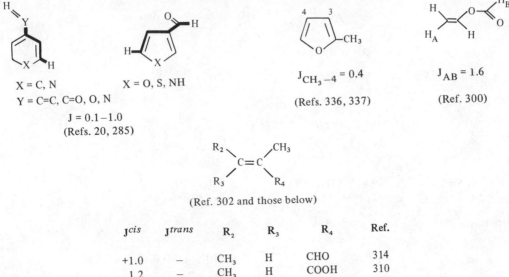

X = C, N
Y = C=C, C=O, O, N
J = 0.1–1.0
(Refs. 20, 285)

X = O, S, NH

$J_{CH_3-4} = 0.4$
(Refs. 336, 337)

$J_{AB} = 1.6$
(Ref. 300)

$R_2(R_3)C{=}C(CH_3)R_4$

(Ref. 302 and those below)

J^{cis}	J^{trans}	R_2	R_3	R_4	Ref.
+1.0	–	CH_3	H	CHO	314
1.2	–	CH_3	H	COOH	310
1.2	–	CH_3	H	$COOCH_3$	310
≈1.2	–	CH_3	H	H	
–	≈1.2	H	CH_3	H	
–	1.6	Br	CH_3	$COOCH_3$	
–	1.5	H	CH_3	COOH	310
–	1.5	H	CH_3	$COOCH_3$	310
–	1.0	C_6H_5	CH_3	$COOCH_3$	308

TABLE 128

Coupling Across One Double and Four Single Bonds, Homoallylic

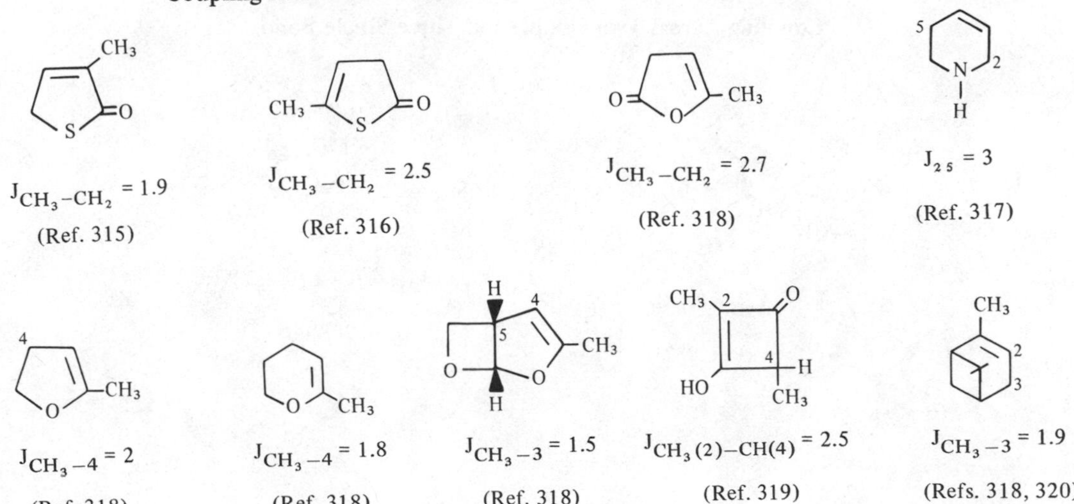

$J_{CH_3-CH_2} = 1.9$
(Ref. 315)

$J_{CH_3-CH_2} = 2.5$
(Ref. 316)

$J_{CH_3-CH_2} = 2.7$
(Ref. 318)

$J_{25} = 3$
(Ref. 317)

$J_{CH_3-4} = 2$
(Ref. 318)

$J_{CH_3-4} = 1.8$
(Ref. 318)

$J_{CH_3-3} = 1.5$
(Ref. 318)

$J_{CH_3(2)-CH(4)} = 2.5$
(Ref. 319)

$J_{CH_3-3} = 1.9$
(Refs. 318, 320)

TABLE 128 (continued)

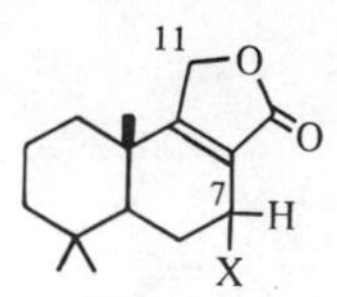

X	J_{7-11}
OH	5 c/s
H	3 c/s

(Ref. 342)

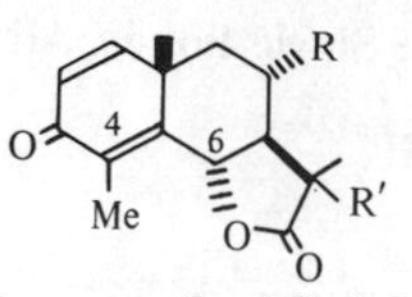

$J_{(CH_3)_4-6}$ = 1.3–1.6 c/s
R = H, –OH, –OAc
R′ = βH, –OH, –OAc

(Refs. 296, 340)

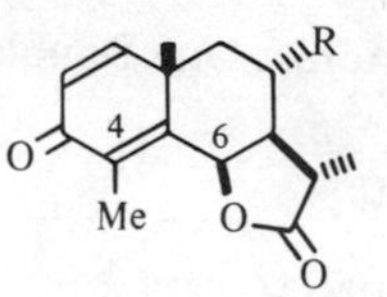

$J_{(CH_3)_4-6} \leqslant 0.5$ c/s
R = –H, –OH, –OAc

(Refs. 296, 340)

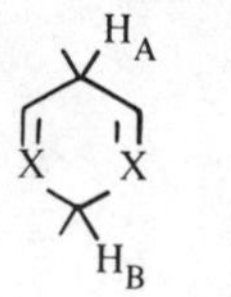

X = CH, N
J_{AB} = (+ ?) 5.5 to (+ ?) 11 Hz

(Refs. 20, 293)

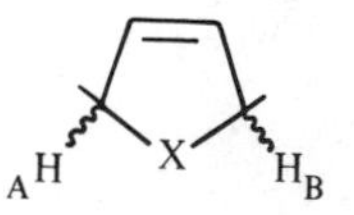

X = 0, NH
J_{AB} = 0.4–7.0 Hz

(Refs. 20, 294)

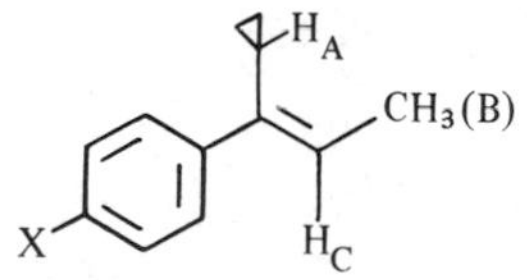

X = H, F, CH_3, OCH_3
J_{AB} = (+ ?) 1.1 Hz

(Ref. 295)

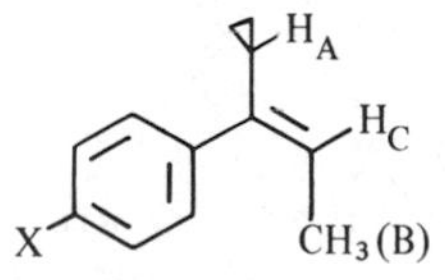

X = H, F, CH_3, OCH
J_{AB} = (+ ?) 0.8 Hz

(Ref. 295)

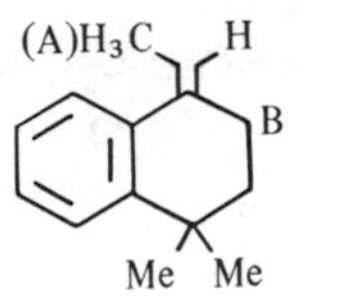

J_{AB} = (+ ?) 1.12 Hz

(Ref. 278)

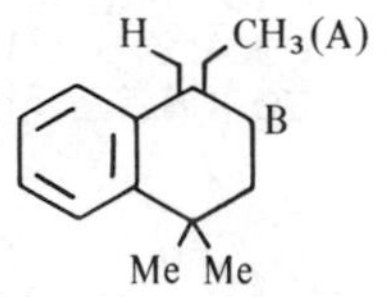

J_{AB} = (+ ?) 1.19 Hz

(Ref. 278)

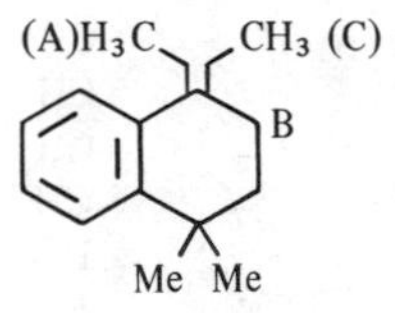

J_{AB} = (+ ?) 1.4 Hz
J_{CB} = (+ ?) 1.1 Hz

(Ref. 278)

TABLE 129

Coupling Across Two Double and Three Single Bonds

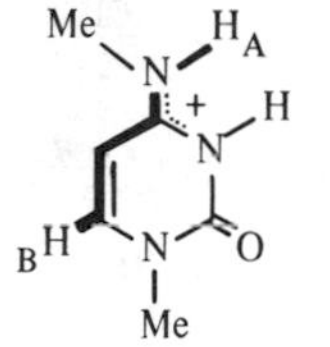

J_{AB} = 0.7 Hz

(Ref. 287)

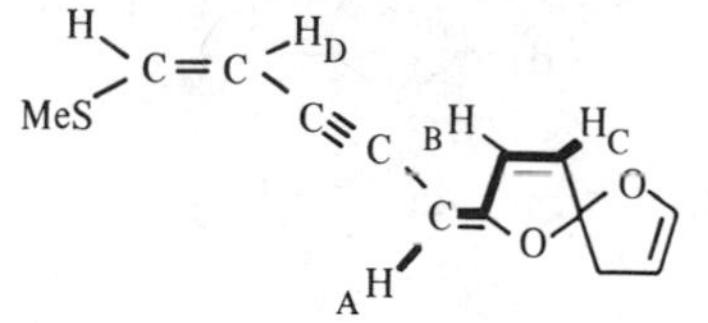

J_{AB} = 0.6, J_{AC} = 1.9, J_{AD} = 2.9 Hz

(Ref. 288)

TABLE 130

Coupling Across Two Bonds of a Benzene Ring and Three Single Bonds

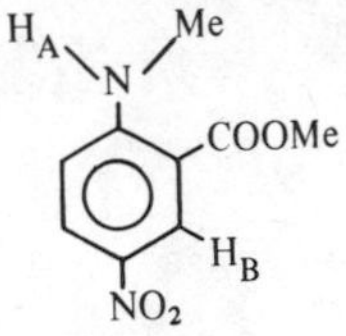

H_A, Me, N, COOMe, H_B, NO_2

$J_{AB} \cong 0.5$ Hz

(Ref. 289)

TABLE 131

Long-range Coupling Constants Coupling Across Six Single Bonds

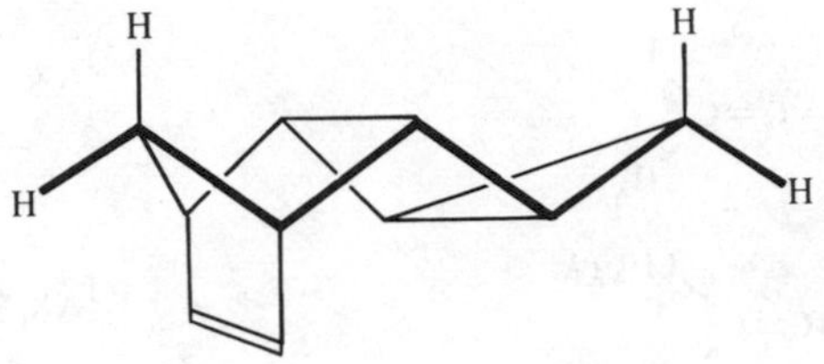

J = 1

(Ref. 385)

TABLE 132

Coupling Across One Double and Five Single Bonds

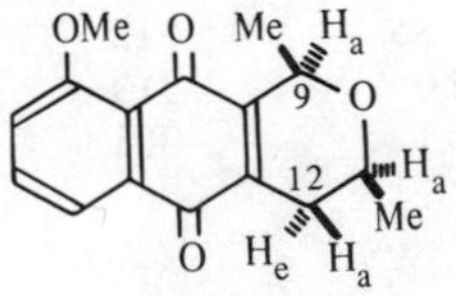

$J_{H_9a-H_{12}a} = 3.5$ c/s
$J_{H_9a-H_{12}e} = 2.9$ c/s

(Ref. 341)

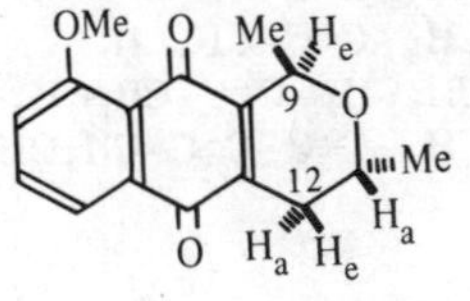

$J_{H_9e-H_{12}a} = 2.0$ c/s
$J_{H_9e-H_{12}e} < 1$ c/s

(Ref. 341)

TABLE 133

Coupling Across Two Double and Five Single Bonds

$J_{CH_3, CH_3} = ca.\ 1$

(Ref. 301)

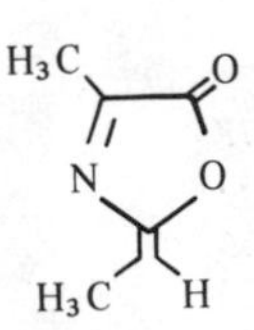

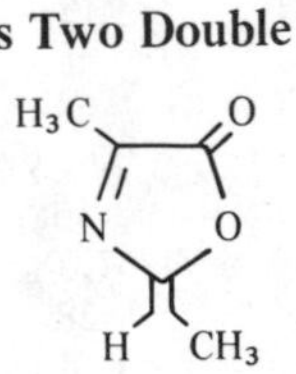

$J_{CH_3, CH_3} = ca.\ 1$

(Ref. 301)

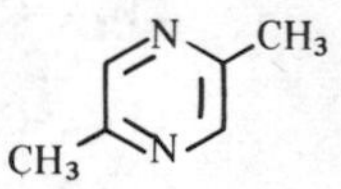

$J_{CH_3-CH_3} = 0.7$

(Ref. 386)

TABLE 134

Coupling Constants in Acetylenes, Cumulenes, and Conjugated Hydrocarbons

Structure	J(Hz)
$H_3C-C\equiv C-H$	2.93
$X-CH_2-C\equiv C-H$, X=Cl, Br, I	2.6–2.8
$H_3C-C\equiv C-CH_3$	2.7
$H-C\equiv C-C\equiv C-H$	2.2
$H_3C-C\equiv C-C\equiv C-H$	1.27
$H_3C-C\equiv C-C\equiv C-CH_3$	1.3
$H_3C-C\equiv C-C\equiv C-C\equiv C-CH_2-OH$	0.4[$J(CH_3, CH_2)$]
$R-CH=C=CH-R$	−5.8 to −6.3
$(CH_3)_2C=C=CH_2$	3.03
(cyclopentene ring, A) $=C=CH_2$ (B)$=C=CH_2$ (B)	4.58 (J_{AB})
$^{X}H^{A}$, H_B, H_A: $C=C=C=C$	$J_{AX} \neq J_{BX} \sim 1-9(?)$
^{X}H, CH_3 (A), CH_3 (B): $C=C=C=C$	$J_{AX} \neq J_{BX} \sim 1$

(Refs. 20, 290)

	J	Ref.
$H-C\equiv C-CH_2OH$	2.4	302
$H-C\equiv C-CH_2CH_3$	−2.4	311
$CH_3-C\equiv C-CH_2OH$	2.4	302
$CH_3-C\equiv C-CH_2Cl$	2.5	302
$CH_3-C\equiv C-CH_2CH_3$	2.55	312
$CH_3CH_2-C\equiv C-CH_2CH_3$	2.0	313
$CH_3-C\equiv C-C\equiv C-CH_2OH$	1.1	302

Molecule	$J_{H_AH_B}$	Ref.
$H_AC\equiv CCH_B=CH_2$	−2.17	374
trans-$CH_{2\,A}=CHCH=CH_{2\,B}$	1.30 (*trans-trans*) 0.60 (*trans-cis*) 0.69 (*cis-cis*)	375
H_A–(cyclohexa-1,4-diene)–H_B	1.11	376
$CH_{2\,A}=CHC\equiv CH_B$	0.8–0.9	374, 377
$CH\equiv CC\equiv CH$	$\|2.2\|$	378
$CH_{2\,A}=C(CH_3)C(CH_3)=CH_{2\,B}$	$\sim \|1.0\|$	363
$CH_{2\,A}=C(CH_3)C\equiv CH_B$	0.28	364
$C_2H=CHCH=CHCH_3$	$\sim \|0.6\|$	363

TABLE 135

Androstanes[212]

The Effect of Substituents on the Chemical Shift of C-18 and C-19 Protons

A star (*) indicates those cases where the shifts are based on measurements of one compound only. Solvent: Chloroform.

Type	19-H ppm	18-H ppm	Ref.
Ring A Substituents			
5-α-Steroids			
5α,14α-Androstane	,0.792	0.692	
5α,14β-Androstane	0.767	,0.992	
1-Oxo	0.375	0.017	
Δ^1*	0.050	0.017	
1α-OH*	0.017	0.017	
1β-OH*	0.050	0.008	
Δ^1-3-Oxo	0.250	0.050	
$\Delta^{1,4}$-3-Oxo	0.458	0.100	
$\Delta^{1,4,6}$-3-Oxo	0.425	0.150	
1α-Oac	0.07	0.00	246
1β-Oac	0.05	0.00	246
1α-,11α-Oxido	0.02	−0.10	249
2-Oxo	−0.025	0.008	
Δ^2*	0	0.042	
2β-OH*	0.250	0.008	
2β-OAc*	0.150	0	
2α-Cl*	0.083	0	239
2α-Br*	0.075	0	239
2β-Br*	0.233	0	239
2α-OH	0.11	0.00	246
2α-Oac	0.13	0.00	246
2α-SH	0.06	0.00	247
2α-SAc	0.12	0.00	247
2β-SH	0.28	0.00	247
2β-SAc	0.13	0.00	247
3-Oxo	0.242	0.042	
3α-OH	0	0.008	
3β-OH	0.033	0.008	
3β-OH(Δ^5)	0.008	0	
3α-OAc	0.025	0.017	
3α-OAc(Δ^4)*	−0.017	0.008	
3β-OAc	0.050	0.008	
3β-OAc(Δ^4)	0.042	0.008	
3β-OAc(Δ^5)	0.017	0	
3β-OCH_3*	0.025	0.008	
3-Ethylene ketal (Δ^5)	0.025	0.017	
Δ^4-3-Oxo	0.417	0.075	
$\Delta^{3,5}$*	0.200	0.058	
$\Delta^{3,5}$-7-Oxo*	0.367	0.075	
3α-SH	0.01	0.00	247
3α-SAc	0.03	0.00	247
3α-CN	0.02	0.00	247
3α-SCN	0.04	0.00	247

TABLE 135 (continued)

Type	19-H ppm	18-H ppm	Ref.
3α-NCS	0.02	0.01	247
3α,4α-Epoxy	−0.01	0.00	247
3α,4α-Epithio	0.03	0.00	247, 248
3β-Et	−0.03	0.00	247
3β-SH	0.02	−0.01	247
3β-SHΔ^5	0.00	0.00	247
3β-SAc	0.02	0.00	247
3β-SAcΔ^5	−0.01	0.00	247
3β-CN	0.05	0.00	247
3β-SCN	0.05	0.01	247
3β-SCNΔ^5	0.04	0.00	247
3β,4β-Epithio	0.20	−0.01	247
3α-O_2C-Ph	−0.05	0.03	249
3β-Br	−0.10	−0.04	249
3β-Cl	−0.10	0.00	249
3α,4α-CCl_2	0.07	0.00	249
3α,4α-CF_2	0.04	0.00	249
$\Delta^{1,4}$-3-Oxo	−0.46	−0.05	249
$\Delta^{1,4,6}$-3-Oxo	0.43	−0.13	249
Δ^4-3-Oxo	−0.41	−0.05	249
$\Delta^{4,6}$-3-Oxo	−0.33	−0.11	249
3α-O_2C-PH	−0.05	0.03	249
4-Oxo	−0.033	0.017	
Δ^4	0.250	0.042	
4β-OH*	0.267	0.008	
4β-OAc*	0.225	0	
4α-Br*	0.075		239
3α,4α-Epoxy	−0.01	0.00	247
3α,4α-Epithio	0.03	0.00	247, 248
3β,4β-Epithio	0.20	−0.01	247
4α-SH	0.06	0.00	247
4α-SAc	0.13	0.01	247
4β-SH	0.24	0.00	247
4β-SAc	0.08	0.00	247
4β-SCN	0.07	0.00	247
3α,4α-CCl_2	0.07	0.00	249
3α,4α-CF_2	0.04	0.00	249
4β-Cl	−0.10	0.09	249
4β-CH_3	−0.07	0.00	249
4α-CH_3	0.10	0.00	249
Δ^5*	0.233	0.042	
5α-OH*	0.058	0.008	
5α,6α-Oxido	0.250		240
5α-CH_3	0.150	0	
5α-Cl	0.250	−0.008	
5α-Br	0.317	0	239
5α-CN*	0.125	0	239
Δ^5-7-Oxo	0.392	0.042	
$\Delta^{5,7}$*	0.142	−0.025	
5α-OAc	0.20	0.00	247
5α-SH	0.25	0.01	247
5α-SAc	0.25	−0.02	247
$\Delta^{5(10)}$		−0.03	249
5α-,6α-Oxido	−0.14	0.06	249
5α-CH_3	−0.15	0.00	249
6-CH_3 (Δ^5)	−0.02	−0.01	249
5β,14α-Androstane	0.925	0.692	

TABLE 135 (continued)

Type	19-H ppm	18-H ppm	Ref.
5β,14β-Androstane	0.900	0.992	
1-Oxo*	0.217	0	
3-Oxo	0.117	0.042	
3α-OH	0.008	0.008	
3β-OH	0.050	0.008	
3α-OAc	0.025	0.008	
3β-OAc	0.058	0.008	
3β,4β-Oxido*	−0.042	0.017	
3-Ethylene ketal	0.033		240
3α-$OCOCH_2CH_2COOCH_3$	0.025	0.017	
4-Oxo	0.200	0	
4α-OH*	0.008	0.008	
5β,6β-Oxido	0.042		240
Rings B and C Substituents			
5-β-Steroids			
5α,14α-Androstane	0.792	0.692	
5β,14α-Androstane	0.925	0.692	
5α,14β-Androstane	0.767	0.992	
5β,14β-Androstane	0.900	0.992	
6-Oxo	−0.050	0.017	
Δ^6	−0.025	0.050	
6α-OH*	−0.008	0.008	241
6β-OH in 5α-Steroids	0.225	0.042	
6β-OH in 5β- and Δ^4-Steroids	0.192	0.042	
6α-OAc*	0.042	0.008	241
6β-OAc in 5α-Steroids	0.183	0.042	
6β-OAc in 5β- and Δ^1-Steroids	0.092	0.050	
6α-CH_3	0	0	
6β-CH_3	0.075	0	242
6α-F*	0.008	0	
6β-Cl	0.317	0.058	
6β-Br	0.250	0.067	239
6β-SH	0.27	0.06	247
6β-SCN	0.09	0.04	247
6β-SAc	0.09	0.03	247
6-OH,6β-CH_3	−0.18	−0.01	249
6β-CN*	0.283	0.050	239
7α-OH,6β-Cl	−0.23		249
5α-,6α-Oxido	−0.14	0.06	249
6β-,19-Oxido		−0.03	249
6α-Cl	−0.04	0.00	249
6β-F	−0.13	−0.04	249
6β-OCH_3	−0.07	0.00	249
6-CH_3 (Δ^5)	−0.02	−0.01	249
6- = CH_2	0.08	−0.01	249
6β-C_2H_5	−0.03		249
7-Oxo	0.275	0.008	
Δ^7	−0.008	−0.117	
7α-OH	−0.008	0.008	
7β-OH	0.025	0.033	
7α-OAc	0.008	0	
7β-OAc	0.042	0.042	241
$\Delta^{7,9}$*	0.092	−0.150	

TABLE 135 (continued)

Type	19-H ppm	18-H ppm	Ref.
Δ^7 & 9α,11α-Oxido	0.183	–0.083	
7,11-Dioxo & 8α,9α-Oxido*	0.408	0.058	
7α-OH,6β-Cl	–0.23		249
7α-OCH_3		0.00	249
$\Delta_8{}^{(9)}$	0.125	–0.083	
$\Delta^{8(14)}$	–0.117	0.175	
8β-OH	0.183	0.183	
8α,14α-Oxido*	0.075	0.300	243
8β,14β-Oxido*	0.100	–0.033	243
$\Delta^{8(9)}$-11-Oxo*	0.283	0.033	
Δ^8	–0.09		249
Δ^8-11-Oxo	–0.29		249
8α-,9α-Oxido	0.10		249
$\Delta^{9(11)}$	0.142	–0.067	
9α-OH	0.142	0	244
9α,11α-Oxido	0.200	0	
9β,11β-Oxido*	0.117	0.183	
9α-F*	0.133	0	
9α-Br (11-Oxo	0.133	0.025	245
$\Delta^{9(11)}$-12-Oxo*	0.267	0.267	
$\Delta^{9(11)}$-11-OH-12-Oxo*	0.300	0.308	
Δ^9-12-Oxo	–0.32		249
8α-,9α-Oxido	0.10		249
9β,11β-Oxido,12α-CH_3	–0.27	–0.27	249
9α-Cl	–0.26	0.01	249
9α-Br	–0.16	–0.04	249
10β-OII		(0.04)	246
10-CO_2H		0.03	249
10-CHO		0.04	249
11-Oxo	0.217	–0.033	
Δ^{11}	–0.033	0.083	
11α-OH	0.117	0.025	
11β-OH	0.258	0.242	
11α-OAc	0.092	0.058	
11β-OAc	0.067	0.117	
11α,12α-Oxido*	0.067	0.133	
11β,12β-Oxido	0.175	0.125	
11α-Br (12-Oxo)*	0.167	0.008	
11β-Br (12-Oxo)*	0.367	0.317	
11β-OH,12α-CH_3	–0.27	–0.35	249
11β-OH,12α-F	–0.27	–0.20	249
11-Oxo,12α-OH	–0.23	0.04	249
11α-OH,12-Oxo	–0.23	–0.37	249
11α-OAc, 12-Oxo	–0.18	–0.40	249
11-Oxo,12α-OAc	–0.28	–0.03	249
Δ^8-11-Oxo	–0.29		249
1α-,11α-Oxido	0.02	–0.10	249
9α-,11α-Oxido	–0.200		249
9β,11β-Oxido	0.117	0	
9β,11β-Oxido,12α-CH_3	–0.27	–0.27	249
11α-Br	–0.18		249
11β-Br	–0.38		249
12-Oxo	0.100	0.375	
12-Oxo & 17β-$COCH_3$*	0.092	0.250	
12-Oxo & 17β-$COOCH_3$	0.092	0.417	
12α-OH	–0.008	0.042	

TABLE 135 (continued)

Type	19-H ppm	18-H ppm	Ref.
12α-OH & 17β-$COOCH_3$	–0.017	–0.042	
12β-OH	0.008	0.067	
12α-OAc	–0.025	0.083	
12β-OAc	0	0	
12α-Br (11-Oxo)	–0.025	0.183	245
11β-OH,12α-CH_3	–0.27	–0.35	249
11β-OH,12α-F	–0.27	–0.20	249
11-Oxo,12α-OH	–0.23	0.04	249
11α-OH,12-Oxo	–0.23	–0.37	249
11α-OAc,12-Oxo	–0.18	–0.40	249
11-Oxo,12α-OAc	–0.28	–0.03	249
$Δ^9$-12-Oxo	–0.32		249
11α-,12α-Oxido	–0.07		249
11β,12β-Oxido	0.175	0.125	
9β,11β-Oxido,12α-CH_3	–0.27	–0.27	249
12α-CH_2O-12β-Oxido	–0.03	–0.27	249
12α-Br	0.02	–0.22	249
12α-CH_3	–0.03	–0.11	249
12-=CH_2	–0.04	–0.30	249
12-=CHBr	–0.07	–0.37	249
12α-CH_2Br	–0.01	–0.33	249
12α-CH_2Cl	–0.05	–0.34	249
Ring D Substituents			
14α-Steroids			
5α,14α-Androstane	0.792	0.692	
5β,14α-Androstane	0.925	0.692	
$Δ^{14}$	0.008	0.250	
14α-OH	0	0.117	
14α,15α-Oxido*	0.025	0.183	
15-Oxo*	0.008	0.075	
15α-OH	0.008	0.033	
15β-OH*	0.033	0.267	
15α-OAc	0	0.067	
15β-OAc*	0.042	0.225	
14α-,15α-Oxido	0.025	0.183	
$Δ^{16}$-17-$COCH_3$	0.017	0.175	
16β-OAc & 17α-OH & 17β-$COCH_3$*	0.008	0.242	
16β-OAc & 17α-OH & 17β-$COCH_2$OAc*	0.008	0.167	
16α,17α-Oxido	0.008	0.417	
16α-CH_3	–0.008	0.008	
16α-CH_3 & 17α-OH & 17β-$COCH_2$OAc	–0.017	0.033	
16α-OH	0.01	0.06	249
$Δ^{16}$	0.01	0.10	247
16α,17α-diOH	0.01	–0.03	249
16α-OAc	0.00	–0.04	249
16β-OAc	–0.02		249
16α,17α-Oxido	–0.01	–0.45	249
16β-Br	–0.12	–0.47	249
17-Oxo	0.017	0.167	
17α-OH & 17β-$COCH_3$	–0.008	–0.008	
17α-OH & 17β-$COCH_2$OAc	–0.008	–0.042	
17α-OH & 17β-$COOCH_3$*	–0.008	–0.017	
17β-OH	0	0.033	

TABLE 135 (continued)

Type	19-H ppm	18-H ppm	Ref.
17β-OH & 17α-CH_3	0.008	0.150	
17β-OAc	0	0.083	
17β-OAc & 17α-CH_3	0.008	0.133	
17β-C_2H_5	–0.008	–0.142	
17β-C_8H_{17}	–0.017	–0.050	
17β-C_9H_{19}*	–0.017	–0.033	
17β-C_9H_{17}	–0.008	–0.033	
17β-C_4H_8COOH	–0.008	–0.042	
17β-$C_4H_8COOCH_3$	–0.008	–0.050	
17β-$C_4H_8COOC_2H_5$*	–0.008	–0.050	
17β-CH(OH(α))CH_3*	–0.008	–0.050	
17β-CH(OH(β))CH_3	–0.008	0.042	
17β-CH(OAc(α))CH_3*	–0.008	–0.033	
17β-CH(OAc(β))CH_3	–0.008	–0.083	
17β-CH(CH_3)$COOCH_3$*	–0.008	–0.033	
17β-$COCH_3$	–0.008	–0.083	
17β-$COCH_2OH$*	–0.008	–0.058	
17β-$COCH_2OAc$*	–0.008	–0.042	
17β-COOH*	–0.008	0.025	
17β-C(OCH_2)$_2CH_3$	–0.008	0.050	
17β-C(=$NNHCONH_2$)CH_3*	0	–0.133	
17α-$COOCH_3$*	–0.017	0.158	
17β-$COOCH_3$	–0.008	–0.050	
17β-$OCOC_2H_5$	0	0.083	
17β-$OCOC_6H_5$*	0	0.225	
17β-$OCOC_6H_{11}$*	–0.008	0.083	
17β-$C_4H_5O_2$	0	–0.017	
17β-$C_4H_3O_2$*	0	–0.067	
17[= (OAc)CH_3]	0	0.100	
17α-OH	0.01	–0.05	249
17α-Me & 17β-OH	0.00	0.15	247
17α-$O_2CC_5H_{11}$	–0.01	0.03	249
17α-$O_2CC_6H_{13}$	–0.01	–0.01	249
17α-OAc	–0.01	–0.01	249
16α,17α-Oxido	–0.01	–0.45	249
17α-OCH_3		–0.10	249
17α-$COCH_3$	–0.01	–0.20	249
Ring D Substituents			
14β-Steroids			
5α,14β-Androstanc	0.767	0.992	
5β,14β-Androstane	0.900	0.992	
14β-OH	0.017	–0.025	
14β-OH & 17β-COOH*	0.025	0.108	
14β-OH & 17β-$COOCH_3$	0.025	–0.017	
14β-OH & 15-Oxo & 17β-$COOCH_3$	–0.017	0.067	
14β,15β-Oxido*	0.050	0.150	
17-Oxo	0.017	0.083	
17β-OH*	0.008	0.025	
17α-$COOCH_3$	–0.008	0.158	
17β-$COOCH_3$	–0.008	–0.067	
17β-$C_4H_5O_2$*	–0.017	–0.025	
17β-$C_4H_3O_2$*	–0.008	–0.100	

TABLE 136

D-Homo-5α-Androstanes

Solvent: CCl_4

	18-Me	19-Me
D-Homo-5α-androstane	0.81	0.77
Ketones		
17a-one	1.066	0.88
17-one	0.77	0.77
16-one	1.025	0.79
Alcohols		
17aβ-ol	0.775	0.775
17aα-ol	0.825	0.78
17β-ol	1.04	0.78
17α-ol	0.82	0.77
16β-ol	0.84	0.78
16α-ol	0.80	0.77
17-en-16α-ol	0.80	0.80
Acetates		
17aβ-OAc	0.866	0.77
17aα-OAc	0.90	0.78
17β-OAc	1.115	0.79
17α-OAc	0.88	0.76
16β-OAc	0.85	0.77
16α-OAc	0.83	0.78
17-en-16α-OAc	0.84	0.80

TABLE 137

Chemical Shifts of Cholestanes[247]

Solvent: $CHCl_3$ or $CDCl_3$

	19-H	18-H	2-H	3-H	4-H	OAc	SAc	Other H	Ref.
5α-Cholestane	0.77	0.65							
3β-Hydroxycholest-1-ene	0.91	0.66							251
3-Oxocholest-1-ene	1.01	0.76							251
3β-Acetoxycholest-1-ene	0.93	0.67							251
2β-Mercapto	1.05	0.65	3.59						
2β-Acetylthio	0.90	0.65	4.05				2.29		
2β-Hydroxy-3α-mercapto	1.00	0.65	3.97	3.24					
2β-Hydroxy-3β-mercapto	0.98	0.64	3.83	2.98					
2β-Hydroxy-3α-thiocyanato	1.02	0.65	4.19	3.75					
2β-Acetoxy-3α-acetylthio	0.92	0.64	4.95	3.87		2.05	2.32		
2β-Acetoxy-3β-acetylthio	0.90	0.63	5.11	3.78		2.03	2.28		
2β-Acetoxy-3α-thiocyanato	0.94	0.65	5.12	3.82		2.05			
2α-Mercapto-3β-hydroxy	0.86	0.64	2.71	3.21					
2β-Mercapto-3α-hydroxy	0.97	0.65	3.23	3.87					
2β-Mercapto-3α,17β-dihydroxy-17α-methyl	1.00	0.84	3.24	3.87				17-Me 2.20	
2β,3α-Dimercapto	1.02	0.65	~3.42	~3.42					
2α-Acetylthio-3β-acetoxy	0.94	0.65	3.72	4.69		2.00	2.29		
2β-Acetylthio-3α-acetoxy	0.87	0.63	3.89	4.83		2.08	2.31		
3β,3α-Diacetylthio	0.91	0.64	~3.94	~3.94			2.32		
2β-Thiocyanato-3α-hydroxy	0.85	0.66	3.75	4.19					
2β-Thiocyanato-3α-acetoxy	0.89	0.65	3.81	5.15		2.09			
2α,5-Episulfide	0.92	0.64	3.61					$H_{1\alpha}$ 1.85, $H_{1\beta}$ 1.31	252
2α,5-*syn*-Episulfoxide	2.3	1.0	3.43					$H_{1\alpha}$ 1.78, $H_{1\beta}$ 1.29	252
2α,5-*anti*-Episulfoxide	1.10	0.67	3.28					$H_{1\alpha}$ 2.84, $H_{1\beta}$ 1.79	252
2α,5-Episulfone	1.00	0.67	2.92					$H_{1\alpha}$ 2.13, $H_{1\beta}$ 1.44	252
2α,5-Oxido	0.94	0.64	4.37					$H_{1\alpha}$ 1.21, $H_{1\beta}$ 1.29	252
5-Hydroxycholest-2-ene	0.88	0.67							252

TABLE 137 (continued)

	19-H	18-H	2-H	3-H	4-H	OAc	SAc	Other H	Ref.
2α,5-Episulfide-3α-exo-hydroxy	0.85	0.65	3.45	3.93	1.26 (α), 2.53 (β)			$H_{1\alpha}$ 1.87, $H_{1\beta}$ 1.18	253
2α,5-Episulfoxide-3α-exo-hydroxy	0.95	0.65	3.63	1.26	2.21 (α), 2.60 (β)			$H_{1\alpha}$ 1.76, $H_{1\beta}$ 1.07	253
2α,5-Episulfide-3α-acetoxy	0.89	0.65	3.57	4.87	1.60 (α), 2.04 2.55 (β)			$H_{1\alpha}$ 1.87, $H_{1\beta}$ 1.30	253
2α,5-Episulfoxide-3α-acetoxy	0.97	0.64	3.66	5.09	2.49 (α), 2.05 2.49 (β)			$H_{1\alpha}$ 1.78, $H_{1\beta}$ 1.28	253
2α,5-Episulfide-3β-endo-hydroxy	1.05	0.65	3.37	4.53	2.03 (α), 2.02 (β)			$H_{1\alpha}$ 1.71, $H_{1\beta}$ 2.04	253
3α,5-Episulfoxide-3β-endo-hydroxy	1.13	0.65	3.48	4.85	2.39 (α), 1.93 (β)			$H_{1\alpha}$ 1.55, $H_{1\beta}$ 2.01	253
2α,5-Episulfide-3β-acetoxy	1.02	0.66	3.65	5.18	2.13 (α), 2.03 1.98 (β)			$H_{1\alpha}$ 1.77, $H_{1\beta}$ 1.82	253
2α,5-Episulfoxide-3β-acetoxy	1.09	0.65	3.75	5.55	2.57 (α), 2.07 2.01 (β)			$H_{1\alpha}$ 1.63, $H_{1\beta}$ 1.72	
2α,5-Episulfide-3β-endo-bromo	1.06	0.66	3.61	4.61	2.27 (α), 2.27 (β)			$H_{1\alpha}$ 1.82, $H_{1\beta}$ 2.20	253
2α,5-Episulfide-3β-endo-bromo	1.14	0.65	3.57	4.89	2.65 (α), 2.27 (β)			$H_{1\alpha}$ 1.73, $H_{1\beta}$ 2.06	253
2α,5-Episulfide-3-oxo	0.99	0.66	3.60		2.42 (α), 2.64 (β)			$H_{1\alpha}$ 2.13, $H_{1\beta}$ 1.63	253
2α,5-Episulfoxide-3-oxo	1.07	0.66	3.83		2.78 (α), 2.58 (β)			$H_{1\alpha}$ 2.09, $H_{1\beta}$ 1.55	253
3β-Ethyl	0.74	0.65							
3α-Hydroxy	0.78	0.66		4.05					
3β-Hydroxy	0.80	0.64		3.59					
3α-Acetoxy	0.79	0.66		5.03		2.06			
3β-Acetoxy	0.82	0.65		4.70		2.02			
3α-Mercapto	0.88	0.65		3.52					
3α-Acetylthio	0.80	0.65		3.00				2.30	
3α-Cyano	0.79	0.65		2.95					
3β-Cyano	0.82	0.65		2.34					
3α,4α-Oxido	0.76	0.65		3.13	2.67				
3α,4α-Epithio	0.80	0.65		3.20	2.58				
3β,4β-Epithio	0.97	0.64							
3α-Hydroxy-4α-mercapto	0.83	0.65		3.78	3.05				
3α-Hydroxy-4β-mercapto	0.97	0.64		3.95	3.09				

TABLE 137 (continued)

	19-H	18-H	2-H	3-H	4-H	OAc	SAc	Other H	Ref.
3α-Hydroxy-4β-thiocyanato	0.81	0.64		4.21	3.50				
3β-Hydroxy-4α-mercapto	0.84	0.65		3.18	2.55				
3β,5α-Dihydroxy	0.98	0.66		4.05					
3β-Hydroxy-5α-mercapto	1.05	0.65		4.33					
3β-Hydroxy-5α-cyano	0.95	0.66		4.12					
3β-Hydroxy-5α,6α-oxido	1.06	0.63		3.83					
3β-Hydroxy-5β,6β-epithio	1.15	0.64		3.81					
3β,6β-Dihydroxy	1.035	0.692							249
3β-Hydroxy-6-oxo	0.75	0.67		3.53					
3β-Hydroxy-6β-mercapto	1.05	0.71		3.64					
3α-Acetoxy-4α-acetylthio	0.93	0.65		5.05	3.76	2.05	2.27		
3α-Acetoxy-4β-acetylthio	0.85	0.65		4.83	3.73	2.07	2.30		
3α-Acetoxy-4β-thiocyanato	0.84	0.65		5.20	3.59	2.09			
3β-Acetoxy-4α-acetylthio	0.94	0.65		4.70	3.62	1.98	2.30		
3β-Acetoxy-5α-hydroxy	1.00	0.66		5.15		2.01			
3β-Acetoxy-5α-mercapto	1.06	0.65		5.46		2.02			
3β-Acetoxy-5α-acetylthio	1.07	0.63		5.30		2.00	2.27		
3β-Acetoxy-5α-chloro	1.10	0.66		5.33					
3β-Acetoxy-5β,6β-oxido	1.02	0.65		4.75		2.03			
3β-Acetoxy-5α,6α-epithio	1.20	0.61		4.94		2.00			
3β,6β-Diacetoxy	1.018	1.692							249
3β-Acetoxy-6-oxo	0.77	0.67		4.68		2.01			
3β-Acetoxy-6β-acetylthio	0.91	0.68		4.73		2.00	2.30		
3α-Thiocyanato-4β-hydroxy	1.04	0.65		3.80	3.80				
3α-Thiocyanato-4β-acetoxy	1.02	0.65		3.82	4.93	2.06			
3β,5α,6β-Trihydroxy	1.19	0.69		4.05					
3β,5α-Dihydroxy-6β-mercapto	1.26	0.71		4.03					
3β,5α-Dihydroxy-6β-thiocyanato	1.08	0.70		4.03					
3β,6β-Diacetoxy-5α-hydroxy	1.16	0.69		5.14		2.01, 2.06			
3β-Acetoxy-5α-hydroxy-6-oxo	0.82	0.65		5.10		2.00			
3β-Acetoxy-6β-acetylthio-5α-hydroxy	1.08	0.68		5.15		2.02			
3β-Acetoxy-5α-hydroxy-6β-thiocyanato	1.08	0.70		5.15		2.05			
3β,5α-Diacetoxy-6β-acetylthio	1.11	0.68		4.75		1.98, 2.09	2.31		
3β-Acetoxy-6β-hydroxy-5α-thiocyanato	1.39	0.70		5.33		2.05			
3β-Acetoxy-5α-bromo-6β-hydroxy	1.33	0.70		5.42		2.04			

TABLE 137 (continued)

	19-H	18-H	2-H	3-H	4-H	OAc	SAc	Other H	Ref.
3-Oxo	1.01	0.68							251
3β-Hydroxycholest-4-ene	1.53	0.69							251
3-Oxocholest-4-ene	1.19	0.72							251
3β-Acetoxycholest-4-ene	1.63	0.68							251
3β-Hydroxycholest-5-ene	1.01	0.67							251
3-Oxocholest-5-ene	1.18	0.72							251
3β-Acetoxycholest-5-ene	1.03	0.68							251
3-Methylene	0.86	0.66							251
3β-Hydroxycholest-6-ene	0.79	0.69							251
3-Oxocholest-6-ene	0.98	0.73							251
3β-Acetoxycholest-6-ene	0.80	0.69							251
3β-Hydroxycholest-7-ene	0.80	0.54							251
3-Oxocholest-7-ene	1.02	0.56							251
3-Acetoxycholest-7-ene	0.82	0.54							251
3β-Hydroxy-6-methylene	0.69	0.65							251
3-Oxo-6-methylene	0.90	0.68							251
3β-Hydroxy-7-methylene	0.94	0.69							251
3-Oxo-7-methylene	1.12	0.71							251
3β-Acetoxy-7-methylene	0.95	0.61							251
3-Oxo-cholest-8-ene	1.14	0.64							251
3β-Acetoxycholest-8-ene	0.97	0.61							251
3β-Hydroxycholest-8(14)-ene	0.70	0.86							251
3-Oxocholest-8(14)-ene	0.91	0.88							251
3β-Acetoxycholest-8(14)-ene	0.71	0.86							251
4β-Acetylthio	0.84	0.65			3.8		2.25		250
4β-Mercapto-5α-hydroxy	1.19	0.65			3.03				
4β-Acetylthio-5α-hydroxy	1.03	0.65			3.67		2.32		
4β-Thiocyanato-5α-hydroxy	1.02	0.65			3.48				
Δ^4	1.08	0.68							251
Δ^5	1.00	0.68						6-H 5.25	
3β-Hydroxycholest-5-ene	1.02	0.68		3.50				6-H 5.34	
3β-Acetoxycholest-5-ene	1.02	0.68		4.59		2.02		6-H 5.34	
3β-Mercaptocholest-5-ene	1.00	0.67		2.58				6-H 5.30	
3β-Acetylthiocholest-5-ene	0.98	0.67		3.30			2.27	6-H 5.34	
3β-Thiocyanatocholest-5-ene	1.04	0.68		3.03				6-H 5.40	
Cholesta-3,5-diene-7-one	1.10	0.70		6.15	6.08			6-H 5.58	252
Cholest-7-ene	0.77	0.54							251
Cholest-8(14)-ene	0.66	0.86							251

TABLE 138

Sapogenins[254]

List of Compounds

No.	Compound	Ref.
1	5α,25D-Spirostane	
2	5α,25D-Spirostan-2-one	
3	5α,25D-Spirost-2-ene	
4	5α,25D-Spirostan-3-one	
5	3α-Hydroxy-5α,25D-spirostane	
6	3β-Hydroxy-5α,25D-spirostane (Tigogenin)	
7	3β-Hydroxy-5α,25L-spirostane (Neotigogenin)	255
8	3α-Acetoxy-5α,25D-spirostane	
9	3β-Acetoxy-5α,25D-spirostane (Tigogenin acetate)	
10	3β-Acetoxy-5α,25L-spirostane (Neotigogenin acetate)	255
11	1α,3β-Diacetoxy-5α,25D-spirostane	
12	5α,25D-Spirost-2-en-11-one	
13	11α-Hydroxy-5α,25D-spirost-2-ene	
14	2α,3β-Dihydroxy-5α,25D-spirostane (Gitogenin)	
15	2α,3β-Dihydroxy-5α,25L-spirostane (Neogitogenin)	
16	2α,3β-Diacetoxy-5α,25D-spirostane (Gitogenin diacetate)	
17	2α,3β-Diacetoxy-5α,25L-spirostane (Neogitogenin diacetate)	
18	2α,3α-Epoxy-11α-hydroxy-5α,25D-spirostane	
19	25D-Spirost-4-en-3-one	
20	5α,25D-Spirostane-3,7-dione	
21	5α,25D-Spirostane-3,11-dione	
22	3α-Hydroxy-5α,25D-spirostan-11-one	
23	3β-Hydroxy-25D-spirost-4-ene	
24	3β-Hydroxy-25D-spirost-5-ene (Diosgenin)	
25	3β-Hydroxyspirost-5,25(27)-diene	
26	3β,27-Dihydroxy-25D-spirost-5-ene (Isonarthogenin)	
27	3β-Hydroxy-5α,25D-spirostan-6-one (Laxogenin)	
28	3β,6α-Dihydroxy-5α,25D-spirostane (Chlorogenin)	
29	3β,6β-Dihydroxy-5α,25D-spirostane (β-Chlorogenin)	
30	3β-Hydroxy-5α,25D-spirost-9(11)-ene	
31	3β-Hydroxy-5α,25D-spirostan-11-one	
32	3β,11β-Dihydroxy-5α,25D-spirostane	
33	11β-Acetoxy-3β-hydroxy-5α,25D-spirostane	
34	3β-Hydroxy-5α,25D-spirostan-12-one (Hecogenin)	
35	3β,12α-Dihydroxy-5α,25D-spirostane	
36	3β,12β-Dihydroxy-5α,25D-spirostane	
37	3α-Acetoxy-11β-hydroxy-5α,25D-spirostane	
38	3β-Acetoxy-25D-spirost-4-ene	
39	3β-Acetoxy-25D-spirost-5-ene (Diosgenin acetate)	
40	3β,27-Diacetoxy-25D-spirost-5-ene (Isonarthogenin diacetate)	
41	3β-Acetoxy-5α,25D-spirost-9(11)-ene	
42	3β-Acetoxy-5α,25D-spirostan-11-one	
43	3β-Acetoxy-23α-bromo-5α,25D-spirostan-11-one	
44	3β-Acetoxy-23β-bromo-5α,25D-spirostan-11-one	
45	3β-Acetoxy-11β-hydroxy-5α,25D-spirostane	
46	3β-Acetoxy-5α,25D-spirostan-12-one (Hecogenin acetate)	
47	3β-Acetoxy-5α,25L-spirostan-12-one (Sisalogenin acetate)	255
48	3β,12α-Diacetoxy-5α,25D-spirostane	
49	3β,12β-Diacetoxy-5α,25D-spirostane	
50	25D-Spirost-1,4-dien-3-one	
51	1β,3β-Diacetoxy-25D-spirost-5-ene (Ruscogenin diacetate)	

TABLE 138 (continued)

No.	Compound	Ref.
52	2α,3α-Dihydroxy-5α,25D-spirostan-11-one	
53	2α,3β-Dihydroxy-5α,25D-spirostan-12-one (Manogenin)	
54	2α,3β-Diacetoxy-5α,25D-spirostan-12-one (Manogenin diacetate)	
55	25D-Spirost-4,6-dien-3-one	
56	6α-Methyl-25D-spirost-4-en-3-one	
57	7α-Hydroxy-25D-spirost-4-en-3-one	
58	3β,4α,5α-Trihydroxy-5α,25D-spirostane	
59	3β-Hydroxy-25D-spirost-5-en-12-one (Gentrogenin)	
60	3β,12α-Dihydroxy-25D-spirost-5-ene (Heloniogenin)	
61	3β,17α-Dihydroxy-25D-spirost-5-ene (Pennogenin)	
62	3β-Hydroxy-5α,25D-spirost-9(11)-en-12-one	
63	3β-Acetoxy-7α-hydroxy-25D-spirost-5-ene	
64	3β-Acetoxy-8β-cyano-5α,25D-spirostan-11-one	
65	3β-Acetoxy-5α,25D-spirost-9(11)-en-12-one	
66	25D-Spirost-1,4-diene-3,11-dione	
67	1α,2α-Dihydroxy-25D-spirost-4-en-3-one	
68	1β,2β-Dihydroxy-25D-spirost-4-en-3-one	
69	1α,2α-Diacetoxy-25D-spirost-4-en-3-one	
70	1β,2β-Diacetoxy-25D-spirost-4-en-3-one	
71	2α,3β-Dihydroxy-5α,25D-spirost-9(11)-en-12-one	
72	2α,3β-Diacetoxy-5α,25D-spirost-9(11)-en-12-one	
73	5β,25D-Spirostane	
74	5β,25D-Spirostan-2-one	
75	5β,25D-Spirost-2-one	
76	2α-Acetoxy-5β,25D-spirostane	
77	2β-Acetoxy-5β,25D-spirostane	
78	3α-Hydroxy-5β,25D-spirostane	
79	3β-Hydroxy-5β,25D-spirostane (Smilagenin)	
80	3β-Hydroxy-5β,25L-spirostane (Sarsasapogenin)	
81	3β-Acetoxy-5β,25D-spirostane (Smilagenin acetate)	
82	3β-Acetoxy-5β,25L-spirostane (Sarsasapogenin acetate)	255
83	5β,25D-Spirostan-7-one	
84	7α-Hydroxy-5β,25D-spirostane	
85	7α-Acetoxy-5β,25D-spirostane	
86	7β-Acetoxy-5β,25D-spirostane	
87	5β,25D-Spirostan-11-one	
88	11α-Hydroxy-5β,25D-spirostane	
89	11α-Acetoxy-5β,25D-spirostane	
90	1β,3β-Dihydroxy-5β,25L-spirostane (Rhodeasapogenin)	
91	1β,3β-Dihydroxy-5β-spirost-25(26)-ene	
92	1β,3β-Dihydroxy-5β-spirost-25(27)-ene (Convallamarogenin)	
93	1β,3β,25β-Trihydroxy-5β-25D-spirostane (Isoreineckiagenin)	
94	1β,3β,25α-Trihydroxy-5β,25L-spirostane (Reineckiagenin)	
95	1β,3β,27-Trihydroxy-5β,25D-spirostane (Isocarneagenin)	
96	3β-Acetoxy-1β-hydroxy-5β,25L-spirostane (Rhodeasapogenin 3-acetate)	
97	1β,3β-Diacetoxy-5β,25D-spirostane (Isorhodeasapogenin diacetate)	
98	1β,3β-Diacetoxy-5β,25L-spirostane (Rhodeasapogenin diacetate)	
99	1β,3β-Diacetoxy-5β-spirost-24-ene	
100	1β,3β-Diacetoxy-5β-spirost-25(27)-ene (Convallamarogenin diacetate)	
101	1β,3β-Diacetoxy-25β-hydroxy-5β,25D-spirostane (Isoreineckiagenin diacetate)	
102	1β,3β-Diacetoxy-25α-hydroxy-5β,25L-spirostane (Reineckiagenin diacetate)	
103	5β,25D-Spirost-2-en-11-one	
104	11β-Hydroxy-5β,25D-spirost-2-ene	
105	11α-Acetoxy-5β,25D-spirost-2-ene	
106	2α-Hydroxy-5β,25D-spirostan-11-one	
107	2α,11β-Dihydroxy-5β,25D-spirostane	

TABLE 138 (continued)

No.	Compound	Ref.
108	2β,3α-Dihydroxy-5β,25D-spirostane (Yonogenin)	
109	2β,3β-Dihydroxy-5β,25L-spirostane (Markogenin)	255
110	2β-Hydroxy-5β,25D-spirostan-11-one	
111	2β,11α-Dihydroxy-5β,25D-spirostane	
112	2β,11β-Dihydroxy-5β,25D-spirostane	
113	2α,3β-Diacetoxy-5β,25D-spirostane	
114	11β-Hydroxy-2α-acetoxy-5β,25D-spirostane	
115	2α-Acetoxy-5β,25D-spirostan-11-one	
116	2β,3α-Diacetoxy-5β,25D-spirostane (Yonogenin diacetate)	
117	2β,3β-Diacetoxy-5β,25D-spirostane (Samogenin diacetate)	
118	2β-Acetoxy-5β,25 D-spirostan-11-one	
119	5β,25D-Spirostane-3,7-dione	
120	7α-Hydroxy-5β,25D-spirostan-3-one	
121	3α-Acetoxy-11β-hydroxy-5β,25D-spirostane	
122	3β,11α-Dihydroxy-5β,25L-spirostane (Neonogiragenin)	
123	3β-Acetoxy-7β-hydroxy-5β,25D-spirostane	
124	3β,11α-Diacetoxy-5β,25D-spirostane (Nogiragenin diacetate)	
125	3β,11α-Diacetoxy-5β,25L-spirostane (Neonogiragenin diacetate)	
126	2β,3α-Diacetoxy-5β,25D-spirostan-1-one	
127	1α,2β,3α-Trihydroxy-5β,25D-spirostane	
128	1β,2β,3α-Trihydroxy-5β,25D-spirostane (Tokorogenin)	
129	3α-Acetoxy-1β,2β-dihydroxy-5β,25D-spirostane (Tokorogenin 3-acetate)	
130	2β-Acetoxy-1β,3α-dihydroxy-5β,25D-spirostane (Tokorogenin 2-acetate)	
131	2β,3α-Diacetoxy-1β-hydroxy-5β,25D-spirostane (Tokorogenin 2,3-diacetate)	
132	1α,2β,3α-Triacetoxy-5β,25D-spirostane	
133	1β,3α-Diacetoxy-2β-hydroxy-5β,25D-spirostane (Tokorogenin 1,3 diacetate)	
134	1β,2β,3α-Triacetoxy-5β,25D-spirostane (Tokorogenin triacetate)	
135	2α,3α-Dihydroxy 5β,25D-spirostan-11-one	
136	2α,3α,11α-Trihydroxy-5β,25D-spirostane	
137	2β,3β-Dihydroxy-5β,25D-spirost-9(11)-ene	
138	2β,3β-Dihydroxy-5β,25D-spirostan-11-one	
139	2β,3β,11α-Trihydroxy-5β,25D-spirostane (Metagenin)	
140	2β,3β-Dihydroxy-5β,25D-spirostan-12-one (Mexogenin)	
141	2α,3α-Diacetoxy-5β,25D-spirostan-11-one	
142	2β,3β-Diacetoxy-5β,25D-spirost-9(11)-ene	
143	2β,3β-Diacetoxy-5β,25D-spirostan-11-one	
144	2β,3β-Diacetoxy-11α-hydroxy-5β,25D-spirostane (Metagenin 2,3-diacetate)	
145	2β,3β,11α-Triacetoxy-5β,25D-spirostane (Metagenin triacetate)	
146	2β,3α-Diacetoxy-5β,25D-spirostan-1-one	
147	3β,4β-Diacetoxy-5β-hydroxy-5β,25D-spirostan-1-one	
148	1α,2β,3α,5β-Tetrahydroxy-5β,25D-spirostane	
149	1β,2β,3α,5β,-Tetrahydroxy-5β,25D-spirostane (Kogagenin)	
150	1β,3β,4β,5β-Tetrahydroxy-5β,25D-spirostane (Kitigenin)	
151	2β,3α-Diacetoxy-1β,5β-dihydroxy-5β,25D-spirostane (Kogagenin 2,3-diacetate)	
152	3β,4β-Diacetoxy-1β,5β-dihydroxy-5β,25D-spirostane (Kitigenin 3,4-diacetate)	
153	1α,2β,3α-Triacetoxy-5β-hydroxy-5β,25D-spirostane	
154	1β,2β,3α-Triacetoxy-5β-hydroxy-5β,25D-spirostane (Kogagenin triacetate)	
155	1β,3β,4β-Triacetoxy-5β,25D-spirostane (Kitigenin triacetate)	
156	5α,22α-Spirostan-3-one	251
157	5α,22α-Spirost-9(11)-en-3-one	251
158	5α,22α-Spirost-11-en-3-one	251
159	11-Methylene-5α,22α-spirostan-3-one	251
160	Spirostan-1,4,6-triene-3-one	257
161	2β,3β-Diacetoxy-5β-25L-spirostane (Markogenin diacetate)	257
162	3β,12α-Dihydroxy-5α,21α,25D-spirost-9(11)-en	258
163	3β,12β-Dihydroxy-5α,21α,25D-spirost-9(11)-en	258

TABLE 138 (continued)

No.	Compound	Ref.
164	3β-Acetoxy-12α-hydroxy-5α,21α,25D-spirost-9(11)-en	258
165	3β-Acetoxy-12β-hydroxy-5α,21α,25D-spirost-9(11)-en	258
166	3β-Hydroxy-12α-methoxy-5α,21α,25D-spirost-9(11)-en	258
167	3β-Hydroxy-12β-methoxy-5α,21α,25D-spirost-9(11)-en	258
168	3β-Hydroxy-12β-ethoxy-5α,21α,25D-spirost-9(11)-en	258
169	3β-Acetoxy-12α-ethoxy-5α,21α,25D-spirost-9(11)-en	258
170	3β-Acetoxy-12β-ethoxy-5α,21α,25D-spirost-9(11)-en	258
171	3β-Hydroxy-12α-chloro-5α,21α,25D-spirost-9(11)-en	258
172	3β-Hydroxy-12β-chloro-5α,21α,25D-spirost-9(11)-en	258
173	3β-Acetoxy-12α-chloro-5α,21α,25D-spirost-9(11)-en	258
174	3β-Acetoxy-12β-chloro-5α,21α,25D-spirost-9(11)-en	258
175	3β-Acetoxy-12α-bromo-5α,21α,25D-spirost-9(11)-en	258
176	3β-Acetoxy-12β-bromo-5α,21α,25D-spirost-9(11)-en	258

TABLE 139

Sapogenins

Chemical Shifts

δ

Compound No.	19-H	18-H	21-H	27-H
1	0.79	0.77	0.96	0.79
2	0.77	0.77	0.95	0.79
3	0.77	0.77	0.96	0.80
4	1.02	0.78	0.96	0.78
5	0.80	0.77	0.97	0.80
6	0.83	0.78	0.96	0.78
7	0.82	0.75	–	–
8	0.80	0.77	0.96	0.79
9	0.83	0.77	0.96	0.78
10	0.82	0.75	1.09	0.98
11	0.89	0.75	0.95	0.78
12	0.99	0.73	0.95	0.79
13	0.90	0.78	0.95	0.78
14	0.87	0.77	0.96	0.79
15	0.87	0.77	1.10	0.98
16	0.93	0.76	0.95	0.78
17	0.93	0.76	1.10	0.97
18	0.92	0.77	0.96	0.79
19	1.20	0.83	0.98	0.78
20	1.30	0.80	0.98	0.78
21	1.23	0.74	0.95	0.79
22	1.01	0.71	0.94	0.80
23	1.08	0.80	0.97	0.78
24	1.03	0.79	0.97	0.78
25	1.03	0.80	0.97	–
26	1.03	0.80	0.98	–
27	0.78	0.78	0.98	0.78
28	0.83	0.76	0.97	0.78
29	1.05	0.80	0.97	0.78
30	0.95	0.71	0.96	0.79
31	1.06	0.72	0.95	0.79
32	1.06	1.00	0.95	0.78

TABLE 139 (continued)

Compound No.	19-H	18-H	21-H	27-H
	δ			
33	0.93	0.82	0.95	0.78
34	0.91	1.05	1.04	0.78
35	0.81	0.83	0.98	0.79
36	0.82	0.75	1.00	0.79
37	0.05	1.01	0.97	0.79
38	1.07	0.79	0.96	0.78
39	1.03	0.79	0.97	0.78
40	1.04	0.79	0.97	–
41	0.97	0.70	0.96	0.79
42	1.05	0.92	0.95	0.79
43	1.05	0.82	0.92	0.80
44	1.05	0.75	1.17	0.83
45	1.08	1.00	0.96	0.78
46	0.92	1.04	1.06	0.79
47	0.92	1.05	1.00	0.90
48	0.84	0.84	0.92	0.78
49	0.86	0.86	1.08	0.78
50	1.25	0.85	0.97	0.79
51	1.17	0.78	0.96	0.78
52	1.04	0.72	0.95	0.79
53	0.95	1.05	1.06	0.79
54	1.00	1.03	1.05	0.79
55	1.13	0.88	0.98	0.81
56	1.20	0.83	0.97	0.79
57	1.20	0.83	0.98	0.79
58	1.00	0.77	–	–
59	1.11	1.09	1.06	0.78
60	1.02	0.83	0.97	0.78
61	1.03	0.83	0.90	0.79
62	1.08	0.93	1.10	0.79
63	1.02	0.78	0.98	0.79
64	1.42	1.11	0.95	0.79
65	1.09	0.93	1.10	0.79
66	1.46	0.81	0.96	0.79
67	1.30	0.83	0.98	–
68	1.34	0.83	0.97	0.78
69	1.42	0.81	0.95	–
70	1.18	0.83	0.97	0.77
71	1.11	0.93	1.10	0.79
72	1.18	0.93	1.08	0.78
73	0.92	0.76	0.96	0.79
74	1.08	0.75	0.95	0.78
75	0.98	0.76	0.94	0.79
76	0.93	0.77	0.97	0.79
77	0.98	0.75	0.97	0.79
78	0.93	0.76	0.97	0.79
79	0.98	0.76	0.97	0.79
80	0.98	0.77	0.99	1.07
81	0.98	0.77	0.97	0.79
82	0.98	0.77	1.08	0.98
83	1.20	0.77	0.97	0.80
84	0.93	0.78	0.97	0.79
85	0.93	0.77	0.97	0.79

TABLE 139 (continued)

Compound No.	19-H	18-H	21-H	27-H
		δ		
86	0.98	0.79	0.97	0.79
87	1.15	0.72	0.94	0.77
88	1.07	0.77	0.97	0.80
89	1.03	0.82	1.05	0.77
90	1.14	0.78	–	–
91	1.12	0.78	0.97	1.55
92	1.13	0.78	0.96	–
93	1.13	0.77	1.00	1.12
94	1.13	0.77	0.97	1.28
95	1.13	0.77	0.98	–
96	1.14	0.78	1.08	0.97
97	1.02	0.77	0.95	0.78
98	1.02	0.77	1.08	0.77
99	1.02	0.78	0.96	1.58
100	1.02	0.78	0.96	–
101	1.02	0.76	1.00	1.10
102	1.02	0.77	0.97	1.30
103	1.21	0.71	0.94	0.79
104	1.21	0.99	0.97	0.79
105	1.08	0.83	0.93	0.77
106	1.15	0.71	0.93	0.79
107	1.18	1.00	0.97	0.79
108	0.97	0.74	0.95	0.78
109	0.98	0.75	–	–
110	1.20	0.71	0.93	0.79
111	1.07	0.77	0.97	0.79
112	1.23	0.99	0.97	0.79
113	0.99	0.76	0.97	0.79
114	1.18	1.00	0.97	0.78
115	1.18	0.72	0.93	0.79
116	0.98	0.75	0.97	0.79
117	1.05	0.77	0.97	0.79
118	1.22	0.71	0.95	0.78
119	1.32	0.80	0.98	0.79
120	1.03	0.82	0.98	0.81
121	1.19	0.99	0.97	0.79
122	1.10	0.77	1.06	0.99
123	1.02	0.79	0.97	0.80
124	1.09	0.82	0.95	0.78
125	1.09	0.83	1.08	0.99
126	1.18	0.75	0.95	0.79
127	1.17	0.77	0.97	–
128	1.12	0.77	0.96	0.78
129	1.14	0.78	0.97	0.79
130	1.10	0.76	0.96	0.78
131	1.12	0.77	0.96	0.79
132	1.03	0.77	0.97	0.78
133	0.96	0.76	0.95	0.78
134	0.96	0.77	0.95	0.79
135	1.14	0.71	0.95	0.79
136	1.06	0.75	0.97	0.79
137	1.12	0.70	0.96	0.78
138	1.23	0.72	0.95	0.79
139	1.11	0.76	0.97	0.79

TABLE 139 (continued)

Compound No.	19-H	18-H	21-H	27-H
		δ		
140	1.07	1.04	1.06	0.78
141	1.17	0.72	0.95	0.80
142	1.17	0.69	0.98	0.79
143	1.27	0.72	0.95	0.79
144	1.16	0.78	0.97	0.78
145	1.13	0.81	0.93	0.78
146	1.17	0.75	0.97	0.79
147	1.22	0.75	0.95	0.78
148	1.62	0.92	1.13	0.70 in pyridine
149	1.50	0.84	1.13	0.71 in pyridine
150	1.30	0.77	–	–
151	1.23	0.77	0.95	0.78
152	1.30	0.78	0.97	0.78
153	1.01	0.76	0.95	0.78
154	1.03	0.77	0.96	0.79
155	1.16	0.78	0.96	0.78
156	1.03	0.80	–	–
157	1.17	0.76	–	–
158	0.98	0.85	–	–
159	1.26	0.71	–	–
160	1.22	0.91	0.97	0.79
161	1.05	0.77	1.05	1.06
162	0.98	0.68	0.98	0.79
163	0.97	0.68	1.02	0.77
164	1.00	0.68	0.98	0.79
165	0.99	0.68	1.02	0.78
166	0.97	0.68	0.98	0.78
167	0.98	0.68	1.00	0.78
168	0.99	0.70	1.00	0.78
169	0.97	0.66	0.97	0.78
170	1.00	0.70	1.02	0.77
171	0.97	0.82	0.98	0.78
172	1.00	0.83	1.07	0.78
173	0.99	0.82	0.98	0.78
174	1.00	0.83	1.07	0.78
175	0.98	0.85	0.99	0.78
176	1.01	0.90	1.13	0.78

REFERENCES

1. Scheinmann, F., *An Introduction to Spectroscopic Methods for the Identification of Organic Compounds,* Vol. 1, Pergamon Press, Oxford, 1970.
1a. Matter, U. E., Pascual, C., Pretsch, E., Pross, A., Simon, W., and Sternhell, S., *Tetrahedron,* 25, 691, 1969.
2. Read, J. M., Jr., Mayo, R. E., and Goldstein, J. H., *J. Mol. Spectrosc.,* 21, 235, 1966.
3. Hayamizu, K. and Yamamoto, O., *J. Mol. Spectrosc.,* 25, 422, 1968.
4. Smith W. B. and Roark, J. L., *J. Am. Chem. Soc.,* 89, 5018, 1967.
4a. Smith, W. B. and Cole, G. M., *J. Phys. Chem.,* 69, 4413, 1965.
5. Crecely, R. W., Read, J. M., Jr., Butler, R. S., and Goldstein, J. H., *Spectrochim. Acta,* 24A, 685, 1968.
6. Martin, J. and Bailey, B. P., *J. Chem. Phys.,* 37, 2594, 1962.
7. Bovey, F. A., *NMR Data Tables for Organic Compounds,* Vol. I, Interscience, New York, 1967.
8. Richards, R. E. and Schaefer, T., *Proc. R. Soc. Lond. Ser. A,* 246, 429, 1958.
9. Cagniant, D., Reisse, A., and Cagniant, P., *Bull. Soc. Chim. Fr.,* p. 2129, 1969.
10. Bhacca, N. S., Johnson, L. F., and Shoolery, J. N., *NMR Spectra Catalog,* Varian Associates, Palo Alto, 1962.
11. Mislow, K., Glass, M. A. W., Hopps, H. B., Simon, E., and Wahl, G. H., Jr., *J. Am. Chem. Soc.,* 86, 1710, 1964.
12. Güsten, H. and Salzwedel, M., *Tetrahedron,* 23, 187, 1967.
13. Güsten, H. and Salzwedel, M., *Tetrahedron,* 23, 173, 1967.
14. Brügel, W., *Nuclear Magnetic Resonance Spectra and Chemical Structure,* Vol. I, Academic Press, New York, 1967.
14a. Smith, W. B. and Chiranjeevi, S., *J. Phys. Chem.,* 70, 3505, 1966.
15. Brügel, W., 8th Eur. Congr. Mol. Spectrosc., Copenhagen, 1965.
16. Dudek, G. O., *Spectrochim. Acta,* 19, 691, 1973.
17. Wells, P. R., *J. Chem. Soc.,* p. 1967, 1963.
18. Pachler, K. J., *J. Chem. Soc.,* p. 2324, 1965.
19. Erichomovitch, L., Ménard, M., Chubb, F. L., Pépin, Y., and Richer, J., *Can. J. Chem.,* 44, 2305, 1966.
20. Jackman, L. M. and Sternhell, S., *Applications of Nuclear Magnetic Resonance Spectroscopy in Organic Chemistry,* 2nd ed., Pergamon Press, Oxford, 1969.
21. Jonathan, N., Gordon, S., and Dailey, B. P., *J. Chem. Phys.,* 36, 2443, 1962.
22. Martin, R. H., DeFay, N., Greets-Evrard, F., and Delavarenne, S., *Tetrahedron,* 20, 1073, 1964.
23. Bavin, P. M. G., Bartle, K. D., and Smith, J. A. S., *Tetrahedron,* 21, 1087, 1965.
24. Martin, R. H., DeFay, N., Greets-Evrard, F., and Figeys, H., *Bull. Soc. Chim. Bèlg.,* 73, 199, 1964.
24a. Martin, R. H., Flammang, R., and Arbaoui, M., *Bull. Soc. Chim. Belg.,* 74, 418, 1965.
24b. Memory, J. D. and Cobb, T. B., *J. Chem. Phys.,* 39, 2316, 1963.
24c. Martin, R. H., DeFay, N., and Greets-Evrard, F., *Tetrahedron,* 20, 1091, 1964.
25. Prinzbach, H., Freudenberger, V., and Scheidegger, U., *Helv. Chim. Acta,* 50, 1087, 1967.
26. Rautenstrauch, V. and Wingler, F., *Tetrahedron Lett.,* p. 4703, 1965; Wittig, G., Rautenstrauch, V., and Wingler, F., *Tetrahedron,* 7(Suppl.), 189, 1966.
27. Nagata, W., Terasawa, T., and Tori, K., *J. Am. Chem. Soc.,* 86, 3746, 1964.
28. Moore, R. E. and Scheuer, P. J., *J. Org. Chem.,* 31, 3272, 1966.
29. Moore, R. E., Singh, H., Chang, C. W. J., and Scheuer, P. J., *Tetrahedron,* 23, 3271, 1971.
30. Bordwell, F. G. and Winn, M., *J. Org. Chem.,* 32, 42, 1967.
31. Smith, W. B. and Shoulders, B. A., *J. Am. Chem. Soc.,* 86, 3118, 1964.
32. Dischler, B., *Z. Naturforsch.,* 20a, 888, 1965; Abraham, R. J. and Bernstein, H. J., *Can. J. Chem.,* 37, 1056, 1959; 39, 905, 1961; Gronowitz, S., Hörnfeldt, A.-B., Gestblom, B., and Hoffman, R. A., *Ark. Kemi,* 18, 133, 1961.
33. Cohen, A. D. and McLauchlan, K. A., *Discuss. Faraday Soc.,* 34, 132, 162.
34. Whipple, E. B. and Chiang, Y., *J. Chem. Phys.,* 40, 713, 1964.
35. Gronowitz, S., Hörnfeldt, A.-B., Gestblom, B., and Hoffman, R. A., *Ark. Kemi,* 18, 133, 1961.
36. Anderson, H. J. and Hopkins, L. C., *Can. J. Chem.,* 44, 1831, 1966.
37. Cohen, L. A., Daly, J. W., Kny, H., and Witkop, B., *J. Am. Chem. Soc.,* 82, 2184, 1960.
38. Elvidge, J. A. and Foster, R. G., *J. Chem. Soc.,* p. 981, 1964.
39. Jardine, R. V. and Brown, R., *Can. J. Chem.,* 41, 2067, 1963.
40. O'Brien, D. F. and Gates, J. W., *J. Org. Chem.,* 31, 1538, 1966.
41. Prugh, J. D., Huitric, A. C., and McCarthy, W. M., *J. Org. Chem.,* 29, 1991, 1964.
42. Reddy, G. S. and Goldstein, J. H., *J. Phys. Chem.,* 65, 1593, 1961; Reddy, G. S., Goldstein, J. H., and Mandell, L., *J. Am. Chem. Soc.,* 83, 1300, 1961.
43. Abraham, R. J. and Bernstein, H. J., *Can. J. Chem.,* 37, 1056, 1959.
44. Abraham, R. J. and Bernstein, H. J., *Can. J. Chem.,* 39, 905, 1961.
45. Gronowitz, S., Sörlin, G., Gestblom, B., and Hoffman, R. A., *Ark. Kemi,* 19, 483, 1962.
46. Rodmar, S., Forsen, S., Gestblom, B., Gronowitz, S., and Hoffman, R. A., *Acta Chem. Scand.,* 19, 485, 1965.
47. Leane, J. B. and Richards, R. E., *Trans. Faraday Soc.,* 55, 518, 1959.
48. Freeman, R. and Whiffen, D. H., *Mol. Phys.,* 4, 321, 1961.
49. Smith, W. B., *J. Phys. Chem.,* 67, 2841, 1963.

50. Schaefer, T., *Can. J. Chem.*, 40, 1678, 1962.
51. Cohen, A. D. and McLauchlan, K. A., *Mol. Phys.*, 7, 11, 1963.
52. Prugh, J. D., Huitric, A. C., and McCarthy, W. C., *J. Org. Chem.*, 29, 1991, 1964.
53. von Hofmann, A., Philipsborn, W. V., and Eugster, C. A., *Helv. Chim. Acta*, 48, 1322, 1965.
54. Reddy, G. S. and Goldstein, J. H., *J. Am. Chem. Soc.*, 84, 583, 1962.
55. Read, J. M., Mathis, C. T., and Goldstein, J., *Spectrochim. Acta*, 21, 85, 1965.
56. Abraham, R. J. and Bernstein, H. J., *Can. J. Chem.*, 37, 2095, 1959.
57. Dischler, B., *Z. Naturforsch.*, 20a, 888, 1965.
58. Grant, D. M., Hirst, R. C., and Gutowsky, H. S., *J. Chem. Phys.*, 38, 470, 1963.
59. Hoffman, R. A. and Gronowitz, S., *Ark. Kemi*, 15, 45, 1959.
60. Mathis, C. T. and Goldstein, J. H., *J. Phys. Chem.*, 68, 571, 1964.
61. Gronowitz, S. and Hoffman, R. A., *Ark. Kemi*, 13, 279, 1958; 15, 499, 1960.
62. Takahashi, K., Sone, T., Matsuki, Y., and Hazato, G., *Bull. Chem. Soc. Jap.*, 38, 1041, 1965.
63. Jakobsen, H. J. and Lawesson, S. -O., *Tetrahedron*, 23, 871, 1967.
64. Chapman, D. and Magnus, P. D., *Introduction to Practical High Resolution Nuclear Magnetic Resonance Spectroscopy*, Academic Press, London, 1966.
65. Brügel, W., *Z. Elektrochem. Ber. Bunsenges.*, 66, 159, 1962.
66. Rao, B. D. N. and Venkateswarlu, P., *Proc. Ind. Acad. Sci.*, 54, 305, 1961.
67. Kowalewski, V. J. and deKowalewski, D. G., *J. Chem. Phys.*, 37, 2603, 1962.
68. Castellano, S. and Bothner-By, A. A., *J. Chem. Phys.*, 41, 3863, 1964.
69. Saika, A. and Gutowsky, H. S., *J. Am. Chem. Soc.*, 78, 4818, 1956.
70. Castellano, S., Günther, H., and Ebersole, S., *J. Phys. Chem.*, 69, 4166, 1965.
71. Kramer, F. A. and West, R., *J. Phys. Chem.*, 69, 673, 1965.
72. Günther, H. and Castellano, S., *Ber. Bunsenges. Phys. Chem.*, 70, 913, 1966.
73. Kowalewski, V. J. and deKowalewski, D. G., *J. Chem. Phys.*, 36, 266, 1962.
74. Kowalewski, V. J., deKowalewski, D. G., and Ferrá, E. C., *J. Mol. Spectrosc.*, 20, 203, 1966.
75. Bernstein, H. J., Pople, J. A., and Schneider, W. G., *Can. J. Chem.*, 35, 65, 1957.
76. Schneider, W. G., Bernstein, H. J., and Pople, J. A., *Can. J. Chem.*, 35, 1487, 1957.
77. Tori, K. and Ogata, M., *Chem. Pharm. Bull.*, 12, 272, 1964.
78. Ito, K., Watanabe, H., and Kubo, M., *J. Chem. Phys.*, 34, 1043, 1961.
78a. Black, P. J. and Heffernan, M. L., *Aust. J. Chem.*, 18, 353, 1965.
78b. Elvidge, J. A. and Foster, R. G., *J. Chem. Soc.*, p. 590, 1963.
78c. Herington, E. F. G. and Lawrenson, I. J., *Spectrochim. Acta*, 21, 1010, 1965.
78d. Jardine, R. V. and Brown, R., *Can. J. Chem.*, 41, 2067, 1963; Cohen, L. A., Daly, J. W., Kny, H., and Witkop, B., *J. Am. Chem. Soc.*, 82, 2184, 1960.
79. Bovey, F. A., *Nuclear Magnetic Resonance Spectroscopy*, Academic Press, New York, 1969.
80. Cavanaugh, J. R. and Dailey, B. P., *J. Chem. Phys.*, 34, 1099, 1961.
81. Allred, A. L. and Rochow, E. G., *J. Am. Chem. Soc.*, 79, 536, 1957.
82. Bothner-By, A. A. and Naar-Colin, C., *J. Am. Chem. Soc.*, 80, 1728, 1958.
83. Lewis, I. C., *J. Phys. Chem.*, 70, 1667, 1966.
84. Yew, F. F., Kurland, R. J., and Mair, B. J., *Anal. Chem.*, 36, 843, 1964.
85. Smith, W. B. and Roark, J. L., *J. Am. Chem. Soc.*, 89, 5018, 1967.
86. Wilk, W. D., Allred, A. L., Koven, B. A., and Marshall, J. A., *J. Chem. Soc.*, B, 565, 1969.
87. Emsley, J. W., Feeney, J., and Sutcliffe, L. H., *High Resolution Nuclear Magnetic Resonance Spectroscopy*, Pergamon Press, Oxford, 1966.
88. Brown, M. P. and Webster, D. E., *J. Phys. Chem.*, 64, 698, 1960.
89. Jungnickel, J. L. and Forbes, J. W., *Anal. Chem.*, 35, 938, 1963.
90. Ebsworth, E. A. V. and Frankiss, S. G., *J. Chem. Soc.*, p. 661, 1963.
91. Biscarini, P., Taddei, F., and Zauli, C., *Boll. Sci. Fac. Chim. Ind. Bologna*, 21, 169, 1963.
92. Sakurai, H. and Ohtsuru, M., *J. Organometal. Chem.*, 13, 81, 1968.
93. Kuntz, I. D., Jr., Schleyer, P. von R., and Allerhand, A., *J. Chem. Phys.*, 35, 1553, 1961.
94. Gibbons, W. A. and Gill, V. M. S., *Mol. Phys.*, 9, 163, 1965.
95. Hofman, W., Stefaniak, L., Urbánski, T., and Witanowski, M., *J. Am. Chem. Soc.*, 86, 554, 1964.
96. Kidd, G., in *Characterization of Organometallic Compounds*, Tsutsui, M., Ed., Interscience, New York, 1971, chap. 8.
97. Van de Vondel, D. F., *J. Organometal. Chem.*, 3, 400, 1965.
97a. Sternhell, S., *Q. Rev.*, 23, 236, 1969.
98. Bothner-By, A. A., in *Advances in Magnetic Resonance*, Vol. 1, Waugh, J. S., Ed., Academic Press, New York, 1965.
99. Abraham, R. J. and Pachler, K. G. R., *Mol. Phys.*, 7, 165, 1964.
100. Niedrich, R. A. and Grant, D. M., *J. Chem. Phys.*, 42, 3733, 1965.
101. Sato, T., Saito, Y., Kainosho, M., and Hata, K., *Bull. Chem. Soc. Jap.*, 40, 391, 1967.
102. Maciel, G. E., McIver, J. W., Jr., Ostlund, N. S., and Pople, J. A., *J. Am. Chem. Soc.*, 92, 4497, 1970.
103. Bernheim, R. A. and Lavery, B. J., *J. Chem. Phys.*, 42, 1464, 1965.

104. Bernstein, H. J. and Sheppard, N., *J. Chem. Phys.*, 37, 3012, 1962.
105. Macdonald, C. G., Shannon, J. S., and Sternhell, S., *Aust. J. Chem.*, 19, 1527, 1966.
106. Niedrich, R. A., Grant, D. M., and Barfield, M., *J. Chem. Phys.*, 42, 3733, 1965.
107. Barfield, M. and Grant, D. M., *J. Am. Chem. Soc.*, 85, 1899, 1963.
108. Macdonald, C. G., Shannon, J. S., and Sternhell, S., *Aust. J. Chem.*, 17, 38, 1964, and references therein.
109. Takahashi, T., *Tetrahedron Lett.*, p. 565, 1964.
110. Schafer, P. R., Davis, D. R., Vogel, M., Nagarajan, K., and Roberts, J. D., *Proc. Natl. Acad. Sci. U.S.A.*, 47, 49, 1961.
111. Pople, J. A. and Bothner-By, A. A., *J. Chem. Phys.*, 42, 1339, 1965.
112. Maciel, G. E., McIver, J. W., Jr., Ostlund, N. S., and Pople, J. A., *J. Am. Chem. Soc.*, 92, 4151, 1970.
113. Godsey, C. E., *Anal. Chem.*, 38, 843, 1966.
114. Henold, K. L., *Chem. Commun.*, p. 1340, 1970.
115. Pascual, C., Meier, J., and Simon, W., *Helv. Chim. Acta*, 49, 164, 1966.
116. Bothner-By, A. A. and Naar-Colin, C., *J. Am. Chem. Soc.*, 83, 231, 1961.
117. Bothner-By, A. A. and Günther, H., *Discuss. Faraday Soc.*, 34, 127, 1962.
118. Brügel, W., Ankel, Th., and Krückeberg, F., *Z. Elektrochem.*, 64, 1121, 1960.
119. Hobgood, R. T., Reddy, G. S., and Goldstein, J. H., *J. Phys. Chem.*, 67, 110, 1963.
120. Bishop, E. O. and Richards, R. E., *Mol. Phys.*, 3, 114, 1960.
121. Whipple, E. B. and Chiang, Y., *J. Chem. Phys.*, 40, 713, 1964.
122. Barnwell, C. N. and Sheppard, N., *Mol. Phys.*, 3, 351, 1960.
123. Kossanyi, J., *Bull. Soc. Chim. Fr.*, p. 704, 1965.
124. Castellano, S. and Waugh, J. S., *J. Chem. Phys.*, 37, 1951, 1962.
125. Banwell, C. N. and Sheppard, N., *Proc. R. Soc. Lond.*, 263A, 136, 1961.
126. Mayo, R. E. and Goldstein, J. H., *J. Mol. Spectrosc.*, 14, 173, 1964.
127. Whipple, E. B., Stewart, W. E., Reddy, G. S., and Goldstein, J. H., *J. Chem. Phys.*, 34, 2136, 1961.
128. Schaefer, T. and Schneider, W. G., *Can. J. Chem.*, 38, 2066, 1960.
129. Martin, G. J. and Martin, M. L., *J. Organometal. Chem.*, 2, 380, 1964.
130. Castellano, S. and Waugh, J. S., *J. Chem. Phys.*, 34, 295, 1961.
131. Hobgood, R. T., Mayo, R. E., and Goldstein, J. H., *J. Chem. Phys.*, 39, 2501, 1963.
132. Freeman, R. J., *J. Chem. Phys.*, 40, 3571, 1964.
133. Murayana, K. and Nukada, K., *Bull. Chem. Soc. Jap.*, 36, 1223, 1963.
134. Reddy, G. S., Goldstein, J. H., and Mandell, L., *J. Am. Chem. Soc.*, 83, 1300, 1961.
135. Faulk, D. D. and Fry, A., *J. Org. Chem.*, 35, 364, 1970.
136. Abraham, R. J., in *Nuclear Magnetic Resonance for Organic Chemists*, Mathieson, D. W., Ed., Academic Press, New York, 1967.
137. Schaefer, T. and Hutton, H. M., *Can. J. Chem.*, 45, 3153, 1967.
138. Laszlo, P. and Schleyer, P. von R., *Bull. Soc. Chim. Fr.*, p. 87, 1964.
139. Doyle, T. D. and Ritter, J. J., *J. Am. Chem. Soc.*, 89, 5739, 1967.
140. Schaefer, T., *Can. J. Chem.*, 40, 1, 1962.
141. Hruska, F., Kotowycz, G., and Schaefer, T., *Can. J. Chem.*, 43, 2827, 1965.
142. Bothner-By, A. A., Castellano, S., Ebersole, S. B., and Günther, H., *J. Am. Chem. Soc.*, 88, 2466, 1966.
143. Cookson, R. C., Crabb, T. A., Frankel, J. J., and Hudec, J., *Tetrahedron*, 7(Suppl.), 355, 1960, and references cited therein.
144. Shapiro, B. L., Kopchik, R. M., and Ebersole, S. J., *J. Chem. Phys.*, 39, 3154, 1963.
145. Shapiro, B. L., Ebersole, S. J., and Kopchik, R. M., *J. Mol. Spectrosc.*, 11, 326, 1962.
146. Fraenkel, G., Adams, D. G., and Williams, J., *Tetrahedron Lett.*, p. 767, 1963.
147. Johnson, C. S., Weiner, M. A., Waugh, J. S., and Seyferth, D., *J. Am. Chem. Soc.*, 83, 1306, 1961.
148. Lynden-Bell, R. M. and Sheppard, N., *Proc. R. Soc. Lond.*, 269A, 385, 1962; Reddy, G. S. and Goldstein, J. H., *J. Mol. Spectrosc.*, 8, 475, 1962; Graham, D. M. and Holloway, C. E., *Can. J. Chem.*, 41, 2114, 1963.
149. Yoshino, T., Manabe, Y., and Kikuchi, Y., *J. Am. Chem. Soc.*, 86, 4670, 1964.
150. Barfield, M. and Grant, D. M., *J. Am. Chem. Soc.*, 83, 4726, 1961; 85, 1899, 1963; *J. Chem. Phys.*, 36, 2054, 1962; Niedrich, R. A., Grant, D. M., and Barfield, M., *J. Chem. Phys.*, 42, 3733, 1965.
151. Banwell, C. N., Sheppard, N., and Turner, J. J., *Spectrochim. Acta*, 16, 794, 1960.
152. Gutowsky, H. S., Karplus, M., and Grant, D. M., *J. Chem. Phys.*, 31, 1278, 1959.
153. Feeney, J., Ledwith, A., and Sutcliffe, L. H., *J. Chem. Soc.*, p. 2021, 1962.
154. Allred, E. L., Grant, D. M., and Goodlett, W., *J. Am. Chem. Soc.*, 87, 673, 1965.
155. Maciel, G. E., McIver, J. W., Jr., Ostlund, N. S., and Pople, J. A., *J. Am. Chem. Soc.*, 92, 4497, 1970.
156. Hobgood, R. T. and Goldstein, J. H., *J. Mol. Spectrosc.*, 12, 76, 1964.
157. Koster, D. F. and Danti, A., *J. Phys. Chem.*, 69, 486, 1965.
158. Bothner-By, A. A. and Harris, R. K., *J. Am. Chem. Soc.*, 87, 3445, 1965.
159. Bishop, E. O. and Musher, J. I., *Mol. Phys.*, 6, 621, 1963.
160. Bothner-By, A. A. and Harris, R. K., *J. Am. Chem. Soc.*, 87, 3451, 1965.
161. Elvidge, J. A., *J. Chem. Soc.*, p. 476, 1959.

162. Englert, G., *Z. Anal. Chem.*, 181, 447, 1961.
163. Whipple, E. B., Goldstein, J. H., and Stewart, W. E., *J. Am. Chem. Soc.*, 81, 4761, 1959.
164. Koster, D. F. and Danti, A., *J. Phys. Chem.*, 69, 486, 1965.
165. Allred, E. L., Grant, D. M., and Goodlett, W., *J. Am. Chem. Soc.*, 87, 673, 1965.
166. Snyder, E. I. and Roberts, J. D., *J. Am. Chem. Soc.*, 84, 1582, 1962.
167. Bertrand, M. and Rouvier, C., *Compt. Rend.*, 263, 330, 1966; Vestin, R., Borg, A., and Lindblom, T., *Acta Chem. Scand.*, 22, 685, 687, 1968; Frankiss, S. G. and Mathsubasa, I., *J. Phys. Chem.*, 70, 1543, 1966; Montijn, P. P., van Boom, J. H., Brandsma, L., and Arens, J. F., *Rec. Trav. Chim.*, 86, 115, 1967.
168. Shoolery, J. N., Johnson, L. F., and Anderson, W. A., *J. Mol. Spectrosc.*, 5, 110, 1960.
169. Hutton, H. M. and Schaefer, T., *Can. J. Chem.*, 41, 2429, 1963.
170. Whipple, E. B., Goldstein, J. H., Mandell, L., Reddy, G. S., and McClure, G. R., *J. Am. Chem. Soc.*, 81, 1321, 1959.
171. Reddy, G. S., Mandell, L., and Goldstein, J. H., *J. Am. Chem. Soc.*, 83, 4729, 1961.
172. Dreeskamp, H., Sackmann, E., and Stegmeier, G., *Ber. Bunsenges.*, 67, 860, 1963.
173. Klinck, R. E. and Stothers, J. B., *Can. J. Chem.*, 44, 45, 1966.
174. van Gorkon, M., *Tetrahedron Lett.*, p. 5433, 1966.
175. Pratt, L. and Smith, B. B., *Trans. Faraday Soc.*, 63, 2858, 1967.
176. Huckerby, T. N., *Annu. Rep. NMR Spectrosc.*, 3, 30, 1970; Drake, J. E. and Goddard, N., *Inorg. Nucl. Chem. Lett.*, 4, 385, 1968; Mackay, K. M., George, R. D., Robinson, P., and Watt, R., *J. Chem. Soc.*, A, 1920, 1968.
177. Takahashi, T., *Tetrahedron Lett.*, p. 565, 1964.
178. Muller, N. and Schultz, P. J., *J. Phys. Chem.*, 68, 2026, 1964.
179. Cahill, R., Cookson, R. C., and Crabb, T. A., *Tetrahedron*, 25, 4711, 1969, and references cited therein.
180. Wiberg, K. B. and Nist, B. J., *J. Am. Chem. Soc.*, 83, 1226, 1961.
181. Watts, V. S. and Goldstein, J. H., *J. Chem. Phys.*, 46, 4165, 1967.
182. Scherr, P. A. and Oliver, J. P., *J. Mol. Spectrosc.*, 31, 109, 1969.
182a. Wiberg, K. B. and Nist, B. J., *J. Am. Chem. Soc.*, 85, 2788, 1963.
182b. Schrumpf, G. and Luttke, W., *Tetrahedron Lett.*, 31, 2635, 1967.
183. Schaefer, T., Hruska, F., and Kotowycz, G., *Can. J. Chem.*, 43, 2827, 1965.
184. Weitkamp, H. and Korte, F., *Tetrahedron*, 20, 2125, 1964.
185. Patel, D. J., Howden, M. E. H., and Roberts, J. D., *J. Am. Chem. Soc.*, 85, 3218, 1963.
186. Longone, D. T. and Miller, O. H., *Chem. Commun.*, p. 447, 1967, on the basis of theoretical calculations, supplemented by experiments by others.
187. Schrumpf, G. and Luttke, W., *J. Mol. Spectrosc.*, 34, 11, 1970.
188. Shono, T., Morikawa, T., Oku, A., and Oda, R., *Tetrahedron Lett.*, p. 791, 1964.
188a. Wittstruck, T. A. and Trachtenberg, E. N., *J. Am. Chem. Soc.*, 89, 3810, 1967.
188b. Wiberg, K. B. and Bartley, W. J., *J. Am. Chem. Soc.*, 82, 6375, 1960.
189. Williamson, K. L., Lanford, C. A., and Nicholson, C. R., *J. Am. Chem. Soc.*, 86, 762, 1964.
189a. Graham, J. D. and Rogers, M. T., *J. Am. Chem. Soc.*, 84, 2249, 1962.
189b. Dauben, W. G. and Wipke, W. T., *J. Org. Chem.*, 32, 2976, 1967.
189c. Hutton, H. M. and Schaefer, T., *Can. J. Chem.*, 41, 1623, 1963.
189d. Perold, G. W. and Hundt, H. K. L., *J. S. Afr. Chem. Inst.*, 21, 144, 1968.
190. Bravo, P., Fronza, G., Gandiano, G., Ticozzi, C., and Zubiani, M. G., *Tetrahedron*, 27, 3563, 1971.
191. Hutton, H. M. and Schaefer, T., *Can. J. Chem.*, 41, 685, 1963.
192. Husher, J. J., quoted in Ref. 189a.
193. Elleman, D. D., Manatt, S. L., and Pearce, C. D., *J. Chem. Phys.*, 42, 650, 1965.
194. Allen, G., Blears, D. J., and Webb, K. H., *J. Chem. Soc.*, p. 810, 1965.
195. Reilly, C. A. and Swalen, J. D., *J. Chem. Phys.*, 32, 1378, 1960; 34, 980, 1961; 35, 1522, 1961.
196. Bothni, A. T. and Roberts, J. D., *J. Am. Chem. Soc.*, 80, 6203, 1958.
197. Brois, S. J., *J. Org. Chem.*, 27, 3532, 1962.
198. Pohland, A. E., Badger, R. C., and Cromwell, N. H., *Tetrahedron Lett.*, p. 4369, 1965.
199. Braillon, B., *J. Mol. Spectrosc.*, 27, 313, 1968.
200. Servis, K. L. and Roberts, J. D., *J. Am. Chem. Soc.*, 86, 3773, 1964.
200a. Wiberg, K. B. and Bath, D. E., *J. Am. Chem. Soc.*, 91, 5124, 1969.
201. Lozac'h, R. and Braillon, B., *J. Chem. Phys.*, 67, 340, 1970.
202. Baggaley, K. H., Erdtmann, H., and Norin, T., *Tetrahedron*, 24, 3399, 1968.
203. Imbach, J. -L., Doomes, E., Rebman, R. P., and Cromwell, N. H., *J. Org. Chem.*, 32, 78, 1967.
204. Fodor, G., Mandava, N., and Weisz, I., *Tetrahedron*, 24, 2357, 1968.
205. Nerdl, F. and Kressin, H., *Annalen*, 707, 1, 1967; Hara, M., Odaira, Y., and Tsutsumi, S., *Tetrahedron Lett.*, p. 2981, 1967; Abraham, R. J., *J. Chem. Soc.*, B, 1730, 1968; Sutcliffe, L. H. and Walker, S. M., *J. Phys. Chem.*, 71, 1555, 1967.
206. Servis, K. L. and Roberts, J. D., *J. Phys. Chem.*, 67, 2885, 1963.
206a. Abell, P. I. and Chiao, C., *J. Am. Chem. Soc.*, 82, 3610, 1960.
206b. Lustig, E. and Moriarty, R. M., *J. Am. Chem. Soc.*, 87, 3252, 1965.

207. Abraham, R. J., *J. Chem. Soc.*, B, 173, 1968.
208. Gianni, M., Saavedra, J., Myhalyk, R., and Wursthorn, K., *J. Phys. Chem.*, 74, 201, 1970.
209. Barrow, K. D. and Spottiswood, T. M., *Tetrahedron Lett.*, p. 3325, 1965.
210. Gamba, A. and Mondelli, R., *Tetrahedron Lett.*, p. 2133, 1971.
210a. Steinmetz, R., Hartmann, W., and Schenck, G. O., *Chem. Ber.*, 98, 3854, 1965.
210b. Krauch, C. H., Farid, S., and Schenck, G. O., *Chem. Ber.*, 99, 625, 1966.
210c. Georgian, V., Georgian, L., and Robertson, A. V., *Tetrahedron*, 19, 1219, 1963.
211. Lustig, E., *J. Chem. Phys.*, 37, 2725, 1962.
212. Bhacca, N. S. and Williams, D. H., *Applications of NMR Spectroscopy in Organic Chemistry*, Holden-Day, San Francisco, 1964.
213. Williams, J. K., Wiley, D. W., and McKusick, B. C., *J. Am. Chem. Soc.*, 84, 2210, 1962.
214. Weitkamp, H. and Korte, F., *Tetrahedron*, 7(Suppl.), 75, 1966.
215. Blomquist, A. T. and Bottomley, C. G., *Annalen*, 653, 67, 1962.
216. Chapman, O. L., *J. Am. Chem. Soc.*, 85, 2014, 1963.
217. Lustig, E., Ragelis, E. P., and Day, N., *Spectrochim. Acta*, 23A, 133, 1967.
218. Mortimer, F. S., *J. Mol. Spectrosc.*, 5, 199, 1960.
219. Brois, S. J. and Beardsley, G. P., *Tetrahedron Lett.*, p. 5113, 1966.
220. Keller, W. D. and Susebrink, T. R., *J. Chem. Phys.*, 44, 782, 1966.
221. Griesbaum, K., Naegele, W., and Wanless, G. G., *J. Am. Chem. Soc.*, 87, 3151, 1965.
222. Gutowsky, H. S., Karplus, M., and Grant, D. M., *J. Chem. Phys.*, 31, 1278, 1959.
223. Hall, E. A. and Roberts, J. D., *J. Am. Chem. Soc.*, 89, 2047, 1967.
224. Lambert, J. B. and Roberts, J. D., *J. Am. Chem. Soc.*, 87, 3891, 1965.
225. Steinmetz, R., Hartmann, W., and Schenck, G. O., *Chem. Ber.*, 98, 3854, 1965.
226. Martin, J. C., Goodlett, V. W., and Burpitt, R. D., *J. Org. Chem.*, 30, 4309, 1965.
226a. Braillon, B., Salaün, J., Gore, J., and Conia, J. -M., *Bull. Soc. Chim. Fr.*, p. 1981, 1964.
227. Krapcho, A. P. and Lesser, J. H., *J. Org. Chem.*, 31, 2030, 1966.
227a. Roth, W. R. and Peltzer, B., *Leibigs Ann. Chem.*, 685, 56, 1965.
227b. Fraenkel, G., Asaki, Y., Mitchell, M. J., and Cava, M. P., *Tetrahedron*, 20, 1179, 1964; Fleming, I. and Williams, D. H., *Tetrahedron*, 23, 2747, 1967.
227c. Dauben, W. G., Koch, K., Smith, S. L., and Chapman, O. L., *J. Am. Chem. Soc.*, 85, 2617, 1963.
227d. Manatt, S. L., Vogel, M., Knutson, D., and Roberts, J. D., *J. Am. Chem. Soc.*, 82, 2645, 1964.
227e. Breslow, R., Kivelivitch, D., Mitchell, M. T., and Wendel, K., *J. Am. Chem. Soc.*, 87, 5132, 1965.
228. Paquette, L. A., Barrett, J. H., Spitz, R. P., and Pitcher, R., *J. Am. Chem. Soc.*, 87, 3417, 1965.
229. Meinwald, J. and Lewis, A., *J. Am. Chem. Soc.*, 83, 2769, 1961.
230. Kaplan, F., Schulz, C. O., Weisleder, D., and Klopfenstein, C., *J. Org. Chem.*, 33, 1728, 1968.
231. Wiberg, K. B., Lowry, B. R., and Nist, B. J., *J. Am. Chem. Soc.*, 84, 1594, 1962.
232. Closs, G. L. and Larrabee, R. B., *Tetrahedron Lett.*, p. 287, 1965.
233. Fleming, I. and Williams, D. H., *Tetrahedron*, 23, 2747, 1967.
234. Mondelli, R. and Gamba, A., *Org. Mag. Res.*, 5, 101, 1973.
235. Booth, H. and Little, J. H., reported by Booth, H., *Prog. NMR Spectros.*, 5, 149, 1969.
236. Ma, J. C. N. and Warnhoff, E. W., *Can. J. Chem.*, 43, 1849, 1965.
236a. Curtin, D. Y., Gruen, H., and Shoulders, B. A., *Chem. Ind.*, p. 1205, 1958.
236b. Russell, G. A. and Ito, A., *J. Am. Chem. Soc.*, 85, 2983, 1963.
236c. Altona, C., Buys, H. R., and Havinga, E., *Rec. Trav. Chim.*, 85, 983, 1966.
237. Sable, H. Z., Ritchey, W. M., and Nordlander, J. E., *J. Org. Chem.*, 31, 3771, 1966; *Carbohydr. Res.*, 1, 10, 1965.
237a. Conia, J. M. and Limasset, J. C., *Bull. Soc. Chim. Fr.*, p. 1936, 1967.
237b. Tsuji, T., Moritani, I., Nishida, S., and Takodoro, G., *Bull Chem. Soc. Jap.*, 40, 2344, 1967; Newsoroff, G. P. and Sternhell, S., R. Aust. Chem. Inst. Symp., Sydney, August 1968.
237c. Klose, G., *Mol. Phys.*, 6, 585, 1963.
237d. Manatt, S. L. and Elleman, D. D., quoted in Ref. 14.
237e. Caserio, M. C., quoted in Ref. 14.
237f. Forsen, S., Gestblom, B., Hoffman, R. A., and Rodmar, S., *J. Mol. Spectrosc.*, 21, 372, 1966.
238. Anteunis, M. and Schamp, N., *Bull. Soc. Chim. Belg.*, 76, 330, 1967.
238a. Cocu, F. G., Wolczunowicz, G., Bors, L., and Posternak, Th., *Helv. Chim. Acta*, 53, 739, 1970.
238b. Nukada, K., *Bull. Chem. Soc. Jap.*, 33, 1606, 1960.
238c. Martin, J.C., *Bull. Soc. Chim. Fr.*, p. 277, 1970.
238d. Abraham, R. J., Parry, K., and Thomas, W. A., *J. Chem. Soc.*, B, 446, 1971.
238e. Cooper, M. A., Elleman, D. D., Pierce, C. D., and Manatt, S. L., *J. Chem. Phys.*, 53, 2343, 1970.
238f. Cort, L. A. and Stewart, R. A., *J. Chem. Soc.*, C, 1386, 1971.
238g. Gagnaire, D. and Vottero, P., *Bull. Soc. Chim. Fr.*, p. 2779, 1963.
238h. Heine, H. W., Peavy, R., and Durbetaki, A. J., *J. Org. Chem.*, 31, 3924, 1966.
238i. Horobin, R. W., McKenna, J., and McKenna, J. M., *Tetrahedron*, 7 (Suppl.), 35, 1966.

238j. Abraham, R. J. and McLauchlan, K. A., *Mol. Phys.*, 5, 195, 513, 1962.
238k. Herr, R. R. and Slomp, G., *J. Am. Chem. Sco.*, 89, 2444, 1967; Slomp, G. and Mackellar, F. A., *J. Am. Chem. Soc.*, 89, 2454, 1967.
238l. Brimacombe, J. S., Foster, A. B., Jones, B. D., and Willard, J. J., *Chem. Commun.*, p. 174, 1965.
238m. Aito, Y., Matsuo, T., and Aso, C., *Bull. Chem. Soc. Jap.*, 40, 130, 1967.
238n. Caspi, E., Wittstruck, T. A., and Piatak, D. M., *J. Org. Chem.*, 27, 3183, 1962.
238o. Anet, F. A. L., *J. Am. Chem. Soc.*, 84, 747, 1962.
238p. Cahill, R., Cookson, R. C., and Crabb, T. A., *Tetrahedron,* 25, 4681, 1969, and references cited therein.
238q. Cookson, R. C. and Crabb, T. A., *Tetrahedron,* 24, 2385, 1968.
238r. Allingham, Y., Cookson, R. C., and Crabb, T. A., *Tetrahedron,* 24, 1989, 1968.
238s. Abraham, R. J., *J. Chem. Soc.*, p. 256, 1965.
238t. Crabb, T. A. and Cookson, R. C., *Tetrahedron Lett.*, p. 679, 1964.
238u. Lemieux, R. U., Stevens, J. D., and Fraser, R. R., *Can. J. Chem.*, 40, 1955, 1962.
238v. Chapman, O. L., *J. Am. Chem. Soc.*, 85, 2014, 1963.
238w. Laszlo, P. and Schleyer, P. von R., *J. Am. Chem. Soc.*, 85, 2017, 1963.
238x. Leonard, N. J. and Laursen, R. A., *J. Am. Chem. Soc.*, 85, 2026, 1963.
238y. Abraham, R. J., Hall, L. D., Hough, L., McLauchlan, K. A., and Miller, H. J., *J. Chem. Soc.*, p. 748, 1963.
238z. Hall, L. D., *Chem. Ind.*, p. 950, 1963.
239. Jacquesy, J. C., Lehn, J.–M., and Levisalles, J., *Bull. Soc. Chim. Fr.*, p. 2444, 1961.
240. Cross, A. D., *J. Am. Chem. Soc.*, 84, 3206, 1964.
241. Kawazoe, Y., Sato, Y., Natsume, M., Hasegawa, H., Okamoto, T., and Tsuda, K., *Chem. Pharm. Bull.* (Tokyo), 10, 338, 1962.
242. Slomp, G. and McGarvey, B. R., *J. Am. Chem. Soc.*, 81, 2200, 1959.
243. Lardon, A. and Reichstein, T., *Helv. Chim. Acta,* 46, 392, 1963.
244. Tori, K. and Kondo, E., *Tetrahedron Lett.*, p. 645, 1963.
245. Cox, J. S. G., Bishop, E. O., and Richards, R. E., *J. Chem. Soc.*, p. 5118, 1960.
246. Tori, K. and Kondo, E., *Steroids,* 4, 713, 1964.
247. Tori, K. and Komeno, T., *Tetrahedron,* 21, 309, 1965.
248. Tori, K., Komeno, T., and Nakagawa, T., *J. Org. Chem.*, 29, 1136, 1964.
249. Zürcher, R. F., *Helv. Chim. Acta,* 44, 1380, 1961; 46, 2054, 1963.
250. Shoppee, C. W., Akhtar, M. I., and Lack, R. E., *J. Chem. Soc.*, p. 877, 1964.
251. ApSimon, J. W., Craig, W. G., Demarco, P. V., Mathieson, D. W., Saunders, L., and Whalley, W. B., *Tetrahedron,* 23, 2357, 1967.
252. Kishi, M., Tori, K., Komeno, T., and Shingu, T., *Tetrahedron Lett.*, p. 3525, 1971.
253. Komeno, T., Kishi, M., Watanabe, H., and Tori, K., *Tetrahedron,* 28, 2767, 1972.
254. Tori, K. and Aono, K., *Annu. Rep. Shionogi Res. Lab.*, No. 14, Osaka, 1964.
255. Kutney, J. P., *Steroids,* 2, 255, 1963.
256. Kirk, D. N., Klyne, W., Peach, C. M., and Wilson, M. A., *J. Chem. Soc.*, C, 1454, 1970.
257. Williams, D. H. and Bhacca, N. S., *Tetrahedron,* 21, 1641, 1965.
258. Green, G. F. H., Page, J. E., and Staniforth, S. E., *J. Chem. Soc.*, B, 807, 1966.
259. Lemieux, R. U. and Stevens, J. D., *Can. J. Chem.*, 44, 249, 1966.
260. Durette, P. L. and Horton, D., *Chem. Commun.*, p. 516, 1969.
261. Holland, C. V., Horton, D., Miller, M., and Bhacca, N. S., *J. Org. Chem.*, 32, 3077, 1967.
262. Horton, D. and Wander, J. D., *Carbohydr. Res.*, 10, 279, 1969.
263. Hall, L. D. and Manville, J. F., *Adv. Chem.*, 74, 228, 1968.
264. Coxon, B., *Tetrahedron,* 22, 2281, 1966.
265. Buss, D. H., Hough, L., Hall, L. D., and Manville, J. F., *Tetrahedron,* 21, 69, 1965.
266. Stevens, J. D. and Fletcher, H. G., Jr., *J. Org. Chem.*, 33, 1799, 1968.
267. Hall, L. D., Steiner, P. R., and Pedersen, C., *Can. J. Chem.*, 48, 1155, 1970.
268. Durette, P. L., Horton, D., and Wander, J. D., *Adv. Chem.*, in press.
269. Horton, D., Jewell, J. S., and Philips, K. D., *J. Org. Chem.*, 31, 4022, 1966.
270. Agahigian, H., Vickers, G. D., von Saltza, M. H., Reid, J., Cohen, A. I., and Gauthier, H., *J. Org. Chem.*, 30, 1085, 1965.
271. Coxon, B., *Tetrahedron,* 21, 3481, 1965.
272. Harris, M. J. and Turvey, J. R., *Carbohydr. Res.*, 15, 57, 1970.
273. Descotes, G., Chizat, F., and Martin, J. C., *Bull. Soc. Chim. Fr.*, p. 2304, 1970.
274. Inch, T. D., Plimmer, J. P., and Fletcher, H. G., Jr., *J. Org. Chem.*, 31, 1825, 1966.
275. Horton, D., Jewell, J. S., and Philips, K. D., *J. Org. Chem.*, 31, 3843, 1966.
276. Bhacca, N. S., Horton, D., and Paulsen, H., *J. Org. Chem.*, 33, 2484, 1968.
277. Emsley, J. W., Feeney, J., and Sutcliffe, L. H., *High Resolution Nuclear Magnetic Resonance Spectroscopy,* Vol. 2, Pergamon Press, Oxford, 1966, chap. 10.12–10.22; Silverstein, R. M. and Bassler, G. C., *Spectrometric Identification of Organic Compounds,* 2nd ed., John Wiley & Sons, New York, 1967, 145.

278. Newsoroff, G. P. and Sternhell, S., *Tetrahedron Lett.*, p. 6117, 1968.
279. Wiberg, K. B., Lampmann, S. M., Ciula, R. P., Connor, D. S., Schertler, P., and Lavanish, J., *Tetrahedron,* 21, 2749, 1965.
280. Barfield, M., *J. Chem. Phys.*, 41, 3825, 1964.
281. Freeman, R. and Gestblom, B., *J. Chem. Phys.*, 47, 2744, 1967; Ernst, R. R., Freeman, R., Gestblom, B., and Lusebrink, T. R., *Mol. Phys.*, 13, 283, 1967.
282. Garbisch, E. W., *Chem. Ind.*, p. 1715, 1964.
283. Tori, K., Ohtsuru, M., Hata, Y., and Tanida, H., *Chem. Commun.*, p. 1096, 1968.
284. Dowd, P. and Sachder, K., *J. Am. Chem. Soc.*, 89, 715, 1967.
285. Feeney, J., Anteunis, M., and Swalen, G., *Bull. Soc. Chim. Belg.*, 77, 121, 1968.
286. Tori, K. and Ohtsuru, M., *Chem. Commun.*, p. 886, 1966.
287. Becker, E. D., Miles, H. T., and Bradley, R. B., *J. Am. Chem. Soc.*, 87, 5575, 1965.
288. Bohlmann, F. and Kapteyn, H., *Chem. Ber.*, 100, 1927, 1967.
289. McCubbin, J. A., Moir, R. Y., and Neville, G. A., *Can. J. Chem.*, 48, 934, 1970.
290. Bertrand, M. and Rouvier, C., *Compt. Rend.*, 263, 330, 1966; Vestin, R., Borg, A., and Lindblom, T., *Acta Chem. Scand.*, 22, 685, 687, 1968; Frankiss, S. G. and Matsubara, I., *J. Phys. Chem.*, 70, 1543, 1966; Montijn, P. P., van Boom, J. H., Brandsma, L., and Arens, J. F., *Rec. Trav. Chim.*, 86, 115, 1967.
291. Göth, H., Gagneux, A. R., Eugster, C. H., and Schmid, H., *Helv. Chim. Acta,* 50, 137, 1967.
292. Fritz, H. P., Schwarzhans, K. E., and Sellmann, D., *J. Organometal. Chem.*, 6, 551, 1966.
293. Mehta, M. D., Miller, D., and Mooney, E. F., *J. Chem. Soc.*, p. 6695, 1965; Garbisch, E. W. and Griffith, M. G., *J. Am. Chem. Soc.*, 90, 3590, 1968.
294. Barbier, C., Gagnaire, D., and Votero, P., *Bull. Soc. Chim. Fr.*, p. 2330, 1968; Katagiri, K., Tori, K., Kimura, Y., Yoshida, T., Nagasaki, T., and Minato, H., *J. Med. Chem.*, 10, 1149, 1967.
295. Ketley, A. D., Berlin, A. J., and Fisher, L. P., *J. Org. Chem.*, 31, 2648, 1966.
296. Sternhell, S., *Rev. Pure Appl. Chem.*, 14, 15, 1964; Ayamizu, K. H. and Yamamoto, O., *J. Mol. Spectrosc.*, 23, 121, 1967.
297. Metlesics, W., Anton, T., and Sternbach, L. H., *J. Org. Chem.*,32, 2185, 1967; Gerig, J. T., *Tetrahedron Lett.*, p. 4625, 1967.
298. Hart, N. K., Johns, S. R., and Lamberton, J. A., *Aust. J. Chem.*, 21, 1321, 1968.
299. von Hofmann, A., Von Philipsborn, W., and Eugster, C. H., *Helv. Chim. Acta,* 48, 1322, 1965.
300. Hruska, F., Hutton, H. M., and Schaefer, T., *Can. J. Chem.*, 32, 1942, 1965.
301. Steiglich, W. and Hurnaus, R., *Tetrahedron Lett.*, p. 384, 1966.
302. Hoffman, R. A. and Gronowitz, S., *Ark. Kemi,* 16, 471, 1960.
303. Alexander, S., *J. Chem. Phys.*, 32, 1700, 1960.
304. Fessenden, R. W. and Waugh, J. S., *J. Chem. Phys.*, 30, 944, 1959.
305. Mortimer, F. S., *J. Mol. Spectrosc.*, 3, 335, 1959.
306. Cohen, A. D. and Sheppard, N.,*Proc. R. Soc. Lond.*, 252A, 488, 1959.
307. Fujiwara, S., Shimizu, H., Arata, Y., and Akahori, S., *Bull. Chem. Soc. Jap.*, 33, 428, 1960.
308. Jackman, L. M. and Wiley, R. H., *J. Chem. Soc.*, p. 2886, 1960.
309. Pople, J. A., Schneider, W. G., and Bernstein, H. J., *High Revolution Nuclear Magnetic Resonance,* McGraw-Hill, New York, 1959, 238.
310. Fraser, R. R., *Can. J. Chem.*, 38, 549, 1960.
311. Narasimhan, P. T. and Rogers, M. T., *J. Chem. Phys.*, 33, 727, 1960.
312. Braillon, B., *J. Chim. Phys.*, 58, 495, 1961.
313. Braillon, B. and Romanet, R., reported at the 1959 Bologna Mol. Spectrosc. Meet.
314. Hoffman, R. A. and Gronowitz, S., *Acta Chem. Scand.*, 13, 1477, 1959.
315. Hörnfeldt, A. and Gronowitz, S., *Acta Chem. Scand.*, 16, 789, 1962.
316. Gronowitz, S. and Hoffman, R. A., *Ark Kemi,* 15, 499, 1960.
317. Shoolery, J. N., *Discuss. Faraday Soc.*, 34, 104, 1962.
318. Gagnaire, D. and Payo Subiza, E., *Bull. Soc. Chim. Fr.*, p. 2623, 1963.
319. Farnum, D. G., Heybey, M. A. T., and Webster, B., *Tetrahedron Lett.*, p. 307, 1963.
320. Sternhell, S., *Rev. Pure Appl. Chem.*, 14, 15, 1964.
321. Bartle, K. D., Jones, D. W., and Matthews, R. S., *Rev. Pure Appl. Chem.*, 19, 191, 1969.
322. Williamson, M. P., Kostelnik, R. J., and Castellano, S. M., *J. Chem. Phys.*, 49, 2218, 1968.
323. Rottendorf, H. and Sternhell, S., *Aust. J. Chem.*, 17, 1315, 1964.
324. Nair, P. M. and Gopakumar, G., *Tetrahedron Lett.*, p. 709, 1964.
325. Bartle, K. D., Jones, D. W., and Matthews, R. S., *Tetrahedron,* 25, 2701, 1969.
326. Bartle, K. D. and Smith, J. A. S., *Spectrochim. Acta,* 23A, 1689,1967.
327. Clar, E., McAndrew, B. A., and Zander, M., *Tetrahedron,* 23, 985, 1967.
328. Ouellette, R. J. and van Leuwen, B. J., *J. Org. Chem.*, 34, 62, 1969.
329. Cagniant, D., *Bull. Soc. Chim. Fr.*, p. 2325, 1966.

330. Clar, E., Sanigok, V., and Zander, M., *Tetrahedron,* 24, 2817, 1968.
331. Dewar, M. J. S. and Fahey, R. C., *J. Am. Chem. Soc.,* 85, 2704, 1963.
332. Bosch, A. and Brown, R. K., *Can. J. Chem.,* 46, 715, 1968.
333. Wells, P. R., *Aust. J. Chem.,* 17, 967, 1964.
334. Brügel, W., paper presented at 8th Eur. Congr. Mol. Spectrosc., Copenhagen, 1965.
335. Martin, R. H., Defay, N., and Greets-Evrard, F., *Tetrahedron,* 21, 2435, 1965.
336. Abraham, R. J. and Bernstein, H. J., *Can. J. Chem.,* 39, 903, 1961.
337. Reddy, G. S. and Goldstein, J. H., *J. Phys. Chem.,* 65, 1539, 1961.
338. Abraham, R. J. and Bernstein, H. J., *Can. J. Chem.,* 37, 1056, 1959.
339. Taurins, A. and Schneider, W. G., *Can. J. Chem.,* 38, 1237, 1960.
340. Pinhey, J. T. and Sternhell, S., *Tetrahedron Lett.,* p. 275, 1963.
341. Cameron, D. W., Kingston, G. I., Sheppard, N., and Lord Todd, *J. Chem. Soc.,* p. 98, 1964.
342. Appel, H. H., Bond, R. P. M., and Overton, K. H., *Tetrahedron,* 19, 635, 1963.
343. Rassat, A., Jefford, C. W., Lehn, J. M., and Waegell, B., *Tetrahedron Lett.,* p. 233, 1964.
344. Ramey, K. C., Lini, D. C., Moriarty, R. M., Gopal, H., and Welsh, H. G., *J. Am. Chem. Soc.,* 89, 2401, 1967.
345. Anet, F. A. L., *Can. J. Chem.,* 39, 789, 1961.
346. Musher, J. I., *Mol. Phys.,* 6, 93, 1963.
347. Meinwald, J. and Meinwald, Y. C., *J. Am. Chem. Soc.,* 85, 2514, 1963.
348. Chalier, G., Rassat, A., and Rousseau, A., *Bull. Soc. Chim. Fr.,* p. 428, 1966.
349. Marchand, A. P. and Rose, J. E., *J. Am. Chem. Soc.,* 90, 3724, 1968, and references cited therein.
350. Bystrov, V. F. and Stepanyants, A. U., *J. Mol. Spectrosc.,* 21, 241, 1966.
351. Bates, R. B. and Thalacker, V. P., *J. Org. Chem.,* 33, 1730, 1968.
352. Kaplan, F., Schulz, C. O., Weisleder, D., and Klopfenstein, C., *J. Org. Chem.,* 33, 1728, 1968.
353. Meinwald, J. and Lewis, A., *J. Am. Chem. Soc.,* 83, 2769, 1961.
354. Wiberg, K. B., Lowry, B. R., and Nist, B. J.,*J. Am. Chem. Soc.,* 84, 1594, 1962.
355. Srinivasan, R. and Sonntag, F. I., *J. Am. Chem. Soc.,* 89, 407, 1967.
356. Masamune, S., *J. Am. Chem. Soc.,* 86, 735, 1964.
357. Schneider, J. J., Crabbé, P., and Bhacca, N., *J. Org. Chem.,* 3118, 1968.
358. Anteunis, M., Schamp, N., and de Pooter, H., *Bull. Soc. Chim. Belg.,* 76, 541, 1967.
359. Abraham, R. J., Gottschalck, H., Paulsen, H., and Thomas, W. A., *J. Chem. Soc.,* p. 6268, 1965.
360. Hall, L. D., Manville, J. F., and Tracey, A., *Carbohydr. Res.,* 4, 514, 1967.
361. De Wolf, M. Y. and Baldeschwieler, J. D., *J. Mol. Spectrosc.,* 13, 344, 1964.
362. Davis, D. R. and Roberts, J. D., *J. Am. Chem. Soc.,* 84, 2252, 1962.
363. Koster, D. F. and Danti, A., *J. Phys. Chem.,* 69, 486, 1965.
364. Hutton, H. M. and Schaefer, T., *Can. J. Chem.,* 45, 1165, 1967.
365. Branwell, C. N. and Sheppard, N., quoted by Hoffman, R. A. and Gronowitz, S., *Ark. Kemi,* 16, 471, 1960.
366. Bothner-By, A. A., Castellano, S., and Günther, H., *J. Am. Chem. Soc.,* 87, 2439, 1965.
367. Garbisch, E. W., *J. Am. Chem. Soc.,* 86, 5561, 1964, and references cited therein.
368. Marchand, A. P. and Rose, J. E., *J. Am. Chem. Soc.,* 90, 3724, 1968, and references cited therein.
369. Elleman, D. D. and Manatt, S. L., *J. Am. Chem. Soc.,* 36, 2346, 1962.
370. Freeman, R., *Mol. Phys.,* 5, 499, 1962.
371. Culvenor, C. C. J., Heffernan, M. L., and Woods, W. G., *Aust. J. Chem.,* 18, 1605, 1965.
372. Bothner-By, A. A., Naar-Colin, C., and Günther, H., *J. Am. Chem. Soc.,* 84, 2748, 1962.
373. Van Binst, G., Nouls, J. C., Stokoe, J., Danheux, C., and Martin, R. H., *Bull. Soc. Chim. Belg.,* 74, 506, 1965.
374. Snyder, E. I., Altmann, L. J., and Roberts, J. D., *J. Am. Chem. Soc.,* 84, 2004, 1962.
375. Hobgood, R. T. and Goldstein, J. H., *J. Mol. Spectrosc.,* 12, 76, 1964.
376. Manatt, S. L., quoted by Barfield, M. and Chakrabarti, B., *Chem. Rev.,* 69, 757, 1969.
377. Hirst, R. C. and Grant, D. M., *J. Am. Chem. Soc.,* 84, 2009, 1962.
378. Snyder, E. I. and Roberts, J. D., *J. Am. Chem. Soc.,* 84, 1582, 1962.
379. Ramey, K. C. and Messick, J., *Tetrahedron Lett.,* p. 4423, 1965.
380. Delman, J. and Duplan, J., *Tetrahedron Lett.,* p. 559, 1966.
381. Anderson, J. E., *J. Chem. Soc.,* B, 721, 1967.
382. Pachler, K. G. R. and Underwood, W. G. E., *Tetrahedron,* 23, 1817, 1967.
383. Pachler, K. G. R. and Wessels, P. L., *J. S. Afr. Chem. Inst.,* 19, 49, 1966.
384. Harris, R. K. and Spragg, R. A., *J. Mol. Spectrosc.,* 23, 158, 1967.
385. Baldwin, J. E. and Pinschmidt, R. K., *J. Am. Chem. Soc.,* 92, 5247, 1970.
386. Cox, R. H. and Bothner-By, A. A., *J. Phys. Chem.,* 72, 1642, 1968.
387. Cocu, F. G., Wolczunowicz, G., Bors, L., and Posternak, Th., *Helv. Chim. Acta,* 53, 1511, 1970.
388. Bauld, N. L. and Rim, Y. S., *J. Org. Chem.,* 33, 1303, 1968.
389. Jochims, J. C. and Taigel, G., *Tetrahedron Lett.,* p. 5483, 1968.
390. Rousselot, M. -M., *Compt. Rend. Acad. Sci.* (Paris), 262C, 26, 1966.
391. Kingsbury, C. A., Egan, R. S., and Perun, T. J., *J. Org. Chem.,* 35, 2913, 1970.

392. Ramey, K. C., Lini, D. C., Moriarty, R. M., Gopal, H., and Welsh, H. G., *J. Am. Chem. Soc.*, 89, 2401, 1967.
393. Anet, F. A. L., *J. Am. Chem. Soc.*, 84, 1053, 1962.
394. Evanega, G. R., Bergmann, W., and English, J., Jr., *J. Org. Chem.*, 27, 13, 1962.
395. Massicot, J. and Marthe, J. P., *Bull. Soc. Chim. Fr.*, p. 1962, 1962.
396. Muller, N. and Schultz, P. J., *J. Phys. Chem.*, 68, 2026, 1964.
397. Segre, A. and Musher, J. I., *J. Am. Chem. Soc.*, 89, 706, 1967.
398. Segre, A., *Tetrahedron Lett.*, p. 1001, 1964.
399. Trager, W. F., Nist, B. J., and Huitric, A. C., *Tetrahedron Lett.*, p. 2931, 1965.
400. Booth, H. and Thornburrow, P. R., quoted by Booth, H., *Progr. NMR Spectrosc.*, 5, 149, 1969.
401. Lemieux, R. U. and Lown, J. W., *Can. J. Chem.*, 42, 893, 1964.
402. Booth, H., Little, J. H., and Feeney, J., quoted by Booth, H., *Progr. NMR Spectrosc.*, 5, 149, 1969.
403. Marchand, A. P., Marchand, N. W., and Segre, A. L., *Tetrahedron Lett.*, p. 5207, 1969.
404. Marchand, A. P. and Rose, J. E., personal communication.
405. Moen, R. V. and Makowski, H. S., *Abstr. 153rd Natl. Meet. Am. Chem. Soc.*, No. Q9, Miami Beach, 1967.
406. Laszlo, P. and Schleyer, P. von R., *J. Am. Chem. Soc.*, 85, 2017, 1963.
407. Tori, K., Muneyuki, R., and Tanida, H., *Can. J. Chem.*, 41, 3142, 1963.
408. Laszlo, P. and Schleyer, P. von R., *J. Am. Chem. Soc.*, 86, 1171, 1964, and references cited therein.
409. Davis, J. C., Jr. and Van Auken, T. V., *J. Am. Chem. Soc.*, 87, 3900, 1965.
410. Thorpe, M. C. and Coburn, W. C., Jr., *J. Org. Chem.*, 34, 2576, 1969.
411. Mortimer, F. S., *J. Mol. Spectrosc.*, 3, 528, 1959.
412. Tori, K., Hata, Y., Muneyuki, R., Takano, Y., Tsuji, T., and Tanida, H., *Can. J. Chem.*, 42, 927, 1964.
413. Snyder, E. I. and Franzus, B., *J. Am. Chem. Soc.*, 86, 1166, 1964.
414. Story, P. R., Snyder, L. C., Douglass, D. C., Anderson, E. W., and Kornegay, R. L., *J. Am. Chem. Soc.*, 85, 3630, 1963.
415. Lehn, J. M. and Seher, R., *Chem. Commun.*, p. 847, 1966.
416. Hutton, H. M. and Schaefer, T., *Can. J. Chem.*, 45, 1165, 1967; Vestin, R., Borg, A., and Lindblom, T., *Acta Chem. Scand.*, 22, 687, 1968.
417. Bovey, F. A., Hood, F. P., Anderson, E. W., and Kornegay, R. L., *J. Chem. Phys.*, 41, 2041, 1964.
418. Anet, F. A. L., *Can. J. Chem.*, 39, 2262, 1961.
419. Eliel, E. L. and Gianni, H. M., *Tetrahedron Lett.*, p. 97, 1962.
420. Booth, H., *Progr. NMR Spectrosc.*, 5, 149, 1969, and references cited therein.
421. Anderson, J. E. and Lehn, J. M., *J. Am. Chem. Soc.*, 89, 81, 1967.
422. Neikam, W. C. and Dailey, B. P., *J. Chem. Phys.*, 38, 445, 1963.
423. Huitric, A. C. and Carr, J. B., *J. Org. Chem.*, 26, 2648, 1961.
424. Bovey, F. A., Anderson, E. W., Hood, F. P., and Kornegay, R. L., *J. Chem. Phys.*, 40, 3099, 1964.
425. Hofman, W., Stefaniak, L., Urbanski, T., and Witanowski, M., *J. Am. Chem. Soc.*, 86, 554, 1964.
426. Eliel, E. L., Gianni, M. H., Williams, T. H., and Stothers, J. B., *Tetrahedron Lett.*, p. 741, 1962.
427. Lemieux, R. U. and Lown, J. W., *Can. J. Chem.*, 42, 893, 1964.
428. Segre, A. and Musher, J. I., *J. Am. Chem. Soc.*, 89, 706, 1967.
429. Trager, W. F., Nist, B. J., and Huitric, A. C., *Tetrahedron Lett.*, p. 2931, 1965.
430. Celotti, J. C., Reisse, J., and Chiurdoglu, G., *Tetrahedron*, 22, 2249, 1966.
431. Premuzic, E. and Reeves, L. W., *J. Chem. Soc.*, p. 4817, 1964.
432. Lichtenthaler, F. W. and Emig, P., *Tetrahedron Lett.*, p. 577, 1967.
433. Feltkamp, H. and Franklin, N. C., *Tetrahedron*, 21, 1541, 1965.
434. Trager, W. F. and Huitric, A. C., *J. Org. Chem.*, 30, 3257, 1965.
435. Feltkamp, H. and Franklin, N. C., *Tetrahedron*, 22, 2801, 1966.
436. Eliel, E. L., *Chem. Ind.*, p. 568, 1959.
437. Marvell, E. N. and Sexton, H., *J. Org. Chem.*, 29, 2919, 1964.
437a. Dudek, G. O. and Holm, R. H., *J. Am. Chem. Soc.*, 84, 2692, 1962.
438. Booth, G. E. and Ouellette, R. J., *J. Org. Chem.*, 31, 544, 1966.
439. Anderson, C. B. and Sepp, D. T., *Chem. Ind.*, p. 2054, 1964.
440. Sweet, F. and Brown, R. K., *Can. J. Chem.*, 45, 1007, 1967.
441. Sweet, F. and Brown, R. K., *Can. J. Chem.*, 44, 1571, 1966.
442. Lambert, J. B. and Keske, R. G., *J. Am. Chem. Soc.*, 88, 620, 1966.
443. Weitkamp, H. and Korte, F., *Chem. Ber.*, 95, 2896, 1962.
444. Anteunis, A., Taverneir, D., and Borremans, F., *Bull. Soc. Chim. Belg.*, 75, 396, 1966.
445. Eliel, E. L. and Knoeber, M. C., *J. Am. Chem. Soc.*, 88, 5347, 1966.
446. Caspi, E., Wittstruck, T. A., and Paitak, D. M., *J. Org. Chem.*, 27, 3183, 1962.
447. Smith, G. V. and Kriloff, H., *J. Am. Chem. Soc.*, 85, 2016, 1963.
448. Chapman, O. L., *J. Am. Chem. Soc.*, 85, 2014, 1963.
449. Anet, F. A. L., *J. Am. Chem. Soc.*, 84, 671, 1962.
450. Harris, R. K. and Spragg, R. A., *Chem. Commun.*, p. 314, 1966.
451. Lambert, J. B. and Keske, R. G., *J. Org. Chem.*, 31, 3429, 1966.

Index

INTRODUCTION TO THE INDEX

Compiled by Paul T. Gilbert

Authors and subjects are indexed together. Every citation throughout the book is indexed by the author's names even though the citation may be by number only. Where an author's name in a bibliography is not easy to locate by page alone, the reference numbers (preceded by R), or the letters in some cases, are given in parentheses. Thus,

Takahashi, K. 358f, 376, 478f (R62, 109)

means that citations of Takahashi's work appear on pp. 358, 359, and 376, and that references are listed on pp. 478 and 479 under numbers 62 and 109.

All compounds are indexed for which information is given on the infrared, Raman, ultraviolet, electron spin resonance, or mass spectra. They are named as far as possible according to the system of the *Handbook of Chemistry and Physics,* 54th edition, with a liberal inclusion of familiar synonyms. If the name in the index differs from that used on the page cited, the latter name appears in parentheses. Thus,

Juglone (1,4-Naphthoquinone, 5-hydroxy-), uv sp 164

means that on p. 164 ultraviolet data are given for this compound under the name in parentheses.

Note the abbreviations ir, esr, uv, nmr; sp = spectrum.

The thousands of compounds in the nuclear magnetic resonance tables are so organized that the reader can probably find what he wants without an alphabetical index. However, many compounds hard to classify are individually indexed, and all compounds are indexed by class or group. In seeking the nmr spectrum of a particular compound, look first for its parent compound (e.g., Benzene, Ethyne, Tetrahydropyran (under Pyran)).

INDEX

A

B

C

D

E

F

G

H

I

J

K

L

M

N

O

P

Q

R

S

T

U

V

W

X

Y

Z